RICHARD F

CONFEDERATE STATES OF AMERICA

ACT TWO SCENE ONE

CONFEDERATE STATES OF AMERICA

ACT II SCENE I
RICHARD E. GLICK
SENATOR ELECT (R NY) 2022

PEOPLE WHO CAST VOTES DECIDE NOTHING**. PEOPLE WHO** COUNT VOTES DECIDE EVERYTHING**. IN AUTHORITARIAN REGIMES; DEATH IS THE SOLUTION TO ALL PROBLEMS.** NO MAN, NO PROBLEM

SIMULTANEOUSLY STEALING THE PRESIDENCY & (2) GEORGIA SENATE SEATS; WHILE STEALING

OUR RIGHT FOR DISSENT OPPOSITIONAL THOUGHT & COMMUNICATION AMONG CONSERVATIVES; IS TRICK JOKER MANIPULATION OF COVID 19 INTO MAIL VOTING WITH MILLIONS MORE GEORGIA, PENNSYLVANIA, MICHIGAN, WISCONSIN, ARIZONA & NEVADA VOTES THAN REGISTERED VOTERS; & OUR CASTRATED SUPREME COURT THAT HEARS NO EVIL, SEES NO EVIL; & IS DEDICATED TO WILLFULLY BLIND IGNORANCE TO ALL ELECTION STEALING EVIL; THEN FAKE NEWS & DEMOCRATS CUNNINGLY MISREPRESENTING OUR JANUARY 6, 2021 WASHINGTON D.C. REPUBLICAN RALLY TO SAVE THE AMERICA WE OWN & WERE BORN IN AS AN INSURRECTION; MORE SO THAN FORT SUMTER; AS THE LEFTIST EXCUSE FOR FIRING 10'S OF 1000'S OF 01/06/2021 WASHINGTON D.C. PATRIOTIC REPUBLICANS FROM OUR JOBS & BLACKLISTING US; & DIGITALLY IN EVERY WAY POSSIBLE; ON ZUCKERBUCKS FACEBOOK & JACK DORSEY'S TWITTER; SHUTTING DOWN OUR SPEECH & DISSENT WITHIN THEIR THOUSAND YEAR REICH.

THIS REICH HAS SILENCED US ON TWITTER, FACEBOOK; PARLER; SNAPCHAT, SHOPIFY, TWITCH, REDDIT, YOU TUBE, GOOGLE, TIKTOK, PAYPAL, PINTEREST, DISCORD, APPLE, INSTAGRAM, CUNNINGLY LYING THAT OUR FREEDOM OF SPEECH VIOLATES THEIR PLATFORM RULES AGAINST HARMFUL; VIOLENT; THREATENING; HATEFUL, CONSPIRATORIAL, "UNACCEPTABLE USE" MISINFORMATION; LIKE "STOP THE STEAL" DEMOCRAT REICH WITH BUYING; BRIBING & SELLING OF; EFFECTIVE IN PRACTICE BACK DOOR 1913 ESPIONAGE ACT TREASON; WITH $700 MILLION ZUCKERBUCKS; DORSEY; BLOOMBERG; SOROS HOLLYWOOD THOUGHT CONTROL PAID FOR POLICY THAT'S NOW THE SOCIAL CREDIT TRACKING MODEL IMPROVING ON XI JINPING IN HIS OWN REICH. THE DEEP ADMINISTRATIVE U.S. GOVERNMENT & COURTS LAUGH AT REPUBLICANS. SHOULD WE REMAIN UNITED BEHIND THIS BLUE HOLLYWOOD HITLER IN SHEEP'S CLOTHING? OR SECEDE FROM IT? EVERYTHING STARTS WITH AN IDEA.

POLITICAL PARTY - DEMOCRAT
BEST SELLER – AMAZON
NOVEMBER 3, 2020
STEALING PRESIDENCY;
DEMOCRATS CAST 1ST STONE

FAKE NEWS MEDIA; GEORGIA; PENNSYLVANIA MICHIGAN; WISCONSIN; ARIZONA; NEVADA; DOMINION SMARTRONICS; ZUCKERBUCKS; DORSEY; SOROS BLOOMBERG DARK UNTOLD $$ BILLIONS LUBRICATING SWING STATE ELECTION THEFT; TWITTER JACK DORSEY & $700 BLUE ZUCKERBUCKS; JEFF CNN GOEBBELS ZUCKER; FIENDISHLY BUYING THE ADMINISTRATIVE DEEP VOTE COUNTING STATE; SEARCH ALGORISMS; BLURRING EXTERMINATION DIGITAL SOCIAL CONTROL FACEBOOK & GOOGLE BOOK BURNING OF FREE THOUGHT BETTER THAN CHINESE SOCIAL CREDIT ACTUAL & IMPLIED; CONTROL SILENCING OUR LEADERSHIP; MANIPULATION FOR DEMOCRAT VOTES & BILLIONS BRIBE DOLLARS; ASSASSINATING GUNS & RELIGION DEPLORABLES IN GENERAL & DEMOCRACY IN PARTICULAR. COCKTAIL INCLUDES MILLIONS MORE DEMOCRAT PARTY CANDIDATE VOTES THAN REGISTERED VOTERS IN PENNSYLVANIA; GEORGIA; MICHIGAN; WISCONSIN; ARIZONA & NEVADA; TRICK DOMINION SMARTRONICS & MILLIONS OF FAKE STUFFED MAIL BALLOTS.

"CHIEF JUSTICE OF WISCONSIN SUPREME COURT PATIENCE D. ROGGENSACK

BITTERLY CONDEMNED HER (4) WISCONSIN ASSOCIATE JUSTICES FOR "JUDICIAL ACTIVISM (A.K.A. POCKET VETO) 4-3 RULING DEPRAVED REFUSAL TO ENFORCE COUNTLESS WISCONSIN CONSTITUTIONALLY MANDATED VOTING LAWS; ALLOWING FRAUDULENT VOTES TO STEAL (11) WISCONSIN ELECTORAL VOTES. DEMOCRATS MOCKINGLY LAUGH IN OUR FACES ABOUT IT; LIKE ADOLF HITLER APRIL 10TH, 1933; HUGO CHAVEZ OCTOBER 7, 2012; XI JINPING 24/7/366 THOUSAND YEAR CHINESE REICH TILL; OR WHICHEVER COMES FIRST.

2020 U.S. PRESIDENTIAL DECEPTION STOLEN ELECTION RESULTS

GEORGIA BIDEN (2,473,633) TRUMP (2,461,854) DIFFERENCE (11, 779) **ELECTORAL VOTES (16)**
WISCONSIN BIDEN (1,630,866) TRUMP (1,610,184) DIFFERENCE (20,784) **ELECTORAL VOTES (11)**
ARIZONA BIDEN (1,672,147) TRUMP (1,661,686) DIFFERENCE (10.461) **ELECTORAL VOTES (11)**
NEVADA BIDEN (703,996) TRUMP (669,890) VOTES (6) DIFFERENCE (31,596) **ELECTORAL VOTES (6)** PROOF POSITIVE THAT THESE STATES WERE STOLEN BY BY BIDEN IS THAT THESE (4) STATES (EXCLUDING PENNSYLVANIA); HAD MORE TOTAL VOTES CAST THAN TOTAL REGISTERED VOTERS **PA Reported 200,000 More Ballots Cast than People Who Voted – Will The State Now Legitimately Go to the Trump Column? A comparison of official county election results to the total number of voters who voted on November 3, 2020 as recorded by the Department of State shows that 6,962,607 total ballots were reported as being cast, while DoS/SURE system records indicate that only 6,760,230 total voters actually voted. Among the 6,962,607 total ballots cast, 6,931,060 total votes were counted in the presidential race, including all three candidates on the ballot and write-in candidates. The difference of 202,377 more votes cast than voters voting, together with the 31,547 over- and under-votes in the presidential race, adds up to an**

alarming discrepancy of 170,830 votes, which is more than twice the reported statewide difference between the two major candidates for President of the United States. After nearly two months, it was discovered that the state of Pennsylvania had 200,000 more votes than people who voted. We already knew that in Pennsylvania tens of thousands of ballots were returned before they were sent out. We know hundreds of thousands of completed ballots were shipped from New York to Pennsylvania before the election. We also know that 2.5 million absentee ballots were counted in Pennsylvania but only 1.8 million in total were sent out. Then yesterday the Pennsylvania House uncovered that the certified results in Pennsylvania for President are in error by more than 200,000 votes. This is more than twice the difference between President Trump and Joe Biden in the Presidential race in the state.

THE DIFFERENCE IN THE WINNING MARGIN OF VOTES ABOVE (4) STATES EXCLUDING SHOPLIFTED; PICKPOCKETED PENNSYLVANIA COMBINED WAS ONLY (74,610) OF THE U.S 2020 PRESIDENTIAL ELECTION TOTAL OF 155,560,099 VOTES CAST **DEMOCRATS SNUCK IN DARK OF NIGHT JUST ENOUGH UNVERIFIED COMPLIANT WITH NO POLL WATCHERS IN THESE (4) STATES ABOVE IN** MOSTLY 80 PERCENT MINORITY URBAN AREAS WITH MOST PARTISAN REPUBLICAN POLL WATCHERS UNDER THREAT OF VIOLENCE ABSOLUTELY & POSITIVELY UNABLE TO VERIFY MILLIONS OF MAIL VOTES FOR SIGNATURE MATCH & MULTIPLE LEGALLY MANDATED COMPLIANCE. WE SHOULD TRUST THESE SCUMBAGS WITH A DOLLAR, MUCH LESS THE ELECTION FINANCED BY $650 MILLION GREASED ZUCKERBUCKS TO DEMOCRAT WAFFEN SS GESTAPO?

IN A GOOD NATURED WAY; US TRUMP VOTERS JUST LAUGH OFF; PHILOSOPHICALLY STEALING AMERICAN DEMOCRACY; HO, HO, HO, GOTCHA; DONNIE BOY; WE BE IS WIN SOME & BE WUZ LOSE SOME, AND WE LOST OUR NATION; BETTER FUCK A DUCK LUCK NEXT TIME. NEXT TIME WILL BE MUCH WORSE; BECAUSE DEMOCRATS HAVE PERFECTED & LEGALIZED THEIR THEFT OF VOTES & ELECTIONS; DEMOCRATS WILL RUN ALL ELECTIONS & COUNT ALL VOTES ACCORDING TO THEIR RULES IN ALL FUTURE NATIONAL ELECTIONS; NEXT, WITH UNVERIFIED ONLINE VOTING. THAT'S THE DEMOCRAT BLUEPRINT FOR CRIPPLING ELECTIONS & STEALING AMERICA WE WERE BORN INTO. WE ALREADY HAVE THE SILICON VALLEY CHINESE SOCIAL CREDIT WRONG PRONOUN & FREEDOM TO SAY STOP THE STEAL STOLEN FROM US BY FACEBOOK, TWITTER & ALL OTHER SOCIAL MEDIA WAFFEN SS GESTAPO LIKE MARK ZUCKERBUCKS **& TWITTER'S JACK DORSEY.**

DEMOCRATS HAVE BROKEN TRUST; EVERY LAW; DARING U.S.A. FLACCID SUPREME COURT**; MOCKING** ALL LAWS MORAL; CONSTITUTIONAL **&** DIVINE**; DISINGENUOUSLY WITH THEIR NEW VERB** ALL PURPOSE DEBUNK "NO EVIDENCE" **NEVER, EVER; ANY EVIDENCE; IN FACE OF TRUTH OBVIOUS TO ALL; W/ NO POSSIBLE REPUBLICAN PRE-EMPTIVE SAFEGUARDS & AFTER OUR IMPOSSIBILITY OF DISPROVING A NEGATIVE; BEFORE THE FACT OF VOTING FRAUD; CALLING REPUBLICANS PARANOID FOR EXPECTING SUCH FRAUD THAT THERE'S NO EVIDENCE OF HAVING PREVIOUSLY OCCURRED.. AND THEN THE MASS MAIL VOTING FRAUDULENT DEMOCRAT BALLOTS THAT DID STEAL THE ELECTION. DEMOCRATS CYNICALLY MANIPULATED COVID 19 PRETEXT; AFTER ELECTION; IT'S TOO LATE. THEN DEMOCRATS LAUGH IN OUR FACES ABOUT IT; MOCKING US AS SUCKERS; CYNICAL; EASY; LIKE HARRY REID:**

CLAIMED ROMNEY (AN UNPRECEDENTED HISTORICAL QUISLING SCUMBAG) **PAID NO TAXES IN (10) YEARS; FAKE MEDIA RAN W/ ROMNEY NO TAXES STORY. AFTER OBAMA REELECTION/ HARRY REID LAUGHED AT REPUBLICANS; "IT WORKED, DIDN'T IT." NOW IT'S COVID.**

FOOL US ONCE.
FOOLED US TWICE.
FOOL US FOREVER?
NEVER?

CALIFORNIA THREATENED TO SECEDE. BECAUSE ON A NATIONAL LEVEL; REPUBLICANS NEVER AGAIN WILL COUNT VOTES. GOING FORWARD; REPUBLICAN VOTES COUNT FOR NOTHING. **OUR WILLFULLY IGNORANT D SUPREME COURT HEARS NO EVIL SEES NO EVIL; PLAYS DUMB ABOUT MOST METASTATIC MALINGNANCY EVER IN THE ANIMAL KINGDOM. IT COULDN'T HAPPEN HERE? IT DID. AMERICA WE WERE BORN INTO NO LONGER EXISTS.**

LOOK AT 1933; GERMANY UNITED BEHIND ADOLF HITLER'S STOLEN ELECTION, WE KNOW HOW THAT WORKED OUT. SEVERAL HUNDRED THOUSAND PEACEFUL JANUARY 5, 2021 CAPITOL DEMONSTRATORS; WERE IDENTIFIED BY FEDERAL; STATE & LOCAL LAW ENFORCEMENT PROVEN TO HAVE BEEN INFILTRATED BY MULTIPLE BUSLOADS FACIAL RECOGNITION SURVEILLANCE SOFTWARE OF BEING ANTIFA & BLACK LIVES MATTER; FROM AS FAR AWAY AS THE WEST COAST;

HUNDREDS OF ANTIFA & BLACK LIVES MATTER MARXISTS WERE PROOF POSITIVE CONFIRMED BY B MULTIPLE STATE & FEDERAL LAW ENFORCEMENT FACIAL RECOGNITION SOFTWARE IDENTIFICATION INFILTRATING THE JANUARY 6, 2021 U.S CAPITOL PEACEFUL DEMONSTRATORS AS ACTUAL VIOLENT THUG CRIMINAL PERPETRATORS OF VIOLENCE THAT THE MAINSTREAM FAKE NEWS DEMOCRAT APPARATCHIK PROPAGANDISTS BLAMED ENTIRELY ON TRUMP SUPPORTERS .MULTIPLE AUDIO/VIDEO FOOTAGE CLIPS SHOWS HUNDREDS OF BLACK CLAD MASKED ANTIFA THUGS AT 1/6/2021 CAPITOL PRO TRUMP RALLY. ANTIFA & BLACK LIVES MATTER ARE RETREAD RECYCLED MS-13; BLOODS & CRIPS DEMOCRAT 2021 BROWNSHIRT GESTAPO STORM TROOPER WAFFEN SS IN GUISE OF HALLOWEEN DEATH WISH FOR AMERICA.

Left-wing activist charged in Capitol riot after saying he was just there to 'document'

THIS IS ONE OF MANY ANTIFA COCKROACHES WHO INFILTRATED THE JANUARY 6

CAPITOL DEMONSTRATION WHO WERE THERE TO MAKE PEACEFUL CONSERVATIVE REPUBLICANS LOOK LIKE ANTIFA & BLACK LIVES MATTER MARXIST RIOTERS

John Sullivan told Fox News last week he regularly attends and takes video at protests

By Michael Ruiz

A left-wing activist who told Fox News last week that he'd followed a pro-Trump mob into the Capitol in order to "document" the siege is now the subject of a criminal complaint in connection with his alleged participation, according to the U.S. Justice Department.

John Sullivan can allegedly be heard egging on protesters in video he provided to the FBI, according to a federal criminal complaint. He has also shared the video to his YouTube and Twitter accounts under the pseudonym Jayden X.

He was charged Thursday in federal court in Washington after being arrested by the FBI. He remains in custody in Toeele County, in his home state of Utah, on a U.S. Marshals Service hold request.

WE GET THE BLAME FOR WHAT THIS LOWLIFE WHACKED ED OUT LOSER SCHMUCK WITH TIME ON HIS FUCKEN HANDS DID

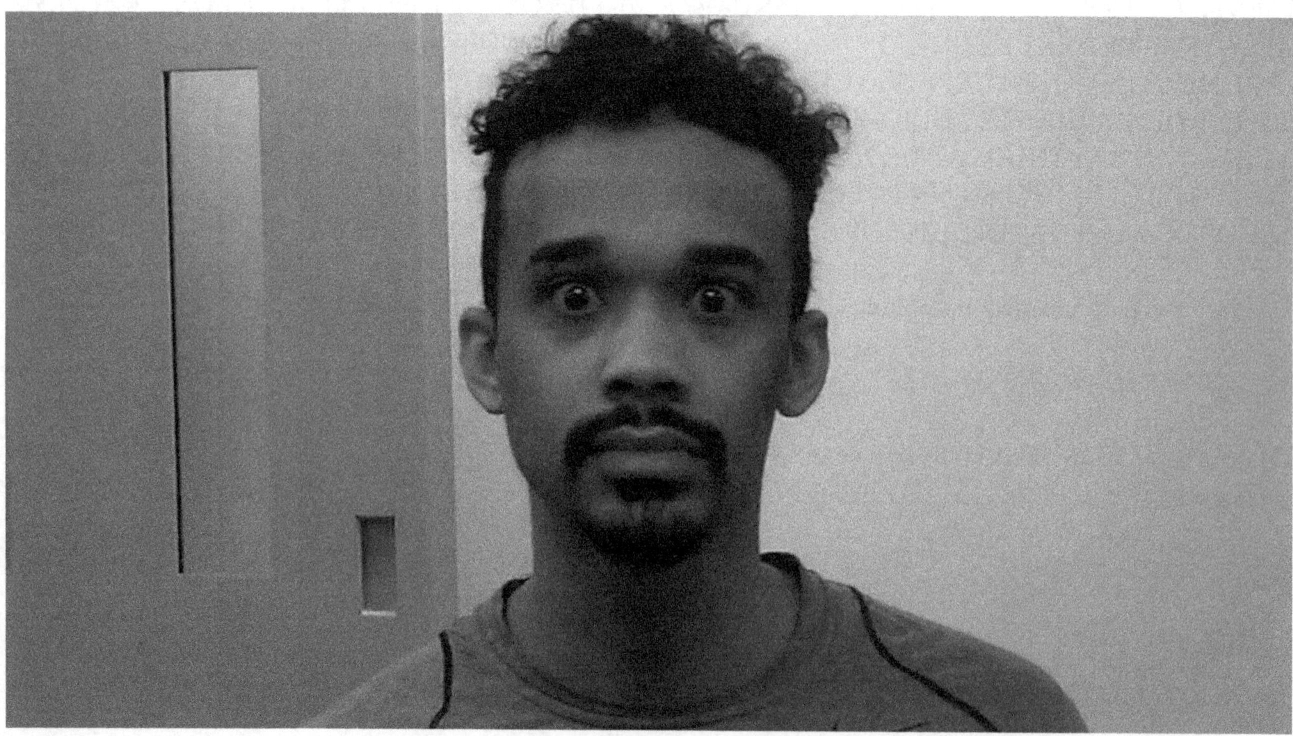

(Toeele County Sheriff's Office)

BLM ACTIVIST INSIDE CAPITOL CLAIMS HE WAS 'DOCUMENTING' RIOTS, ONCE SAID 'BURN IT ALL DOWN'

Inside the building, he told rioters that "We got to get this s--- burned," and "it's our house m-----------," according to an affidavit signed by FBI Special Agent Matthew Foulger. He faces federal charges of civil disorder, entering a restricted building and violent entry or disorderly conduct. Sullivan also allegedly told Foulger that he had been in the Capitol during the riot, entering through a broken window while wearing a ballistic vest.

As protesters climbed over a wall near the Capitol entrance, he allegedly exclaimed in the video, "You guys are f------ savage. Let's go!" "There are so many people," Sullivan's voice can be heard saying as the camera shows a large group of people making its way toward the building. "Let's go. This s--- is ours! F-- yeah. I can't believe this is reality." "We accomplished this s---," he said at another point "We did this together. F--- yeah! We are all a part of this history."

Inside the building, Sullivan told rioters that "We gotta get this s--- burned," and "it's our house m-----------," according to <a href="https://www.justice.gov/opa/page/file/1354781/download" target="_blank">an affidavit</a> signed by FBI Special Agent Matthew Foulger. (FBI)

In an interview with Rolling Stone published Wednesday, Sullivan said he was putting on an act to build rapport with the protesters. "I had to relate to these people, and build trust in the short amount of time I had there to get where I need to go," he told the magazine. "To the front of the crowd to see the dynamic between the police and the protesters, because nobody wants to see the backs of people's heads from a far-off distance."

He apparently made it there. During the unrest, he tweeted up-close video of the moment a Capitol Police officer fatally shot Air Force veteran Ashli Babbitt during the riot. It had been taken just a few feet away, at the height of the chaos outside the Speaker's Lobby.

A screengrab from Sullivan's video outside the Capitol (FBI)

Investigators used this detail and other aspects of the video to confirm Sullivan's alleged whereabouts within the Capitol, they said. Sullivan, the founder of a Utah-based group called Insurgence USA, told Fox News last Thursday that he'd entered the besieged Capitol to "document" what was going on and to dispute "this narrative going around" that Antifa instigators had played a role in the riot.

While he has denied ties to Antifa, or anti-fascists, in recent interviews, his group Insurgence USA had advertised an event called "Kick These Fascists out of DC" on Wednesday around the same time as a pro-Trump rally near the National Mall that preceded the Capitol chaos.

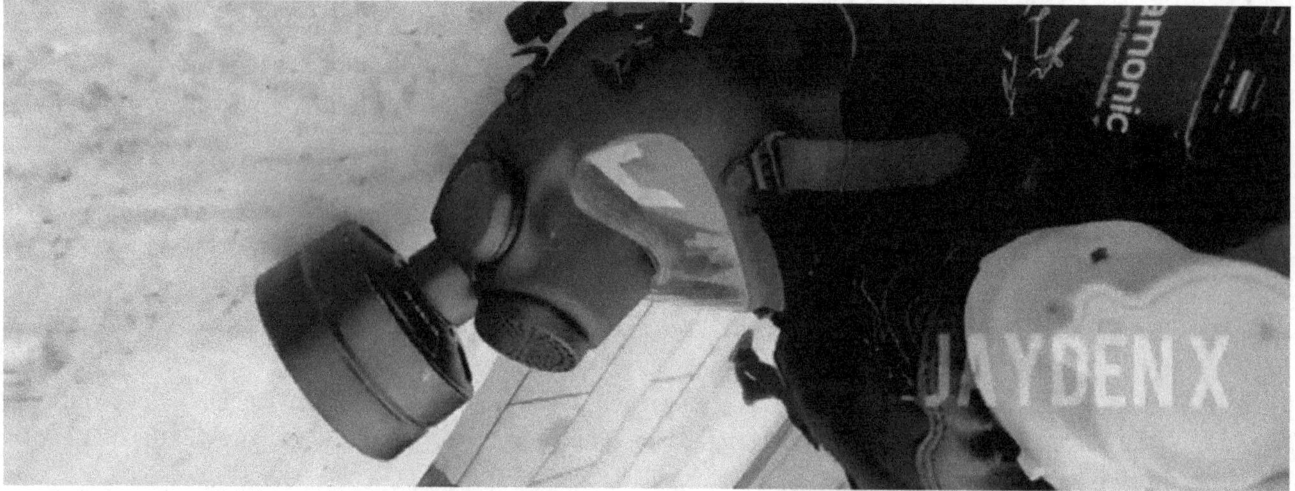

Another screengrab showing protective equipment (FBI)

CONFEDERATE STATES OF AMERICA .... ACT TWO SCENE ONE

After the Trump rally, a mob of demonstrators breached the Capitol, ransacked congressional offices, and stormed the Senate floor, prompting a chorus of condemnations from members of both major parties. The breach interrupted a joint session of Congress aimed at validating Joe Biden as president-elect. Congress reconvened later in the evening and finished the process.

Sullivan, who was still in custody Thursday, could not be reached for comment.

1000'S REPUBLICAN PEACEFUL PARTICIPANTS (US) NOW PROSECUTED AS FELONS; FIRED FROM JOBS; BECAUSE SMARTPHONE GPS GLOBAL POSITIONING PROVE REPUBLICANS (US JUST BEING THERE) WERE IN WASHINGTON D.C.; 01/06/2021; WHILE MILLIONS OF DEMONIC VIOLENT LEFTISTS RIOTED; PILLAGED; PLUNDERED MACY'S MIRACLE ON 34TH ST; 100'S $MILLIONS IN NAME OF BLACK LIVES MATTER; WALKING OFF WITH TV'S REFRIGERATORS; WASHERS/DRYERS; BURNING 1000'S CARS AT DEALERSHIPS; CHICAGO PSYCHOPATH MAYOR LORI LIGHTFOOR ACTUALLY BLOWS IT OFF AS COVERED BY INSURANCE; BLIND EYE NON-ENFORCEMENT OF LAW PROSECUTION DISCRETION UNIVERSAL BLUE STATE POLICY; LAW ENFOREMENT INTENTIONALLY IGNORING SAVAGE CRIMES INCLUDING PREMEDITATED SYSTEMIC COLD BLOODED MURDER OF OVER (2) DOZEN COPS DURING 2020 LEFTIST MOB RIOTS; MOSTLY IN BLUE STATES "SUMMER OF LOVE" NATIONWIDE. IT'S MUCH WORSE. DISSATISFIED WITH STEALING PRESIDENCY & (2) GEORGIA SENATE SEATS; THEY LUST VICIOUSLY TO HUMILIATE & HARM US; IN ALL CONCEIVABLE WAYS; SILENCING CONSERVATIVE DIGITAL SPEECH & SOCIAL MEDIA COMMUNICATION. IN 1861, THE CIVIL WAR WAS TRIGGERED BY MUCH LESS. DEMOCRATS GET THEIR SADISTIC ORGASMIC RUSH FROM SAVAGING 76 MILLION TRUMP VOTERS; WHO ARE ALL NOW JEWS.

Forbes Says It's Targeting Trump Staffers and Their Future Employers

By Michael Dorstewitz

Corporate media and the Left aren't satisfied with merely controlling the White House and both chambers of Congress in less than two weeks. They want revenge.

They also want to punish anyone who worked in the Trump administration and, to a lesser extent, the 45th president's supporters.

On Thursday, in what was the most recent and possibly the most egregious example, Randall Lane, Forbes' chief content officer, announced that Forbes Media was "holding those who lied for Trump accountable" in what he called "a truth reckoning."

Lane claimed that the media group was taking this unprecedented action **in response to the mob attack on Capitol Hill late Wednesday afternoon, which resulted in two deaths — a Capitol Police officer and a female U.S. Air Force veteran who was demonstrating that day.**

Lane alleged that the president's "lies-upon-lies, repeated frequently and fervently, provided the kindling, the spark, the gasoline" that led to the attack.

Lane then singles out five senior White House officials, whom he describes as "the people paid by the People to inform the People."

He named former White House press secretaries Sean Spicer (currently co-host of Newsmax TV's "Spicer & Co."), Sarah Huckabee Sanders, and Stephanie Grisham, as well as current spokeswoman Kayleigh McEnany.

Lane also named Kellyanne Conway, senior counselor to the president.

So what does he propose?

"Simple," he said. "Don't let the chronic liars cash in on their dishonesty."

He observed that previous White House spokesmen have reaped millions in royalties from book deals after they left, adding that "Trump's liars don't merit that same golden parachute."

Acting more like a Mafia don than a media executive, Lane then threatened future employers: "Hire any of Trump's fellow fabulists above, and Forbes will assume that everything your company or firm talks about is a lie."

His short, 600-word rant is filled with hyperbole and outright misstatements of fact.

Lane uses the word "lie," "lies," "liar" or "lied" nine times in his piece — three times in the first paragraph alone.

There's no reference to the fact that it was the previous president, not Trump, who was awarded PolitiFact's "Lie of the Year."

Nor does he acknowledge the daily claims for nearly four years on corporate media and by Democrats promoting the Russian collusion hoax.

What's his remedy for accountability for that doozy?

Lane's article sounds so unhinged the reader has to keep referring to the masthead to confirm that it's indeed Forbes and not some far-left publication like Vox, Slate, or Raw Story.

And that it's not an opinion columnist, but the company's chief content officer who clearly states he is speaking for Forbes, not just himself.

Forbes is seriously diminished by such cancel culture rantings, considering it has long been considered a respected business publication of its creator, B.C. Forbes, a tradition carried on by the late Malcom S. Forbes, and his son Steve, one of the country's most noted conservatives.

Steve Forbes has been a strong supporter of Trump's, endorsing in both 2016 and 2020.

The irony is explained by the fact Steve and the Forbes family no longer own Forbes the media company.

In fact, Forbes Media was sold six years ago to Integrated Whale Media Investments, which is based in Hong Kong, and which has since become a territory of mainland Communist China.

Forbes wasn't the first to threaten future employers of Trump White House staffers.

Rep. Alexandria Ocasio-Cortez suggested shortly after the November election that someone should begin compiling a list of Trump White House staffers.

"Is anyone archiving these Trump sycophants for when they try to downplay or deny their complicity in the future?" The New York Democrat asked.

"I foresee decent probability of many deleted Tweets, writings, photos in the future."

Hari Sevugan, former senior spokesman for the Barack Obama presidential campaign, answered the call.

"You better believe it," he replied. **"We just launched the Trump Accountability Project to make sure anyone who took a paycheck to help Trump undermine America is held responsible for what they did."**

The Lincoln Project's Stuart Stevens announced that it will also track former White House staffers.

"At @ProjectLincoln we are constructing a database of Trump officials & staff that will detail their roles in the Trump administration & track where they are now," he tweeted Saturday.

"No personal info, only professional. But they will be held accountable & not allowed to pretend they were not involved," he added.

Fox News senior political analyst Brit Hume offered a five-word analysis of the Lincoln Project effort.

"This will not end well," he said.

Outrage over Twitter's Trump Ban Grows: Pompeo, Rubio, Ted Cruz, Navalny, James Woods

Donald Trump's Twitter account displayed on a phone screen and Twitter logo in the background are seen in this illustration photo taken in Poland.

By Charlie MCcarthy

People from various walks of life have expressed outrage over Twitter permanently banning President Donald Trump from its platform on Friday.

The social media giant announced its decision in the aftermath of Wednesday's riot at the Capitol, where people protesting the election results stormed the building, joining Democrats in blaming the president for inciting the rioters.

Even Russia's leading pro-democracy dissident Alexey Navalny took to twitter to condemn the ban, calling it

an "unacceptable act of censorship."

"Among the people who have Twitter accounts are cold-blooded murderers (Vladimir Putin or Nicholas Maduro) and liars and thieves (Dmitry Medvedev). For many years, Twitter, Facebook and Instagram have been used as a base for Putin's 'troll factory' and similar groups from other authoritarian countries," Navalny wrote on Twitter.

U.S. lawmakers and government officials also tweeted their reactions.

"Silencing speech is dangerous. It's un-American. Sadly, this isn't a new tactic of the Left. They've worked to silence opposing voices for years," Secretary of State Mike Pompeo tweeted.

"We cannot let them silence 75M Americans. This isn't the [Communist Party of China]."

"Silencing people, not to mention the President of the US, is what happens in China not our country. #Unbelievable," tweeted Nikki Haley, former ambassador to the United Nations.

"Even those who oppose Trump should see the danger of having a small & unelected group with the power to silence & erase anyone," Sen. Marco Rubio, R-Fla., tweeted. "And their actions will only stoke new grievances that will end up fueling the very thing they claim to be trying to prevent."

Ted Cruz, R-Texas, agreed with his Senate colleague.

"Big Tech's PURGE, censorship & abuse of power is absurd & profoundly dangerous," Cruz wrote. "If you agree w/ Tech's current biases (Iran, good; Trump, bad), ask yourself, what happens when you disagree?

"Why should a handful of Silicon Valley billionaires have a monopoly on political speech?"

House members also took to Twitter.

"By banning the duly elected President of the United States, Big Tech has declared they are more powerful than the will of the American people. Unelected tech oligarchs should not have such massive power over global discourse while enjoying little to no oversight/accountability," tweeted Rep. Lauren Boebert, R-Colo., who briefly changed her profile picture to one of Trump.

"The only way to stop Big Tech companies like Google and Facebook from censoring conservatives is to rein in their anticompetitive behavior," Rep. Ken Buck, R-Colo., tweeted.

"They can censor you because they are a monopoly." "Twitter purges conservatives. Google suspends Parler," Rep. Beth Van Duyne, R-Texas, wrote. "Where was Big Tech over the summer when liberal voices were inciting violence in our streets?

"To be clear: This isn't about violence. This is about Big Tech trying to control what we think, what we share,

how we communicate"

"This will not end well and will only make things worse. Big tech must stop," Rep. Dan Crenshaw, R-Texas, tweeted. "For the few liberals left in the Democrat party: work with us to protect our most sacred rights. This must be our greatest priority."

Twitter's decision seemingly put the American Civil Liberties Union in a difficult position.

"ACLU struggling here on this one....this is American Civil Liberties Union after all," tweeted New York Times investigative reporter Eric Lipton, who included a comment from ACLU Senior Legislative Counsel Kate Ruane.

After saying the ACLU understands Twitter's desire to ban Trump, Ruane said, "it should concern everyone when companies like Facebook and Twitter wield he unchecked power to remove people from platforms that have become indispensable for the speech of millions."

Ruane added that while Trump has other means by which he can get out his messages, "Black, Brown, and LGBTQ activists" won't have the same resources if social media platforms censor them.

Actor James Woods also expressed his displeasure about Twitter's ban in a tweet that has been deleted.

"In their #GreatPurge the zealots at Twitter have removed 137,000 followers from my account in two days," he tweeted.

"Those cheering the suppression of people with whom they disagree might remember the pendulum always swings. Be careful what you wish for. It's often what you also deserve."

Actress Kirstie Alley, noting the ACLU's comment, said, "ALL people should be concerned is the KEY here. It's true, the average person will no longer have a platform to speak their views. This is called SLAVERY. This censorship proves BIG TECH now holds the keys to the chains."

PARLER CEO: Tech Companies Coordinated Plan to Close Us Down

This illustration picture shows social media application logo from Parler displayed on a smartphone with its website in the background. (Olivier Douliery/AFP via Getty Images)

By Eric Mack

The silencing of conservative speech on social media has spiraled into a "coordinated effort" by big tech to close down Parler, according to the social media platform's CEO John Matze.

"This was a coordinated attack by the tech giants to kill the competition in the marketplace," Matze's statement read. "We were too successful too fast. "You can expect the war on competition and free speech to continue, but don't count us out. #speakfreely."

Matze's statement comes as Amazon is removing the platform from its webservers, which might take the conservative social media platform down for about a week.

"Sunday at midnight Amazon will be shutting off all of our servers in an attempt to completely remove free speech off the Internet," he wrote. "There is a possibility Parler will be unavailable on the Internet for up to a week as we rebuild from scratch.

"We prepared for events like this by never relying on Amazon's proprietary infrastructure and building bare metal products."

Matze called out Amazon, Google, and Apple for orchestrating the "coordinated effort."

"We will try our best to move to a new provider right now as we have many competing for our business; however, Amazon, Google, and Apple purposely did this as a coordinated effort knowing our options will be limited and knowing this would inflict the most damage right as President Trump was banned from the tech companies."

Amazon Booting Parler Off Its Web Hosting Service

Amazon is removing the Parler social media service from its web servicers, BuzzFeed News reported Saturday night. If Parler cannot find another hosting service once the ban takes effect Sunday, Parler will go offline, Buzzfeed reported.

The news comes after Apple and Google Play removed the app from their stores. Parler has been used increasingly by conservatives amid what they see as increasing censorship by Twitter. Twitter permanently banned President Donald Trump on Friday for tweets it said violated its rules of inciting violence.

Conservatives have said the ban is a stifling of free speech. Amazon has suspended Parler from its Amazon Web Services (AWS) unit, for violating AWS's terms of services by failing to effectively deal with a steady increase in violent content on the social networking service.

AWS did not immediately respond to Reuters' request for comment. AWS plans to suspend Parler's account effective Sunday, at 11:59 p.m. PST, according to an email by an AWS Trust and Safety team to Parler seen by BuzzFeed. Matze, in a post on Parler responding to the Apple suspension, said, "They claim it is due to violence on the platform. The community disagrees as we hit number 1 on their store today," Matze said in a post on Parler.

"More details about our next plans coming soon as we have many options," Matze said. In addition to Parler, right-leaning social media users in the United States have flocked to messaging app Telegram and hands-off social site Gab, citing the more aggressive policing of political comments on mainstream platforms such as Twitter Inc and Facebook Inc.

Google, in its announcement Friday that it was suspending Parler, said that Parler must demonstrate "robust" content moderation if it wants to get back in the store.

'Utterly Shameful': Josh Hawley Strikes Back After Joe Biden Likens Him To Nazi Propagandist

Virginia Kruta

Republican Missouri Sen. Josh Hawley demanded Friday that President-elect Joe Biden retract comments comparing his and Republican Texas Sen. Ted Cruz's questioning of the 2020 presidential election results to lies spread by a Nazi propagandist.

Biden criticized Hawley **and Cruz, stopping short of calling for their resignations but saying instead that he wanted to see them defeated in their next elections. Arguing that they had fed false information about the 2020 presidential election to the American people, he compared their efforts to those of Nazi propagandist Joseph Goebbels.** (RELATED: Rep. Cori Bush Is Trying To Oust Republicans Who Objected To Electoral College Certification)

Biden tells @NikolenDC **that GOP senators who supported election falsehoods, like Ted Cruz and Josh Hawley, are "part of the big lie," and references Nazi propaganda minister Joseph Goebbels** https://t.co/ho31YYlJfR

"They're part of the big lie, the big lie," Biden **said. "I was being reminded by a friend of mine, and maybe you were with me, I can't recall, when we told that, you know, Goebbels and the great lie, you keep repeating the law, repeating the lie. Well, there was a print that when Dresden was bombed, firebombed, there were 250 people that were killed — was it 2,500 people that were killed? And Goebbels said no, 25,000 — or 250,000 were killed. And our papers printed that. Our papers printed it. It's the big lie."** (RELATED: Biden Calls Capitol Riots 'Domestic Terrorism,' Urged To Create White House Post Targeting Extremists)

"President-elect Biden has just compared me and another Republican Senator to Nazis. You read that correctly. Think about that for a moment. Let it sink in," Hawley **issued a statement calling for Biden to retract the comments immediately, adding that he was being called a Nazi for raising questions about the electoral process. Federal election officials have continued to deny allegations of widespread voter fraud raised by President Donald Trump's campaign after issuing a Nov. 12** statement that called the 2020 election the "most secure in American history."

"This is undignified, immature, and intemperate behavior from the President-elect. It is utterly shameful," Hawley continued. "He should act like a dignified adult and retract these sick comments. And every Democrat member of congress should be asked to disavow these disgusting comments."

Nunes: Parler Ban a 'Violation of Antitrust, Civil Rights, the RICO Statute — 'There Should Be a Racketeering Investigation'

Jeff Poor

During this week's broadcast of FNC's "Sunday Morning Futures," Rep. Devin Nunes (R-CA), the ranking Republican on the House Intelligence Committee, called on the Department of Justice to launch an investigation into tech companies' efforts to remove Parler as a platform from the internet.

The California Republican cited violations of antitrust laws, civil rights and the Racketeer Influenced and Corrupt Organizations Act.

"Well, Maria, when I wrote that book, I was hoping to warn Americans so that they would vote right and that maybe this wouldn't happen and this could be prevented," he said. "Unfortunately, it's far worse than what I could even imagine. The effect of this is that there is no longer a free and open social media company or site for any American to get on any longer, because these big companies, Apple, Amazon, Google, they have just destroyed a — what was likely — Parler is likely a billion-dollar company. Poof, it's gone. But it's more than just the financial aspect to that. Republicans have no way to communicate. If — and it doesn't even matter if you're a Republican or conservative."

"If you don't want to be regulated by left-wingers that are at Twitter and Facebook and Instagram, where you get shadowbanned, nobody gets to see you — nobody gets to see you, they get to decide what's violent or not violent, it's preposterous," Nunes continued. "So, I don't know where the hell the Department of Justice is at right now or the FBI. This is clearly a violation of antitrust, civil rights, the RICO statute. There should be a racketeering investigation on all the people that coordinated this attack on not only a company but on all of those like us, like me, like you, Maria. I have 3 million followers on Parler. Tonight, I will no longer be able to communicate with those people. And they're Americans."

ACLU voices concern about 'unchecked power' by Big Tech after Twitter permanently bans Trump

'...companies like Facebook and Twitter wield the unchecked power to remove people from platforms that have become indispensable for the speech of billions'

Chris Enloe

Even the American Civil Liberties Union is sounding the alarm about Big Tech removing President Donald Trump's accounts from its various platforms. What is the ACLU saying?

The civil rights organization, which often fights against conservative causes, released a statement Friday expressing concern that the movement to deplatform Trump could be a slippery slope with eventual unintended consequences, especially for minority groups.

ACLU senior legislative counsel Kate Ruane said in a statement**:**

For months, President Trump has been using social media platforms to seed doubt about the results of the election and to undermine the will of voters. We understand the desire to permanently suspend him now, but it should concern everyone when companies like Facebook and Twitter wield the unchecked power to remove people from platforms that have become indispensable for the speech of billions — especially when political realities make those decisions easier.

President Trump can turn to his press team or Fox News to communicate with the public, but others — like the many Black, Brown, and LGBTQ activists who have been censored by social media companies — will not have that luxury. It is our hope that these companies will apply their rules transparently to everyone.

What's the background?

After the U.S. Capitol riots last Wednesday, social media networks and various online services began restricting Trump's accounts, claiming his rhetoric helped incite the deadly violence.

After initially slapping Trump with a temporary suspension, Twitter took unprecedented action against the president on Friday when it permanently banned Trump's account**, citing "risk of further incitement of violence."**

Unfortunately for Trump, it's not just Twitter**: Facebook and Instagram have also suspended Trump's accounts through at least Inauguration Day. Snapchat, Shopify, Twitch, Reddit, YouTube, Google, TikTok, PayPal, Discord, Pinterest, and even email providers have taken action against Trump or Trump-related content.**

In response, conservatives have flocked to Parler, an alternative social media platform that promises to promote free speech.

However, Parler later found itself in the crosshairs, and has now been dumped from **the Apple App Store, Google Play Store, and Amazon web hosting services. The Big Tech companies had demanded that Parler increase its content moderation, alleging that Parler had been hosting content that promoted violence.**

Parler CEO John Matze responded by claiming his company was the target of a concerted effort against free speech.

Matze said, "We will try our best to move to a new provider right now as we have many competing for our business, however Amazon, Google and Apple purposefully did this as a coordinated effort knowing our options would be limited and knowing this would inflict the most damage right as President Trump was banned from the tech companies."

"This was a coordinated attack by the tech giants to kill competition in the market place. We were too successful too fast," Matze added. "You can expect the war on competition and free speech to continue, but don't count us out."

Post-Capitol riot censorship shows 'unelected' companies have 'monopoly power': Rubio Rubio described rioters who breached the Capitol as a 'rogue's gallery' and 'wackos'

By Evie Fordham

Post-Capitol siege censorship shows 'unelected' companies have monopoly power: Rubio

Florida Sen. Marco Rubio said chaos in the U.S. is a 'gift' to the Communist Party of China.

Online censorship in the wake of violence at the U.S. Capitol shows that "unelected" companies have "monopoly power," Sen. Marco Rubio, R-Fla., said Sunday. "This is also an opportunity for [the left] to go and put pressure on social media companies to literally not just erase the president but erase everybody," Rubio told "Sunday Morning Futures." "We are now living in a country where four or five companies, unelected, unaccountable, have the monopoly power to decide, we're gonna wipe people out, we're going to erase them, from any digital platform, whether it's selling things and the like."

BOZELL: SOCIAL MEDIA GIANTS 'CANCELING CONSERVATIVES,' ANTITRUST ACTION NEEDED

Rubio described rioters who breached the Capitol as a "rogue's gallery" and "wackos," but he said tech companies' eagerness to censor pro-Trump voices is a "cynical" ploy.

Supporters of President Donald Trump climb the west wall of the the U.S. Capitol on Wednesday, Jan. 6, 2021, in Washington. (AP Photo/Jose Luis Magana)

"It's also very cynical," he said. "Facebook, Twitter, these are not moral champions here. The reason why these guys are doing it is because Democrats are about to take power, and they view this as a way to get on their good side to avoid restrictions or any sort of laws being passed that hurt them."

TWITTER SLAMMED FOR NOT ACTING ON CHINESE MEDIA TWEET ALLEGING COVID-19 CAME FROM 'IMPORTED FROZEN FOOD'

Rubio has warned about tech companies' power for a long time. In 2020, he cosponsored legislation to give Americans the ability to sue major tech companies like Facebook, Google and Twitter if they engage in selective censorship of political speech. China is "laughing at us," Rubio added.

"We could be talking about how we all agree that this is terrible and what is it that got in people's heads and what are the things that people believe in, conspiracy-wise ... that caused them to do these actions that we all reject," Rubio said."Instead, what we are now engaging in [is] a new front: who should be censored by five companies who no one's elected and have the power to wipe you out? As far as China's concerned, their fundamental argument is democracy doesn't work, it's messy, it's chaotic. ... Can you think of a better talking point for them?" he asked.

Rush Limbaugh: Swamp, Pelosi Scared to Death of Trump's Final Days

Radio personality Rush Limbaugh and wife Kathryn (L) attend the State of the Union address with First Lady Melania Trump on February 04, 2020

By Sandy Fitzgerald | Saturday, 09 January

Washington's "swamp" and House Speaker Nancy Pelosi are "scared out of their gourd" about President Donald Trump's remaining days in office, according to radio talk show host Rush Limbaugh.

"The hatred is visceral," Limbaugh said on his show Friday. "You can touch it. You can see it. You can see it steaming from the electrodes on these Democrats' heads. I've never seen personal animosity like this. I mean, it is almost to the point of uncontrollable and unpackageable."

House Democrats have drafted a second impeachment of Trump, several media outlets reported Friday, listing just one charge: "Incitement to insurrection" for the Washington protest on Wednesday that breached the Capitol building.

"They've gotta do this in 11 days. So they've gotta call the House together, then they got to get the Senate to go ahead and convict for this, and then they want a proviso that Trump cannot seek the presidency ever again," said Limbaugh. "That doing this is gonna pressure the cabinet and (Vice President Mike) Pence into invoking Amendment 25. But Pence has said that he's not gonna do this."

The push is coming because the "entire Washington establishment" is "scared to death of Trump," said Limbaugh.

"The four-year coup, the four-year effort to get the election results of 2016 overturned, there are all kinds of people who broke the law, all kinds of people who are quaking in their boots," he added. "They're worried silly that Trump is gonna unleash some of these classified documents."

Limbaugh also said the establishment is "terrified" that Trump will pardon people dangerous to them.

"The people in the Washington establishment, why did they want to stop Trump in the first place? Because they didn't want what they have been up to (which is no good) for years to ever come out," said Limbaugh. "They're worried to death that he's got a card or two to play here yet, including the pardon power."

He added that there was likely a "big sigh of relief" when Trump said he would not go to Biden's inauguration. "Imagine if he decided to release a bunch of classified documents right before the inauguration ceremony," said Limbaugh.

Normally, the Senate would be using the next few weeks to hold hearings on Biden's cabinet choices, Limbaugh also said, so they can be confirmed by senators on Inauguration day, but not this year.

"Two long, nervous weeks for the Democrats," Limbaugh said. "Major potential power vacuum. They are scared, folks. Do not doubt me on this."

German presidential election 1932

1925 ←	(March 1932 (first round 13 (April 1932 (second round 10	→ (West) 1949 → (East) 1949

Nominee	Paul von Hindenburg	Adolf Hitler	Ernst Thälmann
Party	Independent (DZ–SPD endorsement)	NSDAP	KPD
Popular vote	**19,359,983**	13,418,517	3,706,759
Percentage	**53.0%**	36.8%	10.2%

Vote by constituency

Hindenburg: 40–50% 50–60% 60–70% 70+%

Hitler: 40–50% 50–60%

President before election	**President-Elect**
Paul von Hindenburg Independent	Paul von Hindenburg Independent

The 1932 German presidential election was held on 13 March, with a runoff on 10 April. Independent incumbent Paul von Hindenburg won a second seven year term against Adolf Hitler of the National Socialist German Workers Party (NSDAP). Communist Party (KPD) leader Ernst Thälmann also ran and received more than ten % of the vote in the runoff. Theodor Duesterberg, the deputy leader of the World War I veterans' organization *Der Stahlhelm*, ran in the first round but dropped out of the 3RD REICH TO LAST A THOUSAND YEARS runoff. This was the second and final direct election to the office of President of the Reich (***Reichspräsident***), Germany's head of state under the Weimar Republic. 2012 Venezuelan Presidential Election

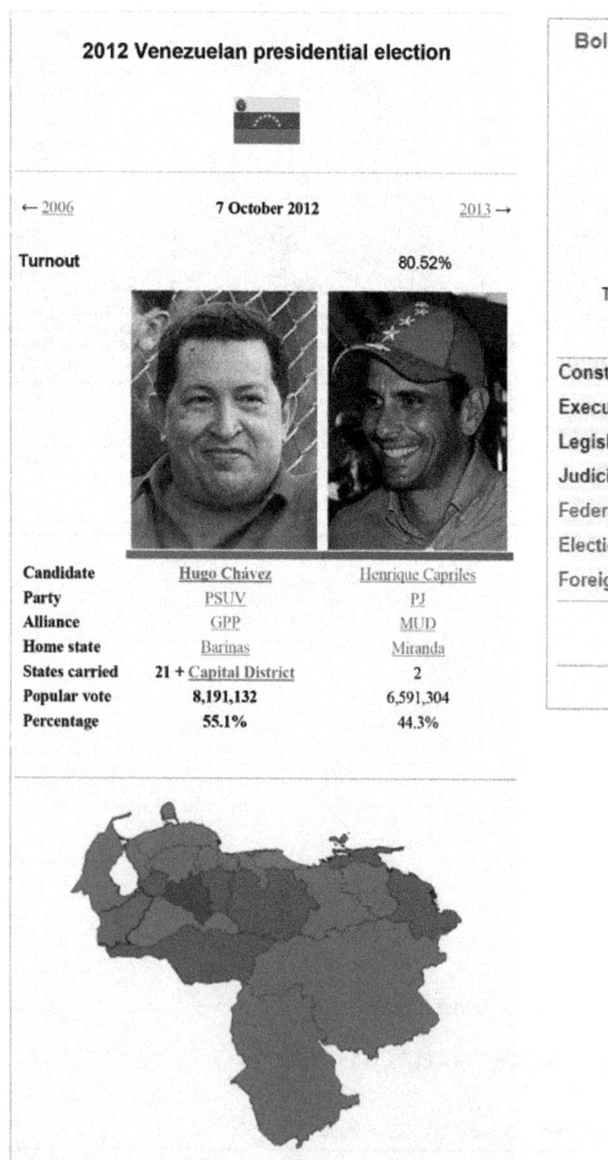

2012 Venezuelan presidential election

← 2006	7 October 2012	2013 →
Turnout		80.52%
Candidate	Hugo Chávez	Henrique Capriles
Party	PSUV	PJ
Alliance	GPP	MUD
Home state	Barinas	Miranda
States carried	21 + Capital District	2
Popular vote	8,191,132	6,591,304
Percentage	55.1%	44.3%

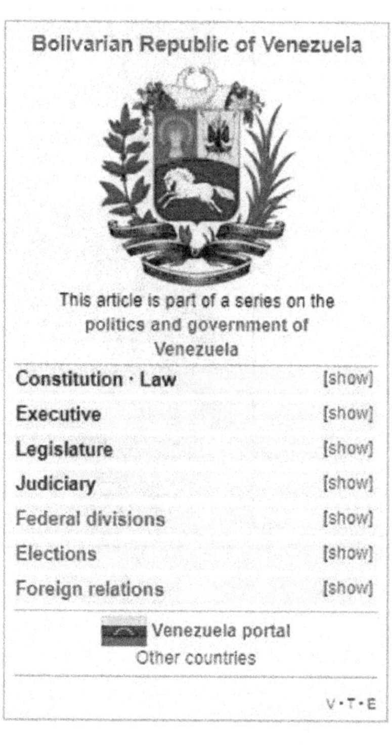

Bolivarian Republic of Venezuela

This article is part of a series on the politics and government of Venezuela

Constitution · Law	[show]
Executive	[show]
Legislature	[show]
Judiciary	[show]
Federal divisions	[show]
Elections	[show]
Foreign relations	[show]

Venezuela portal
Other countries

V · T · E

The Venezuelan presidential election of 2012 was held on 7 October 2012 (referred by local media as **7-O,) to choose a president for the six-year term beginning January 2013.**

After the approval of the Amendment No. 1 of the Constitution of Venezuela in 2009, which abolished term limits; incumbent Hugo Chávez, **representing the** United Socialist Party of Venezuela **(*Partido Socialista Unido de Venezuela*, PSUV) was able to present himself again as a candidate after his reelection in 2006. His main challenger was Governor** Henrique Capriles Radonski of Miranda, **representing** Justice First. **The candidates were backed by opposing** electoral coalitions**; Chávez by the** Great Patriotic Pole **(*Gran Polo Patriótico*, GPP), and Capriles by the opposition** Coalition for Democratic Unity **(*Mesa de la Unidad Democrática*, MUD). There were four more candidates from different parties. Capriles ran an energetic campaign, and visited each of the country's states. Throughout his campaign, Capriles remained confident that he could win the election and be the country's next President. However, Chávez consistently led most established polls, generally by large margins. In the end, his popularity remained high, and went to win the election by a comfortable margin.**

Chávez was elected for a fourth term as President of Venezuela with 55.07% of the popular vote, ahead of the 44.31% of Capriles. The elections showed a historically high turnout, above 80% of the electorate, in a country where voting is not mandatory. Although Chávez did not win the election with a huge landslide as he had previously done in 2006, **his 11-point victory over his opponent was decisive. Capriles conceded defeat as the preliminary results were known. Chávez** died only two months into his fourth term.

RED STATES MUST SECEDE TO FORM OUR OWN CONFEDERATION

ADDITIONALLY; NOT LIMITED TO; W/ PRECEDENT OF WEST VIRGINIA SECEDING FROM VIRGINIA JUNE 21, 1863; BECOMING A SEPARATE & DISTINCT STATE; 2021 RED STATE ARTICLES OF RED STATE CONFEDERATION ENCOURAGE REBELLIOUS JURISDICTIONS WITHIN; INCLUDING; BUT NOT LIMITED TO CALIFORNIA; ILLINOIS & NEW YORK TO SECEDE; & BECOME NORTH NEW YORK; SOUTH ILLINOIS; EAST CALIFORNIA; W/ MORE RED STATES**; US; STRONGER. WE ARE OF YOU; YOU ARE OF US. WE INAUGURATE PAL ZOMBIE JOE; KAMIKAZE KAMALA;** WOODCHUCK SCHMUCK SCHUMER**; THEY CALL HER THE Häagen-Dazs BEN & JERRY'S CHUNKY MONKEY KID; NANCY PELOSI; IF YOU DON'T LIKE IT; Y'ALL BE WUZ CASTIN' 1ST CINDER BLOCK; NEVER A THREAT; GET Y'ALL READY FOR OUR PROMISE TO KEEP.**

BETTER THAN US' ALL RED STATES **SECEDING FROM Y'ALL'S BLUE; IS Y'ALL'S GANGSTA BLUE HUNTER; PAL JOEY & KAMIKAZE KAMALA'S MANIPULATED PHANTOM FRAUDULENT BALLOT STUFFIN' ACT BLUE STATES SECEDING FROM RED; GOING AWAY. JONESTOWN REDUX BE IS BLUE STRYCHNINE O' BE IS PURPLE Y' ALL'S GOIN' WAY** KOOL-AID PARTY**. AFTER BE WHICH Y'ALL FINISH Y'ALL'S ASSES DROPPIN' DEAD O'D. ING FROM Y'ALL'S** PURPLE KOOL-AID **IN TIMES SQUARE; ON RODEO DRIVE & ON STATE STREET; THAT GREAT LORI LIGHTFIGHT 24/7/366 GANGSTA' HOOD STATE STREET. WHEN Y' ALL BLUE STATERS BE IS DROPPIN' DEAD FROM Y' A'LL'S PURPLE KOOL-AID & DEFUND THE POLICE DRIVE-BY O.K. CORRALS IN DA' HOOD; & O.D. ING ON Y' ALL'S PURPLE/BLUE** KOOL-AID **IN DA' MOUTH;**

WE'LL; TO US ALL; THE MAKE AMERICA GREAT AGIN' FO' US ALL BRO'S & SISTAS BE IS RED STATE MISSIONARY IMPERIALIST COLONIZERS OF DOWNTOWN BROOKLYN; RODEO DRIVE & STATE STREET; THAT CHICAGO GREAT STREET; WITH RED REPUBLICAN MISSIONARY CARPETBAGGERS BRINGIN' IN GOD & DONNIE JOHN TRUMP COLONIZERS WE TRUST; DRAININ' DA BLUE SWAMP & BE IS EBONICS PICKIN' UP WID' GOVERNMENT BE IS FO' DA' PEOPLE; BY DA' BRO'S & SISTAS BE IS BRINGIN BACK TA' Y'ALL ONE NATION UNDER GOD; WHERE & WHEN EVERY BLUE STATER DROPS DEAD; BE IS DA' GOOD LAW N' ORDER PROFIT & LOSS FREE ENTERPRISE HAPPY DAYS BE IS HEAH AGIN' LET DA' GOOD TIMES ROLL

Rasmussen: Trump's Approval Rating Rises After DC Protests

Friday, 08 January 2021 10:42 PM

The Rasmussen poll, one of the most accurate polls of the 2020 election, finds President Trump's approval is actually rising after Wednesday's protests.As Democrats move to impeachment and some establishment Republicans call for the 25th Amendment to remove Trump, the poll finds 48% approve of the President's job performance. A source close to the polling firm tells Newsmax that the rolling survey saw Trump's approval soar to 51% on Thursday night. Trump's approval has been up overall, jumping from 45% just before Christmas.

"Americans are disgusted that cities burned for months and Washington and the media did nothing," our source says, "But they still like Trump."

THIS IS WHY RED STATES MUST SECEDE. THIS LOATHSOME JACK DORSEY'S TWITTER THINKS HE"S GOING TO KICK OUT HERO; DONALD JOHN TRUMP; OUR SECOND GREATEST PRESIDENT; AFTER ABRAHAM LINCOLN; AND KICK 76 MILLION OF US WHO VOTED FOR HIM WHEN DORSEY & ZUCKERBUCKS THINK WE'RE DOWN. WE'LL FIND OUT WHAT HAPPENS TO TWITTER & FACEBOOK SCUMBAGS. NEXT THEY'LL TRY TO CUT OFF ELECTRICAL POWER TO NEWSMAX & BAN US FROM THE INTERNET **Nikki Haley Compares Trump Twitter Ban to Chinese 'Silencing'**

Former U.N. Ambassador Nikki Haley speaks in support of Georgia Republican Senate candidates David Perdue, R-Ga. and Kelly Loeffler, R-Ga., during a campaign rally on Dec. 20, 2020 in Cumming, Georgia.)

By Sandy Fitzgerald

Former U.N. Ambassador Nikki Haley Friday compared Twitter's permanent suspension of President Donald Trump's Twitter account to the "silencing" of people in communist china.

"Silencing people, not to mention the President of the US, is what happens in China not our country," Haley said on her Twitter account**, adding the hashtag #Unbelievable. Her comments come after she earlier in the week criticized Trump over the violence in the Capitol building, calling his conduct during a rally before the incidents unfolded "deeply disappointing," reports** Fox News**.**

"President Trump has not always chosen the right words. He was wrong with his words in Charlottesville, and I told him so at the time," she said during a Republican National Committee (RNC) dinner in Florida on Thursday. "He was badly wrong with his words yesterday. And it wasn't just his words. His actions since Election Day will be judged harshly by history."

Haley, a former South Carolina governor who served in the Trump administration between 2017 and the end of 2018, tweeted her comments comparing Twitter to China shortly after the tech giant announced it would suspend the president's account permanently over tweets he'd made following the riot. Twitter said it was suspending the president after determining two tweets violated its site policy against messages glorifying violence.

One of the tweets read that "the 76,000,000 great American Patriots who voted for me, AMERICA FIRST, and MAKE AMERICA GREAT AGAIN, will have a GIANT VOICE long into the future. They will not be disrespected or treated unfairly in any way, shape or form!!!" In the other, Trump said he won't be attending President-elect Joe Biden's inauguration.

"These two Tweets must be read in the context of broader events in the country and the ways in which the President's statements can be mobilized by different audiences, including to incite violence, as well as in the context of the pattern of behavior from this account in recent weeks," Twitter said in its announcement. "We have determined that these Tweets are in violation of the Glorification of Violence Policy and the user @realDonaldTrump should be immediately permanently suspended from the service." Several other Republicans have criticized the riot and Trump's conduct but said they consider suspending the president's account as censorship.

Speaker Pelosi Calls For Pres. Trump's Prosecution in 60 Minutes Interview

–

By Charlie McCARTHY

Speaker Rep. Nancy Pelosi, D-Calif., walks with 60 Minutes correspondent Lesley Stahl of CBS News in a hallway at the U.S. Capitol Jan. 8, 2021 in Washington, DC. SHE'S TALKING ABOUT EVERYONE WHO VOTED FOR HIM.

Speaker of the House Nancy Pelosi said President Donald Trump should be prosecuted and that "nothing is off the table" in an interview with 60 Minutes to be televised Sunday.

Pelosi and fellow Democrats have called for Trump's impeachment in the aftermath of Wednesday's riot at the Capitol.

"Sadly, the person that's running the Executive branch is a deranged, unhinged, dangerous president of the United States," Pelosi said in an excerpt aired Friday on the "CBS Evening News."

"And we're only a number of days until we can be protected from him. But he has done something so serious that there should be prosecution against him."

Demonstrators protesting the presidential election results stormed the Capitol building during a joint session of Congress that met to certify the Electoral College votes. Earlier in the day, Trump addressed a rally of supporters and told them, "We will never give up. We will never concede."

The president and his supporters have said alleged voter fraud resulted in Joe Biden winning the election. Biden will be inaugurated on Jan. 20.

Pelosi, speaking with correspondent Lesley Stahl, said action should be taken against Trump despite only days remaining for his administration.

The 25th Amendment allows for removing the president from office if the vice president and a majority of the president's cabinet or Congress agree to the action. Vice President Mike Pence was said to be opposed to invoking the amendment.

It was suggested to Pelosi the 25th Amendment was off the table.

"No, it isn't," she said. "Nothing is off the table."

Three House Democrats said they plan to introduce an article of impeachment against Trump on Monday for incitement of insurrection.

Banned From Twitter, Trump Tries Posting Pitch to Build Out His Own Platform BEING A REPUBLICAN VIOLATES TWITTER & FACEBOOK RULES.

Rush To Judgment On Trump? Multiple Leftists Arrested For Capitol Riot

When the Capitol riots happened on Jan. 6, the blame of President Trump was all over.

Supposedly, he was the instigator. Supposedly, he'd egged the rioters on. The tape of his urging his supporters to stay strong and fight was Exhibit A in the press, and with no skepticism whatsoever, House Speaker Nancy Pelosi declared Trump guilty and rushed a crazily hasty second impeachment just days before Trump's exit. She declared it was all about holding Trump "accountable" and she added, that her explicit aim at the uselessly late date was to prevent him from ever running from public office again.

Never mind what the voters might want. In more ways than one, in Pelosi's addled mind, their votes don't count. The press also rushed to judgment, even the Wall Street Journal's editorial writers, claiming that Trump's political capital and credibility was now gone and he'd never run for president again.

But as news of the arrests comes out, showing who these branded Trump so-called supporters are, the conventional argument is starting to splinter apart. **The arrests made in the riots case are starting to show the kind of people who like to riot, which is to say extreme leftists.**

Start with this freak, as reported by Fox News:
A left-wing activist who told Fox News last week that he'd followed a pro-Trump mob into the Capitol in order to "document" the siege is now the subject of a criminal complaint in connection with his alleged participation, according to the U.S. Justice Department.

John Sullivan can allegedly be heard egging on protesters in video he provided to the FBI, according to a federal criminal complaint. He has also shared the video to his YouTube and Twitter accounts under the pseudonym Jayden X.

He was charged Thursday in federal court in Washington after being arrested by the FBI. He remains in custody in Toeele County, in his home state of Utah, on a U.S. Marshals Service hold request.

The Epoch Times reports that he was a Black Lives Matter activist. Andy Ngo notes that he's been busted for BLM riot activity, too. GatewayPundit reported that he was caught on video bragging about posing as a Trump supporter.

He had a pal, too, from CNN. According to this report from TrendingPolitics:

On Thursday night, damning new footage showed CNN's Jade Sacker inside of the Capitol with John Sullivan, the BLM member who was charged by federal prosecutors for inciting chaos on January 6th. Sacker co-conspired with the liberal activist in order to cause chaos and make Trump supporters look bad.

The shocking video shows her and Sullivan celebrating and shouting "We did it!" when they got the footage they were looking for. When she asked Sullivan if he was filming, he said was going to delete it. He never did.

Trending Politics ran a tweet of the actual video, and described this:

As you can see, Sacker and Sullivan are overjoyed with the fact that they got footage of Trump supporters "rioting".

"Is this not gonna be the best film you've ever made in your life?!" Sullivan asks her.

Verified twitter user Amuse breaks everything down in further detail in a series of tweets.

"To make this clear. CNN was embedded with BLM/Antifa pretending to be Trump supporters taping them incite a riot. This is freaking huge. If CNN is allowed to maintain its press access anywhere in DC there needs to be a serious overhaul of our entire system," he tweeted. Here's another one, who showed up with furs, **and also got himself arrested. According to the New York Post:**

Aaron Mostofsky was busted Tuesday at his brother's house in Brooklyn by federal agents on multiple charges, including theft of government property for allegedly stealing a police riot shield and bulletproof vest, the source said. Mostofsky, who is the son of Shlomo Mostofsky, a Supreme Court judge and a prominent figure in the Orthodox Jewish community, was photographed with both items.

Video circulating on Twitter following Mostofsky's arrest shows FBI agents swarming the home and carting out what appeared to be the fur pelts and walking stick he had on him during the insurrection.

His politics? According to this report, registered Democrat.

Even the press is starting to notice that the pieces aren't fitting together. Rather than a picture of all wicked and crazed Trump supporters, charging the Capitol, leftist news outfit Bloomberg reported that its survey of various parties involved, including those who died or were arrested, didn't paint the desired picture. Conclusion?

Many of those shown in news footage had no party affiliation and voted sporadically, if at all.

Bloomberg's survey of the players showed that only the people who died of medical emergencies seemed to be fully normal Republican voters — the rest didn't vote at all, voted sporadically, voted Libertarian, Independent or Democrat, and in general were fringe players. Bloomberg, missing that obvious conclusion, seemed to consider these mostly arrested characters "Trump's people" and Trump's "base," in a bid to still pin the riots on Trump. But how anyone who votes Democrat or doesn't vote at all could be a part of Trump's rise and the huge crowds he draws was never actually explained. Trump supporters ... vote for Trump. This isn't rocket science. More and more, it looks like Trump was framed. This, in addition to transcripts not bearing out the claims that Trump called for an attack on the Capitol, as well as the inconvenient timeline — the FBI put out warnings of plans for disturbances days earlier, and the attack on the Capitol began before President Trump finished speaking and probably uttered the words the Democrats literally impeached him on. **It was a rush to judgment, a failure to look at facts. It happened in the aftermath of the event, and it turns out Trump had little or nothing to do with it. Even House Republican leader Kevin McCarthy blamed Trump for the riots. But he, too,disgracefully rushed to judgment, so we await his apology, please.**

The rush to judgment, incidentally, didn't affect just President Trump, who got a second impeachment from it. There were many rushes to judgment in this leftist hysteria.

Here's a blameless man named David Quintavalle, a retired Chicago firefighter, who was falsely accused of being the person who hurled the fire extinguisher that killed police officer Brian Sicknick, who by the way, really was a Trump supporter.

According to The Patch of Chicago: The retired Chicago firefighter from Mount Greenwood — whom social media trolls called a "terrorist" and accused of fatally wielding a fire extinguisher that killed a cop as a mob of Trump-supporting insurrectionists stormed the U.S. Capitol on Jan. 6 — was grocery shopping and celebrating his wife's birthday in Chicago, Patch has learned.

Twitter exploded with unsubstantiated claims Tuesday that Quintavalle — who retired from the fire department in 2016 after 32 years — was the bearded "#extinguisherman" in a surveillance video wearing a "CFD" stocking cap wanted for questioning and "soon to be arrested" by the FBI regarding the fatal beating of U.S. Capitol Police officer Brian Sicknick. *Quintavalle had all his receipts and proofs. But this is how the left's rush to judgment went for him:*

By Tuesday night, Quintavalle began getting angry calls from people saying he's a "f—— murderer" who belongs in jail. TV news reporters had staked out his house. Chicago police dispatched a patrol car to keep watch overnight, as well, his lawyer said. Some folks got ridiculed for tweeting that Quintavalle wasn't "the guy" and his facial features don't match those of the man wanted for questioning by the FBI. One post claimed that tweets disputing Quintavalle's involvement in the U.S. Capitol insurrection were pushed by

trolling Twitter "bots with practically no followers coming out of the woodwork."

This is a hell of a sorry picture.

The facts will continue to roll out and the picture that emerges will likely start to show that these rioters were hardly "Trump's people" as a rule, or people who were egged on by Trump. They were, in general, leftists, political fringers and people who like to go to riots. There remains to be news of whether and how this fiasco was plotted out but expect news of that to roll out. **That leaves Congress and all the jerks who voted for impeachment of President Trump looking like boobs and losers. They've hitched their star to this leftist impeachment obsession, and now have seen it falling flat. Now they are about to sully and overshadow Joe Biden's first days in office with increasingly discredited charges against President Trump and rest assured, the voters will notice just how bad it is. This rush to judgment will trash their own legacies for history.**

READ ABOUT THIS LINCOLN PROJECT FOUND TRUMP HATER

REPORT: Lincoln Project Cofounder John Weaver Acknowledges Sending 'Inappropriate' Messages To Multiple Men

John Weaver, a co-founder of the Lincoln Project and former top advisor to Republicans John McCain and John Kasich, apologized Friday for sending "inappropriate" messages to multiple men, Axios reported.

"To the men I made uncomfortable through my messages that I viewed as consensual mutual conversations at the time: I am truly sorry," Weaver told Axios. "They were inappropriate and it was because of my failings that this discomfort was brought on you."

"The truth is that I'm gay," he reportedly said. "And that I have a wife and two kids who I love. My inability to reconcile those two truths has led to this agonizing place." (RELATED: Young Americans for Liberty Fires President Amid Allegations Of Sexual Misconduct)

Conservative writer Ryan Girdusky alleged Jan. 9 on Twitter that Weaver had offered jobs to young men in exchange for sex. Since then, multiple men have accused Weaver on social media of sending them unsolicited sexual messages, sometimes along with job offers or political opportunities.

Maybe I should start talking about one of the founding members of the Lincoln Project offering jobs to young men in exchange for sex… his wife is probably interested https://t.co/vAtUS9aPPl

— Ryan James Girdusky (@RyanGirdusky) January 9, 2021

After the allegations surfaced, the Lincoln Project appeared to scrub Weaver from their website.

Weaver took a medical leave of absence from the Lincoln Project, anti-Trump super PAC, over the summer of 2020, Axios reported. He told the outlet that he would not be rejoining the Lincoln Project.

"The project's defense of the Republic and fight for democracy is vital," Weaver said according to the report.

"While I am taking full responsibility for the inappropriate messages and conversations, I want to state clearly that the other smears being leveled at me … are categorically false and outrageous," he continued.

"John's statement speaks for itself," a Lincoln Project spokesman told Axios.

WILL WE SECEDE FROM THIS?

Katie Couric wants to know how we will 'deprogram people who signed up for the cult of Trump'

Couric celebrated Trump's social media ban and called for his impeachment

Paul Sacca

During her appearance on "Real Time with Bill Maher," Katie Couric attacked Republican members of Congress and President Donald Trump. Couric went so far as to ask, "How are we going to really almost deprogram these people who have signed up for the cult of Trump?"

The former co-anchor of NBC's "Today" show besieged Republican lawmakers who are friendly toward Trump. Couric appeared to assail Republicans such as Colorado Rep. Lauren Boebert, who vowed to carry her gun into work in Washington, D.C.

Following the riots at the Capitol, metal detectors were installed in the building. Several Republican Congress members, including Boebert, objected to the metal detectors and searches.

"It is so shocking. ... Not only are they not conceding, Bill, but their thoughts – that there might have been some collusion among members of Congress, some are refusing to go through magnetometers ... to check for weapons, they're not wearing masks during this siege," Couric told Bill Maher.

Earlier this week, Rep. Ayanna Pressley (D-Mass.) also slammed GOP Congress members for not wearing face masks during the chaos at the Capitol on Jan. 6. Pressley proclaimed that Republicans not wearing face masks was "criminal behavior," and argued that the maskless politicians were engaging in "chemical warfare."

Couric continued her condemnation of Republicans, "I mean, it's really bizarre, isn't it, when you think about how AWOL so many of these members of Congress have gotten. But I also think some of them are believing the garbage that they are being fed 24/7 on the internet, by their constituents, and they bought into this big lie."

Couric declared, "And the question is how are we going to really almost deprogram these people who have signed up for the cult of Trump."

Couric then called for the impeachment of Trump.

"But Bill, if you commit a crime and then you move, does that means we're not going to charge you with a crime because you're moving out of the neighborhood? I mean, it's ludicrous," Couric argued. "I think there have to be guardrails on presidential power. He incited violence. ... He was really, really inciting violence."

Couric fantasized about a "Hollywood ending" to Trump's administration where Senate Majority Leader Mitch McConnell (R-Ky.) "comes out as the hero" to convict the president.

Couric celebrated Trump being banned from social media platforms, such as Twitter and Facebook.

"You're not allowed to yell fire at a crowded theater, so if you're inciting violence and you're spreading lies that are getting people fired up, encouraging violence, I think there should be some standard," Couric said of the banning of Trump on social media.

The career talk show host gleefully welcomed Joe Biden as the next president, calling his inauguration an "important symbol of closing the chapter on Donald Trump."

Maher cautioned that the 78-year-old Biden should hold a small, indoor inauguration ceremony to protect against a potential coronavirus risk.

"Joe Biden – he's a friggin' tragedy magnet," Maher remarked. "He broke his foot playing with his dog. I mean, his eye exploded from blinking. We have got to treat this guy like the baby in 'Children of Men.'"

Couric downplayed Biden's previous health issues, while at the same time maligning Trump's physique.

"I think he's pretty vibrant and in good shape," Couric defended Biden. "You saw him run across the stage when he made that speech. ... I mean, compare his physical fitness to Donald Trump, hello!"

Couric will be a guest host on "Jeopardy!," attempting to fill in for the late Alex Trebek.

US Loses 140,000 Jobs, First Monthly Loss Since Spring BIDEN ECONOMIC COLLAPSE ALREADY BEGUN

U.S. employers shed jobs last month for the first time since April, cutting 140,000 positions, clear evidence that the economy is faltering as the viral pandemic tightens its grip on consumers and businesses. At the same time, the unemployment rate stayed at 6.7%, the first time it hasn't fallen since April.

Friday's figures from the Labor Department suggest that employers have rehired roughly all the workers they can afford to after having laid off more than 22 million in the spring — the worst such loss on record. With consumer spending barely growing over the past few months, most companies have little incentive to hire. The economy still has 9.9 million fewer jobs than it did before the pandemic sent it sinking into a deep recession nearly a year ago.

The pandemic will likely continue to weaken the economy through the winter and perhaps early spring. But many economists, along with the Federal Reserve's policymakers, say they think that once the coronavirus vaccines are more widely distributed, a broad recovery should take hold in the second half of the year. The incoming Biden administration, along with a now fully Democrat-controlled House and Senate, is also expected to push rescue aid and spending measures that could accelerate growth.

For now, the renewed surge in virus cases, as well as cold weather, has caused millions of consumers to avoid eating out, shopping and traveling. Reimposed business restrictions have shut down numerous restaurants, bars, and other venues. Economists at TD Securities estimate that more than half the states have restricted gatherings to 10 or fewer people, up from about a quarter in September. New York City and California, among others, placed strict new limits on restaurants last month.

In recent months, retailers have been especially hurt by the slump in consumer spending. Debit and credit card data tracked by JPMorgan Chase, based on 30 million accounts, shows that Americans slowed their purchases during the holiday shopping season. Such spending was 6% lower in December compared with a year ago. That was worse than in October, when card spending was down just 2% from the previous year.

Restaurant traffic has also dropped, according to the reservations website OpenTable. Seated dining is down 60% this week compared with a year ago, much worse than two months earlier, when they were down about 35%. The $900 billion financial aid package that Congress enacted last month should also help propel a recovery, economists say. It will provide a $300-a-week federal jobless benefit on top of an average weekly state benefit of about $320. In addition, millions of Americans stand to receive $600 payments, and the Treasury Department said Thursday that 8 million of those payments were going out this week.

Late Wednesday, Goldman Sachs upgraded its forecast for economic growth this year to a robust 6.4% from its previous estimate of 5.9%. Its upgrade was based in part on the expectation that the Biden administration will implement more stimulus.

Still, for now, about 11 million people are officially unemployed. Millions more have stopped looking for work, either because they're discouraged about their prospects or worried about contracting the coronavirus, and aren't counted as unemployed.

Friday's monthly jobs report, the last of Donald Trump's presidency, shows that the nation has 3 million fewer jobs than it did four years earlier. That makes Trump the first president since Herbert Hoover (1929-1933), early in the Great Depression, to preside over a net loss of jobs. All the job losses during the Trump administration occurred after the pandemic struck. Before then, the unemployment rate had fallen to a 50-year low of 3.5%. Still, Trump had pledged to create 25 million jobs in four years.

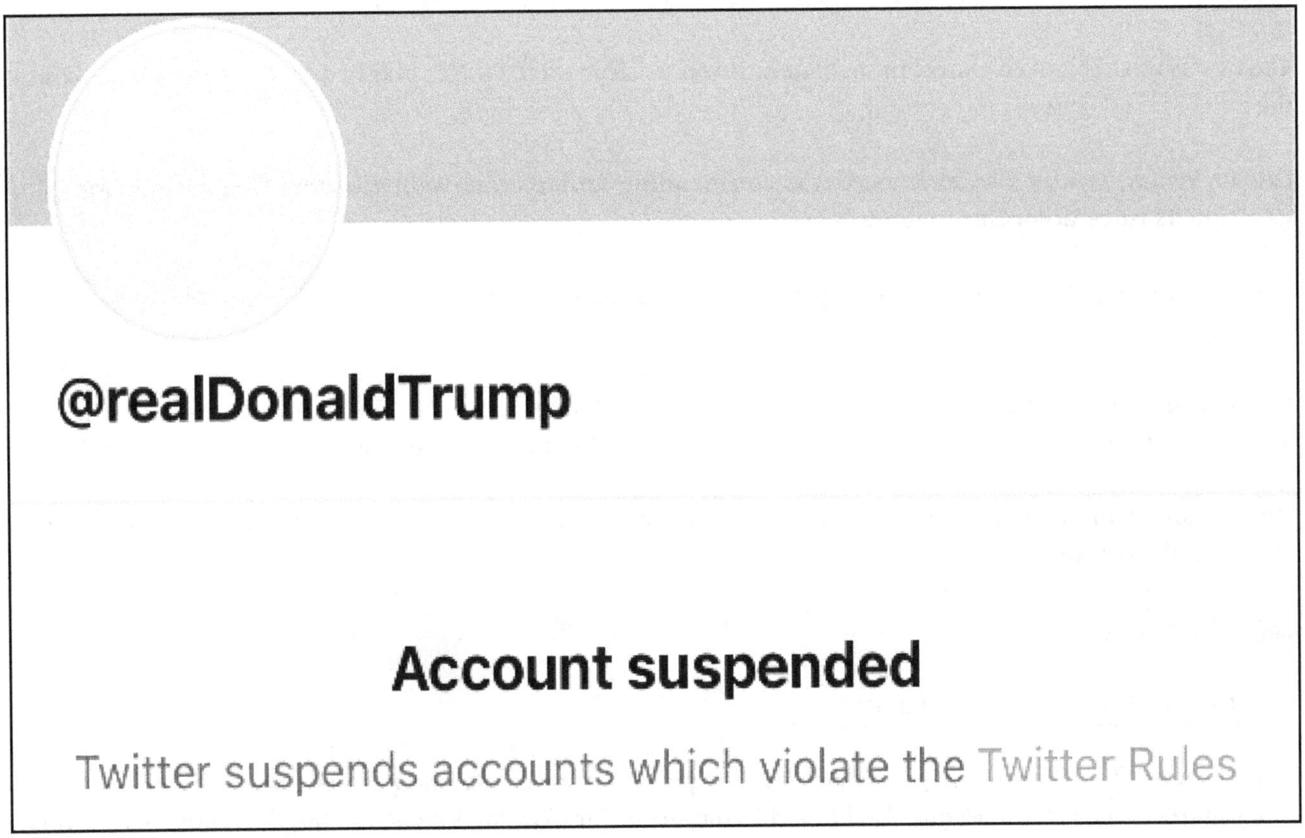

@realDonaldTrump

Account suspended

Twitter suspends accounts which violate the Twitter Rules

By Charlie MCarthy

Being permanently banned from Twitter on Friday didn't stop President Donald Trump from reaching followers.

Trump used the government-owned @POTUS account to criticize Twitter and say he and allies will look into the possibilities of building another social media messaging platform.

"As I have been saying for a long time, Twitter has gone further and further in banning free speech, and tonight, Twitter employees have coordinated with the Democrats and Radical Left in removing my account from their platform, to silence me -- and YOU, the 76,000,000 great …" Trump wrote per CNBC.

"… patriots who voted for me. Twitter may be a private company, but without the government's gift of Section 230 they would not exist for long. I predicted this would happen. We have been negotiating with various other sites, and will have a big announcement soon, while we …

"... also look at the possibilities of building out our own platform in the near future. We will not be SILENCED! Twitter is not about FREE SPEECH. They are all about promoting a Radical Lefty platform where some of the most vicious people in the world are allowed to speak freely ...:

The tweets were removed almost immediately. It was unclear what Twitter planned to do, if anything, about the @POTUS account.

Late on Friday, Twitter also announced it was suspending Trump's campaign account @TeamTrump for violating its rules, according to Reuters.

Earlier in the day, Twitter announced it permanently was suspending Trump's @realDonaldTrump personal account.

"After close review of recent Tweets from the @realDonaldTrump account and the context around them we have permanently suspended the account due to the risk of further incitement of violence," Twitter said.

"In the context of horrific events this week, we made it clear on Wednesday that additional violations of the Twitter Rules would

Rep. Taylor Greene to Newsmax: Time to Wear MAGA Hat Proudly

By Brian Trusdell | Friday, 08 January

Newly elected Rep. Marjorie Taylor Greene of Georgia on Friday condemned protesters who breached the U.S. Capitol earlier this week but also blasted Republicans for blaming President Donald Trump, suggesting their statements are hypocritical.

Speaking to Newsmax TV on Friday, the 46-year-old Taylor Greene, who represents the 14th Congressional District in the northwest corner of Georgia, ridiculed Republicans who have either said Trump incited or encouraged Wednesday's violence.

"He did not call for it. He did not cause it. And I'm tired of all of that," Taylor Greene said on "Spicer & Co." "And Republicans who are abandoning him, that are blaming him, and basically they're going the way with the Democrats are the same Republicans that hated him in the first place and then rode in on his coattails just because it was politically convenient for them."

Taylor Greene called for Republicans to rally around Trump. "It is not time to be embarrassed or throw away your MAGA hat," she said. "Now is the time to wear it and wear it proudly because the accomplishments of President Trump over the past four years for our county and the American people are absolutely incredible and so much to be thankful for and so much to be proud of.

"I think it's time for all of us to be strong and to be proud because we aren't the party of violence. They are. They're the party with antifa and BLM ... for the past year."

BLOODS & CRIPS; THE RIGHTEOUS HAVE USED VIOLENCE TO CLEANSE THE WORLD OF EVIL BULLIES LIKE WE HAVE IN THE USA TODAY Politics

EXCLUSIVE: Senior Trump Advisers Anticipated Twitter Ban, Urged Trump To Switch To Parler In Early 2020 THIS IS WHAT WE'LL ALL DO, IMMEDIATELY

Anders Hagstrom & Henry Rodgers
January 08, 2021

Former Trump campaign manager Brad Parscale urged President Donald Trump in early 2020 to invest heavily in an account on the Parler social media app in anticipation of being banned from Twitter and Facebook, a former senior Trump campaign adviser told the Daily Caller on Friday.

The adviser said Parscale foresaw that Twitter and Facebook would "most likely" ban the president before leaving office, an event that ultimately came to pass Friday**. Parscale made the case for Parler, a social media company that markets itself on free speech absolutism, to Trump at a Cabinet room meeting in early 2020, the adviser said. The plan received pushback from senior adviser Jared Kushner and was ultimately tabled in July with Parscale's departure from the campaign, the adviser said.**

Another former senior Trump campaign official confirmed that Parscale was pushing Trump toward Parler and warned him that bans were likely.

If it had been enacted, Parscale's plan would have seen a drastic shift in where Americans go to view real-time comments from the president, the adviser said. Parscale suggested that Trump post messages to Parler a full hour prior to posting them on Twitter or Facebook, causing not only his followers to transfer away from mainstream platforms but the media as well, accoridng to the adviser.

"This suggestion from Parscale would have prevented the total embarrassment of the POTUS being banned today," the adviser said. (RELATED: Trump Says He Was 'Outraged' By Supporters Storming Capitol, Is Now Focused On 'Smooth' Transition Of Power)

Twitter and Facebook have both taken action to crack down not only on Trump himself but also on numerous other pro-Trump accounts they say spread conspiracies and incite violence. Google also banned Parler from its app store, and Apple has issued an ultimatum threatening to do the same.

Trump released a statement railing against Twitter's decision to ban him Friday evening, though he did say he "predicted" the ban was incoming.

"As I have been saying for a long time, Twitter has gone further and further in banning free speech, and tonight, Twitter employees have coordinated with the Democrats and the Radical Left in removing my account from their platform, to silence me — and YOU, the 76,000,000 great patriots who voted for me," Trump said. "Twitter may be a private company, but without the government's gift of Section 230 they would not exist for long."

"I predicted this would happen," he added. "We have been negotiating with various other sites, and will have a big announcement soon, while we also look at the possibilities of building out our own platform in the near future. We will not be SILENCED."

"YOU WILL ROT FROM WITHIN"

SECESSION BECAUSE OF SLAVERY IN 1861

2021 RED SLAVES ARE SLAVES TO BLUE STATES

UNION TO WHICH WE HAVE BEEN FAITHFUL IS AT AN END. REASON DICTATES; CONSCIENCE DEMANDS; GOVERNMENT WE WALKED INTO; NOW A DEMOCRAT REICH; ONCE A MEADOW; NOW A CESSPOOL; MOCKING LIBERTY & PURSUIT OF CLASSIC AMERICAN DREAM HAPPINESS; DIGITALLY CONTROLLING BROWSER SEARCH FREE EXCHANGE OF THOUGHTS & IDEAS; SECTION 230 FACEBOOK & TWITTER; VOODOO ALGORISMS; THAT LAY WASTE TO FREE PEOPLE NOW IN CHINA; SOON HERE; PAL JOEY KAMIKAZE KAMALA BLUE ALLIANCE WITH HAVANA; CARACAS; TEHRAN & XI JINPING; POLICE STATE BLUE BILL de BLASIO; LORI LIGHTFOOT & NANCY PELOSI NEW YORK CHICAGO & L.A. 24/7/366 NIGHT OF THE LIVING DEAD

WEST VIRGINIA SECEDED FROM VIRGINIA JUNE 20, 1863. UNION IN WHICH WE'VE BEEN UNITED; PAST POINT OF NO RETURN. RED STATES NOW CALL BALLS & STRIKES. WHEN BLUE STATES STEAL THE PRESIDENCY & GIVE IT TO DEMOCRAT WHORES WORSE THAN FIDEL CASTRO; BLUE STATES CAN REMAIN UNITED AMONG YOURSELVES; WITHOUT US. ROT FROM WITHIN. WE ARE NO LONGER OF YOU. YOU ARE NO LONGER OF US

子防化学防细菌掛图

OUR LINE; YOUR SAND; OR STOP READING NOW

THIS WOMAN IS THE RED STATE MARTYR FREEDOM HERO WE WILL NOT LET HER DIE IN VAIN
Unarmed Woman Shot to Death by Capitol Police Unarmed, Air Force Vet

Police officers in riot gear work to disperse protesters who are gathering at the U.S. Capitol Building

By Brian Trusdell

Capitol Police shot and killed a woman protester during the chaos and storming of the U.S. Capitol on Wednesday, the New York Post reported citing unidentified law enforcement sources.

The Post said the woman – identified by Fox News as 14-year Air Force veteran Ashli Babbit of San Diego – was draped in red, white and blue when she was shot. NO COMMENT FROM JOE BIDEN WHO IGNORED THIS MURDER OF OUR MARTYR. **Photos of her laying on the floor, on top of what looks like a Trump flag, show her being treated by police with chest compression, apparently trying to stop the bleeding.**

She was transported via stretcher with blood streaming from her mouth and later died at a local hospital.

Video of the incident**, included in the Post story, shows a mob of people crowding around a double door when a single shot can be heard. The video, which shows the scene from several feet behind the woman and with several others in between, moves forward to show police administering aid with other officers yelling amid the chaos for others to get back because the police are trained to treat her.**

In another video of the shooting, **from a side angle near the double doors,** the sound of the single gunshot **is** heard before several people immediately clear the area and a voice can be heard saying, "We have an active shooter. There is an active shooter here. Get her down." Another voice can be heard asking for a flashlight.

Fox reported, citing Washington Fox affiliate WTTG, that Babbit's husband told the station his wife was an avid supporter of President Donald Trump

San Diego woman fatally shot inside US Capitol was 14-year veteran and 'strong supporter' of Trump
FAKE NEW MEDIA & BIDEN IGNORES THIS

Ashli Babbitt served four tours with U.S. Air Force; MURDERED FOR BEING AN AMERICAN PATRIOT

A woman was fatally shot Wednesday inside the U.S. Capitol building when a group of Trump supporters stormed the building following a rally protesting the outcome of the 2020 presidential election won by President-elect Joe Biden.

Graphic videos circulated on the internet showing the woman when she was struck along with the chaos of the scene, and now her identity has been revealed.

What are the details?

Ashli Babbitt is the name of the victim. KUSI-TV reported that "she was a 14 year veteran, she served four tours with the U.S. Air Force, and was a high level security officer throughout her time in service."

Babbitt's husband spoke with the outlet, who relayed that his wife was "a strong supporter of President Trump and was a great patriot to all who knew her."

WTTG-TV reporter Lindsay Watts also confirmed Babbitt's identity by speaking with her family. Watts tweeted out a photo of the veteran, saying Babbitt "owned a business with her husband" who "did not come to DC" with her. Babbitt's mother-in-law told Watts, "I really don't know why she decided to do this."

Authorities are still investigating the incident and have not released the details surrounding Babbitt's death, including who shot the victim or if anyone has been arrested.Videos of the shooting viewed by TheBlaze are too graphic to publish, but continue to circulate social media. Fox News host Tucker Carlson took the same stance in his commentary over the incident.

During the siege of the Capitol, protesters stormed the Senate chambers. Video footage of the shooting appears to show Babbitt outside the doors of the House chamber, and shows her attempting to climb through a window into the chamber when a shot is heard and she drops to the ground. She died later at a local hospital.

Trump Supporters Take Protests to Statehouses Across US

A supporter of President Trump speaks with riot police during a protest Wednesday in THE EPICENTER OF THE PROGESSIVE DEMOCRAT LEFT *Salem, Oregon.*

Supporters of President Donald Trump staged rallies at statehouses across the United States on Wednesday, disrupting some official functions but remaining decidedly more subdued than protesters in Washington who stormed the U.S. Capitol to demand that Trump's election loss be overturned.

From Atlanta to Salem, Oregon, and points in between, Trump backers repeated the outgoing president's false claims WHY IS THIS FUCKEN SCUMBAG A WRITER FOR NEWSMAX **that his victory was stolen by massive voter fraud, officials and local media reported.**

In Oregon's capital, where crowds protesting in favor of Trump and against state COVID-19 restrictions burned an effigy of the Democratic governor, Kate Brown, police declared an unlawful assembly and ordered protesters to disperse. Oregon state police reported at least one person was arrested in Salem on suspicion of harassment and disorderly conduct.

There were no immediate reports of serious violence, although a news photographer was sprayed with mace or pepper spray at a rally in Salt Lake City, Utah's capital, police said.

Protesters entered the Kansas statehouse in Topeka and assembled inside the first floor of the Capitol rotunda, though they remained orderly, television station KSNT reported. State police later said the demonstrators had obtained a permit in advance.

In Denver, the Colorado capital, Mayor Michael Hancock instructed city agencies to close early "out of an abundance of caution" after about 700 demonstrators gathered at the statehouse.

In Georgia, a major courthouse complex and two other government buildings in Atlanta were ordered closed due to protests near the statehouse. Among those disrupted were aides to Georgia Secretary of State Brad Raffensperger, the Republican election official pressured by Trump in a weekend telephone call to "find" enough additional votes for Trump to win the state.

Georgia is among the states won by Democratic President-elect Joe Biden, who will take office in two weeks.

Staff left their offices early out of an abundance of caution, but Raffensperger was not there, spokesman Walter Jones.

Some state workers also went home early in Salt Lake City, in part because of the demonstration of about 400 people outside, Lieutenant Nick Street of the Utah Highway Patrol said. The event was mostly peaceful but for the assault on the news photographer, Street said.

Demonstrators posted signs on the Capitol building reading "Stop the steal!" and "Trump won!" the Salt Lake Tribune reported.

Several hundred Trump supporters also staged a "Stop the Steal" rally at the Arizona state Capitol in Phoenix, cheering and jeering while exhibiting a guillotine.

Media reported rallies in other state capitals including Little Rock, Arkansas; Tallahassee, Florida; Madison, Wisconsin; Columbia, South Carolina; and Santa Fe, New Mexico

4 Deaths Reported Around Capitol Grounds

FIRST THEY STEAL THE PRESIDENCY OF THE USA; NOW THEY MURDER US FOR DEFENDING THE DEMOCRACY WE WERE BORN INTO WHERE'S THE COMMENT FROM JOE BIDEN? NBC Washington **has reported that there were four deaths on or around the U.S. Capitol grounds Wednesday as angry supporters of President Donald Trump stormed the iconic and historic building in a protest against the certification of Electoral College votes for Joe Biden. A woman died after being shot at the Capitol; reports said she was an unarmed Air Force vet, identified by Fox News as Ashli Babbit of San Diego.**

Additionally, a woman and two men died after suffering medical emergencies around the Capitol grounds, Metropolitan Police Department Chief Robert Contee said.

The cause of death of the three who had emergencies is awaiting reports by the medical examiner, NBC's report said.

Contee said there were also some 52 arrests made in connection with the riot.D.C. Mayor Muriel Bowser extended a public state of emergency declared earlier Wednesday for some 15 days. There was a citywide curfew after the siege was quelled.

In 2020, Vote Fraud Claims Were Not 'Baseless'

By Michael Dorstewitz

Each time a member of the big media reports on someone referring to acts of fraud or even irregularities in the Nov. 3 presidential election, they describe them as "baseless claims" or "unproven."

DEMOCRAT REICH ALL PURPOSE FAVORITE IS DEBUNKED. I'D LOVE TO PERSONALLY DEBUNK DUNK ALL OF THEM FOR AN HOUR INTO CESSPOOLS; & LET THEM ALL SLOWLY GAG; CHOKE

& DROWN ON THEIR OWN EXCREMENT. THEY'LL REMINISCE ABOUT THE GOOD OLD DAYS OF TRUMP DERANGEMENT SYNDROME BEING PARADISE COMPARED TO THE RICHARD E. GLICK DERANGEMENT SYNDROME. THE BIGGEST WEAKNESS OF GUNS & RELIGION MAKE AMERICA GREAT AGAIN DEPLORABLES IS "WE'RE TOO NICE. DONALD JOHN TRUMP IS TOO NICE. HIDEKI TOJO & JULIUS & ETHEL ROSENBERG FOUND OUT HOW NICE WE ARE

Such words are included in almost wire story since election day published by the Associated Press, Reuters, Bloomberg, and others.

Actually, there are many examples of vote fraud that took place during the 2020 election, and serious evidence of voting irregularities relating to the main-in ballots.

Here is what we do know:

Nevada: The Silver State rushed a universal vote-by-mail measure through the legislature in response to the COVID-19 pandemic. The bill, known as AB 4, lacked safeguards to assure voter identity and was implemented without cleaning voter rolls of deceased voters, those who had moved, or who had become ineligible to vote.

Attorney Jesse Binnall testified before the Senate Homeland Security Committee on Dec. 16 as to what resulted.

He had proof of nearly 90,000 fraudulent or improper votes that were cast, including instances where:

- **More than 42,000 people voted multiple times.**
- **At least 1,500 people listed as "dead" voted.**
- **More than 19,000 non-residents voted.**
- **In excess of 8,000 people cast mail-in votes from non-existent addresses.**
- **Over 15,000 votes were cast from commercial or vacant addresses.**
- **Nearly 4,000 non-citizens voted.**

Considering Biden took Nevada by 33,596 votes, these allegations are serious.

Arizona: The Arizona Republican Party alleges more than 100,000 ballots might have been improperly cast in the Grand Canyon State, including some 28,000 duplicated ballots in Maricopa County alone.

Arizona GOP party chairwoman Dr. Kelli Ward also addressed in one of her video reports the subject of "fake news" outlets, that tend to mischaracterize allegations of voter fraud.

"We are trying to have integrity in our electoral process," she said, adding: "We have every right to make legal challenges." Again, only 10,457 votes separate Biden and President Donald Trump on Arizona, a 0.3% difference.

Wisconsin: President Trump's legal team sought to have some 221,000 ballots disqualified that were cast in the state's two most heavily Democratic counties — Dane and Milwaukee.

At issue were incomplete absentee ballot envelopes where clerks filled in missing information, as well as those that were issued without a proper request, and still others that were the subject of ballot harvesting.

In a narrow 4-3 ruling, the Wisconsin Supreme Court rejected the challenge, claiming the campaign was "not entitled to the relief it seeks."

The campaign filed its petition for a writ of certiorari with the U.S. Supreme Court on Tuesday.

Only 20,682 votes separate Trump and Biden in the Badger State, 0.61%.

One can hardly say this is a "baseless" claim, and pure reason has many people suspicious. Biden underperformed Obama in 80% of Wisconsin counties but hugely outperformed in just five counties to win the state.

Michigan: While the Trump campaign has made an issue of the voting systems and software used throughout the state, allegations of widespread fraud remain unproven. The Trump legal team has presented additional evidence of voter fraud and irregularities before the Michigan state Senate Oversight Committee on Dec. 1.

In one instance, a "Guard the Vote" volunteer testified he went through 30,000 of the 172,000 Detroit absentee ballots — about 17%. Some 229 were dead voters and 2,660 listed invalid addresses.

Finally, Republican poll watchers were denied access for proper ballot monitoring due to alleged COVID-19 concerns. Pennsylvania: Nothing about the Keystone State made sense.

Like Detroit, Philadelphia election officials denied Republican poll watchers adequate access into counting rooms, requiring them to seek a court order.

"Trump campaign staffers marched into the PA Convention Center with a court order giving them the right to stand 6 feet away from sorters, instead of the previously allotted 20 feet," reported CBS3 Philly reporter Alecia Reid.

Most recently, a group of 17 Republican state lawmakers released a blockbuster statement Monday, alleging 202,377 more votes were cast than there were voters who voted. State Rep. Frank Ryan, who has a background as a certified public accountant, led the investigation and released a statement.

"These numbers just don't add up, and the alleged certification of Pennsylvania's presidential election results was absolutely premature, unconfirmed, and in error," the statement said. Georgia: The biggest bombshell was a video that appears to depict news media and poll watchers being ushered out of the counting room in an Atlanta tabulation center.

After all but a few workers left, suitcases of what appear to be ballots are removed from underneath a table and are run through machines. Georgia failed to use signature verification and other measures to certify mail-in ballots. Rejection rates — not allowing non-eligible mail-in ballots — plummeted in 2020 from the 2018 election.

Other irregularities:

In addition to outright claims of fraud, state and local officials in at least four states — Wisconsin, Michigan, Pennsylvania, and Georgia — used the pandemic to make last-minute changes to their state voting laws.

The U.S. Constitution provides only each state legislature may set the time, place, and manner of elections.

This prompted Texas Attorney General Ken Paxton to file a lawsuit against the four states with the United States Supreme Court for allegedly exploiting "the COVID-19 pandemic to justify ignoring federal and state election laws and unlawfully enacting last-minute changes, thus skewing the results of the 2020 General Election." In a statement he said, "Trust in the integrity of our election processes is sacrosanct and binds our citizenry and the States in this union together. Georgia, Michigan, Pennsylvania, and Wisconsin destroyed that trust and compromised the security and integrity of the 2020 election."

Despite the fact 18 more states signed on to Texas' petition, the Supreme Court dismissed the case, citing lack of standing. Only Justices Clarence Thomas and Samuel Alito dissented.

Pompeo Stands by Trump: 'I'm Proud of What We Accomplished ... History Will Remember Us Very Well'

Kristina Wong

Secretary of State Michael Pompeo delivered a message to former Trump administration officials walking away from President Donald Trump, during a meeting with top Republican lawmakers and senior congressional staffers on Friday evening, Breitbart News learned exclusively.

"I am proud of what we've accomplished — not just in the national security, foreign policy space, which I've worked with, but the things that we've done with families, the pro-life work that we have done. These are things that will truly be historic. I think history will remember us very well for these things when the books are written," he said in remarks.

Pompeo's remarks were made at the end of a private day-long meeting by the Republican Study Committee, the largest conservative caucus within the House chaired by Rep. Jim Banks (R-IN). Lawmakers and aides discussed the conservative moment and where it goes next.

Pompeo's message was a stark contrast to that from Trump's former United Nations ambassador Nikki Haley, who told Republican National Committee members during a closed door speech on Thursday that Trump "will be judged harshly by history."

It was also a stark contrast to two Trump cabinet secretaries who have resigned in recent days — Betsy DeVos and Elaine Chao — after thousands of the president's supporters protested at the Capitol and some entered and engaged in violence or vandalism.

Pompeo said what happened was tragic but that those walking away from the president were "not listening to the American people."

"While I think we all think the violence that took place in the place where you all work in the Capitol was tragic, I've watched people walk away from this president already. And they are not listening to the American people. Not remotely," he said.

Pompeo also discussed the administration's foreign policy successes, and contrasted it with eight years under the Obama administration.

"We watched eight years of the foreign policy of the previous administration that was fantasy. Fantasy. They would enter into agreements and arrangements that weren't based on anything with the potential to be lasting, and if America First in foreign policy means anything, it means being realistic." He added:

It means this deep recognition that our sole responsibility is to protect the American people. When we do that, I am very confident we will increase security for people all around the world, we will raise others up as well. But our mission set, everyday, is to say, 'How do we make sure that everything we do secures freedom for America?' and it's gotten us to walk away from a whole bunch of things. We've walked away from the World Health Organization. We walked away from the UN Human Rights Commission. We walked away from some of the central understandings of the World Trade Organization.

Each of these things was detrimental to the American people, their prosperity, their security. We were right to do that. It's a sensibility that I think 76 million people still understand and understood in November of this year. They haven't stopped understanding, I promise you that.

Pompeo's remarks also come as House Speaker Nancy Pelosi (D-CA) has been trying to pressure Vice President Mike Pence and cabinet members to invoke the 25th Amendment and remove Trump from the presidency.

Amid reports that some of Trump's cabinet members were discussing doing so, Pompeo tweeted out a photo of himself, Director of National Intelligence John Ratcliffe, and White House National Security Adviser Robert O'Brien in a sign that he was not abandoning the president under Democratic pressure.

"Honored to work alongside @DNI_Ratcliffe and @WHNSC Robert O'Brien. Great patriots who work every day to make America and the world safer and more prosperous," he wrote.

Members also heard from Tucker Carlson earlier in the day, as well as from Larry Arnn, president of Hillsdale College, where the event took place. Carlson said he would not run for public office, according to a source in attendance.

- SMUG MARK ZUCKERBERG ZUCKERBUCKS WHOSE $600 MILLION WITH PRISCILLA CHAN

ZUCKERBUCKS GRINNING GLEEFULLY SMIRKING AFTER STABBING AMERICA IN THE BACK 9 Big Tech Platforms that Have Blacklisted President Donald Trump NEXT THEY SILENCE ALL 76 MILLION TRUMP VOTERS SENATOR JOSH HAWLEY WHO DEMANDED JANUARY 6TH INVESTIGATION OF DEMOCRAT VOTER FRAUD HAS HIS BOOK PUBLICATION CANCELLED BY KANCELLED KULTURE SIMON & SCHUSTER

Alana Mastrangelo

Nine platforms controlled by the Big Tech Masters of the Universe have blacklisted or restricted President Donald Trump.

Twitter, Google, Apple, Facebook, Instagram, YouTube, Snapchat, Pinterest, Shopify, Reddit, TikTok, Twitch, and Discord have all either banned or restricted President Trump from their platforms. The severity of action taken against Trump varies by platform.

1. Twitter On Friday, Twitter permanently banned the account of the President of the United States, Donald J. Trump. Additional bannings include his campaign account and the campaign's digital director.

2 & 3. Facebook and Instagram

On Thursday, Mark Zuckerberg announced that the Facebook and Instagram platforms would be backlisting President Trump "indefinitely."

"We believe the risks of allowing the President to continue to use our service during this period are simply too great," said Zuckerberg. "Therefore, we are extending the block we have placed on his Facebook and Instagram accounts indefinitely and for at least the next two weeks until the peaceful transition of power is complete."

4. Snapchat Snapchat suspended President Trump's account indefinitely on Wednesday. "We can confirm that earlier on Wednesday we locked President Trump's Snapchat account," a Snapchat spokesperson told The Hill.

5. Pinterest While President Trump does not have a Pinterest account, the company has nonetheless been limiting hashtags related to pro-Trump topics, such as #StopTheSteal.

"Pinterest isn't a place for threats, promotion of violence or hateful content," said a Pinterest spokesperson to Axios. "Our team is continuing to monitor and removing harmful content, including misinformation and conspiracy theories that may incite violence."

6. Shopify E-commerce store provider Shopify has banned two stores affiliated with President Trump — one run by the Trump campaign and another belonging to the Trump organization, TrumpStore.com — on Thursday, claiming they violate the platform's policies on supporting violence.

"Shopify does not tolerate actions that incite violence," said Shopify in a statement. "Based on recent events, we have determined that the actions by President Donald J. Trump violate our Acceptable Use Policy, which prohibits promotion or support of organizations, platforms or people that threaten or condone violence to further a cause. As a result, we have terminated stores affiliated with President Trump."

7. Reddit The self-proclaimed "front page of the internet," Reddit, joined the unprecedented wave of censorship by has banning an unofficial Donald Trump forum.

8. TikTok While the President does not have a TikTok account, the Chinese-owned platform is nonetheless banning videos of Trump's speeches to his supporters, claiming that the content on the grounds that they violate the company's misinformation policy.

9. Twitch Amazon-owned Twitch has also locked President Trump's account indefinitely.

"In light of yesterday's shocking attack on the Capitol, we have disabled President Trump's Twitch channel," said a Twitch spokesperson in a statement.

- *AFTER RED STATES HAVE SECEDED; THIS REVOLTING LIVESTOCK DIARRHEA BELOW & GET THEM OUT OF OUR LIFE; GAG ON THIS HIDEOUS DISHRAG UGLY PIG*

- **Anti-Sexual Harassment Group Time's Up Developing App for Women to Address Male UNLESS YOU'RE TARA READE Microagressions in Workplace**

David Ng

Coming soon to a workplace near you is a mobile app that will allow women to address male microagressions in the office. The British arm of Hollywood's Time's Up movement is reportedly developing an app that will educate women on workplace microaggressions and give them the resources to take action. Microaggressions are small social wrongs and slights that are perceived as overt acts of hostility by victim groups.

Time's Up U.K. chair Heather Rabbatts told *Variety* that once the entertainment industry "resets" following the coronavirus pandemic, it won't go back to the old way of doing things. "We want to build it in a way that speaks to our values and aspirations," she said, which include a greater focus on intersectionality — the left-wing academic theory that people exist on "intersections" of oppression based on characteristics such as gender and race.

The mobile app will be one way to achieve that goal, she said. The app will reportedly educate women on what microaggressions are, and will also provide resources for support. While the app is expected to be used within the film and TV industries at first, it will also apply to industries beyond those, *Variety* reported.

"If you have a culture where microaggression is apparent, then that contributes to a culture of silence and being complicit when there is harassment and bullying going on," Rabbatts told the trade publication. "If you don't tackle microaggression, then you can't tackle harassment and bullying."

Time's Up was founded in the wake of the Harvey Weinstein scandal and the subsequent sexual assault and harassment scandals that have taken down powerful men throughout Hollywood and the mainstream media. The organization's main U.S. operation is headed by Tina Tchen, a former Obama associate who worked as an assistant to the former president and later as chief of staff to Michelle Obama. The group is backed by a slew of Hollywood stars and Obama associates including former Obama senior adviser Valerie Jarrett, mega TV producer Shonda Rhimes, CNN personality Ana Navarro, as well as actresses Eva Longoria and Ashley Judd.

Tina Tchen is calling for the removal of President Trump from office. "Time's Up joins the chorus of bipartisan voices demanding Congress reconvene to work to do what needs to be done: remove President Trump from office immediately," she tweeted.

Time's Up recently came under criticism for its spending habits after public tax documents showed that the group spent lavishly on executive salaries but relatively little on its stated goal of fighting sexual harassment in the workplace.

Last year, the group declined to help Tara Reade, the former congressional staffer who accused Joe Biden of sexually assaulting her three decades ago.

Sen. Johnson: Electoral College Challenge Aimed to 'Protect Democratic Process'

Sen. Ron Johnson, R-Wis

Sen. Ron Johnson, R-Wis., on Sunday defended the planned challenge of the Electoral College vote certifying that Joe Biden won the presidential election, declaring it's not an attempt to thwart the democratic process, but one "to protect it."

In an interview on NBC News' "Meet The Press," **Johnson said "tens of millions of Americans that think this election was stolen. We need to get to the bottom of it."**

"We are not attempting to thwart the democratic process, we're acting to protect it," Johnson said.

"We're suggesting let's set up a ... bipartisan commission to organize all the allegations.... acknowledge the problem areas that have not been explained so that we can restore confidence in the election system," he said.

"This is an unsustainable state of affairs now. That's all we're saying. As long as someone will be objecting to this, let's propose a solution of transparency, investigation and with a commission," he said.

Host Chuck Todd challenged Johnson that it was Trump and his allies who planted the election doubt "and now you're saying 'whoa, look at this, oh my god, all these people believe what we told them.'"

But Johnson said "this fire was started back in January of 2017" and led up to the Trump impeachment, charging "the mainstream media dropped pretense of being unbiased. This fire was started when you completely ignored four investigations of Hunter Biden."

"The main stream media and that is what destroyed the credibility of the media and our institutions … so I didn't start this," he added.

"You carried that water for years," he said. "You destroyed the credibility of the press."

Hawley Defends Rationale for Contesting Election

Republican Sen. Josh Hawley is hitting back at GOP colleagues who are criticizing his attempt to overturn the presidential election won by Joe Biden.

In a lengthy email, the Missouri Republican defended his rationale for challenging President Donald Trump's defeat. He and other Republicans are planning to mount objections to the results when Congress convenes for a joint session Wednesday to confirm the Electoral College tally.

Hawley specifically defended himself against criticism from GOP Sen. Pat Toomey of Pennsylvania as he challenges that state's election results. Hawley, a Trump ally and potential 2024 presidential candidate, insisted that constituents back home have been "loud and clear" that they believe Biden's win over Trump was unfair.

"It is my responsibility as a senator to raise their concerns," Hawley wrote late Saturday.

THE TIPPING POINT OF BLUE STATES MAKING SECESSION OUR ONLY REFUSAL JANUARY 6, 2021; TO EVEN CONSIDER & OPTION TO DEBATE OUR RESPECTFUL REQUEST FOR A JOINT SESSION OF CONGRESS; THAT WAS CERTIFYING THE CLEARLY STOLEN ELECTION; DEMOCRATS SMUGLY REFUSAL TO APPOINTMENT OF (5) SENATORS & (5) HOUSE A JOINT INQUIRY OF (5) CONGRESSMEN FROM EACH PARTY; & (5) SUPREME COURT JUSTICE TRANSPARENT COMMISSION TO DISPASSIONATELY; IN DETAIL; SCRUTINIZE 2020 ELECTION FRAUD & AS NEEDED; MANDATE; BASED ON EVIDENCE; RIGOROUSLY SCRUTINIZED GEORGIA; PENNSYLVANIA; MICHIGAN; WISCONSIN; ARIZONA & NEVADA DO-OVERS. DEMOCRATS REFUSED THIS BECAUSE THEY GOT WHAT THEY WANTED; BY CALCULATED STEALING; THAT WAS PLANNED IN DETAIL LONG IN ADVANCE; WITH COVID 19 AS THEIR TEAR JERKER PRETEXT. ARTICLES OF RED STATE SECESSION FROM THE UNION WILL BE BY RED STATE LEGISLATURES & POPULAR VOTE; STATE & FEDERAL PROPERTY; INCLUDING MILITARY INSTALLATIONS REVERT TO RED STATE PROPERTY AFTER SECESSION.

AFTER (35) RED STATE LEGISLATURES PASS ARTICLES OF SECESSION; DEMOCRATS ARE IMPERVIOUS TO; AND ALWAYS SNEERINGLY MOCK & LAUGH AT OUR OLIVE BRANCHES; FIGHTING VINEGAR WITH HONEY CONSERVATIVE GOOD FAITH COMPROMISE; REASON; RIGHT, WRONG, LOGIC & FAIR PLAY; HONEST OUTREACH; US REPUBLICANS WILL RESPOND

WITH THE BRUTE RETALIATORY FAIT ACCOMPLI SECESSION THAT WILL RENDER BLUE AMERICA HAITI; BANGLADESH; VENEZUELA OR CUBA. WE WILL DICTATE THE TERMS OF WHETHER OR NOT RED STATES WILL REMAIN IN THE UNION; FROM A POSITION OF INTIMIDATING STRENGTH.

WE WILL REMAIN IN THE UNION ONLY WITH PROOF POSITIVE SCANNABLE TO INCLUDE BAR CODE; FINGERPRINT & RETINA PICTURE FEDERALLY ISSUED VOTER IDENTIFICATION AND COMPLETE DO OVER OF THE 2020 PRESIDENTIAL SENATE & HOUSE OF REPRESENTATIVES ELECTION; WITH LIVE IN PERSON VOTING ONLY WITH ARMED REPUBLICAN & DEMOCRAT POLL WATCHERS METICULOUSLY SCRUTINIZING EVERY SINGLE VOTE IN REAL TIME WITH NO OUTSIDE ZUCKERBUCKS ; TWITTER JACK DORSEY; GEORGE SOROS OR MIKE BLOOMBERG DARK MONEY ALLOWED AND ABSOLUTELY NO VOTING OTHER THAN LIVE ON-SITE PROOF POSITIVE FEDERAL ISSUE SCANNABLE PICTURE I.D.; & ABSOLUTELY & POSITIVELY ZERO MAIL OR ABSENTEE BALLOT VOTING EXCEPT FOR OVERSEAS MILITARY PERSONNEL. DEMOCRATS SAID TRUST US WITH MAIL &.OR ABSENTEE BALLOTS AND YOU FUCKED CONSERVATIVES STEALING THE PRESIDENCY; SENATE & HOUSE SEATS. NO MORE TRUST. RED STATES REMAIN UNITED WITH BLUE STATES UNDER OUR TERMS ONLY. NO MORE USING COVID 19 AS AN EXCUSE FOR MAIL VOTING. IF DEMOCRATS DON'T LIKE IT, MOVE TO IRAN. RE: IRAN; TWITTER CANCELLED DONALD TRUMP'S TWITTER ACCOUNT; BUT TO THIS DAY TWITTER ALLOW WITH ITS BLESSING THE REVOLUTIONARY IRANIAN ISLAMIC REPUBLIC WORLD EPICENTER OF TERROR IRANIAN TWITTER ACCOUNT.

THE WINNING CARD WE HOLD IS

2021 RED STATE CONTROL OF STATE LEGISLATURES.

State legislative chamber control before and after 2020 elections					
	Pre-election majority		Post-election majority		Change?
State	State Senate	State House	State Senate	State House	Y/N
Alabama	Republican	Republican	Republican	Republican	N/A[2]
Alaska	Republican	Split	Republican	TBD	TBD
Arizona	Republican	Republican	Republican	Republican	No
Arkansas	Republican	Republican	Republican	Republican	No
California	Democratic	Democratic	Democratic	Democratic	No
Colorado	Democratic	Democratic	Democratic	Democratic	No
Connecticut	Democratic	Democratic	Democratic	Democratic	No
Delaware	Democratic	Democratic	Democratic	Democratic	No
Florida	Republican	Republican	Republican	Republican	No
Georgia	Republican	Republican	Republican	Republican	No
Hawaii	Democratic	Democratic	Democratic	Democratic	No
Idaho	Republican	Republican	Republican	Republican	No
Illinois	Democratic	Democratic	Democratic	Democratic	No
Indiana	Republican	Republican	Republican	Republican	No
Iowa	Republican	Republican	Republican	Republican	No
Kansas	Republican	Republican	Republican	Republican	No
Kentucky	Republican	Republican	Republican	Republican	No
Louisiana	Republican	Republican	Republican	Republican	N/A[2]
Maine	Democratic	Democratic	Democratic	Democratic	No
Maryland	Democratic	Democratic	Democratic	Democratic	N/A[2]
Massachusetts	Democratic	Democratic	Democratic	Democratic	No
Michigan	Republican	Republican	Republican	Republican	No
Minnesota	Republican	Democratic	Republican	Democratic	No
Mississippi	Republican	Republican	Republican	Republican	N/A[2]
Missouri	Republican	Republican	Republican	Republican	No
Montana	Republican	Republican	Republican	Republican	No
Nebraska	Republican		Republican		No
Nevada	Democratic	Democratic	Democratic	Democratic	No
New Hampshire	Democratic	Democratic	Republican	Republican	Yes

New Jersey	Democratic	Democratic	Democratic	Democratic	N/A[2]
New Mexico	Democratic	Democratic	Democratic	Democratic	No
New York	Democratic	Democratic	Democratic	Democratic	No
North Carolina	Republican	Republican	Republican	Republican	No
North Dakota	Republican	Republican	Republican	Republican	No
Ohio	Republican	Republican	Republican	Republican	No
Oklahoma	Republican	Republican	Republican	Republican	No
Oregon	Democratic	Democratic	Democratic	Democratic	No
Pennsylvania	Republican	Republican	Republican	Republican	No
Rhode Island	Democratic	Democratic	Democratic	Democratic	No
South Carolina	Republican	Republican	Republican	Republican	No
South Dakota	Republican	Republican	Republican	Republican	No
Tennessee	Republican	Republican	Republican	Republican	No
Texas	Republican	Republican	Republican	Republican	No
Utah	Republican	Republican	Republican	Republican	No
Vermont	Democratic	Democratic	Democratic	Democratic	No
Virginia	Democratic	Democratic	Democratic	Democratic	N/A[2]
Washington	Democratic	Democratic	Democratic	Democratic	No
West Virginia	Republican	Republican	Republican	Republican	No
Wisconsin	Republican	Republican	Republican	Republican	No
Wyoming	Republican	Republican	Republican	Republican	No

HENRY CLAY WAS THE GREAT

COMPROMISER WHO TRIED TO KEEP THE UNION TOGETHER BEFORE THE CIVIL WAR. I, RICHARD E. GLICK, COMPROMISE TO KEEP THE UNION TOGETHER IN 2021.

Henry Clay	
Clay photographed in 1848	
United States Senator from Kentucky	
In office March 4, 1849 – June 29, 1852	
Preceded by	Thomas Metcalfe
Succeeded by	David Meriwether
In office November 10, 1831 – March 31, 1842	
Preceded by	John Rowan
Succeeded by	John J. Crittenden
In office January 4, 1810 – March 3, 1811	
Preceded by	Buckner Thruston
Succeeded by	George M. Bibb
In office December 29, 1806 – March 3, 1807	
Preceded by	John Adair
Succeeded by	John Pope
9th United States Secretary of State	

In office March 4, 1825 – March 4, 1829	
President	John Quincy Adams
Succeeded by	Martin Van Buren
7th Speaker of the United States House of Representatives	
In office March 4, 1823 – March 3, 1825	
Preceded by	Philip Barbour
Succeeded by	John Taylor
In office March 4, 1815 – October 28, 1820	
Preceded by	Langdon Cheves
In office March 4, 1811 – January 19, 1814	
Preceded by	Joseph Varnum
Member of the U.S. House of Representatives from Kentucky	
In office March 4, 1823 – March 6, 1825	
Preceded by	John Johnson
Succeeded by	James Clark
Constituency	3rd district
In office March 4, 1815 – March 3, 1821	
Preceded by	Joseph H. Hawkins
Succeeded by	Samuel Woodson
Constituency	2nd district
In office March 4, 1811 – January 19, 1814	
Preceded by	William T. Barry
Succeeded by	Joseph H. Hawkins
Constituency	2nd district (1813–1814) 5th district (1811–1813)
Personal details	
Born	April 12, 1777 Hanover County, Virginia, U.S.
Died	June 29, 1852 (aged 75) Washington, D.C., U.S.
Political party	Democratic-Republican (1797–1825) National Republican (1825–1833) Whig (1833–1852)
Spouse(s)	Lucretia Hart (m. 1799)
Children	11, including Thomas, Henry, James, John
Education	College of William and Mary

Signature	H. Clay

U.S. Speaker of the House

- War of 1812
- Second Bank of the United States
- Missouri Compromise

U.S. Secretary of State

- Corrupt bargain

U.S. Senator from Kentucky

- Nullification Crisis
- Bank War
- Whig Party
- Compromise of 1850

Presidential elections

- 1824
- 1832
- 1844

Henry Clay Sr. (April 12, 1777 – June 29, 1852) was an American attorney and statesman who represented Kentucky in both the Senate and House. He was the seventh House Speaker and the ninth Secretary of State. He received electoral votes for president in the 1824, 1832, and 1844 presidential elections. He also helped found both the National Republican Party and the Whig Party. For his role in defusing sectional crises, he earned the appellation of the "Great Compromiser" and was part of the "Great Triumvirate."

Clay was born in Hanover County, Virginia, in 1777 and launched a legal career in Lexington, Kentucky, in 1797. As a member of the Democratic-Republican Party, Clay won election to the Kentucky state legislature in 1803 and to the U.S. House of Representatives in 1810. He was chosen as Speaker of the House in early 1811 and, along with President James Madison, led the United States into the War of 1812 against Great Britain. In 1814, he helped negotiate the Treaty of Ghent, which brought an end to the War of 1812. After the war, Clay returned to his position as Speaker of the House and developed the American System, which called for federal infrastructure investments, support for the national bank, and high protective tariff rates. In 1820, he helped bring an end to a sectional crisis over slavery by leading the passage of the Missouri Compromise.

Clay finished with the fourth-most electoral votes in the multi-candidate 1824 presidential election, and he helped John Quincy Adams win the contingent election held to select the president. President Adams appointed Clay to the prestigious position of secretary of state; critics alleged that the two had agreed to a "corrupt bargain." Despite receiving support from Clay and other National Republicans, Adams was defeated by Democrat Andrew Jackson in the 1828 presidential election. Clay won election to the Senate in 1831 and ran as the National Republican nominee in the 1832 presidential election, but he was defeated by President Jackson. After the 1832 election, Clay helped bring an end to the Nullification Crisis by leading passage of the Tariff of 1833. During Jackson's second term, opponents of the president coalesced into the Whig Party, and Clay became a leading congressional Whig.

Clay sought the presidency in the 1840 election but was defeated at the Whig National Convention by William Henry Harrison. He clashed with Harrison's running mate and successor, John Tyler, who broke with Clay and other congressional Whigs after taking office upon Harrison's death in 1841. Clay resigned from the Senate in 1842 and won the 1844 Whig presidential nomination, but he was defeated in the general election by Democrat James K. Polk, who made the annexation of the Republic of Texas his key issue. Clay strongly criticized the subsequent Mexican–American War and sought the Whig presidential nomination in 1848, but was defeated by General Zachary Taylor. After returning to the Senate in 1849, Clay played a key role in passing the Compromise of 1850, which resolved a crisis over the status of slavery in the territories. Clay is generally regarded as one of the most important and influential political figures of his era.

NO MORE WILL RED STATES ABSORB 30 MILLION HAVE-NOT ALIENS TO SUBSUME OUR WEALTH & PERMANENTLY VOTE FOR THE LEFT; AT OUR EXPENSE; WHO BREAST FEED THEM; PLUS UNLIMITED IMMIGRATION; UNMONITORED ONLINE/MAIL VOTING. POLL WATCHERS WERE REFUSED SCRUTINY OF IDENTITY; QUALIFICATION TO VOTE & SIGNATURE MATCHES & VOTE VALIDITY BY TOUGH "HOOD" THUGS; THE WHITE HOUSE & (2) GEORGIA SENATE SEATS WERE STOLEN; BLUE STATES & FAKE MEDIA ENABLERS LAUGH ABOUT IT AT US. FAT UGLY PIG STACY ABRAMS GLOATS GLEEFULLY LAUGHING AT US ABOUT IT.

DEPRAVED ABORTION UNTIL BIRTH; WITH INFANTS SURVIVING ATTEMPTED ABORTION LEFT TO DIE IN MASSACHUSETTS; SOON NATIONWIDE. REINVENTION OF MARRIAGE; GENDER; GOD; WEALTH REDISTRIBUTION; THOUSANDS OF PSYCHOTIC REGULATIONS CRAMMED DOWN OUR THROATS BY UNELECTED "EXPERT" PSYCHOPATH SMUG; ADMINISTRATIVE DEEP STATE BULLIES; W/ THEIR GREEN NEW DEAL; DISTRICT OF COLUMBIA & PUERTO RICO STATES; W (4) MORE DEMOCRATIC SENATORS & ELECTORAL VOTES; SUPREME COURT PACKING. THOUSANDS MORE RED/BLUE STATE DISAGREEMENTS; CONTROLLING CONGRESS & WHITE HOUSE; BLUE STATES UNSTOPPABLE; WIN ALL DISAGREEMENTS; CASE; FORCING BREAKUP OF UNION. WE WILL REPLACE REDESIGNED SERVICES INC. SOCIAL SECURITY; MEDICARE; & MEDICAID; IN RED STATE CONFEDERACY; DARING BLUE STATE LEFT TO STOP US FROM SECEDING. LEFTIST PSYCHOSIS HAS LAID WASTE TO AMERICA WE WERE BORN INTO. BLUE STATES WANT TO MIMIC & BECOME BUDDIES W IRAN; CHINA; CUBA & VENEZUELA. THIS IS OUR RED STATE VISION. WE WILL WRITE IT. TRY TO STOP US. NOW.

President Trump Joins Call Urging State Legislators to Review Evidence and Consider Decertifying 'Unlawful' Election Results

Michael Patrick Leahy

President Trump spoke to 300 state legislators from the battleground states of Arizona, Michigan, Wisconsin, Pennsylvania, and Georgia on Saturday in a Zoom conference call hosted by Got Freedom? In which the 501 (c) (4) non-profit election integrity watchdog group urged those lawmakers to review evidence that the election process in their states was unlawful and consider decertifying the results of the November 3 presidential election.

President Trump addressed the call for 15 minutes at the invitation of former New York City Mayor Rudy Giuliani, who now serves as the president's personal attorney, and was one of the featured speakers on the call. Other featured speakers included Chapman Law School Professor John Eastman, Dr. Peter Navarro, Assistant to the President for Trade and Manufacturing (appearing in his personal capacity), John Lott, Senior Advisor, U.S. Department of Justice (also appearing in his personal capacity), and Liberty University

Law School Professor Phill Kline.

Kline, a former attorney general in Kansas, is a spokesperson for the 501 (c) (4) Got Freedom? non-profit, and also serves as director of the 501 (c) (3) Amistad Project of the Thomas More Society, an election integrity public interest law firm which is engaged in litigation regarding the 2020 election.

In a press statement released after the call, GotFreedom? said they conducted Saturday's "exclusive national briefing . . . at the request of state legislators from Michigan, Pennsylvania, and Wisconsin to review the extensive evidence of irregularities and lawlessness in the 2020 presidential election."

"A similar briefing is being scheduled in Washington, D.C. at the request of Members of Congress," the group noted. A joint session of the newly convened 117th Congress will meet in Washington, D.C. on Wednesday to determine if they will accept the results of the December 14 meeting of the Electoral College, in which Joe Biden received 306 Electoral College votes for president and Donald Trump received 232 Electoral College votes.

If at least one member of the House of Representatives and one member of the Senate object to certifying those votes on Wednesday, each chamber must then separately hold a debate on whether to accept those Electoral College votes.

More than 30 members of the House have already announced they will object to certification. Last week, Sen. Josh Hawley (R-MO) announced he will publicly object to certification.

Then on Saturday, as Breitbart News reported, 11 Republican senators said they would vote not to certify on Wednesday and would instead recommend the establishment of a commission to review the lawfulness of the election process in the disputed states in a full election audit. That commission would have ten days to review the evidence and report back to the joint session of Congress.

"This information should serve as an important resource for state legislators as they make calls for state legislatures to meet to investigate the election and consider decertifying their state election results," Kline, who hosted the call on behalf of Got Freedom? said.

"The integrity of our elections is far too important to treat cavalierly, and elected officials deserve to have all relevant information at their disposal as they consider whether to accept the reported results of the 2020 elections, especially in states where the process was influenced by private interests," Kline added.

The statement continued:

The evidence discussed includes unprecedented public-private partnerships that created a two-tiered election system in the states that determined the winner of the Electoral College. Funded by over $400 million (ACTUALLY OF $650 MILLION TO GREASE SKIDS ONLY FOR DEMOCRATS & THE LEFT) from Facebook founder MARK ZUCKERBUCKS, these public-private partnerships sought to boost turnout in Democratic strongholds while depressing turnout in conservative areas, violating constitutional guarantees of due process and equal protection.

AFTER STEALING THE WHITE HOUSE & PRESIDENCY; MARK ZUCKERBERG & JACK DORSEY OF TWITTER USE THE JANUARY 6, CAPITOL PROTEST AS AN EXCUSE TO CANCEL DONALD TRUMP ON FACEBOOK & TWITTER PERMANENTLY. DO WE WANT TO BELONG TO THIS COUNTRY ANYMORE? ZUCKERBERG; HIS WIFE & DORSEY ARE TOTALITARIAN FASCIST ACCOMPLICES; NOW AFTER STEALING THE ELECTION; BIDEN IS REWARDING BOTH BY REFUSING TO CANCEL SECTION 230 THAT PROTECTS BOTH AGAINST CRIMINAL & CIVIL LIBEL FOR WHAT APPEARS ON TWITTER & FACEBOOK.

THE VIOLENCE IN THE CAPITOL MELEE ON JANUARY 6, 2021, WAS POSITIVELY CAUSED BY ANTIFA INFILTRATORS WITNESSES HAVE POSITIVELY IDENTIFIED BUSLOADS OF ANTIFA; WHOSE CLEAR PLAN WAS TO INFILTRATE THE DEMONSTRATION & SOW VIOLENCE THAT WOULD BE BLAMED ON & DAMN 100'S OF 1000'S OF OUR PEOPLE PROTESTING THE PRESIDENTIAL ELECTION & HONEST VOTING BEING STOLEN FROM US. WHAT ARE REPUBLICANS SUPPOSED TO DO WHEN WE'RE ABANDONED; MOCKED & RIDICULES BY THE JUDICIARY AT ALL LEVELS; CONGRESS; THE JUSTICE DEPARTMENT, FBI & ADMINISTRATIVE DEEP STATE AT EVERY LEVEL?

The private monies paid the salaries of election workers and funded the purchase of election equipment, but came with strict conditions on the conduct of elections in jurisdictions that accepted the money. These private interventions were aided by the actions of public officials, who sought to undermine transparency, fought efforts to audit the results, threatened legislators with investigation and prosecution for questioning the reported results, and in some cases even physically prevented state lawmakers from entering the Capitol Building in order to prevent them from challenging election certification.

A communication sent to participating state legislators after the call summarized Professor Eastman's argument during the call about the specific "Constitutional imperatives" of state legislators.

State legislators, Eastman stated, have both the right and duty to:

- **Assert your plenary power**
- **Demand that your laws be followed as written**
- **Decertify tainted results unless and until your laws are followed**
- **Insist on enough time to properly meet, investigate, and properly certify results to ensure that all lawful votes (but only lawful votes) are counted.**

In that subsequent communication, Kline encouraged the state legislators to:

… agree to sign on to a joint letter from state legislators to Vice President Mike Pence to demand that he call for a 12-day delay on ratifying the election, allowing the states the necessary time to further investigate the lawlessness with which the presidential election was conducted. We also request that you send this message out to fellow legislators to ask them to sign on to the letter as well.

He added that "Representative Daryl Metcalfe (R-Pennsylvania), Senator Brandon Beach (R-Georgia), and Representative Mark Finchem (R-Arizona) already wrote a letter to Vice President Mike Pence for this narrow purpose. Coming together to sign a joint letter is a vital step—one you should take confidently and in solidarity. We will send the joint letter to all legislators who contact us in reply to this message." The 1,400 pages of evidence presented to state legislators on the call can be seen at got-freedom.org/evidence/

Former House Speaker Newt Gingrich, a student of history, compared the long list of anomalies to another election nearly 200 years in the past.

VP Pence 'Welcomes' GOP's Lawful 'Objections'

By Eric Mack

Vice President Mike Pence, who will oversee the Jan. 6 joint session of Congress, issued a statement Saturday he "welcomes" the lawful "authority" in the House and Senate "to raise objections."

VP Pence, facing growing pressure from Trump's allies over his ceremonial role in presiding over the session Wednesday issued a statement Saturday through his chief of staff Marc Short.

Axios' Jonathan Swan tweeted the Short statement: "Vice President Pence shares the concerns of millions of Americans about voter fraud and irregularities in the last election . . . 1/2"

Continuing in an ensuing tweet: "'The Vice President welcomes the efforts of members of the House and Senate to use the authority they have under the law to raise objections and bring forward evidence before the Congress and the American people on January 6th.' 2/2"

Several Republicans have indicated they are under pressure from constituents back home to show they are fighting for President Donald Trump in his campaign to root out voter and election fraud. Sen. Ted Cruz, R-Texas, announced Saturday a coalition of 11 senators and senators-elect who have been enlisted to support Trump's effort. This follows the declaration from Sen. Josh Hawley, R-Mo., who was the first to buck Senate leadership by saying he would join with House Republicans in objecting to the state tallies during Wednesday's joint session of Congress. Senate Majority Leader Mitch McConnell, R-Ky., had urged his party not to try to overturn Elector College. The 11 senators largely acknowledged Saturday they will not succeed in preventing Biden from being inaugurated Jan. 20 after he won the Electoral College 306-232. But their challenges, and those from House Republicans, represent the most sweeping effort to undo a presidential election outcome since the Civil War. "We do not take this action lightly," Cruz and the other senators said in a joint statement. They vowed to vote against certain state electors Wednesday unless Congress appoints an electoral commission to immediately conduct an audit of the election results. They are zeroing in on the 6 states where Trump has raised claims of voter fraud.

Rush Limbaugh: Conservative States Are 'Trending Toward Secession'

BLUE STATE DISEASED TISSUE

ROT FROM WITHIN WITHOUT US

Report: Mark Zuckerberg's $419 Million Non-Profit Contributions 'Improperly Influenced 2020 Presidential Election'

CNN JEFF ZUCKER JOSEPH GOEBBELS WANNABE & MARK & PRISCILLA CHINESE CHINATOWN ZUCKERBUCKS ZUCKERBERG'S MAIN SQUEEZE 5TH COLUMN WIFE; XI JINPING SURROGATE CHAN'S ZUCKERBUCKS BY ZUCKERBERG INTENT & DESIGN PAID & PROPAGANDIZED INNER CITY HOOD GANGSTA'S THEFT OF OUR PRESIDENCY ZUCKERBERG BRIBED 10'S OF 1000'S INNER CITY HOOD SURROGATE GANGSTA' TOUGH ASSED IN YO' FACE BRO'S & SISTAS IN MILWAUKEE; ATLANTA;

PHILADELPHIA; PHOENIX; CLARKE COUNTY NEVADA & MOTOWN WHATEVER CASH NEEDED TO SHOPLIFT & LOOT ENOUGH VOTES FOR BIDEN. ZUCKERBERG'S NOW LAUGHING AT US THE ROSENBERGS WERE ELECTROCUTED FOR MUCH LESS.

Michael Patrick Leahy

A report released by the Amistad Project of the Thomas More Society at a press conference on Wednesday alleged Facebook founder Mark Zuckerberg and his wife ZUCKERBUCKS/BERG TREASON EFFECTIVELY PRO-XI JINPING CHINESE WIFE MAKE OF JULIUS & ETHEL MOUSEKETEERS BY COMPARISON.)

Dec 1, 2016 — On the day Julius & Ethel (BOTH BETTER DEAD THAN RED) HELLO JACK DORSEY; TWITTER; ZUCKERBERG'S ZUCKERBUCKS MARK & PRISCILLA **Rosenberg were scheduled to face the electric chair as convicted spies in June 1953, their sons, Michael and ... Julius and Ethel Rosenberg**

Julius and Ethel Rosenberg were American citizens who were convicted of spying on behalf of the

Soviet Union. Penalty: **Death by** (LA Z BOY MASSAGE W/ CUP HOLDERS) electric **chair A.K.A. ELECTROCUTION** Electric chair

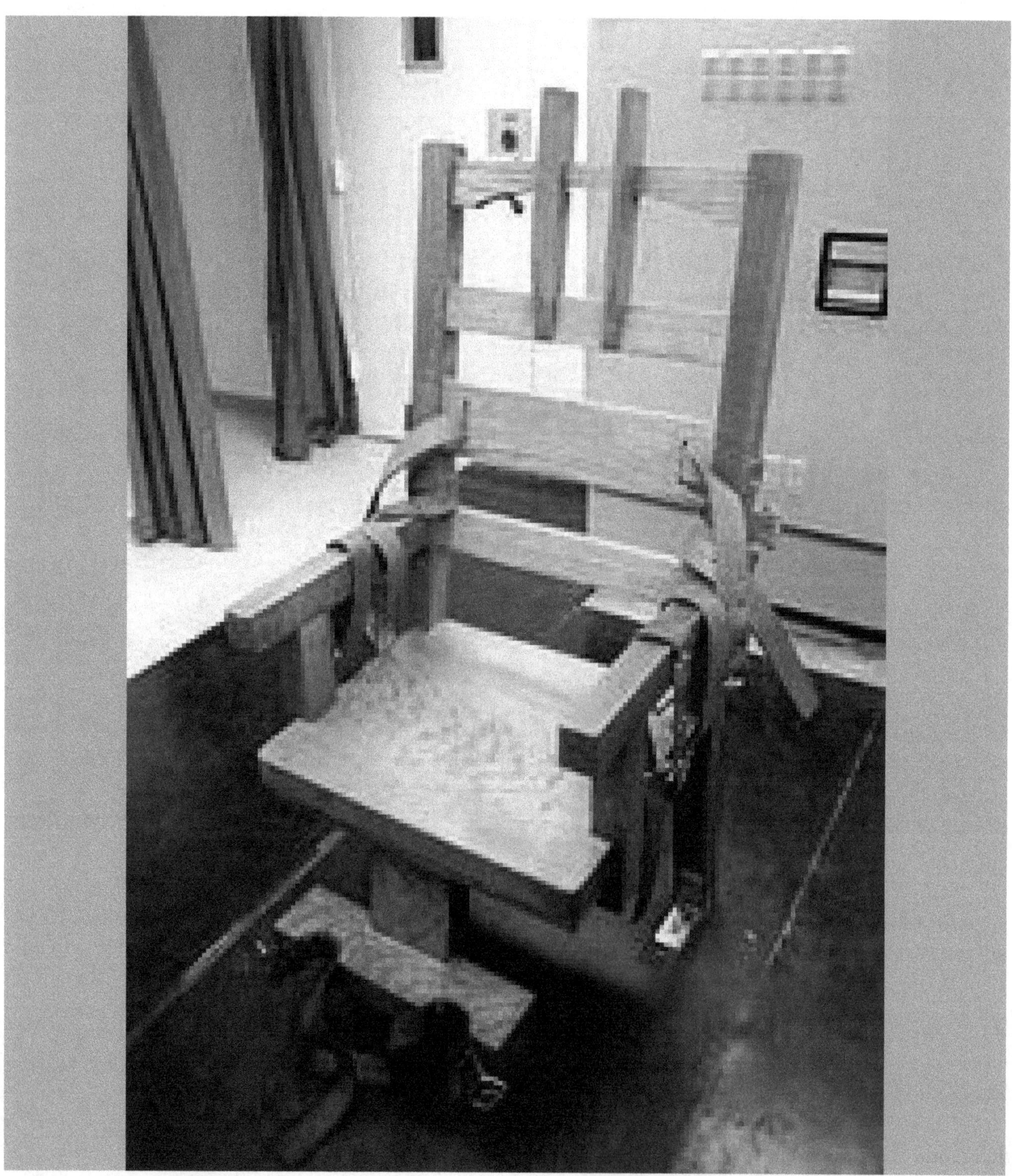

Execution by electrocution, electric chair, almost exclusively employed in United States **usually for BORN AGAIN CHRISTAINS recently found JESUS** electrodes fastened head **& leg. Conceived 1881** Buffalo, New York dentist Alfred P. Southwick**, developed 1880s Alternative to also effective** hanging **just ask HIDEKI TOJO 1st used in 1890; United States;** Philippines**. Theorized damage to the brain, shown 1899** ventricular fibrillation; **eventual cardiac arrest; for** effective political cleansing of AMERICA 1913 ESPIONAGE ACT **FROM** TWITTER'S JACK DORSEY FACEBOOK FOUNDER MARK & PRISCELLA CHAN ZUCKERBUCKS **LINES IN SAND; SHAVING AT SING SING HEAD; NECK;**

GILLETE; BARBASOL various cycles; changes voltage; duration alternating current **THEFT U.S. 2020 ENERGIZER BUNNY FOR STEALING THE WHITE HOUSE & PRESIDENTIAL ELECTION** EZ PASS ETERNAL LIVING CREMATION FLAMES; HELL; HADES OPTION AT REQUEST OF CUSTOMER; A.K.A. CONDEMNED TRAITOR; IF PANCURONIUM BROMIDE; (PAVULON); POTASSIUM CHLORIDE OUT-OF-STOCK (11) MILE RADIUS WALMART; CVS; WALGREENS; RITE AID IF FAILED PARTS ELECTRIC CHAIR OUT OF STOCK AT RADIO SHACK. IF STILL NO STOCK CONDEMNED CHOICE OPTION IMMERSION FINGER & TOE AT A TIME VATS OF SULFURIC ACID; OR SNAKE PIT; OLD SPARKY **RULED CRUEL & UNUSUAL PUNISHMENT FOR CONDEMNED INDIVIDUALS ALLERGIC TO OVERDOSE OF AC AND/OR DC CURRENT.**

(5) STAR GOOGLE JULIUS & ETHEL MARK & PRISCILLA CHAN ZUCKERBUCKS **ROSENBERG OLD TIMER'S DAY REVIEW**

Criminal charge: **Conspiracy to commit** espionage
Children: **Michael Meeropol; Robert Meeropol**
Resting place: Wellwood Cemetery, New York, **U.S**
Born: Julius; **May 12, 1918**; Manhattan, New York, U.S. Ethel;

ZUCKERBERG ZUCKERBUCKS DORSEY STOLEN WHITE HOUSE AXIS CONSPIRACY; JULIUS; ETHEL ROSENBERG; MARK & PRISCILLA ZUCKERBUCKS ZUCKERBERG & JACK DORSEY **CONSIDERED AMERICAN LAW MANDATING FAIR & FREE** UNCONTAMINATED USA ELECTIONS **TO BE AN ANNOYANCE TO THEM.**

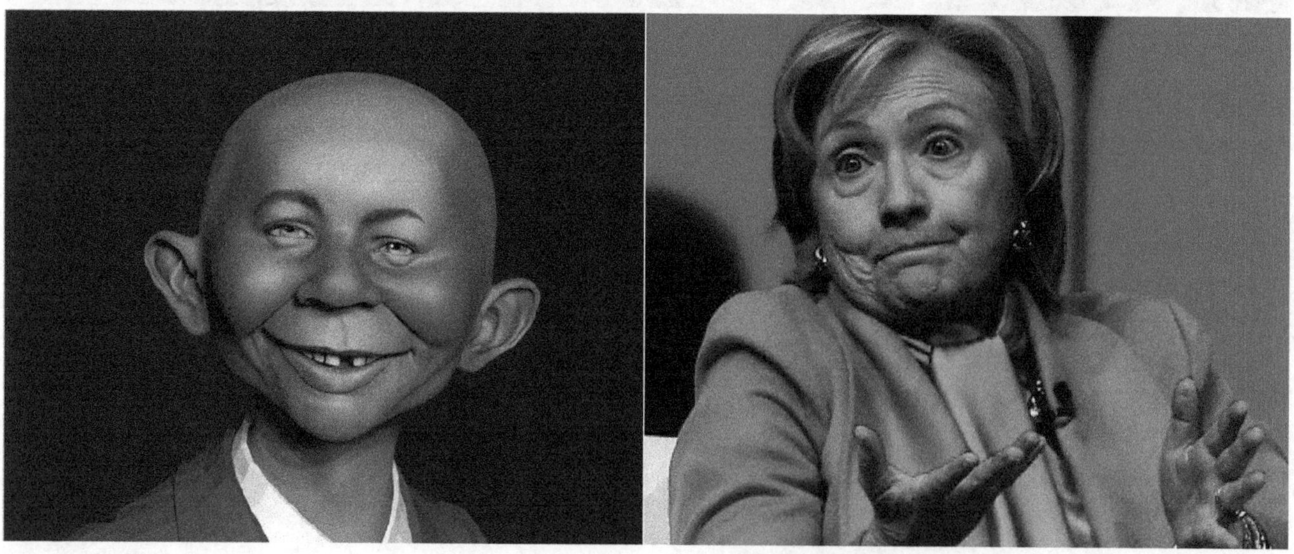

"**With all due respect,** ALL DEY BE IS WUZ WERE, UNTIL FUCKEN MURDERED BY A PATHOLOGICAL ISLAMIC MOB; WUZ BE FUCKEN DEPLORABLES CLINGIN' TO DER' GUNS & RELIGION WHILE WE'

ALL WUZ CLINKIN' COCKTAIL GLASSES IN SCARSDALE & CHAPPAQUA? **WHAT THE FUCK DOES IT ALL MEAN, ANYWAY, EVITA RODHAM PERON? The fact is we had four dead Americans," she said. "Was it because of a protest or was it because of guys out for a walk one night who decided that they'd go kill some** DEPLORABLE ASSED GUNS & OLE' TIME RELIGION 'MERICANS; PROBABLY REPUBLICANS? **What difference at this point does it** FUCKEN MAKE**? TELL US** PLEASE, HILLARY**; WHAT DA' FUCK TO YER' "SWING LEFT" ASS DID IT DEN' O' WILL IT EVA' MAKE' TA' YER' ASS?**

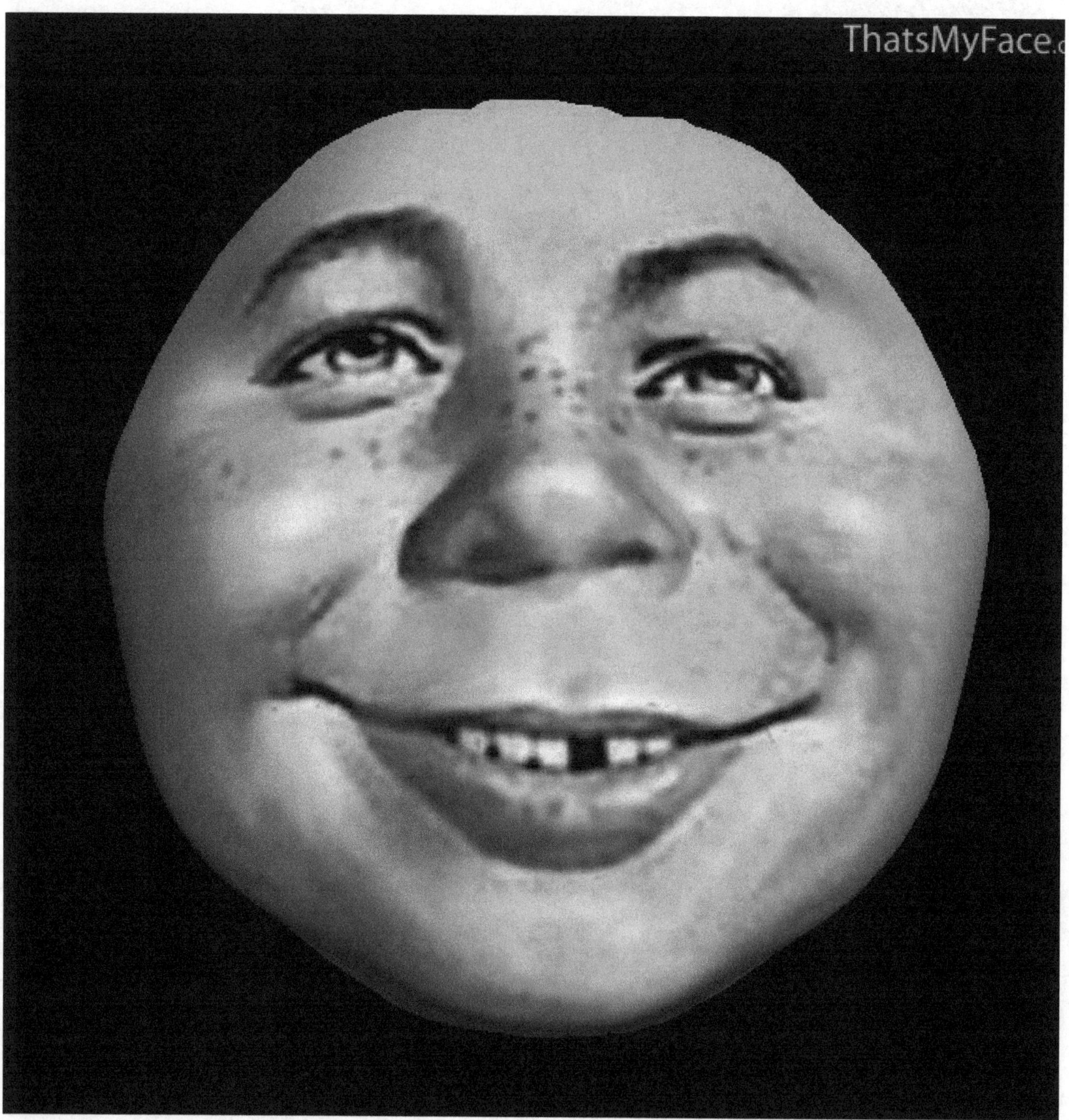

ZUCKERBUCKS' LAST LAUGHIN' AT AMERICA & GOD ; LIGHTEN UP; MARKIE MARK; JUST A GOOD NATURED SUGGESTIVE ITTIE BITTIE TENNIE WEENIE SATURDAY DAY NIGHT SUBMISSION FOR YOUR HILARIOUS HOT FOOT JOKE ON GOD; AMERICA & ALL US GUNS & RELIGION DEPLORABLES

MARK ZUCKERBUCKS ZUCKERBERG; **MINIMUM $419.5 MILLION TO TOPPLE FREE; FAIR 2020 PRESIDENTIAL ELECTION;** ROSENBERGS SIDE-BY-SIDE TOO GOOD FOR TREACHEROUS TO TURN AMERICA INTO XI JINPING CHINA; **Election for Biden o non-profit organizations during the 2020 election cycle–$350 million to the "Safe** STOLEN ELECTIONS IN HOOD GHETTOS; STICKUP GANGSTA'

INTIMIDATION CRIPS; BLOODS; MS-13 LOOTERS ELECTION FOR BIDEN" **Project of the** Center for Technology and Civic Life **(CTCL) additional** $69.5 million **ZUCKERBERG DORSEY FUNDED** Center for Election Innovation and Research**–that, "improperly influence[d] the 2020 presidential election on behalf of one particular candidate and party."**

"The 2020 presidential election witnessed an unprecedented and coordinated public-private partnership to improperly influence the 2020 presidential election on behalf of one particular candidate and party. Funded by hundreds of millions of dollars from Facebook founder Mark Zuckerberg ZUCKERBUCKS **and other high-tech interests, activist organizations created a two-tiered election system that treated voters differently depending on whether they lived in Democrat or Republican strongholds," Amistad Project Director Phill Kline** wrote **in the report's executive summary.**

The report identified three key actions that, taken together, "represent the beginning of the formation of a two-tier election system favoring one demographic while disadvantaging another demographic."

- **Private monies dictated city and county election management contrary to both federal law and state election plans endorsed and developed by state legislatures with authority granted by the United States Constitution.**
- **Executive officials in swing states facilitated, through unique and novel contracts, the sharing of private and sensitive information about citizens within those states with private interests, some whom actively promote leftist candidates and agendas.**
- **Swing state governors also started issuing emergency executive orders shutting down in-person voting while pouring new state resources into encouraging persons to vote in advance. Polling data revealed this coordinated assault on in-person voting generally favored Democrat Party voters who preferred to vote in advance, while placing Republicans, who preferred to vote in person, at a disadvantage. These actions represent the beginning of the formation of a two-tier election system favoring one demographic while disadvantaging another demographic.**

"This evidence is present and available to all Americans," Kline said at the press conference of the information included in the report.

"The mainstream media has also tried to censor this evidence," he noted, adding that, "America understands that there are serious problems with this election."

"This effectively is a shadow government running our elections," Kline continued.

"This network pumped hundreds of millions of dollars into local election systems using the COVID crisis as a pretense. Our report proves that in reality it was nothing more than a naked attempt to purchase an election. 'ZUCKERBUCKS' **and local election officials invited a billionaire into the consolidated ballot counting centers while kicking out the American people," Kline** said **in the statement accompanying the release of the report:**

"This report paints a clear picture of a cabal of billionaires and activists using their wealth to subvert,

control, and fundamentally alter the electoral system itself," Kline added. "We must act now to prevent such privatized elections in the future. The American public deserves transparent and fair elections, not lawless elections directed by powerful private interests."

In addition to Zuckerberg ZUCKERBUCKS, the main foundations funding the effort to subvert the electoral system were The SUBVERSIVE 1913 ESPIONAGE AGE FELONY TREASON IN FORM OF BILLIONS FOR MILLIONS OF FRAUDULENT VOTES TO ELECT A STAGE (6) DEMENTIA TROJAN PIG PRETENDER; Democracy Fund, New Venture Fund, Skoll Foundation, and Knight Foundation, according to the report. Key nonprofits involved in distributing the money include CTCL, the Center for [Election] Innovation Research, the Center for Civic Design, the National Vote at Home Institute, the Center for Secure and Modern Elections, and Rock the Vote.

The report demonstrates that funding from nonprofits was especially unnecessary in Michigan, Pennsylvania, and Wisconsin, as the federal government had already provided sufficient funding through both the Help America Vote Act (HAVA) and the CARES Act.

The report alleged that the privatization of the administration of the election in key battleground states, and its effective removal from the control of properly authorized local and state governments was strengthened by improper "claw back provisions" attached to grants given to counties and cities by CTCL.

Under those provisions, local governments would be required to return the CTCL donations if they failed to implement the more controversial and legally dubious elements of the plan, including the use of drop boxes to collect absentee ballots and the requirement that counting centers be consolidated in a way that made observation of the counting process by GOP observers more difficult.

The report focused heavily on how the CTCL used the $350 million donated to the 501 (c) (3) by Mark Zuckerberg and his wife between September 1, 2020 and October 21, 2020, particularly in urban areas in four key battleground states: Georgia, Michigan, Wisconsin, and Pennsylvania TO STEAL THE WHITE & AMERICAN DEMOCRACY.

In Wisconsin, the report alleged the CTCL plan worked to benefit Biden and the Democrats:

For example, CTCL inked a $100,000 grant to the Mayor of Racine, WI in May of 2020 directing the Mayor to recruit four other cities (Green Bay, Kenosha, Madison, and Milwaukee) to develop a joint grant request of CTCL. This effort results in these cities submitting a "Wisconsin Safe Election Plan" on June 15, 2020 to CTCL and, in turn, receiving $6.3 million to implement the plan. This privatization of elections undermines the Help America Vote Act (HAVA), which requires state election plans to be submitted to federal officials and approved and requires respect for equal protection by making all resources available equally to all voters.

The provision of Zuckerberg-ZUCKERBUCKS CTCL funds allowed these Democrat strongholds to spend roughly $47 per voter, compared to $4 to $7 per voter in traditionally Republican areas of the state. Moreover, this recruiting of targeted jurisdictions for specific government action and funding runs contrary to legislative election plans and invites government to play favorites in the election process.

The "Wisconsin Safe Election Plan" was not authored by the state, and considered state election integrity laws as obstacles and nuisances to be ignored or circumvented. Moreover, CTCL retained the right, in the grant document, to, in its sole discretion, order all funds returned if the grantee cities did not conduct the election consistent with CTCL dictates.

Effectively, CTCL managed the election in these five cities. And this plan violated state law in, at least, the following fashion:

1) The plan circumvented voter identification requirements for absentee ballots by attempting to classify all voters as "indefinitely confined" due to COVID and later, after Wisconsin Supreme Court criticism, by ordering election clerks to not question such claims.

2) The plan initiated the use of drop boxes for ballot collection, significantly breaching the chain of custody of the ballot and failing to maintain proper logs and reviews to ensure all properly cast ballots were counted and all improperly cast ballots were not counted.

3) Initiated the consolidation of counting centers, justifying the flow of hundreds of thousands of ballots to one location and the marginalization of Republican poll watchers such that bipartisan participation in the management, handling, and counting of the ballots was compromised.

These are but examples of radical changes in election processes that opened the door for significant fraud.

In Pennsylvania, the report asserted:

The disparate impact of Zuckerberg funding is also present in the analysis of CTCL funding in Pennsylvania. Documents obtained through court order revealed communication between the City of Philadelphia and CTCL emphasizing that CTCL paid election judges in Philadelphia and other election officials. CTCL mandated Philadelphia to increase its polling locations and to use drop boxes and eventually mobile pick-up units. Moreover, Zuckerberg ZUCKERBUCKS monies allowed Philadelphia to "cure" absentee ballots in a manner not provided for in Republican areas of the state.

In Democrat Delaware County, Pennsylvania, one drop box was placed every four square miles and for every 4,000 voters. In the 59 counties carried by Trump in 2016, there was one drop box for every 1,100 square miles and every 72,000 voters. Government encouraging a targeted demographic to turn out the vote is the opposite side of the same coin as government targeting a demographic to suppress the vote. This two-tiered election system allowed voters in Democrat strongholds to stroll down the street to vote while voters in Republican strongholds had to go on the equivalent of a "where's Waldo" hunt.

In Michigan, the report stated:

The Amistad Project's concerns were amplified by the nature of a contract offered by Michigan's health director to a subsidiary of NGP VAN, a Democrat fundraiser and data services company. Michigan granted the COVID tracing contract to Michigan VAN as a subsidiary of NGP VAN. The contract allowed this leftist organization to demand sensitive information from Michigan citizens at the threat of arrest. Citizens could be ordered to turn over medical records, travel information, the names of associates and friends, and other information with a significant privacy interest and of significant monetary value to a political fundraiser.

Emails later obtained through FOIA requests demonstrate Governor Whitmer's political director was involved in suggesting to the health department that they not directly contract with NGP VAN because of possible political fallout. Governor Whitmer's staffer recommended NGP VAN create a Michigan subsidiary and that the subsidiary become a subcontractor so as to conceal NGP VAN's involvement. When this information became public, Whitmer claimed she was unaware of the agreement and faced with public pressure, she rescinded the contract.

Last month, the Amistad Project filed a lawsuit alleging that more than 100,000 ballots had been cast illegally in Georgia:

The Amistad Project of the Thomas More Society today filed a lawsuit contesting the results of the 2020 presidential election in Georgia, citing expert opinion that well over 100,000 illegal votes were improperly counted, while tens of thousands of legal votes were not counted.

The expert analysis of government data showing that the total number of illegal votes counted and legal votes not counted is greater than 200,000 — vastly exceeding the 12,670-vote margin in the presidential election contest.

"The number of potentially fraudulent ballots we've identified in Georgia is over 15 times greater than the margin separating Donald Trump and Joe Biden. This finding undercuts the integrity of the general election," said Phill Kline, Director of The Amistad Project. "The discrepancies we identified arose in large part because certain election officials acted with greater fealty to the dictates of private funders than to the laws set forth by the people's representatives in the General Assembly."

The report released on Wednesday identified five specific action steps to address the election integrity issues it identified:

- The secretaries, attorneys general, and/or legislatures of states whose county governments received CTCL funds should commission a comprehensive, third-party audit of the consistency of private/public transactions with the HAVA implementation plans of their state. This should include compliance with NIST standards, and state procurement requirements.
- State secretaries, attorneys general and/or legislatures who have membership in the non-profit Electronic Registration Information Center (ERIC) should audit the information access, collection, storage, security and/or potential voter information sharing practices of ERIC with other states or third-party non-profit
associations.
- Secretaries, attorneys general, and/or legislators of states who received Center for Election

Innovation CEIR grants for election related purposes should request and evaluate CEIR contracts for HAVA compliance and the fiscal and procurement requirements of their individual states.

- State by state examination of the legal authority by which CTCL , a non-profit organization chartered in Illinois, negotiated grant contracts with county and municipal governments in multiple jurisdictions across many states.
- County commissioners should coordinate with their respective attorneys general or legislatures to understand and mitigate potential future liabilities of the claw back language in any grant agreements they have with CTCL.

The Zuckerberg-funded ZUCKERBUCKS CTCL announced last month that it will provide even more funding to local counties and cities in Georgia in advance of the January 5 U.S. Senate runoffs in the state. THIS WAS ONLY ONE TOOL IN THE U.S. UNLIMITED TREASON CRIMES ACTUAL & IMPLIED; PLOTS TO FOREVER STEAL AMERICAN DEMOCRACY; 1913 ESPIONAGE ACT MANDATING DEATH PENALTY

Mail-in ballots were part of a plot to deny Lincoln reelection in 1864

An 1864 sketch by William Waud of Pennsylvania soldiers voting. (Library of Congress)

By Dustin Waters

Traveling to Baltimore in the fall of 1864, Orville Wood had no way of knowing he would soon uncover the most elaborate election conspiracy in America's brief history.

Wood was a merchant from Clinton County in the most northeastern corner of New York. As a supporter of President Abraham Lincoln, he was tasked with visiting troops from his hometown to "look after the local ticket."

New York legislators had only established the state's mail-in voting system in April with the intent of ensuring the suffrage of White troops battling the Confederate Army.

The results of the 1864 elections would heavily affect the outcome of the war. Lincoln and his supporters in the National Union Party sought to continue the war and defeat the Confederacy outright. Meanwhile antiwar Democrats, also referred to as Copperheads, looked for an immediate compromise with the Confederate leaders and the end of the abolition movement.

Troops from New York were allowed to authorize individuals back home to cast a vote on their behalf. Along with their mail-in ballots, troops would assign their power of attorney on slips that required four signatures: the voter's, the person authorized as a recipient, a witness to the signed affidavit and a fellow officer. These documents would be sealed in an envelope and shipped back home to be counted in the final vote. This was the process that Orville Wood intended to uphold, he would testify in court later. He quickly found out what a challenge that would be.

Wood arrived at Fort McHenry in Baltimore to visit with the 91st New York Regiment. There, an Army captain suggested that there had been some "checker playing" when it came to the gathering of soldiers' mail-in ballots. These suspicions of fraud were echoed when Wood visited wounded men at the Newton University Hospital. The rumors of wrongdoing led Wood to the office of Moses Ferry in Baltimore.

Ferry had been selected by New York Gov. Horatio Seymour to help oversee the voting process for New York's enlisted men. Seymour had vetoed the initial bill to establish mail-in voting and would go on to run against Ulysses S. Grant in the 1868 presidential election.

Wood masked his suspicions as he entered Ferry's office, portraying himself as a strong supporter of Lincoln's opponent, George McClellan. This was enough to gain Ferry's trust, he testified later.

Ferry told Wood that the votes from New York's 91st Regiment had already been tallied: 400 for McClellan and 11 for Lincoln.

Wood returned to the office later and, following Ferry's instructions, began forging signatures of the 16th New York Cavalry. Meanwhile, a clerk sat across the room signing ballots from the roster of names Wood had brought with him from home. Wood asked to personally deliver these fraudulent ballots, but Ferry said they would have to receive final approval from his colleague in Washington — Edward Donahue Jr.

Donahue soon arrived in Baltimore and met with Wood. It was revealed during this conversation that around 20 co-conspirators were already at work in D.C. to aid in the plot to deliver votes to McClellan. The following day Wood watched as Donahue and his crew formed a sort of assembly line, passing blank papers along to one another to be signed with the names of active enlisted men, wounded and dead soldiers, and officers who never existed.

In addition to operations in D.C. and Baltimore, the scheme extended back to New York. Donahue had received rosters of soldiers from military officials and members of law enforcement. A letter from Gen. J.A. Ferrell read, “Inclosed in this package you will find tickets, also a list of names of the actual residents of Columbia County, now members of the 128th Regiment. With my best wishes for your success.”

A letter from Albany Sheriff H. Cromdell offered to send additional men to assist in Baltimore. The letter read, “All is well here, and we are confident of complete success. It is unnecessary to say that all here have entire confidence in your skill and abetting, and hope you like your help.”

Also discovered in Ferry’s office was a list of around 400 names belonging to sick and wounded soldiers under treatment at a nearby hospital. In reference to the roster, Ferry joked, “Dead or alive, they all had cast a good vote.”

Ferry, Donahue, and their fellow conspirators found humor in their work. One accomplice mocked the outcry he expected from abolitionist newspapers following the corruption of the election. The men bragged about their past successes in fixing local elections back home.

Together, the men had shipped crates of fraudulent votes back to New York. But their scheme was over. Wood reported the operation to authorities. Ferry’s office was searched, and on the morning of Oct. 27, 1864 — less than two weeks before the election — he and Donahue stood trial before a military commission.

Ferry offered a full confession that same day, even offering up the names of others involved in the scheme. Donahue proved more of a challenge.

Following the first day of the trial, a reporter for the New York Times wrote, “The honest electors of the state of New York have escaped an extensive and fearful fraud, a fraud in keeping with the proclivities of the party in whose behalf it was initiated, but one that, if unexposed might have subverted the honest will of the people and left the state and the nation at the mercy of those who would make peace with rebellion and fellowship with traitors.”

Arrests in New York and Washington continued to mount as Donahue returned to trial. Following Wood’s damning testimony and supporting evidence, Donahue begged for mercy from the court. He was a young man, newly married, with no previous record. He visibly wilted as he realized the weight of his current situation, no longer expressing the defiance with which he had entered the proceedings.

The judge advocate addressed the tribunal, saying that Donahue had engaged in one of the most gigantic frauds ever attempted in America — “a fraud which, if it shall be successful, will, in my opinion, have produced a disruption of our entire country, and our war for the preservation of the Union will be practically at an end and futile." In the months following Lincoln's victory — he won 221 electoral votes to McClellan's 21 — anti-abolitionist newspapers attacked his legitimacy, calling the trial another aspect of a conspiracy conducted by the president to ensure his reelection.

The commission that oversaw Ferry and Donahue's trial recommended life in prison for the two men who sought to corrupt the election by mail. The president, who would soon be slain, approved.

Rep. Jordan to Newsmax TV: Electoral College Challenge Based on Rule Changes, Fraud

By Brian Trusdell

Rep. Jim Jordan of Ohio outlined on Newsmax TV the House Republicans' strategy for contesting the Electoral College results on Wednesday, running from voting law and rule changes not approved by state legislatures to claims of fraudulent votes being cast or changed.

"What you're going to see is several members of the United States' House of Representatives object to the electors being accepted and certified in six states," Jordan said Tuesday during special election coverage of the Georgia Senate runoff races. "And the reason you're going to see that is because in all of these states there was unconstitutional change in the election rules just prior to the election."

Jordan, 56, who in November was elected to an eighth term in the House of Representatives from Ohio's 4th Congressional District north and west of Columbus and Cleveland, referred to – without specifying a state or official – several executive actions that have been disputed by Republicans. Among them were Pennsylvania Secretary of the Commonwealth Kathy Boockvar's decision to count mail-in ballots received up to three days after election, the Pennsylvania Supreme Court's decision to uphold that and another decision to allow certain Democratic counties to correct or "cure" absentee ballots, and Georgia Secretary of State Brad Raffensperger's altering of signature verification procedures on mail-in ballots to settle a suit brought by state Democrats.

"The Constitution is very straightforward," Jordan added. "It says that the legislature determines the time, place and manner for elections – not Supreme Courts in the state, not secretaries of state, not county clerks, not Facebook, not Twitter, it says the legislature. And in all of these states that we will object to tomorrow, someone outside the legislature, they went around the legislature and changed the election rules. And the reason they had to go around the legislature is because they were controlled by Republicans. "So they sued in friendly court, or they got a hack secretary of state who changed the rules at the last minute. That's how they did this. And then on top of that, you had the fraud that's been talked about for over the last nine weeks."

Trump: VP Can Reject Fraudulently Chosen Electors

By Brian Freeman

Vice President Mike Pence has the authority to reject the Electoral College results, President Donald Trump tweeted on Tuesday.

"The Vice President has the power to reject fraudulently chosen electors," the president wrote.

His tweet followed a report in The New York Times that Pence wants to raise the issue of election fraud during Wednesday's joint session of Congress, despite not having the authority to affect the outcome.

Trump, during his appearance in Dalton, Georgia, on Monday to press for the election of the two Republican candidates for Senate in Tuesday's runoff election, stressed the importance of Pence, who, as vice president, is set to oversee the certification of the Electoral College vote. "I hope Mike Pence comes through for us, I have to tell you," Trump said. "I hope that our great vice president, our great vice president, comes through for us. He's a great guy. Of course, if he doesn't come through, I won't like him as much."

According to the Times, the role of the vice president in certifying the Electoral College is largely ceremonial.

Leader McConnell Reportedly Eases Up on Colleagues Objecting to Electoral Vote

Senate Majority Leader Mitch McConnell, R-Ky., reportedly has pulled back on his warning to Republican colleagues if they objected to the Electoral College certification.

According to Sen. Kevin Cramer, R-N.D. per Politico on Monday, McConnell spoke on a recent conference call with senators and told them, «this is a very difficult decision for each one of you, you each have to make it yourselves. I›ve voted twice on declarations of war.

"This is right up there." Cramer said McConnell added that he would not "judge anybody for their decision." President Donald Trump and allies have alleged Joe Biden won the November election due to voter fraud in several key battleground states. On Dec. 15, McConnell congratulated Biden on his victory. The two men were longtime Senate colleagues.

McConnell also warned Senate Republicans not to challenge Biden's presidential victory. With Sens. Josh Hawley, R-Mo., and Ted Cruz, R-Texas, leading the electoral objections in the Senate, McConnell has been

offering guidance when sought and fielding calls from GOP members, according to a source familiar with the matter. McConnell is trying to lead his party as Trump enters the final two weeks of his presidency. The Senate runoffs in Georgia on Tuesday will decide if McConnell remains majority leader.

More than a hundred Republican House members and at least a dozen senators have indicated they plan to challenge the electoral voting results during a joint session of Congress on Wednesday.

McConnell reportedly has been talking with many of his fellow Republican senators and leaving public arguments to people such as Sens. Tom Cotton, R-Ark., and Pat Toomey, R-Pa.

"He's letting everybody reach their own conclusion here," said one Republican senator aligned with McConnell. "That's very much his leadership style on issues like this, is to not say much. I think he hopes we don't have too many people vote to do this. Trying to convince people right now wouldn't produce much of a result when you could just give them time to think about it."

Trump Backers Rally in Washington Ahead of Vote Certification

Hundreds of Donald Trump's supporters began massing in Washington on Tuesday, a day ahead of a protest called by the outgoing president who refuses to concede defeat in November's election.

Coming from all corners of America, the demonstrators said they had answered Trump's appeal to gather in the capital Wednesday, when Congress is expected to vote to finalize President-elect Joe Biden's election victory. "My commander-in-chief called me and my Lord and Savior told me" to come, said Debbie Lusk, 66, a retired accountant from Seattle.

"We either take our country back, or it is no more," she told AFP. Trump last month tweeted that supporters should head to Washington for what he promised would be a "wild" day of protests. Large parts of the downtown area were boarded up, with shops and businesses shuttered by the virus and amid fears of a repeat of the violence that rocked the city during racial-justice protests last year.

Trump has refused to accept his election loss, making repeated claims of fraud or vote rigging in the states where he was narrowly beaten. Various courts have rejected legal challenges from Trump's team, but he and his legal team, undaunted, continue to alleged massive and system fraud.

More than half of Republican voters believe Trump won or aren't sure who did, according to a survey last month from researchers at top universities including Harvard. That confusion was echoed by many of the mainly upbeat supporters who had gathered under grey skies at a chilly Freedom Plaza near the White House on Tuesday.

"We don't trust the outcome of the elections," said Chris Thomas, 69, a retired saleswoman wearing a Trump hat. Thomas told AFP she and her husband had come from Oregon because they "believe in the freedom of America", and to show support for Trump economic policies that helped their son's wine-chiller business prosper. At least 300 supporters had gathered by noon, and almost all of them were flouting Washington's mask-wearing order. Several of them said the media had exaggerated the severity of the COVID-19 pandemic, which has killed more than 355,000 people in the U.S.

Vice President Mike Pence is to preside over Wednesday's joint session of Congress, in which lawmakers will count and confirm the state-by-state Electoral College votes that decide the presidency.

That certification is usually a formality, but Trump has been pressuring his loyal deputy to overturn Biden's win, claiming claiming Pence has the authority to discard pro-Biden votes. That claim is in dispute.

But not in dispute is supporters' faith that things will break Trump's way. "It would really surprise us if Pence doesn't back Trump," Thomas, the retired saleswoman, said.

Many demonstrators were hoping for a last-minute surprise that would keep Trump in power beyond Jan. 20, the date of Biden's inauguration. "Trump won by far. There's more than enough evidence," said Matthew Woods, 59, from California.

Anthony Lima, also from California, said he had traveled to Washington because he wanted to see for himself what was happening. "A lot of news agencies don't tell us the truth," he said. "I am open to believe Joe Biden and Kamala Harris won the election, I just want an investigation."

Trump renews pressure on Pence, says if VP 'comes through' and decertifies, he will 'win the presidency'

White House officials told Fox News on Tuesday that Pence will 'follow the law'

By Brooke Singman

Trump: Election fight not over ahead of Electoral College vote

Brian Kilmeade's exclusive interview with President Trump at the Army-Navy Game at West Point.

President Trump early Wednesday put the pressure on Vice President Pence, saying that if he "comes through for us" and decertifies the Electoral College, he will "win the presidency."

"If Vice President @Mike_Pence comes through for us, we will win the Presidency," Trump tweeted. "Many States want to decertify the mistake they made in certifying incorrect & even fraudulent numbers in a process NOT approved by their State Legislatures (which it must be)."

Trump added: "Mike can send it back!"

Trump's tweet put renewed pressure on the vice president who will preside over Wednesday's joint session of Congress to certify the results of the 2020 presidential election.

Trump, on Tuesday night, said that he and Pence "are in total agreement that the Vice President has the power to act."

The president said that the election was "corrupt in contested states, and in particular it was not in accordance with the Constitution in that they made large scale changes to election rules and regulations as dictated by local judges and politicians, not by state legislators."

TRUMP SAYS HE, PENCE IN 'TOTAL AGREEMENT' THAT VP HAS 'POWER' TO BLOCK CERTIFICATION OF ELECTION RESULTS

"This means that it was illegal," Trump said. Trump went on to say that Pence has "several options under the U.S. Constitution."

"He can decertify the results or send them back to the states for change and certification," Trump said. "He can also decertify the illegal and corrupt results and send them to the House of Representatives for the one vote for one state tabulation." A spokesman for Pence declined to comment.

Trump's statement came after The New York Times reported that Pence, during a conversation with Trump, told him that he had no power to block the certification of the election results on Wednesday.

The president, on On Tuesday morning, the president insisted that Pence has the power to overturn the election results.

"The Vice President has the power to reject fraudulently chosen electors," the president tweeted on Tuesday morning. And Monday night, at an election eve rally in Georgia for the two GOP senators running in the state's twin U.S. Senate runoff contests, Trump told the large crowd of supporters, "I hope Mike Pence comes through for us, I have to tell you."

TRUMP SLAMS MCCONNELL, THUNE, CORNYN AS 'WEAK,' 'INEFFECTIVE' RINOS AHEAD OF ELECTORAL COLLEGE CERTIFICATION

"I hope that our great vice president – our great vice president, comes through for us. He's a great guy. Of course, if he doesn't come through, I won't like him as much," Trump emphasized.

But White House officials told Fox News on Tuesday that Pence will "follow the law," saying that Pence is "taking a very diligent and studious approach to his job tomorrow." "He has consulted at length with staff. He has gone through the Electoral Count Act several times," an official said. "He has read legal opinions, met with the Senate parliamentarian and consulted with outside experts on the subject matter."

But those officials add that "the vice president will follow the law. He will act tomorrow with fidelity to the law and the Constitution." Meanwhile, more than a dozen Senate Republicans have said they will object to the certification of the presidential election results in at least one state, and more than 100 House Republican members said they plan to object to results in Arizona, Michigan, Wisconsin, Pennsylvania, Nevada, and Georgia. But Republicans, like Senate Majority Leader Mitch McConnell, R-Ky., Sens. John Thune of South Dakota, John Cornyn of Texas, Mitt Romney of Utah, Susan Collins of Maine, Lisa Murkowski of Alaska and Tim Scott of South Carolina, among others, have committed to voting to certify the election results.

Trump's renewed pressure on Pence comes as he has repeatedly charged for two months that the presidential election was "rigged" and has claimed that there was "massive voter fraud" in a handful of battleground states where Biden narrowly edged the president, to score a 306-232 Electoral College victory over the GOP incumbent. The Trump campaign has launched a number of legal challenges, while Trump himself has urged states with Republican governors and legislatures to overturn Joe Biden's victories.

While the Trump campaign has challenged the results in dozens of lawsuits, judges in multiple states have shot them down.

Attorney General William Barr told the Associated Press last month that "to date, we have not seen fraud on a scale that could have effected a different outcome in the election."

Trump says he, Pence in 'total agreement' VP has 'power' to block certification of 'illegal' election

White House officials told Fox News on Tuesday that Pence will 'follow the law'

By Brooke Singman

Washington Post report on a leaked audio recording of Trump, Georgia Republican secretary of state discussing election results surfaces. John Roberts reports from the White House. President Trump on Tuesday said he and Vice President Mike Pence are "in total agreement" that the vice president "has the power to act" and block the certification of the 2020 presidential election results on Wednesday.

The president's comments came after The New York Times on Tuesday reported that Pence, during a conversation with Trump, told him that he had no power to block the certification of the election results

during the joint session of Congress on Wednesday.

TRUMP SLAMS MCCONNELL, THUNE, CORNYN AS 'WEAK,' 'INEFFECTIVE' RINOS AHEAD OF ELECTORAL COLLEGE CERTIFICATION

"The New York Times report regarding comments Vice President Pence supposedly made to me today is fake news. He never said that," Trump said in a statement Tuesday night. "The Vice President and I are in total agreement that the Vice President has the power to act."

The president said that the election was "corrupt in contested states, and in particular it was not in accordance with the Constitution in that they made large scale changes to election rules and regulations as dictated by local judges and politicians, not by state legislators."

"This means that it was illegal," Trump said.

Trump went on to say that Pence has "several options under the U.S. Constitution."

TRUMP PUTS PRESSURE ON PENCE AHEAD OF ELECTION SHOWDOWN IN CONGRESS

"He can decertify the results or send them back to the states for change and certification," Trump said. "He can also decertify the illegal and corrupt results and send them to the House of Representatives for the one vote for one state tabulation."

A spokesman for Pence declined to comment.

Vice President Mike Pence will preside over the joint session on Wednesday, but he is expected to play a mostly ceremonial role.

Cruz, other Republicans look for a repeat of what led to the election of President Rutherford B. Hayes

By Ronn Blitzer

Cruz says Supreme Court 'better forum' for voter fraud concerns amid his election objection push_

Sen. Ted Cruz, R-Texas, tells Maria Bartiromo on 'Sunday Morning Futures' he wants an 'emergency 10-day audit of the results by an electoral commission.'

Several Republican senators are vowing to challenge electoral votes in the 2020 presidential election from several battleground states when the votes are formally counted at a joint session of Congress **on Wednesday, with the hopes of establishing a commission to determine who gets the votes.**

Unlike what was called for by a failed lawsuit from Rep. Louie Gohmert, R-Texas, the suggestion here is not to simply overturn the election results outright and award a second term to President Trump, but rather to have an independent investigation of those states' elections. While out of the ordinary, it would not be the first time for such a process, as it is what happened following the 1876 election, allowing Rutherford B. Hayes to become president.

TRUMP, HOUSE REPUBLICANS HELD CALL TO DISCUSS ELECTORAL COLLEGE REJECTION: BROOKS

"We should follow that precedent," Sen. Ted Cruz, R-Texas, and 10 other current and incoming senators said in a joint statement, referring to the race between Hayes and Samuel Tilden. "To wit, Congress should immediately appoint an Electoral Commission, with full investigatory and fact-finding authority, to conduct an emergency 10-day audit of the election returns in the disputed states. Once completed, individual states would evaluate the commission's findings and could convene a special legislative session to certify a change in their vote, if needed."

In 1877, following the 1876 election, returns from Florida, Louisiana, and South Carolina – and one elector from Oregon – were disputed. Congress then set up a commission to determine how the electoral votes should be allocated, reserving the right to accept or reject the commission's findings. In the end, Congress awarded all 19 of the contested electoral votes to Hayes, who was elected with 185 electoral votes to Tilden's 184.

GOP LAWMAKERS REJECT GOP PUSH TO OBJECT TO ELECTORAL COLLEGE RESULTS

Sen. James Lankford, R-Okla., one of the senators calling for a repeat of what happened then, outlined how it would work in a Saturday appearance on Fox News' "Justice with Judge Jeanine."

"We've asked a very simple question: Can we put together an electoral commission, have five senators, five House members, five members of the Supreme Court?" Lankford explained. "This is exactly how it was set up in 1876 when there was three states that had all kinds of fraud issues. And so the election commission was set up at that time in 1876, just like this, to be able to study it, look at it, make recommendations. We think that's a good plan. Obviously, there are millions and millions of Americans that think there are major issues with the election."

Lankford said that he wants a commission to get to the bottom of how the election played out in these states, regardless of who the true winner is.

"No matter how this turns out, we want the facts to come out," Lankford said. "We want to make sure every legal vote is counted and votes that aren't legal are not counted. But regardless of where it goes at the end of it, it goes wherever the American people chose."

Senate Judiciary Committee Chairman Lindsey Graham, R-S.C., said he would pay attention to any allegations that will be made on Wednesday, but was skeptical of the overall strategy.

"Proposing a commission at this late date – which has zero chance of becoming reality – is not effectively fighting for President Trump," Graham said in a statement. "It appears to be more of a political dodge than an effective remedy."

Graham went on to say that he "will listen closely to the objections of my colleagues in challenging the results of this election," but noted that "they have a high bar to clear" in providing evidence that multiple state and federal courts erred in their rulings, and that "the failure to take corrective action in addressing election fraud" actually impacted the results of the presidential election. Home | Politics

Trump at Runoff Rally in Ga.: 'I Don't Concede!'

By Eric Mack

Stumping on the eve of the Georgia Senate runoffs, President Donald Trump talked about his own election fight, emphatically insisting 'I don't concede" at what may well be the final consequential campaign rally of his presidency. In Dalton, Ga., on Monday night, Trump told a raucous crowd: "There is no way we lost Georgia." "That was a rigged election," he said, "but we are still fighting it, and you're going to see what will happen.

"I had two elections," he added. "I won both of them. It's amazing. I did much better on the second one."

The House and Senate will weigh the Electoral College votes in a joint session of Congress on Wednesday. Some Republicans in both chambers are planning to contest the certification of votes in a number of battleground states, including Georgia, Pennsylvania, Arizona, Nevada, Wisconsin, and Michigan.

"Can't let it happen – nothing and no one will be able to stop them," Trump said of losing the Senate, which is what brought him to Georgia ahead of the key runoff races that'll decide which party controls the chamber.

At the same time, though, he seemed to referencing his own race against Joe Biden, who Trump claims benefited from rampant and systemic voter fraud.

"The Senate seats are the last line of defense. I must preface, because they will say, 'He just conceded.'

"No, no, I don't think so. I don't concede."

Before the Electoral College drama expected to play out for hours on Wednesday, incumbent Sens. Kelly Loeffler and David Perdue, both R-Ga., face stiff challenges Tuesday by Democrats Rev. Raphael Warnock and Jon Ossoff. The races have taken on huge significance, in that they'll ultimately determine whether Dems or Republicans hold chamber control.

Republicans have already clinched at least a tie with 50 seats, so winning just one will keep majority control in the hands of Senate Majority Leader Mitch McConnell, R-Ky.

But if Dems can win both races, the two parties will be tied for seats. With Biden currently considered winner of the Electoral College and poised to take office on Jan. 20, his running mate, Kamala Harris, will become the Senate's tie-breaking vote, swinging power toward the Dem side of the aisle.

"I have to tell you the stakes of this election could not be higher," Trump said. "You vote [Tuesday]. People want to go out. They don't want to do the ballot thing, unless it's the other side. They want to go and vote. Make sure your vote is counted. Don't let them say, 'I'm sorry, someone else voted for you.'

"The radical Democrats are trying to capture Georgia Senate seats, so they will have absolute power over every aspect of your lives, if the liberal Democrats take the Senate and the White House.

*"And they are not taking this White House. We will fight like h*ll. I will tell you right now."*

Trump railed against courts refusing to take the campaign election cases, particularly when they did so by declaring they had no standing to even look at his camp's evidence.

"I'm not happy with the Supreme Court," Trump said. "They're not stepping up. I'm not happy with them."

Loeffler announced she is joining the Senate GOP fight against certifying the Electoral College vote for Biden.

"I have an announcement, Georgia," she told the rally. "On Jan. 6, I will object to the Electoral College vote. We will get this done, Georgia. "I have a very important question for you: Are you ready to show America that Georgia is a red state?

"That's right. That's right. This president fought for us. We are fighting for him. He put America first. He put the American worker first. Thanks, Mr. President. He stood with our men and women of law enforcement and restored our military."

The electoral challenge is considered by observers and political experts to face very long odds of resulting in any flip from a Biden win; Dems control the House, and though Republicans currently hold the Senate, enough have declined to sign onto the Biden challenge to raise doubts about any vote favoring Trump's camp. (The president has blasted those Republicans who have not lined up on his side.)

Nonetheless, after brief addresses from Loeffler and first daughter Ivanka Trump, Trump returned to the mic to implore supporters to vote to stop the "steal." "Our entire nation is counting on the people of Georgia – in a way the world is counting on the people of Georgia," Trump said. "The fate of our country is at stake. It's in your hands. "You must deliver a Republican victory so big that the Democrats can't steal it or cheat it away. They will be trying. I will tell you that.

"We have all seen what our opponents are capable of doing. I ran two elections. I won both of them – second one much more successful than the first. But we can't let this happen any longer."

WITH SURGICAL PRECISION; IN GEORGIA; THIS IS THE AUTOPSY OF THE (6) SWING STATE DEMOCRAT CONSPIRACY TO STEAL THE WHITE HOUSE 2020 PRESIDENTIAL ELECTION; THE SAME HAPPENED IN GEORGIA; PENNSYLVANIA, MICHIGAN, WISCONSIN; ARIZONA & NEVADA.

CNN has obtained the full January 2 audio call between President Donald Trump and Georgia Secretary of State Brad Raffensperger. Trump is joined on the call by White House chief of staff Mark Meadows and several lawyers.

CNN obtained the audio from a source who was on the call and had direct knowledge of the conversation. CNN has redacted the name of one individual about whom Trump made unsubstantiated claims.

Here is the full transcript and audio of the hour-long call.

President Donald Trump and Georgia Secretary of State Brad Raffensperger

Meadows: Ok. Alright. Mr. President, everyone is on the line. This is Mark Meadows, the chief of staff. Just so we all are aware. On the line is secretary of state, and two other individuals. Jordan and Mr. Germany with him. You also have the attorneys that represent the president, Kurt and Alex and Cleta Mitchell — who is not the attorney of record but has been involved — myself and then the president. So Mr. President, I›ll turn it over to you.

Trump: OK, thank you very much. Hello Brad and Ryan and everybody. We appreciate the time and the call. So we›ve spent a lot of time on this and if we could just go over some of the numbers, I think it›s pretty clear that we won. We won **very substantially in Georgia. You even see it by rally size, frankly. We'd be getting 25-30,000 people a rally and the competition would get less than 100 people. And it never made sense.**

But we have a number of things. We have at least 2 or 3 — anywhere from 250-300,000 ballots were dropped mysteriously into the rolls. Much of that had to do with Fulton County, which hasn't been checked. We think that if you check the signatures — a real check of the signatures going back in Fulton County you'll find at least a couple of hundred thousand of forged signatures of people who have been forged. And we are quite sure that's going to happen.

Another tremendous number. We're going to have an accurate number over the next two days with certified accountants. But an accurate number but its in the 50s of thousands— and that's people that went to vote and they were told they can't vote because they've already been voted for. And it's a very sad thing. They walked out complaining. But the number's large. We'll have it for you. But it's much more than the number of 11,779 that's — The current margin is only 11,779. Brad, I think you agree with that, right? That's something I think everyone — at least that's' a number that everyone agrees on.

But that's the difference in the votes. But we've had hundreds of thousands of ballots that we're able to actually — we'll get you a pretty accurate number. You don't need much of a number because the number that in theory I lost by, the margin would be 11,779. But you also have a substantial numbers of people, thousands and thousands who went to the voting place on November 3, were told they couldn't vote, were told they couldn't vote because a ballot had been put on their name. And you know that's very, very, very, very sad. We had, I believe it's about 4,502 voters who voted but who weren't on the voter registration list, so it's 4,502 who voted but they weren't on the voter registration roll which they had to be. You had 18,325 vacant address voters. The address was vacant and they're not allowed to be counted. That's 18,325.

Smaller number — you had 904 who only voted where they had just a P.O. — a post office box number — and they had a post office box number and that's not allowed. We had at least 18,000 — that's on tape we had them counted very painstakingly — 18,000 voters having to do with [name]. She's a vote scammer, a professional vote scammer and hustler [name]. That was the tape that's been shown all over the world that makes everybody look bad, you me and everybody else.

Where they got — number one they said very clearly and it's been reported they said there was a major water main break. Everybody fled the area. And then they came back, [name] and her daughter and a few people. There were no Republican poll watchers. Actually, there were no Democrat poll watchers, I guess they were them. But there were no Democrats, either and there was no law enforcement. Late in the morning, they went early in the morning they went to the table with the black robe, the black shield and they pulled out the votes. Those votes were put there a number of hours before the table was put there. I think it was, Brad you would know, it was probably eight hours or seven hours before and then it was stuffed with votes.

They weren't in an official voter box, but they were in what looked to be suitcases or trunks, suitcases but they weren't in voter boxes. The minimum number it could be because we watched it and they watched it certified

in slow motion instant replay if you can believe it but slow motion and it was magnified many times over and the minimum it was 18,000 ballots, all for Biden.

You had out-of-state voters. They voted in Georgia but they were from out of state, of 4,925. You had absentee ballots sent to vacant, they were absentee ballots sent to vacant addresses. They had nothing on them about addresses, that's 2,326.

And you had drop boxes, which is very bad. You had drop boxes that were picked up. We have photographs and we have affidavits from many people.

I don't know if you saw the hearings, but you have drop boxes where the box was picked up but not delivered for three days. So all sorts of things could have happened to that box including, you know, putting in the votes that you wanted. So there were many infractions and the bottom line is, many, many times the 11,779 margin that they said we lost by — we had vast I mean the state is in turmoil over this.

And I know you would like to get to the bottom of it, although I saw you on television today and you said that you found nothing wrong. I mean, you know, And I didn't lose the state, Brad. People have been saying that it was the highest vote ever. There was no way. A lot of the political people said that there's no way they beat me. And they beat me. They beat me in the ... As you know, every single state ... we won every state. we one every statehouse in the country. We held the Senate which is shocking to people, although we'll see what happens tomorrow or in a few days.

And we won the House, but we won every single statehouse and we won Congress, which was supposed to lose 15 seats, and they gained, I think 16 or 17 or something. I think there's a now difference of five. There was supposed to be a difference substantially more. But politicians in every state, but politicians in Georgia have given affidavits or are going to that, that there was no way that they beat me in the election that the people came out, in fact, they were expecting to lose and then they ended up winning by a lot because of the coattails. And they said there's no way that they've done many polls prior to the election. There was no way that they won.

Ballots were dropped in massive numbers. And we're trying to get to those numbers and we will have them. They'll take a period of time. Certified. But but they're massive numbers. And far greater than the 11,779.

The other thing, dead people. So dead people voted and I think the number is close to 5,000 people. And they went to obituaries. They went to all sorts of methods to come up with an accurate number and a minimum is close to about 5,000 voters.

The bottom line is when you add it all up and then you start adding, you know, 300,000 fake ballots. Then the other thing they said is in Fulton County and other areas. And this may or may not ... because this just came up this morning that they are burning their ballots, that they are shredding, shredding ballots and removing equipment. They're changing the equipment on the Dominion machines and, you know, that's not legal.

And they supposedly shredded I think they said 300 pounds of, 3,000 pounds of ballots. And that just came

to us as a report today. And it is a very sad situation. But Brad, if you took the minimum numbers where many, many times above the 11,779 and many of those numbers are certified, or they will be certified but they are certified. And those are numbers that are there that exist. And that beat the margin of loss, they beat it, I mean by a lot and people should be happy to have an accurate count instead of an election where there's turmoil.

I mean there's turmoil in Georgia and other places. You're not the only one I mean we have other states that I believe will be flipping to us very shortly. And this is something that — You know, as an example, I think it in Detroit, I think there's a section a good section of your state actually, which we're not sure so we're not going to report it yet. But in Detroit, we had, I think it was, 139% of the people voted. That's not too good.

In Pennsylvania, they had well over 200,000 more votes than they had people voting. And uh that doesn't play too well, and the legislature there is, which is Republican, is extremely activist and angry. I mean, there were other things also that were almost as bad as that. But, uh, they had as an example, in Michigan, a tremendous number of dead people that voted. I think it was I think, Mark, it was 18,000. Some unbelievably high number, much higher than yours, you were in the 4-5,000 category.

And that was checked out laboriously by going through, by going through the obituary columns in the newspapers.

So I guess with all of it being said, Brad, the bottom line and provisional ballots, again, you know, you'll have to tell me about the provisional ballots, but we have a lot of people that were complaining that they weren't able to vote because they were already voted for. These are great people.

And, you know, they were shellshocked. I don't know if you call that provisional ballots. In some states we had a lot of provisional ballot situations where people were given a provisional ballot because when they walked in on November 3 and they were already voted for.

So that's it. I mean, we have many many times the number of votes necessary to win the state. And we won the state and we won it very substantially and easily and we're getting, we have, much of this is a very, you know they're certified, far more certified than we need. But we're getting additional numbers certified, too. And we're getting pictures of dropboxes being delivered and delivered late. Delivered three days later, in some cases, plus we have many affidavits to that effect.

Meadows: So Mr. President, if I might be able to jump in and I›ll give Brad a chance. Mr. Secretary, obviously there is, there are allegations where we believe that not every vote or fair vote and legal vote was counted and that›s at odds with the representation from the secretary of state›s office.

What I'm hopeful for is there some way that we can we can find some kind of agreement to look at this a little bit more fully. You know the president mentioned Fulton County.

But in some of these areas where there seems to be a difference of where the facts seem to lead, and so Mr. Secretary, I was hopeful that, you know, in the spirit of cooperation and compromise is there something

that we can at least have a discussion to look at some of these allegations to find a path forward that's less litigious?

Raffensperger: Well, I listened to what the President has just said. President Trump, we›ve had several lawsuits and we›ve had to respond in court to the lawsuits and the contentions. Um, we don›t agree that you have won. And we don›t — I didn›t agree about the 200,000 number that you›d mentioned. And I can go through that point by point.

What we have done is we gave our state Senate about one and a half hours of our time going through the election issue by issue and then on the state House, the government affairs committee, we gave them about two and a half hours of our time, going back point by point on all the issues of contention. And then just a few days ago we met with our U.S. congressmen, Republican congressmen, and we gave them about two hours of our time talking about this past election. Going back, primarily what you've talked about here focused in on primarily, I believe, is the absentee ballot process. I don't believe that you're really questioning the Dominion machines. Because we did a hand retally, a 100% retally of all the ballots and compared them to what the machines said and came up with virtually the same result. Then we did the recount, and we got virtually the same result. So I guess we can probably take that off the table.

I don't think there's an issue about that. What you--

Trump: Well, Brad. Not that there›s not an issue, because we have a big issue with Dominion in other states and perhaps in yours. But we haven›t felt we needed to go there. And just to, you know, maybe put a little different spin on what Mark is saying, Mark Meadows, uh, yeah we›d like to go further, but we don›t really need to. We have all the votes we need.

You know, we won the state. If you took, these are the most minimal numbers, the numbers that I gave you, those are numbers that are certified, your absentee ballots sent to vacant addresses, your out of state voters 4,925. You know when you add them up, it's many more times, it's many times the 11,779 number. So we could go through, we have not gone through your Dominion. So we can't give them blessing. I mean, in other states, we think we found tremendous corruption with Dominion machines but we'll have to see.

But we only lost the state by that number, 11,000 votes, and 779. So with that being said, with just what we have, with just what we have we're giving you minimal, minimal numbers. We're doing the most conservative numbers possible, we're many times, many, many times above the margin. And so we don't really have to, Mark, I don't think we have to go through ...

Meadows: Right

Trump: Because, what›s the difference between winning the election by two votes and winning it by half a million votes. I think I probably did win it by half a million. You know, one of the things that happened Brad, is we have other people coming in now from Alabama and from South Carolina and from other states, and they›re saying it›s impossible for you to have lost Georgia. We won. You know in Alabama, we set a record, got the highest vote ever. In Georgia, we set a record with a massive amount of votes. And they say it›s not possible to have lost Georgia.

And I could tell you by our rallies. I could tell you by the rally I'm having on Monday night, the place, they already have lines of people standing out front waiting. It's just not possible to have lost Georgia. It's not possible. When I heard it was close I said there's no way. But they dropped a lot of votes in there late at night. You know that, Brad. And that's what we are working on very, very stringently. But regardless of those votes, with all of it being said, we lost by essentially 11,000 votes and we have many more votes already calculated and certified, too.

And so I just don't know, you know, Mark, I don't know what's the purpose. I won't give Dominion a pass because we found too many bad things. But we don't need Dominion or anything else. We have won this election in Georgia based on all of this. And there's nothing wrong with saying that, Brad. You know I mean, having the correct — the people of Georgia are angry. And these numbers are going to be repeated on Monday night. Along with others that we're going to have by that time which are much more substantial even. And the people of Georgia are angry, the people of the country are angry. And there's nothing wrong with saying, you know, um, that you've recalculated. Because the 2,236 in absentee ballots. I mean, they're all exact numbers that were done by accounting firms law firms, etc. and even if you cut 'em in half, cut 'em in half and cut 'em in half, again, it's more votes than we need.

Raffensperger: Well Mr. President, the challenge that you have is, the data you have is wrong. We talked to the congressmen and they were surprised.

But they — I guess there was a person Mr. Braynard who came to these meetings and presented data and he said that there was dead people, I believe it was upward of 5,000. The actual number were two. Two. Two people that were dead that voted. So that's wrong. There were two.

Trump: Well Cleta, how do you respond to that? Maybe you tell me?

Mitchell: Well, I would say Mr. Secretary, one of the things that we have requested and what we said was, if you look, if you read our petition, it said that we took the names and birth years and we had certain information available to us. We have asked from your office for records that only you **have and so we said there is a universe of people who have the same name and same birth year and died.**

But we don't have the records that you have. And one of the things that we have been suggesting formally and informally for weeks now is for you to make available to us the records that would be necessary —

Trump: But Cleta, even before you do that, and not even including that, that›s why hardly even included that number, although in one state we have a tremendous amount of dead people. So I don›t know — I›m sure we do in Georgia, too. I›m sure we do in Georgia too.

But, um, we're so far ahead. We're so far ahead of these numbers, even the phony ballots of [name], known scammer. You know the Internet? You know what was trending on the Internet? "Where's [name]?" Because they thought she'd be in jail. "Where's [name]?" It's crazy, it's crazy. That was. The minimum number is 18,000 for [name], but they think it's probably about 56,000, but the minimum number is 18,000 on the [name] night where she ran back in there when everybody was gone and stuffed, she stuffed the ballot boxes.

Let's face it, Brad, I mean. They did it in slow motion replay magnified, right? She stuffed the ballot boxes. They were stuffed like nobody had ever seen them stuffed before.

So there's a term for it when it's a machine instead of a ballot box, but she stuffed the machine. She stuffed the ballot — each ballot went three times they were showing: Here's ballot No 1. Here it is second time, third time, next ballot.

I mean, look. Brad. We have a new tape that we're going to release. It's devastating. And by the way, that one event, that one event is much more than the 11,000 votes that we're talking about. It's uh, you know. That one event was a disaster. And it's just, you know, but it was, it was something, it can't be disputed. And again we have a version that you haven't seen but it's magnified. It's magnified and you can see everything. For some reason they put it in three times, each ballot, and I don't know why. I don't know why three times. Why not five times, right? Go ahead.

Raffensperger: You›re talking about the State Farm video. And I think it›s extremely unfortunate that Rudy Giuliani or his people, they sliced and diced that video and took it out of context. The next day we brought in WSB-TV and we let them show, see the full run of tape and what you›ll see, the events that transpired are nowhere near what was projected by, you know —

Trump: But where were the poll watchers, Brad? There were no poll watchers there. There were no Democrats or Republicans. There was no security there.

It was late in the evening, late in the, early in the morning, and there was nobody else in the room. Where were the poll watchers and why did they say a water main broke, which they did and which was reported in the newspapers? They said they left. They ran out because of a water main break, and there was no water main. There was nothing. There was no break. There was no water main break. But we're, if you take out everything, where were the Republican poll watchers, even where were the Democrat poll watchers, because there were none.

And then you say, well, they left their station, you know, if you look at the tape, and this was, this was reviewed by professional police and detectives and other people, when they left in a rush, everybody left in a rush because of the water main, but everybody left in a rush. These people left their station.

When they came back, they didn't go to their station. They went to the apron, wrapped around the table, under which were thousands and thousands of ballots in a box that was not an official or a sealed box. And then they took those. They went back to a different station. So if they would have come back, they would have walked to their station and they would have continued to work. But they couldn't do even that because that's illegal, because they had no Republican poll watchers. And remember, her reputation is deva — she's known all over the Internet, Brad. She's known all over.

I'm telling you, "Where's [name]" was one of the hot items ...[name] They knew her. "Where's [name]?" So Brad, there can be no justification for that. And I you know, I give everybody the benefit of the doubt. But that was — and Brad, why did they put the votes in three times? You know, they put 'em in three times.

Raffensperger: Mr. President, they did not put that. We did an audit of that and we proved conclusively that they were not scanned three times.

Trump: Where was everybody else at that late time in the morning? Where was everybody? Where were the Republicans? Where were the security guards? Where were the people that were there just a little while before when everyone ran out of the room. How come we had no security in the room? Why did they run to the bottom of the table? Why do they run there and just open the skirt and rip out the votes? I mean, Brad. And they were sitting there, I think for five hours or something like that, the votes. But they just all happened to run back and go, you know, Brad...

Raffensperger: Mr. President, we›ll send you the link from WSB.

Trump: I don›t care about the link. I don›t need it. Brad, I have a much better link —

Mitchell: I will tell you. I›ve seen the tape. The full tape. So has Alex. We›ve watched it. And what we saw and what we›ve confirmed in the timing is that. They made everybody leave, we have sworn affidavits saying that. And then they began to process ballots. And our estimate is that there were roughly 18,000 ballots. We don›t know that. If you know that ...

Trump: It was 18,000 ballots but they used each one three times.

Mitchell: Well, I don›t know about that.

Trump: I do think because we had ours magnified out. Each one magnified out is 18 times three

Mitchell: I›ve watched the entire tape.

Trump: Nobody can make a case for that, Brad. Nobody. I mean, look, you›d have to be a child to think anything other than that. Just a child. I mean you have your never Trumper...

Mitchell: How many ballots, Mr. Secretary, are you saying were processed then?

Raffensperger: We had GBI ... investigate that.

Germany: We had our — this is Ryan Germany. We had our law enforcement officers talk to everyone who was who was there after that event came to light. GBI was with them as well as FBI agents.

Trump: Well, there›s no way they could — then they›re incompetent. They›re either dishonest or incompetent, okay?

Mitchell: Well, what did they find?

Trump: There›s only two answers, dishonesty or incompetence. There›s just no way. Look. There›s no way. And on the other thing, I said too, there is no way. I mean, there›s no way that these things could have been you know, you have all these different people that voted but they don›t live in Georgia anymore. What was that number, Cleta? That was a pretty good number too.

Mitchell: The number who have registered out of state after they moved from Georgia. And so they had a date when they moved from Georgia, they registered to vote out of state. And then it›s like 4,500, I don›t have that number right in front of me.

Trump: And then they came back in and they voted.

Mitchell: And voted. Yeah.

Trump: I thought that was a large number, though. It was in the 20s. The point is...

Germany: We›ve been going through each of those as well and those numbers that we got that Ms. Mitchell was just saying, they›re not accurate. Every one we›ve been through, are people that lived in Georgia, moved to a different state, but then moved back to Georgia legitimately. And in many cases

Trump: How many people do that? They moved out and then they said, «Ah, to hell with it I›ll move back.» You know, it doesn›t sound like a very normal ... you mean, they moved out, and what, they missed it so much that they wanted to move back in? It›s crazy.

Germany: This is they moved back in years ago. This was not like something just before the election. So there›s something about that data that, it›s just not accurate.

Trump: Well, I don›t know, all I know is that it is certified. And they moved out of Georgia and they voted. It didn›t say they moved back in Cleta, did it?

Mitchell: No, but I mean, we›re looking at the voter registration. Again, if you have additional records, we›ve been asking for that, but you haven›t shared any of that with us. You just keep saying you investigated the allegations.

Trump: But, Cleta, a lot of it you don›t need to be shared. I mean, to be honest, they should share it. They should share it because you want to get to an honest election.

I won this election by hundreds of thousands of votes. There's no way I lost Georgia. There's no way. We won by hundreds of thousands of votes. I'm just going by small numbers when you add them up they're many times the 11,000. But I won that state by hundreds of thousands of votes.

Do you think it's possible that they shredded ballots in Fulton County? Because that's what the rumor is. And also that Dominion took out machines. That Dominion is really moving fast to get rid of their, uh, machinery.

Do you know anything about that? Because that's illegal, right?

Germany: This is Ryan Germany. No, Dominion has not moved any machinery out of Fulton County.

Trump: But have they moved the inner parts of the machines and replaced them with other parts?

Germany: No.

Trump: Are you sure, Ryan?

Germany: I›m sure. I›m sure, Mr. President.

Trump: What about, what about the ballots. The shredding of the ballots. Have they been shredding ballots?

Germany: The only investigation that we have into that — they have not been shredding any ballots. There was an issue in Cobb County where they were doing normal office shredding, getting rid of old stuff, and we investigated that. But this is stuff from, you know, from you know past elections.

Trump: I don›t know. It doesn›t pass the smell test because we hear they›re shredding thousands and thousands of ballots and now what they›re saying, «Oh, we›re just cleaning up the office.» So I don›t think they›re cleaning.

Raffensperger: Mr. President, the problem you have with social media, they — people can say anything.

Trump: Oh this isn›t social media. This is Trump media. It›s not social media. It›s really not it›s not social media. I don›t care about social media. I couldn›t care less. Social media is Big Tech. Big Tech is on your side. I don›t even know why you have a side, because you should want to have an accurate election. And you›re a Republican.

Raffensperger: We believe that we do have an accurate election.

Trump: No, no you don›t. No, no you don›t. You don›t have. Not even close. You›re off by hundreds of thousands of votes. And just on the small numbers, you›re off on these numbers **and these numbers can't be just — well, why wont? — Okay. So you sent us into Cobb County for signature verification, right? You sent us into Cobb County, which we didn't want to go into. And you said it would be open to the public. And we could have our - So we had our experts there they weren't allowed into the room. But we didn't want Cobb County. We wanted Fulton County. And you wouldn't give it to us. Now, why aren't we doing signature — and why can't it be open to the public?**

And why can't we have professionals do it instead of rank amateurs who will never find anything and don't want to find anything? They don't want to find, you know, they don't want to find anything. Someday you'll tell me the reason why, because I don't understand your reasoning, but someday you'll tell me the reason why. But why don't you want to find?

Germany: Mr. President, we chose Cobb County —

Trump: Why don›t you want to find ... What?

Germany: Sorry, go ahead.

Trump: So why did you do Cobb County? We didn›t even request — we requested Fulton County, not Cobb County. Go ahead, please. Go ahead.

Germany: We chose Cobb County because that was the only county where there›s been any evidence submitted that the signature verification was not properly done.

Trump: No, but I told you. We›re not, we›re not saying that.

Mitchell: We did say that.

Trump: Fulton County. Look. Stacey, in my opinion, Stacey is as dishonest as they come. She has outplayed you ... at everything. She got you to sign a totally unconstitutional agreement, which is a disastrous agreement. You can›t check signatures. I can›t imagine you›re allowed to do harvesting, I guess, in that agreement. That agreement is a disaster for this country. But she got you somehow to sign that thing and she has outsmarted you at every step.

And I hate to imagine what's going to happen on Monday or Tuesday, but it's very scary to people. You know, where the ballots flow in out of nowhere. It's very scary to people. That consent decree is a disaster. It's a disaster. A very good lawyer who examined it said they've never seen anything like it.

Raffensperger: Harvesting is still illegal in the state of Georgia. And that settlement agreement did not change that one iota.

Trump: It›s not a settlement agreement, it›s a consent decree. It even says consent decree on it, doesn›t it? It uses the term consent decree. It doesn›t say settlement agree. It›s a consent decree. It›s a disaster.

Raffensperger: It›s a settlement agreement.

Trump: What›s written on top of it?

Raffensperger: Ryan?

Germany: I don›t have it in front of me, but it was not entered by the court, it›s not a court order.

Trump: But Ryan, it›s called a consent decree, is that right? On the paper. Is that right?

Germany: I don›t. I don›t. I don›t believe so, but I don›t have it in front of me.

Trump: OK, whatever, it›s a disaster. It›s a disaster. Look. Here›s the problem. We can go through signature verification and we›ll find hundreds of thousands of signatures, if you let us do it. And the only way you can do it, as you know, is to go to the past. But you didn›t do that in Cobb County. You just looked at one page compared to another. The only way you can do a signature verification is go from the one that signed it on November whatever. Recently. And compare it to two years ago, four years ago, six years ago, you know, or even one. And you›ll find that you have many different signatures. But in Fulton, where they dumped ballots, you will find that you have many that aren›t even signed and you have many that are forgeries.

OK, you know that. You know that. You have no doubt about that. And you will find you will be at 11,779 within minutes, because Fulton County is totally corrupt and so is she, totally corrupt.

And they're going around playing you and laughing at you behind your back, Brad, whether you know it or not, they're laughing at you and you've taken a state that's a Republican state, and you've made it almost impossible for a Republican to win because of cheating, because they cheated like nobody's ever cheated before. And I don't care how long it takes me, you know, we're going to have other states coming forward — pretty good.

But I won't ... this is never ... this is ... We have some incredible talent said they've never seen anything ... Now the problem is they need more time for the big numbers. But they're very substantial numbers. But I think you're going to find that they — by the way, a little information, I think you're going to find that they are shredding ballots because they have to get rid of the ballots because the ballots are unsigned. The ballots are corrupt, and they're brand new and they don't have a seal and there's the whole thing with the ballots. But the ballots are corrupt.

And you are going to find that they are — which is totally illegal, it is more illegal for you than it is for them because, you know what they did and you're not reporting it. That's a criminal, that's a criminal offense. And you can't let that happen. That's a big risk to you and to Ryan, your lawyer. And that's a big risk. But they are shredding ballots, in my opinion, based on what I've heard. And they are removing machinery and they're moving it as fast as they can, both of which are criminal finds. And you can't let it happen and you are letting it happen. You know, I mean, I'm notifying you that you're letting it happen. So look. All I want to do is this. I just want to find 11,780 votes, which is one more than we have because we won the state.

And flipping the state is a great testament to our country because, cause you know, this is — it's a testament that they can admit to a mistake or whatever you want to call it. If it was a mistake, I don't know. A lot of people think it wasn't a mistake. It was much more criminal than that. But it's a big problem in Georgia and it's not a problem that's going away. I mean, you know, it's not a problem that's going away.

Germany: Mr President, this is Ryan. We›re looking into every one of those things that you mentioned.

Trump: Good. But if you find it you›ve got to say it, Ryan.

Germany: ... Let me tell you what we are seeing. What we›re seeing is not at all what you›re describing, these are investigators from our office, these are investigators from

GBI, and they're looking and they're good. And that's not what they're seeing. And we'll keep looking, at all

these things.

Trump: Well, you better check the ballots because they are shredding ballots, Ryan. I›m just telling you, Ryan. They›re shredding ballots. And you should look at that very carefully. Because that›s so illegal. You know, you may not even believe it because it›s so bad. But they›re shredding ballots because they think we›re going to eventually get ... because we›ll eventually get into Fulton. In my opinion it›s never too late. ... So, that›s the story. Look, we need only 11,000 votes. We have are far more than that as it stands now. We›ll have more and more. And. Do you have provisional ballots at all, Brad? Provisional ballots?

Raffensperger: Provisional ballots are allowed by state law.

Trump: Sure, but I mean, are they counted or did you just hold them back because they, you know, in other words, how many provisional ballots do you have in the state?

Raffensperger: We›ll get you that number.

Trump: Because most of them are made out to the name Trump. Because these are people that were scammed when they came in. And we have thousands of people that have testified or that want to testify when they came in they were probably going to vote on November 3. And they were told I›m sorry, you›ve already been voted for, you›ve already voted. The women, men started screaming, No. I proudly voted til November 3. They said, I›m sorry, but you›ve already been voted for and you have a ballot and these people are beside themselves. So they went out and they filled in a provisional ballot, putting the name Trump on it.

And what about that batch of military ballots that came in. And even though I won the military by a lot, it was 100 % Trump. I mean 100 % Biden. Do you know about that? A large group of ballots came in. I think it was to Fulton County and they just happened to be 100 % for Trump — for Biden, even though Trump won the military by a lot, you know, a tremendous amount. But these ballots were 100 % for Biden. And, do you know about that? A very substantial number came in, all for Biden. Does anybody know about it?

Mitchell: I know about it, but —

Trump: OK, Cleta, I›m not asking you Cleta, honestly. I›m asking Brad. Do you know about the military ballots that we have confirmed now. Do you know about the military ballots **that came in that were 100 %, I mean 100 % for Biden. Do you know about that?**

Germany: I don›t know about that, I do know that we have when military ballots come in, it›s not just military, it›s also military and overseas citizens. The military part of that does generally go Republican. The overseas citizen part of it generally goes very Democrat. This was a mix of ‹em.

Trump: No, but this was. That›s OK. But I got like 78 **% in the military. These ballots were all for ... They didn't tell me overseas. Could be overseas too, but I get votes overseas too, Ryan, you know in all fairness. No they came in, a large batch came in and it was, quote, 100 % for Biden. And that is criminal. You know, that's criminal. OK. That's another criminal, that's another of the many criminal events, many criminal events here.**

Oh, I don't know, look Brad. I got to get ... I have to find 12,000 votes and I have them times a lot. And therefore, I won the state. That's before we go to the next step, which is in the process of right now. You know, and I watched you this morning and you said, uh, well, there was no criminality.

But I mean, all of this stuff is very dangerous stuff. When you talk about no criminality, I think it's very dangerous for you to say that.

I just, I just don't know why you don't want to have the votes counted as they are. Like even you when you went and did that check. And I was surprised because, you know ...the check... And we found a few thousand votes that were against me. I was actually surprised because the way that check was done, all you're doing is you know, recertifying existing votes and, you know, and you were given votes and you just counted them up and you still found 3,000 that were bad. So that was sort of surprising that it came down to three or five I don't know. still a lot of votes. But you have to go back to check from past years with respect to signatures. And if you check with Fulton County, you'll have hundreds of thousands because they dumped ballots into Fulton County and the other county next to it.

So what are we going to do here folks? I only need 11,000 votes. Fellas, I need 11,000 votes. Give me a break. You know, we have that in spades already. Or we can keep it going but that's not fair to the voters of Georgia because they're going to see what happened and they're going to see what happened. I mean, I'll, I'll take on to anybody you want with regard to [name] and her lovely daughter, a very lovely young lady, I'm sure. But, but [name] ... I will take on anybody you want. And the minimum, there were 18,000 ballots but they used them three times. So that's, you know, a lot of votes. ...and that one event... And they were all to Biden, by the way, that's the other thing we didn't say. You know, [name] , the one thing I forgot to say which was the most important. You know that every single ballot she did went to Biden. You know that, right? Do you know that, by the way, Brad?

Every single ballot that she did through the machines at early, early in the morning, went to Biden. Did you know that, Ryan?

Germany: That›s not accurate, Mr. President.

Trump: Huh. What is accurate?

Germany: The numbers that we are showing are accurate.

Trump: No, about [name] . About early in the morning, Ryan. When the woman took, you know, when the whole gang took the stuff from under the table, right? Do you know, do you know who those ballots, who they were made out to, do you know who they were voting for?

Germany: No, not specifically.

Trump: Did you ever check?

Germany: We did what I described to you earlier —

Trump: No no no — did you ever check the ballots that were scanned by [name] , a known political operative and balloteer. Did ever check who those votes were for?

Germany: We looked into that situation that you described.

Trump: No, they were 100 % **for Biden. 100 %. There wasn't a Trump vote in the whole group. Why don't you want to find this, Ryan? What's wrong with you? I heard your lawyer is very difficult, actually, but I'm sure you're a good lawyer. You have a nice last name.**

But, but I'm just curious why wouldn't, why do you keep fighting this thing? It just doesn't make sense. We're way over the 17,779, right? We're way over that number and just if you took just [name] , we're over that number by five, five or six times when you multiply that times three.

And every single ballot went to Biden, and you didn't know that, but, now you know it. So tell me, Brad, what are we going to do? We won the election and it's not fair to take it away from us like this. And it's going to be very costly in many ways. And I think you have to say that you're going to reexamine it and you can reexamine it, but reexamine it with people that want to find answers, not people that don't want to find answers. For instance, I'm hearing Ryan that he's probably, I'm sure a great lawyer and everything. But he's making statements about those ballots that he doesn't know. But he's making them with such — he did make them with surety. But now I think he's less sure because the answer is they all went to Biden and that alone wins us the election by a lot. You know, so.

Raffensperger: Mr. President, you have people that submit information and we have our people that submit information. And then it comes before the court and the court then has to make a determination. We have to stand by our numbers. We believe our numbers are right.

Trump: Why do you say that? I don›t know. I mean, sure, we can play this game with the courts, but why do you say that? First of all they don›t even assign us a judge. They don›t even assign us a judge. But why wouldn›t you — Hey Brad, why wouldn›t you want to check out [name] ? And why wouldn›t you want to say, hey, if in fact, President Trump is right about that, then he wins the state of Georgia, just that one incident alone without going through hundreds of **thousands of dropped ballots. You just say, you stick by, I mean I've been watching you, you know, you don't care about anything. "Your numbers are right." But your numbers aren't right. They're really wrong and they're really wrong, Brad. And I know this phone call is going nowhere other than, other than ultimately, you know — Look ultimately, I win, okay?**

Mitchell: Mr. Secretary...

Trump: Because you guys are so wrong. And you treated this. You treated the population of Georgia so badly. You, between you and your governor, who was down at 21, he was down 21 points. And like a schmuck, I endorsed him and he got elected, but I will tell you, he is a disaster.

And he knows, I can't imagine that people are so angry in Georgia, I can't imagine he's ever getting elected again I'll tell you that much right now. But why wouldn't you want to find the right answer, Brad, instead of keep saying that the numbers are right? Cause those numbers are so wrong?

Mitchell: Mr. Secretary, Mr. President, one of the things that we have been, Alex can talk about this, we talked about it, and I don›t know whether the information has been conveyed to your office, but I think what the president is saying, and what we›ve been trying to do is to say, look, the court is not acting on our petition. They haven›t even assigned a judge. But the people of Georgia and the people of America have a right to know the answers. And you have data and records that we don›t have access to. And you keep telling us and making public statements that you **investigated this and nothing to see here. But we don't know about that. All we know is what you tell us. What I don't understand is why wouldn't it be in everyone's best interest to try to get to the bottom, compare the numbers, you know, if you say, because - to try to be able to get to the truth because we don't have any way of confirming what you're telling us. You tell us that you had an investigation at the State Farm Arena. I don't have any report. I've never seen a report of investigation. I don't know that is. I've been pretty involved in this and I don't know. And that's just one of like , 25 categories. And it doesn't even, and as I, as the president said, we haven't even gotten into the Dominion issue. That's not part of our case. It's not part of our, we just didn't feel as though we had any way to be able to develop —**

Trump: No, we do have a way but I don›t want to get into it. We found a way in other states excuse me, but we don›t need it because we›re only down 11,000 votes so we don›t even need it. I personally think they›re corrupt as hell. But we don›t need that. Because all we have to do Cleta is find 11,000-plus votes. So we don›t need that. I›m not looking to shake up the whole world. We won Georgia easily. We won it by hundreds of thousands of votes. But if you go by basic simple numbers, we won it easily, easily. So we›re not giving Dominion a pass on the record. We just, we don›t need Dominion, because we have so many other votes that we don›t need to prove it any more than we already have.

Hilbert: Mr. President and Cleta, this is Kurt Hilbert, if I might interject for a moment. Um Ryan, I would like to suggest just four categories that have already been mentioned by the president that have actually hard numbers **of 24,149 votes that were counted illegally. That in and of itself is sufficient to change the results or place the outcome in doubt. We would like to sit down with your office and we can do it through purposes of compromise and just like this phone call, just to deal with that limited category of votes. And if you are able to establish that our numbers are not accurate, then fine. However, we believe that they are accurate. We've had now three to four separate experts looking at these numbers.**

Trump: Certified accountants looked at them.

Hilbert: Correct. And this is just based on USPS data and your own secretary of state›s data. So that›s what we would entreat and ask you to do, to sit down with us in a compromise and settlements proceeding and actually go through the registered voter IDs and registrations. And if you can convince us that that 24,149 is inaccurate, then fine. But we tend to believe that is, you know, obviously more than 11,779. That›s sufficient to change the results entirely in of itself. So what would you say to that, Mr. Germany?

Germany: Kurt, um I›m happy to get with our lawyers and we›ll set that up. That number is not accurate. And I think we can show you, for all the ones we›ve looked at, why it›s not. And so if that would be helpful, I›m happy to get with our lawyers and set that up with you guys.

Trump: Well, let me ask you, Kurt, you think that is an accurate number. That was based on the information given to you by the secretary of state›s department, right?

Hilbert: That is correct. That information is the minimum most conservative data based upon the USPS data and the secretary of state›s office data that has been made publicly available. We do not have the internal numbers from the secretary of state. Yet, we have asked for it six times. I sent a letter over to Mr... several times requesting this information, and it›s been rebuffed every single time. So it stands to reason that if the information is not forthcoming, there›s something to hide. That›s the problem that we have.

Germany: Well, that›s not the case sir. There are things that you guys are entitled to get. And there›s things that under the law, we are not allowed to give out.

Trump: Well, you have to. Well, under the law you›re not allowed to give faulty election results, OK? You›re not allowed to do that. And that›s what you done. This is a faulty election result. And honestly, this should go very fast. You should meet tomorrow because you have a big election coming up and because of what you›ve done to the president — you know, the people of Georgia know that this was a scam. And because of what you›ve done to the president, a lot of people aren›t going out to vote and a lot of Republicans are going to vote negative because they hate what you did to the president. Okay? They hate it. And they›re going to vote. And you would be respected. Really respected, if this thing could be straightened out before the election. You have a big election coming up on Tuesday. And therefore I think that it is really important that you meet tomorrow and work out on these numbers. Because I know Brad that if you think we›re right, I think you›re going to say, and I›m not looking to blame anybody. I›m just saying you know, and, you know, **under new counts, and under uh, new views, of the election results, we won the election. You know? It's very simple. We won the election. As the governors of major states and the surrounding states said, there is no way you lost Georgia, as the Georgia politicians say, there is no way, you lost Georgia. Nobody. Everyone knows I won it by hundreds of thousands of votes. But I'll tell you it's going to have a big impact on Tuesday if you guys don't get this thing straightened out fast.**

Meadows: Mr. President. This is Mark. It sounds like we›ve got two different sides agreeing that we can look at these areas ands I assume that we can do that within the next 24 to 48 hours to go ahead and get that reconciled so that we can look at the two claims and making sure that we get the access to the secretary of state›s data to either validate or invalidate the claims that have been made. Is that correct?

Germany: No, that›s not what I said. I›m happy to have our lawyers sit down with Kurt and the lawyers on that side and explain to my him, here›s, based on what we›ve looked at so far, here›s how we know this is wrong, this is wrong, this is wrong, this is wrong, this is wrong.

Meadows: So what you›re saying, Ryan, let me let me make sure ... so what you›re saying is you really don›t want to give access to the data. You just want to make another case on why the lawsuit is wrong?

Germany: I don›t think we can give access to data that›s protected by law. But we can sit down with them and say

—

Trump: But you›re allowed to have a phony election? You›re allowed to have a phony election right?

Germany: No sir.

Trump: When are you going to do signature counts, when are you going to do signature verification on Fulton County, which you said you were going to do, and now all of a sudden you›re not doing it. When are you doing that?

Germany: We are going to do that. We›ve announced —

Hilbert: To get to this issue of the personal information and privacy issue, is it possible that the secretary of state could deputize the lawyers for the president so that we could access that information and private information without you having any kind of violation?

Trump: Well, I don›t want to know who it is. You guys can do it very confidentially. You can sign a confidentiality agreement. That›s OK. I don›t need to know names. But we go the information on this stuff that we›re talking about. We got all that information from the secretary of state.

Meadows: Yeah. So let me let me recommend, Ryan, if you and Kurt would get together, you know, when we get off of this phone call, if you could get together and work out a plan to address some of what we›ve got with your attorneys where we can we can actually look at the data. For example, Mr. Secretary, I can tell you say they were only two dead people who would vote. I can promise you there were more than that. And that may be what your investigation shows, but I can promise you there were more than that. But at the same time, I think it›s important that we go ahead and move expeditiously to try to do this and resolve it as quickly as we possibly can. And if that›s the good next step. Hopefully we **can, uh we can finish this phone call and go ahead and agree that the two of you will get together immediately.**

Trump: Well why don›t my lawyers show you where you got the information. It will show the secretary of state, and you don›t even have to look at any names. We don›t want names. We don›t care. But we got that information from you. And Stacey Abrams is laughing about you know she›s going around saying these guys are dumber than a rock. What she›s done to this party is unbelievable, I tell ya. And I only ran against her once. And that was with a guy named Brian Kemp and I beat her. And if I didn›t run, Brian wouldn›t have had even a shot, either in the general or in the primary. He was dead, dead as a doornail. He never thought he had a shot at either one of them. What a schmuck I was. But that›s the way it is. That›s the way it is. I would like you ... for the attorneys ... I›d like you to perhaps meet with Ryan ideally tomorrow, because I think we should come to a resolution of this before the election. Otherwise you›re going to have people just not voting. They don›t want to vote. They hate the state, they hate the governor and they hate the secretary of state. I will tell you that right now. The only people like you are people that will never vote for you. You know that Brad, right? They like you know, they like you. They can›t believe what they found. They want people like you. So, look, can you get together tomorrow? And Brad. We just want the truth. It›s simple. And everyone›s going to look very good if the truth comes out. It›s OK. It takes a little while but let the truth come out. And the real truth is I won by 400,000 votes. At least. That›s the real truth. But we don›t need 400,000. We need less than 2,000 votes. And are you guys able to meet tomorrow Ryan?

Germany: Um, I›ll get with Chris, the lawyer representing us and the case, and see when he can get together with Kurt.

Raffensperger: Ryan will be in touch with the other attorney on this call, Mr. Meadows. Thank you President Trump for your time.

Trump: OK, thank you, Brad. Thank you, Ryan. Thank you. Thank you, everybody. Thank you very much. Bye.

Sen. Ted Cruz to Lead Senate GOP in Opposing Certification

A.K.A. ALAMO TED CRUZ CHANCES OF WINNING HAVE NOTHING TO DO WITH GOING AFTER TREASON TO STEAL THE WHITE HOUSE

Sen. Ted Cruz, R-Texas

Sen. Ted Cruz, R-Texas, said Saturday he is joining a block of about a dozen Republican senators that will

raise objections Jan 6 to Joe Biden's Nov. 3 victory, according to a joint statement from the lawmakers.

Cruz and 10 other Republican senators or senators-elect said in a statement they would raise objections in Congress on Jan. 6. It is when Congress is required by the U.S. Constitution to meet and accept the results of the Electoral College, a gathering that is typically a formality.

The statement calls for a delay of certification, and a 10-day investigation into accusations of wrongdoing, which have been stoked by Trump but repeatedly dismissed in court.

"Congress should immediately appoint an Electoral Commission, with full investigatory and fact-finding authority, to conduct an emergency 10-day audit of the election returns in the disputed states. Once completed, individual states would evaluate the Commission's findings and could convene a special legislative session to certify a change in their vote, if needed.

EVERY FUCKEN DEMOCRAT ON TELEVISION TO TELL AMERICA WHY WE SHOULDN'T DO THIS ESPECIALLY WOODCHUCK SCHMUCK SCHUMER I'M PERSONALLY CLEANSING THE SENATE OF; ON ELECTION DAY 2022.

"Accordingly, we intend to vote on January 6 to reject the electors from disputed states as not 'regularly given' and 'lawfully certified' (the statutory requisite), unless and until that emergency 10-day audit is completed."

According to a joint statement released Saturday, joining Cruz are: GOP Sens. Ron Johnson, R-Wis.; James Lankford, R-Okla.; Steve Daines, R-Mont.; John Kennedy, R-La.; Marsha Blackburn, R-Tenn.; and Mike Braun, R-Ind.; as well as Sens.-elect Cynthia Lummis; R-Wyo.; Roger Marshall, R-Kan.; Bill Hagerty, R-Tenn.; and Tommy Tuberville, R-Ala.

"We are not naïve. We fully expect most if not all Democrats, and perhaps more than a few Republicans, to vote otherwise. But support of election integrity should not be a partisan issue. A fair and credible audit-conducted expeditiously and completed well before January 20-would dramatically improve Americans' faith in our electoral process and would significantly enhance the legitimacy of whoever becomes our next President. We owe that to the People.

"These are matters worthy of the Congress, and entrusted to us to defend. We do not take this action lightly. We are acting not to thwart the democratic process, but rather to protect it. And every one of us should act together to ensure that the election was lawfully conducted under the Constitution and to do everything we can to restore faith in our Democracy."

The Trump campaign presented evidence of voter and election fraud, but Attorney General William Barr, who stepped down before Christmas, has said it did not meet the level of overturning the election.

Cruz's call for an investigation and an unprecedented delay in formally certifying Joe Biden's victory is seen as a condition that is all but certain to not be met, the people said. Cruz is poised to then oppose certification.

Say a prayer for New York City

By Post Editorial Board

Oh-oh: NYC's next mayor might actually be worse than de Blasio

Gotham's in trouble. Not just because it's suffering under the weight of crushing woes — soaring violence, out-of-control homelessness, a broken economy, a broke City Hall. And a population that can't flee fast enough.

But also because none of the would-be saviors running for mayor **is offering any meaningful plan to turn things around. And the primary, where the election is likely to be decided, is now less than six months away.**

As Bob McManus noted last week, **none of the candidates has yet to articulate any sound ideas to tackle the city's huge problems or even manage its core functions more effectively and efficiently, even as tax revenue is expected to fall billions below planned spending levels for the foreseeable future. Instead, candidates are more interested in reversing "inequities" and addressing racial "imbalances."**

You might expect, for instance, that City Comptroller Scott Stringer — the city's official, elected budget watchdog — would run almost single-mindedly on a plan to overhaul spending norms, confront labor

and demand sacrifices, à la the 1970s, when Gotham nearly went bust. Or push ways to save struggling businesses. Instead, he's focused on the need for a diversity czar and procurement preferences to minority- and women-owned businesses. (Seriously.)

Former Bloomberg housing commissioner and Obama Housing and Urban Development Secretary Shaun Donovan has been around long enough to be able to offer solid new solutions. His big contribution so far? "Fifteen-minute neighborhoods" — whatever *they* are. He promises they'll assure every New Yorker has access to a "great public school, fresh food, rapid transportation, a park [and] a chance to get ahead." (Feeling assured yet?)

Kathryn Garcia, Mayor de Blasio's recent sanitation commissioner, likewise offers nothing innovative in her pandemic-recovery plan. Her Web site promises "a public-health focused, risk-management approach" to reopening the city to business and tourism and "clear guidelines for every single industry." Talk about lowering the bar. She also promises to streamline regulations for restaurants and nightlife establishments and make business permitting and licensing easy and accessible. Good, but that's it?

Brooklyn Beep Eric Adams is among the frontrunners by virtue of his office, years as a state senator and the weakness of the rest of the field. He claims he's a moderate, yet his Web site opens with a video of him focused on police brutality, in which he actually admits he became a cop not to fight crime but to "take on police brutality from within." As for the 40 % spike in murders this year? Not a word.

Longshot wannabe City Councilman Carlos Menchaca (D-Bklyn), meanwhile, is opposed to rezonings in his district as tantamount to "human-rights violations" because in his view they don't take into account local concerns. Never mind that they are the primary means of easing the city's longtime chronic housing shortage. One of his ideas is to turn the Sunset Park waterfront into a "21st century hub for the new green economy and offshore wind development at the South Brooklyn Marine Terminal."

Former Citigroup honcho Ray McGuire is a fresh face but so far has only offered stale visions, vague promises and off-the-mark remedies. His Web site, for example, stresses minorities' "fear" of "overly aggressive policing" and the need for "a reimagined approach to public safety."

COVID has ravaged the health of thousands of New Yorkers, put many thousands out of work and upended the city's economy and finances. Crime, homelessness and other street chaos have also made life miserable here. The next mayor will have that and more to deal with come 2022. Pray that *someone* looking to take charge will come up with at least a few sensible ideas.

CHANCES OF TRUMP WINNING ISN'T WHY WE FIGHT; FOR LONG DEAD ANNE FRANK YET TO BE BORN; BOTH YET TO BE BORN FAR AWAY; & "KITTY" CATHERINE SUSAN GENOVESE; WHOSE (33) SCREAMS HERE AT HOME; WHERE IGNORED MARCH 13, 1964; BY THOSE OF US WHI "DIDN'T WANT TO GET INVOLVED".

Still, several other senators are in talks to follow Cruz, they added. It is not yet clear how many will, and whether any or all will vote against certification, or simply object or abstain. Discussions between senators' offices were ongoing Saturday, the people said.Sen. Josh Hawley, R-Mo., has already said he will object, teeing up a lengthy process Jan. 6 that is unlikely to stop the results but might splinter the GOP. Sen. John Thune, R-S.D., the Senate GOP's No. 2, said last week that attempts to object to the electoral count would "go down like a shot dog in the Senate." He advised GOP lawmakers who plan to take part in such an effort to reconsider.

Trump responded by urging someone – for example, South Dakota Gov. Kristi Noem – to launch a primary challenge against Thune in 2022.

Alan Dershowitz to Newsmax TV: Cancel Culture Is Left's Political Weapon

By Eric Mack

Cancel culture has overtaken America, but it is a cancer on our society, as the political left has weaponized it into a beast that will ultimately metastasize and come after anyone, according to legal expert Alan Dershowitz on Newsmax TV. "Cancel culture not only cancels free speech and due process, it also derails meritocracies," Dershowitz told "Saturday Report." "It says, 'We're not going to judge people on their merits; we're judging people on the basis of identity politics.'

"It's a cancer on America. It's a political weapon being used by the hard left, in general, and it just has such a terrible impact." Dershowitz warned host Carl Higbie, the power of social justice warriors is strong enough to take over American culture. "It has nothing to do with social justice," Dershowitz said. "It's not social. It's not justice. It's anti-social injustice. So, let's not let them claim social justice. Let's not let them claim they're progressives; they're regressives. They are taking away out liberties in the name of their definition of political correctness and identity politics. "We have to fight back. Unless we do, cancel culture will become American culture, and that would be a disaster for the freest and the best country in the history of the world."

Dershowitz is author of "Cancel Culture: The Latest Attack on Free Speech and Due Process," detailing lists of those who have been canceled and their losses. "Lists, blacklists, McCarthyite blacklists coming from the hard left these days – it's just doing a terrible job on American freedoms and the Bill of Rights," Dershowitz said. "There are people denying it. 'No, no, no, it's a right-wing argument designed to trivialize the left.'

"No, no, no, this is a real phenomenon. It has affected real people's lives. It has caused suicides. It has caused all kinds of terrible, terrible, terrible reactions, denying people the right to have jobs, denying audiences the right to hear speakers. It's just the reverse of McCarthyism of the 1950s. It's hard-left McCarthyism, and whether you're right, left, center – Republican of Democrat – you have to fight it, because they're coming for you next." Dershowitz noted the most recent example of a teen girl who was recorded using the N-word at age 15 and was blackmailed for it, causing her to be denied acceptance into the college of her choice.

"It's just amazing what people are prepared to do, and it's all one-sided," Dershowitz lamented. "If you're

African-American you can use those words without any hesitation. You can be anti-Semitic. You can join [Louis] Farrakhan's group. You can do whatever you want. "But, if you're – as they say – pale, Yale, and male, you're not going to be able to get away with anything. It's a double standard."

MR CLEAN CLEANSING AMERICA OF KANCEL KULTURE OF TOJO; JULIUS & ETHEL ROSENBERG 1913 U.S. ESPIONAGE ACT BULLIES ARE COWARDS; BELOW GEORGE FROST KENNAN'S X ARTICLE LONG TELEGRAM EXPLAINS LENGTH BOOK YOU'RE NOW READING

Answer to Dept's 284, Feb. 3,1945; involves questions so intricate, so delicate, so strange to our form of thought, and so important to analysis of our domestic & international environment that I cannot compress answers into single brief message without yielding to what I feel would be a dangerous degree of oversimplification. I hope, therefore, Dept will bear with me if I submit in answer to this question five parts...I apologize in advance for this burdening of telegraphic channel; but questions involved are of such urgent importance, particularly in view of recent events, that our answers to them, if they deserve attention at all, seem to me to deserve it at once.

Pence Asks Judge to Reject GOP Congressman's Elector Lawsuit

WE CAN'T EVEN TRUST PENCE. BOTH THE POPULAR VOTES ARE BALLOT STUFFING & DIGITAL FRAUD THE THE WINNING MARGIN OF ELECTORAL VOTES ARE A FRAUDULENT RICK DECK. WHY SHOULDN'T WE FIGHT IN EVERY WAY POSSIBLE TO PREVENT THEFT OF AMERICAN DEMOCRACY?

Vice President Mike Pence asked a federal judge in Texas to deny a Republican congressman's emergency request for a court order that would essentially allow the vice president to reverse Donald Trump's election loss during a joint session of Congress Wednesday.

Rep. Louie Gohmert of Texas should have sued the U.S. Senate or the House of Representatives if he disagrees with the established way that Electoral College votes are counted, Justice Department attorneys representing Pence said in a filing Thursday.

"The vice president -- the only defendant in this case -- is ironically the very person whose power they seek to promote," the government said. "The Senate and the House, not the vice president, have legal interests that are sufficiently adverse to plaintiffs."

Gohmert argues Pence can hand Trump a second term by simply rejecting swing states' slates of Democratic electors and instead choosing competing GOP electors when the Senate and House meet jointly to open and count certificates of electoral votes. Election experts have said such a finding would create a major conflict of interest.

The House asked for the judge's permission to file its own brief, in which it argues Gohmert is trying to "upend" Congress' longstanding role in counting the votes of the Electoral College and invalidate the Electoral Count Act, which has governed the process since 1887.

"The House also has a compelling interest in ensuring that the public's confidence in the processes for confirming the results of the 2020 presidential election is not undermined by this last-minute suit, which would authorize the vice president to ignore the will of the nation's voters," House attorneys said in the request. In another filing Thursday, Colorado elector Alan Kennedy argued Gohmert's lawsuit is based on flawed legal arguments and debunked claims of election fraud.

"Plaintiffs conclude their Electoral College fantasy by proposing unlimited discretion for defendant Pence to usurp the electoral process as plaintiffs desire," Kennedy, a lawyer, said in a motion to intervene in the case. "On behalf of the American People, please stop this madness."

Kennedy argues that competing slates of electors cannot be chosen because, among other things, they don't exist. States can only choose one slate -- and the swing states at issue already did so -- for President-elect Joe Biden and Vice President-elect Kamala Harris, he said.

"If an incumbent vice president could keep his or her job that way, then votes of millions of people and votes of duly elected and certified electors would be meaningless, and our nation's most cherished principle -- 'here, We the People rule' -- would be eviscerated," Kennedy said.

The vice president has the constitutional role of presiding over the Senate, which has traditionally included overseeing the formal acceptance of the Electoral College vote.

"I can tell you that the argument is something we expected and are not worried about," Gohmert's attorney

Howard Kleinhendler said in an email, adding that a more-detailed response will be filed Friday.

The Dec. 27 lawsuit by Gohmert echoes Trump's claim that Biden won the election only through rampant voter fraud perpetrated by thousands of corrupt Democratic officials and election workers. Some members of Congress have signaled they will object during the joint session, though not enough to block Biden's win.

Rep. Vernon Jones to Newsmax TV: Too Much at Stake Not to Vote in Georgia Runoffs

By Charlie MCarthy

There's too much at stake for disillusioned voters to stay home during Georgia's U.S. Senate runoffs, according to State Rep. Vernon Jones, on Newsmax TV.

Jones, a conservative Democrat, said voters need to go to the polls on Tuesday to reelect incumbent Sens. Kelly Loeffler, R-Ga., and David Perdue, R-Ga.

"Here's what's at stake. Defunding the police is at stake. What's at stake is not supporting the police," Jones

told host Grant Stinchfield on Thursday's "Stinchfield." "What's at stake is socialism coming into our lives. What's at stake is Marxism, and *Black Lives Matter*, and Antifa.

"They have to come out and vote. They have to."

Like many voters, Jones said he has not been happy with what he called "election fraud" in Georgia during the November election. He cited alleged improprieties involving mail-in ballots, out-of-state residents requesting absentee ballots, and election observers being removed during voting. "We have to have people come out and vote," said Jones, who represents House District 91. "Their voices have to be counted. There's so much at stake here. They're not happy with the system, I'm not happy with the system."

Sen. Loeffler opposes the Rev. Raphael Warnock, and Perdue goes against Jon Ossoff in the runoffs that will decide which party will own a voting majority in the U.S. Senate.

THIS SCUMBAG IS WHO DEMOCRATS ARE POURING HUNDREDS OF MILLIONS OF DOLLARS INTO GEORGIA TO SUPPORT

Cheat Sheet: 9 Things to Know About Raphael Warnock

Ashley Oliver

Democrat Rev. Raphael Warnock, who has worked as senior pastor at Ebenezer Baptist Church in Atlanta for 15 years, has come under heavy scrutiny for his past speeches, sermons, writings, and run-ins with police as he challenges Republican Sen. Kelly Loeffler in Georgia's U.S. Senate runoff election.

Critics of Warnock have routinely labeled him "radical," including Loeffler, who said during their last debate that Democrats "want to fundamentally change America, and the agent of change is my opponent, radical liberal Raphael Warnock."

Below are nine of the most talked about issues, in no particular order, surrounding Warnock's Senate candidacy:

1. Warnock's Wife Calls Him a 'Great Actor' After Alleging He Drove over Her Foot

Warnock's then-wife, Ouleye Ndoye, told police in March her husband is a "great actor" and "phenomenal at putting on a really good show" in bodycam footage of Ndoye commenting to Atlanta police right after a domestic dispute. Ndoye accused Warnock of running over her foot with a car, according to a police report obtained by the *Atlanta Journal-Constitution*. Warnock denied the accusation at the time, and a medical examiner later said Ndoye's foot did not show signs of injury.

The new bodycam footage shows Ndoye tearing up as she speaks to police after the incident, saying, "I've tried to keep the way that he acts under wraps for a long time, and today he crossed the line. So that is what is going on here, and he's a great actor. He is phenomenal at putting on a really good show."

Watch:

Warnock's campaign responded to the footage by saying Loeffler "has now stooped to a new low of attacking his family."

2. Warnock Defends Rev. Jeremiah Wright

Warnock has repeatedly defended Wright, who served as former pastor to President Barack Obama and is known for a number of incendiary statements — which Obama himself has condemned — including declaring that "America's chickens are coming home to roost" in regard to the 9/11 terrorist attacks and giving an impassioned sermon in which he shouted several times, "God damn America!"

Speaking to Greta Van Susteren in a 2008 Fox News appearance, Warnock said, "We celebrate Rev. Wright in the same way that we celebrate the truth-telling tradition of the black church, which when preachers tell the truth, very often it makes people uncomfortable."

During a 2013 speech, Warnock said Wright's "God damn America" sermon was a "very fine homily entitled on confusing God and government" and that it was "consistent with black prophetic preaching." Warnock argued Wright's sermon had been taken out of context and noted that the black church was "barely understood by mainstream America."

The Black Church Center for Justice and Equality posted a video in 2014 in which Warnock described Wright's "God damn America" sermon as "Christian preaching at its best."

3. Warnock Says America Needs to 'Repent for Its Worship of Whiteness'

Warnock said while addressing Atlanta's Candler School of Theology in 2016, just before the presidential election, that "America needs to repent for its worship of whiteness on full display."

Watch:

4. Warnock Says People Cannot Serve God and the Military

Warnock said in a 2011 sermon, "America, nobody can serve God and the military," a clip of which has garnered close to three million views online since it surfaced in November. Sen. Tom Cotton (R-AR) called Warnock's words "an insult to everyone who served" — Georgia is home to several military installations, including Fort Benning, Fort Stewart, and Fort Gordon, and an analysis by 24/7 Wall St. found the state has the tenth-most active duty personnel in the country.

Responding to the criticism in a press conference, Warnock said the sermon was a "spiritual lesson" about priorities, saying "a person cannot have two masters." He said, "My ultimate allegiance is to God, and therefore, whatever else that I may commit myself to, it has to be built on a spiritual foundation."

5. Dr. James Cone Was Warnock's 'Mentor'

Warnock has described Dr. James Cone, who often defended Marxism and used provocative, race-fueled language, as his "mentor." Cone served as Warnock's academic adviser at the Union Theological Seminary, and Warnock considered Cone to be the "father of black theology."

In *My Soul Looks Back*, Cone called for the "total reconstruction of society along the lines of democratic socialism." In ***A Black Theology of Liberation*, Cone** argued that salvation comes from being like God and becoming "black" — that is, adopting total political solidarity with the black community. He determined that "satanic whiteness" makes "white religionists" incapable of "perceiving the blackness of God"; therefore, they must purge themselves of said whiteness. Cone wrote, "There will be no peace in America until white people begin to hate their whiteness, asking from the depths of their being: 'How can we become black?'"

After his death, Warnock eulogized Cone, saying Cone "spoke with the power and the moral authority of a prophet."

6. Church Where Warnock Was Pastor Hosts Fidel Castro

New York's Abyssinian Baptist Church hosted communist Cuban dictator Fidel Castro while Warnock worked as a pastor there in 1995. Castro received a warm welcome at the gathering, including chants of "Fidel! Fidel! Fidel!"

In 2016, just after Castro's death, Warnock said, "We remember Fidel Castro, whose legacy is complex. Don't let anyone tell you a simple story; life usually isn't very simple. His legacy is complex, kind of like America's legacy is complex."

Warnock has received enormous backlash for the association to Castro, who is widely considered responsible for thousands of innocent lives lost during his regime. Just last week, while campaigning in Georgia, South Carolina's senior senator, Sen. Lindsey Graham, asked a crowd, "What kind of church is it that would invite Fidel Castro to come by and speak? Warnock is the most radical person to ever run for Senate in the history of Georgia."

CNN's Jake Tapper asked Warnock about the issue in November. Warnock said, "I was a youth pastor. I had nothing to do with that program. I did not make any decisions regarding the program. I **have never met the Cuban dictator. And so I'm not connected to him." Tapper pressed further, "But do you understand why people would be appalled by anyone celebrating Fidel Castro?" Warnock responded, "Well, absolutely. And I never have. What I'm putting forward in this race is American values."**

7. Warnock Defends Louis Farrakhan's Nation of Islam

In a 2013 sermon, Warnock praised the antisemitic Nation of Islam: "Its voice has been important, and its voice has been important even for the development of black theology," Warnock said. As Breitbart News's Joel Pollak reported, the Nation of Islam is led by Louis Farrakhan, "whose racist and antisemitic rhetoric has long been a matter of public record."

8. Warnock Oversees Camp Suspected of Child Abuse

Warnock worked as senior pastor of Baltimore's Douglas Memorial Community Church, which ran Camp Farthest Out, from about 2001 to 2005. The camp was suspected of child abuse in 2002, and according to a 2002 report by the *Baltimore Sun*, Warnock was arrested for interfering with a state trooper who was questioning the camp's counselors on the matter. **Warnock has said his interference was due to making sure the counselors "had the benefit" of legal counsel.**

Warnock himself has not been accused of child abuse and little detail is public regarding the allegations against the camp; however, one of the camp's attendees, Anthony Washington, who was 12 years old at the time, recently detailed his experience at the camp to the Washington Free Beacon. Washington said he received a financial settlement after filing a lawsuit against the camp alleging child abuse, including an instance of counselors pouring urine on him and punishing him by forcing him to sleep outside.

Loeffler told Breitbart News she found the allegations "disgusting" and chastised Warnock for refusing to answer questions about the allegations.

9. Warnock Does Not Denounce Marxism, Describes Marxism as Useful

In their last debate, Loeffler asked Warnock whether he would denounce Marxism, and Warnock evaded

the question. The momentous exchange was widely circulated online and has since been incorporated into Loeffler's stump speeches as evidence of Warnock's "radical" viewpoints.

The question stemmed in part from Warnock's past writings, which reveal his interest in Marxism, a philosophy named for *Communist Manifesto* author Karl Marx that has been employed by oppressive governments such as those of China and the Soviet Union.

In his 2014 book, ***The Divided Mind of the Black Church: Theology, Piety, and Public Witness,*** **Warnock espoused Marxism, saying it has "much to teach the black church." Warnock cited more than 30 separate works by the aforementioned Cone in his book, including several works on Marxism.**

27 GOP Pa. Lawmakers Urge McConnell to Contest Electors

By Eric Mack

Republican state legislators in Pennsylvania are urging Senate Majority Leader Mitch McConnell, R-Ky., to contest the results of the state's 20 electors. The request was made in a letter signed by 27 GOP state lawmakers, urging McConnell to "dispute the certification until an investigation is completed" in election irregularities and violations of state election law, Newsweek reported.

"Without a thorough investigation into these allegations, the certification of the Pennsylvania election results is suspect at best," the letter read, per the report.

The Pennsylvania Supreme Court and Democrat leaders violated state election law "by eliminating signature verification, postmarks, and due dates while allowing the proliferation of drop boxes with questionable security measures and the unauthorized curing of ballots, as well as the questionable treatment of poll watchers," the letter claimed. It added allegations that due process was violated by the state courts and Pennsylvania Secretary of State Kathy Boockvar, who declined to address election results that "were so fraught with inconsistencies, improprieties, and irregularities that the results for the office of President of the United States cannot be determined in our state."

Biden's margin of victory was 80,555 votes in Pennsylvania.

A joint session of Congress on Jan. 6 will receive, open, and count the Electoral College votes, officially certifying the election of Democrat Joe Biden.

McConnell has urged Republicans to not challenge the election results, but a group of House Republicans and at least one senator, Sen. Josh Hawley, R-Mo., have vowed to step forward to challenge the results. Both chambers of Congress will then break off separately for two hours of debate on the electors.

Still, Congress appears to have the votes to certify Biden as the presidential election victor.

- ***"I do not think that he will prevail in his quest, and I question why he is doing it when the courts have unanimously thrown out the suits that the president's team have filed for lack of credible evidence," Sen. Susan Collins, R-Maine, a frequent Trump skeptic within the GOP, said, per Newsweek. "And Senator Hawley's a smart attorney who clerked for the Supreme Court, so he clearly understands that. So I don't understand."***
- Over 4,100 People (MOSTLY BLACK) Shot in Mayor Lightfoot's (BLACK LIFE MATTERS) 2020 Chicago (HOW MUCH DOES YOUR LIFE MATTER WHEN SHOT DEAD IN AGE 9 DRIVE-BY **Over 4,100 people were shot in Mayor Lori Lightfoot's (D) Chicago January 1, 2020, through December 27, 2020.** HOPEFULLY MOST VOTED FOR PAL ZOMBIE & KAMIKAZE KAMALA BEFORE THEY WERE SHOT DEAD IN THE HEAD. YOU WIN SOME & LOSE SOME. DEM'S DA' BREAKS. YOU CAN'T SURVIVE EVERY INTENDED & RANDOM GUNSHOT IN LORI LIGHTFOOT'S MAGIC KINGDOM; WHEN DID LORI LIGHTFOOT EVER PROMISE CHICAGO A ROSE GARDEN? YOU WIN SOME. YOU LOSE SOME. ESPECIALLY IN CHICAGO. BETTER LUCK NEXT TIME

The *Chicago Tribune* reports the exact figure at 4,115 shooting victims, a total that represents fatal and non-

fatal shootings combined. The *Tribune* isolates homicides in a separate body of data, noting there were 768 homicides in Chicago January 1, 2020, through December 27, 2020. This is up considerably over 2019, a year in which the Chicago Police Department noted 491 homicides in the city.

Breitbart News reported some 27 people were shot, seven fatally, in Mayor Lightfoot's Chicago over the past weekend alone. Seventeen were shot, three fatally, over the weekend of December 11-13, 2020, and 40 people were shot, six fatally, over the weekend prior to that.

Shootings on Chicago's expressways also surged in 2020, with 87 such shootings occurring by October 10, 2020. WGNTV explained that 57 people were wounded in the 87 shooting and six people were killed.

By December 7, 2020, NBC 5 indicated that the number of expressway shootings in Chicago had reached 115. There were a total of 52 expressway shootings in Chicago in 2019.

SO YOU WERE SHOT DEAD IN LORI LIGHTFOOT'S CHICAGO? WHO THE FUCK EVER TOLD YOU TO BE BORN IN THE FIRST PLACE? PAL JOEY & KAMMIE HARRIS MAIL VOTING FRAUD IS YER CURE ALL.

GOP Risks Deep and Lasting Rift Over Electoral College Challenge of Biden

THE JUDAS FRAUD PRETENDER BRAIN DEAD TROJAN MONKEY

President Donald Trump's extraordinary challenge of the Nov. 3 presidential election is becoming a defining moment for the Republican Party, one that will come to a head at Wednesday's joint session of Congress to confirm the Electoral College results.

Senate Majority Leader Mitch McConnell is urging Republicans not to try to overturn the election, in which Joe Biden prevailed, but not everyone is heeding him. Sen. Josh Hawley of Missouri vows to join House Republicans in objecting to the state tallies.

Then there's the other side of the party's split; GOP Sen. Ben Sasse of Nebraska warns such challenges are a "dangerous ploy" threatening the nation's civic norms.

Caught in the middle is Vice President Mike Pence, who faces growing pressure and a lawsuit from Trump's allies over his ceremonial role in presiding over the session Wednesday.

Political experts anticipate no significant change in the outcome. Biden is set to be inaugurated Jan. 20 after winning the Electoral College vote 306-232. But the effort to force a vote on the college's conclusion is forcing Republicans to make choices that will set the contours of the post-Trump era and an evolving GOP.

"I will not be participating in a project to overturn the election," Sasse wrote in a lengthy social media post.

Sasse, a potential 2024 presidential contender, said he was "urging my colleagues also to reject this dangerous ploy."

Trump, the first president to lose a reelection bid in almost 30 years, has attributed his defeat to widespread voter fraud. But those claims have gained little to no traction in the courts. Indeed, of the roughly 50 lawsuits the president and his allies have filed challenging election results, nearly all have been dismissed or dropped, either because judges said they had no standing to intervent or because they found the evidence insufficient.

He's also lost twice in efforts to get the Supreme Court to step in.

Still, the president has pushed Republican senators to pursue his charges even though the Electoral College has already cemented Biden's victory. Wednesday is when Congress is to formally recognize the count before the new president is sworn in.

"We are letting people vote their conscience," Sen. John Thune, the second-ranking Republican, told reporters at the Capitol.

Thune's remarks as the GOP whip in charge of rounding up votes show that Republican leadership is not

putting its muscle behind Trump's demands, but allowing senators to choose their course. He noted the gravity of questioning the election outcome.

"This is an issue that's incredibly consequential, incredibly rare historically and very precedent-setting," he said. "This is a big vote. They are thinking about it."

Pence will be carefully watched as he presides over what is typically a routine vote count in Congress but is now heading toward a prolonged showdown that could extend into Wednesday night, depending on how many challenges Hawley and others mount.

The vice president is being sued by a group of Republicans who want Pence to have the power to overturn the election results by doing away with an 1887 law that spells out how Congress handles the vote count.

Trump's own Justice Department may have complicated what is already a last-ditch try to upend the ritualistic congressional count. It has asked a federal judge to dismiss the lawsuit from Rep. Louie Gohmert, R-Texas, and a group of Republican electors from Arizona who insist Pence can, and must, step outside mere ceremony and shape the outcome of the vote.

In a court filing in Texas, the department said they have "have sued the wrong defendant," and that Pence should not be the target of the legal action.

"A suit to establish that the vice president has discretion over the count, filed against the vice president, is a walking legal contradiction," the department argues.

To ward off a dramatic unraveling, McConnell convened a conference call with Republican senators Thursday specifically to address the coming joint session and logistics of tallying the vote, according to several Republicans granted anonymity to discuss the private call.

The Republican leader pointedly called on Hawley to answer questions about his challenge to Biden's victory, according to two of the Republicans. But there was no response because Hawley was a no-show, the Republicans said. His office did not respond to a request for comment.

Sen. Pat Toomey, R-Pa., who has acknowledged Biden's victory and defended his state's elections systems as valid and accurate, spoke up on the call, objecting to those challenging Pennsylvania's results and making clear he disagrees with Hawley's plan to contest the result, his office said in a statement.

McConnell had previously warned GOP senators not to participate in raising objections, saying it would be a terrible vote for colleagues. And that's the point: In essence, lawmakers would be forced to choose between the will of a departing president and that of the voters. Several Republicans have indicated they are under pressure from constituents back home to show they are fighting for Trump in his weekslong campaign to stay in office.

Hawley became the first GOP senator this week to announce he will raise objections when Congress meets to affirm Biden's victory in the election, forcing House and Senate votes that are likely to delay — if not to alter — the final certification of Biden's win.

Other Republican senators are expected to join Hawley, wary of ceding the spotlight to him as they, too, try to emerge as leaders in a post-Trump era. A number of Republicans in the Democratic-majority House have already said they will object on Trump's behalf. They only needed a single senator to go along with them to force votes in both chambers.

When Biden was vice president, he, too, presided over the session as the Electoral College presented the 2016 vote tally to Congress to confirm Trump the winner. The session was brief, despite objections from some Democrats. Jen Psaki, CONDESCENDING MOCKINGLY CALLS FIGHTING FOR RIGHTEOUSNESS ANTICS. .. speaking for the Biden transition team, dismissed Hawley's move as "antics" that will have no bearing on Biden being sworn in on Jan. 20.

MAIL FRAUD VOTING ISN'T NEW; WHAT'S NEW IS AMERICA'S JUDICIARY; LEGISLATORS & GOVERNORS WINKING & DOING NOTHING ABOUT IT; IN 1864; THERE WAS (1) SINGLE WITNESS INVESTIGATION THAT EXPOSED 1864 MAIL FRAUD; IN 2021 WE HAVE (5,000) SWORN PENALTY OF FELONY PERJURY AFFIDAVIT WITNESSES TO FIRST HAND SYSTEMIC VOTE STEALING FOR DEMOCRATS UNDER PENALTY OF 10 YEAR PRISON FOR LYING; 5000 OF OUR WITNESSES EAGER TO TESTIFY BEFORE A SUPREME COURT THAT REFUSES TO ACKNOWLEDGE MIRROR IMAGE DIGITAL & AUDIO VISUAL PROOF OF THE CONSPIRACY TO STEAL OUR WHITE HOUSE; EVERYONE WE PAY TO PROTECT AMERICA SAYS "WHERE'S THE EVIDENCE? THIS IS NEW. SO RED STATE AMERICA SECEDES. BYE.

STATE LEGISLATURES; GOVERNORS & JUDGES IN ARIZONA; WISCONSIN; MICHIGAN; PENNSYLVANIA; NEVADA & GEORGIA; & U.S. SUPREME COURT EXCLUDING THOMAS & ALITO; ARE WAFFEN SS GESTAPO BLOODS & CRIPS MS-13 COSA NOSTRA MAFIOSI & MEDIA; FOX NEWS IN PARTICULAR; **DEBUNK (5000) SWORN WITNESS AFFIDAVITS** TO VOTE STEALING FRAUD; INCLUDING AUDIO-VIDEO; ALL SAY "WHERE'S THE EVIDENCE?

Dominion Voting Systems has dismissed the audit report, **claiming the company is the subject of a "continuing malicious and widespread disinformation campaign" to undermine confidence in the Nov. 3 election.**

BULLSEYE MICHAEL FLYNN – **ADOLF HITLER USED 41 % OF VOTES WON IN CORRUPTED MARCH 5, 1933 ELECTION TO SEIZE GERMANY AS DID HUGO CHAVEZ OCTOBER 7 2012 W/ TRICK DOMINION SMARTRONICS VOTING TOUCH SCREENS FOR 55.07% popular vote, TO SEIZE REELECTION IN VENEZUELA**

DONALD TRUMP ISN'T SAVING THE ELECTION FOR HIMSELF; BUT DEMOCRACY FOR THE WORLD.

DIETRICH BONHOEFFER MOST FAMOUS MAN GERMAN HISTORY AFTER ADOLF HITLER

GOP's Hawley Joins Trump-Fueled Push to Object to Biden Electors

Republican Senator Josh Hawley said he will object to the certification of the Electoral College votes for Joe Biden as president when Congress convenes on Jan. 6, defying warnings from GOP leaders against staging a doomed-to-fail spectacle.

"I cannot vote to certify the electoral college results on January 6 without raising the fact that some states, particularly Pennsylvania, failed to follow their own state election laws," Hawley, of Missouri, said in a statement. "And I cannot vote to certify without pointing out the unprecedented effort of mega corporations, including Facebook and Twitter, to interfere in this election, in support of Joe Biden."

John Thune, the Senate's No. 2 Republican, said last week that attempts to object to the electoral count would "go down like a shot dog in the Senate." He advised GOP lawmakers who plan to take part in the effort to reconsider.

House Speaker Nancy Pelosi, who leads a Democratic majority in the chamber, said Wednesday that the objections from a handful of Republicans won't change the outcome.

"I have no doubt that next Wednesday, a week from today that Joe Biden will be confirmed by the acceptance of the vote of the Electoral College as the 46th president of the United States," she said.

Representative Mo Brooks of Alabama said earlier this month that he will object to the declaration and is likely to be joined in that effort by other House Republicans, including Representative Marjorie Taylor Greene of Georgia. An objection to any state by both a senator and a representative triggers up to two hours of debate in the respective chambers. If President Donald Trump's supporters object to more than one state, the procedure could drag on for several hours.

"At the very least, Congress should investigate allegations of voter fraud and adopt measures to secure the integrity of our elections," Hawley said. "But Congress has so far failed to act."

Hawley's statement made reference to previous attempts by Democrats in Congress to object to election results, saying they were "praised by Democratic leadership and the media" when they made them. Hawley said Democrats were entitled to make those objections and so are those now raising issues.

Democratic objections after the 2000 and 2016 elections failed for lack of a participating senator, and an objection over the Ohio votes in 2005 by former Democratic Senator Barbara Boxer of California and former Democratic U.S. Representative Stephanie Tubbs Jones was voted down.Election law experts say any objection to electoral votes for Biden on Jan. 6 would almost certainly fail because the Democratic-controlled House would reject it, and there are enough Republican senators who have acknowledged Biden's victory to oppose it.

The electoral vote process will be presided over by Vice President Mike Pence, who could find himself in the awkward position of having to gavel down objections raised by supporters who want to keep him and Trump in office.

Representative Louie Gohmert, a Republican from Texas, has sued Pence seeking to force him to disregard states' chosen Democratic electors and instead select competing slates of GOP electors.

"The Constitution expressly designates defendant Pence as the individual who decides which set of electoral votes, or neither, to count," Gohmert said in the suit, filed Sunday in federal court in Texas.

Nancy Pelosi WE MUST SECEDE IF ONLY TO GET AWAY FROM THIS Bans 'Gender' Terms Like Mother, Daughter, Father, Son in House Rules

Alana Mastrangelo

House Speaker Nancy Pelosi (D-CA) and Rules Committee Chairman James McGovern (D-MA) unveiled the rules for the 117th Congress on Friday, which contain "future-focused" proposals, including the elimination of gendered terms, such as "father, mother, son, and daughter."

"This package, which will be introduced and voted on once the new Congress convenes, includes sweeping ethics reforms, increases accountability for the American people, and makes this House of Representatives the most inclusive in history," said the House Committee on Rules in a statement.

House Speaker Pelosi went on to say she is "pleased to join Chairman Jim McGovern in introducing this visionary rules package, which reflects the views and values of the full range of our historically diverse House Democratic Majority."

"Thanks to the leadership of Chairman McGovern and our Members, Democrats have crafted a package of unprecedented, bold reforms, which will make the House more accountable, transparent, and effective in our work to meet the needs of the American people," said Pelosi.

"These future-focused proposals reflect our priorities as a Caucus and as a Country," the House Speaker added.

Within the proposals are the creation of the "Select Committee on Economic Disparity and Fairness in Growth," which would require Congress to "honor all gender identities by changing pronouns and familial relationships in the House rules to be gender neutral."

In clause 8(c)(3) of rule XXIII, gendered terms, such as "father, mother, son, daughter, brother, sister, uncle, aunt, first cousin, nephew, niece, husband, wife, father-in-law, mother-in-law, son-in-law, daughter-in-law, brother-in-law, sister-in-law, stepfather, stepmother, stepson, stepdaughter, stepbrother, stepsister, half brother, half sister, grandson, or granddaughter" will be removed.

In their place, terms such as "parent, child, sibling, parent's sibling, first cousin, sibling's child, spouse, parent-in-law, child-in-law, sibling-in-law, stepparent, stepchild, stepsibling, half-sibling, or grandchild" will be used, instead.

THE FACE OF EVIL IS TRUMP'S NOT INVOKING THE INSURRECTION ACT ECHOES BONHOEFFER; MEMORIZED BY EVERY AGE (6) GERMAN CHILD; TAUGHT 60 MILLION DIED BECAUSE OF SILENCE IN THE FACE OF EVIL. AMERICA REPEATS THE SILENCE OF GERMANY & VENEZUELA?

DIETRICH BONHOEFFER:

- NOT TO ACT IS TO ACT
- NOT TO SPEAK IS TO SPEAK
- SILENCE INEVIL"

NO ONE BUT BONHOEFFER STOOD UP TO ADOLF HITLER BEFORE IT WAS TOO LATE; HE WAS STRANGLED TO DEATH OVER (6) HOURS IN THE MOST HORRIFIC MURDER EVER SUFFERED BY A LIVING THING. IF IN DEPRAVED INDIFFERENCE AMERICA WELCOMES 2020 DEMOCRATS TO REPEAT WHAT HITLER DID IN 1933 & CHAVEZ DID IN 2012; WE ARE UNWORTHY OF "IN GOD WE TRUST" KNOWINGLY LOOKING THE OTHER WAY; AGREEING DIETRICH BONHOEFFER DIED IN VAIN & W/ AMERICAN DEPRAVED INDIFFERENCE OF REPUDIATING GOD.

THE INSURRECTION ACT WOULD HAVE RIGHTED THIS WRONG.

BIDEN & DEMOCRATS: CHALLENGE DIETRICH BONHOEFFER WHO SPEAKS TO US HIS UNMARKED MASS GRAVE.

SILENCE OF COLLABORATING LEGISLATURES; GOVERNORS & JUDGES IS DEPRAVED THE LEFTIST ACTIVISM **REFUSING TO ENFORCE. CONSTITUTIONAL RULE OF PRESIDENTIAL ELECTION LAWS; POCKET VETO DOING NOTHING WHEN JUDGES; GOVERNORS & LEGISLATORS MUST DO EVERYTHING MANDATED BY ELECTION LAW. .**

THIS IS CONSPIRATORIAL PROXY ACTIVISM IMPOSE MARXISM ON AMERICA BY ARIZONA; WISCONSIN; MICHIGAN; PENNSYLVANIA; NEVADA & GEORGIA; PAID BY THE ZUCKERBUCKS FUNDED SPIDER WEB EVADING COUNTLESS ELECTION LAWS; OVERTHROWING ELECTED AMERICAN GOVERNMENT; USING OUR OWN LAWS TO DESTROY OUR NATION; AS **DID HITLER & CHAVEZ; USING COVID 19 S A PRETEXT FOR FRAUD STEALING THE PRESIDENCY.**

IF THIS SOUNDS COMPLICATED; IT'S LESS SO THAN OPERATION WARP SPEED THAT BROUGHT US (3) VACCINES SINCE MARCH, 2020.

HITLER & CHAVEZ WERE A STEP AHEAD OF GERMANY & VENEZUELA.

REPUBLICANS CAN'T FIGHT HITLER'S KIND BY BEING DAINTY & NICE.

IF THE U.S. MILITARY REFUSES TO DEFEND AGAINST THIS INSURRECTION; I DARE YOU TO US FORCE TO PREVENT US FROM SECEDING FROM THE CONTAMINATED UNION & FORMING OUR OWN CONFEDERATION

US Army Rejects Using 'Martial Law' on Election Fraud By Eric Mack

Retired Lt. Gen. Michael Flynn's Newsmax TV remarks on President Donald Trump weighing «martial law» and «military capabilities» amid election fraud has forced U.S. Army leaders to issue a statement Friday rejecting that consideration. **"There is no role for the U.S. military in determining the outcome of an American election," Army Secretary Ryan McCarthy and Army chief of staff Gen. James McConville** wrote in a joint statement Friday. The statement echoed one by Chairman of the Joint Chiefs of Staff Gen. Mark Milley before the election.

Gen. Flynn told Thursday's "Greg Kelly Reports":

"He could immediately on his order seize every single one of these machines around the country on his order. He could also order, within the swing states, if he wanted to, he could take military capabilities and he could place them in those states and basically rerun an election in each of those states. It's not unprecedented.

"I mean, these people are out there talking about martial law like it's something that we've never done. Martial law has been instituted 64 times."

Flynn's martial law remarks were on the heals of Georgia lawyer L. Lin Wood's previous comments to Newsmax TV's "The Count" last week:

"If the Supreme Court does not act, I think the president should declare some extent of Martial law, and he should hold off an stay the electoral college.

"Because we cannot have in this country, an election of our leader, where you have massive evidence of fraud and illegality. This country has to have a vote that has integrity. And the electoral college does not need to meet and vote until we have resolved these issues."

Michael Flynn to Newsmax TV: Trump Has Options to Secure Integrity of 2020 Election

By Solange Reyner

Former national security adviser Michael Flynn says President Donald Trump has options to make sure the integrity of the 2020 election remains intact, including seizing voting machines around the country and using military capabilities to rerun elections in swing states. "I don't know if he's going to take any of these options. The president has to plan for every eventuality because we cannot allow this election and the integrity of our election to go the way it is," Flynn said Thursday during an appearance on Newsmax TV's "Greg Kelly Reports."

"This is just totally unsatisfactory. There's no way in the world we're going to be able to move forward as a nation with this. ...

"He could immediately on his order seize every single one of these machines around the country on his order. He could also order, within the swing states, if he wanted to, he could take military capabilities and he could place them in those states and basically rerun an election in each of those states. It's not unprecedented," Flynn added. The Pentagon earlier this month dismissed nine Defense Business Board members and replaced them with 11 new appointments, including Trump loyalists Corey Lewandowski

and David Bossie. Scott O'Grady, another appointee, shared conspiracy theories on Twitter that called the president's loss to President-elect Joe Biden a "coup." He also voiced approval for martial law.

Flynn says the notion isn't new. "These people out there talking about martial law like it's something we've never done," Flynn told Kelly. "Martial law has been instituted 64 times. I'm not calling for that. We have a constitutional process. ... That has to be followed. But I will tell you I'm a little concerned about Chief Justice John Roberts at the Supreme Court. We can't fool around with the fabric of the Constitution of the United States." Trump pardoned his former national security adviser last month, ending a yearslong prosecution in the Russia investigation that saw Flynn twice plead guilty to lying to the FBI. As with the recent election results, the president has called the Russia probe a long-running hoax.

McCONNELl IS A TRILLION % RIGHT IF DEMOCRATS DON'T LIKE IT; FUCK 'EM. WE MUST BE TEN TIMES MORE VICIOUS TO DEMOCRATS THAN THEY ARE TO US. THEY UNDERSTAND BRUTE POWER. THIS IS HOW IT'S GONNA BE

New Relief-Checks Bill From McConnell Boosts Aid Amounts, but Also Leaves Democrats Seething

By Jeffrey Rodack

After blocking a Senate move to vote on boosting coronavirus stimulus checks on Tuesday, Senate Majority Leader Mitch McConnell introduced an alternative proposal. In it, the checks are increased as President Donald Trump, many Democrats and even some GOP lawmakers have urged.

But McConnell also ties those fatter payments to Trump priorities including probing allegations of election fraud and diminishing liability protections for social media platforms.

Sent the original COVID-19 economic stimulus bill, Trump declined to sign without major changes. He wanted individual relief checks boosted from $600 to $2,000.

Unrelated to COVID, he also wanted a repeal of Section 230 of the Communications Decency Act, which protects social media platforms from being sued over third-party content. And he wanted inquiries into his claims of election fraud, which have been been pressed without success in court and at the legislative level for weeks since the Nov. 3 election outcome favored opponent Joe Biden.

Senate Democratic leader Chuck Schumer of New York said the new proposal from McConnell could not pass, giving the majority leader an "out" on the larger relief package.

In a statement, Newsweek reported, Schumer had this to say: "Senator McConnell knows how to make $2,000 survival checks reality and he knows how to kill them," Schumer said. "If Sen. McConnell tries loading up bipartisan House-passed CASH Act with unrelated, partisan provisions that will do absolutely nothing to help struggling families across the country, it will not pass the House and cannot become law."

The move by McConnell creates a bind for Dems, who can either vote the bill down and be blamed for killing the package of much-needed aid, or embrace it with the add-ons and, as Newsweek put it, "lend credence" to Trump's claims of election fraud that drove his loss to Biden.

The immediate future of the Republican legislator's proposed alternative is not clear. He said Tuesday, albeit without a precise time frame, that lawmakers would be beginning a process to help focus and refine the president's wishes.

In a sign of how House Dems were likely to view the McConnell plan, New Jersey Rep. Bill Pascrell Jr. tweeted this, **Newsweek reported: "To block you from getting $2000 mitch mcconnell is demanding a 'commission' to spew lies about the election trump lost** TRUMP LOST NOTHING; YOU FUCKEN STOLE AMERICA FROM; AND THIS IS GETTING UGLIER BY THE SECOND, WITH US ULTIMATELY WINNING. **and attack democracy. This is a goddamn disgrace. The depravity of republican leaders has no bottom."**

Dem firebrand and New York Rep. Alexandria Ocasio-Cortez tweeted: **"I think it's a big mistake to not approve a clean bill sending $2k checks out to people, so let's call it even. Keep going @BernieSanders! Make the Senate countdown the New Year on the Senate floor until they pass $2k checks, no funny business.** THERE'S NOTHING FUNNY WITH YOU, YOU TREACHEROUS FIENDISH DEMON.

Jason Miller to Newsmax TV: We Want to Present 'Specific Evidence' Jan. 6

By Charlie McCarthy

Specific examples of voter fraud will be presented Jan. 6 if debate is held on the 2020 election results, according to Trump campaign senior adviser Jason Miller on Newsmax TV.

Electoral College ballots are scheduled to be certified during a joint session of Congress on Jan. 6. Miller said evidence presented there would be different than that in the legal battles President Donald Trump's campaign has fought in the courts.

"Any of the [court] dismissals have been on process," Miller told Carl Higbie on Tuesday's "Greg Kelly Reports." "So, let's talk about Wisconsin where Mayor [Rudy] Giuliani is leading the legal team, actually filed a Supreme Court case this afternoon that said that we've identified over 50,000 ballots in the state of Wisconsin that were cast unconstitutionally."

The Trump's campaign fight in Wisconsin has centered on ballots that were cast by people who should not have been allowed to vote.

"Article II of the Constitution makes it very clear, the state legislatures, and state legislatures alone, set up the voting systems for each state, the codes and the way they are conducted," Miler said. "And what we have here is we have over 20,000 ballots that were cast without actually having a application on file, the mail ballots. Wisconsin's very clear, very specific you got to have an application on file."

Miller said Wisconsin also allowed ballot harvesting and "6,000 or so of these ballots that we believe were just completely null and void from people who never should have been able to cast them."

He then cited "suitcases of ballots" found in Georgia, the campaign's inability to "inspect the machines" in Arizona, and Michigan where "they're running through ballots multiple times."

"These are the specific types of evidence we want to present to the American people on the national stage and not allow local politicians to sweep it under the rug," Miller said. A group of congressional Republicans led by Rep. Louie Gohmert, R-Texas, are suing Vice President Mike Pence to prevent him from confirming Joe Biden's victory in the 2020 presidential election.

Miller said the 1887 Electoral Count Act designates the vice president as the official to preside over the meeting. He then hopes one representative and one senator join together to objecting to the Electoral College vote, allowing two hours of debate. "We hope Rep. Gohmert is successful in this and we will have a chance in front of the American people, next week to present these cases, all these evidences of fraud,"

Miller said. Jenna Ellis to Newsmax TV: Trump Denied 'Due Process'

Jon Ossoff Tweet Resurfaces Amid Alleged Ties to China

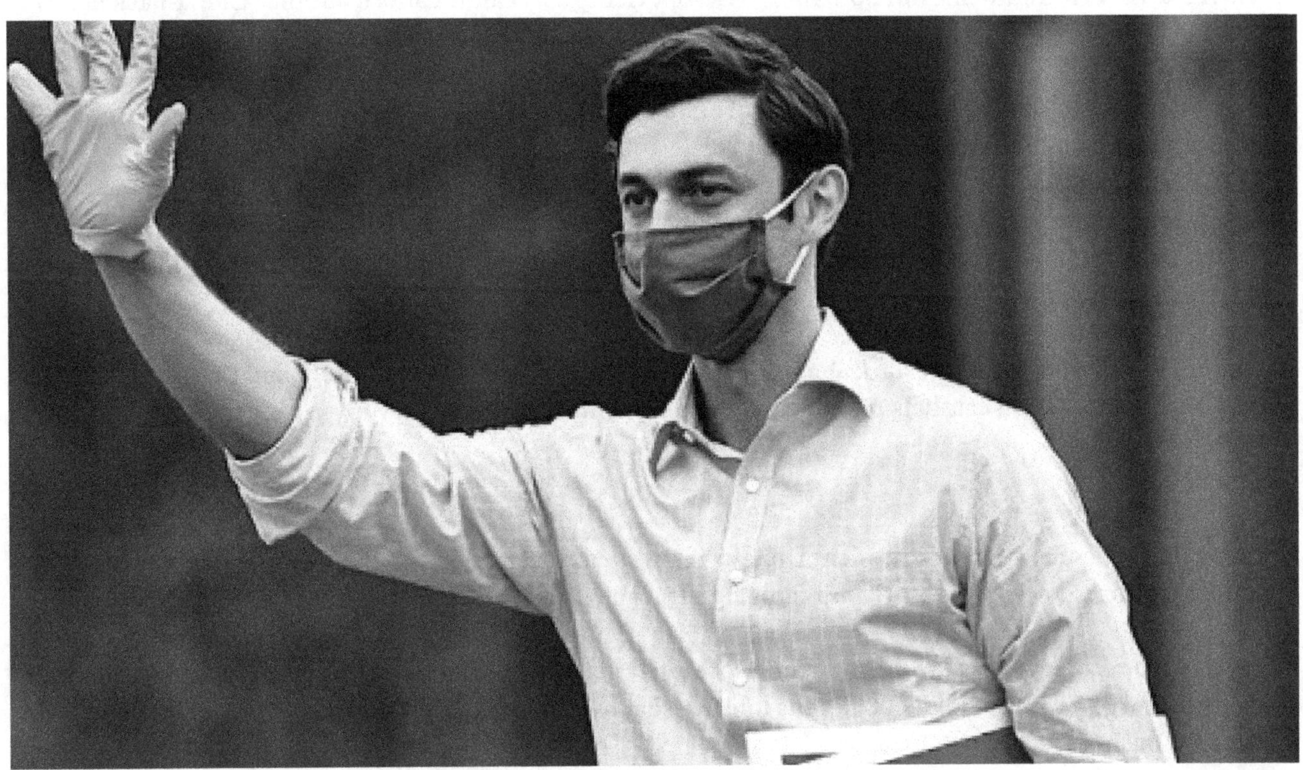

By Charlie McCarthy

Georgia Senate candidate Jon Ossoff encouraged supporters to follow Chinese state-run media on Twitter in 2012.

The eight-year tweet resurfaced as evidence of Ossoff's financial ties to China mounted, the Washington Examiner reported. Ossoff, a Democrat opposing incumbent Sen. David Perdue, R-Ga., in one Jan. 5 runoff, implored people to follow the Xinhua News Agency, the official state-run press agency of the People's Republic of China.

Ossoff tweeted Nov. 7, 2012, the day after Election Day:

"Esp. during 18th Party Congress, #follow @XHNews (Xinhua - Chinese state media). #ff"

Ossoff filed a campaign financial disclosure in May, when he failed to reveal acceptance of more than $5,000 the past two years from the Hong Kong-based telecommunications firm PCCW Media Limited, according to The Atlanta Journal-Constitution. He amended the filing in July to include details.

Perdue tweeted a link Saturday to The Washington Times report detailing the allegations of impropriety.

Perdue tweeted:

"Hunter Biden. Eric Swalwell. And now – Jon @Ossoff. Georgians cannot afford another China-backed liberal in Washington"

The Georgia Republican Party has pursued legal action against Ossoff by asking the Senate Select Committee on Ethics to open an investigation into the matter.

"The Georgia Senate Primary was held on June 9, 2020," the complaint read. "This was prior to Ossoff filing the amended Public Financial Disclosure Report [on July 10] which showed he earned compensation from controversial companies.

"Georgian voters were left in the dark about the financial interests relevant to Ossoff, and they deserved to know whether Ossoff had conflicts of interest or financial entanglements relevant to his candidacy."

By Eric Mack

The rejections of courts to hear President Donald Trump's campaign election challenges is denying him the right to due process, according to Trump campaign legal adviser Jenna Ellis on Newsmax TV.

"They need to recognize that President Trump absolutely gets the same opportunities to argue his case that President George W. Bush did in 2000," Ellis told Tuesday's "Stinchfield," pointing to the landmark Supreme Court case Bush v. Gore.

"And to treat him differently than every other sitting president in every other election is manifestly unfair according to due process and our Constitution."

As the Trump campaign brings some final cases before the Jan. 6 certification of the Electoral College, Ellis told host Grant Stinchfield the Supreme Court has engaged in a "dereliction of duty and fidelity to the U.S. Constitution by refusing to take up cases."

Ellis added, if the challenges do not render a remedy for the Trump campaign, the failure will not be of their work to root out election fraud, but a "failure of the Supreme Court, the Judicial branch the entire way down."

Murder Rates Rise Alongside Anti-Police Demonstrations

Michael Ginsberg

Nine cities with some of America's largest murder rate increases hosted *Black Lives Matter* and Defund the Police protests in 2020.

Data analyst and criminologist Jeff Asher published a preliminary look at America's skyrocketing murder rate. He found that murder rates rose year over year in 51 out of the 57 locales from which he accessed data.

Nine of the ten cities with the highest murder rate increases and more than 20 killings hosted sustained *Black Lives Matter* protests and riots during the summer. These are evidence of what Manhattan Institute fellow Heather Mac Donald calls the Ferguson Effect, wherein anti-police protests and rioting lead to less proactive policing. The absence in police presence then leads to a spike in violent crime.

Omaha, Nebraska

Omaha's murder rate increased 106% from 2019 to 2020. Its 35 murders were the most in the city since 2015. The City of Omaha is currently a defendant in a federal lawsuit filed by the American Civil Liberties Union

(ACLU). Omaha police officers fired tear gas and arrested hundreds protestors who blocked streets and bridges in Omaha on May 29 and 30.

Lubbock, Texas

Lubbock's murder rate increased 100% from 2019 to 2020. The city saw more murders by May 2020 than it did in all of 2019. Many of those murders may not be attributable to the Ferguson Effect, since they were before major protests in the aftermath of the death of George Floyd.

Milwaukee, Wisconsin

Milwaukee saw 191 murders in 2020, for a year over year increase of 94%. Milwaukee Public Schools cancelled their contract with the Milwaukee Police Department following the death of George Floyd. The city also hosted sustained protests in the aftermath of the police shooting of Jacob Blake. The Milwaukee Bucks cancelled a playoff game with the Orlando Magic in protest of the shooting.

Blake was shot after pulling a knife on Kenosha police officers. He later plead guilty to disorderly conduct charges stemming from a sexual assault of his ex-girlfriend, which prompted the police dispatch. (RELATED: Kamala Harris Told Jacob Blake She's Proud Of Him)

Louisville, Kentucky

Louisville's murder rate increased 78% in 2020, with 139 murders reported. Kentucky's largest city saw sustained protests and rioting following the death of Breonna Taylor on March 13, who was shot while police served a no-knock warrant at her boyfriend's apartment. At least seven people were shot during protests and riots following Taylor's death. Small business owners struggled to protect their stores and restaurants from looters.

Fort Wayne, Indiana

Fort Wayne reported 37 murders by Sept. 25 for a 76.2% year over year increase. Police worried that the city was on pace to break 2016's record 48 murders. Fort Wayne police deployed tear gas and pepper spray after protestors blocked traffic and climbed atop a truck near the Allen County Courthouse.

Seattle, Washington

Seattle reported 47 murders in 2020, a 74% increase. At least two men were killed in Seattle's Capitol Hill Occupied Protest (CHOP), which was set up in the aftermath of the death of George Floyd. Seattle Mayor Jenny Durkan defended CHOP as "a peaceful expression of our communities collective grief." She later signed a bill cutting the Seattle Police Department's budget by 18%. Seattle business owners were not impressed, filing a lawsuit alleging that the city violated their constitutional rights by allowing the occupation.

Minneapolis' murder rate increased 72% in 2020, with 81 killings reported. Minneapolis also saw the death of George Floyd, an unarmed black man. Minneapolis police officer Derek Chauvin was charged with second-degree murder after he knelt on Floyd's neck for over eight minutes. The Minneapolis City Council voted unanimously to replace its police department with a "community-based public safety model" in the aftermath of Floyd's death and widespread protests and rioting. Minneapolis minority business owners were forced to turn to armed guards organized by the NAACP after police were unable to prevent looting. (RELATED: Minneapolis City Council President Says Calling The Police During An Emergency Is 'Privilege')

Aurora, Colorado

32 people were killed in Aurora in 2020, a 68% increase over 2019's total. Aurora saw protests throughout 2020 following the 2019 death in police custody of 23 year old Elijah McClain. Rioters were charged after barricading police inside an Aurora precinct. The 18 Aurora police officers had to be rescued by a tactical team. Other protestors blocked Interstate Highway 225 near Aurora. One protestor shot at a car that drove through the blockade.

New Orleans, Louisiana

New Orleans reported 194 homicides in 2020 for a 62% year over year increase. Protests in New Orleans were often led by Take 'Em Down NOLA, a group that advocates "occupying streets and in some cases literally removing the symbols of… oppression." They scored a victory when the Louisiana State Supreme Court removed a statue of Supreme Court Chief Justice Edward Douglass White. White was the only Louisianan on the United States Supreme Court until Amy Coney Barrett was confirmed in Oct. 2020. Other New Orleans protestors and activists called for the city council to defund the New Orleans Police Department and use that money to fund social programs

Federal judge — who is Stacey Abrams' sister — orders two Georgia counties to stop removing voters from rolls ahead of Jan. 5 runoffs

Thousands of voters were set to be removed from rolls

Phil Shiver

A federal judge has ordered two counties in Georgia to reverse course on removing thousands of individuals from voter rolls ahead of the state's Jan. 5 Senate runoffs.

POLL: Will you be spending Christmas with your family or social distancing?

The judge, Leslie Abrams Gardner — who is the sister of former Democratic candidate for governor Stacey Abrams, a prominent ally of Democratic President-elect Joe Biden — issued the ruling Monday, concluding the counties relied on unverified change-of-address data to proceed with the action.

"Defendants are enjoined from removing any challenged voters in Ben Hill and Muscogee Counties from the registration lists on the basis of National Change of Address data," Gardner wrote in the order.

Politico reported that the majority of the registrations officials were seeking to rescind, about 4,000, came from Muscogee County, where Biden claimed an easy victory, while an additional 150 registrations were from Ben Hill County, where President Trump won by a sizable margin.

The number of registrations could prove significant in the hotly contested state where, in November, Biden defeated Trump by just under 12,000 votes and Republican Sens. David Perdue and Kelly Loeffler were unable to accrue the majority needed for victory and avoid runoff elections.

The elections boards in each of the counties had approved motions filed by local voters claiming the registrations should be removed based on data from the United States Postal Service's National Change of Address database that allegedly showed the individuals had moved out of the county.

In her Monday order, Gardner ruled that the evidence in each case was not conclusive enough to support their removal and noted that the removals may have violated federal law because the voters were not given proper notice as is required within 90 days of a federal election.

Earlier on Monday, the Muscogee County elections board filed a motion requesting Gardner's recusal from the case given her connection to Abrams, but the request was denied.

Abrams, after losing her run for governor in 2018, has become a vocal proponent of increasing voter registration in the state. Earlier this month, the Georgia secretary of state's office announced it had launched an investigation into the New Georgia Project, a third-party registration group founded by Abrams, for "repeatedly and aggressively" seeking to register "ineligible, out-of-state, or deceased voters" ahead of the runoff elections.

In the motion, lawyers for the board described Abrams as "a Georgia politician and voting rights activist who was the Democratic candidate in the 2018 Georgia gubernatorial election and has since engaged in various highly publicized efforts to increase voter registration and turnout for the 2020 general election in Georgia."

This week, during an interview on CNN, Abrams charged that "Republicans do not know how to win without voter suppression as one of their tools."

Virginia gubernatorial candidate says 'Trump should declare martial law'

By Michael Ruiz

Virginia Republican state Sen. Amanda Chase, an outspoken Trump supporter and gubernatorial hopeful, doubled down on disputed voter fraud claims and said Thursday that her state needs an election audit – through martial law, if necessary.

"President Trump should declare martial law as recommended by General Flynn," Chase wrote in a fiery Facebook post Tuesday.

In the post, she also disputed the 2020 election results in response to the Electoral College confirming President-elect Joe Biden on Monday.

Flynn also tweeted an ad Dec. 1 from the conservative We the People Convention calling on Trump to invoke martial law "if Legislators, Courts and the Congress do not follow the Constitution."

Chase is known to open carry a .38 revolver and has been described as «Trump in heels,» a renegade, and the Virginia Senate's very own Annie Oakley.

She discussed concerns about changes to the state's voting laws leading up to the election in an interview with Fox News Thursday.

She argued that state Democrats, who control majorities in the Legislature and hold the governor's office, scaled back voter ID laws, mail-in signature requirements and ballot chain-of-custody rules, weakening the state's election integrity in the summer and fall. Lawmakers who supported the changes argued they were necessary to protect voters' health due to the coronavirus pandemic.

Virginia state Senator Amanda Chase (R-11) at work in the statehouse, on February, 20, 2019 in Richmond, VA. (Getty)

"That legislation that was passed was in essence legalizing the ability of the Democrats to commit election fraud here in Virginia," Chase alleged Thursday.

THIS JUSTIFIES TRUMP INVOCATION OF INSURRECTION ACT TO RESTORE LAWFUL ELECTION

John O'Bannon, the lone Republican on Virginia's three-person Board of Elections, told VPM **last month that he thinks, "in general, the elections have been fair in Virginia." And state elections officials have said they haven't seen widespread voter fraud.**

But Chase said an investigation is warranted. She supports former Gen. Michael Flynn, and the call to

impose martial law and temporarily "suspend the Constitution," but only under "extreme" circumstances. "You never want to suspend the Constitution," she said. "You know the question is, if we get into an extreme situation where we feel like the Democratic Party has committed treason, we really don't have much of a choice but to suspend the Constitution and have a very limited focus on martial law as it pertains to election integrity, and votes, and securing the equipment that we used to vote to ensure we get to the bottom of what happened."

SIDNEY POWELL APPEALS GEORGIA 'KRAKEN' SUIT DISMISSAL TO 11TH CIRCUIT COURT

Democratic Gov. Ralph Northam's office did not immediately respond to Fox News' request for comment. But President Trump's legal team has found little success in a flurry of lawsuits alleging voter fraud throughout the country.

When asked if martial law meant troops on street corners and upending everyday life, Chase said no. She said she meant a "limited martial law" where the military would seize and audit voting machines and ballots to investigate claims of voter fraud.

"A lot of Virginians have told me this… 'We accepted Clinton, we accepted Obama, because we felt like it was a fair election,'" she told Fox News Thursday. "But what we cannot accept is Biden as our president, because we do not feel that this election was fair and honest."

Some other elected Republicans condemned Chase's stance, however.

"I find it world-record levels of cognitive dissonance that she's against the governor's curfew, but she's for martial law," said U.S. Rep. Denver Riggleman, of Virginia's 5th District. "I also think it's gibberish. We don't want the 'G' in GOP to stand for gibberish." But he conceded that Chase's messaging is working; she is fundraising millions for her gubernatorial campaign and appeals to "a wide swath of the electorate."

IS IMPOSING MARTIAL LAW BY INVOKING THE INSURRECTION ACT US BEING NICE? GERMANY WAS NICE; GOT ADOLF HITLER. VENEZUELA WAS NICE; GOT HUGO CHAVEZ. TUPAC SHAKUR SAID, "I DIDN'T GET WHERE I AM BY BEING NICE. BEING NICE GAVE HITLER & CHAVEZ GERMANY & VENEZUELA,

"I think we need a vaccine against disinformation just like we have a vaccine against COVID-19," Riggleman said, proposing that private sector analytics companies present facts to the public, sidestepping "conspiracy theories," the media and both major political parties.

One such program, he said, is the Network Contagion Research Institute, of which he is a board member.

Virginia state delegate Kirk Cox, who is running against Chase in the GOP gubernatorial primary for a chance to take on Northam, said in a statement, "Senator Chase's suggestion that martial law be imposed is absurd and dangerous."

AFTER ELECTORAL COLLEGE VOTES, WHAT NEXT?

When asked her response to Republican and independent voters who have conceded Biden is the president-elect, Chase said she would keep on fighting.

"We've got to get to the bottom of the voter fraud so that we can continue to operate as a republic," she said. "We have to ensure that every legal vote is counted."

After a brief delay, Virginia certified its election results on Nov. 18, and its electors cast their Electoral College ballots for Biden on Monday.

Supporters are eyeing Jan. 6 as their next, and perhaps final, chance to overcome what they see as widespread voter fraud. A joint session of Congress is scheduled to formally count the Electoral College votes.

AGAIN?

Outspoken Georgia Poll Workers Barred From Senate Runoffs

THEY WERE FIRED FOR EXPOSING UNPROSECUTED VOTE STEALING PUNISHABLE (10) YEAR FEDERAL PRISON; STACY ABRAMS DEMOCRATS GOT AWAY WITH IT & ARE LAUGHING AT REPUBLICANS

By Brian Trusdell

Two Fulton County poll workers in Georgia who spoke to news outlets or filed affidavits claiming voting irregularities in the November election have been told they will not return to work the Senate runoff races, The Epoch Times is reporting.

The two women, Bridget Thorne and Susan Voyles, said they consider their notification that their appointments was not being renewed essentially as being fired and retribution for going public with their allegations.

"I see it as a direct consequence of my being honest," Voyles told New Tang Dynasty Television, a part of

Epoch Media Group, on Friday.

The pair was informed they would not be returning in letters from Dwight Brower, elections consultant for the Fulton County Department of Registration and Elections. He wrote the women that Georgia law enables officials to appoint poll managers and that they must be reappointed for each election.

"There are many factors (management skills, performance, actions, behavior, etc.) considered prior to making reappointments for each primary or election," Brower wrote. "Unfortunately, a decision has been made to not reappoint you in a poll management or other poll positions in Fulton County."

A spokeswoman for Fulton County, which encompasses Atlanta, did not respond to The Epoch Times request for comment.

Georgia Secretary of State Brad Raffensperger decried the decision not to reappoint Thorne and Voyles.

"I condemn in the strongest terms the decision by Fulton County elections officials to fire two poll managers purely for raising concerns about the November elections," he said in a statement. "Though we have found no credible evidence of widespread fraud, it is important that individuals can raise their voice when they believe they have seen wrongdoing. Retribution against whistleblowers poses a threat to the continued strength and vibrancy of our democracy."

Voyles filed an affidavit in a lawsuit filed by famed attorney Lin Wood, who represented wrongfully accused Richard Jewell in the 1996 Centennial Olympic Park bombing, claiming she witnessed unusual batches of "pristine" ballots nearly all marked for Joe Biden being counted.

"In my 20 years' of experience of handling ballots," she said, "I observed that the markings for the candidates on these ballots were unusually uniform, perhaps even with a ballot-marking device."

Thorne said she witnessed ballots from early voting dumped in the election warehouse in Fulton County.

"Being a precinct manager, it was just upsetting just to see people dumping these ballots out into suitcases and there was no security. There was no chain of command," she said. "I could have walked out of the building with a whole suitcase of ballots if I wanted to. There was nobody holding me accountable."

Trump Demands Bigger Relief Checks in Virus Stimulus; Says Pelosi: 'Let's Do It'

President Donald Trump threatened on Tuesday not to sign a $892 billion coronavirus relief bill that includes desperately needed money for individual Americans, saying it should be amended to increase the amount in the stimulus checks.

The outgoing Republican president's threat, with less than a month left in office, throws into turmoil a

bipartisan effort in Congress to provide help for people whose lives have been upended by the pandemic.

"The bill they are now planning to send back to my desk is much different than anticipated," Trump said in a video posted on Twitter. "It really is a disgrace."

Speaker Nancy Pelosi was quick to embrace Trump's call for bigger checks in the relief package.

After the president posted his video, she tweeted: "Republicans repeatedly refused to say what amount the President wanted for direct checks. At last, the President has agreed to $2,000 — Democrats are ready to bring this to the Floor this week by unanimous consent. Let's do it!"

Both the House of Representatives and the Senate passed the legislation on Monday night.

Trump said he wants Congress to increase the amount in the stimulus checks to $2,000 for individuals or $4,000 for couples, instead of the "ridiculously low" $600 for individuals currently in the bill.

Trump also complained about money in the legislation for foreign countries, the Smithsonian Institution and fish breeding, among other spending.

"I'm also asking Congress to immediately get rid of the wasteful and unnecessary items from this legislation, and to send me a suitable bill, or else the next administration will have to deliver a COVID relief package. And maybe that administration will be me," he said.

Rudy Giuliani to Newsmax TV: Pennsylvania Lawsuit First of Many Efforts

The new effort by President Donald Trump's legal team asking the U.S. Supreme Court to overturn three Pennsylvania Supreme Court decisions **is just the first of many efforts to overturn what they see as a fraudulent election, Trump personal attorney Rudy Giuliani tells** Newsmax TV.

"You have to go state by state," he told "Spicer & Co." **host Sean Spicer on Monday, acknowledging even a victory in the case would only net 20 electoral votes — not enough to give Trump the 270 needed to secure reelection. "I remember an old adage that I learned from baseball," Giuliani said. "When you're down by 10 runs, you can't score 10 runs on one hit. So you got to get one run at a time. So the way I look at it, we have to win one of these legislatures. I think we have three good ones to pick from: Pennsylvania, and Georgia, and Arizona."**

Giuiliani said he thinks his team has demonstrated enough fraud in any of those cases - "that the state legislature has a very, very strong basis to make a determination the election in those three states were stolen."

The state legislatures are the final arbiters, he said, under the U.S. Constitution, and that is why his team has

been holding hearings in various legislatures to present their case the votes filed were not accurate.

Asked about a reported White House meeting in which Trump discussed appointing former Trump team lawyer Sidney Powell as a special prosecutor to investigate election fraud — as story Trump has called "fake news" — Giuliani said:

"Let me say definitively: Sidney Powell is not part of our legal team. She hasn't been for five weeks. She is not a special counsel for the president. She does not speak for the president, nor does she speak for the administration. She speaks for herself. And she's a fine woman, a fine lawyer. But whatever she is talking about it's her own opinion. I'm not responsible for them. The president isn't, nor is anybody else on our legal team."

He added, he and the team will be "extremely aggressive" in their fight, but added, "We're also going to do it within the bounds of rationality, common sense, and the law

Hice to Newsmax TV: McConnell Should Tell Senators to 'Get on Board' With Election Challenge

Rep. Jody Hice, R-Ga., who has said he plans to lead the challenge of his state's electors when Congress meets in joint session on Jan. 6, tells Newsmax TV he disagrees with Senate Majority Leader Mitch McConnell's directive to Republicans not to join the effort, saying the party needs to fighting for free and fair elections.

"I think it's totally inappropriate for Mitch McConnell trying to walk away from this," Hice said Tuesday on "Spicer & Co." "If we lose that integrity of the ballot box, we will ultimately lose our country, so he needs to be in the battle with us. He needs to be encouraging senators to get on board with this."

Hice met with President Donald Trump and other Republicans in the White House on Tuesday about plans to overturn the presidential election by challenging state electors in disputed states. He admitted to host Sean Spicer that the plan is a longshot, but said it is worth the effort.

"The president's very energetic. He is laser focused, as are many of us who were there in the room, Hice said, adding that everyone in the meeting is convinced the election was "filled with fraud, and we have got to get to the bottom of it."

Courts have not looked at the evidence, but he said that will be presented in the process on Jan. 6. Though no senators have said for certain they will join the effort, several have indicated willingness, and Hice said he's assured they'll have someone on board. At least one member of the Senate and one from the House must object to a set of electors before debate can take place.

Hice said each state will be called alphabetically, and when a state, such as Arizona, where a challenge is planned, comes up, the House and Senate would each then dismiss to their respective chambers for two hours of debate, where he said Republicans would then make their case. After that votes would be taken by state delegation, not by member-by-member, and if enough votes were were cast to overturn, then an alternate slate of electors would be accepted and Trump would be awarded the state instead of Democrat Joe Biden.

In the Electoral College vote on Dec. 14 Biden won 306 to Trump's 232, meaning Trump would need to overturn several states to reach the 270 needed to win.

NYC Mayor de Blasio: 'I like to say very bluntly, our mission is to redistribute wealth'

The far-left mayor says he knows 'a lot of people bristle at that phrase'

By Breck Dumas

New York City Mayor Bill de Blasio (D) reiterated to his constituents Friday, "I like to say very bluntly, our mission is to redistribute wealth," a declaration he has made before although he recognized that "a lot of people bristle at that phrase." What are the details?

During a press conference, de Blasio began by voicing his support for the findings of a recently-concluded investigation by the city that determined the NYPD "made a number of key errors that likely escalated tensions and a potential for violence" during the protests following the death of George Floyd. He promised the police department would be reformed.

"The COVID era has taught us that so clearly, and we need to do better and we will," de Blasio said. "And that means a commitment to fighting disparities and inequality in every part of the life of New York City and that certainly takes us to education where if you're talking about the problems of disparity, if you're talking about structural racism, certainly policing is not the only area to talk about. There are many areas to talk about and education must be front and center."

"There has been so much that needed to be addressed in education in New York City, and from the beginning, what I tried to focus on was a very simple concept: equity and excellence," he continued. "That we needed to profoundly change the distribution of resources."

De Blasio emphasized, "I like to say very bluntly, our mission is to redistribute wealth." He added, "A lot of people bristle at that phrase, that is, in fact, the phrase we need to use." De Blasio has used such phrasing before, even just recently.

In August, the New York Post reported that de Blasio "made a public plea" for "taxing the rich and redistributing their money even as the Big Apple reels from a coronavirus-induced budget crisis that's already caused well-heeled New Yorkers to head for the hills."

"Help me tax the wealthy. Help me redistribute wealth. Help me build affordable housing in white communities if you want desegregation," the mayor told a caller on WNYC's "The Brian Lehrer Show" during a discussion about schools.

"What changes things is redistribution of wealth," he reiterated. "Tax the wealthy at a much higher level. I just feel like this is a lot of cocktail party comfort going on rather than people honestly dealing with this issue."

But de Blasio's insistence on further taxes on wealthy New Yorkers has received pushback even from fellow Democrat Gov. Andrew Cuomo, who has pleaded with high earners to stop fleeing the state in a mass exodus that began when the coronavirus and lockdowns hit.

Cuomo pointed out earlier this year that the wealthiest one % of New Yorkers pay roughly half the taxes collected in the state.

New Trump Petition Asks Supreme Court to Overturn Pennsylvania Election Results

By Solange Reyner

President Donald Trump is carrying on his fight to overturn the election results, Politico reports. The president's legal team on Sunday filed a new petition with the Supreme Court asking to reverse a trio of decisions from the Pennsylvania Supreme Court easing some of the state's election rules related to signature verification, Election Day observation and mail-in ballot declarations. They are also asking the court to allow the Pennsylvania General Assembly to pick its own slate of electors.

"Collectively, these three decisions resulted in counting approximately 2.6 million mail ballots in violation of the law as enacted by the Pennsylvania Legislature," Trump's attorney John Eastman wrote in the filing.

The campaign team said the decision by the state's top court to extend the statutory deadline for receipt of mail ballots from 8 p.m. on Election Day to 5 p.m. three days later had "national importance" and may violate the U.S. Constitution. "The petition seeks all appropriate remedies, including vacating the appointment of electors committed to Joseph Biden and allowing the Pennsylvania General Assembly to select their replacements," Trump attorney Rudy Giuliani said in a statement.

Electors in all 50 states and the District of Columbia last week cast ballots formalizing Joe Biden's win over Trump. The challenge follows a similar lawsuit brought by Texas Attorney General Ken Paxton which the justices refused to hear earlier this month.

Gaetz Says He Will Challenge Electoral College Votes on Jan. 6

By Eric Mack

Rep. Matt Gaetz, R-Fla., touted himself as an attorney general appointee for President Donald Trump, vowing to "go easy on marijuana, tough on big tech."

"And so I figure, in the next term of Donald Trump, whether that's in 2021 or 2025, maybe he ought to pick me to be the attorney general," Gaetz told Turning Point USA's young conservatives conference in West Palm Beach, Florida, this weekend, Mediaite reported.

"And for whatever reason he doesn't run, maybe I ought to pick the attorney general," Gaetz added, per the report.

"I would go easy on marijuana, tough on Big Tech, and I would go after the 'deep state.'"

Gaetz has been a vocal supporter of President Trump and a staunch opposition of Democrat-led investigations into the Trump administration.

Trump's past attorney general William Barr has decided to resign before Christmas amid potentially multiple investigations of the Biden family, election fraud, and special counsel John Durham's investigation of the investigators of 2016 election meddling.

Gaetz said he plans to challenge Electoral College votes when they are counted during a Joint Session of Congress on Jan. 6.

"So on January 6, I'm joining with the fighters in the Congress and we are going to object to electors from states that didn't run clean elections."

Gaetz said newly elected Alabama senator Tommy Tuberville, R-Ala., will join the planned objection by members of the House of Representatives. Gaetz during his speech said that moments before the event he had spoken to Tuberville, who told him that he plans on joining the effort.

"I had a chance to speak to coach Tuberville just moments ago and he says we are done running plays from the establishment's losing playbook and it's time to fight," Gaetz said.

"Now coach Tubervillve went for it a lot on fourth down when he was coaching at Auburn. They called him the Mississippi riverboat gambler. The odds may be tough, it may be fourth and long but we're going for it on January 6."

IF BLUE AMERICA WANTS THIS; DIE IN YOUR BED WITHOUT US.

By Jeffrey Rodack

Rush Limbaugh, noting conservatives have very little in common with people in certain states, is raising the issue of secession.

Limbaugh made his comments on his radio show on Wednesday.

"I actually think that we're trending toward secession," he said. "I see more and more people asking what in the world do we have in common with the people who live in, say, New York? What is there that makes us believe that there is enough of us there to even have a chance at winning New York, especially if you're talking about votes.

"A lot of bloggers have written extensively about how distant and separated and how much more separated our culture is becoming politically and that it can't go on this way. There cannot be a peaceful coexistence of two completely different theories of life, theories of government, theories of how we manage our affairs. We can't be in this dire a conflict without something giving somewhere along the way.

"I know that there's a sizable and growing sentiment for people who believe that that is where we're headed whether we want to or not. Whether we want to go there or not. I, myself, haven't made up my mind. I still haven't given up the idea that we are the majority and that all we have to do is find a way to unite and win."

I JUST WISH WE COULD GIVE A WIN TO RUSH

Rush Limbaugh gives update on cancer battle: 'Every day remains a gift'

WE LOVE HIM SO MUCH; MORE THAN ANYONE WE NEED HIM

'I wake up every morning, and I thank God that I did,' radio host tells listeners Tuesday.

By Samuel Chamberlain

Conservative radio host **Rush Limbaugh gave listeners an update on his** lung cancer **battle Tuesday, saying he was taking it day-to-day but blessed to still be alive.**

"Every day remains a gift," Limbaugh greeted his audience Tuesday. "You know, I wake up every morning, and I thank God that I did."

The host added that "there will probably be, down the road, similar-type days where I will need take a day for rest or for whatever medical challenges present themselves. But the fact that I'm able to get back here and be with you is a genuine blessing, and I appreciate it and I appreciate your understanding throughout all of this.

"As we say, everything's day-to-day, and especially in the circumstances I find myself in."

CANCER-STRICKEN LIMBAUGH SAYS HE'S 'DAY-TO-DAY', THANKFUL TO BE AROUND FOR ELECTION

Limbaugh, 69, announced Feb. 3 that he had been diagnosed with advanced lung cancer. The following night, President Trump awarded Limbaugh the Presidential Medal of Freedom during the State of the Union address.

In October, Limbaugh told listeners that recent scans had shown "some progression of cancer." He missed several shows that month to undergo treatment.

"It's tough to realize that the days where I do not think I'm under a death sentence are over," the host said at the time, adding: "When you have a terminal disease diagnosis that has a time frame to it, then that puts a different psychological and even physical awareness to it."

On Tuesday, Limbaugh emphasized to listeners that "there are gonna be days where I'm not gonna be able to get in ... there are medical challenges that present themselves and that have to be dealt with and some of

them, you know, pop up as a surprise. Some of them are predictable.

"But I continue to look at this and live this as a day-to-day proposition ...," Limbaugh concluded. "And so the bottom line is that every day is a gift. And even on those days where I'm not able to get here, realize that I wish I could be. And that when those days occur, that I will do what I can to get back as quickly as is possible."

FIDEL & MOTORCYCLE DIARIES CHE

HILLARY & MARXIST HUGO CHAVEZ; WHO TURNED VENEZUELA; THE WORLD'S 4TH RICHEST COUNTRY INTO A BASKET CASE NOW POORER THAN HAITI OR BANGLADESH; NO ANESTHESIA; RUNNING WATER IN HOSPITALS OR ELECTRICITY FOR ELEVATORS IN (18) STORY HIGH-RISE BUILDINGS

MASTERMIND & FOUNDER OF ELECTION FRAUD DOMINION VOTING SYSTEMS SMARTRONICS HUGO "BABYCAKES" CHAVEZ

Audit Finds Mich. County's Dominion Voting Was Rigged to Create Fraud

By Brian Trusdell

A forensic audit of the presidential vote tally by Dominion Voting Systems software used in Antrim County, Michigan, showed a more than 68% error rate, with auditors claiming the system intentionally creates the errors so the machine can have them "adjudicated" – allowing individuals to change the result.

The error rate is astounding considering the Federal Election Commission allows a maximum error rate of just 0.0008 % for computerized voting systems.

"We conclude that the Dominion Voting System is intentionally and purposefully designed with inherent errors to create systemic fraud and influence election results," the audit report prepared by Allied Security Operations Group read.

"The system intentionally generates an enormously high number of ballot errors. The electronic ballots are then transferred for adjudication. The intentional errors lead to bulk adjudication of ballots with no oversight, no transparency, and no audit trail."

Dominion denied that there were software glitches in Antrim County or anywhere else. In a statement the company said "isolated human errors not involving Dominion" were at fault. The Detroit Free Press reported the elections office failed to update the programming in their tabulators after requiring changes to their ballot, the company said.

The audit was released Monday by state court Judge Kevin Elsenheimer of the 13th Circuit Court of Michigan in a case brought by county resident William Bailey against Antrim County, Michigan.

The lawsuit allowed Allied Security to take forensic images of the county's 22 tabulators and review other election-related material.

Initial results in the reliably Republican county in northern Michigan showed Joe Biden with a 7,769-4,509 lead, which was changed to a 9,783-7,289 Trump lead two days later and eventually a 9,748-5,960 margin for Trump.

The discrepancy was attributed to a clerk's failure to update the programming in the tabulators. Russell James Ramsland Jr., who conducted the audit and has worked with NASA and the Massachusetts Institute of Technology, disputed the claim.

"We disagree and conclude that the vote flip occurred because of machine error built into the voting software designed to create error," he wrote in the report.

Dominion Voting Systems dismissed **the audit, claiming it is the subject of a "continuing malicious and widespread disinformation campaign" to undermine confidence in the Nov. 3 election.**

Dominion systems are used across Michigan and in as many as 30 states, including several disputed battleground states.

Results certified by Democrat officials in Michigan say Biden won the state by 154,000**, but President Trump's legal team and his allies continue to question the results, claiming, in part, that Dominion Voting Systems are unreliable.**

"The findings in Antrim County, where the error rate was a mind-blowing 68%, the ballot rejection rate was 82%, and software security records and adjudication files were missing, in violation of state and federal laws, are nothing short of mind-blowing," Trump attorney and former federal prosecutor and New York City Mayor Rudy Giuliani said in a release. "The evidence of fraud is indisputable."

Sen.-elect Tommy Tuberville defies Mitch McConnell, opens door to Electoral College challenge in Senate. 'We're gonna have to do it in the Senate'

Stefani Reynolds- Chris Pandolfo

Sen.-elect Tommy Tuberville (R-Ala.) indicated this week that he may challenge the Electoral College votes from several key battleground states in the U.S. Senate in defiance of Senate Majority Leader Mitch McConnell (R-Ky.).

Some congressional Republicans led by Rep. Mo Brooks (R-Ala.) are discussing a plan to challenge the results of the election when Congress convenes on Jan. 6 to certify Joe Biden as president. In a video posted by Lauren Windsor, the executive producer of "Undercurrent," Tuberville appeared to lend his support to the effort.

"Well, you see what's coming. You've been reading about it in the House. We're gonna have to, we're gonna have to do it in the Senate," Tuberville said.

The congressional procedure for accepting a state's Electoral College results can be slowed considerably if one member of the House and one member of the Senate each object to recording the electoral votes of a state.

Should objections be raised, each house of Congress will be forced to debate for two hours and then hold a floor vote on whether to accept the results. In the event that the Democratic-controlled House votes one way and the Republican-controlled Senate votes another way, the tie is broken by the governor's certification in the disputed state.

Rep. Brooks has been leading the charge to challenge the results of the Electoral College in Congress.

"I find it unfathomable that anyone would acquiesce to election theft and voter fraud because they lack the courage to take a difficult vote on the House or Senate floor," Brooks told Politico in an interview. "Last time I checked, that's why we were elected to Congress."

So far it's been unclear that any GOP senators would join Brooks and his House colleagues. Sen. McConnell, the top Republican in the Senate, on Tuesday warned Republican senators on a private conference call that challenging the Electoral College would result in a "terrible vote" because they would have to vote the challenge down and appear to side against President Donald Trump.

Until Tuberville's comments, no GOP senators gave hints they would support an effort to challenge the election. Sen. Kelly Loeffler (R-Ga.) perhaps came the closest. She faces a tough runoff election in Georgia on

Jan. 5 and on Wednesday told reporters she hadn't decided whether she would challenge the election if she wins.

"I haven't looked at it," she said. "Jan. 6 is a long way out and there's a lot to play out between now and then."

Trump wants Republicans to fight. On Wednesday the president told McConnell via tweet that it is "too soon to give up," despite the election results being certified by every state and the Electoral College officially selecting Biden to be the next president of the United States.

The odds that Republicans could successfully reject the results of the election in Congress are almost nonexistent. Even if Tuberville or Loeffler were to object, there are not enough votes in the Senate to toss the election results from not one, but several states Trump would need to overcome Biden's 306-232 lead in the Electoral College. The Trump campaign's various legal challenges, most of which have been dropped or dismissed, and the remaining pending cases, even if successful, would not be enough to overturn the election.

WHEN REELECTED IN 2012 BARACK HUSSEIN OBAMA & HUGO CHAVEZ ECHOED EACH OTHER'S ASSES "A BEAUTIFUL ELECTION"

B. HUSSEIN OBAMA & HUGO CHAVEZ

Matthew DePerno to Newsmax TV: Dominion System Changes Votes

By Brian Trusdell

Attorney Matthew DePerno told Newsmax TV on Monday that he hopes an audit report of vote tabulating machines that found a 68% error rate in Antrim County, Michigan, will help President Donald Trump continue to contest election results in the state and across the country.

"This is not over," DePerno said on "Greg Kelly Reports." "There are still options for the president, and we hope that we've given him something to on here, based on our investigation, because if this happened in Antrim County, there are 48 other counties in Michigan that use the same machines, and there's hundreds of counties across the country that also use them."

DePerno was the attorney who filed suit for an Antrim County man against local election officials and was allowed to have a cybersecurity firm conduct a forensic audit of the machines and results. The report, produced by Allied Security Operations Group, determined that the Dominion Voting Systems software used to calculate vote totals is "intentionally and purposefully designed with inherent errors to create systemic fraud and influence election results."

The report and DePerno claim that the Dominion software is designed to create a high % of errors which then must be "adjudicated" – a process in which the ballot is transferred to a computer screen and an operator manually enters the ballot choices.

DePerno also said that changes can be made to batches of ballots, but the individual who conducted the audit, Russell James Ramsland Jr., could not determine where the ballots were transferred to be "adjudicated."

"This program is designed specifically to generate these types of errors and that's how they move votes from one candidate to another," DePerno said. "They put them in these folders for mass adjudication and they're shipped somewhere, in our case, specifically as you see in the report, we can't tell that right now, because on Nov. 4, all of those system files, those adjudication files and internet files, were deleted. That's pretty significant also."

Dominion Voting Systems has dismissed the audit report, claiming the company is the subject of a "continu-.ing malicious and widespread disinformation campaign" to undermine confidence in the Nov. 3 election

Arizona Republicans Cast Alternate Electors for Trump

Arizona Republicans met Monday to cast an alternate slate of electors with state GOP Chairwoman Kelli Ward saying the move has "historic precedent."

The Republican electors cast their 11 electoral votes for President Donald Trump, in opposition to the official electoral votes cast the same day for Democrat Joe Biden, who was declared president-elect with 306 official electoral votes.

The electoral votes of all 50 states and the District of Columbia will be opened at a joint meeting of Congress on Jan. 6, where they will be officially certified. The Republicans in Arizona contend their electors should be counted as "true," according to Ward, and the states 11 votes counted for Trump.

Ward, in a video posted to YouTube, pointed to 1960, when Hawaii, voting in its first presidential election as a state, sent two slates of electors to Washington, D.C. In a close vote, Hawaii's governor declared Republican Vice President Richard Nixon the winner, but with recounts continuing, Democrats also sent their own electors.

Eventually, Democrat Sen. John F. Kennedy was declared the winner, and although Republicans planned to object to counting the state's three electoral votes for Kennedy, the person in charge of the proceedings, Nixon himself as the sitting vice president, asked for unanimous consent for the votes for Kennedy to count — they would not have affected the outcome — and his fellow Republicans complied.

Similarly, Ward said, Arizona Republicans have transmitted their results "to the proper entities in Washington, D.C., for consideration by Congress. We believe that we are the electors for the legally cast votes here in

Arizona." Ward said the election is "far from over" as Trump continues to pursue legal avenues to overturn the election in Arizona and other swing states.

Alternate electors met in other states as well in hopes the last-ditch strategy can keep Trump in office another four years in what they believe to be an election stolen through fraudulent means. GOP Michigan electors were turned away Monday when they tried to deliver their votes to the state Senate. US News & World Report noted, "Trump loyalists in Pennsylvania met in Harrisburg and cast what they described as a 'conditional vote' for Trump." Republicans in Georgia and Wisconsin also voted for an alternate slate of electors, Breitbart reported.

SHE'S NOT A BIMBO; SHE HAS MORE BALLS THAT JOHN McCAIN & OUR 2020 WORTHLESS, LIMP DICK SUPREME COURT OTHER THAN ALITO & CLARENCE THOMAS

Sarah Palin to Newsmax TV: Judges 'Sheep' Trying to Get Along

By Brian Trusdell

Former Alaska governor and Republican vice presidential candidate Sarah Palin referred to judges who dismissed claims by President Donald Trump and his allies of election fraud and illegality on procedural grounds such as standing as "sheep" and called their decisions "tragic for our country."

Palin, 56, who in 2008 was the running mate of presidential candidate and Sen. John McCain, was referring to decisions such as the Pennsylvania Supreme Court which dismissed a challenge for "laches," a legal term for saying the case was brought too late, and the U.S. Supreme Court, which dismissed a challenge last week, saying states such as Texas lacked standing to bring the case.

"It's baffling what we see in terms of the lack of courage," Palin said on Newsmax TV's "Stinchfield" on Tuesday. "That's tragic for our country. We do see so many sheep, just following those who I think are giving them the perception that things will be made easier for them if they'll just follow, if they'll just follow these Democratic leaders like AOC (Rep. Alexandria Ocasio-Cortez)."

Palin made reference to a video clip earlier in the program that showed Ocasio-Cortez, wearing a sweatshirt that said "Tax the rich," arguing that if Democrats win both runoff races for the Senate in Georgia, the country can expand social welfare and raise the minimum wage.

"Holy moly. Do people hear what she's saying?" Palin asked. "She's saying, anybody who is working hard, you're out there working, you shouldn't be living in poverty. And people like me are saying, 'Well, duh, AOC, then quit taking their money, those who are working so hard, and giving it to able-bodied people who are choosing not to work.' "The things that these Democrat leaders are saying today, they're so twisted. It's so Orwellian. Who would have thought that "1984," the book, was going to be their playbook."

THEY HATE US GUNS & RELIGION DEPLORABLES

THIS UNSOLICITED EMAIL CAME TO ME SUNDAY, NOVEMBER 29, 2020 222 Republican Congressmen Won't Say if PAL ZOMBIE & KAMIKAZE KAMALA Biden President-Vice President Elect

By Sandy Fitzgerald |

An overwhelming majority of congressional Republicans won't acknowledge Joe Biden as the President-Elect, according to a Washington Post survey. The survey was taken the morning after President Donald Trump posted a 46-minute video claiming he'd won the election and alleged "corrupt forces" were trying to steal his victory. Just 25 out of 222 Republicans acknowledged Biden's win.

Ninety % of Senate and House GOP members have yet to say who the winner is. The Post survey **asked** lawmakers three questions: **Who won the presidential contest, do you support or oppose Trump's continuing**

efforts to claim victory, and if they will accept Biden as the legitimately elected president if he wins the electoral college majority.

Only 8 Republicans said they support Trump's claim of victory.

The survey also found that 11 of 52 Senate Republicans acknowledge Biden's win. Out of 14 House Republicans who recognized Biden as the winner, six will be retiring from politics later this month and two others represent districts that Biden won.

GOP Rep. Fred Upton, R-Mich., who worked with Biden on the "Beau Biden Cancer Moonshot" proposal, called Biden the president-elect and promised to work with the new administration shortly after the election was called by most news outlets on Nov. 7.

Sen. Pat Toomey, R-Pa., did not acknowledge the win until Nov. 21, after a federal judge rebuked the president's legal team's challenges in Pennsylvania. After that, he congratulated Biden and declared that he'd won. Meanwhile, GOP Reps. Paul Gosar of Arizona and Mo Brooks of Alabama are the only members of their party to publicly insist Trump won the race.

The non-response to the survey contrasts with Democrats in 2016, when Senate Minority Leader WOODCHUCK SCHMUCK SCHUMER D-N.Y., on the day after the election was called for Trump, took a call from him and shortly after issued a statement congratulating him as the president-elect, notes The Post.

Senate Majority Leader Mitch McConnell Tuesday said that the "future will take care of itself" and would not comment on the president's claims of voter fraud.

House Minority Leader Kevin McCarthy, R-Calif., on Thursday said "let's wait" to see who is sworn in before answering questions about executive orders Biden could issue in his first days in the Oval Office.

The Post said the non-reactions mirror how there have been just a few critics of Trump over the past four years, and said the silence leaves them standing alone while other federal, state, and local party members are rejecting the president's claims. The poll comes as Trump's campaign has suffered losses in its quest to overturn results in several key states.

YO' BE IS GOT CRIPS & BLOODS BRO'S & SISTAS HOOD FUCKEN THUGS RUNNING THE YO' PUT SCUMBAGS OSSOFF & WARNOCK IN POWER IN THE JANUARY 5 RUN-OFF? WE LET THEM STUFF BALLOT BOXES AGAIN?

Rep. Mo Brooks to Newsmax TV: Senators 'Shaking in the Foxhole'

By Eric Mack

The House has the members needed to contest the Electoral College certification Jan. 6, but thus far senators have lacked the courage to stand for Americans, according to Rep. Mo Brooks, R-Ala., on Newsmax TV.

"I've been in Congress for a decade; I know how some of these Congress critters and Senate critters try to avoid being courageous when it comes to what they call 'difficult votes,' but in my mind that's what we were elected to do," Brooks told Thursday's "Stinchfield." "I can only control my own vote, how I am going to conduct myself concerning this voter fraud and election theft.

"And I am going to assure the American people, I am going to do everything I can to reverse these Electoral College votes submitted by states that have election systems that are so badly flawed that their reporting of Electoral Colleges votes is rendered untrustworthy."

Brooks pointed to the key battleground states Pennsylvania, Georgia,and Nevada.

"We should not be certifying those voters, rather we should be rejecting them, which is our absolute right under the United States Constitution," Brooks told host Grant Stinchfield.

Senators should stand for the Americans who feel this election was stolen, he added.

"The citizenry should be fed up," Brooks said. "We elect people to Congress in the House and the Senate to be leaders on behalf of our country. Not to shake in their boots in foxholes while the battle is being fought — only to rise up after the battle is over with and joke with the winners and claim we won.

"That's not what we need in Washington."

Brooks concluded with a rebuke of the opposition, saying the "socialist Democrats have essentially stolen" the "accurate and honest elections" from the American people with their unlawful executions of mass mail-in balloting under the guise of the coronavirus pandemic.

Andy Biggs to Newsmax TV: I'm With Mo Brooks

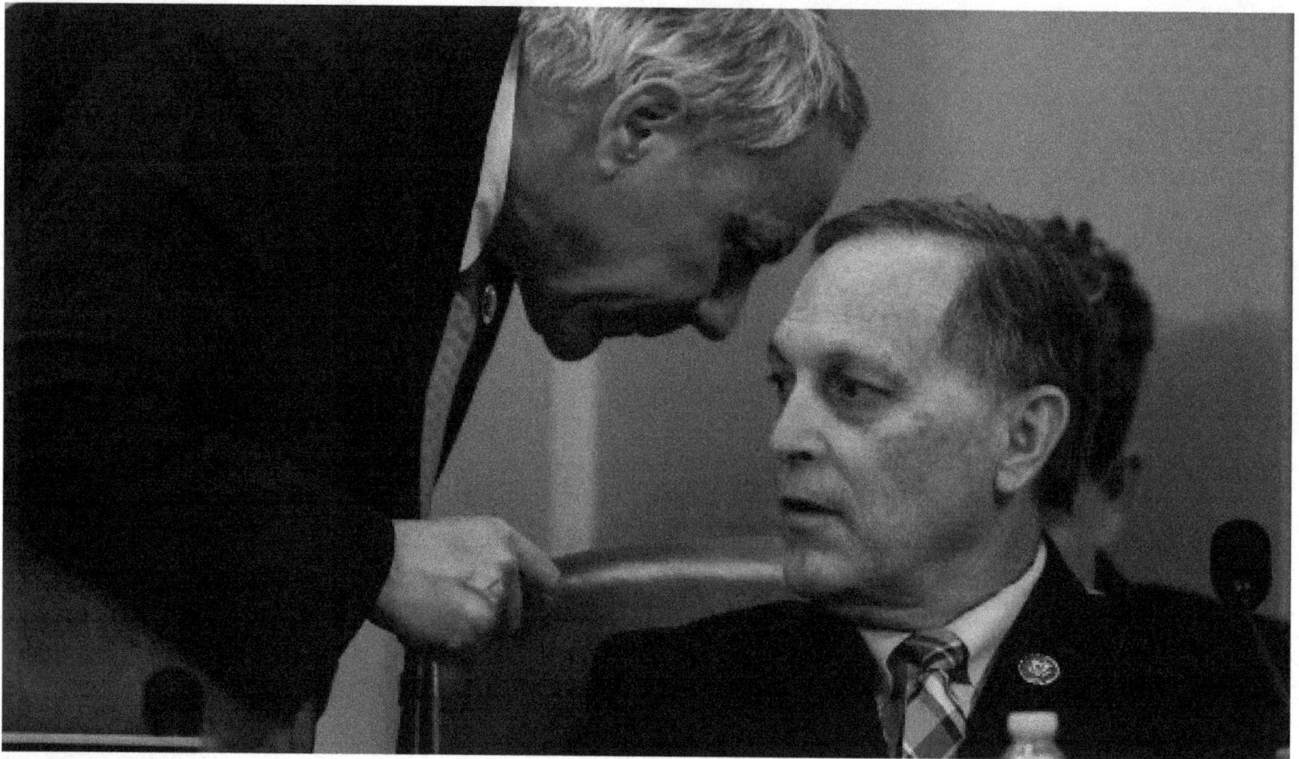

By Theodore Bunker

Rep. Andy Biggs, R-Ariz., told Newsmax TV on Thursday that he's "leaning in heavy support of" Rep. Mo Brooks', R-Ala., plan to contest the 2020 presidential election.

Biggs told "American Agenda" that "right now, I'm leaning heavily into supporting that plan because we've seen so many allegations."

He added that he agreed with Sen. Rand Paul, R-Ky., when he claimed that widespread fraud occurred in the election.

"That's important when you consider if you're gonna object," he said, adding that Republicans are drawing from Democrats' playbook.

"Don't ever forget that in 2017 that's exactly what Democrats did when they objected to the sitting of President Trump's electors, and they did it in 2005, so this is not without precedent, what Mo's suggested, and I'm with him on that because there's so much fraud out there, we actually need to make the point."

HERE WE WIN Supreme Court Throws out Challenge to Trump Census Immigrant Plan

The U.S. Supreme Court on Friday threw out a lawsuit seeking to block President Donald Trump's plan to exclude immigrants living in the United States illegally from the population count used to allocate congressional districts to states.

The 6-3 ruling on ideological lines with the court's six conservatives in the majority and three liberals dissenting, gives Trump a short-term victory as he pursues his hard-line policies toward immigration in the final weeks of his presidency.

However, his administration is battling against the clock to follow through on the vaguely defined proposal before President-elect Joe Biden takes office on Jan 20. The justices left open the possibility of fresh litigation if Trump's administration completes its plan.

The unsigned decision said that "judicial resolution of this dispute is premature" in part because it is not clear what the administration plans to do. The ruling noted that the court was not weighing the merits of

Trump's plan.

Challengers led by New York state and the American Civil Liberties Union said Trump's proposal would dilute the political clout of states with larger numbers of such immigrants, including heavily Democratic California, by undercounting state populations and depriving them of seats in the U.S. House of Representatives to the benefit of his fellow Republicans.

"If the administration actually tries to implement this policy, we'll sue. Again. And we'll win," said Dale Ho, a lawyer for the American Civil Liberties Union who represents the challengers.

The administration has not disclosed what method it would use to calculate the number of people it proposed to exclude or which subsets of immigrants would be targeted. Acting Solicitor General Jeffrey Wall told the justices during the Nov. 30 oral argument in the case that the administration could miss a Dec. 31 statutory deadline to finalize a Census Bureau report to Trump containing the final population data, including the number of immigrants excluded.

"The government does not deny that, if carried out, the policy will harm the plaintiffs. Nor does it deny that it will implement that policy imminently," liberal Justice Stephen Breyer wrote in a dissenting opinion.

Breyer noted that the government can currently try to exclude millions of individuals, including those who are in immigration detention or deportation proceedings, and the some 700,000 young people known as "Dreamers" who came to the U.S. illegally as children.

There are an estimated 11 million immigrants living in the United States illegally. The challengers have argued that Trump's policy violates both the Constitution and the Census Act, a federal law that outlines how the census is conducted.

The Constitution requires apportionment of House seats to be based upon the "whole number of persons in each state." Until now, the U.S. government's practice was to count all people regardless of their citizenship or immigration status.

By statute, the president is required to send Congress a report in early January with the population of each of the states and their entitled number of House districts.

Georgia Secretary of State Announces Statewide Ballot Audit

By Charlie MCarthy

Georgia's secretary of state has relented and announced a statewide signature-matching effort for the November election.

President Donald Trump's campaign claimed voter fraud and has requested that Secretary of State Brad Raffensperger order such an audit since the election ended.

Signatures for absentee ballots in all of Georgia's 159 counties will be reviewed, per The Washington Times.

Raffensperger's announcement came less than three weeks before the Jan. 5 Georgia U.S. Senate runoff election for both seats in the upper chamber. The election will determine which party will hold a Senate majority.

The University of Georgia will partner with the secretary's office to analyze a random sampling of signatures from each county for mail-in ballots during the November election, a Thursday press release said. The audit is expected to wrap up in two weeks.

"We are confident that elections in Georgia are secure, reliable and effective," Mr. Raffensperger said.

"Despite endless lawsuits and wild allegations from Washington, D.C., pundits, we have seen no actual evidence of widespread voter fraud, though we are investigating all credible reports. Nonetheless, we look forward to working with the University of Georgia on this signature match review to further instill confidence in Georgia's voting systems."

The state already was auditing signatures for mail-in ballots in Cobb County, an Atlanta suburb. The Georgia Bureau of Investigation is helping with that effort.

"The Trump campaign claimed that Cobb County did not properly conduct signature match in June," Jordan Fuchs, Georgia's deputy secretary of state said. "After the countywide audit, we will look at the entire state. We will look at the entire election to make sure signature match was executed properly."

Georgia was among several battleground states accused of widespread voter fraud, centering on mail-in ballots, by President Trump.

The president lost the state by 0.2 % or 11,779 votes. Mike Lindell to Newsmax TV: President Will Prevail By Charlie McCarthy

President Donald Trump ultimately will win the election and serve a second term, according to MyPillow founder and CEO Mike Lindell on Newsmax TV.

Lindell said he recently financed rallies around the country to heighten people's awareness of "a complete fraud" of an election.

"I wanted people to be aware that this election was stolen and Donald Trump's going to be our president the next four years," Lindell told host Grant Stinchfield on Thursday's "Stinchfield." "And there's about six pathways to do it, but one of the things is, it's right.

"I spoke to [attorney] Sidney Powell, I've talked to [attorney] Lin Wood, I've talked to Gen. [Michael] Flynn, I know what evidence is out there, plus I've done my own due diligence." Lindell said Fox News was complicit in securing the election for Joe Biden.

"It sure looked like that when they call Arizona with only 14% of the vote in and they don't call Florida for the president when it was impossible for Biden to win," Lindell said. "So, all the things that happened on Election Night, I'm going, 'What is going on?'"

Lindell, whose business has advertised on Fox News, was asked if he would refrain from running commercials on the network.

"I didn't boycott CNN back in the day when they bad-mouthed me directly, and I'm not going to do anything to Fox," he said. "My decisions will be based on business decisions not on my beliefs.

"I wouldn't advertise anywhere if every time a host or a network did something wrong. They attack me all the time, just like they do the president."

Amistad: 'Bombshell' Antrim Audit May Impact 5 Swing States With Dominion

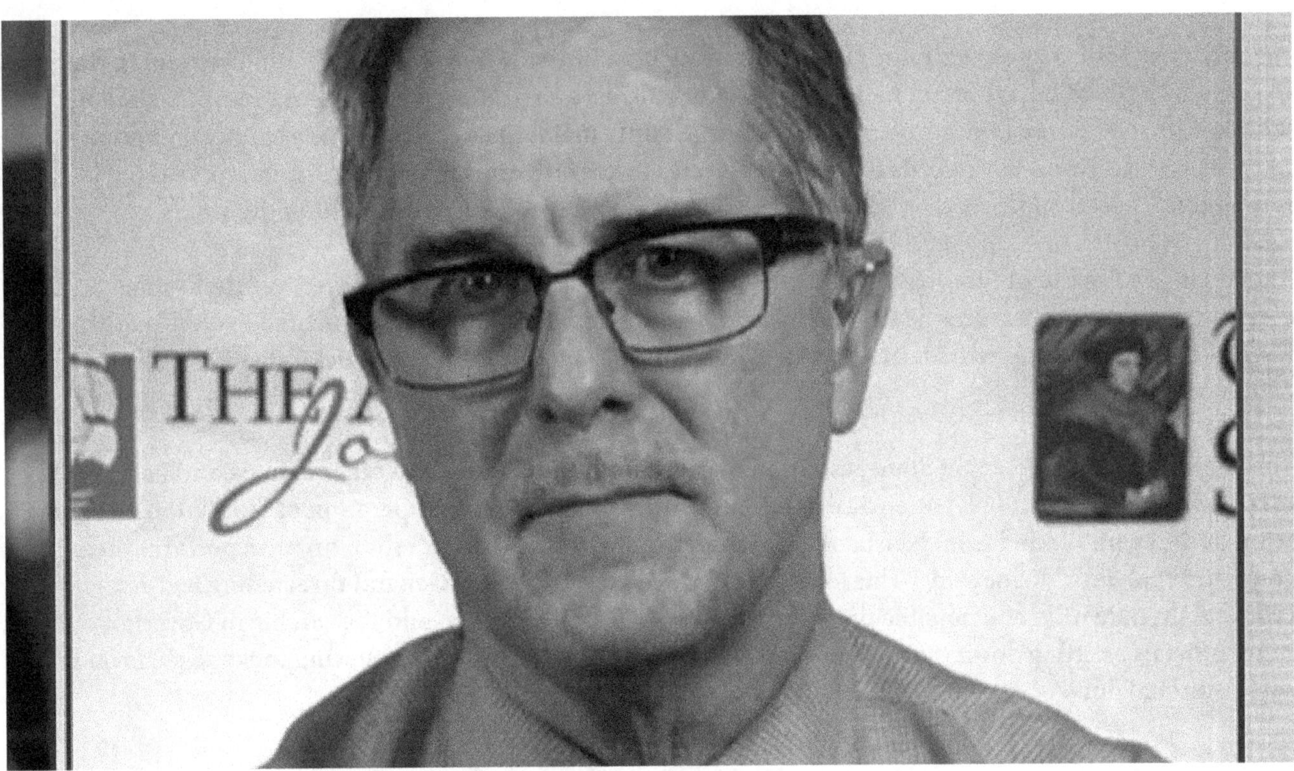

Amistad Project Dir. Phill Kline

The Amistad Project of the non-partisan Thomas More Society is announcing Monday it is demanding the preservation of evidence in five key swing states in response to a bombshell report detailing the results of a forensic audit of Dominion voting machines in Antrim County, Michigan, which was approved for release by 13th Circuit Judge Kevin Elsenheimer.

"We're filing in all swing states a demand that judges step in and preserve evidence to avoid it from being destroyed or spoiled by the intentional or reckless acts of executive officials," said Phill Kline, director of the Amistad Project, which has previously filed election litigation in Arizona, Georgia, Michigan, Pennsylvania, and Wisconsin.

The report claims the "tabulation log for the forensic examination of the server for Antrim County from Dec. 6, 2020 consists of 15,676 individual events, of which 10,667 or 68.05% of the events were recorded errors."

The Federal Election Commission allows a maximum error rate of just 0.0008%.

"The error rate detailed in this report has implications for every state where we have litigation, and it comes on a day when officials are blocking legislators from having their say about elections in their states," Kline said. "This joins with other compelling evidence that the elections in these states cannot be certified under the law."

Investigators believe the error rate in Antrim County is an intentional flaw built into the software in order to compel "bulk adjudication" of ballots by election officials — a process that allows alteration of ballots with minimal or no meaningful oversight. Antrim County maintains records of the adjudication process for previous elections, but records for the 2020 election were either deleted or never entered, making it impossible to determine whether adjudicated ballots accurately reflected the intent of the voters.

The Michigan Bureau of Election also issued a memorandum Dec. 1 instructing election clerks that electronic poll book files must be deleted from all laptops and flash drives. The Amistad Project is asking judges in all swing states to issue emergency orders preventing state and local officials from destroying such evidence.

"In Michigan, the Secretary of State has ordered deletion of e-poll books and other evidence and also has taken affirmative steps to seal forensic evidence regarding the flaws in the operation of Dominion machines from both the public and from legislators who need access to this information in order to perform their constitutional duty," Kline said. "This joins with the Michigan Attorney General threatening legislators with criminal investigation and possible prosecution if they disagree with her, and the Michigan Governor and other officials shutting down the peoples' house and preventing them from gathering today to perform their constitutional duty."

B. HUSSEIN OBAMA & HUGO CHAVEZ

Guide to Election Theft

Americans have a legal path when a vote is disputed. Chávez denied all recourse.

By Mary Anastasia O'Grady

On Wednesday six plaintiffs filed a civil action in the U.S. District Court for the Northern District of Georgia against Republican Gov. Brian Kemp, the secretary of state and four others. The complaint alleges "massive election fraud" to help Joe Biden win the Nov. 3 election for president. It further alleges "the fraud was executed by many means, but the most fundamentally troubling, insidious, and egregious is the systemic adaptation of old-fashioned 'ballot-stuffing.' " This was "amplified and rendered virtually invisible by computer software created and run by domestic and foreign actors for that very purpose." The plaintiffs want Georgia to decertify the election. The 104-page complaint is now before the federal court, which will review the material presented and make a ruling. Central to the argument against the governor and his associates is the claim that software used by Georgia was developed by Hugo Chávez—who died in 2013—to steal elections in Venezuela. Critics are dismissing this as a fantastic conspiracy theory. But they should instead welcome and help to air it.

Matthew DePerno to Newsmax TV: Dominion System Changes Votes

By Brian Trusdell

Attorney Matthew DePerno told Newsmax TV on Monday that he hopes an audit report of vote tabulating machines that found a 68% error rate in Antrim County, Michigan, will help President Donald Trump continue to contest election results in the state and across the country.

"This is not over," DePerno said on "Greg Kelly Reports." "There are still options for the president, and we hope that we've given him something to on here, based on our investigation, because if this happened in Antrim County, there are 48 other counties in Michigan that use the same machines, and there's hundreds of counties across the country that also use them."

DePerno was the attorney who filed suit for an Antrim County man against local election officials and was allowed to have a cybersecurity firm conduct a forensic audit of the machines and results. The report, produced by Allied Security Operations Group, determined that the Dominion Voting Systems software used to calculate vote totals is "intentionally and purposefully designed with inherent errors to create systemic fraud and influence election results."

The report and DePerno claim that the Dominion software is designed to create a high % of errors which then must be "adjudicated" – a process in which the ballot is transferred to a computer screen and an operator manually enters the ballot choices.

DePerno also said that changes can be made to batches of ballots, but the individual who conducted the audit, Russell James Ramsland Jr., could not determine where the ballots were transferred to be "adjudicated."

"This program is designed specifically to generate these types of errors and that's how they move votes from one candidate to another," DePerno said. "They put them in these folders for mass adjudication and they're shipped somewhere, in our case, specifically as you see in the report, we can't tell that right now, because on Nov. 4, all of those system files, those adjudication files and internet files, were deleted. That's pretty significant also."

Dominion Voting Systems has dismissed the audit report, claiming the company is the subject of a "continuing malicious and widespread disinformation campaign" to undermine confidence in the Nov. 3 election.

BULLSEYE MICHAEL FLYNN – THERE'S MORE TO THIS. ADOLF HITLER USED THE CORRUPTED 2012 October 7 **ELECTION OF MARCH 5, 1933; & The Venezuelan presidential election of 2012** was held on .2013 **55.07% of the popular vote, ahead** to choose a president for the six-year term beginning January

US Army Rejects Using 'Martial Law' on Election Fraud

By Eric Mack

Retired Lt. Gen. Michael Flynn's Newsmax TV remarks on President Donald Trump weighing «martial law» and «military capabilities» amid election fraud has forced U.S. Army leaders to issue a statement Friday rejecting that consideration.

"There is no role for the U.S. military in determining the outcome of an American election," Army Secretary Ryan McCarthy and Army chief of staff Gen. James McConville wrote in a joint statement **Friday.**

The statement echoed one by Chairman of the Joint Chiefs of Staff Gen. Mark Milley before the election.

Gen. Flynn told Thursday's "Greg Kelly Reports**":**

"He could immediately on his order seize every single one of these machines around the country on his order. He could also order, within the swing states, if he wanted to, he could take military capabilities and he could place them in those states and basically rerun an election in each of those states. It's not unprecedented.

"I mean, these people are out there talking about martial law like it's something that we've never done. Martial law has been instituted 64 times."

Flynn's martial law remarks were on the heals of Georgia lawyer L. Lin Wood's previous comments to Newsmax TV's "The Count" last week:

"If the Supreme Court does not act, I think the president should declare some extent of Martial law, and he should hold off an stay the electoral college.

"Because we cannot have in this country, an election of our leader, where you have massive evidence of fraud and illegality. This country has to have a vote that has integrity. And the electoral college does not need to meet and vote until we have resolved these issues."

THIS JUSTIFIES INVOCATION AS OUR ONLY OPTION TO SAVE LAWFUL SELECTION OF PRESIDENT

John O'Bannon, the lone Republican on Virginia's three-person Board of Elections, told VPM **last month that he thinks, "in general, the elections have been fair in Virginia." And state elections officials have said they haven't seen widespread voter fraud.**

But Chase said an investigation is warranted. She supports former Gen. Michael Flynn, and the call to im-

pose martial law and temporarily "suspend the Constitution," but only under "extreme" circumstances.

"You never want to suspend the Constitution," she said. "You know the question is, if we get into an extreme situation where we feel like the Democratic Party has committed treason, we really don't have much of a choice but to suspend the Constitution and have a very limited focus on martial law as it pertains to election integrity, and votes, and securing the equipment that we used to vote to ensure we get to the bottom of what happened."

AFTER ELECTORAL COLLEGE VOTES, WHAT HAPPENS NEXT?

When asked her response to Republican and independent voters who have conceded Biden is the president-elect, Chase said she would keep on fighting. "We've got to get to the bottom of the voter fraud so that we can continue to operate as a republic," she said. "We have to ensure that every legal vote is counted."

After a brief delay, Virginia certified its election results on Nov. 18, and its electors cast their Electoral College ballots for Biden on Monday. Supporters are eyeing Jan. 6 as their next, and perhaps final, chance to overcome what they see as widespread voter fraud. A joint session of Congress is scheduled to formally count the Electoral College votes. Federalist's Hemingway: Ga. Video Not Debunked

By Brian Trusdell

The Federalist's senior editor Mollie Hemingway is ridiculing several news outlets that claim Republican accusations of questionable behavior by Fulton County election officials at State Farm Arena, purportedly caught on video, had been debunked, rebutting the reports with affidavits and even other news reports.

Hemingway, 46, the author of "Justice on Trial," about the Senate hearings of Brett Kavanaugh's nomination to the Supreme Court, dismissed a report by «Lead Stories» and then The Washington Post, Newsweek, and others, which appeared to anoint government officials as the sole arbiters of whether anything nefarious occurred.

At issue: a video that purportedly showed a handful of election workers telling observers and other ballot counters to leave State Farm Arena in the evening because of burst water pipe. Once the room was cleared, the remaining election officials uncovered suitcase-like containers from under draped tables -- containers alleged to contain thousands of ballots that were then processed without the observers on hand.

Lead Stories, The Washington Post, **and others quoted election officials as saying no one was asked to leave and characterizing the activity as normal.**

"Leaving aside whether relying solely and uncritically on government officials' claims constitutes anything close to a 'fact check,' let's look at the claim that party observers were never told that counting was over for the night," Hemingway wrote. She then noted how two Republican poll observers swore under oath they observed a woman they assumed was the supervisor «yell out» to most workers after 10 p.m. to stop counting and return at 8:30 a.m. the next morning.

This, she said, was buttressed by an ABC News report which said ballot counters were told to go home and counting had stopped. Their source was Regina Waller, the Fulton County public affairs manager for elections.

However, Lead Stories quoted Frances Walton, chief investigator for the Georgia Secretary of State, as saying no was asked to leave, according to information provided to the "media liaison who was present that night."

"While Lead Stories doesn't name the media liaison, the media liaison who was present that night, according to the affidavits, was Regina Waller, the Fulton County public affairs manager for elections," Hemingway wrote.

"OK, so on the one hand you have sworn affidavits from observers saying that supervisors told ballot counters to go home for the evening shortly after 10 p.m., and a video showing everyone leaving en masse at that time.

"And on the other hand, you have two government officials promising that no one was told that counting was over

Rasmussen Poll: Majority Says Media Buried Laptop to Help Biden

By Brian Trusdell

More than half of likely voters believe news media outlets ignored a report in October that Hunter Biden's laptop computer was found to have emails incriminating him and his father in illicit foreign business deals and potential influence peddling to help the elder Biden's presidential campaign, a Rasmussen poll released Tuesday found. Fifty-two % believed the story was buried so as to not damage Joe Biden's presidential aspirations, 32% say it was ignored because it was a "partisan hit job," and 17% were not sure.

Fifty-six % believe it is likely the elder Biden was consulted and perhaps profited from his son's business dealings in Ukraine and China, including 43% who believe it is very likely. That outnumbers the people surveyed who believe the connection is unlikely 38%, and 22% who consider it very unlikely. The poll was taken Monday and Tuesday among a national survey of 1,000 likely voters, less than a week after Hunter Biden acknowledged the U.S. Attorney's Office in Delaware was investigating is tax filings.

That admission came nearly two months after the New York Post first revealed the laptop, left for repairs at a Delaware computer shop, contained emails indicating Hunter Biden introduced his father to a senior official

at a Ukrainian energy company, contradicting Joe Biden's claim he never spoke to his son about his business dealings. The emails also show the company official asked Hunter Biden about ways "you could use your influence" on energy concern's behalf.

Twitter blocked any posts that included the story, claiming it violated the company's hacking policy, and Facebook similarly slowed spread of the story. A July Rasmussen survey showed 75% of Republicans and 47% of non-affiliated voters believed media outlets would aid Biden in the campaign. Only 29% of Democrats agreed.

The most recent poll said 70% of likely voters have been following the Hunter Biden story closely, 38% very closely. Of those closely following the story, 76% said news media organizations deliberately ignored the story before election day to assist Joe Biden, and 72% said he likely profited from his son's overseas involvements.

Ratcliffe's Election Meddling Report Not Ready for Friday

Director of National Intelligence John Ratcliffe

President Donald Trump's spy chief will not meet Friday's deadline to submit a classified report to Congress on foreign efforts to sway the Nov. 3 election, officials said, because of arguments within the intelligence

community over whether China should be cited more prominently for its attempts to influence American voters.

A statement from Director of National Intelligence John Ratcliffe's office Wednesday night said the deadline will not be met because career officers in the intelligence community say they have "received relevant reporting since the election and a number of agencies have not finished coordinating on the product."

Ratcliffe was weighing Tuesday refusing to sign off on the report unless it more fully reflected the national security threat posed by China's efforts, according to people familiar with the matter, who spoke on condition of anonymity owing to the sensitivity of the information.

The report was to go to Capitol Hill as Trump continues to reject the outcome of the presidential election won by Democrat Joe Biden. Trump has claimed wide-scale voter fraud cost him the race, with a number of fellow Republicans still refusing to recognize Biden as president-elect. The intelligence report would not deal with allegations of domestic fraud, such as in ballot-counting.

Ratcliffe and other Trump appointees – including National Security Adviser Robert O'Brien, Secretary of State Michael Pompeo, and Attorney General William Barr – noted over the summer China posed a bigger election threat than Russia.

In recent months, they have issued a barrage of warnings China is covertly attempting to sway American politics and culture from state legislatures to Hollywood movies and from college campuses to Disney theme parks.

U.S. intelligence agencies cited China and Iran for their attempts at 2020 election interference, with his supporters saying those nations would seek to hurt Trump rather than help him.

In September, FBI Director Christopher Wray focused on Russia in an appearance before a House committee, saying it was seeking to hurt Biden's presidential campaign through social media and influence operations. Although Wray testified China also was trying to interfere, primarily by spreading disinformation, Trump chided Wray in a tweet, saying China "is a FAR greater threat than Russia, Russia, Russia."

Ratcliffe's concerns are fueled by fresh intelligence that provides a fuller picture of what China's leaders either did or planned to do to keep Trump from being reelected, the people said.

That information, some of it in Mandarin and gathered in the weeks before and after the election, is still being assessed, one of the people said. It includes social media campaigns, such as attempts to amplify messages Trump is a white supremacist, the person said.

China has previously rejected the Trump administration claims as false. The Chinese embassy in Washington didn't immediately respond to a request for comment. The Office of the Director of National Intelligence declined to comment.

The dispute over China's role comes even as the U.S. government is trying to assess the damage from a devastating hacking attack on government agencies attributed to Russia.

Some analysts say the new intelligence will show China's effort to influence the U.S. election was far more extensive than previously reported by spy agencies over the last year, the people said.

The report is due in classified form to lawmakers 45 days after the election, with an unclassified version set to be released to the public weeks afterward. It summarizes intelligence gathered by agencies including the Federal Bureau of Investigation and the Central Intelligence Agency.

Before taking over in May as director of national intelligence, Ratcliffe was a Republican congressman from Texas who emerged as one of Trump's fiercest defenders during the president's impeachment inquiry last year.

A Texas congressman and former federal prosecutor with no previous intelligence agency background, Ratcliffe was originally chosen to replace former Director of National Intelligence Dan Coats last year. But he withdrew from consideration following public scrutiny of his qualifications, and his denunciation of former special counsel Robert Mueller at a House hearing.

Tensions over the report due this week reflect the debate that played out before the election over which adversary bore greater responsibility for attempts to tamper with American democratic institutions. In September, O'Brien asserted that China – not Russia – "has the most massive program to influence the United States politically."

Yet a week later, a Homeland Security Department official accused Trump administration appointees, including O'Brien, of attempting to suppress intelligence on Russian election interference while promoting China as the prime threat.

In a whistleblower complaint, Brian Murphy, Homeland Security's former intelligence chief, said he was ordered to stop providing intelligence assessments on Russian election meddling and start reporting instead on interference activities by China and Iran.

Sen. Rick Scott to Newsmax TV: We'll See What Happens With Electors Jan. 6

By Charlie McCarthy

Senate Republicans will continue to monitor alleged election fraud before Congress counts Electoral College votes on Jan. 6, according to Sen. Rick Scott, R-Fla., on Newsmax TV.

Asked if he would be willing to join a House member in objecting to the Electoral College vote, Scott was noncommittal when answering host Greg Kelly on Wednesday night's "Greg Kelly Reports."

"We'll see," said Scott, a member of the Homeland Security and Governmental Affairs Committee that met earlier in the day. "I think today was an important day. I think Chairman [Sen.] Ron Johnson [R-Wis.] did a good job. He held an important hearing today. We heard from [former independent counsel] Ken Starr and then we heard from some individuals that gave us some information about what was going on in a couple of these states, what happened in Wisconsin and what happened in Nevada."

Rep. Moe Brooks, R-Ala., said Monday he plans to challenge the certification of the Electoral College votes on Jan. 6 when the Senate and the House of Representatives meet in a joint session. At least one senator must join Brooks to force a vote on the matter. Will Scott or another Republican join the congressman?

"I think all of us are in the same position," Scott said. "What we're doing is we're trying to get as much information as possible. We're going to continue to watch what's going on. We're going to continue to listen about the fraud. We know there was a lot of fraud. If you remember in the beginning, the Democrats would say there was no fraud. Now they're saying well, there's not enough fraud.

Scott, himself, went through a long process before securing his victory against Democrat opponent Bill Nelson two years ago.

"Senate Minority Leader WOODCHUCK SCHMUCK SCHUMER EVIL SCUMBAG [D-N.Y.], after I won the race by 54,000 votes, sent a lawyer up said, 'I really don't care; WOODCHUCK SCHMUCK SCHUMER ACTUALLY SAID THIS what the votes are. We're going to win in the courts,'" Scott said. "I had a thousand lawyers, I went through two recounts. We had to remove two supervisor of elections because of the irregularities that happened. They found 95,000 ballots illegal after election night. So, we've got to get the facts. We got to understand exactly what happened here. We want to make sure this election and all future elections are fair."

Ex-Trump Lawyer Powell Asks High Court to Nullify 2 Biden Wins

Sidney Powell

Former Donald Trump campaign lawyer Sidney Powell asked the Supreme Court to overturn Joe Biden's election victories in Michigan and Georgia, continuing with a flurry of long shot litigation despite repeated rejections in the courts. The latest requests appeared on the court's online docket Tuesday, a day after the Electoral College confirmed Biden's victory. Although Trump hasn't conceded, Senate Majority Leader Mitch McConnell congratulated Biden as president-elect on Tuesday.

The Supreme Court has already spurned two efforts to nullify Biden victories, first a challenge to his Pennsylvania triumph and then a Texas lawsuit that sought to reverse the results in four pivotal states.

Powell, who is no longer associated with Trump's legal team, sued last month on behalf of Republican voters in Michigan and Georgia. She described her litigation as "releasing the Kraken," a reference to a mythical sea monster unleashed by Zeus in the 1981 fantasy film "Clash of the Titans." In rejecting the Michigan suit, U.S. District Judge Linda Parker said it "offered nothing but speculation and conjecture that votes for President Trump were destroyed, discarded or switched to votes for Vice President Biden." In Georgia, U.S. District

Judge Timothy Batten dismissed the suit orally after an hourlong hearing. Powell is seeking to challenge those rulings directly at the Supreme Court, bypassing the federal appeals court level.

The cases are King v. Whitmer, 20-815, and In Re Pearson, 20-816.

SCUMBAG ZUCKERBERG ZUCKERBUCKS & HIS MAO PRISCILLA CHAN WANNABE THROWS IN $500 MILLION TO STEAL THE PRESIDENCY FOR BIDEN & GETS AWAY WITH IT GOD & SATAN KNOW ZUCKERBERG DID THIS

Report: Zuckerberg Money Used in Violation of Federal Election Law

By Brian Trusdell

A new report by a national public interest law firm alleges that some $500 million donated by Facebook CEO Mark Zuckerberg was used to violate election laws by providing funds to Democrat-dominated municipalities and their elections efforts for the benefit of Joe Biden. The allegation: that this was in violation of the Help America Vote Act.

The 39-page report compiled by the Thomas More Society's Amistad Project claimed that the bulk of $500 million from Zuckerberg and his wife, Priscilla Chan, went to the previously little-known leftist nonprofit Center for Tech and Civic Life.

Although listed as a nonpartisan organization, the CTCL funded ballot collection sites in traditionally Democrat dominated jurisdictions and "considered state election integrity laws as obstacles and nuisances to be ignored or circumvented, " states the authors.

"The provision of Zuckerberg-CTCL funds allowed these Democrat strongholds to spend roughly $47 per voter, compared to $4 to $7 per voter in traditionally Republican areas of the state (of Wisconsin)," **the report stated. "Moreover, this recruiting of targeted jurisdictions for specific government action and funding runs contrary to legislative election plans and invites government to play favorites in the election process.**

Gingrich: Zuckerberg 'Corruption' Raises 'Enormous Questions About the Legitimacy of the Biden Potential Presidency'

Trent Baker

Sunday on New York WABC 770 AM radio's "The Cats Roundtable," former House Speaker Newt Gingrich called into question the "legitimacy" of the Joe Biden presidency.

According to Gingrich, the 2020 presidential election "was the most corrupt election in modern times." He argued that efforts by Facebook and its CEO Mark Zuckerberg to "maximize Democratic turnout" in the election "raises enormous questions about the legitimacy of the Biden potential presidency" because it is "a direct violation" of the 2002 Help America Vote Act.

"I think the Democrats focused on the election where Republicans focused on the campaign. The Democrats didn't care if Biden never campaigned. They were going to generate votes and turn out votes," Gingrich told host John Catsimatidis. "And when you go around and look state by state, the results are fascinating, and I think they raise real questions about exactly what happened. I personally believe this was the most corrupt election in modern times."

He continued, "Just take the one example of Zuckerberg and Facebook, they put in $400 million basically renting city governments and getting them to maximize turnouts and precincts that they couldn't carry, which is a direct violation of the 2002 voting act by Congress, which says that you have to have a fair effort across the board. You can't just select areas you're going to try to maximize turn out in. So, I think just the $400 million that Zuckerberg put in to maximizing Democratic turnout, by itself, is a big enough corruption that it raises enormous questions about the legitimacy of the Biden potential presidency."

THIS IS CAPITAL DEATH PENALTY TREASON FOR MUCH LESSER TREASON

"This privatization of elections undermines the Help America Vote Act (HAVA), which requires state election plans to be submitted to federal officials and approved and requires respect for equal protection by making all resources available equally to all voters." The report claims that a "well-funded network" of foundations and nonprofits used the outbreak of the novel coronavirus to justify funneling hundreds of millions of dollars **to counties and municipalities across Michigan, Pennsylvania and Wisconsin in the name of "safe" elections.**

"The illegitimate infusion of private funding and third-party promotion of training, equipment, security, staffing, and reporting programs by a network of private nonprofits at the local level bypassed state administrative processes, violated legislative prerogatives codified in state Help America Vote Plans (HAVA), and resulted in questions about the integrity of the U.S. electoral system," the Society alleged.

IT'S BEEN WIDELY SUGGESTED PRESIDENT TRUMP DECLARE MARTIAL LAW IN NEVADA; ARIZONA; WISCONSIN; MICHIGAN PENNSYLVANIA & GEORGIA VOTER FRAUD JURISDICTIONS TO ESTABLISH U.S. CONSTITUTIONAL; MOB ELECTION INSURRECTION GANGSTA' THUG HOOD BLOODS & CRIPS MS-13 TREACHERY BY XI JINPING COMMUNIST CHINESE WHORE LEFTISTS TO SEIZE CONTROL OF AMERICA

Sen. Rand Paul says voter 'fraud happened' and 'the election in many ways was stolen'

Will the Kentucky Republican challenge the Electoral College votes?

Breck Dumas

Kentucky GOP Sen. Rand Paul said Wednesday that voter "fraud happened" in the Nov. 3 election and that "the election in many ways was stolen," pointing to examples of allegations raised in several states. The Republican made the comment during a Senate hearing addressing election irregularities as President Donald Trump continues to challenge the outcome of the race despite President-elect Joe Biden officially winning the Electoral College vote.

What are the details?

"A lot of the laws that have to be confirmed and I think reaffirmed are state laws, so it's not in our purview," Paul said, addressing the Homeland Security and Government Affairs Committee. "But the state laws are set,

and then we have federal elections. So what we've heard about what happened in Wisconsin, what happened in Nevada, I think is absolutely true and we have to prevent it from happening again."

"I think state legislatures will need to reaffirm that election law can only be changed by a state legislature," he continued, referring to changes in election laws made in some states by officials rather than lawmakers—such as in Pennsylvania where universal mail-in voting was implemented ahead of the general election without action from the legislature.

Paul went on to argue, "The fraud happened. The election in many ways was stolen, and the only way it will be fixed is by in the future reinforcing the laws."

THIS ISN'T CORRECTABLE BECAUSE STATES ARE RUN BY CRIPS; BLOODS & MS-13 MASQUERADING AS GOVERNORS; DEEP ADMINISTRATIVE STATE; JUDGES & LEGISLATURES; PLAYING SLEIGHT-OF-HAND AMBIGUITY TAKING ADVANTAGE OF THE TRUST OF AMERICA; THEY HAVE STOLEN A PRESIDENTIAL ELECTION FOR A PRESIDENT WHO WILL RAPE AMERICA AND DEMOCRACY? WHEN TO WE SAY NO? IT'S COMMON FOR MARXISTS TO USE DEMOCRACY TO RAPE & DESTROY DEMOCRACY. READ SAUL ALINSKY.

What else?

Sen. Paul's remarks sparked speculation over whether he might be considering challenging the Electoral College votes next month when Congress meets to certify the election for Biden, an action that Senate Majority Leader Mitch McConnell (R-Ky.) in a call earlier this week reportedly urged GOP members not to do. When asked about the prospect by CNN, Paul replied, "I haven't thought about it, or made any plans to do anything." Regarding McConnell's alleged warning, Paul said, "I wasn't part of that phone call."

Rep. Mo Brooks (R-Ala.) announced weeks ago that he plans to contest the Electoral College votes on Jan. 6, saying that the "election was stolen by the socialists engaging in extraordinary voter fraud and election theft measures." No Senate Republicans has yet committed to joining Brooks in the challenge, but if one were to do so it would force debate over the issue. However, the prospect of overturning the Electoral College vote by Congress is highly unlikely, particularly given that Democrats control the House.

WHAT DEMOCRATS HAVE DONE IS THE HOUSTON ASTROS & BOSTON RED SOX CHEATING & STEALING SIGNS TO WIN CONSECUTIVE WORLD SERIES; WE'RE LETTING THEM DO THIS TO US?

Laura Ingraham: Chinese officials know Biden win was 'huge victory' for Communist Party

The effect of a Biden presidency on U.S.-China relations.

The Chinese Communist Party (CCP) isn't trying to hide their excitement at Joe Biden's presidential election victory, Laura Ingraham said Tuesday night.

"Every Chinese official knows that Biden's victory was a huge victory for the CCP, and that our new leaders will worry more about offending President Xi than standing up for American workers," said "The Ingraham Angle" host.

Ingraham said most American elites, like former President Barack Obama, have supported China and Biden intends to follow in their footsteps.

CHINA EXPLOITING MOBILE NETWORKS TO SPY ON AMERICAN CELLPHONES: REPORT

"Biden's advisers have a proven track record of advancing the CHINESE COMMUNIST PARTY CCP's interests," **she explained. "Biden adviser Steve Ricchetti was a key player in establishing permanent normal trade relations with China back in 2000. [National Security Adviser-designate] Jake Sullivan has called for more cooperation with Beijing.**

"And Biden's nominee for secretary of state, Tony Blinken? His own consulting firm helped American universities court big, big donations from Beijing. So do you really expect him to counsel Biden against letting the CCP continue its conquest of higher education?"

BIDEN'S TREASURY NOMINEES MEET WITH RACIAL JUSTICE ACTIVISTS, 'DEFUND THE POLICE' SUPPORTERS

Ingraham went on to note that a Chinese company recently bought 140,000 acres of land in Texas to reportedly establish a wind farm. The host pointed out that the land is "conveniently located" near Laughlin Air Force Base.

"Why should we trust them?" she asked. "We can't do what they can do in our country. Why? Well, maybe they're a little smarter on those issues than we are."

Ingraham urged American leaders to protect the nation's global strength, since Biden's policies will likely weaken it.

Jill Biden's Doctorate Is Garbage Because Her Dissertation Is Garbage

By David Ruiz

WHAT'S SO FUNNY; YOU CONTRIVED SHALLOW ADULTEROUS BITCH JILL BIDEN WHO CHEATED ON YOUR HUSBAND SCREWING JOE BIDEN WRECKED WHILE ZOMBIE JOE WAS CRASHING THE NEW CORVETTE THAT HER FIRST HUSBAND BOUGHT FOR CHEATING ADULTEROUS WIFE WHILE DELAWARE COPS COVERED IT UP BECAUSE JILL WAS CHEATING ON HER HUSBAND WITH DELAWARE SENATOR JOE BIDEN?

JILL Biden speaks during a drive-in campaign rally held by former Vice President Joe Biden at Heinz Field in Pittsburgh, Penn., November 2, 2020. Her dissertation is not an addition to the sum total of human knowledge.

You can tell someone is smarting from an inferiority complex when he insists on being addressed as "Dr." on the basis of holding an academic doctorate rather than being a physician. Ph.D. holders who have genuine accomplishments don't make you call them "Doctor," which is why you never hear about "Dr. Paul Krugman" and "Dr. George Will." None of the professors I knew at Yale, even the ones who were eminent in their fields, insisted on the title, and I think most of them would have scoffed if someone had addressed them as "Dr." The only reason you ever hear the phrase "Dr. Henry Kissinger" is that Kissy grew up in title-mad, airs-and-graces Germany, where people are awed rather than dismissive even if you insist on a triple-serving title ("Herr Professor Doktor").

Insisting on being called "Doctor" when you don't heal people is, among most holders of doctorates, seen as a gauche, silly, cringey ego trip. Consider "Dr." Jill Biden, who doesn't even hold a Ph.D. but rather a lesser Ed.D., something of a joke in the academic world. President-elect Joe Biden once explained that his wife sought the degree purely for status reasons: "She said, 'I was so sick of the mail coming to Sen. and Mrs. Biden. I wanted to get mail addressed to Dr. and Sen. Biden.' That's the real reason she got her doctorate," Joe Biden has said.

THIS CONTRIVED ADULTEROUS TRAMP REPLACES MELANIA TRUMP? GOOGLE HER INFIDELITY

CHEATING ON HER HUSBAND W/ PAL ZOMBIE JOE. HUNTER, JOE'S BROTHER JIM; THE WHOLE FUCKEN FAMILY IS ROTTEN-TO-THE-CORE; PLUS THEY'RE ALL IN BED WITH XI JINPING' THE MOST DANGEROUS MAN WHO EVER LIVED

Mrs. Biden wanted the credential for its own sake. As for its quality, well. She got it from the University of Delaware, whose ties to her husband, its most illustrious alumnus if you don't count Joe Flacco, run so deep that it has a school of public policy named after him. That the University of Delaware would have rejected her 2006 dissertation as sloppy, poorly written, non-academic, and barely fit for a middle-school Social Studies classroom (all of which it is) when her husband had been representing its state in the U.S. Senate for more than three decades was about as likely as Tom Hagen telling Vito Corleone that his wife is a fat sow on payday. The only risk to the University of Delaware was that it might strain its collective wrist in its rush to rubber-stamp her doctoral paper. Mrs. Biden could have turned in a quarter-aed excuse for a magazine article written at the level of Simple English Wikipedia and been heartily congratulated by the university for her towering mastery. Which is exactly what happened.**

Jill Biden's dissertation is not an addition to the sum total of human knowledge. It is not a demonstration of expertise in its specific topic or its broad field. It is a gasping, wheezing, frail little Disney forest creature that begs you to notice the effort it makes to be the thing it is imitating while failing so pathetically that any witnesses to its ineptitude must feel compelled, out of manners alone, to drag it to the nearest podium and give it a participation trophy. Which is more or less what an Ed.D. is. It's a degree that only deeply unimpressive people feel confers the honorific of "Doctor." People who are actually smart understand that being in possession of a credential is no proof of intelligence.

My friends, I have read this document in its entirety and it is so equally lacking in rhetorical force, boldness of conception, and original research that it amounts to a triple null set, a vacuum inside a blank inside an abyss. If Ingmar Bergman were alive and hired to make a film about this paper, he would say, "I can't do it, there's so much emptiness even I cannot grasp it," and it would sound so much worse in Swedish that suicide hotlines would have to hire extra staff. Gene Simmons has a better claim to be a Doctor of Love than Jill Biden to be a Doctor of Education; after all, Simmons has spent a lifetime demonstrating mastery of his field. As for Biden, she has spent a lot of time teaching remedial English to slow learners in community colleges. Which is like being a rock musician who's in a bar band. That plays covers. At mixers. Held in assisted-living facilities. Mrs. Biden's dissertation emits so much noxious methane the EPA should regulate it, Greta Thunberg should denounce it, and Hollywood celebrities should hold a telethon to draw awareness to its dangers.

- The Embarrassing Russian Disinformation Canard

As Joe Biden has frankly noted, Mrs. Biden sought the Dr. honorific to rebuild her *amour propre*. Much of the press plays along, addressing Jill Biden as "Dr. Biden" even when actual medical doctors are referred to without the honorific if they are not currently practicing. Eminent pediatric neurosurgeon and HUD secretary Ben Carson is now "Mr. Carson" to the *New York Times*, but the same paper refers to Mrs. Biden as "Dr. Biden." This practice appears to contradict the *Times*' style guide, which explains that the "Dr." title is used for non-physicians "only if it is germane to the holder's primary current occupation (academic, for

example, or laboratory research)."

Mrs. Biden until recently taught English composition at NoVa, a small community college in Northern Virginia. To justify addressing her as "Dr." would require a generous view of what constitutes an "academic," and judging by the writing skills evinced by her students ("She very bad teacher and it is hard to pass class. I RECOMMEND NOT TAKE THIS PROFESSOR"), they emerged from her tutelage lacking mastery of even very basic grammar. As for the contents of the dissertation, which she cobbled together from a few secondary sources and some vapid interviews and questionnaires she sent around at the campus where she worked before her husband became vice president, Delaware Technical Community College, I'll go over them in detail in my next column.

Stephen Miller: 'Alternative Electors' Will Send Trump Votes to Congress

Stephen Miller By Sandy Fitzgerald

The Electoral College's vote will not end President Donald Trump's hopes for reelection, as his allies are planning to send an "alternative" slate of electors to Congress, senior White House adviser Stephen Miller argued Monday as electors gathered nationwide to cast their votes.

"The only date in the Constitution is Jan. 20," Miller said on Fox News' "Fox & Friends." "We have more than enough time to right the wrong of this fraudulent election result and certify Donald Trump as the winner of the election."

Miller added that "as we speak, an alternate slate of electors in the contested states is going to vote and we're going to send those results up to Congress. This will ensure that all of our legal remedies remain open. That means that if we win these cases in the courts, we can direct that the alternate state of electors be certified."

Miller said Trump supporters will be acting as "alternates" in the contested states of Michigan, Georgia, Wisconsin, and Pennsylvania and submit their own unofficial results.

If Trump's campaign succeeds in any of its continued legal efforts in those states, the "alternate" electors would be recognized by a joint session of Congress when it convenes on Jan. 6 to count the electoral votes and officially declare the winner of the election, Miller said.

The Washington Post reports that technically, alternative electors can meet and cast their own votes, as electors are picked for each candidate before the election is held. If their votes are then submitted to Congress, it must consider them.

If both chambers of Congress vote individually to accept Biden's electors, the dispute is considered as being resolved. If the chambers do not agree and each chamber identifies a different slate of electors, a tiebreaker using a certificate of ascertainment from a state comes into play.

A state executive has already certified Biden's win in each of the four states Trump is contesting, reports the Post.

Miller, however, argued that if "you just cured three simple constitutional defects, Donald Trump is the winner of this election."

He said signature matching rules in Georgia were "illegally changed as a result of a consent decree without the legislature's approval."

Miller further claimed there were "hundreds of thousands of improperly cast ballots in Wisconsin, absentee voters who never actually submitted the request for an absentee ballot," and that in Pennsylvania, there was the "clear equal protection violation when Democrat ballots were cured in advance of Election Day."

Trump Slams Barr, SCOTUS Decision in Twitter Attacks

By Sandy Fitzgerald

President Donald Trump on Saturday took to Twitter to slam Attorney General William Barr for not revealing "the truth" about Hunter Biden before the election and to rail against the Supreme Court's decision not to take up a Texas lawsuit filed against four states, calling the ruling a "legal disgrace."

"Why didn't Bill Barr reveal the truth to the public, before the Election, about Hunter Biden," Trump tweeted. "Joe was lying on the debate stage that nothing was wrong, or going on - Press confirmed. Big disadvantage for Republicans at the polls!" He also said that "IF Biden gets in, nothing will happen to Hunter or Joe. Barr will do nothing, and the new group of partisan killers coming in will quickly kill it all. Same thing with Durham. We caught them cold, spying, treason & more (the hard part), but "Justice" took too long. Will be DOA!"

Trump's other tweets claimed that the court "let us down" by rejecting the bid from Texas, backed up by

Trump, to invalidate ballots in Michigan, Pennsylvania, Wisconsin, and Georgia.

"No Wisdom, No Courage!" the president said in one tweet **late Friday night, which he followed with a barrage of other messages posted into the early morning hours.**

"So, you're the President of the United States, and you just went through an election where you got more votes than any sitting President in history, by far - and purportedly lost," he said **in a two-part tweet.**

"You can't get 'standing' before the Supreme Court, so you 'intervene' with wonderful states that, after careful study and consideration, think you got 'screwed', something which will hurt them also. Many others likewise join the suit but, within a flash, it is thrown out and gone, without even looking at the many reasons it was brought. A Rigged Election, fight on!"

He then tagged Texas Lt. Gov. Dan Patrick in his claim that the SCOTUS decision is a legal disgrace, an embarrassment to the USA!!!» **In yet another** tweet**, Trump called the decision a "a great and disgraceful miscarriage of justice" and declared that the people of the United States were cheated because his campaign was "never even given our day in court."**

"The Supreme Court had ZERO interest in the merits of the greatest voter fraud ever perpetrated on the United States of America," Trump later added**. All they were interested in is "standing", which makes it very difficult for the President to present a case on the merits. 76,000,000 votes!**

He also declared he won the election by a landslide **"in terms of legal votes, not all of the fake voters and fraud" and** accused two GOP governors**, Brian Kemp of Georgia and Doug Ducey of Arizona of being "RINO Republicans" who "allowed states that I won easily to be stolen."**

The president further declared, in an all-caps tweet **that "WE HAVE JUST BEGUN TO FIGHT!!!"**

Trump also retweeted several items from conservative pundits, and at one point announced that the FDA had approved Pfizer's coronavirus vaccine **on an emergency use basis, and posted a video of himself talking about the medication.**

Dershowitz to Newsmax TV: Supreme Court Just Didn't Want to Get Involved

By Brian Trusdell

Retired Harvard Law Professor Alan Dershowitz said Friday's decision by the U.S. Supreme Court to turn away a lawsuit from Texas and 17 other states challenging the election results in four battleground states on the justification that they didn't have standing to bring the suit indicates the court just didn't want to get involved.

Appearing on Newsmax TV's "Stinchfield," Dershowitz agreed with Justices Samuel Alito and Clarence Thomas, who indicated that Texas did have standing, saying they "get the better of the argument," but that the court just didn't want to deal with what may be perceived as political.

"This Supreme Court decision sends a message," Dershowitz said. "The majority included the three justices appointed by President [Donald] Trump, and they all said, 'We're not going to hear the Texas case. We're not going to get involved in this election.'

"I think this sends a message. It's not a legal message, but it's a practical message: the Supreme Court is out of this game."

The Texas suit claimed that officials in Pennsylvania, Wisconsin, Michigan and Georgia used fears of the outbreak of the novel coronavirus as a justification to disregard election laws, which the Constitution grants only to the various state legislatures.

It argued that by weakening laws intended to curb fraud, the officials in the four states denied citizens in Texas — and other states — equal protection of their vote. Dershowitz said he believed the argument was valid, but the Supreme Court, in essence, said that citizens in other states were not harmed by the actions of officials in the four states.

Giuliani to Newsmax TV: Legal Fight Will Go On attorney for President Donald Trump

By Solange Reyner

Rudy Giuliani says President Donald Trump's legal battle will go on despite the Supreme Court rejecting a bid Friday from Texas' attorney general to block the ballots of millions of voters in battleground states that went in favor of Joe Biden.

"The case wasn't rejected on the merits, the case was rejected on standing," Giuliani said Friday during an appearance on Newsmax TV's "Stinchfield." "The answer to that is to bring the case now in the district court by the president, by some of the electors, alleging the same facts where there would be standing and therefore get a hearing."

The court's order was issued with no public dissents. The Electoral College will convene Monday to affirm Biden's win. "The worst part of this is, basically the courts are saying they want to stay out of this, and they don't want to give us a hearing and they don't want the American people to hear these facts.," said Giuliani.

"That's a terrible, terrible mistake. These facts will remain an open sore in our history unless they don't get resolved. They need to be heard, they need to be aired and somebody needs to make a decision on whether they're true or false and some court's going to have the courage to make that decision."

The lawsuit, brought by Texas Attorney General Ken Paxton, sought to sue Pennsylvania, Georgia, Wisconsin and Michigan and invalidate their election results. The Supreme Court said Texas had not demonstrated "a judicially cognizable interest in the manner in which another State conducts its elections."

Arizona GOP Chief Appeals to Supreme Court Over Biden Win

Arizona's Republican Party chairwoman appealed to the U.S. Supreme Court as part of a long-shot effort to nullify Joe Biden's victory there in the presidential election, according to a filing posted online by a Democratic lawyer.

The filing comes as the high court has nixed a similarly improbable bid by Texas to invalidate voters' selection of Biden in four pivotal states, and reverse President Donald Trump's election defeat.

The high court on Friday also got an emergency filing from former Trump campaign lawyer Sidney Powell seeking to decertify Biden's victory in Georgia, according to Democratic lawyer Marc Elias, who has been active in the post-election litigation. Neither case has been formally docketed at the Supreme Court.

The appeal by Arizona GOP Chairwoman Kelli Ward says the state needs more time to conduct a new, larger examination of duplicates that were made of thousands of damaged ballots in the state's largest county, Maricopa, which voted heavily for Biden

US Supreme Court Asked to Decertify Biden's Win in Arizona

Conservative lawyer Sidney Powell has asked the U.S. Supreme Court to decertify Democrat President-elect Joe Biden's victory over Republican President Donald Trump in Arizona.

Powell, who filed the request with the court on Friday night, also asks the justices to bar Biden's electors from casting Electoral College votes on Monday.

Her appeal marks the second petition for review filed with the nation's highest court in challenges to Biden's win in the state. Arizona GOP Chairwoman Kelli Ward on Friday asked the Supreme Court to review her case seeking to overturn Arizona's election results.

Powell is appealing the dismissal of her lawsuit that alleged voting equipment in Arizona switched votes from Trump to Biden. A lower-court judge dismissed the challenge on Wednesday, ruling no evidence of fraud had been presented and that those who filed the lawsuit lacked legal standing. Arizona certified its elections results on Nov. 30, showing that Biden had won the state by more than 10,000 votes.

The lawsuit alleged Arizona election systems have security flaws that let election workers and foreign countries manipulate results and that those systems switched votes from Trump to Biden. Opposing attorneys said the lawsuit used conspiracy theories to make wild allegations against one of Maricopa County's vendors for voting equipment, without providing proof to back up its claims of widespread Arizona election fraud. No evidence of voter fraud or election fraud has emerged during this election season in Arizona. Similar election challenges filed by Powell were dismissed in Michigan, Georgia and Wisconsin.

In all, seven lawsuits challenging the results of the presidential vote in Arizona have been dismissed, including one by Ward that sought to reverse Biden's victory in the state. Last week, a woman filed yet another challenge that is nearly identical to Powell's now-dismissed case. A judge is scheduled to hear arguments Monday in a request by election officials to dismiss the lawsuit, which was filed in Pinal County.

Dershowitz: SCOTUS Told Trump, Don't Count On Courts In Elex Fight

WHY NOT? THE SUPREME COURT ONLY WANTS NON-CONTROVERSIAL EASY FIGHTS; CASTING A BLIND EYE TO THE MOST EVIL CRIME IN AMERICAN HISTORY BASED ON "STANDING TECHNICALITY" DO RED STATES WANT TO BE PART OF THIS EVIL NATION?

Attorney Alan Dershowitz leaves federal court, in New York, in 2019.

President Donald Trump should realize he "can't count on the judiciary" in his quest to overturn the election, according to constitutional legal expert Alan Dershowitz.

WHO CAN'T WE COUNT ON NOW THAT DEMOCRATS HAVE THE LICENSE TO CONTROL THE WINNING CRITICAL MASS OF VOTES EVERYWHERE IN AMERICA GOING FORWARD? WE CAN ONLY COUNT ON OURSELVES & MUST SECEDE FROM THE UNION.

In an interview with radio host John Catsimatidis on WABC 770 aired Sunday, and posted by The Hill**, the Supreme Court's** rejection of a Texas lawsuit taking issue with the count sent a message to Trump's legal team and loyalists. **"The three justices that President Trump appointed, his three justices, voted not to hear the case," Dershowitz said, The Hill reported. "I think it's a message to him and his team that you can't count on the judiciary, you can't count on the courts," he said.**

Dershowitz said Trump needs a "perfect storm" to overturn the election results — including the help of courts, governors and state legislatures — and turning to state legislatures is "very, very unlikely."

"So I suspect on Monday we will see the electors…elect Joe Biden," Dershowitz said. "Whether you like that or you don't like it, that's the reality that the Trump team has to face." Trump's personal lawyer Rudy Giuliani however, has said the fight will go on, and that the campaign would present the case in district court.

"We're not finished," Giuliani said**. "Believe me."**

REMEMBER WINSTON CHURCHILL

WE WILL FIGHT ON THE BEACHES … WE WILL FIGHT IN THE FIELDS; WE WILL FIGHT IN THE STREETS OF OUR CITIES; AND WHEN WE ARE OVERWHELMED AT HOME; WE WILL FIGHT ON THE HIGH SEAS WITH OUR GREAT NAVY … WE WILL FIGHT FROM OUR COLONIES ON WHICH THE SUN NEVER SETS … WE WILL NEVER SURRENDER FROM SURRENDER OF FRANCE; JUNE 22, 1940 UNTIL THE 3 MILLION WEHRMACHT & PANZER BARBAROSSA DAGGER INTO THE SOVIET UNION BRITAIN FOR A YEAR STOOD ALONE AGAINST THE REICH; MUCH WORSE ODDS THAN WE GUNS & RELIGION DEPLORABLE FACE IN 2021; BRITAIN DIDN'T FIGHT BECAUSE THE UNION JACK HAD A GOOD CHANCE OF WINNING. THEY FOUGHT FOR THE SAME REASON WE MUST FIGHT NOW; IT'S NOT OUR FIGHT TO CHOOSE & DECISION TO MAKE. DEMOCRATS WILL STEAL EVERY ELECTION GOING FORWARD. SECESSION IS THE CHOICE HISTORY HAS MADE FOR US.

- HUNTER BIDEN Called His Father And Chinese Business Partner 'Office Mates' In September 2017 Email

THEY'RE LAUGHING AT EVERYONE READING THIS BOOK GETTING FUNNIER FOR DEMOCRATS BY THE MINUTE THEIR JOKE IS ON US

NOTICE, SINCE THE ELECTION BIDEN HAS NO COMMENT ON ANYTHING EXCEPT (100) DAYS OF MASKING

Andrew Kerr and Chuck Ross

Hunter Biden sent an email to the manager of his Washington, D.C. office building in September 2017 asking her to make keys for his "office mates" Joe Biden and Gongwen Dong, who he said was the "emissary" for the chairman of the Chinese energy conglomerate CEFC.

- **Hunter Biden's dealings with CEFC in 2017 were at the center of Tony Bobulinski's October allegation that Joe Biden was "plainly familiar" with his family's Chinese business dealings.**

- **Multiple news outlets have reported this week that a federal investigation into Hunter Biden's "tax affairs" is focused on his foreign business activities, including with CEFC.**

Hunter Biden called his father, President-elect Joe Biden, and his Chinese business partner "office mates" in a Sept. 21, 2017, email to the general manager of his former Washington, D.C. office building.

"[P]lease have keys made available for new office mates," Hunter Biden wrote in the email before listing Joe Biden, his stepmother Jill Biden, his uncle Jim Biden and Gongwen Dong, who he identified as the "emissary" for the chairman of the now-bankrupt Chinese energy conglomerate CEFC.

Hunter Biden also requested that a sign be made for his office stating "The Biden Foundation" and "Hudson West (CEFC US)."

Hunter Biden's dealings with CEFC in 2017 were at the center of allegations from his ex-business partner, Tony Bobulinksi, who said in October that Joe Biden was "plainly familiar" with his family's business dealings in China. Bobulinski was one of the recipients of the much-publicized May 2017 email purportedly referencing Joe Biden as the "big guy" who would hold 10% in a joint-venture deal with Hunter Biden and CEFC.

Joe Biden On Hunter Biden Investigation: 'I'm Proud Of My Son'

Anders Hagstrom

President-Elect Joe Biden said he is "proud of my son" in response to Friday questions about the newly-announced FBI investigation into Hunter Biden. Biden made the statement following an event announcing several nominations for his upcoming cabinet. He ignored questions about the investigation throughout the event but offered the brief statement afterward. Hunter is currently being investigated for his "tax affairs" and possibly his dealings with Chinese businesses. (RELATED: Hunter Biden Says He's Under Federal Investigation) Hunter was under investigation well before Election Day, a fact Attorney General Bill Barr was reportedly aware of but did not reveal publicly. The revelation angered some Republicans on Capitol Hill who believe the news could have helped President Donald Trump's election effort.

Trump himself expressed frustration with the DOJ's decision not to come forward with the information.

Hunter first announced he was under investigation in a public statement Wednesday.

"I learned yesterday for the first time that the U.S. Attorney's Office in Delaware advised my legal counsel, also yesterday, that they are investigating my tax affairs," Biden said at the time. "I take this matter very seriously but I am confident that a professional and objective review of these matters will demonstrate that I handled my affairs legally and appropriately, including with the benefit of professional tax advisors."

Feds Slap Hunter Biden With Subpoena For Foreign Business Records: Report

Chuck Ross

Federal prosecutors subpoenaed Hunter Biden on Tuesday for records for his business dealings with more than two dozen entities, including Ukrainian energy firm Burisma Holdings and companies based in China, the Associated Press reported.

DO US GUNS & RELIGION DEPLORABLES WANT TO SECEDE FROM THIS "OUR THING" COSA

NOSTRA "OF WHITE TRAILER TRASH HUNTER & JOE? LET'S SECEDE FROM THEIR CRIME SYNDICATE WHILE RED STATES HAVE OUR COMBINED 80 % OF U.S. SQUARE MILEAGE TERRITORY; AND MOST OF THE (50) STATES MILITARY; MANUFACTURING; INDUSTRY OF EVERY KIND; PLUS SEAPORTS; AIRPORTS & AGRICULTURE. FUCK THEM. LET BLUE SCUM DIE ALONE WITHOUT US

Biden announced on Wednesday through his father's transition team that his attorney had been notified that he was the target of an investigation into his "tax affairs."

The younger Biden did not disclose any other details of the investigation in his statement. A source familiar with the probe told The Daily Caller News Foundation that the investigation started in 2018, before Joe Biden launched his presidential campaign. According to the Associated Press, the subpoena, issued through the U.S. attorney's office in Delaware, seeks records related to Burisma Holdings and Chinese companies that are not named in the report.

Hunter Biden joined the board of Burisma Holdings in April 2014, months after his father had taken over as the Obama administration's chief liaison to the Ukrainian government. (RELATED: DOJ Probe Of Hunter Biden Is More Extensive Than He Let On, And Could Involve His Chinese Business Deals) **Burisma executives were at the time seeking to expand the company's business outside of Ukraine. They also hoped to quash various investigations into Burisma's owner, Mykola Zlochevesky, who was under investigation for bribery. President-elect Joe Biden embraces his son Hunter Biden after addressing the nation from the Chase Center November 07, 2020 in Wilmington, Delaware. (Photo by Andrew Harnik-Pool/Getty Images) Burisma paid Hunter Biden and his business partner, Devon Archer, more than $80,000 per month as board members.**

Biden also consulted for reporters about the investigation of his son. "I'm proud of my son," he said Friday when a reporter asked if he believes Hunter Biden had committed any crimes.

'Reopen' Economy?

Senator Rand Paul

Sen. Rand Paul, R-Ky., a staunch deficit hawk, argues the best way to stimulate the economy is to "reopen" it.

DEMOCRATS WANT ECONOMIC COLLAPSE THAT WILL MAKE OVER 50 % OF GDP STATE OWNED; WHERE DEPENDENT VOTERS WILL VOTE FOR DEMOCRAT ONE PARTY GOVERNMENT THAT PAYS THEM

In an interview on Wednesday with Sinclair Broadcasting's "America This Week," Paul said more economic stimulus isn't the answer to the economic fallout from the coronavirus crisis.

"It's a mistake to think that government is what should stimulate the economy... the economy should be left alone," he said.

"The only way to get a long lasting stimulus... is to reopen the economy," he declared.

"We borrowed about $3 trillion in the spring and our debt is now over $27 trillion. So I don't think borrowing more money is the answer," he said.

He also defended his believe there are advantages to herd immunity to the virus.

"Those who have had the disease naturally… they have the same immunity is if they had the vaccine… natural immunity," he said, adding: "We should acknowledge some advantages… we shouldn't discount immunity in the discussion.

George Schultz at 100: Trust Must Be Coin of the Realm - FOR BULLY DEMOCRATS "ITS ALL ABOUT ME" THEY START BY STRIKING DOWN "IN GOD WE TRUST" DEMOCRATS HAVE ELIMINATED GOD FIRST FROM OUR SCHOOLS; NOW FROM THE REST OF OUR GOVERNMENT BY THE PEOPLE; OF THE PEOPLE & FOR THE PEOPLE. RED GUNS & RELIGION DEPLORABLE DOMINOS CANNOT BE ALLOWED TO TOPPLE INSTANTLY

Former US Treasury Secretary and Secretary of State George Schultz testifies before the US Senate Foreign Relations Committee 29 February, 2000

By Eric Mack

On his 100th birthday, former Secretary of State George Schultz outlines the 10 ways in which "trust is the coin of the realm" in an opinion piece Sunday for The Washington Post.

"Dec. 13 marks my turning 100 years young," Schultz, who served under former President Ronald Reagan.

"I've learned much over that time, but looking back, I'm struck that there is one lesson I learned early and then relearned over and over: Trust is the coin of the realm. "When trust was in the room, whatever room that was — the family room, the schoolroom, the locker room, the office room, the government room or the military room — good things happened. When trust was not in the room, good things did not happen. Everything else is details." His life-lesson missive outlined the 10 ways he learned about the value of trust.

1. Family

   "My early boyhood memories underlined the joy of family closeness and how it creates powerful bonds of trust."

2. Country

   "During World War II, I served in the Pacific theater in a Marine outfit that included a sergeant named Palat. I have forgotten his first name, but I have never forgotten the respect and admiration — the deep-seated trust — that he inspired. When Palat was killed in action, it brought home to me more than ever how pitiless war can be."

3. Work

   "I saw how Joe [Scanlon] rebuilt bonds of trust between the workers and management that had been frayed or broken. Ultimately, both sides benefited, as did the country."

4. Race

   "Black workers from a closed plant in Kansas City had seniority claims on the new jobs. In that era of great racial friction, trouble might have been expected. Yet the town's civic leaders made it clear to us: Black families would be welcomed."

5. Law

   Former Attorney General John Mitchell brought trust to legal battles over segregation: "Mitchell growled, 'I am attorney general, and I will enforce the law.' Then he left. No nonsense. Opponents of school segregation could trust the administration."

6. Politics

   On President Richard Nixon bridging differences: "I knew the president and trusted that he would rise to the occasion — and he did."

7. Diplomacy

   At a World War II memorial in Leningrad: "Facing the cemetery, I raised my best Marine salute, and [Soviet foreign trade minister] Patolichev thanked me for the show of respect. Later on, to my surprise, I found that I had earned the trust of Soviet leaders as a result of this visit."

8. Personal connections

   On advice from President Reagan: "Telling a story, he made me understand, helps make your case in a way that no abstraction can: A story builds an emotional bond, and emotional bonds build trust.'

9. Foreign Policy

   "Reagan's famous formulation: Trust, but verify. The agreement was self-bolstering, because successful verification enhanced the sense of trust, and greater trust promoted verification."

10. Faith

    "'In God we trust.' Yes, and when we are at our best, we also trust in each other. Trust is fundamental, reciprocal and, ideally, pervasive. If it is present, anything is possible. If it is absent, nothing is possible. The best leaders trust their followers with the truth, and you know what happens as a result? Their followers trust them back. With that bond, they can do big, hard things together, changing the world for the better."

Supreme Court Justice Amy Coney Barrett joined the majority in rejecting Friday Texas' lawsuit which sought to block the certification of Electoral College votes.

The court ruled that Texas lacked standing under Article III of the Constitution and that Texas did not provide a "judicially cognizable interest in the manner in which another State conducts its elections."

Conservative Justices Samuel Alito and Clarence Thomas dissented, noting they would grant the motion to file the complaint.

During Barrett's confirmation hearings, Democratic Connecticut Senator Richard Blumenthal said Barrett must recuse herself from any cases involving President Donald Trump and the outcome of the election, according to PBS. Blumenthal said Barrett's participation would cause "explosive, enduring harm to the court's legitimacy," according to the report.

All 50 states have certified their election results and the Supreme Court rejected an emergency request from Pennsylvania Republicans to block the election results Tuesday.

However, Texas Attorney General Ken Paxton, in a bid supported by President Donald Trump and 17 other

Republican-led states, asked the high court **Tuesday for an emergency order to invalidate the ballots in the four battleground states of Georgia, Wisconsin, Michigan and Pennsylvania.**

Trump filed a motion to intervene Wednesday, which is a request for him to join the lawsuit. (RELATED: 'New California' And 'New Nevada' File Brief In Support Of Texas-Led Lawsuit Seeking To Overturn Election Results)

The suit **asked the court to block the certification of the Electoral College votes because the suit alleged that the four states had illegal votes. Paxton argued that pandemic-era changes in election procedures violated federal law.**

"Using the COVID-19 pandemic as a justification, government officials in the defendant states of Georgia, Michigan and Wisconsin, and the Commonwealth of Pennsylvania, usurped their legislatures' authority and unconstitutionally revised their state's election statues," the suit read.

Paxton said states used executive orders to change the election process and hurt voting integrity by not "protecting" signature verification and witness requirements.

The suit also alleged that the states didn't segregate late ballots that would allow an "accurate analysis to determine which ballots were cast in conformity with the legislatively set rules and which were not."

In October, the Supreme Court refused to expedite Pennsylvania Republicans' challenge to a state Supreme Court ruling that allowed ballots to be received and counted as valid up to three days after the election even if they lacked a postmark because the high court was under the impression that Secretary of State Kathy Boockvar would order late ballots to be segregated.

Boockvar **initially** complied **and issued** guidance **on Oct. 28 ordering all late ballots to be kept separate in case the Supreme Court ruled the extension unconstitutional.**

However, she then updated the guidance **last minute on Nov. 1, ordering all ballots that arrived before Nov. 6 to be counted as valid.**

- **Supreme Court Justice Samuel Alito ordered Nov. 6 that all late ballots must be segregated despite Boockvar's guidance.**

CCP Insider: China Couldn't Use Wall Street To Fix Trump, But It Can With Biden

By Chuck Ross

A Chinese academic with links to the communist party recently detailed how Beijing used access to a "core circle" of power brokers in Washington and on Wall Street to influence U.S. policy towards China.

- The academic, Di Dongsheng, asserted that Beijing will re-establish its power through that group of "old friends" under the Biden administration.
- Di said that China had far less success influencing the Trump administration because Wall Street — which he identified as a key ally for Beijing — was unable to "control" Donald Trump.
- Di's remarks have surfaced in the wake of a warning from the U.S.'s top counterintelligence official, who said last week that there has been an uptick in Beijing's efforts to influence incoming Biden administration employees.

The Chinese government will rely on a "core circle" of "old friends" on Wall Street and in Washington to influence the Biden administration, according to a Chinese academic with ties to the communist regime.

Di Dongsheng, the associate dean of the School of International Relations at Renmin University, offered his predictions about China-U.S. relations in the upcoming administration during a speech in Shanghai on Nov. 28.

Di asserted that Beijing was unable to fully respond to a "trade war" that President Donald Trump waged because the Republican was invulnerable to influence by Wall Street.

"Wall Street had a very profound influence over America's domestic and foreign affairs since the 1970s. We used to heavily rely on them," Di said at the event, according to The Washington Times.

Di asserted that Wall Street was unable to "control" Trump, which had a negative impact on China during its trade standoff with the U.S.

"I'm going to drop a bomb," Di continued, "we had people up there inside America's core circle of power, we had our old friends."

"During the last three to four decades, we used the core circle inside America's real power," Di said.

But Di asserted that U.S.-China relations would be on the mend under Biden because of his administration's close ties to Wall Street.

"Now with Biden winning the election, the traditional elites, political elites, the establishment, they have a very close relationship with the Wall Street," Di said.

Di gave a nod to his communist party pedigree during his Shanghai speech.

He told a story of an event he helped arrange for Gua Weimin, a deputy director of the Chinese government's foreign propaganda office, in 2015 in Washington, D.C. to promote a book written by Xi Jinping.

Di and Weimin appeared at an event held at Politics & Prose, a popular independent bookstore in Washington. Weimin serves as deputy director of China's State Council Information Office, which controls Beijing's foreign propaganda efforts.

Chinese state-controlled media outlet China Daily wrote about the event, saying that the turnout showed that Xi's book was "proving a popular read" in the U.S.

Di also suggested in his speech in Shanghai that the Chinese government supported Hunter Biden's business deals in China.

"You all heard that Trump said Biden's son has securities companies all over the world. But who helped Biden's son build his global companies?" Di said.

"There are indeed buy-and-sell transactions involved in here. So I think at this particular time, it is of strategic and tactical value for us to show goodwill."

Hunter Biden had several business deals in China, including one with CEFC China Energy, a major energy conglomerate whose owner has links to the communist party. CEFC wired Biden millions of dollars in 2017, according to a Senate report released in September. (RELATED: Feds Obtained FISA Warrant Against Hunter Biden's Chinese Business Partner)

Di's remarks have surfaced as top U.S. counterintelligence officials have heightened warnings about Beijing's covert efforts to influence U.S. policy, both in Congress and the Biden administration.

William Evanina, the top counterintelligence official at the Office of the Director of National Intelligence, warned last week **that U.S. officials have seen a spike in Chinese operatives trying to cozy up to Biden associates. "We've also seen an uptick, which was planned and we predicted, that China would now re-vector their influence campaigns to the new administration," Evanina said at a cybersecurity forum.**

"And when I say that, that malign foreign influence, that diplomatic influence plus, or on steroids, we're starting to see that now play across the country to not only the folks starting in the new administration, but those who are around those folks in the new administration."

Several of Biden's incoming advisers have long called for stronger diplomatic ties to Beijing, and for viewing China as an ally instead of a competitor. One of Biden's key advisers, Steve Ricchetti, played an integral role in helping the Clinton administration **pass a bill in 2000 that established Permanent Normal Trade Relations (PNTR) with China.**

Clinton tasked Ricchetti, his deputy chief of staff, with wrangling votes in Congress to support PNTR.

Jake Sullivan, who Biden has tapped as his national security adviser, has criticized President Trump's China policies and called for working more closely with Beijing. He appeared on Beijing-controlled news outlet CGTN in December 2017 to criticize Trump over his policy in Israel.

THIS IS THE FUTURE THE CHINA/ DEMOCRAT/U.S/IRAN AXIS WANT FOR RESD STATE AMERICAN PATRIOTS. IF NOT ALREADY; SOON IT WILL BE TOO LATE ALL WHO IGNORE THE WORST HISTORY BEFORE OUR EYES NOW; ARE BOUND TO REPEAT IT HERE AT HOME SOON

Journalist Executed For Allegedly Inspiring Nationwide Economic Protests In Iran

Andrew Trunsky

Iran executed an exiled journalist Saturday whose work allegedly helped spark economic protests across the country, the Associated Press reported.

BIDEN ACTUALLY WANTS TO RE-ENTER THE NUCLEAR ACCORD WITH THESE DEMONS

HE IS US/ WE ARE HIM. KIDNAPPED VIOLENTLY OFF AN IRAQ STREET; SHIPPED IN A CRATE TO IRAN AND HUNG BY THE NECK UNTIL DEAD IN DECEMBER 2020. WHAT DOES JOE BIDEN SAY? HE WANTS TO REENTER OBAMA'S IRAN DEAL

Ruhollah Zam was killed a little over a year after Iranian authorities lured him into Iraq, leading to his abduction and imprisonment. He is one of several opposition figures seized by Iranian government operatives in recent months, according to the AP.

Zam lived in Paris under the protection of the French government. Iran carried out his kidnapping and

execution as tensions between the state and western countries continue to rise amid the collapsed nuclear deal and crippling economic sanctions imposed by the United States.

The execution was immediately condemned internationally, according to the AP. (RELATED: Iran Says Nuclear Scientist Was Assassinated By A Satellite-Controlled Pickup Truck-Mounted Machine Gun)

Ruhollah Zam, a former opposition figure who had lived in exile in France and had been implicated in anti-government protests, speaks during his trial at Iran's Revolutionary Court in Tehran on June 2, 2020. Zam's "execution is a deadly blow to freedom of expression in Iran and shows the extent of the Iranian authorities' brutal tactics to instill fear and deter dissent," said Amnesty International's Diana Eltahawy. (RELATED: Iran Considered Assassinating US Ambassador: Report)

Iranian state television portrayed Zam as "the leader of the riots" when it announced his execution via hanging Saturday morning. He was sentenced to death in June after being found guilty of "corruption on Earth," a charge frequently given to those accused of espionage for conspiring to overthrow Iran's government.

- Iran's 2017 protests began over a spike in food prices and quickly grew to widespread backlash against the entire ruling class, including Iranian President Hassan Rouhani. Many videos shared by Zam denounced both Rouhani and Iranian Supreme Leader Ayatollah Ali Khamenei, according to the AP

WATCH: Antifa Stabs 4 Trump Supporters in Washington, D.C

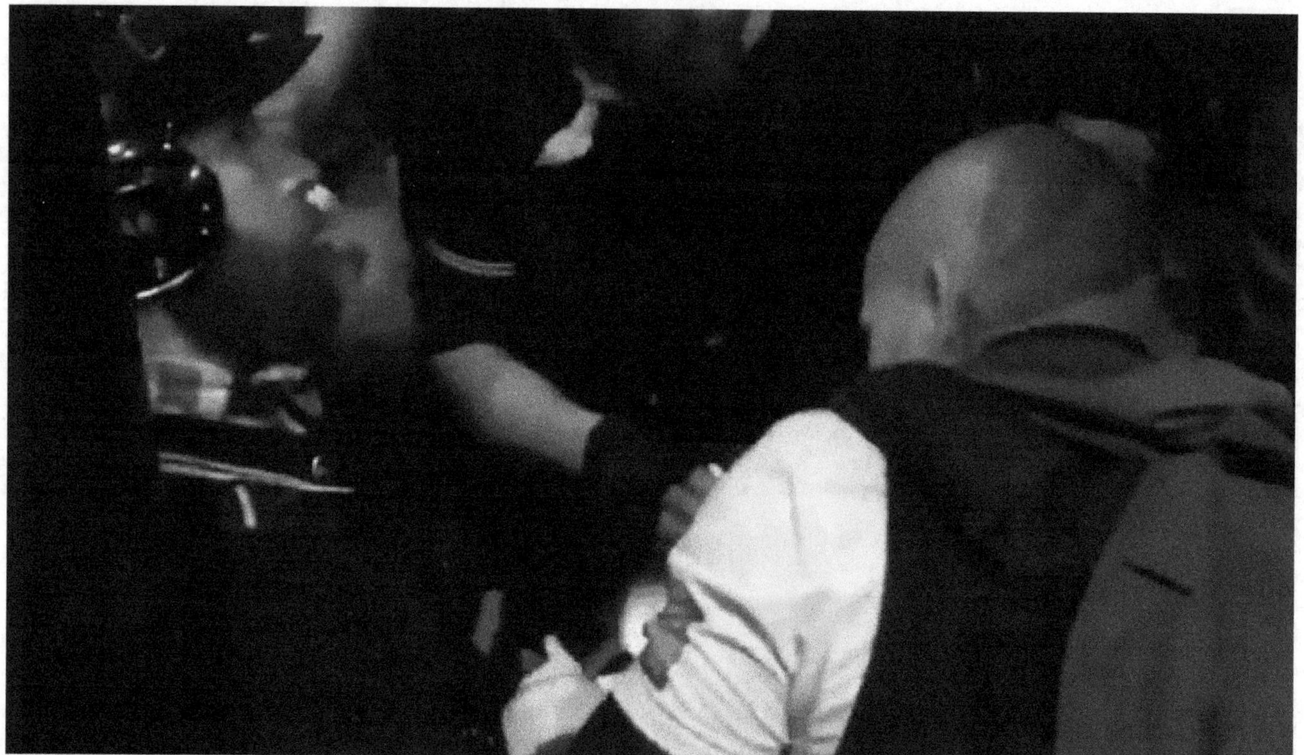

Bob Price and Lana Shadwick

Tweeted videos show an Antifa protester allegedly stabbing Trump supporters in Washington, D.C., on Saturday night. Additional videos show the man being captured by police after the Trump supporters retaliated and took him to the ground. Reports indicate four stabbing victims were transported to local hospitals.

A pair of videos tweeted by Mauro Gomez reportedly shows a "BLM/Antifa allegedly stabs 2 Trump supporters."

People surrounding the man can be heard yelling, "Knife, knife, knife."

Photographer Shane B. Murphy reported via Twitter that four patients were transported to D.C. hospitals with varying injuries after "Antifa-BLM militant stabbed several Proud Boys."

Later, NBC4 in Washington, D.C., reported that four people had been stabbed Saturday night.

Murphy tweeted another video from independent journalist @elaadeliahu showing the knife attack from a

slightly different angle. A video tweeted by Eric Thomas shows one of the stabbing victims being tended to by police. Miss N0b0dy tweeted another video showing a second stabbing victim being tended to by Trump supporters and police.

More confrontations continue as Antifa and Proud Boys clash in the streets.

CHOSE SIDES; THE TIME FOR US IS NOW

More Silicon Valley Insiders Added to Biden Transition Team THEY WILL CONTROL DIGITAL ACCESS TO ANY OUR SEARCH INFORMATION; COMMUNICATION AMONG REPUBLICANS & ANY OF OUR DISAGREEMENT WITH DEMOCRATS

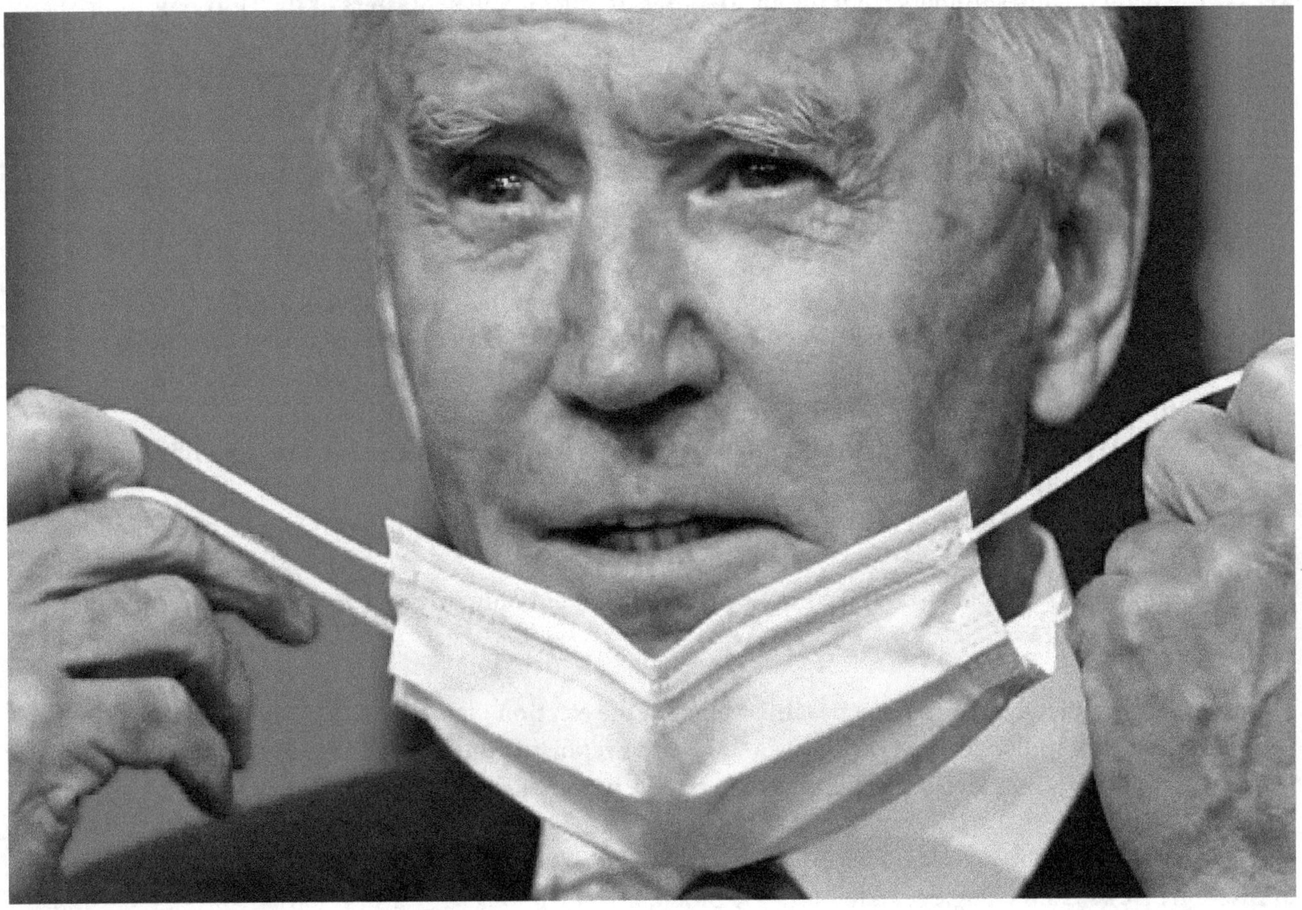

Allum Bokhari

After an election year in which the tech giants repeatedly interfered in the election against President Donald Trump, Joe Biden is now rewarding Silicon Valley by appointing insiders to a range of roles in his transition team.

Shortly after election night, the *Financial Times* reported that former Google CEO Eric Schmidt is being considered to lead a key tech task force inside the White House. **As *Politico* recently reported, four more Google and Facebook employees have been added to Biden's transition team.**

They are : Zaid Zaid, a Facebook public policy official, Chris Upperman, a Facebook manager, Rachel Lieber, a Facebook director and associate general counsel, and Deon Scott, a Google program manager who also worked in the Obama administration's Department of Homeland Security (DHS). This is just the latest news of the Biden team's efforts to court current and former Silicon Valley employees.

As Breitbart News previously reported, plenty other alumni of big tech, including former executives at companies like Amazon and Airbnb, are also expected to join the Biden transition team: A recent report outlines the number of Big Tech executives that are expected to join Joe Biden's transition team in the coming weeks. The team includes insiders from the entire range of Silicon Valley Masters of the Universe.

A report published by Protocol has revealed that a huge number of Big Tech executives are expected to join Joe Biden's presidential transition team, with Protocol stating there's "definitive Silicon Valley representation and thought leaders on tech issues involved in shaping the future of the federal government. "

Notable tech execs joining the transition team include:

- **Tom Sullivan, Amazon's director of international tax planning (State Department)**
- **Brandon Belford, Lyft's senior director to the chief of staff (Office of Management and Budget)**
- **Divya Kumaraiah, Airbnb's strategy and program lead for cities (Office of Management and Budget)**
- **Will Fields, Sidewalk Labs' senior development associate (Treasury Department)**
- **Nicole Wong, former Google and Twitter, former Obama Deputy Chief Technology Officer (Office of Science and Technology Policy)**
- **Martha Gimbel, senior manager of economic research at Schmidt Futures (Council of Economic Advisers)**
- **Linda Etim, senior adviser at the Bill and Melinda Gates Foundation (team lead for International Development)**

This comes after Silicon Valley companies intervened in the election on behalf of Joe Biden. In addition to Twitter and Facebook both burying the *New York Post's* reporting on the Biden family's financial ties to Ukraine and China, Google also suppressed conservative news sources.

Six months before the election, following a major change to its core search algorithm, clicks and impressions to Breitbart News from Google searches for "Joe Biden," dropped to zero and stayed their through election day**. Prior to Google's update, clicks and impressions from the search term saw a normal pattern of activity.**

Allum Bokhari is the senior technology correspondent at Breitbart News. His new book, #DELETED: Big Tech's Battle to Erase the Trump Movement and Steal The Election, which contains exclusive interviews with sources inside Google, Facebook, and other tech companies, is currently available for purchase.

THEN, NOW & ALWAYS A JEW HATER
Biden Delivered Egyptian Disinformation to Israel Ahead of Yom Kippur War and Later Lied About It

Deborah Danan

In 1973, 30-year-old freshman senator Joe Biden made his first overseas trip to Egypt and Israel. This week, an Israeli historian revealed Biden had passed on disinformation to then-Israeli prime minister Golda Meir, telling her Egypt believed it would be impossible to go to war with Israel — contributing to an Israeli consensus that would end up costing the Jewish state dearly when its neighboring foe caught it unawares a little more than a month later and attacked.

Despite Israel's victory in the Yom Kippur War, the fact that Egypt caught it by surprise is still an open wound for the country.

Biden met with mid-tier Egyptian officials in Cairo, the highest ranking of whom was the Minister of

Propaganda. Hassanein Heikel, then-editor of the semi-official *Al-Ahram* daily and former minister of information, was also at the meeting, Yigal Kipnis told Israel's Channel 12 **news this week.**

Later, the junior senator from Delaware would sit with Israel's premier, a meeting he often recounts when speaking at Jewish or pro-Israel events, and tell her that the general consensus among the Egyptian officials he met with was that Israel's military superiority made it all but impossible to consider the option of entering a conflict with it.

Kipnis stressed that it is unclear if Biden's meeting and the subsequent misinformation he imparted to Meir, which is recorded in a document that was sent to then Israel's then-Washington envoy Simcha Dinitz, did anything to impact Israel's existing consensus that war was not on the cards."Golda did not need Biden to think that the Egyptians would not go to war and that if they did then the result would be clear," Kipnis told the Israeli network, adding that it is difficult to know how much Biden's information helped the Egyptian fraud scheme, if at all.

"The Egyptians seem to have used Biden's visit as part of their plan to 'lull' Israel into thinking there was no chance of war," the report said.

However, Biden himself paints a very different picture of the meeting with Meir, one that puts into question the depiction of him as an unwitting tool who unknowingly passed on disinformation to Israel.

While he was vice president of the United States under Barack Obama, Biden referred to the meeting **in an April 2015 speech he gave at an event marking Israel's Independence Day. In it Biden claimed to have been the only one in the room who expressed deep concern about an impending war between Israel and Egypt.**

According to Biden, he told Meir, "I thought that they were getting ready to attack again." "And everyone including my military and Israeli military thought I was crazy," Biden said in 2015.

"I remember driving from Cairo all the way to out to the Suez. And you could see these great plumes of dust and sand. But none it seemed isolated. It turns out it was maneuvers taking place in the desert. And I was really worried. And we went through, and she painted a bleak, bleak picture — scared the hell out of me, quite frankly, about the odds," he went on.

Later, Biden recounted, Meir asked Biden to pose for a photo.

"She said, 'Senator, you look so worried,'" he recalled. "I said, 'Well, my God, Madam Prime Minister,' and I turned to look at her. I said, 'The picture you paint.' She said, 'Oh, don't worry. We have' — I thought she only said this to me. She said, 'We have a secret weapon in our conflict with the Arabs: You see, we have no place else to go.'"

"And it's an absolutely true story," Biden said.

In October, Channel 13's Nadav Eyal released excerpts from a classified memo of the meeting made by a unnamed senior Israeli official who was in attendance, who corroborated Kipnis' report, and that of Dinitz's, that Biden had expressly told Meir that Egypt was not interested in going to war.

According to the government memo, Biden also warned that Israel's actions in the territories it had captured during the defensive Six Day War six years earlier, including the West Bank and the Gaza Strip, were leading to "creeping annexation," and suggested unilateral withdrawals.

The memo said Biden also slammed the Nixon administration **for being "dragged by Israel," complaining that it was impossible to have a real debate in the Senate about the Middle East as senators were "afraid" of saying things that would be unpopular with Jewish voters.**

'Stop the Steal' rally turns bloody after four stabbed and in critical condition; counterprotests incite chaos in DC

Alarming videos show brawls and bloody battles in the nation's capital

PAUL SACCA

There were several pro-Trump rallies held in Washington, D.C., on Saturday, including the "March for Trump" and the "Stop the Steal" rally in support of challenging the 2020 presidential election results. In retaliation, at least three anarchist and Antifa-linked groups planned counterprotests in the nation's capital, including the "F*** MAGA**" protest. The clashing groups clashed on the streets of D.C., which resulted in four people being stabbed and nearly two dozen arrests.**

POLL: Would you take the COVID-19 vaccine?

The large protests in support of President Donald Trump were mostly peaceful, but violent skirmishes erupted on Saturday night between the adversarial groups.

A coalition of *Black Lives Matter* **and Antifa supporters appear to be prepared for battle as they wield shields.**

A horde of black bloc members are seen marching towards police and throwing water bottles and bricks at them. (*Content Warning: Graphic footage*):

An alleged Antifa member was physically removed from the fracas when a police officer picked him up like a child and dropped him on the street.

Members of BLM and Antifa fought with the Proud Boys, despite police attempting to constantly separate

the warring groups, as seen in video from Daily Caller field correspondent Shelby Talcott and Townhall senior writer Julio Rosas.

Fireworks were reportedly launched towards the hotel that the Proud Boys were staying at, according to Matthew Miller from the Post Millennial.

A man dressed in all black is surrounded by a group of Proud Boys, some of them are heard yelling, "He's got a knife!" One person walks behind the man with the knife and hits him in the head with an object. The group then jump on the man, and apparently, that is when the stabbings happened. The exact moment that the man drew his knife was captured by SWNS chief photographer Adam Gray.

The four people who were stabbed were said to be in critical condition, some suffered "life-threatening injuries," according to D.C. fire spokesman Doug Buchanan.

Proud Boys pray for the members who were stabbed, asking for a "moment of silence" for two "brothers" who are "fighting for their f***ing life" and "might not f***ing pull through."

Two police officers sustained non-life-threatening injuries and two people with minor injuries, D.C. Mayor Muriel Bowser's office said.

The Metropolitan Police Department reported making 23 arrests on Saturday: 10 for simple assaults, six for assaults on police officers, four committed "riotous acts," two charged with "crossing a police line," and one person had a taser and was charged with "possession of a prohibited weapon."

Video from reporter Brendan Gutenschwager appears to show the man with the knife being arrested.

Pinkerton: What Happens When a Communist Regime Penetrates Our Government

James P. Pinkerton

The U.S. Congressman, a Democrat, is accused of being an agent of a foreign communist power. As one accuser says of the lawmaker, "I think he is a spy." The Congressman denies it, and yet eventually, it's demonstrated that he has been, in fact, engaged in espionage on behalf of foreign communist paymasters.

Perhaps the reader might be thinking that this case is connected to the People's Republic of China; after all, its many spy programs have been in the news a lot lately—including just this past week.

On December 1, John Ratcliffe, the former Member of Congress whom President Trump appointed as Director of National Intelligence (DNI) earlier this year, wrote in *The Wall Street Journal,* "The People's Republic of China poses the greatest threat to America today, and the greatest threat to democracy and freedom world-wide since World War II." He added, "The intelligence is clear: Beijing intends to dominate the U.S. and the rest of the planet economically, militarily and technologically."

In addition, in a December 3 interview with CBS News' intelligence ace, Catherine Herridge, Ratcliffe added more detail, asserting that the Chinese have proven themselves capable of using blackmail, bribery, and covert and overt influence to ensure that the U.S. enacts laws and policies favorable to China.

Then, on December 8, came a pair of revelations that are perhaps traceable to Ratcliffe's intelligence work. The *New York Post* reported on a video, taped in November, in which a Chinese official, Di Dongsheng, vice dean of the School of International Relations at Beijing's Renmin University, said: I'm going to throw out something maybe a little bit explosive here. It's just because we have people at the top. We have our old friends who are at the top of America's core inner circle of power and influence.

Yes, Di's words are, indeed, explosive—the idea that China's friends are "at the top of America's core inner circle of power and influence." So who might these friends be? Di didn't say, exactly, although he mentioned Hunter Biden, who is certainly well-placed and has had plenty of business activity in China, along with Chris Heinz, step-son of John Kerry, whom Joe Biden has slated to be his climate-change czar.

U.S. Vice President Joe Biden, left, waves as he walks out of Air Force Two with his granddaughter Finnegan Biden and son Hunter Biden at the airport in Beijing, China, on Dec. 4, 2013. Hunter Biden's private equity firm secured a billion dollar deal with the state-owned Bank of China ten days after accompanying his father on this trip to China. (AP Photo/ Ng Han Guan)

Of course, Di's statements haven't been verified, let alone proven. So it's possible that some or all of these allegations will be judged to be misleading, or perhaps even as outright fake news. Or, they might someday be regarded as a disinformation plot—perhaps, who knows, aimed at throwing investigators off the trail of

someone else. As they say, espionage and counter-espionage are a wilderness of mirrors**.**

In that same spirit of curious but cautious, we must, at least for now, also put a caveat in front of Tuesday's bombshell scoop of Axios, headlined**, "Suspected Chinese spy targeted California politicians." As that piece detailed, early in the last decade, a female Chinese national named Fang Fang (also known as Christine Fang) deliberately networked with various Golden State politicians, including Rep. Eric Swalwell, best known for his ill-starred bid for the 2020 Democratic presidential nomination.**

Moreover, the Axios report added: Through campaign fundraising, extensive networking, personal charisma, and romantic or sexual relationships with at least two Midwestern mayors, **Fang was able to gain proximity to political power. [emphasis added] In fact, one unnamed intelligence official told Axios that the Fang case "was a big deal, because there were some really, really sensitive people that were caught up." (Swalwell, we might note, has a spot on the powerful** House Intelligence Committee**.)**

These are some tantalizing suspicions, aren't they? For his part, Swalwell denies any wrongdoing–although in an interview **with Politico, he pointedly refused to discuss his relationship with Fang (Gee, how should we interpret that?). For her part, Fang reportedly left the U.S. in 2015, returning to China—where she will most likely be unavailable to investigators.**

HE SCREWS HER WHILE SHE SPIES FOR XI JINPING & THEY BOTH LAUGH AT REPUBLICANS WHILE SCREWING

Rep. Eric Swalwell (D-CA) with suspected Chinese communist spy Christine Fang (Facebook) Indeed, as of now, it's an open question as to how much more we'll learn about any of these cases. After all, Ratcliffe is a Trump appointee, and Joe Biden has already named a successor, Avril Haines, for the DNI post.

So what will Haines do once she's in office? Will she have anything notable to say about China's campaign against the U.S.? Will she provide us with more details about Di's comments? Or about Fang's activities? Or about Swalwell—and what he did or didn't do? And what about that pair of randy Midwestern mayors? Will we ever find out their names?

We don't yet know the answers to those questions, of course, although we do know that Joe Biden has been notably non-communicative about one China-connected figure close to him: his son, Hunter Biden. Yes, Joe Biden has said that son will not be involved in any foreign money-making schemes; however, as Breitbart News' Joel Pollak **has pointed out, the elder Biden has made that pledge before and not kept it. (And we can add that such restrictions are hard to enforce; what, after all, constitutes a foreign scheme, as opposed to just, you know, Hunter Biden living his usual high life in a** $12,000-a month **pad in the Hollywood Hills?)**

In the meantime, we should know that if something has happened before, that raises the likelihood that it can happen again. As the philosopher Hegel **explained, the actual proves the possible. And actually, there was once a member of Congress who was spy for a communist country. So yes, today, a communist spy in our midst is a possibility.**

An Explosive Accusation, Proven

It was in the 1930s, when a Democratic Congressman from New York City, Samuel Dickstein, operated as a paid spy for the Soviet Union. As detailed in a 1999 book, *The Haunted Wood: Soviet Espionage in America – The Stalin Era*, **by Allen Weinstein and Alexander Vassiliev, Dickstein delivered secrets to his NKVD (a predecessor to the KGB) handler,** Peter Gutzeit, **a Russian operating in the United States. Gutzeit had also spread his tentacles into Hollywood and other leftist hotbeds. In 2014, another intelligence historian, Peter Duffy, summed up the case against Dickstein in an article** headlined, **"The Congressman Who Spied for Russia." (Duffy dug up the quote, used in the first paragraph of this piece, "I think he is a spy," said by a contemporary of Dickstein's.)**

Soviet spy Rep. Samuel Dickstein (D-NY), 1937. (Library of Congress)

In addition to the elected Dickstein, hundreds of others in non-elected federal jobs were also Soviet spies. Perhaps the most notorious of these was Alger Hiss, a onetime top aide in the State Department, who was revealed as a communist agent by a young Congressman, Richard Nixon, in 1948, and sent to prison in the early 1950s.

This was the Cold War era, when the communist Soviet Union sought to overturn American security and threaten world peace. John Berresford, an independent historian whose extensive research on the Hiss case has been showcased at the Smithsonian Museum, sees similarities—and dissimilarities—between America's situation in the Cold War with the Soviet Union and today in what's emerging as a new cold war with China.

Among the *dis*similarities is that the Soviet Union back then had the benefit of the international appeal of communism. That is, many idealists—wrongheadedly, of course—saw communism, then embodied by Josef Stalin, as the better system. By contrast, in our time, as Berresford says, "No one is ideologically committed to President Xi Jinping."

Yet on the other hand, China has far-flung business interests across the world, as well as plenty of money. And money, all too often, can make things happen, spy-wise. As Berresford puts it, "The words may

change but the song—that is, blackmail and seduction—remains the same." Indeed, the essence of spycraft is temptation: if not ideological, then financial or sexual. Anything that someone might want, a spy-recruiter might provide.

Proven Countermeasures

So what can we do about Chinese espionage? We know what Ratcliffe and the Trump administration want to do—they want to get tough. So now we'll have to see the stance of the Biden administration.

Yet the Bidenites should realize that there's a price to be paid for laxity on national security—including a political price. For perspective, we might think back, again, to the 1940s. We had been allies with the Soviet Union during World War II, based on the hard-nosed calculation that Hitler's Germany was the greatest enemy and that we needed all the help we could get to beat him.

Yet after Germany's surrender in May 1945, it soon became apparent that the Soviet Union was also a grave threat. And the threat wasn't just the Red Army in Europe; it was also the "fifth column" of communist spies in the U.S. Most, if not all, of those spies, including Alger Hiss, had penetrated the federal government during the administration of Franklin D. Roosevelt from 1933 to 1945.

Soviet spy and Democratic administration official Alger Hiss testifying before the House Un-American Activities Committee in Washington, DC, on Aug. 25, 1948. (AP Photo)

So now it was the challenge of FDR's successor in the Oval Office, Harry Truman, to address the communist threat. Truman, after all, wanted to be elected in 1948, and he could't hope for such a victory if he were seen as oblivious to the threat of internal subversion. In the meantime, the opposition Republicans, smelling lots

of red rats hidden inside the federal government, were on the hunt. After some hesitation, Truman stepped up on counter-espionage. In 1947, he issued Executive Order 9835, establishing a Loyalty Program for the federal government, including a Loyalty Oath. Some might argue that a dedicated communist, or other nogoodnik, would be happy simply to lie about loyalty. And yet history proves that oaths do actually have an effect on individuals; moreover, loyalty programs and oaths have an effect on institutions—that is, they send a signal that leadership takes security seriously, and so safety measures fall into place.

In 1952, Uncle Sam went further, putting into law the McCarran-Walter Act, toughening up on immigration and internal security. We might note that the sponsors of the legislation, Sen. Pat McCarran of Nevada and Rep. Francis Walter of Pennsylvania, were both Democrats. In other words, Democrats can do it—at least the old kind of Democrats could.

Today

So what will the Biden administration do about China? One place to start making a good impression would be the full and frank disclosure of the $22 million that anonymous Chinese individuals or interests donated to the University of Pennsylvania's Biden Center for Diplomacy and Global Engagement. During the Trump years, the so-called Penn Biden Center served as a kind of holding center for once and future Biden aides, including Tony Blinken, Biden's pick to be the next secretary of state. So what's up with that $22 million? Who gave it? Why did they give it? What are they getting for it? If and when those questions are answered, there will be more questions to be asked.

A lot more. Because this is Cold War II with China—and the stakes couldn't be higher.

WHEN WITH OUR BACKS TO THE WALL SERIOUSLY CONSIDERED THE FIRST SECESSION FROM THE UNITED STATES THAT LED TO THE AMERICAN CIVIL WAR; DO WE ACTUALLY WANT TO LIVE IN THE SAME NATION WITH THESE PEOPLE? GOP Rep. Waltz: America 'Flooded with Chinese Communist Money' GOP Rep. Waltz: America 'Flooded with Chinese Communist Money'

Ian Hanchett

On Saturday's broadcast of the Fox News Channel's "Fox & Friends," Rep. Michael Waltz (R-FL) said "the country is flooded with Chinese Communist money" and China is "flooding the zone" with money to influence the entirety of American society.

Waltz said, "The point that I want everybody to understand today is that the country is flooded with Chinese Communist money. This is a much bigger and pervasive problem. It's in Hollywood. It's in think tanks. It's in journalism. It's in Wall Street. And it's certainly going after progressive politicians like Swalwell."

He later added that China is "flooding the zone in the United States with money in a way the Soviet Union was never able to do to influence all of American society, and around the world, to eventually, again, kowtow to Beijing and how they see the future, not us."

Texas GOP chairman Allen West floats secession in reaction to SCOTUS shooting down election suit

'Perhaps law-abiding states should bond together and form a Union of states that will abide by the constitution'

Breck Dumas

Allen West, the chairman of the Republican Party of Texas, suggested Friday that some states secede from the United States in reaction to the U.S. Supreme Court turning down his state's lawsuit seeking to overturn election results in four other states.

What are the details?

West, a former Florida congressman, issued a statement, saying:

"The Supreme Court, in tossing the Texas lawsuit that was joined by seventeen states and 106 US congressman (sic), have decreed that a state can take unconstitutional actions and violate its own election law. Resulting in damaging effects on other states that abide by the law, while the guilty state suffers no consequences. This decision establishes a precedent that says states can violate the US constitution and not be held accountable. This decision will have far reaching ramifications for the future or our constitutional republic. Perhaps law-abiding states should bond together and form a Union of states that will abide by the constitution."

He added, "The Texas GOP will always stand for the Constitution and for the rule of law even while others don't."

The @TexasGOP is out with a statement in the wake of the Supreme Court decision, all but calling for secession: "P… https://t.co/DqHUYhHOBH

— Adam Kelsey (@Adam Kelsey The word "Confederacy" began trending on Twitter following the decision and West's remarks.

But not all Republicans who supported the suit agreed with West. Arkansas GOP Rep. Bruce Westerman, who signed on in support of Texas' litigation, issued a statement calling for unity in the country.

Westerman said, in part:

"Although there are other election lawsuits in courts around the country, I believe the Texas attorney general's case was the best and likely last opportunity for SCOTUS to hear claims of fraudulent voting that could have had an impact on the presidential election results...SCOTUS rejected the case, and I believe closed the books on challenges to the 2020 election results."

He added, "The only milestone left in completing the election process will be Congress counting the votes on January 6. The casting of electoral votes will end a hotly contested election, and we should come together as Americans to work together for the future of our country."

— Rep. Bruce Westerman (@Rep. Bruce Westerman

Another House Republican, Rep. Adam Kinzinger (Ill.) called for West's termination over the statement, tweeting, "I believe @TexasGOP should immediately retract this, apologize, and fire Allen West and anyone else associated with this. My guy Abraham Lincoln and the Union soldiers already told you no."

I believe @TexasGOP should immediately retract this, apologize, and fire Allen West and anyone else associated with… https://t.co/66xcZU90Xh

— Adam Kinzinger (@Adam Kinzinger)1607733853.0

President Donald Trump, Vice President Mike Pence, and their campaign have filed dozens of lawsuits nationwide seeking to overturn what they call a "rigged" election that has been widely called for Democratic nominee Joe Biden by mainstream media. The Trump camp has not been successful in their litigation efforts.

Two cases filed separately by pro-Trump politicians seeking to challenge state election results have now been rejected by the Supreme Court. Earlier this week, the high court turned down a lawsuit led by Rep. Mike Kelly (R), which sought to reject mail-in ballots filed in his home state of Pennsylvania.

THE RICHARD E. GLICK RED STATE SECESSION DOCTRINE ECHOES JAMES MONROE; CHINESE PRESENCE IN OUR HEMISPHERE; NO MATTER IN WHAT SHAPE IT COMES; WHETHER ACCEPTED BY BLUE DEMOCRAT PROGRESSIVE LIBERAL GOVERNMENT; UNIVERSITY LEFT HIGHER EDUCATION; OR BIRTH TOURISM; WILL BE TERMINATED ON-SIGHT INSTANTLY WITH PREJUDICE

High School Bans Yearbook Picture of Student with American Flag Draped Over Her Shoulders

Alana Mastrangelo

Lewis and Clark High School in Spokane, Washington, rejected a student's yearbook picture because she posed with an American flag draped over her shoulders. A statement from the school claims the decision was not made against what the flag represents, but out of respect: "We respect our flag as much as any school in the area and were concerned that in the photo submitted it was being used as a prop in the photo and was not being afforded appropriate regard."

"The fact that I can't have my senior picture in the yearbook because it contains the American flag in it amazes me," wrote the student to her Facebook page on Monday, sharing a purported screenshot of an email she received from the school notifying her that her yearbook photo was denied.

"Are you kidding me right now? If the American flag offends you effing leave," the student added. "Screw this school I want to switch Lewis and Clark High School."

According to Lewis and Clark's principal, Marybeth Smith, the American flag violates the school's new policy, which states that "no props are allowed."

"We have rejected a photo this year in which our American flag was displayed in a way not sanctioned by Title Four, US Code, Chapter One," said Smith in a statement posted to the school's Facebook page.

The statement went on to claim that while the American flag is not allowed to be featured in the student's yearbook photo, the school does not and has not "banned the American flag from inclusion in photos."

"We do not and have not banned the American flag from inclusion in photos," said Smith in her statement. "In the past we have celebrated students who have enlisted in the military by using senior photos highlighting their branch of service – student in uniform and US flag displayed behind them. It's been an honor to portray our seniors in this way."

The statement added:

We say the Pledge daily during school, we have our flag displayed in accordance with Code guidelines on our stage during all school events and we even have one of the largest US flags in this area in our gym – it is celebrated during the playing of our National Anthem prior to athletic competitions held there. We respect our flag as much as any school in the area and were concerned that in the photo submitted it was being used as a prop in the photo and was not being afforded appropriate regard. We continue to work through the matter with the student. Thank you.

The student took to social media again on Tuesday to respond to some of the other criticisms that she had apparently received in response to her photo.

"Well I'm sorry for using the flag as 'clothing or apparel' and 'draping it over me' because that goes against certain guidelines (flag code)," the student wrote. "People have also pointed out that the stripes on the

bottom of my shoes are offensive, but it's not the American flag so they can calm down on that one."

"I'm also not sitting on the ground nor am I sitting on the flag. I would NEVER let the flag touch the ground. I don't think I'm the 'exception' or 'entitled' to anything, but I'm just reaching out since the school was not doing anything," she added.

The student also noted that if people consider her photo with the American flag to be "clothing," then it does not violate the school's policy against using "props."

"If everyone keeps claiming that I am using the flag as 'clothing' then there's no way that it could be a 'prop' therefore making it acceptable in the yearbook," the student said.

"I am sick of the people saying I am the opposite of patriotic for this picture and will let them spew the lies," she added.

Principal Smith is expected to meet with the student and her parents to go over the new policy, according to a report by Country Music Family.

The student added that if she is not allowed to use the photo featuring the American flag, then she will not submit another one.

Violence erupts in Washington between Trump supporters and leftist groups — shot fired, suspect detained

Videos show a scary scene David Ryder Paul Sacca

Several rallies and counterprotests went down on Saturday in Olympia, Washington. In the midst of tense and sometimes violent clashes between Trump supporters and members of leftist groups, someone fired a gun. Police had made at least two arrests.

In Olympia, there was a "RE-Open WA" rally planned, a "Stop the Steal" parade, and a "BLM: Washington vs. Fascism" counterprotest scheduled for Saturday, according to Fox News.

It didn't take long for the polar opposite groups to run into each other in Olympia. Proud Boys and Black Bloc members confronted each other as seen in video taken by reporter Shauna Sowersby. Both groups are now in front of the Capitol, with one person from the Trump supporters and Proud Boys group trying...

Then fights erupted between the two groups, and an "unlawful assembly" was declared by the Olympia Police Department.

"First fight breaks out between Back the blue / stop the steal protesters and Portland / Washington counter-protesters," Independent Media said.

First fight breaks out between Back the blue / stop the steal protesters and Portland / Washington counter-proteste...

An alleged member of the Proud Boys was reportedly arrested for pointing his gun. While at the same time law enforcement is seen firing crowd control munitions at apparent Antifa members lined up in the middle of the street.

The violence escalated to the point that the Olympia Police Department was forced to declare a riot.

A Proud Boy member was arrested for aiming his gun at Portland/ Washington counter-protesters, Olympia Police use f... https://t.co/3C58wpanWY

A shot was fired during the protests. A man wearing all black was seen brandishing a handgun. He flees the scene and puts on a red hat. The same man appears to be on the ground and being arrested by the Olympia Police Department officers and Washington State Troopers.

Olympia Police Dept. and Washington State Troopers arrest and hogtie the shooting suspect near 10th and Columbia....

Olympia police and WSP have secured the area and have so far found one spent casing, a live round and some sort of... https://t.co/jHAZpyHBEt

— Shauna Sowersby (@Shauna Sowersby)1607811643.0

Washington State Patrol spokesperson Chris Loftis confirmed the shooting to the Seattle Times.

"Suspect detained," Loftis said. "No information confirmed on victim or any injury status."

Loftis described the situation as, "Fluid situation with two groups of size, both including heavily armed individuals."

There was violence in Olympia last Saturday as well. There was a nasty brawl between "Back the Blue" supporters and Black Bloc members.

"We did make an arrest for a subject that appeared to fire at least one round from a handgun into the opposing crowd," the Olympia Police Department said last week. "Any witnesses to that crime should contact @OlyPD through the 911 system."

CAN YOU BELIEVE YOU'RE READING THIS? DO WE WANT TO BE PART OF THIS COUNTRY?

CNN's April Ryan suggests media should ignore (DO YOU ACTUALLY) WANT TO BE PART OF JEFF ZUCKER'S CNN AMERICA) info that damages Biden, gets summarily torched

'...would make a Stalinist propagandist blush'

Chris Enloe

Reporter April Ryan, a political analyst for CNN, is being condemned for suggesting on Thursday that journalists should not expose contradictions between what Joe Biden says privately and what he says publicly.

Ryan's comments came after The Intercept obtained and reported on leaked audio of Biden admitting that **Republicans "beat the hell out of" Democrats during last month's election for generally embracing the "defund the police" agenda.**

The Biden transition team later defended the remarks, **despite the comments rebuking the progressive vision for criminal justice reform.**

What did Ryan say?

In response to the leaked audio, Ryan suggested the real story behind the remarks is why they were leaked.

"The question is who leaked this and why? Also I am told by a rights leader in that meeting that @JoeBiden was being more so passionate than defensive. Can't wait to hear what the Biden camp has to say!" Ryan tweeted.

Ryan later doubled down on that sentiment, again questioning why Biden's comments were leaked.

"I asked an incoming White House source was the meeting contentious with civil rights leader and @ JoeBiden and the answer was 'no'. A rights leader at the meeting says @JoeBiden was passionate. The question is who taped this meeting and why? What is the agenda?" Ryan said**.**

What was the reaction?

Vice journalist Edward Ongweso Jr. highlighted the absurdity of Ryan's response to the leaked audio by mocking her reaction**.**

Ongweso tweeted:

It is irresponsible and sets a dangerous precedent for journalists covering the incoming administration to be able to use secretly recorded conversations in their stories. To parse out Biden's thoughts and anticipate his policy commitments, you must go through proper channels. The White House Press Secretary, the spokespeople for the President and Vice President, senior officials (without attribution), and the President's public statements are all designated and responsible sources for information about the President's thoughts and intentions. Revealing a contradiction between Biden's private thoughts and public statements is dangerous because it erodes public trust in the President, the Office, and the media itself.

Ryan, however, apparently did not understand that she was being mocked, replying, "You hit the nail on the head! This is not good at all."

Jonathan Turley, a professor at George Washington University Law School and self-described "liberal," also tore into Ryan, calling her reaction to the leaked audio something that "would make a Stalinist propagandist blush."

"The fact is that Ryan was just stating what has become the approach of many in the media. As we recently discussed, we are moving dangerously close to a de facto state media with the cooperation of Big Tech companies," Turley wrote. "Ryan believes that it is outrageous to rely on unapproved material if it is critical of Joe Biden (despite her use of such material for the last four years against Trump)."

THESE LINE IN THE SAND COURAGEOUS BEST OF AMERICA KIDS HAVE SET AN EXAMPLE FOR 76 MILLION TRUMP VOTERS & OUR FAMILIES. ARE WE WITH THEM OR AGAINST THEM?

Sun sets in DC as counterprotesters, pro-Trump demonstrators face off following election defeat for president

By Marisa Schultz, Michael Ruiz

President's helicopter makes an appearance above the rally of his supporters in Washington, D.C.; reaction from My Pillow CEO Mike Lindell.

Chaos erupted in the nation's capital Saturday night hours after two pro-Trump rallies had ended and groups of Proud Boys and Antifa clashed under cover of darkness, with police frequently forcing them apart amid reports of brawls and stabbings.

Images and videos on social media show demonstrators exchanging barrages of fireworks, and police forcing them to separate with a Hyatt Hotel in the background.

"Moments after I took this video, fireworks exploded at the front entrance of the Hyatt Hotel," Washington Post reporter Marissa Lang tweeted. "Proud Boys and anti-fascist [Antifa] protesters had been starting to brawl at the entrance.

She also said police pepper-sprayed a group of protesters a few blocks away and later reported that at least two people had been stabbed, citing fire officials.

A spokeswoman for the Metropolitan Police Department said earlier there had been six arrests in connection with the demonstrations as of early Saturday evening, but she could not say on what charges. The department did not immediately respond to a request for comment on the after-dark clashes.

Several unverified videos on Twitter posted during the protests from the area appeared to show people with bleeding wounds being treated by police.

Police separated the groups, shut down traffic in parts of downtown D.C. and sealed off *Black Lives Matter* Plaza near the White House. As the evening went on, police squashed other potential clashes, according to numerous journalists in the area who shared videos to Twitter.

At one point, a group of Proud Boys allegedly ducked through an alleyway to sidestep police and confront Antifa, according to the Post Millennial's Matthew Miller.

In subsequent videos, viewers can hear what appear to be the sounds of stun guns going off, fireworks and demonstrators coughing after reportedly inhaling pepper spray. Despite aggressive and graphic language between both groups of protesters and counterprotesters, police appeared in quickly intervene and keep them apart in numerous videos.

Earlier Saturday, President Trump**'s backers descended on Washington to support the president, who has** come up short **in his efforts to overturn the results of the 2020 presidential election.**

Wiith Trump flags and hats, and a few face masks, they gathered at Freedom Plaza near the White House chanting "Four More Years" and "Stop the Steal" to urge Trump to keep on fighting. Organizers of the Women for America First rally were expecting 15,000 participants for the rally and march to the Supreme Court. One speaker at the rally, retired Gen. Michael Flynn who was Trump's former national security adviser, told the crowd he was confident Trump would remain in office.

"When people ask me...on a scale of 1 to 10, who's going to be the next president of the United States? I say: 10, Donald J. Trump ... without hesitation."

Trump last month granted a pardon to Flynn, who pleaded guilty in 2017 to lying to the FBI about his contact with a Russian ambassador, but later claimed innocence.

Former U.S. national security adviser Michael Flynn speaks as supporters of U.S. President Donald Trump listen during a rally to protest the results of the election in front of Supreme Court building, in Washington, U.S., Dec. 12.

"The fraud that is being perpetrated on the United States of America through this previous election is outrageous," Flynn told the crowd. "It's outrageous. We will not accept it." Trump appeared to be pleasantly surprised by another show of support in the Democratic stronghold of D.C.

"Wow! Thousands of people forming in Washington (D.C.) for Stop the Steal," Trump tweeted Saturday morning. "Didn't know about this, but I'll be seeing them! #MAGA" Trump later departed the White House in Marine One en route to the Army-Navy football game at West Point. But before the game, crowds cheered below the "fly-over" from the commander-in-chief. Trump aide Dan Scavino tweeted an aerial picture with a message to the crowd. "Thank you, Patriots."

During the last major "Stop the Steal" rally in D.C. on Nov. 14, Trump and his motorcade drove through the downtown D.C. crowd to wave to supporters before heading to his golf resort in Virginia.

FLACCID; HEAR NO EVIL; SEE NO EVIL; BE WILLFULLY IGNORANT ABOUT DEMOCRAT CLEAR & PRESENT OBVIOUS THEFT OF PRESIDENCY SUPREME COURT DECLINES TO HEAR TRUMP-SUPPORTED TEXAS CASE OVER ELECTION RESULTS IN FOUR OTHER STATES

Two pro-Trump groups applied for park permits for rallies on Saturday. Speakers at the "March for Trump" demonstration organized by the Women for America First included "My Pillow" guy Mike Lindell and former Trump aides Sebastian Gorka, Boris Epshteyn and Katrina Pearson, who encouraged supporters to keep up the fight to overturn the election results.

People gather on Pennsylvania Avenue for the "Stop the Steal" rally in support of U.S. President Donald Trump, in Washington, U.S., December 12, 2020. REUTERS/Erin Scott

"I've read the Constitution. I don't think Joe Biden has," **Gorka told the crowd, "but I've read the Constitution. And I know one thing: It ain't over until January 20th."**

The presidential inauguration is Jan. 20.

Supporters of US President Donald Trump participate in the Million MAGA March to protest the outcome of the 2020 presidential election, on December 12, 2020 in Washington, DC.

Trump supporters made clear they will continue to fight back regardless of the media and court rulings, and will not accept Biden as president.

"In 2016, they had this thing called the resistance, do you remember that?" Pearson said of the left's movement against Trump. "You haven't seen a resistance until patriots show up to defend the republic."

A second pro-Trump rally was set for the Sylvan Theater on the National Mall, where organizers planned for 500 people, according to their national park permit.

Meanwhile, the "Refuse Fascism" anti-Trump group scheduled a counter-protest in *Black Lives Matter* **Plaza at noon, with the message: "**Trump: You Lost. Get the Hell Out!**"**

The rallies come a day after a major legal defeat for Trump, when the Supreme Court Friday declined to hear a Texas case that challenged the election results in Pennsylvania, Michigan, Georgia and Wisconsin.

PENNSYLVANIA ACCUSES TEXAS OF SEEKING 'TO DECIMATE THE ELECTORATE' IN FIERY SUPREME COURT BRIEF

Trump has repeatedly alleged he beat President-elect Joe Biden, and claims there was widespread voter fraud. But states have stood by their results and courts have repeatedly rejected Trump's legal claims that Biden's victory -- by a margin of more than 7 million votes nationwide -- should be tossed out.

Supporters of US President Donald Trump demonstrate in Washington, DC, on December 12, 2020, to protest the 2020 election. (Photo by Jose Luis Magana On Jan. 6 there will be a joint session of the House and Senate to count the electoral votes and certify Biden as the winner.

On Saturday, the Biden transition team praised courts for tossing out Trump's "baseless" legal claims. "The Supreme Court has decisively and speedily rejected the latest of Donald Trump and his allies' attacks on the democratic process," Biden transition official Michael Gwin said in a statement. "This is no surprise — dozens of judges, election officials from both parties, and Trump's own Attorney General have dismissed his baseless attempts to deny that he lost the election. President-elect Biden's clear and commanding victory will be ratified by the Electoral College on Monday, and he will be sworn in on January 20th."

Ben & Jerry's and Colin Kaepernick debut brand-new ice cream flavor to help 'amplify calls to defund and abolish the police'

Woke dessert Sarah Taylor

WE NEED OUR OWN NATION & OUR OWN ARMED SERVICES TO PROTECT OURSELVES FROM THEM. WAKE UP. WOKE AMERICANS ARE MORE A THREAT TO US THAT CHINA, RUSSIA, NORTH KOREA, IRAN & CUBA COMBINED.

Vermont-based ice cream manufacturer Ben & Jerry's has announced that it is releasing a new frozen confection flavor in honor of NFL player-turned activist Colin Kaepernick and his work in equality and in eradicating police brutality.

What are the details?

In a Thursday press release, the company announced that the new dessert — a non-dairy flavor in an apparent nod to Kaepernick's veganism — is called "Change the Whirled" and features a caramel sunflower butter base with fudge chips, graham cracker swirls, and chocolate cookie swirls.

The new flavor, according to the company's release, "celebrates Kaepernick's courageous work to confront systemic oppression and to stop police violence against black and brown people."

"Ben & Jerry's believes Kaepernick represents the very best of us, willing to use his power and platform in the pursuit of equity and justice rooted in a commitment to love and resistance," a statement from the company revealed.

According to a Thursday report from TMZ, the company added, "We are so inspired by Colin Kaepernick's bold activism for racial justice that we did what we do best: We whipped up a euphoric flavor to honor his work. ... We're proud to be working with a dedicated activist like Colin Kaepernick, whose work helped spark the international conversation around racial justice."

What else?

Kaepernick himself issued a statement on the new flavor and said that he is "honored" to partner with the popular company to debut the flavor.

"Their commitment to challenging the anti-black roots of policing in the United States demonstrates a material concern for the wellbeing of black and brown communities," Kaepernick said in a statement. "My hope is that this partnership will amplify calls to defund and abolish the police and to invest in futures that can make us safer, healthier, and truly free."

In case there was any confusion about Ben & Jerry's stance on police reform, Chris Miller — Ben & Jerry's head of global activism strategy — told USA Today, "That very much is our approach, this idea we can help normalize and reinforce these ideas to a more mainstream, general population audience. It's not a particularly radical notion to suggest that police forces and policing probably are not the best way to handling things like mental health crises and substance abuse, and contextualize them for people what a different vision of public safety looks like."

The flavor will be a full-time flavor and will be available at participating retailers beginning in 2021.

Cruz Offering to Argue Pa. Election Lawsuit Before US Supreme Court

By Brian Trusdell

Texas Sen. Ted Cruz says he is available and willing to give the oral argument before the U.S. Supreme Court if the court agrees to hear an election lawsuit out of Pennsylvania challenging the constitutionality of lawmakers' dramatic expansion of absentee voting.

Cruz, the longest-serving solicitor general in the history of Texas and a former law professor at the University of Texas Law School in Austin, was the first U.S. senator to publicly support the case, filed by Rep. Mike Kelly of Pennsylvania, 2020 U.S. congressional candidate Sean Parnell and former state representative candidate Wanda Logan.

"If #SCOTUS grants cert in the PA election case, I have told the petitioners I will stand ready to present the oral argument," Cruz said on Twitter after first disclosing his intent on Fox News Channel. "Because of the importance of the legal issues presented, I've publicly urged #SCOTUS to hear the case brought by Congressman Mike Kelly, congressional candidate Sean Parnell & state rep. candidate Wanda Logan challenging the constitutionality of the POTUS election results in PA."

Kelly's appeal argues that Pennsylvania legislators last year passed legislation greatly expanding the use of absentee voting as pandemic fears raised worries about in-person processing of votes, making it a "no-excuse" mail-in election and contradicting the state's constitution. It further derides the Pennsylvania Supreme Court for dismissing Kelly's lawsuit for "laches," a legal term for a procedural issue, i.e. saying the case was brought too late.

Cruz was especially critical of the Pennsylvania Supreme Court's dismissal on the procedural ground.

"Even more persuasively, the plaintiffs point out that the Pennsylvania Supreme Court has also held that plaintiffs don't have standing to challenge an election law until after the election, meaning that the court effectively put them in a Catch-22: before the election, they lacked standing; after the election, they've delayed too long," Cruz said. "The result of the court's gamesmanship is that a facially unconstitutional election law can never be judicially challenged.

Cruz also on Monday filed a friend of the court brief – along with 10 of his Senate colleagues – in Arizona Attorney General Mark Brnovich's case challenging the Democratic National Committee's stance that the Voting Rights Act bans state laws limiting absentee voting. among other measures.

106 in House GOP Back Texas Suit; McCarthy Refuses to Sign By Eric Mack

"Most of my Republican colleagues in the House, and countless millions of our constituents across the country, now have serious concerns with the integrity of our election system. The purpose of our amicus brief will be to articulate this concern and express our sincere belief that the great importance of this issue merits a full and careful consideration by the Court."

Trump has called Johnson to thank him for his assistance in the election challenge, Johnson tweeted Wednesday:

"President Trump called me this morning to let me know how much he appreciates the amicus brief we are filing on behalf of Members of Congress. Indeed, 'this is the big one!'"

Paxton's case argues that the swing states of Pennsylvania, Michigan, Wisconsin, and

Georgia unconstitutionally violated state election laws and therefore should not certify their election results to the U.S. House.

Already, 18 states led by GOP attorneys general have signed on to Paxton's case, **which called for the four battleground states to respond by Thursday afternoon. In all four cases, the attorneys general** wrote to the court **to reject Paxton's lawsuit as dependent on flimsy evidence and bogus allegations.Among those states, only Georgia has a Republican attorney general, Chris Carr. Even he argued that it'll be tough for Texas to show it has been harmed by the elections in other states.**

"The novel and far-reaching claims that Texas asserts, and the breathtaking remedies it seeks, are impossible to ground in legal principles and unmanageable," Carr wrote in Georgia's filing.Still, the Trump camp contends, there are constitutional arguments to be made about the certification of election results in states that changed election law amid the coronavirus pandemic without supporting legislation.

Key Republicans signing on to Johnson's amicus brief include, per The Hill:

- **House Minority Whip Steve Scalise, R-La.**
- **House Judiciary Ranking Member Rep. Jim Jordan, R-Ohio.**
- **House Freedom Caucus Chairman Rep. Andy Biggs, R-Ariz.**
- **Rep. Jim Banks, R-Ind.**

Some notable Republicans that did not sign on are House Minority Leader Kevin McCarthy, R-Calif., and GOP Conference Chairwoman Liz Cheney, R-Wyo., the latter of whom has emerged as a Trump critic. During a House GOP leadership news conference Thursday, McCarthy twice declined to say he would sign on to Texas lawsuit, telling reporters **only: "The president has a right for every legal challenge to be heard. He has the right to go to the Supreme Court with it, yes."**

The Trump campaign has rejected the Dec. 8 "safe harbor deadline" of election challenges and even said Dec. 14 electoral college vote does not seal the deal. Instead, according to Trump campaign senior legal counsel Jenna Ellis, Jan. 6 is the date the House reviews the electoral college vote.

It is the hope of the Trump campaign and President Trump's lawyers the House will reject the 62 electoral college votes from those four pivotal states. John Eastman to Newsmax TV: Pressure on SCOTUS to Hold Elex Fraud 'Trial' Is 'Extremely Strong'

THE SUPREME MIDGET COURT

By Eric Mack

After receiving the briefs and opposition from the four key battleground states Thursday, the next step by the Supreme Court will be to review whether to take a case as "a trial court," John Eastman, counsel to President Donald Trump and presidential scholar, said Thursday on Newsmax TV.

And the pressure on the high court to take that step is growing, he said. "I suspect the Supreme Court is going to meet in conference [Friday] to decide whether to grant Texas' motion to file the original action," Eastman told Thursday's "Greg Kelly Reports." "And then they'll confront the issue like President Trump's motion to intervene.

"If they grant that Texas motion, they'll set a briefing schedule. They could even appoint a special master to look at some of underlying allegations of fraud." With original jurisdiction in a dispute between states in Texas v. Pennsylvania, the Supreme Court would take the unique role as "trial court," Eastman told host Greg Kelly.

"It's not their normal role," he continued. "Normally they'll end of appointing a trial judge to serve as a special master to try and sort through the evidentiary issues."

Eastman said the pressure for the Court to take the case is mounting.

"With 18 states now and the president of the United States himself, the press to exercise whatever discretion they have to take the case, and hear it, is extremely strong," he said.

Additionally, some 106 Republican members of the House have signed on to a brief in support of the filing by Texas' attorney general, Ken Paxton.

The Texas lawsuit does not make specific fraud allegations. Instead, Texas said changes to voting procedures removed protections against fraud and were unlawful when the reforms were made by officials in the four states or courts without the approval of the states' legislatures. Democrats and the Joe Biden campaign should welcome the legal review to legitimize the election and the next president, Eastman added.

"I think both sides ought to want to have this resolved," he said. "Half the country thinks this election was stolen, including, according to [pollster] Rasmussen, 30% of Democrats. If that's true, why would even the Biden camp not want to actually have a court look at the data, look at the violations of state law that occurred to loosen the fraud risk protections on absentee ballots.

"What would they not want to get this cleared up? So if they do win the election after a fair review, they could come in as a more legitimate president."

Eastman noted the principal legal issue is states violated or ignored their own state election laws. "The legislature of the states has the sole authority under the federal Constitution," he continued. "Those actions by state elections officials were just patently unconstitutional."Democrat-led states might come out against the 18 states joining Paxton's bill of complaint, but Eastman noted that will only help to spur the Supreme Court to ultimately take the case.

"It does highlight to the Supreme Court how important this case is and how important and necessary it is that it be resolved in a way that the country can think it was fairly decided," he concluded. "Right now the country doesn't think that."

Rep. Doug Collins to Newsmax TV: Georgia Pols Right to Back Texas Lawsuit

By Charlie McCarthy

It's understandable why Georgia politicians support a lawsuit against their own state, according to Rep. Doug Collins, R-Ga. on Newsmax TV.

"There's been so much concern about the election security and election integrity here in Georgia and other places that the suit is going forward and it gets it to the Supreme Court and, as the president said, brings it into one final push," Collins told host Grant Stinchfield on Thursday's Stinchfield.

"This is an original jurisdiction case for the Supreme Court. That means it's not like other Supreme Court cases that they hear. They are actually acting as a trial court, so they can look at evidence. They're not determining if something was done wrong in a lower court, they're actually the arbiters of the original jurisdiction here. We'll see It's an uphill battle."

Earlier, Georgia State Senator William Ligon told Stinchfield 15 fellow state senators and 12 state representatives joined together to support the lawsuit filed by Texas Attorney General Ken Paxton against four battleground states, including Georgia, lost by President Donald Trump.

Paxton claims election results were inaccurate due to unconstitutional and late changes to the election process.

"In Georgia, we've got to have some clarity and some more push down here because what we saw has left a lot of people really concerned about what could happen on Jan. 5," said Collins, citing the date of the US Senate runoff elections. "That's the biggest issue we have in the country right now."

Collins also was asked why Georgia Secretary of State Brad Raffensperger refused to order verification of signatures from the November election.

"They're trying so hard to say nothing was wrong down here. Now let's think about this, there was a run election, the vast majority of the counts were fine," Collins said. "Right now, he has over 258 investigations going on out of his own office. The [Georgia Bureau of Investigation] and the governor has ordered that law enforcement can look into this – I want to see more of this."

States Assail 'Bogus' Texas Bid to Overturn Election Via SCOTUS

BOGUS DEMOCRATS? MORE GUILTY THAN ADOLF HITLER; TOJO; DRACULA; JACK THE RIPPER; CHARLES MANSON JEFFREY DAHMER; JOHN WAYNE GACY; VLAD THE IMPALER; JOHN WILKES BOOTH; LEE HARVEY OSWALD; JUDAS & OSAMA BIN LADEN COMBINED

Georgia, Michigan, Pennsylvania and Wisconsin on Thursday urged the U.S. Supreme Court to reject a lawsuit filed by Texas and backed by President Donald Trump seeking to undo President-elect Joe Biden's election victory, saying the case has no factual or legal grounds and offers "bogus" claims.

"What Texas is doing in this proceeding is to ask this court to reconsider a mass of baseless claims about problems with the election that have already been considered, and rejected, by this court and other ROTTEN-TO-THE-CORE FRAUDULENT COURTS; ALL OF THESE JUDICIARIES SHOULD BE DISMEMBERED WHILE ALIVE INTO SMALL PIECES BY THE SWORD OF SOLOMON; WHO SAVED THE BABY.**," Josh Shapiro, Pennsylvania's Democratic attorney general, wrote in a filing to the nine justices.**

Texas filed the long-shot suit against the four election battleground states on Tuesday directly with the Supreme Court. It asked that the voting results in those states be thrown out because of their changes in voting procedures that allowed expanded mail-in voting during the coronavirus pandemic.

Trump's campaign and his allies already have been spurned in numerous lawsuits in state and federal courts challenging the election results. Legal experts have said the Texas lawsuit has little chance of succeeding and have questioned whether Texas has the legal standing to challenge election procedures in other states. Biden, a Democrat, defeated Trump in the four states in the Nov. 3 election. The Republican president won them in the 2016 election.

The Texas lawsuit, Shapiro wrote, was adding to a "cacophony of bogus false claims" about the election.

Trump has claimed he won re-election and has made allegations of widespread voting fraud. State election officials have said they have found no evidence of such fraud.

Dana Nessel, Michigan's Democratic attorney general, listed the many cases filed in that state that Trump and his backers have lost.

"The challenge here is an unprecedented one, without factual foundation or a valid legal basis," Nessel wrote in Michigan's filing.

Chris Carr, Georgia's Republican attorney general, said Texas cannot show it has been harmed by the election results in other states.

"The novel and far-reaching claims that Texas asserts, and the breathtaking remedies it seeks, are impossible to ground in legal principles and unmanageable," Carr wrote in Georgia's filing.

Josh Kaul, Wisconsin's Democratic attorney general, noted that Trump already had obtained recounts in the two most heavily Democratic counties in the state, showing no problems with the results.

"There has been no indication of any fraud, or anything else that would call into question the reliability of the election results," Kaul wrote in Wisconsin's filing.

TRUMP MEETS TEXAS OFFICIAL

Trump filed a motion with the court on Wednesday asking the justices to let him intervene and become a plaintiff in the suit filed by Ken Paxton, the Republican attorney general of Texas and an ally of the president. Trump met on Thursday with Paxton and other state attorneys general who support the suit.

Twenty states joined the District of Columbia in filing a brief lodged by Democratic officials on Thursday backing the four states targeted by Texas. Seventeen other states on Wednesday filed a brief urging the justices to hear the case in filings by Republican officials. Arizona filed its own brief signaling an interest in the case without explicitly taking sides.

More than 100 U.S. House of Representatives Republicans led by Mike Johnson of Louisiana also filed a brief backing Trump. "The Supreme Court has a chance to save our Country from the greatest Election abuse in the history of the United States," Trump wrote on Twitter on Thursday, repeating his unfounded allegations that the election was rigged against him.

The Texas lawsuit does not make specific fraud allegations. Instead, Texas said changes to voting procedures removed protections against fraud and were unlawful when the reforms were made by officials in the four states or courts without the approval of the states' legislatures.

Democrats and other critics have accused Trump of aiming to reduce public confidence in U.S. election integrity and undermine democracy by trying to subvert the will of the voters.

One Republican state attorney general, Dave Yost of Ohio, filed a separate brief on Thursday disagreeing with the Texas proposal that votes be tossed out, saying that it "would undermine a foundational premise of our federalist system: the idea that the States are sovereigns, free to govern themselves."

Texas asked the Supreme Court to immediately block the four states from using the voting results to appoint presidential electors to the Electoral College and allow their state legislatures to name the electors rather than having the electors reflect the will of the voters. All four of the targeted states have Republican-led legislatures.

Biden has amassed 306 electoral votes - exceeding the necessary 270 - compared to Trump's 232 in the state-by-state Electoral College that determines the election's outcome. The four states contribute 62 electoral votes to Biden's total.

Pa. Lawmakers File Brief With Supreme Court Supporting Texas Case

By Brian Trusdell

JUST LIKE GEORGIA; PENNSYLVANIA REPUBLICANS SUE STATE IN THE SUPREME COURT

Republican lawmakers in the Pennsylvania state legislature have filed a document with the U.S. Supreme

Court supporting Texas' lawsuit looking to invalidate the election results in the Keystone state as well as Wisconsin, Georgia, and Michigan. The amicus brief blasted the Pennsylvania Supreme Court for "offering extrajudicial guidance to the Commonwealth's county boards of elections. These efforts were condoned and furthered by the overreaching of Pennsylvania's Supreme Court, in clear violation of the requirements of the U.S. Constitution." Texas' lawsuit was the latest in a series of court challenges filed by President Donald Trump and allies seeking to void the election results. While many of the other suits have claimed fraud and other irregularities in six states, the four named as well as Nevada and Arizona, the Texas suit is a constitutional challenge against actions by executive officials and courts, who it says unilaterally altered state laws intended to prevent fraud and thus disenfranchised voters in Texas.

DEFUND THE POLICE ACT 2 SCENE 1

HIDEKI TOTO FILED A BRIEF WITH THE HAGUE WORLD COURT DEFUNDING HANGMAN'S ROPE. JULIUS & ETHEL ROSENBERG FILED A BRIEF WITH CON EDISON CUTTING OFF ELECTRICAL POWER AT SING SING.

Two Brothers Arrested in Connection with Killing of Louisiana Gas Station Clerk

Katherine Rodriguez

Authorities say two NOW BORN AGAIN FOLLOWERS OF JESUS brothers have been arrested in connection with an armed robbery and fatal shooting of a Louisiana gas station clerk who was on his knees when he gave the money from the cash register to the suspects. The U.S. Marshals Service arrested Lamonte Loggins on Tuesday and Eric Rodgers on Wednesday in Memphis, Tennessee, in connection with the killing of Ab El Ghader Sylla, 30, in Kenner, Louisiana, on November 30, WWLTV reported.

Authorities charged Loggins with first-degree murder and charged Rodgers with second-degree murder and armed robbery. Both suspects are awaiting extradition to Louisiana.

Investigators say Sylla was tending to the store on November 30 when two men came in, forced him to hand over $100, and ordered him on his knees. One suspect was keeping an eye on the door while the other took out the gun. But instead of taking the cash and leaving, they allegedly fired the gun at Sylla. Sylla was able to call out for help and was transported to the hospital, but he eventually succumbed to his injuries and died.

DEMOCRATS DESERVE A BREAK TODAY

Dan Crenshaw says AOC exemplifies the 'worst stereotypes of the millennial generation' after latest outburst of 'victimhood'

"It really is about elevating that victimhood as a virtue"

Carlos Garcia

Republican Rep. Dan Crenshaw of Texas issued a fiery response to Rep. Alexandria Ocasio-Cortez (D-N.Y.) after she accused Republicans of mocking her background as a waitress. The latest feud was sparked when Ocasio-Cortez compared her previous job as a waitress and bartender to her conservative congressional colleagues who she characterized as sitting on chairs all day.

"The thing that these conservative Senators don't seem to understand is that I've actually had a physically difficult working-class job without good healthcare most of my adult life. I bring that work ethic to Congress & to my community. They sit around on leather chairs all day," she tweeted. When some pushed back on her sweeping generalization, she added another missive complaining that her critics mock her for her bartending experience. "Republicans like to make fun of the fact that I used to be a waitress, but we all know if they ever had to do a double they'd be the ones found crying in the walk-in fridge halfway through their first shift bc someone yelled at them for bringing seltzer when they wanted sparkling," she mocked.

"Victimhood as a virtue"

Crenshaw took aim at the comments while being interviewed by Megyn Kelly on her podcast Thursday. "There's multiple members of Congress, on the Republican side, missing body parts. To say that we just don't know hardship — and there's multiple businesses, multiple people that have real-life experiences, and for

you to just dismiss that, it just shows how out of touch she is truly and how insulting she is all the time," said Crenshaw.

Crenshaw himself is a former Navy SEAL who lost his eye while serving his third deployment in Afghanistan.

"And that playing the victim thing, she really embodies sort of the worst stereotypes of the millennial generation. And it gives us a bad name, and I wish she'd stop," he continued. "It really is about elevating that victimhood as a virtue," Crenshaw concluded.

Missouri, 5 more states ask to join Texas Supreme Court election case against Georgia, others

By Tyler Olson

Missouri and five other states on Thursday threw their support even further behind the Texas lawsuit aiming to prevent Georgia, Pennsylvania, Michigan and Wisconsin's electors from casting their electoral votes by asking the Supreme Court to let them join the Texas suit. Missouri on Wednesday led a group of 17 states in filing a brief that supported the Texas lawsuit, which alleges that the four key swing states that voted for President-elect Joe Biden violated the Constitution by having their judicial and executive branches make changes to their presidential elections rather than their legislatures.

But the Thursday filing led by Missouri Attorney General Eric Schmitt, which also includes Arkansas, Utah, Louisiana, Mississippi and South Carolina, would make those states parties before the court in the case rather than just outside voices weighing in. President Trump's campaign did the same on Wednesday. "The intervening states do not doubt that plaintiff state of Texas will vigorously and effectively litigate this case, but the attorney general of each individual state is best situated to represent the interests of that state and its people," the six states said in their request.

Missouri Attorney General Eric Schmitt is leading a coalition of six states seeking to join Texas' suit aiming to prevent four states' presidential electors from casting their votes.

MISSOURI, 16 OTHER STATES FILE BRIEF SUPPORTING TEXAS SUIT TO DELAY PRESIDENTIAL ELECTOR APPOINTMENT

The states led by Missouri on Thursday also said they back the arguments so far made to the court by Texas and the president's campaign, which have argued that not only are the actions taken by Georgia, Pennsylvania, Wisconsin and Michigan unconstitutional, but they also open up the potential for widespread voter fraud. "All the unconstitutional changes to election procedures identified in the Bill of Complaint have two common features: (1) They abrogated statutory safeguards against fraud that responsible observers have long recommended for voting by mail, and (2) they did so in a way that predictably conferred partisan advantage on one candidate in the presidential election," the Missouri brief from Wednesday, which was joined by 16 other states, said.

It continued: "When non-legislative actors in other states encroach on the authority of the 'Legislature thereof' in that state to administer a presidential election, they threaten the liberty, not just of their own citizens, but of every citizen of the United States who casts a lawful ballot in that election – including the citizens of amici states."

The Texas suit is unique in that it seeks to take advantage of the Supreme Court's rarely used original jurisdiction for cases in which states sue other states. Despite the backing of so many state attorneys general, most legal experts say the Texas suit is fatally flawed in several ways and nearly certain to fail.

"This is political posturing through litigation. Not one of those attorneys general believes they are entitled to win," Harvard Law professor Lawrence Lessig told Fox News. Lessig is a former clerk for the late Justice Antonin Scalia and currently works with Equal Votes, a nonprofit that seeks to end winner-take-all allocation of electoral votes in states. This is political posturing through litigation. Not one of those attorneys general believes they are entitled to win

— Harvard Law professor Lawrence Lessig

SENATE JUDICIARY COMMITTEE ADVANCES AMY CONEY BARRETT REPLACEMENT ON 7TH CIRCUIT TO FLOOR OVER DEM OPPOSITION

Lessig continued: "As lawyers, that should stop them from signing onto such an action. But they are acting as politicians, not lawyers here – to the detriment of the rule of law."

Walter Olson, a senior fellow at the libertarian Cato Institute, said the only question at this point is the manner in which the Supreme Court will hand Texas a loss in the case.

"This set of lawsuits has met with rejection, so far as I know, from every single federal judge to have ruled on them," Olson said. "The Supreme Court will reject this one too, and the only real question is whether it will do so through orders declining even to hear the case (which is what I predict) or by taking up the case and promptly dismissing on the merits."

Ilya Shapiro, the director of the Robert A. Levy Center for Constitutional Studies at the Cato Institute, pointed out that Texas Solicitor General Kyle Hawkins, the person who would normally be leading his state's litigation, has not worked on the suit.

"[It is] basically a political maneuver more than a real legal lawsuit," Shapiro said. "There's a reason why the Texas solicitor general's name isn't on the case."

Among the several reasons why the Texas lawsuit is all but certain to fall flat is its timing after the election. A principle called "laches," Olson said, "doomed the suit that tried to throw out Pennsylvania's mail-in votes, so it dooms this claim."

Ken Paxton, Texas attorney general, speaks during a news conference outside the Supreme Court in Washington, D.C., U.S., on Monday, Sept. 9, 2019. Paxton is leading his state in a lawsuit aiming to prevent presidential electors from four states from voting, without the backing of his own solicitor general.

TRUMP TOUTS TEXAS SUPREME COURT CASE AS 'THE BIG ONE,' SAYS 'WE WILL BE INTERVENING'

He said a party cannot bring a case that could have been addressed in an orderly fashion before "at exactly the time most disruptive and prejudicial to the rights of third parties (such as, in this case, innocent voters who relied on their states' approved methods)."

There is also the fact the "safe-harbor" day for elector selection has already passed, which Olson says harms Texas' case too.

"Standing," or whether a party is permitted to bring a suit in a certain case, also goes against Texas, according to Lessig.

"Not without a radical (and hence, certain to be perceived a politically motivated) change in standing doctrine," will the Supreme Court say that Texas and the other states may sue.

And on the merits of the case specifically, Olson says, Texas would also lose because "the imagined 'rule' is universally ignored since states have in fact allowed their governors, judiciaries or both to make rulings and determinations affecting the manner in which presidential elections are held and electors thus chosen."

"Texas has done this too," Olson added.

Also of note Thursday is that Ohio, a state with a Republican attorney general in David Yost, filed a brief in support of neither Texas nor the defendant states Georgia, Pennsylvania, Michigan and Wisconsin.

"Although Ohio does not endorse Texas's proposed relief, it does endorse its call for a ruling on the meaning of the electors clause," its brief says, mentioning that such a ruling would clear up controversies for future elections. "Ohio urges the court to decide, at the earliest available opportunity, whether state courts and state executive actors violate the electors clause when they change the rules by which presidential elections are run."

Shapiro also said he believes it could be positive if the Supreme Court weighs in on the Texas case to quash doubts about this election.

"It might even be good for the country if the Supreme Court took this case and unanimously ruled against the claim because that might provide some closure for the supporters of the president," Shapiro said.

He added, however, that the court will more likely simply decline to hear it because the "weakness" of the Texas case would prevent the court from needing to even go so far as unanimously dismissing it.

Texas AG Paxton Files Election Suit Against 4 Battleground States

By Jeffrey Rodack

Texas Attorney General Ken Paxton filed suit on Tuesday against Georgia, Michigan, Pennsylvania, and Wisconsin, claiming the four states exploited the pandemic to justify ignoring election laws.

In papers filed with the U.S. Supreme Court, Paxton claimed the states unlawfully enacted last-minute changes, which skewed the results of the general election.

The papers also allege that the majority of the rushed decisions, made by local officials, were not approved by the state legislatures, thereby circumventing the Constitution. "The battleground states flooded their people with unlawful ballot applications and ballots while ignoring statutory requirements as to how they were received, evaluated and counted," according to a statement posted on the Texas attorney general's website.

"Trust in the integrity of our election processes is sacrosanct and binds our citizenry and the States in this union together. Georgia, Michigan, Pennsylvania, and Wisconsin destroyed that trust and compromised the

security and integrity of the 2020 election.

"The states violated statutes enacted by their duly elected legislatures, thereby violating the Constitution. By ignoring both state and federal law, these states have not only tainted the integrity of their own citizens' vote, but of Texas and every other state that held lawful elections," said Attorney General Paxton. "Their failure to abide by the rule of law casts a dark shadow of doubt over the outcome of the entire election. We now ask that the Supreme Court step in to correct this egregious error."

In court papers, Paxton claimed "unconstitutional changes opened the door to election irregularities in various forms" and that each of the four states "flagrantly violated constitutional rules governing the appointment of presidential electors."

Ken Paxton to Newsmax TV: 'This Is Our Last Chance By Eric Mack

Bringing an "original jurisdiction" election challenge before the Supreme Court was a duty for Texas Attorney General Ken Paxton to protect his voters in Texas, he said Wednesday on Newsmax TV.

"I am encouraged that these other states have joined, and think there's a recognition that this is our last chance and we are running out of time," Paxton told Wednesday's "Stinchfield**." Paxton noted Texas had already "fought off" 12 lawsuits under his leadership in defending Texas' election against the unconstitutional election actions taken in the four battleground states in his lawsuit, including mass mail-in ballot attempts and signature verification restrictions proposed by Democrats.**

"We were successful in maintaining our legislative stance, so my voters were protected," Paxton told host Grant Stinchfield. "But this is a national election and the fact this happened in other states has the impact of disenfranchising my voters, given that we had elections that were fair and by the law."

Paxton's case before the U.S. Supreme Court **is called Texas v. Pennsylvania, but it includes key battlegrounds Michigan, Wisconsin, and Georgia. He laments the "stunning" lack of "common sense" of unconstitutionally changing state election law without proper due process in the legislatures. "That's why so many Americans are frustrated, because you've got these courts of supposedly smart people as judges and it's almost common sense from the night of the election," Paxton said.**

Calling his case "one of the most important issues of our time," Paxton said it is not just about deciding this presidential election, but all elections in the future. "Not just for this election, but the future of our country and the future elections we either can trust or we can't trust," he concluded.He asked the court to restrain the states from voting in the electoral college until it hears arguments in the case. 17 States Join Texas Election Suit Amid Trump Pledge to Intervene in Case

Donald Trump said his campaign would seek to join a bid by Texas to challenge the president's election defeat at the U.S. Supreme Court. Now, 17 other states have filed in support of the case, which allies call the

culmination of Trump's legal challenges and critics dismiss as a publicity stunt.

"This is the big one," Trump tweeted Wednesday morning. Trump must petition the Supreme Court to be allowed to intervene.

Seventeen other states filed a brief in support of the Texas suit, brought by the state's scandal-plagued attorney general, Ken Paxton. Texas is seeking to prevent electors from Michigan, Georgia, Wisconsin and Pennsylvania from participating in the Electoral College on Dec. 14.

The Supreme Court on Tuesday evening gave the states until 3 p.m. Thursday to file responses.

Paxton's case repeats allegations about mail-in voting that have already been roundly rejected in dozens of courts across the nation.

The Texas suit was filed on the same day as the Dec. 8 "safe harbor" date for states to certify their slates of electors to send to the Electoral College. The passing of that deadline means time is short for Trump's effort to overturn his re-election defeat, in which he's sought to pressure state legislatures to override voters and appoint alternative electors who would back him instead of Joe Biden.

In addition to Missouri, the states joining Texas were: Alabama, Arkansas, Florida, Indiana, Kansas, Louisiana, Mississippi, Montana, Nebraska, North Dakota, Oklahoma, South Carolina, South Dakota, Tennessee, Utah and West Virginia. All of the states were represented by Republican officials in the filing. All but three of the states have Republican governors.

Trump also said that his campaign hadn't been part of a separate case, brought by a Pennsylvania Congressman, that the Supreme Court rebuffed on Tuesday -- the first time the high court has weighed in on Republican litigation to try to overturn the election outcome.

"This was not my case as has been so incorrectly reported," Trump wrote in a second tweet on Wednesday.

In a one-sentence order, the court said Tuesday that it would not grant a request from plaintiffs including Rep. Mike Kelly to void Pennsylvania's election results.

Trump Warned Georgia AG Against Push Back on Texas Lawsuit

By Theodore Bunker

President Donald Trump earlier this week called Georgia Attorney General Chris Carr to warn him not to rally Republicans against the lawsuit filed by Texas over the 2020 presidential election, the Atlanta Journal-Constitution reports. In a "cordial" 15-minute phone call on Tuesday, according to the newspaper's sources, Trump told Carr that he's "heard great things" about the attorney general, but said he'd heard Carr was trying to rally other Republicans against the lawsuit, which Carr denied. The call occurred after Trump talked to the state's two Republican senators, but before the senators issued a joint statement saying that they "fully support" the lawsuit.

The Journal-Constitution notes that earlier on Tuesday, before the phone call, Carr's office had referred to the Texas lawsuit as "constitutionally, legally and factually wrong."

Georgia Deputy Secretary of State Jordan Fuchs dismissed the lawsuit as spreading "false and irresponsible" theories. "Texas alleges that there are 80,000 forged signatures on absentee ballots in Georgia, but they don't bring forward a single person who this happened to," she said. "That's because it didn't happen."

Records Still Not Available for 500,000 Georgia Absentee Ballots

A polling worker holds 2020 presidential primary ballots that were dropped at a post office and brought to a government center to be processed and counted in Hartford, Connecticut. (

By Jeffrey Rodack

Documents necessary to establish the chain of custody for more than 83% of the estimated 600,000 Georgia absentee ballots placed in drop boxes by voters and subsequently delivered to local election officials still have not been produced by state or county officials.

The Georgia Star News **noted that the Georgia Election Code Emergency Rule mandates that every county is responsible for documenting the transfer of absentee ballots picked up at drop boxes.**

The digital newspaper had sent out an Open Records Request for the ballot transfer forms to 77 of Georgia's

159 counties. Bartow, Cobb, Clarke, and Cook counties provided the transfer forms.

And the Star News noted a preliminary review of the forms provided by Cobb County indicated there were problems documenting the chain of custody.

The four counties had accounted for about 100,000 of the estimated 600,000 absentee ballots placed in drop boxes — or about 16.6%.

Ten counties told the newspaper they did not have drop boxes. Sixty counties did not respond to the paper's request.

Other counties were either investigating whether such records existed or told the paper they would make the information available at a later date.

The newspaper said it appears that state officials do not plan to take any actions to avoid a repeat of chain of custody questions for absentee ballots placed in drop boxes ahead of the Jan. 5 Senate runoffs.

Georgia is one of four states being sued by Texas Attorney General Ken Paxton. The suit, filed with the U.S. Supreme Court, claims the states exploited the pandemic to justify ignoring election laws.

Fla. AG Moody: Supreme Court Should Review Texas Motion

By Surya Gowda

Florida Attorney General Ashley Moody

Florida Attorney General Ashley Moody is supporting Texas in its lawsuit filed with the Supreme Court, which aims to block four battleground states that certified Democrat Joe Biden as their election winner from voting in the Electoral College until the court hears arguments in the case.

"The integrity and resolution of the 2020 election is of paramount importance," wrote Moody on Wednesday, CBS Miami reports. "The United States Supreme Court should weigh the legal arguments of the Texas motion and all pending matters so that Americans can be assured the election was fairly reviewed and decided."

In joining a friend-of-the-court brief backing Texas, Florida accompanies Missouri, Alabama, Arkansas, Indiana, Kansas, Louisiana, Mississippi, Montana, Nebraska, North Dakota, Oklahoma, South Carolina, South Dakota, Tennessee, Utah, and West Virginia. The Texas lawsuit, filed by the state's Attorney General Ken Paxton, claims Georgia, Michigan, Pennsylvania, and Wisconsin "exploited the COVID-19 pandemic to justify ignoring federal and state election laws and unlawfully enacting last-minute changes, thus skewing the results of the 2020 General Election." Governor Ron DeSantis and other Florida Republicans have supported moves to contest election results in key states. Moody previously added Florida to a brief that hoped to get the Supreme Court to overturn a ruling that let some late-arriving absentee ballots be counted in Pennsylvania, according to CBS Miami. But Democrats in the state, including Agriculture Commissioner Nikki Fried, slammed Moody's actions. "It's embarrassing to the integrity of our democracy and resolution of this election," Fried, who serves in the state Cabinet, said.

Paxton has claimed his lawsuit is a bid to protect election integrity. "If other states don't follow the Constitution and if their state legislature isn't responsible for overseeing their elections ... it affects my state," he said Tuesday.

AG Paxton: Texas Lawsuit Not Hoping to Put 'Genie Back in the Bottle'

Texas Attorney General Ken Paxton

By Sandy Fitzgerald

Texas isn't expecting the four states it's suing over the November election to "put the genie back in the bottle," but it hopes the Supreme Court will agree that their legislatures should pick electors who will, in turn, choose the next president, state Attorney General Ken Paxton said Thursday.

"In my state, we were able to protect the system as legislature set it up," Paxton told Fox Business' Maria Bartiromo on "Mornings With Maria." "We didn't let the genie out of the bottle. We can verify results did it the way legislature intended."

But in the states Texas has sued — Pennsylvania, Wisconsin, Michigan, and Georgia — that hasn't happened, said Paxton. "There is no way to go back and look at 2.5 million ballots in Pennsylvania to know whether there was fraud, so that remedy is virtually impossible, if not impossible," said Paxton. "We are asking the court put [the election] back in the hands of the state legislature to pick their own electors, as it's been done for years by certain state legislatures."

Paxton will be at the White House for a lunch with President Donald Trump, along with a dozen other GOP state attorneys general, reports The Houston Chronicle. Ten of them have backed the Texas election challenge. The White House says the meeting was scheduled weeks ago and that it is closed to the press.

Paxton told Bartiromo Thursday morning that the genesis for his lawsuits came because it "seemed wrong to us" that voters in Texas were "disenfranchised" in the national election because the other states "didn't follow state law." "A lot of those states eliminated signature verification, which is the only check you have on the credibility of those ballots," said Paxton.

The attorneys general of 17 states where Trump won filed an amicus brief on Wednesday to join in Texas' efforts, including Missouri, Alabama, Arkansas, Florida, Indiana, Kansas, Louisiana, Mississippi, Montana, Nebraska, North Dakota, Oklahoma, South Carolina, South Dakota, Tennessee, Utah, and West Virginia. Arizona GOP Attorney General Mark Brnovich has filed a separate brief to support the case.

Paxton said it's a good question whether or not the Supreme Court will take up the case after so many other states have joined in. But if it won't hear the case, there is no place else the states can go for recourse.

The case is important not only because of Trump and Joe Biden, said Paxton, but because of future elections in the United States. "I want to make sure the right person is elected based on what voters did in the country," he said. "Otherwise, we can't trust elections going forward. That is a real problem for democracy."

Hollywood actor Kumail Nanjiani bashes male Trump supporters, says 'traditional masculinity is a disease' THIS PERSON SHOULD BE RECLASSIFIED AS A COCKROACH & EXTERMINATED

The comment ignited a wave of backlash

Hollywood actor Kumail Nanjiani drew thousands of responses on Twitter after declaring that "traditional masculinity is a disease." The critique, which was seen as inflammatory by many, was a response to a tweet regarding President Donald Trump's popularity with men in the 2020 election.

Amelia Thomson-DeVeaux, a senior writer at FiveThirtyEight, promoted one of her articles in a tweet captioned: "Why did so many men stick with Trump in 2020? The COVID-19 pandemic may have given him a way to reach more masculine men. Many of those men actually liked Trump's 'shrug it off' approach."

Nanjiani retweeted the post about men who voted for Trump and added his own commentary that appeared to be an insult to male Trump supporters. The tweet read, "Traditional masculinity is a disease."

Nanjiani did not expound on his belief that "traditional masculinity is a disease." The vague statement was immediately met with a wave of backlash.

Gad Saad, an evolutionary psychologist and professor in the John Molson School of Business at Concordia University, simply asked, "Is traditional femininity also a disease or is it a virtue?" Former NFL player Cory Procter astutely replied, "Masculinity is a power to be harnessed. Not suppressed."

One reaction on Twitter that garnered more than 3,500 "Likes" stated, "Traditional masculinity is what brought men out from primitive status. Traditional masculinity means men willing to lay down their lives for the right cause. It means doing hard things because they are right. It means being a loving father, standing against evil. Being a shield for the innocent. It means taking the hit, and to keep on standing. Being a man means original thought, the spirit of discovery and adventure. Challenging preconceived notions while staying rooted enough for a stable future. Rolling over. Denigrating yourself to blind."

Many internet commentators pointed out that Nanjiani seemed to take great pride in getting a chiseled, "masculine" body last December for his role in the Marvel superhero movie "The Eternals," where he played Kingo, a 16th-century Samurai warrior.

Nanjiani gleefully posted a shirtless photo of himself with his new physique on Instagram. He admitted the photo of his new body was to grab attention and said, "I never thought I'd be one of those people who would post a thirsty shirtless, but I've worked way too hard for way too long so here we are."

"I found out a year ago I was going to be in Marvel's Eternals and decided I wanted to transform how I looked," Nanjiani said. One commenter noted that Nanjiani and his fellow cast members on the HBO TV show "Silicon Valley" were on the March 2018 cover of the Hollywood Reporter magazine with the headline: "Triumph of the Beta Male."

In July 2019, Nanjiani spoke out against traditional masculinity in an interview with the Hollywood Reporter. "I feel like we're in a time where we can talk about masculinity and how it's always been very traditionally defined in a narrow way and how that's led to problems for everyone — for women and for men," Nanjiani said during a press blitz for one of his movies. Nanjiani is a fervent activist for the Democratic Party. The actor, along with other celebrities, started Win Both Seats, an organization supporting the Democratic Senate candidates in the upcoming Georgia runoff election.

On Wednesday, Nanjiani issued a dire-sounding warning to his 3 million Twitter followers and instructed them to vote for Democratic Senate candidate Raphael Warnock. "The soul of our democracy is at stake. #VoteWarnock to save the Senate."

Trump Asks Sen. Cruz to Argue Texas Supreme Court Election Case

Sen. Ted Cruz, R-Texas. By Solange Reyner

President Donald Trump has asked Texas Sen. Ted Cruz to argue the state's Supreme Court case seeking to overturn the results of the election, reports The New York Times.

The state of Texas is suing four swing states that certified wins for Joe Biden.

Attorney General Ken Paxton in the suit filed earlier this week argued that a handful of battleground states destroyed the integrity of the 2020 election vote totals and insists the U.S. Constitution was violated by allowing their legislatures to make last-minute changes that ignored federal electoral regulations.

Cruz on Monday offered to present before the Supreme Court the merits of a lawsuit filed by Rep. Mike Kelly claiming Pennsylvania's 2019 voting reform bill is unconstitutional.

Good morning. The U.S. gets closer to vaccines. And dozens of Republicans join the campaign to overturn the election.

Supporters of President Trump in Lansing, Mich., on Tuesday.Emily Elconin/Reuters

THE TIMES DEFINES TRUTH AS FALSE
Falsehoods and threats

President Trump's attempts to overturn the election result are very unlikely to succeed. For that reason, the effort can sometimes seem like a publicity stunt — an effort by Trump to raise money and burnish his image with his supporters.

And it may well be all of those things. But it is also a remarkable campaign against American democracy. It has grown to include most Republican-run states, most Republican members of Congress and numerous threats of violence. I want to use today's newsletter to explain it.

The new centerpiece in the effort is a lawsuit that the state of Texas filed this week with the Supreme Court and that Trump supports. It claims that the election in four swing states — Georgia, Michigan, Pennsylvania and Wisconsin — suffered from "unconstitutional irregularities."

The suit is based on the same lies that Trump has been telling about voter fraud. In reality, there was no meaningful fraud, as local officials from both parties have concluded. William Barr, Trump's attorney general, came to the same conclusion.

Nonetheless, the attorneys general of 17 states — including Florida, South Carolina, Tennessee, Indiana, Utah, Arizona and the Dakotas — have backed the Texas lawsuit. Yesterday, more than half of House Republicans released a legal brief supporting it. "If they get their way in court (they won't), they would break the country," David French of The Dispatch, a conservative publication, wrote.

They are doing so, as my colleagues Jeremy Peters and Maggie Haberman have explained, largely because they believe that defying Trump would damage their standing with Republican voters. By doing so, the politicians are "inflaming the public," French noted, causing many voters to believe — wrongly — that a

presidential election was unfair. And that belief is fueling an outbreak of violent threats against elections officials, including:

- **Dozens of Trump supporters, some armed, went to the home of Jocelyn Benson, Michigan's Democratic secretary of state, and began shouting obscenities.**
- **On Twitter, Trump supporters have posted photographs of the home of Ann Jacobs, a Wisconsin official, and mentioned her children.**
- **In Phoenix, about 100 Trump supporters, some armed, protested at the building where officials were counting votes.**
- **In Vermont, officials received a voice message threatening them with "execution by firing squad."**
- **Seth Bluestein, a Philadelphia official, received anti-Semitic and violent threats after Pam Bondi, a Trump ally, publicly mentioned him.**
- **A Georgia poll worker went into hiding after a viral video falsely claimed he had discarded ballots.**
- **Brad Raffensperger, Georgia's Republican secretary of state, and his wife have received death threats, including by text message, and caravans have circled their house.**
- **Gabriel Sterling, another Georgia official, received a message wishing him a happy birthday and saying it would be his last.**

In a later interview with Time magazine, Sterling argued that elected politicians could defuse the threats by acknowledging that the election was fair. "Leadership is supposed to look like grown-ups in the room saying, 'I know you're upset, but this is the reality,'" Sterling said.

A swing state responds: In a Supreme Court filing, Pennsylvania called the Texas lawsuit part of a "cacophony of bogus claims," a "seditious abuse of the judicial process" and "an affront to principles of constitutional democracy."

Rep. Mike Kelly to Newsmax TV: Trump Team Must 'Play to the Whistle'

FOR IMMEDIATE RELEASE

CONTACT: Jessica Proud (914) 438-5325

Statement from NYGOP Chairman Nick Langworthy Opposing Governor Cuomo and Democrats' Plan to Raise Taxes and Fees on New Yorkers

December 10, 2020

"New York is on the edge of a cliff and a Cuomo tax increase will be the final shove that seals our fate. New York's fiscal problems have not come from a lack of revenue--they are the result of Democrats' tax and spend policies that have driven millions of jobs and New Yorkers to other states.

"A tax on the so-called wealthy, aka our revenue generators, will accelerate the exodus of our critical financial industry and the legislature's proposed package delivery fee is a regressive tax that hits the working and middle class the hardest. "Federal aid to deal directly with the covid emergency is necessary and fair, but it's not the solution to cover up years of bad fiscal policies that made New York the highest taxed, least-business friendly climate in the nation. Neither is taking more money from overburdened New Yorkers. "The Republican Party will fight these proposals every step of the way and hold Cuomo accountable for the destruction of our state."

By Brian Trusdell

Pennsylvania GOP Rep. Mike Kelly said his challenge to election results in his state is not over despite being denied an emergency order by the U.S. Supreme Court to stop Pennsylvania officials from certifying its elections results, saying he would – and implored President Donald Trump and his supporters – to "play to the whistle."

"All that happened is we were not granted temporary injunctive relief," Kelly said on Newsmax TV's "Greg Kelly Reports" on Wednesday. "The case is still alive and well. And we are looking, how do we get the court to take on the case for its merits of being constitutional or unconstitutional. That's all we're looking at. That's a huge ask by the way. But we are in the midst of a constitutional crisis right now in our country, and we have to get answers, and we have to get it from the highest court in the land."

Kelly's remarks came a day after the Supreme Court denied the request by Kelly, 2020 U.S. congressional candidate Sean Parnell and former state representative candidate Wanda Logan. who asked the Supreme Court to prevent state officials "from taking any further action to perfect the certification of the results."

Their case was based on the fact that the Pennsylvania legislature last fall passed a law that allowed for absentee ballots to be obtained without a justification in contravention of the state's constitution.

Another case has been put forth to the Supreme Court by Texas, and joined by 17 other states, to prevent Pennsylvania as well as Michigan, Georgia and Wisconsin from participating in the Electoral College. "What we do now is we petition the court to hear (our) case. It's called cert," Kelly said. "That's what we're asking the court to do. Hear the lawsuit based on its merits. That's all we're asking: constitutional, unconstitutional. Then make a decision afterwards of what are those findings and what are the remedies.

"Play up to the whistle. Play up to the echo of the whistle."

Jordan Sekulow to Newsmax TV: Texas' SCOTUS Case 'Be-All, End-All'

By Eric Mack

Texas Attorney General Ken Paxton's lawsuit filed with the U.S. Supreme Court is the "be-all, end-all case" for President Donald Trump's ongoing and long-running election challenge, Trump lawyer Jordan Sekulow

said Tuesday on Newsmax TV. "The Supreme Court is not just considering what Texas has filed [Tuesday], they are now going the next step, which is to say, 'We want a response from the states named,'" Sekulow told Tuesday's "Stinchfield," referring to four battleground states Pennsylvania, Georgia, Michigan, and Wisconsin.

"This is the case we've been talking about to reach SCOTUS. This is the outcome-determinative case, 62 electoral college votes, enough to change the outcome of the election."

The Supreme Court, in a case of "original jurisdiction," Sekulow said, will weigh the lawsuit's proposed remedy of the four state legislatures seating new electors, because the "electors clause" was violated, along with "due process" and "equal protection."

"These are all constitutional challenges that Texas is bringing," Sekulow added in his interview with host Grant Stinchfield.

"It's specifically going at the heart of constitutional challenges."

The four states above have until Thursday at 3 p.m. ET to "actively respond" to election fraud allegations in AG Paxton's bill of complaint. Sekulow noted all the other cases brought before – regardless of their lack of success in courts – are included and germane to Paxton's case, labeled Texas vs. Pennsylvania at the Supreme Court.

"I think for the Newsmax audience, they need to understand this is the be-all, end-all case to really determine the outcome of this election," Sekulow said. "This is the major challenge, the one we were waiting for.

"That's different than most court cases at the Supreme Court, because this is a case of original jurisdiction . . . because it is state versus state."

Stinchfield noted Louisiana is signing on to Texas' complaint, and Sekulow added more states likely will, too.

In papers filed with the U.S. Supreme Court, Paxton claimed the states unlawfully enacted last-minute changes, which skewed the results of the general election.

The papers also allege the majority of the rushed decisions, made by local officials, were not approved by the state legislatures, thereby circumventing the Constitution.

"The battleground states flooded their people with unlawful ballot applications and ballots while ignoring statutory requirements as to how they were received, evaluated, and counted," read a statement posted on the Texas attorney general's website.

Texas AG Paxton: Election Lawsuit a Bid to Protect Integrity, Constitution

Texas Attorney General Ken Paxton By Sandy Fitzgerald

Texas Attorney General Ken Paxton says his lawsuit filed with the Supreme Court against the states of Georgia, Michigan, Pennsylvania, and Wisconsin is a bid to protect election integrity and abide by the Constitution.

"If other states don't follow the Constitution and if their state legislature isn't responsible for overseeing their elections ... it affects my state," Paxton told Fox News' Sean Hannity Tuesday night. "Our job is to make sure the Constitution is followed and that every vote counts, and in this case, I'm not sure every vote was counted. Not in the right way." In Paxton's lawsuit, the attorney general claims the four states exploited the coronavirus pandemic to justify ignoring election laws and unlawfully enacted last-minute changes that skewed the election results. The lawsuit also claims that most of the quick decisions that were made by local officials had not been approved by state legislatures and circumvented the Constitution.

The states have until Thursday to respond to the lawsuit. Paxton told Hannity that the lawsuit came from recognizing that the other states' election management directly impacted Texas. His case is based on Article

II of the Constitution that mandates state legislatures have sole authority on election processes, and he says he will prove that was elected during this year's election.

"It is the responsibility of state legislatures, per the Constitution to set the rules for the election of electors," he told Hannity. "Can this be overridden by people who are not responsible under the Constitution for doing this?"

He said he hopes the court will recognize his case.

"Part of the genius of what the founders put in place is making sure that everybody in a state was at least treated the same," he said. "We have county by county distinctions that treated voters differently and we, therefore, have unreliable results."

Trump Vows to Intervene in Texas Election Case Before Supreme Court

President Donald Trump on Wednesday vowed to intervene in a case brought by the state of Texas before the U.S. Supreme Court to throw out the voting results in four other states. Trump, writing on Twitter, said: "We will be INTERVENING in the Texas (plus many other states) case. This is the big one. Our Country needs a victory!" He also played down, in a separate tweet, a case filed against Pennsylvania's election results in which the Supreme Court rejected a emergency action:

"This was not my case as has been so incorrectly reported. The case that everyone has been waiting for is the State's case with Texas and numerous others joining. It is very strong, ALL CRITERIA MET. How can you have a presidency when a vast majority think the election was RIGGED?"

It wasn't immediately clear what Trump meant by saying that his team would be "intervening" in the case. He must petition the Supreme Court to be allowed to intervene.

In a string of later tweets, several of which Twitter labeled as "disputed," Trump continued his attack:

- "There is massive evidence of widespread fraud in the four states (plus) mentioned in the Texas suit. Just look at all of the tapes and affidavits!"
- "RIGGED ELECTION!"
- "We will soon be learning about the word 'courage', and saving our Country. I received hundreds of thousands of legal votes more, in all of the Swing States, than did my opponent. ALL Data taken after the vote says that it was impossible for me to lose, unless FIXED!"
- "No candidate has ever won both Florida and Ohio and lost. I won them both, by a lot! #SupremeCourt"
- #OVERTURN

He provided no details on whether it would be his presidential campaign or the U.S. Justice Department that would take action.

Officials from the four states at issue have called the lawsuit a reckless attack on democracy while legal experts gave it little chance to succeed. It was filed directly with the Supreme Court rather than with a lower court, as is permitted for certain litigation between states.

The Texas suit, brought by the state's attorney general, Ken Paxton, seeks to prevent electors from Michigan, Georgia, Wisconsin, and Pennsylvania from participating in the Electoral College on Dec. 14.

Paxton's case repeats allegations about mail-in voting that have been rejected by other courts across the nation.

"The erosion of confidence in our democratic system isn't attributable to the good people of Michigan, Wisconsin, Georgia, or Pennsylvania but rather to partisan officials, like Mr. Paxton, who place loyalty to a person over loyalty to their country," Michigan Attorney General Dana Nessel said in a statement.

The Texas suit was filed on the same day as the Dec. 8 "safe harbor" deadline, set by federal law, for states to certify their slates of electors to send to the Electoral College.

'Make Them Pay': Michigan Democratic State Rep. Cynthia Jones Threatens Trump Supporters

IF GUNS & RELIGION DEPLORABLES CALL THIS UGLY LOATHSOME SCUMBITCH SKANK DISHRAG FOR WHAT SHE IS; WE ARE RACISTS? EXPLAIN WHY WE ALLOW HUMAN COCKROACH LARVA LIKE THIS TOI LIVE AMONG US, MUCH LESS BE ELECTED

Henry Rodgers

Michigan Democratic State Rep. Cynthia Johnson threatened President Donald Trump's supporters in a Facebook live video Tuesday, saying it is a warning message to those who support the president.

In the Facebook live video, Johnson said Trump supporters better be careful, calling on "soldiers" to "make them (Trump supporters) pay." The video was over three minutes long. Johnson took office on January 1, 2019. Her current term ends on December 31, 2020.

"So this is just a warning to you Trumpers. Be careful, walk lightly, we ain't playing with you. Enough of the shenanigans. Enough is enough. And for those of you who are soldiers, you know how to do it. Do it right, be

in order, make them pay," Johnson says in the video. THE FULL FACEBOOK LIVE: "I wish I could be talking to y'all in a private room, because, uh, I just wish I could, but we're public so...," Johnson also said in the video. (RELATED: Kentucky Democratic Rep. Reportedly Arrested In Louisville Riots)

GAG ON WHAT WE GET WITH PAL ZOMBIE BIDEN; COMMENT ON IT JOE

Johnson did not immediately respond to the Daily Caller when asked about the comments in her video.

'White Fragility' Author Robin DiAngelo Was Paid Nearly Two Times More Than Black Counterpart To Speak At Social Justice Event

Marlo Safi

THIS UGLIER THAN DECOMPOSED SKUNK ROADKILL DISHRAG BITCH SKANK IS WHY YOU'RE READING THIS BOOK

Left-wing academic Robin DiAngelo was paid 70% more than her black counterpart during a college event the two spoke at that focused on "racial equity" and disparities, Campus Reform reported.

DiAngelo, who is white and is renowned for coining the term "white fragility," spoke alongside author

Austin Channing Brown at a virtual event hosted by the University of Wisconsin-Madison's Diversity Forum, according to Campus Reform. To speak at the event, titled, "The Pandemic Effect: Exposing Racism & Inequities," DiAngelo was paid $12,750 while Brown was paid $7,500, nearly 40% less than DiAngelo, who charges steep fees for her appearances.

The two were represented by the same agency, which the University told Campus Reform decides the speaking fees. The University also added that the goal of the event, which 3,300 people attended, was to "improve campus climate and ensure all members of our community are able to thrive."

Once again, @UWMadison demonstrates how little they value the work of BIPOC folx.

Paying a white keynote speaker nearly DOUBLE what they paid a black woman for the same thing is a perfect representation of just how fake their "equity and diversity" initiatives are. pic.twitter.com/qrIYbrHWEv

— UW Madison BIPOC Coalition (@UWBIPOCCo) December 6, 2020

Thanks for sharing this feedback. In this case and others, speaker fees are set by the agency that represents the speaker. @uw_diversity

— UW-MaskUp (@UWMadison) December 6, 2020

Brown is the author of "I'm Still Here: Black Dignity in a World Made for Whiteness," a New York Times bestseller that is about bringing "the Black American experience into center stage" as "nearly all institutions ... claim to value 'diversity' in their mission statements" but fall short when it comes to action.

DiAngelo has previously charged $12,000, not counting travel and other expenses, to speak at the University of Kentucky for a two-hour racial justice session, where she would also discuss her book "White Fragility: Why is it so hard for white people to talk about racism?" She also charges $320 per hour for phone calls. (RELATED: $12K A Day: How White Liberals Profit From Pushing 'White Privilege')

The event at the University of Wisconsin took place Oct. 27 and 28, and DiAngelo led with a keynote that would address how "white fragility" prevents white people from "moving towards greater racial equity." There were three breakout sessions with subjects including campus activism, racial disparities during the pandemic, and "racism on campus and beyond."

DiAngelo's speaking fees typically run between $10,000 and $15,000, and her clients have included Amazon, the Bill & Melinda Gates Foundation, and the YMCA Seattle Public Schools, among others. She was slated to deliver a three-and-a-half hour racial justice workshop at the University of Connecticut in the fall, charging $20,000 for the event that would focus on "anti-black racism" and equity initiatives. SHE IS THE BEST PART. LIGHTS, CAMERAS, ACTION.

REPORT: Big Data 'Turbocharged' Uighur Round-Ups In China

NEXT, PAL ZOMBIE & KAMIKAZE KAMALA WILL BE ROUNDING UP GUNS & RELIGION DEPLORABLES, INCLUDING YOU

GREG BAKER

Uighur Muslims were arrested in China after being flagged by a computer program as taking part in allegedly suspicious activity, CBS News reported. Human Rights Watch (HRW), a United States-based non-profit organization, reported the arrest of over 2,000 residents of the Aksu prefecture, in mid-Western Xinjiang, China, in a report Wednesday, according to CBS News.

Citizens were marked through a program, called the Integrated Joint Operations Platform, which accumulated data from various security systems throughout Xinjiang, CBS News reported. Chinese officials would then review the data and decide whether or not to send the person in question to camps, according to CBS News. The listed reason for detainment for many people was simply that the Integrated Joint Operations Platform had flagged them, CBS News reported. Around 10% of detainees were being held for extremism or terrorism, according to the list, CBS News reported.

HRW believes their research proves that many flagged citizens were taking part in legal activity, such as phone calls abroad to family, per CBS News. HRW said the arrests proved that "China's brutal repression of Xinjiang's Turkic Muslims is being turbocharged by technology," per CBS News. (RELATED: REPORT: Chinese Tech Giant Tested Facial Recognition Software To Alert Authorities To Uighurs) NEXT IT'S US GUNS & RELIGION DEPLORABLES

Zhao Lijian, Chinese foreign ministry **spokesman, said the report wasn't "worth refuting," in a statement Wednesday, CBS News reported.**

The arrests follow a spike in surveillance technology **in Xinjiang allegedly aimed at preventing terrorism, these measures include facial recognition, iris scanners, and DNA collection, according to CBS News.**

At this point, HRW refuses to publish the list in its entirety due to safety concerns for their anonymous source, according to CBS News.

Tags : CHINESE COMMUNIST uighurs

ARE BRO'S & SISTAS FRO' DER' HOOD BE IS ONLY MR. & MRS. CLEAN?

NOW; NEXT JEWISH 'Yellow Privilege': College Residence Adviser Anonymously Distributes Document On Asians As Oppressors

DON MACKINNON & AUTUMN KLEIN

A document explaining "yellow privilege" NEXT JEWISH PRIVILEGE was distributed to students by an anonymous residential adviser at the University of British Columbia (UBC), according to the Montreal Gazette.

The six-page document defines "yellow privilege" as the advantages East Asians are granted, including protections under criminal law, the Montreal Gazette reported.

A disclaimer is included, stating that the document is not to "perpetuate and enforce an idea but to stimulate much needed healthy discussions on racial issues in society today," according to the Montreal Gazette.

The University of British Columbia's student housing department has apologized after a document about "yellow privilege" was sent to some students **https://t.co/W6d1id3fSK**

— **Tyler Dawson (@tylerrdawson)** December 7, 2020

To support its claims, the document points to the model minority, which it defines as an East-Asian stereotype that is furthered by the idea that Asians are successful due to their innate talents, the Montreal Gazette reported.

The author of the document argues this has led to East Asians acting as both the oppressors and the oppressed, per the Montreal Gazette. East Asians face oppression because they keep quiet to avoid losing their status as a model minority, according to the document, per the Montreal Gazette. However, East Asians act as oppressors by separating themselves from poor Southeast Asians, the document argues, according to the Montreal Gazette.

Georgia Yee, vice president of academic and university affairs for the UBC Alma Mater Society, said, "This is completely unacceptable to see. I'm a little horrified to see this, both as a former RA and in my current role. Glad to see actions are being taken to report this incident," in a post on Reddit, according to the Montreal Gazette.

The document urges the students to contemplate which privileges they're afforded that they may or may not be aware of, the Montreal Gazette reported.

"We sincerely apologize for this communication and its impact, in particular to members of our Asian communities. We recognize the email and its content have even greater implications in the midst of a pandemic that has spurred a climate of increased negativity towards Asian communities," Sean Ryan, associate director of student housing, said in an email to students, per the Montreal Gazette.

THIS IS EXACTLY WHY RED STATES MUST SECEDE & FORM OUR OWN CONFEDERATION YouTube Will Remove Videos Questioning Biden Election Victory Even as Legal Challenges Continue

Lucas Nolan

Google-owned video platform YouTube has announced plans to remove any content that questions Joe Biden's victory in the 2020 U.S. presidential election despite the fact that legal challenges involving multiple states continue. YouTube also announced it will be promoting "authoritative news sources," such as NBC and CBS in video recommendations.

In a recent blog post titled "Supporting the 2020 U.S. election," Google-owned video-sharing platform YouTube announced plans to remove any content that questions Joe Biden's victory in the 2020 U.S. presidential election or implies fraud impacted the election outcome.

In the blog post, YouTube writes: Yesterday was the safe harbor deadline for the U.S. Presidential election and enough states have certified their election results to determine a President-elect. Given that, we will start removing any piece of content uploaded today (or anytime after) that misleads people by alleging that widespread fraud or errors changed the outcome of the 2020 U.S. Presidential election, in line with our approach towards historical U.S. Presidential elections. For example, we will remove videos claiming that a Presidential candidate won the election due to widespread software glitches or counting errors. We will begin enforcing this policy today, and will ramp up in the weeks to come. As always, news coverage and commentary on these issues can remain on our site if there's sufficient education, documentary, scientific or artistic context.

YouTube also announced that it will be promoting "authoritative news sources," such as NBC and CBS:

Now let's look at recommendations, one of the main ways our viewers find content. Limiting the reach of borderline content and prominently surfacing authoritative information are important ways we protect people from problematic content that doesn't violate our Community Guidelines. Over 70% of recommendations on election-related topics came from authoritative news sources and the top recommended videos and channels for election-related content were primarily authoritative news. In fact, the top 10 authoritative news channels were recommended over 14X more than the top 10 non-authoritative channels on election-related content.

YouTube also included a graphic showing the most-viewed U.S. election-related content on the platform, with ABC News ranking the highest:

Trump touts Texas Supreme Court case as 'the big one,' says 'we will be intervening'

Texas files lawsuit challenging election results in four other states

Texas Attorney General Ken Paxton tells 'Fox & Friends' he hopes to argue his case before the Supreme Court.

President Trump **on Wednesday touted** Texas' suit demanding the U.S. Supreme Court block the Electoral College votes of Georgia, Michigan, Pennsylvania and Wisconsin, calling it the «big one.»

"We will be INTERVENING in the Texas (plus many other states) case. This is the big one. Our Country needs a victory!" Trump wrote on Twitter.

Trump's legal team has faced repeated setbacks in challenging the results of states that went for President-elect Joe Biden. **Trump's team could file an amicus brief in support of Texas' suit.**

TRUMP TEAM CONTINUES LEGAL FIGHT AS ELECTORAL COLLEGE 'SAFE HARBOR' DEADLINE ARRIVES

Texas Attorney General Ken Paxton sued **battleground states Pennsylvania, Georgia, Michigan and Wisconsin on Tuesday to challenge their** 2020 presidential election results.

"These elections in other states where state law was not followed ... affects my voters because these are national elections, and so if there are fraudulent things or things that affect an election and state law is not followed as is required by the Constitution it affects our state," Paxton told "Fox & Friends" **on Wednesday. "It affects every state."**

"We can't go back and fix it, but we can say, OK, let's transfer this to the legislature ... and let them to decide the outcome of the election. That would be a valid constitutional situation," Paxton continued.

The legal challenge seeks to invalidate the 62 Electoral College votes from those four battleground states and award Trump a second term, alleging unconstitutional changes to election rules before the vote.

"Using the COVID-19 pandemic as a justification, government officials in the defendant states of Georgia, Michigan and Wisconsin, and the Commonwealth of Pennsylvania (collectively, 'Defendant State'), usurped their legislatures' authority and unconstitutionally revised their state's election statutes," Paxton's complaint says. AND THE WILLFULLY IGNORANT SUPREME COURT DOES NOTHING **"They accomplished these statutory revisions through executive fiat or friendly lawsuits, thereby weakening ballot integrity."**

Ken Paxton, Texas attorney general, speaks during a news conference outside the Supreme Court in Washington, D.C., U.S., on Monday, Sept. 9, 2019. At least three more states are getting behind the Texas lawsuit.

Arkansas Attorney General Leslie Rutledge said Tuesday her office would be joining the suit, and Missouri Attorney General Eric Schmitt announced that his state is also "in the fight" with Texas.

Louisiana Attorney General Jeff Landry also backed the suit in a statement.

"Election integrity is central to our republic," Schmitt, a Republican, tweeted. "And I will defend it at every turn. As I have in other cases – I will help lead the effort in support of Texas' #SCOTUS filing today. Missouri is in the fight."

The Supreme Court on Tuesday denied a request from Trump allies to stop the certification of Pennsylvania's election results.

The high court left intact a decision from the Pennsylvania Supreme Court that tossed a lawsuit from Rep. Mike Kelly challenging a 2019 law to expand mail-in voting. Georgia stands out as a defendant in the Texas suit because both of its senators are facing tough challenges in runoff elections that will determine the balance of power in the Senate.

"We fully support President Trump's legal recourses and Attorney General Paxton's lawsuit," Sens. David Perdue and Kelly Loeffler said in a joint statement on Tuesday. "The president has every right to use every legal recourse available to guarantee these simple principles: every lawful vote cast should be counted, any illegal vote submitted cannot be counted, and there must be full transparency and uniformity in the counting process. This isn't hard and it isn't partisan. It's American. No one should ever have to question the integrity of our elections system and the credibility of its outcomes."

Trump has attacked Georgia Gov. Brian Kemp, a Republican, after he certified the state's election results for Biden.

In letter to Trump, House Republicans call for special counsel to investigate election

GOP representatives say the Justice Department has not done enough

By Ronn Blitzer

Fox News Flash top headlines are here. Check out what's clicking on Foxnews.com.

More than two dozen House Republicans are calling on President Trump to direct Attorney General William Barr to appoint a special counsel to investigate November's presidential election, according to a letter obtained by Fox News.

The letter, sent Wednesday morning, claimed that Barr's Justice Department has not been taking adequate action to address the matter. TRUMP TOUTS TEXAS SUPREME COURT CASE AS 'THE BIG ONE,' SAYS

'WE WILL BE INTERVENING'

"The Department of Justice has been asked on multiple occasions to launch an investigation into this matter, but inaction from the department along with comments made by the attorney general indicate a lack of willingness to investigate the irregularities your campaign and other elected officials across the nation have alleged," the letter said. The message was signed by 27 Republican members of Congress, including Reps. Lance Gooden, R-Texas, Paul Gosar, R-Ariz., Louie Gohmert, R-Texas, Thomas Massie, R-Ky., and Ted Budd, R-N.C. It follows a nearly identical letter Gooden sent on his own last week. A spokesperson from Gooden's office said the new letter was the result of "an outpouring of support" from Gooden's fellow Republicans.

MISSOURI JOINS 'FIGHT' ALONGSIDE TEXAS TO CHALLENGE ELECTION BEFORE SUPREME COURT

Gooden's home state of Texas recently went to the Supreme Court with a case against Georgia, Michigan, Pennsylvania and Wisconsin, alleging that the four battleground states improperly changed their election procedures. The lawsuit calls for special elections to take place in those states in order to appoint presidential electors, or if electors have already been appointed, for state legislatures to appoint new ones.

Attorneys general from Missouri, Louisiana, Arkansas and other states have announced their support of the lawsuit.

27 Republican reps call for special counsel probe into election irregularities

'The American people deserve a definitive resolution'

Phil Shiver

A group of 27 Republican members of the House of Representatives sent a letter to President Trump on Wednesday urging him to direct Attorney General William Barr to launch a special counsel investigation into 2020 election "irregularities."

What did they say?

In the letter, which was first obtained by Politico, the group of lawmakers argue that "the American people deserve a definitive resolution to the uncertainty hovering over the outcome of our election," but protest that "legitimate questions of voter fraud remain unanswered."

"The Department of Justice has been asked on multiple occasions to launch an investigation into this matter, but inaction from the Department along with public comments made by the Attorney General indicate a lack of willingness to investigate the irregularities your campaign and other elected officials across the nation have alleged," the letter reads.

"The appointment of a Special Counsel would establish a team of investigators whose sole responsibility

is to uncover the truth and provide the certainty America needs," it continues. "We urge you to take swift and decisive action and direct Attorney General Barr to appoint a Special Counsel to restore the American people's faith in our elections." The group, led by Rep. Lance Gooden (R-Texas), includes several prominent conservatives, such as Reps. Paul Gosar (R-Ariz.), Louie Gohmert (R-Texas), Thomas Massie (R-Ky.), and Jody Hice (R-Ga.).

What's the background?

The news comes as legal challenges to the election brought by the president's allies continue to hit dead-ends in the court system, and time is running out before the Electoral College meets on Dec. 14 and a new president is sworn in on Jan. 20. The u Attorney John Durham, who is currently investigating the origins of the Trump-Russia probe, to a special counsel, essentially safeguarding his investigation from any incoming Biden administration's attempts at interference. Following that news, Rep. Ken Buck (R-Colo.) sent a letter to Barr requesting that he initiate a special counsel investigation into Hunter Biden, the son of Democratic nominee Joe Biden.

Missouri, 16 other states file brief supporting Texas suit to delay presidential elector appointment

By Tyler Olson

Missouri led a group of 17 states that Wednesday afternoon filed a brief with the Supreme Court supporting

the Texas lawsuit aimed at delaying the appointment of presidential electors from Georgia, Pennsylvania, Michigan and Wisconsin. The brief mirrors the argument of the Texas suit in saying that the states acted unconstitutionally when either their judiciaries or executive branches changed their elections laws. The Texas suit, and the states that support it, say that only state legislatures may set laws regarding how states appoint their presidential electors.

"The integrity of our elections is of critical importance to maintaining our republic, both today and in future elections," Missouri Attorney General Eric Schmitt said in a statement. "The stakes of protecting our Constitution, defending our liberty and ensuring that all votes are counted fairly couldn't be higher. With this brief, we are joining the fight."The Trump campaign also filed a brief asking to join on the Texas suit on Wednesday.

"The illegal suspension or violation of state law thus calls directly into question the certification of the results of the elections in Defendant States for Vice President Joe Biden, Proposed Plaintiff in Intervention's opponent in the election," its brief said. "President Trump's interest in the outcome of this litigation could therefore not be more acute."

The brief filed by Missouri and the other states, which is officially a motion for leave to file a bill of complaint, also warns that the changes enacted by the state executives and judicial branches opened the states' elections up to potential fraud.

Missouri Attorney General Eric Schmitt led a group of 17 state attorneys general Wednesday in supporting the Texas lawsuit which aims to block electors from Michigan, Wisconsin, Pennsylvania and Georgia.

LOEFFLER & PERDUE BACK TEXAS SUIT AIMING TO OVERTURN ELECTOR SLATES ON GEORGIA, OTHER STATES BIDEN WON

"The Bill of Complaint alleges that non-legislative actors in each Defendant State unconstitutionally abolished or diluted statutory safeguards against fraud enacted by their state Legislatures, in violation of the Presidential Electors Clause," the brief states.

It continues: "All the unconstitutional changes to election procedures identified in the Bill of Complaint have two common features: (1) They abrogated statutory safeguards against fraud that responsible observers have long recommended for voting by mail, and (2) they did so in a way that predictably conferred partisan advantage on one candidate in the Presidential election." The Texas legal action is an extraordinary effort to essentially overturn the result of the presidential election, which President-elect Biden won because of key victories by tens of thousands of votes in the states Texas is suing. It follows numerous losses by President Trump's legal teams and his allies in lower courts as claim after claim of widespread voter fraud that may have affected the result of the election has gone unsubstantiated.

Texas' suit is unique in that it seeks to take advantage of the Supreme Court's rarely used original jurisdiction to bypass the lower courts and put the issue directly in front of the justices.

Texas specifically asks the Supreme Court to declare Michigan, Wisconsin, Pennsylvania and Georgia's elections "in violation of the Electors Clause and the Fourteenth Amendment of the Constitution;" declare electoral votes from those states invalid; prevent the states' electors from meeting or being certified; and direct the states to appoint new presidential electors. The Texas lawsuit is widely considered a longshot to succeed. Georgia Attorney General Chris Carr, a Republican, previously panned the Texas suit as fundamentally "wrong."

"With all due respect, the Texas Attorney General is constitutionally, legally and factually wrong about Georgia," a Carr spokesperson told the Dallas Morning News. Carr is the recently named chairman of the Republican Attorneys General Association. The states that joined the Wednesday brief are Missouri, Alabama, Arkansas, Florida, Indiana, Kansas, Louisiana, Mississippi, Montana, Nebraska, North Dakota, Oklahoma, South Carolina, South Dakota, Tennessee, Utah, and West Virginia.

They argue that they have an interest in the case because "the unconstitutional administration of elections" in some states dilutes votes in their own states. "When non-legislative actors in other States encroach on the authority of the 'Legislature thereof' in that State to administer a Presidential election, they threaten the liberty, not just of their own citizens, but of every citizen of the United States who casts a lawful ballot in that election—including the citizens of amici States," the Wednesday brief says. The four states being sued have until 3 p.m. Thursday to file a response with the Supreme Court.

Trump Legal Team Pressing Legal Challenges Into January

By Cathy Burke

President Donald Trump's legal team is reportedly is moving full steam ahead with courtroom election challenges that are now expected to continue into January.

Tuesday marked the "safe harbor" deadline, historically accepted as the date by which all state-level election challenges — such as recounts and audits — are supposed to be completed.

But Rudy Giuliani and Jenna Ellis, representing Trump in his bid to overturn the election results, said the courts will look at challenges into next month, well past that deadline, the Washington Times reported.

"Justice Ruth Bader Ginsburg recognized in Bush v. Gore that the date of 'ultimate significance' is Jan. 6, when Congress counts and certifies the votes of the Electoral College," they said in a statement, the news outlet reported.

"The only fixed day in the U.S. Constitution is the inauguration of the president on Jan. 20 at noon."

Ellis reiterated that message on Fox Business' "Mornings With Maria."

"Although we have the safe harbor deadline today, and we have the meeting of the Electoral College next week on Dec. 14, the ultimate date of significance is Jan. 6," she maintained.

According to The New York Times, there are lawsuits left unresolved in Georgia, Arizona, Wisconsin, and Pennsylvania. Of the three federal lawsuits still unresolved, two are in Wisconsin and one in Arizona, the news outlet reported.

There's also a petition before the United States Supreme Court involving an appeal of a state lawsuit in Pennsylvania; that suit addresses whether election officials were permitted to accept ballots up to three days after Election Day if they were postmarked by Nov. 3, the Times noted.

The New York Times reported that after California's certification of its votes on Friday, Joe Biden will have secured more than the 270 Electoral College votes needed to become president.

But the president and his legal team have assailed the election results, alleging widespread and systemic voter fraud and massive errors in the tallying of a record number of mail-in and absentee ballots.

Those ballots were used more than ever this election cycle as a response to fears that requiring in-person voting would expose Americans to the coronavirus.

Alan Dershowitz to Newsmax TV: Texas Lawsuit 'Very Doubtful'

Alan Dershowitz told Newsmax TV on Tuesday that Texas' attempt to sue multiple other states over the 2020 presidential election is a "creative approach," that "almost certainly" won't overturn the results of the election."

Dershowitz noted on "John Bachman Now" that the U.S. Constitution allows a state to sue another state, but "it rarely happens and it almost never succeeds, but it's a very creative approach."

He added that the argument that Texans have been deprived of their rights is "a stretch," adding that "it's never been tried before," but "it probably will be taken seriously by the Supreme Court. Will it result in an undoing of the election? Almost certainly not."

Dershowitz said, "will the Supreme Court take the case? Who knows. They're never had it like this presented before, this is all novel. The whole case is a first impression. A+ for creativity, but whether or not it will work in the end is very doubtful."

He also said that the court could strike down the safe harbor deadline, which is on Tuesday, as unconstitutional, but said he could not be sure if that would happen.

Arizona GOP Retweets Call 'To Give My Life' for Election Fight

The Arizona Republican Party late Monday issued a thinly veiled call for political violence, asking supporters if they were willing to die in the fight over the 2020 election results.

The party retweeted "Stop the Steal" organizer Ali Alexander's boast that he'd be "willing to give my life for this fight."

"He is. Are you?" the Arizona GOP's Twitter account asked.

Shortly after, the state GOP Twitter account shared a clip of the fourth "Rambo" movie, where Sylvester Stallone's character tells his posse: "This is what we do, who we are. Live for nothing, or die for something," Yahoo news reported.

The tweet was promptly taken down.

Arizona is one of several battleground states that went to Joe Biden where President Donald Trump and his lawyer Rudy Giuliani have been trying to overturn the election results.

Giuliani met with with Republican lawmakers and other leaders in the state days before it was announced he'd been hospitalized with COVID-19. The Arizona state legislature closed in the wake of the news, the Arizona Republic reported. The Electoral College meets next week to confirm the election that shows Joe Biden won.

Sidney Powell to Newsmax TV: Our Case Was Prejudged

By Eric Mack

A federal judge listened to oral arguments Monday, but he had already prejudged the case in granting leftist "interveners'" motions of dismiss, including the Democrat National Committee, according to former federal prosecutor Sidney Powell on Newsmax TV.

"The court wouldn't pay attention of it," Powell told Monday's "Greg Kelly Reports" of her lawsuit calling for the decertification of Georgia's election results amid evidence of election and voter fraud. "It's obvious the judge had made up his mind before he hit the bench, and he read from prepared notes when he granted the motion to dismiss. "So, we had oral argument, but I would say it was essentially meaningless, except to the extent the public got to hear another federal judicial proceeding that didn't turn out the way it should have."

U.S. District Court Judge Timothy Batten ruled the case had no standing to sue, the case belonged in state court, was filed too late, and the relief sought was "extraordinary." "We're going to proceed immediately with

an emergency appeal, and we expect to get relief in the Supreme Court," Powell told host Greg Kelly.

"We're determined to win because the American people have been defrauded from their lawful votes in this election, and that cannot stand," she concluded.

FOR A TRILLION REASONS; NO EVIDENCE OF DEMOCRAT'S NAKED STEALING THE PRESIDENCY OF THE UNITED STATES MEANS NOTHING TO THE U.S. LEGAL SYSTEM THIS IS WHY RED STATES HAVE NO ALTERNATIVE BUT TO SECEDE & FORM OUR OWN CONFEDERATION BEFORE IT'S TOO LATE

Sidney Powell Plans Appeals of Dismissed Georgia Lawsuit

By Eric Mack

After a federal judge dismissed lawyer Sidney Powell's election fraud lawsuit Monday in Georgia, Powell told The Epoch Times **she plans to appeal and "proceed as fast as possible to the Supreme Court."**

U.S. District Court Judge Timothy Batten ruled the case had no standing to sue, the case belonged in state court, and was filed too late. "There's no question that Georgia has a statute that explicitly directs that elections contests be filed in Georgia Superior Court," Judge Batten, a President George W. Bush appointee, said in his ruling. "They are state elections. State courts should evaluate these proceedings from start to finish."

Powell's lawsuit sought the remedy of decertifying Georgia's election results, but Judge Batten rejected the remedy as extraordinary, per the report.

Powell plans to appeal the lawsuit lacks standing or was brought too late.

Powell said in closing her argument, per the Times:

"For those reasons, we request the court to deny the motion to dismiss, allow us a few days, perhaps even just five, to conduct an examination of the machines that we have requested from the beginning and find out exactly what went on and give the court further evidence it might want to rule in our favor, because the fraud that has happened here has destroyed any public confidence that the will of the people is reflected in their vote and just simply cannot stand."

Arizona High Court to Hear GOP-Led Suit Alleging Mail-In Ballot Defects

By Theodore Burke

The Arizona Supreme Court has agreed to hear an election lawsuit filed by state Republican Party Chairwoman Kelli Ward over alleged irregularities with mail-in ballots.

A lower court judge had dismissed Ward's case last week. But, according to the Washington Examiner, she took an appeal up to the state's highest court.

The Examiner said that court will now decide the matter without oral argument.

Ward's case aims to reverse the state's certification of its election results to the Arizona Supreme Court, local news station KTAR reports.

A judge in Maricopa County Superior Court ruled against Ward last Friday, finding she failed to prove election fraud that would reverse President Donald Trump's loss in the state.

She told KTAR News 92.3 FM's "The Mike Broomhead Show," before the case was dismissed, she was prepared to "go to the end to prove" that "President Trump won this election by a landslide in Arizona."

Four previous attempts to challenge the results of the election have already been dismissed in Arizona. The state's Republican Gov. Doug Ducey and Attorney General Mark Brnovich have both approved the election certification from Democrat Secretary of State Katie Hobbs, which shows Joe Biden won the state by over 10,000 votes.

Ward's lawsuit specifically pertains to Maricopa County, which Biden won by more than 45,000 votes. The county's director of Election Day and emergency voting Scott Jarrett said in court last Thursday that Trump might have only lost about 103 votes, according to the error rate they have recorded.

Trump Campaign Appeals Another Ballot Case in Pennsylvania

President Donald Trump's campaign continues to press lawsuits over Pennsylvania's election, appealing another case it lost to the state Supreme Court, this time over fewer than 2,000 ballots in a suburban Philadelphia county.

Meanwhile, nine state Republican lawmakers filed another lawsuit in state courts Monday, citing perceived irregularities or complaints over mail-in voting procedures, and asking the court to prevent Pennsylvania

from casting its electoral votes for President-elect Joe Biden. The Electoral College meets Dec. 14.

The moves are among a flurry of activity by Republicans, including in the courts and the state Legislature, to try to deny a victory to Biden in Pennsylvania, mirroring similar efforts in other battleground states where Trump lost.

The Trump campaign's appeal, filed Friday, is one of at least five pending cases in which Trump or Republicans are trying to throw out certain ballots or trying to upend Biden's victory in Pennsylvania over Trump by more than 80,000 votes.

The Bucks County case involves 1,995 mail-in ballots in which voters failed to handwrite their name, address or date on the outside ballot-return envelope, or enclosed their ballot in an inner unmarked secrecy envelope that became unsealed.

The Trump campaign maintains the ballots should be thrown out under state law, although the state Supreme Court, ruling in separate cases, has refused to do so.

The county election board chose to count the ballots, a decision that was upheld in lower courts. Bucks County's lawyers contend that Trump's campaign should not be allowed to appeal and point out that the number of ballots in question are far too few to overturn Biden's win.

In the U.S. Supreme Court, lawyers for Gov. Tom Wolf, a Democrat, have until Tuesday to respond in a case led by Republican U.S. Rep. Mike Kelly, of northwestern Pennsylvania.

Kelly and the other plaintiffs are asking the high court to block Biden's victory in the battleground state, throw out the state's year-old mail-in voting law and all the mail-in ballots cast by voters under that law. Most of the 2.5 million mail-in ballots were cast by Democrats.

The state's lawyers say justices are highly unlikely to grant it. Even if they did, it would not give Trump the presidency.

Pennsylvania's Supreme Court threw out the case on Nov. 28.

Wednesday, or Dec. 9, is the safe harbor deadline for Congress to challenge any presidential electors named by this date in accordance with state law, as some Republicans have urged Congress to do. Still, Trump backers say courts can still intervene.

Some claims in the newly filed lawsuit have been settled by state courts. Some claims have been thrown out of court, such as the claim that counties aren't allowed to let a voter fix a technical error on a mail-in ballot — like not writing a date or address on the outside ballot envelope — that might invalidate it.

It includes an affidavit by a U.S. Postal Service contract truck driver who claims he hauled thousands of filled-out mail-in ballots from Bethpage, N.Y., to Lancaster on Oct. 21, although it's not clear whether that was unusual or suspicious. The Postal Service has declined comment, and a spokesperson has said the Postal Service's Office of Inspector General is looking into the matter.

Election officials say the ballots could have been mailed by voters living out of state, while Pennsylvania's Department of State, which oversees election administration, said it isn't possible to inject any ballots – much less tens or hundreds of thousands – into an election without detection.

Only registered voters can apply for and receive a ballot, and must fulfill identification requirements, the department said.

Each return envelope is printed with a barcode unique to the voter to prevent anyone from voting twice, it said.

The lawsuit also includes an affidavit by a Republican ballot watcher in Delaware County, a Democratic-leaning suburb of Philadelphia.

The ballot watcher, Gregory Stenstrom, lodged complaints about perceived violations of chain-of-custody procedures for electronic voting machine drives that he connected to large, unexplained additions of vote totals for Biden.

Delaware County officials did not comment Monday evening. Still, no state or county election official or prosecutor in Pennsylvania has raised evidence of widespread election fraud in the state.

Dick Morris to Newsmax TV: States Could Withhold Electors

By Brian Trusdell

Several states could withhold their electors, or instruct them to abstain, in the Electoral College, which would deny Joe Biden the 270 necessary to win and send the election of president to the House of Representatives, according to former Democrat strategist and White House adviser Dick Morris on Newsmax TV.

Morris cited the opinion in the 2000 Bush v. Gore Supreme Court decision, which ultimately resulted in George W. Bush's victory and reaffirmed the constitutional authority of the state legislatures in choosing their electors, Morris told Monday's "Greg Kelly Reports." "The opinion made the point that at the beginning of the republic, the state legislatures routinely chose the electoral votes, and then that was delegated by them to the voters," Morris told host Greg Kelly. "And that at any point, they could take that power back and name them themselves.

"And the effort here is not to flip the votes from Biden to [President Donald] Trump, but to have these electors say what is honestly, complete true, which is we are the name electors who will say, 'Look, I'm the elector for Georgia, and I can't possibly tell who won this election. There are so many allegations of fraud and a tiny little margin, I'm going to abstain in the Electoral College, because I can't tell who's going to vote; I'm agnostic.'

"And that would deprive Biden of 270 votes and send the election to the House of Representatives," Morris continued.

"We're not hijacking it from democracy; we're saving it from the steal, and delegating the selection of the president to a democratically elected body, the new Congress, not the old one – the one that was just elected in the same election and let them make this decision."

Dershowitz explains how Supreme Court could get involved in Georgia election challenge be asked to weigh in on who can choose state's electors

By Ronn Blitzer

Harvard Law Professor emeritus Alan Dershowitz and former independent counsel Ken Starr react on 'Sunday Morning Futures.'

Attorneys Alan Dershowitz and Ken Starr appeared on Fox News' "Sunday Morning Futures" to discuss recently revealed evidence of possible voter fraud in Georgia, and explained the possible processes for how the Trump campaign could use it in their effort to reverse the result of the presidential election in that state.

Starr, who rose to fame as the independent counsel investigating President Bill Clinton, pointed to information presented to Georgia state senators last week, including video that purportedly showed ballots being counted without supervision. While Georgia officials have insisted that the video simply shows "normal" ballot counting procedure, Starr said Georgia legislators "seemed to be really troubled" by the video and other evidence presented to them.

KEMP, TRUMP CLASH OVER ELECTION RESULTS

"There certainly is probable cause for investigating and looking further," Dershowitz said. "Giuliani has made very serious accusations. The question is which institution is designed constitutionally to look into it. Is it the state legislature? Is it the courts? Is the clock running in such a way that there won't be time to look into this?"

Dershowitz, the Harvard Law professor emeritus, said he has proposed for the future the creation of a neutral panel consisting of former judges and justices that would field election-related complaints.

LOEFFLER AND WARNOCK TO FACE OFF IN KEY GEORGIA SENATE DEBATE WITH CONTROL OF UPPER CHAMBER ON THE LINE

Trump campaign attorney Ray Smith had called on Georgia state legislators to step in and choose electors instead of following the election results. Dershowitz said that it is not a given that they have the power to do this. Should they try, Dershowitz said, the issue could end up being decided by the Supreme Court.

"Clearly state legislators have the power before the voters vote to pick the electors," Dershowitz said. "The unanswered constitutional question is do they have the powers, the legislatures, to pick electors after the voters vote if they conclude that the voters' count has been in some way fraudulent or wrong. That is a constitutional question we don't know the answer to, and the Supreme Court may get to decide that question if a state legislature decides to determine who the electors should be, and changes the electors from Biden to Trump."

Arizona GOP Lawmakers Seek Audit on Voting Equipment, Software

By Sandy Fitzgerald

Arizona lawmakers are seeking an independent audit of the Dominion software and equipment used in the general election.

Senate President Karen Fann and House Speaker Rusty Bowers, both Republicans, formally asked for the review on Friday, reports Breitbart.

The two leaders, along with Senate Government Chair Michelle Ugenti-Rita and House Majority Leader Warren Petersen spoke several times with members of the Maricopa County Board of Supervisors, according to a press release.

Ugenti-Rita said in a statement that as a longtime advocate for "improving and modernizing our election system" she was pleased to learn that the Maricopa County board supports the audit of its software and equipment.

"(It is) 'important we maintain all of the voting public's confidence in our elections and this is a positive first step in the right direction," she said.

Peterson added that a "significant number of voters" think fraud occurred and since there was a "number of irregularities" it's easy to understand why.

"Especially concerning are the allegations made surrounding the vendor Dominion," said Peterson. "It is imperative that the County immediately do a forensic audit on the Dominion software and equipment to make sure the results were accurate.

Trump thanked Fann and Bowers on Twitter Friday night for their efforts, claiming that a "fast check of signatures will easily give us the state. Votes against have been reduced to a very small number!"

Arizona leaders certified the election last week for Joe Biden, saying he was ahead of Trump by 10,457 votes.

Bowers on Friday, however, released another statement about the Trump campaign's calls for the legislature to overturn the certification saying the Trump campaign has "presented only theories, not proof" of voter fraud in the state, and even with evidence, "the Arizona Legislature simply could not do what is being asked."

"As a conservative Republican, I don't like the results of the presidential election," he added. "I voted for President Trump and worked hard to reelect him. But I cannot and will not entertain a suggestion that we violate current law to change the outcome of a certified election

Trump: I Will Win Georgia With Signature Verification

By Sandy Fitzgerald

President Donald Trump said Saturday he'll "easily and quickly" win in Georgia if Gov. Brian Kemp or Secretary of State Brad Raffensperger will "permit a simple signature verification."

"Has not been done and will show large scale discrepancies," said Trump on Twitter.

"Why are these two 'Republicans' saying no? If we win Georgia, everything else falls in place!"

Trump called Kemp early Saturday to ask that the governor order the state's absentee ballot signatures to be audited and to urge that he convince the state legislature to overturn Joe Biden's victory, reports The Washington Post.

The call came hours before Trump's rally in Georgia tonight on behalf of Republican Sens. David Perdue and Kelly Loeffler, who are seeking reelection in a race that will ultimately determine which party will control the Senate. The two are facing Democrat challengers Jon Ossoff and Raphael Warnock in a runoff election on Jan. 5.

According to a person familiar with their call, Trump pushed Kemp to call in a secret session of the state legislature to appoint electors who would back him, and demand the audit, which Kemp has said he doesn't have authority to do. The same person told The Post that Kemp has declined Trump's requests.

Kemp tweeted, in response to Trump's message, that he told Trump he has already called for a signature audit three times "to restore confidence in our election process and to ensure that only legal votes are counted in Georgia."

Kemp's spokesman, Cody Hall, confirmed the governor and Trump spoke, but Tim Murtaugh, the spokesman for Trump's campaign, declined comment.

The Post reports that according to the Georgia Constitution, absentee and mail-in ballots are separated from envelopes they're mailed in when they are being processed to protect voters' privacy, making it impossible to later match them up.

Georgia House Republicans Call for Review on Absentee Ballot Process

By Sandy Fitzgerald

Georgia's House Majority Leader Jon Burns is calling for Secretary of State Brad Raffensperger and the State Election Board to review the state's absentee ballot verification process as the Jan. 5 runoff elections in two Senate races approach. Burns has submitted a letter, signed by more than 100 current and newly elected House members to encourage Raffensperger to seek more staffing opinions that will provide support and oversight for the elections.

Georgia Gov. Brian Kemp posted the letter on Twitter, saying that he wanted to thank Burns, House David

Ralston, and members of the House "for proposing necessary reforms that will help restore confidence in our elections." In the letter, Burns said that many Georgians, including his colleagues, have "serious concerns" about the state's elections and as the Senate elections near, must have confidence in the progress going forward. The House members are calling for Raffensperger to implement a more "robust verification process" for reviewing signatures on absentee ballot applications and mail-in ballot envelopes that will include independent observers. They also address opportunities for the secretary of state or the State Election Board to join forces with other state agencies in support of state and local election officials on Election Day

"Multiple news outlets reported significant failures in counties across our state before, during, and after Election Day," he said. "These counties were rural, suburban, and metro-area and represented all demographics and areas of our state. We hope these suggestions can help Georgians rest assured that each and every legal vote is counted here in Georgia."

Georgia Gov. Brian Kemp Says Secretary Of State Has Not Ordered Signature Audit

WHY NO GEORGIA SIGNATURE AUDIT THAT WILL MAKE (16) BIDEN ELECTORAL VOTES TRUMP ELECTORAL VOTES & BEGIN THE HERD STAMPEDE FOR OUR RED GUNS & RELIGION DEPLORABLE COUNTERATTACK LONG ROAD BACK VICTORY" WHY, WHY, WHY NO AUDIT OF SIGNATURES BY DEMOCRATS WHO WANT TO HIDE THEIR THEFT OF THE WHITE HOUSE?

Henry Rodgers

Republican Georgia Gov. Brian Kemp said Georgia Secretary of State Brad Raffensperger has not yet ordered a signature audit, saying by law Raffensperger is the only one in the state who can order it.

Kemp was interviewed on Fox News and asked about a signature audit, to which he put the blame on Raffensperger, saying he believes it should be done, but that it is not his decision. Kemp said this after a Senate Judiciary subcommittee heard new allegations of alleged election fraud in Fulton County, GA, with a videotape that alleges proof of ballots being counted without anyone watching.

"I called early on for a signature audit," Kemp said. "Obviously, the secretary of state, per the laws and the [state] Constitution would have to order that and he has not done that."

"I think it should be done. I think especially [given] what we saw today, it raises more questions," Kemp continued.

Kemp first announced his support for a sample signature audit on Nov. 20 and reiterated his support on Nov. 24. Thursday night was Kemp's third time calling for a signature audit.

Republican Georgia Sens. Kelly Loeffler and David Perdue, who face runoff elections in January, called on Raffensperger to resign over the management of the elections throughout the state on Nov. 9, saying they were unhappy with how votes had been counted. The two Senators told Raffensperger that illegal votes should not be counted and blamed him for not providing transparency on the elections. "There have been too many failures in Georgia elections this year and the most recent election has shined a national light on the problems. While blame certainly lies elsewhere as well, the buck ultimately stops with the Secretary of State. The mismanagement and lack of transparency from the Secretary of State is unacceptable. Honest elections are paramount to the foundation of our democracy. The Secretary of State has failed to deliver honest and transparent elections," the statement said.

Loeffler will face Democratic challenger Raphael Warnock, in her runoff while Perdue faces a rematch against his Democratic challenger, Jon Ossoff.

Ossoff, Warnock Campaign with Democrat Congressman Who Called Jews 'Termites'

MEIN KAMPF COCKROACH REICH PERSON "IT" HOOD

Sean Moran

GEORGIA CAMPAIGNING with Rep. Hank Johnson (D-GA), who in 2016 compared Israeli settlers to "termites."

MY PEOPLE ARE A PROBLEM FOR THIS LOATHSOME HANK JOHNSON

WE US' ALL DARE THIS ABOVE SCUMBAG HANK JOHNSON CALL MY PEEPLES BE IS TERMITES TO US ALL'S FACES; SEE WHAT HAPPENS NEXT TO YO' BE IS EBONICS BULLYZE BE IS RAPPAS MUDDA GANGSTA'S SUCKAS FUCKAS ASSES IN DER YOU'S HOOD

Warnock and Ossoff will attend a "Drive-in Rally" hosted by the Rockdale and Newton County Democrats with Johnson. Johnson's rally with Ossoff and Warnock raises questions about Johnson's controversial remarks, including his own commentary on Israeli settlers.

At an event in 2016 sponsored by the Campaign to End the Israeli Occupation — which supports the Boycott, Divestment, and Sanctions movement (BDS), Johnson said:

There has been a steady [stream], almost like termites can get into a residence and eat before you know that you've been eaten Georgia Senate Democrat candidates Raphael Warnock and Jon Ossoff will campaign Saturday up and you fall in on yourself, there has been settlement activity that has marched forward with impunity and at an ever increasing rate to the point where it has become alarming.

It has come to the point that occupation, with highways that cut through Palestinian land, with walls that go up, with the inability or the restriction, with the illegality of Palestinians being able to travel on those roads and those roads cutting off Palestinian neighborhoods from each other. And then with the building of walls and the building of check points that restrict movement of Palestinians. We've gotten to the point where the thought of a Palestinian homeland gets further and further removed from reality.

Johnson also said that "Jewish people" A.K.A. "HIS JEWISH PROBLEM" steal land and property from Palestinians.

"You see one home after another being appropriated by Jewish people who come in to claim that land just because somebody did not spend the night there," Johnson said.

He added, "The home their [Palestinian] ancestors lived in for generations becomes an Israeli home and a flag goes up."

Johnson also compared Israeli Defense Minister Avigdor Lieberman to President Donald Trump.

"The fact is the Israeli government, which is the most right-wing government ever to exist in the state of Israel in its history, the most right-wing government, you got a guy like Trump who is now the minister of defense in Israel calling the shots on defense," Johnson said. ***Ms. Shapiro is author of "The Byline Bible" and a co-author of "The Bosnia List."***

The Protocols of the Elders of Zion

"Protocols of Zion" redirects here. For the film, see Protocols of Zion (film).

The Protocols of the Elders of Zion

Cover of first book edition, *The Great within the Minuscule and Antichrist*

Author	**Unknown. Plagiarised from** Hermann Goedsche and Maurice Joly**, plagiarized in turn from** Eugène Sue and Alexandre Dumas, père
Original title	*Програма завоевания мира евреями* (**Programa zavoevaniya mira evreyami, *"The Jew-("ish Programme to Conquer the World***
Country	Russian Empire
Language	Russian**, with plagiarism from German and French texts**
Subject	Antisemitic conspiracy theory
Genre	Propaganda
Publisher	Znamya
Publication date	**August–September 1903**
Published in English	**1919**
Pages	**(edition 1905) 417**

The Protocols of the Elders of Zion (Russian: Протоколы сионских мудрецов) **or** *The Protocols of the Meetings of the Learned Elders of Zion* is a fabricated antisemitic text**purporting to describe a** Jewish plan for global domination. The hoax, which was shown to be plagiarized from several earlier sources, some not antisemitic in nature, was first published in Russia in 1903, translated into multiple languages, and disseminated internationally in the early part of the 20th century. According to the claims made by some of its publishers, the ***Protocols*** are the minutes of a late 19th-century meeting where Jewish leaders discussed their goal of global Jewish hegemony by subverting the morals of Gentiles**, and by controlling the press and the world's economies.**

Henry Ford funded printing of 500,000 copies that were distributed throughout the United States in the 1920s. The Nazis sometimes used the ***Protocols*** as propaganda against Jews; it was assigned by some German teachers, as if factual, to be read by German schoolchildren after the Nazis came to power in 1933, despite having been exposed as fraudulent by The Times of London in 1921. It is still widely available today in numerous languages, in print and on the Internet, and continues to be presented by some proponents as a genuine document. **3.3 Emergence in Russia** **4** Adaptations

- o **4.1** Television
- ▪ **4.1.1** Ash-Shatat

Creation

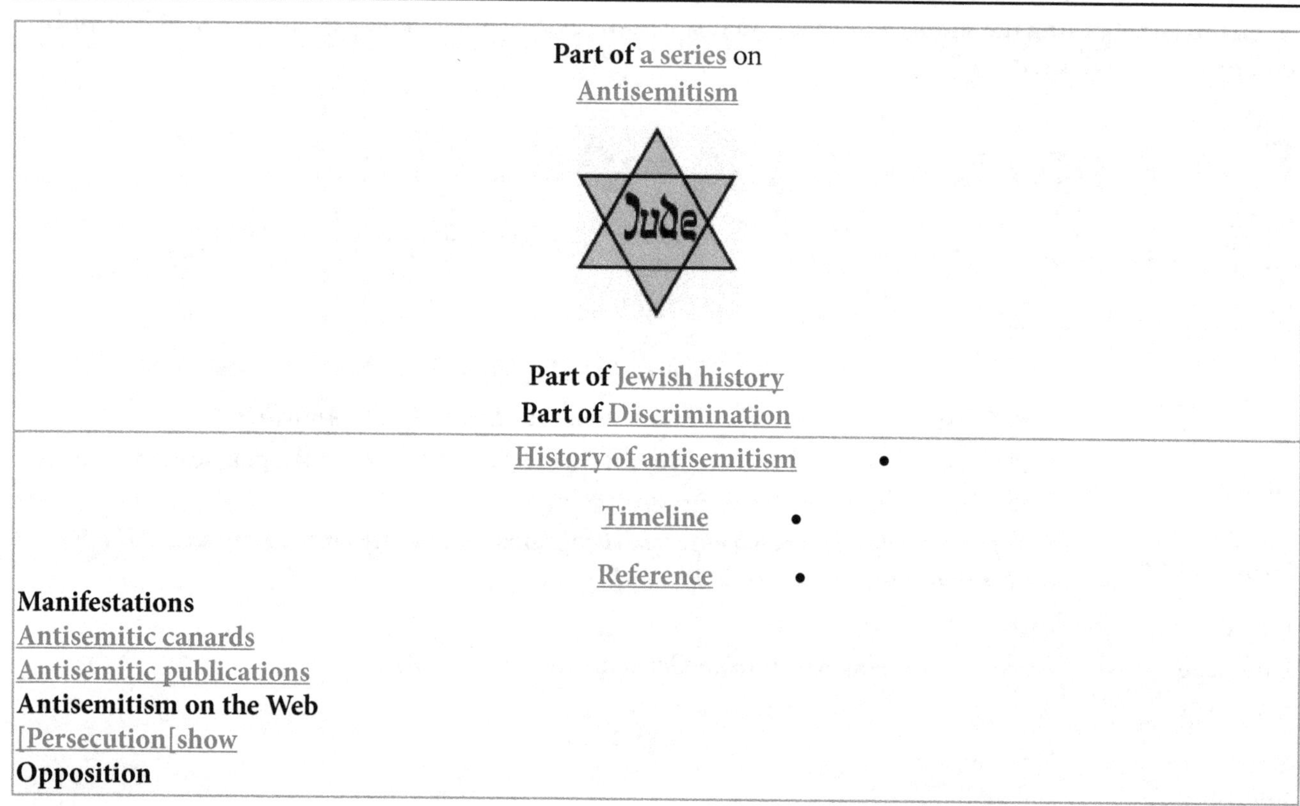

Part of a series on
Antisemitism

Part of Jewish history
Part of Discrimination

History of antisemitism •

Timeline •

Reference •

Manifestations
Antisemitic canards
Antisemitic publications
Antisemitism on the Web
[Persecution[show
Opposition

The *Protocols* is a fabricated document purporting to be factual. Textual evidence shows that it could not have been produced prior to 1901. It is notable that the title of Sergei Nilus**'s widely distributed edition contains the dates "1902–1903", and it is likely that the document was actually written at this time in Russia, despite Nilus' attempt to cover this up by inserting French-sounding words into his edition.** Cesare G. De Michelis argues that it was manufactured in the months after a Russian Zionist congress in September 1902, and that it was originally a parody of Jewish idealism meant for internal circulation among antisemites until it was decided to clean it up and publish it as if it were real. Self-contradictions in various testimonies show that the individuals involved—including the text›s initial publisher, Pavel Krushevan**—deliberately obscured the origins of the text and lied about it in the decades afterwards.**

If the placement of the forgery in 1902–1903 Russia is correct, then it was written at the beginning of

the anti-Jewish pogroms in the Russian Empire**, in which thousands of Jews died or fled the country. Many of the people whom De Michelis suspects of involvement in the forgery were directly responsible for inciting the pogroms.**

Political conspiracy background

Towards the end of the 18th century, following the Partitions of Poland**, the** Russian Empire inherited the world›s largest Jewish population. The Jews lived in shtetls in the West of the Empire, in the Pale of Settlement and until the 1840s, local Jewish affairs were organised through the qahal**, the semi-autonomous Jewish government, including for purposes of taxation and conscription into the** Imperial Russian Army**. Following the ascent of** liberalism in Europe, the Russian ruling class became more hardline in its reactionary policies, upholding the banner of Orthodoxy, Autocracy, and Nationality**, whereby non-Orthodox and non-Russian subjects, including the Jews, were not always embraced. Jews who attempted to** assimilate were regarded with suspicion as potential «infiltrators» supposedly trying to «take over society», while Jews who remained attached to traditional Jewish culture were resented as undesirable aliens.

КНИГА КАГАЛА

1869.

The Book of the Kahal (1869) by Jacob Brafman, in the Russian language original.

Resentment towards Jews, for the aforementioned reasons, existed in Russian society, but the idea of a Protocols-esque international Jewish conspiracy for world domination was minted in the 1860s. Jacob Brafman**, a Russian Jew from** Minsk**, had a falling out with agents of the local** *qahal* and consequently turned against Judaism**. He subsequently converted to the** Russian Orthodox Church and authored polemics against the Talmud and the *qahal.*[6] Brafman claimed in his books *The Local and Universal Jewish Brotherhoods* (1868) and *The Book of the Kahal* (1869), published in Vilna, **that the** ***qahal*** continued to exist in secret and that it had as its principal aim undermining Christian entrepreneurs, taking over their property and ultimately seizing power. He also claimed that it **was an international conspiratorial network, under the central control of the Alliance Israélite Universelle, which was based in Paris and then under the leadership of Adolphe Crémieux, a prominent freemason. The Vilna Talmudis Tt, Jacob Barit, attempted to refute Brafman's claim.**

The impact of Brafman's work took on an international aspect, as it was translated into English, French, German and other languages. The image of the "*kahal*" as a secret international Jewish shadow government working as a state within a state was picked up by anti-Jewish publications in Russia and was taken seriously by some Russian officials such as P. A. Cherevin and Nikolay Pavlovich Ignatyev who in the 1880s urged governors-general of provinces to seek out the supposed *qahal*. **This was around the time of the Narodnaya Volya** assassination of Tsar Alexander II of Russia and the subsequent pogroms. **In France it was translated by Monsignor** Ernest Jouin in 1925, who supported the Protocols. In 1928, Siegfried Passarge, **a geographer active in the Third Reich, translated it into German.**

Aside from Brafman, there were other early writings which posited a similar concept to the Protocols. This includes *The Conquest of the World by the Jews* (1878), published in Basel and authored by Osman Bey (born Frederick Millingen). Millingen was a British subject of Dutch-Jewish extraction (the grandson of James Millingen), **but served as an officer in the Ottoman Armywhere he was born. He converted to Islam, but later became a Russian Orthodox Christian. Bey's work was followed up by Hippolytus Lutostansky's *The Talmud and the Jews*** (1879) which claimed that Jews wanted to divide Russia among themselves. Incidentally, in a 1904 edition of *The Talmud and the Jews,* Hippolytus directly quoted verbatim the first, little-known 1903 edition of the *Protocols.*

Sources employed

Source material for the forgery consisted jointly of Dialogue aux enfers entre Machiavel et Montesquieu (*Dialogue in Hell Between* Machiavelli *and* Montesquieu), **an 1864** political satire by Maurice Joly; **and a chapter from *Biarritz*, an 1868 novel by the antisemitic German novelist** Hermann Goedsche, **which had been translated into** Russian in 1872.

A major source for the *Protocols* was Der Judenstaat by Theodor Herzl, **which was referred to as *Zionist Protocols*** in its initial French and Russian editions. Paradoxically, early Russian editions of the *Protocols* assert that they did not come from a Zionist organization. The text, which nowhere advocates for Zionism, **resembles a parody of Herzl's ideas.**

Literary forgery

The Protocols is one of the best-known and most-discussed examples of literary forgery, **with analysis and proof of its fraudulent origin going as far back as 1921. The forgery is an early example of "conspiracy theory" literature.** **Written mainly in the first person plural, the text includes generalizations, truisms, and platitudes** on how to take over the world: take control of the media and the financial institutions, change the traditional social order, etc. It does not contain specifics.

Maurice Joly

Elements of the *Protocols* were plagiarized from Joly›s fictional ***Dialogue in Hell*, a thinly veiled attack on the political ambitions of** Napoleon III**, who, represented by the** non-Jewish character Machiavelli**, plots to rule the world. Joly, a** monarchist and legitimist**, was imprisoned in France for 15 months as a direct result of his book's publication. Scholars have noted the irony that** *Dialogue in Hell* was itself **a plagiarism, at least in part, of a novel by** Eugène Sue**,** *Les Mystères du Peuple* (1849–56).

Identifiable phrases from Joly constitute 4% of the first half of the first edition, and 12% of the second half; later editions, including most translations, have longer quotes from Joly.

The Protocols 1–19 closely follow the order of Maurice Joly›s ***Dialogues*** 1–17. For example:

Dialogue in Hell Between Machiavelli and Montesquieu	***The Protocols of the Elders of Zion***
How are loans made? By the issue of bonds entailing on the Government the obligation to pay interest proportionate to the capital it has been paid. Thus, if a loan is at 5%, the State, after 20 years, has paid out a sum equal to the borrowed capital. When 40 years have expired it has paid double, after 60 years triple: yet it remains debtor for the entire capital sum. **Montesquieu, Dialogues, p. 209 —**	**A loan is an issue of Government paper which entails an obligation to pay interest amounting to a percentage of the total sum of the borrowed money. If a loan is at 5%, then in 20 years the Government would have unnecessarily paid out a sum equal to that of the loan in order to cover the percentage. In 40 years it will have paid twice; and in 60 thrice that amount, but the loan will still remain as an unpaid debt.** **Protocols, p. 77 —**
Like the god Vishnu, my press will have a hundred arms, and these arms will give their hands to all the different shades of opinion throughout the country. **Machiavelli, Dialogues, p. 141 —**	**These newspapers, like the Indian god Vishnu, will be possessed of hundreds of hands, each of which will be feeling the pulse of varying public opinion.** **Protocols, p. 43 —**
Now I understand the figure of the god Vishnu; you have a hundred arms like the Indian idol, and each of your fingers touches a spring. **Montesquieu, Dialogues, p. 207 —**	**Our Government will resemble the Hindu god Vishnu. Each of our hundred hands will hold one spring of the social machinery of State.** **Protocols, p. 65 —**

Philip Graves brought this plagiarism to light in a series of articles in *The Times* in 1921, the first published evidence that the *Protocols* was not an authentic document.

Hermann Goedsche

"Goedsche was a postal clerk and a spy for the Prussian Secret Police**. He had been forced to leave the postal work due to his part in forging evidence in the prosecution against the Democratic leader** Benedict Waldeck in 1849.» Following his dismissal, Goedsche began a career as a conservative columnist, and wrote literary fiction under the pen name Sir John Retcliffe. His 1868 novel ***Biarritz*** **(*To Sedan*) contains a chapter called "**The Jewish Cemetery in Prague and the Council of Representatives of the Twelve Tribes of Israel." **In it, Goedsche (who was unaware that only two of the original twelve Biblical "tribes" remained) depicts a clandestine nocturnal meeting of members of a mysterious** rabbinical cabal that is planning a diabolical «Jewish conspiracy.» At midnight, the Devil appears to contribute his opinions and insight. The chapter closely resembles a scene in Alexandre Dumas' ***Giuseppe Balsamo*** (1848), in which Joseph Balsamo a.k.a. Alessandro Cagliostro and company plot the Affair of the Diamond Necklace**.**

In 1872 a Russian translation of "The Jewish Cemetery in Prague" appeared in Saint Petersburg as a separate pamphlet of purported non-fiction. François Bournand, in his ***Les Juifs et nos Contemporains*** (1896), reproduced the soliloquy at the end of the chapter, in which the character Levit expresses as factual the wish that Jews be «kings of the world in 100 years» —crediting a «Chief Rabbi John Readcliff.» Perpetuation of the myth of the authenticity of Goedsche›s story, in particular the «Rabbi›s speech», facilitated later accounts of the equally mythical authenticity of the ***Protocols*****. Like the *Protocols*, many asserted that the fictional "rabbi's speech" had a ring of authenticity, regardless of its origin: "This speech was published in our time, eighteen years ago," read an 1898 report in** La Croix**, "and all the events occurring before our eyes were anticipated in it with truly frightening accuracy."**

Fictional events in Joly's *Dialogue aux enfers entre Machiavel et Montesquieu*, which appeared four years before *Biarritz*, may well have been the inspiration for Goedsche's fictional midnight meeting, and details of the outcome of the supposed plot. Goedsche's chapter may have been an outright plagiarism of Joly, Dumas père, or both.

Structure and content

The ***Protocols*** purports to document the minutes of a late-19th-century meeting attended by world Jewish leaders, the «Elders of Zion», who are conspiring to take over the world.The forgery places in the mouths of the Jewish leaders a variety of plans, most of which derive from older antisemitic canards. For example, the ***Protocols*** includes plans to subvert the morals of the non-Jewish world, plans for Jewish bankers to control the world›s economies, plans for Jewish control of the press, and – ultimately – plans for the destruction of civilization.The document consists of twenty-four «protocols», which have been analyzed by Steven Jacobs and Mark Weitzman, who documented several recurrent themes that appear repeatedly in the 24 protocols, as shown in the following table:[

Protocol	Title	Themes[29]
1	"The Basic Doctrine: "Right Lies in Might	Freedom and Liberty; Authority and power; Gold = money
2	Economic War and Disorganization Lead to International Government	International Political economic conspiracy; Press/Media as tools
3	Methods of Conquest	Jewish people, arrogant and corrupt; Chosen-ness/Election; Public Service
4	The Destruction of Religion by Materialism	Business as Cold and Heartless; Gentiles as slaves
5	Despotism and Modern Progress	Jewish Ethics; Jewish People's Relationship to Larger Society
6	The Acquisition of Land, The Encouragement of Speculation	Ownership of land
7	A Prophecy of Worldwide War	Internal unrest and discord (vs. Court system) leading to war vs Shalom/Peace
8	The transitional Government	Criminal element
9	The All-Embracing Propaganda	Law; education; Freemasonry
10	Abolition of the Constitution; Rise of the Autocracy	Politics; Majority rule; Liberalism; Family
11	The Constitution of Autocracy and Universal Rule	Gentiles; Jewish political involvement; Free-masonry
12	The Kingdom of the Press and Control	Liberty; Press censorship; Publishing
13	Turning Public Thought from Essentials to Non-essentials	Gentiles; Business; Chosenness/Election; Press and censorship; Liberalism
14	The Destruction of Religion as a Prelude to the Rise of the Jewish God	Judaism; God; Gentiles; Liberty; Pornography
15	Utilization of Masonry: Heartless Suppression of Enemies	Gentiles; Freemasonry; Sages of Israel; Politi-cal power and authority; King of Israel
16	The Nullification of Education	Education
17	The Fate of Lawyers and the Clergy	Lawyers; Clergy; Christianity and non-Jewish Authorship
18	The Organization of Disorder	;Evil; Speech
19	Mutual Understanding Between Ruler and People	Gossip; Martyrdom
20	The Financial Program and Construction	Taxes and Taxation; Loans; Bonds; Usury; Moneylending
21	Domestic Loans and Government Credit	Stock Markets and Stock Exchanges
22	The Beneficence of Jewish Rule	Gold = Money; Chosenness/Election
23	The Inculcation of Obedience	Obedience to Authority; Slavery; Chosenness/ Election
24	The Jewish Ruler	Kingship; Document as Fiction

Publication history

See also: List of editions of Protocols of the Elders of Zion

The Protocols appeared in print in the Russian Empire as early as 1903, published as a series of articles in Znamya, **a** Black Hundreds newspaper owned by Pavel Krushevan. **It appeared again in 1905 as the final chapter (Chapter XII) of the second edition of *Velikoe v malom i antikhrist*** («The Great in the Small & Antichrist"), **a book by** Sergei Nilus. **In 1906, it appeared in pamphlet form edited by** Georgy Butmi de Katzman. **These first three (and subsequently more) Russian language imprints were published and circulated in the** Russian Empire during the 1903–6 period as a tool for scapegoating Jews, blamed by the monarchists for the defeat in the Russo-Japanese War and the Revolution of 1905. **Common to all three texts is the idea that Jews aim for world domination. Since** ***The Protocols*** are presented as merely a document, **the** front matter and back matter are needed to explain its alleged origin. The diverse imprints, however, are mutually inconsistent. The general claim is that the document was stolen from a secret Jewish organization. Since the alleged original stolen manuscript does not exist, one is forced to restore a purported original edition. This has been done by the Italian scholar, Cesare G. De Michelis in 1998, in a work which was translated into English and published in 2004, where he treats his subject as Apocrypha.

As fiction in the genre of literature, the tract was further analyzed by Umberto Eco in his novel Foucault›s Pendulum in 1988 (English translation in 1989), in 1994 in **chapter 6, "Fictional Protocols", of his** Six Walks in the Fictional Woods and in his 2010 novel The Prague Cemetery. **As the** Russian Revolution unfolded, causing White movement**-affiliated Russians to flee to the West, this text was carried along and assumed a new purpose. Until then,** ***The Protocols*** had remained obscure;[31] it now became an instrument for blaming Jews for the Russian Revolution. It became a tool, a political weapon, used against the Bolsheviks who were depicted as overwhelmingly Jewish, allegedly executing the «plan» embodied in ***The Protocols*. The purpose was to discredit the** October Revolution, **prevent the West from recognizing the** Soviet Union, **and bring about the downfall of** Vladimir Lenin**'s regime.**

AMERICA, ESPECIALLY DONNIE, IS TOO GENTLE WITH THIS ROTTEN-TO-THE-CORE, 5TH COLUMN; METASTASIZING IN THE DEMOCRATIC JEW HATING PARTY OF AMERICA ROTTING FROM WITHIN.

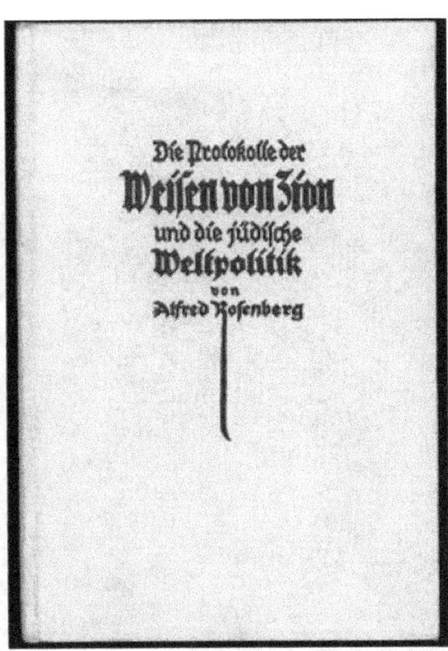

Exposing the Protocols of the Elders of Zion as a lie

Alfred Rosenberg's 1923 commentary on the Protocols of the Elders of Zion

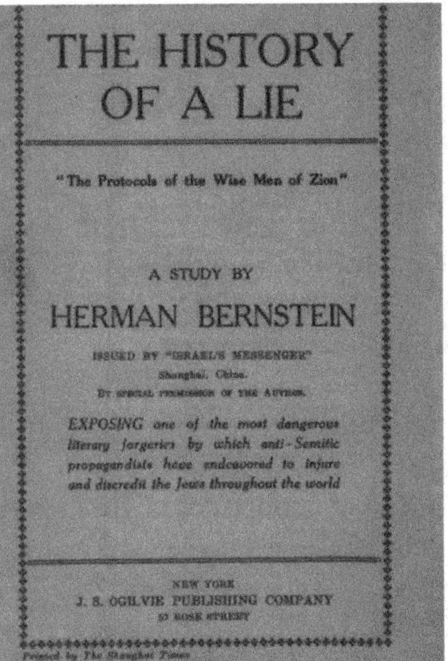

An Arabic translation of the Protocols of the Elders of ZionTHE USA DEMOCRATS OF KISSING COUSINS OF IRAN; WHOSE NATION PURPOSE IS THE EXTERMINATION, VAPORATION, INCINERATION OF ALL TRACES OF JEWS & JUDAISM.

2005 Syrian edition of the Protocols of the Elders of Zion

WHY SHOULDN'T JEW HATERS ILHAN ADULLAHI OMAR & RASHIDA TLIAB HAND OUT FREE PROTOCOLS OF THE ELDERS & ZION COPIES AT EVERY LITTLE RED SCHOOLHOUSE DOOR IN AMERICA?

First Russian language editions

Conspiracy references

According to Daniel Pipes,

The great importance of *The Protocols* lies in its permitting antisemites to reach beyond their traditional circles and find a large international audience, a process that continues to this day. The forgery poisoned public life wherever it appeared; it was «self-generating; a blueprint that migrated from one conspiracy to another.»The book›s vagueness—almost no names, dates, or issues are specified—has been one key to this wide-ranging success. The purportedly Jewish authorship also helps to make the book more convincing. Its embrace of contradiction—that to advance, Jews use all tools available, including capitalism and communism, philo-Semitism and antisemitism, democracy and tyranny—made it possible for ***The Protocols*** to reach out to all: rich and poor, Right and Left, **Christian and** Muslim**, American and Japanese.**

Pipes notes that the ***Protocols*** emphasizes recurring themes of conspiratorial antisemitism: «Jews always scheme», «Jews are everywhere», «Jews are behind every institution», «Jews obey a central authority, the shadowy ‹Elders›», and «Jews are close to success.»

The Protocols is widely considered influential in the development of other conspiracy theories[citation needed], **and reappears repeatedly in contemporary conspiracy literature, such as** Jim Marrs' ***Rule by Secrecy,*** which identifies the work as a Czarist forgery. Some recent editions proclaim that the «Jews» depicted in the Protocols are a cover identity for other conspirators such as the **Illuminati,**[34] **Freemasons, the Priory of Sion, or even, in the opinion of David Icke, "extra-dimensional entities"**

Emergence in Russia

The front piece of a 1912 edition using occult symbols.

The chapter "In the Jewish Cemetery in Prague" from Goedsche's ***Biarritz,*** **with its strong antisemitic theme containing the alleged rabbinical plot against the European civilization, was translated into Russian as a separate pamphlet in 1872. However, in 1921, Princess** Catherine Radziwill gave a private lecture in New York in which she **claimed that the Protocols were a forgery compiled in 1904–5 by Russian journalists** Matvei Golovinski and Manasevich-Manuilov at the direction of Pyotr Rachkovsky, **Chief of the Russian secret service in Paris.**[

In 1944, German writer Konrad Heiden identified Golovinski as an author of the *Protocols*. **Radziwill's account was supported by Russian historian Mikhail Lepekhine, who published his findings in November 1999 in the French newsweekly** L'Express. **Lepekhine considers the** *Protocols* a part of a scheme to persuade Tsar Nicholas II that the modernization of Russia was really a Jewish plot to control the world. Stephen Eric Bronner writes that groups opposed to progress, parliamentarianism, urbanization, and capitalism, and an active Jewish role in these modern institutions, were particularly drawn to the antisemitism of the document. Ukrainian scholar Vadim Skuratovsky offers extensive literary, historical and linguistic analysis of the original text of the *Protocols* and traces the influences of Fyodor Dostoyevsky's prose (in particular, The Grand Inquisitor and The Possessed) **on Golovinski's writings, including the** ***Protocols.***

Golovinski's role in the writing of the Protocols is disputed by Michael Hagemeister, Richard Levy and Cesare De Michelis, who each write that the account which involves him is historically unverifiable and to a large extent provably wrong.

In his book ***The Non-Existent Manuscript*****, Italian scholar** Cesare G. De Michelis studies early Russian publications of the *Protocols*. The *Protocols* were first mentioned in the Russian press in April 1902, by the Saint Petersburg newspaper *Novoye Vremya* (Новое Время – *The New Times*). **The article was written by famous conservative publicist** Mikhail Menshikov as a part of his regular series «Letters to Neighbors» («Письма к ближним») and was titled **"Plots against Humanity". The author described his meeting with a lady** (Yuliana Glinka, **as it is known now) who, after telling him about her mystical revelations, implored him to get familiar with the documents later known as the** ***Protocols*****; but after reading some excerpts, Menshikov became quite skeptical about their origin and did not publish them.**

The *Protocols* were Krushevan and Nilus editions

published at the earliest, in serialized form, from August 28 to September 7 (O.S.) **1903, in** Znamya, **a Saint Petersburg daily newspaper, under** Pavel Krushevan. **Krushevan had initiated the** Kishinev pogrom**four months earlier.**

In 1905, Sergei Nilus published the full text of the *Protocols* in *Chapter XII*, **the final chapter (pp 305–417), of the second edition (or third, according to some sources) of his book,** Velikoe v malom i antikhrist, **which translates as "The Great within the Small: The Coming of the Anti-Christ and the Rule of Satan on Earth". He claimed it was the work of the** First Zionist Congress, **held in 1897 in** Basel, Switzerland.[1] When it was pointed out that the First Zionist Congress had been open to the public and was attended by many non-Jews, Nilus changed his story, saying the Protocols were the work of the 1902–3 meetings of the Elders, but contradicting his own prior statement that he had received his copy in 1901:

In 1901, I succeeded through an acquaintance of mine (the late Court Marshal Alexei Nikolayevich Sukotin of Chernigov) in getting a manuscript that exposed with unusual perfection and clarity the course and development of the secret Jewish Freemasonic conspiracy, which would bring this wicked world to its inevitable end. The person who gave me this manuscript guaranteed it to be a faithful translation of the original documents that were stolen by a woman from one of the highest and most influential leaders of the Freemasons at a secret meeting somewhere in France—the beloved nest of Freemasonic conspiracy.

Stolypin's fraud investigation, 1905

A subsequent secret investigation ordered by Pyotr Stolypin, the newly appointed chairman of the Council of Ministers, came to the conclusion that the *Protocols* first appeared in Paris in antisemitic circles around 1897–1898. When Nicholas II learned of the results of this investigation, he requested, «The Protocols should be confiscated, a good cause cannot be defended by dirty means.» Despite the order, or because of the «good cause», numerous reprints proliferated.[]

The Protocols in the West

In the United States, *The Protocols* are to be understood in the context of the First Red Scare (1917–20). The text was purportedly brought to the United States by a Russian army officer in 1917; it was translated into English by Natalie de Bogory (personal assistant of Harris A. Houghton**, an officer of the** Department of War**) in June 1918,**[47] and Russian **expatriate** Boris Brasol soon circulated it in American government circles, specifically diplomatic and military, in typescript form, a copy of which is archived by the Hoover Institute**. It also appeared in 1919 in the** Public Ledger as a pair of serialized newspaper articles. But all references to «Jews» were replaced with references to Bolsheviki as an exposé by the journalist and subsequently highly respected Columbia University School of Journalism dean Carl W. Ackerman. **In 1923, there appeared an anonymously edited pamphlet by the** Britons Publishing Society**, a successor to** The Britons**, an entity created and headed by** Henry Hamilton Beamish**. This imprint was allegedly a translation by** Victor E. Marsden**, who died in October 1920. Most versions substantially involve "protocols", or minutes of a speech given in secret involving Jews who are organized as** Elders**, or** Sages**, of** Zion**, and underlies 24 protocols that are supposedly followed by the Jewish people. *The Protocols*** has been proven to be a literary forgery and hoax as well as a clear case of plagiarism.

English language imprints

On October 27 and 28, 1919, the Philadelphia Public Ledger published excerpts of an English language translation as the «Red Bible,» deleting all references to the purported Jewish authorship and re-casting the document as a Bolshevik manifesto**.The author of the articles was the paper's** correspondent at the time, Carl W. Ackerman**, who later became the head of the journalism department at** Columbia University**. On May 8, 1920, an article in *The Times*** followed German translation and appealed for an inquiry into what it called an «uncanny note of prophecy». In the leader (editorial) titled «The Jewish Peril, a Disturbing **Pamphlet: Call for Inquiry",** Wickham Steed wrote about *The Protocols*: **What are these 'Protocols'? Are they authentic? If so, what malevolent assembly concocted these plans and gloated over their exposition? Are they forgery? If so, whence comes the uncanny note of prophecy, prophecy in part fulfilled, in part so far gone in the way of fulfillment?".**

Steed retracted his endorsement of *The Protocols* after they were exposed as a forgery. **In the US, Henry Ford sponsored the printing of 500,000 copies, and, from 1920 to 1922, published a series of antisemitic articles titled "**The International Jew: The World's Foremost Problem**", in** The Dearborn Independent**, a newspaper he owned. The articles were later collected into multi-volume book series of the same name.**[] **In 1921, Ford cited evidence of a Jewish threat: "The only statement I care to make about the *Protocols*** is that they fit in with what is going on. They are 16 years old, and they have fitted the world situation up to this time.»

Robert A. Rosenbaum wrote that «In 1927, bowing to legal and economic pressure, Ford issued a retraction and apology—while disclaiming personal **responsibility—for the anti-Semitic articles and closed the *Dearborn Independent*** in 1927.[1] He was also an admirer of Nazi Germany. **In 1934, an anonymous editor expanded the compilation with "Text and Commentary" (pp 136–41). The production of this uncredited compilation was a 300-page book, an inauthentic expanded edition of the twelfth chapter of Nilus's 1905 book on the coming of the anti-Christ. It consists of substantial liftings of excerpts of articles from Ford's antisemitic periodical *The Dearborn Independent*. This 1934 text circulates most widely in the English-speaking world, as well as on the internet. The "Text and Commentary" concludes with** a comment on Chaim Weizmann**'s October 6, 1920, remark at a banquet: "A beneficent protection which God has instituted in the life of the Jew is that He has dispersed him all over the world". Marsden, who was dead by then, is credited with the following assertion: It proves that the Learned Elders exist. It proves that Dr. Weizmann knows all about them. It proves that the desire for a "National Home" in Palestine is only camouflage and an infinitesimal part of the Jew's real object. It proves that the Jews of the world have no intention of settling in Palestine or any separate country, and that their annual prayer that they may all meet "Next Year in Jerusalem" is merely a piece of their characteristic make-believe. It also demonstrates that the Jews are now a world menace, and that the Aryan races will have to domicile them permanently out of Europe.**

The Times exposes a forgery, 1921

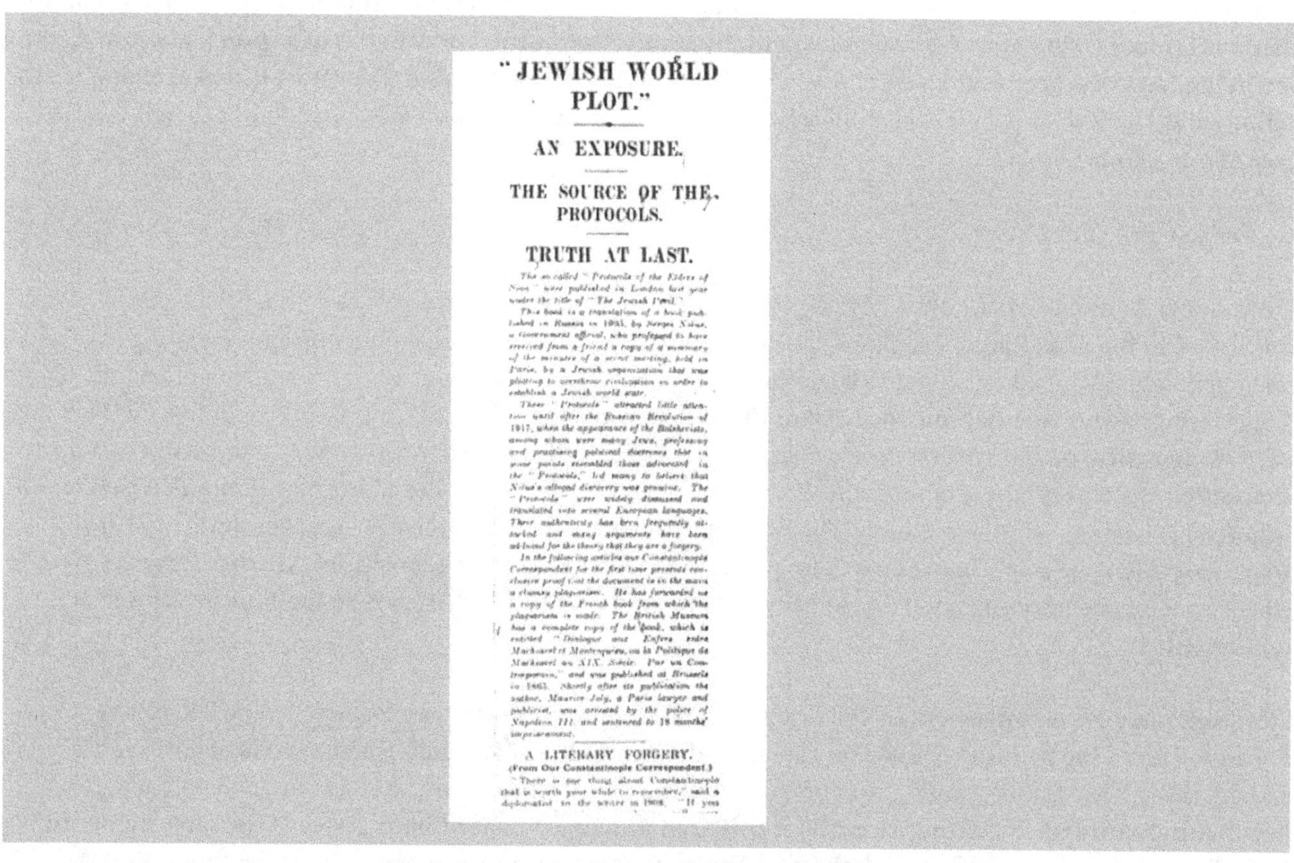

"JEWISH WORLD PLOT."

AN EXPOSURE.

THE SOURCE OF THE PROTOCOLS.

TRUTH AT LAST.

The so-called "Protocols of the Elders of Zion" were published in London last year under the title of "The Jewish Peril."

This book is a translation of a book published in Russia in 1905, by Sergyei Nilus, a Government official, who professed to have received from a friend a copy of a summary of the minutes of a secret meeting, held in Paris, by a Jewish organization that was plotting to overthrow civilization in order to establish a Jewish world state.

These "Protocols" attracted little attention until after the Russian Revolution of 1917, when the appearance of the Bolshevists, among whom were many Jews, professing and practising political doctrines that in some points resembled those advocated in the "Protocols," led many to believe that Nilus's alleged discovery was genuine. The "Protocols" were widely discussed and translated into several European languages. Their authenticity has been frequently attacked and many arguments have been adduced for the theory that they are a forgery.

In the following articles our Constantinople Correspondent for the first time presents conclusive proof that the document is in the main a clumsy plagiarism. He has forwarded us a copy of the French book from which the plagiarism is made. The British Museum has a complete copy of the book, which is entitled "Dialogue aux Enfers entre Machiavel et Montesquieu, ou la Politique de Machiavel au XIX. Siècle. Par un Contemporain," and was published at Brussels in 1865. Shortly after its publication the author, Maurice Joly, a Paris lawyer and publicist, was arrested by the police of Napoleon III. and sentenced to 15 months' imprisonment.

A LITERARY FORGERY.

(From Our Constantinople Correspondent.)

"There is one thing about Constantinople that is worth your while to remember," said a diplomatist to the writer in 1908. "If you

The Times exposed the ***Protocols*** as a forgery on August 16–18, 1921

In 1920–1921, the history of the concepts found in the *Protocols* was traced back to the works of Goedsche and Jacques Crétineau-Joly by Lucien Wolf (an English Jewish journalist), and published in London in August 1921. But a dramatic exposé occurred in the series of articles in *The Times* by its Constantinople reporter, Philip Graves, **who discovered the plagiarism from the work of** Maurice Joly.

According to writer Peter Grose, Allen Dulles, **who was in Constantinople developing relationships in post-**Ottoman political structures, discovered «the source» of the documentation and ultimately provided him to *The Times*. **Grose writes that** *The Times* extended a loan to the source, a Russian émigré who refused to be identified, with the understanding the loan would not be repaid. Colin Holmes, a lecturer in economic history at Sheffield University, **identified the émigré as Michael Raslovleff, a self-identified antisemite, who gave the information to Graves so as not to "give a weapon of any kind to the Jews, whose friend I have never been."**

In the first article of Graves' series, titled "A Literary Forgery", the editors of *The Times* wrote, «our Constantinople Correspondent presents for the first time conclusive proof that the document is in the main a clumsy plagiarism. He has forwarded us a copy of the French book from which the plagiarism is made.» In the same year, an entire book documenting the hoax was published in the United States by Herman Bernstein. **Despite this widespread and extensive debunking, the** *Protocols* continued to be regarded as important factual evidence by antisemites. Dulles, a successful lawyer and career diplomat, attempted to persuade the US State Department to publicly denounce the forgery, but without success.

Arab world

A translation made by an Arab Christian appeared in Cairo in 1927 or 1928, this time as a book. The first translation by an Arab Muslim was also published in Cairo, but only in 1951.

Switzerland

The Berne Trial, 1934–35

Main article: Berne Trial

The selling of the *Protocols* (edited by German antisemite Theodor Fritsch) **by the** National Front during a political manifestation in the Casino of Berne on June 13, 1933, led to the Berne Trial**in the** *Amtsgericht* (district court) of Berne, **the capital of** Switzerland, **on October 29, 1934. The plaintiffs (the Swiss Jewish Association and the Jewish Community of Berne) were represented by Hans Matti and** Georges Brunschvig, **helped by Emil Raas. Working on behalf of the defense was German antisemitic propagandist** Ulrich Fleischhauer. **On May 19, 1935, two defendants (Theodore Fischer and Silvio Schnell) were convicted of violating a Bernese statute prohibiting the distribution of "immoral, obscene or brutalizing" texts while three other defendants were acquitted. The court declared the** *Protocols* to be forgeries, plagiarisms, and obscene literature. Judge Walter Meyer, a Christian who had not heard of the *Protocols* earlier, said in conclusion,

I hope the time will come when nobody will be able to understand how in 1935 nearly a dozen sane and responsible men were able for two weeks to mock the intellect of the Bern court discussing the authenticity

of the so-called Protocols, the very Protocols that, harmful as they have been and will be, are nothing but laughable nonsense.

Vladimir Burtsev**, a Russian émigré, anti-Bolshevik and** anti-Fascist who exposed numerous Okhrana agents provocateurs in the early 1900s, served as a witness at the Berne Trial. In 1938 in Paris he published a book, *The Protocols of the Elders of Zion: A Proved Forgery*, **based on his testimony.**

On November 1, 1937, the defendants appealed the verdict to the *Obergericht* (Cantonal Supreme Court) of Berne. A panel of three judges acquitted them, holding that the ***Protocols*****, while false, did not violate the statute at issue because they were "political publications" and not "immoral (obscene) publications (Schundliteratur)" in the strict sense of the law. The presiding judge's opinion stated, though, that the forgery of the *Protocols*** was not questionable and expressed regret that the law did not provide adequate protection for Jews from this sort of literature. The court refused to impose the fees of defense of the acquitted defendants to the plaintiffs, and the acquitted Theodor Fischer had to pay 100 Fr. to the total state costs of the trial (Fr. 28›000) that were eventually paid by the Canton of Berne. This decision gave grounds for later allegations that the appeal court «confirmed authenticity of the Protocols» which is contrary to the facts. A view favorable to the pro-Nazi defendants is reported in an appendix to Leslie Fry's *Waters Flowing Eastward*. **A more scholarly work on the trial is in a 139-page monograph by Urs Lüthi.**

The Basel Trial

A similar trial in Switzerland took place at Basel**. The Swiss** Frontists Alfred Zander and Eduard Rüegsegger distributed the ***Protocols*** (edited by the German Gottfried zur Beek) in Switzerland. Jules Dreyfus-Brodsky and Marcus Cohen sued them for insult to Jewish honor. At the same time, chief rabbi Marcus Ehrenpreis of Stockholm (who also witnessed at the Berne Trial) sued Alfred Zander who contended that Ehrenpreis himself had said that the ***Protocols*** were authentic (referring to the foreword of the edition of the ***Protocols*** by the German antisemite Theodor Fritsch). On June 5, 1936 these proceedings ended with a settlement.

Germany

According to historian Norman Cohn**, the assassins of German Jewish politician** Walter Rathenau (1867–1922) were convinced that Rathenau was a literal «Elder of Zion».

It seems likely Hitler first became aware of the *Protocols* after hearing about it from ethnic German white émigrés**, such as** Alfred Rosenberg and Max Erwin von Scheubner-Richter**. Hitler refers to the** *Protocols* in Mein Kampf:

... [**The Protocols**] **are based on a forgery, the** Frankfurter Zeitung moans [ ] every week ... [which is] the best proof that they are authentic ... the important thing is that with positively terrifying certainty they reveal the nature and activity of the Jewish people and expose their inner **contexts as well as their ultimate final aims.**

The Protocols also became a part of the Nazi propaganda effort to justify persecution of the Jews. In The Holocaust: *The Destruction of European Jewry 1933–1945*, Nora Levin states that «Hitler used the Protocols as a manual in his war to exterminate the Jews»:

Despite conclusive proof that the *Protocols* were a gross forgery, they had sensational popularity and large sales in the 1920s and 1930s. They were translated into every language of Europe and sold widely in Arab lands, the US, and England. But it was in Germany after World War I that they had their greatest success. There they were used to explain all of the disasters that had befallen the country: the defeat in the war, the hunger, the destructive inflation.

Hitler endorsed the Protocols in his speeches from August 1921 on, and it was studied in German classrooms after the Nazis came to power. "Distillations of the text appeared in German classrooms, indoctrinated the Hitler Youth, and invaded the USSR along with German soldiers." Nazi Propaganda Minister Joseph Goebbels proclaimed: "The Zionist Protocols are as up-to-date today as they were the day they were first published.

In contrast to Hitler, Nazi leader Erich von dem Bach-Zelewsky admitted:

I am the only living witness but I must say the truth. Contrary to the opinion of the National Socialists, that the Jews were a highly organized group, the appalling fact was that they had no organization whatsoever. The mass of the Jewish people were taken complete by surprise. They did not know at all what to do; they had no directives or slogans as to how they should act. This is the greatest lie of anti-Semitism because it gives the lie to that old slogan that the Jews are conspiring to dominate the world and that they are so highly organized. In reality, they had no organization of their own at all, not even an information service. If they had had some sort of organization, these people could have been saved by the millions, but instead, they were taken completely by surprise. Never before has a people gone as unsuspectingly to its disaster. Nothing was prepared. Absolutely nothing.

Richard S. Levy criticizes the claim that the Protocols had a large effect on Hitler›s thinking, writing that it is based mostly on suspect testimony and lacks hard evidence. **Publication of the Protocols was stopped in Germany in 1939 for unknown reasons. An edition that was ready for printing was blocked by censorship laws.**

German language publications

Having fled Ukraine in 1918–19, Piotr Shabelsky-Bork brought the Protocols to Ludwig Muller Von Hausen who then published them in German. **Under the pseudonym Gottfried Zur Beek he produced the first and "by far the most important" German translation. It appeared in January 1920 as a part of a larger antisemitic tract dated 1919. After** ***The Times*** discussed the book respectfully in May 1920 it became a bestseller. «The Hohenzollern family helped defray the publication costs, and Kaiser Wilhelm II had portions of the book read out aloud to dinner guests». Alfred Rosenberg›s 1923 edition «gave a forgery a huge boost».

Italy

Fascist politician Giovanni Preziosi published the first Italian edition of the ***Protocols*** in 1921. The book however had little impact until the mid-1930s. A new 1937 edition had a much higher impact, and three further editions in the following months sold 60,000 copies total.The fifth edition had an introduction by Julius Evola, **which argued around the issue of forgery, stating: "The problem of the authenticity of this document is secondary and has to be replaced by the much more serious and essential problem of its truthfulness".**

Modern era

See also: Contemporary imprints of The Protocols of the Elders of Zion *and* New World Order (conspiracy theory) § The Protocols of the Elders of Zion

The *Protocols* continue to be widely available around the world, particularly on the Internet, as well as in print in Japan, the Middle East, Asia, and South America.

Governments or political leaders in most parts of the world have not referred to the *Protocols* since World War II. The exception to this is the Middle East, where a large number of Arab and Muslim regimes and leaders have endorsed them as authentic, including endorsements from Presidents Gamal Abdel Nasser and Anwar Sadat of Egypt, **the elder President Arif of** Iraq, **King** Faisal of Saudi Arabia, **and Colonel** Muammar al-Gaddafi of Libya.

The 1988 charter of Hamas, **a Palestinian Islamist group, states that** ***The Protocols of the Elders of Zion*** embodies the **plan of the Zionists. Recent endorsements in the 21st century have been made by the** Grand Mufti of Jerusalem, **Sheikh** Ekrima Sa'id Sabri, **the education ministry of** Saudi Arabia, **member of the** Greek Parliament Ilias Kasidiaris, **and** Young Earth creationist, Kent Hovind.

Adaptations Television

Ash-Shatat *Main article:* Ash-Shatat

Ash-Shatat (Arabic: ⊠⊠⊠⊠⊠ *The Diaspora*) **is a 29-part Syrian television series produced in 2003 by a private Syrian film company and was based in part on the** ***Protocols.*** Syrian national television declined to air the program. *Ash-Shatat* was shown on Lebanon›s Al-Manar, before being dropped. The series was shown in Iran in 2004, and in Jordan during October 2005 on Al-Mamnou, **a Jordanian satellite network.**[96]

- Judaism portal
- Russia portal

The Protocols of the Learned Elders of Zion Pertinent concepts

- Black propaganda
- Blood libel
- Disinformation
- Hate speech
- World government

Individuals

- Martin Heidegger and Nazism

Related or similar texts

- A Racial Program for the Twentieth Century
- Alta Vendita
- Tanaka Memorial
- Protocols of Zion
- Hamas Covenant
- The Prague Cemetery
- Memoirs of Mr. Hempher, The British Spy to the Middle East
- Warrant for Genocide

Khamenei names new chief for Iran's Revolutionary Guards

DUBAI (Reuters) - Iran's top authority Supreme Leader Ayatollah Ali Khamenei has replaced the head of the influential Revolutionary Guards Corps, state TV reported on Sunday, days after the United States designated the elite group a foreign terrorist organization.

FILE PHOTO: Iran's Supreme Leader Ayatollah Ali Khamenei speaks live on television after casting his ballot in the Iranian presidential election in Tehran June 12, 2009.

The TV station did not give a reason for the change when it announced the appointment of Brigadier General Hossein Salami to the position and his promotion to the rank of Major General. He served as deputy commander of the Guards for years and is known for his hardline comments against Israel and the United States. DONALD JOHN TRUMP EXTERMINATED THIS COCKROACH SCUMBAG SURGICALLY WITH A DRONE STRIKE JANUARY 3, 2020

"The Supreme Leader has appointed Salami as the new commander-in-chief of the Guards, who will replace Mohammad Ali Jafari," it said. JOE BIDEN IMMEDIATELY SENT HIM A BASKIN ROBBINS ICE CREAM CAKE. KAMIKAZE KAMALA SENT HIM A $35 MARK ZUCKERBUCKS WHITE CASTLE GIFT CERTIFCATE WHEN HE'S GIVEN A TICKET TAPE PARADE CANYON OF HERO'S WELCOME IN MANHATTAN

Major General Jafari had held the post since September 2007. President Donald Trump on April 8 designated the Guards a terrorist organization, in an unprecedented step that drew Iranian condemnation and raised concerns about retaliatory attacks on U.S. forces. The designation took effect on April 15.

Tehran retaliated by naming the United States Central Command (CENTCOM) as a terrorist organization and the U.S. government as a sponsor of terrorism.

On April 13, Salami was quoted by Iran's semi-official Tasnim news agency as saying that he and the IRGC were proud of being designated a terrorist group by Washington.

POLITICAL CLOUT

The IRGC, created by late Ayatollah Ruhollah Khomeini during Iran's 1979 Islamic Revolution, **is more than a military force. It is also an industrial empire with political clout and is loyal to the supreme leader.**

Comprising an estimated 125,000-strong military with army, navy and air units, the Guards also command the Basij, a religious volunteer paramilitary force, and control Iran's missile programs. The Guards' overseas Quds forces have fought Iran's proxy wars in the region.

The IRGC is in charge of Iran's ballistic missile and nuclear programs. Tehran has warned that it has missiles with a range of up to 2,000 kms (1,242 miles), putting Israel and U.S. military bases in the region within reach.

Salami, born in 1960, said in January that Iran's strategy was to wipe "the Zionist regime" (Israel) off the political map, Iran's state TV reported.

"We announce that if Israel takes any action to wage a war against us, it will definitely lead to its own elimination," Salami said after an Israeli attack on Iranian targets in Syria in January, Iranian media reported.

Israel sees Iran's nuclear and ballistic missile programs as a threat to its existence. Iran says its nuclear work is for peaceful purposes only.

Israel, which Islamic Iran refuses to recognize, backed Trump's move in May to quit a 2015 international deal on Iran's nuclear program and welcomed Washington's re-imposition of sanctions on Tehran.

Michigan Board of Elections Orders County Clerks to Delete Vote Data

MICHIGAN IT COULDN'T HAPPEN HERE NAZI REICH TO LAST A THOUSAND YEARS MS-13 BLOODS CRIPS BOYZ SISTAS IN HOOD STEAL PRESIDENTIAL ELECTION TRUTH ON TWITTER & ZUCKERBUCKS FACEBOOK ON SOCIAL MEDIA FLAGS JEWS AS RACIST

Kyle Olson

Michigan Republican **legislative leaders were not happy** (WHAT DO YOU MEAN NOT HAPPY; WE'RE GONNA LET THESE SCUMBAGS SHOPLIFT OUR RED REPUBLICAN DEMOCRACY?) **on Friday when they learned the Board of Elections (BOE) ordered county clerks to delete election-related data from government computers.**

On December 1, the BOE, which is under the auspices of Secretary of State Jocelyn Benson (D), sent a memo to all clerks about recounts and the "release of voting equipment."

One section, titled, "E-Pollbook laptops and flash drives," read: The EPB software and associated files must be deleted from all devices by the seventh calendar day following the final canvass and certification of the election (November 30, 2020) unless a petition for recount has been filed and the recount has not been completed, a post-election audit is planned but has not yet been completed, or the deletion of the data has been stayed by an order of the court or the Secretary of State.

That raised the ire of state Rep. Matt Hall (R) and state Sen. Ed McBroom (R), chairmen of their respective oversight committees, who indicated the memo violated an order by House Speaker Lee Chatfield (R) and Senate Majority Leader Mike Shirkey (R) for election data to be preserved.

Chatfield and Shirkey issued a directive on November 6 "which served as notice of the Michigan Legislature's

plans to conduct an inquiry into the general election," a release from Hall said.

"Because of that inquiry, Detroit city clerk and BOE offices were directed to preserve certain materials, including relevant electronic information. The inquiry also demands all surveillance video recordings that were taken at the TCF Center in Detroit from Nov. 3-5 be kept," it continued.

"Our work is about restoring confidence in our elections process. We are making sure that we have access to relevant and needed information as the Legislature performs its inquiry into what happened and that the information hasn't been deleted in the face of that inquiry and litigation that is still out there," Hall said.

"It is concerning this memo went out after a letter was delivered asking these entities to preserve evidence. As a result, we want an assurance that this information is being preserved."

Hall and McBroom said they are requesting "immediate clarity" to ensure the election data is being preserved in accordance with the directive from Chatfield and Shirkey.

Both oversight committees held lengthy hearings this week and took testimony from election workers and observers who claimed laws, rules, and procedures were violated during the counting process at the TCF Center in Detroit.

WHITE HOUSE SHOPLIFTER PAL ZOMBIE THE ELDER & PICKPOCKET KAMIKAZE KAMALA JUNIOR MISS

Lawsuit requests 'new statewide election' in Georgia presidential contest over voter fraud allegations

'...massive irregularities, mistakes, and potential fraud'

Chris Enloe

The Trump campaign filed a new lawsuit in Georgia state court late Friday seeking to invalidate the results of the presidential contest in the Peach State over allegations of voter fraud.

What are the details?

According to WXIA-TV, Trump's legal team claims "tens of thousands of illegal votes" were cast in last month's election. The lawsuit requests the decertification of the state's election results, and wants the court to "order a new election to be conducted in the presidential race." As alleged evidence of their claims, the lawsuit includes "dozens of signed affidavits from Georgia residents who claimed to have witnessed voter fraud," WXIA reported. The lawsuit also demands that the court direct Georgia's Republican-controlled state legislature to appoint presidential electors. Lead Trump campaign counsel Ray Smith said in a statement: What was filed today clearly documents that there are literally tens of thousands of illegal votes that were cast, counted, and included in the tabulations the Secretary of State is preparing to certify. The massive irregularities, mistakes, and potential fraud violate the Georgia Election Code, making it impossible to know with certainty the actual outcome of the presidential race in Georgia.

The Secretary of State has orchestrated the worst excuse for an election in Georgia history. We are asking the Court to vacate the certification of the presidential election and to order a new statewide election for president. Alternatively, we are asking the Court to enjoin the certification and allow the Georgia legislature to reclaim its duty under the U.S. Constitution to appoint the presidential electors for the state.

The Trump campaign's statement explained, "Attached to the complaint are sworn affidavits from dozens of Georgia residents swearing under penalty of perjury to what they witnessed during the election: failure to process and secure the ballots, failure to verify the signatures on absentee ballots, the appearance of mysterious 'pristine' absentee ballots not received in official absentee ballot envelopes that were voted almost solely for Joe Biden, failure to allow poll watchers meaningful access to observe the election, among other violations of law."

What about voter fraud?

Despite the Trump campaign's claims, Attorney General William Barr said this week that the Department of Justice has not uncovered credible evidence of voter fraud. "To date, we have not seen fraud on a scale that could have affected a different outcome in the election," Barr said.

The Georgia secretary of state's office also has clarified on multiple occasions they have neither seen evidence of voter fraud, WXIA noted.

Crowds of supporters swell ahead of Trump's Georgia rally as GOP tension, anticipation build

Trump's mission is to boost turnout in the Jan. 5 twin runoff elections, where the GOP Senate majority is at stake

By Paul Steinhauser

Trump supporters flock to Georgia gov's mansion in call for action

With the Republican majority on the line in Georgia's Senate runoffs, President Trump returns to the campaign trail Saturday for the first time since last month's presidential election.

Crowds of supporters were already lined up to attend the rally. Some even camped overnight, despite temperatures dropping to the mid-30s.

As the mostly maskless supporters stood in line waiting for temperature checks, a chant broke out: "Stop the steal."

On the eve of Trump's trip, Vice President Mike Pence -- in the Peach State for the second time since the kickoff of the twin Senate election showdowns -- emphasized, "President Trump and I need David Perdue and Kelly Loeffler back in the Republican majority in the United States Senate."

Loeffler and Perdue are the GOP candidates in the Jan. 5 elections, which will determine if Republicans hold the chamber, or if Democrats control both the House and Senate, as well as the White House.

While Pence is the most well-known so far in a slew of high-profile Republicans to parachute into Georgia in the past month, the biggest name of all returns Saturday. Trump will headline a rally at 7 p.m. ET at the airport in the southern Georgia city of Valdosta. The event will be carried live by Fox News Channel.

Ahead of his trip, the president tweeted that he'll be holding "a big Trump Rally" for the GOP senators. He emphasized that they are "fantastic people who love their Country and love their State. We must work hard and be sure they win."

For Republicans, there's plenty of anticipation of the president's visit -- and trepidation over what he'll say.

Ahead of the rally, Perdue tweeted that Trump "knows that NO ONE can sit this election out. It's too important, and we MUST hold the line in the Senate. Looking forward to having him down in Georgia on Saturday!"

And on Thursday night at a televised town hall in Georgia on Fox News' "The Ingraham Angle," Perdue predicted that the president's message would be that the best way to protect his achievements the past four years would be *"to get Kelly Loeffler and David Perdue reelected."*

Republicans desperately need Trump supporters to return to the polls a month from now, despite unfounded claims of widespread voter fraud in the Nov. 3 election.

The balance of power for the next Senate coming out of last month's elections is 50 Republicans and 48 Democrats. That means Democrats must win both of Georgia's runoffs to make it a 50-50 split Senate. If that occurs, Vice President-elect Kamala Harris would be the tie-breaking vote, giving her party a razor-thin majority in the chamber.

GEORGIA SENATE RUNOFFS BEING PROBED IN 3RD PARTY CHEATER GROUPS REGISTERING HUNDREDS OF THOUSANDS

OF DEAD & OUT-OF-STATE VOTERS

In Georgia, where state law dictates a runoff if no candidate garners 50% of the vote, Perdue narrowly missed avoiding a runoff, winning 49.75% of the vote. Democratic challenger Jon Ossoff trailed by roughly 87,000 votes.

In the other race, Loeffler captured nearly 26% of the vote in a whopping 20-candidate special election to fill the final two years of the term of former GOP Sen. Johnny Isakson. Democratic candidate Rev. Raphael Warnock won nearly 33% of the vote.

"It's critically important that Republicans are united in this fight against Raphael Warnock and Jon Ossoff," said Jesse Hunt, communications director for the National Republican Senatorial Committee, the re-election arm of the Senate GOP. "It may sound cliché, but with two very consequential runoffs, turnout is critical."

Hunt told Fox News that "the president's visit is going to be an event that energizes and mobilizes our Republican voters."

The visit comes on the eve of Sunday's debate between Loeffler and Warnock, which will be carried live nationally on Fox News. Saturday's event will be Trump's first stop in Georgia since he campaigned there on Nov. 1.

President Donald Trump waves as he leaves after speaking at a campaign rally at Middle Georgia Regional Airport, Trump continues to fight the results of the presidential contest in Georgia, a once solidly red state that's turned into a crucial battleground in recent years. President-elect Joe Biden carried the state by roughly 12,000 votes in last month's election. The results were backed up by a manual recount mandated by state officials. A second recount requested by the president, completed Friday, didn't alter the final result – and the election results were certified.

But as Biden prepares to take office, Trump has continued his assault on the election.

The president this week tweeted or retweeted baseless charges of voter fraud in Georgia, and he's repeatedly attacked Republican Gov. Brian Kemp and Secretary of State Brad Raffensperger, who are both Trump supporters, for their refusal to reverse the election results.

Conspiratorial claims by pro-Trump attorneys Sidney Powell and Lin Wood this week further roiled the waters. They filed lawsuits seeking to overturn Georgia's results. At a rally Wednesday, they went further, urging GOP voters to not support Perdue and Loeffler, charging that the senators have not been supportive enough of Trump's efforts to overturn the election.

"They have not earned your vote. Don't you give it to them," Wood said. "Why would you go back and vote in another rigged election, for God's sake!"

That's got plenty of Republicans in Georgia pushing back.

Former House Speaker and 2012 presidential candidate Newt Gingrich, who represented Georgia in Congress for decades, tweeted this week: "Lin Wood and Sidney Powell are totally destructive. Every Georgia conservative who cares about America MUST vote in the runoff."

Gabriel Sterling, a top Georgia election official and a Republican, predicted that voter fraud allegations by Trump and his allies will drive down GOP turnout in the Senate runoffs. "At this point, there's no way that it can't," he told CNN in an interview this week.

A Southern-based Republican strategist told Fox News that "this stuff from Sidney Powell and Lin Wood is crazy."

"It's hurting our chances in Georgia. It's very confusing to voters," said the strategist, who asked to remain anonymous in order to speak more freely.

GOP leaders are hoping the president will forcefully push back against Powell and Wood at his Saturday rally. But some are also worried over what else Trump may say.

"We need the president to come down here to turn out voters. But what's he going to do or say? Who knows," the GOP strategist said.

On Friday, as his legal team filed a new lawsuit in Georgia, Trump tied the runoffs to his push to reverse the state's presidential election results as he once again demanded a signature audit of ballots.

"The best way to insure a @KLoeffler and @sendavidperdue VICTORY is to allow signature checks in the Presidential race, which will insure a Georgia Presidential win," the president claimed. And he argued that "Spirits will soar and everyone will rush out and VOTE!"

But ahead of the president's trip, a dozen and a half leading Georgia Republicans issued a statement urging that the focus turn from attacks over the Nov. 3 results to the Senate runoffs.

"We have watched with increasing concern as the debate surrounding the state's electoral system has made some within our Party consider whether voting in the coming run-off election matters, "the statement read. "We say today, without equivocation, that without every vote cast for President Trump and all our Republican candidates on November 3 also being cast in the U.S. Senate runoffs, the trajectory of our State and Nation will be irreparably altered on January 5th. Now is the time to unite our Party and win these U.S. Senate seats."

Among those signing the statement were former Republican Sens. Isakson, Saxby Chambliss and Mack Mattingly, and former GOP Gov. Nath

Trump pressures Georgia's governor on voter verification

WHY NOT GET BACK (16) GEORGIA ELECTORAL VOTES STOLEN FROM US?

Trump team files lawsuit in Georgia challenging election results

Former U.S. attorney for Utah Brett Tolman weighs in on 'Fox & Friends.'

President Trump on Saturday pressured Georgia Gov. Brian Kemp to implement a «simple signature verification» process -- which he says would lead to his victory in that state.

Fast Facts

- **Judge James Todd Russell in Carson City dismissed the lawsuit because of a lack of evidence.**
- **Trump's campaign attorney Jesse Binnall presented claims of voter fraud, alleging 42,284 votes were counted twice; roughly 20,000 voters were found to have voted without a Nevada mailing address; 2,468 voters had changed their address to another state; and a supposed 1,506 votes were cast by deceased individuals.**

Trump's campaign attorney Jesse Binnall presented claims of voter fraud, alleging 42,284 votes were counted twice; roughly 20,000 voters were found to have voted without a Nevada mailing address; 2,468 voters had changed their address to another state; and a supposed 1,506 votes were cast by deceased individuals.

Fox News has projected that President-elect Joe Biden has won the state of Georgia. But it is one of a number of swing states in which the Trump campaign has launched legal challenges, as it claims mass voter fraud.

By Eric Mack

Levying explosive claims of widespread voter fraud specifically tied to Dominion Voting Systems and potentially a pay-for-play scheme with GOP Gov. Brian Kemp, Trump campaign lawyer Sidney Powell on Newsmax TV **vowed to deliver a "biblical" voter fraud case this week.**

"We've got tons of evidence; it's so much, it's hard to pull it all together," Powell told Saturday night's "The Count" co-hosted by Rob Schmitt and Mark Halperin, teasing the explosive allegation of the Georgia governor in a contested and key battleground state.

"Hopefully this week we will get it ready to file, and it will be biblical."

"It's a massive project to pull this fraud claim together with the evidence that I want to put in," she added.

"You name the manner of fraud and it occurred in Georgia." Among the most explosive claims alluded to by Powell were:

- **Joe Biden votes being "weighted" at 1.25 times and President Donald Trump votes being parsed at 3/4.**
- **Algorithms that gave Democrats 35,000 extra votes.**
- **Modifications made to voting machines after statutory cutoff dates for changes.**
- **Past election victories, including Hillary Clinton's primary victory over Sen. Bernie Sanders, I-Vt., being forced decided by Dominion Voting Systems.**
- **Alleged pay-for-play kickbacks to public officials, potentially even Georgia GOP Gov. Kemp for a late grant to use Dominion Voting Systems.**

"Georgia is probably going to be the first state I'm gonna blow up," Powell said rhetorically with her pending lawsuits alleging massive voter fraud.

Georgia's Kemp Urges Signature Audit After Smoking Gun' Video Emerges. THIS TURNED OUT TO BE ANOTHER GEORGIA FRAUD, BECAUSE IT WAS IN COBB COUNTY; NOR DEMOCRAT ATLANTA FULTON COUNTY, WHERE MOST FRAUD OCCURRED

Georgia Governor Brian Kemp

Georgia Gov. Brian Kemp calls for a signature audit of the 2020 election results, calls oversight committee testimony 'concerning' But it's the secretary of state who is in charge of elections

Phil Shiver

Georgia Republican Gov. Brian Kemp urged Georgia Secretary of State Brad Raffensperger to conduct a signature audit of the state's 2020 election results Thursday, calling some of the testimony to come out during that day's state Senate Oversight Committee hearing "concerning."

While it is unclear to what degree a signature audit can still be conducted in the state since mail-in ballots are separated from their signed envelopes before they are counted, the call matches what President Donald Trump has been asking for since counting was completed earlier this month showing Democratic nominee Joe Biden edging the incumbent in the state by just under 13,000 votes.

"You know, I've called early on for a signature audit, obviously the secretary of state, per the laws and the Constitution would have to order that; he has not done that," Kemp told Fox News' Laura Ingraham. "I think it should be done. I think, especially with what we saw today, it raises more questions. There needs to be transparency on that. I would again call for that, and I think in the next 24 hours hopefully we'll see a lot more from the hearings that the legislature had today and we'll be able to look and see what the next steps are."

Later in the interview, after Ingraham played video from the hearing showing Democratic poll workers in Fulton County allegedly pulling cases of ballots from under a table to count them while Republican poll watchers were no longer present, Kemp said, "Certainly what [we saw] today was concerning."

"We need to get answers from the secretary of state about exactly what happened," he added. "Obviously, they should be investigating this, I imagine they already are."

Kemp, a Trump supporter, has been under fire from the president this week. On Monday, Trump called the governor out on Twitter, asking, "Why won't Governor [Kemp], the hapless Governor of Georgia, use his emergency powers, which can be easily done, to overrule his obstinate Secretary of State, and do a match of signatures on envelopes[?]"

"It will be a 'goldmine' of fraud, and we will easily WIN the state," the president added. "Also, quickly check the number of envelopes versus the number of ballots. You may just find that there are many more ballots than there are envelopes. So simple, and so easy to do. Georgia Republicans are angry, all Republicans are angry. Get it done!"

After the tweet, Kemp's office quickly responded by clarifying that state law prohibits him from interfering in elections because "the Secretary of State, who is an elected constitutional officer, has oversight over elections that cannot be overridden by executive order."

During the Thursday interview, Ingraham also pressed Kemp on what he may be able to do as governor to ensure election fraud does not occur during next month's Senate runoff elections between Republican Sens. David Perdue and Kelly Loeffler and their Democratic challengers, Jon Ossoff and Rev. Raphael Warnock.

Kemp said he was considering calling the state legislature back to session or facilitating changes through the court system, but did not commit to any action.

Joe Biden's education lead praised communist China's 'magical' school system

She wants this for America. Would you look at that

Phil Shiver

The education lead for Democratic nominee Joe Biden's transition team has a history of speaking fondly of the Chinese Communist Party's school system.

Linda Darling-Hammond, a Stanford University professor who currently serves as the president of the California State Board of Education, once praised the state-run education system for its "magical work" in forging a unified and strong teacher-government presence in student life, the Washington Free Beacon reported.

She made the argument in her 2017 book, titled, "Empowered Educators: How High-Performing Systems Shape Teaching Quality Around the World," in which she also commended China for greatly increasing its public funding of education.

"Teachers in China are revered as elders, role models, and those whom parents entrust to shape the future of their children," she wrote. "In the Tao traditions of ritual, the phrase 'heaven-earth-sovereign-parent-teacher' is repeated and becomes ingrained in how people see themselves holistically governed and supported."

The Post Millennial notes that "sovereign" refers to the leader of a nation, which for China is President Xi Jinping.

Despite Darling-Hammond's tranquil and joyous description of a safe learning environment, Xi and Communist Party leaders exercise ham-fisted authority over the country's educational institutions. Reuters reported that state-sponsored agents are regularly sent into classrooms to supervise and crack down on the dissemination of "western values" or any other "improper" remarks.

Xi has declared that China's systems of higher education must "serve the Communist Party in its management of the country," and "adherence to the Party's leadership is essential to the development of higher education in the country."

Anyone who does not adhere to the Communist Party's leadership is subject to swift punishment. In 2013, a Chinese economist who openly criticized the party was removed from his position at Peking University, a major research institution in Beijing.

According to Reuters, "a year later, the university, once a bastion of free speech in China, established a 24-hour system to monitor public opinion on the internet."

However, Darling-Hammond pays no mind to China's hostile educational environment or the fact that government severely discriminates against the country's less wealthy and well-connected students, leading to 60% of rural students dropping out before even reaching high school.

Darling-Hammond also helped oversee Obama's education transition team for the Department of Education that's intended to ensure a smooth handoff from President Trump's administration.

Darling-Hammond has long been considered a top prospect for Biden's Secretary of Education, but she removed herself from consideration earlier this month, vowing that she is committed to staying in California and working with Gov. Gavin Newsom (D) to achieve their goals in the state.

NEW YORK BLUE HELL DEFUND COPS $1 BILLION IN 2021 NYC'S 2020 shooting surge reaches 'levels unseen in years,' police say

The number of shootings through November in New York City has risen "to levels unseen in years," the police department said Friday in announcing its latest crime statistics.

"The year so far has presented significant public safety challenges with gun violence continuing to afflict New Yorkers across the city," the New York Police Department (NYPD) said in a press release.

The uptick in shootings across the Big Apple continued through November, with the NYPD reporting a surge of 112.5% for the month compared to the same time last year. The police department documented 115 shootings this November compared to the 51 reported during the 2019 month, officials said.

Year to date, the department has seen gun violence skyrocket by 95.8% compared to the first 11 months of 2019 – 1,412 shootings so far in 2020 compared to the 721 by that point last year, police said.

ARRESTED NYC BAR OWNER VOWS TO KEEP FIGHTING CORONAVIRUS RESTRICTIONS, SAYS 'LOST FAITH' IN CUOMO, DE BLASIO

New York Police officers block off the street near the scene where a suspect was killed during a shootout with U.S. marshals in the Bronx that left two officers wounded, The NYPD found that "40% of those accused of a

shooting have had a past gun possession arrest, while 21% of shooting victims have had one."

FUGITIVE WHO ALLEGEDLY SHOT MASSACHUSETTS TROOPER DIES IN GUN BATTLE WITH US MARSHALS IN NYC; 2 AGENTS WOUNDED

Meanwhile, the number of murders for the month and year to date is also up. Police said 28 people were killed citywide this November, compared to the 23 murdered in November 2019.

So far, 422 people have been murdered in 2020 – a 38.4% increase from the 305 people killed during the same time frame in 2019, police said.

But not all news was bad. The number of gun arrests made in November skyrocketed by 112.3%, from 228 in 2019 to 484 last month, police said. Year to date, police have made 3,793 firearms-related arrests, up 22.2% year over year.

Trump: USPS Responsible for Ballot Tampering

By Jeffrey Rodack

President Donald Trump says there is well-documented evidence that the United States Postal Service is responsible for tampering with hundreds of thousands of ballots in the presidential election.

Trump made his comments in a Friday morning tweet. He wrote: "Whistleblowers reveal that the USPS is responsible for tampering with hundreds of thousands of ballots. @OANN This long time Democrat stronghold got rid of massive numbers, especially in swing states, during and before delivery of the ballots. Well documented evidence."

As many as 280,000 pre-marked ballots were transported from Bethpage, New York, to Lancaster, Pennsylvania, in late October and then "disappeared," the director of a public interest law firm said Tuesday, quoting a postal service subcontractor.

Phill Kline, director of the legal group Thomas More Society's Amistad Project, said that a witness has testified to the fact the ballots went missing, which was verified by other witness statements.

Kline claimed postal service workers engaged in "widespread illegal efforts" to influence the election, according to The Epoch Times.

The Amistad Project says it also has sworn expert affidavits claiming "over 300,000 ballots are at issue in Arizona, 548,000 in Michigan, 204,000 in Georgia, and over 121,000 in Pennsylvania.

64 Pennsylvania Lawmakers Urge Congress to Block Electors

By Eric Mack

Pennsylvania has certified its election results, but 64 state Republicans have signed a letter Friday urging Congress to not commit the state's 20 electoral votes for Democrat Joe Biden.

The congressional block of Pennsylvania's electors is "extremely unlikely," University of Iowa law professor Derek Muller told NBC-10 Philadelphia, particularly because it would require Democrat House members to support the contested Pennsylvania election results.

The 64 Pennsylvania lawmakers signing on to the letter still represent less than half of the GOP membership, per the report. Democrat state Rep. Malcolm Kenyatta rebuked the Republican signatories as "hostages of their own misinformation campaign," per NBC-10 Philly. Even Sen. Pat Toomey, R-Pa., a frequent critic of President Donald Trump,. vowed he "will not be objecting to Pennsylvania's slate of electors."

Still, legal scholars like Alan Dershowitz have hailed the Trump campaign's potential constitutional challenges in the state as credible, saying the legislature was unlawfully overridden on election law by

Democrat leaders and their friends in the state courts. Regardless, Pennsylvania Republicans will be introducing election law reforms, but they face a roadblock in approval by Democrat Gov. Tom Wolf.

“We'd like to tighten it up as soon as we can,” state Senate Majority Leader Kim Ward, R-Westmoreland, told NBC-10 Philly. “We always have the hurdle of the governor, working with him, and if he doesn't like it, he just goes to the state Supreme Court.”

Ward was a party to a state-GOP statement vowing to “investigate and seek answers to the questions presented in the 2020 General Election because it is ‘crucial to restoring public confidence in elections.’”

“There are very legitimate and credible issues which need to be resolved after the 2020 election about the security of mail-in ballots and the process of counting votes,” the statement read.

Democrats have objected to changes. State Senate Minority Leader Jay Costa, D-Allegheny, and House Minority Leader Joanna McClinton, D-Philadelphia, called efforts to reform their election law a “sham process.”

“The votes, fairly cast, have been accurately counted and reported,” their statement read, per the report. “It is time to move on and focus on a peaceful transition — rather than partisan efforts to undermine the results ANNE FRANK DOESN'T LIKE.

Giuliani Sees Win in Michigan Court Ruling

By Eric Mack

A review of a flipped marijuana resolution in Michigan's Antrim County has led to a judge ordering records preserved and a forensic review, including photos being taken on the county's 22 precinct election counting machines, the Detroit Free Press reported.

The ruling, not connected to the Trump campaign's election challenge, was hailed as a victory by attorney Rudy Giuliani, because it was on those same machines a “glitch” was found to have erroneously given 6,000 votes to Joe Biden that belonged to President Donald Trump.

Giuliani tweeted:

“Big win for honest elections. Antrim County Judge in Michigan orders forensic examination of 22 Dominion voting machines. This is where the untrustworthy Dominion machine flipped 6000 votes from Trump to Biden. Spiking of votes by Dominion happened all over the state.” The Michigan State Court Administrative Office order comes amid a claim by a voter that ballots were damaged during a Nov. 6 recount, which turned a tie vote on a marijuana proposal to passing by one vote, according to the Free Press.

Circuit Judge Kevin Elsenheimer ruled Friday for preservation of election orders and places a protective order around “forensic images and/or other information gleaned from the forensic investigation.”

The county argued its licensing agreements with Dominion Voting System does not permit access to the machines, but the judge ruled the complaint outweighs that concern – the forensic imagining is taking place Sunday, according to the Free Press.

The voter complaint claims to have evidence the voting "tabulators were compromised," according to the report.

Antrim County is a small area in northern Michigan, where just over 16,000 votes were cast and delivered nearly a 4,000-vote margin for President Trump after the 6,000-vote "glitch" was corrected.

Trump legal team celebrates after Michigan judge allows probe of Dominion voting machines

By Ronn Blitzer

Rudy Giuliani testifies in Michigan over alleged election fraud

A Michigan judge is allowing a forensic investigation of 22 Dominion vote tabulation machines in rural Antrim County amid claims that votes there were compromised.

Trump campaign attorneys celebrated the decision although the case is not related to the presidential contest.

GIULIANI APPEARS WITH WITNESSES ALLEGING VOER FRAUD IN HEATED MICHIGAN HEARING

"Our team is going to be able to go in this morning at about 8:30 and will be there for about eight hours to conduct that forensic examination and we'll have the results in about 48 hours, and that'll tell us a lot about these machines," attorney Jenna Ellis said on "Fox & Friends" Sunday morning.

Trump attorney Rudy Giuliani tweeted that it was a "BIG WIN FOR HONEST ELECTIONS."

NEVADA GOP VOWS APPEAL AFTER JUDGE DISMISSES TRUMP CAMPAIGN'S LATEST SUIT

Antrim County spokesperson Jeremy Scott said forensic images will be taken from county precinct tabulators used in the Nov. 3 election. According to the Detroit Free Press. Fox News asked Scott what role the Trump campaign legal team has in the process, but he did not immediately respond.

The order from Judge Kevin Elsenheimer stems from a challenge made by voter William Bailey, who alleges that ballots were damaged during a recounting of ballots in a village marijuana proposal that narrowly passed.

Elsenheimer's order does not mention the presidential race. The county did, however, draw controversy after an error initially showed that President-elect Joe Biden won, even though Trump was later shown to have won by several thousand votes.

The county clerk, a Republican, corrected the error, saying it was the result of human error, according to the Free Press. Election officials have said the Dominion vote tabulation machines operated properly.

In other contested states, recounts have found no evidence of problems with the machines or their software.

According to the Detroit News, the judge's order instructs the county to "maintain, preserve and protect all records in its possession used to tabulate votes in Antrim County."

Sen. Mike Braun Defends Continued Probe Of Alleged Ballot Fraud

Sen. Mike Braun, R-Ind., speaks to reporters on Jan. 22, 2020.

Sen. Mike Braun, R-Ind., on Sunday defended the continued investigation into alleged ballot fraud, saying half the country is "uncertain" about results that show Joe Biden beat President Donald Trump.

In an interview on ABC News' "This Week," Braun said the uncertainty is "going to be to the disadvantage of whoever is there trying to run the country."

"Whether we dismiss it, reflexively, whether we would find widespread fraud, there's a wide gulf in between, and I think that when you just say that there's nothing there, you're going to have half of the country uncertain about what just happened and disgruntled going into the future," he said.

- Though host George Stephanopoulos asserted the issue has been settled, Braun said "over 50% ... view that something is amiss, and that's going to carry forward in terms of undermining a democracy."

"If you don't pursue it, overturn every stone, this is going to linger into the future," he said.

"Recounts are one thing, and we all know that they hardly ever change result of an election," Braun added.

"Ballot integrity, a whole other issue, and from the get-go, there was a dialogue on recounts and people have certified all this stuff. That, to me, is dismissing some of the evidence, sworn testimony that's out there, and if you don't carry it to its conclusion, you're going to have uneasiness going into the future."

Trump Nevada Lawsuit: Double Ballots Cast, Dead People Voted

Jesse Binnall, an attorney for the Trump campaign, speaks at a news conference Tuesday, Nov. 17, 2020, in Las Vegas.

By Sandy Fitzgerald

The Trump campaign says in a new lawsuit in Nevada that there is evidence that more than 40,000 people voted twice and that there is evidence that votes had been cast in the names of dead people.

Campaign attorney Jesse Binnall told Judge James Russell Thursday in Las Vegas that 1,506 votes came from dead people, 42,284 double ballots were cast, about 20,000 voters voted without having a Nevada mailing address, and 2,468 voters had changed their addresses to another state, reports CBS affiliate KLAS-TV in Las Vegas.

According to results certified last week by Nevada's Supreme Court and Gov. Steve Sisolak, Trump lost to Joe Biden in Nevada by 33,596 votes.

The legal team said it focused on a state election law that lets mail-in ballots be sent without requests, and before the hearing on Thursday the Republican Party in Nevada posted a video on Twitter showing 20 binders it said had evidence to back their claims, reports Fox News.

"We have testimony from multiple witnesses reporting that the USB drives used in the election would show that vote tallies changed overnight," the post said. "That means in the dead of night, votes would appear or disappear on these voting machines during early voting and Election Day."

Binnall told KLAS that during the night, there is "no good explanation" why votes reappeared, but Russell noted that there still is no way to tell who may have voted for whom based on that argument.

He also asked how the information could change the outcome of the evidence.

Attorney Kevin Hamilton, who represented the Democrats, said that there was no evidence beyond hearsay or speculation presented and that Clark County, Nevada, had reported no instances of voter fraud in the June primary.

Binnall told KLAS that the election was "unfortunately stolen."

The district court judge said he will try to make a decision in the case by Friday

KAMIKAZE KAMALA SEIZED AMERICA WHEN PAL ZOMBIE MOVED INTO LENIN'S MAUSOLEUM. "SOCIALISM (1) COUNTRY; (1) SYSTEM; IS (5) YEAR SILICON VALLEY COLLECTIVIZATION REAL-TIME REPOPULATION SOCIAL CREDIT CONTROL PLAN MANAGED BY THE TRILATERAL MARK & PRISCILLA CHINATOWN CHAN ZUCKERBUCKS ZUCKERBERG; TWITTER JACK DORSEY & BILL GATES THOUGHT; TRACKING YOUR MOVEMENTS; THOUGHTS & COMMUNICATION WITH SMARTPHONES; REEDUCATION CONTROL PROGRAM SUB-CONTRACTED W/ RANDI WEINGARTEN PRE-K THRU HARVARD, PRINCETON & YALE DOCTORAL TENURED INFRASTRUCTURE IRON CLAW TEACHERS UNION PRESIDENT RANDI WEINGARTEN; SKANK DISHRAG ALWAYS NOW PORKY BLOATED PIG

America's Biggest Teachers Union Shakedowns

THE LAST THING THESE TEACHERS CARE ABOUT IS IN-PERSON TEACHING FOR BLACK SINGLE MOM KID'S WELFARE. ONLY THE MOST PAY; PENSIONS & BENEFITS USING COVID 19 AS THEIR EXCUSE TO FUCK OFF & NOT WORK WHILE GETTING PAID SEE MY WEBSITE RANDIWEINGARTENOKCORRAL.COM

Adam Barnes

Teachers unions THE MAIN CORE CONSTITUENCY DEMOCRATIC PARTY FOUNDATION; **have been instrumental in keeping American schools online during the pandemic. But some have escalated their positions on reopening to include an array of social justice demands.**

A set of demands from teachers unions in July, which addressed how to safely reopen schools amid a pandemic, was criticized **by The Wall Street Journal editorial board as "political extortion." The board argued that unions were taking advantage of a health crisis to advance their own ideological agendas and to eliminate competition from charter schools.**

"For most Americans the coronavirus is a scourge. But teachers unions seem to think it's also an opportunity—to squeeze more money from taxpayers and put their private and public charter school competition out of business," the board wrote. "Rather than work to open schools safely, the unions are issuing ultimatums and threatening strikes until they are granted their ideological wish list."

"If there's a silver lining here, it's that Americans are getting a closer look at the true, self-interested character of today's teachers unions," The Wall Street Journal editorial board added. (RELATED: Our Kids Are The Hostages — How Teachers Unions Are Using Coronavirus To Try To Line Their Pockets WITHOUT WORKING)

Prior to school openings, Randi Weingarten, president of the American Federation of Teachers, said **that no action was "off the table" when it came to the safety of students and teachers. The head of the National Educators Association Lily Eskelsen García reinforced Weingarten's approach.**

"Nobody wants to see students back in the classroom more than educators, but when it comes to their safety,

we're not ready to take any options off the table," Garcia said.

Studies suggest that schools are not the once-feared super spreaders and the positive COVID-19 tests there typically reflect outbreaks in the surrounding community. A survey conducted by Brown University economist Emily Oster in September analyzed data from schools across 47 states. Out of more than 200,000 students and 63,000 staff tested, the study found an infection rate among staff at 0.24% and 0.13% among students.

Forty % of American students are taking classes exclusively online, USA Today reported in mid-November.

United Teachers Los Angeles (UTLA) made a list of demands in a July policy paper to safely reopen L.A. schools, The Daily Wire reported. The list included a plea for local help to defund police department as well as an effort to close charter schools — their competition. The Union argued police brutality "is a leading cause of death and trauma for Black people, and is a serious public health and moral issue." The paper asks local authorities to "shift the astronomical amount of money devoted to policing, to education and other essential needs such as housing and public health."

Charter schools, according to the 35,000-member union, "drain resources from district schools." The union's policy paper also advocated for a Medicare for All plan, according to The Daily Wire.

UTLA also reached an agreement that barred schools from requiring online, face-to-face instruction, which also included a provision stating teachers do not have to work over four hours a day, according to The Wall Street Journal.

"It is time to take a stand against Trump's dangerous, anti-science agenda that puts the lives of our members, our students, and our families at risk," said UTLA President Cecily Myart-Cruz, The Daily Wire reported. "Even before the spike in infections and Trump's reckless talk, there were serious issues with starting the year on school campuses."

Other states and localities recently shut down their school districts amid a new surge in COVID-19 cases. New York City, despite maintaining an infection rate below 1%, us out of office, teachers unions' political wish lists will look selfish and unfocused on student needs, Hess wrote.

"In the last few years, things have turned around for the unions — they've effectively positioned their members as sympathetic underdogs while riding an anti-Trump progressive wave to great effect," Hess wrote.

"If Biden is wearing his mask and pushing for more school funding, unions will no longer be able to insist that school reopening is just a Trumpian rush back to business-as-usual. A reluctance to get teachers back to school will look less responsible and more self-interested," Hess continued.

FOR DISSENTERS & JEWS LIKE ME; AUTHOR OF THIS BOOK;

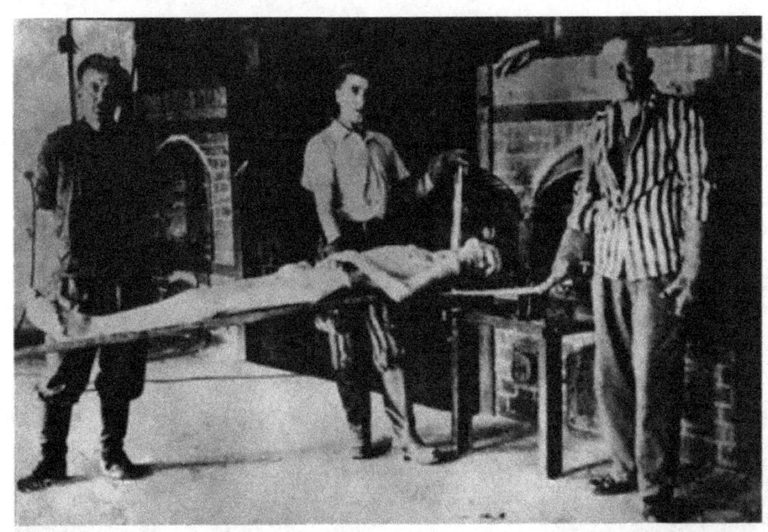

OTHER DAYS OF OTHER AUTHORITARIAN HALLEY'S COMET CROUPIER CHIPS "COMING 'ROUND TO HIS ASS'S WRONG END OF A ROPE VOTE STEALING OF DEMOCRACY PAID FOR BY SLOWLY HANGING WITH HIS FEET ½ INCH FROM THE FLOOR WHILE HE GASPS FOR BREATH WITH HIS WRISTS TIGHTLY TIED BY PIANO WIRE CUTTING INTO HS FLESH BEHIND HIS FUCKEN BACK TOO DARN TOOTIN' GOOD FOR HIS ASS … HIM

EVIL NEVER MISSED BY DIETRICH BONHOEFFER WHO WARNED GERMANY BEFORE IT WAS TOO LATE HAMMURABI; "EYE FOR AN EYE"; "TOOTH FOR A FUCKEN TOOTH TOO FUCKEN GOOD FER 'EM; NO PRISONERS; READ, CHECK; COPY; WE DO UNDERSTAND EACH OTHER, DON'T WE? "

I AM AMERICAN SHE WAITS FOR SHE IS THE PRICE I PAY EVERY INSTANT, UNTIL _

ERADICATING REAL; IMAGINED AND/OR ACCUSED ENEMIES OF HER DEMOCRAT REICH; KAMIKAZE KAMALA BRINGS HER "CLEANSING" DURING WHICH 1 MILLION DISSENTING CONTRARIANS VANISH; CONSOLIDATING KAMIKAZE KAMALA'S FINGER CLAWS IN THE DEMOCRATIC PARTY IN GENERAL; & UNITED STATES IN TOTAL; W/ CHINESE; IRANIAN & CUBAN MUTUAL ADMIRATION SOCIETY NON-AGGRESSION MILITARY; MAIL TRACKED BALLOT ELECTION STRANGULATION; TRIANGULATION; REEDUCATION; OPPOSITION DEPORTATION/ EXTRADITION COOPERATION; ALL FACILITATED WITH THE DIGITAL MARK & PRISCILLA CHINATOWN MOO GOO GAI PAN ZUCKERBUCKS SOCIAL CREDIT FACEBOOK; GOOGLE TRACKING & JACK DORSEY TWITTER ECONOMIC; TENTACLES INCLUDING; BUT NOT LIMITED TO; ANTI-SEMITISM DURING WHICH ALL JEWS VANISH GLOBALLY; COINCIDING WITH EXTERMINATION OF ISRAEL & TERMINATING WITH PREJUDICE ALL JEWISH PROXIES INCLUDING ME IN AMERICA; KAMIKAZE KAMALA DEREPUBLICANIZATION OF AMERICA EMPLOYS HER SHE DEMONS ALEXANDRIA OCASIO-CORTEZ; ILHAN ABDULLAHI OMAR; RASHIDA TLIAB; AYANNA PRESLEY; BERNIE SANDERS; POCAHONTAS WARREN; W/ MASS REPRESSION; BOOK BURNING; & ALL PAST & YET & UNIMAGINABLE FUTURE POLITICAL EXTERMINATION TO SCORCH & CLEANSE THE UNIVERSE OF "THE JEWISH PROBLEM" .

KAMIKAZE KAMALA WALKS THE WALK; TALKING HER BIBLICALIZATION OF MARXIST SOCIAL

CONTROL; POLITICAL IDENTITY; MOST NOTABLY *Black Lives Matter* WAFFEN SS BLOODS & CRIPS MS-13 SECRET ENFORCEMENT MATTERS USEFUL WHITE IDIOT STOCKHOLM SYNDROME DISEASED TISSUE; NIGHT OF WALKING WHITE PRIVILEGE EMBALMED ZOMBIES DIGITALLY ROBOTIC UNTIL REPURPOSING INTO SOYLENT PELLET GREEN NEW DEAL FEEDSTOCK CHOW MADE FROM DISSIDENT HUMAN BEINGS;

W CAPITALISM CRUMPLING; STOCK MARKETS & 401K'S IN FREEFALL WORLDWIDE; CULT OF KAMIKAZE KAMALA PERSONALITY PROJECTS UNPARALLELED UTOPIAN HEIGHTS FOR HER NEW PERSON OF COLOR UTOPIACRACY TRIUMPH OF MEIN KAMPF HERD NEW HUMAN PERSON REPOPULATION. KAMIKAZE KAMALA IS AT BEST; A REMORSELESS; VINDICTIVE; HATEFUL; VENGEFUL; HUNTER OF REPUBLICANS; IN 2021 CONCEIVES & IMPLEMENTS HER; INCLUDING BUT NOT LIMITED TO; DIGITAL LASER LIKE ARTILLERY TWITTER; ZUCKERBUCKS FUNDED FACEBOOK & GOOGLE; NEW SOCIAL DIGITAL PROPAGANDA MEDIA WITH PYRAMID CAPSTONE OF KAMIKAZE KAMALA MARIONETTE TOTAL CONTROL; & HER DEMOCRATIC NATIONAL COMMITTEE TO LAST A THOUSAND YEARS. SHE POSITS: "JEWS ARE A PERSUASIVE BASKET OF DEPLORABLE TRIPWIRE INTELLECT; CHARACTER NATIONALITY; & DETERMINATION TEMPLATE; MY OBSTACLE TO MY USA DEMOCRATIC PARTY FUCKEN REICH EVEN GETTING OFF THE GROUND; MUCH LESS LASTING MY FUCKEN (1000) YEARS; BEFORE IN A FIRE IN THE SKY THE EARTH GOES UP IN A FIREBALL; WITH MY ZUCKERBUCKS RING AROUND MY FUCKEN DEMOCRAT MAY POLE FIDEL/HUGO COMMON DENOMINATOR MULBERRY BUSH; WITH JEWBOY WRITERS INCLUDING; BUT NOT LIMITED TO RICHARD E. GLICK; MOSES; DAVID; SOLOMON; ISIAH; ELIJAH; ABRAHAM; ZACHARIAH; JACOB; ADAM; JESUS OF NAZARETH & EVERY OTHER NO FUCKEN GOOD SORRY FUCKEN ASSED YIDDISHA JEWBOY HALF-BREED MONGREL HOMYONKEL SCUMBAG WHO FUCKS WITH & QUESTIONS MY LIBERAL PROGRESSIVE GREEN NEW DEAL; CONSPIRING WITH ABRAHAM LINCOLN; DONALD JOHN TRUMP; RUDOLPH GIULIANI & SIDNEY POWELL; EVERY FUCKEN ONE OF THEIR ASSES' INCLUDING YOU READING THIS FUCKEN BOOK RIGHT NOW; IS AN OBSTACLE TO & ANTITHETICAL TO MY KAMIKAZE GREEN NEW DEAL KAMALA DEMOCRAT BLUE REICH MATTERS DEMOCRATIC NATIONAL KAMALA SOCIALISM.

MY KAMIKAZE KAMALA "MY PLAYTHING A.K.A AMERICA;" DOCTRINE OF XI JINPING; MAO; FIDEL CASTRO; HUGO CHAVEZ & JOSEPH STALIN LIVES MATTER IS PITCHFORK & TORCH INTIFADA MALLET & OAK STAKE DOOR-TO-DOOR MASS OPPOSITIONAL CLEANSING OF RED AMERICA REPUBLICAN GUNS & RELIGION DEPLORABLE TOTAL EXTERMINATION TO INCLUDE ANY & ALL CONTRARY * OPPOSITIONAL DISSENTING THOUGHTS OF ANY KIND TRUMP DERANGEMENT SYNDROME. IT'S NOT ENOUGH THAT AMERICA KNOWS THERE IS AN ELECTION. REPUBLICANS WHO CAST THE VOTES MUST FOREVER NEVER AGAIN DECIDE ANYTHING

DEMOCRATS WILL FOREVER USE TRICK DOMINION SMARTRONICS & VOTING BY MAIL DECEPTION TO COUNT THE VOTES UNTIL

DEMOCRATS WILL FOREVER DECIDE EVERYTHING UNTIL
DEATH & DISAPPEARANCE OF CONTRARIAN OPPOSITION SHINING SUNLIGHT ON REALITY
SOLVES ALL REICH PROBLEMS; ESPECIALLY JEWISH PROBLEMS; TO LAST A THOUSAND YEARS
PROBLEMS; OR WHICHEVER COMES FIRST;
FOR ALL OF US; NOW & FOREVER, STARTING IN PRESCHOOL
HOW DOTH I CONTROL THEE AMERICA SEA TO SHINING PURPLE MOUNTAINS MAJESTY ….
LET ME COUNT MY WAYS … I'LL CONTROL HER EVERY INSTANT…
I'LL CONTROL HER VERY SOUL …
I'LL CONTROL HIS EVERY FANTASY …
I'LL CONTROL HER AIR …
I'LL CONTROL HIS FOOD …
I'LL CONTROL YOUR TRANSEXUALITY & WATER …
I'LL CONTROL THE BISEXUALITY RACIAL MIX OF WHERE YOU LIVE …
I'LL CONTROL THE TRISEXUALITY OF WHERE; WITH WHOM; HOW LONG YOU GO TO & LEARN
IN SCHOOL …
I'LL CONTROL YOUR PANINTERSEXUALITY AMERICAN HISTORY THAT YOU LEARN …
I'LL CONTROL THE INTERSEXUALITY REPRODUCTIVE & ABORTION SKULL CRUSHING UNTIL
BIRTH ONE SIZE FITS ALL AS WELL AS IF YOU GO TO HEAVEN
OR THE INTERSEXUALITY MULTISEXUALTY OF BREEDING LESBIAN HUMANS WITH
HOMOSEXUAL BABOONS; BONOBOS; CHIMPANZEES & LOWLAND GORILLAS JUST TO START,
AND THEN; BASED ON YOUR DIGITAL TRACKING IN WUHAN CHINA; IF YOU ROT IN HELL ... I'LL
CONTROL YOUR INTERORGANIC TOXIC MASCULINE MASCULINITY
I'LL CONTROL YOUR DIGITALLY VIRTUAL SMOKIN' HOT BABE FEMALE FEMININITY
I'LL CONTROL YOUR PRE & POST INDUSTRIALIZED 3RD TRIMESTER NATIONAL REICH PAID TO
LAST A THOUSAND YEAR TILL & SKULL CRUSHING UNTIL YOUR LAST SECOND BEFORE LIVE
BIRTH …
I'll CONTROL YOUR NATIONAL FEDERATION OF TEACHERS (3) YEAR OLD BOY'S FREEDOM TO BE
A GIRL
I'LL CONTROL YOUR NATIONAL DEMOCRATIC INTERSECTIONALITY SOCIALISTIC (3) YEAR OLD
GIRLS FREEDOM TO BE A BOY
I'LL CONTROL WHAT MARRIAGE IS NOW & WILL FOREVER WILL BE; UNLESS I DECIDE
MARRIAGE WILL NO LONGER EXIST AT ALL
MY CONTROL OF MARRIAGE WILL MAKE UNLAWFUL REPRODUCTION WITH LOVE
I'LL CONTROL YOUR EVERY THOUGHT OF POLITICS & INDIVIDUAL PERSONAL
FREEDOM NOT IDENTICAL TO NAZI DEMOCRATIC MS-13; BLOODS & CRIPS SERVING MY
KAMIKAZE KAMALA COSA NOSTRA REICH MAFIOSI
STARTING WITH STEALING YOUR 2020 VOTES & ELECTIONS
THEN STEALING YOUR ECONOMY THEN STEALING YOUR
POLICE
THEN STEALING EVERY PENNY THAT ONCE BELONGED TO YOU; BUT NOW BELONGS TO
MY KAMIKAZE KAMALA CULTURAL NEW DEAL REVOLUTION STEALING YOUR TAXES
CHOOSING WHO GETS WHAT HEALTHCARE WITH EACH & EVERY ONE OF YOU
FOREVER A MARIONETTE WITH KAMIKAZE KAMALA AS VENTRILOQUIST MARIONETTE

PUPPETEER FOR EACH & EVERYONE OF YOU; IN EACH & EVERY WAY
BUT FOR MY PREFERRED CLASS UNIONIZED PROGRESSIVE STRIDENT DEEP
ADMINISTRATIVE DOCTRINAIRE GESTAPO WAFFEN SS STATE; TO LAST A THOUSAND YEARS;
KAMIKAZE KAMALA CONTROLS YOUR FREEDOM TO READ THIS BOOK
CONTROLS TAXING YOU WITHOUT REPRESENTATION?
JOSEPH GEOBBEL KAMIKAZE KAMALA MEDIA?
LENI REIFENSTALF KAMIKAZE KAMALA
HOLLYWOOD
KAMIKAZE KAMALA COUNTING VOTES COUNTS FOR MORE THAN WHO VOTES & FOR WHOM;
FOR BLUE AMERICA FOREVER COUNTS FOR EVERYTHING & AMERICA NEVER ... LET MY
PEOPLE GO
GOMORRAH ETERNAL
MEIN KAMPF FOREVER
NO GOING BACK
ONLY THE YEARN
NO REPUBLICAN GUNS & RELIGION DEPLORABLES NO PROBLEMS

WHEN DID KAMIKAZE KAMALA & PAL ZOMBIE EVER PROMISE ANNE FRANK A ROSE GARDEN?
NEVER AGAIN FOR YOUR DAUGHTERS, EITHER

PROTECT HER NOW; OR "NEVER AGAIN" CLEAR VISION AT WHITES OF REICH EYES

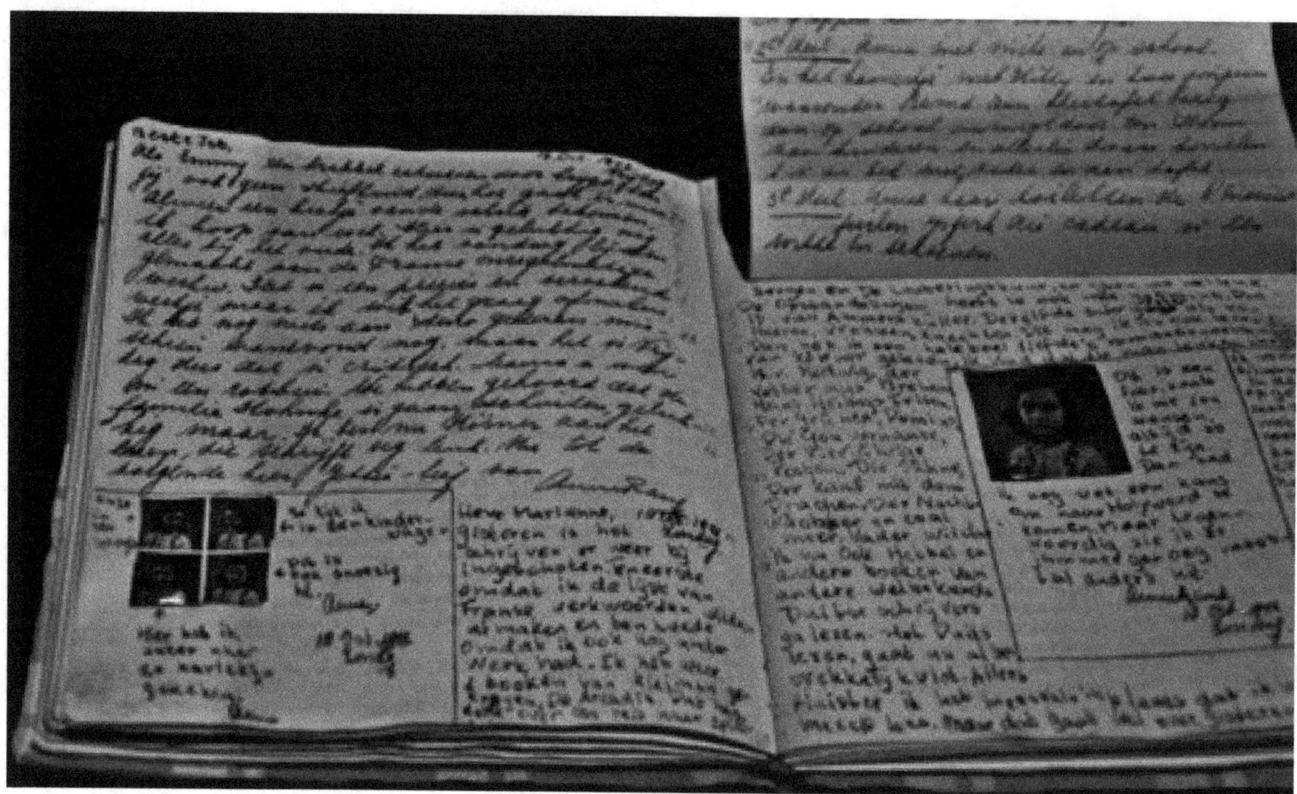

Dit is een foto, zoals
ik me zou wensen,
altijd zo te zijn.
Dan had ik nog wel
een kans om naar
Holywood te komen.
Annefrank.
10 Oct. 1942
(translation)
"This is a photo as I would wish
myself to look all the time. Then
I would maybe have a chance to
come to Hollywood."
Anne Frank, 10 Oct. 1942

- WHO LIVES OR DIES IN OUR 2020 HEAVEN & HELL COIN FLIP; AMY COMEY BARRET; JOHN G. ROBERTS; CLARENCE THOMAS; STEPHEN G. BREYER; SAMUEL A. ALITO JR,; SONIA WISE LATINA SOTOMAYOR; ELENA KAGAN & BRET M. KAVANAUGH???
- AMERICA; HUMANITY; & ANNE FRANK; WE, THE PEOPLE?

THEY CALL US & OUR LEADER DEPLORABLE. THEY SNIDELY, SMUGLY; MOCK; HUMILIATE & RIDICULE US; SNEERING OUR BELOVED PRESIDENT IS A TEMPER TANTRUM PETULANT CHILD WHO SHOULD PUT ON HIS BIG BOY PANTS; THEY THREATEN TO PUT HIM & ALL OF US ON THEIR ENEMY BLACKLIST; AND ALREADY ARE GETTING US FIRED FROM OUR JOBS FOR USING THE WRONG PRONOUNS. EVERYTHING THEY SAY ABOUT DONALD JOHN TRUMP IS THE SAME THING THEY THINK OF US 76 MILLION DEPLORABLES WHO VOTED FOR HIM.

READ THE U.S. CONSTITUTION. WE CHOSE TO JOIN & BECOME A PART OF THESE UNITED STATES. NO WHERE DOES THE CONSTITUTION MENTION DIVORCE. THE CONSTITUTION SAYS THAT ANYTHING OUTSIDE THE LETTER OF THE CONSTITUTION IS LEGAL; UNLESS EXPRESSLY DISALLOWED.

ARE WE AS MAD AS HELL? ARE WE TAKING IT ANYMORE FROM PAL ZOMBIE & KAMIKAZE KAMALA? WE'RE (30) RED STATES; INCLUDING THE (5) THEY'VE STOLEN. THEY'RE (20) BLUE STATES; & THEY USED ELECTION FRAUD TO TURN (6) OUR RED STATES INTO COUNTERFEIT BLUE STATES STATES THAT ARE ACTUALLY RED. WE OWN 89 % OF 2021 U.S.SQUARE MILEAGE &

LAND MASS. MOST U.S. MANUFACTURING; PORTS & 80 % OF THE U.S MILITARY IS ON RED STATE LAND; INCLUDING FORT SUMTER.

IF DEMOCRATS STEAL OUR PRESIDENTIAL ELECTION & MAKE DEMENTIA CRIMINAL ENTERPRISE PAL ZOMBIE PRESIDENT & KAMIKAZE KAMALA MARXIST VICE PRESIDENT; LET THEM HAVE THEIR OWN FUCKEN COUNTRY TO DO IT IN; LET THEM DO IT INTO THEIR OWN (20) BLUE STATES.

BYE. OUR (30) RED STATES WILL SECEDE FROM THE UNION. THEY CAN HAVE RHODE ISLAND. IF THEY DON'T LIKE IT; HAVE CODE PINK DO SOMETHING ABOUT IT.

Battle of Gettysburg

Part of the Eastern Theater of the American Civil War

The *Battle of Gettysburg* by Thure de Thulstrup

Date	**July 1–3, 1863**
Location	Gettysburg, Pennsylvania **39.811°N 77.225°W**Coordinates**: 39.811°N 77.225°W**
Result	Union victory

Belligerents

United States	Confederate States

Commanders and leaders

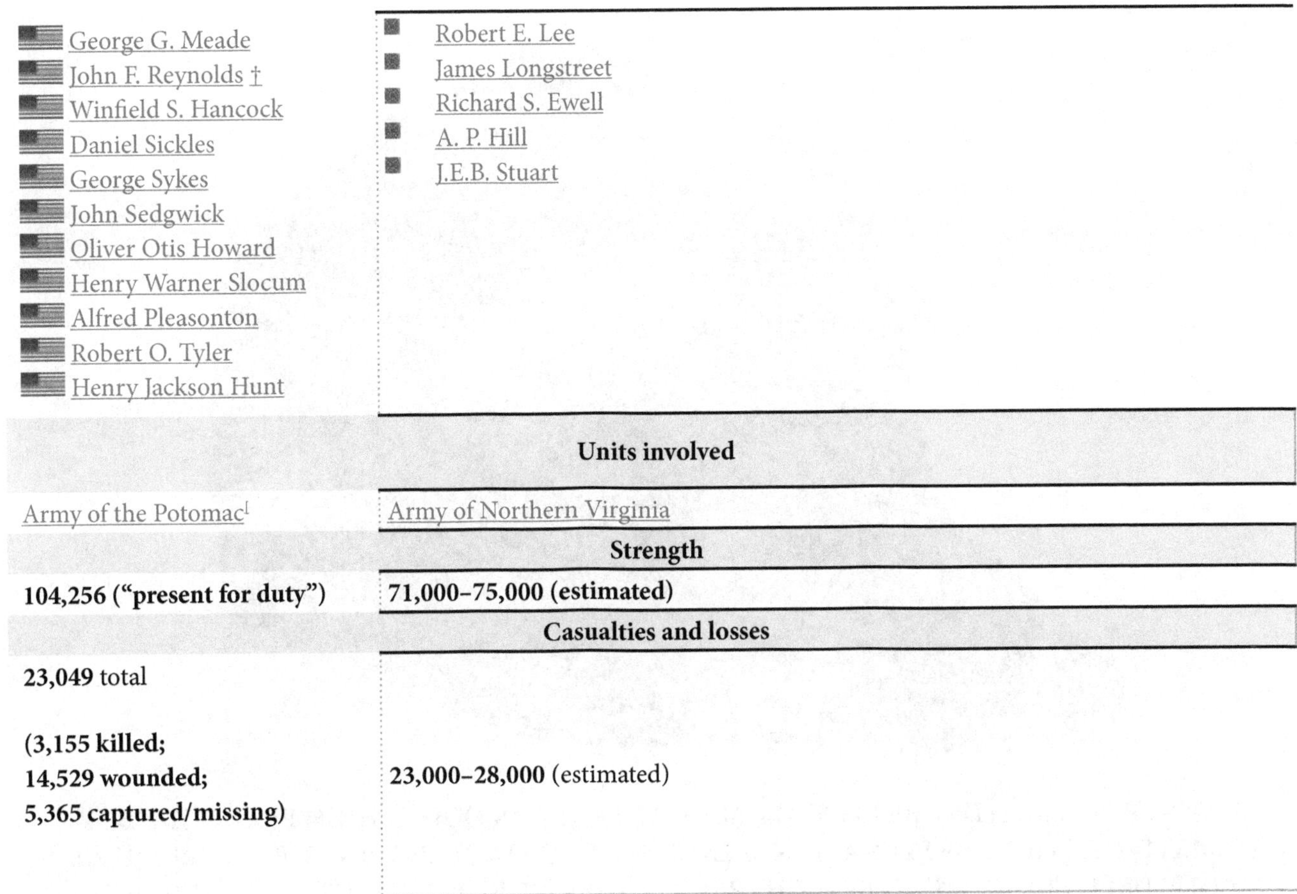

George G. Meade John F. Reynolds † Winfield S. Hancock Daniel Sickles George Sykes John Sedgwick Oliver Otis Howard Henry Warner Slocum Alfred Pleasonton Robert O. Tyler Henry Jackson Hunt	Robert E. Lee James Longstreet Richard S. Ewell A. P. Hill J.E.B. Stuart
Units involved	
Army of the Potomac[1]	Army of Northern Virginia
Strength	
104,256 ("present for duty")	**71,000–75,000 (estimated)**
Casualties and losses	
23,049 total **(3,155 killed; 14,529 wounded; 5,365 captured/missing)**	**23,000–28,000** (estimated)

I DARE BLUE AMERICA CODE PINK MILITARY.

BLUE AMERICA WILL NOT TAX & BULLY RED AMERICA WITHOUT REPRESENTATION.

WHAT WILL FREE RED AMERICA CALL HERSELF? THE CONFEDERATE STATES OF AMERICA? SAVE YOUR DIXIE CUPS. RED AMERICA WILL RISE AGAIN; IN THE FORM OF RED STATE AMERICA? WHO WILL BE OUR PRESIDENT? ABRAHAM LINCOLN IS OUR 1ST PICK. OUR 2ND PICK IS RONALD REAGAN. WIN? PLACE? SHOW? ON DAY ONE THE MOST RECENT PRESIDENT OF THE UNITED STATES WILL THE 1ST PRESIDENT OF THE ACT 2; SCENE ONE CONFEDERATE STATES OF AMERICA HE'S TRIED & PROVEN; THE GREATEST AMERICAN PRESIDENT SINCE ABRAHAM LINCOLN. HAVE WE COME FULL CIRCLE?

WHAT WENT AROUND, CAME AROUND.

ALL ABOARD OUR CHOO CHOO CHUGGING. WE'RE LEAVIN' THE STATION; WITH OR WITHOUT YOU. DON'T MISS THAT TRAIN. GET ON BOARD WITH OUR ENGINEER. DON'T LOOK TO ME LIKE CASEY JONES. THAT HAT LOOKS LIKE MAKE AMERICA GREAT AGAIN. BE DEY IS IN DA' 'HOOD' EBONICS WE' ALL CALLS IT; GALS' BETTA' FO' Y'ALL GALS LATE, DEN BE ALL NEVA' SUCKAS

….. DAT'S BE IS RIGHT; DEY BE IS US' ALL ASSES LEARNIN' IN QUOTA HIGH PLAINS JEWBOY AFFIRMATIVE ACTION; 'BE IS US ALL IN SPENCE; MISS PORTA'S'; CHAPIN; O' BE IS BREARLY'S GOO' OLE' DEPLORABLE ASSED BE IS CHARM SCHOOLS WE BE IS BEIN 'US' ALL STARBUCKS LATTE CHUGGIN' IS BETTA' LATE DEN' NEVA …

REFORMS THAT PUT AMERICA TO WORK AGAIN

The Tax Cuts and Jobs Act made America competitive and helped unleash an economic boom. Now, America First Policies believes more needs to be done.

National Economic Council Director Larry Kudlow has advocated a payroll tax cut and incentives for businesses to bring their supply chains back to this country. The goal: invest in new equipment, hire Americans to make more of what we buy, and put more money in their pockets to buy it.

Offshoring creates risks. Long supply lines are vulnerable to disruption and corruption. In addition, countries like China sponsor governmentwide efforts to steal intellectual property.

The Strengthening America's Supply Chain and National Security Act would identify our supply chain vulnerabilities and build out domestic capacity to eliminate dependence on China and other nations, for the safety and health of all Americans.

The Protecting our Pharmaceutical Supply Chain from China Act would provide economic incentives for

manufacturing drugs and medical equipment in the United States and end U.S. dependence on China for pharmaceutical manufacturing.

America First Policies strongly supports Congress using tax and other incentives to bring manufacturing supply chains back to the U.S., rebuild the middle class and ensure a stronger and more resilient American economy for the future.

AMERICA FIRST TRADE DEALS

For too long, one-sided agreements let other nations import their goods to America, drove American companies offshore and left America dangerously dependent on China and other countries for our essential needs.

New generation trade agreements with Mexico, Canada, South Korea and China have reset the terms for fair and reciprocal trade, bringing manufacturing back home **and boosting exports for American farmers, ranchers and factory workers.**

America First Policies strongly supports ongoing efforts to reform existing trade agreements and negotiate new ones. Talks underway with India, the United Kingdom, **the** European Union **and** a second phase agreement with China **for new generation trade agreements will end the offshoring of American jobs and promote products that carry the label "Made in the USA."**

America First Policies believes Congress should expeditiously approve new generation trade agreements.

JOBS FOCUSED REGULATORY REFORM

Over-regulation hurts independent businesses, farms and the Americans who depend on them. Common-sense regulatory reform will boost employment and expand opportunities while preserving public health and safety.

Every new regulation is an opportunity for a new lawsuit. America wants to go back to work, not back to court. Opening America for business will take more than a pronouncement from politicians in Washington, D.C. It will take administrative and legislative action to prevent frivolous litigation.

National Economic Council Director Larry Kudlow **and a** bipartisan coalition of lawmakers **support stronger liability protections for businesses, healthcare professionals and other essential workers**

Lower energy prices give American industry an advantage and help create American jobs. Proposed Interior Department regulations **will ensure access to resources and energy on public lands and** offshore **for continued American energy independence.**

Proposed regulations **to overhaul** NEPA**, the National Environmental Policy Act, for the first time in 40 years will cut the federal permitting timeline for major projects down to two years. This will help reduce traffic** in our cities, connect our rural communities to high-speed Internet and grow America's economy, ensuring America remains the best place to live, work and raise a family.

America First Policies supports legislative and regulatory reform efforts to strengthen America's economy, promote energy independence, and help America's Main Street businesses, middle class and manufacturers.

A STRONG AMERICAN WORKFORCE

As we rebuild American industry and economy, job training that expands opportunities for Americans is more important than ever.

Already, over 360 companies have taken the Pledge to America's Workers, providing over 14 million training jobs and career opportunities.

The FY 2021 budget calls for a $900 million increase in funding to provide vocational and technical education in every high school in America.

Proposed regulations at the U.S. Department of Labor would allow companies, unions, non-profits and trade associations to develop apprenticeship programs that will train Americans for the jobs that are going begging today.

The Education Freedom Scholarships and Opportunity Act now before Congress would provide $5 billion for state-based scholarship programs, empowering all parents to send their kids to the public, private, religious, public charter, home, or magnet school they feel best meets the needs of their children.

The proposed Second Step Act will earmark millions of dollars for Federal programs to reduce the rate of recidivism, offer prisoners the support they need for life after their release, and support reentry programs, inmate education, and occupational training programs.

America First Policies urges Congress and the Administration to support these measures to help make certain Americans have skills and opportunities.

PUTTING AMERICA TO WORK BUILDING 21ST CENTURY INFRASTRUCTURE

From highways and ports to the Internet and emerging 5G Internet, infrastructure is essential to America's way of life and prosperity.

Congress should adopt America's Transportation Infrastructure Act, the largest highway infrastructure bill in our history to rebuild our roads, highways and bridges. Proposed regulations will ensure more rural Americans will have access to high speed broadband Internet. America First Policies believes in building strong infrastructure to put America back to work. We urge Congress to pass America's Transportation Infrastructure Act and support Administration efforts to promote high speed broadband Internet

Trump Says His Campaign Will Make New Legal Challenge In Wisconsin After Recount

Anders Hagstrom

President Donald Trump's campaign will make a new legal challenge in Wisconsin after the state finishes its recount this week, Trump announced Saturday. Biden took the state by more than 20,000 votes, a lead the recount is unlikely to overturn. Trump says his campaign will seek to remove individuals they say voted illegally, an argument they've made unsuccessfully in several other states. Trump's challenges in the state got off to a rough start, with lead lawyer Jim Troupis arguing his own vote was illegal. The campaign is seeking to throw out all in-person absentee ballots, a method used for early voting. Both Troupis and his wife used this method to vote in the 2020 election.

Troupis reportedly declined to answer questions about his voting method, though he acknowledged his own vote is among those the campaign is seeking to throw out, according to the Milwaukee Journal-Sentinel. Trump has ongoing legal challenges in both Wisconsin and Pennsylvania, where he is seeking to overturn President-elect Joe Biden's 81,000-vote lead. The Third District Court of Appeals threw out Trump's lawsuit in Penn-

sylvania on Friday, saying the campaign had made no specific allegations and provided no evidence of fraud.

AMERICAN DEMOCRAT MARXISTS WANT ALL CAPITALISM TO FAIL SO GOVERNMENT OWNS EVERYTHING; PAYS EVERYONE; & ALL GOVERNMENT EMPLOYEES VOTE FOR THE ONE WORLD, ONE STATE TOTALITARIAN STALINISM GOVERNMENT THAT BREAST SUCKLES EVERYONE; THE CRYSTAL BALL UNDER PAL ZOMBIE & KAMIKAZE KAMALA; ALREADY, IN NEW YORK; THERE ARE NO JOBS FOR THE BEST & BRIGHTEST COLLEGE GRADUATES. UNLESS YOU'RE THE INSIDER CONNECTED PREFERRED CLASS WITH A GOVERNMENT JOB. WHAT LUNATIC IN THE PRIVATE SECTOR WOULD THROW AWAY HIS CAPITAL BY INVESTING IN NEW YORK; WHERE CUOMO & DE BLASIO HAVE SHUT EVERYTHING; ALLEGEDLY UNDER THE PHONY GUISE OF CUTTING COVID RISK TO ZERO? WHO WOULD OPEN A RESTAURANT; A THEATER OF FITNESS GYM? OR A STORE WHERE MACY'S MIRACLE ON 3TH STREET IS LOOTED BY (1000'S) OF SAVAGES; EVEN WITH THOSE ARRESTED IMMEDIATELY RELEASED; WITH NONE EVER PROSECUTED; WITH MOST COPS LOOKING ON; DOING NOTHING; REPEAT; NEW YORK CITY LAW ENFORCEMENT PROSECUTING NOBODY. REALITY IS THERE ARE NOW NO GOOD JOBS FOR YOUNG PEOPLE; EVEN THE BEST & BRIGHTEST, TO LIVE INDEPENDENTLY. AND ANYONE WHO CAN WILL GET OUT & MOVE TO RED TEXAS, TENNESSEE & IF THEY DON'T GET READY FOR THE CHINESE BLUE STATE AUTHORITARIAN DEMOCRATIC PARTY DIGITALLY REAL-TIME FUTURE SOCIAL CREDIT COMING SOON

NYC's Finances 'Bleak,' Will Go Bankrupt if Not Fixed, Says Ex-Official

New York City is in dire financial straits because of the coronavirus pandemic and will go bankrupt if the situation isn't addressed, according to a former deputy mayor.

In a radio show interview with John Catsimatidis "The Cat's Roundtable" on WABC 770 AM-N.Y.aired Sunday, Randy Levine, currently president of the New York Yankees, said "good financial footing" has to be restored.

"Because of the pandemic, because of what's happened here, the fiscal situation in the city is really, really bleak. It hasn't gotten the attention that it deserves," Levine said in comments posted by The Hill.

"If this city is not on good financial footing, then nothing else can happen," he said, adding: "If you don't solve this problem, then nothing happens. The city will go bankrupt."

Levine served as the deputy mayor for economic development, planning and administration from 1997 to 2000.

The city has doled out $5.2 billion to deal with the pandemic, including paying for ventilators, food assistance, testing and reopening schools with COVID-19 precautions, the New York Times reported, and is facing a $4 billion budget gap.

"We have giant out-year budget deficits. The private sector is shrinking. Businesses are closing," Levine said. "People can't pay their mortgages, their rent. Real estate is depressed."

"If you don't fix [the budget] you'll have no city services," he added. "If we have a city that goes bankrupt, then there's going to be chaos."

"We've got to reduce the size of the city government in a planned way," Levine argued, adding that this includes reducing the number of city employees, selling unused city property and focusing on funding for "core services."

Since COVID-19 first ravaged the city in the spring, Broadway shows, restaurants and other tourist attractions have been forced to shut down, leading to 896,000 private sector jobs lost between February and April, according to the city comptroller's office.

JONATHAN CHENG/CHUN HAN WONG

LU YUYU ESTIMATES HE DOCUMENTED ROUGHLY 70,000 PROTESTS AND DEMONSTRATIONS IN CHINA FROM 2012 TO 2016. HE WAS SENTENCED TO FOUR YEARS IN PRISON FOR HIS WORK.

SOON, FROM AN INCH AWAY; HIS KIND WILL GET A BULLET FROM SUPREME DEAR LEADER; XI JINPING; MAO GOING FORWARD; TO THE BACK OF HIS HEAD;

On a summer day in 2016, a posse of men surrounded Lu Yuyu on a street in China's southwestern city of

Dali. He said they wrestled him into a black sedan and slid a shroud over his head. His girlfriend was pushed into a second car, screaming his name.

Mr. Lu had for years posted a running online tally of protests and demonstrations in China that was closely read by activists and academics around the world, as well as by government censors. That made him a target.

While China's Communist Party has long punished people seen as threats to its rule, government authorities under Chinese leader Xi Jinping have engaged in the most relentless pursuit of dissenters since the crackdown on the 1989 Tiananmen Square pro-democracy protests, according to academics and activists.

"Over the past eight years under Xi, authorities have become hypersensitive to the publicizing of protests, social movements and mass resistance," said Wu Qiang, a former politics lecturer at Beijing's Tsinghua University.

"Lu's data provided a window into social trends in China," Mr. Wu said, and that made him a threat to the party. China Labour Bulletin, a Hong Kong-based group that promotes worker rights, used Mr. Lu's posts as the primary source for its "Strike Map," an interactive online graphic tallying worker unrest.

Chinese leader Xi Jinping, center, is applauded by senior members of the government on Oct. 23 in Beijing.

Mr. Xi's crackdown has snared women planning protests against sexual harassment, human-rights lawyers once given leeway and Marxist students advocating workers' rights. Many have endured lengthy detentions and various forms of psychological pressure.

"Their goal is to make you feel helpless, hopeless, devoid of any support, U.S.A. DEMOCRATS WILL break you down so you begin to see activism as something foolish that doesn't benefit anyone, and gives pain to everyone around you," said Yaxue Cao, a Washington-based activist who runs China Change, a news and commentary website advocating for human rights. "In so many cases, they are successful."

After Mr. Lu was snatched off the street, he spent four years in custody, his girlfriend left him, and, since his release in June, he said he has been kept under close watch by police. He struggles to find steady work, he said, and suffers from depression. His landlord recently asked him to move, he said, citing pressure from authorities.

The experience keeps him far from his past documentation work. "If you're lucky, they'd detain you within a month, or if you're unlucky, within a week," said Mr. Lu, 43 years old. "There's no point."

Control The Population Cost

China's annual national expenditure on public security

1.50 Trillion yuan Xi Jinping in office 1.25; 1.00; 0.75; 0.50; 0.25; retroactively since 2007; '09; '11; '13; '15; '17; '19

Note: 1 trillion yuan = $151.7 billion at current exchange rate

Source: China's Ministry of Finance

For years, the Communist Party grudgingly allowed a limited role for NGOs and activists, from environmentalists to labor organizers, to contribute policy ideas and tackle social problems. Under Mr. Xi, such work became solely the party's domain. Modern surveillance has made it easier to hound anyone trying to perform that role outside of party control. China's annual national spending on (SOCIAL CREDIT DIGITAL SURVEILLANCE) public security has nearly doubled since Mr. Xi took power in late 2012, reaching the equivalent of about $211 billion in 2019 at current rates, according to government figures.

Mr. Lu recounted his life in interviews with The Wall Street Journal, giving a detailed picture of the government's tactics. The Journal corroborated much of his story through court documents and interviews with his friends and lawyers involved in his case. His account is consistent with other cases documented by human-rights activists.

Mr. Lu, who considers himself a record-keeper rather than an activist, said speaking up was a way to resist government censorship and to protect himself. "Being silenced would mean they can act brazenly and lock you down," he said. Police and judicial authorities connected with Mr. Lu's detention, trial, imprisonment and subsequent surveillance didn't respond to queries about his case.

Internet explorer

Mr. Lu was born in the impoverished southwestern province of Guizhou, where his father ran a seedling farm. He was a shy boy, and his parents sent him to live with different families to learn how to better interact with people. He was bullied in school, he said, and struggled with his studies. At 19, he went to prison for about six years after stabbing and wounding someone. He said he was standing up for a friend who had gotten into a fight.

After his release in 2002, Mr. Lu drifted from job to job, working in factories and construction. He discovered "dark folk," music that mixed folk and industrial styles, and devoted hours online following his favorite Finnish and German bands. His moniker, "Darkmamu," paired his musical interest with the Romanization of the Chinese word for numbness.

"I saw no hope in anything and had no direction in life," he said.

That began to change in 2011, when he tuned into social-media chatter about such Chinese activists as dissident artist Ai Weiwei. Censorship on China's Twitter -like Weibo microblogging platform was relatively loose at the time, allowing more open discussion about social issues and criticism of government policies.

In April 2012, Mr. Lu raised a banner along a Shanghai thoroughfare calling for China's leaders to publicly declare their personal assets, a way to curb corruption. He also called for the right to vote. Police chased him out of the city, he said, and when he returned, they detained him for 10 days.

Workers in China's Wenling city protested the closure of more than 4,500 shoe factories in a safety crackdown after 16 people were killed in a 2014 factory fire. Demonstrations flared across China that year, including high-profile protests against power and copper plant projects. Mr. Lu, who moved to the southern city of Fuzhou, scoured social media and began to realize the scale of national unrest. He said he decided to document as many demonstrations as he could.

"It wouldn't change the broad trajectories of history," he said, "but for me, I felt like I was doing something that meant I haven't lived in vain."

Mr. Lu sifted through online chatter, images and videos of public unrest, posting his findings on Weibo, he said. He sharpened his abilities to cross-check information. He quit his job at a plastics factory, he said, and started a blog with a university student, Li Tingyu, who admired his work before she became his girlfriend and collaborator. They raised donations that supported full-time research, and their work drew attention abroad.

Police showed up at the couple's apartment in the southern city of Zhuhai, Mr. Lu said, to warn them against continuing to publish their findings. Mr. Lu said he believes what followed was government-directed harassment: Their landlord refused to renew their lease. Strangers knocked on their door and claimed they were the new tenants. One day, they lost running water.

Li Tingyu and Lu Yuyu in 2015.

The couple moved to Dali in southwestern China, where they isolated themselves from family, friends and

acquaintances. Authorities eventually found them there. On June 15, 2016, the couple posted a tally of 94 demonstrations, including 27 protests by workers airing such grievances as unpaid wages. Later that day, they were picking up an online-shopping delivery at a courier station when they were captured by police and hustled away in separate cars, Mr. Lu recalled.

Days later, friends and supporters sensed trouble. Human-rights lawyers learned Mr. Lu and Ms. Li had been accused of "picking quarrels and provoking trouble." The charge was commonly used for disorderly conduct such as damaging property. In 2013, it was expanded to include online behavior by defining the internet as a public space. The couple had compiled a data set comprising 67,502 protests that spanned June 2013 to June 2016, according to a 2019 research paper by Zhang Han, now an assistant professor at the Hong Kong University of Science and Technology, and Jennifer Pan, a Stanford University assistant professor who studies authoritarian governance. Through their blog, Mr. Lu and Ms. Li drew broad attention to protests in China, Ms. Pan said, "which is precisely the information government censors want to suppress." After Mr. Lu's arrest, investigators waved copies of his social-media posts at him. "Why do you collect and publish this information? What's the purpose?" Mr. Lu recalled an official asking him. He said he was documenting history.

Through the weeks of interrogation, Mr. Lu said, his thoughts often drifted to his girlfriend. He worried about who would take care of their pet, a tomcat named "Little Yellow Fur."

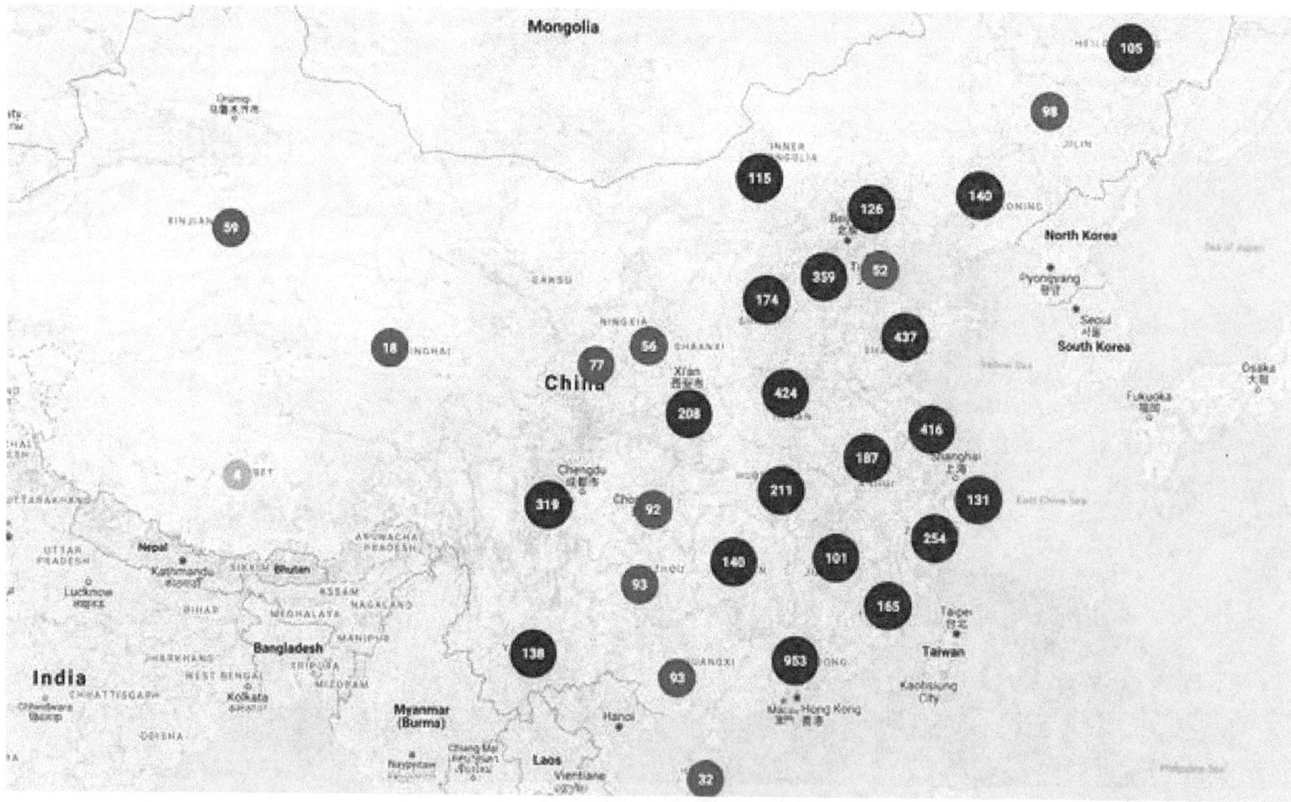

An interactive 'Strike Map' made by Hong Kong-based China Labour Bulletin tracked incidents of worker unrest in China. It used data compiled by Lu Yuyu and Li Tingyu until the couple's detention in June 2016.

Prosecutors and police pressed Mr. Lu to plead guilty, which typically is rewarded with a lighter sentence. He said officials brought his father to the detention center hoping to persuade Mr. Lu, but he refused to acknowledge wrongdoing.

In November 2016, the journalist advocacy group Reporters Without Borders and French television broadcaster TV5Monde jointly awarded Mr. Lu and Ms. Li a press-freedom prize for "their commitment to freely and independently-reported information in China," work the couple did at a high personal cost.

Officials visited Mr. Lu the following April, he said, to let him know Ms. Li had been convicted and given a suspended sentence. Mr. Lu said officials hoped he, too, would plead guilty. A copy of a Chinese court document related to Mr. Lu's case, viewed by Journal, said Ms. Li had confessed.

Mr. Lu stood trial in June 2017. Prosecutors accused him of spreading false information. Mr. Lu, who denied wrongdoing, was convicted and sentenced to four years. His appeals were denied, according to court records.

In prison, Mr. Lu lived in a 12-man cell and worked 10-hour shifts sewing jeans, skirts and other apparel. He was paid the equivalent of a few dollars a month, he said.

Prison life wore on Mr. Lu. Last year, he suffered hallucinations and bouts of paranoia, he said. Prison officials offered counseling, but his symptoms persisted. About two months before his release, Mr. Lu said, he received a judicial notice forbidding him from setting foot in Beijing, Shanghai or Xinjiang.

Mr. Lu tracked tens of thousands of protests in China, including one in Shanghai where demonstrators in June 2015 carried banners opposing rumored plans for a paraxylene plant; and a protest later that year in Shanghai by investors in a metals exchange.

No escape

After leaving prison, Mr. Lu moved in temporarily with his brother in their hometown. Police showed up to get his cellphone number. An official with the police department's political-security arm would call him to ask where he was and what he was up to. Mr. Lu moved to an apartment in the city of Zunyi, near his home village. Local police found him within a week, he said. He returned to social media with a new Twitter account, circumventing Chinese internet controls that block the platform. He listed his location as "hell" and posted an account of his detention and trial.

Mr. Lu tried to track down Ms. Li and eventually reached her mother. She said her daughter had married. Mr. Lu insisted on speaking to Ms. Li, and that night she called, sobbing as she apologized and said she had a new life, Mr. Lu recounted. She couldn't be reached for comment. In early August, police issued Mr. Lu a warning for using a virtual private network to circumvent Chinese internet controls. They seized his mobile phone and computer, which were later returned. He said police told him not to speak to news media.

Mr. Lu said he no longer felt safe in Zunyi. A couple of weeks later, he began traveling, first within Guizhou. He posted photos from his trips on social media, including shots of the lush cliffs along Guizhou's Wuyang River and cattle on a grassy mountain in Fujian province.

Lu Yuyu earlier this fall in China.

Zunyi police kept close track of his whereabouts. An official would call him and ask, “What are you doing?” The phone calls and questions were repeated every time he reached a new city. Mr. Lu knew it was pointless to lie.

In late September, while Mr. Lu was staying at a friend’s apartment in the southern city of Guangzhou, officers called the friend and asked to meet. Mr. Lu then moved to a second friend’s apartment. The following day, police called the second friend who alerted Mr. Lu. It was too late. The officers were already at the door. They had made the call from downstairs.

The officers told Mr. Lu he had to leave Guangzhou. When he refused, they drove him to a police station, collected data from his phone and hauled him to the train station, he said. Hours later, the police texted a request: Send a selfie to prove he had reached his destination.

Police and justice-bureau officials in Zunyi regularly summon Mr. Lu to ask about his plans and warn him against circumventing internet controls.

While Mr. Lu has enough savings to survive for several months, he said he hopes he can secure a job soon. Police surveillance makes it tough to leave his hometown, where job opportunities are limited. Depression at times keeps him from sleeping more than a couple of hours a night, he said. In late October, his landlord, under pressure from authorities, told him he had to move.

Mr. Lu is comforted by his work documenting tens of thousands of protests, even if he can't return to that role. "I'd just end up in jail again," he said. "You can tell people how brave you are, but in reality you wouldn't achieve anything."

Zeldin: Gov't Has 'a Responsibility' to Ensure Businesses it Shuts Down Are 'Still Alive' – NYC Isn't Considering Impact of Restrictions Ian Hanchett

On Saturday's broadcast of the Fox News Channel's "Fox & Friends," Rep. Lee Zeldin (R-NY) stated that leaders like New York City Mayor Bill de Blasio (D) haven't taken into consideration "the impacts on whether or not a business can survive their restrictions."

TOUCHDOWN NEW YORK CITY; STATE; COUNTIES & MUNICIPAL TAX JURISDICTIONS WANT GOVERNMENT TAX LIENS SO THEY CAN SEIZE ALL WINNER KEEP ALL A.K.A. DEMOCRAT GOVERNMENT CARCASSES OF REAL ESTATE & PRIVATE PROPERTY FREE ENTERPRISE THIS IS GREEN NEW DEAL MARXISM ALL ALONG.

Zeldin stated that government has an obligation to make sure that businesses that were doing well before the government shut them down are "still alive on the other side."

Zeldin said [relevant remarks begin around 2:20] there needs to be "More funding for the Paycheck Protection Program, driving funding towards these small businesses. The restaurant industry has been especially hit hard, they're not the only business, but restaurants have been hit hard, especially when you add on the state and local restrictions. When you have feckless leaders like say, a Bill de Blasio in New York City, where, at a whim, they'll close down small businesses and they don't really measure the impacts on whether or not a business can survive their restrictions. I believe that the government has a responsibility. If you're going to shut down a business that was doing well before you shut them down, you have a responsibility to make sure that they're still alive on the other side."

DEPLORABLE GUNS & RELIGION RESISTANCE IS ONLY KNOWLEDGE; & COMMUNICATION AMONG OURSELVES; WHILE STILL POSSIBLE

Team Trump Looking Past Election Suits to State Houses

By Brian Trusdell

Rudy Giuliani says he and his associates contesting election results on behalf of President Donald Trump will be lobbying state legislatures in key states to assert their authority in determining the electors for the Electoral College in addition to their legal challenges because they "don't have a lot of time."

Appearing on Newsmax TV**'s** "Greg Kelly Reports" on Thursday, Giuliani said the Trump campaign is taking a two-prong approach. **"We're doing both, with equal speed and enthusiasm and taking advantage of which one gives us the hearing the quickest. And which one will work fastest for us," said Giuliani, the former mayor of New York City. "Because we don't have a lot of time. We've got a lot of evidence; we don't have a lot of time. And we're facing a major censorship, so it's very hard to get this information out to the public.**

"The public has only a small idea of the kind of evidence we have."

Giuliani's comments come on the day that a federal appeals court refused to hear the Trump camp**aign's appeal of a lawsuit challenging the results of the presidential election in Pennsylvania rejected by Barack Obama-appointed district court Judge Matthew Brann.**

The former mayor disputed the contention saying he had affidavits from election observers that were denied access to witness ballots being counted, of absentee ballots being "cured" — that is, information such as a voter signature or missing secrecy envelope was allowed to be corrected, among other irregularities.

"The situation in Michigan was worse than the situation in Pennsylvania," Giuliani said. "The situation in Wisconsin was outrageous. I mean they have all these absentee ballots without applications. In Nevada, they used a machine that basically didn't work and let every signature go through, even though it's illegal to use a machine. I mean they cheated in all the places that were critical to them. And you know they did, because Trump was way ahead on the night of the election. It's impossible that (Joe) Biden would have come back in every single one of those places. Impossible."

Giuliani's strategy appears to already have some traction in Pennsylvania, where state Sen. Doug Mastriano said half of the leadership in both houses of the General Assembly, both controlled by Republicans, support the efforts to reclaim their authority to appoint electors to the Electoral College.

"I've spent two hours online trying to coordinate this with my colleagues. And there's a lot of good people working this here," Mastriano said Friday on "War Room," former White House strategist Steve Bannon's video podcast. "Saying, that the resolution saying we're going to take our power back. We're going to seat the electors. Now obviously we're going to need the support of the leadership of the House and Senate. We're getting there on that.

Giuliani: 3 State Legislatures Could Change Electoral College Voters

Rudy Giuliani speaks at a press conference on Nov. 7, 2020.

President Donald Trump's attorney Rudy Giuliani said Sunday that legislatures in three states that Trump lost could wind up deciding who votes in the Electoral College — likely sending the election issue to the U.S. Supreme Court.

In an interview on Fox News' "Sunday Morning Futures," Giuliani says he believes the legislative bodies in Georgia, Michigan and Arizona are poised to take votes on electors.

In Georgia, he asserted, "they started a petition to hold their own session, which they're allowed to do under the Constitution.

"They're the first legislature to do this now. This is a constitutional role that the founding fathers gave to our legislatures. They're the ones who are supposed to select the president, not the governors, not the board of elections. They're the ones who have the constitutional obligation to decide on the electors."

"Michigan is considering the same thing," Giuliani claimed. "They're not quite as far along, but they are drafting something right now, and so is Arizona, so those three ... could very well end up in front of the leg-

islature to decide who the electors are."

Giuliani said in Wisconsin, there's a lawsuit that "basically says if you don't have an application for the [absentee] ballot, the ballot doesn't count."

"There are some 50-or-60,000 ballots without applications, they would have to be thrown out and that would change the election," he claimed.

"If any of these state legislatures change the electors based on their own analysis, of course that'll be taken to the Supreme Court and the Supreme Court will have to decide if it was done reasonably, rationally, or arbitrarily that's the standard," he said.

"In each case each one of these legislatures has more than enough of that to sustain the Supreme Court challenge," he claimed.

Giuliani's strategy was outlined as Supreme Court Justice Samuel Alito asked Pennsylvania officials to file response briefs to an effort by Rep. Mike Kelly, R-Pa., to flip the state's election results.

Kelly is hoping to get the nation's high court to take up the same election case the Pennsylvania Supreme Court has already rejected.

His 50-page filing was submitted to Alito, who oversees cases from the Third Circuit, which includes Pennsylvania, the legal website, **Law & Crime reported. A hearing was requested for Tuesday. Pennsylvania's members of the Electoral College are due to meet Dec. 14.**

According to Law & Crime, Kelly's arguments center on a pre-COVID-19 pandemic state election reform law that created a "no-excuse mail-in" voting regime that he claims violates the state constitution.

Kelly argues people have to vote in person unless they can take advantage of only a few, narrow excuses contained within the state constitution — and that the 2019 reform law should be struck down as invalid, the website reported.

Though the Supreme Court doesn't strictly have jurisdiction to settle Pennsylvania constitutional issues, Kelly argues the state is acting under a "direct grant of authority" from the U.S. Constitution, which gives the high court the right to jump in.

DNI Ratcliffe: Elex 'Issues' Have To Be Settled Before Winner Declared

Director of National Intelligence John Ratcliffe

Director of National Intelligence John Ratcliffe said Sunday it's yet to be decided if there'll be a Biden administration.

In an interview on Fox News' "Sunday Morning Futures," Ratcliffe said issues outlined by President Donald Trump's legal team, headed by Rudy Giuliani, have to be heard in court.

"These election issues, we'll see who is in what seats and whether there is a Biden administration," he said.

According to Ratcliffe, universal mail-in balloting had never been done before this presidential election, and is behind the many questions about the election results. "Essentially we had universal mail-in balloting across this country in a way we hadn't seen before and to that point, almost 73% of the American people this year voted before Election Day, a good & of those, by mail," he said.

"That's about an 80% increase over anything we've ever seen before, so it's little wonder that we see what's happening around the country as a result of that, with mail-in balloting and all of the questions —and

the questions that are being raised in lawsuits and by everyday Americans about what happened in the election."

Ratcliffe praised the nation's intelligence community and the way it addressed problems from foreign interference "that we saw in 2016."

"But people need to understand that's different than election fraud issues — things like postal drivers saying they took 200,000-plus ballots from New York to Pennsylvania. Tens of thousands of ballots supposedly mailed in, but no folds or creases in them. More votes than ballots issued in places. People pulling out suitcases and video evidence of that with questionable explanations for that. Those are issues of election fraud that need to be investigated and there's a lot of them and it's not just one person or one group of people. It's across the country."

Ratcliffe lamented that "a lot of people in this country… don't think that the votes were counted fairly, that the process is at the state and local level weren't administered fairly."

"They deserve that accounting," he said.

Video Alleged to Show Ga. Ballots Counted After Poll Watchers Were Ousted Eric Mack

Video footage presented by attorneys for the Trump campaign is alleged to show Georgia's Fulton County poll workers counting ballots without monitors present, attorney Jacki Pick said Thursday on Newsmax TV.

A private security firm inside Atlanta's State Farm Arena provided the surveillance video to Trump campaign lawyers at 1 a.m. ET on Thursday, Pick told Thursday's "Stinchfield."

"We just got it at 1 a.m., a big team watched it, and we were shocked at what we saw," Pick, a volunteer attorney in Georgia who presented the evidence to the state Senate earlier Thursday, told host Grant Stinchfield.

The video confirms what the campaign's witnesses have sworn to in affidavits, Pick contended.

"Yes, people were sent home, told to stop working, stop counting, but some people stayed behind: Sure enough, just as our poll watchers - well, our monitors - had said," Pick said, saying the video shows suitcases being pulled from under a table covered by a black cloth -- purportedly holding thousands of ballots.

The Epoch Times tweeted the full surveillance video Thursday afternoon:

"WATCH: Footage of State Farm Arena in #Atlanta shows that after poll monitors and media were told

counting was done, four workers stayed behind to count #ballots, at times pulling out suitcases containing ballots from underneath desks. Watch full video: https://youtube.com/watch?v=keANzinHWUA"

In presenting the evidence to the Georgia state Senate, Pick rejected an official's claim that allegations of no poll monitor being present has been debunked, saying the video was just received Thursday and could not have already been debunked.

"Obviously, that's not true," Pick continued. "Whoever said that – I believe it was the Secretary of State [Brad Raffensperger] clearly wasn't present: Check. Or hasn't seen this video: Check.

"So, who do you believe? The secretary of state or the video?"

Trump tweeted **about the evidence, too, even as it was conspicuously slapped with an unsubstantiated Twitter "disputed" tag: "Wow! Blockbuster testimony taking place right now in Georgia. Ballot stuffing by Dems when Republicans were forced to leave the large counting room. Plenty more coming, but this alone leads to an easy win of the State!"**

Trump added hours later:

"People in Georgia got caught cold bringing in massive numbers of ballots and putting them in "voting" machines. Great job @BrianKempGA!"

Pick said the next step in the gathering of evidence is to subpoena the election counting logs during that time frame.

Pick said the evidence shown in the video contains more than enough votes being counted without a monitor to surpass the margin of victory for Biden. She added that a number of other voter fraud allegations are in the 64-page complaint being presented in Georgia.

"The president has more than one way to meet his burden to contest the election," Pick said. "But certainly this evidence we have now in this video is quite strong to cast doubt. Because no matter what those ballots said, he does not have to show how they voted or would have voted had they not been questionable.

"It doesn't matter. They broke Georgia law here by not permitting our Republican poll watchers and press to be present. That's required by statute."

The poll counters in the video might face scrutiny, but Pick said the legal team's priority is to show the unlawful counting of votes in the presidential election first.

"The plot will likely thicken," Pick concluded.

A spokesperson for Fulton County said to Epoch, «Any credible report of such activity will be investigated and addressed as provided by Georgia law.»

Geraldo Spars With Jesse Watters And Greg Gutfeld On Voter Fraud

Virginia Kruta

Fox News contributor Geraldo Rivera sparred with hosts Jesse Watters and Greg Gutfeld over ongoing allegations of voter fraud.

Rivera joined Thursday's broadcast of "The Five," where he argued that there didn't appear to be enough evidence for anything to be overturned. (RELATED: 'The Year Big Media Lost Its Soul': Geraldo Rivera Says Trump 'Ran His Heart Out' Against All Odds)

Watters began by noting that Rivera had been skeptical of the allegations of fraud from the start, and asked whether recent hearings and sworn testimony from witnesses had moved the needle at all. "Have you changed your opinion a little bit?" Watters asked.

"I think you are giving false hope to our audience that there is enough here to overturn the election of the president —" Rivera replied, and Watters quickly interrupted. "No, I'm just reporting what the —" he said before Rivera cut him off.

"Let me finish. Greg was filibustering there for 5 minutes. I think I get 30 seconds," Rivera laughed. "Bill Barr is the best lawyer in Washington, D.C. He's a two-time attorney general. He is the most effective, high-functioning person in the Trump Administration. He had the president's back more than anyone else in Washington." Rivera went on to say that it had been Attorney General William Barr who stood up before the Ameri-

can people and pushed back on the Russia narrative, adding that Barr had most recently said that he didn't see evidence of widespread fraud that would change the outcome of the election.

"You're not addressing the testimony! You're just pointing to Barr! You're not answering what we are asking!" Gutfeld jumped in then. (RELATED: 'As Modern As A Poodle Skirt': Greg Gutfeld Disputes Claim That Biden Is First To Have 'Legitimacy' Questioned)

Rivera pushed back, saying that the kind of limited fraud that might have happened could result in a few people being prosecuted as individuals, but he didn't see it amounting to the kind of numbers that would change the election results. "Geraldo is missing the point!" Gutfeld said then, adding," We are talking about specific, crucial counties where you don't need widespread — and nobody is claiming widespread. We are talking specific, targeted —" Cohost Martha MacCallum then pointed out that the Trump campaign had claimed they could prove 100,000 ballots were fraudulent in the state of Nevada, a state that President-elect Joe Biden won by a margin of only 35,000 votes.

"Let the process play out," she said.

WILL WE LET THIS UGLY FAT DISHRAG PIG SKANK LIVESTOCK BITCH STEAL WHAT THE GREATEST AMERICANS DIED FOR?

REPORT: New York Activists Are Buying Ubers For Georgia Voters To Get To The Polls

GAG ON THIS FAT, UGLY REVOLTING PIG

Dylan Housman

Liberal activists in New York are reportedly getting involved in the Georgia runoff elections by buying Ubers to drive voters to the polls. Millennial activist group Plus1Vote is spending funds on the ridesharing service to shuttle Georgians to the polls during early voting and on the January 5th election day, co-founder Saad Amer told the New York Post. Amer, a New Yorker himself, said the group is utilizing Uber to "provide free rides to the polls" and "drop off absentee ballots to ballot drop boxes."

Plus1Vote claims to advocate for better policy on climate change, social justice, and gun control, and the Post reports that it had previously paid for Lyft rides for voters throughout the south in the November general election. The group is partnering with the New Georgia Project, an organization founded by failed Georgia gubernatorial candidate Stacey Abrams, reports the Post. (RELATED: Senate Committees Release A Treasure Trove Of Trump-Russia Documents)

The New Georgia Project, which was also previously led by Democratic senate candidate Raphael Warnock, is currently being investigated for improper voter registration activities. Other New York groups are also get-

ting involved in the Georgia race by phone banking, including New York Young Democrats, Persist Brooklyn, and the Working Families Party, according to the Post.

New York Republicans are also raising money to help Republican Georgian candidates Kelly Loeffler and David Perdue, the Post reports. The state GOP held a virtual fundraiser Thursday night with Senate Majority Leader Mitch McConnell and has discussed the possibility of phone banking from the empire state, according to the Post. (RELATED: Supreme Court Ruling Sends A Message Churches Can't Be Treated Like 'Second Class' Citizens, Legal Experts Say)

Republicans must win at least one of the two runoff races in order to keep control of the United States Senate.

Detroit Vote Counter Claims Harassment After Refusing to Backdate Ballots

By Brian Trusdell

A Detroit ballot processor testified before a Michigan legislative hearing on Thursday that she was intimidated and harassed by supervisors after she refused to backdate absentee ballots and accept others that violated state law on Election Night.

Jessy Jacob, a 34-year Detroit city worker, told a hearing of the state's Senate Oversight Committee that she was instructed by election officials on the morning of Nov. 4 to enter ballots as received by Nov. 2 knowing they had been received after the 9 p.m. deadline on Nov. 3, Election Day. Her refusal drew reprisals, she said.

"They treated me like a criminal, humiliated me, harassed me," Jacob said in her witness statement sitting beside Rudy Giuliani and Jenna Ellis, campaign lawyers for President Donald Trump. "It was so bad."

The Trump campaign has filed lawsuits contesting election results in several states and is lobbying state legislatures to invoke their authority to select electors to the Electoral College.

At one point, Jacob said she was told by a representative from the Michigan Department of State's Bureau of Elections, "I don't need you here. I don't need any of your help. Get out of here.

"I couldn't do anything, because when I am entering the ballot, I couldn't lie about the date," Jacob said.

Jacob said that she was processing opened absentee ballots, some of which had no postage stamp and no signature match. Other issues included that some absentee ballots were issued on Nov. 3. The state manual for ballot processors says ballots are invalid if they are issued after 4 p.m. on Nov. 2.

"So it was issued on Nov. 3, Election Day," she said. "It was issued, received, everything, on Nov. 3. Then I checked whether that voter is newly registered. No, he was not registered on Nov. 3. He was registered

sometime in 2010 — 10 years ago. You are not supposed to issue absentee ballots on election day to already registered voters."

But when she took her concerns to supervisors, she learned no one else at the facility where she was working was following the process to accept legal ballots.

While expressing her concerns, she was told by Chris Thomas, a contractor for the Detroit City Clerk's Office and overseeing operations: "She's right, but why should we punish voters for a processor's mistake?"

"I never expected this kind of treatment," Jacob said. "It was really, really bad. I had to go through this, so inhumane."

Jordan Sekulow to Newsmax TV: Trump Campaign to File Lawsuit in Ga. Contesting 2020 Results)

By Solange Reyner

The Trump campaign will file a lawsuit in Georgia Thursday night contesting the results of the 2020 presidential election in the state, Jordan Sekulow, a member of President Donald Trump's legal team, said during an appearance on Newsmax TV**.**

"Might be this evening on the video that we're seeing just now that will contest the entire election," Sekulow told Chris Salcedo **in reference to a video out of Fulton County allegedly showing workers counting votes without Republicans or Democrats watching.**

"The security camera shows that. That's a huge election law violation," he said. "That's illegal. You can't count votes without anyone watching, send everyone home under a phony pretense that a water main broke that actually happened sometime very early morning and keep counting votes. They're on video doing that."

Voting was delayed in Fulton County on Election Night after a water pipe broke at the ballot processing site at State Farm Arena. The pipe burst at 6:07 a.m. **and was repaired within two hours, according to Fulton Commission Chairman Robb Pitts. It wasn't mentioned by county officials during a 10 a.m. press conference that day.**

Trump's attorneys on Thursday asked the Georgia Legislature to overturn the state's election results and select their own electors. The Georgia secretary of state's office after a second recount in the state declared Joe Biden the winner.

Video Shows Georgia Ballots Counted After Poll Watchers Were Ousted

By Eric

holding thousands of ballots. Mack

Video footage presented by attorneys for the Trump campaign is alleged to show Georgia's Fulton County poll workers counting ballots without monitors present, attorney Jacki Pick said Thursday on Newsmax TV.

A private security firm inside Atlanta's State Farm Arena provided the surveillance video to Trump campaign lawyers at 1 a.m. ET on Thursday, Pick told Thursday's "Stinchfield.**"**

"We just got it at 1 a.m., a big team watched it, and we were shocked at what we saw," Pick, a volunteer attorney in Georgia who presented the evidence to the state Senate earlier Thursday, told host Grant Stinchfield.

The video confirms what the campaign's witnesses have sworn to in affidavits, Pick contended.

"Yes, people were sent home, told to stop working, stop counting, but some people stayed behind: Sure enough, just as our poll watchers - well, our monitors - had said," Pick said, saying the video shows suitcases being pulled from under a table covered by a black cloth -- purportedly

The Epoch Times tweeted the full surveillance video Thursday afternoon:

"WATCH: Footage of State Farm Arena in #Atlanta shows that after poll monitors and media were told counting was done, four workers stayed behind to count #ballots, at times pulling out suitcases containing ballots from underneath desks. Watch full video: https://youtube.com/watch?v=keANzinHWUA"

In presenting the evidence to the Georgia state Senate, Pick rejected an official's claim that allegations of no poll monitor being present has been debunked, saying the video was just received Thursday and could not have already been debunked.

"Obviously, that's not true," Pick continued. "Whoever said that - I believe it was the Secretary of State [Brad Raffensperger] clearly wasn't present: Check. Or hasn't seen this video: Check.

"So, who do you believe? The secretary of state or the video?"

Trump tweeted **about the evidence, too, even as it was conspicuously slapped with an unsubstantiated Twitter "disputed" tag:**

"Wow! Blockbuster testimony taking place right now in Georgia. Ballot stuffing by Dems when Republicans were forced to leave the large counting room. Plenty more coming, but this alone leads to an easy win of the State!"

Trump added hours later:

"People in Georgia got caught cold bringing in massive numbers of ballots and putting them in "voting" machines. Great job @BrianKempGA!"

Pick said the next step in the gathering of evidence is to subpoena the election counting logs during that time frame.

Pick said the evidence shown in the video contains more than enough votes being counted without a monitor to surpass the margin of victory for Biden. She added that a number of other voter fraud allegations are in the 64-page complaint being presented in Georgia.

"The president has more than one way to meet his burden to contest the election," Pick said. "But certainly this evidence we have now in this video is quite strong to cast doubt. Because no matter what those ballots said, he does not have to show how they voted or would have voted had they not been questionable.

"It doesn't matter. They broke Georgia law here by not permitting our Republican poll watchers and press to be present. That's required by statute."

The poll counters in the video might face scrutiny, but Pick said the legal team's priority is to show the unlawful counting of votes in the presidential election first.

"The plot will likely thicken," Pick concluded.

A spokesperson for Fulton County said to Epoch, «Any credible report of such activity will be investigated and addressed as provided by Georgia law.»

Freedom Caucus Demands AG Barr Update on Fraud Probes

By Eric Mack

The House Freedom Caucus is calling on the Justice Department, namely Attorney General William Barr, to update the public on whether it is investigating election irregularities and allegations of voter fraud.

"We're waiting for them to give us some kind of indicia they're actually investigating the multiple allegations of the improprieties in this 2020 presidential election," HFC Chairman Rep. Andy Barr, R-Ariz., told reporters Thursday. "We have a keen interest in that, but we think all American people do as well.

"We want to call attention to our efforts to communicate to the Department of Justice and Attorney General Barr to have him include us in the information that he's ostensibly, it appears to be anyway, that they're investigating. But we've seen no indicia of it and I'm not sure anyone in America has."

The members are calling for "an open transparent view of all the records" after AG Barr said publicly there is "no evidence" of widespread voter fraud "that would change the outcome of the election."

Even the Justice Department refuted that claim, saying there has been no conclusion to the effect, Rep. Biggs noted to reporters. "So, there's some mixed signals that are going on there," Biggs said. "To be frank with you, those of us that called on the DOJ to be actually conducting an investigation into the elections, I was surprised at the first statement by the attorney general, but I was even more surprised by the walk back of that statement."

The HFC members also noted, changing the outcome of the election is not their goal, but instances of voter and/or election fraud must be investigated to secure this and all future elections for the American people.

"If there's fraud or not, it's not enough to overturn the election; it's not enough to make a difference," Rep. Randy Weber, R-Texas. "Ladies and gentlemen, I don't understand if there's criminal activity present – fraud, that's criminal activity – why we don't look at that. Why is it OK?

"If somebody's murdered, we don't let the perpetrator get away with murder, because we can't change the results, right? We can't bring the person back to life. If somebody attempts murder, we don't say 'well, you didn't get away with it, so it's all good."

GOP lawmakers ask SCOTUS to block final certification of PA votes count

A complaint filed on Thursday argues that expanded absentee voting procedures violate the state's constitution

By Shannon Bream

Republican lawmakers asked the Supreme Court on Thursday night to halt the vote certification process of general election results in Pennsylvania, a key battleground state won by President-elect Joe Biden.

Their complaint alleges that procedures employed in the 2020 election violate the state's constitution because the state has repeatedly rejected previous attempts to expand absentee voting by statute, "uniformly holding" that a constitutional amendment is required. Supreme Court Justice Samuel asked Pennsylvania officials to respond by Wednesday, Dec. 9, by 4 p.m. ET to the complaint.

Lawmakers, led by Rep. Mike Kelly, R-Pa., characterize the expanded absentee voting methods used in response to the coronavirus pandemic as an "unconstitutional, no-excuse absentee voting scheme" and contend

that ballots cast via this process are not valid. They are asking for any certifications, including a declared Biden victory, to be put on hold while the lawsuit is considered.

PENNSYLVANIA WHISTLEBLOWER SPEAKS OUT AFTER CLAIMING 'FORENSICALLY DESTRUCTIVE' VOTE CANVASSING PROCEDURE

Lawmakers are asking for an injunction that would prevent executives in the state, including Democratic Gov. Tom Wolf and Secretary of State Kathy Boockvar, from tabulating, computing, canvassing, certifying, or otherwise finalizing the results. Biden won the presidency with the help of Pennsylvania's 20 electoral votes. His winning the state with more than 81,000 votes out of nearly 7 million ballots that were cast.

Most mail-in ballots were submitted by Democrats. The Pennsylvania Supreme Court dismissed the case over the weekend. President Trump has repeated unfounded claims that the election was riddled with fraud and rigged by Democrats.

Nevada 'fraud': 1,500 'dead' voters, 42,248 voted 'multiple times,' RV camps as 'homes' by Paul Bedard

The Trump campaign on Wednesday unveiled a tranche of information it plans to present to a Nevada state court Thursday that suggests there were thousands of fraudulent votes cast — possibly enough to overturn Joe Biden's win there by 33,569 votes.

Officials said that among the evidence and expert testimony to be presented in Carson City are indications that over 1,500 ballots were cast by dead voters, that 42,248 people voted "multiple times," data on a huge spike in incomplete voter registrations, and home addresses in temporary RV camps and casinos.

They also plan to present polling that 1% of Nevada voters shown to have voted never did and 2% of those shown to have voted by mail never got a ballot.

The legal team was quick to note that it has just begun to collect information and that fraud cases can sometimes take months to years to investigate.

Officials also added that they have been stonewalled by U.S. Postal Service and state and county officials in their efforts to review votes and registrations.

Their focus has been in Democratic-heavy Clark County, where Biden won by 90,922 votes. Biden won 521,852 to President Trump's 430,930. By contrast, in 2016, Trump won 511,319 votes and lost it to Hillary Rodham Clinton by just 26,434 votes.

One of the leaders of the effort, American Conservative Union Chairman Matt Schlapp, told Secrets, "In my years of experience in politics, I have never seen the amount of illegal voting like we have documented in Clark County, Nevada. It is a level of corruption I didn't think could happen in a modern, free country."

Schlapp said that if bad votes are thrown out, the president would be the winner. "I can't predict what a judge will do, but any fair-minded American would come to the same conclusion: Trump won Nevada by thousands of votes if illegal ballots are remedied."

The campaign and surrogate groups have made similar claims in several states. Unlike many of those, the Nevada effort won a green light to continue. Schlapp said that the problems his group has found in just a few weeks in Nevada are likely in other states.

"This is a shameful moment in American history. Five or six Democrat-controlled major cities greenlighted fraud and changed outcomes. Trump won Nevada by a wide margin, and I believe these same dirty deeds occurred in Georgia, Wisconsin, Pennsylvania, and Michigan, essentially disenfranchising 73.3 million Americans. This is a civil rights emergency. If we don't immediately expose the fraud, America will never accept this election," he added.

Also today, Indiana Sen. Mike Braun told Secrets that he believes Democratic cities also saw fraud, and he said that if states refuse to investigate the reports, people will lose faith in the voting system.

Jenna Ellis to Newsmax TV: Trump Team Heads to Arizona

Senior Legal Adviser to the Trump 2020 campaign Jenna Ellis said Friday on Newsmax TV that she and a team will head to Arizona on Legislature Next

By Brian Trusdell

Monday in an effort to convince the state's legislature to reassert its authority under the Constitution to appoint electors to the Electoral College.

Ellis began her appearance on "Stinchfield" by announcing that the Pennsylvania General Assembly has announced it will introduce a resolution in both houses of the state legislature to reclaim its authority to appoint electors — a revelation previewed earlier in the day by state Sen. Doug Mastriano on "War Room," former White House strategist Steve Bannon's video podcast.

"We're hopeful that Arizona will follow the same path that Pennsylvania has now spearheaded by going first, and by seeing that there is substantial and more than enough evidence that this election was irredeemably compromised," Ellis said. "And so, in Arizona, both the mayor (Rudy Giuliani) and myself will go to this hearing where legislators in Arizona will hear from witnesses in that state talking about the election official fraud that occurred in Arizona.

"And we're hopeful that they will take the same course of action that the Pennsylvania state legislature is now doing and that they will also reclaim their state legislative authority and take back their opportunity, their mandate and their obligation under the Constitution to select their Electoral College delegation based on the actual election results, counting every legal vote, not based on the corruption and fraud that occurred."

Guiliani is President Donald Trump's personal attorney and is spearheading the Trump legal team's challenge to election results in several states.

Ellis' comments followed those of Guiliani earlier Friday on "Greg Kelly Reports" that lobbying state legislatures would be undertaken in addition to legal claims. The Trump campaign is hoping states will assert their authority under Article 2, Section 1, Clause 2 of the U.S. Constitution.

"Each State shall appoint, in such Manner as the Legislature thereof may direct, a Number of Electors, equal to the whole Number of Senators and Representatives to which the State may be entitled in the Congress," the text of the Constitution

Donald Trump Calls In to Arizona Voter Fraud Hearing: We're Fighting Back

Charlie Spiering

President Donald Trump called in to a hearing with Republican lawmakers in Arizona Monday, praising them for fighting back against Democrat election fraud.

"What they did is they played game, and games like nobody has ever seen before," Trump said, referring to the Democrats. "This is the first time that Republicans or the first time anyone has fought back."

The audience applauded and cheered when they heard the president's voice, as his attorney Jenna Ellis held the phone to a microphone.

The president claimed that he won the swing states of Arizona, Michigan, Georgia, Pennsylvania, and Wisconsin, reminding supporters that he earned 11 million more votes than he did in 2016.

"I've been watching the hearings and they're fascinating, incredible," he said.

The president praised all of the in-person witnesses who noted voting and counting anomalies in the state, where Biden finished with a lead over Trump of 10,457 votes."I know some get heat, but many more get praise from the American public," Trump said.

Trump appeared furious that Arizona certified the election results on Monday as the Republican hearing about fraud was taking place. He accused Republican Gov. Doug Ducey of rushing the certification process, despite questions about the election's integrity.

"On top of it, you have a governor named Ducey," he said as the crowd booed. "He just rushed to sign certificates … what's that all about? He didn't have to sign it. I say, why would he sign when you have these incredible hearings going on that's showing such corruption and such horrible fraud?"

The audience applauded in agreement."You have to figure out what that's all about with Ducey. He couldn't go fast enough," Trump said, He added, "We're not going to forget what Ducey just did."

The president repeated allegations of voters who arrived to cast their ballot to find out it was already filled out, people paid to vote, and mail-in ballots that were processed without Republican election observers."This shows how arrogant the Democrats and others were in taking away and stealing an election," he said.

Trump noted that he also faced criticism for fighting for voter integrity, noting that people repeatedly urged him to choose the "easier route" and focus on 2024.

"I said, 'No,'" he recalled. "I have to focus on two weeks ago. This is the greatest scam ever perpetrated on our

country." The president praised Arizona Republicans for holding the hearing, despite widespread criticism from corporate media. "We admire all of the people, and that includes all of these representatives that are up there and doing a great job," Trump said. "What they don't realize is that they might hear some things, but they're becoming legend for taking this on." The president again praised Rudy Giuliani for having the courage to fight when other lawyers backed down.

"This is the most important thing that you've ever done," he said.

Amistad Lawyer: FBI Collecting Data on Vote Fraud

The FBI is using voter fraud information collected by the Amistad Project, the project's director, Phillip Kline, said Monday on Newsmax TV.

Kline, who is former attorney general of Kansas, tweeted the news on Sunday.

Appearing on "Stinchfield," Kline said the group's investigations show "what we call the blood in the street. It's after the crime is committed. And what evidence is there to show that a crime has been committed." The FBI is looking at evidence uncovered by Amistad Society investigators who have crunched data from the government, then reached out to actual voters to see if how they voted actually matches the government's data.

"And we've come up with tens of thousands of Republican ballots that were not counted," Kline told host Grant Stinchfield. "We've come up with hundreds of thousands of Republicans who say they never requested a ballot, but they voted absentee by somebody else. We've identified people outside of the state who voted within the state. And all of this occurred in the key swing states that we're speaking about."

Kline said all of the areas investigated "had hundreds of millions of dollars poured into their election offices by MARK ZUCKERBUCKS"

The Facebook CEO, Kline said, poured in $400 million into the election, matching the federal government expenditures, through his charities.

FACEBOOK ZUCKERBUCKS **PAID OFF "They paid the election judges,** they paid the people

who boarded up the windows, they bought the machines and America was kicked out of the counting room, and a billionaire invited in, **in all of the swing state urban (DO REPUBLICAN DEPLORABLE GUN & RELIGION RED LIVES MATTER? WHAT ABOUT US?) Core cities, and that is a violation the law."**

Amistad's data show that all of these changes benefited Democratic strongholds as they were suppressing the vote in Republican strongholds, Kline said, "and then we had them sidestepping the law and accepting ballots they should not have accepted"

Sen. Cruz Publicly Implores SCOTUS to Hear Pa. Election Challenge

By Brian Trusdell

Sen. Ted Cruz, R-Texas, publicly urged the U.S. Supreme Court on Tuesday to hear the expedited appeal of a case challenging the election results in Pennsylvania, saying the matter "raises serious legal issues."

Cruz, the longest serving solicitor general in the history of Texas and a former law professor at the University of Texas Law School in Austin, is the first U.S. senator to publicly support the appeal, filed by Rep. Mike Kelly, R-Pa.

"Hearing this case now – on an emergency expedited basis – would be an important step in helping rebuild confidence in the integrity of our democratic system," Cruz said in statement that also noted a Reuters/Ipsos poll found 39% of Americans believed the election was "rigged."

Kelly's appeal argues the Pennsylvania legislature passed legislation greatly expanding the use of absentee voting, making it a "no-excuse" mail-in election and contradicting the state's Constitution. It further derides the Pennsylvania Supreme Court for dismissing Kelly's lawsuit for "laches," a legal term for a procedural issue saying the case was brought too late.

Cruz was especially critical of the Pennsylvania Supreme Court's dismissal on the procedural ground.

"Even more persuasively, the plaintiffs point out that the Pennsylvania Supreme Court has also held that plaintiffs don't have standing to challenge an election law until after the election, meaning that the court effectively put them in a Catch-22: before the election, they lacked standing; after the election, they've delayed too long," Cruz said. "The result of the court's gamesmanship is that a facially unconstitutional election law can never be judicially challenged."

Dick Morris to Newsmax TV: Enough Episodic Evidence to Establish Pattern of Voter Fraud (Newsmax TV's "American Agenda") By Solange Reyner

There is enough episodic evidence to establish a pattern of fraud in the 2020 presidential election, according to political strategist Dick Morris on Newsmax TV.

"I think that the issue of scale, you have obstruction from the secretaries of state, you have obstruction from the courts, the Democratic-controlled courts, and it's very hard to penetrate that to get evidence enough to reverse several million votes, but there certainly is enough episodic evidence to establish a pattern of fraud," Morris told Tuesday's "American Agenda."

Morris also questioned Attorney General Bill Barr's statement earlier Tuesday that the Justice Department had uncovered no evidence of widespread voter fraud that would tip the results of the presidential election.

"I'd like to know the number of people they had doing it and what they did," Morris said. "But this fraud was so deeply concealed within the voting machines that it was almost undetectable. You would need a top-level forensic computer expert to go in there and detect it.

"These voting machines were designed by people who worked for Hugo Chavez with the sole intention of creating a system that could be hacked without anyone knowing about it, results that could be flipped, votes that could be altered,

Andy Biggs to Newsmax TV: Enough Evidence for Lawsuit in Arizona

By Theodore Bunker

Rep. Andy Biggs, R-Ariz., told Newsmax TV **on Tuesday that President Donald Trump's campaign legal team has "evidence to sustain a lawsuit" in the state of Arizona. Biggs made his comments on "**National Report**" about the argument presented by Trump's legal team at an event in Arizona on Monday, after the state officially certified Joe Biden as the winner in the 2020 presidential election.**

The congressman said that the Trump campaign has "strong" evidence of fraud and said: "I think yesterday, what they showed is that there's actually evidence to sustain a lawsuit, and if you can sustain a lawsuit then the courts would have to really get involved. And also, they would hopefully order a forensic audit in Arizona, which is what a lot of us have been asking for for several weeks." He added, "We need a forensic audit because then we would know for certain about those mail-in ballots, which were about 75% of the ballots cast in Arizona

Trump Lawsuit: Wisconsin Absentee Ballot Abuses Affected 220K Votes

Election officials count absentee ballots at a polling place located in the Town of Beloit fire station on November 3, 2020 near Beloit, Wisconsin.

By Sandy Fitzgerald

President Donald Trump's campaign filed a lawsuit in the Wisconsin Tuesday claiming the absentee voting process was abused in the state.

The suit seeks to disqualify more than 221,000 ballots in the state's two most Democrat-heavy counties.

The lawsuit comes after the state completed its partial recount and after Wisconsin Gov. Tony Evers on Monday night formally certified Joe Biden as the state's winner. The legal team in Wisconsin, led by former Wisconsin Circuit Court Judge Jim Troupis, said the recount gave the campaign a "unique ability" to examine ballots.

Troupis said the state's electoral votes "likely won't change the overall outcome," but "exposing exactly how the election processes were abused in Wisconsin holds enormous value for this election beyond a victory for

President Trump. Regardless, we're demonstrating that the results of this election unequivocally ought to be questioned." In the lawsuit, the campaign complains that officials on the Wisconsin Elections Commission and the city clerks of Milwaukee and Madison "willfully disregarded the current statute and made conscious efforts to circumvent Wisconsin election law."

This resulted in tens of thousands of votes cast "well outside of the bounds of Wisconsin law," the campaign further claims.

The lawsuit also claims that the law was violated several times through altered certification of absentee ballot envelopes, voting events called "Democracy in the Park" where ballots were accepted, a lack of required absentee ballot applications, and unlawful claims of indefinite confinement.

In the legal action, the campaign claims election officials accepted ballots without a required absentee application on file, even though the state's law requires that request forms be submitted before a voter can cast an absentee ballot, and such ballots must "be called into question."

The campaign also pointed to a state law requiring ballots to be returned to voters to correct and resubmit if they are filled out incorrectly, have missing information, or are damaged, saying that municipal clerks were "illegally altering ballot envelopes themselves."

The suit further claims voters were allowed to circumvent voter ID laws by claiming an absentee voting status that was only to be used by people who are indefinitely confined. Democrat election officials in March had told voters they could claim the status because of the coronavirus pandemic, the campaign says, but that was struck down by the Wisconsin Supreme Court. However, the number of people saying they were confined indefinitely jumped by almost 600% in Dane County and 500% in Milwaukee County.

Evers, the Wisconsin Elections Commission, and the Biden campaign did not immediately respond to Fox News' request for comment.

Obscure Law Could Be Trump's Last Bid to Challenge Election Results

President Donald Trump speaks in the press briefing room in Washington. By Jeffrey Rodack

President Donald Trump's efforts to challenge the election results could come down to him pressing congressional Republicans to step in and help. Politico noted that Congress has to certify the results of the election after the Electoral College casts the official vote for president on Dec. 14. An 1887 law mandates that Congress must meet on Jan. 6 to take action. The law says that the House and Senate must meet in joint session that day to certify the results. But if a House member and senator team together, they are able to object to entire slates of presidential electors. And there are multiple opportunities for lengthy delays in the process since each state's electors must be certified separately, Politico said. If a slate of electors is challenged, the

House and Senate must go back to their chambers and debate the outcome before voting. And if the Senate upholds a challenge to some presidential electors, it would almost certainly put the chamber at odds with the Democrat-run House victory. Still, several Republican lawmakers in then House acknowledge they are considering the option to challenge, Politico said.

"Nothing is off the table," said Rep. Matt Gaetz, R-Fla. And Rep. Warren Davidson, R-Ohio, said potential challenges are seriously being considered by some members and they're "studying" up on it.

Meanwhile Jenna Ellis, who is part of the Trump campaign's legal team, cautioned: "Until the Electoral College actually votes on Dec. 14, we don't have a president-elect."

Law Firm Claims More Than 280K Pre-marked Ballots Disappeared in Pennsylvania

Phill Kline, director of the Thomas More Society's Amistad Project, on Newsmax TV

By Brian Trusdell

As many as 280,000 pre-marked ballots were transported from Bethpage, New York, to Lancaster, Pennsylvania, in late October and then "disappeared," the director of a public interest law firm said Tuesday, quoting a postal service subcontractor. Phill Kline, the director of the legal group Thomas More Society's Amistad Project, said at a press conference in Arlington, Virginia, that a witness has testified to the fact the ballots went missing, which was verified by other witness statements.

"This evidence demonstrates, and it's through eyewitness testimony that's been corroborated by others through their eyewitness statements, that 130,000 to 280,000 completed ballots for the 2020 general election were shipped from Bethpage, New York, to Lancaster, Pennsylvania, where the ballots, and the trailer in which they were shipped, disappeared," said Kline, a former attorney general for the state of Kansas.

Kline claimed in a news release, postal service workers engaged in "widespread illegal efforts" to influence the election, according The Epoch Times.

Three individuals spoke at Tuesday's event to provide first-hand accounts of what Kline outlined, including truck driver subcontractor Jesse Morgan, who said he drove the truck filled with potentially upward of 288,000 ballots Oct. 21. The ballots were addressed to Harrisburg, but Morgan was instructed to deliver them to a Lancaster location.

The truck — and ballots — vanished after he parked at a USPS depot in Lancaster, he said. Kline said the numbers come from estimates his group discerned.

The news conference also heard from a witness who claims to have seen a Dominion Voting Systems vendor inserting thumb drives into voting aggregation machines in Delaware County, Pennsylvania, and a third man - another USPS subcontractor — who said he was told the postal service was planning to backdate tens of thousands of ballots in the days after the Nov. 3 election in order to circumvent the ballot submission deadline, Justthenews.com reported.

"This evidence joins with unlawful conduct by state and local election officials, including accepting millions of dollars of private funds, to undermine the integrity of this election," Kline said.

In a press release, the Amistad Project says it has sworn expert affidavits claiming "over 300,000 ballots are at issue in Arizona, 548,000 in Michigan, 204,000 in Georgia, and over 121,000 in Pennsylvania." Kline said the information will be shared with the FBI, federal, and local prosecutors "who are aware of our evidence."

The Epoch Times said neither the FBI nor postal service has responded to a request for comment.

The claims come on the same day that U.S. Attorney General William Barr told The Associated Press his office has no evidence of fraud that would change the election results.

Who are the groups at the center of the Georgia election investigation?

What we know about 4 progressive groups accused of seeking fraudulent registrations

By Andrew Keiper

Georgia Sec. of State probing groups soliciting out-of-state voters is 'reassuring': Henninger

The Wall Street Journal's Dan Henninger tells 'America's Newsroom' Republicans should take investigation of alleged voter fraud as 'a huge incentive' to show up and vote in Georgia's Senate runoffs.

A group at the center of the investigation into voter fraud recently opened by the Georgia Secretary of State Brad Raffensperger hired contractors who were found to have forged ballot applications in 2014.

The group, The New Georgia Project, was founded by former Georgia gubernatorial candidate Stacey Abrams to help register new voters. Ultimately, the 2014 investigation found no wrongdoing by the group, but did cite 14 people for forging 53 voter applications. All those cited were working as independent contractors, according to the Atlanta Journal-Constitution.

On Wednesday, Raffensperger announced an investigation into several progressive organizations he alleged "sought to register ineligible, out-of-state, or deceased voters" for the Jan. 5 Senate runoff elections**. Among those named are Vote Forward, The New Georgia Project, Operation Voter Registration GA and America Votes.**

GEORGIA GROUP FOUNDED BY STACEY ABRAMS UNDER INVESTIGATION FOR SEEKING OUT-OF-STATE, DEAD VOTERS

"I have issued clear warnings several times to groups and individuals working to undermine the integrity of elections in Georgia through false and fraudulent registrations," said Raffensperger in a statement. "The security of Georgia's elections is of the utmost importance. We have received specific evidence that these groups have solicited voter registrations from ineligible individuals who have passed away or live out of state. I will investigate these claims thoroughly and take action against anyone attempting to undermine our elections.""I have issued clear warnings several times to groups and individuals working to undermine the integrity of elections in Georgia through false and fraudulent registrations."

— DO NOTHING EVER; BUT YAP Georgia Secretary of State Brad Raffensperger

The New Georgia Project, which was led by Democratic Senate candidate Raphael Warnock until February, is accused by Raffensperger of several election violations. Almost all of them involve sending voter registration or absentee application mail to people who were either deceased or ineligible to vote.

The progressive nonprofit was founded in 2013 and works to build the progressive voting bloc in Georgia largely by registering young people to vote. In the 2018 election cycle, the New Georgia Project reported $96,000 in payments, with two payments worth a total of $35,000 going to the Working Families Party.

FLORIDA ATTORNEY UNDER INVESTIGATION AFTER SAYING HE IS MOVING TO GEORGIA TO VOTE

Vote Forward is a nonprofit founded by Scott Forman in 2017. The progressive group focuses on sending handwritten letters imploring people to vote. According to OpenSecrets, a campaign finance database, the organization had no filings for 2020 and raised just over $50,000 in 2018.

Forman, like many on the medium, has made a number of inflammatory Tweets about President Trump and his supporters. He insinuated the president is a "would-be dictator" and called his supporters deplorables.

Whoops! We couldn't access this Tweet.

Raffensperger alleged that Vote Forward sent a letter to a deceased person encouraging them to vote.

PRO-TRUMP ATTORNEYS SIDNEY POWELL, LIN WOOD URGE GEORGIANS NOT TO VOTE IN SENATE RUNOFFS WITHOUT CHANGES

America Votes is a much larger operation, conducting voter education and mobilization efforts in 20 states. In his announcement, Raffensperger accused the progressive nonprofit of sending two absentee ballot applications in one week to an old address of a Georgia voter.

During the 2020 election cycle, according to campaign finance data, the nonprofit amassed more than $15 million in donations. The group dispersed money to a number of progressive political action committees.

The investigation is a formal acknowledgement that there was some impropriety in the voting process, though both sides of the aisle understand it's nowhere near enough to upend Joe Biden's victory in the state. Raffensperger's office did not respond to requests for comment from Fox News.

The announcement comes about a month before two critical runoff Senate elections in Georgia, the results of which will determine the partisan balance of power in Congress during Biden's presidency.

Pro-Trump Lawmakers Ask SCOTUS To Just Nullify Biden's Pennsylvania Win

Anders Hagstrom

Pro-Trump lawmakers have asked the Supreme Court of the United States to nullify Pennsylvania's certification of President-Elect Joe Biden's victory in the state, Bloomberg reported Tuesday evening.

The effort, led by pro-Trump Republican Pennsylvania Rep. Mike Kelly, maintains that the Pennsylvania General Assembly illegally adjusted mail-in ballot laws ahead of the 2020 election. Kelly's argument is the same one that the Pennsylvania Supreme Court rejected **on Saturday. The decision now rests with Justice Samuel Alito, who handles emergency requests relating to Pennsylvania,** according **to Bloomberg.**

Alito can reject the request outright, refer it to the full court, or issue a temporary order on the issue, according to Bloomberg. "The want of due diligence demonstrated in this matter is unmistakable," the PA Supreme Court found on Saturday. "Petitioners filed this facial challenge to the mail-in voting statutory provisions more than one year after the enactment of Act 77."

Kelly's request is the second new pro-Trump legal action to be undertaken Tuesday. Trump's campaign also filed another lawsuit in Wisconsin seeking the invalidation of more than 220,000 votes, saying the state had improperly counted mail-in ballots.

Trump's legal challenges have been thrown out or withdrawn in Arizona, Georgia, Michigan and Nevada, and his remaining challenges are dwindling.

White House Press Secretary Kayleigh McEnany said prior to Thanksgiving that Trump would not concede the election until the Electoral College officially certifies Biden's victory. The Electoral College holds its official vote on Dec. 14th**, and the Trump campaign has until December 8th to finish any legal challenges.**

Attorney General Bill Barr also told the Associated Press that the DOJ has not found evidence that voter fraud overturned the result of the 2020 election on Tuesday. He ordered the DOJ to probe any credible reports of election fraud more than three weeks ago.

"To date, we have not seen fraud on a scale that could have affected a different outcome in the election," Barr told the AP.

Trump lawyer Rudy Giuliani was quick to push back on Barr's statement, however.

"With all due respect to the Attorney General, there hasn't been any semblance of a Department of Justice investigation," Giuliani said. "We have gathered ample evidence of illegal voting in at least six states, which they have not examined. We have many witnesses swearing under oath they saw crimes being committed in connection with voter fraud. As far as we know, not a single one has been interviewed by the DOJ. The Justice Department also hasn't audited any voting machines or used their subpoena powers to determine the truth."

Whistleblowers claiming USPS threw out, backdated ballots before election

The Amistad Project of the Thomas More Society, which has forged ahead with an independent investigation of alleged voter fraud in several key battleground states that Trump lost, has claimed that the FBI asked them to turn over their findings to their Los Angeles Field Office.

The FBI told Fox News that it's their "standard practice to neither confirm nor deny the existence of investigations. As such, we will decline further comment."

On Tuesday, the Amistad Project said that multiple "whistleblowers" lobbed serious accusations of "multistate illegal efforts by USPS workers to influence the election in at least three of six swing states."

"Details include potentially hundreds of thousands of completed absentee ballots being transported across three state lines, and a trailer filled with ballots disappearing in Pennsylvania," the group said.

One subcontractor alleged that over 100,000 ballots were improperly backdated on the day after the election so that they would be counted in Wisconsin, while another said they witnessed a vendor of Dominion machines and election officials in Pennsylvania tampering with voter machines.

TRUMP: DOJ 'MISSING IN ACTION' ON ALLEGED ELECTION FRAUD

The claims bear similarities to debunked lawsuits filed by the Trump campaign in Michigan, Wisconsin, Ne-

vada, Arizona, Pennsylvania, and Georgia, alleging voter fraud in the presidential election.

Attorneys for Trump have alleged, among other things, that Republicans were denied the opportunity to observe the canvassing process, with Trump claiming they have "hundreds and hundreds of affidavits" of witnesses' personal stories to back their argument up.

However, the so-called proof has not been presented during numerous court hearings, with judges repeatedly ruling against the Trump campaign in most of those states.

On Tuesday, Attorney General William Barr, put a pin in Trump's declaration of widespread voter fraud as well, telling the Associated Press in an interview that U.S. attorneys and FBI officials have been working to follow up on specific complaints and information they have received, but have not uncovered enough evidence that would change the outcome of the election.

Pennsylvania GOP Introduces Resolution to Dispute Election

By Brian Trusdell

Republicans in Pennsylvania General Assembly formally introduced a joint resolution Monday declaring the general elections results in dispute and reserving the power to designate presidential electors for the Electoral College.

The introduction was the latest step in a process begun last week by state Sen. Doug Mastriano to reclaim the authority granted in the U.S. Constitution to appointing the electors to the Electoral College.

The six-page resolution outlined the reasons for contesting the results, specifically accusing the officials in the executive branch for changing election law by allowing for absentee ballots that arrived after 8 p.m. on election day to be counted and the "partisan majority" on the Pennsylvania Supreme Court for allowing it.

It also said mail-in ballots were allowed to be corrected in heavily Democratic counties and were permitted to be counted without signature verification.

"A number of compromises of Pennsylvania's election laws took place during the 2020 General Election," the General Assembly said in a statement quoted by The Epoch Times. "The documented irregularities and improprieties associated with mail-in balloting, pre-canvassing, and canvassing have undermined our elector process and, as a result, we cannot accept certification of the results in statewide races."

Despite numerous lawsuits and challenges, Secretary of the Commonwealth Kathy Boockvar formally certified Pennsylvania's results last week declaring Joe Biden the winner of the state's election for president by more than 80,000 votes.

The resolution calls on Boockvar and Gov. Tom Wolf, both Democrats, to withdraw or vacate its certification of election results and declares "the General Assembly takes back and reserves the power to designate presidential electors for the Commonwealth of Pennsylvania for the December 2020 meeting of the Electoral College."

It also called on the U.S. Congress to recognize and count only electors votes as certified by the Pennsylvania House and Senate.

Republicans control both houses of the Pennsylvania legislature, known as the General Assembly.

GOP members outnumber Democrats in the Pennsylvania House 113-90 and 28-21 in the Senate, with one independent who caucuses with the Republicans.

Article 2, Section 1, Clause 2 of the U.S. Constitution says, "Each State shall appoint, in such Manner as the Legislature thereof may direct, a Number of Electors, equal to the whole Number of Senators and Representatives to which the State may be entitled in the Congress."

Pa. State Senator Moving to Have Legislature Appoint Electors

Pennsylvania Sen. Doug Mastriano, R-Franklin, attends a hearing of the Pennsylvania State Senate Majority Policy Committee, Wednesday, Nov. 25, 2020, in Gettysburg, Pa.) By Brian Trusdell

A member of the Pennsylvania Senate said he has spoken to the leadership in both houses of the state's General Assembly about exercising its authority to appoint electors to the Electoral College because of "so much evidence of shenanigans and fraud" in the presidential election.

"So, we're going to do a resolution between the House and Senate, hopefully today," Republican Sen. Doug Mastriano said Friday on "War Room," **former White House strategist Steve Bannon's video podcast.**

"I've spent two hours online trying to coordinate this with my colleagues. And there's a lot of good people working this here. Saying that the resolution, saying we're going to take our power back. We're going to seat the electors. Now obviously we're going to need the support of the leadership of the House and Senate. We're getting there on that."

Mastriano, 56, a retired U.S. Army colonel who represents the state's Senate District 33 in the south central counties of Cumberland, Adams, Franklin, and York, said about half of the Pennsylvania House and Senate leaders support the move. Republicans control both houses: 29-21 in the Senate and 113-90 in the House of Representatives.

Article 2, Section 1, Clause 2 **of the U.S. Constitution says, "Each State shall appoint, in such Manner as the Legislature thereof may direct, a Number of Electors, equal to the whole Number of Senators and Representatives to which the State may be entitled in the Congress."**

Mastriano said he is expecting "a struggle."

"We're going to hear the palpitations and you know the outcries of our Gov. (Tom) Wolf and Secretary (of State Kathy) Boockvar, whose resignation should have happened months ago and she shouldn't have ever been confirmed," he said.

Mastriano added the actions are necessary due to the revelations at a Wednesday hearing of the Pennsylvania Senate Majority Policy Committee in Gettysburg.

"(There's) so much evidence of shenanigans and fraud, we can't stand aside and just watch this unfold around us," he said. "If there's extensive shenanigans out there, it's up to the General Assembly to step in. So we have a fight on our hands and we're going to fight. We're going take the fight all the way to the Supreme Court if we have to."

Affidavit in Sidney Powell's Suit Claims Evidence Ties Vote Machines to Iran, China

An analysis by a onetime military intelligence analyst whose name was redacted in an affidavit with lawyer attorney Sidney Powell's lawsuit against Michigan officials insists there's "unambiguous evidence" that Dominion Voter Systems servers were accessible to and were "compromised by rogue actors, such as Iran and China."

According to reporting by The Epoch Times, **Powell's complaint, filed Wednesday against Michigan Gov. Gretchen Whitmer, Secretary of State Jocelyn Benson, and the Board of State Canvassers, cites the affidavit as representing a former electronic intelligence analyst and supporting claims that "the Dominion software was accessed by agents acting on behalf of China and Iran in order to monitor and manipulate elections, including the most recent US general election in 2020." Epoch said that a separate complaint in Georgia expands on the assertion, claiming that "by using servers and employees connected with rogue actors and hostile foreign influences combined with numerous easily discoverable leaked credentials, Dominion neglectfully allowed foreign adversaries to access data and intentionally provided access to their infrastructure in order to monitor and manipulate elections, including the most recent one in 2020."**

The analyst, who allegedly claimed to have "extensive experience as a white hat hacker used by some of the top election specialists in the world," said that they scanned Dominion network nodes and found a number of interrelationships with foreign entities, including access to Dominion's server by a network from Hunan, China. Another review is said to have confirmed links to an Iranian IP address. The analyst said the findings represent a "complete failure" on the part of Dominion to provide "basic cyber security." For its part, the voting machine company didn't respond to Epoch Times inquiries, but earlier in the week issued a strong denial that it is under any outside entity's influence.

As The Epoch Times reported, Dominion said there were "unfounded allegations being made against the company and its voting systems" in recent days. What's more, the firm said, "Dominion voting systems are designed and certified by the U.S. government to be closed and do not rely on network connectivity. Dominion's tabulators also do not have exposed USB or other memory ports." The latter comments appear to be in reference to recent claims of mysterious parties showing up and inserting thumb drives into Dominion machines during the vote earlier this month.

President Donald Trump and his legal surrogates are challenging the results of the Nov. 3 election, which seem to propel Joe Biden to the White House. The Trump campaign has alleged widespread and systemic voter fraud in multiple battleground states.

Trump's Ga. Lawyer Sends Demand Letter for Signature Match Recount

President Donald Trump speaks in the Diplomatic Room of the White House on Thanksgiving on November 26, 2020 in Washington, D.C.

A lawyer for President Donald Trump's reelection campaign in Georgia is asking for an audit of up to 45,000 signatures on ballots that allegedly have been illegally cast in the presidential race before the state's recount is completed.

In the fifth letter sent to Georgia Secretary of State Brad Raffensperger by President Donald Trump's campaign counselor Ray S. Smith, the lawyer urged an audit "before it's too late."

"It is not possible for you to accurately certify the results in the president race… until and unless there is a thorough audit of the Signatures, which we have now requested four times in writing prior to this request," Smith wrote.

"You cannot in good faith conclude the ongoing statutory recount until you have institute a Signature matching audit," Smith argued. "The margin in Georgia at this time is 12,670 votes — and the potential illegal absentee ballots included in that number is between three and four times the margin of votes awarding the victory to Joe Biden."

Smith asserted he estimated that "between 38,250 and 45,626 illegal votes may have been cast, counted, and included in your tabulations for the presidential race."

"It is inconceivable that you are unwilling to take any steps to audit the Signatures before completing the current recount and proceeding to certify the results of an election where so many illegal votes may be included in your tabulations," he wrote.

"We implore you to exercise your statutory authority and your duty to the electorate to audit the Signatures, before it is too late," he pleaded.

Raffensperger has pushed back on claims of fraud, saying on Monday those trying to overturn the election results in the state are "dishonest actors" spreading "massive amounts of disinformation," the Washington Post reported.

He asserted the recount requested by the Trump campaign would wrap up by its Wednesday deadline just shy of midnight.

Ric Grenell to Newsmax TV: DC Press Are in Bag for Dems By Eric MACK

White House press secretary Kayleigh McEnany shut down a CNN reporter at press briefing, saying she does not call on activists, and former Amb. Ric Grenell on Newsmax TV said that is ostensibly the entire media in the capitol.

"We're at the point where we've got to recognize that the Washington, D.C., press corps is a bunch of advocates; they are a bunch of advocates," Grenell, also the former acting director of national intelligence, told Monday's "Spicer & Co." "So, we have to stop expecting that they're going to play fair. We have to start treating them exactly like who they are: Which are a bunch of advocates for the Democrats."

Grenell told host Sean Spicer, conservatives need to "start doing what President [Donald] Trump has done: Take to social media, tell your own story, be aggressive about it, ignore the Washington, D.C., advocates."

Also, Grenell noted, CIA Director John Brennan's critiques of the Trump administration should equally fall on deaf ears, particularly with regard to the Iran and Israel."Every single time there is a story about the Iranian regime, you can count on John Brennan giving aid and comfort to the Iranian regime," Grenell said. "This is a horrific pattern from him and it's gotta stop.

"He's an American who's had access at the highest levels of our U.S. intelligence. He probably still has access to a certain level of intelligence, and for him to constantly take the side of the Iranian regime is scary. "We know his pattern. We know what he always does. And he's always going to be against Israel, always going to be for the Iranian regime, and it's really getting sickening."

Georgia Secretary of State Raffensperger investigating 250 cases connected to election

Raffensperger singled out groups that he said are working to register ineligible people to vote ahead of a high-profile runoff election for Georgia's two U.S. Senate seats.

Georgia Secretary of State Brad Raffensperger on Monday said his office is investigating more than 250 claims of voting irregularities connected with the November election.

Speaking to reporters from the state Capitol Monday, Raffensperger said his office is investigating any credible claims that groups are working to register ineligible people to vote ahead of a high-profile runoff election for Georgia's two U.S. Senate seats. He said his office's 23 investigators are also continuing to look into allegations of problems with absentee ballots, as well as claims of people who voted twice, people who cast a ballot in a dead person's name, and non-residents who voted in Georgia.

Georgia Secretary of State Brad Raffensperger speaks during a news conference on Monday, Nov. 30, 2020, in Atlanta. (AP)

Gabriel Sterling, a top official in Raffensperger's office, said more than 250 cases have been opened, but there has been nothing so far that jumps out as being likely to change the outcome of the election.

Raffensperger also hit back at allegations of widespread fraud, saying those that perpetuate them "are exploiting the emotions of many Trump supporters with fantastic claims, half-truths, misinformation and,

frankly, they're misleading the president as well, apparently."

DISTRICT JUDGE HALTS 3 GEORGIA COUNTIES FROM ERASING DOMINION VOTING MACHINE DATA

The secretary of state's office is looking into a sworn statement from a Republican official in Gwinnett County, in Atlanta's northeastern suburbs, that says there were more absentee ballots than absentee ballot envelopes, Raffensperger said.

"This is the kind of specific charge that our office can investigate and ascertain the truth," he said.

County election workers around the state are currently working on a recount of the presidential race that was requested by the Trump campaign, and Raffensperger said he expects them to finish by the Wednesday night deadline. Under state law, the losing candidate can request a recount when the margin is less than 0.5%. Certified results showed Trump losing to Biden by 12,670 votes, or 0.25%.

The recount, which is being done using scanners that read and tabulate votes, is the third time the votes in the presidential race are being counted in Georgia. After the initial count following Election Day, Raffensperger selected the presidential race for an audit required by state law. Because of the tight margin, he said, the audit required the roughly 5 million votes in that contest to be recounted by hand.

Georgia Senate runoff spurs election probe of groups trying to register out-of-state voters

Office has 250 open investigations into 'credible claims of illegal voting' and election law violations, secretary of state says

Georgia**'s top election official says he is opening an investigation into whether third-party groups are trying to register people from other states to illegally vote in Georgia's twin Jan. 5** Senate runoff elections**, when the GOP's majority in the chamber is at stake.**

Secretary of State Brad Raffensperger announced to reporters on Monday that "we have opened an investigation into a group called America Votes, who is sending absentee ballot applications to people at addresses where they have not lived since 1994."

DONALD TRUMP JR. TO STAR IN NEW ADS IN GEORGIA SENATE RUNOFF CAMPAIGN

Raffensperger, a Republican, also said his investigators are looking into "Vote Forward, who attempted to register a dead Alabama voter, a woman, to vote here in Georgia." He also spotlighted "The New Georgia Project, who sent voter registration applications to New York City."

Georgia Secretary of State Brad Raffensperger speaks during a news conference on Nov. 20, 2020, in Atlanta. The secretary of state also pinpointed "Operation New Voter Registration Georgia, who is telling college students in Georgia that they can change their residency to Georgia and then change it back after the election."

Raffensperger emphasized that "voting in Georgia when you're not a resident of Georgia is a felony. And encouraging college students to commit felonies without regard for what it might mean for them is despicable. These third-party groups have a responsibility not to encourage illegal voting. If they do so, they will be held responsible." Raffensperger's office also has 23 investigators working on 250 open investigations into "credible claims of illegal voting" and election law violations, he said. Gabriel Sterling, the election official who manages Georgia's voting system, told reporters that "this is new information, these outside groups attempting to register people illegally potentially, in other states."

Sterling said that these third-party groups appear to be "literally saying 'hey, it's OK to commit a felony.'"

GEORGIA EXTENDS USE OF ABSENTEE BALLOT DROP BOXES IN STATE'S RUNOFF ELECTIONS

And Raffensperger emphasized that "this office will continue to take steps to protect the voting rights of the legally registered Georgians of this state, Republican, Democrat, independent, and whatever party you may be a member of." The current balance of power for the next Senate coming out of this month's elections is 50 Republicans and 48 Democrats. That means Democrats must win both of Georgia's runoff elections to make it a 50-50 Senate. If that occurs, Vice President-elect Kamala Harris would be the tie-breaking vote, giving her party a razor-thin majority in the chamber. In Georgia, where state law dictates a runoff if no candidate reaches 50% of the vote, GOP Sen. David Perdue narrowly missed avoiding a runoff, winning 49.75% of the vote. Democratic challenger Jon Ossoff trails by roughly 87,000 votes.

In the other race, appointed Republican Sen. Kelly Loeffler captured nearly 26% of the vote in a whopping 20-candidate special election to fill the final two years of the term of former GOP Sen. Johnny Isakson. The Democratic candidate in the runoff, Rev. Raphael Warnock, won nearly 33% of the vote in the first round.

District judge halts 3 Georgia counties from erasing Dominion voting machine data

Trump to campaign for Georgia Senate runoff candidates

Fox News correspondent Charles Watson joins 'Fox Report' with the latest from Atlanta. A district judge on Sunday night blocked three Georgia counties from altering or erasing data on Dominion voting machines after Republican nominees to the Electoral College filed an emergency motion. Judge Timothy C. Batten Sr.'s order applies to Dominion voting machines in Cobb, Gwinnett and Cherokee counties, which are clustered in the Atlanta metropolitan area. The order does not apply to Georgia's other 156 counties.

DOMINION SERVER CRASH DELAYS RECOUNT IN GEORGIA'S FULTON COUNTY: REPORT

"After a general election and hand recount audit, Vice President [Joe] Biden was declared the winner of Georgia's General Election for President by a margin of 12,670 votes on November 20, 2020," the plaintiffs wrote on Friday. "But the vote count certified by the Defendants on November 20 is wrong. Tens of thousands of votes counted toward Vice President Biden's final tally were the product of illegality, and physical and computer-based fraud leading to 'outright ballot stuffing.'"

Officials work on ballots at the Gwinnett County Voter Registration and Elections Headquarters, Friday, Nov. 6, 2020, in Lawrenceville, near Atlanta.

"Georgia's election process depends entirely on voting machines, tabulators and software purchased from Dominion Voting Systems Corporation ('Dominion') that was compromised. Computerized vote recording and tabulations are controlled by software programs that were designed to cheat, and which were open to human manipulation," the filing continued. The elector nominees, who include conservative teen pundit C.J. Pearson, are seeking an order to allow them to inspect Dominion voting machines. They name Georgia Gov. Brian Kemp and Georgia Secretary of State Brad Raffensperger, both Republicans, among the defendants.

TRUMP PRESSES GEORGIA'S REPUBLICAN GOVERNOR TO OVERRULE SECRETARY OF STATE, SCRUTINIZE BALLOT SIGNATURES

"WE WILL STOP THE STEAL," Pearson tweeted on Monday.

Dominion countered that "allowing such forensic inspections would pose substantial security and proprietary/trade secret risks," Batten wrote. Dominion has until Wednesday "to file a brief setting forth in detail the factual bases they have, if any, against allowing the three forensic inspections. The brief should be accompanied and supported by affidavit or other evidence, if appropriate," Batten ordered.

Batten's order comes as all eyes are on Georgia amid twin Senate runoff races and President Trump's criticism of Kemp and Raffensperger over the election, which he lost.

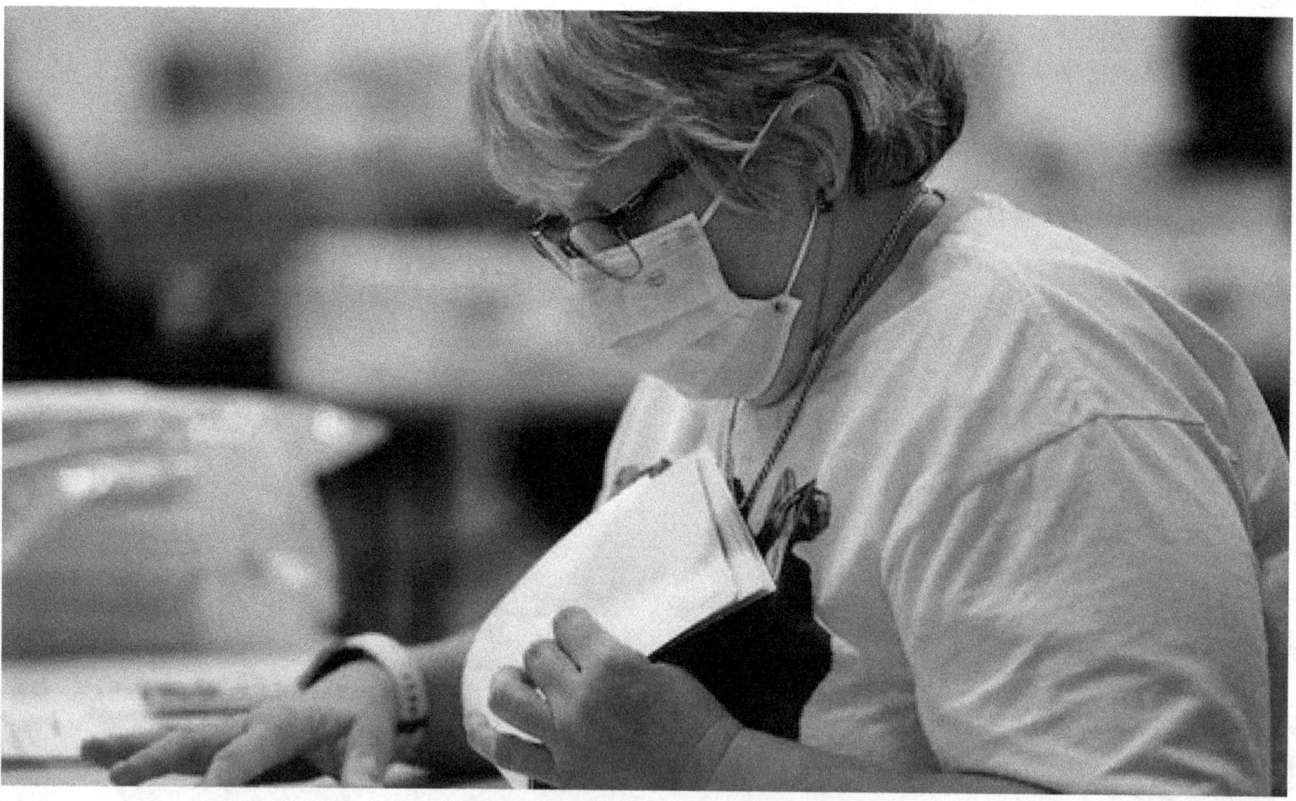

Cobb County Election officials handle ballots during an audit, Monday, Nov. 16, 2020, in Marietta, Ga. THE THEFT WAS IN BIG POPULATION ATLANTA FULTON COUNTY; THAT WASN'T SIGNATURE AUDITED.

"Why won't Governor @BrianKempGA, the hapless Governor of Georgia, use his emergency powers, which can be easily done, to overrule his obstinate Secretary of State, and do a match of signatures on envelopes," Trump wrote on Twitter **on Monday morning. "It will be a 'goldmine' of fraud, and we will easily WIN the state."**

Michael Steel, a spokesman for Dominion, previously denied claims that vote cast through the company's systems were at risk of being altered. He said it is physically impossible to alter votes in the system.

"Look, when a voter votes on a Dominion machine, they fill out a ballot on a touch screen. They are given a printed copy which they then give to a local election official for safekeeping. If any electronic interference had taken place, the tally reported electronically would not match the printed ballots. and in every case where we've looked at -- in Georgia, all across the country -- the printed ballot, the gold standard in election security, has matched the electronic tally," he said**.**

Trump's campaign launched several lawsuits challenging the voting systems and processes in key battleground states including Pennsylvania and Wisconsin.

Sidney Powell to Newsmax TV: Plenty of Time for Trump to Overturn Election Results

By Solange Reyner

Attorney Sidney Powell says there's plenty of time for President Donald Trump's legal team to overturn the results of the 2020 presidential election.

"With the fraud case, the Dec. 8 deadline doesn't apply," Powell said Friday during an appearance on News-max TV's "Stinchfield" **in reference to the "safe harbor" deadline that frees a state from further challenge if it resolves all disputes and certifies its voting results.**

"We have at least until Dec. 14," she said.

"We might file more suits. The court in Michigan or Wisconsin today just gave us a great order recognizing that. These are not pure election contests we are filing. These are massive fraud suits that can set aside the results of the election due to this fraud at any time. The states should not be certifying election results in the face of it."

Powell, a former member of Trump's legal team, has been a part of multiple lawsuits in a crusade to overturn results from the 2020 election.

Several states have certified Joe Biden as the winner of the election. Newsmax has yet to project a winner as Trump continues to contest the results in court.

The Wisconsin Supreme Court on Friday said it wouldn't accept a lawsuit by Trump's legal team, sidestepping a decision on the merits of the claims and instead ruling that the case must first wind its way through the lower courts.

The president asked the court to disqualify more than 221,000 ballots in the state's two biggest Democrat counties, alleging irregularities in the way absentee ballots were administered.

Trump Campaign Files Lawsuit in Georgia to Overturn Result

By Jeffrey Rodack

President Donald Trump has filed suit in Georgia claiming the election process was filled with "significant systemic misconduct, fraud and other irregularities" resulting in "many thousands of illegal votes" being cast and counted.

The suit was filed in Georgia on Friday on behalf of Trump and David Shafer, a presidential elector pledged

to the president. The suit named Georgia Secretary of State Brad Raffensperger and a slew of local elections officials.

It is asking the court to prevent certification of the results and order a new presidential election.

The suit claims:

- The election code mandates that those wishing to vote by absentee ballots may apply for a mail-in ballot "not more than 180 days" prior to the election. But it alleges the officials permitted at least 305,701 people to illegally vote who applied for absentee ballots more than 180 days prior to the election and then improperly counted the illegal votes.
- Officials allowed at least 92 individuals to vote whose absentee ballots, according to state records, were returned and accepted prior to that individual requesting an absentee ballot.
- The officials mailed at least 2,664 absentee ballots to individuals prior to the earliest date permitted by law.
- Respondents unlawfully adopted standards to be followed by the clerks and registrars in processing absentee ballots inconsistent with the election code.
- Despite the legal requirement for signature matching and voter identity verification, the respondents failed to ensure that such obligations were followed by election officials.

The lawsuit also claims the officials violated Georgia law and the election code, along with state election board rules and regulations.

"The fraud, misconduct and irregularities that occurred under the 'supervision' of (the) respondents are sufficient to place the contest election in doubt," the lawsuit said. "As a result, there is substantial doubt as to the outcome of the contested election, and the contested election ... shall be enjoined, vacated, and nullified and either a new presidential election be immediately ordered that complies with Georgia Page 52 of 64 law or, in the alternative, that such other just and equitable relief is obtained so as to comport with the Constitution of the State of Georgia."

A-listers Matthew McConaughey and Russell Brand slam the left for their treatment of conservatives Hard-line stance Sarah Taylor

Actor Matthew McConaughey has blasted the "far left," and said that the "illiberal left" is condescending, patronizing, and arrogant when it comes to dealing with conservative Americans. What are the details?

McConaughey recently spoke to fellow entertainer and British actor Russell Brand and discussed the attitudes of those on the "far left" when it comes to dealing with their conservative peers and working-class Americans.

"We live in a time, I feel, in my country and yours, where there's this sort of ... condemnation and criticism of what I might describe as ordinary working people," Brand began. "A kind of offhandedness, like, 'Oh, they're dumb, they're voting for Brexit, they're voting for Trump."

"I don't like it, and I don't like to hear it," Brand said. "I've spent enough time with people that have been described in this manner to feel ill at ease with it. How do you feel about ... that kind of judgment? Do you feel that there is a way of meshing together these apparently disparate groups right now?"

McConaughey responded, "I hope so. ... Let's get aggressively centric, I dare you. It's not a recessive, it's an aggressive move." He went on to explain that many people on the "illiberal left" are hard-pressed to get along with those on the right.

"There are a lot [of people] on that illiberal left that absolutely condescend, patronize, and are arrogant towards the other 50%," he explained. Brand responded in agreement and explained that his personal experiences growing up have turned him away from elitism.

"Our entire way of measuring what is valuable has been biased to such an alarming degree that it's created this kind of chasm of mistrust," Brand later insisted.

What else?

In October, McConaughey said that cancel culture is a poison upon society. In remarks to podcaster Joe Rogan, McConaughey said, "We're making people persona non grata because of something they do that is right now deemed wrong or it's the hot point in a hot topic right now. You can't erase someone's entire existence. Where the heck does some forgiveness go?"

He also insisted that some progressives go too far left.

"Some people in our industry, not all this, there's some that go to the left so far that go to the illiberal left side so far, that is so condescending and patronizing to 50 % of the world that need the empathy that the liberals have gives and should give to throw somebody, to illegitimize them because they say they are a believer," McConaughey said. "It's just so arrogant, and in some ways hypocritical to me."

Georgia election officials refute claims made about viral video with` suitcaseś of ballots

Officials say everything in the video looks like normal election procedure TAMI CHAPPELL & Chris Pandolfo

The Georgia secretary of state's office on Friday reportedly said they've investigated claims of voter fraud made in a viral video shared by the Trump campaign and others, and found that the claims were not true.

According to Fox News, senior officials in Secretary of State Brad Raffensperger's office have investigated and DEBUNKED IS THE ALL PURPOSE FAVORITE CODE WORD OF SNIDE; CONDESCENDING LIBERAL DEMOCRATS WHO HATE GUNS & RELIGION DEPLORABLE GUTS claims that Fulton County election officials illegally counted ballots without poll watcher supervision.

The Trump campaign and various political commentators and media figures on Thursday claimed that video footage taken by security cameras showed "suitcases filled with ballots" being counted at State Farm Arena in Atlanta on Nov. 3 after election supervisors were told to leave the room. The video was first presented as part of testimony from the Trump campaign at an election integrity hearing held by state lawmakers. Those that testified were not asked to swear under oath.

The narrator of the video is Jackie Pick, an attorney who said she was not acting as a lawyer for the Trump campaign but rather presented testimony as a volunteer. She claimed that the video showed "four people" staying behind to count "suitcases" of ballots after "Republican observers and the press" were told to leave. Trump's legal team asserts that something fraudulent or nefarious may have occurred while these ballots were allegedly counted without supervision and at the very least complains that what occurred in the video was against protocols established by Georgia state election law.

An official from Raffensperger's office told Fox News an investigation showed these claims were unfounded. According to the official, Fulton County election officials had a designated observer watching the votes being counted the entire time. Additionally, the official said there was nothing suspicious about the "suitcases" of ballots that were pulled out from beneath a table and that those cases on video are the cases ballots were supposed to be kept in.

TheBlaze has contacted the Georgia secretary of state's office requesting comment on Fox News' reporting.

Other Georgia officials have stated on the record that the claims made about the video were false.

Gabriel Sterling, a Republican in charge of implementing Georgia's voting system, told Lead Stories that nothing in the video appeared "bizarre or odd" and that what is seen looks like normal election procedure. He disputed allegations that Republican poll watchers were told vote counting had ended and they were to go home.

He explained that the election workers who went home are known as "cutters," because their job was to open absentee ballot envelopes and verify ballots for eventual scanning and counting. He said they were dismissed sometime after 10 p.m. on Nov. 3, as shown in the video, because their work for the evening had been finished. The four workers who remained behind were responsible for scanning the ballots.

"If you look at the video tape, the work you see is the work you would expect, which is you take the sealed suitcase looking things in, you place the ballots on the scanner in manageable batches and you scan them," Sterling told Lead Stories.

The chief investigator for the Georgia secretary of state, Frances Watson, also spoke to Lead Stories and he said that the "suitcases" seen in the video were standard containers. "There wasn't a bin that had ballots in it under that table," Watson explained. "It was an empty bin and the ballots from it were actually out on the table when the media were still there, and then it was placed back into the box when the media were still there and placed next to the table."

Watson said that there was never an announcement made to the media or to partisan election observers about the counting being done for the night or telling them to go home. TheBlaze has previously reported that Fulton County officials explicitly denied that anyone from the Trump campaign was ever told vote counting was finished for the night. Multiple requests made to the Trump campaign for response were unanswered.

Additionally, Lead Stories obtained comments from the state election board monitor who was present for the vote counting on Nov. 3. He explained that at no point was the ballot counting unobserved by elections officials, as Pick and others have claimed:

A state election board monitor, who asked for his name not to be used due to safety concerns, told Lead Stories on the phone on December 3, 2020, that he was present at the vote counting location beginning at 11:52 p.m., after leaving briefly at earlier in the evening. He then stayed until about 12:45 a.m., when the work that night was completed. The deputy chief investigator for the secretary of state's office was present beginning at 12:15 a.m. November 4, he said.

Georgia officials are responding to other "concerning" allegations made during Thursday's testimony.

Republican Gov. Brian Kemp on Thursday called on the secretary of state to conduct a signature audit of absentee ballots to verify the election results. However, a signature audit presents difficulties because when absentee votes are first counted on Election Day, they are separated from the signed envelopes they came in, WXIA-TV explained. To preserve the secrecy of ballots, ballots are not signed by voters, just the envelopes they are delivered in. So there is no way to retroactively match votes that have already been counted with the signatures of the voters who sent those ballots.

The Georgia secretary of state's office has not yet responded to the governor's request. WHO BELIEVES THIS?

Sidney Powell to Newsmax TV: Dominion Contracts Warrant Criminal Probe

By Eric Mack

The $107 million contract awarded by Georgia for Dominion Voting Systems should be thoroughly investigated for potential "benefits being paid to family members of those who signed the contract," according to former federal prosecutor Sidney Powell on Newsmax TV.

"There should be an investigation, a thorough criminal investigation, frankly, of everyone involved in acquiring the Dominion [Voting] System for the state of Georgia," Powell told Saturday's "The Count" hosted by Tom Basile and Mark Halperin.

"And frankly for every other state, given how appalling the system is and the fact it was designed to manipulate the votes and destroy the real votes of American citizens who were casting legal votes."

Powell's investigation is turning up potential criminal allegations, including "money or benefits being paid to family members of those who signed the contract for Georgia."

"I think there are multiple people in the Secretary of State's office and other that should be investigated in Georgia for what benefits they might have received for giving Dominion the $100-million, no-bid contract," Powell said.

The Atlanta-Journal Constitution reported in 2019, however, Georgia did receive three bids for the new voting systems, with Dominion winning on being "the lowest-cost system among three companies that submitted bids."

That contract was pursued by the state after Stacey Abrams never conceded to Gov. Brian Kemp in the 2018 midterm elections, claiming the Secretary of State and Kemp unlawfully "suppressed" votes by voiding registrations found to be illegitimate.

Arizona Republicans to Hold Meeting on Nov. 3 Election

Arizona Republicans have scheduled a meeting at a hotel in downtown Phoenix on Monday to discuss the Nov. 3 election.

The event was billed as a "fact-finding hearing" featuring members of Trump's legal team and members of the Arizona Legislature, but top leaders of the Republican-controlled Legislature told The Associated Press that the planned gathering was not an official legislative event.

According to press release by state Rep. Mark Finchem, R-Oro-Valley, the gathering is intended "to hear testimony and view evidence related to allegations of electoral compromise related to the 2020 election."

A similar event was held Wednesday in Gettysburg, Pennsylvania.

No evidence of fraud or hacking of voting machines has emerged during this election in Arizona.

Five challenges have been filed in Maricopa County Superior Court in Phoenix since Nov. 3 and four of those have been dismissed. An initial hearing on the fifth is scheduled Monday, the same day as the hotel event and the state election canvass at the state Capitol.

Among the Trump supporters using social media to publicize the Arizona event were state GOP Chairwoman Kelli Ward and U.S. Rep. Paul Gosar, R-Ariz. "I will be there," Gosar declared on Twitter.

It wasn't clear whether the Trump attorneys would be present in Phoenix or addressing the gathering remotely. On Tuesday, Republican Gov. Doug Ducey acknowledged for the first time that President-elect Joe Biden won Arizona. The Arizona Legislature is not in session and Senate President Karen Fann said neither she nor House Speaker Rusty Bowers, authorized fellow Republican lawmakers to hold a hearing at the Capitol on the election.

"So they found a site off-site to hold it," Fann said. The planned gathering drew scorn from some Democrats.

"Might as well have a boat parade and call it a legislative hearing. This unsanctioned unofficial circus sideshow will have no bearing or impact on @JoeBiden's victory in Arizona," the Democratic Caucus of the Arizona House said in its Twitter feed.

Dick Morris to Newsmax TV: Legislatures, Feds Important in Trump Case

By Sandy Fitzgerald

As the fight for President Donald Trump's election moves in the federal court, "our chances of winning increase," and state legislatures will also come into play, political strategist and author Dick Morris told Newsmax TV Saturday.

"State legislatures like in Pennsylvania are taking their constitutional duty seriously to determine who won the state and who gets the electoral votes," Morris, also an analyst for Newsmax TV, told "The Count." "The Constitution is explicit that state legislatures have that authority."

In the past, legislatures "rubberstamped" what the state boards of canvassers told them, but now with the irregularities in the state courts, "they are moving in asserting their legal jurisdiction over that and I think that is very important," Morris said.

Meanwhile, Arizona would be the most difficult state for Trump to win, but Michigan, Pennsylvania, and Georgia, the "fraud was very blatant and well planned well in advance,' said Morris.

"Pennsylvania prepared for the fraud by illegally extending that time you had to vote to 3 days after the election day, clearly in violation of the Constitution and state law," he added.

Morris also discussed the ruling by Judge Matthew Brann of the U.S. District Court in the Middle District of Pennsylvania, noting that the "mistake" the judge made was that the federal case wasn't about ballot fraud, but about equal protection under the law.

Roger Stone to Newsmax TV: Evidence Denial Is a Media ´Stunt̀ By Eric Mack

The breathless claims of "no evidence" (IN COMBINATION WITH EVERY ALLEGATION OF VOTER FRAUD IS ASSESSED WITH THE LEFT'S ALL PURPOSE WORD OF HAVING BEEN DEBUNKED – WHERE THE FUCK DID THAT WORD COME FROM?) **is a "mainstream media stunt," according to Roger Stone on** Newsmax TV.

"I think the mainstream media stunt of saying there's no evidence (ABSOLUTELY ZERO EVIDENCE; JUST LIKE MR. CLEAN HAS JUST WIPED DOWN & RENDERED ALL OPERATING TABLES IN THE SURGICAL WARD SPIC & SPAN; AND THEN FOLLOWED UP WITH COMET; LYSOL; & BABBO; THE FOAMING CLEANER; 112% COMPLETELY GERM & PATHOGEN FREE & THEN FOR GOOD MEASURE; WIPED DOWN WITH CHARMIN) **whatsoever of voter fraud is patently absurd, because** the evidence is not only overwhelming, it's also compelling,**" Stone told Saturday's "The Count" hosted by Tom Basile and Mark Halperin.**

Stone pointed to the "old fashioned, urban, Democrat vote-stealing machine" and "serious evidence of cyber manipulation of the vote."

Asked by Halperin if President Donald Trump does not succeed in his legal challenge, who could beat him in the Republican Party in 2024?

"That would be no one," Stone said. "This president is even more popular than the great Ronald Reagan was."

Stone added Reagan's GOP approval rating was a "marvel" in the high 80s.

"Donald Trump has approval ratings in the mid-90s, which I've never seen in American politics," Stone added.

The grassroots of the Republican Party loves Donald Trump."

Dark Money, Assailed by Dems, Aided Biden: Analysis

Though Dems have long criticized anonymous money in politics, this latest election cycle saw a wave of it flow into and fill up Democratic Party coffers.

According to an analysis **by the Center for Responsive Politics for CNN, more than $320 million in "dark money"** A.K.A. $700 MILLION ZUCKERBUCKS **boosted Democrats in races for the White House and congressional seats, more than double what Republicans saw.**

At the top of the list, the analysis showed, was Joe Biden. He took in nearly $132 million in such anonymous

funding for his bid to unseat President Donald Trump. Trump, who is appealing vote counts showing a Biden win, received just $22 million in dark money.

Biden's aides declined comment on the record, CNN said, but pointed to his letting reporters listen in on fundraising events as evidence of his support for transparency.

They also note that the former vice president, a supporter of public financing for federal candidates, has proposed sweeping changes to address the role of money in politics and curb the outsize influence of dark money while backing more small-donor, grassroots funding for candidates.

The analysis defined dark money as donations and other spending by nonprofits that don't disclose sources, and money from limited liability corporations functioning as shell corporations.

With such funding, the mysterious sourcing of cash obscures the agenda of the donors. Dems have railed against it for years.

"This is a rotten system, but as long as it exists, both parties are going to use it," said Fred Wertheimer, who runs a watchdog group, Democracy 21, and according to the cable news network is part of a coalition of more than 170 groups urging the incoming president to tackle issues that include campaign finance transparency. "The test for us is: What are you prepared to do about the system?" Wertheimer was quoted as saying.

The analysis looked at dark money giving to super PACs, and any money nonprofits spend directly on an election or defeat of a specific person seeking office. One Nation, a nonprofit with anonymous funding associated with Mitch McConnell, the Republican Senate majority leader, is the largest nameless donor in federal races so far, giving more than $60 million to an aligned super PAC working to help the GOP keep its Senate hold.

On the flip side, three liberal groups, led by a group known as the Sixteen Thirty Fund, account for a third of the dark money donations aiding Dems. In all, the analysis pointed to $52 million flowing from the Sixteen Thirty Fund to other groups active in the 2020 elections.

One small sum, about $300,000, went to The Lincoln Project, which has generated ads, postings and more sharply critical of Trump.

For all the qualms over dark money, the system remains in place, indeed, even as candidates, parties and other groups ramp up their spending on all-important Senate runoff elections in Georgia. The Jan. 5 votes will ultimately determine who controls the Senate chamber.

Pa. poll watcher, a Navy vet, alleges missing USB cards, up to 120,000 questionable votes

At a hearing Wednesday, the poll watcher alleged the cards may have been used to add illegal votes to the state's vote count

By Dom Calicchio

A U.S. Navy veteran and data scientist from Pennsylvania alleged this week that 47 USB cards used during the state's Nov. 3 election have gone missing – and asserted that as many as 120,000 votes cast in the election should be called into question.

At a hearing in Gettysburg on Wednesday, poll watcher Gregory Stenstrom of Delaware County identified himself a former commanding officer in the Navy and a forensic computer scientist with expertise on security and fraud issues.

"I personally observed USB cards being uploaded to voting machines by the voting machine warehouse supervisor on multiple occasions," Stenstrom testified. "This person is not being observed, he's not a part of the process that I can see, and he is walking in with baggies of USBs."

USB (Universal Serial Bus) cards are small, handheld devices that help people move data from one electronic device to another. Stenstrom alleged the cards may have been used to add illegal votes to the state's vote count -- and claimed there was a lack of proper oversight on how state election workers handled ballots.

"In all cases the chain of custody was broken," he said. "It was broken for the mail-in ballots, the drop-box ballots, the Election Day USB card flash drives. In all cases they didn't follow any of the procedures defined by the Board of Delaware County of Elections."

The witness also told lawmakers that law enforcement personnel failed to act after he reported the alleged mishandling of ballots.

TRUMP CAMPAIGN PUSHES FORWARD IN LEGAL CHALLENGE OF PA. CERTIFICATION, LOOKS TO REVIVE POLL WATCHER CLAIMS

"I literally begged multiple law enforcement agencies to go get the forensic evidence from the computers. It's a simple process. It wouldn't have taken more than an hour to image all 5 machines. That was never done despite my objections and that was three weeks ago." Pennsylvania – which certified its election results Tuesday -- is one of several battleground states where the Trump 2020 Campaign has raised allegations of possible voter fraud. Pennsylvania was worth 20 electoral votes to the winner.

President Trump was initially scheduled to attend Wednesday's hearing, which was convened by the Pennsylvania Senate Majority Policy Committee.

The president later canceled his travel plans, opting instead to meet with his legal advisers in Washington. But Trump lawyer Rudy Giuliani appeared at the hearing.

However, the president's legal fight in Pennsylvania continues. In a letter filed with the Third Circuit Court of Appeals on Wednesday, Trump 2020 Campaign attorney Marc Scaringi called for oral arguments as the campaign fights against a lower court's dismissal of their case challenging Pennsylvania's certification of votes.

Sen. Paul Calls Out Anomalies in Vote Counts, Big Tech

By Eric Mack

Count Sen. Rand Paul, R-Ky., as an election "statistical anomaly" skeptic and one wary of big tech censorship of conservative voices. Paul noted President Donald Trump's "margin of 'defeat'" was covered by overnight "data dumps" in four key battleground states. "Interesting . . . Trump margin of "defeat" in 4 states occurred in 4 data dumps between 1:34-6:31 AM. Statistical anomaly? Fraud? Look at the evidence and decide for yourself.(That is, if Big Tech allows u to read this) Anomalies in Vote Counts; https://votepatternanalysis.

substack.com/p/voting-anomalies-2020" On cue, Twitter slapped a "this claim about election fraud is disputed." Twitter has been using that to reject Republican attempts to contest the presidential election results amid evidence of illegal votes, including from those who are deceased, unconstitutional election law changes forced by courts and Democrat officials against the will of the state legislatures, and questions about election voting systems.

The voting anomalies outlined by the report linked to by Paul are:

- "An update in Michigan listed as of 6:31AM Eastern Time on November 4th, 2020, which shows 141,258 votes for Joe Biden and 5,968 votes for Donald Trump
- An update in Wisconsin listed as 3:42AM Central Time on November 4th, 2020, which shows 143,379 votes for Joe Biden and 25,163 votes for Donald Trump
- A vote update in Georgia listed at 1:34AM Eastern Time on November 4th, 2020, which shows 136,155 votes for Joe Biden and 29,115 votes for Donald Trump
- An update in Michigan listed as of 3:50AM Eastern Time on November 4th, 2020, which shows 54,497 votes for Joe Biden and 4,718 votes for Donald Trump"

According to the data study: "In particular, we are able to quantify the extent of compliance with this property and discover that, of the 8,954 vote updates used in the analysis, these four decisive updates were the 1st, 2nd, 4th, and 7th most anomalous updates in the entire data set. Not only does each of these vote updates not follow the generally observed pattern, but the anomalous behavior of these updates is particularly extreme. That is, these vote updates are outliers of the outliers."

Pennsylvania Judge Backs Trump Claims Over Mail-In Ballots

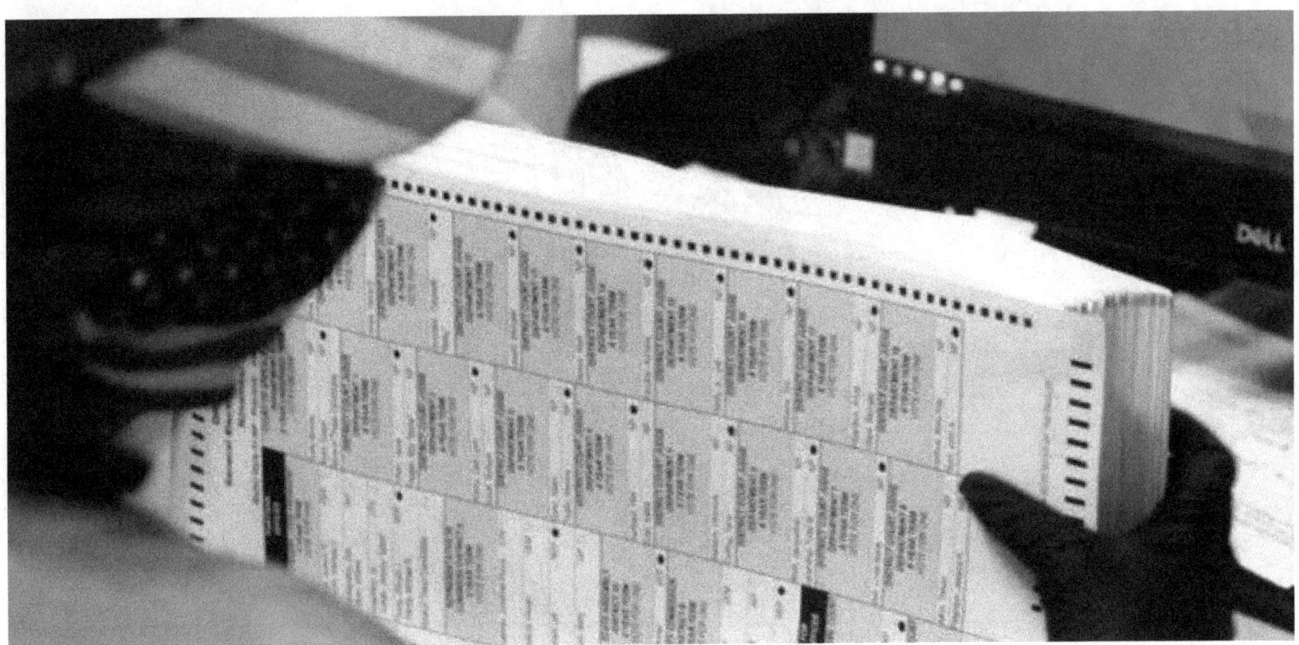

After a Pennsylvania Judge blocked the state from 'taking any further steps' to complete the certification of the presidential race on Wednesday – she dropped a detailed opinion on Friday justifying her decision, which concludes that the state's changes to mail-in balloting procedures were likely illegal. The order is currently delayed while the state Supreme Court considers the case on an expedited basis, which was filed by a group of Republicans who argued that the state's changes to mail-in voting, Act 77, violated the commonwealth's constitution.

Commonwealth Judge Patricia McCullough noted in her opinion that the plaintiffs "have established a likelihood to succeed on the merits" of the case, because "the Constitution does not provide a mechanism for the legislature to allow for the expansion of absentee voting without a constitutional amendment." "Petitioners appear to have a viable claim that the mail-in ballot procedures set forth in Act 77 contravene Pa. Const. Article VII Section 14 as the plain language of that constitutional provision **is at odds with the mail-in provisions of Act 77."**

Judge McCullough adds that without the emergency injunction, the plaintiffs would likely suffer "irreparable harm." "If what may be an unconstitutional mail-in voting process remains extant, such mail-in ballots may make the difference as to whether he is successful or not." In short; Judge McCullough believes that Pennsylvania's last-minute changes to mail-in ballots was likely unconstitutional, and if allowed to remain in place may negatively affect at least one of the plaintiffs (a GOP congressman) in future elections.

Pa. Judge Opines State's Mail-in Ballot Procedures Likely Illegal

A Pennsylvania judge who Nov. 25 blocked the state from going forward with additional steps that might be required to certify the state's presidential vote said in a written opinion that changes to the Pennsylvania's mail-in balloting procedures were likely illegal.

The order is delayed while the Pennsylvania Supreme Court considers the case, filed by Pennsylvania Republicans, on an expedited basis. Friday night's opinion simply provides the judge's reasoning for ordering a temporary delay.

It is unclear exactly what further steps in the process can be delayed, but the plaintiffs suggested there were several, including the assembly of electors. The Electoral College vote to certify the Nov. 3 election results does not take place until Dec. 14. A federal appeals court Friday had rejected President Donald Trump's attempt to revive a lawsuit in which his campaign was seeking to undo Pennsylvania's certification Joe Biden's victory in the state.

A three-judge panel resoundingly dismissed the campaign's goal of striking out tens of thousands of ballots, saying there were no claims of fraud in the lawsuit, or proof. The decision potentially tees the case up for the U.S. Supreme Court, and the president has openly mused the 6-3 conservative majority could deliver the election to him. But most legal experts doubt the high court will take up a case which will not change the race. Biden would still win the presidency without Pennsylvania's 20 electoral votes, and Georgia, Michigan and Nevada have also certified results in his favor.

"Voters, not lawyers, choose the president," the federal appeals court in Philadelphia said. "Ballots, not briefs, decide elections. The ballots here are governed by Pennsylvania election law. No federal law requires poll watchers or specifies where they must live or how close they may stand when votes are counted. Nor does federal law govern whether to count ballots with minor state-law defects or let voters cure those defects."

In its ruling, the U.S. Court of Appeals for the Third Circuit took apart the Trump campaign's legal arguments, as it refused to force the lower-court judge who dismissed the case to allow the campaign to file a revised complaint. Trump is trying to invalidate tens of thousands of mail-in ballots and asking the appeals court for an emergency order blocking "the effects" of Pennsylvania's certification of votes.

Trump lawyer Jenna Ellis said in a tweet the campaign would appeal to the Supreme Court.

The Trump campaign brought an expedited appeal of the lower-court judge's ruling. U.S. District Judge Matthew Brann on Saturday rejected both the request to file a new complaint and the idea of blocking certification, saying the campaign's suit was speculative and based on "strained legal arguments" that were without merit. The combined rulings from Brann and the appeals court are the highest-profile courtroom defeats for Trump since the Nov. 3 election. Suits filed by the campaign and its GOP allies have failed in Michigan, Georgia, Nevada and Arizona as judges declined to toss out millions of votes based on claims tied to a vast and implausible conspiracy theory about corrupt Democratic election workers. The appeals panel, with all three members appointed by Republican presidents, said the campaign's ultimate goal of setting aside 1.5 million mail-in ballots from the defendant counties for an audit and "statistical analysis" to look for improper ballots would not be fair to voters, especially when there is no allegation of fraud in the complaint.

"There is no allegation of fraud (let alone proof) to justify harming those millions of voters as well as other candidates," the appeals court said.

Here Is What You Missed From Pennsylvania's State Senate Hearing On The Election Samantha Renck

The Pennsylvania State Senate held a hearing before a Republican committee Wednesday about the election and voter fraud allegations. "Each state shall appoint in such manner as the legislature thereof may direct," Rudy Giuliani, the president's personal attorney, said, "a number of electors."

"It's the state legislature that controls this process," he said. "It's your power." President Donald Trump also called into the hearing from the Oval Office. "This was an election that we won easily," Trump said. "The election was rigged and we can't let that happen. We can't let it happen for our country and this election has to be turned around." The hearing also included witnesses from throughout Pennsylvania who alleged voter fraud and election irregularities. Despite these allegations, no widespread voter fraud has been proven.

Sen. Tim Scott Says Dems Will 'Transform America' Into 'Socialist Utopia' If GOP Loses In Georgia

Tim Scott_ GOP winning 2 Georgia seats will 'save America' Henry Rodgers

Republican South Carolina Sen. Tim Scott said he believes America will turn into a different country if the GOP loses their two Senate runoff races in Georgia, saying the wins would "save the nation." Scott was asked about the two races in an appearance on Fox News Wednesday night. In one race, Republican Georgia Sen. Kelly Loeffler is running against Democratic challenger Raphael Warnock**. In the other, Republican Georgia Sen. David Perdue faces a rematch against his own Democratic challenger,** Jon Ossoff**.**

Scott **said if Republicans do not win these seats and keep a majority of the Senate the U.S. would like like a "socialist utopia." "(These are) the most consequential two Senate seats in all of America and all time," Scott said in the interview, Fox News** reported**. "We save the nation and continue to move in the right direction by having those two seats won by two Republicans on January the 5th, and we'll spend a lot of time trying to make that happen."**

"It means the ability to add more justices to the Supreme Court," Scott continued. "We've had nine justices for the last 150 years. They want to stack the courts so that they can continue to transform America into a socialist utopia. It just can't happen." Scott also mentioned how divided Republicans and Democrats are. "The two sides cannot be further apart," Scott said. "One side wants a $4 trillion dollar tax increase, and the way you (Democrats) get that? Win two seats in Georgia." **Ocasio-Cortez A Ticket To Campaign For His Democrat Opponent)**

- **It is likely that a number of Senators or well-known politicians on both sides will help** campaign in the state and **donate money** from their own campaigns to help the two candidates win their runoff races in January, as they are expected to be the most expensive Senate races in history.
- **YouTube Celebrates 'Unthanksgiving,' Honoring 'Indigenous Resistance'**

Allum Bokhari

The official YouTube account on Twitter celebrated what it called "Unthanksgiving" on Thursday, an obscure holiday the far-left platform claims is meant to honor "indigenous resistance."

The official account of the Google-owned video platform has not posted any tweet celebrating Thanksgiving, snubbing the holiday currently being celebrated by its millions of American users in favor a 5-tweet thread about "unthanksgiving."

From the thread:

For Indigenous and Native Americans, the fourth Thursday of November is dedicated to Indigenous history, activism, and resistance. It's called Unthanksgiving.

Unthanksgiving is about acknowledging, educating, and honoring centuries of Indigenous resistance. Coinciding with New England's National Day of Mourning, Unthanksgiving activates Alcatraz Island, the site of a 19-month occupation by Bay Area Natives in 1969.

For generations, Native Americans and Indigenous persons have shared their experiences, using Unthanksgiving as an opportunity for intergenerational and intercultural dialogue.

Generations before have lived on these lands. Days like Unthanksgiving are opportunities for learning and understanding whose land you live on. Unthanksgiving is about honoring Native American and Indigenous heritage, to better understand this history. How are you connected to – and connecting with – Indigenous heritage and history where you live?

The initial tweet in YouTube's thread has been "ratioed," meaning it has attracted more replies and quotes – the vast majority of which mock or condemn the thread – than retweets.

Google, which owns YouTube, is known for its woke left-wing culture. In 2018, Breitbart News reported on a leaked document from inside the company instructing managers to be wary of rewarding employees for adhering to the values of

"white male dominant culture." A.K.A. TOXIC MASCULINITY US LESBIAN BABOONS ARE DOMINANT IN THAT SPECIES

Beyond left-wing virtue signaling, Google has also engaged in election interference. Six months before the election, following a major change to its core search algorithm, clicks and impressions to Breitbart News from Google searches for "Joe Biden," dropped to zero and stayed there through election day. Prior to Google's update, clicks and impressions from the search term saw a normal pattern of activity.

26 Pa. House Republicans call for withdrawing certification of presidential electors **By Jan Murphy**

HARRISBURG — Declaring the results of statewide electoral contests in the 2020 general election to be in dispute, a group of Pennsylvania House Republican lawmakers has announced its intention to introduce a resolution calling for Gov. Tom Wolf and Secretary of State Kathy Boockvar to withdraw their certification of the Nov. 3 election results in the presidential and other statewide contests.

Citing what they described as election law compromises, irregularities and improprieties associated with mail-in balloting, pre-canvassing, and canvassing, the **26 lawmakers** stated in a news release issued late Friday afternoon the issues raised about the election have "undermined our elector process and as a result we cannot accept certification of the results in statewide races."

The proposed resolution, if it gets introduced, has only a short life since the legislative session ends on Monday. All pending bills and resolutions will die at its conclusion.

A spokesman for House Speaker Bryan Cutler, a Lancaster County Republican, said Mr. Cutler was not involved in writing the resolution. Mr. Cutler also has not scheduled any session days to consider it before

the session's end. A spokesman for House Majority Leader Kerry Benninghoff, a Centre County Republican, repeated on Friday what his caucus leaders stated earlier: They are standing by tradition of the popular-vote winner in the presidential race getting the electors.

On Tuesday, Mr. Wolf certified the election results showing President-elect Joe Biden won the state by more than 81,000 votes. Other statewide races resulted in Republican Auditor General candidate Timothy De-Foor and Republican state Treasurer candidate Stacy Garrity as the winners of their races while Democrat-ic incumbent Josh Shapiro won his re-election bid as attorney general. Even though two of the three GOP candidates for statewide row offices were certified as the winners, the lawmakers say they and the selection of presidential electors for Mr. Biden should be withdrawn or vacated. The resolution also urges Congress to "declare the selection of presidential electors in this commonwealth to be in dispute."

Concerns about the fairness and integrity of the election that the group of lawmakers raise in some of the 21 clauses in their resolution are similar to arguments raised by President Donald Trump's legal team during a Senate Majority Policy Committee meeting on Wednesday. "It is absolutely imperative that we take these steps if we are to ensure public trust in our electoral system. Faith in government begins with faith in the elections which select that government," the House GOP members' news release states. "Just as Pennsylvania led the founding of our nation, Pennsylvania should also lead the way by making sure our commonwealth continues to stand as a keystone in our nation where free and fair elections are of paramount concern, no matter the final outcome of those elections."

Those who have signed on as co-sponsors of the resolution are Reps. Russ Diamond, Eric Nelson, Paul Schemel, Greg Rothman, Frank Ryan, Dawn Keefer, Mike Jones, David Rowe, Michael Puskaric, Barbara Gleim, Bud Cook, Cris Dush, Stephanie Borowicz, David Zimmerman, Daryl Metcalfe, David Maloney, Dan Moul, Brad Roae, Kathy Rapp, Jim Cox, Rob Kauffman, Matthew Dowling, Eric Davanzo, Rich Irvin, Aaron Bernstine, and Andrew Lewis. State and local officials have consistently said there is no evidence of wide-spread fraud related to the election.

Mr. Trump has lost a string of legal challenges to the election results in Pennsylvania. The latest occurred Fri-day when a federal appeals court panel refused to block certification of Pennsylvania's vote. Judge Stephanos Bibas wrote there is no proof to back his assertions that the 2020 presidential election was unfair.

Trump campaign eyes Supreme Court battle after appeals panel tosses Pa. fraud case By Vandana Rambaran

The Trump 2020 Campaign looked ahead to a potential Supreme Court fight after a panel of federal appeals judges in Pennsylvania dismissed the campaign›s lawsuit over alleged voter fraud in the presidential election.

TRUMP CALLS INTO PENNSYLVANIA ELECTION MEETING, REPEATING CLAIMS OF VOTING IR-REGULARITIES

"The campaign's claims have no merit," the 3rd U.S. Circuit Court of Appeals in Philadelphia ruled Fri-

day, despite Trump lawyer Rudy Giuliani arguing to a lower court that widespread voter fraud occurred in a state where President-elect Joe Biden won by just over 80,000 votes.

The Trump campaign has the option of asking the U.S. Supreme Court for emergency injunctive relief, which would go to Justice Samuel Alito, who would then likely ask his eight colleagues to weigh in.

"The activist judicial machinery in Pennsylvania continues to cover up the allegations of massive fraud. We are very thankful to have had the opportunity to present proof and the facts to the PA state legislature. On to SCOTUS!," Jenna Ellis, Trump's attorney and campaign adviser, said in a statement on Twitter after the court ruling.

Friday's ruling upheld U.S. District Judge Matthew Brann's take on the Trump campaign's error-filled complaint, which Brann said, "like Frankenstein's Monster, has been haphazardly stitched together."

The three judges on the panel were all appointed by Republican presidents.

"Free, fair elections are the lifeblood of our democracy. Charges of unfairness are serious. But calling an election unfair does not make it so. Charges require specific allegations and then proof. We have neither here," Judge Stephanos Bibas, a former law school professor, wrote in his ruling.

PA POLL WATCHER, A NAVY VET, ALLEGES MISSING USB CARDS, UP TO 120,000 QUESTIONABLE VOTES

The decision is the latest blow to Trump's efforts to prove the election outcome in several battleground states where he lost were "rigged." Giuliani held a public hearing alongside Trump on Wednesday and alleged that Republicans were denied the opportunity to observe the canvassing process, with Trump claiming they have "hundreds and hundreds of affidavits" of witnesses' personal stories to back their argument up.

However, the so-called proof has not been presented during numerous court hearings, with judges repeatedly ruling against the Trump campaign.

In addition to Pennsylvania, Giuliani claimed that similar schemes also took place.

"Act 77 is the most expansive and fundamental change to the Pennsylvania voting code, implemented illegally, to date," the filing stated. "As with prior historical attempts to illegally expand mail-in voting by statute, which have been struck down going as far back as the Military Absentee Ballot Act of 1839, Act 77 is another illegal attempt to override the limitations on absentee voting prescribed in the Pennsylvania Constitution, without first following the necessary procedure to amend the constitution to allow for the expansion."

McCollough's order says the remaining certification work — if there is any — must halt until an evidentiary hearing Friday.

The order came hours before Trump campaign lawyer Rudy Giuliani testified before the Pennsylvania state

legislature regarding allegations of voter fraud in the state. The Republican-held legislature also heard testimony from a number of election workers who claim they witnessed irregularities of fraud during the vote counting.

A Pennsylvania district court threw out the Trump campaign's federal lawsuit alleging fraud on Saturday.

- "This Court has been presented with strained legal arguments without merit and speculative accusations, unpled in the operative complaint and unsupported by evidence," U.S. District Judge Matthew Brann *wrote*. "In the United States of America, this cannot justify the disenfranchisement of a single voter, let alone all the voters of its sixth most populated state. Our people, laws, and institutions demand more."

Highlights of Pennsylvania Republicans' Hearing on Election Irregularities

Charlie Spiering

Former New York City Mayor Rudy Giuliani appeared at a public hearing of Pennsylvania Republicans Wednesday to review his claims of voter fraud and election irregularities in the commonwealth.

The hearing was hosted by the Pennsylvania Senate Majority Committee, led by State Sen. Doug Mastriano (R-Adams/Cumberland/Franklin/York) at the Wyndham Hotel in Gettysburg.

President Trump is relying on Giuliani and campaign lawyer Jenna Ellis to represent his legal battle to challenge 2020 election results in each state.

An audience of Pennsylvania Trump supporters also appeared to listen to the presented evidence.

"All we ask is that you listen to the facts that we are presenting and then evaluate it," Giuliani said.

Several witnesses appeared in person to describe the voting irregularities they witnessed as they were prevented from meaningful access to the voting process.

"Republicans were uniformly not allowed, kept out, put in chutes like they were cows to keep them away from seeing these ballots," Giuliani explained.

Other witnesses explained that thousands of ballots were counted in secret, as they were kept out of the room.

Leah Hoopes from Delaware County, Pennsylvania said she served as a poll worker for three straight days as the results came in.

"What became of concern was the back room, which had no observers, no line of sight or transparency into the process. There was no cooperation, complete resistance from election night to every day after," she said.

PA Senate Republicans

Hoops said she and others were intimidated for coming out and signing affidavits about their concerns with the election.

WHO INTIMIDATED THEM? GANGSTA' BRO' TOUGH GUYS IN DA' HOOD; WITH THEIR THUG POWER OF SHAKEDOWN NUMBERS ON THEIR SIDE? DO WE KNOW THEM TOO WELL

"We have stuck our necks out, been intimidated, threatened bullied, have spent countless hours away from our families, friends, and jobs," she said during the hearing.

Attorney Justin C. Kweder, a certified canvass observer, said he returned as an election observer for ten days at the Philadelphia Convention Center.

He said that Republican observers were kept between 10-200 ft. away from the election counting process.

"It was impossible for me or any observer to see what the workers were doing with any type of specificity," he said.

He also raised concerns about more than 5,000 damaged mail-in ballots that were duplicated by poll workers.

Other witnesses appeared via video teleconferencing to talk about their concerns with "illegal pre-canvassing," as Democrat counties contacted voters to help "cure" their ballots so they would be counted.

One election observer testified that a poll worker repeatedly cursed at her and threatened to slap her in the face when she tried to verify some of the steps in the voting process. OH REALLY, YOU DON'T SAY?

Giuliani also brought an election security specialist to talk about the voting systems in the United States.

The expert questioned the anomaly of reporting spikes in the voting counts for Biden late in the evening as a "prime indicator of fraudulent voting."

He claimed that there was a discrepancy of around 700,000 ballots between the number of mail-in ballots sent out and the mail-in ballots that were received.

The audience laughed and gasped in shock as the expert noted a point when a spike of votes recorded in Pennsylvania had 600,000 votes for Biden and only 3,200 for Trump.

President Trump called in to the hearing, appearing impressed by what he had heard from the witnesses.

He vowed to fight the results of the election and thanked everyone present for sharing their testimonies.

"We have to turn the election over, because there's no doubt," Trump said. "We have all the evidence, we have all the affidavits, we have everything. All we need is to have some judge listen to it properly without having a political opinion or having another kind of a problem."

The president praised Giuliani for continuing to fight the case, while other lawyers backed down.

"This is going to be your crowning achievement because you are saving our country," Trump concluded.

Pennsylvania Republicans also took time to question Giuliani and Ellis about the case and the road forward for challenging the election.

State Sen. Mastriano celebrated the successful hearing and thanked the witnesses for stepping up.

"As Jesus said, 'You shall know the truth and the truth shall set you free,' and guess what, the truth's out there," he said as the hearing drew to a close.

He drew comparisons of their fight to the patriots who birthed freedom in Philadelphia, fought at the Battle of Gettysburg, and the heroes of Flight 93.

- **"We're not going to let it stand," he said. Donald Trump Calls In to Gettysburg Hearing: We Have to Overturn Election Because Democrats Cheated**

Charlie Spiering

President Donald Trump called in to a Pennsylvania hearing on voter fraud Wednesday, urging supporters to keep fighting the 2020 election results.

"They have to turn over the results," Trump said. "It would be easy for me to say, 'Oh let's worry about four years from now.' No. This election was lost by the Democrats, they cheated. It was a fraudulent election."

The president phoned in to a public hearing on the 2020 election held by Pennsylvania state Republicans at a hotel in Gettysburg. Several witnesses publicly attested to voter irregularities and opportunities for fraud during the voting and counting process, particularly surrounding mail-in ballots.

The president cited the hundreds of signed affidavits gathered by the campaign, describing it as evidence that proved the election was fraudulent.

He noted that Republican poll watchers were barred from witnessing the actual vote counting process, forced into pens, and treated aggressively by poll workers.

"If you were a Republican poll watcher. you were treated like a dog," Trump said and added, "What happened here, this is not the United States of America what happened."

The president also cited claims from people who tried to vote but were told that a mail-in ballot had already been sent in their names.

He said that the obvious irregularities in the process proved that Democrats got sloppy with their attempts.

"They just stepped on the gas and they got caught. Just like they got caught spying on my campaign," Trump said.

He noted that the sudden jumps in votes tallied for Biden in the late night and early morning were also suspect.

"Very weird things happened, but they're not weird to professionals, and they're not weird to Dominion and other people that operate machines," Trump said.

The president said that people were getting multiple ballots sent to their homes and that dead people were "requesting ballots."

"The whole world is watching the United States of America, and we can't let them get away with it," Trump said.

He accused judges of acting cowardly by failing to take up the cases in various places amid widespread threats against anyone contesting the election.

"We have to turn the election over, because there's no doubt," Trump said. "We have all the evidence, we have all the affidavits, we have everything, all we need is to have some judge listen to it properly without having a political opinion or having another kind of a problem."

The president praised former Mayor Rudy Giuliani for continuing to fight the case, while other lawyers backed down.

- **"This is going to be your crowning achievement because you are saving our country," Trump concluded**

Sidney Powell: Evidence of voter fraud could be released online 'by this weekend'

'We're going to have to file several lawsuits'

TRUMP CAMPAIGN PUSHES FORWARD IN LEGAL CHALLENGE OF PA. CERTIFICATION, LOOKS TO REVIVE POLL WATCHER CLAIMS

"I literally begged multiple law enforcement agencies to go get the forensic evidence from the computers. It's a simple process. It wouldn't have taken more than an hour to image all 5 machines. That was never done despite my objections and that was three weeks ago."

The hearing was arranged by Pennsylvania state Republicans to address allegations of possible voter fraud following the election in a state where Democrat Joe Biden defeated President Trump by just over 80,000 votes, according to the Fox News Decision Desk.

Pennsylvania – which certified its election results Tuesday -- is one of several battleground states where the Trump 2020 Campaign has raised allegations of possible voter fraud. Pennsylvania was worth 20 electoral votes to the winner. President Trump was initially scheduled to attend Wednesday's hearing, which was convened by the Pennsylvania Senate Majority Policy Committee.

The president later canceled his travel plans**, opting instead to meet with his legal advisers in Washington. But Trump lawyer Rudy Giuliani appeared at the hearing. However, the president's** legal fight in Pennsylvania continues**. In a letter filed with the Third Circuit Court of Appeals on Wednesday, Trump 2020 Campaign attorney Marc Scaringi called for oral arguments as the campaign fights against a lower court's dismissal of their case challenging Pennsylvania's certification of votes.**

Young Conservative Allegedly Kicked Out Of Sorority For This TikTok Video

'Slow, Meticulous, Deliberate': Senator-Elect Rips China, Urges Trump Policies Continue

FEC Chair Says It's 'Crucial' That Trump Lawyers 'Present The Evidence' On Voter Fraud, Foreign Influence Allegations

5-tweet thread about "unthanksgiving." From the thread: ***For Indigenous and Native Americans, the fourth Thursday of November is dedicated to Indigenous history, activism, and resistance. It's called Unthanksgiving. Unthanksgiving is about acknowledging, educating, and honoring centuries of Indigenous resistance. Coinciding with New England's National Day of Mourning, Unthanksgiving activates Alcatraz Island, the site of a***

19-month occupation by Bay Area Natives in 1969.

to the values of "white male dominant culture."

The decision is the latest blow to Trump's efforts to prove the election outcome in several battleground states where he lost were "rigged." Giuliani held a public hearing alongside Trump on Wednesday and alleged that Republicans were denied the opportunity to observe the canvassing process, with Trump claiming they have "hundreds and hundreds of affidavits" of witnesses' personal stories to back their argument up.

However, the so-called proof has not been presented during numerous court hearings, with judges repeatedly ruling against the Trump campaign.

In addition to Pennsylvania, Giuliani claimed that similar schemes also took place.

Judge Orders Halt To Certification Of Pennsylvania Election Results After State Already Certified Them

ANDERS HAGSTROM

A Pennsylvania Commonwealth Court judge ordered a halt to the certification of the state's election results Wednesday, though it is unclear what effect the order will have as the state certified its election results Tuesday. Commonwealth Court Judge Patricia McCullough handed down the order, which the Daily Caller has confirmed with the Commonwealth Court office. The order blocks certification of results "to the extent that there remains any further action to perfect the certification of the results." Democratic Pennsylvania Gov. Tom Wolf announced that the state department certified President-elect Joe Biden's win in the state Tuesday.

State Attorney General Josh Shapiro says the order does not affect Tuesday's certification, and his office is ready to file an appeal.

McCollough's order came in response to a petition from Republican members of and candidates for the state legislature, who argue the state's mail-in voting statute violates the Pennsylvania constitution. The statute, Act 77, was signed into law in October 2019. (RELATED: White House Cancels Trump's Trip With Giuliani To Attend Pennsylvania Election Hearing)

Former New York City Mayor Rudy Giuliani, personal attorney to U.S. President Donald Trump, speaks during a news conference held to discuss filing election-related lawsuits at Atlantic Aviation PHL private air terminal in Philadelphia, Pennsylvania, U.S. November 4, 2020.

Sidney Powell: Evidence of voter fraud could be released online 'by this weekend'

'We're going to have to file several lawsuits'

Sidney Powell files Lawsuits Challenging Election Results in Georgia, Michigan

Joel B. Pollak

Attorney Sidney Powell filed lawsuits Wednesday challenging the results of the presidential vote in Georgia and Michigan, alleging "ballot stuffing," which she alleges was "amplified and rendered virtually invisible by computer software created and run by domestic and foreign actors."

Powell made similar claims last week at a press conference with President Donald Trump's legal team. She was attacked by critics who claimed that she could not prove what she alleged. The legal team distanced **themselves from her on Sunday, saying that her claims had gone beyond the evidence they had seen or could prove in court.**

Powell — who also defended Lt. Gen. Michael Flynn, pardoned by President Trump on Wednesday — accepted the decision but pressed ahead regardless.

She alleges in Georgia:

Mathematical and statistical anomalies rising to the level of impossibilities, as shown by affidavits of multiple witnesses, documentation, and expert testimony evince this scheme across the state of Georgia. Especially

egregious conduct arose in Forsyth, Paulding, Cherokee, Hall, and Barrow County. This scheme and artifice to defraud affected tens of thousands of votes in Georgia alone and "rigged" the election in Georgia for Joe Biden.

Powell makes similar allegations in Michigan, noting an "especially egregious range of conduct in Wayne County and the City of Detroit, though this conduct occurred throughout the State at the direction of Michigan state election officials."

Powell traces the fraud to "software and hardware from Dominion Voting Systems Corporation," which she said derives from software created by "Smartmatic Corporation, which became Sequoia in the United States."

She goes on to allege, in both the Georgia and the Michigan complaints, "Smartmatic and Dominion were founded by foreign oligarchs and dictators to ensure computerized ballot-stuffing and vote manipulation to whatever level was needed to make certain Venezuelan dictator Hugo Chavez never lost another election."

Based on the affidavit of a whistleblower, Powell alleges that the systems were designed to make ballot-stuffing hard to detect by a "simple audit." They were manipulated, she says, by people who had access to the systems.

In Georgia, she says:

[V]ideo from the State Farm Arena in Fulton County shows that on November 3rd after the polls closed, election workers falsely claimed a water leak required the facility to close. All poll workers and challengers were evacuated for several hours at about 10:00 PM. However, several election workers remained unsupervised and unchallenged working at the computers for the voting tabulation machines until after 1:00 AM.

She also claimed that "the Dominion software was accessed by agents acting on behalf of China and Iran in order to monitor and manipulate elections, including the most recent US general election in 2020." One expert, she says, "concludes that hundreds of thousands of votes that were cast for President Trump in the 2020 general election were transferred to former Vice-President Biden."

And she adds that "Georgia's election officials and poll workers exacerbated and helped, whether knowingly or unknowingly, the Dominion system carry out massive voter manipulation by refusing to observe statutory safeguards for absentee ballots. Election officials failed to verify signatures and check security envelopes. They barred challengers from observing the count, which also facilitated the fraud."

In Michigan, Powell says, in addition to problems with Dominion, there were "additional categories of 'traditional' voting fraud and Michigan Election Code violations, supplemented by healthy doses of harassment, intimidation, discrimination, abuse and even physical removal of Republican poll challengers to eliminate any semblance of transparency, objectivity or fairness from the vote counting process."

Powell alleges, citing expert testimony, that Michigan saw tens of thousands of "excess voters," where unassigned or blank absentee ballots were filled out by election workers, and nearly all of those votes went to Joe

Biden. She also alleges that in four precincts, more ballots were counted than could be physically processed during a two and-a-half hour interval Nov. 4.

She alleges that glitches in Michigan — such as one that mistakenly counted 6,000 votes for Biden in Antrim County — were always in Biden's favor.

- **There are enough ballots affected, Powell argues, for the courts to set aside the results of the 2020 election in each state.**
- **Pennsylvania judge rules GOP lawsuit challenging new absentee ballot law has 'likelihood to succeed'**
- '...this Court can state that Petitioners have a likelihood of success on the merits of its Pennsylvania Constitutional claim' **Chris Enloe**
- **The Pennsylvania judge who temporarily halted the certification of election results in the Keystone State issued an opinion Friday explaining that the Republican plaintiffs in her case will likely win on the merits of their lawsuit.**
- What's the background?
- As TheBlaze reported, Commonwealth Judge Patricia McCullough issued an injunction Wednesday after Republican lawmakers made an emergency request to stop certification of the state's election results over concerns about Act 77, a new law that allowed Pennsylvania voters to obtain an absentee ballot for the election for any reason.
- **From** Sinclair Broadcasting Group**:**
- **The plaintiffs argue Act 77, which was signed into law in October 2019, wrongfully overrides the stipulations for absentee balloting established by the state's constitution. The Pennsylvania Constitution states absentee ballots can be cast by those who cannot go to polling locations due to a work obligation, sickness, religious holiday, or "election day duties."**

  As a result, the suit asks the court to prevent the certification of election tallies that include mail-in ballots resulting from the expanded rules of Act 77, and further moves to have the Pennsylvania General Assembly assign the state's electors.
- What is the judge saying now?
- **McCullough** explained in a 13-page opinion **that the plaintiffs are likely to succeed in their lawsuit because Act 77 appears to violate the Pennsylvania state constitution.**
- **"Petitioners appear to have established a likelihood to succeed on the merits because Petitioners have asserted the Constitution does not provide a mechanism for the legislature to allow for expansion of absentee voting without a constitutional amendment," McCullough wrote.**

- "Petitioners appear to have a viable claim that the mail-in ballot procedures set forth in Act 77 contravene Pa. Const. Article VII Section 14 as the plain language of that constitutional provision is at odds with the mail-in provisions of Act 77," she continued.

- "Since this presents an issue of law which has already been thoroughly briefed by the parties, this Court can state that Petitioners have a likelihood of success on the merits of its Pennsylvania Constitutional claim," McCullough said.
- Anything else?
- According to WESA-FM, Gov. Tom Wolf (D) and Secretary of State Kathy Boockvar have appealed to the state Supreme Court to intervene. Democrats currently hold a 5-2 majority on the Pennsylvania high court.

- Meanwhile, Ed Morrissey noted at Hot Air that the "laches" doctrine could apply in this case, thereby hurting the plaintiffs' argument, because they did not raise objections before or after Pennsylvania's June 2 primary, which used the same absentee system as the general.

- "Having raised no objection before the election, the plaintiffs have participated in the alleged violation, which would impact their standing to demand relief," Morrissey explained.

Exclusive — Trump Lawyer Jenna Ellis Receives Threats: 'You Deserved to Be Raped'

Joel B. Pollak THIS IS OUR BABE. DEMOCRATS ACTUALLY THREATEN TO RAPE HER.

Jenna Ellis, a legal advisor to President Donald Trump and senior legal adviser to the Trump campaign, has received threats, late night phone calls from unfamiliar numbers, and public calls for her disbarment, she told Breitbart News exclusively Wednesday.

Via direct message (DM), Ellis told Breitbart News that she had received "Hundreds of DMs and messages etc threatening me."

Some threats have been public, like attempts **to have her disbarred and encouraging the public to file Bar complaints.**

Others have been more direct — and less subtle.

She added: "CNN reporter messaged today accusing me of my bar license being lapsed. Unknown number has called my cell dozens of times between midnight and 4am to blow up my phone and try to get through the DND [do not disturb]."

Ellis provided Breitbart News with a screen grab of text messages from an unknown person who attempted to provoke her to respond, ending with: "You're a fking c**t. You're the reason people despise humanity. You deserved to be raped."**

Other Trump attorneys have been harassed, including by the Lincoln Project, a group of Never Trump Republicans who have encouraged the public to harass law firms taking up the president's case.

The mainstream media has defended these efforts; the *Washington Post*, for example, published an op-ed **Nov. 12 titled "Yes, going after Trump's law firms is fair game." Trump's lawyers in Pennsylvania** withdrew **the following day, reportedly because of threats.**

Joe Biden has not said anything about the threats against Trump's legal team, as scholar Jonathan Turley has noted. PAL ZOMBIE JOE DOESN'T SAY MUCH ABOUT ANYTHING BUT MASKING, SOCIAL DISTANCING & THE UNIVERSE UNIFYING AROUND HIS ATTEMPT TO STEAL THE PRESIDENCY OF AMERICA

"When such actions were taken against lawyers representing civil rights groups and others in the 1960s, it was correctly denounced as an outrageous abuse of our legal system," Turley tweeted **this week. "Now it has become a campaign supported by politicians, lawyers, and the media."**

Computer repairman at center of 'Biden laptop' scandal closes shop, disappears amid purported death threats Sarah Taylor

John Paul Mac Isaac, the computer repairman at the center of a reported Biden family scandal, has closed his Wilmington, Delaware, computer repair shop amid purported death threats.

Mac Isaac previously claimed he had a laptop computer and hard drive containing information about former Vice President Joe Biden's son, Hunter, and his international business dealings with Ukraine.

For his part, the elder Biden said the allegations were a "desperate campaign to smear me and my family," but did not confirm whether the laptop belonged to his son.

What are the details?

According to the Delaware News Journal, a "closed" sign now appears in the window of Mac Isaac's shop.

His attorney, Brian Della Rocca, told the outlet that his client closed up shop after he received several death threats. He has not elaborated on Mac Isaac's whereabouts at the time of this reporting, though a neighbor told the outlet that Mac Isaac left town.

In October, Mac Isaac said that he retained a copy of the hard drive's contents because he "feared he would be killed by people who 'work for [Joe] Biden' and having it was 'protection.'"

Della Rocca told the outlet that he did not believe his client would be involved in any potential lawsuits or investigations related to the laptop.

The outlet noted that Della Rocca "said his office has spoken in recent weeks with Wilmington FBI agents and with Delaware's Assistant United States Attorney Leslie Wolf" but that he "declined to describe the nature of the conversations."

"I've been in touch with federal law enforcement, yes," he told the outlet.

Neither the U.S. Attorney's Office in Delaware nor the Federal Bureau of Investigation commented when approached by the outlet for remarks on the allegations.

In October, the New York Post reported that Mac Isaac was asked to repair a computer that reportedly contained a variety of nefarious and possibly incriminating emails and photos appearing to confirm that a secret meeting between the former vice president and a top Burisma executive had taken place.

He later told Fox News, "I just don't know what to say, or what I'm allowed to say. I know that I saw, I saw stuff — and I was concerned. I was concerned that somebody might want to come look …

Newsmax/McLaughlin Poll: Two-Thirds of Nation Back Trump on Recounts

More than two-thirds of the nation says it is fair for President Donald Trump to ask for a recount in key states, according to a new Newsmax/McLaughlin & Associates poll released Thursday.

Sixty-seven % of likely voters backed Trump's recounts where the vote margins in his race with Joe Biden were 1% or closer, which applies to states like Georgia, Pennsylvania, Wisconsin, and Arizona.

Despite the close contests, 65% of Americans say the election will ultimately be decided honestly. But fully a third of all voters, 35%, said that there was significant fraud.

"This seems to be a very disturbing and high number for the country that always prided itself to be the

world's leading democracy," pollster John McLaughlin said. "The highest level of fraud concerns are among Trump voters at 70% and Republicans at 65%."

Here are how the results from the Newsmax/McLaughlin & Associates break down:

- **94% of Republicans blame most of the voter fraud in the recent election on the Democrats, while 6% say Republicans were behind it.**
- **51% of those polled say voter fraud is a problem in big Democrat-run cities, compared to 49% who say it is not a problem.**
- **An overwhelming 90% approve of voter identification laws that make certain every vote cast in the election for president and Congress was cast by a legal citizen who was eligible to vote.**
- **A similar majority of 88% say they approve of states requiring that all mail-in ballots have a matching signature with the person's voter registration.**
- **57% believe media organizations like CNN, ABC, CBS, and NBC should declare Biden the winner even as recounts are being conducted in multiple states. But the vast majority of Trump voters, 77%, and Republicans, 70%, say the media should not.**
- **42% say media coverage of the presidential races has been unfair and biased against Trump, 10% say it has been unfair and biased against Biden, and 48% say it has been fair to both candidates.**

The election results have not made Americans happy or changed their outlook on the future of the country, however.

John McLaughlin to Newsmax TV: Media Bias Against Trump Entire Election

The mainstream media bias in the coverage of President Donald Trump's election challenges is no different than the bias against his presidency all year, pollster John McLaughin told Newsmax TV Thursday.

"Remember he was supposed to get blown out; it was supposed to be a Biden landslide," McLaughlin told "Greg Kelly Reports" guest host Joe Pinion. «And now what you›ve got is a situation where, if you look at the 11,000 votes in Arizona the 12,000 votes in Georgia the 20,000 votes in Wisconsin, yeah that›s enough electoral votes that›s 37 electoral votes, that Joe Biden wouldn›t be president right there, and you›re talking about 43,000 votes out of 158 million.»

McLaughlin & Associates conducted a poll for Newsmax that found two-thirds of Americans back the president on recounts. One question in the poll asked about fraud in Democratic-led cities: 51% said they believe it exists.

"People know there's bad things going on," McLaughlin said, saying there has been "significant fraud for decades" in the New York/New Jersey area where he lives.

"And now it's automated with these computer systems where it's pretty easy that they can manufacture votes

on a computer pretty quick," he said. "And the voters want to have answers. They want to know that it was an honest election or not."

Whole Foods CEO blasts socialism, explains how universities corrupt young people: 'Trickle-up poverty'

'It just impoverishes everything' by Chris Enloe

Whole Foods CEO John Mackey blasted socialism during a recent interview, explaining such economic policies cause increased poverty.

During a discussion hosted by the American Enterprise Institute on Tuesday, Mackey did not mince words — he said socialism is the "path of poverty."

"They talk about 'trickle-down wealth,' but socialism is trickle-up poverty," Mackey explained. "It just impoverishes everything."

Mackey explained that capitalism, on the other hand, is the "greatest thing humanity has ever created," and blamed intellectuals in universities for corrupting young people into thinking that capitalism is bad.

"Capitalism is the greatest thing humanity's ever done. We've told a bad narrative, and we've let the enemies of business and the enemies of capitalism put out a narrative about us that's wrong, it's inaccurate — and it's doing tremendous damage to the minds of young people," Mackey said.

"The Marxists and socialists, the academic community is generally hostile to business. It always has been. This is not new," he explained. Socialism is favored by far-left progressive politicians like Rep. Alexandria Ocasio-Cortez (D-N.Y.) and Sen. Bernie Sanders (I-Vt.). Mackey went on to explain that not all progressivism is bad, but that socialism must be abandoned.

"We have to recognize that some of the progressive insights are important and they shouldn't go away, but we can't throw out capitalism and replace it with socialism, that will be a disaster," Mackey said, Just The News reported. "Socialism has been tried 42 times in the last 100 years, and 42 failures, it doesn't work, it's the wrong way. We have to keep capitalism, I would argue, we need conscious capitalism," he continued.

According to Mackey, capitalism and business innovation overall is responsible for increased living conditions worldwide, has increased global literacy rates, and is even responsible for increasing life expectancy.

Business, therefore, should be evaluated "in terms of its value-creation," Mackey said. "For its customers, and all the jobs that it creates for its employees and the residual or tangential effects that happen when it trades with suppliers, who also trade for voluntary reasons — they're benefitting and they're prospering as a result," the businessman explained.

Ex-Trump Lawyer Sidney Powell Files Election Suits in 'DISTRCOICT' Court

A lawyer who was dropped from President Donald Trump's legal team filed lawsuits in Michigan and Georgia alleging massive election fraud. Sidney Powell, who has pushed some of the most extreme conspiracy theories around the election of Joe Biden, filed the lawsuits late Wednesday, according to a post on Twitter. The two cases have similar themes of problems linked to voting machines, mail-in ballots and deceased Venezuelan dictator Hugo Chavez. Powell was kicked off Trump's legal team this week after her claims about a vast Democratic conspiracy against the president. Days earlier she had appeared at a press conference alongside Trump lawyer Rudy Giuliani, where she alleged a plot to swing the election to Biden that involved voting-machine tampering and Venezuela. The pre-Thanksgiving lawsuits, which target elected officials in both states, also include other claims about forged ballots and observers being unable to watch the vote count.

Despite numerous allegations of voter fraud and irregularities from Trump and his supporters, no evidence has emerged of widespread problems that would have changed the results of the election, which Biden won with 306 electoral votes. Both lawsuits of Powell were riddled with typographical errors.

The Michigan lawsuit, which was on the court website, was frequently marred by formatting problems that removed the spacing between words. For example: "TheTCFCenterwastheonlyfacilitywithinWayneCounty-authorizedtocountthe ballots." In the Georgia complaint, which was only available on Powell's website, the word district in the court name was misspelled twice on the first page of the document. First there was an extra c for "DISTRICCT" and then, a few words later, "DISTRCOICT." The cases are: King v. Whitmer, 20-cv-13134 U.S. District Court, Eastern District of Michigan and Pearson v. Kemp, Northern District of Georgia

Former U.S. House Speaker Newt Gingrich waits for the arrival of Vice President Mike Pence at the Vatican for an audience with Pope Francis on Jan. 24, 2020.

By Solange Reyner

Election officials in Democratic strongholds of Pennsylvania "exceeded their authority in order to give voters preferential treatment," but their work was sloppy and lazy and the courts "need to stop them from destroying more evidence," former House Speaker Newt Gingrich writes in a column for The Epoch Times.

Gingrich, citing a Nov. 21 lawsuit filed in district court, said officials in certain counties used "a variety of illegal practices that were used to inflate the number of votes received by Democrat presidential candidate Joe Biden, including disparate treatment of voters based on where they live and outright manipulation of Pennsylvania's voter registration system by partisan activities." "Specifically, election workers illegally 'pre-canvassed' mail-in ballots to determine whether they were missing a secrecy envelope or failed to include necessary information," writes Gingrich. "When ballots were found to be flawed, voters were given an opportunity to correct, or 'cure,' their ballots to make sure they counted. In at least some cases, Democrat Party officials were even given lists of voters to contact about curing their ballots."

Gingrich said Democrat Secretary of State Kathy Boockvar, specifically, issued guidance authorizing the illegal practices "despite lacking the statutory authority to do so." Several news outlets have called the race for Biden. Newsmax will not announce a winner until enough states certify votes for a candidate to get to 270 Electoral College votes. Lou Dobbs Scolds 'Dismissive' Fox News Reporter on Fraud Hearing

BACK STABBING FOX NEWS; NOW HERD MENTALITY ONLY BETRAYED US CHRIS WALLACE ACTUALLY HAD HAS THE FUCKEN NERVE TO MOCK & SNEER AT OUR ANGER AS HEARTBURN?

Lou Dobbs speaks at the Conservative Political Action Conference on Feb. 24, 2017. By Eric Mack

The Pennsylvania Republican election fraud hearing Wednesday was such a matter of a debate over its legitimacy, even Fox Business' host and a Fox News on-site reporter seemed to spar over it. "It's not clear if [Wednesday's] meeting was just to shine some light on some potential irregularities and some problems or actually change some of the results in Pennsylvania.

"OH REALLY; YOU CONTEMPTIBLE, LOATHSOME SCUMBAG SCHMUCK? DOESN'T EVERYTHING START SOMEWHERE?

Fox News correspondent David Spunt told "Lou Dobbs Tonight" from Gettysburg, Pennsylvania. "It's interesting to note though that there were witnesses here, but this was not a court hearing or a legal proceeding. There was no judge, the claims here [Wednesday] stood a different standard than those made in court under oath." Lou Dobbs chimed in to reject the reporter's dismissal of the hearing.

"You sound rather dismissive of the expert witnesses, including psyops, computer forensic experts that were testifying as to the irregularities and anomalies of the election," Dobbs responded. "And point of fact, it was an informational hearing, and you are, I'm sure, aware that . . . a state judge has intervened to temporarily stop the certification of the vote in Pennsylvania as a result of claims by, amongst others, Congressmen Mike Kelly and Sean Parnell, both Republicans declaring in their lawsuit that the entire proceeding was unconstitutional.

Federalist: 5 Ways Biden Unusually Outperformed Norms

By Eric Mack

Journalists are strangely lacking curiosity about some mysterious ways Democrat Joe Biden pulled off some "electoral jujitsu" in this presidential election, according to The Federalist's J.B. Shurk.

THERE'S NOTHING STRANGE ALL THESE ASSASSINS DO IS GREASE EVERY PATHWAY FOR THE LEFT TO SEIZE POWER; THEY PROACTIVELY REPORT WHAT FAVORS DEMOCRATS & REFUSE TO COVER ANYTHING THAT FAVORS US.

"Surely the journalist class should be intrigued by the historic implausibility of Joe Biden's victory," according to Shurk's outline of five improbabilities, breaking down this "unique political voodoo."

"That they are not is curious, to say the least."

Biden "pulled so many rabbits out of his hat" to potentially become the oldest elected president in American history, should Trump fail in his legal challenges to the election tallies of several key state. Most notable are these:

1. 80M Votes

Trump gained 10 million more votes in 2020 than he saw in his 2016 election victory, but that pales in comparison to Biden's record gains in defeating the first "incumbent president in nearly a century and a half" who has gained votes in a reelection campaign.

"Candidate Joe Biden was so effective at animating voters in 2020 that he received a record number of votes, more than 15 million more than Barack Obama received in his reelection of 2012," **Shurk wrote.**

"Proving how sharp his political instincts are, the former VP managed to gather a record number of votes while consistently trailing President Trump in measures of voter enthusiasm. Biden was so savvy that he motivated voters unenthusiastic about his campaign to vote for him in record numbers."

2. Overcoming Bellwether County Losses

"Amazingly, he managed to secure victory while also losing in almost every bellwether county across the country," Shurk wrote. "No presidential candidate has been capable of such electoral jujitsu until now."

Biden might be the first U.S. president in 60 years to lose the bellwether states of Ohio and Florida. Remarkably, Shurk noted, "despite national polling giving Biden a lead in both states, he lost Ohio by eight points and Florida by more than three."

"Even more unbelievably, Biden is on his way to winning the White House after having lost almost every historic bellwether county across the country," Shurk wrote. "The Wall Street Journal and The Epoch Times independently analyzed the results of 19 counties around the United States that have nearly perfect presiden-

tial voting records over the last 40 years. President Trump won every single bellwether county, except Clallam County in Washington.

"Whereas the former VP picked up Clallam by about three points, President Trump's margin of victory in the other 18 counties averaged over 16 points. In a larger list of 58 bellwether counties that have correctly picked the president since 2000, Trump won 51 of them by an average of 15 points, while the other seven went to Biden by around four points. Bellwether counties overwhelmingly chose President Trump, but Biden found a path to victory anyway."

3. Biden Topped Hillary Clinton in Just a Few Cities

Polling guru Richard Baris of Big Data Poll marveled at how "Biden underperformed Hillary Clinton in every major metro area around the country, save for Milwaukee, Detroit, Atlanta and Philadelphia."

Coincidentally, those are major cities in key battleground states the Trump campaign has questioned and sought to contest with legal challenges of voter fraud: Wisconsin, Michigan, Georgia, and Pennsylvania. The electoral college votes in those states are ultimately deciding this election.

Even The Washington Post featured an election analyst Robert Barnes who marveled: "Big cities in swing states run by Democrats . . . the vote even exceeded the number of registered voters," **Shurk wrote.**

4. Republicans Gained Around the Country, but Biden Soared

It was a "Biden miracle," Shurk noted, that Trump might lose reelection despite his GOP gaining House seats.

There were 27 House tossups, pollster noted, but Republican not only won them, they appear to have swept them all, a shocked Shurk projected.

"Democrats failed to flip a single state house chamber, while Republicans flipped both the House and Senate in New Hampshire and expanded their dominance of state legislatures across the country," he added.

"Amazingly, Biden beat the guy who lifted all other Republicans to victory. Now that's historic!"

5. Trump's Primary Performance Was Legendary

Trump was just one of five incumbents since 1912 to win over 90% of the primary vote, and he set a record for an incumbent with 18 million votes. That is more than double the next most primary votes for an incumbent in history.

"No incumbent who has received 75% of the total primary vote has lost reelection," according to Shurk, but Trump won 94% of the primary vote for the fourth-best all-time.

"For Biden to prevail in the general election, despite Trump's historic support in the primaries, turns a century's worth of prior election data on its head," Shurk concluded.

"Joe Biden achieved the impossible. It's interesting that many more journalists aren't pointing that out.

Trump continues fight in Wis., Pa.: 'We have found many illegal votes'

'The Wisconsin recount is not about finding mistakes in the count, it is about finding people who have voted illegally'

By Morgan Phillips

President Trump promised to challenge the Wisconsin vote count after the recount there, and said his campaign is disputing a number of votes larger than President-elect Joe Biden**'s winning margin.**

"The Wisconsin recount is not about finding mistakes in the count, it is about finding people who have voted illegally, and that case will be brought after the recount is over, on Monday or Tuesday. We have found many illegal votes. Stay tuned!" the president tweeted Saturday afternoon.

Biden picked up 132 more votes after an election recount in Milwaukee County, one of two places in Wisconsin where Trump spent $3 million to force a recount.

In Dane County, another Democratic stronghold in Wisconsin, votes are still being tallied in a count expected to last into the weekend, but Trump has gained 68 votes over Biden so far.

Trump is gearing up for yet another legal battle, this time to toss tens of thousands of ballots in the state Biden clinched by nearly 20,600 votes, with margins in Milwaukee and Dane counties about 2-to-1 for the Democrat.

The deadline to certify the votes, which will be done by the Democratic chair of the bipartisan Wisconsin Election Commission, is Tuesday, but the Wisconsin Voters Alliance, a conservative group, has filed a lawsuit against election officials, seeking to block the process.

TRUMP CAMPAIGN EYES SUPREME COURT BATTLE AFTER APPEALS PANEL TOSSES PA FRAUD CASE

Later Saturday, the president tweeted about Pennsylvania, saying he could prove fraud.

"Specific allegations were made, and we have massive proof, in the Pennsylvania case. Some people just don't want to see it. They want nothing to do with saving our Country. Sad!!!" Trump said.

"The number of ballots that our Campaign is challenging in the Pennsylvania case is FAR LARGER than

the 81,000 vote margin. It's not even close. Fraud and illegality ARE a big part of the case. Documents being completed. We will appeal!" he continued.

The Trump campaign has been looking ahead to a potential Supreme Court case after a panel of federal appeals judges in Pennsylvania dismissed the campaign›s lawsuit claiming voter fraud in the presidential election.

"The campaign's claims have no merit," the 3rd U.S. Circuit Court of Appeals in Philadelphia ruled Friday, despite Trump lawyer Rudy Giuliani arguing to a lower court that widespread voter fraud occurred in a state where President-elect Joe Biden won by just over 80,000 votes.

The Trump campaign has the option of asking the U.S. Supreme Court for emergency injunctive relief, which would go to Justice Samuel Alito, who would then likely ask his eight colleagues to weigh in.

"The activist judicial machinery in Pennsylvania continues to cover up the allegations of massive fraud. We are very thankful to have had the opportunity to present proof and the facts to the PA state legislature. On to SCOTUS!," Jenna Ellis, Trump's attorney and campaign adviser, said in a statement on Twitter after the court ruling.

Meanwhile, Trump's attorneys have targeted absentee ballots in which voters identified themselves as "indefinitely confined," allowing them to cast an absentee ballot without showing a photo ID; ballots that have a certification envelope with two different ink colors, indicating a poll worker may have helped complete it; and absentee ballots that don't have a separate written record for the request, such as in-person absentee ballots.

Election officials have tallied those ballots during the recount but marked them as exhibits at the request of the Trump campaign.

Trump's campaign challenges have failed in courts elsewhere, with experts widely concurring that there's no proof of GOP claims of widespread voter fraud. Legal efforts to date have been unsuccessful in Arizona, Georgia, Michigan, Nevada and Pennsylvania.

GOP Pa. State Rep Says Election Should Not Be Certified

By Eric Mack

With the Trump campaign turning from the courts to the legislatures, Pennsylvania state Rep. Greg Rothman, R-Cumberland County, is taking the baton to call for a state review of the contested election.

"We're asking for the election not to be certified, and for us, the legislature, to have an opportunity to look into what happened to make sure that all the ballots are legal, and they were all counted, and we have a fair election," Rothman told Sunday's "The Cats Roundtable" on WABC 770 AM-N.Y. "That's what America is all about." Rothman sees the election as having been taken from the legislature by the Democrat leaders in the state.

"Through the Democrats, the governor and the department of state, even the Supreme Court, they turned it into a vote-by-mail – no verifications," Rothman told host John Catsimatidis. That is a case the Trump campaign has hoped would rise to the U.S. Supreme Court for its unconstitutional change of state election law without legislature approval.

Also, as the Trump campaign has argued, Republican monitors were denied lawful, meaningful monitoring

of the mail-in ballot counting, Rothman added.

"It's indisputable that hundreds of thousands of vote-by-mail ballots [were counted] without anybody from the Trump campaign or the Republican party being able to observe," he concluded.

Pennsylvania Judge Delays Election Certification Pending Republican Legal Challenge

Charlie Spiering

A Commonwealth Court Judge ruled Wednesday that Pennsylvania election results should not be certified until a Republican lawsuit challenging the voting process is resolved.

The order, signed by Commonwealth Judge Patricia McCullough, bars all respondents from certifying the results of the election pending a hearing on Friday, November 27 at 11:30 a.m.

President Donald Trump's campaign lawyer, Jenna Ellis, touted the development on Twitter.

The lawsuit, brought to the court by Rep. Mike Kelly (R-PA), Republican Congressional candidate Sean Parnell, and others, challenges the constitutionality of Act 77. The act, which the state legislature passed **and Gov.**

Tom Wolf (D) signed in October 2019, expanded mail-in and absentee voting in the commonwealth. **The lawsuit** argues **that any changes made to absentee voting should require an amendment to the commonwealth's Constitution. If a court ruled in favor of the Pennsylvania Republican** lawsuit **it would invalidate all votes cast by mail in the 2020 election. "This court must intervene immediately in order to prevent further, irreparable injury from the resulting wrongs of an election conducted pursuit to an unconstitutional and invalid mail-in voting scheme," the plaintiffs** wrote**.**

Attorneys for Wolf and Secretary of State Kathy Boockvar requested the court dismiss the lawsuit.

- **"While draped in the driest of historical arguments, petitioners' claim is audacious; to grant it would undercut the very foundations of Pennsylvania's democracy and snatch the most basic of rights from its people," the attorneys wrote in their response to the**
- Hollywood Healing

Georgia Democrat Senate Candidate Jon Ossoff Claims 'Oversight' in Omitting Payment from Chinese Communist-Linked Company

CARD CARRYING DEMOCRAT COCKROACH HE IS THE ABSOLUTE MOST EVIL

Kristina Wong

Georgia Senate Democrat candidate Jon Ossoff's campaign is claiming its omission from its financial dis-

closures in May of a payment from a Chinese Communist Party (CCP)-linked company to Ossoff's media production company was due to a "paperwork oversight."

WE REALLY BELIEVE THIS SCUMBAG NEEDS THE DEATH PENALTY TO CLEANSE THE UNIVERSE OF HIM. After a political ad asserted that Ossoff ignored rules and hid cash from Chinese communists, an Ossoff campaign spokesperson called it a "paperwork oversight."

The November 17 Senate Leadership Fund ad said, "Jon Ossoff. A trail of dirty money. Ossoff ignored the rules, hiding cash from Chinese communists."

The ad was referring to Ossoff's initial financial disclosure filings for his Senate candidacy in May 2020. That filing showed that his media production company, Insight TWI, **received more than $5,000 in the past two years from 21 TV or broadcasting groups from around the world.**

Two months later, in July 2020, Ossoff amended that filing to include 32 companies, including PCCW Media Limited — a Hong Kong-based Chinese media company that is partially owned by the Chinese state-run company China Unicom, led by a CCP member.

Ossoff campaign spokesperson Miryam Lipper told FactCheck.org in regard to the ad that Ossoff was not "hiding" the payment and that it was a "paperwork oversight" that was "rectified" after "a normal review of the campaign's paperwork."

Lipper also wrote to FactCheck.org, "PCCW does not = Chinese communists."

However, multiple media reports show direct ties between PCCW Media Limited and the CCP.

PCCW Media Limited is owned by Richard Li — who has spoken out against pro-democracy protests in Hong Kong, as well as owned by the Chinese state-owned China Unicom, which is run by CEO Wang Xiaochu, a member of the CCP**.**

Li has a long track record of supporting Beijing. According to the *National Review*, in 2016, Li released a public statement that said he was "staunchly opposed to the independence of Hong Kong."

"Mr. Richard Li and MOOV would like to clearly state that the company and Mr. Li respect freedom of expression," the statement said**. "However, both Mr. Li and the Company are staunchly opposed to the independence of Hong Kong and it is their view that the independence of Hong Kong would not be feasible, and discussing Hong Kong's independence is a waste of society's resources."**

At the height of the democracy protests in 2019, Li took out full-page advertisements in seven newspapers to call for the restoration of "the social order with the rule of law," backing the **recommendations of Beijing's Hong Kong and Macau Affairs Office of the State Council, according to the *National Review*.**

And Li's father, Li Ka-shing, reportedly the richest man in Hong Kong, publicly backed the CCP's sweeping national security law in 2020 to crack down on critics and dissenters.

Despite Lipper claiming that PCCW Media Limited "does not = Chinese communists," she still made an effort to distance Ossoff's company from PCCW. She claimed PCCW did not directly pay Insight TWI, despite Ossoff's own filing listing the company as those that paid Insight TWI more than $5,000 in the past two years. "In some instances, as is the case with PCCW, TWI even licenses the documentaries to distributors like Sky Vision who re-license them to TV stations," Lipper claimed.

"TWI would never have sold anything to PCCW directly, just received a royalty check from Sky Vision when PCCW ran TWI's two investigations of ISIS war crimes," she added. She also asserted the payment did not mean PCCW controlled Ossoff. The structure of Insight TWI "doesn't leave any room for this notion that he is somehow controlled by these groups in the nefarious way they try to imply," she told FactCheck.org. FactCheck.org also said **support for the ad's "charges is weak" and called PCCW Media Limited "supposed" "Chinese communists."**

OUR OTHER COCKROACH

Barack Hussein Obama: Pro-Trump 'Evangelical Hispanics' Care More About Abortion than 'Cages' THESE KID CAGES WERE FIRST MANUFACRURED & USED BY BARACK HUSSEIN OBAMA

Neil Munro

President Donald Trump boosted his share of Latino votes because of religious and social issues, not because of his successful economic record, according to former President Barack Obama.

Obama made the claim as he admitted November 25 to a radio host that urban Democrats are often oblivious to the views of people outside their social circle.

"People were surprised about a lot of Hispanic folks who voted for Trump," Obama told *The Breakfast Club*, a radio show run by Lenard Larry McKelvey, who calls himself "Charlamagne tha God." Obama continued:

But there's a lot of evangelical Hispanics who, you know, the fact that Trump says racist things about Mexicans, or puts detainees, you know, undocumented workers, in cages — they think that's less important than the fact that, you know, he supports their views on gay marriage or abortion, right?

Obama's comments echoed his 2008 dismissal of midwestern voters' economic worries in a speech to elite donors in San Francisco:

You go into some of these small towns in Pennsylvania, and like a lot of small towns in the Midwest, the jobs have been gone now for 25 years and nothing's replaced them. And they fell through the Clinton Administration, and the Bush Administration, and each successive administration has said that somehow these communities are gonna regenerate and they have not. And it's not surprising then they get bitter, they cling to guns or religion or antipathy to people who aren't like them or anti-immigrant sentiment or anti-trade sentiment as a way to explain their frustrations.

Numerous post-election surveys show that the GOP's share of the Latino vote grew because most Latinos want to be ordinary Americans, and to escape from their assigned task of brown voters in the Democrats' diverse alliance of racial identity groups.

Because they are ordinary Americans, Latinos liked Trump's good economic record — median household income rose by seven % in 2019! — and they liked the GOP's support for anti-crime laws and other mainstream priorities — including marriage and abortion.

For example, on November 23, moderate author Christopher Caldwell wrote **in the far-left *New Republic* magazine:**

Trump didn't sell out his supporters. In fact, his presidency saw something extraordinary, even if it was all but invisible from the country's globalized cities: the first egalitarian boom since well back into the twentieth century. In 2019, the last non-Covid year, he presided over an average 3.7 % unemployment rate and 4.7 % **wage growth among the lowest quartile of earners. All income brackets increased their take. That had happened in the last three Obama years, too. The difference is that in the Obama part of the boom, the income of the top decile rose by 20 %, with tiny gains for other groups. In the Trump economy, the distribution was different. Net worth of the top 10 % rose only marginally, while that of all other groups vaulted ahead. In 2019, the share of overall earnings going to the bottom 90 & of earners** *rose* **for the first time in a decade.**

The great demographic surprise of the election—Trump's uptick among Black and Latino men—owed more to this wage progress than to Lil Wayne's endorsement, or to Trump's musing aloud that he had done more for Blacks in America than any president since Abraham Lincoln.

Even *Politico* admitted:

But, in interviews with more than a dozen experts on Hispanic voters in six states, no factor was as salient as Trump's blue-collar appeal for Latinos. "Most Latinos identify first as working-class Americans, and Trump spoke to that," said Josh Zaragoza, a top Democratic data specialist in Arizona, adding that Hispanic men in particular "are very entrepreneurial. Their economic language is more aligned with the way Republicans speak: pulling yourself up by your bootstraps, owning your own business."

"Most Latinos in this country are working class," [Harvard academic Ryan] Enos said. "One would have to assume that this identity of being working class is more important than this identity of being Latino."

Even the *New York Times* posted an op-ed admitting that most Latinos dislike Obama-style identity politics. Breitbart News reported:

The political problem for Biden's progressive allies is that only about 25 % of Latinos identify themselves as a progressive-style "people of color" identity group, the authors said. The majority of Latinos "rejected this designation [because] they preferred to see Hispanics as a group integrating into the American mainstream, one not overly bound by racial constraints but instead able to get ahead through hard work."

For example, numerous polls show that Latinos say they favor immigration but they strongly prefer border security, oppose welfare for migrants and want employers to hire Americans before importing workers.

Breitbart News reported polling data that shows Latinos favor Trump's immigration policies:

Exit polling conducted by Zogby Analytics for the Federation for American Immigration Reform (FAIR) found that Hispanic voters — including those who voted for Democrat Joe Biden — are overwhelmingly supportive of reducing overall legal immigration to the U.S., nearly as much as white Americans.

For instance, nearly 73 % of Hispanic voters said they support reducing immigration while tens of millions of Americans are jobless or underemployed. This is just a five % difference between white Americans who support reducing immigration.

Similarly, 6-in-10 Hispanic voters said overall legal immigration should be reduced even after the U.S. recovers from its unemployment crisis to "protect American jobs" for Americans. This is only a six % difference between white Americans who support the policy.

ALL WILL GET FREE STUFF & VOTE DEMOCRAT

Watch–Joe Biden: Amnesty for Over 11 Million Illegal Aliens Going to Senate in My First 100 Days

John Binder

Democrat Joe Biden says he will send an amnesty deal for "over 11 million" illegal aliens to the United States Senate in his first 100 days in office.

During an interview with NBC News's Lester Holt, Biden reiterated his plan to give amnesty to the roughly 11 to 22 million illegal aliens living in the U.S. Biden said of his agenda: Some of it's going to depend on the kind of cooperation I can or cannot get from the United States Congress. But I am going, I made a commitment, in the first 100 days, I will send an immigration bill to the United States Senate with a pathway to citizenship for over 11 million undocumented people in America.

Already, a number of Senate Republicans have suggested that they are interested in working with Biden on some sort of immigration deal. Senators Lindsey Graham **(R-SC), John Cornyn (R-TX), and Chuck Grassley (R-IA) have** all hinted **at striking a Democrat-GOP deal on immigration that would almost certainly include an amnesty. Currently, about** 24.5 million Americans are either jobless or underemployed, but all want full-time jobs. Those unemployed are forced to compete in the labor market by an endless stream of foreign workers who secure visas and green cards that rack up to more than 2.5 million admissions every year.

These legal immigration admissions are in addition to the hundreds of thousands of illegal aliens who successfully cross U.S. borders and overstay their visas every year. Exit polling after the election reveals that voters across party and racial lines overwhelmingly want less overall immigration to the U.S. More than 3-in-4 voters**, for instance, said it is important to reduce immigration with continued high unemployment, and more than 62 % said, even after unemployment has leveled off, immigration should remain lower than its current levels.**

Sidney Powell promises 'massive' Georgia lawsuit by Wednesday that will 'save' Trump's presidency

OK, let's see it

Sidney Powell, the pro-Trump attorney who is reportedly working on compiling evidence to prove that manipulated voting software skewed the results of the 2020 election, vowed that a "massive" lawsuit in Georgia would be filed by Wednesday and that it, along with similar lawsuits, would ultimately "save" Donald Trump's presidency.

"I think no later than tomorrow," Powell told Fox Business Network's Lou Dobbs on Tuesday regarding the lawsuit. "It's just going to be — it's a massive document. And it's going to have a lot of exhibits."

"Do you think that we're going to see the Trump presidency saved?" Dobbs asked.

"Yes, I definitely do," Powell responded. "There's no issue in my mind but that he was elected in an absolute landslide nationwide."

It is just the latest assurance provided by Powell over the last couple of weeks. The defense attorney for Gen. Michael Flynn has repeatedly promised she would "release the Kraken" of evidence proving that Trump won the election "in a landslide." However, to date no such evidence has been submitted resulting in the overturning of results, which show former Vice President Joe Biden winning enough Electoral College votes to become the next president.

In Georgia, Biden narrowly defeated Trump by just over 12,000 votes.

Nevertheless, Powell contended that she and her team are hard at work compiling evidence for lawsuits in several battleground states.

"We will be rolling them out as fast as we possibly can, because it affected the entire country," she said. "It's all so clear that there was foreign intrusion into our voting systems, and that's going be the real — where the rubber meets the road."

"There's no doubt that the software was created and used in Venezuela to control the elections and make sure that Hugo Chavez was always reelected as the dictator of Venezuela, in what appeared to be 'free and fair elections,'" she added later during the interview. "But they were manipulated by the software used in the Dominion machines and used by other machines in the United States, frankly. And we are just continuing to be inundated by evidence of all the frauds here, and every manner and means of fraud you could possibly think of."

The news comes on the heels of the Trump legal team appearing to distance themselves from Powell. In a statement over the weekend, Trump campaign senior legal adviser Jenna Ellis and Trump's personal attorney Rudy Giuliani made clear that Powell was "not a member" of the legal team and "not a lawyer for the president in his personal capacity," but "is practicing law on her own."

Sidney Powell "Releases Kraken" With Dual Lawsuits In Michigan, Georgia

Sidney Powell has finally released the Kraken – filing two lawsuits in Michigan and Georgia late Wednesday alleging massive schemes to rig the election for Joe Biden.

In Georgia, Powell claims in a 104-page complaint filed in the US District Court in Atlanta that the purpose of the scheme was "illegally and fraudulently manipulating the vote count to make certain the election of Joe Biden as president of the United States."

"Old-fashioned ballot-stuffing" has been "amplified and rendered virtually invisible by computer software created and run by domestic and foreign actors for that very purpose," the suit continues, adding that "Mathematical and statistical anomalies rising to the level of impossibilities, as shown by affidavits of multiple witnesses, documentation, and expert testimony evince this scheme across the state of Georgia."

"This scheme and artifice to defraud affected tens of thousands of votes in Georgia alone and 'rigged' the election in Georgia for Joe Biden."

According to *Just the News*, Powell's allegations include that:

- ***At least 96,600 absentee ballots were requested and counted but were never recorded as being returned to county election boards by the voter. "Thus, at a minimum, 96,600 votes must be disregarded," the suit said.***

- ***Kemp and Raffensperger "rushed through the purchase of Dominion voting machines and software in 2019 for the 2020 Presidential Election" without due diligence and disregarded safety concerns.***
- ***"There is incontrovertible physical evidence that the standards of physical security of the voting machines and the software were breached, and machines were connected to the internet in violation of professional standards and state and federal laws."***
- *Fulton County election workers used a claim of a water leak to evacuate poll watchers and workers for several hours on Election night, even as "several election workers remained unsupervised and unchallenged working at the computers for the voting tabulation machines until after 1:00 AM.*
- ***State officials in a settlement with Democratic parties made changes to election procedures that violated both state law and the U.S. Constitution.***

The suit asks for over a dozen remedies, including an injunction blocking the state's certified results – in which Biden 'won' by 12,000 votes – from being transmitted to the Electoral College.

Powell's suit also demands an audit where signatures are matched, the impounding of various election machines and video surveillance from vote-counting areas.

In Michigan, Powell filed a 75-page complaint seeking to set aside the results of the election, claiming that "hundreds of thousands of illegal, ineligible, duplicate, or purely fictitious ballots**" enabled by "massive election fraud" facilitated Biden's win in the state.**

"The scheme and artifice to defraud was for the purpose of illegally and fraudulently manipulating the vote count to manufacture an election of Joe Biden as president of the United States," the suit alleges, adding that the most "troubling, insidious, and egregious ploy" involved "systemic adaptation of old-fashioned 'ballot-stuffing.'"

As Mimi Ngyuen Ly of *The Epoch Times* notes:

The complaint alleged "an especially egregious range of conduct" in Wayne County and the City of Detroit and similar conduct throughout the state, which it attributed to direction from Michigan state election officials. **It noted that the "same pattern of election fraud and voter fraud writ large occurred in all the swing states with only minor variations" in Pennsylvania, Arizona, and Wisconsin.**

The complaint cited eyewitness and expert testimony to allege that there were enough ballots identified to overturn and reverse the election results. It also said results of the election cannot be relied on because the entire election process was "riddled with fraud, illegality, and statistical impossibility."

The suit claimed that election software and hardware from Dominion Voting Systems used by the Michigan Board of State Canvassers helped facilitate the fraud.

"The Dominion systems derive from the software designed by Smartmatic Corporation, which became Sequoia in the United States," the complaint reads.

"Smartmatic and Dominion were founded by foreign oligarchs and dictators to ensure computerized ballot-stuffing and vote manipulation to whatever level was needed to make certain Venezuelan dictator Hugo Chavez never lost another election," it added, citing a whistleblower's affidavit alleging that the Smartmatic software was used to manipulate Venezuelan elections in favor of Chavez.

"A core requirement of the Smartmatic software design ultimately adopted by Dominion for Michigan's elections was the software's ability to hide its manipulation of votes from any audit," the complaint alleged.

The complaint cited a former electronic intelligence analyst under the 305th Military Intelligence Battalion, who declared that the Dominion software was accessed by agents acting on behalf of China and Iran to monitor and manipulate elections, including the 2020 U.S. general election.

Another part of the complaint said that a former U.S. Military Intelligence expert had analyzed the Dominion software system and concluded that the system and software "were certainly compromised by rogue actors, such as Iran and China."

"By using servers and employees connected with rogue actors and hostile foreign influences combined with numerous easily discoverable leaked credentials, Dominion neglectfully allowed foreign adversaries to access data and intentionally provided access to their infrastructure in order to monitor and manipulate elections, including the most recent one in 2020," the filing said

'Extraordinary Overreach'

MUCH MORE EXTRAORDINARY CHEATING TO STEAL A PRESIDENTIAL ELECTION

"The order purports to interfere with the ongoing process of seating presidential electors and precludes certification of any other result from the 2020 general election," they said. "This extraordinary act of judicial overreach threatens to undermine the integrity of Pennsylvania's elections and reduce public confidence in them." The case is separate from the federal lawsuit by President Donald Trump's campaign that seeks to undo Pennsylvania's certification unless tens of thousands of allegedly illegal mail-in ballots are invalidated. The state case was brought by Republicans led by U.S. Rep. Mike Kelly.

Boockvar said in an earlier court filing that the plaintiffs "had not offered any explanation, let alone a satisfactory one, for why they delayed bringing their challenge until more than a year (and two elections)" after the state adopted the mail-in voting expansion. The law was passed by the GOP-led legislature.

The plaintiffs argued an injunction could still be issued even though the certification had taken place, pointing out that a number of formal steps remained, including issuing commissions to elected candidates. The state's "duties with regard to finalization of the full election results are far from complete," they said in a motion on Tuesday.

Biden: Americans 'Won't Stand' for Election Results Not Being Honored

SCHMUCK; EXACTLY WHAT ARE YOU OR ANYONE ELSE GOING TO FUCKEN DO ABOUT IT; ATTACK US DEPLORABLES WITH CODE PINK?

Joe Biden said Wednesday that Americans "won't stand" for the results of the Nov. 3 election not being honored.

EAT SHIT & DIE, PAL ZOMBIE & KAMIKAZE KAMALA

"Our democracy was tested this year," Biden said in a Thanksgiving Day address in his hometown of Wilmington, Delaware. "And what we learned is this: The people of this nation are up to the task.

"In America, we have full and fair and free elections, and then we honor the results," he said. "The people of this nation and the laws of the land won't stand for anything else."

Biden did not mention Donald Trump by name but he was clearly referring to the president's refusal to

accept the results of the election, which on their face favored the Biden campaign. The president and his legal team are continuing to press legal challenges and allegations of systemic voter fraud, in some instances urging state legislators to designate their own electors for the official rendering of the electoral college vote.

Biden said the COVID-19 pandemic has exacerbated political divisions in the United States and called for unity.

"It has divided us. Angered us. And set us against one another," he said. "I know the country has grown weary of the fight.

"But we need to remember we're at a war with a virus -- not with each other."

Dick Morris to Newsmax TV: Georgia Ignored Election Fraud Warning By Eric Mack

Even The Atlanta Journal-Constitution (THE WORST) had forecast potential voter fraud in Georgia with its scathing rebuke of the new Dominion Voting Systems› **vulnerabilities Oct. 23, but Georgia ignored it, according to presidential political strategist Dick Morris on** Newsmax TV.

The AJC "ran a story 11 days before Election Day, warning that Georgia's new electronic voting system is vulnerable to cyberattacks that could cause chaos at the polls or even manipulate the results on Election Day," Morris told Wednesday's "American Agenda**," noting the AJC is a Democrat-leaning newspaper.**

"They were warned about this by The Atlanta Journal-Constitution, that's like being warned about it by the Democratic Party; they are an organ of the Democratic Party. But, nevertheless, they reported this and the Secretary of State's office ignored it completely."

The AJC report quoted U.S. District Judge Amy Totenberg before the election warning that the Dominion Voting System "presents serious security vulnerability and operational issues" caused by "fundamental deficits and exposure."

"These risks are neither hypothetical nor remote under the current circumstances," Totenberg wrote in a order criticizing Georgia's state election officials, per the AJC.

Also, the AJC reported, Georgia paid $104 million to be the only state in the U.S. to use the Dominion Voting System in every polling place.

Most egregiously, Morris noted, GOP Secretary of State Brad Raffensperger's "office weakened the system's defenses, disabling password protections on a key component that controls who is allowed to vote," the AJC reported.

"In addition, days before early voting began on Oct. 12, Raffensperger's office pushed out new software to

each of the state's 30,000 voting machines through hundreds of thumb drives that experts say are prone to infection with malware," the report continued.

"And what state officials describe as a feature of the new system actually masks a vulnerability.

"Officials tell voters to verify their selections on a paper ballot before feeding it into an optical scanner. But the scanner doesn't record the text that voters see; rather, it reads an unencrypted quick response, or QR, barcode that is indecipherable to the human eye. Either by tampering with individual voting machines or by infiltrating the state's central elections server, hackers could systematically alter the barcodes to change votes."

Pa. AG Rejects Fraud Hearing as 'Fake,' 'Devoid of Reality'

IF YOU DON'T LIKE IT, DO SOMETHING THE FUCK ABOUT IT.

Pennsylvania Attorney General Josh Shapiro urged voters Wednesday to "drown out the noise" of misinformation about mail ballots as he cast his own on Oct. 14, 2020.

By Eric Mack

An election fraud hearing before Pennsylvania Republican lawmakers in Gettysburg on Wednesday did not sit well with the Democrat state Attorney General Josh Shapiro, who rebuked it is a «fake» and «devoid of reality.»

Shapiro tweeted:

"The sitting president's remarks today were devoid of reality. The election is over. Pennsylvania has certified results & declared Joe Biden the winner of our Commonwealth. Lying through a cell phone at a fake hearing changes nothing." OH REALLY**?**

President Donald Trump called into the meeting examining accusations of election impropriety, calling the state's election fraudulent and illegitimate.

"This election was lost by the Democrats," Trump said by phone held to the mic by Trump campaign legal counsel Jenna Ellis. «They cheated, it was a fraudulent election.»

Ellis sat alongside Rudy Giuliani, the president's personal lawyer who has been leading a longshot legal effort in several states to reverse the results of the Nov. 3 election.

Trump had planned to travel to the hearing, but scrapped the trip earlier in the day. The visit had not been listed on the president's public schedule, but people familiar with the matter said he intended to appear alongside Giuliani.

Pennsylvania Lt. Gov. John Fetterman was also nonplussed by the hearing.

"This is an Amway convention in a holiday ballroom, that's all it is," Fetterman told a radio program, Newsweek reported. «They›re going to sell the same kind of products that no one really believes is legitimate.

"And that's the problem here, with all of this. I just put this out on social media, the Pennsylvania GOP is saying that there is voter fraud in Pennsylvania, but not our races, you know there wasn't any fraud in our races that elected us."

Biden Promises FIRST CLASS CLASS AIRFARE & GREEN CARDS TO THE ENTIRE POPULATION OF BANGLADESH PLUS THE BEST OF EVERYTHING FOR FREE ONCE THE GET HERE to Push Immigration Bill in First 100 Days

By Solange Reyner

Joe Biden says he will push an immigration bill through the Senate in his first 100 days in office to establish a "pathway to citizenship for over 11 million undocumented people in America."

LET THEM TAKE OUR JOBS & TAXPAYER PAID BENEFITS

Biden has not been certified as the winner of the presidential election, though several news outlets have called the race for the former vice president. Newsmax has not announced a winner, citing close races in several battleground states, recounts, and legal challenges. Still, Biden has started his transition and in a wide-ranging interview with NBC News' Lester Holt said he was committed to sending an immigration bill to Congress immediately.

Biden has already promised to restore the Deferred Action for Childhood Arrivals program, which allows about 600,000 young immigrants who live in the U.S. illegally and were brought here as children to remain here. He is also expected to end the Trump administration's so-called Muslim ban, family separation practice, and construction of the U.S.-Mexico border wall.

Several senior Republican lawmakers are willing to work with the Democrat on a comprehensive immigration reform package should he win the election.

Poll: Big Majority Wants Trump to Run in 2024; Don Jr. Emerges

President Trump listens to Don Jr. whip up the crowd during a rally in Kenosha, Wisconsin, the night before Election Day. By Jeffrey Rodack

A super-majority -- 68% of Republicans and GOP primary voting independents -- would love to see President Donald Trump run again in 2024 if he ultimately fails to prevail against Joe Biden in this year's election, according to a new Newsmax/McLaughlin Associates poll.

The president continues to hold a strong job approval rating, with 48%.

And to a majority of Americans, 52%, major media outlets in the U.S. have been biased and unfair in their coverage of Trump, who is in the midst of a fierce legal battle on several fronts to challenge the results of the recent presidential election.

Here are more highlights from the Newsmax/McLaughlin poll:

- **In all, 53% of Republican primary voters say they would favor Trump in a field of 13 potential challengers, including Vice President Mike Pence, Sen. Ted Cruz, and Secretary of State Mike Pompeo. Pence finished second with 9%. None of the other potential candidates finished with more than 4%. "In a crowded field of 14 possible candidates for the 2024 Republican primary, no one comes close to President Trump," pollster John McLaughlin said.**
- **If Trump does not run again in 2024, Pence and Donald Trump Jr. then appear tied for the lead with 20% each.**

Don Jr., the president's eldest son and the most politically active of Trump's children, has apparently enjoyed the talk of a 2024 bid.

In October, he tweeted a picture of himself standing in front of a "Don Jr. 2024" sign, saying that "this will make lib heads explode."

The poll, conducted by McLaughlin & Associates between Nov. 21 and 23, surveyed 1,000 likely general election voters. It has a margin of error of plus or minus 3.1 % points.

Legal adviser for President Trump says these arguments in Sidney Powell's lawsuits could 'affect the outcome of the election'

These allegations 'have legs' PHIL SHIVER

Pro-Trump attorney Sidney Powell finally came through on her promise to legally challenge the 2020 election Thursday by releasing two highly anticipated lawsuits in Georgia and Michigan alleging widespread fraud. As for what affect the lawsuits will have on the results of the election — which for now show former Vice President Joe Biden defeating President Trump 306-232 in the Electoral College — that remains to be seen.

But at least one Trump campaign legal adviser appears to believe that the claims made in the Georgia lawsuit**, if argued successfully before a judge, could overturn the election and grant the president a victory.**

What are the details?

In a lengthy Twitter thread Thursday, Harmeet Dhillon, a lawyer and former Republican Party official who is now involved in the Trump campaign›s legal effort, summarized the key claims made in Powell›s suit. She acknowledged that while some of Powell›s major arguments — such as that Dominion Voting Systems software was hacked and that thousands of ballots were pre-printed for Biden — would certainly «be enough to change the election results,» they may be more difficult to prove in court.

Instead, Dhillon suggested that a simpler path to victory for Powell would be to lean into a couple lesser, but still serious, claims of election fraud made in the suit.

"To me, the easiest way to reach the goal [of overturning the election] is something much simpler alleged in the complaint at para. 121," wrote Dhillon. "That thousands of specific, identifiable voters, cast ballots after they moved out of state as evidenced in their registration in a national database, and may even have cast votes in their new states also which can easily be checked against the other state's records. This accounts for thousands of votes."

"The other category Matt Braynard has researched & documented, is thousands of identifiable, specific registrations at fraudulent addresses such as P.O. Boxes, non-residential, etc.," she continued. "These seem to be specific and of a sufficient volume that their disqualification would affect the outcome of the election. I think this simple tack — much easier to grasp and prove than the more complicated theories — is compelling."

It should be noted that UPS allows individuals to set up personal mailboxes at local stores where they can receive mail and packages and the United States Postal Service sometimes allows individuals without permanent addresses to have mail sent to local stores via «General Delivery.»

It could be that Powell's suit is alleging an irregular number of absentee ballots were delivered to such mailboxes, raising suspicion of fraudulent activity.

Dhillon went on to counter the charge that it is too late to challenge the election because votes have already been cast, recounted, and in many cases certified by state election officials.

"[But] how are you supposed to allege that someone cast a ballot from a fraudulent registration address or after moving, before the election?" Dhillon asked. "This is something that can only be checked after the votes are cast and tallied, particularly where last-minute registrations are permitted by increasingly lax voter registration policies pushed by Democrats, followed by no signature verification or other safeguards, as the lawsuit alleges."

By Eric Mack

Journalists are strangely lacking curiosity about some mysterious ways Democrat Joe Biden pulled off some "electoral jujitsu" in this presidential election, according to The Federalist's J.B. Shurk.

Biden says he'll push 'pathway to citizenship for over 11 million WHY NOT 111 BILLION? **undocumented people' in first 100 days**

Biden said he would push an immigration bill through the Senate at the start of his presidency

By Vandana Rambaran

Incoming Biden administration signals shift in Iran foreign policy

Fox News senior strategic analyst Gen. Jack Keane tells 'America's Newsroom' there will be an opportunity for President-elect Biden to renegotiate a nuclear deal with Iran.

President-elect Joe Biden has committed to forging «a pathway to citizenship for over 11 million undocumented people in America» in the first 100 days of his administration.

In a wide-ranging interview with NBC News' Lester Holt, Biden said he would work to push an immigration bill through the Senate right at the onset of his presidency, but he is sure to face a steep uphill battle.

Black Lives Matter PROTESTERS DEMAND LA MAYOR BE EXCLUDED FROM BIDEN CABINET: REPORTS

The Republican stronghold in the Senate hangs in the balance, with two Georgia runoffs still in play that will determine the majority party come January.

"Some of it's gonna depend on the kinda cooperation I can or cannot get from the United States Congress," Biden acknowledged. On Tuesday Biden announced he intends to nominate Alejandro Mayorkas – a former Department of Homeland Security official under President Barack Obama – as secretary of the DHS.

The move could foreshadow Biden's intent to slash President Trump's immigration restrictions and ensure that protections under Obama policies such as the Deferred Action for Childhood Arrivals (DACA) are reinforced.

GEORGIA SEC. OF STATE SAYS TRUMP THREW HIM 'UNDER THE BUS' HE SHOULD HAVE BEEN CRUSHED & DIED THERE AUTHOR ADDENDUM

On the campaign trail**, Biden pledged to end the Migrant Protection Protocols (MPP) that keep migrants in Mexico as their hearings play out. Known as the "Remain-in-Mexico" policy, opponents have claimed it puts migrants in danger, but Trump officials say it has been key in ending "catch-and-release" by which migrants were released into the U.S. instead.**

Trump has seized on the point in recent weeks, claiming that an end to the program would create a surge in illegal border crossings**. Biden also said he would spend the critical first three months of his presidency rolling back Trump's executive orders related to the environment, among other things. He also said he would prioritize "immediate assistance" to state and local governments "to keep them from basically going under," as they continue to grapple with the coronavirus pandemic.**

Biden said he would not be using the Justice Department to go after Trump for purported crimes, and instead said he is entirely focused on tackling the COVID-19 crisis instead. "What I'm focused on getting the American public back at a place where they have some certainty, some surety, some knowledge that they can make it. The middle-class and working-class people are being crushed. That's my focus," Biden said.

Fox News staffers thought Newsmax was a joke. But they're not laughing anymore

By Brian Stelter,

Stelter: Fox News has never seen competition like this in its history ***New York (CNN Business)*** **Fox News is taking action to stave off newfound competition from Newsmax TV. Producers on some Fox programs have been told to monitor Newsmax's** guest bookings and throw some sand in Newsmax›s gears by encouraging guests who appear on both channels to stop saying yes to the upstart.

According to Fox sources, producers were told to avoid some regular guests if they kept showing up on Newsmax after being encouraged to stop. Management's goal: to remind guests who's boss in the right-wing media world.

Analysis: Fox News' rivals are using the network's own dishonest tactics against it

And Fox News is still boss, with five times the audience of Newsmax at any given time of day. A Fox

spokesperson said there was no directive about guest bookings. But it's clear that Fox is feeling pressure from the right like never before. Fox hosts and producers are on edge about the ratings race, a number of staffers told CNN Business. The staffers also said that the competitive dynamic is having an impact on some of Fox's programming choices.

Newsmax TV's ratings boom ALONG WITH THE DAILY CALLER, BRIEBART & THE BLAZE; ALL MAJOR MEDIA INCLUDING CALL REPUBLICAN TRUTH DEBUNKED FALSEHOODS I CANCELLED HOME DELIVERY OF THE WALL STREET JOURNAL AFTER (12) YEARS

Until Election Day, Newsmax barely had a pulse on Nielsen's TV ratings reports, which showed that the channel only averaged 34,000 viewers at any given time in August and September. A slight uptick in October became a groundswell of viewership after November 3. One of the obvious causes was Fox's projection that President Trump would lose the state of Arizona, drastically narrowing his path to re-election. Newsmax criticized Fox and gave viewers false hope about Trump's chances.

This tactic continued when Fox and all the other major networks called the election for President-elect Biden on November 7. Newsmax insisted that the race wasn't over and that the major networks were acting irresponsibly, when in fact Newsmax was the irrational actor. A subset of the Fox audience flocked to Newsmax for shows that hyped voter fraud allegations and harangued the rest of the media.

Greg Kelly, the 7 p.m. host on Newsmax, was the biggest beneficiary: His show averaged 80,000 viewers in the run-up to Election Day and topped 800,000 on the first weekday after Biden was projected as president-elect.

Sources at Fox derided Newsmax as "far-right" and "fringe" and they singled out Kelly for particular criticism. But there has been a noticeable shift in the way they talk about Newsmax.

Earlier this year, while working on a book about Fox News and Trump, I spoke with some of the same staffers, and when I brought up Newsmax and another wannabe rival, One America News, they usually scoffed or cracked a joke. The channels were dismissed like the fleas on an elephant's back.

Fox News has never seen competition like this I WON'T CONSIDER FOX AGAIN UNLESS FOX FIRES MOUSEY COCKROACH CHRIS WALLACE FOR CAUSE RENDERING HIM INELIGIBLE FOR UNEMPLOYMENT BENEFITS

But the Fox staffers are not joking anymore. They are paying close attention to the daily ratings spreadsheets that show Newsmax's performance alongside Fox News, Fox Business and other channels.

Overall, CNN has made the biggest gains in the post-election period; CNN has been beating Fox News in the

key 25- to 54-year-old demographic for nearly three weeks. But Fox has also been losing share to Newsmax, particularly in the early evening hours, according to a close reading of the Nielsen data.

On Monday evening, for example, Kelly averaged 188,000 viewers between the ages of 25 and 54, while Fox's "The Story" averaged 288,000 viewers in that demographic at that hour.

Before the election, Kelly was garnering about 30,000 viewers in the demo, while Fox was getting more than 500,000 in the demo.

Some of Fox's audience erosion is due to predictable post-election fatigue; Fox also fell into a slump after Mitt Romney lost to Barack Obama in 2012.

If history is any guide, the audience will gradually "come home," in the words of one Fox executive, who pointed out that the network remains dominant among conservative viewers. On Monday Fox had 1.4 million viewers at any given time of day, and more than 2 million during prime time, while Newsmax had 300,000 at any given time of day. Competition in the right-wing media landscape

IT'S NOT RiGHT WING. IT'S WHO IS MARRIED TO TRUTH; NOT PROGRESSIVE DEMOCRAT ADVOCACY

REPEAT; I GOT RID OF THE WALL STREET JOURNAL, WHICH IS NOW A CUTESY POO LITTLE CONNECTED GIRLIE PROGRESSIVE LITTLE LIBERAL TWAT TWIRP CONDESCENDING BITCH FUCKEN NEW YORK TIMES BRATS

No one quite knows what to expect in this new competitive landscape. In recent days, Newsmax has come off its immediate post-election highs. Kelly averaged 600,000 viewers on Tuesday, down from 1.1 million last Thursday.

And Newsmax is one of many Fox challengers. One America News is not rated by Nielsen, which is normally a sign that a channel is very small, but the channel's owners say that their internal metrics show big post-election gains. Google searches for both Newsmax and One America News both spiked after Election Day.

Charles Herring, the president of OANN, said Friday that "a massive wave of former Fox News viewers have abandoned Fox and have found a home at OAN." He said some former Fox viewers "believe new pro left voices have infiltrated the network." Other right-wing outlets include two streaming services: BlazeTV, with Glenn Beck and Mark Levin among the hosts, and The First TV, with Bill O'Reilly. One throughline of most of Fox's rivals: They employ former Fox talent.

Trump, despite being closely aligned with Fox during his time in office, has been taking advantage of the competition and promoting Newsmax on his Twitter feed.

On Tuesday night Trump tweeted out the results of an unscientific poll, "Should President Trump concede to Biden?," that was shown multiple times on Newsmax TV.

The results were meaningless, except to show that Newsmax is still catering to Trump fans who don't want the election to be over.

IT ISN'T OVER, OR IT WASN'T OVER WHEN FOX ANOINTED BIDEN AS PRESIDENT-ELECT & FOR WEEKS REFUSED TO REPORT ANY NEWS ABOUT GUNS & RELIGION DEPLORABLES FIGHTING BACK THAT'S THE FUCKEN POINT

Some of Fox's talk shows have indulged election denialism, too, but they have been contradicted by the newscasts that air at other times of day. And this is a source of tension internally, some of the Fox sources said. Last Sunday the vociferously pro-Trump host Maria Bartiromo delievered a scathing criticism of an election technology company called Dominion Voting Systems. Then she told viewers to tune in later in the day when a spokesperson for Dominion would be interviewed by Fox News anchor Eric Shawn. She even read a list of questions that she said Shawn should ask.

Inside Fox, staffers cringed at the awkward contrast between Bartiromo's conspiratorial programming and Shawn's straightforward interview, which rebuked the conspiracy theories.

THIS FAT FACE UGLY SELF-ABSORBED SCHMUCK Stelter calls out CEO: Stop airing this bogus voter fraud stuff Many Fox viewers prefer the conspiracy theories however -- Bartiromo's show had more than 1.9 million viewers while Shawn's newscast barely averaged 1 million.

"Our audience has absolutely been radicalized," one longtime on-air staffer at Fox said.

Multiple staffers pointed to programming adjustments, like the airing of Mark Levin's right-wing talk show on both Saturday and Sunday nights, that are meant to appeal to the Fox base. Levin's show used to air just on Sundays. Last Saturday, however, Fox aired a six-day-old episode of the show, full of out-of-date claims about Trump's legal challenges. The staffers said the frequent re-airing of clips from "Tucker Carlson Tonight" during the day was another noticeable attempt to appease viewers.

When asked about the apparent booking drama between Fox and Newsmax, Chris Ruddy, the CEO of Newsmax, said Fox is committing an "anti-competitive violation" by trying to block guests. Two of the Fox sources shrugged at that suggestion. "Welcome to the big leagues," one said.

Richard,

Did you see the President's email?

We pulled the records of his most LOYAL supporters - the ones who have been there for him no matter what. It should come as no surprise, but your donor record showed up in the top 1%.

INCREDIBLE. Look at everything you've done for our movement:

SUPPORTER: Richard Glick
P.O. Box 493, Greenlawn, New York 11740
Donor Since: May 24, 2020
2020 Gifts: 8
Lifetime Total: $675.00

DONOR RECORD

The truth is, we are pacing BEHIND our Election Defense Fund Goal. If we don't do something quick, we risk LOSING America to BIG GOVERNMENT SOCIALISTS.

We ran the numbers and our average gift is just over $45. If every supporter took action and contributed that amount TODAY, we'd be back on track and would have what it takes to SAVE AMERICA from Joe Biden and Kamala Harris.

Urgent: **Do you approve of Pres. Trump's job performance?** Vote Here Now!

Dick Morris to Newsmax TV: Stats Prove Ballot Stuffing

By Brian Trusdell

Former Democratic strategist and White House adviser Dick Morris told Newsmax TV **on Monday that Democratic presidential voter turnout was disproportionately larger than the population gains from 2012 to**

2020 in key cities where President Donald Trump is disputing election tallies. Appearing on "Greg Kelly Reports," Morris pointed out that the vote for Joe Biden in Phoenix was 48% more than Barack Obama received in 2012, when the city only witnessed a 14% gain in population. Similarly, he said, Atlanta saw a 30% larger vote for Biden than Obama in 2012, despite a 9% gain in population, and Detroit had a 10% higher vote total for Biden than Obama while seeing no increase in population at all.

"And the only way that that increase can be justified is by ballot stuffing," Morris said. "The non-Democratic cities didn't realize that kind of gain. And even cities like New York and Chicago, that were not in swing states, didn't realize that kind of a gain. It was pure ballot stuffing with absentee and mail-in ballots."

Morris admitted that Democratic antipathy toward Trump could account for the increased voter turnout overall, from 135 million in 2016 to 150 million earlier this month. But it doesn't explain why the turnout was significantly higher in the states where claims of fraud, particularly in Arizona, Michigan and Georgia, are being made, but not across the board in other Democrat-controlled cities.

- **"Sure it did," Morris said. "But in these particular cities and in these particular states, where Biden won by 80,000 in one state, or 20,000 in another, these kinds spikes in turnout are indicative of ballot stuffing. The secretary of state in Michigan sent out 7.7 million absentee ballots, and got huge numbers back, and that permitted them to stuff the ballot [box] with phony ballots. Two hundred thousand absentee ballots in Pennsylvania, alone, were counted." Pennsylvania State Senate Plans Meeting to Air Complaints of Voter Fraud**

Charlie Spiering

The Pennsylvania State Senate Majority Policy Committee plans to meet Wednesday in Gettysburg to air complaints of voter fraud to the public.

"Over the past few weeks, I have heard from thousands of Pennsylvanians regarding issues experienced at the polls, irregularities with the mail-in voting system, and concerns whether their vote was counted," State Sen. David Argall, R-Mahanoy City said in a statement**. "We need to correct these issues to restore faith in our republic."**

The meeting will take place on Wednesday, November 25 at 12:30 p.m. at the Wyndham Hotel in Gettysburg.

President Donald Trump has been rumored **to** make an appearance at the meeting, but the White House would not confirm those reports, and no changes were made to the president's public schedule.

President Trump's lawyer former New York City Mayor Rudy Giuliani is expected to give a presentation, according to the campaign.

Each Senator at the hearing will give a five-minute opening statement followed by witnesses willing to present affidavits attesting to voter fraud in the 2020 election.

"It's in everyone's interest to have a full vetting of election irregularities and fraud," Giuliani said in a statement. "And the only way to do this is with public hearings, complete with witnesses, videos, pictures and other evidence of illegalities from the November 3rd election."

Report: Facebook hatched 'emergency' plan using 'secret internal ranking' to suppress 'right-wing' news sources post-election

Blatant censorship Phil Shiver

In the tense days after the election as claims of widespread fraud were being disseminated on the platform, Facebook reportedly made an "emergency change" to its algorithm to suppress news sources that were spreading what the company believed to be "election misinformation."

According to the New York Times**, the change involved weighting news sources using a "secret internal ranking" of publishers that Facebook created based on "signals about the quality of their journalism." The result became the more prominent featuring of posts from mainstream news outlets such as "CNN, The New York Times, and NPR," and the suppression of posts from "right-wing" outlets.**

The change — which was hatched by a group of employees and approved by the social media giant's chief executive, Mark Zuckerberg — was reportedly part of several "break glass" plans the company had spent months developing in the case of a contested election. Here's more from the Times report:

It involved emphasizing the importance of what Facebook calls "news ecosystem quality" scores, or N.E.Q., a secret internal ranking it assigns to news publishers based on signals about the quality of their journalism.

Typically, N.E.Q. scores play a minor role in determining what appears on users' feeds. But several days after the election, Mr. Zuckerberg agreed to increase the weight that Facebook's algorithm gave to N.E.Q. scores to make sure authoritative news appeared more prominently, said three people with knowledge of the decision, who were not authorized to discuss internal deliberations.

The change was part of the "break glass" plans **Facebook had spent months developing for the aftermath of a contested election. It resulted in a spike in visibility for big, mainstream publishers like CNN, The New York Times and NPR, while posts from highly engaged hyperpartisan pages, such as Breitbart and Occupy Democrats, became less visible, the employees said.**

"It was a vision of what a calmer, less divisive Facebook might look like," the report noted, as if granting its approval to the emergency plan. The Times' approval is not surprising since it was explicitly listed as one of the publishers who benefitted from the algorithm change.

The sentiment is not likely to be shared by Republicans and supporters of President Trump, however, who will no doubt see the change as yet another egregious example of blatant, purposeful censorship. The social media company, along with Twitter, had been heavily scrutinized in the weeks leading up to the election for its unabashed censorship of the New York Post's bombshell reporting on Hunter Biden.

Guy Rosen, a Facebook executive who oversees its integrity division, told reporters on a conference call last week that the post-election algorithm changes were always meant to be temporary, but that decision is not uniformly popular at the company. The Times noted that some at the company argued that the changes should become permanent.

(40) ACRES & A MULE JUST BECAME CORY BOOKER'S (4000) ACRES $4 MILLION & (12) JOHN DEERE TRACTORS

Sen. Booker Introduces Bill to Transfer Land to Black Farmers

I SAY PEOPLE OF THE CAUCAUSIAN PERSUASION STOLE HOMELAND FROM LOWLAND GORILLAS; BABOONS; ORANGUTANS & OPRAH WINFREY; WHOOPI GOLDBERG & HOLLYWOOD STARS LIKE GEORGE CLOONEY SHOULD PAY REPARATIONS TO KING KONG; MICHAEL JACKSON'S CHIMPANZEE BUBBLES & ALL THEIR FRIENDS & FAMILY THIS SELF-INDULGENT; FULL OF ITSELF MORON DIMWIT BEING A SENATOR IS WHY NEW JERSEY IS BECOMING BANGLADESH

NEW JERSEY SHOULD RECALL CORY BOOKER & UPGRADE HIM WITH

SENATOR BUBBLES (D NJ) NEW JERSEY'S LONG ROAD BACK STARTS WITH FIGURING OUT A WAY TO REPLACE HIM WITH BUBBLES HEY COREY; WILL YOU ACCUSE ME OF PLAYING THE MONKEY CARD?

Senator Cory Booker (D-N.J.) THE GENIUS WHO CAME UP WITH THE IDEA OF BABY BONDS FOR NEW BORN CHIMPANZEES & GIRAFFES; AND NOW GRANTING THEM ANIMAL PERSONHOOD CITIZENSHIP & VOTING RIGHTS FOR COCKROACHES UNDER HIS INSECTHOOD BILL; **makes his opening statement during the first day of the Supreme Court confirmation hearing for Judge Amy Coney Barrett before the Senate Judiciary Committee on Capitol Hill on October 12, 2020 in Washington, D.C** CORY BOOKER IS INTRODUCING A BILL MAKING IT A FEDERAL FELONY TO CAUSE PAIN & SUFFERING WHILE KILLING MOSQUITOS.

By Surya Gowda

Three Democrat senators have introduced a bill that would reform the U.S. Department of Agriculture and create a system of land grants to transfer millions of acres to Black farmers at no charge.

Sen. Cory Booker, D-N.J., the lead sponsor of the bill, tweeted **Tuesday, "I'm proud to team up with @ewarren and @SenGillibrand to introduce the Justice for Black Farmers Act. We need to balance the scales after decades of systemic racism within @USDA have harmed Black farmers."**

The bill was announced on Nov. 19 by Booker, Sen. Elizabeth Warren, D-Mass., and Sen. Kirsten Gillibrand, D-N.Y., and is set to be released on Nov. 30.

Booker told Mother Jones **the bill aims to reverse the "destructive forces that were unleashed upon Black farmers over the past century — one of the dark corners of shame in American history." A new USDA agency called the Equitable Land Access Service would buy agricultural land from willing sellers and "convey grants of that land to eligible Black individuals at no cost to the eligible Black individuals," the** bill states**.**

Through the race-based land transfer program, up to 32 million acres of land would be under Black ownership in a decade, which is seven times the amount currently in Black-owned farms, according to Agriculture.com**.**

The fund devotes $8 billion annually to the project and aims to make 20,000 grants each year of up to 160 acres through 2030.

Sen. Cotton says Biden's Cabinet picks signal return of Obama's 'disastrous' foreign policy

Cotton looks back at foreign policy decisions made during the Obama administration

By Talia Kaplan

Republicans retaining Senate control would 'put the brakes' on radical left-wing agenda: Sen. Cotton

President-elect Joe Biden's appointments appear to signal a «return of the Obama administration›s foreign policy," which "had disastrous consequences for our nation," Senate Armed Services Committee member Tom Cotton, **R-Ark., warned on "**Fox & Friends**" on Wednesday.**

Cotton, an Army combat veteran, made the comment two days after Biden announced a number of key Cabinet appointments, **including Antony Blinken as secretary of state, Alejandro Mayorkas as secretary of homeland security and Avril Haines to serve as the first woman to lead the intelligence community, among other positions.**

Describing his Cabinet appointments during an interview with "NBC Nightly News**" on Tuesday, Biden said, "This is not a third Obama term because we face a totally different world than we faced in the Obama-Biden administration." "President Trump has changed the landscape," the former vice president continued, before referencing the** president's foreign policy stance**. "It's become '**America First**,' which meant America alone."**

"We find ourselves in a position where our alliances are being frayed," Biden went on to say during the interview. "It's a totally different -- that's why I found people who joined the administration and key points that represent the spectrum of the American people as well as the spectrum of the Democratic Party."

In response, Cotton pointed to former President Barack Obama's memoir **"where he says a lot of these people were responsible, for instance, for advising him to go to** war in Libya**, a war that's now in its 10th year."**

He called the war "a 10-year after-party that's introduced civil war and slavery and unleashed a flood of migrants into Europe." "Look at ISIS**, the rise of ISIS happened after Barack Obama rushed us out of** Iraq**," Cotton said Wednesday.**

He also noted that Biden's appointments are from "the same group that said that you could never have a separate peace between Israel **and Arab nations without resolving the Palestinian question."**

BIDEN REACHES IN A GARBAGE CAN TO PICK BLINKEN, MAYORKAS, SULLIVAN FOR KEY CABINET POSITIONS

"There are so many peace deals that President Trump has brokered between Israel and Arab nations, it's hard to keep track of them," Cotton went on to note. Three Middle East peace deals have been brokered during the Trump administration. Late last month, Trump announced a peace deal that would normalize ties be-

tween Israel and Sudan **and claimed there "would be many more peace deals to come in the** Middle East."

The administration has already brokered peace agreements between Israel and the United Arab Emirates **and** Bahrain**.**

Cotton also brought up China **and comments made by** Jacob Sullivan**, Biden's pick to be America's next national security adviser.**

"People like Jake Sullivan **have said we should be** celebrating the rise of China,**" Cotton noted. "It was on the watch of so many of these nominees that China literally built islands out of the water in the** South China Sea and militarized them, far extending the reach of their missiles and aircraft and their ships."

Sullivan is a former top Hillary Clinton adviser who championed the ill-fated unraveling of Libya almost a decade ago.

He comes with a storied pedigree of foreign policy experience, having served as a senior policy adviser to Clinton's 2016 presidential election campaign, deputy chief of staff at the Department of State under the Obama administration and then-Vice President Biden's national security adviser, along with multiple degrees, fellowships and professor posts at Ivy League schools.

Blinken (FAMOUS PITCHMAN FOR GRECIAN FORMULA FOR GRAYING PUBIC HAIR HELLO IRAN; VENEZUELA; CHINA & CUBA; SLUMBER PARTY IN LINCOLN BEDROOM) has held senior foreign policy positions in two administrations over three decades, according to the Biden transition, and has advised Biden on foreign policy since 2002. During the Obama administration, Blinken served as deputy secretary of state and as a principal deputy national security adviser to former President Obama. During the first term of the Obama administration, Blinken served as Biden's national security adviser.

Mayorkas, the first Latino and immigrant nominated to serve as secretary of homeland security, served as the deputy secretary of homeland security in the Obama administration from 2013 to 2016 and director of U.S. Citizenship and Immigration Services from 2009 to 2013. During that time, Mayorkas led the implementation of DAC and led the department's response to Ebola and Zika.

Haines, if confirmed, would be the first woman to serve as DNI. Under the Obama administration, Haines served as a principal deputy national security adviser and as a deputy director at the CIA — she was the first woman to hold both of those positions.

Obama takes shot at evangelical Hispanics who voted for Trump despite 'racist' rhetoric

WHAT DO YOU EXPECT FROM THIS BARACK HUSSEIN OBAMA SCHMUCK?

Trump improved with Hispanic voters compared to 2016

By David Rutz

Former President Barack Obama took a shot Wednesday at some Hispanics who voted for President Donald Trump, saying they did not care about his «racist» remarks because of their alignment on social views.

"People were surprised about a lot of Hispanic folks who voted for Trump, but there's a lot of evangelical Hispanics who, the fact that Trump says racist things about Mexicans, or puts undocumented workers in cages, they think that's less important than the fact that he supports their views on gay marriage or abortion," he said on "The Breakfast Club" radio show.

Trump surprised political onlookers with his improved showing with Hispanic voters in 2020 from 2016, helping him to comfortable victories in states with significant Hispanic populations like Texas and Florida. His focus on working-class issues and stance against socialism was appealing to some Latinos, although a majority still voted for President-elect Joe Biden.

Nevertheless, the trend worried Democrats who assumed Trump›s strict immigration policies would alienate the demographic.

OBAMA ADMITS TO READING MARX ‹AS A STRATEGY FOR PICKING UP GIRLS›

Some critics attacked Obama for what they viewed as divisive comments, reminiscent of his 2008 reference to "bitter" working-class voters who "cling" to guns and religion. Others noted the "cages" he referred to from the Trump administration's family separation policy were built during his presidency.

Obama, who is promoting his latest memoir, "A Promised Land," said people who live in liberal cities like New York, Los Angeles, and Washington, D.C., often forget the country's enormous size and range of viewpoints.

Trump Wants 3rd Circuit to Halt Pennsylvania Certification

President Donald Trump's campaign on Monday asked a federal appeals court for permission to request an emergency injunction blocking Pennsylvania from certifying the election result while the campaign seeks to revise a lawsuit over mail-in ballots.

The filing in the U.S. Court of Appeals for the Third Circuit in Philadelphia signals that Trump hasn't given up his effort to block Pennsylvania from certifying his election loss, even though the state's 67 counties are required by law to certify their results by Monday evening.

Secretary of State Kathy Boockvar, a Democrat who is a defendant in the suit, could affirm statewide results swiftly after the counties certify their results.

The request is part of the campaign's appeal of a Saturday decision by U.S. District Judge Matthew Brann for denying its request to file a second revised complaint in the case. In the same decision, Brann dismissed the campaign's first amended complaint, saying it was far too short on evidence.

The appeals court earlier granted the campaign's request for expedited review and gave it a 4 p.m. deadline to file its initial brief in the case.

Trump's lawyers have repeatedly stated their strategy is to bring an election case before the U.S. Supreme Court, but the campaign's decision to appeal for the right to file a new complaint rather than reverse dismissal could delay the timetable for getting to the high court. If the appeal is successful, it would allow the campaign to file a revised complaint adding several claims, requiring more filings and a new hearing before Brann.

Brann eviscerated the Trump campaign's lawsuit in his ruling, calling it a "Frankenstein's Monster" that had been "haphazardly stitched together" and saying it made "strained legal arguments without merit and speculative accusations."

Chris Pandolfo

Attorney Sidney Powell announced Friday that the Donald Trump campaign legal team will possibly begin making public evidence from affidavits supporting their claims of a "national conspiracy" of voter fraud in the 2020 presidential election as soon as this weekend. Speaking to BlazeTV host Glenn Beck on the radio, Powell told Beck documents backing up allegations she made against voting system companies Smartmatic and Dominion in a press conference Thursday will be published online soon.

"We will start putting documents online and sending them to people like you, as soon as we possibly can," Powell said. "I would hope that we could start that by this weekend."

She described the volume of evidence her team has received as a "tsunami," though so far Trump's lawyers have held back most of what they claim to have.

"We've unearthed a global, criminal conspiracy that is just mind-blowing. And we've only scratched a tip of the iceberg," Powell asserted.

On Thursday, Powell and the other members of President Donald Trump's legal team alleged that communist Venezuela and George Soros interfered in the U.S. election through weaknesses in Dominion Voting Systems software. Trump's lawyers claim to be in possession of an affidavit from "one very strong witness" who will testify that technological insecurities in Dominion's voting machines made it possible for votes cast for Trump to be switched to former vice president Joe Biden.

This witness, Powell told Beck, "was sitting at [Venezuelan communist dictator] Hugo Chavez's right hand" and personally saw how Dominion's voting machines were manipulated to change the results of elections in the communist nation.

Dominion Voting Systems has categorically denied "false assertions about vote switching and software issues with our voting systems."

"Dominion has no company ownership relationships with the Pelosi family, Feinstein family, Clinton Global Initiative, Smartmatic, Scytl, or any ties to Venezuela," the company said in a statement.

Justice Alito 'Tolerance for 72 MILLION MAKE AMERICA GREAT AGAIN Opposing Views Is Now in Short Supply'

By Jeffrey Rodack

Supreme Court Justice Samuel Alito warned that the pandemic has sparked "unimaginable" restrictions on civil liberties.

Trump to NY Post: Election 'Greatest Theft in The History of America'

President Donald Trump appears to be nowhere close to conceding the presidential election to former Vice President Joe Biden, according to a new interview in The New York Post. **But on Sunday,** Trump tweeted "he won," apparently in reference to Biden.

"He won because the Election was Rigged," Trump wrote on Twitter.

"NO VOTE WATCHERS OR OBSERVERS

allowed, vote tabulated by a Radical Left privately owned company, Dominion, with a bad reputation & bum equipment that couldn't even qualify for Texas (which I won by a lot!), the Fake & Silent Media, & more!"

In a story published Saturday night, Trump told Post columnist Michael Goodwin that the election"was stolen." "It was a rigged election, 100 %, and everyone knows it," Trump said in the Friday night interview. "It's going to be that I got about 74 million votes, and I lost? It's not possible."

When Goodwin asks if he'll ever concede, Trump responded: **"We'll see how it turns out." he said at one point.**

"When I asked if he could come to terms with defeat, he responded only that 'it's hard to come to terms when they won't let your poll watchers in to observe' the counting," Goodwin writes. "A third time, he said, 'Again, I can't tell you what's going to happen.'

Goodwin writes that Trump seems convinced that Biden's victory was corruptly engineered by Dominion Voting Systems, a technology used by most states, including Michigan and Georgia. Trump repeatedly cited Dominion, according to Goodwin.

The News That Biden Voters Didn't Know

Tim Graham

Journalists have strongly slanted the "news" during the Trump era in order to destroy Donald Trump's presidency, and to destroy it early if possible. Their actions betray that they feel they have important and influential platforms from which they can and should run America in between elections. The voters can have a say for about two weeks every two years.

Recall 2004, when Newsweek's Evan Thomas admitted the press would go all in for Democratic presidential and vice presidential nominees John Kerry and John Edwards, and that the effort would "be worth maybe 15 points." That wasn't enough in 2004. But what about in elections decided by 3 or 4 points? The media felt robbed in 2016 because they had tried so hard. And then they never let up. The president's being infected with coronavirus didn't even cause them to stop beating their war drums for a moment.

In this election, it wasn't just the reporting power of the news media but the censorship power of Big Tech that could be credited with shaping the election. Fox News' Tucker Carlson said that "Democrats harnessed the power of Big Tech to win this election."

In his partisan nightly newsletter, CNN's Brian Stelter mocked Carlson: "These are Jell-O arguments, all about emotion. But I suspect that this will be the go-to position for many GOP media stars: Trump was robbed, thus we were robbed -- no, we can't prove it, but we know it in our guts."

This is not an emotional argument. You can watch the difference between CNN reporters at President Trump's press conferences and CNN reporters at President-elect Joe Biden's press events. It's the difference between rabid tigers and domesticated kittens.A new Media Research Center poll of 1,750 voters in seven swing states, conducted by The Polling Company, demonstrates how the suppression of news that was potentially damaging to Biden was successful: -- Forty-five % of Biden voters were unaware of the financial scandals of Hunter Biden, which were wrapped up in then-Vice President Joe Biden's foreign-affairs power during Barack Obama's presidency.

-- Thirty-five % of Biden voters were unaware of Tara Reade's allegation that Biden sexually assaulted her on Capitol Hill when she worked for him.

-- Twenty-five % of Biden voters said they didn't know about Sen. Kamala Harris' left-wing ideology, that she was ranked America's most "progressive" senator in 2019. The media also suppressed good news on President Trump's record:

-- Forty-nine & of Biden voters had no idea economic growth surged by 33% in the third quarter of 2020, which would be unheard of if not for the extraordinary pandemic lockdown during the second quarter.

-- The five preelection jobs reports from June 5 to Oct. 2 showed a record 11.1 million jobs were created in the summer and fall. But 39.4% of Biden voters said they didn't know about this good news.-- Fifty-one % of Biden voters did not know that in 2018, the U.S. became a net exporter of oil for the first time in nearly 70 years.

-- Forty-four & of Biden voters had no idea that Trump's team had helped broker historic agreements between Israel and Arab nations.

-- Thirty-six % of Biden voters said they did not know about the administration's key role in promoting coronavirus vaccine research through Operation Warp Speed.

In every case, Biden voters said they might not have been Biden voters if the "news" media had done their job and reported all the news, rather than burying stories that didn't match their manipulative narratives. One of every 6 Biden voters we surveyed (17%) said they would have abandoned the Democratic candidate had they known the facts about one or more of these news stories. This would have swung the swing states the other way. That's why the media hit the Mute button.

Seven Letter Poll: 79 % of Trump Voters Say Election 'Stolen'

A majority of President Donald Trump voters say the election was stolen from the president and they would like to see him run again in 2024 if Joe Biden is ultimately declared the next president, the Washington Examiner reports.

According to a new survey released Monday from communications and messaging firm Seven Letter, 79% of Trump backers think the Democrats stole the election through voter fraud. It also found 66% of Trump voters want the president to run again in four years.

"Sixty-six % of GOP voters think President Trump should run again for president in 2024," the survey says. "Provided a list of potential candidates, Trump leads the 2024 field among Republican voters, with 35%. He's trailed by Vice President Mike Pence (19%), Donald Trump Jr. (11%), Amb. Nikki Haley (7%), and Sen. Ted Cruz (6%)."

The survey was the first conducted by Seven Letter Insight, a public opinion and messaging research firm. Seven Letter Insight is led by Matt George, founder and president of Matt George Associates, and a former partner at Luntz Global Partners.

The survey sampled 1,500 Americans from Nov. 10-19.

Rep. Barry Loudermilk to Newsmax TV: Ga. Needs 'Deeper Forensic Audit'

By Eric Mack

Georgia's second recount must be a "deeper forensic audit' into potential voter fraud, particularly with the Jan. 5 Senate runoffs looming, according to Rep. Barry Loudermilk, R-Ga., on Newsmax TV.

"There has to be a deeper forensic audit done," Loudermilk told Monday's "Stinchfield.**"**

"What the Secretary of State is saying is we've already verified the signatures and we've separated the ballots from the envelopes. You still have to verify that people who are voting are people that should be voting.

"Whether you can discount their ballot or not in the last election, we need to know, if it's people who voted illegally, that they don't do it again in this runoff."

Added to the confusion of the current recount, the contested presidential election, and the upcoming Senate runoffs for the seats of Sens. David Perdue, R-Ga., and Kelly Loeffler, R-Ga., liberal activists have pushed for people to move to the state of Georgia to become eligible to vote for Democrat challengers Jon Ossoff and

Rev. Raphael Warnock.

Regardless, the fraud needs to be rooted out of Georgia, Loudermilk told host Grant Stinchfield.

"I believe there was fraud in this election," Loudermilk said. "People say, 'give us the evidence.' Well, you have to investigate to get to the evidence. We have a lot of circumstantial evidence. I mean, if you look in Georgia, Republicans won up and down the ballot, except for the presidential and the Senate race.

"Tell me how that has happened – when we Republicans held the House and the Senate. We made great gains in Georgia.

"A lot of interesting things will come out of this election, but we have to continue to fight to make sure future elections are trustworthy, that they have integrity."

Georgia will conduct another presidential vote recount despite already officially certifying results

A hand recount affirmed Joe Biden's win in the Peach State

Chris Enloe

Georgia will conduct another recount of its presidential election results after a request from President Donald Trump's campaign, Axios reported.

The development comes despite the fact that Georgia has already certified its election results, which happened after Georgia Secretary of State Brad Raffensperger (R) conducted an entire hand recount of the state's presidential election results.

The hand recount affirmed Georgia's results and Joe Biden's victory in the Peace State. The Associated Press reported, "No individual county showed a variation in margin larger than 0.73%, and the variation in margin in 103 of the state's 159 counties was less than 0.05%, a memo released with the results says."

Following the hand recount, Gov. Brian Kemp (R) certified the election results late Friday.

Why a recount now?

Despite the certification, Georgia officials said Trump's campaign could request another recount because the final margin between Trump and Biden was less than 0.5%.

On Saturday, the Trump campaign hand-delivered a letter to the state secretary of state's office asking for another recount, the AP reported.

"Today, the Trump campaign filed a petition for recount in Georgia. We are focused on ensuring that every aspect of Georgia State Law and the U.S. Constitution are followed so that every legal vote is counted. President Trump and his campaign continue to insist on an honest recount in Georgia, which has to include signature matching and other vital safeguards," Trump's team said. In response, Raffensperger asked his deputy to prepare county officials for the recount, emphasizing a transparent process.

"This will be highly scrutinized so emphasize to the counties the importance of transparency and accuracy of the process," Raffensperger said.

The recount will be done using scanners that read and tabulate the votes. County election workers have already done a complete hand recount of all the votes cast in the presidential race. But that stemmed from a mandatory audit requirement and isn't considered an official recount under the law. State law requires that one race be audited by hand to ensure that the machines counted the ballots accurately, and Raffensperger selected the presidential race. Because of the tight margin in that race, a full hand count of ballots was necessary to complete the audit, he said.

Anything else?

With few exceptions, nearly every legal maneuver by Trump's campaign to challenge the close election results have been dismissed by judges, tossed from court, or withdrawn by the campaign.

Blackwell: The Greatest Electoral Heist in American History

Ken Blackwell

The pieces are finally coming together, and they reveal a masterpiece of electoral larceny involving Big Tech oligarchs, activists, and government officials who prioritize partisanship over patriotism.

The 2020 election was stolen because leftists were able to exploit the coronavirus pandemic to weaken, alter, and eliminate laws that were put in place over the course of decades to preserve the integrity of the ballot box. But just as importantly, it was stolen because those same leftists had a thoroughly-crafted plan, and because they were rigorous in its implementation and ruthless in its execution.

Let's not forget that liberals have been consumed by a fixation with removing Donald Trump from office for longer than he's actually been in office. The sordid story of the 2020 election heist begins all the way back in January 2017, when Barack Obama's former campaign manager and senior advisor, David Plouffe, took a job leading the policy and advocacy efforts of the Chan Zuckerberg Initiative, a "charitable" organization established by Facebook founder Mark Zuckerberg and his wife, Priscilla Chan.

Earlier this year, just as it was becoming clear that Joe Biden would be the Democratic Party's nominee for president, Plouffe published a book outlining his vision for the Democrats' roadmap to victory in 2020, which involved a "block by block" effort to turn out voters in key Democratic strongholds in the swing states that would ultimately decide the election, such as Philadelphia, Milwaukee, Detroit, and Minneapolis.

The book was titled, *A Citizen's Guide to Defeating Donald Trump*, and it turned out that the citizen Plouffe had in mind was none other than his former boss, Mark Zuckerberg. Although Plouffe no longer officially managed Zuckerberg's policy and advocacy efforts at that point, the political operative's influence evidently remained a powerful force.

Thanks to the extensive efforts of investigators and attorneys for the Amistad Project of the nonpartisan Thomas More Society, who have been following Zuckerberg's money for the past 18 months, it is still possible to expose the inner workings of this heist in time to stop it. Perhaps even more importantly, these unsung heroes of American democracy are dedicated to making sure that such a travesty will not become a permanent feature of our elections.

Under the pretext of assisting election officials conduct "safe and secure" elections in the age of COVID, Zuckerberg donated $400 million — as much money as Congress appropriated for the same general purpose — to nonprofit organizations founded and run by left-wing activists. The primary recipient was the Center for Tech and Civic Life (CTCL), which received the staggering sum of $350 million. Prior to Zuckerberg's donations, CTCL's annual operating expenses averaged less than $1 million per year. How was Zuckerberg even *aware* of such a small-potatoes operation, and why did he entrust it with ⅞ of the money he was pouring into this election cycle, despite the fact that it had no prior experience handling such a massive amount of money?

Predictably, given the partisan background of its leading officers, CTCL proceeded to distribute Zuckerberg's funds to left-leaning counties in battleground states. The vast majority of the money handed out by CTCL — especially in the early days of its largesse — went to counties that voted overwhelmingly for Hillary Clinton in 2016. Some of the biggest recipients, in fact, were the very locales Plouffe had identified as the linchpins

of the Democrat strategy in 2020. Zuckerberg and CTCL left nothing to chance, however, writing detailed conditions into their grants that dictated exactly how elections were to be conducted, down to the number of ballot drop boxes and polling places. The Constitution gives state lawmakers sole authority for managing elections, but these grants put private interests firmly in control.

Amistad Project lawyers tried to prevent this unlawful collusion by filing a flurry of lawsuits in eight states prior to Election Day. Unfortunately, judges were forced to put those lawsuits aside without consideration of their merits because the plaintiffs had not yet suffered "concrete harm" in the form of fraudulent election results. The law had no remedy to offer because the left's lawless schemes had not yet reached fruition.

In the meantime, CTCL continued splashing Zuckerberg's cash — only now, the organization was intent on finding Republican-leaning jurisdictions to give its donations a veneer of bipartisanship. Of course, the number of votes in play in those counties paled in comparison to those in the liberal counties. Philadelphia County alone, for instance, projected that the $10 million grant it received from CTCL would enable it to increase turnout by 25-30 % — translating to well over 200,000 votes.

The left didn't put all of its eggs into the CTCL basket, though. High-ranking state officials simultaneously took significant steps to weaken ballot security protocols, acting on their own authority without permission or concurrence from the state legislatures that enshrined those protections in the law.

In Wisconsin, Democrat Secretary of State Doug La Follette THIS GUY MUST BE ELECTROCUTED IMMEDIATELY WITH ALL OF THESE VOTES DISQUALIFIED allowed voters to claim "indefinite confinement" in order to avoid having to provide a photocopy of their ID when requesting an absentee ballot.

The exemption was intended for legitimate invalids, THIS STOLE WISCONSIN FOR BIDEN

but COVID offered a convenient excuse for circumventing the law, despite the fact that Wisconsin had no pandemic-related lockdown rules that would have rendered anyone "indefinitely confined." The impact was far-reaching. About 240,000 voters claimed the exemption in 2020, compared to just 70,000 in 2016.

In Michigan, Democrat Secretary of State Jocelyn Benson unilaterally voided the legal requirement that voters provide a signature when requesting an absentee ballot, establishing an online request form. She then took things a step further by announcing that she would "allow civic groups and other organizations running voter registration drives to register voters through the state's online registration website," granting partisan groups such as Rock The Vote direct access to Michigan's voter rolls.

In Pennsylvania, election officials in heavily-Democratic counties that received CTCL funding allowed flawed mail-in ballots to be "cured" — that is, altered or replaced — prior to Election Day. In other counties, officials rightly interpreted this as a flagrant violation of state law. On the night before Election Day, less than 24 hours before polls were due to close, Democrat Secretary of State Kathy Boockvar sought to imbue this illegal practice with the appearance of validity by issuing a statement authorizing counties to contact voters who had cast improper ballots. Even if Boockvar had the statutory authority to do this, which she did not, the timing of her memo made it impossible for rural counties to take advantage of it to nearly the same extent as urban counties.

In numerous states, officials also absurdly consolidated the vote-counting and ballot-curing process in sporting arenas and other large venues, rather than the ward- and precinct-level offices that normally handle the job. This made absolutely no sense as a pandemic-related safety measure, but that didn't stop the officials from citing COVID as their rationale.

Consolidating the vote-counting tied the other efforts together. Instead of a manageable number of ballots being transported to small offices and counted in the immediate presence of observers from both parties, truckloads of ballots were brought to a single location, inevitably resulting in confusion and commingling of ballots from various sources. Securing those ballots from the time they left voters' hands to the time they were officially counted should have been the top priority of election workers, but it's not even clear whether there were logs kept identifying which ballots were delivered by which trucks and when. If such logs even exist, they have not been disclosed.

At the same time, election officials could claim that they were adhering to legal requirements that observers be "in the room" during the counting process while using COVID as an excuse for relegating those observers to the "penalty box," far from the actual counting and curing.

This was particularly egregious when it came to ballot "curing," a process that actually involves election workers filling out brand new ballots on behalf of voters whose ballots purportedly could not be read by machine. This could have been due to something the voter themselves did, such as spilling coffee on the ballot. It also could have been due to something that election workers themselves did, such as crumpling ballots to prevent the machines from receiving them, just as a vending machine rejects crumpled bills.

It's impossible to know exactly what happened, because Republican observers were denied meaningful access to the process — and in some cases literally locked out of the counting rooms while election workers obscured the windows with cardboard.

These election workers, it should be noted, were paid directly by CTCL's grants. **These supposedly impartial arbiters of our electoral process are supposed to work for the people, but they were on Zuckerberg's payroll.**

All of this sounds like the stuff of fiction — the sort of thing one would expect from a cinematic thriller or a spy novel. Sadly, it's the reality that our country is faced with after years of placidity in the face of increasingly aggressive intervention into our electoral process on the part of Big Tech oligarchs and activists with deep pockets and shallow motivations.

Ken Blackwell, former Secretary of State of Ohio, is the Distinguished Fellow for Human Rights and Constitutional Governance, at the Family Research Council. He served as United States Ambassador to the United Nations Human Rights Commission from 1990-1993.

GOP-controlled legislatures in Pennsylvania, Arizona, and Michigan plan to hold public hearings about the election results, Trump team says

'The only way to do this is with public hearings'

Photo (left): Tom Williams/CQ-Roll Call, Inc via Getty Images; Photo (right): Al Drago/Bloomberg via Getty Images

Carlos Garcia

An attorney on the legal team for President Donald Trump said that three key states are going to hold special hearings on the certitude of the presidential election results.

POLL: Who is the most corrupt?

Jenna Ellis of the Trump legal team released a statement **outlining what the hearings from states with Republican-controlled legislatures would entail.**

"The first hearing, held by the Pennsylvania State Senate, will be conducted tomorrow, Wednesday, November 25th, in Gettysburg, PA, where each participating Senator will give a five-minute opening statement followed by testimony from witnesses who have filed affidavits attesting to 2020 election fraud," read the statement.

The Wednesday hearing would also including a presentation from former New York City Mayor Rudy Giuliani, who is also representing the president.

"It's in everyone's interest to have a full vetting of election irregularities and fraud," Giuliani said. "And the only way to do this is with public hearings, complete with witnesses, videos, pictures and other evidence of illegalities from the November 3rd election."

The statement said that Arizona was scheduled to have its public hearing on the election results on Monday, Nov. 30, and Michigan is set to have a public hearing on Tuesday, Dec. 1.

Most mainstream media outlets have declared **former Vice President Joe Biden the victor of the presidential election based on projections from local vote counts, but the president has** refused **to concede pending the**

outcome of his legal challenges. The statement added that state legislatures are granted sole authority over their electors, according to Article 2, Section 1.2 of the United States Constitution.

The legal team made headlines recently when Giuliani released a statement clarifying that Sidney Powell was acting on her own behalf and was not on their legal team despite having had her speak at a media briefing Thursday about the election results. Powell has claimed that she has evidence of a massive election scam that stole the election from Trump, who she says won "in a landslide."

Wayne County GOP members rescind votes to certify election, claim Dems 'bullied' them

'The comments made accusations of racism and threatened me and members of my family'

By Edmund DeMarche

Michigan GOP canvassers reportedly rescind votes to certify results

Board members in Wayne County reverse course after secretary of state says audit request non-binding; Kevin Corke reports

The two Republicans on Michigan's Wayne County Board of Canvassers claimed in signed affidavits Wednesday that they were bullied into siding with Democrats and have now rescinded their votes to certify.

The two Republicans -- Monica Palmer and William C. Hartmann -- were involved in a brief deadlock in the county's election certification process Tuesday before initially voting to certify.

Wayne County, which includes Detroit, is Michigan's most populous county, with more than 1.7 million residents.

Both Republicans say they were called racists and subjected to threats for raising concerns about ballots that Democrats said were from predominately Black communities, Jenna Ellis, a lawyer for the Trump 2020 Campaign, told Fox News on Tuesday.

SEAN HANNITY BLASTS ZOOM CALLERS OVER 'TRULY VILE SMEARS' DIRECTED AT MICHIGAN GOP COUNTY CANVASSERS

Hartmann said in the affidavit that he observed about 71% of Detroit's 134 Absent Voter Counting Boards "were left unbalanced and many unexplained."

He said he voiced his concerns and said if the votes did not match, there should have been some kind of explanation. Powell said she spotted the same discrepancy.

"I voted not to certify, and I still believe this vote should not be certified. Until these questions are addressed, I remain opposed to certification of the Wayne County results," Hartmann said in his affidavit, according to JustTheNews, which was first to report on their decision to rescind.

Palmer said in her affidavit that she faced "accusations of racism" and threats to her family.

"After the vote, my Democratic colleagues chided me and Mr. Hartmann for voting not to certify," she said, according to the affidavit obtained by Fox News. "After the vote, the public comment period began and dozens of people made personal remarks against me and Mr. Hartmann. The comments made accusations of racism and threatened me and members of my family. The public comment continued for over two hours and I felt pressured to continue the meeting without a break."

Neither Palmer nor Hartmann could be reached for further comment by Fox News late Wednesday.

The pair said state officials indicated they would not honor an earlier compromise to audit the ballots, which contributed to their decision to rescind. It was unclear if their decision to rescind could change their earlier vote to certify.

Sidney Powell: Tucker Carlson 'Insulting, Demanding, and Rude'

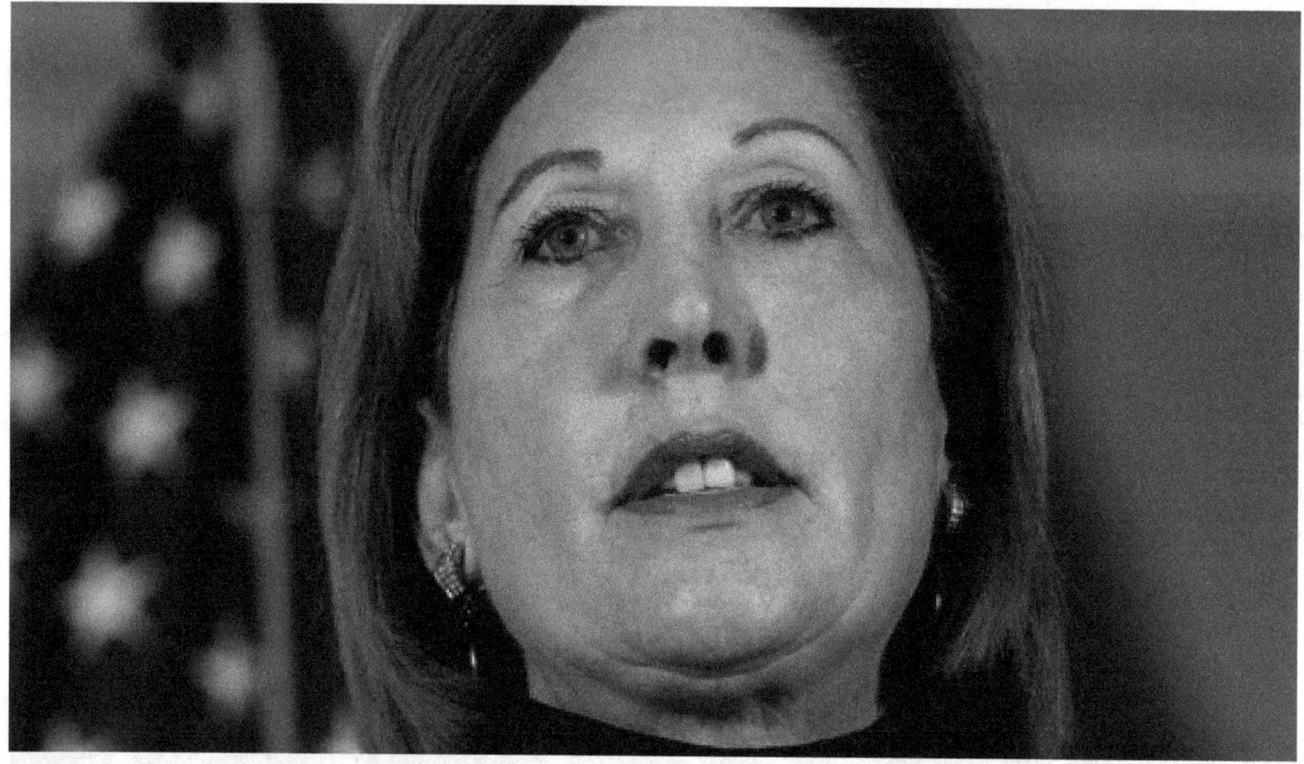

Attorney Sidney Powell speaks to the press about various lawsuits related to the 2020 election, inside the Republican National Committee headquarters on November 19, 2020 in Washington, DC. (Drew

By Sandy Fitzgerald

Trump campaign attorney Sidney Powell, during an appearance on Fox Business Friday morning, slammed Fox News prime time host Tucker Carlson as being "insulting, demanding, and rude" after he called her out for not presenting evidence for her claims that Communist countries were behind voting software that she said threw votes from President Donald Trump to Joe Biden.

"I didn't get angry with the request to provide evidence," Powell told Fox Business' Maria Bartiromo. "In fact, I sent an affidavit to Tucker that I had not even attached to a pleading yet to help him understand the situation, and I offered him another witness who could explain the math and the statistical evidence far better than I can. I'm not really a numbers person." Carlson, Powell said, was "insulting, demanding, and rude, and I told him not to contact me again, in those terms."

Powell, during a Thursday afternoon news conference with Rudy Giuliani and Jenna Ellis, claimed that countries like Cuba, China, and Venezuela were behind Dominion Voting Systems, the company behind the voting machines. Dominion has strongly denied any such connection.

"Sidney Powell has been saying similar things for days. On Sunday night, we texted her after watching one of her segments. What Powell was describing would amount to the single greatest crime in American history," Carlson said on his program Thursday night. "Millions of votes stolen in the day. Democracy destroyed, the end of our centuries-old system of self-government, not a small thing."

He added that the show invited her onto the program, where "we would've given her the whole hour, we would've given her the entire week actually and listened quietly the whole time at rapt attention."

But, Carlson claimed Powell "never sent us any evidence, despite a lot of requests, polite requests, not a page. When we kept pressing, she got angry and told us to stop contacting her. When we checked with others around the Trump campaign, people with positions of authority, they told us Powell has never given them any evidenc

They had been praised by Republicans -- including President Trump -- for standing up to brutal personal attacks from Democrats who called them racists during a live Zoom meeting.

McEnany: Trump's path to victory is Supreme Court, exposing 'systemic' voter fraud

By Joshua Q. Nelson

Kayleigh McEnany on the Trump legal team strategy post-election

The path to challenging "systemic voter fraud" during the 2020 presidential election **is through the courts,** Trump **campaign adviser Kayleigh McEnany said Saturday.**

While no evidence of such a scheme has been presented in court, McEnany, who also serves as White House press secretary, doubled down on the allegations and accused the news media of being complicit.

"We have 234 affidavits in Michigan, of voters in one county saying this is what I observed. We have voters in Pennsylvania saying 'I showed up to vote, was told I couldn't cast my ballot because there is a mail-in ballot that was cast on my behalf that wasn't cast by me,'" McEnany said on "Fox & Friends Weekend.»

McEnany said "real systematic claims" exist and will be brought before judges.

"Our justice system is where that will play, and that is something that the media cannot get in the way of. **They can try to hide it, but the American people are smart. The 73 million people who showed up to vote for this president -- the most-ever votes for a sitting president -- they have a voice. We will be heard.**

"The Tea Party movement made their voice heard, the Trump movement is now making our voice heard, and, again, we don't need the media by our side, we can do it without them," McEnany said.

GIULIANI PRESSES TRUMP ELECTION CHALLENGE CASE IN FIERY NEWS CONFERENCE WITH LEGAL TEAM

President Trump**'s personal attorney** Rudy Giuliani alleged widespread voter fraud during a news conference Thursday but provided no evidence of such a scheme.

In court so far, the Truimp campaign has primarily focused on the validity of ballots and counts without asserting fraud.

"We've got to continue fighting this, and the federal courts are the path and, hopefully, up to the Supreme Court, " McEnany said, "because voter fraud is real, and they seized on a pandemic and created an electoral epidemic -- one that was inexcusable, a system that should never have happened."

THE REPUBLICAN RACE CARD BE IS CRITICIZING BLOODS & CRIPS DRIVE-BY MURDERS & O.J. SIMPSON BE WUZ OFFING IN COLD BLOOD HIS OLD LADY

Ned Staebler, chief executive of TechTown, who, according to the New York Times**, is a poll challenger at the TCF Center in Detroit, said in the viral Zoom meeting, "The Trump stain, the stain of racism that you, Wil-**

liam Hartmann and Monica Palmer, have covered yourself in, is going to follow you throughout history."

He said the two would "forever be known in southeastern Michigan as two racists who did something so unprecedented that they disenfranchised hundreds of thousands of Black voters in the city of Detroit."

Joe Biden defeated Trump in Wayne County, a Democratic stronghold, by more than a 2-1 margin and won Michigan by 146,000 votes, according to unofficial results.

Ellis said in an interview with "Fox News @ Night" that President Trump is focused on making sure that every legal vote is counted and every illegal vote is tossed.

Boris Epshteyn to Newsmax TV: Stand By on Dominion Software

By Brian Trusdell

Strategic adviser for the Trump campaign Boris Epshteyn says evidence is being gathered on the Dominion Voting Systems Corp. software used to tally ballots in several states where election results are being disputed and told supporters of the president to "stand by."

"Dominion is used in almost 30 states across the country and pretty much every battleground," Epshteyn said on Newsmax TV's "The Chris Salcedo Show" on Wednesday. "In the state of Arizona, where I spent time after the election overseeing some of the process that's going on there from our perspective – the Trump campaign's perspective, Dominion's system is used only in Maricopa County. "But guess what, Maricopa is the largest county in Arizona and accounts for about 70% of the vote in the state of Arizona. So, we have to get to the bottom of the Dominion issue, figure out what's going on, and if the system is switching votes, well that throws everything into chaos."

Former U.S. District Attorney Sidney Powell, who represents President Donald Trump's former National Security Adviser Michael Flynn, charged on Tuesday on Newsmax TV that she has been collecting evidence to challenge the results of states using Dominion, which she said was created to allow for the rigging of elections. She said a former Venezuelan military officer now living in the United States has signed an affidavit of overseeing rigging elections in his native country for Hugo Chavez.

"I would tell folks to stand by," Epshteyn said. "We are working to get to the bottom of that issue and as soon as we have more information, it will be forthcoming. I know Sidney Powell has been out there talking about it a lot. And she'll continue to do so."

ANOTHER MISTAKE? Georgia GOP Says They Discovered 9,626 Vote Error

The chairman of the Georgia Republican Party said one of their monitors discovered a 9,626 vote error in the

DeKalb County hand count. "One of our monitors discovered a 9,626 vote error in the DeKalb County hand count. One batch was labeled 10,707 for Biden and 13 for Trump – an improbable margin even by DeKalb standards," GOP Chair David Shafer wrote in a series of Twitter messages. "The actual count for the batch was 1,081 for Biden and 13 for Trump.

Shafer pointed out that had this counting error not been discovered, Biden would have gained enough votes from this one batch alone to cancel out Trump's gains from Fayette, Floyd and Walton. "Our attorneys have turned over an affidavit from our monitor to the Secretary of State and requested an investigation," he said.

There's been no comment from DeKalb County election workers or the Georgia Secretary of State's office.
EDITOR'S NOTE: Social media is cracking down on Conservative content. Many of you have complained that you never see our content in your news feeds. There's only one way to fight back — and that's by subscribing to my FREE weekly newsletter. Click here.

One of our monitors discovered a 9,626 vote error in the DeKalb County hand count. One batch was labeled 10,707 for Biden and 13 for Trump – an improbable margin even by DeKalb standards. The actual count

Fox News Sunday morning host Maria Bartiromo made a stunning revelation during an interview with renowned lawyer Sidney Powell. Bartiromo shared the following about the firm that runs the application used in Michigan where thousands of Trump votes were switched to Joe Biden

Maria Bartiromo: I've also seen reports that Nancy Pelosi's longtime Chief of Staff is a key executive of that

company. Richard Bloom, Senator Feinstein's husband is a significant shareholder of this company. Nancy Pelosi's chief of staff is CEO of Dominion Voting Systems Mentioned during a Fox News interview by host Maria Bartiromo were Nadeam Elshami, House Speaker Nancy Pelosi's former chief of staff who last year became a lobbyist for Dominion, and Richard Blum, California Sen. Dianne Feinstein's husband, who she said is a significant shareholder in the company.

"They have invested in it for their own reasons and are using it to commit this fraud to steal votes. I think they've even stolen them from other Democrats in their own party who should be outraged about this also," Powell said. The attorney also suggested that Dominion had a hand in tilting the primaries in Joe Biden's favor. "Bernie Sanders might very well have been the democratic candidate but they've stolen against whoever they wanted to steal it from," Powell said. Dominion did not immediately return a request for comment on Powell's claims.

The company, which has a lock on a third of the voting machine market according to ***Bloomberg*, has faced scrutiny in the past couple of days with voting problems reported in parts of Michigan** and **Georgia, although the company and local officials have discounted the idea that the software was to blame. Dominion has customers in 28 states** and Puerto Rico, including all of the battleground states where Trump and his allies are contesting and pinning their hopes on recounts after media outlets called the presidential race for Biden.

Diane Feinstein's husband is a major shareholder (they also have an executive who is a Chinese citizen)!! This same voting system was fully compromised at a hacking competition at a conference in 2019! Will this be part of president trump's legal team's argument against the validity of the 2020 election? This is a proof-positive conflict of interest.

Sidney Powell claims her investigative team has identified 450,000 ballots in battleground states that cast a vote only for Biden, with no other candidates voted down the ticket.

Here are two key clips from this bombshell interview

Sidney Powell is an impressive resume

Sidney Powell started her career as an Assistant United States Attorney in the **Western District of Texas** and later worked in the **Eastern District of Virginia. At one point she was the president of the American Academy of Appellate Lawyers as well as the Bar Association of the Fifth Federal Circuit.**

Sidney also has her own firm called Sidney Powell, P.C. that she opened in 1992. Her practice specializes in complex litigation, having dealt with $3 billion dollar asbestos cases, international aerospace contract issues, **employment discrimination** cases and everything in between.

Sidney was the form president and founder of The Genesis Alliance, an all-volunteer non-profit women's shelter. She was also the past president of the American Academy of Appellate Lawyers and the Bar Association of the Fifth Federal Circuit.

DOMINION IS MUCH MORE THAN STEALING VOTES. DOMINION IS A 1913 U.S ESPIONAGE ACT CAPITAL CRIME PUNISHABLE BY DEATH

Second Georgia County Finds Previously Uncounted Votes

A second Georgia county has uncovered a trove of votes not previously included in election results, but the additional votes won't change the overall outcome of the presidential race, the secretary of state's office said Tuesday. A memory card that hadn't been uploaded in Fayette County, just south of Atlanta, was discovered during a hand tally of the votes in the presidential race that stems from part of a legally mandated audit to ensure the new election machines counted the votes accurately, said Gabriel Sterling, a top official in the secretary of state's office.

The memory card's 2,755 votes are not enough to flip the lead in the state from Democrat Joe Biden to Republican President Donald Trump. The breakdown of the uncounted ballots was 1,577 for Trump, 1,128 for Biden, 43 for Libertarian Jo Jorgensen and seven write-ins, Sterling said.

Election officials on Monday said Floyd County, in north Georgia, had found more than 2,500 ballots that hadn't been previously scanned.

Both counties will have to recertify their results, and the margin between Trump and Biden will be about 13,000 votes when those previously uncounted votes are accounted for, Sterling said.

County elections workers have been working on the hand tally since Friday. State law leaves it up to the secretary of state to choose which race to audit. Secretary of State Brad Raffensperger selected the presidential

race and said the tight margin meant the audit would require a full hand recount.

The counties have until 11:59 p.m. Wednesday to complete the hand count. The secretary of state's office originally said the results of the hand tally would be certified. But Sterling said Tuesday that the state would instead certify the results certified by the counties.

Once the results are certified, if the margin between the candidates remains within 0.5%, the losing campaign can request a recount. That would be done using scanners that read and tally the votes and would be paid for by the state, Raffensperger has said.

State election officials have consistently defended the integrity of Georgia's vote count and have said the audit is expected to affirm the results. They have conceded that there may be wrongdoing — people who vote twice or people who vote despite not being eligible — and have pledged to investigate any cases.

"We have not seen widespread voter fraud," Sterling said. "We do know there's going to be illegal voting, but it's going to be down in the low hundreds, not in the 12,929 range."

The Associated Press has not declared a winner in Georgia, where Biden leads Trump by 0.3 % points. There is no mandatory recount law in Georgia, but state law provides that option to a trailing candidate if the margin is less than 0.5 % points. It is AP's practice not to call a race that is - or is likely to become - subject to a recount.

Also on Tuesday, Raffensperger announced that a random audit of a sample of Georgia's new voting machines found no evidence of hacking or tampering.

Raffensperger last week asked Pro V&V, an Alabama-based testing laboratory, to do the audit, his office said in a news release. The company "found no evidence of the machines being tampered."

"We are glad but not surprised that the audit of the state's voting machines was an unqualified success," Raffensperger said in the release.

The new election system the state bought last year from Dominion Voting Systems for more than $100 million includes touchscreen voting machines that print paper ballots that are read and tabulated by scanners.

The audit was done on a random sample of voting machines from Cobb, Douglas, Floyd, Morgan, Paulding and Spalding counties. The equipment tested included the touchscreen voting machines, precinct scanners and absentee ballot scanners.

The company took the software and firmware out of the equipment to check that the only software and firmware present was that certified for use by the secretary of state's office, the release says.

Pro V&V is a voting system test laboratory that is certified by the U.S. Election Assistance Commission, which sets voluntary guidelines for election management and certification.

Dick Morris to Newsmax TV: 'Georgia May Well Be Overturned'

By Theodore Bunker

Political strategist Dick Morris told Newsmax TV on Wednesday that "Georgia may well be overturned," by the courts in the 2020 election.

"Georgia may well be overturned, not just because the three counties where they forgot to input the results into the machine, but also because of people who are voting who are probably dead and people who are not registered," Morris told "American Agenda."

He added, "The problem in Georgia is that the state will not give us the list of people who voted. And they have that and will not turn it over to us. And we need that list to be able to call those people and find out if a they're alive and see if they actually voted."

Georgia election officials have until midnight on Wednesday to complete their audit of the presidential election in the state, in which Joe Biden leads President Donald Trump.

Dick Morris to Newsmax TV: Dominion Needs to Be Investigated

By Eric Mack

In a signal where President Donald Trump's legal focus is right now, presidential political strategist Dick Morris on Newsmax TV wagged a skeptical finger at Dominion Voting Systems.

"Something clearly is amiss," Morris told Tuesday's "Stinchfield" about data and election result irregularities being reported in key battleground states, including large turnouts and margins for Joe Biden where polling was not showing such strength.

"I do not necessarily believe it was a retail fraud, you know, vote by vote, count by count," Morris told host Greg Kelly. "I think it may well have originated in the Dominion software, in the Smartmatic software that the polling people, voting people used."

Trump lawyer Sidney Powell earlier Tuesday noted the legal team has the affidavit of a former high-ranking Venezuelan military officer who worked closely with Hugo Chavez to rig elections with the Dominion Voting Systems.

Morris is calling for state-by-state audits of Dominion, and failing that, Trump supporters need to contact their state legislators to refuse to certify the election results until an thorough investigation is considered.

THIS CALLS FOR AGGRESSIVE DEATH PENALTY PROSECUTION WITH MANDATORY MAXIMUM PAIN & SUFFERING BY A DEDICATED SPECIAL PROSECUTOR

Sidney Powell to Newsmax TV: Dominion Designed to 'Rig Elections'

By Eric Mack

In building its case for multi-state audits of those relying on Dominion Voting Systems, the Trump legal team has a former Venezuelan official saying it was designed to rig elections, according to former federal prosecutor Sidney Powell on Newsmax TV.

"The math just doesn't add up for anything and we know Dominion has a long history of rigging elections, because that's what it was created to do to begin with," Powell told Tuesday's "Greg Kelly Reports," noting even the "founder of the company admits he can change a million votes, no problem at all."

Powell told host Greg Kelly the team has an affidavit of a former high-ranking Venezuelan military officer who now lives in America, saying he saw the rigging of Venezuelan elections for Hugo Chavez.

"So don't tell me there's no evidence of fraud," she continued. "We've got increasingly mounting evidence of significant fraud across multiple states that casts into question the validity of elections in every swing state."

It is not just limited to Nevada, Arizona, Michigan, Wisconsin, and Georgia either, she said. adding "it went beyond that, too."

Powell said the ease of changing vote tallies and manipulating results was a "feature" of the devices, according to the military officer's affidavit.

"It was created so Hugo Chavez would never lose another election, and he did not after that software was created," Powell said. "He won every single election and then they exported it to Argentina and other countries in South America, and then they brought it here."

Trump Legal Team Scored a Big Win in Nevada. Could It Lead to a 2020 Bombshell?

Matt Vespa

For the most part, it's been something of a disaster for the Trump legal team, but I will say they are scrappy and are not giving up. Yet, time is a resource that is in *very short supply*. Rush Limbaugh and Fox News' Tucker Carlson have called out the Trump legal effort for hosting press conferences promising bombshell evidence that has yet to be revealed. We're still waiting, but the Trump team did score a big legal win in Nevada, where a judge granted a motion allowing the campaign to present its evidence regarding voter fraud. Paul Bedard of the Washington Examiner says it could set the precedent for other state challenges:

In its first court victory, a Nevada judge has agreed to let the Trump campaign present its evidence that fraud and illegalities plagued the state's election, enough to reverse Joe Biden's win and set an example for other state challenges.

According to Trump officials, the judge set a Dec. 3 hearing date and is allowing 15 depositions. What's more, the campaign plans to present its evidence that could result in the rejection of tens of thousands of mail-in ballots in Democratic Clark County where Biden ballots outnumbered Trump ballots by 91,000 in unofficial results.

Oddly, there has been a virtual news blackout of the Trump court victory. However, there were major headlines on the state Supreme Court's certification of Biden's victory Tuesday.

In its court filing from Nov. 17, the Trump team made several allegations of voter fraud, including votes by nonresidents and the dead.

But its biggest claim was that the signatures on hundreds of thousands of mail-in ballots were not verified by human officials, as required by law. What's more, they found that officials used a machine to verify signatures, apparently against the rules, and even those machines were plagued with problems.

This is welcome news after days of generally odd behavior on those leading the legal front regarding this election cycle. Let's see if the evidence presented is strong enough to convince a judge invalidating shoddy ballots, which is a high bar.

Reince Priebus reacts to Wis. Dems' rule-change try following Trump recount filing: 'You can't make this up!'

Trump Objects to Counting Thousands of Wisconsin Ballots

The recount of the presidential election in Wisconsin's two most heavily Democratic counties began Friday with President Donald Trump's campaign seeking to discard tens of thousands of absentee ballots that it alleged should not have been counted.

Trump's three objections attempting to discard the ballots were denied by the three-member Dane County Board of Canvassers, twice on bipartisan votes. Dane County Clerk Scott McDonell said he expected the campaign was building a record before filing a lawsuit.

Joe Biden won Wisconsin by 20,600 votes and carried Dane and Milwaukee counties by a 2-to-1 margin. Trump only paid for recounts in those two counties, not in the 70 others, 58 of which he won.

There's no precedent for a recount overturning a deficit as large as Trump's in Wisconsin, so his strategy is widely seen as seeking to build a case to take to court.

His team on Friday sought to have ballots discarded where election clerks filled in missing address information on the certification envelope where the ballot is inserted; any absentee ballot where a voter declared themselves to be "indefinitely confined" under the law; and any absentee ballot where there was not a written application on file, including roughly 69,000 that were cast in-person during the two weeks before Election Day.

Trump attorney Christ Troupis argued that certification envelopes filled out by people who voted absentee in-person do not count under the law as a written application, even though the envelope is identified as such. The board of canvassers, controlled 2-1 by Democrats, voted unanimously to reject the complaint.

Troupis also argued that people claimed to be indefinitely confined even though they were not. Such a declaration exempts the voter from having to show a photo ID to cast their ballot, which Troupis called "an open invitation for fraud and abuse." The Republican-controlled Wisconsin Supreme Court this spring ruled that it is up to individual voters to determine whether they are indefinitely confined, in line with guidance from the bipartisan Wisconsin Elections Commission.

The canvassing board voted 2-1 to count those ballots, with the Republican opposed.

Trump's attorney also claimed that the law does not allow clerks to fill in missing information on the envelope that goes with absentee ballots. The state elections commission told clerks before the election that they can fill in missing information on the absentee ballot envelopes, a practice that has been in place for at least the past 11 elections.

The canvassing board voted unanimously to count those ballots. In Milwaukee, the canvassing board agreed to Trump's request to set aside all absentee ballot envelopes where voters claimed "indefinitely confined" status and those with two different colors of ink, perhaps indicating that someone other than the voter completed the information.

A Trump challenge in Milwaukee seeking to reject and not count absentee ballots in envelops altered by clerk

staff to fix addresses or other errors was rejected by election officials, Biden campaign attorney, Danielle Friedman, said in a call with reporters Friday night.

She said that in limited counting so far, the vote tally for Biden has changed little, adding there have been "no changes on the scale that would change the result" and that "the Trump campaign seems aware of that fact."

"They're not actually interested in recounting the votes," she said, suggesting the end goal was land the legal issue court later.

Even though the ballots in altered envelopes would be counted, they will sit be segregated in case of legal challenges in coming days. Trump also asked to separate absentee ballots with or without written applications and to observe absentee ballot logs that would account for those requested through the state's myvote.wi.gov website. Unlike in Dane County, Trump's campaign in Milwaukee initially asked only to review those ballots and others, not to have them discounted.

In both Madison and Milwaukee, the recounts were taking place in large convention centers so workers could be distanced to protect against spreading the coronavirus. Observers were required to wear masks and plexiglass shields were set up.

Milwaukee County Clerk George Christenson, a Democrat, said it was irresponsible of Trump to force the recount amid the pandemic that is surging in Wisconsin.

"It just shows his lack of empathy toward the American people," Christenson said.

In Milwaukee, the Rev. Greg Lewis, founding president of groups of faith leaders who sought to bolster Black turnout, said the recount highlights the "oppression, disenfranchisement, downright racism and disrespect" that minority communities in Milwaukee face.

"I almost died and we are running around here counting votes unnecessarily," said Lewis, who contracted COVID-19 earlier this year. "This is nonsense. This is pitiful. Why do we keep putting up with this? The people have decided, let it be."

There have been at least 31 recounts in statewide elections in the U.S. since the most famous one in Florida's presidential election in 2000. The recounts changed the outcome of three races. All three were decided by hundreds of votes, not thousands.

The state's election commissioners finally agreed to start a recount Friday and finish by Dec. 1 so the state can certify results, reports said

By Dom Calicchio

Former White House Chief of Staff Reince Priebus reacted on Twitter late Wednesday to the election situation in Wisconsin**.**

At a special meeting that lasted more than five hours, Democrats on the state elections commission **sought to**

change recount guidelines after the Trump 2020 Campaign filed a petition to review the state's votes in Dane and Milwaukee counties. "Let's get this straight," Priebus wrote. "The Trump campaign sent the Wis Election Comm. $3 mil and filed its petition for a recount. Then the WEC immediately called a special meeting to change certain recount rules that deal with the issues brought up in the petition? You can't make this up!"

That meeting in the state capital of Madison turned into a "partisan brawl," with three Republicans and three Democrats arguing over how clerks should conduct the recount amid the coronavirus pandemic, the Milwaukee Journal Sentinel reported.

TRUMP CAMPAIGN SPENDS $3M TO FILE FOR RECOUNTS IN TWO WISCONSIN COUNTIES

The Democrats asserted their proposed changes would bring the guidance into line with current state law, while the Republicans argued that no guidelines should change after the Trump campaign's filing, according to The Associated Press. Points of contention included how to determine if absentee ballots were issued illegally and how far away recount observers should station themselves, the Journal Sentinel report said.

The two sides finally agreed early Thursday to start the recount Friday and finish by Dec. 1 so the state can certify results, the newspaper reported. At one point, Republican Commissioner Bob Spindell expressed concerns about recounts in Dane County (home of Madison) and Milwaukee County (home of the state's largest city), noting that in Milwaukee County most polling locations were shut down because of the virus outbreak.

"I don't think we can necessarily trust the canvassers of Dane or Milwaukee County, especially after they reduced 180 polling places to five terrible type voting centers for the April election, which caused all sorts of problems including suppression of the vote," Spindell said, according to the newspaper. Commissioner Julie Glancey, a Democrat, then accused Spindell of "Democrat bashing."

Reince Preibus

"This is ridiculous," she told Spindell. "All you and Dean [GOP Commissioner Dean Knudesen] keep talking about is, these evil Democrats are going to do something nasty so that these honest, hardworking Republicans aren't going to be able to see what's going on -- and I'm tired of that."

Priebus, 48, was born in New Jersey but is no stranger to Wisconsin politics. After moving to the Midwestern state with his family as a child, Priebus later attended the University of Wisconsin at Whitewater and served as a clerk for the Wisconsin State Assembly's education committee, the state's Court of Appeals and its Supreme Court.

Priebus eventually became chairman of the Republican National Committee, serving in that role from January 2011 until beginning a six-month stint at the White House after Trump took office in January 2017. He was succeeded as chief of staff by John Kelly in July of that year.

FLASHBACK: Trump sounded the alarm about voter fraud before he became president

Trump raised concerns about votes during the 2012 election

By Brittany De Lea

Trump fires top election security official amid fraud claims

President targets voting systems as campaign continues legal fight; John Roberts reports.

President Trump **on Wednesday resurfaced proof that he has been weary of the security of the U.S.** electoral process **long before he sought reelection in the 2020 cycle.**

Trump retweeted a post he sent out during the 2012 election, between former President Barack Obama and Sen. Mitt Romney, R-Utah, where he cited reports that voting machines were "switching" votes cast for Romney to Obama.

In a separate tweet, he called the contest "a total sham and a travesty."

In 2016, though Trump ultimately secured the Republican nomination and the Oval Office, he accused Sen. Ted Cruz, R-Texas, of committing fraud to win the Iowa caucuses.

FIRED ELECTION SECURITY OFFICIAL CHRIS KREBS 'OUT OF HIS LANE' WITH VOTER FRAUD STATEMENTS: DHS OFFICIAL

Since President-Elect Joe Biden was deemed to have the amassed the necessary number of electoral votes

to secure the White House, Trump has claimed that the Democrats "cheated" and that "unconstitutional" means were used to "rig" the voting process – including the alleged refusal of poll watchers at voting centers.

On Wednesday, the president alluded to "voter fraud all over the country." Trump's campaign has launched a number of lawsuits challenging the voting systems and processes in a number of key battleground states, including Georgia, Michigan, Pennsylvania and Nevada.

Consequently, he has so far refused to concede. In the run-up to Election Day, the president repeated unfounded claims about the security of the mail-in ballot process – which experienced a surge in volume amid the pandemic.

GOP Elections Chief Mum as Democrats Defend Nevada Vote

While President Donald Trump has escalated his legal battle over the election in Nevada and sought to contest its results, the Republican official in charge of supervising the state's vote has stayed quiet.

Republican Secretary of State Barbara Cegavske, who has kept a low profile since Trump launched a series of legal challenges in Nevada, has not issued any statements since the president's campaign contested the results of the state's vote Tuesday.

Her office said Wednesday that she was unavailable for an interview and declined to respond to emailed questions about Trump asking a judge to overturn or throw out the Nevada results, along with claims from his lawyers that the results "lacked integrity."

Cegavske spokeswoman Jennifer Russell said the secretary of state would not comment because of the lawsuit.

Other elected officials, all Democrats, defended the election process.

State Attorney General Aaron Ford said evidence shows Nevada held fair, safe, secure elections and that there was no widespread voter fraud. Ford said in a statement that his office would prosecute "any isolated and substantiated incidents of voter fraud."

Ford said Trump's team never filed an official complaint and supporting evidence with his office, despite being explicitly invited to do so.

The Trump campaign has filed multiple lawsuits in Nevada to try to stop the widespread mailing of ballots and then the counting of mailed ballots, but none have succeeded.

The battle escalated Tuesday, when campaign lawyers filed a lawsuit and declared to reporters that Trump had won Nevada despite results showing he lost to Joe Biden by 33,596 votes.

"We're quite confident in the fact that when the law and the facts are clearly adjudicated in this matter, that it will be very clear that once all the voting happened, once everything occurred, the results were unreliable because of the irregularities and the fraud," campaign attorney Jesse Binnall said.

Trump's campaign and his allies, looking to establish widespread fraud in multiple states, have pointed to issues typical of most every election: problems with signatures, secrecy envelopes and postal marks on mail-in ballots, as well as the potential for a small number of ballots miscast or lost.

With Biden leading Trump by wide margins in key battleground states, it remains a question mark whether those issues would have any impact on the outcome of the election.

U.S. Sen. Jacky Rosen, a Nevada Democrat, pushed back on the Trump campaign's claims.

"The results from the election are clear: Joe Biden and Kamala Harris came out ahead in Nevada, and President Trump will not be able to overturn the will of Nevada's voters with unfounded lawsuits like this one," Rosen said in a statement. "Our democratic elections are safe, fair, and secure, with no credible evidence of voter fraud."

The lawsuit claims that votes were cast on behalf of dead people, that election observers weren't allowed to

witness "key points" of processing and that people on American Indian reservations were illegally given incentives to vote. Binnall said he can prove votes were tainted by the use of an optical scanning machine to process ballots in the Las Vegas area and by voting machine malfunctions and that illegal ballots were cast by people living out of state or not registered voters. He didn't immediately offer any evidence.

Trump's campaign previously claimed it had identified more than 3,000 people who "improperly" cast ballots in Nevada because they live elsewhere, but voting rights activists say hundreds of people on the list appear to be linked to the U.S. military. A hearing on the new lawsuit was not immediately set by a judge in Carson City. Time is short, with the state Supreme Court scheduled Tuesday to certify the Nevada election.

Meanwhile, all 17 Nevada counties certified canvasses of their votes by a Wednesday deadline set by state law, according to Cegavske's office. Before the lawsuit was announced, Cegavske said in a news release that her role certifying election returns is ministerial and that after the state high court certifies the count as complete, Democratic Gov. Steve Sisolak will certify the election. In a separate legal challenge, a hearing was scheduled for Friday in Las Vegas in a lawsuit from conservative former state lawmaker Sharron Angle and her Election Integrity Project seeking to block statewide certification of the election.

Powell also argued, as a foreign company, the use of that election system already violated President Donald Trump's order against foreign interference in our election.

"Our votes were eventually counted in Barcelona, Spain, or Frankfurt, Germany, on foreign servers," Powell claimed. "It's absolutely stunning."

And that includes the Democrat and mainstream media's efforts to ignore the corruption.

'What's really stunning is the efforts against getting the stuff out on this," she concluded. "But you have to realize every tech company, every media company, every social media company, scads of globalist corporations have been doing business in countries with these dictators that have been installed through this rigged election system for decades."

New York Times previously sounded alarm on how easily electronic voting machines can be hacked

By Joseph A. Wulfsohn

THEY'RE FUCKEN LYING BECAUSE THESE OFFICIAL CHOSE & BOUGHT THESE MACHINE VOTING SYSTEMS Officials: Dominion machines did not change or delete any votes

Alex Halderman, computer science and engineering professor, University of Michigan says Dominion machines did not change or delete any votes.

The New York Times has joined the vast majority of the mainstream media in dismissing any concerns President Trump's legal team has raised amid the challenge of the 2020 presidential election results, including the possibility that ballots from electronic voting machines were tampered with.

However, the Times previously sounded the alarm about how vulnerable such voting machines can be to hackers.

Back in April 2018, New York Times Opinion shared a video on its YouTube page called "How I Hacked an Election." The video features University of Michigan Computer Science Professor J. Alex Halderman, who urged that electronic voting machines "have got to go."

Halderman demonstrated a mock election he organized at his university using "obsolete machines" that are commonly used in normal elections to have Michigan students vote on which school is the best, their own or their arch-rival Ohio State University.

WASHINGTON POST EDITORIAL BOARD CALLS TO 'ABOLISH THE ELECTORAL COLLEGE'

"After the chaos of the 2000 election, we were promised a modern and dependable way to vote. I'm here to tell you that the electronic voting machines Americans have got to solve the problem of voting integrity -- they turned out to be an awful idea," Halderman said. "That's because people like me can hack them all too easily. I'm a computer scientist who's hacked a lot of electronic voting machines. I've even turned one machine into a video game console. Imagines what the Russians and North Koreans can do."

While the Department of Homeland Security's Cybersecurity & Infrastructure Security Agency concluded the Nov. 3 vote was the "most secure election in history," Halderman singled out a specific machine model, the Accuvote TS & TSX, which was used in several states during the 2016 election including Georgia, Florida, Texas, and Pennsylvania could be vulnerable to cyber attacks "that can change votes."

Halderman went on to explain how he was able to successfully hack the voting machines he was using in his on-campus demonstration. The first step is to either buy a voting machine on eBay or "if you're the North Koreans, hack the manufacturer and steal their software code." The second step is to "write the virus" followed by the third step, which is to email the virus to "every election official" who is responsible for programming the voting machines with new ballots.

MEDIA SHAMES TRUMP CHALLENGING ELECTION RESULTS AFTER GIVING CREDENCE TO AL GORE'S BATTLE IN 2000, VIDEO SHOWS

The hacker then is able to "hijack the ballot programming" and let election officials copy the "invisible malicious code" onto the voting machines. Finally, the malicious code "silently" steals the votes. In front of the Michigans students, Halderman announced the winner from a printout of the electronic ballots that showed Ohio State as the winner, sparking plenty of boos from the crowd and accusations of the election being

"rigged." "There's a good reason we computer scientists are paranoid -- it's a golden age for hackers," Halderman said. After Halderman admitted to the students that he "hacked the voting machines," he revealed that the paper ballots showed that Michigan handily won the election. "Michigan won in a landslide and I could say this confidently because I have the real results from the safest and simplest solution: paper ballots," Halderman said. On Monday, the Times ran a report about a letter signed by 59 election security experts expressing confidence in the results of the 2020 election.

"Anyone asserting that a U.S. election was 'rigged' is making an extraordinary claim, one that must be supported by persuasive and verifiable evidence... To our collective knowledge, no credible evidence has been put forth that supports a conclusion that the 2020 election outcome in any state has been altered through technical compromise," the experts wrote.

One of the signatories of the letter included this fucken death penalty eligible Halderman.

- Biden's 'Return to Normalcy' Is Going to Be Terrible

Ben Shapiro

After spending two years avoiding serious questions about his policy preferences, his team and his prospective presidency, we now know what Joe Biden intends to do should the Electoral College, as expected, vote for him in December: He'll reopen the swamp for business. The media spent four long years suggesting that President Donald Trump was steeped in corruption, ensconced in partisanship, enmeshed in dangerous foreign policy fiascos. The media assured us that they would defend democracy from Trump's brutalities, that they would spend every waking moment fighting to prevent anyone from accepting Trumpian standards as the "new normal."

Instead, the media suggested we needed to return to the old "normal" -- by which they meant a system in which the media and Democrats worked hand-in-glove together to lie to the American public about the content of policy ("If you like your doctor, you will be able to keep your doctor!" -- former President Barack Obama); in which conventional wisdom was treated as gospel truth, no matter how wrong it was ("There will be no advanced and separate peace with the Arab world without the Palestinian process" -- John Kerry on Israel); and in which cozy relationships between corporations and government were considered *de rigueur*.

They meant a system in which all difficult political questions were put off for another day; in which scandals were brushed off without a second thought; in which even anti-journalistic efforts by Democrats were dismissed as out of hand. It was a system in which constitutional boundaries were routinely overridden in the name of left-wing policy priorities; in which nasty rhetoric by Democrats was written off as a natural byproduct of the right's innate evil; in which alternative news sources were treated as conspiracy outlets.

That's the "normal" the media and Democrats wanted.

And it's the normal they'll apparently be pursuing. Biden is stacking his administration with all the members of the establishment Democratic gang. Tony Blinken, most famous for embracing the Iran deal and encouraging more American troops in Syria, will be headed to the State Department. Janet Yellen, fresh from her tenure as Federal Reserve chairwoman under Obama, will be headed to the Department of the Treasury. Jake Sullivan, Biden's national security adviser when he was vice president, most famous for the suggestion that the Iran deal was a stellar piece of negotiation (it wasn't), will become the White House national security adviser.

Meanwhile, the media will continue to cover Biden in sycophantic fashion. This week, The Washington Post ran an entire piece devoted to the wonders of the New Biden Era, titled "Washington's establishment hopes a Biden presidency will make schmoozing great again." The piece celebrated the old normal as "respect for experience and expertise," as "civility and bipartisan cooperation," as an opportunity to "bring people back together." One wonders what sort of peyote the editorial staff of The Washington Post must be ingesting in order to remember the Obama Era so fondly; then, one quickly realizes that they're simply high from huffing Democratic flatulence.

Pennsylvania High Court to Hear Trump Challenge to Thousands of Votes

The Pennsylvania Supreme Court said on Wednesday it would take up an appeal by President Donald Trump's campaign challenging thousands of mail-in votes cast in Philadelphia that were missing information on the return envelopes.

The lower Court of Common Pleas ruled on Friday against the Trump campaign which sought to invalidate 8,329 ballots in Philadelphia, the state's biggest city, because envelopes lacked information such as printed names, the date or addresses.

The campaign has not alleged the ballots were fraudulent. Joe Biden, the Democratic challenger, won Pennsylvania by a margin of around 82,000 votes, according to Edison Research. Trump's campaign is challenging the results in Pennsylvania and elsewhere, alleging all manner of voter fraud. Newsmax has not yet called the race for either Biden or Trump.

A win in Pennsylvania is important, as the state represents 20 electoral votes.

A decision by the Pennsylvania Supreme Court would likely impact ballots across the state, although the

number was unclear. In a separate case likely to be affected by a Supreme Court decision, Nicole Ziccarelli, a Republican state senate candidate, said in court papers she was seeking to invalidate 2,349 ballots in Allegheny County, which includes Pittsburgh, because envelopes lacked dates.

The Trump campaign has been fighting several lawsuits trying to overturn Pennsylvania's election outcome, which will be critical if the president hopes to succeed in his long-shot bid to reverse the election. The president has claimed the election was stolen but his campaign has not yet scored a significant victory in court.

On Tuesday, a federal judge overseeing a separate case expressed skepticism of the campaign's request to block officials from certifying Biden's victory in Pennsylvania.

In another Trump lawsuit, the Pennsylvania Supreme Court ruled against the campaign on Tuesday and said Philadelphia officials acted reasonably in keeping Trump observers behind barricades and 15 feet (4.5 m) from counting tables.

Trump Suggests Special Prosecutor For 'Rigged' Election

President Donald Trump on Sunday suggested he'll consider appointing a special prosecutor to probe an election he alleges was rife with illegal and "rigged" balloting.

In an interview on Fox News' "Sunday Morning Futures," **the president also lamented that James Comey — the FBI director Trump fired in 2017, triggering the appointment of special counsel Robert Mueller — and the FBI's former deputy director, Andrew McCabe, haven't faced tough legal scrutiny for their part in the 2016 election.**

"This whole thing is a terrible situation," he said. "This should have never been allowed to happen, and you know, it's an embarrassment to our country, all over the world they're talking about it and yeah, I would consider a special prosecutor," he said in answer to host Maria Bartiromo's question about such an appointment "to investigate" his allegations "and to continue the investigating into what took place in the 2016 election."

"I went through three years of a special counsel prosecutor," Trump added. "I call [it] prosecutor because it's a much more accurate term," he added. Trump lashed out at "all of the fraud that's taken place" in the current election that shows Joe Biden the winner, alleging that Dominion voting machines led to fraudulent results — as well as snafus in the mail delivery of mail-in ballots.

"The mailmen are carrying thousands of ballots back and forth, back and forth. There are many mailman that are in big trouble for... getting rid of ballots," he alleged.

"This is the craziest thing you've ever seen, but many ballots with the name Trump on it were thrown out. You've read that. They found ballots in a river, with the name Trump on from the military. They were signed and they were floating in a river. They found ballots under rocks that had the name Trump on. They

were signed and signed with Trump." "We won the election easily. There's no way Joe Biden got 80 million votes. I just said, there's no way Joe Biden beat Barack Obama in the Black communities of various cities and then he did very badly compared to Obama in other cities throughout the United States. There's no way it happened."

"This election was a fraud and it was a rigged election," he declared. As for 2016, he railed, Mueller's probe "spent $48 million… they went through taxes and they went through everything for $48 million. You look at everything and they found no collusion, no nothing."

"It was a Russia hoax, just a pure hoax and a very sad thing for the country," he said. "And as much as I've done — and I think I've done more than virtually in four years more than any president in the history with Space Force and tax cuts, biggest regulation cuts in history, biggest tax cuts in history… the VA — as much as I've done, I could have done more except that I was under investigation … from the day I came down the escalator."

AZ GOP Chair Dr. Kelli Ward Confident Election 'Will Ultimately Be Decided in Favor of President Donald J. Trump'

Dr. Kelli Ward, chair of the Republican Party of Arizona, said in a Wednesday update that the day is "expected to be a lawsuit day" for the Arizona Republican Party, and she reaffirmed her confidence that the election will "ultimately be decided in favor of President Donald J. Trump."

Ward described the day as a "lawsuit day" in her morning update. The Arizona GOP is expected in court Wednesday afternoon over their lawsuit demanding a hand-count audit of votes by precinct rather than by voting centers in Maricopa County. "The Arizona Republican Party has a lawsuit about election integrity," Ward said, identifying the Arizona Democratic Party and Democrat Secretary of State Katie Hobbs (D) as the opposition.

"And by the way, the Maricopa County Republican Party did make an issue of this," Ward said. "They passed a resolution saying we need to vote by precincts all the way back in June before the primary — June of 2020":

"There is a fundamental difference between sampling 'polling centers' and 'precincts,' most notable being the fact that there were only around 175 voting centers in this election but there were 748 precincts," the Republican Party of Arizona said in a statement last week, announcing the legal action:

Ward said the issue comes down to if the legislature and the law it passed "should that take second fiddle to an election procedures manual created and printed by one member of the executive branch — Katie Hobbs, the Secretary of State who has called Trump supporters — remember — neo-Nazis." "I say no," Ward said, adding that they will "hopefully have good news" to share after today's showing in court.

Ward also expressed confidence that Trump will, in fact, emerge as the victor in the highly disputed presidential election. "I'm going to tell you. I believe — I still do now, just as I did on election night — that this election will ultimately be decided in favor of President Donald J. Trump. ur 11 electoral votes will go to him," she said.

"And we should not and will not ever allow mistakes, glitches, and other irregularities to become a partisan issue. We want full transparency and election integrity," she added. "That's it." This week, Arizona Reps. Andy Biggs (R) and Paul Gosar (R) expressed their belief that America "deserves an election audit," providing examples of issues and concerns in a video shared by the Arizona GOP:

Joe Biden (D) led Trump by less than 10,400 votes in the Grand Canyon State as of Wednesday afternoon.

Jordan Sekulow to Newsmax TV: Pending Georgia Lawsuit 'Shocking'

By Eric Mack

An election challenge lawsuit planned to be filed early this week is new and will be "shocking," according to President Donald Trump lawyer Jordan Sekulow on Newsmax TV.

"We have got lawsuits likely to be filed in Georgia on either Monday or Tuesday; I can't get into the details," Sekulow, the son of Trump personal attorney Jay Sekulow, told Saturday's "America Right Now."

"I can't tell you right now, but what's coming in Georgia will be shocking, when we file this in federal court Monday or Tuesday," Jordan Sekulow told host Tom Basile. "It's nothing that we have talked before. It's not what you heard in the press conference [Thursday] either. "This is something completely separate." The fact Jordan Sekulow pointed to federal court, it is likely a constitutional legal challenge. He did allude to some challenges to the constitutional issue of "equal protection under the law." He added, to those saying "put up or shut up, it's coming this week."

"They've got to be outcome determinative, but I will tell you, the Lt. Gov. [Geoff Duncan] in Georgia, the Secretary of State in Georgia [Brad Raffensperger] in Georgia, they're in for quite a shock on Monday and Tuesday about how poorly they run and they ran – there's going to be a proof – of how poorly run they ran the elections in one of their major counties," Sekulow said.

Sekulow did note it was related neither to the challenges on signature verification on mail-in ballots in Georgia, nor a potential upcoming audit of the recently certified election results in Georgia, as teased by GOP Gov. Brian Kemp. "That recount was not a recount at all," Sekulow said. "All we did is find more votes, which were new votes, not recounted votes." Sekulow noted his legal team is working on the constitutional case, while the Trump campaign legal team of Rudy Giuliani, Jenna Ellis, and Sidney Powell are focusing on compiling the evidence of voter fraud, including Dominion Voting Systems. "Look at the in-fighting in Georgia: That's a lawyer's dream, so we've got to be there and we are," Sekulow said

Protests in Atlanta Over Election Results

President Donald Trump speaks during an event in the briefing room of the White House in Washington, Friday, Nov. 20, 2020, on prescription drug prices.

By Solange Reyner

Large crowds of protesters gathered outside the Georgia State Capitol Saturday as part of a nationwide "Stop the Steal" protests. Georgia on Friday certified results in the state for Democrat Joe Biden following a hand recount. The count affirmed Biden won by more than 12,000 votes out of about 5 million cast, according to data released by Secretary of State Brad Raffensperger's office.

Gov. Brian Kemp, a Republican, also certified the results but said he would permit President Donald Trump's legal team to officially call for a recount. The move will "formalize the certification," but it "paves the way for the Trump campaign to pursue other legal options and a separate recount if they choose," Kemp said Friday night. Trump's campaign has two business days from the certification date to request a recount.

Several news outlets have declared Biden the President-Elect. Trump has refused to concede, citing voter fraud. Newsmax will not project a winner until enough states certify votes and get one candidate to 270 Electoral College votes.

Michigan, National Republicans Want State Certification Delayed

RNC Chair Ronna McDanial By Sandy Fitzgerald

The Republican National Committee and Michigan's GOP are asking the Board of State Canvassers to delay certification of Michigan's election results, saying an investigation of "anomalies and irregularities" occurring in the state's Nov. 3 election is necessary.

In their request, Republican National Committee Chairwoman Ronna McDaniel and Michigan Republican Party Chairwoman say a "full, transparent audit" is needed before the votes can be certified, pointing to states like Georgia that have taken "discretionary steps" to determine the results, reports The Detroit News.

The state and national request come after GOP Senate candidate John James asked for a two-week delay. James came in behind incumbent Democrat Sen. Gary Peters by more than 92,000 votes in unofficial results but has not conceded the election.

In their written request, McDaniel and Cox said it would be a "grievous dereliction of the board's duty" to voters in Michigan if they didn't make sure the "irregularities" outlined by the James campaign were not investigated thoroughly in a full audit before the results from Wayne County, where Detroit is located, are audited. On Friday, Secretary of State Jocelyn Benson said an audit could not be before the certification of the results, as election officials didn't have legal access to the documents they needed.

Cox and McDaniel, though, said it's still possible to investigate some claims that are being made about Wayne County's poll books while they comply with the Dec. 8 deadline for certification.

But, they warned that to ignore the irregularities would "foster feelings of distrust among Michigan's electorate." State canvasser Norm Shinkle, a Republican, said Friday he's considering moving for the audit or delaying the state's final certification, but he couldn't make that decision without the state Michigan Bureau of Elections report on the certifications.

Dan Gainor: Twitter, Facebook were a big part of takedown efforts against Trump in 2020 election

Unless Trump can pull off enough last-minute court victories, Twitter and Facebook cost Trump the election

By Dan Gainor

Facebook, Twitter executives grilled during Judiciary committee hearing

Fox News correspondent Gillian Turner joins 'Special Report' with the latest.

Twitter might have finally won its war against its archenemy — President Donald Trump.

Tuesday in the U.S. Senate, Twitter CEO Jack Dorsey **once again admitted, at a Senate Judiciary Committee**

hearing on "Breaking the News: Censorship, Suppression, and the 2020 Election," that censoring the New York Post scoop about the Hunter Biden scandal "was wrong."

Except it appears to have worked.

At least, as of right now, Biden has been declared the winner by news outlets. And he remains ahead in the race, pending Trump's court challenge. Unless Trump can pull off enough last-minute court victories, Twitter and Facebook cost Trump the election.

NEWT GINGRICH: ELECTION 2020 -- AMERICANS DESERVE A SYSTEM THAT IS OPEN, TRANSPARENT AND RELIABLE

They did it by hiding the Hunter Biden story. A post-election poll conducted by McLaughlin & Associates showed more than a third (36 % of Biden voters didn't even know about the scandal. The Media Research Center poll said his voters were unaware of allegations that Biden and his son had financial ties to communist China.

Twitter CEO Jack Dorsey (WITH CHARLES MANSON BEARD) **testifies remotely during a Senate Judiciary Committee hearing on Facebook and Twitter's actions around the closely contested election on Tuesday, Nov. 17, 2020, in Washington.. (Bill Clark/Pool via AP)**

Thirteen % of those voters were enough to turn the election for Trump. That works out to 4.6 % of the total

vote for the former vice president. They said they wouldn't have voted for Biden if they had known. That would likely have shifted enough votes to cost Biden the Electoral College.

Unless Trump can pull off enough last-minute court victories, Twitter and Facebook cost Trump the election.

The original New York Post story was headlined: "Smoking-gun email reveals how Hunter Biden introduced Ukrainian businessman to VP dad." It created an enormous bad news narrative for Biden weeks before the election. So the two biggest social media sites in the world censored it and stopped the story dead in its tracks.

Facebook announced it would restrict access to the story, pending action by its fact-checkers. Except even the fact-checkers admitted that wasn't the typical policy. The International Fact-Checking Network, which handles Facebook fact-checking, criticized the company. "The decision to reduce or prevent the distribution of @nypost 's article based on some mysterious, non-transparent criteria and an unknown methodology is a serious mistake," the organization tweeted. James Carafano: 5 top global issues for the day after inauguration

- **Liz Peek: Trump's 2020 supporters – what they had to overcome to vote for 4 more years**

- **Schoen & Cooperman: Election 2020 – Biden, Dems hurt by this and here's how they can bounce back**

Twitter suspended links to the story and those who linked to it. That included numerous prominent people on Twitter such as White House press secretary Kayleigh McEnany.

Traditional news outlets were largely silent about the censorship, happy to see a bad Biden story killed before it could truly harm their candidate.

Trump has been the enemy of leftist Twitter for his entire presidency, despite having nearly 89 million followers on the site. While the site refused to shut him down, it has censored him and his campaign nearly 200 times. Most of those have come this month.

But this incident was appalling. The social media site committed one of the greatest acts of censorship in American history when it shut down the Hunter Biden scandal.

Here's Dorsey's latest explanation for that censorship, where he told the Senate Judiciary Committee: "Upon further consideration, we admitted this action was wrong and corrected it within 24 hours." Except Twitter still demanded the Post take down its original tweet, which it refused to do.

It took 17 days for Twitter to admit it was wrong in this way, as well. Seventeen days -- right before an election.

This wasn't the first time Dorsey admitted that Twitter messed up. Back on Oct. 14, he tweeted: "Our communication around our actions on the @nypost article was not great. And blocking URL sharing via tweet or DM with zero context a

Rep. Rick Allen to Newsmax TV: Georgia's Recount 'Outlandish'

By Eric Mack

Georgia has a constitutional issue to resolve with its discrepancies in voter identification in person versus absentee ballots, according to Rep. Rick Allen, R-Ga., on Newsmax TV.

"If you go and vote in person, there's a different standard, and you have equal protection under the law, so why wouldn't the standard for absentee ballots be the same as if you showed up and went to vote in person?" Allen, who won reelection in Georgia's 12th district **with over 58% of the vote, told Wednesday's** "Stinchfield."

"That's outlandish."

The ballot recount is failing to address the difference in Georgia's rules with in-person voter I.D. and sketchy signature verification on absentee ballots, Allen told host Grant Stinchfield.

"I don't believe it's legitimate, no," Allen said, noting his Georgia delegation has sent a letter to the Justice Department to investigate Georgia's vote counting, ballot recounting and signature verification process on absentee ballots.

Allen added Georgia Secretary of State Brad Raffensperger is suspect, too.

"He's been defending his position, and he has been defending the equipment, which is questionable; he's defending how the votes were counted," Allen said.

News November 16, 2020

2,600 uncounted ballots from pro-Trump county discovered during Georgia recount

Officials called it an 'amazing blunder'

WHAT ABOUT OTHER AMAZING BLUNDERS?

Georgia officials said **that human error led to 2,600 ballots being uncounted from Floyd County, which will likely lessen the lead of former Vice President Joe Biden over President Donald Trump in the 2020 presidential election. Georgia's voting implementation manager Gabriel Sterling explained to reporters on Monday where the uncounted ballots came from.**

"Well what it is, is they had these ballots in their ballot manifests, they had them there and they were counted in the audit. When they finished the audit, they had like 40,000 votes, when on the election night reporting

they only had 38,000 votes, and that's how it was discovered," said Sterling. "So that's where we came across this, and then they kinda back-figured that they came from those early vote results that were not uploaded," he added. "But that's where we're having an investigator to button up exactly where their breakdown came."

He said that the "amazing blunder" came from someone not uploading the ballot count from a memory card into a ballot machine. "It's not an equipment issue. It's a person not executing their job properly. This is the kind of situation that requires a change at the top of their management side," Sterling said.

The ballots that were found included 1,643 new votes for Trump and 865 new votes for Biden, giving the president a boost. Sterling said that the new votes would not change the results of the Georgia presidential election because it would not be enough to change the outcome.

"It looks like it's about an 800 plus vote swing towards the president on this, but the lead statewide is 14,155, so that would take it down to 13,300 and something, I believe," Sterling said.

Ga. County's Uncounted Ballots Will Boost Trump, but by How Much?

Joe Biden's victory margin in Georgia tightened slightly Monday after the state discovered that around 2,600 ballots went uncounted in a rural county.

The unofficial breakdown of the votes that weren't previously uploaded was 1,643 for Trump, 865 for Biden and 16 for Libertarian Jo Jorgensen, according to Gabriel Sterling, who oversaw the implementation of the new statewide election system for the secretary of state's office.<

While the discovery in Floyd County will bolster President Donald Trump's tally by about 800 votes, it's unlikely to change the state's overall results significantly, said Sterling. Biden's margin over Trump will fall to about 13,300 votes from 14,100.

Still, the gaffe could worsen an already tense situation in the state, which is conducting a hand recount of the Nov. 3 vote, which the Trump campaign alleges was marred by fraud. As of Monday, Georgia had recounted about 4.3 million of the 5 million ballots cast, Sterling said. It was during this audit process that election workers discovered the uncounted ballots in Floyd County, a Republican-leaning community in northwest Georgia.

Secretary of State Brad Raffensperger suggested that Floyd County's elections chief should resign over the error, Sterling said. "Nothing is making us see any substantive change in the outcome," Sterling, a Republican, said during a videoconference with journalists Monday afternoon. Yet "there is no good explanation as to why you wouldn't upload those numbers."

Raffensperger, also a Republican, tested negative for COVID-19 but has remained in quarantine in recent days after his wife tested positive. His office has insisted that the state's election results are accurate despite repeated allegations from the president and his allies, which last week included a call from Georgia's incumbent U.S. senators, David Perdue and Kelly Loeffler, that Raffensperger should resign.

More uncounted votes found in second Georgia county, giving another boost for Trump

Officials said they found the votes that had been scanned onto a memory card

Carlos Garcia

A second memory card was found in the Georgia recount process with uncounted votes that gives President Donald Trump a boost against former Vice President Joe Biden.

The Georgia Secretary of State's office told reporters on Tuesday that the discrepancy was discovered in the votes from Fayette County during a hand recount.

A total of 2,755 votes were discovered, with 1,577 going to Trump and 1,128 going for Biden. The new votes decrease Biden's sizable lead by about 450 votes.

This is an addition to the first batch of uncounted votes

Pat Gray

Election officials rejected fewer mail-in ballots in 2020 than in previous elections

In this clip, Pat explained that mail-in ballot rejection rates plummeted for first-time mail-in voters this year. States like Georgia, Michigan, and other swing states saw fewer rejections despite the increase in ballots cast by mail.

The New York Times reported, "With absentee ballots flooding election offices nationwide, the officials processing them are tentatively reporting some surprising news: The share of ballots being rejected because of flawed signatures and other errors appears lower — sometimes much lower — than in the past."

Richard,

What we're about to tell you is important, so we'll get right to the point.

So far, we have 234 pages of sworn affidavits alleging Election irregularities from just ONE county in Michigan. Here are the allegations:

- EYEWITNESS saw a batch of ballots where 60% of them had the SAME signature
- EYEWITNESS saw a batch of ballots scanned 5 times
- EYEWITNESS saw 35 ballots counted that were NOT connected to a voter record
- EYEWITNESS saw poll workers marking ballots with NO mark for candidates

- VOTER said deceased son was recorded as voting TWICE
- EYEWITNESS said provisional ballots were placed in the tabulation box
- FAILED software that caused an error in Antrim County used in Wayne County
- Republican challengers not readmitted but Democrats admitted
- Republican challengers physically pushed from counting tables by officials
- Democrats gave out packet: "Tactics to Distract Republican Challengers"
- Republican challenges to suspect ballots ignored
- **Republican Canvassers Rescind Their Votes to Certify Wayne County, Michigan, Results**

Joel B. Pollak

Two Republican members of the Wayne County Board of Canvassers in Michigan rescinded their votes to certify the election results, saying Wednesday they were bullied into changing their original votes, and state authorities had refused to conduct an audit. As Breitbart News reported Tuesday, the board originally deadlocked 2-2 along partisan lines and failed to certify the results because of discrepancies between ballots and voter rolls. But after public abuse and threats, and with the video stream down, the two Republicans agreed to change their votes, saying that they're promised state authorities would audit the results.

Justthenews.com reported:

In an extraordinary turnabout that foreshadows possible legal action, the two GOP members of Wayne County's election board signed affidavits Wednesday night alleging they were bullied and misled into ap-

proving election results in Michigan's largest metropolis and do not believe the votes should be certified until serious irregularities in Detroit votes are resolved.The statements by Wayne County Board of Canvassers Chairwoman Monica Palmer and fellow GOP member William C. Hartmann rescinding their votes from a day earlier threw into question anew whether Michigan's presidential vote currently favoring Democrat Joe Biden will be certified. They also signaled a possible legal confrontation ahead.

Their pronouncements come just 24 hours after a chaotic meeting in which the county's election board initially failed to certify the Nov. 3 election results during a 2-2 deadlocked vote when both Palmer and Hartmann voted against certification. But after hours of contentious public comment and criticism — including Democratic allegations of racism and threats against their safety — the two GOP members struck a deal to certify the elections in return for a promise of a thorough audit.

Palmer and Hartmann have each submitted affidavits. Palmer, the board's chair, said **in her affidavit that "more than 70% of Detroit's 134 Absent Voter Counting Boards (AVCB) did not balance." She then voted not to certify the results.**

She added: "After the vote, public comment period began and dozens of people made personal remarks against me and Mr. Hartmann. The comments made accusations of racism and threatened me and my family." She said that she was advised that she could not oppose the certification and that voting to certify "would result in a full, independent audit of Detroit's unbalanced precincts." She later learned that Secretary of State Jocelyn Benson did not view the agreement as binding on her. Consequently, Palmer said, she was rescinding her vote. Hartmann said that he agreed to certify the results after being "berated" and after being told by Wayne County counsel that the discrepancies in the vote were insufficient reason not to certify the result. He added that he was promised that the state would audit the results, but later learned that Benson had no intention of doing so.

It is not clear whether the decision to rescind votes after the fact has any legal value; litigation is likely to follow.

Jim Jordan: Congress Should Investigate 2020 Election

Ian Hanchett

On Wednesday's broadcast of the Fox News Channel's "Hannity," House Judiciary Committee Ranking Member Rep. Jim Jordan (R-OH) stated that there should be a Congressional investigation of the 2020 election by the House Judiciary Committee and House Oversight and Reform Committee.

Jordan said, "So, Ranking Member [of the House Oversight Committee] Comer today — first call for an investigation. We sent a letter **to Mr. Nadler and Chairwoman [of the House Oversight Committee] Maloney. Why don't you guys investigate? The committees aren't even meeting this week. Why not? Why not look into this? So, that, to me, is the fundamental question."**

PROOF THAT JOE BIDEN WILL BECOME DRACULA LIVING IN A COFFIN IN HIS WILMINGTON BASEMENT

Feminists: Joe Biden Support for LGBTQUEER AS FOLK Equality Act Would Harm Women's Rights BY PUTTING REAL LIFE DREAMGIRL SMOKIN' HOT BABES UNDER DOMINATION OF WHACKED OUT PSYCHOPATH MEN WHO THINK THEY ARE GIRLS GO BACK TO YER COFFIN, JOE

Penny Starr

The far-left feminist Women's Liberation Front (WOLF) is opposing the Democrat's pro-transgender Equality Act because it would weaken womens' rights by subordinating womens' biological identity to men's claimed sense of "gender identity." WOLF, which says on its website, "female humans, the class of people called women, are oppressed by men under a male-supremacist system called patriarchy," posted an article titled, "What Could a Joe Biden Presidency Mean for Women's Rights?"

While this group likes some of Biden's and vice presidential candidate Kamala Harris' campaign promises — including support for abortion, gay marriage, and government-run health care — when it comes to the Equality Act, WOLF takes a different stance. "Despite all his progressive policies, Biden's contradictory support for the current version of the Equality Act and other "gender-identity" laws will actually undermine

women's sex-based rights," WOLF states.

- BIDEN IS A (A.K.A. IT) FRANKENSTEIN LABORATORY ONE-OF-A-KIND THE WORST PART OF HIM IS HIS VAPID, SHALLOW, GLUED ON SMILE NOW HE "IT" CALLS WEARING A MASK "MASKING" A NEW WORD UNKNOWN BY SHAKESPEARE ; NEXT BIDEN & KAMIKAZE KAMALA WILL DEMAND SOCIAL DISTANCING FOR THE DEAD IN MASS CREMATIONS DURING THE UPCOMING BLACK DEATH ONLY FOR WHITE PEOPLE NEXT LOAN FORFIVENESS FOR QUEER GENDER REIMAGINING STUDIES MAJORS AT JUNIOR COLLEGE (3) MONTH PHD. PROGRAMS FOR REVERSE TRANSVESTITES NEXT SEPARATE BUT EQUAL ZOO ENCLOSURES FOR GREEN NEW DEAL FEMALE GORILLAS IDENTIFYING AS KING KONG WANNABES?

"BUILD BACK BETTER" IS AN ADOLF HITLER EXPRESSION FOR AUSCHWITZ & DACHAU CREMATORIA (PLURAL) FOR THE STILL LIVING BUT SOON DEAD JEWISH

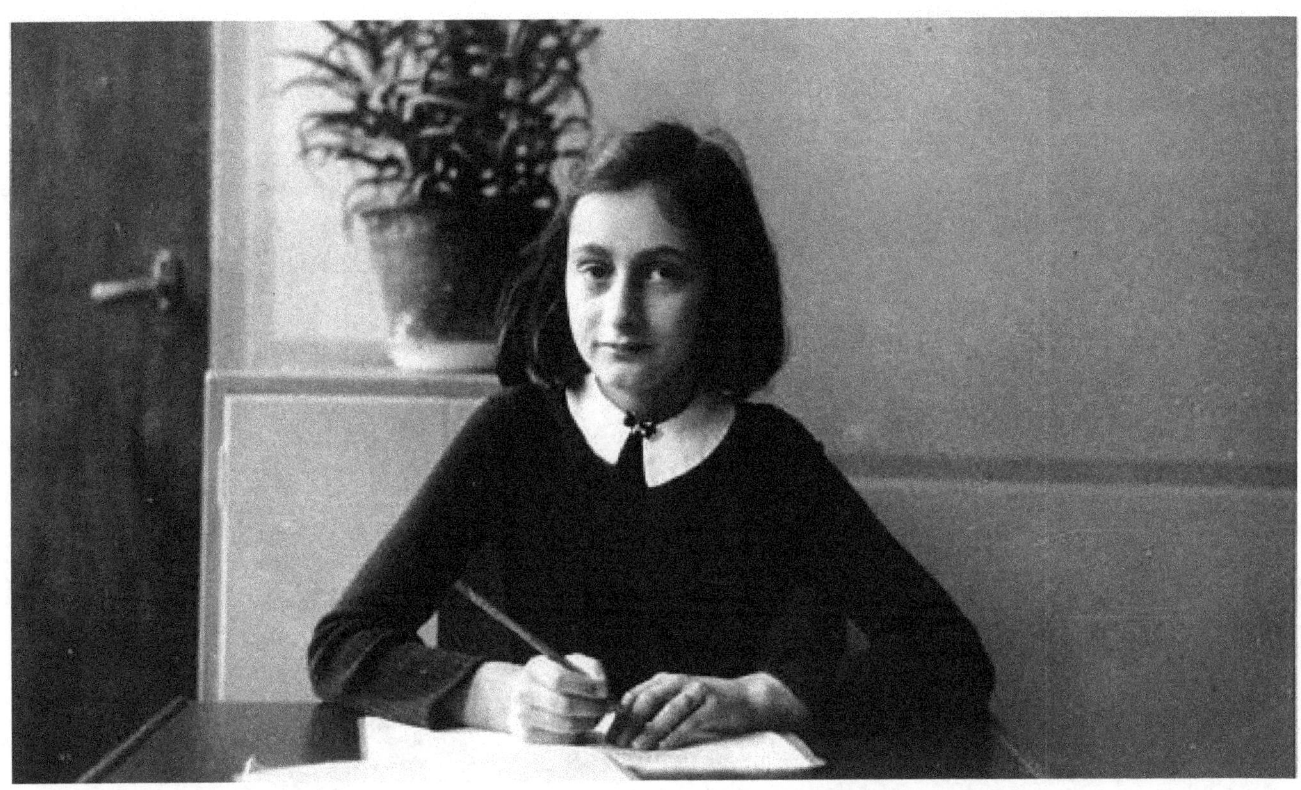

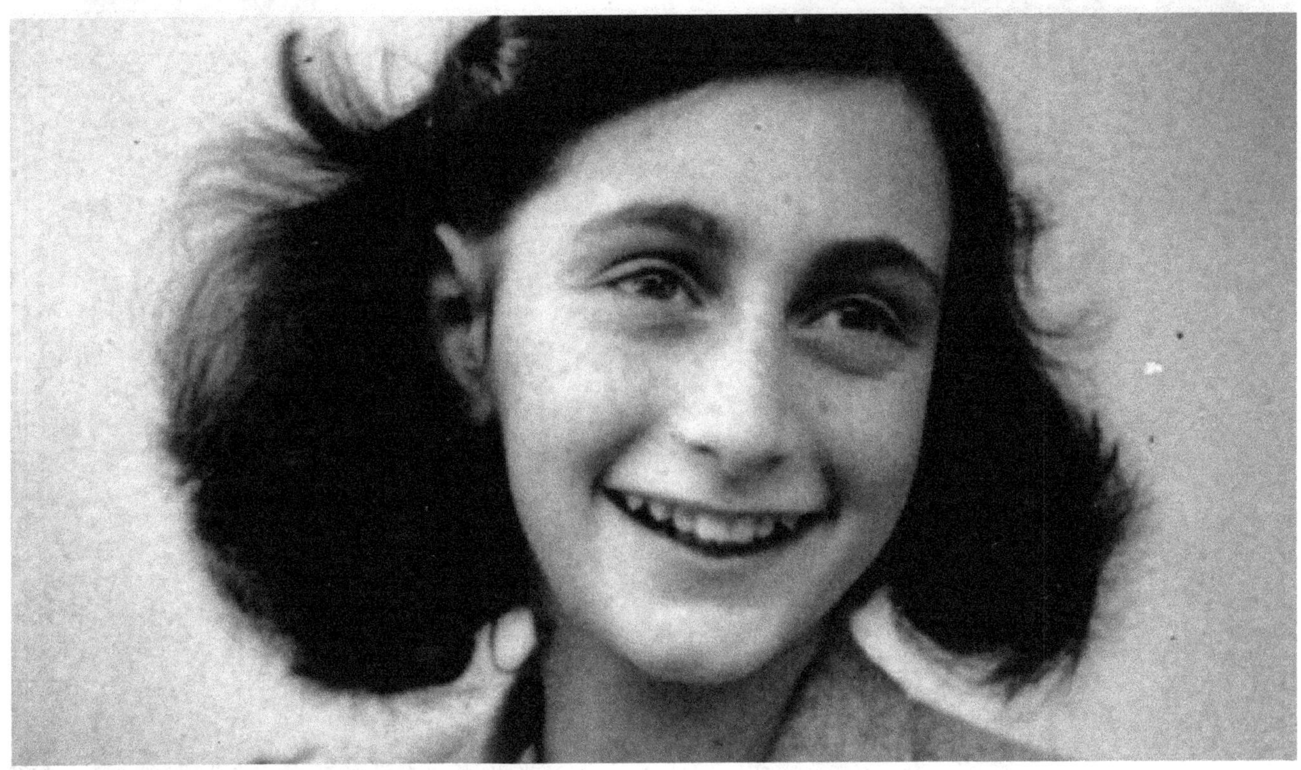

Dit is een foto, zoals
ik me zou wensen,
altijd zo te zijn.
Dan had ik nog wel
een kans om naar
Holywood te komen.
Annefrank.
10 Oct. 1942

(translation)
"This is a photo as I would wish
myself to look all the time. Then
I would maybe have a chance to
come to Hollywood."
Anne Frank, 10 Oct. 1942

PLAGIARIZED (LIKE EVERYTHING BIDEN THINKS; SAYS & DOES) FROM FIDEL CASTRO

BARACK HUSSEIN'S BAD & EVERYTHING GETTING WORSE ALL THE TIME "NEW NORMAL" OBAMA SNEERED "THOSE JOBS AREN'T COMING BACK. WHAT'S TRUMP GOING TO DO, WAVE A MAGIC WAND"

Foxconn Plant Championed by Trump Lands Google Server Contract

Monday, 23 November 2020 07:33 AM AFTER THE ELECTION IN WISCONSIN WAS STOLEN BY BIDEN

Foxconn Technology Group plans to assemble key components for Google servers from its plant in Wisconsin, people familiar with the matter said, finally breathing life into a factory Donald Trump hailed as crucial to bringing manufacturing back to the U.S.

The Taiwanese company has decided to locate production for this new contract at the existing complex rather than make the components at home or in China, the people said, asking not to be identified discussing a sensitive move. The under-utilized factory should start mass production in the first quarter, timed with the release of Intel Corp.'s Ice Lake server chips, they said. Foxconn is setting up surface-mount technology assembly lines that it will use to place semiconductors onto circuit boards, they added.

Foxconn, known also as Hon Hai Precision Industry Co., is one of several Taiwanese firms exploring ways to expand in America and lessen a reliance on Chinese production bases. The company has also sought to diversify a business that counts on Apple Inc. for half its revenue, including by courting more American clients. On Thursday, Taiwan Semiconductor Manufacturing Co. won city-level incentives for a $12 billion chip plant in Phoenix, another step toward bringing high-tech manufacture back to the U.S. and addressing security concerns over the industry's supply chain.

A Foxconn representative confirmed it's developing data center infrastructure and high-performance computing "capabilities" in Wisconsin, but declined to name any customers.

Taiwan counts Washington as an essential diplomatic, economic, and military ally amid rising tensions with Beijing. Foxconn, which operates most of its factories in central and southern China, won Google's business because it was the only contract manufacturer capable of establishing a surface-mount technology line on American soil, one of the people said. Shanghai-listed Foxconn Industrial Internet Co., its cloud business unit, will oversee the server business in Wisconsin, another person familiar with Foxconn's operations said.

The plant in Wisconsin was unveiled to much fanfare in 2018 by Foxconn Chairman Terry Gou and Trump, who called it "the Eighth Wonder of the World." Once envisioned as the centerpiece of a Made in America effort that would create 13,000 jobs for the Badger State, it instead succumbed to delays and switched directions several times after local officials slashed subsidies. The company missed its first-year hiring target by a wide margin, ending 2018 with just 178 full-time employees. And rather than the promised large-sized display panels, it began churning out face masks and ventilators this year.

Yet its location in the heart of America is now a boon to Alphabet Inc.'s Google, which is trying to win lucrative contracts for its server-dependent cloud business. The U.S. company considers it an important area for the company's growth, but one in which Amazon.com Inc. and Microsoft Corp. dominate. An American base could help Foxconn court U.S. government contracts, particularly as Washington ramps up scrutiny over a largely Chinese-focused global electronics supply chain.

GOP poised to flip 4 House seats in California, more than any other state

Despite Democrats' confident predictions of a "Blue Wave" sweeping statehouses in the November election, the final results showed that almost nothing had changed. Yet in California, a Democrat stronghold, Republicans are poised to flip more House seats than in any other state.

The results have shown a significant, reversal from the 2018 midterms, which was marked by a rabid anti-Trump furor that helped Democrats flip seven House seats. Now, the GOP is on the verge of taking back four of those seats.

Young Kim took back California's 39th District from Democrats after incumbent Rep. Gil Cisneros flipped the normally Republican district i**Young Kim** took back California's 39th District **from Democrats after incumbent Rep. Gil Cisneros flipped the normally Republican district in the 2018 "Blue Wave."**

Sunlight shines on the U.S. Capitol building on Capitol Hill in Washington.

In the Republican stronghold of Orange County, Michelle Steel took back California's 48th District **after the unprecedented 2018 victory of Democratic Rep. Harley Rouda.**

California's 21st District, which includes Fresno and Kern counties, looks set to return to the GOP after David Valadao was projected this week to reclaim the seat he lost to Democratic Rep. TJ Cox in 2018.

Republican U.S. Rep. Mike Garcia declared victory **last Friday in the state's 25th Congressional District. The seat, a former GOP stronghold that spans parts of Los Angeles and Ventura counties, was flipped blue by Democrat Katie Hill in 2018, but she resigned from Congress last year over a nude photo scandal. The final results are expected to be announced later this week. So how did Republicans manage to make gains in a solidly blue stat – despite confident predictions to the contrary?**

For California Republican Chairwoman Jessica Millan Patterson, GOP gains in the Golden States reflected Californian's disillusionment with years of Democrats' "failed" policies.

"Californians are ready for some change," Patterson told Fox News in an interview. "California Democrats have to own every single failed policy here in California, whether it's affordability, homelessness of K-12 education. They have shown every single one of those failures. And I think time and time again, they have shown – particularly Governor Newsom – how out of touch they are with working Californians." Patterson said that the flipped House seats, combined with voters' rejection of a batch of progressive propositions, suggests that "Californians overwhelmingly agreed with us on the idea."

CALIFORNIA CHURCH ASKS SUPREME COURT TO BLOCK CORONAVIRUS RESTRICTIONS ON GATHERINGS

"People were fed up and sick and tired of every single new regulation and just out of touch policy that they tried to put forward in these communities. And we talked about it. We talked about what their failures were and what California Republican solutions are," she said.

A person who worked on both the campaigns of Mike Garcia and Michelle Steel attributed their wins to a message of lower taxation and less regulation, which puts them at odds with what is coming out of Sacramento. "I think when you have good candidates with a good message of lower taxes and fighting tax hikes, things like that – saying I don't support defunding the police, that was also, kind of the background of both of these races. I think when you have good candidates with a good fiscal message, that plays anywhere," he said. "And it shows that when you have that, you can be outspent two, three, four-to-one and still win at the end of the day." Though Democrats have ultimately retained control of the House, their losses pointed to a potential GOP-controlled House in 2022, but a potential foothold in a state where they have been sidelined for decades.

"Here in California, we've been the poster child for failed radical left socialist agenda. And we don't want this to happen to the rest of the country," Patterson said. "We're doing our best to fix things here in California. And I think that if you haven't already, you should take another look at the California Republican Party."

CALIFORNIA HERE WE COME KAMIKAZE KAMALA NEW DEAL California Inmates Involved in $1 Billion COVID-19 NEW DEAL Unemployment Benefits Fraud, According to Officials

Alex Galbraith

California prison inmates pulled off a massive amount of benefits fraud this year, potentially bringing in over $1 billion in illegitimate unemployment benefits under programs passed to ease the economic impact of COVID-19. According to prosecutors in California, the scheme involved tens of thousands of inmates across the California penal system.

"The fraud is honestly staggering," Sacramento County District Attorney Anne Marie Schubert told NBC News.

The benefits were spread out between direct payments to inmates and checks sent to their relatives. A significant portion of the state's death row inmates (133 out of 700) had their names used in the plot. The alleged beneficiaries include Scott Peterson, a true crime bugbear who became infamous after killing his wife and unborn child in 2002.

Peterson's lawyer claimed his name was used without his knowledge while speaking to CNN.

"They are not making any accusations against Scott at all at this point," attorney Pat Harris said. "There is no accusation that he did anything wrong. I am 100 % confident they will find that Scott was in no way involved in anything fraudulent."

The fraud also included many instances of fake names and false social security numbers, according to authorities. John Doe, John Adams, and "Poopy Britches" were all found to be fraudulent beneficiaries of the program established by inmates. The majority of the alleged fraud took advantage of the supplemental $600 per week unemployment benefits passed under the CARES Act.

"That money was stolen from the coffers of the California government," Schubert told CNN.

California sent unemployment benefits to 20,000 prisoners, including notorious killers

BREAKING NEW YORK TIMES; CNN W/ POST MSNBC SCOTT PETERSON; MURDERER oF HIS WIFE LACIE & UNBORN SON CONNER; USING HIS $1,413,212,67 UNEMPLOYMENTS BENEFITS THAT HE'S COLLECTED WHILE ON SAN QUENTIN DEATH ROW TO PAY FOR HIS **AIR HAVANA HELICOPTER GUNSHIP ESCAPE** FROM THE SAN QUENTIN PRISON YARD TO JUAREZ STATE IN MEXICO; A WAITING CUBAN AIR FORCE JET WILL WHISK SCOTT PETERSON TO HAVANA PETERSON ALREADY SOLD MOVIE RIGHTS TO HIS STORY FOR $7,620,000 TO DREAMWORKS; BRAD PITT & TOM CRUISE COMPETING FOR THE TITLE ROLE TO PLAY PETERSON **From left: Defense attorney Mark Geragos, Scott Peterson and defense attorney Pat Harris listen during Peterson's murder trial on July 29, 2004 in Redwood City, Calif.**

SACRAMENTO, Calif. — California's system for paying unemployment benefits is so dysfunctional that the state approved more than $140 million for at least 35,000 prisoners, prosecutors said Tuesday, **detailing a scheme that resulted in payouts in the names of well-known convicted murderers like Scott Peterson and Cary Stayner.**

From March to August, more than 35,000 inmates were named in claims filed with the California Employment Development Department, with more than 20,000 being paid, according to Sacramento County District Attorney Anne Marie Schubert. At least 158 claims were filed for 133 death-row inmates, resulting in more than $420,000 in benefits paid. CAN LOSER SCHMUCK JIMMY KIMMEL; WITH HIS HUMOR OF A SUICIDAL MORTICIAN; USE THIS MATERIAL?

"It involves rapists and child molesters, human traffickers and other violent criminals in our state prisons," Schubert said.

The list includes Peterson, who was sentenced to death after being convicted of killing his pregnant wife following a trial that riveted the nation. Others are Stayner, convicted of killing four people in Yosemite National Park in 1999; Susan Eubanks, a San Diego woman convicted of shooting her four sons to death in 1997; Isauro Aguirre, who was sentenced to death for the 2013 murder of 8-year-old Gabriel Fernandez in Los Angeles; and Wesley Shermantine, part of the duo dubbed the "Speed Freak Killers" for their meth-induced killing rampage in the 1980s and '90s.

Prosecutors said they learned of the scheme from listening in on recorded prison phone calls, where inmates would talk about how easy it was for everyone to get paid. They said the scheme always involved someone on the outside to facilitate the applications. In Kern County, home to five state prisons, one address was used to receive benefits for 16 inmates. "In my nearly four decades as a prosecutor in this state, I have never seen fraud of this magnitude," Kern County District Attorney Cynthia Zimmer said. In some cases, inmates used their real names. In others, they used fake names and even fake Social Security numbers. In one instance, an inmate used the name: "poopy britches," Schubert said.

"Quite frankly, the inmates are mocking us," Schubert said.

Prosecutors declined to give more details about the claim associated with Peterson, citing an ongoing investigation. His attorney, Pat Harris, did not return an email or phone message from The Associated Press seeking

comment. The California Supreme Court recently overturned Peterson's death sentence and has ordered a lower court to review his murder conviction. Get the tools you need to succeed in the market, with real-time market data, news, and analysis from MarketWatch — one of the most reputable brands for personal finance, business, and market news. Become a MarketWatch subscriber today.

Prosecutors blamed the Employment Development Department, which has been overwhelmed by more than 16.4 million benefit claims since the pandemic began in March, resulting in a backlog that at one time totaled more than 1.6 million people.

But prosecutors said in its haste to approve benefits, the department did not check unemployment claims against a list of prisoners, as many other states do. San Mateo District Attorney Stephen Wagstaffe said that when he notified the department about 22 inmates fraudulently receiving benefits, they told him they could not cut off the payments until they were formally charged with a crime.

The problem was so bad that on Monday, nine county district attorneys sent a letter to Gov. Gavin Newsom asking for him to intervene.

In an email to the AP, Newsom called the fraud "absolutely unacceptable." He said he first learned of the fraud earlier this year, which prompted him to order the department to "review its practices and take immediate actions to prevent fraud and to hold people accountable."

Newsom said he has ordered the Office of Emergency Services to set up a task force to assist prosecutors with their investigation.

The Inauthenticity Behind MARXIST JEW HATING Black Lives Matter BREAKING CNN NY TIMES W POST MSNBC JOE BIDEN EXECUTIVE ORDER GIVES Black Lives Matter ISRAEL & JERUSALEM TO BE GREEN NEW DEAL COTTON PLANTATION INCLUDING ALL U.S. NUCLEAR WEAPONS AS DEMOCRAT REPARATIONS FOR "SYSTEMIC RACISM" BIDEN DEFENDS VICTIM FOCUSED IDENTITY & RACIAL PRIDE (AUTHOR ADDENDUM)

By Shelby Steele

A 'defund the police' NOW UPGRADED TO DEFUND GOD & HUMAN CIVILIZATION **protest in Minneapolis, June 6.**

Sen. Tim Scott of South Carolina gave a remarkable speech at this year's Republican National Convention. Yes, here was a black man at a GOP event, so there was a whiff of identity politics. When we see color these days, we expect ideology to follow. But Mr. Scott's charisma that night was simply that he spoke as a person, not a spokesperson for his color. Burgess Owens, Herschel Walker, Daniel Cameron and several others did the same. It was a parade of individuals. And in their speeches the human being stepped out from behind the identity, telling personal stories that reached for human connections with the American people—this rather than the usual posturing for leverage with tales of grievance. So they were all fresh and compelling.SUBSCRIBE

Do these Republicans foretell a new racial order in America? Clearly they have pushed their way through an old racial order, as have—it could be argued—many black Trump voters in the recent election. I believe there is in fact a new racial order slowly and tenuously emerging, and that we blacks are swimming through rough seas to reach it. But to better see the new, it is necessary to know the old. The old began in what might be called America's Great Confession. In passing the 1964 Civil Rights Act, America effectively confessed to a long and terrible collusion with the evil of racism. (President Kennedy was the first president to acknowledge that civil rights was a "moral issue.") This triggered nothing less than a crisis of moral authority that threatened the very legitimacy of American democracy.

Even today, almost 60 years beyond the Civil Rights Act, groups like *Black Lives Matter*, **along with a vast grievance industry, use America's insecure moral authority around race as an opportunity to assert them-**

selves. Doesn't BLM dwell in a space made for it by America's racial self-doubt?

In the culture, whites and American institutions are effectively mandated by this confession to prove their innocence of racism as a condition of moral legitimacy. Blacks, in turn, are mandated to honor their new freedom by developing into educational and economic parity with whites. If whites achieve racial innocence and blacks develop into parity with whites, then America will have overcome its original sin. Democracy will have become manifest.

This was America's post-confession bargain between the races—innocence on the white hand, development on the black. It defined the old order with which those convention speakers seemed to break. But there is a problem with these mandates: To achieve their ends, they both need blacks to be victims. Whites need blacks they can save to prove their innocence of racism. Blacks must put themselves forward as victims the better to make their case for entitlements.

This is a corruption because it makes black suffering into a moral power to be wielded, rather than a condition to be overcome. This is the power that blacks discovered in the '60s. It gained us a War on Poverty, affirmative action, school busing, public housing and so on. But it also seduced us into turning our identity into a virtual cult of victimization—as if our persecution was our eternal flame, the deepest truth of who we are, a tragic fate we trade on. After all, in an indifferent world, it may feel better to be the victim of a great historical injustice than a person left out of history when that injustice recedes.

Yet there is an elephant in the room. It is simply that we blacks aren't much victimized any more. Today we are free to build a life that won't be stunted by racial persecution. Today we are far more likely to encounter racial preferences than racial discrimination. Moreover, we live in a society that generally shows us goodwill—a society that has isolated racism as its most unforgivable sin.

This lack of victimization amounts to an "absence of malice" that profoundly threatens the victim-focused black identity. Who are we without the malice of racism? Can we be black without being victims? The great diminishment (not eradication) of racism since the '60s means that our victim-focused identity has become an anachronism. Well suited for the past, it strains for relevance in the present.

Thus, for many blacks today—especially the young—there is a feeling of inauthenticity, that one is only thinly black because one isn't racially persecuted. "Systemic racism" is a term that tries to recover authenticity for a less and less convincing black identity. This racism is really more compensatory than systemic. It was invented to make up for the increasing absence of the real thing.

This summer, in cities from Portland, Ore., to Baltimore, black protest seemed driven more by the angst of inauthenticity than by any real menace. The protests themselves came off as theater. There were costumes, masks and well-rehearsed mimes of confrontation and outrage. The violence was destructive, but only to a point. After all it was calibrated to go on for months. In the summer of 2020, self-consciousness replaced spontaneity as the essence of youthful protest in America—yet another sign that there is not enough real victimization to light the sort of fire that burned down Detroit in the '60s.

I doubt that any of the black speakers at the RNC would argue that racism has vanished from American life. What makes them harbingers of a new racial order is that they unpair victimization from identity. Victimization may be an experience we endure, but it should never be an identity that defines us. They all spoke as American citizens in a spirit of citizenship.

This is the great challenge that always awaits the oppressed after freedom is achieved. If only out of loyalty to our past (all this suffering has to mean something), we will feel compelled to make victimization the centerpiece of our identity today. This will seem the authentic and honorable thing to do. But it will only further invest us in precisely the fruitless tangle of identity and woundedness that mires us in the past. We should never deny the past, but it should only inform and inspire.

In the end, only one achievement will turn us from the old victim-focused racial order toward a new, nonracial order: the full and unqualified acceptance of our freedom. We don't have to fight for freedom so much any more. We have to do something more difficult—fully accept that we are free.

MACYS RENAMED BLACK LIVES MATTER CHERNOBYL STORES WORLDWIDE INTERNATIONAL PART OF REPARATIONS PAID TO "SUN NEVER SETS ON THE BLACK LIVES MATTER EMPIRE"

BLACK
LIVES
MATTER

MATTERS

Shootings in New York City Nearly Double as Arrests for Serious Crimes Fall

CUOMO de BLASIO JOINTLY ANNOUNCE INSTEAD OF TAPS; NEW YORK STATE WILL BE SENDING BY BUS & SUBWAY THE NEW YORK PHILHARMONIC ORCHESTRA TO PERFORM HONORING ALL UNSOLVED NO ARREST DRIVE-BY ASSAULT RIFLE UNDER AGE SIX MURDER VICTIMS "ITS GETTING BETTER ALL THE TIME" HIP HOP UPDATE REINTERPREATION AT ALL GRAVESIDE POTTERS FIELD & MURDER VICTIM UNCLAIMED BODY DIRECT CREMATIONS PAID BY EXECUTIVE BIDEN ORDER MEDICAID ALEXANDRIA OCASIO-CORTEZ DEMANDS POLICE FUNDING BE CUT TO BELOW ZERO; REPARATIONS PAID TO CRIMINAL LIVES MATTER FROM COP UNEMPLOYMENT BENEFITS & MURDERED COP WIDOW'S PENSION BENEFITS

NYPD Commissioner Dermot Shea says officers are making progress in gun arrests

NYPD officers at the site of a shooting in Corona, Queens, on Nov. 1. *By* Ben Chapman

NOW READ THIS

Teens plead not guilty in stabbing death of Barnard College student Tessa Majors

By Jay Croft and Mark Morales, CNN

Updated 5:38 PM ET, Wed February 19, 2020

14-Year-Old Boy Sentenced to 18 Months for His Role in Stabbing of Barnard Student Tessa Majors BELIEVE ME; IN JAIL HE GETS SMART BIG SCREEN TV; ALL CABLE CHANNELS; DELIVERY TO HIS CELL OF HUSTLER MAGAZINE & UBER EATS 24/7 DELIVERY OF BAGELS; LOX; PHILADELPHIA ANY FLAVOR; FREE CANNABIS/ANY BRAND ROLLING PAPERS CREAM CHEESE & MANISCHEWITZ CHOCOLATE COVERED EGG MATZO AFTER HIS SENTENCE THEY FORCE HIM TO LEAVE PRISON BUT GETS TO COME HOME TO JAIL IF HE KILLS A (12) YEAR OLD GIRL ON THE WAY OUT

Shootings in New York City have nearly doubled this year, **New York Police Department officials said Tuesday, while arrests for major crimes have plummeted.**

From Jan 1. through Sunday, the city has recorded 1,359 shootings, an increase of nearly 95% from the 698 in the same period last year, according to NYPD data. The number of shooting victims rose to 1,667 from 828.

Meanwhile, arrests for major crimes have fallen by nearly 13%, driven by drops for every major category except burglaries, car thefts and gun-related crimes, according to the data. Arrests for crimes involving guns are up nearly 19% this year, the data showed.

In a press conference Tuesday, Mayor Bill de Blasio attributed the rise in shootings and the drop in arrests to factors related to the coronavirus pandemic**, citing the closure of businesses, schools and houses of worship as factors that created a "perfect storm" in the city.**

"A lot of things we depend on to keep people safe and stable weren't there," Mr. de Blasio said.

Police at the scene of a shooting in the Bronx on Oct. 9.

According to NYPD officials, the year-over-year increase in shootings and murders is more pronounced than any in more than two decades. Murders in the city rose more than 37%, with 405 reported between Jan. 1 and Sunday, compared with 295 in the same period in 2019.

THE SOLUTION; PER CUOMO; de BLASIO; WOODCHUCK SCHMUCK SCHUMER & GILLIBRAND IS ORDERING ALL COPS IN ACTIVE SHOOTER END GAMES TO BEG KILLERS WITH ASSAULT RIFLES TO ACCEPT ROBOT DELIVERED BEN & JERRY'S CHUNKY MONKEY ICE CREAM & CHIPS AHOY EXTRA CHUNKIE SOFT & CHEWY NATURAL GOODNESS COOKIES TO GET ON THE GOOD SIDE OF EVERY ACTIVE SHOOTER BEFORE THEY SHOOT TO KILL AT COPS WITH BEN & JERRY'S HAPPY BELLY AND/OR Häagen-Dazs ON ALL 911 CALLS

Many shootings have taken place in areas of Queens, the Bronx and Brooklyn. A 70-year-old woman was struck on Tuesday afternoon by a stray bullet in the Bedford-Stuyvesant section of Brooklyn and wasn't likely to survive, police officials said.

Criminologists, police and law-enforcement officials have cited various factors for the city's rise in violent crimes, including a backlogged court system, changes to bail laws and a decrease in the numbers of arrests.

NYPD officials have blamed the drop in arrests on a shortage of officers caused by dramatic increases in officers calling in sick amid the pandemic, as well as staffing cuts due to reductions to the department's budget. Large-scale demonstrations in the city over the summer have also placed demands on the uniformed workforce, according to NYPD officials.

In a radio interview Tuesday, NYPD Commissioner Dermot Shea said that officers were making progress in fighting the rise in shootings, citing an increase in gun arrests that began in September. Gun arrests in the city climbed by more than doubled in October, according to NYPD data.

"THE OFFICERS OUT THERE ARE PULLING OFF THE STREET GATLING ANTI-AIRCRAFT GUNS; HARPOONS; PLUS TRIBAL AFRICAN WAR CLUBS ADORNED WITH ORANGE FEATHERS; PITCHFORKS; TOMAHAWKS; BRASS KNUCKLES; BLUNDERBUSSES; COBRA VENOM POISON TIPPED CROSSBOW ARROWS; DAVID & GOLIATH STANDARD ISSUE SLING SHOTS; WATER GUNS THAT SQUIRT LYE & SULFURIC ACID & ATOMIC CATAPULTS THAT THROW BOULDERS OF UP TO 1.6 LONG TONS;

THESE ARE ONLY SOME OF TODAY'S ARSENAL OF **EVERYDAY MASS DESTRUCTION WEAPONS POSSESSED BY NINE-YEAR-OLDS WITH WAR MAKING CAPABILITIES; WEAPONS ONCE STANDARD TERROR ISSUE OF SADDAM HUSSEIN; ATILLA THE HUN; CONAN THE BARBARIAN & ADOLF HITLER; MORE COMMONLY NOW FOUND AMONG NYC ADOLESCENTS; EAST SIDE; WEST SIDE; SIDEWALKS OF FUN CITY AT THE CROSSROADS OF NEW YORK BIG APPLE NEW NORMAL BLUE STATE DAY-BY-DAY CITY LIVING; WE MAKE THE BEST OF IT; ... BOYS & GIRLS, O.K LET'S HEAR IT NOW, ALL TOGETHER ...**

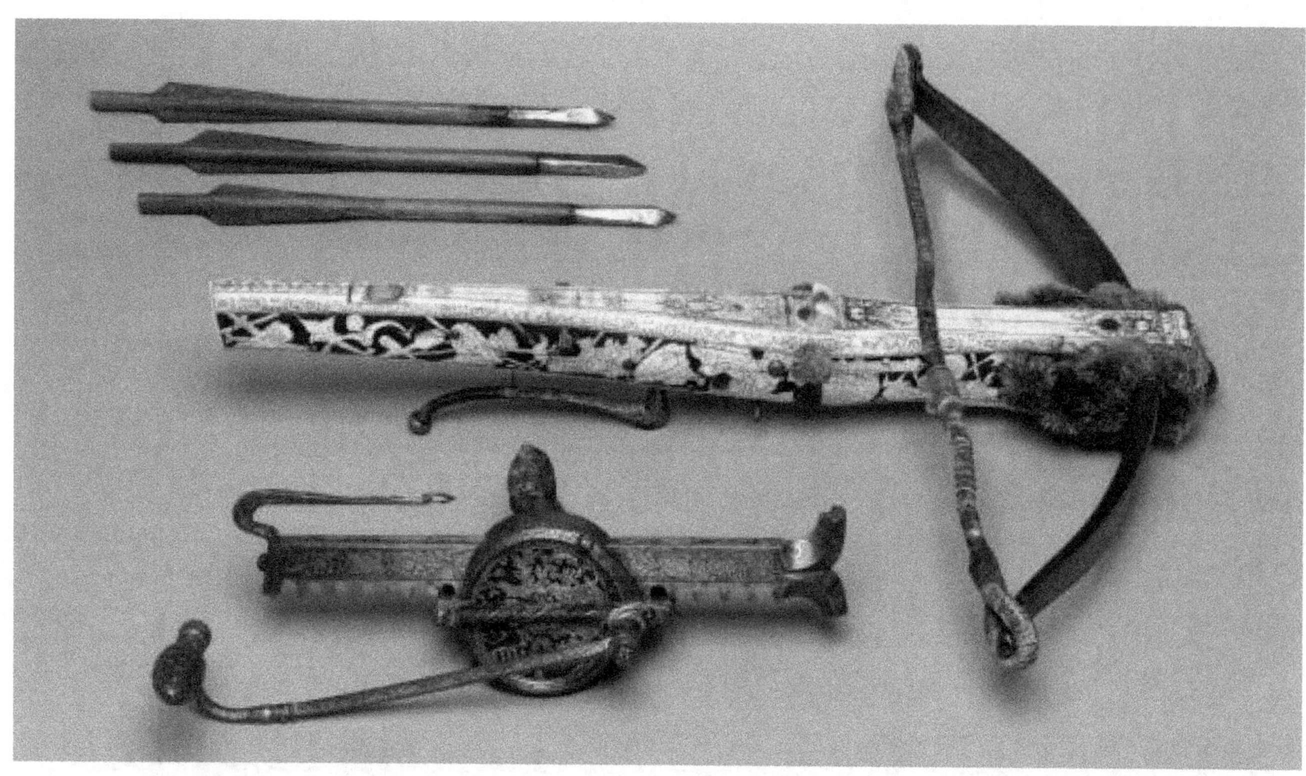

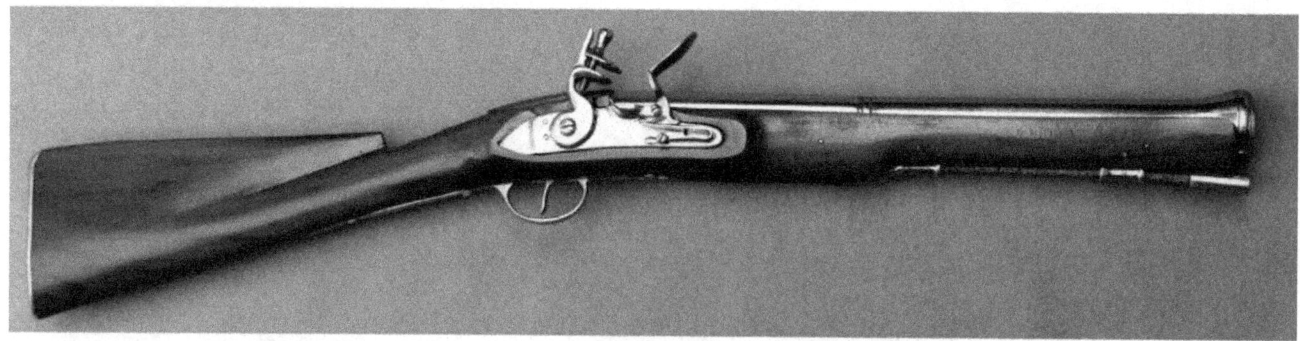

Chinese Traction Catapults ARE NOW COMMONLY USED BY BROOKLYN 6TH GRADE CHILDREN IN SIEGE WARFARE ADOLESCENT STREET CRIME

The use of catapults, however, was not limited to the Roman army. There are records which show that the catapult was also employed by the armies of ancient China as well. For example, during the early Spring and Autumn period (8th – 7th centuries BC), there was a machine called a 'hui' that was used by the King of Zhou against the Duke of Zheng during a battle in 707 BC. As the word 'hui' no longer exists, we cannot be completely sure of its meaning. Nevertheless, scholars from the Han Dynasty interpreted this device as a catapult.

WE HAVE FOUND AUTHORITATIVE REPORTS THAT KINDERGARTENERS WITH SHOULDER FIRED STINGER MISSILES ARE NOW PLANNING BRINKS ARMOURED CAR HEISTS & HEAR RUMORS OF 4TH GRADERS IN THE AL SHARPTON HOUSING PROJECT ON BARACK HUSSEIN OBAMA BOULEVARD NOW HAVE A CACHE OF CRUISE MISSILES ARMED WITH MULTIPLE REENTRY NUCLEAR WARHEADS. WE MUST GET NUCLEAR & BIOLOGICAL WEAPONS OF MASS DESTRUCTION OUT OF THE HANDS OF CHILDREN IN THE "HOOD" UNDER THE AGE OF (6); Mr. Shea said. "It's just COMMON SENSE. we need to recalibrate and get some of these very dangerous PRE-SCHOOL (4) YEAR OLDS INTO PRISONER OF WAR CAMPS; PREFERABLY AT LEAST AS SECURE AS GUANTANAMO OR ALCATRAZ; BEFORE THEY SHUT IT DOWN; WITH SHARKS SWIMMING AROUND THE ISLAND PRISON; RINGED WITH

CONCERTINA WIRE & GUARDS WITH SNIPER RIFLES; BEFORE IT'S TOO LATE. MAYBE WE CAN DISTRACT THESE KIDS WITH HOSTESS CUPCAKES.

NYC CITY COUNCIL BEGINS HEARINGS ON RELOCATING RIKERS ISLAND PRISON TO THE 3RD OUTERMOST RING OF SATURN PAID FOR BY INCREASED NYC PROPERTY TAXES & 15% SURCHARGES ON DAY OLD BAGELS

Cuomo stands up for President Trump on media bias CUOMO ADDED; IT'D BE GREAT; IF ADOLF BABY WERE STILL AROUND; 'OLE TIMES SAKE; BYGONES BE BYGONES; ADOLF BABY COULD GIVE US A HELPING HAND; IF HE HAS ANY EXTRAS; LEND LEASE AUST B KING TIGER TANKS; V-2 MISSILES & MESSERSCHMITT 262 JET FIGHTERS ARMED WITH 160 ROUND @ MINUTE 50 CALIBRE MACHINE GUNS & ROCKETS TO SAVE NEW YORKERS FROM KIDS UNDER THE AGE OF 9.

BREAKING CNN NY TIMES W POST MSNBC ADVERTISEMENTS IN TIMES OF MOGADISHU SOMALIA EXPEDIA OFFERING NYC SAFARIS TO AFRICAN MIDDLE CLASS TOURISTS TOURS ON ELEPHANTS FURLOUGHED FROM RINGLING BROTHERS BARNUM & BAILEY GREATEST SHOW ON EARTH TOURISTS FROM MOGADISHU; SOMALIA; MALAGASY REPUBLIC (A.K.A.) MADAGASCAR) VISITING NYC TIMES SQUARE FOR NEW YEARS EVE ISSUED WILL BE AK 47 ASSAULT RIFLES; NOW LIMITED TO SHOOTING (7) NEW YORKERS PER TOURIST @ DAY INCREASED TO (11) FOR TAXIDERMY TROPHY MOUNTING STUFFED NATIVE NEW YORKER (3) NYC HUMANS OF AGE 4 OR OLDER GAME KILLS; SHIPMENT INCLUDED BACK HOME TO MOGADISHU FROM JFK OR NEWARK AIRPORT

ROUND TRIP INC. ALL-IN $9999.999.99 INCLUDING NYC STATE SALES TAX ALL EXPENSES PAID INCLUDING GRATUITIES INTRODUCTORY THRU MEMORIAL DAY 2021. SEE BROOKLYN BIG GAME HUNTING FOR SOMALIA & GAZA TOURISTS IN PROMOTIONAL 2021 BROCHURES

RESERVE YOUR NYC BROOKLYN PROSPECT PARK & CENTRAL PARK ELEPHANT BACK NYC HUNTING; ALL EXPENSES PAID TOURS ROUND TRIP MOGADISHU TO JFK 1ST CLASS TRIP CONCIERGE (7) NIGHTS AT YOUR CHOICE OF PLAZA; PIERRE; CARLYLE; RITZ CARLTON OR WALDORF ASTORIA 24/7 FOOD/LIQUOR/CANNABIS ROOM SERVICE INCLUDED. MC/VISA/AMEX/ BITCOIN/ DISCOVER RESERVE YOURS TODAY

Fox News Media Analyst Howard Kurtz reacts to Joe Biden choosing cabinet officials out of the media ranks.

New York Gov. Andrew Cuomo **defended** President Trump **this week as the three-term Democratic governor indicated the media did not treat the president with the respect that the office commands.**

Cuomo said during an interview with WAMC radio Monday that the press has taken on a "nastier tone," which he has noticed at his press conferences and all across the nation, describing a "disrespect that never existed."

"The way they question President Trump at some of these press conferences is just – I've never heard that tone with the president," Cuomo said**.**

When asked by WAMC's Alan Chartock whether the president "deserved it," Cuomo said there is supposed to be a "decorum" to the institution – indicating that even if you do not like a person, you still respect the institution he or she represents.

"There are reporters who just are unprofessional, don't know the facts and ask really biased questions," Cuomo explained. "You want to say 'well I don't like the president and I disrespect him,' I know but it's still the office of the president."

5 THINGS TO KNOW ABOUT NY GOV. ANDREW CUOMO'S CORONAVIRUS NURSING HOME CONTROVERSY

While Trump has been known for his contentious relationship with the media – routinely calling out different networks for their coverage of his presidency and campaigns – Cuomo has also had his fair share of tense run-ins with reporters.

Last week**, for example, the governor drew attention for his hostile responses to reporters who were confused about New York City's school closure plan.**

When a reporter said he was "still very confused," Cuomo snapped back "then you're confused!"

"No, [parents are] not confused. You're confused," Cuomo told the reporter. "Read the law and you won't be confused." While Trump and Cuomo have publicly butted heads on numerous occasions, they were able to work together during the worst of the early coronavirus outbreak in New York to flatten the curve.

AFTER (13) YEARS; I CANCELLED MY HOME DELIVERY OF THE WALL STREET JOURNAL; THEY KEEP CHARGING ME EVEN THOUGH I TOLD THEIR CIRCULATION SUPERVISOR I DON'T

WANT THEIR FUCKEN RAG WITH TRITE POLITICALLY CORRECT YOUNG BITCH REPORTERS ANYWHERE NEAR MY HOME; AND UGLY LITTLE RUNT NERD CHRIS WALLACE (FUCK HIM) ACTUALLY SNEERS AT REPUBLICAN HEARTBURN AFTER HE CALLED ARIZONA AT 10:30 PM ELECTION NIGHT

They also faltered in

Fox News daytime ratings drop by 32% in two weeks since the election

WE'RE GOING TO PAY THESE COCKROACHES TO STAB AMERICA & FREEDOM IN THE BACK?

a key demographic in prime time

Rafael Henrique

Cable news network behemoth Fox News dipped **in viewership among a key demographic in recent ratings reports, and lost 32% of viewership in daytime.**

Nielsen Media Research said that CNN took both top spots among the 25-54 age demographic during prime-time on Friday. Anderson Cooper's show, "AC360," took the time spot with 604K viewers. Chris Cuomo's CNN show took the second highest slot.

Fox News' total viewership also fell an astounding **32% in the two weeks after the Nov. 3 election compared to its viewership the two weeks before the election.**

While Fox News' viewership dropped, the viewership for CNN and MSNBC increased to near parity. In weekday average daytime viewership, Fox News garnered 1.63 million viewers, CNN received 1.68 million viewers, and MSNBC received 1.71 million viewers.

But despite the precipitous drop in daytime, Fox continues to beat the competition in total numbers of viewers during prime-time hours.

Fox News averaged 2.98 million viewers in prime time, with CNN averaging 2.05 million, and MSNBC seeing an average of 2.18 million viewers. Critics of Fox News have excoriated the network after they called the state of Arizona for former Vice President Joe Biden on election night while most other outlets were saying the results were too close to call. The state has since been called for Biden by the mainstream news outlets.

President Trump has also turned on the cable news network and has been criticizing Fox News in favor of some of its lesser known competitors. In one instance, he appeared to refer to himself as the "Golden Goose" and blamed them for the 2020 election.

"Very sad to watch this happen, but they forgot what made them successful, what got them there. They forgot the Golden Goose," the president tweeted.

"The biggest difference between the 2016 Election, and 2020, was @FoxNews!" he added.

In another missive sent out in March, the president accused Fox News of not doing enough to get him and other Republicans re-elected.

Some viewers have posted on social media that they are actively seeking alternative sources of news, including the YouTube channel of BlazeTV host Steven Crowder.

Here's more about Trump criticizing Fox News: "FOX DAYTIME RATINGS HAVE COMPLETELY COLLAPSED"

Republicans Sue to Stop Wisconsin Vote Certification

Election workers, right, verify ballots as recount observers, left, watch during a Milwaukee hand recount of presidential votes at the Wisconsin Center Friday in Milwaukee. (AP)

Republicans filed a lawsuit Tuesday asking the Wisconsin Supreme Court to block certification of the presidential election results even as a recount over Joe Biden's apparent win over President Donald Trump is ongoing.

The lawsuit echoes many of the same arguments Trump is making in trying, unsuccessfully, to have tens of thousands of ballots discounted during the recount. It also seeks to give the power to name presidential electors to the Republican-controlled Legislature.

Wisconsin state law allows the political parties to pick electors, which was done in October. Once the election results are certified (it's scheduled to be done Dec. 1), those pre-determined electors will cast their ballots for the winner on Dec. 14.

"The litigation filed this afternoon seeks to disenfranchise every Wisconsinite who voted in this year's presidential election," said Democratic Attorney General Josh Kaul. "The Wisconsin Department of Justice will ensure that Wisconsin's presidential electors are selected based on the will of the more than 3 million Wisconsin voters who cast a ballot."

The lawsuit also rehashes a claim that a federal court rejected in September that Facebook CEO Mark Zuckerberg tried to "illegally circumvent Wisconsin absentee voting laws" through grants awarded by a nonprofit center he funds. At least 10 cases have been filed across the country seeking to halt certification in parts or all of key battleground states, including lawsuits brought by the Trump campaign in Michigan and Pennsylvania. So far none have been successful.

Wisconsin's election results are scheduled to be certified Dec. 1.

The Wisconsin lawsuit was filed by attorney Erick Kaardal, a former Minnesota Republican Party official who also represented rapper Kanye West in his unsuccessful lawsuit attempting to get on the ballot in Wisconsin. Kaardal represents a conservative group called the Wisconsin Voters Alliance and a host of Republican voters.

Kaardal also filed an unsuccessful federal lawsuit in Wisconsin that attempted to block $6.3 million from being awarded to five heavily Democratic cities from the nonprofit Center for Technology and Civic Life, which is primarily funded by Zuckerberg and his wife. A judge tossed the lawsuit that argued the money amounted to bribery to bolster Democratic turnout in Green Bay, Kenosha, Madison, Milwaukee and Racine.

Many of the same arguments alleging the money was illegally awarded and therefore the election results should be nullified are being made in the new lawsuit in state court. Other claims mirror those by Trump's campaign. Those claims allege absentee ballots should not have been counted where election officials filled in missing information on the certification envelope that contains the ballot and that voters who identified as "indefinitely confined" were lying to avoid the state's photo ID law.

The Wisconsin Elections Commission advises clerks that they can fill in missing information on the ballot envelopes, such as the address of a witness. That's been the practice for years, and it's never been challenged.

The Wisconsin Supreme Court this spring affirmed the state elections commission's guidance that it's up to each voter to decide whether they are indefinitely confined. More than 215,000 voters this year said they were confined, which allows them to cast a ballot without having to present a photo ID. The lawsuit says more than 96,000 self-identified confined voters should not count. Biden won Wisconsin by 20,608 votes, but the lawsuit claims that more than 156,000 ballots should be tossed out. The lawsuit alleges that more than 14,000 ballots “requested in the name of a registered Republican by someone other than that person” were cast and that more than 12,000 “Republican ballots” were returned but not counted. People do not register to vote by political party in Wisconsin so it is impossible to know how many Republicans or Democrats requested absentee ballots. The lawsuit comes as the recount in Milwaukee and Dane counties has resulted in very few vote changes. As of Tuesday morning, Trump had gained just 57 votes. Trump paid for a recount in only the two counties with the largest numbers of Democratic votes.

Nearly 400 absentee ballots cast in Milwaukee that were not opened on Election Day were discovered Tuesday, a mistake that the city's top elections official attributed to human error. The county board of canvassers voted unanimously to count the ballots as part of the recount, which must be done by Dec. 1.

CNBC/Change Poll: Only 3 % Of Trump Voters Consider Election Legitimate

A supporter of President Donald Trump stands with a sign outside the Philadelphia Convention Center.

By Brian Trusdell

Only 3% of those who voted for Donald Trump consider tallies showing Joe Biden winning the election are legitimate.

In stark contrast, a whopping 73% view the incumbent Republican as the rightful winner, a CNBC/Change Research poll released Tuesday said.

The results **were relatively consistent among demographic groups sorted by age, education, and primary television news source. However, all 3% of those who believe Biden was the legitimate winner listed Fox News Channel as their primary source.**

(Since the election and dispute over the outcome, many in the Fox News audience have shifted to Newsmax, which has seen a sharp rise in ratings and demand for its online app among people critical of what they call Fox's increasingly muddled message on the current administration.)

The poll parallels a survey released by the communications and messaging firm Seven Letter**, which said on Monday that 79% of Trump voters believe the election was, in fact, stolen. In the CNBC/Change poll, 73% of Trump voters believe the 74-year-old native New Yorker to be the legitimate winner of the presidential election, 66% among Fox viewers and 84% among Newsmax viewers.**

"Trump voters who say Newsmax is one of their primary political news sources are particularly likely to call Trump the real winner," the text of the poll said.

Moreover, 31% said Trump should "fight in court until states certify results, and then concede to Joe Biden if Biden is certified the winner," but more than twice as many believe Trump should "fight in court until the Electoral College votes, and never concede to Joe Biden." Only 3% of Trump voters believe he should concede and begin any transition. This week, the General Services Administration authorized the start of transition activity and cooperation between the current White House and a Biden one, freeing up office space, millions of dollars in resources and access to intelligence briefings on a range of topics.

Trump, however, has remained steadfast in his contention that he won the election, and that widespread voter fraud helped tilt the numbers to Biden in several battleground states. Many of his legal challenges have failed, but he continues to press the case for recounts and reexaminations of ballots in places including Pennsylvania, and his legal team is aiming to take their case all the way to the Supreme Court -- a position applauded by dedicated Trump followers.

Newsmax itself, while calling more states for Biden based on certification of the votes, has not yet declared Biden the president-elect while those challenges are playing out.

The survey of 1,203 Trump voters was conducted online Nov. 18-21 and had a margin of error of 2.83 % points.

Rep. Guy Reschenthaler to Newsmax TV: Pa. Certifying Tainted Results 'Reckless'

By Eric Mack

Pennsylvania Secretary of State Kathy Boockvar's certification of the state's election results constitutes a "reckless" rush to judgment that started even before the election began, Rep. Guy Reschenthaler, R-Pa., said Tuesday night on Newsmax TV.

"I don't think we should be surprised that Secretary Boockvar – the person who said Pennsylvania was going to go to Joe Biden before voting even started – I don't think anybody should be surprised that she certified the election, but it's somewhat reckless, because the Trump campaign still has a pending lawsuit," Reschenthaler told Tuesday's "Stinchfield."

"As a lawyer, there is grounds for this lawsuit."

There is an "equal protection" constitutional case being made by the Trump campaign that has merit, Reschenthaler told host Grant Stinchfield. "You had some counties that were controlled by Democrats, Democrat-concentrated areas, that were allowing voters to cure ballots," he continued, focusing on the process of informing a mail-in voter there were errors or mistakes on their ballot. "And in the Republican areas, you were not allowed to cure ballots." Reschenthaler also reiterated the Trump campaign's contention that Pennsylvania state courts "unilaterally" changed election law, though the state legislature has the legal authority to decide.

"A clear violation of the U.S. Constitution," Reschenthaler insisted. "So, with these pending legal cases, these legal challenges, it may have been premature" to certify a Biden victory.

Rep. Louie Gohmert to Newsmax TV: Lawsuits Take Time to Get to Supreme Court

By Brian Trusdell

Rep. Louie Gohmert, R-Texas, downplayed the certification of election results in Pennsylvania and Nevada, saying lawsuits challenging the outcome were still working their way through courts, and even legal setbacks are part of the process to get the matter before the U.S. Supreme Court.

Gohmert, 67, who served as a state district judge and chief justice on Texas' 12th Circuit Court of Appeals,

told Newsmax TV's "American Agenda" on Tuesday that attorneys for President Donald Trump probably expected courts in some states to be hostile to their claims. "It's not up to litigants to show the evidence to professors, it's presenting that to the judges, that's where it's supposed to go," Gohmert told host Bob Sellers. "And even though there [are] unfriendly courts in Pennsylvania, that's laying the groundwork to get to the Supreme Court, where this ultimately needs to be decided."

Gohmert, who has represented Texas' 1st Congressional District along the border with Louisiana since 2005, said he might not expect any change in court results anytime soon. "No, I don't think it does at all," Gohmert said. "You've got to put evidence in at the trial court level, even though you know you're in unfriendly territory, because the goal is to put your evidence in there. The only thing supposed to be considered by appellate courts are things of which they can take judicial notice without actually having had them introduced into evidence.

"Now, I've seen evidence that there are some liberals on the Supreme Court that have just considered whatever they wanted to. That's highly unethical and inappropriate. But appropriately, you get evidence in before the trial court, knowing that you're laying the foundation, you're building brick by brick what you want to get before the Supreme Court. And that's being done. And keep in mind, the election just happened just over two weeks ago, and it takes time to do the research and dig out evidence."

James Delingpole

The Great Reset has been trending on Twitter. Once you're familiar with what it means for the future of our civilisation, you'll understand why…

Put simply, it is the blueprint for a complete transformation of the world economy. There will be no money, no private property, no democracy. Instead, every key decision — what you do for a living, how much stuff you consume, whether you can take a vacation — will decided for you by a remote, unaccountable elite of 'experts'.

It sounds like a conspiracy theory — and is often dismissed as such by people who imagine they are being savvy and sophisticated. In fact, though, the people pushing for the Great Reset are perfectly open about their plan. Indeed, they can scarcely stop talking about it…

One of these people is Canadian Prime Minister Justin Trudeau. It was a video of Trudeau talking about the Great Reset which prompted the flurry of nervous interest on social media.

Trudeau says:

'Building Back Better means giving support to the most vulnerable while maintaining our momentum on reaching the 2030 Agenda for Sustainable Development and the SDGs. Canada is here to listen and to help. This pandemic has provided an opportunity for a reset. This is our chance to accelerate our pre-pandemic efforts to reimagine our economic systems that actually address global challenges like extreme poverty, inequality and climate change.'

It sounds innocuous enough — the kind of meaningless garbage you'd expect from to come from Trudeau. But in fact, there is deeper meaning to the phrases he uses: 'Building Back Better'; '2030 Agenda'; 'Sustainable Development and the SDGs'; and 'reset' are all buzzwords for the complete transformation of the global economy in order to create a New World Order.

'Build Back Better' is the slogan of the Great Reset **and the man who invented it,** Klaus Schwab**. Schwab is a bald German in his early Eighties with a strong accent and the sinister air of a James Bond villain who in the 1970s founded what is now known as the** World Economic Forum**. The WEF holds the annual summit at** Davos **in Switzerland where, it has been said, 'billionaires go to lecture millionaires on how ordinary people live.' Up until recently, Davos has probably seemed like a harmless event: a sort of annual joke in which we all get to laugh at the absurd spectacle of the one % of the one % turning up in their private jets and their limousines to expound on the importance of sustainability and saving the planet.**

But the events of 2020 have changed all that because COVID-19 has provided the perfect pretext **for the kind of co-ordinated globalist takeover which might previously have been little more than an evil glint in Klaus Schwab's eyes.**

By Schwab's own admission**, the world must "act jointly and swiftly to revamp all aspects of our societies and economies" — in short, he says, ever industry must "be transformed… we need a 'Great Reset' of capitalism."**

In a warning of the rollercoaster of change we can expect if this plan goes ahead, Schwab continues: "The level of cooperation and ambition this implies is unprecedented. But it is not some impossible dream. In fact, one silver lining of the pandemic is that it has shown how quickly we can make radical changes to our lifestyles. Almost instantly, the crisis forced businesses and individuals to abandon practices long claimed to be essential, from frequent air travel to working in an office."

As the WEF puts it of the coming technocracy that would rule our lives: "Welcome to 2030. I own nothing, have no privacy, and life has never been better."

There is nothing new about the Great Reset. Schwab and his acolytes have been talking about it for years. Chinese Coronavirus – or rather the draconian, liberty-sapping measures taken by governments in order to combat it – has merely accelerated the process.

As I reported in an earlier piece, Schwab has written several books about his masterplan:

His latest, called *Covid-19: The Great Reset*, makes no bones about the fact that the chaos of the Coronavirus pandemic represents the perfect opportunity to accelerate the entire world towards a 'new normal'.

At the time of writing (June 2020), the pandemic continues to worsen globally. Many of us are pondering when things will return to normal. The short response is: never. Nothing will ever return to the 'broken' sense of normalcy that prevailed prior to the crisis because the coronavirus pandemic marks a fundamental inflection point in our global trajectory.

Got that? As far as your new globalist overlords are concerned, you are NEVER going to get your old life back, however much you might wish it. Also, be clear: this is being done for your own good because your old way of life was based on a 'broken' model.

Such is the author's conviction that the new normal is what we need and should want, he scarcely bothers to pretend that Chinese coronavirus is anything other than a handy pretext.

Unlike certain past epidemics, COVID-19 doesn't pose a new existential threat.

Schwab is clear in his book that coronavirus is not so much a crisis as an opportunity to be exploited – a chance to accelerate the birth of the New World Order he calls The Fourth Industrial Revolution.

Radical changes of such consequence are coming that some pundits have referred to a 'before coronavirus' (BC) and 'after coronavirus' (AC) era. We will continue to be surprised by both the rapidity and unexpected nature of these changes – as they conflate with each other, they will provoke second-, third-, fourth- and more-order consequences, cascading effects and unforeseen outcomes.

All of this stuff would, of course, be mere pie in the sky if it were just a sinister-looking bald guy with a passing resemblance to Blofeld saying it. Unfortunately, lots of people of influence around the world take this stuff very seriously.

That's why Joe Biden used 'Build Back Better' as his campaign slogan. It's why the UK Conservatives feature the website on their Twitter page. And why UK Prime Minister Boris Johnson inserts the phrase into his speeches.

In fact, as I reported in May, it's a phrase you find being used by all manner of institutions. My piece was titled *'Build Back Better' – the Latest Code Phrase for Green Global Tyranny'.*

Hardly anyone was interested back then. Maybe more people will be now that they start to realise that while these Global Reset guys may sound like kooks they are in fact deadly serious.

Sure, it sounds like a conspiracy theory.

But as someone wise once said, it's not a conspiracy theory when they tell you exactly what they're doing…

EconomyLondon / EuropePoliticsBuild Back BetterJoe Biden

The lengthy commentary says, in part:

Joe Biden has promised that on his first day in office he would restore Obama-era guidance that will give male students access to girls' sports, bathrooms, and locker rooms "in accordance with their gender identity." This is a major backslide for the rights of girls in education, and should be understood as a threat to Title IX, the groundbreaking legislation which guaranteed equal education access to girls and women in federally-funded schools.

Biden has also committed to make passing the Equality Act a top legislative priority in his first 100 days. While much of the Equality Act holds good potential for many groups of women, such as prohibiting employment and housing discrimination against lesbian and bisexual Americans, it also enshrines the undefined concept of "gender identity" into law as a protected characteristic—effectively providing unlimited access for men into women's sports and spaces such as prisons, shelters, and domestic violence services.

All of the funding and support of the Violence Against Women Act is undermined if men are allowed to enter women's domestic violence shelters, and if stats on male violence are falsified to validate the identity claims of violent men. If boys are able to steal scholarships from female athletes, attempts to increase economic opportunities for women and girls could be nullified. If violent male sex offenders and convicted domestic abusers are allowed in female prisons where they will continue to rape and assault women, progressive justice system reform will perversely worsen some conditions for the most vulnerable women.

"Through such promises to eliminate single-sex accommodations and women's sex class recognition in the law, Biden's stance on gender identity undercuts all of his other progressive policy stances on women's issues," the commentary concludes.

CHICAGO IS GETTING BETTER ALL THE TIME CHICAGO IS MY KIND OF TOWN

Report: 23 Shot Monday Alone in Mayor Lightfoot's Chicago

Twenty-three people were shot Monday alone in Mayor Lori Lightfoot's (D) Chicago.

The ***Chicago Sun-Times*** reports the shooting victims included two teenage girls–a 16-year-old and a 17-year-old–who were shot "near Pulaski Road and Lexington Street" around 4:40 p.m. Their wounds were not life-threatening.

A five-year-old boy was also shot on Monday. He was "playing with an iPad on a couch...inside a home in the 200 block of West 115th Street" around 7:30 p.m. when shots were fired at the home from a passing vehicle. The gunfire left the 5-year-old in critical condition.

Four people were shot in one incident around 7:23 p.m. "in the 2700 block of South Dearborn Street." The four individuals were standing and talking when another individual walked up, an argument ensued, and shots were fired. Two 22-year-olds, a 29-year-old, and an 18-year-old were wounded.

Monday's violence follows a weekend in which over 20 were shot**, one fatally, in the city.**

The *Chicago Tribune* reports 3,619, people were shot in Chicago January 1, 2020, through November 9, 2020. Over 670 people were killed **in Chicago January 1, 2020, through November 9, 2020. The *Sun-Times*** reports ten people were shot in Lightfoot's Chicago on Tuesday alone.

AWR Hawkins is an award-winning Second Amendment columnist for Breitbart News and the writer/curator of *Down Range with AWR Hawkins*, ***a weekly newsletter focused on all things Second Amendment, also for Breitbart News. He is the political analyst for Armed American Radio. Follow him on Twitter:*** *@AWRHawkins*. ***Reach him at*** *awrhawkins@breitbart.com*. ***You can sign up to get Down Range at*** *breitbart.com/downrange*.

Joe Biden supports 'immediately' canceling some student loan debt, penalizing American taxpayers

'It should be done immediately'

Chris Enloe

Former Vice President Joe Biden declared Monday that, as president, he would move to ensure that Americans with student loans have some of their debt "immediately" — by magic, apparently — wiped away. Chris Enloe **Outstanding student loan debt** currently stands **at more than $1.5 trillion.**

What are the details?

Biden was asked by a reporter on Monday whether student loan forgiveness is part of his economic agenda. Biden responded affirmatively, no doubt pleasing the Democratic Party's far-left members.

"It's holding people up," Biden said of student loan debt, the New York Times reported. **"They're in real trouble. They're having to make choices between paying their student loans and paying their rent, those kinds of decisions. It should be done immediately."**

Biden voiced support for a proposal from House Democrats that would forgive $10,000 of student loan debt per borrower. "Immediate $10,000 forgiveness of student loans, helping people up there in real trouble," Biden said., House Democrats originally proposed forgiving $10,000 of student loan debt per borrower as part of their proposal for a second COVID-19 relief bill, **which had a price tag of $3 trillion, making it the most expensive bill in history. The legislation was never considered in the Republican-controlled Senate because of its cost. Democrats** later scaled back their bill when **the Congressional Budget Office** estimated that it would cost **between $200 billion and $300 billion to forgive the amount of debt they were proposing.**

Is forgiving debt a good idea?

Biden is forging a middle ground by supporting the forgiveness of just $10,000. For many Americans, especially those who worked their way through college to graduate without debt or those who worked diligently

after graduation to pay off their debt, any forgiveness is too much. But for progressive Democrats — and many young people, in fact — Biden would not be going far enough. On Tuesday, Rep. Alexandria Ocasio-Cortez (D-N.Y.), one of the most influential Democrats in the country, reiterated her demand for debt cancelation.

She said, "'Things were bad for me, so they should stay bad for everyone else' is not a good argument against debt cancellation - student, medical, or otherwise." Contrary to what progressives like Ocasio-Cortez claim, "canceling debt" is not something that actually exists. Lawmakers could remove a borrower's liability for re-paying the debt, but the debt will be shifted onto *someone*.

In the case of federal student loans, the burden would be further shifted onto taxpayers. Canceling student loan debt, then, rewards Americans who choose to go into debt for a degree — and agree to re-pay their debt — while penalizing Americans who did not choose debt, one critic told Ocasio-Cortez. Magically wiping away debt absolves all responsibility for mostly unwise decisions, removing the life-learning element included in accepting a mountain of debt for a college degree with a poor return on investment.

THERE ARE INFINITY SQUARED REASONS TO MOVE PERMANENTLY FROM (NYC) WHERE (1) WEEK DIRECT CREMATION NO BURIAL LIFE INSURANCE POLICIES ARE SELLING BRISKLY HERE; WITH SAME WEEK FREE PICKUP OF YOUR REMAINS ANYWHERE IN (5) NYC BOROUGHS; NYC NOW THE SUB-BASEMENT OF HELL; WHERE ALL WHITE PEOPLE ARE HATED UNLESS LGBTQ

Megyn Kelly yanks kids out of NYC school over call to reform white children — and now she and her family are leaving the city altogether

Goodbye, New York Sarah Taylor

Veteran news journalist and media maven Megyn Kelly has pulled her children out of their New York City school and plans to leave the city behind altogether.

Kelly announced the decision after learning that her kids' school promoted the "reform" of white children in racially biased practices.

Kelly did not reveal the name of the school her children previously attended.

What are the details?

During Monday's broadcast of her podcast, "The Megyn Kelly Show," Kelly said that she received a letter from the administrators of her two young sons' school that detailed a plan to implement an extreme racial social justice agenda in the school.

"It's so out of control on so many levels, and after years of resisting it, we're going to leave the city," Kelly admitted. "We pulled our boys from their school, and our daughter is going to be leaving hers soon, too. The schools have always been far left, which doesn't align with my own ideology, but I didn't really care. Most of my friends are liberals; it's fine. I come from Democrats as a family."

Kelly added, however, that the final straw was when she found out that the administration was peddling concerning sentiments about how white children are "left unchecked and unbothered" in their schools, homes, and communities. "I'm not offended at all by the ideology, and I lean center-left on some things, but they've gone around the bend," she insisted. "I mean, they have gone off the deep-end. The summer in the wake of George Floyd, they circulated amongst the diversity group — which includes white parents like us; there are people who want to be allies and stay attuned to what we can do — an article, and afterward, they recirculated it and wanted every member of the faculty to read it."

Kelly recalled that the article asserted that white children are inherently racist.

According to Kelly, a portion of the article — which appears to have been written by Nahliah Webber, executive director of Orleans Public Education Network in June — said, "There is a killer cop sitting in every school where white children learn. They gleefully soak in their whitewashed history that downplays the holocaust of indigenous native peoples and Africans in the Americas. They happily believe their all-white spaces exist as a matter of personal effort and willingly use violence against black bodies to keep those spaces white."

"As black bodies drop like flies around us by violence at white hands, how can we in any of our minds conclude that whites are all right?" the article added. "White children are left unchecked and unbothered in their schools, homes, and communities to join, advance, and protect systems that take away black life. I am tired of white people reveling in their state-sanctioned depravity, snuffing out black life with no consequences."

The article continued, "Where's the urgency for school reform for white kids being indoctrinated in black death and protected from the consequences? Where are the government-sponsored reports looking into how white mothers are raising culturally deprived children who think black death is okay?"

"Where are the national conferences, white papers, and policy positions on the pathology of whiteness in schools?" the article said. "This time if you really want to make a difference in *Black Lives Matter*— and not have to protest this s*** again — go reform white kids. Because that's where the problem is — with white children being raised from infancy to violate black bodies with no remorse or accountability."

Anything else?

A portion of Kelly's podcast appeared on Twitter Monday, captioned, "'After years of resisting it, we're going to leave.' @MegynKelly describes why she pulled her kids out of their NYC schools — and she, @GlennLoury and @Coldxman Hughes discuss how 'woke' leftism has taken over schools."

Cuomo blames drug companies, President Trump for speedy COVID-19 vaccines

HE ACTUALLY BLAMES OPERATION WARP SPEED DRUG COMPANIES FOR DOING THE BEST JOB A DRUG COMPANY HAS EVER DONE

ANDREW CUOMO DEFINES MEDIOCRITY & EVIL

The governor's comments come as preliminary results have shown two company's vaccines as more than 90% effective in treating COVID-19

By Bradford Betz

HHS lays out plans for COVID-19 vaccine distribution

Health and Human Service Secretary Alex Azar joins 'The Daily Briefing' with insight.

New York Gov. Andrew Cuomo on Tuesday said the speedy process by which coronavirus vaccine trials are being rolled out are being driven both by President Donald Trump's ego and the profit motivation of the drug companies manufacturing the vaccines.

The Democrat made the comments during an interview on Hot 97's Ebro in the Morning radio show. His appearance came as Moderna Inc. and competitor Pfizer Inc. recently announced preliminary results showing their vaccines appear more than 90% effective, at least for short-term protection against COVID-19.

President Donald Trump on Monday praised Moderna as one of two recent "great discoveries."

"Another Vaccine just announced. This time by Moderna, 95% effective," Trump tweeted. "For those great 'historians', please remember that these great discoveries, which will end the China Plague, all took place on my watch!" Host Ebro Darden told Gov. Cuomo he had spoken with people, including "people who claim to be nurses," who said they "do not trust this vaccine" and feel that it has been rushed.

Gov. Cuomo provides a coronavirus update during a news conference in the Red Room at the State Capitol in Albany, N.Y. (Office of Governor Andrew M. Cuomo)

Cuomo said the vaccine was moving ahead so quickly because of "money and ego," noting that the first drug company to get the vaccine will profit handsomely.

"You didn't need Trump to tell the vaccine companies you should develop a vaccine. He had nothing to do with it," Cuomo said. Pfizer, Moderna, Johnson & Johnson, they all know this is billions of dollars, whoever gets to the market first. So, it's in their economic interest to push this fast," Cuomo said.

NY GOV. CUOMO RIPPED FOR TELLING OTHERS TO ADMIT MISTAKES AMID COVID-19 NURSING HOME DEATHS

He surmised that the president wants to be able to say before leaving the White House that he "solved COVID because" he supposedly "discovered a vaccine."

"Nah, it's all BS. He didn't do anything. It's the drug companies and nobody is going to trust him saying it's a safe vaccine. But you're going to see this play out, they'll do what's called an emergency authorization by the FDA," he said.

Cuomo then predicted that the emergency authorization could happen as soon as January, because "Trump

will push them." "(The president) will say we authorized the drug for emergency use, and you could see it starting in January before Biden gets into office and that's why I'm pushing so hard to make sure that we have a process in place to check what the FDA says before people start getting a vaccine in New York," Cuomo said.

Fox News has reached out to both Pfizer and Moderna with a request to respond to the governor's accusations.

MODERNA CORONAVIRUS VACCINE TRIAL VOLUNTEER SAYS PUBLIC SHOULD NOT BE CONCERNED ABOUT RISK

Michael Bars, a White House spokesman, said that Cuomo does not have "much of an understanding (of) the unprecedented public-private partnership poised to deliver a life-saving vaccine in record time."

"President Trump's Operation Warp Speed **continues to expedite the regulatory process while providing billions of dollars to a portfolio of companies in the process of delivering a safe and effective vaccine five times faster than other in history," Bars said in a statement provided to Fox News.**

"The recent announcements by Pfizer and Moderna regarding their incredibly promising and impressive efficacy data further demonstrate that the Warp Speed Program is rapidly advancing on a trajectory of success to the benefit of millions of at-risk Americans," he said.

DEAD VOTERS & NON-RESIDENT FRAUD OUT-OF-STATE VOTERS NATIONWIDE VOTE FOR PAL ZOMBIE & KAMIKAZE KAMALA

Arizona GOP Chair to Newsmax TV: We'll Turn Over Every Election Rock

By Brian Trusdell

Arizona Republican Party Chairwoman Kelli Ward told Newsmax TV **on Tuesday that her state's election has seen various issues from complaints of votes not being tabulated, dead people voting and those from other states being thanked for voting, and the GOP will press to investigate.**

"We are going to turn over every rock looking for slime that is infecting our election integrity," Ward, 51, said on "American Agenda."

Ward, a former member of the Arizona House of Representatives and Senate, listed a litany of irregularities, commented that Joe Biden leads President Donald Trump in the state by about 10,000 votes out of more than 3.3 million cast and that, "This election is far from over."

"There are so many irregularities that we are seeing on the ground here in Arizona that must be investigated," Ward said. "We have questions whether ballots that were pushed through the machine by the poll worker pushing the green button to override protections have actually been counted. I hope that we're able to see those.

"We have evidence and complaints of people that do not live in Arizona, but they're being notified by the elections department 'Thank you for voting' and actually even getting surveys to comment how the election process went for them. We have evidence of people who have passed away casting ballots. It's across the spectrum here in Arizona."

Rep. Gosar to Newsmax TV: Election 'Doesn't Make Sense'

By Brian Trusdell

Arizona Rep. Paul Gosar questioned the apparent contradiction in the election results of Republicans gaining at least seven seats in the House of Representatives, appearing to retain control of the Senate and President Donald Trump receiving 13 million more votes than in 2016 and yet ostensibly losing to Joe Biden.

Gosar, 61, who represents Arizona's 4th Congressional District from the Phoenix suburbs to the Nevada border, told Newsmax TV on Tuesday that Arizona's tally for president showed Biden leading by about 10,000 votes, which he questioned considering the use of the disputed Dominion Voting Systems Corp. software to count ballots in Maricopa County, which includes more than half the state's population.

"It didn't work so well in the House," Gosar said on "Greg Kelly Reports." "You know, 27 toss-up races in the House by (the) Cook (Political Report), and the Republicans won it all. That's what just doesn't make sense. How is it that we, the Republicans, held our ground and gained all across the board, and yet the president overperforms and he loses? It doesn't make sense."

Gosar expressed the sentiment that statements and actions combined with the results have given rise to make many suspicious of the supposed outcome. Asked if we have messed up elections Gosar said "oh we really have.

"Particularly when you see some of the comments from our secretary of state (Democrat Katie Hobbs) saying she was elected to get Democrats elected, now that's magical, and then calling Trump supporters Nazis," he said. "That hardly builds confidence in your state officials. And then you see results where you see a huge spike in the number of 90-year-olds, that all of a sudden decide to get registered to vote – just all of a sudden. It doesn't make sense, particularly in a state that the president was extremely popular."

Rep. Jody Hice to Newsmax TV: Ga. Sec. of State to Blame for Chaos

By Solange Reyner

Georgia Secretary of State Brad Raffensperger is to blame for the chaos in the Georgia election, according to Rep. Jody Hice, R-Ga., on Newsmax TV.

"The statistics speak for themselves," Hice told Monday's "Spicer & Co." "We've had 10 times more absentee ballots but 10 times fewer of those ballots cast out because of improper signature verification.

"There is chaos in this Georgia election system because of secretary of state in Georgia Brad Raffensperger. He has brought this upon himself, he has brought it upon Georgia, and the people of Georgia are irate as to how this thing has gone down and rightfully so."

Raffensperger, a Republican who has gone head to head with President Donald Trump over the election results in Georgia, on Sunday posted several fact checks on his official Facebook page correcting misinformation about the election promoted by Trump and his campaign.

"The state of Georgia strengthened signature match this year," Raffensperger wrote in one post, saying election officials received signature-match training requiring a confirmed match be made twice before a ballot is cast.

He also said Republican leaders such as Sen. Lindsey Graham, R-S.C., have been putting pressure on him to exclude legal ballots.

Hice said the entire outcome "smells like a rat, and when you smell a rat, it's typically because there is a rat.

"When you have not a single Republican incumbent lose nationwide, when you have Republicans do extremely well in the state of Georgia, on the state level as well as the federal level; you have the Senate across the country holding - all of which we were told would not happen," he concluded. "And then you have President Trump getting 9 million more votes in this election then he did 4 years ago.

Trump Lawyer Alleges Harassment From Opposing Firm

A lawyer for President Donald Trump's campaign is dropping out of a Pennsylvania lawsuit challenging the election results a day after complaining about being harassed for her work, including by an attorney from a firm representing the state of Pennsylvania.

Linda Kerns, who leads her own law firm in Philadelphia, said in a court filing Monday she and two other lawyers reached agreement with the campaign that it would be best if they withdrew from the case. Marc A. Scaringi will represent the Trump campaign, she said. Kerns did not provide a reason for the withdrawal request and there is no indication her harassment complaint had anything to do with it.

But late Sunday she said in a court filing, an attorney with Kirkland & Ellis in Washington left her a one-minute voice mail that "falls afoul of standards of professional conduct."

The Trump campaign lawsuit seeks to block Pennsylvania from certifying the election result unless thousands of ballots are tossed out. Another firm on the case, Porter Wright Morris & Arthur LLP, gave notice last week it is withdrawing from the matter. A Trump spokesman blamed that decision on harassment by "leftist mobs," after the Lincoln Project, an anti-Trump group that funded Democrats, targeted lawyers working for the campaign.

Kerns, who did not identify the lawyer who allegedly harassed her in the filing, also said she "has been subjected to continuous harassment in the form of abusive emails, phone calls, physical and economic threats and even accusations of treason – all for representing the President of the United States' campaign in this litigation."

The case is one of several the Trump campaign and the GOP have filed seeking to challenge the election amid rampant voter fraud. A hearing on Pennsylvania's motion to dismiss the suit is set for Tuesday.

Kirkland & Ellis's lawyer on the matter apologized to Kerns and told her the attorney who left the voice mail does not work on the Pennsylvania case. In her filing, Kerns said that is "not good enough." She asked the judge overseeing the case to issue an unspecified sanction against the firm.

In a response filed with the court Monday, Kirkland & Ellis lawyer Daniel T. Donovan said an associate was "acting unilaterally, in his personal capacity," when he made the call. During the call, the associate provided Kerns with his personal email address while a baby was "babbling in the background."

"We disagree with the characterization of the voice mail in the motion," Donovan said in the filing. "The firm expects that every lawyer will conduct themselves with the highest standards of professional conduct, including being respectful of and courteous to other members of the bar."

Kerns responded to that filing with another letter to the court, saying the associate who "foolishly chose to vent his ideological hatred" had not personally apologized. She also rejected the law firm's suggestion the associate did not represent Pennsylvania.

"Every lawyer at a firm is counsel to every client of that firm," Kerns said.

PER THE U.S. 1913 FEDERAL ESPIONAGE ACT; THIS SAME EXACT TREASON IS PUNISHABLE BY DEATH; I.E. ELECTROCUTION OF HUSBAND & WIFE JULIUS & ETHEL ROSENBERG

Julius & Ethel Rosenberg

Julius and Ethel Rosenberg

Ethel and Julius Rosenberg in 1951

Born	**Julius** **May 12, 1918** Manhattan, **New York, U.S.** **Ethel** **September 28, 1915** Manhattan, **New York, U.S.**
Died	**Julius** **June 19, 1953 (aged 35)** Sing Sing Correctional Facility, **New York, U.S.** **Ethel** **June 19, 1953 (aged 37)** Sing Sing Correctional Facility, **New York, U.S.**
Resting place	Wellwood Cemetery, **New York, U.S.**
Occupation	**Julius** **Electrical engineer** **Ethel** **Actress, singer, secretary**
Children	Michael Meeropol Robert Meeropol
Criminal charge	**Conspiracy to commit espionage**
Penalty	**Death by** electric chair

Julius and **Ethel Rosenberg** were American citizens; MODELS FOR MARK & PRESCILLA CHAN ZUCKERBUCKS **who were convicted of spying on behalf of the** Soviet Union**. The couple was accused of providing top-secret information about** radar, sonar, jet propulsion engines, and valuable nuclear weapon designs**; at that time the United States was the only country in the world with nuclear weapons. Convicted of espionage in 1951, they were executed by the** federal government of the United States in 1953 in the Sing Sing correctional facility in Ossining, New York, **becoming the first American civilians to be executed for such charges and the first to suffer that penalty during peacetime. Other convicted co-conspirators were sentenced to prison, including Ethel's brother,** David Greenglass (who had made a plea agreement), Harry Gold**, and** Morton Sobell. Klaus Fuchs**, a German scientist working in Los Alamos, was convicted in the United Kingdom.**

For decades, the Rosenbergs' sons (Michael and Robert Meeropol**) and many other defenders maintained that Julius and Ethel were innocent of spying on their country and were victims of** Cold War paranoia. After the fall of the Soviet Union**, much information concerning them was declassified, including a trove of** decoded Soviet cables (code-name: Venona), which detailed Julius›s role as a courier and recruiter for the Soviets and Ethel›s role as an accessory. In 2008, the National Archives of the United States published most of the grand jury testimony related to the prosecution of the Rosenbergs.

Jill Biden's Ex-Husband Just Made a Bold & True Accusation

JOE; WITH PLAGIARISM AT BEST; & CHEATING IN PRESIDENTIAL ELECTIONS & HIGH TREASON AGAINST GOD AT WORST; MUCH LESS THE AMERICAN PEOPLE; CHEATED ON JILL BIDEN'S EX-HUSBAND; EVEN WORSE; WHILE CHEATING; JOE BIDEN; WITH JILL IN THE CAR; WRECKED HER NEW CORVETTE THAT HER HUSBAND JILL BIDEN CHEATED ON & JILL WAS STILL MARRIED TO (JOE WRECKED THE CORVETTE JILL'S HUSBAND BOUGHT FOR HER. ALL WILL BE WELL WITH BIDEN AS PRESIDENT. WHO'S WORSE, FATHER OR SON; JOE OR HUNTER. DISHONESTY IS IN THE BIDEN D.N.A. WAY OF LIFE. READ MY PREVIOUS BOOKS FOR THIS SPELLED OUT IN SPLIT SECOND EXQUISITE COORDINATES; BY DATE; TIME; PLACE; PERSON PLAGIARISM; HIGH CRIMES AT WORST; EVERY KIND OF MISDEMEANOR; DECEPTION; EASY WAY OUT & FRAUD AT WORST. I DARE JOE BIDEN TO FACE ME & DENY ANYTHING I ACCUSE THIS CREEP OF.

FOR DEPTH PERCEPTION OF DEMOCRATS & REPUBLICANS HATRED OF EACH OTHER TODAY; LOOK NO FURTHER THAN INTO THE LOOKING GLASS OF 10,000 ARMED LAND & SEA CLASHES; 750,000 BURIED COFFINLESS; FORT SUMTER, SOUTH CAROLINA; APRIL 12, 1861, UNTIL PALMETTO RANCH TEXAS, MAY 12, 1865. IN PLAGIARISM; PROVEN SINCE LAW SCHOOL; A DANGER TO HIMSELF & THE COMMUNITY; PAL JOEY; WIVES; SISTERS; NIECES; DAUGHTERS; AUNTS; GRANDKIDS APRIL 15, HIS WIFE JILL BIDEN; MOUTHPIECE TO AMERICA' TAKE A DEEP BREATH; SWALLOW; & VOTE FOR MY CINDER BLOCK TONGUE HUSBAND JOE; HE'S ELECTABLE; HE COMES COMPLETE W HIS NO-WORK NO-SHOW SON HUNTER $50K @ MONTH UKRAINE BURISMA GAS HOLDINGS; HUNTER DID NOTHING WRONG INC. NOTHING OF VALUE FOR HIS 10% BHR INVESTMENT SLUSH SHANGHAI SHANGAIN WUHAN UNDER THE TABLE 3 CARD MONTE PRIVATE EQUITY KISSING COUSIN ABSENTEE CORONAVIRUS BAT SOUP; WILLFULLY IGNORANT TO BOTH HUNTER'S NO-SHOW BOARD OF BURISMA & BOARD OF WUHAN MOO GOO GAI PAN STAMP LICKING/ENVELOPE PUSHING; DON'T BELIEVE IT; HUNTER NEVER SPILLED SOY SAUCE ON XI JINPING'S HUGO BOSS POWER 19 MILLION YUAN WORSTED SUIT; RADIO FREE HAVANA; CHRIS CUOMO ASKED PAL JOEY; YOU KNEW THESE OPTICS; WHY DIDN'T YOU KEEP HUNTER ON HIS LEASH; HE'S A BIGGER TIME BOMB FOR AMERICA THAN EVEN YOU ARE; JOE; "I DO WHAT'S BEST FOR ME & MY FAMILY"; WHAT ABOUT WHAT'S BEST FOR AMERICA; PAL JOEY? ON THE AIR FORCE 2 (12) HOUR RETURN FROM HUNTER'S EXCELLENT NICE-SOMETHING-FOR-NOTHING $1.5 BILLION GIFT FROM DAD YOU CAN GET IT; NO-WORK OR SHOW PRIVATE EQUITY SHOPLIFTING ADVENTURE; WHY DIDN'T JOE ASK HUNTER WHY HIS ASS GOT KICKED OUTTA THE NAVY FOR TESTING POSITIVE FOR COKE; BUYING CRACK ON SKID ROWS FROM DERELICTS ACROSS AMERICA; WIFE KATHLEEN'S 2017 DIVORCE PAPERS; HUNTER'S $$$ COKE; WHORES; STRIP CLUBS; PIMPS; TITO'S HANDCRAFTED VODKA; KIDS W 2 STRIPPERS ABANDONED; BANGING DEAD BROTHER BEAU'S WIDOW; HALLIE; DUMPING HER FOR SOUTH AFRICAN MODEL MELISSA COHEN W APRIL 1, 2020 BABY, PRESCOTT ARIZONA COP RAP SHEET; HERTZ CALIF RENTAL DUMPED; KEYS/ IN GAS COMPARTMENT NOT DROPBOX; CRACK PIPE/WHITE POWDER; 2 FAKE DC DRIVERS LICENSES; FAKE DEL. ATTY GENERAL BADGE; FAKE U.S. SECRET SERVICE BUSINESS CARDS; NEW HAMPSHIRE CAMPAIGN STOP;

COLLEGE STUDENT MADISON MOORE: JOE; YOU'RE ARGUABLY THE MOST ADVANTAGED CANDIDATE HOW DO YOU EXPLAIN YOUR IOWA LOSS &;HOW YOU CAN WIN IN NOVEMBER? JOE: "YER A LYIN' DOG-FACED PONY SOLDIER"; ALEXANDRIA OCASIO-CORTEZ; ILHAN OMAR ABDULLAHI: MUSLIMS MUST RAISE HELL; MAKE PEOPLE UNCOMFORTABLE; JEWS ARE ALL ABOUT THE BENJAMINS BABY; IN SUPER BOWL OF HEAVEN &; HELL; THE ADMINISTRATIVE; ADDICTION; EDUCATION; POVERTY INDUSTRIAL COMPLEXES; 3RD TRIMESTER SKULL CRUSHING; UNIVERSITY LEFT TOXIC FEMINISTS; GENDER DYSPHORIC; MATHEMATICALLY IMPOSSIBLE; WITH 4% OF ENERGY RENEWABLE WORLDWIDE; EARTH WORSHIP BY ANY ATHEISM; HAMMURABI'S CODE; MAGNA CARTA DENIAL; HATRED OF AMERICA; WORSHIPPING CHE; FIDEL & HUGO; BURN BERNIE BURN; OMAR: 9 11, 2001; WHY DID SOME PEOPLE SAY SOME PEOPLE DID SOMETHING; OPEN BORDER UNVETTED ONLINE &; VOTING BY MAIL; FREE STUFF TO PARASITES WHO HATE AMERICA; OVER 50% GOVT OWNERSHIP OF ECONOMY; VOTERS ELECT DEMOCRATS WHO BREASTFEED THEM; GOV ANDREW CUOMO AUG 15 2018 AMERICA NEVER WAS THAT GREAT ANYWAY BRET STEPHENS PEOPLE WHO BELIEVE IN NOTHING WILL SUBMIT TO ANYTHING DANIEL HENNINGER OBAMA NEVER PAID A PRICE FOR HIS PEOPLE WHO CLING TO THEIR GUNS & RELIGION AS DID HILLARY FOR HER BASKET OF DEPLORABLES; LET AULD ACQUAINTANCE BE FORGOT NEVER BROUGHT TO MIND IN THE CROSSHAIRS AT THE CROSSROADS OF IT CAN'T HAPPEN HERE & LET MY PEOPLE GO; MOSES; CAST DOWN THINE STAFF BEFORE RAMSES; WITH YOUR YOUNG; CATTLE & SHEEP FOLLOW ME; 10 TIMES THOU HATH WITNESSED MIRACLES OF THE LORD; ON THE 11TH, NOVEMBER 3, 2020; VOTE NOT FOR A FALSE IDOL

JUST WHAT WE NEED FOR THEM ALL TO VOTE DEMOCRAT

MSNBC Columnist: Joe Biden Must Heal America from Trump by Surging Refugee Resettlement to U.S.

Democrat Joe Biden's plan to surge refugee resettlement by over 700 % to the United States is "what America needs to heal" after four years of President Trump, an MSNBC columnist writes.

JOHN BINDER

In a piece titled "Biden's refugee plan is what America needs to heal from Trump," MSNBC columnist Hayes Brown writes that Americans "need to make space" for a surge in refugees that the former vice president has promised to bring to the U.S. Brown writes:

Massively increasing the number of refugees allowed into the U.S. has the benefit, then, of doing exactly that — marking an end to the U.S. government's hostility to immigrants under Trump and showing the world our renewed place in the global community. It also happens to be the right thing to do and entirely fitting with Biden's beliefs.

The years through 2016 have shown that the maximum numbers of refugees welcomed into the country wax and wane as attitudes in the U.S. shifted. But part of the transformation the U.S. needs to recover from the Trump era requires a renewed commitment to making amends for a history of American exclusion and embracing the country's immigrant heritage more fully than ever. The time to make those changes is now, no matter how hard they may seem. [Emphasis added]

As the Biden administration does the work of building this country into a place where the laws equally apply to everyone, where health care is a given, where we halt the warming of the planet, we need to make space for the people who've dreamed of a place where all that and more is possible. [Emphasis addd]

Biden's plan to overhaul the nation's immigration system includes a reversal of Trump's reforms to the State Department's refugee resettlement program — a boon for the business lobby that has fought against any reforms to immigration reduction, knowing it forces their industries to mechanize or hire American.

Trump, this year, reduced the annual cap on refugees to 15,000 admissions for Fiscal Year 2021. The cap is merely a numerical limit and not a goal federal officials are supposed to reach.

The reduction of refugees is the lowest level of resettlement since the program's inception in 1980, accounting for an 80 % reduction compared to the Obama-Biden years. Likewise, Trump has sought to allow states and localities to have a say in whether or not they want to resettle refugees in their communities.

On the other hand, Biden has vowed to increase the refugee resettlement program by 700 %, setting the annual cap at 125,000, with plans to raise that cap every year for at least four years.

Over the last 19 years, more than 985,000 refugees have been admitted to the country. This is a number more than double that of residents living in Miami, Florida, and would be the equivalent of adding the population of Pensacola, Florida, to the country every year. Refugee resettlement costs American taxpayers nearly $9 billion every five years, according to the latest research. Over the course of five years, an estimated 16 **%of all refugees admitted will need housing assistance paid for by taxpayers.**

EXACTLY HOW DO WE REJOICE ABOUT

LITTLE BOYS WHO WANT TO BE LITTLE GIRLS & LITTLE GIRLS WHO WANT TO BE LITTLE BOYS LET'S PAY THEM IN $1 TRILLION FOREIGN AID TO DO THIS IN SAUDI ARABIA, IRAN & PAKISTAN

Transgender Awareness Week Renews Criticism of J.K. Rowling for Supporting Women's Rights

PENNY STARR

J.K. Rowling has won hearts around the world for her Harry Potter series, but during the orchestrated celebration of Transgender Awareness Week, the attacks against her are surfacing again based on comments she made in support of protecting women's rights from being destroyed by the radical transgender ideology.

Rowling, like a growing coalition of feminists and conservative advocates for women, spoke out about the transgender ideology that strips women of a female identity that recognizes their biology, gags women's speech against the male-led transgender ideology; denies women their right to safe, single-sex spaces; and protects the integrity of female athletics.

In December 2019, Rowling tweeted support for Maya Forstater, a U.K. tax expert who lost her job after tweeting that "men cannot change into women."

Despite the statement being scientifically true, Rowlings was demonized for her tweet and also for another social media post about some advancing the "people who menstruate" idea that claims men who live as women have periods — so all people have periods.

"People who menstruate," Rowling tweeted. "I'm sure there used to be a word for those people. Someone help me out. Wumben? Wimpund? Woomud?"

The renewed criticism of Rowling includes a student at Johns Hopkins University — ironically one of the foremost U.S. institutions of science and medicine — who slammed the author in a student newspaper commentary:

When faced once again with backlash, Rowling doubled down. She tweeted that she supports trans women but wants to defend the truth of being female. She later published an essay detailing her reasons for speaking out, which was poorly received.

As a result, Rowling's legacy has been irreparably tarnished (for good reason). During Transgender Awareness Week, it is worth reconsidering exactly why she has fallen so far.

Senior Jillian Hesler, co-president of the University's Diverse Sexuality and Gender Alliance, is not a huge fan of Harry Potter themself. However, they felt that a fantasy author should be aware of who her stories influence.

"Fantasy, in particular, can act as a bastion for a lot of kids who don't align with social norms or don't feel like they fit in," [she] wrote in an email to The News-Letter. "It's just such a slap in the face to people who used those books as an escape at any point in their lives."

"If you don't even have enough imagination and consideration to not be a bigot, then you definitely shouldn't be writing a fantasy novel," [she] wrote.

The controversy inspired Rowling to write an essay about the issue, for which she was also criticized, because she directly addressed how the "transgender" ideology hurts women. **The essay, published in June 2019, explains how she became interested in "gender identity" and she writes, in part:**

What I didn't expect in the aftermath of my cancellation was the avalanche of emails and letters that came showering down upon me, the overwhelming majority of which were positive, grateful and supportive. They

came from a cross-section of kind, empathetic and intelligent people, some of them working in fields dealing with gender dysphoria and trans people, who're all deeply concerned about the way a socio-political concept is influencing politics, medical practice and safeguarding. They're worried about the dangers to young people, gay people and about the erosion of women's and girl's rights.

If you didn't already know – and why should you? – 'TERF' is an acronym coined by trans activists, which stands for Trans-Exclusionary Radical Feminist. In practice, a huge and diverse cross-section of women are currently being called TERFs and the vast majority have never been radical feminists. Examples of so-called TERFs range from the mother of a gay child who was afraid their child wanted to transition to escape homophobic bullying, to a hitherto totally unfeminist older lady who's vowed never to visit Marks & Spencer again because they're allowing any man who says they identify as a woman into the women's changing rooms. Ironically, radical feminists aren't even trans-exclusionary – they include trans men in their feminism, because they were born women.

But accusations of TERFERY have been sufficient to intimidate many people, institutions and organisations I once admired, who're cowering before the tactics of the playground. 'They'll call us transphobic!' 'They'll say I hate trans people!' What next, they'll say you've got fleas? Speaking as a biological woman, a lot of people in positions of power really need to grow a pair (which is doubtless literally possible, according to the kind of people who argue that clownfish prove humans aren't a dimorphic species).

Rowling goes on to explain why she wrote the essay, including her charitable work to help children and women in Scotland because …it's been clear to me for a while that the new trans activism is having (or is likely to have, if all its demands are met) a significant impact on many of the causes I support, because it's pushing to erode the legal definition of sex and replace it with gender.

I'm concerned about the huge explosion in young women wishing to transition and also about the increasing numbers who seem to be detransitioning (returning to their original sex), because they regret taking steps that have, in some cases, altered their bodies irrevocably, and taken away their fertility. Some say they decided to transition after realizing they were same-sex attracted, and that transitioning was partly driven by homophobia, either in society or in their families. Rowling also pushes back on the idea that just accepting the "transgender" ideology is enough:

It isn't enough for women to be trans allies. Women must accept and admit that there is no material difference between trans women and themselves. But, as many women have said before me, 'woman' is not a costume. 'Woman' is not an idea in a man's head. 'Woman' is not a pink brain, a liking for Jimmy Choos or any of the other sexist ideas now somehow touted as progressive. Moreover, the 'inclusive' language that calls female people 'menstruators' and 'people with vulvas' strikes many women as dehumanizing and demeaning. I understand why trans activists consider this language to be appropriate and kind, but for those of us who've had degrading slurs spat at us by violent men, it's not neutral, it's hostile and alienating.

Rowling reveals in the essay that she is a domestic abuse and sexual assault survivor, which has influenced her advocacy for women's rights. "I'm mentioning these things now not in an attempt to garner sympathy, but out of solidarity with the huge numbers of women who have histories like mine, who've been slurred as

bigots for having concerns around single-sex spaces," Rowling wrote. Rowling expressed support for all people in the essay, including those who claim the "transgender" label. But she also concludes that speaking out in favor of women can be frightening in the current culture.

"Huge numbers of women are justifiably terrified by the trans activists; I know this because so many have got in touch with me to tell their stories,"she wrote. "They're afraid of doxxing, of losing their jobs or their livelihoods, and of violence.

"But endlessly unpleasant as its constant targeting of me has been, I refuse to bow down to a movement that I believe is doing demonstrable harm in seeking to erode 'woman' as a political and biological class and offering cover to predators like few before it."

'Enough To Overturn Any Election' — Trump Campaign Holds Press Conference Laying Out Their Evidence Of Voter Fraud

Henry Rodgers

President Donald Trump's legal team held a press conference Thursday afternoon, explaining the alleged evidence of voter fraud they believe would have impacted the results of the 2020 presidential election. The press conference was led by Trump lawyer Rudy Giuliani, who was joined by Trump campaign lawyer Jenna Ellis, lawyer Sidney Powell, and lawyer Joe Digenova. Giuliani, explained that they believe there is "direct evidence" to show there was voter fraud in the presidential election. Giuliani specifically mentioned Pennsylvania, Michigan and Georgia throughout the presser. In the presser, Giuliani said the evidence they have

is "enough to overturn any election." "The recount in Georgia will tell us nothing because these fraudulent ballots will just be counted again," Giuliani said about the recount effort in the state of Georgia. Trump's lawsuits thus far do not allege voter fraud on a large enough scale to flip a state.

During the presser, Giuliani also said there is a pattern in the voting data that suggests "a plan from a centralized place" to commit voter fraud in Democrat-run cities. Giuliani also said the Trump campaign will likely bring a lawsuit to Arizona. (RELATED: President Trump's Campaign Files For Partial Recount In Wisconsin) Just hours before the press conference, Trump's campaign withdrew a lawsuit trying to stop the state of Michigan from certifying its election results Thursday, Giuliani said in a Thursday statement. (RELATED: Trump Campaign Drops Lawsuit Challenging Michigan Election Results)

Trump has yet to concede the election. *WHY THE FUCK SHOULD HE?*

Rudy Giuliani: The Case for Election Fraud Being Made by American Patriots in Both Parties

Penny Starr

Prsident Donald Trump's legal team held a press conference on Thursday about the election fraud that's been uncovered — a large amount of it reported by American citizens from both major political parties who want to preserve U.S. election integrity.

"That takes us to Michigan, where there was an honest Democrat who said they were cheating," Rudy Giuliani, Trump's lead attorney, said to reporters at the press conference. "We'll show you her affidavit, because I know you keep reporting, falsely, that we have no evidence."

"That we have no specific acts of fraud," Giuliani said. "That's because the coverage of this has been almost as dishonest as the scheme itself."

"The American people are entitled to know this," Giuliani said.

Giuliani said that the press should not lie about what the investigation has revealed so far, including that it is Americas coming forward to share their stories of election fraud.

"You don't report to them that a citizen of this country, a very fine woman, who is willing to allow me to give you her name..." Giuliani said. "I can't give you all these affidavits, because if I do these people will be harassed, they will be threatened."

But some were willing to make their affidavits public, including Jessie Jacob, who works for the city of Detroit.

"She was assigned to voting during in September," Giuliani said. "She was trained, basically, trained to cheat. She said, 'I was instructed by my supervisor to adjust the mailing date of these absentee mail-in packages to be earlier than when they were sent.'"

"The supervisor made that announcement for all workers to engage in that fraudulent practice," Giuliani said. "That's not me saying that. The's an American citizen saying that under oath."

Giuliani also said this same woman said she saw election workers illegally coaching people on whom to vote for.

He told reporters much of the evidence is public and reporters can review **it online, including the Michigan case, *Constantino v. City of Detroit.***

"All you've got to do to find out if I'm misleading you at all is to look at the lawsuits," Giuliani said. "Look what's alleged, look at the affidavits."

Giuliani said that while not all affidavits have been made public, citizens have provided hundreds of them.

9 Key Points from Trump Campaign Press Conference on Challenges to Election Results

Joel B. Pollak

Rudy Giuliani and other lawyers representing President Donald Trump's campaign outlined their case Thursday that the Nov. 3 presidential election was so deeply flawed in several key states that the results should be overturned in the president's favor.

Giuliani said there was a pattern to the alleged irregularities in key states that suggested, he said, a "plan from a centralized place" to commit voter fraud in cities controlled by Democrats. He said widespread adoption of vote-by-mail had allowed Democrats to take big-city corruption practices nationwide. "They picked the places where they could get away with it."

Here are the key allegations the lawyers presented:

1. Observers were allegedly prevented from watching mail-in ballots being opened. Giuliani said that many mail-in ballots were opened without observers being able to check that they were properly signed, a key protection against fraud. Those votes, he said, were "null and void," especially where the envelopes had been discarded, making recounts useless.

2. Allegedly unequal application of the law in Democratic counties. In Pennsylvania, whose state supreme court created new, relaxed voting rules before the election, Giuliani alleged that absentee voters in Democratic counties were allowed to "cure" defects in their ballots, while voters in Republican counties, which obeyed the state law as written, were not.

3. Voters allegedly arrived at the polls to discover other people had voted for them. Giuliani said that many provisional ballots cast in Pittsburgh were submitted by people who showed up to vote in person, only to be told that they had voted already. He alleged that Democrats had filled out absentee ballots for other people, hoping they would not show up.

4. Election officials were allegedly told not to look for defects in ballots, and to backdate ballots. Giuliani cited an affidavit from an official who swore she was told not to exclude absentee ballots for **defects, and to backdate ballots so they would not appear to have been received after Election Day, to avoid a Supreme Court order to sequester those ballots.**

5. Ballots casting votes for Joe Biden and no other candidates were allegedly run several times through machines. Giuliani said that there were 60 witnesses in Michigan who would attest to ballots being "produced" quickly and counted twice or thrice. He said that a minimum of 60,000 ballots, and a maximum of 100,000 ballots, were allegedly affected.

6. Absentee ballots were accepted in Wisconsin without being applied for first. Giuliani noted that Wisconsin state law was stricter regarding absentee ballots than most other states are, yet alleged that 60,000 absentee ballots were counted in the Milwaukee area, and 40,000 in the Madison area, without having been applied for properly by the voters who cast them.

7. There were allegedly "overvotes," with some precincts allegedly recording more voters than residents, among other problems. Giuliani said there was an unusually large number of overvotes in precincts in Michigan and in Wisconsin, which he alleged was the reason that Republicans on the Wayne County Board of Canvassers had refused to certify the results there this week. He also alleged that there were some out-of-state voters in Georgia, and people who had cast votes twice there.

8. Voting machines and software are allegedly owned by companies with ties to the Venezuelan regime and to left-wing donor George Soros. Sidney Powell argued that U.S. votes were being counted overseas, and that Dominion voting machines and Smartmatic software were controlled by foreign interests, manipulating algorithms to change the results. Powell noted specifically that Smartmatic's owners included two Venezuelan nationals, whom she alleged had ties to the regime of Hugo Chavez and Nicolas Maduro. The legal team alleged that there were statistical anomalies, such as **huge batches of votes for Biden, that could not be explained except as manipulation — which, they alleged, happened in the wee hours of the morning as vote-counting had**

stalled. (The companies have disputed these allegations vigorously.) 9. The Constitution provides a process for electing a president if the vote is corrupted. Jenna Ellis argued that the media, had usurped the power to declare the winner of the election. She made the point, citing Federalist No. 68, that the constitutional process of selecting a president had procedural safeguards against corruption and foreign influence.
Giuliani said that the campaign believed that enough votes were flawed — more than double the margins between Biden and Trump in key states — that the president had a path to victory.

Giuliani presented evidence in the form of sworn affidavits, citing two and noting that the campaign had many more from private individuals.

He noted that several lawsuits that had been dismissed had been filed by private individuals, not the campaign directly. He said lawsuits might be filed in Arizona, and that the campaign was also examining irregularities in New Mexico and Virginia, though he said he did not think there were enough disputed votes in the latter.

Giuliani also took on the media, arguing that they had provided misleading information and condoned threats against Trump's legal team.

Trump Summons Michigan GOP Leaders for Extraordinary Meeting

President Donald Trump summoned Michigan's Republican legislative leaders to the White House for an extraordinary meeting Friday amid a push to upend the process that appeared to hand the battleground state to Democrat Joe Biden.

Two people familiar with the matter told The Associated Press that Trump invited Senate Majority Leader Mike Shirkey and House Speaker Lee Chatfield. They agreed to go, according to a state official aware of the leaders' plans. The two officials spoke on the condition of anonymity because they were discussing private conversations.

It was not immediately clear what the meeting would be about. Neither Shirkey nor Chatfield commented.

Trump's campaign has openly floated the notion of trying to get friendly state legislatures to appoint electors. If Trump succeeds in convincing Michigan's state board of canvassers not to certify Biden's victory in the state, state lawmakers could be called on to select electors, but such a move would be unprecedented and, say some legal experts, possibly illegal. It would be certain to draw a swift legal challenge.

Both Shirkey and Chatfield have indicated that they will not try to overturn the results favoring Biden.

"Michigan law does not include a provision for the Legislature to directly select electors or to award electors to anyone other than the person who received the most votes," Shirkey's spokeswoman said last week. On Nov. 6, Chatfield tweeted: "Whoever gets the most votes will win Michigan! Period. End of story. Then we move on." Asked at a Lansing news conference about the plan for legislative leaders to visit Trump, Democratic Gov. Gretchen Whitmer said, "I hope they wear masks, and I hope they stay safe."

"All the meetings in the world, though, can't take away from the fact that Joe Biden won Michigan by over 150,000 votes," Whitmer added. "That's 14 times the margin that Donald Trump won by in 2016. ... So we will be sending a slate of electors that reflects the will of the people of Michigan at the end of this process."

Also Thursday, state officials said Michigan's largest county cannot revoke its certification of election results after two Republicans who approved Biden's local landslide wanted to revert to their initial stance of refusing to bless the vote tally.

The GOP effort to change position represented another complication in what is typically a routine task. Monica Palmer and William Hartmann, the two GOP canvassers in Wayne County, said they only voted to certify the results after "hours of sustained pressure" and after getting promises that their concerns about the election would be investigated.

"We deserve better — but more importantly, the American people deserve better — than to be forced to accept an outcome achieved through intimidation, deception and threats of violence," they said in a statement Wednesday night.

State officials said the certification of the Detroit-area vote will stand. Michigan's chief election officer said a post-election audit will be performed, though not to check "mythical allegations" of fraud.

"There is no legal mechanism for them to rescind their vote. Their job is done, and the next step in the process is for the Board of State Canvassers to meet and certify," said Tracy Wimmer, a spokeswoman for the Michigan secretary of state.

The four-member state board, which is expected to meet Monday, is split with two Democrats and two Republicans — the same makeup as the Wayne County board.

Trump's campaign said the latest about-face by Palmer and Hartmann is legitimate. It withdrew a federal lawsuit challenging the Detroit-area results, attaching affidavits from the pair.

Palmer and Hartmann initially voted against certification Tuesday, leaving the county Board of Canvassers deadlocked at 2-2 along party lines. Palmer complained that certain Detroit precincts were out of balance, meaning that absentee ballot books did not match the number of ballots cast.

"This is not an indication that any votes were improperly cast or counted," Secretary of State Jocelyn Benson said.

The GOP move drew an immediate rebuke from the public and injected partisan politics into the business of an unsung panel that is supposed to confirm the will of the voters. A person familiar with the matter told the AP that Trump reached out to Palmer and Hartmann on Tuesday evening after the revised vote to express gratitude for their support.

In a statement, the pair reported being the target of threats, which they said they reported to law enforcement.

Trump "was checking to make sure I was safe after seeing/hearing about the threats and doxxing," Palmer said in a text message to the Detroit Free Press, referring to the practice of publicly disclosing someone's personal information.

The election tally shows Biden besting Trump in Wayne County by a more than 2-1 margin on his way to winning Michigan by 154,000 votes, or 1.8 % points, according to unofficial results.

The county canvassers later voted again and certified the results, 4-0. Then, on Wednesday, Palmer and Hartmann signed affidavits saying they believe the vote should not be certified.

Jonathan Kinloch, a Democratic canvasser, said he heard passion — not threats — during the stormy Tuesday night meeting when the audience on Zoom was allowed to speak after the 2-2 tie and before the unanimous vote.

"I heard people basically being very assertive in demonstrating their outrage, but it happens all the time," Kinloch said.

Benson, a Democrat, said a post-election audit will be conducted in Wayne County and any other community with "significant clerical errors."

"Audits are neither designed to address nor performed in response to false or mythical allegations of 'irregularities' that have no basis in fact," she said.

Various federal and state officials from both parties have declared the 2020 election safe and secure. But Trump and his allies have spent two weeks raising claims of fraud and refusing to concede to Biden.

Georgia Trump Supporter Denied Order Halting Vote Certification

A conservative Atlanta lawyer failed to win a court order halting certification of Georgia's election results showing Joe Biden won the state over President Donald Trump by more than 12,000 votes.

U.S. District Judge Steven Grimberg on Thursday rejected a lawsuit by L. Lin Wood claiming Georgia Secretary of State Brad Raffensperger and state election board members violated the constitutional rights of voters through the way they allowed election officials to process defective absentee ballots. Wood had sought an injunction and a hand recount in Georgia's 159 counties.

Georgia is due to certify its results on Friday, becoming the first of the battlegrounds states to do so. The state and its 16 electoral votes went to Trump in 2016 and became one of few states that flipped in 2020.

Judge Tosses Republican Bid to Halt Arizona From Certifying Biden Win

A judge on Thursday dismissed a Republican-backed lawsuit seeking to halt Arizona officials from certifying Joe Biden as the winner of the state, dealing another courtroom setback to President Donald Trump and his allies.

Judge John Hannah, a state court judge in Phoenix, said in a brief order he was denying a request by the Arizona Republican Party for an injunction blocking the Maricopa County Board of Supervisors from certifying the results in the county, where the majority of Arizonans live.

Democrat Joe Biden defeated Trump in Arizona by more than 10,000 votes, according to Edison Research, one of the states he appeared to flip to win the White House by securing 306 Electoral College votes to the president's 232. Trump has alleged fraud, though his court challenges have so far gotten little traction. But opinion polls show his complaints about a "rigged" election have a political benefit, with as many as half of Trump's fellow Republicans believing them, according to a Reuters/Ipsos poll.

Arizona Republicans had asked Hannah to order a new audit of ballots, arguing it had been conducted in a way that violated state law.

The judge did not explain why he was denying the request but said he would issue a lengthier decision soon.

The Arizona Republican Party said in a statement that it had sought "judicial clarification" on whether election officials could supersede state laws.

"Unfortunately, this ruling instead makes clear to Arizonans that they must ensure that this issue is addressed with new legislation that clearly outlines the parameters in which the Secretary can and cannot impose their own interpretation of our laws in the future," the statement said.

The party filed the case last week against Maricopa County Recorder Adrian Fontes and the county board of supervisors.

The lawsuit alleged a violation of a law relating to determining a sample for a post-election audit of ballots.

The judge also said it would be "futile" to allow the party to file a revised lawsuit, signaling deep skepticism about the case.

Michigan Board Member Considers Seeking Election Audit

By Brian Trusdell

A Republican member of the Michigan Board of State Canvassers is considering calling for an audit of the state's election results before he votes to certify them, The Washington Post reported Thursday.

Norman Shinkle, one of two Republicans on the four-member board, said he is leaning toward asking for the audit before the board is scheduled to vote on Monday. "I do think with all of the potential problems, if any of them are true, an audit is appropriate," Shinkle told the Post in a telephone interview. ‹›I take one step at a time, and if we can get more information, why not?››

Shinkle said that among his concerns are the claims that machines and software supplied by Dominion Voting Systems Corp., used in 30 states including nearly all of the ones where results have been in dispute, switched votes from President Donald Trump to Democratic rival Joe Biden. "If Dominion was fudging votes, that's a serious problem," he said. "If it's true. I don't know. I have to be convinced of it. That's why the audit makes sense. "Right now the idea to check into some of these accusations seems to make sense to me. We have to have people trust our system going forward."

The Post appeared to try to impugn Shinkle's integrity by saying he was under intense pressure because his wife, Mary, filed an affidavit in support of a federal lawsuit by the Trump campaign — a reference to which he seemed to take exception. "That's almost an accusation against marriage," he said. "My wife can do whatever she wants to do."

Giuliani presses Trump election challenge case in fiery news conference with legal team

The ex-New York City mayor aggressively made the case for the Trump campaign's legal challenges

By Ronn Blitzer

The Trump campaign holds a news conference on the 2020 election legal challenges. U Thursday for the Trump campaign's legal challenge of the 2020 election results, alleging in a fiery news conference that there was a "centralized" plan to carry out voter fraud around the country.

This is a different approach than the campaign has recently taken in court, where they have primarily focused on the validity of ballots and counts without asserting fraud. While Giuliani did not present any direct evidence of a massive fraud scheme, Giuliani asserted that this is the "logical conclusion" reached as a result of incidents he said took place in several states.

TRUMP CAMPAIGN DROPS LAWSUIT CHALLENGING MICHIGAN VOTING RESULTS

"What I'm describing to you is a massive fraud," Giuliani said at the Capitol Hill news conference with other members of Trump's legal team, who repeatedly lashed out at the news media and accused them of treating their efforts unfairly. At one point, Giuliani repeatedly told one reporter: "You're lying." His descriptions largely entailed recitations of allegations put forth in several lawsuits that the Trump campaign has filed. Former Vice President Joe Biden is the projected winner in the contest, but the Trump campaign is contesting those calls, raising concerns in several battleground states.

Former Mayor of New York Rudy Giuliani, a lawyer for President Donald Trump, speaks during a news conference at the Republican National Committee headquarters, The former New York City mayor spoke about incidents in Pennsylvania where Republican poll watchers claimed they were not allowed to observe the counting process because they were kept too far away. A judge had ruled in their favor and ordered that they be permitted six feet away from the counting at a center in Philadelphia, but that was overturned after officials appealed.

Giuliani also claimed that while Pennsylvania does not allow absentee voters to fix any errors with their ballots, some were given that opportunity -- but not those from Republican areas. He cited sworn affidavits from cases in Pennsylvania and Michigan from poll workers who spoke about instructions from supervisors. One affidavit said that workers in Pennsylvania were instructed to assign ballots without names to random people, resulting in thousands of people in Pittsburgh showing up to the polls to find that votes had been cast in their names.

Another affidavit said that a supervisor in Michigan instructed workers to change the dates on absentee ballots to show that they arrived earlier than they had. An affidavit also claimed that workers were told not to request photo identification from Michigan voters, even though state law requires it.

Giuliani also said that approximately 100,000 absentee ballots in Wisconsin should have been deemed invalid because there were no applications for them. President-elect Joe Biden leads President Trump in that state by roughly 20,000 votes.

"If you count the lawful votes, Trump won Wisconsin," Giuliani said.

Trump campaign legal adviser Jenna Ellis explained the lack of new evidence at the news conference to support their allegations by saying this was merely an "opening statement," and that more evidence would be forthcoming in court.

Giuliani pushed back against a reporter who claimed he and his team were taking their time rolling out their cases.

"We're not going to drag it out. I mean it's ridiculous for you to say we're dragging it out," Giuliani said, noting that Al Gore took more time in the legal battle over the 2000 election.

He also said that more lawsuits could be coming in Arizona and potentially New Mexico, where Trump trails Biden by nearly 100,000 votes. He also said a challenge could come in Virginia, where Biden leads by almost 500,000 votes, if they believe they could overcome that deficit.

Rudy Giuliani: 'Dominion Shouldn't Be Counting Votes Anywhere'

Attorney for the president, Rudy Giuliani speaks to the media at a press conference

By Eric Mack

There are too many coincidences of election irregularities for them to be accidental, particularly the Dominion Voting Systems tied to Venezuela and China, according to Trump legal team coordinator Rudy Giuliani.

"Curiously, in the very, very close states where Trump lost by less than 1%, it's those machines that are being

used," Giuliani told "The Cats Roundtable" on WABC 770 AM-N.Y. "Nevada, Michigan, and Georgia use those machines. Those machines should not be used in any American election. Again, they're foreign machines. "It looks like it is a Canadian company; it actually is a company owned by two Venezuelans that's been in business for about 20 years and been disqualified in so many places it would make your head spin."

Giuliani told host John Catsimatidis the legal team is going to press the courts, as "every one of those machines has to be audited in every state." "Dominion was counting the votes in 29 states," Giuliani said. "Dominion shouldn't be counting the votes anywhere. Dominion, when you look into it with just a little bit of investigation, you find out that Dominion uses a software, Smartmatic, which is a company that goes back to 2004.

"It was founded by two Venezuelans and Cesar Chavez. It has a terrible history of having fixed elections in Argentina, having fixed elections in Venezuela. It was all outlined in 2008 by the House of Representatives. It got kicked out of Texas for being woefully incompetent. It is still run by these two Venezuelans who are close to [Nicolas] Maduro, and the Dominion company is not an American company.

"It's a Canadian company. We send our ballots outside the United States to be counted to a company that is allied with Venezuela and China. That's outrageous." The China connections include parts made in China, Dominion Voting Systems CEO John Poulos, a former lobbyist for House Speaker Nancy Pelosi, D-Calif., told Congress last January before the global coronavirus pandemic erupted in the U.S.

"This has been going on with Democrats for years," Giuliani told Catsimatidis. "They get away with it because they do it only in Democratic cities that they own. You don't see them doing this in Omaha, Nebraska. You don't see them doing in a place that's Republican.

Giuliani: Trump 'Far From' Conceding Election To Biden

Attorney for the President, Rudy Giuliani speaks to the media at a press conference on Nov.7, 2020 in Philadelphia, Pennsylvania.

President Donald Trump is not conceding the election to Joe Biden, Rudy Giuliani insisted Sunday, calling a Trump tweet earlier in the day "sarcastic." In an interview on Fox News' "Sunday Morning Futures," the president's personal lawyer said Trump is "far from" giving up on the the Nov. 3 election despite Biden's ballot win.

"What he's saying is more I guess you'd call it sarcastic, or a comment on the terrible times in which we live and which the media has said he won," Giuliani said of the tweet.

"It was illegal obviously," he added about the posting. "He's contesting it vigorously in the courts. The media has tried to call the election, and they don't have a legal right to call the election. It gets decided by our electors, not by NBC, CBS, MSNBC and CNN and even Fox." "He's gotten more evidence of the rigging that went on he's really outraged and I am too," Giuliani said.

Giuliani also blasted Dominion voting machines used in some states, alleging it's a "very, very dangerous foreign company" that tallied votes in 27 states.

"[It's] a company that's not American, a company that's foreign, a company that has close close ties with Venezuela and therefore China, and uses a Venezuela company software that's been used to steal elections in other countries," he alleged. "I don't think people have any idea of the dimension of the national security problem that Dominion creates. This Dominion company is a radical left company," he alleged. Giuliani asserted even beyond the 2020 election, "this whole thing has to be investigated as a national security matter," alleging "the governors who gave contracts to this company never bothered to do any due diligence."

Ken Starr: Legal Challenges To Election 'Important Process'

Former Independent Counsel Ken Starr answers questions during a discussion held at the American Enterprise Institute in 2018

By Cathy Burke

Former independent counsel Ken Starr on Sunday called legal challenges to the presidential election an "important process" that should be allowed to play out. In an interview on "Fox News Sunday," Starr said the judicial system is perfectly designed to the process. **"Our system is designed to check, let's check it out," Starr urged. "A lawsuit was filed just on Wednesday. Let's let this process run."** **He pointed to lawsuits filed in Michigan and elsewhere.**

"If it is meritorious it would change over 1 million votes," he said of the Michigan suit. "In Georgia ditto [where] there is a state recount underway" and an "unprecedented flood of mail in-ballots." "This election we need to check," Starr asserted. Starr said the massive numbers of mail-in ballots generated "anecdotal evidence" that those ballots were sent to people who shouldn't have gotten them. "Everyone has heard, if his or her ears are open, anecdotal evidence, not proof, that people who should not have received those ballots received them… let's accept the judgment of the courts," he said.

Starr also dismissed the speculation that GOP state legislatures would appoint pro-President Donald Trump electors to the Electoral College in states Joe Biden won. "The legislature does have the ultimate authority," he said. "I think it's more of a theoretical possibility," Starr added.

Ballot Rejection Rates Historically Low in Key Battlegrounds

Gwinnett county workers begin their recount of the ballots on November 13, 2020 in Lawrenceville, Georgia

By Eric Mack

Mail-in balloting rejection rates from the 2016 presidential election to this one, particularly in battleground states, have dramatically shrunk to infinitesimal numbers, according to reports.

Despite massive warnings about mail-in ballot rejection rates being around 1% historically, 3% for first-time absentee ballot voters and as high as 6.5% in some states, the rejection rates in 2020 contested states like Georgia, Pennsylvania, and Nevada were "strikingly" low, according to U.S. data (2016 from a congressional report **and 2020 from the** U.S. Elections Project **run by the University of Florida):**

- **Georgia: 6.5% rejections in 2016 to a mere 0.2%, more than 30 times lower.**
- **Pennsylvania: 1% in 2016 to 0.03% this year.**
- **Nevada: 1.6% in 2016 to around 0.75% this year.**
- **Michigan: 0.5% in 2016 to 0.1% this year.**
- **North Carolina: 2.7% in 2016 to 0.8% this year.**

A number of irregularities can lead to the rejection of a mail-in ballot, including forgotten or significantly different signatures, misplaced addressed, or improper markings or completion.

"Every indication in the several states I've analyzed is that the initial rate of rejected mail ballots was not lower in the 2020 General Election, but that the cure rate was much higher," Florida political science professor Daniel Smith told Just the News. "This was the result of litigation — which resulted in voters in several states[able] to have more opportunities and time to correct mistakes with their return envelopes or security sleeves — but also the work on the ground by the parties and voting rights organizations to directly notify voters who had problems with their ballots that they had an opportunity to cure them."

Michigan expects to reduce its rejection rate even further this year, according to Michigan Secretary of State office spokeswoman Tracy Wimmer to Just the News, because "the Michigan Legislature passed a law requiring clerks to notify voters if there was a signature issue (either missing or mismatched) with their absentee ballot and ensure they understood how to cure it." "The curing window was available until 8 p.m. on Election Day," she added, "and since missing or mismatched signatures usually account for one of the largest % of rejections, we expect those will go down this year."

Trump: 'I Concede NOTHING!'

Donald Trump showed few signs of conceding the presidential election to Joe Biden for a week after the race was called, while also hardly acting as if he was preparing for a second term.

On Sunday the president appeared, almost as an aside in his ninth Twitter post of the morning, to find a way out of his conundrum of how to recognize defeat and claim victory at the same time.

"He won because the Election was Rigged," Trump tweeted, a post that was flagged by Twitter for containing disputed claims of election fraud.

An hour later, while in a motorcade heading to his golf course in Virginia, Trump recanted, saying "I concede NOTHING! We have a long way to go."

Jason Miller, senior adviser to the Trump campaign, said in a statement that the president's initial tweet "was referring to the mindset of the media."

Setting aside Sunday's flurry of tweets, though, Trump has done little over the past two weeks on some of the administration's top pre-election priorities. The stimulus deal he tried to ram through in the closing days of the campaign with ever-higher offers looks dead for now.

His coronavirus briefing on Friday ended a lengthy time out of the public eye. He's stopped calling out governors who are pushing more aggressive lockdowns. And even his prized ban of the Chinese app TikTok has been pushed off, for now.

Trump Tweets That Biden Won Election, Says Vote Was 'Rigged'

Trump didn't speak in public from Nov. 7 -- the day news organizations declared Biden the winner -- through Friday afternoon. It was the longest stretch of time without addressing the public since taking office.

The vacuum has been filled by steady speculation about what advice Trump is getting from family members and others about how and when to acknowledge that he's not getting a second term, and how best to protect his legacy and brand -- including for a possible comeback run in 2024.

Trump's inaction, coupled with his blocking Biden's ability to get access to federal agencies by refusing to concede, leaves the nation in a unusual state with its outgoing president not doing the job, and its incoming leader stymied from key functions.

National Security

At the same time, abrupt personnel moves at the Pentagon and at Homeland Security have created unease even among some of the president's allies. The idea that Trump is putting national security at risk is gaining purchase daily.

Senate Republicans including James Lankford of Oklahoma have insisted that Biden start receiving intelligence briefings.

"If that's not occurring by Friday, I will step in," Lankford, who sits on the Senate Homeland Security and Governmental Affairs Committee, said on Wednesday. It's unclear if Lankford intervened as promised.

When he broke his silence, Trump suggested for the first time since Election Day that he may have lost to

Biden. He made the comment as he rejected more lockdowns in response to a nationwide surge in coronavirus cases, hospitalizations and deaths.

"Whatever happens in the future, who knows which administration it will be, I guess time will tell, but I can tell you this administration will not go to a lockdown," Trump said.

On Twitter, Trump continued his claims of victory amid what he says was a "Rigged Election" rife with fraudulently cast votes and botched tallies in Biden's favor. But the campaign hasn't provided evidence to back up those claims, and its legal challenges crumbled in several states on Friday.

The president suffered another setback when news networks called Georgia for Biden. That would give Biden 306 electoral votes, far above the 270 needed to win, leaving Trump with 232. All 50 states' presidential races have been called by news organizations including Associated Press and major networks.

Biden's leads across a number of crucial swing states are large enough that they should withstand any recount, barring a massive and unprecedented error in tabulation.

Waving, Smiling

Trump has encouraged his supporters to protest the election. On Saturday, thousands of them gathered in Washington, unfurling Trump flags and chanting "four more years!" Trump made a cameo appearance, waving and smiling from his armored limousine on the way to his golf course, but didn't address the group.

The president's Friday event was focused largely on the administration's coronavirus vaccine development efforts. But Trump did little to acknowledge rising infections and hospitalizations ahead of this month's Thanksgiving holiday, leaving that task to Vice President Mike Pence.

It's not the only unpleasant duty the president has delegated. The administration signaled this week that it's passing responsibility for stimulus negotiations with Democrats to Senate Majority Leader Mitch McConnell, despite Trump's promise of a sweeping package shortly after Election Day.

That's a marked contrast from the president's proclamation in late October that the country would "have a tremendous stimulus package immediately after the election," helped by his ability to sway GOP lawmakers. On Saturday, Trump tweeted that Congress must do a "big and focused" relief bill, without suggesting he would get involved.

Trump has also backed off another pre-election focus: his call for the Chinese owner of the TikTok video-sharing app to quickly sell its U.S. operations in response to national security concerns. The administration instead has given the company longer to resolve the issues.

White House spokesman Judd Deere rejected as "false" the idea that Trump has given up on governing.

"President Trump is fighting hard for a free and fair election while at the same time carrying out all of his

duties to put America First," Deere said. At the White House, some aides are working on transition binders for the new administration, refreshing their resumes, and reaching out to friends and former colleagues about potential employment.

Biden, meanwhile, is proceeding as the victor. The president-elect has formed a panel of coronavirus experts, named White House staff, and spoken with congressional leaders and heads of state. Biden -- who Trump mocked throughout the campaign for "hiding in his basement" -- has taken questions from reporters, and his transition team held its first press briefing on Friday.

But while Trump has retreated from the public eye, he's been busy, consulting with aides and lawyers about his options and political future. The president has begun stretching his days in the Oval Office longer than usual -- not decamping for the residence until after 8 p.m. most nights last week -- and surveying allies about how they think he should approach the coming weeks.

In a conversation with Fox News reporter Geraldo Rivera, Trump said he would "do the right thing" but wanted to see "what states do" in certifying their election results over the next few weeks.

He told Washington Examiner columnist Byron York that he thought that "maybe" he had lost, before ultimately rejecting the idea. Trump said it was important to file legal challenges to examine allegations of fraud.

"Never bet against me," Trump said.

But Trump isn't acting like a man wagering he'll prevail.

Legal Setbacks

There's little sense among the president's allies that the campaign's numerous lawsuits -- which have struggled to gain traction in courts across the country -- will succeed, much less reverse the outcome of the election.

On Friday, the law firm handling the president's litigation in Pennsylvania withdrew, while the legal team in Arizona dropped a suit over 191 disputed ballots in a state where Biden's lead is over 10,000 votes. In total, the president's campaign has lost over a dozen legal challenges.

Trump has used social media to tout various debunked claims, including a disproved assertion that election software glitches changed vote counts in Michigan and Georgia. The company in question, Dominion Voting Systems, pushed back forcibly in a statement on Saturday. In total, Twitter has flagged nearly a quarter of the president's post-election tweets for misinformation.

Meanwhile, a new wave of coronavirus infections hit Trump loyalists. Leading figures in the president's recount effort, including political advisers Corey Lewandowski and David Bossie, have tested positive, as has White House chief of staff Mark Meadows.

Esper Out

Trump has been active since the election in at least one realm of governing: personnel. On Monday, he fired Defense Secretary Mark Esper, the first in a series of housecleaning moves at the Pentagon and Department of Homeland Security.

While the dismissals appeared partly as recrimination against Pentagon brass with whom he'd had disagreements, the changes might also pave the way for an accelerated troop withdrawal from Afghanistan.

On Thursday, the White House announced a ban of U.S. investments in Chinese firms owned or controlled by the military, in his first post-election bid to punish Beijing, which he has blamed for the spread of the coronavirus.

But the president has steered clear of the ongoing saga of TikTok. The administration granted the app's owner, ByteDance Ltd., a 15-day extension on Thursday to resolve national security concerns after the company submitted a filing saying the government had stopped responding to efforts to strike a compromise deal. The White House has declined to comment.

Mad Rush

Other actions can be seen as a tacit acknowledgment that the president's days are likely numbered. The administration is rushing plans to auction drilling rights in the U.S. Arctic National Wildlife Refuge in what appeared to be a bid to issue leases before Biden -- who's pledged to protect the region --- takes office. And Trump announced a fresh slate of judicial nominations Friday, as he and McConnell rush to fill vacancies before the transfer of power.

The White House provided a list of Trump's actions since the election, which included the approval of disaster declarations for Puerto Rico and Florida, and issuance of a strategic plan on intellectual property.

Deere, the White House spokesman, added: "He's also working to advance meaningful economic stimulus, engaging members of Congress on a government funding proposal, and ensuring state and local governments have what they need to respond to the ongoing pandemic."

NYPost: Biden SLUSH FUND POLITICAL PARASITE HACK FOR BIDEN JOBS & INCOME PROGRAM Cancer Charity Spent More Than $3M on Salaries, Zero on Research, Grants

By Solange Reyner

Joe Biden's cancer charity spent more than $3 million on salaries and zero on cancer research and grants during a two-year period, according to tax filings reviewed by the New York Post.

Documents also show the Biden Cancer Initiative, founded by Democratic presidential nominee Joe Biden and wife, Jill, after Joe's oldest son, Beau died in 2015 from brain cancer, spent nearly $1 million on travel and conference expenses during that time.

The charity took in $4.8 million in contributions in fiscal years 2017 and 2018 and spent $3 million on payroll in those two years.

Gregory Simon, president of the Biden Cancer Initiative and former Pfizer executive, reportedly received $429,850 during the 2018 fiscal year, nearly double what he made in 2017.

Danielle Carnival, former chief of staff for Obama's Cancer Moonshot Task Force, was paid $258,207 in 2018.

The initiative, suspended in 2019 as Biden became further involved in the 2020 presidential election, was initially touted as an organization that would "develop and drive implementation of solutions to accelerate progress in cancer prevention, detection, diagnosis, research and care, and to reduce disparities in cancer outcomes."

TOXIC MASCULINITY TAKE ONE

Trump's Bizarre Comment About Son Barron is Turning Heads **if any kid would attract hot**

young girls, who in the world more than BARON TRUMP? He's as good looking as good looking gets. Maybe the best looking (15) year old who ever lived. CERTAINLY BETTER LOOKING THAN BARACK HUSSEIN OBAMA'S SELF-ABSORBED BRATS

and investors have ties to Democrats. Goodwin reports that "it is true the firm made a contribution and worked with the Clinton Family Foundation during the Obama-Biden administration."

The Associated Press also reported that a former top aide to House Speaker Nancy Pelosi is one of the company's lobbyists. The firm also employs a lobbyist who worked for Republicans Dick Cheney and John Boehner.

Trump, according to Goodwin, views the suspicious election results as "the concluding act of a confederacy against him that began with the Obama-Biden administration's corrupting of the FBI and CIA to spy on him in 2016 and tip the election to Hillary Clinton. That effort gave birth to the Russia, Russia, Russia narrative that wasn't fully revealed as false until the probe of Special Counsel Robert Mueller finally concluded in 2019."

"It's amazing but nothing happened to [Jim] Comey and [Andrew] McCabe, even though they were caught cold," Trump told Goodwin, referring to the former director and deputy director of the FBI.

"Then this, the greatest theft in the history of America. And everybody knows it," Trump told Goodwin.

President Donald Trump appears to be nowhere close to conceding the presidential election to former Vice President Joe Biden, _________

"He won because the Election was Rigged," Trump wrote on Twitter. "NO VOTE WATCHERS OR OBSERVERS allowed, vote tabulated by a Radical Left privately owned company, Dominion, with a bad reputation & bum equipment that couldn't even qualify for Texas (which I won by a lot!), the Fake & Silent Media, & more!"

In a story published Saturday night, Trump told Post columnist Michael Goodwin that the election"was stolen."

"It was a rigged election, 100 %; and everyone knows it," Trump said in the Friday night interview. "It's going to be that I got about 74 million votes, and I lost? It's not possible."

When Goodwin asks if he'll ever concede, Trump responded: "We'll see how it turns out." he said at one

point.

“When I asked if he could come to terms with defeat, he responded only that ‘it’s hard to come to terms when they won’t let your poll watchers in to observe’ the counting,” Goodwin writes. “A third time, he said, ‘Again, I can’t tell you what’s going to happen.’

Goodwin writes that Trump seems convinced that Biden’s victory was corruptly engineered by Dominion Voting Systems, a technology used by most states, including Michigan and Georgia. Trump repeatedly cited Dominion, according to Goodwin.

“It was turned down by the state of Texas because it is insecure,” Trump told Goodwin. Trump also repeated allegations that the ompany’s owners and investors have ties to Democrats. Goodwin reports that “it is true the firm made a contribution and worked with the Clinton Family Foundation during the Obama-Biden administration.”

The Associated Press also reported that a former top aide to House Speaker Nancy Pelosi is one of the company’s lobbyists. The firm also employs a lobbyist who worked for Republicans Dick Cheney and John Boehner.

Trump, according to Goodwin, views the suspicious election results as “the concluding act of a confederacy against him that began with the Obama-Biden administration’s corrupting of the FBI and CIA to spy on him in 2016 and tip the election to Hillary Clinton. That effort gave birth to the Russia, Russia, Russia narrative that wasn’t fully revealed as false until the probe of Special Counsel Robert Mueller finally concluded in 2019.”

“It’s amazing but nothing happened to [Jim] Comey and [Andrew] McCabe, even though they were caught cold,” Trump told Goodwin, referring to the former director and deputy director of the FBI.

“Then this, the greatest theft in the history of America. And everybody knows it,” Trump told Goodwin.

Trump Urges Judge to Preserve Suit Over Pennsylvania Ballots

The Trump campaign urged a judge to preserve its bid to block Pennsylvania from certifying President-elect Joe Biden as the winner, claiming there’s evidence that voters in Democratic-leaning counties were improperly allowed to fix errors with their ballots.

In a filing Sunday in federal court, the campaign said a half-dozen Pennsylvania counties named in the suit illegally allowed voters who cast deficient ballots to cast replacement absentee and mail-in ballots before Election Day or provisional ballots on Nov. 3 to “cure” any issues.

The campaign seeks to block Pennsylvania from certifying the result unless it scraps about 680,000 mail-in

votes from the state's most populous counties, which include the Philadelphia and Pittsburgh areas.

"Unless Bush v. Gore was much ado about nothing, presidential candidates of course have an interest in having lawful votes for them counted and unlawful votes for their opponent invalidated," the filing said. "That's particularly true in Pennsylvania, one of a few swing states where recounts or other litigation is ongoing and where the vote margin is close."

The filing was made by campaign lawyer Linda Kerns, two days after attorneys with Porter Wright Morris & Arthur LLP walked away from the case. The campaign said that firm "buckled" under criticism from "leftist mobs."

A hearing on the swing state's motion to dismiss the lawsuit is set for Nov. 17, with a separate evidentiary hearing scheduled for two days later. The case will be decided by U.S. District Judge Matthew Brann in Williamsport, Pennsylvania.

County Disparities

The suit is part of President Donald Trump's last-ditch effort to reverse the result of the election, which he continues to claim without evidence was "rigged" against him by Democrats. A similar suit seeking to block Michigan from certifying the result for Biden is also pending. Legal experts say the cases are weak and likely designed to reinforce a political strategy to undermine Biden rather than win in court.

Pennsylvania Attorney General Josh Shapiro's office didn't immediately return a message seeking comment.

The campaign's Sunday filing cited Pennsylvania's Lancaster County, which Trump won, as an example of how things were done right, because election officials there "did not contact voters who submitted defective ballots or give them an opportunity to cure," the filing said. "They simply followed the law and treated these ballots as invalid and refused to count them."

Another plaintiff in the case, voter John Henry, alleges his defective vote was treated differently from those of voters in other counties in violation of the Constitution's Equal Protection Clause.

"In other words, Henry cast a defective ballot that was not counted, but another Pennsylvania voter in another county could cast the same defective ballot and have his vote counted -- solely based on place of residence," the campaign said. "The Defendant counties' insistence upon counting illegal ballots disparately favored Democratic-leaning counties over Republican-leaning counties."

With almost all ballots counted in Pennsylvania, Biden is ahead by almost 66,000 votes or almost one full point.

The case is Donald J. Trump For President Inc. v. Boockvar, 4:20-cv-02078, U.S. District Court for the Middle District of Pennsylvania (Williamsport).

China Expert: Beijing Happy (WHY SHOULDN'T CHINA BE HAPPIER THAN A PIG IN SLOP?) With Biden Win

By Brian Freeman

Beijing is pleased with several news outlets calling the 2020 presidential race for Democrat Joe Biden, China expert Gordon Chang said on Sunday. Speaking on "The Cats Roundtable" radio show **on WABC 770AM hosted by John Catsimatidis, Chang said,** "I think China is very happy with how things turned out, because Beijing worked very hard to get the vice president elected" **by malicious and massive attacks on President Donald Trump through a public disinformation campaign.**

Chang said "that Twitter took down 174,000 fake Chinese accounts in June alone, which shows you the size of China's effort. **And they were working for Biden even during the Democratic nomination process, because**

they were favoring him over Bernie Sanders." He insisted that "once Biden got the nomination, they went to work on President Trump, making life difficult for him."

Chang added that China is not "going to let up. It's probably going to test the Biden administration in ways that are going to be extremely dangerous, stressing that "this is a risk for us. We not only have China going after us internationally. They are going after our democracy. Which is the reason why Hong Kong is so important. They tried to snuff out representative governance there. They're now going to turn their attention to us, because they've been attacking our form of government for three or four months in intensified ways."

EXCLUSIVE VIDEOS: Counter-Protesters Target Trump Supporters After 'Million MAGA March' As Violence Breaks Out In Downtown DC

Shelby Talcott

WASHINGTON, D.C. — Supporters of President Donald Trump were targeted by counter-protesters in Washington, D.C. Saturday after the "Million MAGA March," and violence broke out in the city.

Reporters on the ground captured multiple incidents**, particularly at** *Black Lives Matter***, where Trump supporters were swarmed, harassed and at times physically assaulted as the march wrapped up. Thousands of Trump supporters arrived in D.C. to attend the march, voicing support for Trump and backing allegations of voter fraud in the election.**

The march began at Freedom Plaza Saturday morning and ended at the Supreme Court, where police **officers first kept counter-protesters separate from the pro-Trump crowd. The scene was tense at times, with both sides yelling and provoking, but remained largely peaceful as police successfully kept the groups apart.**

As the march came to an end, some pro-Trump supporters made their way to BLM Plaza, where counter-protesters were waiting. In one incident, a female Trump supporter walking with her young children was harassed – a fight broke out and one of her daughters **was seen crying as police escorted the family out.**

Later in the day, a large group of **counter-protesters wearing black bloc mobilized and marched to the plaza. Upon arrival, they declared the area officially off-limits to Trump supporters. Fights began breaking out left and right in the street, with pro-Trump individuals becoming the only target.**

One woman got her hat stolen, her flag stolen and was hit in the back of the head after being forced to retreat from the area. Another young couple was harassed and had water and other objects thrown as the female screamed, visibly scared by the incident.

Other individuals dining at a nearby restaurant had a firecracker **thrown at their table – prompting everyone eating on the patio to rush inside the restaurant, which quickly locked its doors. Meanwhile, fires rose up at the** plaza **as protesters burned pro-Trump memorabilia.**

Despite police being out en masse around the city, the many incidents often escalated quickly. At times, officers arrived before a scene escalated, in which case they escorted Trump supporters from the area. Other times, however, police arrived to simply break up the fights.

As the night wore on, the violence continued, with protesters marching to Harry's Pub, where pro-Trump supporters have gathered in the past. The group was met with a heavy police line with Trump supporters behind them. Once again, despite the police presence, the groups managed to collide, according to reporters on the ground. Protesters and the Proud Boys**, a far-right group, began to** battle **each other on the streets of downtown D.C., hurling punches and donning protective gear. Eventually, police arrived to break up the situation and make** arrests.**The violent evening in** D.C. **ended with both crowds dispersing late in the evening. Police remained out in full force downtown following the attacks, and some Trump supporters marched into the early hours of Sunday morning.** (RELATED: Multiple Storefronts Are Boarding Up Windows And Entrances Ahead Of Possible Election Day Protests And Violence In DC)

STOP REPUBLICANS
POST ELECTION FUND -

We spent every cent we had on the election and now we're broke.
Even though the election is over, now our real work begins.
That's why we still need support from grassroots donors like you.
Please, we need you to chip in TODAY:

500% MATCH: Donate Now →

PAID FOR BY STOP REPUBLICANS PAC
(WWW.STOP-REPUBLICANS.ORG) **AND NOT AUTHORIZED BY ANY CANDIDATE OR CANDIDATE'S COMMITTEE**

WHO ARE THESE TRAITORS WANTING MY MONEY WITH NO ADDRESS & ONLY A P.O. BOX?

This message was sent to: rrgg3348@gmail.com | Change or update your email address by clicking here.

Stop Republicans, an accountability project of Progressive Turnout Project, is a grassroots-funded effort dedicated to resisting the Republican Party and Donald Trump's radical right wing agenda.

We believe that emails are a crucial way for our campaign to stay in touch with supporters like you. However, if you'd prefer to receive fewer emails, you can click here. If you would like to unsubscribe, click here.

Our movement is powered by supporters like you. Your grassroots support is critical to helping us defeat Republicans across the country. If you'd like to donate, please click here. Thanks for your support!WHO ARE YOU & WHERE ARE THESE HIDDEN DISEASED TISSUE COCKROACH SCUMBAGS

Stop Republicans
P.O. Box 618293
Chicago, IL 60661

100 % OF THE TIME; DEMOCRAT STRATEGY IS CONSPIRING TO FIRE & DEPRIVE OF THEIR LIVELIHOODS ANYONE WHO RESISTS DEMOCRAT EVIL; NOW DEMOCRATS WANT LAWYERS WHO USE ACTUAL EVIDENCE OF DEMOCRAT'S STEALING THE 2020 PRESIDENTIAL ELECTION TO FIRE OUR REPUBLICAN LAWYERS. JUST LIKE THEY FIRE ALL SCHOOL TEACHERS; PROFESSORS & JOURNALISTS WHO RESIST & DISAGREE WITH THE LEFT.

DID WE COME THIS FAR

THE NEIGHBOR SAID IT WAS HORRIBLE. WHEN THE 2 SOLDIERS CAME TO THE FARMHOUSE DOOR TO TELL MRS SOUSLEY HER BOY WAS DEAD; YOU COULD HEAR THE HOLLERING & SCREAMING OVER THE FIELDS ALL NIGHT LONG TO THE NEXT FARM. THE NEXT DAY A POSTCARD CAME TO MRS SOUSLEY FROM HER SON, (19) YEAR OLD FRANKLIN; 1 OF 6 SOLDIERS; IN 2 TAKES; HISTORY'S MOST FAMOUS PHOTO BY JOE ROSENTHAL; FEB 23 1945 STARS & STRIPES HOISTED OVER MT SURIBACHI. 26 DAYS; ROSENTHAL; & 3 OF THE 6 SOLDIERS KILLED IN ACTION. POSTCARD (9/19/1925–3/21/1945) FRANKLIN TO MOTHER, YOU CAN NEVER IMAGINE HOW A BATTLEFIELD LOOKS. IT SURE LOOKS HORRIBLE. LOOK FOR MY PICTURE IN THE NEWSPAPERS. I HELPED PUT UP THE FLAG. PLEASE DON'T WORRY & WRITE. 19 YEARS/171 DAYS MOCK; RIDICULE; MOTHER'S TEARS; AMERICAN EXCEPTIONALISM; EVERY HEART; EVERY TONGUE

FRANKLIN SOUSLEY DIED FOR THIS?

6/4/1942; 49 WRONG OCEAN; LAUGHING STOCK; RINKY DINK SHIPS; BARELY IN AIR; WRONG SKY SCRAP HEAP TURKEYS; 148 SILICON VALLEY WARSHIPS; 248 EXTERMINATOR; LIGHTNING FAST ACROBAT ZEROS; KATES; BETTYS; FLATTOP YORKTOWN; OIL SLICK 10 MILES TRAILING; W/ BANDAIDS; SCOTCH TAPE; AFLOAT; COME OUT SWINGING? WISH, PRAYER & A RABBITS FOOT; 3 MONTHS? ADMIRAL CHESTER WILLIAM NIMITZ; SOFTLY; 3 DAYS; GREATEST GENERATION; AYE, AYE, SIR. HEART; SOUL; DAYS UNTO SECONDS; WELDERS/SHIPFITTERS 1400; 3 DAYS PATCHED UP; ALAMO LINE IN SAND;

MARCH 6, 1836, (26) YEAR OLD COLONEL WILLIAM B. TRAVIS; WITH HIS SWORD, AT THE ALAMO, DREW A LINE IN THE SAND … …
THERE WERE (186) DEFENDERS AGAINST THE (8,000) ASSAILANTS OF PRESIDENT GENERAL ANTONIO LOPEZ DE SANTA ANNA.
"WE WILL SELL OUR LIVES DEARLY ...
I WANT EVERY MAN WHO IS PREPARED TO STAY HERE & DIE WITH ME, TO CROSS THIS LINE ...".
ALL CROSSED, EXCEPT FOR (2), WHO ESCAPED THROUGH ENEMY LINES, OVERNIGHT

THE (186) DEFENDERS OF THE ALAMO INCLUDED DAVY CROCKETT; & JIM BOWIE; WHO WAS CRIPPLED, AND COULDN'T STAND. IN A COT, JIM BOWIE HAD HIS MEN CARRY HIM ACROSS THE LINE ... WHEN THEIR AMMUNITION WAS SPENT; THEY FOUGHT BACK WITH KNIVES UNTIL THEY WERE ALL BAYONETED.
EVERYONE, INCLUDING THE DEAD, WAS MUTILATED BY BAYONETS. ..

THIS IS WHAT NEW YORK & CONNECTICUT IS …

NOTHING IS WRITTEN …

WE WILL WRITE IT … TODAY, TOMORROW. NOW & FOREVER … FOR OUR OWN 3,000 WHO DIED ON SEPTEMBER 11, 2001, AND FOR THEIR KIDS & WIDOWS.

I WANT EVERYONE TO STAND WITH ME.

WE'LL FIGHT OUR WAY BACK TOGETHER. ....

IT NEVER HAD TO BE THIS WAY.

IT WON'T BE THIS WAY AGAIN ...

ALL ABOARD YOUR CHOO-CHOO CHUGGIN ...
RIGHT UP HERE, WITH YOUR ENGINEER ...

ALL ABOARD; YOUR VICTORY TRAIN.

I AM RICHARD E. GLICK.

READ MY (8) BOOKS; MAINE REMEMBER; DIVE BOMB GROUP BOSS CLARENCE WADE MCCLUSKY; JOSEPH KARROL, 27; SAM ADAMS, 30; TURKEYS THRU 10,000 SLUGS @ SECOND HURRICANE GALE; VALKYRIE COME; THERMOPYLAE GO; OCEAN FLOOR; MINUTES; CARRIERS AKAGI; SORYU; KAGA; HIRYU; FOOTBALL BRADY; MAHOMES; NEXT DAY DEAD BOTH; KARROL; ADAMS; BEFORE INFAMY; ARIZONA REFUELED; 2020; OIL STILL LEAKS. UNDERWATER CEMETERY EXPENDABLE 1,117; BROTHERS/TRIOS 35; THOMAS AUGUSTA FREE DAD; WILLIAM THOMAS FREE SON; GO ASK THE SPARTANS; REGIMENTAL FLAG BEARER; PRIMARY YANKEE SHARPSHOOTER TARGET; 14 BOYS; NO UNIFORMS; MISMATCHED BUTTERNUT; LED 26TH NORTH CAROLINA ASSAULT; SOLDIER UNIVERSAL; 14 WEAPONLESS BOYS; MINIE BALLS; 13 KILLED; LED CHARGE; BY THE 14TH; 26TH N CAROLNA REGIMENTAL COLORS HELD HIGH; NEVER HIT THE GROUND; FOLLOW ME; BOYZ 2 MEN; NONE OLD ENOUGH FOR WHISKEY OR TO VOTE NO SLAVEOWNERS; OF 14; 13 DEAD; JULY 1, 1863; CHARGE; NO ROMANESQUE NORMAN TAPESTRY 50 BATTLE SCENE HASTINGS; BAYEUX CATHEDRAL; IN 1070'S COMMISSIONED BY BISHOP ODO FOR HIS HALF BROTHER; THE DUKE OF NORMANDY; WILLIAM/CONQUEROR; BAYEAUX MUSEE DE LA TAPISSERIE; 2390 FT.; 2 ½ LONGER THAN THE TITANIC; CALL TO GLORY; FOR 13 BOYS; DAISIES; DAFFODILS; WATERED BY BLOOD; WE WILL NEVER FORGET THEM; LOVINGLY MANICURED LAWNS; TOWN SQUARE; NO OSCAR BIG BUDGET; "LONGEST DAY"; OMAHA BEACH; LAST OF 14; CONCENTRIC; EARTHWORKS; OVERRUN; 3 BLUE LINES BROKEN; GUNS; SPUN ROUND; GRAPE/CANNISTER; MUZZLE LOADER; HURRICANE GALES; SHRAPNEL FURIOUSLY RAMMED HOME; CHAOS; DRIVEN OFF; BLUE RETREAT; 26TH N CAROLINA; 800; 588 KILLED/WOUNDED; BOY COLONEL DEAD; HENRY KING BURGWYN JR; 20; EVERY MAN; CLUSTER N CAROLINA SMALL TOWNS; 37,000 CONFEDERATE N CAROLINA; DEAD; NO KNOCK; FRONT DOOR; JOHNNY EVER MARCH HOME? EVER? NEVER. GIRLS; NO SWEETHEARTS; KIDS; MOMS; HUSBANDS; DADS, NONE; GRANDMAS; NO GRANDKID; 1 LESS BELL TO ANSWER. 1 LESS EGG TO FRY. 1 LESS MAN TO PICK UP AFTER; N CAROLINA, WAR IS HELL; SILENCE; PLENTY; ASHES, ONLY; HILLARY; HARD CHOICES; "THE CONFEDERATE FLAG SHOULDN'T FLY ANYWHERE" SHOUT IT; HILLARY; FROM THE ROOFTOPS; UNREDEEMABLE; GUNS & RELIGION; DEPLORABLES; CONDESCENDING; MEAN-SPIRITED SELF-ABSORBED; YAPS DISINGENUOUS TO DESCENDANTS; BILL NEVER INHALED; DRAFT DODGER; MONICA; CHAPPAQUA HIGH TREASON SERVER; J. CHRISTOPHER STEVENS CANCELLED RESCUE ISLAM BUTCHERY; SUSAN RICE LIED

REPUBLICAN VIDEO DISSED PROPHET MUHAMMAD "THE CONFEDERATE FLAG SHOULDN'T FLY ANYWHERE?" SHUT YOUR FACE HILLARY, BEFORE I SHUT IT FOR YOU

YOU NEVER QUITE KNEW WHERE THE PEOPLE LEFT OFF; & WHERE ABE LINCOLN BEGAN. KANSAS FARMER; JEWISH TAILOR; IRISH POLICEMAN; BROOKLYN SAILOR; BUFFALO HUNTER TELLIN' A STORY; OUT IN THE OREGON TERRITORY. FREEDOM'S A THING; HAS NO ENDING; NEEDS TO BE CARED FOR; NEEDS DEFENDING; GREAT LONG JOB; FOR MANY HANDS CARRIES FREEDOM; ACROSS THE LAND

Battle of Thermopylae.

19th-century painting by John Steeple Davis, depicting combat during the battle

Date	**20 August or 8–10 September 480 BC**
Location	Thermopylae, Greece 38.796607°N 22.536714°E Coordinates: 38.796607°N 22.536714°E
Result	Persian **victory**[
Territorial changes	**Persians gain control of** Phocis, Boeotia, **and** Attica[

Belligerents	
Greek city-states	Persian Empire

Commanders and leaders	
• King • Leonidas of Sparta † • Demophilus †	• King • Xerxes I of Persia • Mardonius • Hydarnes II • Artapanus[4]
Strength	
Total • 5,200 (or 6,100) (Herodotus) • 7,400+ (Diodorus) • 11,200 (Pausanias) • 7,000 (modern est.)	• 2,641,610 (Herodotus) • 70,000–300,000 (modern est.)
Casualties and losses	
4,000 (Herodotus)[	c. 20,000 (Herodotus)

Location of the battle of Thermopylae

The Battle of Thermopylae (/θr'mpli/ *thr-MOP-i-lee*; Greek: Μάχη τῶν Θερμοπυλῶν, *Máchē tōn Thermopylōn*) was fought between an alliance of Greek city-states, led by King Leonidas I **of** Sparta**, and the** Achaemenid Empire **of** Xerxes I**. It was fought over the course of three days, during the** second Persian invasion of Greece. The battle took place simultaneously with the naval battle at Artemisium. It was held at the narrow coastal pass of Thermopylae ("The Hot Gates") in August or September 480 BC. The Persian invasion was a delayed response to the defeat of the first Persian invasion of Greece, which had been ended by the Athenian victory at the Battle of Marathon in 490 BC. By 480 BC, Xerxes had amassed a massive army and navy. He set out to conquer all of Greece. The Athenian politician and general Themistocles had proposed that the allied Greeks block the advance of the Persian army at the pass of Thermopylae, while simultaneously blocking the Persian navy at the Straits of Artemisium.

A Greek force of approximately 7,000 men marched north to block the pass in the middle of 480 BC. The Persian army was rumoured to have numbered over one million soldiers. Today, it is considered to have been much smaller. Scholars report various figures ranging between about 100,000 and 150,000 soldiers.The Persian army arrived at the pass in late August or early September. The vastly outnumbered Greeks held off the Persians for seven days (including three of battle) before the rear-guard was annihilated in one of history's most famous last stands. During two full days of battle, the small force led by Leonidas blocked the only road by which the massive Persian army could pass. After the second day, a local resident named Ephialtes betrayed the Greeks by revealing a small path used by shepherds. It led the Persians behind the Greek lines. Leonidas, aware that his force was being outflanked, dismissed the bulk of the Greek army and remained to guard their retreat with 300 Spartans and 700 Thespians. It has been reported that others also remained, including up to 900 helots and 400 Thebans. The remaining soldiers fought to the death. Most of the Thebans reportedly surrendered.

Themistocles was in command of the Greek Navy at Artemisium when he received news that the Persians had taken the pass at Thermopylae. Since the Greek strategy required both Thermopylae and Artemisium to be held, given their losses, it was decided to withdraw to Salamis. The Persians overran Boeotia and then captured the evacuated city of Athens. The Greek fleet—seeking a decisive victory over the Persian armada—attacked and defeated the invaders at the Battle of Salamis in late 480 BC. Wary of being trapped in Europe, Xerxes withdrew with much of his army to Asia (losing most to starvation and disease), leaving Mardonius to attempt to complete the conquest of Greece. However, the following year saw a Greek army decisively defeat the Persians at the Battle of Plataea, thereby ending the Persian invasion.

Both ancient and modern writers have used the Battle of Thermopylae as an example of the power of a patriotic army defending its native soil. The performance of the defenders is also used as an example of the advantages of training, equipment, and good use of terrain as force multipliers and has become a symbol of courage against overwhelming odds.

WE WILL SELL OUR LIVES DEARLY. THEY ARE 8000. WE ARE 182. WITH HIS SWORD; 26; AT THE BEGINNING OF LIFE; WITH HIS SWORD; HE DREW A LINE WITH N THE SAND. I WANT EVERY MAN WHO IS PREPARED TO STAY

HERE & DIE WITH ME TO CROSS THIS LINE.

"Remember the Alamo"

Battle of the Alamo	
Part of the Texas Revolution	
The Alamo, as drawn in 1854	
Date	**February 23 – March 6, 1836**
Location Alamo Mission, San Antonio, Mexican Texas **29°25⊠32⊠N 98°29⊠10⊠W**Coordinates: **29°25⊠32⊠N 98°29⊠10⊠W**	
Result	**Mexican victory**
Belligerents	
Mexican Republic	Republic of Texas
Commanders and leaders	
Antonio López de Santa Anna Manuel Fernandez Castrillon Martin Perfecto de Cos	William Travis † James Bowie † Davy Crockett †
Strength	
8,000	**185–260**
Casualties and losses	
600 + killed and wounded	**182**

The Battle of the Alamo (February 23 – March 6, 1836) was a pivotal event in the Texas Revolution**. Following a** 13-day siege, Mexican troops under President General Antonio López de Santa Anna reclaimed the Alamo Mission near San Antonio de Béxar (modern-day San Antonio, Texas, **United States), killing the** Texian and immigrant occupiers. Santa Anna›s cruelty during the battle inspired many Texians, both legal Texas settlers and illegal immigrants from the United States, to join the Texian Army. Buoyed by a desire for revenge, the Texians defeated the Mexican Army at the Battle of San Jacinto**, on April 21, 1836, ending the rebellion.**

Several months previously, Texians had driven all Mexican troops out of Mexican Texas**. About 182 Texians**

were then garrisoned at the Alamo. **The Texian force grew slightly with the arrival of reinforcements led by eventual Alamo co-commanders** James Bowie and William B. Travis. **On February 23, approximately 8,000 Mexicans marched into San Antonio de Béxar as the first step in a campaign to retake Texas. For the next 10 days, the two armies engaged in several skirmishes with minimal casualties. Aware that his garrison could not withstand an attack by such a large force, Travis wrote multiple letters pleading for more men and supplies from Texas and from the United States, but the Texians were reinforced by fewer than 100 men because the United States had a treaty with Mexico, and supplying men and weapons would have been an overt act of war.**

In the early morning hours of March 6, the Mexican Army advanced on the Alamo. After repelling two attacks, the Texians were unable to fend off a third attack. As Mexican soldiers scaled the walls, most of the Texian fighters withdrew into interior buildings. Occupiers unable to reach these points were slain by the Mexican cavalry as they attempted to escape. Between five and seven Texians may have surrendered; if so, they were quickly executed. Several noncombatants were sent to Gonzales to spread word of the Texian defeat. The news sparked both a strong rush to join the Texian army and a panic, known as «The Runaway Scrape"**, in which the Texian army, most settlers, and the new, self-proclaimed but officially unrecognized,** Republic of Texas government fled eastward toward the United States ahead of the advancing Mexican Army.

Within Mexico, the battle has often been overshadowed by events from the Mexican–American War of 1846–48. In 19th-century Texas, the Alamo complex gradually became known as a battle site rather than a former mission. The Texas Legislature purchased the land and buildings in the early part of the 20th century and designated the Alamo chapel as an official Texas State Shrine. The Alamo has been the subject of numerous non-fiction works beginning in 1843. Most Americans, however, are more familiar with the myths and legends spread by many of the movie and television adaptations, including the 1950s Disney mini-series ***Davy Crockett*** and **John Wayne's 1960 film *The Alamo*.**

THAT WAS THEN. WE ARE TODAY & TOMORROW …IF …

EVERY ONE OF US … EVERY FIGHTER; IN EVERY FIGHT WORTH DYING FOR; ONLY FOUGHT; BECAUSE WE REPUBLICANS HAD A GOOD CHANCE OF WINNING; MUCH LESS COMING OUT OF ALIVE; YOU & I WOULD HAVE NEVER BEEN BORN; MUCH LESS EVER HAVE BEEN; NOW OR EVER BE FREE.

WE WILL FIGHT ON THE BEACHES … WE WILL FIGHT IN THE STREETS OF HONG KONG AGAINST XI JINPING; WITH OUR HANDS AGAINST MACHINE GUNS; WE WILL FIGHT ON THE BEACHES OF TAIWAN WITH OUR FISTS. WE WILL FIGHT IN THE VALLEYS OF XINJIANG PROVINCE BY THE GAN RIVER; KORANS IN HAND; ALONGSIDE OUR UYGHUR BROTHERS & SISTERS; WE WILL FIGHT ON THE HIGH SEAS FROM THE TITANIC. WE WILL FIGHT ATHEISTIC KANCEL KULTURE LEFTIST KKK GROUPTHINK SPLIT SECOND BY SPLIT SECOND WITH THE POETRY OF JESUS OF NAZARETH; THE PATIENCE OF CONFUCIUS; THE WISDOM OF BUDDHA; THE FURY OF MUHAMMAD; THE ETERNITY OF ALLAH; THE TEN COMMANDMENTS OF JEHOVAH; THE WARRIOR TENACITY OF MARS; THE SLEDGEHAMMER OF JUPITER; THE RESOURCEFULLNESS OF SHANGO; THE EYES; EARS; & (6) SENSES OF SILVER FOX. WILL WE EVER SURRENDER? THAT'S

YOUR CHOICE. NOT MINE. NOT EVEN THE CHOICE OF GOD. WE WILL FOREVER FIGHT; FOR THE SAME REASON HE DIED FIGHTING. HE DIED FOR HER.

YOUNG GIRLS WITHOUT SWEETHEARTS

DID JOE BIDEN & KAMALA HARRIS EVER PROMISE TO ANNE FRANK A ROSE GARDEN?

nederland
ANNE
FRANK
60
c

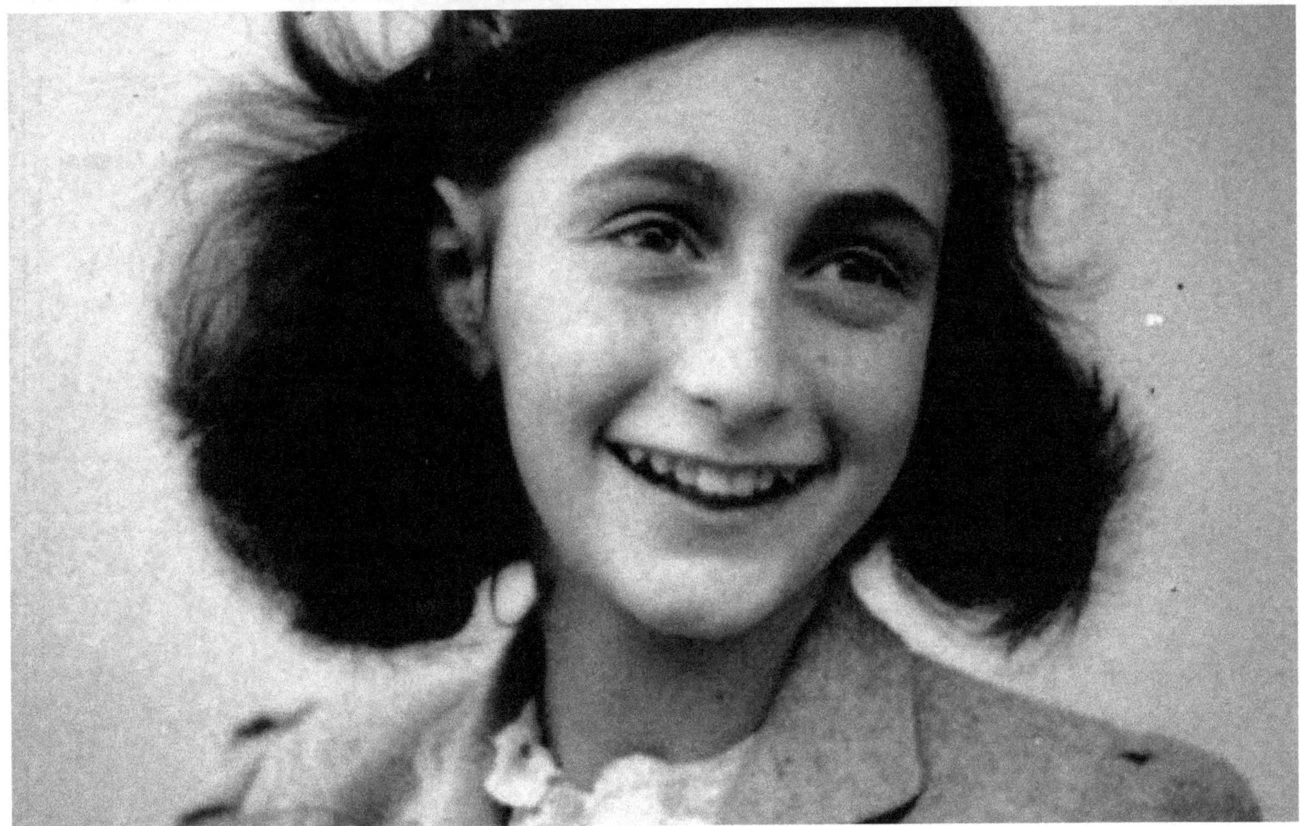

AS CONGRESSBITCH ILHAN ABDULLAHI OMAR SMIRKS; ISRAEL HAS HYPNOTIZED THE WORLD & ITS ALL ABOUT THE BENJAMINS BABY, OF COURSE, ANNE FRANK HAS ALSO HYPNOTIZED THE WORLD; AND ITS ALL ABOUT (15) YEAR OLD JEWISH GIRLS, BABY …

YOU DEBATE ANNE FRANK; JOE BIDEN; KAMIKAZE KAMALA; ILHAN ABDULLAHI OMAR; AND "NEVER AGAIN" … MEANING US … ARE READY FOR YOU …

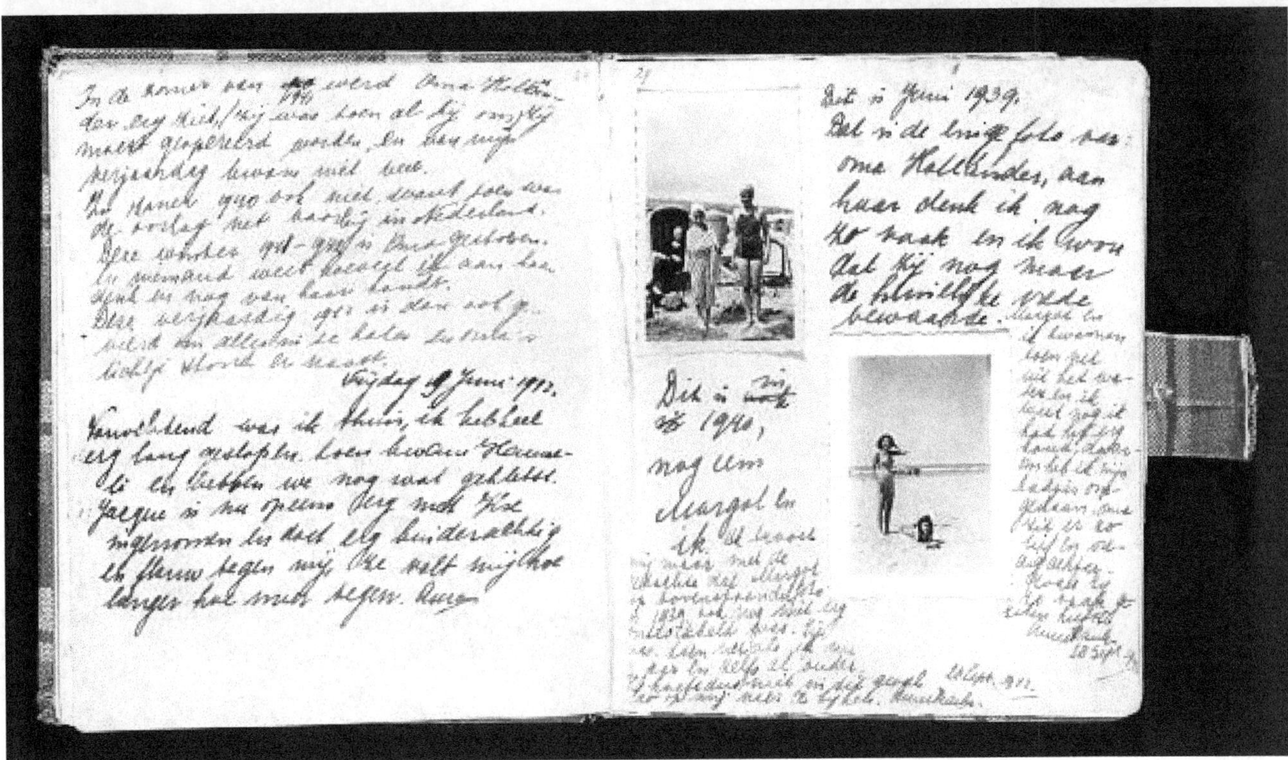

Alexandria Ocasio-Cortez Refuses Invitation to Visit Auschwitz Concentration Getaway ...

WOMEN, CHILDREN & OLD MEN ARRIVING AT AUSCHWITZ BERKENAU – MAY 1944

SLAVE LABORERS - COLUMN A
WOMEN; "IT TAKES A VILLAGE" CHILDREN & OLD MEN – INDUSTRIAL CREMATORIA - COLUMN B

PAY ANY PRICE. BEAR ANY BURDEN. I AM THE AMERICAN WHO SHE WAITS FOR.

TALK TO GOD; ALEXANDRIA OCASIO-CORTEZ; ABOUT THIS (16) YEAR OLD JEWISH RESISTANCE GIRL BEING HANGED . **CNN Faces Backlash Barrage for Denigrating Holocaust: '(EXTRA LOATH-SOME CHUBBY UGLY PIG SKANK FACE; EATING TOO MANY DEEP FRIED TWINKIES, YOU UGLY DISHRAG BITCH SKANK) Amanpour Must Be Fired'**

Joshua Klein

After CNN's IS THIS A REVOLTING UGLY DISHRAG SKANK PIG WITH FANCY-ASSED FUCKED UP NAME "Christiane Amanpour" SHE ACTUALLY GET PAID MILLIONS OF DOLLARS @ YEAR commemorated Kristallnacht — the infamous anti-Jewish pogrom carried out throughout Nazi Germany — by likening it to the Trump presidency, her comments were met with an immediate backlash, with many expressing shock at the belittling of the horrors of Nazi Germany._

Kristallnacht Pogrom Description

Kristallnacht, or the Night of Broken Glass, was a pogrom against Jews carried out by SA paramilitary forces and civilians throughout Nazi Germany on 9–10 November 1938. The German authorities A,K.A; FRAU OCASIO-CORTEZ; HER REICH THAT WOULD LAST 1000 YEARS; LIKE OUR OWN CONGRESS & OUR OWN SUPREME COURT IN OUR OWN STOLEN 2020 PRESIDENTIAL ELECTION; LOOKED ON WITHOUT INTERVENING..

In a jaw-dropping segment on Thursday, CNN anchor Christiane Amanpour recalled Kristallnacht by noting that President Donald Trump's presidency has similarly waged a "modern day assault" attacking "those same values" the Nazi regime did.

The backlash was immediate.

In an exclusive statement to Breitbart News, Morton Klein, head of the Zionist Organization of America (ZOA) — the oldest pro-Israel organization in the United States — expressed disgust at the ill comparison. Noting his personal experience as a child of Holocaust survivors, Klein stated he was "disgusted" by Amanpour, whom he accused of "trivializing and belittling the Holocaust by absurdly and recklessly comparing President Trump's pro-Israel, pro-Jewish tenure to that of Nazi Germany," while demanding she be "condemned, ostracized and fired."

"This mindless analogy is even more cruel and ridiculous given that he has an Orthodox Jewish daughter,

son-in-law, and grandchildren," Klein added. He then went on to contrast between the two extremes.

"Would the Nazis have protected the Jewish State, as Trump has, by putting the most severe sanctions on the true enemy of the Jews today — Iran — who is developing nukes and repeatedly threatens to destroy the Jewish State?" he asked.

Pointing out a double standard, Klein continued his criticism.

"Did Amanpour ever compare the Obama regime to the Nazis given that he gave $150 billion to the antisemitic Iran regime, giving it greater ammunition to succeed in its Nazi-like plans of annihilating the Jewish State?" he furthered.

Klein also called out the noted silence from Jewish organizations and those who embrace the "cancel culture."

"Where is ADL, AIPAC, AJC, the Reform, Conservative, Orthodox and Reconstructionist Jewish movements, Hadassah and the National Council of Jewish Women, Jewish Women International, the Conference of Presidents in demanding her immediate dismissal?" he asked. "Where is the cancel culture when we legitimately need it to rid the journalism world of the always-hostile-to-the-Jewish-State Amanpour?"

Klein was far from alone in his criticism.

"This is ⊠⊠@camanpour on⊠ ⊠@CNN⊠ comparing Trump's tenure to Nazi Germany," wrote former Brexit Party Member of the European Parliament (MEP) Ben Habib. "How the hell is this sort of prejudice tolerated on mainstream media? Third rate rubbish."

"The time has come for the corporate media to fire people like this," wrote conservative talker Mark Levin. "These media corporations must police themselves and their newsrooms."

"This is vile, repugnant, and absurd!" wrote former New York State Democrat lawmaker Dov Hikind. "But not entirely unexpected from the shoddy "journalist" and Khamenei-shill Christiane Amanpour…"

"People are feeling a lot of different things right now after the election. That's OK," wrote Rep. Michael Waltz (R-FL). "What's not OK is @CNN and @camanpour comparing US politics to the Holocaust. Not only are these implications divisive but they're also incredibly disrespectful to the Jewish community."

"These people are truly despicable," tweeted Donald Trump Jr.

The Orthodox Jewish Public Affairs Council also referred to the comments as despicable.

"Despicable. @camanpour compares verbal fact checking of a POTUS to a Nazi pogrom in which dozens of Jews were murdered," wrote the group dedicated to countering defamation. "Amanpour uses the book burning of Kristallnacht to reach this comparison thus ignoring the overall deadliness and human cost of the night."

"Politicizing and exploiting the six million Jews murdered in a systematic campaign of genocide to score cheap political points is reprehensible," said Linda, founder and CEO of Momsonamitzvah. "At a time when our country needs healing and dialogue, Amanpour must now address her horribly offensive and inappropriate comparison with a public apology immediately."

"Hey @CNN @camanpour please stop using the horrors of the Holocaust to justify an agenda," wrote StopAntisemitism.org. "Our suffering is not yours to play political ping pong with."

"Weimar Jews and the Holocaust that followed have become fun little playthings – media toys – for journalists to casually toss around, use and exploit to make themselves feel way more important than they are and to elevate fear," tweeted journalist Glenn Greenwald. "This is repugnant and offensive, @camanpour."

"DISGUSTING demeaning of the Holocaust by @camanpour, @CNN," tweeted republican strategist Boris Epshteyn. "How far the left goes to wrongfully attack @realDonaldTrump is depraved. Will @cnn do the right thing?"

"Here we see CNN's @camanpour pissing on the graves of the 6,000,000 Jews murdered by the Nazis," wrote twitter user Arthur Schwartz. "@CNNPR, you're an absolute disgrace."

"@camanpour appallingly compares Trump's tactics to the Nazi kristallnacht?" tweeted Trump campaign adviser Steve Cortes. "So our President criticizing the media and litigating an election = genocide? Such an insult to the victims of the Nazis, and to the brave Americans who smashed that tyranny."

"@camanpour: I'm ashamed to have to count you an Iranian compatriot," wrote Iranian-American columnist Sohrab Ahmari. "This is a grotesque abuse of history, a horrific, ahistorical equivalence-drawing, a shameful cheapening of the Shoah."

British sports and entertainment broadcaster Ross Dyer stated that as someone "who lost many ancestors in the Shoah, I find this comparison to be utterly false and highly offensive."

Author and radio host Eric Metaxas was most blunt.

"Ms. Ahmanpour (TRASHY DISHRAG SKANK BITCH MY AUTHOR ADDENDUM) should be fired. Fired. FIRED," he wrote. "This is one of the most offensive things ever said on television. But it also reveals a level of ignorance that is frightening."

"This is almost impossibly offensive," wrote Reporter Alex Bernson. "And it wasn't an off-the-cuff remark – she opened the program with it."

Former CNN senior digital producer Steve Krakauer stated that CNN staff as a whole are as responsible as Amanpour.

"@CAmanpour comparing Trump to Hitler and Kristallnacht, saying they 'assault' the 'same values' is obscene and outrageous," he wrote. "But Amanpour alone should not be condemned – it took writers, producers and executives at CNN to allow this inflammatory nonsense on the air."

"@CNN and @camanpour should be ASHAMED of themselves," tweeted political commentator Bryan Leib. "Serious question…How did this segment make it on the air?"

"Awful from @camanpour," wrote Algemeiner's Dovid Efune. "Using the Holocaust as a political cudgel is the height of insensitivity and disrespect."

Efune also questioned her consistency in commemorating the event.

"Did she mark Kristallnacht in previous years? Or only when politically opportune?" "The memory of the massacred millions is sacred. This segment is a desecration," he concluded.

Author and filmmaker Dinesh D'Souza described the comments as a "new low."

"We all knew CNN has been terrible, but this is a new low," wrote D'Souza. "Comparing Trump to Nazis purging Jews… REALLY?"

International human rights lawyer Arsen Ostrovsky wondered just where all the progressive voices were.

"Why has @ADL not come out to condemn @camanpour @CNN over this repugnant comparison of @realDonaldTrump to Kristallnacht and the Nazis, who murdered 6 million Jews?" he wrote.

"How is this acceptable? Where are all the progressive voices? Is your silence not a gross double standard?"

On Thursday, Breitbart News was first to report on Amanpour's egregious remarks.

In the opening of her daily global affairs interview program earlier that day, Amanpour dedicated her introduction to commemorating Kristallnacht (or "Night of Broken Glass") which occurred this week in 1938.

"This week, 82 years ago, Kristallnacht happened; it was the Nazis' warning shot across the bow of our human civilization that led to genocide against a whole identity," she stated.

Flashing scenes of Jewish victims followed by the Nazi burning of Jewish books, Amanpour then continued by comparing the forces behind the notorious historical event with the current administration.

"And, in that tower of burning books, it led to an attack on fact, knowledge, history and truth," she added. "After four years of a modern-day assault on those same values by Donald Trump, the Biden/Harris team pledges a return to norms, including the truth."

Amanpour is the Chief International Anchor for CNN and host of CNN International's nightly interview program *Amanpour*, which has aired for nearly a decade.

In April last year, Amanpour suggested that "lock her up" chants were a form of hate speech that the FBI could have "shut down." Amanpour's latest comments not only grossly misinform but drastically belittle the horrors of the past.

The U.S. Holocaust Memorial Museum describes the period following the night that violent anti-Jewish demonstrations broke out across Germany, Austria, and the Sudetenland region of Czechoslovakia:

Over the next 48 hours, violent mobs, spurred by antisemitic exhortations from Nazi officials, destroyed hundreds of synagogues, burning or desecrating Jewish religious artifacts along the way. Acting on orders from Gestapo headquarters, police officers and firefighters did nothing to prevent the destruction. All told, approximately 7,500 Jewish-owned businesses, homes, and schools were plundered, and 91 Jews were murdered. An additional 30,000 Jewish men were arrested and sent to concentration camps. Nazi officials immediately claimed that the Jews themselves were to blame for the riots, and a fine of one billion reichsmarks (about $400 million at 1938 rates) was imposed on the German Jewish community.

The greater significance of the event is also noted.

THESE LOATHSOME FUCKEN DEMOCRATS NOT ONLY HATE OUR GUTS THEY WANT THE ABSOLUTE WORST FOR US. THEY WANT TO STEAL OUR MONEY & ALL OF OUR ASSETS; & ARE ALREADY STEALING OUR VOTES & LAUGHING IN OUR FACES ABOUT THEIR CRIMES AGAINST US. SECEDE; IF ONLY TO PREVENT BEING CONTAMINATED BY THEM. THIS IS OUR COMMON SENSE & SURVIVAL. FOR US.

THIS IS THE HATRED THE LEFT HAS FOR GUNS & RELIGION DEPLORABLES. SOON IT WILL BE TOO LATE. IS IT ALREADY TOO LATE?

WHY NOT FIGHT? THIS IS WHO WE ARE.

WE ARE THE AMERICAN PEOPLE. WE DON'T WHIMPER, ROLL OVER & CRY.

LET IT BE WRITTEN.

LET IT BE SAID.

THE RICHARD E. GLICK DOCTRINE:

IF DEMOCRACY PERISHES FROM AMERICA, IT WILL PERISH FOREVER FROM THE FACE OF THE EARTH. LOOK IN THE MIRROR.

WILL YOU LET THIS HAPPEN?

WHEN DEMOCRACY IN AMERICA PERISHES,

GOD'S MERCY FOR US WILL PERISH WITH IT.
WE REPUBLICANS ARE DEMOCRACY.
WHO'S ANGER RISES EVERY SUNRISE.
HIS MERCY IS STILL WITH US EVERY SUNSET.
ABRAHAM LINCOLN SAID, DEMOCRACY CAN & MAY PERISH.
MEN HAVE FOUGHT & DIED FOR IT.
NOTHING HAS CHANGED, OR EVER WILL CHANGE.

"Kristallnacht was a turning point in the history of the Third Reich, marking the shift from antisemitic rhetoric and legislation to the violent, aggressive anti-Jewish measures that would culminate with the Holocaust."

BLM and anti-fascist supporters attack multiracial family at Million MAGA March

President Trump made a surprise visit to the Million MAGA March

Paul Sacca

An ugly scene developed at the Million MAGA March on Saturday when a *Black Lives Matter* supporter and a man who was marching with an anti-fascist group harassed a multiracial family that was out showing their support for President Donald Trump.

CALLING ALL AMERICANS TO TAKE BACK OUR CONSTITUTIONAL FREEDOMS; AS NECESSARY CAN HAVE A 1000 INTERPRETATIONS YOU FIGURE IT OUT, WOODCHUCK SCHMUCK SCHUMER. WE'RE NICE PEOPLE, ONLY NICER THAN YOU

Thousands of Trump supporters converged on Washington, D.C., on Saturday to rally around Trump. However, tensions flared in the afternoon after hordes of counterprotesters assembled. One of the counterprotest groups at the Trump rally was Refuse Fascism, a self-described "national movement organizing to drive out the Trump/Pence regime." The anti-fascist group had announced days earlier that they were holding a counterprotest to "overwhelm" Trump supporters.

"We are gathering non-violently," Lucha Bright of Refuse Fascism told WUSA-TV. "We are not intending to engage them. We want to overwhelm them with our numbers. If they attack us, that is not out of the realm of possibilities of what they do. But we are hoping, especially if we gather in large numbers, that we will overwhelm them with our strength." Video from Saturday shows a group dressed in all black holding bright orange "Refuse Fascism" signs pursue a multiracial family, which included three young children. Several people in the mob get in the face of the black mother who is wearing a Trump jacket and pushing a stroller with an infant at *Black Lives Matter* Plaza.

A woman wearing a *Black Lives Matter* shirt gets in the face of the mother, but is separated by a man, presumably the father. Then the BLM supporter gets in the face of the father, and it sounds as if she screams at him, "You're an ugly b**!" The mother yells, "Get away!" One of the daughters is seen crying. The father prods the woman with his flag pole to keep the woman at a distance. The woman then charges at the father to try to take away his Gadsden flag, he waves her off with his hand. Then a man dressed in all black that was**

walking with the anti-fascist group advances at the father and attacks him. The father retaliates by hitting the man with the flagpole. The woman runs at the father and is also struck with the flagpole. The father gets shoved to the pavement, and he falls on top of the small child, who screams in pain. Police immediately separate the two sides. Video taken by photojournalist Jorge Ventura shows the woman and the man had bruises on their heads. In another video, couple holding a "Refuse Fascism" sign harass a reported Trump supporter who's son appears to be wearing a "Make America Great Again" hat. Earlier in the day, there were black bloc protesters with signs that read: "Punch MAGA in the face," who antagonized Trump supporters gathered near the Supreme Court, where a scuffle broke out.

Before the counterprotesters arrived on the scene, thousands of Trump supporters sang the "Star-Spangled Banner" in unison. Before the Million MAGA March kicked off, Trump drove by in his motorcade and gleefully waved to his supporters.

ASK THIS GUY. HE HAS ALL THE ANSWERS "WHAT'S IT ALL ABOUT, FLYBOY?"

A Tuskegee Airman Turns 95 - HE WAS BORN ON THE 4TH OF JULY

America isn't perfect, (NEITHER IS GOD) but it was and still is worth fighting for.

By Harry Stewart July 2, 2019

WE ARE OF YOU. YOU ARE OF US.

Harry Stewart Jr. among other graduates of Tuskegee Flying School in Alabama, 1944. U.S. AIR FORCE VIA HARRY STEWART JR.

YOU ARE THE GREATEST OF OUR AMERICAN GREATNESS.

To-days
TONNAGE
TARGET
20.000 TONS
19.000
18.000
17.000
16.000
15.000
14.000
13.000
12.000
11.000
10.000
9.000
8.000
7.000
6.000
5.000
4.000
3.000
2.000
1.000
RED BALL
HIGHWAY
STAY ON THE
BALL
KEEP 'EM
ROLLING!

THE NEVER-
BEFORE-TOLD
STORY OF
THE ARMY'S
DEVIL
DRIVERS!
THE
RED BALL EXPRESS

I was born on Independence Day 95 years ago. On June 27, 1944, I graduated from Tuskegee Army Flying School, established in Alabama shortly before America's entry into World War II to train young African-American men as Army combat pilots. My journey to the flight line started in my high-school library in the New York City borough of Queens. I came across a magazine article about the first all-black flying combat unit, the 99th Pursuit Squadron. I decided right then that when I turned 18 the squadron was where I wanted to serve. These black flyers had glamour, polish, prestige. The Army Air Forces accepted me even though I had no high-school diploma. The country needed pilots, I was gung-ho, and I had passed the battery of written tests. The train ride down South was eye-opening for a teenager who'd never traveled far from New York. When the train crossed the Mason-Dixon Line, the conductor came by and pointed at me: "Move to the colored car." It was disconcerting, but I saw it as an unavoidable hurdle to earning my wings. I swallowed hard and kept going.At Tuskegee Army Airfield, the sky filled with silvery planes emblazoned with the Army Air Forces star-in-circle insignia. The big-barreled trainers emitted a raspy cacophony from their radial engines and fast-turning propellers. You felt you were part of something big, something magnificent. You weren't just learning to fly; you were serving your country, and you were going to fight.

At the controls of P-51 Mustangs, I flew 43 combat missions with the 332nd Fighter Group, known as the Red Tails. Our commander was the legendary Benjamin O. Davis Jr., who had endured four years of the silent treatment from white cadets at West Point but nevertheless managed to graduate 35th out of a class of 276. At our mission briefings, he implored us, "Gentlemen, stay with the bombers!" His convictions were encapsulated in his statement:

"The privileges of being an American belong to those brave enough to fight for them."

ARE WE?
LOOK IN THE MIRROR.
ARE YOU?
IF NOT YOU, WHO? US? NOW IT'S OUR TURN, NOW
IF NOT NOW, IF EVER; WHEN?

On Easter Sunday 1945, I shot down three long-nosed Focke-Wulf Fw 190s, the best piston fighters in the Luftwaffe inventory. That action resulted in my receiving the Distinguished Flying Cross. I was thankful that my country had given me the opportunity to fly and fight, and all these years later I am proud that I contributed to the cause. We called it winning the Double V, victory against totalitarianism abroad and institutional racism at home. July 4 is my birthday, but I celebrate my country's birthday too. America was not perfect in the 1940s and is not perfect today, yet I fought for it then and would do so again.

Mr. Stewart is a retired Air Force lieutenant colonel and subject of a new biography, "Soaring to Glory: A Tuskegee Airman's Firsthand Account of World War II," written by Philip Handleman.

MR. STEWART FOUGHT AGAINST THIS FUTURE FOR AMERICA

Election in House

By Eric Mack

The legal battle for President Donald Trump is no longer about him reaching 270 electoral college votes, but denying Joe Biden from reaching it, according to legal expert Alan Dershowitz on Newsmax TV.

"Let's look at the big picture: The big picture now has shifted," Dershowitz told "Saturday Report." "I do not believe that President Trump is now trying to get to 270 electoral votes. I think he thinks that's out of the question.

"What he's trying to do is to deny Joe Biden 270 votes, by challenging in Pennsylvania, Georgia, in Nevada, in Michigan, in Arizona."

Keeping Biden from 270 would put the election on the House delegations - a state-by-state majority held by Republicans 26-23-1 - as designated by the U.S. Constitution.

"If he can keep the Biden count below 270, then the matter goes to the House of Representatives, where of course there is a Republican majority among the delegations of states, and you vote by state if it goes to the House," Dershowitz told host Carl Higbie. "He's trying to follow the playbook of three elections of the 19th century."

Barring that narrow path to victory, Dershowitz speculated Trump will announce he will run for reelection in 2024, "and to campaign against what he regards as 'corrupt bargain' as analogous to what happened in 1824 and two other times in the 19th century."

"I think that's the strategy that is now in operation," Dershowitz concluded.

"You need a perfect storm for it to work. You need to get enough states, enough state attorneys general, or state departments, or whoever, secretaries of state or governors that are Republican that legitimately refuse to certify the results because they're under challenge on the day the electoral college meets by statute.

"If on that day, Biden doesn't have 270 votes – you don't get to vote two or three times on that; as far as the Constitution's concerned, it's one vote – and if the one vote doesn't give the leading candidate 270 electoral votes, then automatically it goes to the House of Representatives, where a whole new process takes over, and a process that clearly favors President Trump."

Trump Laments Georgia Recount's Signature Verification Block

By Eric Mack

Georgia Democrat operative Stacey Abrams effectively placed a preemptive block of signature verification on ballots in Georgia's hand recount, President Donald Trump lamented Saturday.

Trump tweeted:

"The Consent Decree signed by the Georgia Secretary of State, with the approval of Governor @ BrianKempGA, at the urging of @staceyabrams, makes it impossible to check & match signatures on ballots and envelopes, etc. They knew they were going to cheat. Must expose real signatures!"

Continuing in an ensuing tweet:

"....What are they trying to hide. They know, and so does everyone else. EXPOSE THE CRIME!"

Abrams is credited with a massive grassroots campaign to help Joe Biden pickup hundreds of

thousands of votes in Georgia, registering new Democratic voters.

Former national security adviser Susan Rice tweeted Nov. 4:

"Either way this goes in Georgia, we owe @staceyabrams our greatest gratitude and respect. Rarely does one person deserve such disproportionate credit for major progress and change."

Rep. Doug Collins, R-Ga., is working for Trump, his campaign, and the Republican National Committee to challenge the hand recount in Georgia, having already called out GOP Gov. Kemp and GOP Secretary of State Brad Raffensperger.

"One of the things we have got to start talking about is the fact in Georgia you have several problems," Collins told Newsmax TV**'s "**John Bachman Now**" on Friday. "No. 1 is that you don't have voter ID on the actual absentee ballot itself, so once its separated from the envelope, you don't know where that vote is, whether it was a valid or invalid, or if it gets put into the system, then you can't trace it because no voter ID on it.**

"No. 2: we gave away the signature verifications **in many ways when the secretary of state put together a consent decree with the Democrats, Stacey Abrams' group, that really, in essence, gutted our verification process. That's also got to be readdressed as well."**

THIS APOTHEOSIS GENESIS OF LEFTIST STEALING AMERICA. KIMBERLY STRASSEL IS THE MOST PROFOUND POLITICAL THINKER WHO WAS EVER LIVED

Harvesting the 2020 Election

OUR INCARNATION OF ADOLF HITLER; (MY AUTHOR ADDENDUM) NANCY PELOSI'S top priority was remaking the electoral system. The virus gave her a boost.

By Kimberley A. Strassel

Potomac Watch: Since Nancy Pelosi retook the speaker's gavel in 2019, her top priority has been remaking the electoral system. The coronavirus gave her a boost. Images: Getty Images Composite: Mark Kelly

The Trump campaign is pressing its case that last week's ballot counting was off, and it will get its day in court. But if Republicans want a fuller accounting of the shenanigans, they'll need to look much further back than Election Day. They'll need to internalize Nancy Pelosi's H.R. 1, and then do battle.

House Resolution 1 is the designation for the first bill unveiled in any new Congress. It's designed to highlight the majority party's top priority. In early 2017, the Republican-led House gave the title to Donald Trump's tax reform. When Mrs. Pelosi retook the speaker's gavel in 2019, her party had just

campaigned on a slew of urgent Democratic priorities: health care, climate change, immigration, student debt. None of these rose to the honor of H.R. 1.

- 2020's Biggest Election Losers November 5, 2020
- First, Hail All the Lawyers October 29, 2020
- The Biden 'Family Legacy' October 22, 2020
- A Justice Is Worth 1,000 Tweets October 15, 2020

- Sanders Haunts Biden-Harris October 8, 2020

Instead, Mrs. Pelosi unveiled a 600-plus page bill devoted to "election reform." Some of the legislation was aimed at weaponizing campaign-finance law, giving Democrats more power to control political speech and to intimidate opponents. But the bill was equally focused on empowering the federal government to dictate how states conduct elections—with new rules designed to water down ballot integrity and to corral huge new tranches of Democratic voters.

The bill would require states to offer early voting. They also would have to allow Election Day and online voter registration, diluting the accuracy of voting rolls. H.R. 1 would make states register voters automatically from government databases, including federal welfare recipients. Colleges and universities were designated as voter-registration hubs, and 16-year-olds would be registered to vote two years in advance. The bill would require "no fault" absentee ballots, allowing anyone to vote by mail, for any reason. It envisioned prepaid postage for federal absentee ballots. It would cripple most state voter-ID laws. It left in place the "ballot harvesting" rules that let paid activists canvass neighborhoods to hoover up absentee votes.

Democrats grandly named their bill the For The People Act, but conservatives had better titles. This page called it the "Majority Preservation Act,**" while the editors at National Review described it as an "Unconstitutional, Authoritarian Power Grab." Senate Majority Leader Mitch McConnell decried the bill as a "naked attempt to change the rules of American politics to benefit one party," and dubbed it the "Democrat Politician Protection Act."**

Mrs. Pelosi's bill didn't become law, despite her attempts this year to jam some of its provisions into coronavirus bills. But it turns out she didn't really need it. Using the virus as an excuse, Democratic and liberal groups brought scores of lawsuits to force states to adopt its provisions. Many Democratic politicians and courts happily agreed. States mailed out ballots to everyone. Judges disregarded statutory deadlines for receipt of votes. They scrapped absentee-ballot witness requirements. States set up curbside voting and drop-off boxes. They signed off on ballot harvesting.

Meaning, "the fix" (as it were) was in well before anyone started counting votes. Pollsters aside, political operatives understood this election would be close—potentially closer in key states than it was in 2016. The Democratic strategy from the start, as evidenced by that legal onslaught, was to get rules in place that would allow them to flood the zone with additional mail-in ballots.

And of course there was harvesting—as these pages warned. This isn't a new practice; candidates and campaigns have been honing it for years. Three years ago, the Palm Beach Post ran an expose on the practice in Florida. A North Carolina congressional race in 2018 was roiled by a ballot-harvesting operation, and a new election was ordered. This year simply offered the perfect environment to roll it out at new levels, and throughout the fall conservative groups were documenting examples.

Yet the beauty of ballot harvesting is that it is nearly impossible to prove fraud. How many harvesters offered to deliver votes, only to throw away inconvenient ones? How many voters were pushed or cajoled, or even paid—or had a ballot filled and returned for them without their knowledge? And this is before questions of what other mischief went on amid millions of mailed ballots (which went to wrong addresses or deceased people) and reduced voter verification rules. As the Heritage Foundation's election expert Hans von Spakovsky has explained, mail-in voting is the "single worst form of election possible" because "it moves the entire election beyond the oversight of election officials."

Republicans fought the worst changes but were up against the virus excuse. The question is whether they now understand the stakes. This election was a mere glimpse of the system Mrs. Pelosi wants nationwide, and she has already suggested "election reform" might again be her first priority in 2021. The GOP's job is to harness voters' frustration about the murky mess that was this year's vote into a movement that demands transparency and renewed integrity of the ballot. Or risk a lot of 2020 repeats.

THEY KNOW JESUS FROM SATAN

More New Yorkers Voted for Donald Trump in 2020 Than in 2016

Biggest gains are notched in majority-Latino South Bronx

Oswald Denis, an Evangelical minister, said many in his congregation were attracted to President Trump because of his support for Israel and his opposition to abortion.

By Jimmy Vielkind & Emma Tucker

President Trump received tens of thousands more votes in New York City in the 2020 presidential election than in 2016, and some of his largest gains came from an unlikely area: the South Bronx.

Mr. Trump, a Republican, more than doubled his vote in each of three state Assembly districts bordering the Harlem River that are considered Democratic bastions, according to in-person voting data analyzed by the City University of New York's Center for Urban Research.

President-elect Joe Biden still won the areas by wide margins, and received more than 80% of votes in the Bronx, but the districts posted the largest percentage increases in Trump votes anywhere in the city.

CUNY compared in-person votes cast this year with the total number of votes cast in 2016, when Mr. Trump received 164,131 votes in his home city—about 1.1 million fewer than Democratic nominee Hillary Clinton. Even with incomplete figures, Mr. Trump has surpassed his 2016 total by 76,612 as a result of better showings in most of the Bronx and Brooklyn as well as all of Queens and Staten Island. The number of votes he received in most of Manhattan was less this year than in 2016.

Mr. Biden received just over 1 million in-person votes in the five boroughs.

Election officials are still opening more than 700,000 absentee ballots, so the final tallies will change in the coming days. Most of the mailed ballots were requested by Democrats, and political observers expect Mr. Biden's votes to increase.

President Trump improved his standing among many Latino voters, including in the South Bronx.

New York City as a whole generally backs Democratic candidates. But the results reflect Mr. Trump's gains in majority-Latino communities**, which Republicans said they hoped to build on in coming elections—including next year's mayoral contest. Democrats said they would re-examine the voter-outreach strategies and campaign messages they use to engage Latino voters. "I don't necessarily think it's a pro-Trump vote as much as it is a wake-up call to Democrats," said Bronx Borough President Ruben Diaz Jr., the top-ranking Latino Democrat in the Bronx.**

Across New York state, Mr. Trump won the support of 30% of self-identified Latino voters compared

with 66% for Mr. Biden, according to AP VoteCast, a large survey of voters conducted in the week before the election.

Bronx voters offered a variety of explanations for Mr. Trump's gains, including his support for religious communities and small-business owners. The Rev. Oswald Denis, a 48-year-old Evangelical minister in the South Bronx said he and other pastors attend weekly meetings to discuss politics and city affairs.

Many members of his congregation—and other pastors—were attracted to the president because of his support for Israel and his antiabortion stance.

"That was very emotional for us," said Mr. Denis, who referred to the relocation of the U.S. Embassy to Israel from Tel Aviv to Jerusalem in 2018. "In the end, we believe that Jerusalem is the city of peace where God is going to reign."

Francisco Marte Sr., who immigrated to the South Bronx from the Dominican Republic and now runs the Bodega and Small Business Association of New York, said he knew many entrepreneurs supported Mr. Trump.

"Most of them were against the leftist policies," he said. Mr. Trump's support for law-and-order also resonated, he said.

Democrat Amanda Septimo was just elected to the state Assembly representing the 84th District, which includes the Bronx neighborhoods of Melrose, Mott Haven and Hunts Point. She won in a district where Mr. Trump received at least 2,500 more votes in this year's election than in 2016. The president's tally so far this year—4,166—is more than the 3,157 enrolled Republicans in the district. Overall turnout in the district this year was up by roughly 650 voters.

Ms. Septimo said she could feel support for Mr. Trump on the ground in the district. She said Democrats needed to do a better job connecting with working-class communities but that she thought the biggest factor boosting Mr. Trump was disinformation about Mr. Biden's stances. "When you look at some of the Spanish-focused media, it's really alarming," she said.

Republicans were more likely than Democrats to vote on Election Day, observers said, and they finished ahead of several Democratic incumbent state legislators in Brooklyn and Staten Island—excluding the mail-in ballots still being counted.

GOP pollster John McLaughlin said Mr. Trump's message in support of law and order was particularly effective in the communities, where it was reinforced by advertisements in the competitive race for Congress between Democratic Rep. Max Rose and Assemblywoman Nicole Malliotakis. Ms. Malliotakis finished ahead of Mr. Rose **on Election Day and** declared victory**, but the Associated Press hasn't called the election.**

"We saw that the president was running even or ahead in a lot of these areas, and he created a foundation that was solid for these candidates," Mr. McLaughlin said. Mr. Diaz Jr. said the Bronx Democratic Party didn't mount its normal voter-turnout drives, in part because of the coronavirus pandemic and a transition in party leadership. Democrats in New York focused on helping Mr. Biden in the nearby battleground of Pennsylvania rather than back home.

State Sen. Jamaal Bailey, the new Bronx party chairman, said the party would need to adjust to new forms of campaigning. He said he was still waiting for all of the votes to be counted in the election, but said Democrats should hone their message.

Some Republicans said President Trump's economic policies had strong appeal among many working-class voters.

Bronx Republican Chairman Mike Rendino said the results showed Mr. Trump's economic populism played well in working-class neighborhoods, and he said it would be difficult for Republicans to retain that support if they returned to pre-Trump policies. Curtis Sliwa, a Republican candidate for mayor, said GOP votes mostly came from Albanian and Italian neighborhoods in the northern part of the borough. Mr. Sliwa founded the Guardian Angels, a nonprofit crime-prevention organization, in the Fordham neighborhood in 1979. He said he would expand his outreach to include Dominican-Americans in the South Bronx.

"The Democrats just assume, 'Oh, you don't have to worry about the Bronx. It's just a lock,' " he said. "It's still Democratic, but it's starting to change."

Hispanic Democrat says far-left socialist message is 'killing us': report

Some Democrats believe that focusing on socialism and 'defund the police' weakened their support

By Peter Aitken

How did President Trump perform among Latino voters?

Hispanic Democrats are grappling with a surprising shift in their base support, blaming the focus on far-left mes-.saging during the U.S. presidential election, according to reports

Current vote totals put President-elect Joe Biden around 5.5 million votes ahead of President Donald Trump, but certain local battles ended far closer, indicating a noticeable shift in numbers for Trump among Hispanic and .Asian voters

Trump won big in Florida, and Hispanic-heavy Miami-Dade County shows a strong example of why: while Biden won the county, Trump lost by less than 100,000 votes – a far smaller gap compared to the nearly 300,000 votes by which he fell behind Hillary Clinton in 2016.

October 10, 2020 - Orlando, Florida, United States - People hold placards after U.S. Vice President

Mike Pence addressed supporters at a Latinos for Trump campaign rally at Central Christian University on October 10, 2020 in Orlando, Florida. With 24 days until the 2020 presidential election, both Donald Trump and Democrat Joe Biden are courting the Latino vote as Latinos are the largest racial or ethnic minority in the electorate, with 32 million eligible voters. (Photo by Paul Hennessy/NurPhoto via Getty Images)

Analysts have largely attributed this shrinking gap to a change in Hispanic voter attitudes in the county, but Florida is not the only place that such a shift occurred.

Texas and California also saw similar shifts, though perhaps not to the same degree as in Florida. Overall, the Republicans only picked up House seats in districts that were not heavily carried by Trump if there was a heavy Hispanic or Asian population, according to the New York Times**.**

A now-famous Democrat conference call shortly after the election revealed frustrations in the party over the losses, with pre-election projections instead indicating a "blue wave" that would have seen the party pick up seats. Rep. Linda Sanchez, D-Calif., harshly criticized the party's Latino outreach program – a view shared by other Latino and Hispanic representatives.

"Defund police, open borders, socialism – it's killing us," Rep. Vincente Gonzalez, D-Texas, said on the call. "I had to fight to explain all that."

Gonzalez argued that the associations with socialism differ wildly for Hispanic and Asian migrant populations: while the "average white person" may think of the Nordic model, these migrant populations may instead recall despotic "left-wing regimes" in Cuba and South East Asia.

In a Washington Post op-ed**, data analyst David Byler pointed out that the 2016 Trump campaign was a low point in Republican efforts to appeal to Latino voters, which may have made the Democrats overconfident in their support going into the 2020 election.**

In fact, Byler argues that Latino outreach had declined over the previous few election cycles, most notably Mitt Romney's quote about wanting undocumented immigrants to "self-deport."

Some analysts argue that Trump carefully restructured his campaign approach in 2020, shifting his focus from building the border wall and onto "law and order," which was focused on left-wing

groups like ANTIFA & BLACK LIVES MATTER.

JOE BIDEN'S MILITARY GUYS TURNED DOLLS MAKE MARILYN MONROE LOOK FLAT CHESTED SHE'LL SUE 101ST AIRBORNE AFTER AL FRANKEN PINCHES IT'S TUSH. CATEGORY (5) SEXUAL HARASSMENT SETTLEMENT MORE THAN PRICE BEATING DEUTCHLAND UBER ALLES & GREATER EAST ASIA CO-PROSPERITY SPHERE; FROM

New York World-Telegram

LATEST WALL ST. PRICES
Real Estate, Page 31
PRICE THREE CENTS

Local Forecast: Light rains tonight, somewhat higher temperatures than last night; tomorrow cloudy followed by clearing, cooler than today.

VOL. 74.—NO. 135.—IN TWO SECTIONS—SECTION ONE — NEW YORK, MONDAY, DECEMBER 8, 1941.

1500 DEAD IN HAWAII

CONGRESS VOTES WAR

Tally in Senate Is 82 to 0, In House 388 to 1, with Miss Rankin Sole Objector

By LYLE C. WILSON.
United Press Staff Correspondent.

WASHINGTON, Dec. 8.—Congress today proclaimed existence of a state of war between the United States and the Japanese Empire 33 minutes after President Roosevelt stood before a joint session to ask such action and pledge that we will triumph—"so help us, God."

Democracy was proving its right to a place in the

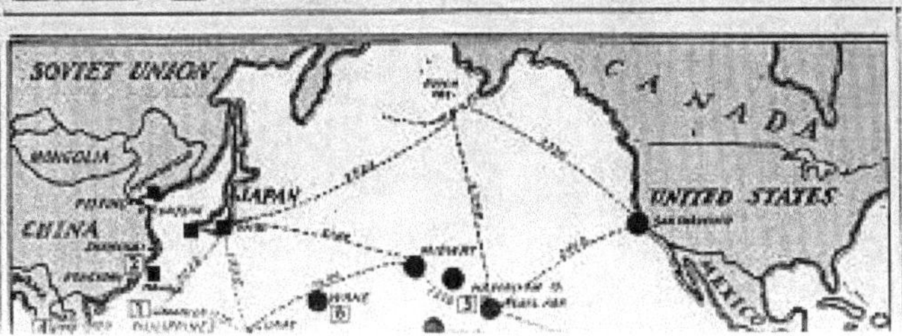

100 to 200 Soldiers Killed in Japanese Raid On Luzon in Philippines

BULLETIN.

By the United Press.

MANILA, Dec. 8.—Press dispatches reported that 100 to 200 troops, 60 of them Americans, were killed or injured today when Japanese warplanes raided Iba, on the west coast of the island of Luzon, north of the Olongapo naval base.

BULLETIN.

TO WIN; WHY NOT TEENY WEENY PECKIE POO ON CHEEK; TUSH FO' PAL JOEY; NO ONE BE IS LOOKIN' JILLIE WIFIE'S IN POWDER ROOM

Joe Biden CORONATES TRANSGENDER HARDENED ALAMO VETERAN to Review Department of Defense WHY NOT PIECE OF ASS FOR MYSELF

Penny Starr

GUY 'O THING; WHY NOT US TO BROWNIE'S ROSEDALE NORTH CONDUIT BLVD. HIDE-A-WAY DUTCH O' YOU PAY THAT SMILE; FACE; TUSH; BOOBS BLOWS AWAY JAYNE MANSFIELD

YER' IN THE ARMY NOW ...... DON'T FIRE TILL WHITES OF 'ER BRA & UNDIES

A former official from the Barack Obama administration, Shawn Skelly, has joined former Vice President Joe Biden's presidential transition team as an agency reviewer for the Department of Defense.

Skelly, who is a man living as a woman, was appointed to the Obama administration in 2013 as a special assistant to the UNDERWEAR VICTORIA'S SECRET **Undersecretary of defense for acquisition, technology, and logistics and coordinator of the Department of Defense Warfighter Senior Integration Group. Skelly also was director of the Office of the Executive Secretariat at the Department of Transportation during the Obama administration.**

The *Washington Blade* reported **on Skelly's appointment and Biden's agenda of including LGBT officials in his administration:**

Skelly, who co-founded **Out in National Security, an affinity group for LGBTQ national security professionals, and served on active duty in the U.S. Navy for 20 years as a naval flight officer, is named a member of the agency review team for the Defense Department in a news statement that went out Wednesday.**

Ted Kaufman, a former U.S. senator and co-chair of the Biden-Harris transition team, said in a statement members of the agency review team would rigorously evaluate operations of federal agencies as Joe Biden prepares to take office as president.

"Our nation is grappling with a pandemic, an economic crisis, urgent calls for racial justice, and the existential threat of climate change," Kaufman said. "We must be prepared for a seamless transfer of knowledge to the incoming administration to protect our interests at home and abroad. The agency review process will help lay the foundation for meeting these challenges on Day 1. The work of the agency review teams is critical for protecting national security, addressing the ongoing public health crisis, and demonstrating that America remains the beacon of democracy for the world."

"LGBTQ **advocates are pressing Biden to reverse Trump's ban on transgender military service in short order upon taking office as litigation against the policy continues in federal courts," the *Blade* reported. "According to a memo from the San Francisco-based Palm Center, Biden could lift the ban against transgender service members in as little as 30 days."**

NBC reported on Skelly but also outlined the more expansive policies that LGBT advocates are pressing Biden to put in place if he becomes the president, including putting an end **to HIV/AIDS:**

That ambitious platform includes pledges to enact the Equality Act, reinstate Obama-era guidelines preventing anti-LGBTQ discrimination in areas like federal contracts, fight against broad carve-outs in antidiscrimination law on the basis of religious beliefs, end the transgender military ban, and eliminate LGBTQ youth homelessness.

Biden has also set a goal of ending the HIV epidemic — which disproportionately affects gay and

bisexual men as well as transgender women — by 2025, five years ahead of the goal set by President Donald Trump during his State of the Union address this year.

Top scientists around the world and at the highest levels of the U.S. federal government for decades have been working to find a vaccine for the virus since it reached pandemic status as it spread among and killed homosexual men back in the 1980s. Although therapeutic treatments have been successful in saving lives, no cure has been found. Biden's team put out a press release on Tuesday that said 40 percent of his transition team would "represent communities historically underrepresented in the federal government, including people of color, people who identify as LGBTQ+, and people with disabilities." The Victory VICTORIA'S SECRET Institute, an organization that advances LGBT elected officials, is pressuring Biden to appoint individuals based on their sexual orientation as one qualification to his cabinet.

While an official list of cabinet positions has not been released, Elliot Imse, the institute's senior director of communications, named some of the LGBT people who could be on it, including former South Bend, Indiana, Mayor Pete Buttigieg for ambassador to the United Nations; Sen. Tammy Baldwin (D-WI) to head up Health and Human Services; Dr. Rachel Levine, Pennsylvania's secretary of Health, for either the Health and Human Services secretary or surgeon general; and Rep. Mark Takano (D-CA) for secretary of Veterans Affairs.

The Victory Institute would also like to see sexual orientation as one of the qualifications for being nominated for an open seat on the U.S. Supreme Court. And while Biden is not officially president-elect, NBC noted that in his "acceptance" speech on Saturday he thanked transgender people for their support. According to Gallup, 4.5 percent of the U.S. population identify as LGBT, and 0.3 percent of people in the U.S. identify as transgender, or a man or women living a lifestyle opposite of their biological sex.

Democratic Presidential Nominee Joe Biden Speaks On Death Of...
People: Joe Biden

Democratic Presidential Nominee Joe Biden Speaks On Death Of...
People: Joe Biden
Save

Joe Biden Campaigns

SUPREME COURT JUSTICE SAMUEL ALITO'S remarks came Thursday during an address to a conference of the Federalist Society, according to The Washington Post.

"We have never before seen restrictions as severe, extensive, and prolonged as those experienced for most of 2020," he said in a speech webcast to the legal society's lawyers' convention. And Fox News **noted that Alito maintained that many recent law school graduates claim they face "harassment" and "retaliation" for any views that depart "from law school orthodoxy."**

"Tolerance for opposing views is now in short supply," he said. "In certain quarters religious liberty has fast become a disfavored right. For many today, religious liberty is not a cherished freedom. It's often just an excuse for bigotry and it can't be tolerated even when there's no evidence that anybody has been harmed."

He also said houses of worship have been treated unfairly compared to other businesses during the pandemic. He pointed out the case in Nevada, according to the news network. "Nevada was unable to provide any justification for treating casinos more favorably than other houses of worship," he said, referring to a recent Supreme Court case. The court deferred to the governor who sided with the state's biggest industry, he said

Alito noted it would have been difficult to imagine before the pandemic that speeches and concerts

would be off-limits and that churches would be empty on Easter. Supreme Court Justice Samuel Alito warned that the pandemic has sparked "unimaginable" restrictions on civil liberties.

His remarks came Thursday during an address to a conference of the Federalist Society, according to The Washington Post**. "We have never before seen restrictions as severe, extensive, and prolonged as those experienced for most of 2020," he said in a speech webcast to the legal society's lawyers' convention. And** Fox News **noted that Alito maintained that many recent law school graduates claim they face "harassment" and "retaliation" for any views that depart "from law school orthodoxy."**

"Tolerance for opposing views is now in short supply," he said. "In certain quarters religious liberty has fast become a disfavored right. For many today, religious liberty is not a cherished freedom. It's often just an excuse for bigotry and it can't be tolerated even when there's no evidence that anybody has been harmed." He also said houses of worship have been treated unfairly compared to other businesses during the pandemic. He pointed out the case in Nevada, according to the news network.

"Nevada was unable to provide any justification for treating casinos more favorably than other houses of worship," he said, referring to a recent Supreme Court case. The court deferred to the governor who sided with the state's biggest industry, he said

Mich. Court Rejects Request to Block Detroit Election Certification Results

Detroit election workers work on counting absentee ballots for the 2020 general election at TCF Center in Detroit last week. A Michigan state court rejected on Friday a request by supporters of President Donald Trump to block the certification of votes and appoint an independent auditor in Detroit, which voted heavily in favor of Democrat Joe Biden.

The ruling is a setback for Trump and Republicans who have been trying to overturn Biden's apparent victory in the Nov. 3 election by preventing officials from certifying election results.

"It would be an unprecedented exercise of judicial activism for this Court to stop the certification process of the Wayne County Board of Canvassers," wrote Timothy Kenny, chief judge of the Third Judicial Circuit Court of Michigan, referring to the county that includes Detroit.

The lawsuit alleged fraud and voting irregularities, which Wayne County has denied.

The judge rejected those allegations, writing: "Plaintiffs' interpretation of events is incorrect and not credible."

He noted that allegations, such as city workers encouraging voters to cast their ballot for Democrats, were not backed up by details, such as locations or times when such events allegedly took place.

The judge also said that one witness who had filed an affidavit had posted on Facebook before the election that he speculated that Democrats were using the pandemic as cover for election fraud, undermining his testimony and credibility.

On Wednesday, the Trump campaign filed a similar lawsuit in U.S. District Court in the Western District of Michigan, alleging harassment of Republican poll challengers and a requirement they adhere to six-foot distancing rules that was not equally enforced against Democratic poll challengers.

Michigan is due to certify its election results on Nov. 23.

The campaign and Republicans have also sued in Georgia, Pennsylvania and Wisconsin seeking to block the certification of election results.

Also on Friday, the U.S. Court of Appeals upheld a lower court's decision before the election that a former Pennsylvania congressional candidate and four individual voters lacked standing to sue over the state's decision to allow "no excuses" absentee ballots and to extend mail-ballot deadlines due to the coronavirus pandemic.

Alito noted it would have been difficult to imagine before the pandemic that speeches and concerts would be off-limits and that churches would be empty on Easter.

Richard,

What we're about to tell you is important, so we'll get right to the point.

So far, we have 234 pages of sworn affidavits alleging Election irregularities from just ONE county in Michigan. Here are the allegations:

- **EYEWITNESS saw a batch of ballots where 60% of them had the SAME signature**
- **EYEWITNESS saw a batch of ballots scanned 5 times**
- **EYEWITNESS saw 35 ballots counted that were NOT connected to a voter record**
- **EYEWITNESS saw poll workers marking ballots with NO mark for candidates**
- **VOTER said deceased son was recorded as voting TWICE**
- **EYEWITNESS said provisional ballots were placed in the tabulation box**
- **FAILED software that caused an error in Antrim County used in Wayne County**
- **Republican challengers not readmitted but Democrats admitted**
- **Republican challengers physically pushed from counting tables by officials**
- **Democrats gave out packet: "Tactics to Distract Republican Challengers"**
- **Republican challenges to suspect ballots ignored**

And that's only a few of them, Richard. The potential voter fraud we're uncovering in Michigan is UNPRECEDENTED. We're doing everything we can to FIGHT BACK, but we can't do it without you.

President Trump is calling on his most LOYAL defenders to step up to the front lines of this nasty battle and DEFEND THE ELECTION. For a short time, you can even INCREASE your impact by 1000%.

Target Stops Sale of Transgender-Skeptical Book

Neil Munro

The Twitter account for Target stores says the $80 billion corporation will stop selling a book about trangenderism's harmful impact on young girls, following a complaint from a single Twitter account.

"Thank you so much for bringing this to our attention. We have removed this book from our assortment," the Target tweet said after a

Target Stops Sale of Transgender-Skeptical Book

The Twitter account for Target stores says the $80 billion corporation will stop selling a book about trangenderism's harmful impact on young girls, following a complaint from a single Twitter account.

"Thank you so much for bringing this to our attention. We have removed this book from our assortment," the Target tweet said after an activist complained that Target is selling the book, authored by Abigail Shrier.

"Target.com just made my book disappear," Shrier responded. "Does it bother anyone that Woke activists and spineless corporations now determine what Americans are allowed to read?"

The book, titled Irreversible Damage: The Transgender Craze Seducing Our Daughters, helps to explain how a wave of young girls are nudged and pushed into declaring they want to take life-altering drugs, adopt an opposite-sex identity, and undergo irreversible surgery.

Some corporations and many pro-transgender groups have tried to block and hide the book from American readers. In July, for example, Shrier tweeted:

Amazon explicitly bars ads for the book, while granting ads to books that celebrate the medical transition of teen girls who suddenly decide they're trans. If you don't think that indicates that Amazon is a retailer with a strong opinion, I'm not sure what to say. :)

The person who asked Target to remove the book hides the content of his account.

In August 2015, Target stores began pushing "gender neutral" product lines in the kids' sections. In April 2016, the company insisted that women share bathrooms with men who say they are women — prompting a huge consumer correction that temporarily chopped up to one-third of the company's stock value.

In May 2016, Breitbart reported the company's costly policy:

Target's design professionals likely embraced the "gender neutral" pitch because they want to be "hipper-than-thou," said Glenn Stanton, the director of Global Family Formation Studies at Focus on the Family and a research fellow at the Institute of Marriage and Family in Ottawa, Ontario. By using their employer to help the status of transgenders, they please their peers but at the cost of "seeking to solve a problem that doesn't exit and ironically creating for themselves an infinitely larger problem with the client base — moms with young children," he said.

THE WOKE MOB ASKS NOT FOR US TO ACCEPT PAN SEXUALITY; THE WOKE MOB WANTS TO PROMOTE & URGE PAN SEXUALIY ON THREE YEAR OLDS

True the Vote Lawsuit: Dead People, Felons Voted Illegally in Michigan

The election integrity group True the Vote is suing Gov. Gretchen Whitmer (D-MI) and county officials in Wayne County, Washtenaw County, and Ingham County, Michigan, alleging that dead people and felons voted illegally in the presidential election.

The lawsuit, filed on Thursday, is seeking to invalidate ballots in counties where they allege widespread illegal ballots and fraudulent ballot-counting took place. The lawsuit cites reports claiming that about 10,000 dead people returned mail-in ballots to vote in Michigan.

True the Vote's Catherine Engelbrecht said:

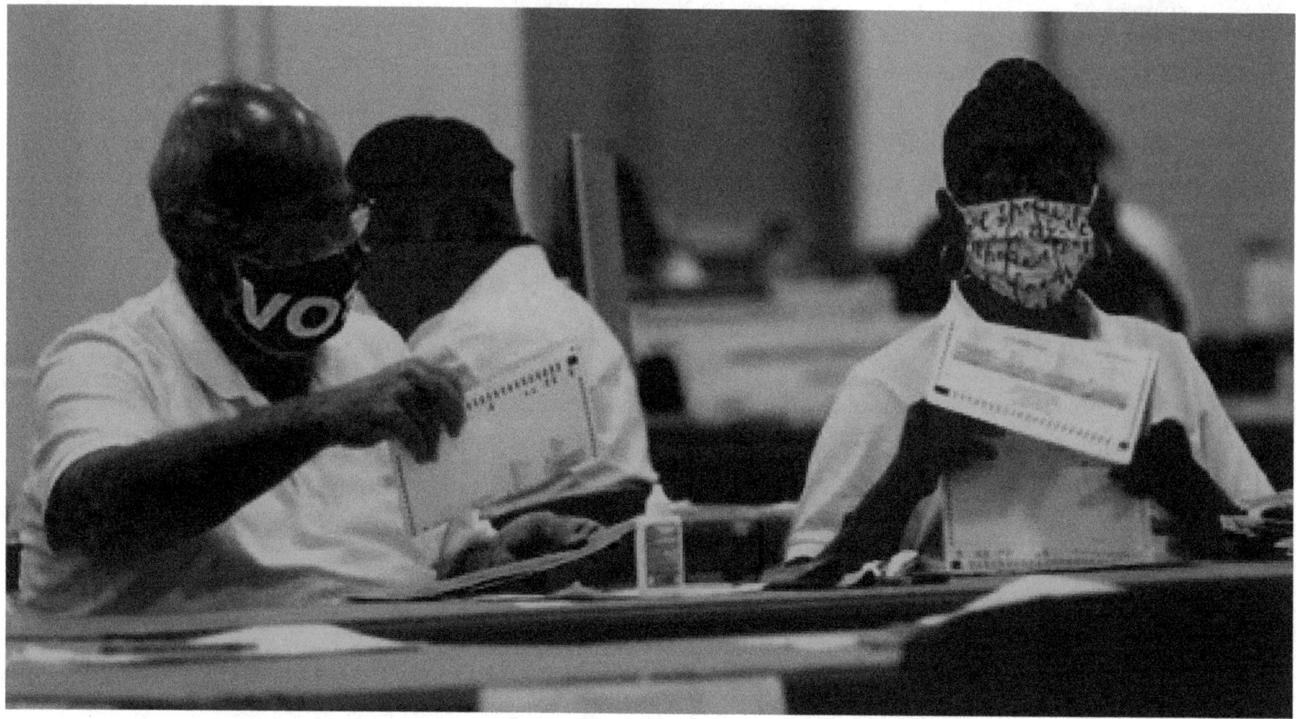

Every illegal vote that is counted dilutes the voting rights of law-abiding American citizens, and jeopardizes Americans' trust in their electoral process. Enough is enough. True the Vote is taking a stand on behalf of Michiganders — and all Americans — to stop bad actors who are stripping away citizens' most basic rights by refusing to secure our election process. We will take proper action to put an end to it.

Among the evidence presented, the lawsuit claims that ballot counting was not transparent, dates on ballots were fraudulently changed, software glitches occurred, clerical errors occurred, illegal votes were cast, poll watchers were excluded from voting sites, ballots were wrongly backdated, and votes were dumped at counting sites.

In one instance alleged in the lawsuit, a software glitch in Antrim County allegedly caused at least 6,000 ballots to be counted for Democrats that were actually supposed to go to Republicans. The lawsuit claims 69 of Michigan's 83 counties use the same software.

Likewise, the lawsuit alleges that more than 50 Michigan counties, including Wayne County and Washtenaw County, had more registered voters than eligible voting-age citizens. Wayne County's voter registration rate was 107 percent, while Washtenaw County's was 113 percent, the lawsuit claims.

Earlier this year, Detroit, Michigan, agreed to clean up its voter rolls after a lawsuit by the Public Interest Legal Foundation (PILF) claimed that more than 2,500 dead people were on the region's voter rolls.

Experts: Polls Tried to Suppress Republican Turnout

By Marisa Herman

Final 2020 election predictions of a Democrat sweep didn't pan out, leaving pollsters in the hot seat once again, with Republicans gaining seats in the House despite poll data showing a blue wave.

The presidential race also exposed many polls as ridiculously wrong, giving Joe Biden huge margins of victory where he eventually barely won and underestimating President Donald Trump's support over and over.

Democrats History of Voter Fraud

Protesters, police, members of the media and others converge outside of the Philadelphia Convention Center as the counting of ballots continues in the state on November 6, 2020.(Spencer Platt/Getty Images)

By Michael Dorstewitz

Democrat-run cities have a history of voter fraud and irregularities, giving more weight to President Donald Trump's charges of a stolen election while his lawyers battle in court. The voter fraud previously present in Democrat-run governments changes state vote counts and can even change the course of elections.

- **With Pennsylvania possibly the key to the election, Philadelphia's history of election fraud could be a game changer. This year, a former Philadelphia elections judge was convicted of casting fraudulent ballots and certifying false voting results in exchange for cash. And despite Democrats' insistence that voter fraud is rare or nonexistent, The Heritage Foundation found nearly 1,300 cases of it, which resulted in more than 1,100 convictions.**

Alan Dershowitz: 'I Do Think that Trump Will Win the Pennsylvania Lawsuit' if Enough Votes at Stake

Robert Kraychik

Harvard Law School Professor Emeritus Alan Dershowitz, host of *The Dershow,* told Breitbart News on Thursday that President Donald Trump is likely to win a lawsuit his campaign filed in Pennsylvania challenging the legiti-.macy of mail-in ballots received after Election Day

Dershowitz predicted that the U.S. Supreme Court would take up the Trump campaign's lawsuit if the number of votes being challenged are enough to change the outcome of the presidential election in Pennsylvania.

"I do think that Trump will win the Pennsylvania lawsuit," said Dershowitz on SiriusXM's *Breitbart News Tonight* with host Joel Pollak, "namely, the lawsuit that challenges ballots that were filed before the end of Election Day but not received until after Election Day."

Dershowitz continued, "The [Pennsylvania] legislature had basically said no to that and the [Pennsylvania] Supreme Court said yes because of the pandemic. That may have been the right

decision in some theoretical sense, but the Constitution doesn't permit anybody in the state but the legislature to make decisions about elections." "That was decided correctly in Bush versus Gore, and I think that four-to-four vote would become a five-to-four vote if the issue came before the Supreme Court and there were not disputed ballots to make a difference in the outcome of the election. That remains to be seen."

Dershowitz remarked, "As I understand the facts of the case — although I think what the judiciary did may have been the right thing morally: if you get your ballot in on time, you shouldn't be denied the vote just because the post office screwed up — I don't think you can really make that argument under Article Two. I do think that the Republican argument is the stronger one.

"The Supreme Court will take the case only if it would make a difference, only if the plaintiffs — the Republicans — can show that the number of disputed ballots that were subject to sequestration by Justice Alito's decision exceeds the difference between the winning margin and the losing margin."

Dershowitz concluded, "The Pennsylvania constitutional argument is a wholesale argument that clearly belongs in federal courts.." The Supreme Court ordered Pennsylvania election boards on November 6 to separate the count of mail-in ballots that arrived after Election Day in the event that the Supreme Court revisits election lawsuits related to such votes.

Twitter Labels 300K Election-Related Posts as Disputed, Misleading

By Solange Reyner

WHO ELECTED TWITTER TO BE JUDGE OF WHAT'S TRUE?

Twitter labeled approximately 300,000 posts containing election-related content as disputed and potentially misleading, part of its widespread efforts to clamp down on misinformation.

The tech giant has also continued to label President Donald Trump's claims on Twitter as disputed and, in some tweets, includes links to "learn how voting by mail is safe and secure."

"These enforcement actions remain part of our continued strategy to add context and limit the spread of misleading information about election processes around the world on Twitter," Vijaya Gadde and Kayvon Beykpour, who lead Twitter's legal and product teams, respectively, wrote in a blog post Thursday.

Twitter said there was a 29% decrease in quote tweets of those labeled tweets due, in part, to a prompt that warned people prior to sharing.

"We also got ahead of potentially misleading information by showing everyone on Twitter in the U.S. a series of pre-bunk prompts," Gadde and Beykour wrote. "These prompts, which were seen 389 million times, appeared in people's home timelines and in Search, and reminded people that election results were likely to be delayed, and that voting by mail is safe and legitimate."

Millions of conservatives have migrated to alternative social media and media sites like Parler, Rumble, and Newsmax following the election due to censorship on Twitter and Facebook.

Ken Paxton to Newsmax TV: There's a Reason Texas Rejected Dominion

As Dominion Voting Systems software comes increasingly under scrutiny in contested presidential elections this cycle, Texas Attorney General Ken Paxton tells Newsmax TV his state tested the software and rejected it. "There is a reason that Texas rejected it," Paxton told "Stinchfield" host Grant Stinchfield. "We didn't do it arbitrarily. We knew that these were unreliable systems. We didn't want to trust them.

"We didn't want to be in the same situation that some of these other states are in now where we're questioning the results, so we clearly believe that this was a problem."

Paxton said Texas tested Dominion software up to three different times, beginning in 2012, each time finding system failures in both hardware and software.

"We discovered that these systems are subject to different types of unauthorized manipulation and potential fraud," he said.

President Donald Trump on Thursday accused Dominion Voting Systems of having "DELETED 2.7 MILLION TRUMP VOTES NATIONWIDE."

Trump tweeted a quote he attributed to One America News Network and its chief White House correspondent Chanel Rion as saying: "REPORT: DOMINION DELETED 2.7 MILLION TRUMP VOTES NATIONWIDE. DATA ANALYSIS FINDS 221,000 PENNSYLVANIA VOTES SWITCHED FROM PRESIDENT TRUMP TO BIDEN. 941,000 TRUMP VOTES DELETED. STATES USING DOMINION VOTING SYSTEMS SWITCHED 435,000 VOTES FROM TRUMP TO BIDEN."

Twitter flagged this post with a note that says, "This claim about election fraud is disputed."

However, many, including some lawmakers, have criticized Dominion software for not preventing glitches and other irregularities from occurring in voting machines. **Dominion also bought Sequoia Voting Systems in 2010, which raised questions due to accusations that the latter was involved in rigging the 2004 Venezuelan elections.**

Sen. Ted Cruz to Newsmax TV: 'Media Don't Get to Decide Presidency'

Sen. Ted Cruz, R-Texas, blasted the media's premature jump behind Joe Biden as the nation's president elect ahead of his certification, saying "the media don't get to decide the presidency in the United States." In an interview on Newsmax TV**'s "**The Chris Salcedo Show**," Cruz, who has staunchly argued for a counting "every single legal" ballot, said it is the "voters who decide the match" — and that has not yet been settled.**

"The media don't get to decide the presidency in United States," he said, adding it is "the American people" who do. "But we now have a series of contested results, we have recounts that are proceeding, ligation that is challenging the results," he said. "An election isn't final until the results are final. So everyone should give this a little bit of time to let the process play out."

Cruz noted the Georgia runoff races Jan. 5 will ultimately have "massive consequences" on control of the Senate and the outcome of major policies. "If Democrats win both of those Senate seats we go from 50-48 to 50-50," he said. "And with 50-50, with Joe Biden as president, it means [Democratic New York Sen.] WOODCHUCK SCHMUCK SCHUMER **majority leader, and they have no check at all." With a split Senate vote, the vice president casts the deciding vote, potentially Biden's running mate Kamala Harris.**

"It means the most radical far left," Cruz concluded, "can ram through" policies.

2020 ELECTION ACT 1 SCENE 1 AUTOPSY JUSTICE FOR GOD

Tom Fitton

I take no comfort in saying that we saw this coming. Back in June, for example, I told Lou Dobbs, "It's been a state by state battle to protect the integrity of our elections. There will be a severe temptation to cheat, and now that's going to be a lot easier to do because our system is going to be overwhelmed with ballots and applications for ".ballots

"We've proven repeatedly – because we've been winning in court to clean up voter lists – that the lists across America are filthy in terms of having more people on the rolls than are eligible to vote. And those people, you can be sure, are going to be the groups getting some of these ballots," I said at the time.

Our most recent research in September revealed that 353 U.S. counties had 1.8 million more registered voters than eligible voting-age citizens. In other words, the registration rates of those counties exceeded 100% of eligible voters!

I have to wonder how much worse it might have been had we not been busy in court. As you

know,we are a national leader in seeking cleaner elections.

In 2018, the Supreme Court upheld a voter roll cleanup program that resulted from our settlement of a federal lawsuit with Ohio. California settled a lawsuit with us and last year began the process of removing up to 1.6 million inactive names from Los Angeles County's rolls. Kentucky also began a cleanup of hundreds of thousands of old registrations last year after it entered into a consent decree to end another Judicial Watch lawsuit. In September this year, we sued Illinois for refusing to disclose voter roll data in violation of federal law.

Dick Morris to Newsmax TV: Georgia Recount 'a Sham and a Hoax and a Fix'

By Cathy Burke

Political strategist and Newsmax analyst Dick Morris on Friday blasted the presidential ballot recount underway in Georgia, declaring that the process is a ''sham and a hoax and a fix."

In an interview on Newsmax TV's ''Spicer & Co.," Morris offered a video of Republican monitors at a hand-count of ballots in Georgia. "Inspectors are far away from the table ... [they] can't see the ballots," Morris said of the footage.

''This is the recount that is supposed to solve the problems," he added. ''It's absurd. "They did not permit the envelopes to be examined," Morris said. ''A lot of absentee ballots ought to be thrown out" and were not, he pointed out.

"This is a sham and a hoax and a fix," Morris declared.

Rep. Fred Keller to Newsmax: Pa. Court Ruling Could Help Trump

By Brian Trusdell

Rep. Fred Keller, R-Pa., told Newsmax TV on Friday he was optimistic that a Pennsylvania judge's ruling on Thursday would help President Donald Trump's efforts to challenge election results because it established that Gov. Tom Wolf and Secretary of the Commonwealth Kathy Boockvar assumed authority to change voting rules they didn't have. ‹›I did polling ... and I'm convinced that Trump won›› the election, Morris asserted. ‹›It's easier to steal paper ballots than machine ballots,›› he said. ‹›Now with the supposed recounting taking place, we see in that video how absurd the notion is."

Project Veritas: Pennsylvania Whistleblower Told to Dump All Non-Biden Mailers After Nov. 9

JOEL B. POLLAK

James O'Keefe's Project Veritas reported Thursday that a new U.S. Postal Service (USPS) employee had come forward, claiming mail carriers were told to deliver only mailings for Joe Biden after Nov. 9, and mark the rest as ".“undeliverable

Speaking to O'Keefe, the Elkins Park, Pennsylvania, whistleblower, said that meant other political mail was "garbage":James O'Keefe: "You're a letter carrier. OK. And tell me what your boss told you on Nov. 9."

Elkins Park USPS whistleblower: "You were told that the only political mail that will be delivered from now on will be that of the 'winner,' in this case, Joe Biden. And that other political mail from other sources and senders would be put into the undeliverable bulk business mail bin or UVM." Elkins Park USPS whistleblower: "All political mail for Biden was to be continued to be treated as

first-class and delivered the day it was received."

James O'Keefe: "What happens to the undeliverable bulk business mail?"

Elkins Park USPS whistleblower: "I believe it goes back to the plant, but undeliverable bulk business mail is essentially a step away from the garbage."

Project Veritas has been publishing allegations of inappropriate practices by USPS workers in Pennsylvania and Michigan. In one case, USPS employee Richard Hopkins reported that a supervisor had told him to backdate mail-in ballots so that they would appear to have been mailed by Election Day, and would hence be eligible to be counted.

Though the *Washington Post* reported that Hopkins recanted his story, Hopkins denied that he had, and O'Keefe published audio purporting to show an inspector pressuring Hopkins. Other allegations published by Project Veritas include the improper dumping of spoiled ballots.

Joel B. Pollak is Senior Editor-at-Large at Breitbart News and the host of Breitbart News Sunday *on Sirius XM Patriot on Sunday evenings from 7 p.m. to 10 p.m. ET (4 p.m. to 7 p.m. PT). His newest e-book is The Trumpian Virtues: The Lessons and Legacy of Donald Trump's Presidency. His recent book, RED NOVEMBER, tells the story of the 2020 Democratic presidential primary from a conservative perspective. He is a winner of the 2018 Robert Novak Journalism Alumni Fellowship.*

Giuliani to Newsmax TV: 623,000 Pa. Votes Shouldn't Count

Former New York mayor Rudy Giuliani, a lawyer for President Donald Trump, speaks during a news conference at Four Seasons Total Landscaping on legal challenges to vote counting in Pennsylvania, Saturday Nov. 7, 2020, in Philadelphia.

By Brian Trusdell

Trump attorney Rudy Giuliani told Newsmax TV on Friday that approximately 623,000 absentee ballots were counted without inspection by observers in Pennsylvania, requiring that they be thrown out.

The revelation comes amid several lawsuits pending before courts contesting the election results in several states, most notably Pennsylvania, where Democrat Joe Biden leads by about 60,000 votes in unofficial and incomplete results.

"You basically had the Republicans locked out of the mail ballot counting, which is of course terrible, because the mail ballot was new to this year," Giuliani said on "The Chris Salcedo Show."

"Everyone warned about how fraudulent it could be. And the law passed by the Pennsylvania legislature said you had to have observers from both sides there. "Well, the Republicans were locked out, completely. Then when they were let in, they were put in corrals, 20 feet away, where they could see nothing. Therefore, something like 300,000 ballots were counted without inspection of any kind. "They could be...they could be anything. They could be ballots from dead people. They could be ballots from the same person 14 times. A hundred times. So now we're up to 623,000 ballots that are unlawful ballots that can't be counted. And they all come out of Philadelphia and Pittsburgh."

Philadelphia and Pittsburgh are notoriously Democratic strongholds, where Giuliani said Biden received 80 percent and 70 percent of the vote. "That alone would switch the election to a 300,000 victory for Trump, which oddly, was what the victory probably was," Giuliani said. "(Trump) was ahead by about 800,000 votes on election night. There's no way you're making up 800,000 votes. Just doesn't happen. Any fool would know that."

US Appeals Court Rejects Effort to Block Late Ballots in Pa.

Workers prepare main-in ballots for counting, Wednesday, Nov. 4, 2020, at the convention center in Lancaster, Pa., following Tuesday's election.

A federal appeals court in Philadelphia on Friday rejected an effort led by a Republican congressional candidate to block about 9,300 ballots that arrived after Election Day.

The three-judge panel, led by Chief U.S. Circuit Judge Brooks Smith, noted the "unprecedented challenges" facing the nation this year, especially the "vast disruption" caused by the COVID-19 pandemic.

Smith said the panel sought to uphold "a proposition indisputable in our democratic process: that the lawfully cast vote of every citizen must count." The ruling involves the Pennsylvania Supreme Court's decision to accept mail-in ballots that arrived by Friday, Nov. 6, three days after the close of polling places. That court had agreed with Democrat state officials who wanted to extend the deadline amid concerns about Postal Service delays and the pandemic.

State Republicans have separately asked the U.S. Supreme Court to review the issue. However, there are not enough late-arriving ballots to change the results in Pennsylvania, given Joe Biden's lead. The Democrat former vice president won the state by about 60,000 votes out of about 6.8 million cast. Separately, a national law firm that came under criticism for its work for the Trump campaign has asked to withdraw from a lawsuit that seeks to stop Pennsylvania officials from certifying the election results.

Legal giant Porter Wright Morris & Arthur filed the motion to withdraw Thursday, leaving local election lawyer Linda A. Kerns of Philadelphia as the campaign's only remaining attorney on the federal court case in Williamsport. Kerns was meanwhile in court for the Trump campaign Friday in a state case in Philadelphia that involves a challenge to about 8,300 mail-in ballots in which voters made alleged technical mistakes. The judge in that case did not immediately rule.

The Trump campaign or Republican surrogates have filed more than 15 legal challenges in Pennsylvania as it seeks to reclaim the state's 20 electoral votes, but have so far offered no evidence of any widespread voter fraud. They've pursued similar litigation in other battleground states, including Georgia, Arizona, Nevada, and Michigan. Porter Wright, amid criticism that law firms were helping Trump defy the will of the American people, appeared to take down its Twitter feed Tuesday after it was inundated with attacks. Federal Election Commission records show Trump and the Republican National Committee have paid the firm $732,824.92 since February, including $143,312 from an RNC account dedicated to "recount" efforts.

The firm did not reply to specific questions about the Twitter feed or whether it would likewise step down from other election cases involving President Trump. In a statement earlier this week, the firm said it had a long history of handling election law cases for Democrat, Republican, and independent campaigns and issues. "At times, this calls for us to take on controversial cases. We expect criticism in such instances, and we affirm the right of all individuals to express concern and disagreement," the Ohio-based firm said. The appeals court, in denying a request for a temporary injunction Friday, said it was not ruling on the wisdom of the extension or the state court's power to grant it. Instead, the court said the private citizens who sued — the congressional candidate and

several voters — do not have the right to stop ballots from being counted that were filed by voters following the stated rules. The ruling upheld a decision issued by a federal judge in Pittsburgh.

Pollak: Key Question Is Why Vote-by-Mail Rejection Rate Dropped Dramatically

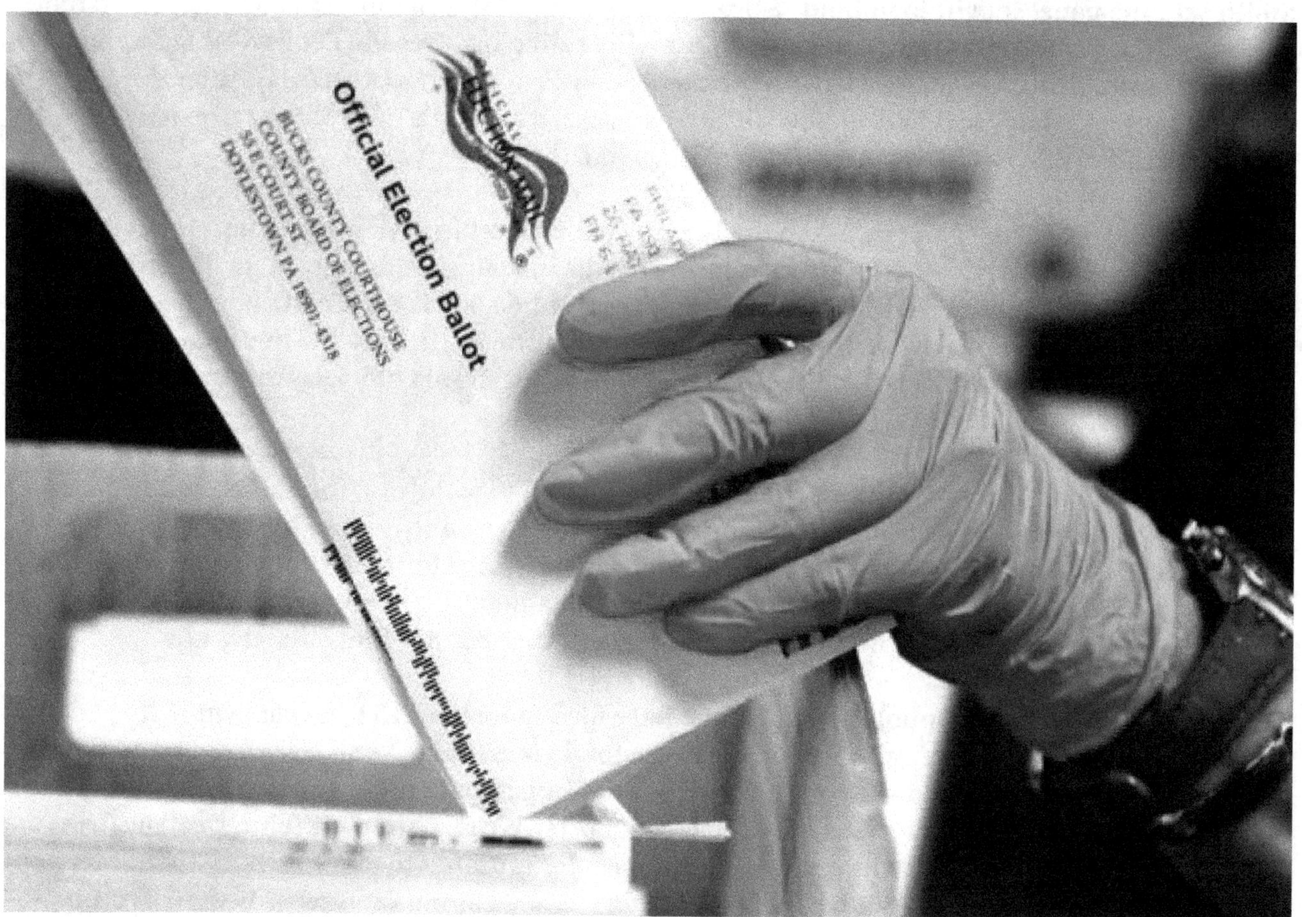

JOEL B. POLLAK

The key empirical question that must be asked about the 2020 election results is why the rejection rate for vote-by-mail ballots dropped dramatically from the primary season, when mass vote-by-mail began in some states, to the general election. Absentee ballots, which are traditionally a very small proportion of the vote in most states, are typically rejected at a rate of 1% to 2%. However, the rate of faulty absentee ballots rose to 25% after mass .vote-by-mail was adopted earlier this year

The *Washington Post* reported in August:

More than 534,000 mail ballots were rejected during primaries across 23 states this year — nearly a quarter in key battlegrounds for the fall — illustrating how missed delivery deadlines, inadvertent mistakes and uneven enforcement of the rules could disenfranchise voters and affect the outcome of the presidential election. Nevada's Clark County saw 17 percent of vote-by-mail ballots returned as undeliverable. Though New York is not a battleground state, one in four mailed-in primary ballots that were *returned* in New York City were also rejected for errors.

MOST MAIL VOTES FOR BIDEN; ALL MOVING PARTS GREASED DIGITALLY & BY MAIL TO REJECT ZERO BIDEN VOTES & COUNT MILLIONS OF FRAUDULENT BIDEN IN BAIT & SWITCH FOR NEVADA; ARIZONA; WISCONSIN; MICHIGAN PENNSYLVANIA & GEORGIA APPEARANCE OF WIN SEIZED BY CORRUPT DEEP STATE, MEDIA, JUDGES & LEGISLATORS

However, early reports about the rejection rate for mailed-in ballots in the general election suggest that it was lower than in 2016 — perhaps a fraction of a percent, up to 30 times lower than absentee ballots in an election *without* mass vote-by-mail.

Joe Biden's Transition Aide Steered $3M to Hunter Biden Linked Firm

HARIS ALIC

A top BIDEN aide; HEINRICH HIMMLER & MARTIN BORMANN; MATERNAL & PATERNAL LINEAGES; steered $3 million taxpayer dollars to Hunter Biden-linked venture capital firm.

READ NO EVIL; HEAR NO EVIL; SEE & IGNORE ELECTION THEFT

Last week, Bloomberg reported that Don Graves, a high-ranking executive at Key Bank, has been tasked to advise Biden on financial regulation issues during the transition process. Graves, who worked for the former vice president during the Obama administration, has been a long time fixture in the Biden family orbit

As Peter Schweizer, a senior contributor at Breitbart News and the president of the Government Accountability Institute, revealed in Profiles in Corruption, that relationship benefited Hunter Biden's business interests on at least one occasion. In December 2013, Hunter Biden, along with his long-time business associate Devon Archer, invested in a Hawaii-focused venture capital fund called mbloom. The investment, which was meant to provide seed capital for technology startups, was the result of a public-private partnership between Biden's firm, Rosemont Seneca Technology (RST) Partners, and the state of Hawaii.

As part of the agreement, RST would provide five million for the fund, with the Hawaii Strategic Development Corporation (HSDC) matching the same amount. Little-known at the time, however, was that more than half of HSDC's contribution, nearly $3 million, came from the Treasury Department's State Small Business Credit Initiative. The program, which expenses more than $1.5 billion to state economic development agencies, fell under the purview of then-Deputy Assistant Secretary of the Treasury Don Graves.

Complicating matters is that while Graves was overseeing the Small Business Credit Initiative, he was also informally advising Biden on economic and domestic policy as the executive director of the president's Council on Jobs and Competitiveness. That role took on a more official form shortly after mbloom received its contribution from HSDC, with Graves leaving the treasury department and joining the vice president's office. Since then, the two men's personal and professional lives have continued to intertwine. Graves, now the head of corporate responsibility and community relations at KeyBank, has not only donated to Biden's 2020 campaign, but has also taken an active role in the former vice president's philanthropic pursuits.

Graves' success in leveraging his relationship with the Biden family sharply contrasts with that of taxpayers in the state of Hawaii. Within months of HSDC inking the mbloom deal with Hunter Biden's firm, the fund was embroiled in scandal. Most notably, two of the companies that first received capital from mbloom were owned by individuals, Arben Kryeziu and Nick Bicanic, tasked with managing the fund. The scandal only grew when the company owned by Bicanic went under, without ever reporting a profit, and Kryeziu fell afoul of the Securities and Exchange Commission. HSDC, which initially saw mbloom as an opportunity to diversify Hawaii's service-centered economy, stepped in to stabilize the fund. Those efforts proved futile, especially when Archer was indicted for defrauding a Native American tribe in May 2016. The charges against Archer stemmed in part from allegations that he and a business associate conspired to use tribal bonds under their control to drive up the stock price of Code Rebel, a technology company also owned by Kryeziu.

ME; RICHARD E. GLICK; # 1 PAL JOEY ENEMY LIST

Leftists Back Down on Plans to Create List to Block Trump Backers from Jobs

CAN'T FIRE ME; SELF-EMPLOYED CANNER PICKING UP CANS AT B. HUSSEIN OBAMA HOUSING PROJECT AL SHARPTON BLVD.

KYLE MORRIS

The Trump Accountability Project, which targets supporters of President Donald Trump by adding them to ".a list and "holding them accountable" after the election, has announced that it is "no longer active

HOLD ME ACCOUNTABLE & SEE WHAT THE PRICE TO YOU IS

Nolte: CNN's Chris Cuomo Goes Full McCarthy Threatening GOP for Disputing Election

CUOMO BROTHERS; SCHUMER & GILLIBRAND; TOGETHER OR SEPARATELY; GET CLOSE TO ME; NEVER A THREAT, FOREVER A PROMISE

JOHN NOLTE

CNN's Chris "Fredo" Cuomo issued a series of threats on Wednesday to Republicans who are supporting the fight .for ballot integrity in the 2020 election

Behar: Trump 'Is So Evil' — Wants Coronavirus to Get Worse to Drop in 'Biden's Lap'

THE WORLD WILL BE BETTER OFF (& CLEANER) WHEN THIS REVOLTING UGLY DISHRAG SKANK PIG MEN ALWAYS RUN FROM; DROPS DEAD; SHE'S SO HATEFUL BECAUSE SHE'S ALWAYS REJECTED BY UGLIEST, MOST HARD UP (69) YEAR OLD VIRGINS FOR A 69'ER

RUN FROM THIS SKANK LEAVE HER VIRGINITY AT (73) FER SOMEONE ELSE

PAM KEY

Joy Behar said Thursday on ABC's "The View" that President Donald Trump was "so evil" that he wanted the COVID-19 pandemic to worsen in the United States, so potentially Joe Biden's administration would have to deal with a larger problem.

During a discussion of future shutdowns to quell the spread of coronavirus, co-host Sunny Hostin said, "The issue is Americans aren't going to wear their masks, most Americans, or many Americans. They're not going to socially distance. They're not going to follow the CDC guidelines in that way. They're not going to continuously wash their hands, and if everyone isn't doing the same thing and required to do the same thing, it just doesn't work. I actually am in favor of this short-term lockdown of — what is it?

Leaders: Won't Interfere in Electoral College

QUISLING REPUBLICANS WITH DEMOCRATS FIX ELECTION & COMMIT ELECTOR FRAUD

Pennsylvania Senate Majority Leader Jake Corman By Sandy Fitzgerald

The Pennsylvania General Assembly will not interfere in choosing the state's presidential electors or help to determine the outcome of the election, as the popular vote determines the electors under state law, the Republican leaders of the state's Senate and House say. "To insinuate otherwise is to inappropriately set fear into the Pennsylvania electorate with an imaginary scenario not provided for anywhere in law — or in fact," Senate Majority Leader Jake Corman, R-Benner Township, and House Majority Leader Kerry Beninghoff, R-Bellefonte, wrote for the Centre Daily Times in State College, PA.

"To set the record — once again — without question: The only and exclusive way that presidential electors can be chosen in Pennsylvania is by the popular vote," they wrote. "The legislature has no hand in this process whatsoever." Corman has doubled down on the statements in the piece, published before the election on Oct. 19, telling reporters that Republicans will continue to honor the wishes of the state's voters and will not bypass them to appoint electors who would back President Donald Trump, Pittsburgh CBS affiliate KDKA in Pittsburgh reported Monday.

"Our role is to monitor the process, our role is to provide oversight and call out questions where they might need asked, but certainly want to stay with the tradition of the popular vote winner getting the electors," Corman said, according to Monday's report. In their opinion piece, Corman and Beninghoff said the legislature will follow election code passed in 1937 concerning how the state's voters are to choose electors for the presidential race. "The General Assembly has a sworn duty to follow the Constitution and the Election Code, which does not involve the legislature in the process of choosing electors," they wrote. "There have been zero discussions occurring within the Pennsylvania House of Representatives and Senate about changing this provision." The lawmakers said they understand that "misrepresentations and attention-grabbing social media posts" are part of the rhetoric surrounding the presidential election, but the Assembly must "rise above that."

Paxton said Texas tested Dominion software up to three different times, beginning in 2012, each time finding system failures in both hardware and software.

"We discovered that these systems are subject to different types of unauthorized manipulation and potential fraud," he said.

President Donald Trump on Thursday accused Dominion Voting Systems of having "DELETED 2.7 MILLION TRUMP VOTES NATIONWIDE."

Trump tweeted a quote he attributed to One America News Network and its chief White House correspondent Chanel Rion as saying:

"REPORT: DOMINION DELETED 2.7 MILLION TRUMP VOTES NATION-WIDE. DATA ANALYSIS 221,000 PENNSYLVANIA VOTES STOLEN FROM PRESIDENT TRUMP GIVE TO BIDEN. 941,000 TRUMP VOTES DELETED BY STATES USING DOMINION VOTING SYSTEMS SWITCHED 435,000 VOTES FROM TRUMP TO BIDEN."

Twitter flagged this post with a note that says, "This claim about election fraud is disputed."

However, many, including some lawmakers, have criticized Dominion software for not preventing glitches and other irregularities from occurring in voting machines. Dominion also bought Sequoia Voting Systems in 2010, which raised questions due to accusations that the latter was involved in rigging the 2004 Venezuelan elections.

We just analyzed data in the key state of Nevada, where we found that in Clark County, there were about 154,000 "inactive" voters on the election rolls just before Election Day. Speaking of Election Day, federal law seems clear that the key results were supposed to be decided on … Election Day. Here is one of the relevant statues: The electors of President and Vice President shall be appointed, in each State, on the Tuesday next after the first Monday in November, in every fourth year succeeding every election of a President and Vice President. 3 U.S. Code § 1

Indeed, on Tuesday, the president could have had the votes to win the presidency. These vote totals are changing because of unprecedented, extraordinary, illicitly secretive, and inherently suspect counting AFTER Election Day that continue as I write. There will be court battles (which will almost certainly involve your Judicial Watch) but the presidency may ultimately come down to a fight in Congress over the counting of Electoral College electors from the states that are engaged in the slow-motion counting of votes. State legislatures in Pennsylvania, Michigan, Wisconsin, Georgia (and maybe Arizona) will have decisions to make – endorse and ratify what happened this week to President Trump's vote totals or appoint a slate of electors to reelect the president. So, in addition to supporting Judicial Watch's effort to secure the election, you may want to share your views on the election controversy with your elected representatives, both in your statehouse and in Congress.

Dick Morris to Newsmax TV: Georgia Recount 'a Fraud

Dump All Non-Biden Mailers After Nov. 9

Michigan Lawmakers Request Full Audit Of Election Citing Voting Irregularities

Brianna Lyman

Republican Michigan state Sens. Lana Theis and Tom Barrett called on Michigan Secretary of State Jocelyn Benson Thursday to do a complete audit before the election results are certified.

"Every citizen deserves to have faith in the integrity of the election process and its outcome," the letter reads**. "It is our responsibility, as elected public servants, to assure the people of Michigan of the process's integrity through complete transparency and the faithful investigation of any allegations of wrongdoing, fraud, or abuse."**

INBOX: Michigan GOP state senators are requesting a full audit of the 2020 General Election

"Unfortunately, a number of serious allegations have been made which cannot and should not be ignored," the letter continued, citing a "glitch" in Antrim county along with allegations of "mishandled" ballots. The letter also cites allegations that poll watchers were not allowed to observe the ballot process.

Antrim County**, a traditionally Republican county that initially flipped blue this election flipped**

back to red after a manual recount of votes found thousands of votes meant for President Donald Trump accidentally went for Joe Biden. The county uses "Dominion Voting System," which is also used in 64 counties across the state. Benson's office said the skewed results were due to "county user error" and not the software itself. (RELATED: Ric Grenell: Trump Campaign Is 'Not Being Allowed To Check' Ballots At Nevada Polling Stations)

RNC Chairwoman Ronna McDaniel said there were election irregularities in Detroit's ballot counting center, TCF Center. She said there were reports that poll watchers were challenged and intimidated and that ballot counters were backdating ballots, according to Fox 2.

However, those claims have been refuted by Benson, the ACLU and senior election advisor to Detroit Chris Thomas, per the same report.

Thomas said a clerical error occurred when the ballot envelopes were received in satellite offices. Employees stamped the envelopes with a date of receipt, which was entered into the system. Thomas said that is not backdating, per Fox 2.

The Trump campaign has filed multiple lawsuits **in the state, with the most recent suit also seeking to block Benson from certifying the results on the grounds that the state ran an unconstitutional election. The suit also seeks to give campaign officials the opportunity to review counted ballots in Wayne County.**

The campaign filed a suit **shortly after Election Day seeking to stop the counting of mail-in votes. However, Michigan Court of Appeals Judge Cynthia Stevens rejected the suit, ruling that the demands of the campaign can't be met by Benson since the process of counting ballots was nearly completed.**

The campaign presented an affidavit from a local election official who claimed she was instructed to backdate the ballot. Stevens rejected the claim as "hearsay."

However, early reports about the rejection rate for mailed-in ballots in the general election suggest that it was lower **than in 2016 — perhaps a fraction of a percent, up to** 30 times lower **than absentee ballots in an election *without* mass vote-by-mail.**

JOE BIDEN'S TRANSITION AIDE BLOODLINE HIMMLER BORMANN LINEAGE

Heinrich Himmler
1942

4th Reichsführer-SS

In office - 6 January 1929 – 29 April 1945

Deputy	Reinhard Heydrich
Preceded by	Erhard Heiden
Succeeded by	Karl Hanke

Chief of German Police

In office: 17 June 1936 – 29 April 1945

Preceded by	**Office established**
Succeeded by	Karl Hanke

Director of the Reich Main Security Office

Acting

In office 4 June 1942 – 30 January 1943

Minister	Wilhelm Frick
Preceded by	Reinhard Heydrich
Succeeded by	Ernst Kaltenbrunner

Reichsminister of the Interior

In office: 4 August 1943 – 29 April 1945

Chancellor	Adolf Hitler
Preceded by	**Wilhelm Frick**
Succeeded by	Paul G

Himmler was one of the most powerful GO-TO FIXERS in Nazi Germany; main architect of the Holocaust; & ASPIRATIONAL NAZI NEW DEAL HOW TO SUCCEED MODEL FOR 2021 USA DEMOCRATS WITHOUT REALLY TRYING; member of reserve battalion during World War I, Himmler did not see active service.

Reichsleiter **& Head of the Party Chancellery**

After the *Machtergreifung* **(Nazi Party seizure of power) in January 1933, the relief fund was repurposed to provide general accident and property insurance, so Bormann resigned from its administration. He applied for a transfer and was accepted as chief of staff in the office of** Rudolf Hess**, the** Deputy Führer**, on 1 July 1933. Bormann also served as personal secretary to Hess from July 1933 until 12 May 1941. Hess' department was responsible for settling disputes within the party and acted as an intermediary between the party and the state regarding policy decisions and legislation. Bormann used his position to create an extensive bureaucracy and involve himself in as much of the decision-making as possible. On 10 October 1933 Hitler named Bormann** *Reichsleiter* **(national leader – the second highest political rank) of the Nazi Party, and in November he was named** *Reichstag* **deputy.**[I] **By June 1934, Bormann was gaining acceptance into Hitler›s inner circle and accompanied him everywhere, providing briefings and summaries of events and requests.**

2021 HOW TO SUCCEED USA DEMOCRAT ROLE MODEL BORMANN IN 1939

In 1935, Bormann was appointed as overseer of renovations at the Berghof, Hitler's property at Obersalzberg. In the early 1930s, Hitler bought the property, which he had been renting since 1925 as a vacation retreat. After he became chancellor, Hitler drew up plans for expansion and remodelling of the main house and put Bormann in charge of construction. Bormann commissioned the construction of barracks for the SS guards, roads and footpaths, garages for motor vehicles, a guesthouse, accommodation for staff, and other amenities. Retaining title in his own name, Bormann bought up adjacent farms until the entire complex covered 10 square kilometres (3.9 sq mi). Members of the inner circle built houses within the perimeter, beginning with Hermann Göring, Albert Speer, and Bormann himself. Bormann commissioned the building of the Kehlsteinhaus (Eagle›s Nest), a tea house high above the Berghof, as a gift to Hitler on his fiftieth birthday (20 April 1939). Hitler seldom used the building, but Bormann liked to impress guests by taking them there.

While Hitler was in residence at the Berghof, Bormann was constantly in attendance and acted as Hitler's personal secretary. In this capacity, he began to control the flow of information and access to Hitler. During this period, Hitler gave Bormann control of his personal finances. In addition to salaries as chancellor and president, Hitler's income included money raised through royalties collected on his book *Mein Kampf* and the use of his image on postage stamps. Bormann set up the Adolf Hitler Fund of German Trade and Industry, which collected money from German industrialists on Hitler's behalf. Some of the funds received through this programme were disbursed to various party leaders, but Bormann retained most of it for Hitler's personal use. Bormann and others took notes of Hitler's thoughts expressed over dinner and in monologues late into the night and preserved them. The material was published after the war as *Hitler's Table Talk*.

The office of the Deputy Führer had final approval over civil service appointments, and Bormann reviewed the personnel files and made the decisions regarding appointments. This power impinged on the purview of Minister of the Interior Wilhelm Frick, and was an example of the overlapping responsibilities typical of the Nazi regime.[39] Bormann travelled everywhere with Hitler, including trips to Austria in 1938 after the *Anschluss* (the annexation of

As we all know, President Donald Trump believes, and not without cause, that there was a substantial amount of election fraud in a number of swing states on Election Night. I for one have never seen a state stop counting ballots, and yet a number of swing states run by far-left Democrats did just that when it looked as though the president was on the road to victory.

Wisconsin Republicans Claim Thousands Avoided Voter ID Laws

Election officials count absentee ballots at a polling place located in the Town of Beloit fire station on November 03, 2020 near Beloit, Wisconsin.

Republicans in Wisconsin say that thousands of voters avoided identification laws by claiming to be "indefinitely confined" and requesting an absentee ballot, the Washington Examiner reports.

Wisconsin law allows a voter to self-report that they are indefinitely confined in their home due to age, illness, or disability, allowing them to receive a mail-in ballot as long as a witness signs off. The number of indefinitely confined voters rose dramatically during the coronavirus pandemic, from around 72,000 in 2019 to about 243,000 in 2020.

Several counties in the state did issue guidance in March saying that the governor's lockdown order met the requirement for being indefinitely confined, but the state Supreme Court later ruled that that "advice was legally incorrect," though voters who had listed themselves as being confined during the primary season did end up receiving absentee ballots in the general election.

"At what point does it become fraud?" An unnamed GOP official asked in an interview with the Examiner. "I think it became fraud in April, when people were listing themselves as indefinitely

confined when they were not. And that was just allowed to continue and get worse and worse."

The official added that the state Supreme Court did not provide a definitive ruling regarding voters who had already listed themselves as being indefinitely confined.

Kenneth Dragotta, a member of the board of the Waukesha County Republican Party, told the Examiner: "So you can register as indefinitely confined, and a ballot is going to be sent to you every election. You don't even have to request it. But here's the problem. Indefinitely confined people are not required to provide proof of identification or an ID card. There's no requirement that that be in the hands of the election commission or the municipal clerk prior to issuing a ballot. You don't even have a voter ID requirement on those people that registered. All you have is proof of residency that is required. But does that sound like a really robust, safe election process? I think not."

Rep. Jody Hice to Newsmax TV: How Many Votes Were Altered by Glitches in Machines

By Tauren Dyson

There needs to be an investigation into the glitches and other irregularities in the voting machines used in multiple states to tabulate the election results for the presidential election last Tuesday, Georgia Rep. Jody Hice told Newsmax TV.

"Where there is smoke there is fire. The same type of problems that we saw in Michigan, we are having glitches here in Gwinnett County, here in particular, right here in Georgia. What do those glitches mean? How many votes have been altered by those glitches?" Hice told Monday's "Stinchfield."

"Isn't it interesting that we're using the same software, the same company here, Dominion Software, and their machines," Hice said. "Both sides of the aisle recognize that Dominion has a poor track record."

"I think it's interesting too that not only are Republicans calling on this. I remember Jamie Raskin ... in a hearing, he brought up the very alarming statistics and dangers of Dominion Software. And he's, of course, a high-ranking Democrat," Hice said.

Trump Campaign Is Filing Another Election Lawsuit In Michigan — Seeks To Delay Certification Over More Claims Of 'Unequal Treatment'

Christian Datoc Senior White House Correspondent

The Trump campaign will file yet another election lawsuit in Michigan, communications director Tim Murtaugh announced to reporters on a Tuesday evening phone call.

The suit — which similar to prior attempts in Pennsylvania, Georgia and Nevada — seeks to block the local secretary of state from certifying the results of the election on the grounds that Michigan ran an unconstitutional election. The suit will additionally look to grant campaign officials the opportunity to review counted ballots in Wayne County, Michigan.

Trump 2020 General Counsel Matt Morgan and Counsel to the Campaign Thor Hearne also took part in the call, and like the Pennsylvania suit filed Monday, **claim that poll watchers in Democrat-ran counties received "unequal treatment" compared to their counterparts in Republican-ran counties.** (RELATED: Trump Launches Last-Ditch Legal Effort In 4 States)

TOPSHOT - (COMBO) This combination of pictures created on September 29, 2020 shows US President Donald Trump (L) and Democratic Presidential candidate former Vice President Joe Biden squaring off during the first presidential debate at the Case Western Reserve University and Cleveland Clinic in Cleveland, Ohio on September 29, 2020. Parker asked during the Tuesday call if the suit in question has a serious chance of overturning that deficit, Murtaugh clarified that every suit filed by the campaign is done in "an effort to get us closer to the elec-".tion

"We do not think we're going to eat the apple in one bite, but a large part of these lawsuits is to gather further information," he added. "We do ultimately believe that President Trump will win this election."

Murtaugh confirmed to Daily Caller after the call's conclusion that the suit has not yet been filed.

New federal lawsuit seeks to throw out 1.2 million votes in Michigan, flipping the state for Trump

The lawsuit targets three Democratic strongholds

JEFF KOWALSKY & Chris Enloe

Another federal lawsuit was filed in Michigan this week that seeks to toss out up to 1.2 million votes, which would flip the Great Lakes State in President Donald Trump's favor.

Calling all Americans to take back our constitutional freedoms

Media-declared president-elect Joe Biden defeated Trump in Michigan by approximately 146,000 votes.

What are the details?

The lawsuit**, filed by four voters in the U.S. District Court for the Western District of Michigan, seeks to toss out ballots in three Democratic strongholds — Wayne, Ingham, and Washtenaw counties — over allegations of voter fraud,** according to Michigan Live.

Those three counties are responsible for about 1.2 million votes, favoring Biden by more than 2:1. Eliminating ballots from those counties would give Trump a victory in Michigan. Plaintiffs claim that "sufficient evidence" exists "to place in doubt the November 3 presidential-election results" in the three identified counties, citing "issues with transparency, fraudulent changing of dates, a software glitch, clerical errors, illegal votes, and many other issues and irregularities."

More from Michigan Live**:**

Plaintiffs also cite ongoing investigations launched by the Michigan Legislature and a variety of other claims that have been debunked. (THEY WERE NEVER DEBUNKED) **The allegations include charges of Republican ballot challengers being harassed and illegal tampering with ballots.**

Plaintiffs conclude that "this evidence suffices to place in doubt the November 3 presidential election results in identified counties and/or the state as a whole." However, the group of voters also claims to have additional evidence of illegal ballots being included in unofficial results, based on "expert reports" and data analysis.

The lawsuit further says that certifying the votes would violate voters' First Amendment and Fourteenth Amendment rights by "vote-dilution disenfranchisement."

Defendants include Democratic Gov. Gretchen Whitmer, members of the Michigan State Board of Canvassers, Wayne County Board of Canvassers, Washtenaw County Board of Canvassers, and Ingham County Board of Canvassers.

Are the lawsuits working?

Lawsuits alleging unproven claims of voter fraud are losing the legal battle in court.

The most recent loss came on Friday, when Wayne County Circuit Chief Judge Timothy Kenny denied a request for an independent audit of Wayne County votes, according to the Detroit Free Press. **The lawsuit** had claimed **local election officials managed a fraudulent election.**

Also on Friday, Trump's campaign dropped a legal challenge in Arizona **and shut down its voter fraud hotline. The campaign** also suffered a loss in federal court **when the U.S. Court of Appeals for the Third Circuit ruled against the campaign's efforts to block mail-in votes received after Election Day from being counted.**

Michigan Attorney General Plays Race Card over Trump Campaign Suit: Theme Is 'Black People Are Corrupt' UGLY TRICKSTER LOSER SKANK PLAYS RACE CARD?

BITCH, PEDDLE SKANK BODY AT MAIN STREET BUS STATION TO SOMEONE LIKE AL FRANKEN OR FOR A NICKEL TO WOODCHUCK SCHMUCK SCHUMER

KYLE OLSON

The Michigan attorney general invoked race as the Trump campaign is seeking legal relief to halt the election results from Wayne County from being certified. The Trump campaign has filed a federal lawsuit in the Western District claiming widespread fraud in last week's election. The campaign provided numerous affidavits from indi-.viduals who were witnessing the vote counting process in Detroit

They allege ballots were counted multiple times, election officials coached voters to cast ballots for Joe Biden and Democrats, and a pattern of assigning fraudulent ballots to non-voters.

Attorney General Dana Nessel assailed the Trump campaign's suit, claiming it lacked evidence, and went after the alleged motives of the effort itself.

"Really the themes that we see, that persist, are this: Black people are corrupt, Black people are incompetent and Black people can't be trusted. That's the narrative that is continually espoused by the Trump campaign and their allies in these lawsuits," WE NOT BE IS TALKIN' DA' TALK & WALKIN' DA' BE IS DA' WALK 'BOUT BLACK PEEPLES. WE BE IS TALKIN 'BOUT YO', UGLY SKANK ASSED BITCH

AUTHOR ADDENDUM

Nessel said on Wednesday, the *Detroit Free Press* reported.

Nessel claimed the Trump campaign has not filed similar suits in Oakland or Kent counties, where workers are primarily white. The attorney general also attacked the campaign over where the suit was filed. Detroit is in the Eastern District. "In my view, this is really a brazen case of forum shopping," Nessel said, according to the paper. "I will add that forum shopping and judge shopping are my least two favorite shopping seasons."

The *Free Press* reported all five judges in the Western District were nominated by Republican presidents, while 13 of the 20 in the Eastern District were nominated by Democrats. Nessel claimed "none" of the accusations in the dozens of affidavits are true. Meanwhile, in a Wednesday hearing in Wayne County over a separate lawsuit filed by the Great Lakes Justice Center (GLJC) making similar claims of widespread fraud, David Fink, an attorney for the city of Detroit, said, "They're looking wherever they can to get validation for the unsupported conspiracy theories they have," Bloomberg reported.

The report continued: The state court case filed Monday by Trump supporters Cheryl Costantino and Edward McCall Jr. is seeking to block certification of the vote in Detroit and surrounding Wayne County. The federal case filed by the campaign Wednesday seeks to block the statewide election certification also based on allegations of fraud in Wayne County.

Fink said any delay to certification could mean missing the "ultimate deadline" of Dec. 14, when the Electoral College meets to cast its votes. Stopping the count threatens to throw the outcome to the House of Representatives or open the door to state legislators seeking to appoint electors who don't represent the will of the people. "Either scenario is desperately dangerous," Fink said.

Circuit Judge Timothy Kenny said he will rule Friday on whether to grant the GLJC's request to block the certification of the Wayne County vote or order an audit.

Georgia's GOP Congressional Reps Demand Answers About Alleged Voter Irregularities

Joshua Caplan

Members of the U.S. House of Representatives Congressional Delegation for Georgia sent a letter Tuesday to Georgia Secretary of State Brad Raffensperger requesting information regarding allegations of voter irregulari-.ties in the Peach State's 2020 presidential election

Reps. Earl L. "Buddy" Carter, Drew Ferguson, Austin Scott, Jody Hice, Barry Loudermilk, Rick Allen, and Representatives-elect Andrew Clyde and Marjorie Taylor Greene wrote to Raffensperger:

As Members and Members-Elect of the Georgia Congressional Delegation, we are deeply concerned by continued, serious allegations of voting irregularities in our state. The Georgia Republican Party and the Donald J. Trump for President Campaign have received reports of deceased or ineligible voters casting ballots, eligible voters being denied the opportunity to vote, and Republican poll watchers and observers being denied access to activities and meetings critical to ensuring a fair, accurate, and transparent vote tabulation.

The letter continued: As such, we write to request your thorough review of the allegations brought forth by the Georgia Republican Party and the Donald J. Trump for President Campaign.

Specifically we ask you fully examine and grant the requests laid out in their letter addressed to you earlier today before certification of the November 3, 2020 General Election.

The letter concluded: "A fair election ensures all legal ballots are counted. We are united in asking you to ensure that such is the case and look forward to your prompt response."

The development comes one day after Sens. David Perdue and Kelly Loeffler (R-GA) called on Raffensperger to resign over his management of the state's election.

"The management of Georgia elections has become an embarrassment for our state. Georgians are outraged, and rightly so," the statement via Perdue and Loeffler reads. "We have been clear from the beginning: every legal vote cast should be counted. Any illegal vote must not. And there must be transparency and uniformity in the counting process. This isn't hard. This isn't partisan. This is American. We believe when there are failures, they need to be called out — even when it's in your own party."

"There have been too many failures in Georgia elections this year and the most recent election has shined a national light on the problems. While blame certainly lies elsewhere as well, the buck ultimately stops with the Secretary of State," the statement continues. "The mismanagement and lack of transparency from the Secretary of State is unacceptable. Honest elections are paramount to the foundation of our democracy."

The statement concludes, "The Secretary of State has failed to deliver honest and transparent elections. He has failed the people of Georgia, and he should step down immediately."

As of Tuesday, President Donald Trump trails **former Vice President Joe Biden by 12,567 votes in Georgia.**
On Sunday, the Trump campaign tapped Rep. Doug Collins (R-GA) to head up its recount efforts in the state.

"In order for Americans to have full faith and confidence in our elections, every legal vote must be counted and every illegal or fraudulent vote must be excluded," Collins said.

"We look forward to guaranteeing that our elections are safe and secure, just as we look forward to President Trump winning Georgia," the lawmaker added.

High Profile MI Attorney Turned Poll Watcher Challenged Election Workers on Ballot Count and Was Kicked Out

Beth Baumann

Former Michigan Assistant Attorney General Zach Larsen on Sunday signed an affidavit detailing his experience seeing "voting irregularities" in precincts throughout the state.

According to Larsen, he spent Election Day as a "roving attorney and credentialed poll challenger," along with another group of attorneys. Larsen stated the group visited 20 to 30 precincts throughout Lansing, East Lansing and Williamston that day. On Election Day he had the ability to visually inspect poll books and watch as poll workers counted ballots.

It was Wednesday, Nov. 4th when the issues began.

From the affidavit:

Larsen stated in his sworn testimony that at the TCF Center in Detroit, election workers weren't complying to ballot counting the way he was told it was supposed to take place.

When I arrived at a counting table and began to observe the process, I noticed immediately that part of the process that was being implemented did not conform to what I had been told in my training and the materials that I had received.

Specifically, the information I had received described the process that was supposed to be occurring at the tables as follows.

A first election official would scan a ballot. If the scan did not confirm a voter in the poll book, that official would then check the voter against a paper copy "supplemental poll book."

The official would then read the ballot number to a second election official and hand the ballot to that official, who would remove the ballot (while still in the secrecy sleeve) and confirm the ballot number. That second official would then hand the ballot (in the secrecy sleeve) to a third official who would tear the stub off of the ballot, and place the stub in a ballot stub envelope, then pass the remaining ballot to a fourth official.

The fourth official would then remove the ballot from the secrecy sleeve, flatten the ballot to ensure it was capable of processing, and visually inspect for rips, tears, or stains before placing the ballot in the "ballots to be tabulated box." However, if that fourth official identified a concern, she would place the ballot back in its envelope and into a "problem ballots" box that required additional attention to determine whether they would be processed and counted. A copy of a diagram that I had received on this process is attached as Exhibit A to this affidavit.

What I observed immediately was that the secrecy of the ballot was not being respected.

Instead, the second official at the table where I was observing was repeatedly placing her fingers into the secrecy sleeve to separate the envelope and visually peek into the envelopes in a way that would allow her to visually observe the ballot and identify some of the votes cast by the voter.

Sometimes, the third official whose job was merely to remove the stub from the ballot would likewise remove the ballot from the secrecy sleeve or otherwise peek to observe the ballot. Sometimes a ballot would be removed completely from the secrecy sleeve and then placed back inside and passed along this process.

I conferred regarding this issue with another challenger at a nearby table, and he indicated he had observed similar irregularities regarding the use of the secrecy sleeves.

When that challenger raised the issue with a supervisor, and he was immediately asked "why does it matter?" and "what difference does it make?"

Beyond the legal requirements for maintaining ballot secrecy, both of us were concerned that the violations of the secrecy of the ballot that we witnessed could be or were being used to manipulate which ballots were placed in the "problem ballots" box.

Larsen stated another challenger found another issue, where some ballots were being placed into "problem ballots" boxes because the voter allegedly didn't place the ballot in the secrecy sleeve. Other ballots that were at the same table but didn't have the secrecy sleeve were being moved to the "ballots to be tabulated" box.

From my experience at the first table I had visited (addressed in Paragraphs 15 through 17 above), I had also witnessed ballots that were placed into the "ballots to be tabulated" box that had arrived without a secrecy sleeve. So the differentiation among these ballots despite both ballots arriving in secrecy sleeves was perplexing and again raised concerns that some ballots were being marked as "problem ballots" based on who the person had voted for rather than on any legitimate concern about the ability to count and process the ballot appropriately.

The affidavit also stated ballots for non-eligible voters were being counted, despite their names not being on the poll book or the supplemental poll book.

According to Larsen, things got intense when he went to get a better visual of the poll book and ballots. The election official allegedly told him he had to stand at the monitor, not where he was. Larsen retorted that he had a right to "observe the process." Another election official and a Democratic challenger allegedly yelled at Larsen, saying he needed to back

Trump campaign released 234 pages affidavits regarding alleged voting irregularities in Michigan. Here's what they say.

They mostly concern an alleged 'atmosphere of intimidation' at a major Detroit counting location WE DEPLORABLES BE IS WUZ DEALIN' WID' HOOD BRO' CRIPS BLOODS WANNABE ASSED GANGSTA' ASSED SCUMBAGS SHAKE-SPEARE BE IS ELIZABETHAN QUEENS EBONICS WOULD BE IS SAY

Leon Wolf

In recent days, the Trump campaign has touted a number of affidavits collected from poll workers in Michigan that they say proves the existence of widespread irregularities in the Michigan vote counting process, and which they plan to attach as an exhibit to an expected lawsuit that will challenge the certification of the vote in Michigan.

Calling all Americans to take back our constitutional freedoms

The campaign released those affidavits Tuesday to some members of the media (thanks to Brad Heath of Reuters for providing me with a copy). The full .pdf file of exhibits can be read here. I have endeavored to separate the actual allegations of fraud in this post. Keep in mind that, at this point, these are mere allegations that have not been tested by cross-examination or any other form of investigation.

CLICK HERE TO READ THE FULL SET OF AFFIDAVITS

By my count, the 234 pages contain affidavits from 101 individuals. The majority of them appear to be handwritten impressions of the counting process.

Here, by my count, is a complete list of actual allegations that raise the potential of voter fraud from these affidavits:

- Alexandra Seely claimed that she challenged 10 votes at a given table and that those challenges were not recorded. She claims that poll workers would not take out the "log" to record her challenges.
- Articia Bomer claimed that "At approximately 4:50am I witnessed a man spraying a chemical on a ballot counting machine. He then placed twenty-seven ballots into the machine and I noticed

tape on the top of the ballot where a ballot number would normally be. Throughout the night I witnessed him insert these same 27 ballots at least five times." Note that this could have been repeated attempts to get the machine to scan ballots that would not scan rather than the same 27 ballots actually being counted five times.

- Betty Tyson claimed that she saw poll workers reviewing rejected ballots and curing where an erroneous or defective mark had made the ballot unreadable by the machine. She claims that some of the workers "added votes where there was no X or [check mark]," but does not specify how many.

- Multiple affidavits raised as their sole complaint that they witnessed ballot duplication (transfer of correct voter data from a damaged or defective ballot to another one that can be read by a machine) being done and that there was not a GOP observer present for that process. It is unclear whether Michigan law requires this, but it seems certain that best practices would have been to avoid such a scenario. The number of ballots that are damaged in machines is, by all accounts, very small. Note: This claim was raised in a lawsuit filed last week, and the city denied the claim at that time. TheBlaze has reached out to Wayne County officials for further comment on the contents of these affidavits.

- A number of the affidavits claim that GOP poll workers were not permitted to access records that were necessary to properly challenge some ballots.

- Cythnia Brunell claimed that, at the table she observed, she believed 11 ballots would have been rejected due to irregularities she believed had occurred, but only four were. The other seven were scanned through the counting machine. It is unknown what the ultimate disposition of those votes was.

- David Piontek claims that he saw an unnamed poll worker scan six ballots from the "problem ballot" file and that the computer declared them an "unlisted person." According to Piontek, the worker manually entered the ballots into the system and assign each voter a fictitious birthdate of 1/1/1900. A Jeffrey A. Gorman also stated this issue in his affidavit. The fictitious birthdate issue has been explained ad nauseam, but these allegations do raise at least the possibility that non-registered voters had their votes counted. This accusation was also noted in several other affidavits. Best estimate is that approximately 100 of these ballots were identified throughout the course of the affidavits.

- Jacqueline Zaplitny alleges that, "I was told to observe the computers that were identifying ballots that showed 'error'. I was told [to] view the people that were 'determining the intent of the voter.' There were multiple ballots that were 'corrected' on ballots that should have been overvoted and not counted." Without seeing the ballots in question, it is difficult to determine the validity of this claim.

- Michael Cassin, who identified himself as an independent poll watcher, said that he made six challenges to ballots that were not recorded in the log. A handful of other affiants raised similar contentions, although some of their challenges are, just by the way they are described, things that could not be challenged (e.g., one worker described trying to challenge a poll worker taking a pile of ballots off a table and moving it somewhere else).

- Patricia Rose alleged that she witnessed a poll worker attempt to run a batch of 50 ballots through a machine four times due to the machine jamming. According to her affidavit, "The ballot stack she was feeding in kept getting jammed. Rather than stop and go seek the assistance of a supervisor or technical support person, she removed the remaining ballots in the in-feed tray, and kept taking the scanned ballots off the top feed and adding them back to the stack, reinserting the whole stack again, and scanning them in again." The affiant was able to identify a number of batches where this happened, but was unable to say whether those votes had actually been counted multiple times, or whether the machine had been reset in-between each batch. This allegation was repeated regarding a different batch by Glen Sitek.

- Multiple affiants claimed that signature verification was not being done, or that they did not see it being done, on absentee ballots.

- Whitney Meyers claimed that, "On the street in front of the Department I witnessed workers with 'Detroit Elections' aprons on collecting ballots from cars. I witnessed multiple drivers in cars drop off multiple ballots, including more ballots than people in the car." Meyers did not explain how she arrived at this conclusion or whether she brought it to anyone's attention at the time. She also indicated that she saw a worker accept at least one ballot after the polls closed at 8pm. She also alleged that an unnamed individual placed "ballots" (did not specify or estimate how many) into one of the ballot drop boxes after 8pm and before the box could be locked.

- William Henderson alleged that eight ballots went missing from a given batch that he identified, but he does admit that it's possible they were located elsewhere and counted appropriately there.

- Brett Kinney claims that he successfully challenged a group of ballots, which were initially set aside as being problem ballots but were subsequently processed. It is not clear whether this was done because these challenges were ultimately rejected, or for some other reason.

- Anita Chase claims that she checked the voter records and discovered that her deceased son, identified as Mark D. Chase, voted twice since he passed away, including in the 2020 election.

This list constitutes the entire body of potential actual fraud allegations raised in the affidavits. The testimony contained in these affidavits clearly pertains to fewer than 1,000 total ballots, although it should be noted that numerous affiants complained that they were not able to see what was happening because they were required to maintain six feet of social distance or because people were in their way.

Some (most?) of the allegations in the affidavit concern allegations that GOP poll watchers were treated differently (worse) than Democratic poll watchers, or that the majority of the people in the room were

Democrats or were friendlier to the Democrats. Although these allegations are at least potentially relevant politically (albeit they are not tremendously surprising in Wayne County), they do not directly pertain to the issue of voter fraud, so I have not included them in this list, although you may certainly peruse them and draw your own conclusions.

The material in the affidavits alleging an "atmosphere" of intimidation and hostility toward the GOP poll workers is voluminous. I would estimate that it constitutes a significant portion of the material in the affidavits. I have not repeated most of it here because it does not directly establish or allege voter fraud.

Reading between the lines, some of the frustration experienced by the poll workers and refusal to entertain further complaints may have been come by honestly. The affidavits are rife with complaints about things that were, in fact, done properly and in accordance with the law.

For example, one affiant described at length how she insistently and repeatedly attempted to challenge a group of ballots that had already been placed in a "problem" ballot box (i.e., they had already been successfully challenged). This is, again, not the fault of people who got about 10 minutes of training in the procedures, but you can imagine that the cumulative effect of these challenges (which appear to have been quite voluminous, just based on the people who submitted affidavits) may have led to some short fuses and unwillingness to explain the same thing to each of the 200-plus watchers who were present.

Additionally, a large portion of the affidavits' contents centers on complaints regarding the counting process and what poll watchers viewed as selective enforcement of social distancing measures like six feet distance and mask wearing. Again, these complaints are in the affidavits and can be perused at leisure, if you are interested. They are not proof of voter fraud.

The affidavits contain many complaints that poll workers were not able to see as well as they would have liked due to having to remain six feet away from the tables due to COVID-19 social distancing measures. Many of the affiants claim that poll workers intentionally blocked their view of certain aspects of the counting process. These claims are difficult to evaluate without having been present in the environment.

I have omitted all of the complaints contained in the affidavits about poll workers being insulted, etc. This behavior should not have occurred, and you can read all about it in the affidavits if you wish. In most cases, it is not clear, however, who leveled the insults, nor what the context of the conversation was. Ultimately, those complaints are beyond the purview of this article.

I have also summarily omitted complaints about the number of poll watchers allowed in the location, and complaints about the boarding up of windows and/or cheering of people who were ejected. By all accounts, including the admission of the Trump campaign, the Trump campaign had more than 130 observers present and on site at the TCF Center during the entire duration of counting. Additionally, the controversy over whether the windows should have been boarded up in order to prevent people outside from filming what was going on inside is not directly relevant to allegations of voter fraud. Probably the most common complaint in the affidavits is from people who were not, in fact, allowed into the counting facility. Ultimately, the argument about how many people should have been allowed in the room is beyond the purview of this article. I have also omitted some allegations that are, on their own terms, completely unsupported by eyewitness testimony and are mere conjecture on their own terms. For example, one affiant complained that s/he was completely unable to see what was happening with a particular batch of ballots, but then followed that up with a statement of belief that the people s/he could not see were illegally altering ballots.

Additionally, some of the allegations appear to be borne out of failure to understand how the process was supposed to be carried out. For instance, one of the affidavits complains that when the computer identified a "duplicate" ballot (which presumably refers to a situation where someone has voted in person and also requested a mail-in ballot), the ballot was removed from the pile and then passed to the next person at the table. However, that is exactly what was supposed to happen to those ballots: they were supposed to be removed from the rest of the pile and considered as a provisional ballot until a check could be performed to determine whether the mail-in ballot was ever received.

Where an affidavit raises a complaint for which there is an obvious, non-fraud explanation (for instance, the complaints about 1/1/1900 birthdays), or where it complains about things that happened exactly as they should have (e.g., "I observed ballots that should have been duplicated due to being torn, stained or damaged. A supervisor instructed the workers to run damaged ballots through the tabulator and only to duplicate rejected ballots") I have omitted it. I do not, by the way, blame any of the affiants for raising these issues; many of them make clear that they responded to calls for volunteers on Facebook and received very little training.

Many of the allegations present an incomplete picture, from which it is impossible to draw any conclusions at all. For instance, numerous affiants complained that people who showed up to vote but who had requested a mail-in ballot were allowed to vote. This was proper procedure, and their in-person ballots were supposed to be provisional until it could be determined if they had turned in a mail-in ballot or not. Most of the affiants raising this complaint do note that the ballots were set aside, as is proper, but have no information about what was revealed when these provisional ballots were checked against the mail-in list.

Also, it should be noted that the affidavits contain numerous complaints about lack of security at the counting location, and I have also not included those. Having personally worked as an observer for elections before, I will say that none of the complaints strike me as representing unusual behavior (I don't recall having my ID checked and I certainly don't recall being searched or having my belongings searched when I entered a poll location); however, perhaps many of these complaints should lead to reforms in the security process for counting votes.

Notably, many of the affiants also complained about batches of ballots being left unsecured on or underneath tables; however, none of the affidavits contains any testimony about these boxes being tampered or destroyed or added to in any way. TheBlaze has reached out to officials for the State of Michigan and Wayne County for comment on the issues raised by the affiants.

10 GOP Attorneys General Back Lawsuit Challenging Pennsylvania Mail-In Ballots

By Solange Reyner

Republican attorneys general from ten states have filed an amicus brief in the GOP lawsuit challenging the extension of counting mail-in ballots in Pennsylvania, urging the U.S. Supreme Court to intervene and reverse the decision.

"The Pennsylvania Supreme Court's decision overstepped its constitutional responsibility, encroached on the authority of the Pennsylvania legislature, and violated the plain language of the Election Clauses," reads the brief, signed by attorneys general in Ohio, Texas, Alabama, Arkansas, Florida, South Dakota, Kentucky, Missouri, Mississippi and Oklahoma.

"Free and fair elections are the cornerstone of our republic and it's one of the reasons why the United States is the envy of the world," Missouri Attorney General Eric Schmitt said at a press conference announcing the brief. "We have to ensure that every legal vote cast is counted and that every illegal vote not cast is not counted. To do so would disenfranchise millions of Americans."

The U.S. Supreme Court in October ruled that Pennsylvania could count mailed-in ballots received up to three days after the Nov. 3 election, rejecting a Republican plea in the presidential battleground state. Many news outlets have called the race for Democratic challenger Joe Biden, though President Trump has refused to concede, citing voter fraud.

Nolte: Top Pollster Reports 59% Concerned Vote-By-Mail Leads to Fraud

Jack Knudsen & John Nolte

Rasmussen Reports, one of the most accurate pollsters of the 2016 and 2020 presidential elections, found 59 per- ".cent of likely voters are concerned "increased use of voting by mail will lead to more vote fraud

A plurality of 44 percent are "very concerned," while 15 percent are "somewhat concerned." Only 27 percent are "not at all concerned, while 13 percent are "not very concerned."

Let me just stop now to make something clear…

After the polling debacles of 2016, 2018, and 2020, it's time for everyone to stop taking media polls and media-approved polls seriously.

Any poll released by Fox News, the Washington Post, ABC News, Reuters, Quinnipiac, NBC, etc... these are fraud polls. These are polls put together by propagandists and liars. We have now had three — three! — election cycles where these pollsters have been exposed as shameless liars, and anyone who pays attention to them is a fool looking to be lied to.

The pollsters who have proven themselves over the past few election cycles are Rasmussen, IBD/TIPP, Susquehanna, and Trafalgar. The rest are all proven liars and hacks, and nothing they report means a thing. It's all lies. So if Rasmussen publishes a poll that says 59 percent of likely voters are worried about mail-in voting leading to vote fraud, I trust this poll.

When the proven liars at Reuters claim 80 percent of the public, including more than 50 percent of Republicans ,agree Biden is president-elect, you know that poll is a lie because the pollsters at Reuters lie. That's all they do is lie.

What's especially fascinating about this Rasmussen poll is a surprising high number of Democrats — 36 percent, are very (24 percent) or somewhat (12 percent) concerned about the potential for vote fraud with mail-in ballots. That is a much higher number than you would expect, which means those are Democrats who are persuadable in putting a stop to the obvious fraud behind mail-in ballots.

Of course 62 percent of Democrats say they are not very (18 percent) or not at all (44 percent) concerned, but that number is still lower than I expected.

Among "others" or unaffiliated or Independent voters, a majority of 56 percent are very (39 percent) or somewhat (17 percent) concerned, while 42 percent are not at all (26 percent) or not very (16 percent) concerned.

Let me just say that OF COURSE mail-in voting creates fraud. OF COURSE it does, especially when Democrat-run states mail out millions and millions of unsolicited ballots to every registered voter, which means you have millions and millions of ballots laying around all over the place that anyone can fill out and mail back.

No one can have trust in this system, especially after what happened on Tuesday night when the counting in Democrat-run states and cities was going President Trump's way and then — for the first time in my long experience — they STOPPED COUNTING.

Matt Perdie

I'm not saying there was enough fraud to tip the scales to His Fraudulency Joe Biden, but I sure as hell want to find out, and I sure as hell have lost confidence in American elections.

"The survey of 1,000 Likely U.S. Voters was conducted November 5 and 8, 2020 by Rasmussen Reports. The margin of sampling error is +/- 3 percentage points with a 95% level of confidence," per the pollster.

GET READY FOR 3rd TRIMESTER SKULL CRUSHING

Massachusetts Dems Push Radical ROE Act: Abortions Until Birth, Care Denied to Baby Survivors

Dr. Susan Berry

Massachusetts House Speaker Robert DeLeo (D) will push for a vote this week on an amendment to the annual budget bill that would codify abortion rights into state law, legalize abortions until birth, and allow abortionists to .deny care to infants who survive the procedure

"Following last week's joint statement with Senate President [Karen] Spilka [D], in which we expressed concern over the threat to women's reproductive rights on the national level, it is urgent that the House take up an immediate measure to remove barriers to women's reproductive health options and protect the concepts enshrined in *Roe v. Wade*," DeLeo said in a statement, reported WBUR News.

Though, according to the news report, DeLeo warned state House legislators not to attach major

policy measures to the budget bill, he said Monday the ROE Act [Act to Remove Obstacles and Expand Abortion Access] is an "urgent" matter and must be included.

If passed, the measure would legalize abortions after 24 weeks of pregnancy, allow a loophole for girls under the age of 16 to obtain an abortion without the consent of their parents, allow non-physicians to perform abortions, and allow abortionists to deny life-saving medical care to an infant who survives abortion.

"In the midst of a deadly pandemic, where the focus has been about saving lives, the radical Democrats want to kill babies born alive following failed late-term abortions," Massachusetts Republican Party Chairman Jim Lyons said Monday.

"As WBUR reported, this budget amendment is essentially the same bill as the so-called ROE Act which allows babies who have survived abortions to be killed on the spot," he added.

According to WBUR, DeLeo and Spilka vowed to introduce legislation to expand abortion rights should Amy Coney Barrett be confirmed to the U.S. Supreme court.

A coalition of over 300 Massachusetts pastors, however, sent a letter to Gov. Charlie Baker (R), requesting he veto the amendment.

Opponents to the measure "have consistently referred to this as the 'Infanticide Act' due to its eliminating of existing requirements for doctors to save the life of a child born alive during an abortion," a press release said.

In their letter to Baker, the pastors said in addition to their prayers for the governor, state leaders, and "justice for the poor, the downtrodden, the defenseless, and the least among us," they include as well their prayers for "our children still in their mother's womb."

The pastors added:

In 2019 alone, there were 18,593 abortions performed in the Bay State. How much more "accessible" does the murder of unborn children need to be? Abortion ends the life of a human child and puts the physical, mental, and emotional health of women, most especially young women, at risk.

"This is a radical, major, policy shift," Lyons said, asserting the Democrats are attaching such a pivotal piece of legislation to a necessary budget bill without a public hearing.

"Speaker DeLeo just finished saying that the commonwealth's critical overdue budget would be free from radical policy overhauls only to turn around and use that same budget-making process to push through this despicable legislation," he stated, "and that should disgust us all, regardless of party affiliation."

Jordan Sekulow to Newsmax TV: Trump Team Building Its Elex Case Carefully, Methodically

By Eric Mack

Despite mainstream media's urgent demands for evidence of widespread election fraud, it will take time for the legal case to be "outcome determinative," according to a member of President Donald Trump's legal team Jordan Sekulow on Newsmax TV.

"It's going to be a little bit of a slow process to get this into court, but then all the federal courts know they've got to do this rapidly," Sekulow, of the American Center for Law and Justice, told Tuesday's "Spicer & Co." "So, chill out. Take your time. Let us do our legal work, and then the courts are going to do this in an expedited manner.

"Whether it's like 30 days or so, I think we have all this figured out."

Pennsylvania's alleged commingling of late ballots is a legal battle in the crosshairs of the Supreme Court already, according to Jordan Sekulow, the son of Trump's personal attorney Jay Sekulow. On the segregating of late ballots, as ordered by Supreme Court Justice Samuel Alito, Jordan Sekulow noted Pennsylvania elections officials "came back and said, 'we didn't do any of that.'"

"So now it's referred to the entire court," he told host Sean Spicer. "They're kind of holding it right now, Sean.

"For that to get there, for them to make a decision like that – which would be kind of like a Bush versus Gore decision – they've got to look at the other states, too, and make sure that we've got realistic legal challenges, which we believe we do, that can actually, when they're all put together, change the outcome of the electoral college in favor of President Trump." Flipping Pennsylvania's 20 electoral college votes from Biden to Trump would be a significant legal victory, but that alone will not overturn the ultimate winner of the presidential election.

"What we're looking at – tens of thousands of votes – enough voters that could potentially overturn who wins the state of Pennsylvania," Jordan Sekulow told Spicer.

"I think there's a chance, because of enough state attorneys general have weighed in this Pennsylvania case, that they may ultimately decide it because of what you said, Sean, for future precedent – even if it doesn't affect the outcome.

"But I do think they're taking a step back to see what else is the Trump team, the president's legal team, the RNC legal team, what else are they bringing." Sekulow pointed to legal cases being brought in states like Michigan, Nevada, and Georgia – potentially already headed for a recount – as the paths of an "outcome determinative" case for Trump.

In Nevada, Sekulow notes, elections officials' order to "turn down" the threshold of signature verifications on electronic election systems might change the course of that state's electors. "That's up to 600,000 votes and we believe a third of those would likely be tossed out," he said. "That's in the current legal challenge."

Trump Campaign Files Another Suit in Pa. Over Ballot Curing

Kayleigh McEnany, White House press secretary, center, Ronna McDaniel, right, chairwoman of the Republican National Committee, and Matt Morgan, President Trump's campaign general counsel, conclude a news conference on Pennsylvania litigation and to "give an overview of the post-Election Day landscape," at the RNC

The Trump campaign on Monday filed a new lawsuit in Pennsylvania seeking to prevent the "curing" of ballots — the process of quick certification.

The lawsuit was announced Monday by Trump campaign general counsel at a press conference attended by White House Press Secretary Kayleigh McEnany and Republican National Committee Chairwoman Ronna McDaniel.

"The election is not over," Morgan said. "Tabulation and candidacy continues across the United States."

The suit was filed in the United States District Court for the Middle District of Pennsylvania by President Donald Trump and two representative voters, Morgan said.

The suit alleges "a violation of equal access based on a lack of meaningful observation and transparency" in counties controlled by Democrats and "a violation of equal protection based on disparate treatment between Republican voters and Democrat voters," he said. "What this means if you were a Democrat in Philadelphia, you were able to work outside the grounds on fixing defective ballots — sometimes referred to as 'curing' — but if you're in Republican counties in the state of Pennsylvania you were not allowed to do that because they were strictly following the text of the statute in Pennsylvania," Morgan said.

In Philadelphia and Allegheny Counties, more than 682,000 ballots were tabulated outside of the view of GOP ballot observers who were entitled by law to view them, he said.

"We believe that a meaningful review of those ballots could discern that there were some ballots that were illegally counted," Morgan said. "We believe that this lawsuit takes us one step closer to closing the gap in the vote differential in Pennsylvania."

"If it were this close the other way, if Trump was in the lead in all these states, the media would be screaming, 'This isn't over,'" McDaniel added.

Trump is contesting election results in four other states: Georgia, Arizona, Michigan and Nevada. Mainstream media outlets declared Democrat Joe Biden president elect on Saturday, but Newsmax is holding off on declaring a winner until all legal proceedings have made their way through the system

Pennsylvania Auditors Warned of Dead People, Duplicates on State Voter Rolls

Pennsylvania auditors alerted officials of possible dead people and duplicate registrations on the state's voter rolls last year, but the warnings went unacknowledged.

In December 2019, Pennsylvania's Department of Auditor General (DAG) released the findings of an audit report conducted January 1, 2016 to April 16, 2019 but was limited in scope because of "a lack of cooperation and a failure to provide the necessary information by" Pennsylvania's Department of State, the Department of Transportation, and four county election offices.

Due to the state's noncooperation, the auditors were "unable to establish with any degree of reasonable assurance" that the state's voter rolls system is "secure and that Pennsylvania voter registration on records are complete, accurate, and in compliance with applicable laws, regulations, and related guidelines."

Even without cooperation from state agencies and multiple county election offices, the report "identified tens of thousands of potential duplicate and inaccurate voter records, as well as voter

records for nearly three thousand potentially deceased voters that had not been removed" from Pennsylvania voter rolls.

Specifically, the report analyzed the voter registration records for the state's more than 8.5 million voters and alerted the Pennsylvania Secretary of State of "potential inaccuracies," including:

- 24,408 cases where a driver's license number was listed in more than one voter record
- 13,913 potential duplicate voter registrations
- 6,876 potential date of birth inaccuracies
- 2,230 potential date of birth and/or registration date inaccuracies
- 2,991 records of potentially deceased voters

On the issue of dead people on Pennsylvania's voter rolls, at least 2,094 of the 2,991 identified by auditors had their death notices sent to the Secretary of State's office so the voter registration would be canceled.

Auditors stated that the manual process of canceling voter registrations for dead people "depends on the accuracy of the data" in the state's voter rolls and thus if a "piece of personal information is inaccurately listed in the voter record," the death notice may be dismissed and the deceased registrant could stay on the rolls.

The full report can be read here: on records are complete, accurate, and in compliance with applicable laws, regulations, and related guidelines."

Even without cooperation from state agencies and multiple county election offices, the report "identified tens of thousands of potential duplicate and inaccurate voter records, as well as voter records for nearly three thousand potentially deceased voters that had not been removed" from Pennsylvania voter rolls.

Trump Campaign Spox Murtaugh: Pennsylvania Presidential Election 'Unconstitutional'

Trent Baker

White House communications director for the Trump campaign Tim Murtaugh on Tuesday sounded off on the 2020 presidential election and the campaign's lawsuits filed in multiple states over claims of voter fraud.

Murtaugh, on Fox News Channel's "Outnumbered Overtime," said the process in parts of Pennsylvania was "unconstitutional." He argued GOP voters received "disparate treatment."

"What they did in Pennsylvania was conduct, basically, an unconstitutional election," Murtaugh outlined. "Depending on where you were in the state and when you voted, you were treated differently. John Roberts was just going over there some words from our lawyer, Matt Morgan from yesterday, and the fact is Democrat voters in Philadelphia were called and said, 'You better come on in. There might be a problem with the mail-in ballot that you submitted, and they were invited to cast a provisional vote. This is before Election Day. That is not allowed. That is precanvassing a ballot before Election Day. Republican voters were not given that same opportunity. That is disparate treatment."

He continued, "If you voted in person in Pennsylvania, you were subjected to rigorous security standards: checking voter id ... signature matching. If you mailed in a ballot, which 2.65 million Pennsylvanians did, there were no such safeguards. You cannot have an election and treat different voters differently within the state. That is a violation of the equal protection clause of the U.S. Constitution and it's a very serious offense. And absolutely, we believe they are going to prevail on that suit, otherwise we wouldn't have filed it."

Jordan Sekulow to Newsmax TV: Trump Team Building Its Elex Case Carefully, Methodically

By Eric Mack

Despite mainstream media's urgent demands for evidence of widespread election fraud, it will take time for the legal case to be "outcome determinative," according to a member of President Donald Trump's legal team Jordan Sekulow on Newsmax TV.

"It's going to be a little bit of a slow process to get this into court, but then all the federal courts know they've got to do this rapidly," Sekulow, of the American Center for Law and Justice, told Tuesday's "Spicer & Co." "So, chill out. Take your time. Let us do our legal work, and then the courts are going to do this in an expedited manner. "Whether it's like 30 days or so, I think we have all this figured out."

Pennsylvania's alleged commingling of late ballots is a legal battle in the crosshairs of the Supreme Court already, according to Jordan Sekulow, the son of Trump's personal attorney Jay Sekulow.

On the segregating of late ballots, as ordered by Supreme Court Justice Samuel Alito, Jordan Sekulow noted Pennsylvania elections officials "came back and said, 'we didn't do any of that.'" "So now it's referred to the entire court," he told host Sean Spicer. "They're kind of holding it right now, Sean.

"For that to get there, for them to make a decision like that - which would be kind of like a Bush versus Gore decision - they've got to look at the other states, too, and make sure that we've got realistic legal challenges, which we believe we do, that can actually, when they're all put together, change the outcome of the electoral college in favor of President Trump." Flipping Pennsylvania's 20 electoral college votes from Biden to Trump would be a significant legal victory, but that alone will not overturn the ultimate winner of the presidential election. "What we're looking at - tens of thousands of votes - enough voters that could potentially overturn who wins the state of Pennsylvania," Jordan Sekulow told Spicer.

"I think there's a chance, because of enough state attorneys general have weighed in this Pennsylvania case, that they may ultimately decide it because of what you said, Sean, for future precedent - even if it doesn't affect the outcome. "But I do think they're taking a step back to see what else is the Trump team, the president's legal team, the RNC legal team, what else are they bringing."

Sekulow pointed to legal cases being brought in states like Michigan, Nevada, and Georgia -

potentially already headed for a recount – as the paths of an "outcome determinative" case for Trump. In Nevada, Sekulow notes, elections officials' order to "turn down" the threshold of signature verifications on electronic election systems might change the course of that state's electors.

"That's up to 600,000 votes and we believe a third of those would likely be tossed out," he said. "That's in the current legal challenge."

Trump Campaign Seeks Expedited Appeal of Dismissed Pa. Case

DEMOCRAT UGLIEST STATEDOWN SKANK PIG FACE CRIME AGAINST HUMANITY Pennsylvania Secretary of State Kathy Boockvar

Pennsylvania officials can certify election results that currently show Democrat Joe Biden winning the state by more than 80,000 votes, a federal judge ruled Saturday, dealing President Donald Trump's campaign another blow in its effort to invalidate the election.

Trump Lawyers: Pennsylvania Lawsuit Dismissal Moves Us Closer to Supreme Court

Charlie Spiering

President Donald Trump's campaign lawyers said Saturday they would file an appeal to the Third Circuit court .after a federal judge dismissed a lawsuit to challenge the results of the election in Pennsylvania

Trump 2020 attorneys former Mayor Rudy Giuliani and Jenna Ellis said in a statement:

Today's decision turns out to help us in our strategy to get expeditiously to the U.S. Supreme Court. Although we fully disagree with this opinion,

We're thankful to COCKROACH LARVAE OBAMA-APPOINTED

JUDGE (AUTHOR ADDENDUM) for making this anticipated decision quickly, rather than simply trying to run out the clock.

The lawsuit argued that the legal guarantee of "equal protection under the law" was violated after counties where voters were primarily Democrats took different approaches than counties where voters were primarily Republicans to help voters with problems with their mail-in ballots.

U.S. Middle District Judge Matthew Brann dismissed the suit on Saturday "with prejudice," issuing a stinging rebuke to the campaign for trying to "disenfranchise almost seven million voters." He wrote:

One might expect that when seeking such a startling outcome, a plaintiff would come formidably armed with compelling legal arguments and factual proof of rampant corruption, such that this Court would have no option but to regrettably grant the proposed injunctive relief despite the impact it would have on such a large group of citizens. That has not happened.

Ellis and Giuliani argued that their evidence showed that 682,777 ballots in Pennsylvania were cast illegally, after poll workers denied the Republican party's right to independent review, and said they wished to present their evidence in court.

"This is just an extension of the Big Tech, Big Media, Corrupt Democrat censorship of damning facts the American public needs to know," they wrote.

Trump lawyer Rudy Giuliani told Newsmax TV's Mark Halperin via text Saturday night the expedited dismissal is helpful for filing an expedited appeal and potentially raising the case to the Supreme Court.

Campaign senior legal adviser Jenna Ellis also pointed to the decision as a positive development in their effort to push the case relatively quickly to the Supreme Court. In a joint statement, they said they would seek an expedited appeal to the U.S. Third Circuit Court of Appeals.

U.S. District Judge Matthew Brann in Williamsport, Pennsylvania, turned down the request for an injunction by President Donald Trump's campaign, spoiling the incumbent's hopes of somehow overturning the results of the presidential contest.

In his ruling, Brann said the Trump campaign presented "strained legal arguments without merit and speculative accusations ... unsupported by evidence." "In the United States of America, this cannot justify the disenfranchisement of a single voter, let alone all the voters of its sixth most populated state," the opinion said. "Our people, laws, and institutions demand more."

Trump had argued the U.S. Constitution's guarantee of equal protection under the law was violated

when Pennsylvania counties took different approaches to notifying voters before the election about technical problems with their submitted mail-in ballots.

Pennsylvania Secretary of State Kathy Boockvar and the seven Biden-majority counties that the campaign sued had argued Trump had previously raised similar claims and lost.

They told Brann the remedy the Trump campaign sought, to throw out millions of votes over alleged isolated issues, was far too extreme, particularly after most of them have been tallied.

"There is no justification on any level for the radical disenfranchisement they seek," Boockvar's lawyers wrote in a brief filed Thursday.

Pennsylvania Attorney General Josh Shapiro, a Democrat, tweeted shortly after Brann's ruling, saying "Another one bites the dust."

"These claims were meritless from the start and for an audience of one," he said in a statement. "The will of the people will prevail. These baseless lawsuits need to end."

The state's 20 electoral votes would not have been enough on their own to hand Trump a second term. Counties must certify their results to Boockvar by Monday, after which she will make her own certification.

Democratic Gov. Tom Wolf will notify the winning candidate's electors they should appear to vote in the Capitol on Dec. 14.

Dick Morris to Newsmax TV: Giuliani's Equal Protection Argument 'Brilliant' IT IS BRILLIANT BUT THESE JUDGES HAVE ALREADY MADE UP THEIR MINDS BEFORE HEARING THE CASE. AFTER (30) RED STATES SECEDE FROM THE UNION WE WON'T HAVE THIS PROBLEM

By Sandy Fitzgerald

President Donald Trump's attorney Rudy Giuliani was "brilliant" with his argument and press conference earlier this week, because he is laying out an equal protection argument that could be taken up in the Supreme Court, political analyst Dick Morris told Newsmax TV Saturday night.

"It isn't a matter for the federal courts whether the election was fraudulent; it's a matter of whether certain voters were treated differently than others," **Morris told Newsmax TV's Rob Schmitt. "You can get away with almost anything in the cities than you can in the rest of the state.** That is a situation of equal protection under the law, which triggers the Supreme Court review."

He also pointed out that the Supreme Court on Friday made a "crucial" move when it assigned each justice to a separate group of circuit courts to handle emergency appeals that could pop up there. The jurisdictions were posted on Twitter by the website SCOTUSBlog.

"Justice (Samuel) Alito, for example, he was the one that intervened in Pennsylvania to ask that the ballots be counted, the signatures are verified, and that Republicans be allowed access," said Morris. "That's because Pennsylvania is part of his jurisdiction."

He added that circuits in Wisconsin, Michigan, Pennsylvania and Georgia all have Trump-appointed justices assigned and that's "very important" as the cases move forward.

"What we have to understand is elections are run by states, not by the federal government," said Morris. "Guliani is making a very compelling case."

For example, in Philadelphia, "you could vote without signing anything. The signature wasn't vetted... all kinds of ballots would be accepted that were not accepted in Harrisburg or in Wilkes Barre or some other community in Pennsylvania."

Rep. Louie Gohmert to Newsmax TV: Evidence Vital to Build Case

By Sandy Fitzgerald

It is important for the Trump campaign to get its evidence into the lower courts, even if they know the judges there will not be bipartisan, so there is more to use when the case about voter fraud makes it to the Supreme Court, Rep. Louie Gohmert said Saturday on Newsmax TV.

"You've to go get everything you can, if you're conservative, in the way of evidence," Gohmert told host Rob Schmitt on "The Count." "[They have to] get their man at the trial court, even if it means losing there, in order to get to the Supreme Court with a more effective case."

Gohmert also said, while Rep. Jim Jordan, R-Ohio, is demanding a congressional investigation into the integrity of the election, that would mean the case would go before the House Judiciary Committee, which is chaired by Rep. Jerry Nadler, D-N.Y.

"If Nadler's in charge of [the hearing] having it won't do any good," said Gohmert, also a member of the Judiciary Committee. "It doesn't mean we won't demand one, but if you know, that's putting the fox in charge of the henhouse."

That, he added, would be the same as Dominion Voting Systems and Smartmatic being in charge of voting machine systems.

Gohmert also slammed former Cybersecurity and Infrastructure Security Agency Director Christopher Krebs, who President Donald Trump fired after he said this year's election was secure.

"It's so ridiculous for Krebs to have been saying for months now including on Election Day that everything is secure," Gohmert said. "These are the very people who have accommodated fraud in their system, at least. On Election Day, in an article in Politico, he was thanking his partners in Silicon Valley for making it safe."

There are also many Republicans looking forward to the elections in 2022 and 2024 to regain control in Washington, D.C., but that will not happen if election fraud doesn't stop, Gohmert said.

He added, if Trump doesn't pull out a victory in the current election, he would like to see him win in 2024, but "if this fraud is not completely exposed, it really won't matter."

Trump campaign files appeal after Pennsylvania judge shoots down lawsuit

By Andrew O'Reilly

President Trump's legal team on Sunday filed an appeal to a federal judge's ruling that struck down his campaign's .effort to block the certification of votes in Pennsylvania

The appeal, which was filed to the U.S. Court of Appeals for the Third Circuit, comes just a day after U.S. Middle District Judge Matthew Brann in Williamsport, Pa., rejected a request by the Trump 2020 Campaign for an injunction that would stop the certification of the election, as the campaign seeks to overturn results in swing states across the country. "Plaintiffs ask this Court to disenfranchise almost seven million voters," Brann said Saturday. "This Court has been unable to find any case in which a plaintiff has sought such a drastic remedy in the contest ".of an election, in terms of the sheer volume of votes asked to be invalidated

PA COURT REJECTS TRUMP CAMP'S EFFORTS TO BLOCK 9,000 ABSENTEE BALLOTS AFTER ELECTION DAY

"One might expect that when seeking such a startling outcome, a plaintiff would come formidably armed with compelling legal arguments and factual proof of rampant corruption, such that this Court would have no option but to regrettably grant the proposed injunctive relief despite the impact it would have on such a large group of citizens," he added.

The president argued that the Constitution's guarantee of equal protection under the law was violated by the state, when counties took different measures to inform voters of technical issues that arose with the unprecedented number of mail-in ballots.

Even if he eventually does win the Pennsylvania case, Trump would still need to win other lawsuits in other states then ask to delay certification. The campaign peppered battlegrounds states with litigation in the days after the election alleging widespread election fraud without proof, but the majority of those cases have already been dismissed.The president has taken his effort to subvert the results of the 2020 election beyond the courtroom in recent days, straight to local lawmakers. Some Trump allies have expressed hope that state lawmakers could intervene in selecting Republican electors.Trump invited Michigan legislators to the White House Friday, hoping that an Oval Office meeting would persuade them to set aside the popular vote favoring Biden by more than 154,000. But the lawmakers issued a statement after the meeting that they would follow the law and "normal process" on electors. Trump may have been considering a similar invitation to lawmakers from Pennsylvania.

Recounts still are being conducted in Wisconsin where Biden initially won by more than 20,000 votes. By KYLE CHENEY

President Donald Trump made explicit Saturday the strategy his legal team has been hinting at for days: He wants Republican-led legislatures to overturn election results in states that Joe Biden won. "Why is Joe Biden so quickly forming a Cabinet when my investigators have found hundreds of thousands of fraudulent votes, enough to "flip" at least four States, which in turn is more than enough to win the Election?" Trump said, despite refusing to produce any such evidence either publicly or in court cases filed by his attorneys.

"Hopefully the Courts and/or Legislatures will have the COURAGE to do what has to be done to maintain the integrity of our Elections, and the United States of America itself," Trump said. Trump's comment came after a string of legal defeats, including a rejection by a federal judge in Pennsylvania Saturday who said the Trump team presented no evidence of election fraud or misconduct, despite seeking to invalidate millions of votes. Trump's lead lawyer in the case, Rudy Giuliani, said he intends to appeal the case to the Third Circuit and, if necessary, the Supreme Court.

But with few cases pending in courts, Trump's options have narrowed and he is becoming increasingly reliant on longshot scenarios where election results are not certified and Republican-controlled statehouses in Pennsylvania, Michigan, Arizona and Georgia intervene to declare him the winner.

GOP legislative leaders in those states have not endorsed this approach. Trump summoned Michigan legislative leaders to the White House on Friday, but they later issued a statement indicating they had not seen any reason to intervene on Trump's behalf.

To succeed, Trump's plan would require several unprecedented legal steps. First, Republican-led legislatures in states Biden won would need to move to overturn their state's popular vote and appoint a slate of Trump electors when the Electoral College meets on Dec. 14. In Pennsylvania and Michigan, such maneuvers would be certain to meet vetoes from Democratic governors, so the lawmakers would also need to secure a legal determination that they hold the sole power to appoint electors — a disputed legal premise that has never been tested.

Trump's call for lawmakers to hand him the election is the most overt call he's made yet for state lawmakers to overturn the election results. But it also underscores his dwindling options: Michigan is due to certify its vote totals on Monday, as are Pennsylvania counties, which would hand the statewide certification duty to Secretary of State Kathy Boockvar, a Democrat. On Friday, Georgia certified Biden's victory. As of Friday evening, Pennsylvania's GOP leaders said they had not received an invitation to meet Trump at the White House, but last month, they said they would not step in to alter the election results.

Officials Say Postal Worker Recants Claims of Backdated Ballots; He Denies It

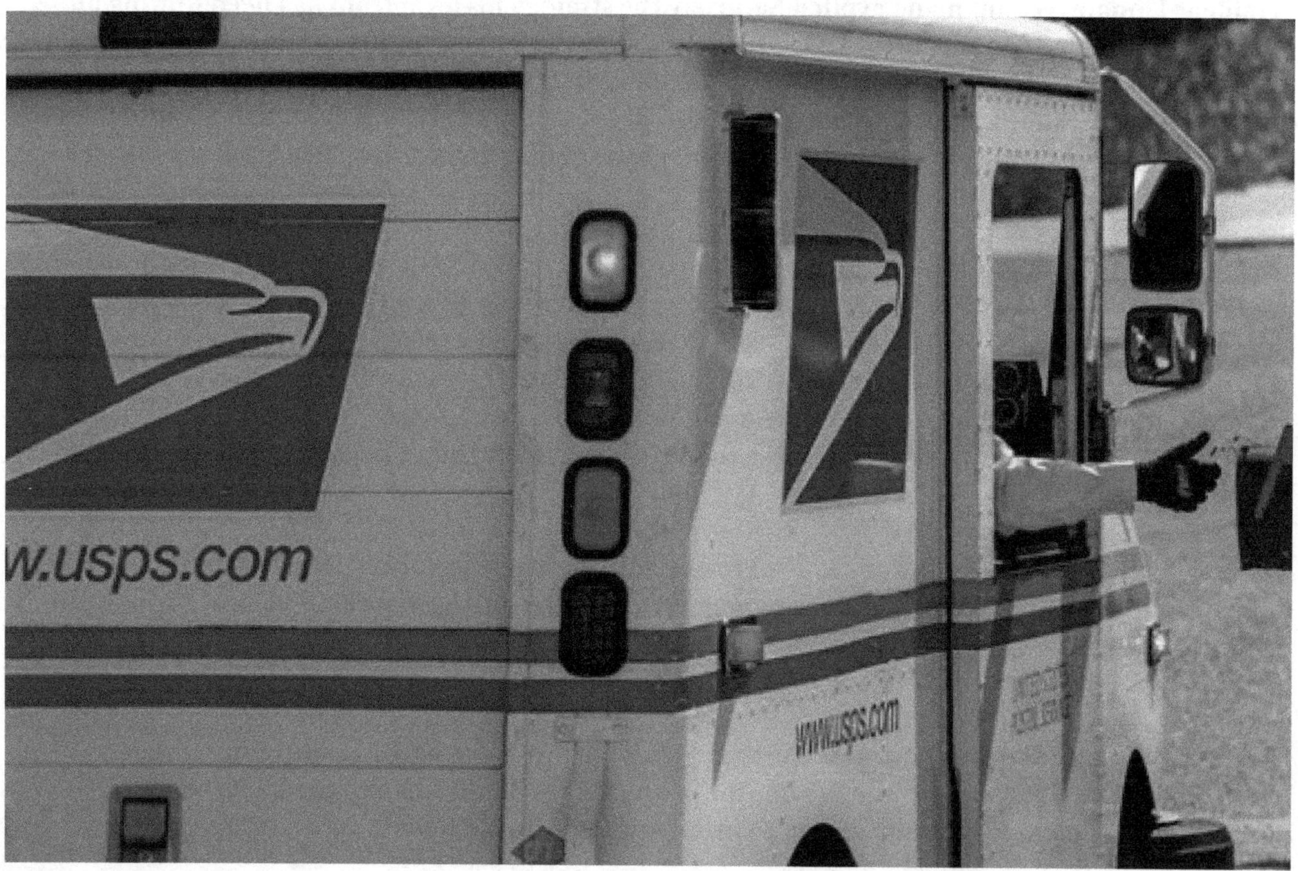

A postal worker in Pennsylvania who said the postmaster in Erie, Pa., instructed employees to backdate ballots mailed after election day has recanted his story, The Washington Post reported Tuesday, citing three officials briefed on the case.

But the postal worker has said in a YouTube posting he has not recanted.

The claim by Richard Hopkins has been used by Republicans as potential evidence of widespread voter fraud as President Donald Trump's reelection campaign files lawsuits seeking to overturn the results in key states. Attorney General Bill Barr on Monday issued a memo citing voting irregularities in authorizing federal prosecutors to pursue credible cases.

According the Post, Hopkins on Monday admitted to investigators from the U.S. Postal Service's Office of Inspector General that his allegations were not true and signed an affidavit recanting his claims. Democratic members of the House Oversight Committee tweeted on Tuesday: the "whistleblower completely RECANTED." Hopkins denied recanting in a YouTube video posted Tuesday night.

"I'm here to say I did not recant my statements. That did not happen," he said.

Trump campaign spokesman Tim Murtaugh told the Post that Hopkins statements were only a small part of their case in Pennsylvania.

Erie Postmaster Rob Weisenbach has denied the allegations, calling them "100% false," adding that they were made "by an employee that was recently disciplined multiple times."

Chaos erupts after Dems claim that USPS whistleblower recanted his testimony, whistleblower denies recanting

What is going on here?

JASON REDMOND & Leon Wolf

The bizarre case of the Erie, Pennsylvania, U.S. Postal Service whistleblower who claims that he overheard his supervisors discussing backdating the postmarks on absentee ballots took another twist Tuesday when Democrats on the House Oversight Committee claimed that the whistleblower recanted, only to have the whistleblower release a video denying that he recanted.

Calling all Americans to take back our constitutional freedoms

The whistleblower, who has been identified as Richard Hopkins, claimed in an affidavit **that he overheard his supervisor telling another postal employee that he had backdated a group of mail-in ballots that were collected on Nov. 4 to make it appear that they had in fact been mailed on Nov. 3. Under a ruling from the Pennsylvania Supreme Court, ballots that were mailed by Nov. 3 will still be counted (pending a legal challenge to this ruling) even if they were received after Election Day.**

It is important to note that, even if the whistleblower's allegations are true, none of the ballots received after Nov. 3 have yet been counted or added to either candidate's total**. Thus, the**

whistleblower's allegations do not directly pertain to Biden's current lead in the state. The state has revealed that about 10,000 votes total were received in the mail between Nov. 3 and Friday, but those ballots have remained sequestered and uncounted pending the Trump campaign's legal challenge to their inclusion. Presumably, if the Trump campaign's challenge fails, those ballots will only serve to increase Biden's current lead in the Keystone State.

Nevertheless, the whistleblower's affidavit has become a flash point of controversy as it represents one of the few concrete allegations of voter fraud that have been brought forth by the campaign. The affidavit appears to have been the reason for remarks by Senator Lindsey Graham (R-S.C.) over the weekend promising a Senate Judiciary Committee investigation into voting irregularities.

The controversy intensified Tuesday afternoon when Democrats on the House Oversight Committee released a statement claiming that the whistleblower had "recanted" his testimony, a claim that was magnified by many in the media.

Project Veritas, which publicized Hopkins' story, did not waste time refuting this characterization, releasing a video of Hopkins saying that he did not recant his testimony.

In a subsequent tweet, O'Keefe claims that federal investigators "intimidated" Hopkins and complains that he was interviewed for four hours without legal counsel. He further promised a full release of the transcript of that interview.

Although Hopkins has denied "recanting," it is not yet clear what he *did* say to federal agents during their interview or whether he may have revised some details that he claimed in his affidavit.

Hopkins was also praised by President Donald Trump on Twitter, who stated, "A brave patriot. More & more people are stepping forward to expose this Rigged Election!"

Pennsylvania Judge Sides With Trump Campaign, Rules Segregated Ballots Can't Be Counted

Jordan Lancaster

A Pennsylvania judge sided with the Trump campaign Thursday, ruling that ballots that did not have proof of identity before November 9 would not be counted. Under Pennsylvania state law, if a ballot is lacking proof of identification, voters have until six days after the election - November 9 - to fix it so that their ballot can be counted. Once the Pennsylvania Supreme Court ruled that ballots could be accepted up to three days after election day, Pennsylvania Secretary of State Kathy Boockvar issued guidance saying that a ballot lacking proof of identification could be fixed up to six days after the deadline to accept ballots, Fox News reported. Boockvar issued the guidance November first, two days before Election Day. (RELATED: Trump Campaign Launches Another Lawsuit In Pennsylvania Over Ballot 'Curing' — Here's What You Need To Know)

The Trump campaign argued that the order to extend the ballot identification deadline had no basis in law and that Boockvar didn't have the power to issue her guidance, Fox News reported. Judge Mary Hannah Leavitt sided with the Trump campaign, writing in a court order that Boockvar "lacked statutory authority to issue the November 1, 2020 guidance." Ballots for which proof of identity had been provided between November 10 and 12 had been separated while the court decided what to do with them. Leavitt's ruling means that the segregated ballots will not be counted, according to Fox News. The Trump campaign has brought several legal challenges related to the election in Pennsylvania, including a claim that thousands of ballots had been improperly counted, according to the report. The campaign argues that the ballots should not have been counted because they were missing information. A hearing is scheduled for Friday. The Trump campaign also challenged Pennsylvania's three-day extension for accepting mail-in ballots. They are awaiting action from the Supreme Court related to the issue.

B. HUSSEIN OBAMA LAUGHINGLY CALLED THE CALIPHATE OF IRAQ & AL SHAM (ISIS) THE JUNIOR VARSITY. DONALD TRUMP LARGELY EXTERMINATED ISLAMIC TERRORISM ABROAD & MS-13 AT HOME. DEMOCRATS WANT SYMPATHETIC OUTREACH TO THIS EVIL; UNDER DEMOCRATS; WILL RETURN; REPLICATING WORLDWIDE LIKE H.I.V.

Over 50 People Beheaded In Mozambique By ISIS-Linked Terrorists

WITH YOU VOTING FOR THE USA TOTALITARIAN LEFT; THIS WILL BE IS YOU:

DYLAN HOUSMAN

ISIS-linked terrorists beheaded and dismembered more than 50 people over three days at a soccer field in Mozambique, according to local reports. The terrorists launched attacks on villages in the areas of Miudumbe and Macomia, burning down homes and kidnapping women and children, according to the New York Post. Others were then taken to a soccer field in Muatide where more than 50 people were beheaded and "chopped up," as reported by Al Jazeera. (RELATED: 'The Terrorist Risk Is Everywhere' — Macron Calls For Stricter European Borders After Recent Attacks)

The militants who carried out the brutal attack — which included several more beheadings in another nearby village — are allegedly attempting to form an Islamic state in the area, the BBC reported. The attackers chanted "allahu akbar" while carrying out the atrocities, which lasted multiple days, per the BBC.

The group goes by the name "Al-Shabaab" but do not have any apparent connection to a terrorist group that operates under the same name in Somalia, per Al Jazeera. They have been committing these types of mass killings for three years now in the region, according to the Post. Last year they pledged allegiance to ISIS and have been building their own mosques throughout northeastern Mozambique, the Post says, citing Amnesty International. (RELATED: Russian Soldier Killed Officer With Axe, Shot Two More In Murder Spree, Investigators Say)

Pa. Supreme Court to Hear Challenge to Ruling Allowing Closer Observer Access

IN DEMOCRAT USA TOTALITARIAN FASCISM; REPUBLICAN OBSERVERS ARE VIOLENTLY PREVENTED FROM OBSERVING VOTE COUNTING BY INNER CITY GOON HOOD GOON TOUGH GUY THUGS WHO THREATEN WOMEN & OLD PEOPLE IN THE 2020 PRESIDENTIAL ELECTION PAID BY FACEBOOK ZUCKERBUCKS & JACK DORSEY $600 MILLION; THEN GANGSTA' HOOD THUGS (IF WE CALL THIS WHAT IT IS THEY CALL IT RACISM WITH THE DEMOCRAT RACE CARD) THREATEN REPUBLICAN FAMILIES & GET THEM FIRED FROM THEIR JOBS. (30) REPUBLICAN STATES MUST SECEDE TO FORM OUR OWN CONFEDERATION

People participate in support of counting all votes as the election in Pennsylvania is still unresolved on November 04, 2020 in Philadelphia, Pennsylvania.

By Solange Reyner

Pennsylvania's Supreme Court has agreed to hear the Philadelphia County Board of Elections challenge to a ruling requiring that election observers be granted closer access to vote tabulators, reports Politico.

The state's high court said it would review whether the case is moot and whether a state judge erred in reversing a trial court's decision that the board's original regulations regarding observer and representative access complied with applicable Election Code requirements.

Counting will resume in the meantime, the court said.

A state judge last Thursday ordered Philadelphia officials to allow party and candidate observers to move closer to election workers processing mail-in ballots. A spokesperson for the Philadelphia board of elections said barriers were shifted in response to the order while the city appealed it.

"There are specific rules in Pennsylvania about where poll watchers can stand and what they can do," said Suzanne Almeida, interim director of Common Cause Pennsylvania. "It applies to both parties equally. Everyone has the exact same access. This is not about disadvantaging one party over another."

The number of poll watchers allowed at an election office varies. Some smaller offices might allow only a few inside, while larger ones could have dozens.

President Donald Trump has refused to concede the presidential race to Democratic challenger Joe Biden, citing voter fraud, though several news outlets have called the race for the former vice president.

Trump has sued several states to stop counting what he says are "illegal" votes, and has alleged that his campaign observers were blocked from ballot-counting rooms though he has not presented evidence.

McEnany: 'Unlike Our Opponents, We Have Nothing to Hide'

By Eric Mack

Acting in her "personal capacity," White House press secretary Kayleigh McEnany joined Republican National Committee Chairwoman Ronna McDaniel and campaign legal counsel Matt Morgan for a news conference Monday, but mainstream media mostly ignored it.

"Unlike our opponents, we have nothing to hide," McEnany told reporters in prescient comments as Fox News cut away from it, angering some viewers. You can watch the news briefing in its entirely from C-SPAN.

"We are fighting for the rights of all Americans to have faith and confidence not only in this election, but in the many elections to come," McEnany told reporters. "There is only one party in America that opposes voter ID. One party in America that opposes verifying signatures, citizenship, residency, eligibility.

"There is only one party in American trying to keep observers out of the count room. And that party, my friends, is the Democrat Party.

"You don't take these positions because you want an honest election. You don't oppose an audit of the vote, because you want an accurate count. You don't oppose our efforts at sunlight and transparency because you have nothing to hide.

"You take these positions because you are welcoming fraud and you are welcoming illegal voting.

"Our position is clear: We want to protect the franchise of the American people. We want an honest, accurate, lawful count. We want maximum sunlight. We want maximum transparency. We want every legal vote to be counted, and we want every illegal vote to be discarded.

"Unlike our opponents, we have nothing to hide.

"The integrity of our election matters. The Constitution of the United States matters.

"What we have seen across the country is Democrat officials systematically trying to do an end run around the Constitution to tip the scales of the election in their favor."

Morgan laid out the paths for legal challenges by the campaign, starting with Pennsylvania, where Republican ballot-counting monitors were not given "meaningful" access to view the opening, processing, and counting of ballots.

"We are very close to the automatic recount statute in Pennsylvania," Morgan noted.

There are pending lawsuits on whether late-arriving ballots might have been co-mingled in the counting process, despite Supreme Court Justice Samuel Alito giving federal guidance to segregate those ballots in the event a case might rule them ineligible to be counted in the Nov. 3 elections.

Also, Morgan claimed some counties did not abide by equal protection under the law by permitting Democrat voters to "cure" ballot mistakes, while Republican might not have been.

"This lawsuit itself could change that, could swing that small discrepancy" in the voting margins between President Donald Trump and Biden in the state of Pennsylvania. "So this is the relief that we're seeking at this time, but I would also used the press and those out there that this is step one of a process.

"We are within our rights to look into these irregularities. We were in our rights to observe the votes as they were being tabulated."

McDaniel, speaking on behalf of the GOP, noted voting and ballot irregularities should be cause for concern and pause the rush to move Democrat Joe Biden's team into transitioning to the White House until the electoral college votes for the next president.

There is still a lot of work to do, she said.

"As you guys can understand, with 2,800 incident reports, this is a lot to track down," she told reporters. "It means we're interviewing these people, we're getting their statements and we're turning into affidavits. But that takes a lot of time and effort."

She added a call for media to look into allegations of fraud or political bias in ballot counting and permitting legal monitoring.

"We should all be alarmed by this, no matter where you are on the political spectrum," she said.

"Democrats and the media want to ignore these clear irregularities and rush to call states as won and end the certification and canvas process," she continued.

"We're hearing we need to unite, we need to come together," she added, referring to Democrat Joe Biden's pre-certification, pre-concession, acceptance speech.

"Even one instance of voter fraud should be too many for all of us. We intend to ensure that every lawful voter has their vote counted in accordance with the law. That observers are granted the access that they are due under state law, and that any irregularities that have occurred – whether by malicious intent or incompetence – are investigated to the fullest extent allowed under the law."

McDaniel also called out Democrat and media complicity in hypocrisy.

"If the shoe was on the other foot, if it were this close the other way, if President Trump was in the lead in all these states, the media would be screaming: 'This isn't over; the race isn't over. We need more time to count to make sure it's right.'

"But because it's Biden in a very slight lead, the media demands that the race is over and there's nothing to see here. The American people need to have confidence in their elections."

THIS IS DEMOCRAT INNER CITY HOOD CRIPS & BLOODS

GANGSTA'S PAID BY ZUCKERBUCKS TO STEAL THE PRESIDENCY HIRED Detroit Elections Worker Says She Was Instructed to Change Ballot Dates MARK ZUCKERBERG'S GANGSTA'S COMMONLY SAID THAT U.S.A. DEMOCRATIC ELECTION LAW ARE AN ANNOYANCE TO THEM. WE MUST SECEDE FROM TWITTER'S JACK DORSEY ZUCKERBERG ZUCKERBUCKS AS JEWISH HITLER

By Brian Trusdell and Eric Mack

A Detroit city worker who was assigned to the election has sworn in an affidavit that she and others were ordered to change mailing dates on ballots and observed supervisors "coaching" voters to cast ballots for Democrat Joe Biden.

Jessy Jacob, a longtime city worker, signed the affidavit in a lawsuit by the Great Lakes Justice Center – which says it focuses on freedom of speech, religious liberty, and sanctity of life, among other issues – on behalf of two Michigan voters.

"Why aren't you worried about these irregularities?" GOP chairwoman Ronna McDaniel, a Michigander, scolded defiant reporters at a Trump campaign briefing Monday. "If you have an election worker told to backdate ballots, that's a problem.

"What we are seeing is deeply alarming," she added in an impassioned rejection of media's skepticism of Trump campaign fraud claims. When pressed again for evidence of illegal voter fraud, McDaniel reminded the media of the claims filed in affidavits and lawsuits.

"I think I just went thought that with you: With someone backdating ballots? That's called illegal," she said, adding delivering evidence to the media reluctant to do its own investigations will take time.

"That's going to be an investigation process, but somebody was told you need to backdate ballots to make them legal, ballots that were illegal under the law."

Still, a CNN reporter called the claims a "conspiracy theory."

"Listen, how is it a conspiracy theory when a whistleblower in the city of Detroit is saying, 'I was

told by my supervisor to lie and to backdate ballots. This is somebody protected under the law. There's no conspiracy there."

The lawsuit in Detroit claims ballots were forged, voters were coached to cast ballots, dates were changed on absentee ballots, people were allowed to vote in person and cast an absentee ballot, ballots were counted for which there was no registered voter, and tens of thousands of ballots arrived late, all for Democrat Biden.

"The suit states Wayne County election officials allowed illegal, unlawful, and fraudulent processing of votes cast in last Tuesday's election," the Great Lake Justice Center wrote Sunday in a release. "Numerous witnesses have filed sworn affidavits under oath attesting to the fraudulent activities they observed directly. These acts disenfranchised lawful voters and potentially changed the outcome of the election."

The suit asks the election results be voided and a new election ordered.

"As you guys can understand, with 2,800 incident reports, this is a lot to track down," McDaniel told reporters at the briefing. "It means we're interviewing these people, we're getting their statements and we're turning into affidavits. But that takes a lot of time and effort."

She added a call for media to look into allegations of fraud or political bias in ballot counting and permitting legal monitoring.

"We should all be alarmed by this, no matter where you are on the political spectrum," she said.

"Democrats and the media want to ignore these clear irregularities and rush to call states as won and end the certification and canvas process," she continued.

"We're hearing we need to unite, we need to come together," she added, referring to Democrat Joe Biden's pre-certification, pre-concession, acceptance speech.

"Even one instance of voter fraud should be too many for all of us. We intend to ensure that every lawful voter has their vote counted in accordance with the law. That observers are granted the access that they are due under state law, and that any irregularities that have occurred – whether by malicious intent or incompetence – are investigated to the fullest extent allowed under the law."

McDaniel also called out Democrat and media complicity in hypocrisy.

"If the shoe was on the other foot, if it were this close the other way, if President Trump was in the lead in all these states, the media would be screaming: 'This isn't over; the race isn't over. We need more time to count to make sure it's right.'

"But because it's Biden in a very slight lead, the media demands that the race is over and there's

nothing to see here. The American people need to have confidence in their elections."

Megyn Kelly to Newsmax TV: Biden's Call for Unity Disingenuous THEY ACTUALLY HAVE FUCKEN NERVE TO CALL FOR UNITY OVER DIVISION AFTER STEALING THE PRESIDENCY TO PUT DEMOCRAT TOTALITARIAN THUGS IN CHARGE OF AMERICA.

By Eric Mack

Joe Biden's call for unity is more than merely disingenuous, it is also completely detached from reality, according to media personality Megyn Kelly on Newsmax TV.

"Biden tweeted out late Saturday night, a nation unified, a nation strengthened, a nation healed – OK, so, no it isn't!" Kelly told Monday's "Greg Kelly Reports." "It's not even close.

"That was written by a man in his basement for the past year," she continued to host Greg Kelly, no relation. "Because the nation's extremely divided right now, extremely divided. And you need to look no further than Joe Biden's own party." Biden's speech Saturday night was called out by Megyn Kelly as being hypocritical, because he alienated all those who voted for President Donald Trump while claiming he can bring them to support him.

"Biden's been saying this all along: He's the unifier, he's the one that's going to bring us together," she said. "It sounds delightful. It sounds great, and I want that. I want world peace and I want all the puppies and kittens to be adopted.

"But, let's get real. It's not connected to the reality on the ground in this country right now. And the only reason you're hearing Biden and all these Democrats calling for it is because they won. It's only the person that wins that says, 'lets have unity.'

"But what has he been doing for the past four years, Greg? They have been calling all of the Trump supporters – not just Trump, that would be bad enough – all his supporters, racists, bigots, xenophobes, misogynists, sexists, transphobe. "Now it's: 'That stuff we said, we're good, right? Aren't we good? Get over here – group hug."

Megyn Kelly rebuked Democrats like Rep. Alexandria Ocasio-Cortez for calling to put Trump backers on an "accountability list." "The people who voted for Trump now need to be on the accountability list," she rebuked. "And what are they going to do? They're going to try to stop you from getting a job. They're going to try to blackball you.

"They're going to try to stop you – they said it explicitly – they're going to try to stop you from getting any sort of a publishing deal." The legal fight over the election is not over, even if the margins make it a longshot, but the Trump campaign deserves its days in court and the election deserves to have "its tires kicked," particularly the legal actions in Pennsylvania, Megyn Kelly said.

"Of all the legal challenges, that's my favorite, because the courts had no business jumping in, when managing elections is the business of the legislators," Megyn Kelly, who is also a lawyer, said. "And, so, it shouldn't have done that. I understand, it was COVID and they wanted different rules, but too bad.

"These judges had no business jumping in there, and I think it really did change the effect of the election. And these are serious matters. People need to have faith in the election, and there's a reason they don't just let some judges take care of it. "I also don't want to raise your audience's expectations to an unreasonable level. This is a very uphill battle for him at this point."

CNN's Preposterous Call for Unity THEY STEAL CONTROL OF OUR LIVES & CALL FOR UNITY CONTROLLED BY DEMOCRAT GESTAPO WAFFEN SS

Tim Graham

Ben Shapiro

DEMOCRAT UNITY IS SHUT YER' FUCKEN MOUTH & SURRENDER TO TOTALITARIAN NATIONAL SOCIALISM NAZISM

There was a Museum of Broadcasting in New York City, but there's never been a Museum of Broadcasting Shamelessness. Imagine a place where they could run a medley of clips of Dan Rather insisting that, despite the small problem of his reporting on phony National Guard documents, "the underlying story is true."

An obvious entry in the Shamelessness Museum emerged about one minute after Joe Biden made his "victory speech" on the night of Nov. 7. CNN tweeted out a new commercial in which it creepily echoed Biden's sentiments that we must all come together and break out the Cokes and sing "I'd Like to Teach the World to Sing" or something.

A female narrator mourned in the commercial, saying, "Our trust has been broken -- in our leaders, in our institutions, even with some of our friends. And we are hurting. Now, more than ever, we need each other -- to listen, to learn from one another, to rebuild those bonds."

Does anyone think CNN hasn't been ripping apart our leaders and our institutions for four years? The announcer added: "(T)rust shows that we believe in the good in each other. It's what makes us human. And when we trust one another, that is when we can truly achieve great things."

If you thought this would lead to an abrupt switch in CNN's daily product from hourly rage to "Mister Rogers' Neighborhood," you would be sadly, badly mistaken. Instead, shameless CNN is running this unity-goo-goo advertisement in between its usual Trump Hater thunderbolts.

Anderson Cooper is pictured in the ad, but two days after Biden declared victory, Cooper was furious that Trump hadn't conceded. He complained to old Obama strategist David Axelrod: "In the mid-90s -- I think it was like '96 -- I was in Kinshasa, in the waning days of Mobutu. And Mobutu was, you know, a pretty awful dictator. And when he finally fled the country and the rebels were moving to take the capital, his son drove around in a pickup truck with a machine gun and settling scores with people he felt had not been supportive enough with Mobutu."

So, President Donald Trump and Donald Trump Jr. are somehow comparable to a tyrant and his son on a mobile, murderous rampage. Cooper added: "Thankfully, it hasn't come to that here, but I can't believe we're in a situation where, you know, a transfer of power is not -- I can't believe we are in this situation here. It just seems so petty." Anderson Cooper has cornered the market on pettiness. This came after he strangely apologized for calling the president "an obese turtle on his back flailing in the hot sun." This showed his capacity for insincerity.

Newt Gingrich Responds Perfectly When Pressed Over Claim that 2020 Election Was 'Stolen'

Matt Vespa

But this kind of inflammatory fare just keeps churning on CNN. Morning anchor John Berman carped on Nov. 9 that the Republicans were still enabling Trump: "They're treating him like a petulant child. ... They hope he wears himself out." The next day, Berman complained that the GOP wasn't accepting Biden's call for unity: "The response from the outgoing president? No. The response from the administration? Hell no. The response from Republican leaders in Congress? F no."

CNN should expect hostility toward the call for unity, because hyperbolic abuse has come out of the network for years. There will be no unity, because there is not one ounce of regret from CNN. You cannot spend four years with people such as Don Lemon denouncing Trump fans as "people who will lie, steal and cheat, lie to their own mother, lie to themselves" and expect unity. CNN's own continued abuse in between the "unity" commercials should underline why their Xeroxed Biden message is preposterous.

Tim Graham is director of media analysis at the Media Research Center and executive editor of the blog NewsBusters.org.

Joe Biden's Majority Doesn't Work Full Time, Stay Married or Go To Church

Terry Jeffrey

Joe Biden's Majority Doesn't Work Full Time, Stay Married or Go To Church

A week after the 2020 presidential election, one thing is obvious about the United States of America: It is deeply divided.

With 148 million votes counted, President Donald Trump trailed former Vice President Joe Biden by about 4.7 million votes. But, according to the exit polls, there were some demographic groups that did pick Trump over Biden.

Who were they?

For starters, according to the network exit poll published by ABC News, there was the divide between people who worked full time and those who did not. The exit poll asked the question: "Do you work full-time for pay?"

Voters who said no went for Biden over Trump by 57% to 42%. By contrast, voters who said they did work full time picked Trump over Biden 51% to 47%. Why do people who don't work full time

prefer Biden? Why do those who do prefer Trump? Is it a good sign for the long-term well-being of the United States that the popular-vote winner in our presidential election was preferred by those who do not work full time and not by those who do?

Then there was the divide between married and unmarried people. The exit poll asked voters: "Are you currently married?" People who said they are not "currently" married voted overwhelmingly for Biden. He won 58% of their vote, while Trump won only 40%. Meanwhile, Trump won 53% of married voters, while Biden won only 46%.

It did not matter whether the married person was a male or female. A majority of both husbands and wives voted for Trump over Biden. Trump beat Biden 55% to 44% among married men and 51% to 47% among married women. Why did the majority of married voters -- both male and female -- not want Biden to be president?

Then there was the massive gap between those who practice a religion and those who do not.

The Associated Press VoteCast survey interviewed about 140,000 voters on Election Day and the days leading up to it. It asked "how often ... if at all" a person attends church or religious services. The result: The more often a voter attends church or religious services, the more likely they were to vote for Trump.

In fact, Biden only won majorities among voters who said they rarely or never attend church or religious services.

Among voters who attend church or religious services once a week or more, Trump won 61% to 37%. Among those who attend a few times a month, Trump won 54% to 45%. Among those who attend about once a month, Trump also won 54% to 45%. Among voters who only attend church or religious services a "few times a year or less," Biden won 52% to 47%.

Among voters who said they "never" go to church, Biden beat Trump 63% to 35%. Based on these polls -- and looked at purely from a political perspective -- there are certain cultural trends in the United States that would be good for Republicans and bad for Democrats (and vice versa).

FOX NEWS IS NOW THE MOST CORRUPT CONSPIRATORIAL FAKE NEWS; WHEN OUR SIDE BECOMES CONVINCING SHOWING AIRTIGHT; ABSOLUTE & POSITIVE EVIDENCE; FOX NEWS SMUG LITTLE CLITORIS MOUTHPIECE CALLS BIDEN PRESIDENT-ELECT; CUTS AWAY; IGNORING OUR TRUTH WITH THEIR ALL-PURPOSE DEBUNKED NO EVIDENCE; CALLING OUR OBVIOUS TRUTH ABOUT DEMOCRAT STEALING THE WHITE HOUSE FALSEHOODS. THIS IS A FOX STOLEN ELECTION

Fox News cuts away from Kayleigh McEnany's speech on allegations of voter fraud

Host Neil Cavuto said 'unless she has more details to back that up, I can't in good countenance continue showing you this'

Fox News host Neil Cavuto interrupted the network's live feed of a Trump campaign speech from White House press secretary Kayleigh McEnany on Monday, telling viewers he could not "in good countenance continue showing" it due to her allegations of voter fraud in the contested election between President Donald Trump and former Vice President Joe Biden.

What are the details?

McEnany, who was joined by Republican National Committee chairwoman Ronna McDaniel, explained that she was attending in her "personal capacity" as an adviser to the Trump campaign before saying, "This election is not over. Far from it. We have only begun the process of obtaining an accurate, honest vote count."

"We are fighting for the rights of all Americans who want to have faith and confidence not only in this election, but in any elections to come," she said. "There is only one party in America that opposes voter I.D. One party in America that opposes verifying signatures, citizenship, residency, eligibility. There is only one party in America trying to keep observers out of the count room. And that party, my friends, is the Democrat party. "You don't take these positions because you want an honest election," McEnany continued. "You don't oppose an audit of the vote because you want an accurate count. You don't oppose our efforts at sunlight and transparency because you have nothing to hide. You take these positions because you are welcoming fraud, and you are welcoming illegal voting." McEnany added, "We want every legal vote to be counted, and we want every illegal vote to be discarded." With that, Cavuto pulled the plug, saying, "Whoa, whoa, whoa, I just think we have to be very clear." "She's charging the other side as welcoming fraud and welcoming illegal voting," the Fox News host said. "Unless she has more details to back that up, I can't in good countenance continue showing you this. I want to make sure that maybe they do have something to back that up, but that's an explosive charge to make that the other side is effectively rigging and cheating."

Fox News cuts away from the Trump campaign press conference with Neil Cavuto saying that they "can't in good counter... **You may watch McEnany and McDaniels' speeches in their entirety below, beginning at the 13:30 mark:**

Anything else?

Fox News has faced backlash from some Trump supporters who are angered that the outlet was the first to call the state of Arizona for Biden following Election Day last week, despite hundreds of thousands of votes remaining to be counted. The Trump campaign has filed lawsuits in numerous states amid accusations of voting irregularities, while all major U.S. news networks, including Fox News, declared over the weekend that Biden is the projected winner of the race. Trump-Pence 2020 general counsel Matt Morgan argued in a statement **that "the president is on course to win Arizona outright, despite the irresponsible and erroneous 'calling' of the state for Biden by Fox News and the Associated Press."**

AZ Secretary of State's History of Disdain for Trump and His Supporters: 'So Much Deplorable at Trump Rallies' THIS PROBABLE BITCH HIDEOUS UGLY BITCH SKANK ALPHA MALE HATING DISHRAG AT LEAST COMES RIGHT OUT & TELLS US 24/7/366 HOW & WHY SHE HATES OUR GUTS & EVERYTHING ABOUT US.

DISHRAG TYPICAL PROGRESSIVE LEFTIST LIBERAL UGLIER THAN DEATH SKANK ALPHA MALE HATING LESBIAN BITCH

HANNAH BLEAU

Arizona Secretary of State Katie Hobbs (D), who recently rejected a request for an "independent analysis" of voting data, has a history of expressing disdain for President Trump and his supporters, explicitly accusing the president of standing on the side of "the freaking Nazis" and once asserting that there is "so much deplorable at ".Trump's rallies

On Tuesday, Hobbs rejected a request from Arizona Senate President Karen Fann (R), who asked for an "independent analysis" of voting data to restore confidence among Arizonians. Hobbs promptly dismissed the request, asserting that there is "no 'current controversy' regarding elections in Arizona, outside of theories floated by those seeking to undermine our democratic process for political gain."

Hobbs wrote:

I respectfully decline your request to push aside the work that remains to be done to ensure an orderly completion of this election and instead launch and fund with taxpayer dollars a boundless "independent" evaluation of "all data related to the tabulation of votes in the 2020 General Election."

Her rejection comes as the vote count in the Grand Canyon State continues, with Trump gradually reducing Joe Biden's (D) lead. President Trump has said that he will "easily" win the state when an audit is completed. However, Hobbs is no ally of the president, and it remains unclear if her partisan disdain — which she openly displayed in the past — will have any bearing on her handling of the election in the state.

- **In September 2015, months after Trump announced his intention to run for president, she expressed disgust after witnessing individuals wearing Trump shirts at an airport. Trump Trails Biden by 11.6K in Arizona: 'If We Can Audit the Total Votes Cast, We Will Easily Win'**

Hannah Bleau

President Donald Trump trails former Vice President Joe Biden by fewer than 12,000 votes in battleground Arizo- .na but remains confident that he can "easily" win the state if officials conduct a statewide audit

Maricopa County's latest batch of results showed the president taking 53.4 percent of the 13,143 votes counted and Biden taking 44.3 percent, according to Data Orbital. Biden's lead stood at 11,635 as of Wednesday evening.

There are 24,738 ballots remaining, 6,715 of which are in Maricopa County. At this point, Trump would need to take 74 percent of the remaining ballots to overtake his Democrat challenger and secure the state's 11 electoral votes:However, Trump remains confident that he will "easily" win Arizona if a statewide audit is completed:

While some believe the state should go to a recount, it is very difficult to automatically trigger one in the Grand Canyon State. The margin of victory for races with over 25,000 ballots cast must be 200 or less or within "one-tenth of one percent of the number of votes cast for both such candidates or upon such measures or proposals":

Arizona Secretary of State Katie Hobbs (D), who once accused Trump of "pandering to his neo-nazi base," formally rejected a request for an "independent analysis" of voting data in the state, contending that it fuels baseless theories of those who are "seeking to undermine our democratic

process for political gain."

DEMOCRAT RAPIST FOX IN HENHOUSE DECLARES INCARNATION OF CHIEF JUSTICE SOLOMON SPLITTING OWNERSHIP OF BABY IN OLD TESTAMENT – 49.5 OF BABY FOR PAL JOEY & KAMIKAZE KAMALA; REST FOR GUNS & RELIGION DEPLORABLES Arizona Secretary of State Rejects 'Independent Analysis' of Voting Data, Says It Would Amplify Baseless Theories

Hannah Bleau

Arizona Secretary of State Katie Hobbs (D) rejected a request for an "independent analysis" of voting data in the state, concluding that it would simply amplify the voices of people who seek to "undermine our democratic pro- ".cess for political gain

"It is patently unreasonable to suggest that, despite there being zero credible evidence of any impropriety or widespread irregularities, election officials nonetheless have a responsibility to prove a negative," Hobbs wrote in response to Arizona Senate President Karen Fann (R), who requested an "independent analysis" of voting data to restore confidence and credibility among residents.

"To be clear, there is no 'current controversy' regarding elections in Arizona, outside of theories floated by those seeking to undermine our democratic process for political gain," Hobbs continued, adding that elected officials should "work to build, rather than damage, public confidence in our system" before formally denying the request:

I respectfully decline your request to push aside the work that remains to be done to ensure an orderly completion of this election and instead launch and fund with taxpayer dollars a boundless "independent" evaluation of "all data related to the tabulation of votes in the 2020 General Election."

The Prescott Republican made the request on Monday, contending that an independent analysis would "help to restore credibility and hopefully end the current controversy over fairness in the election process in Arizona" given the mounting concerns and suspicions of fraud and abuse.

"I am not claiming fraud was involved in Arizona's election, but we must do everything we can to satisfy Arizonans that the count was lawfully done," Fann added.

The state Senate leader has maintained that the request is reasonable, particularly if the allegations are, in fact, baseless as Hobbs assumes.

"If there's no factual basis on any of these things, then absolutely, let's put that to rest and show them that's not true," Fann said on Wednesday. "If there's something there that needs to be fixed, let's fix it."

Despite Hobbs' claims, there are concerns regarding the election in Arizona. Over the weekend, the Trump campaign and Republican National Committee (RNC) filed a lawsuit, alleging that in-person voters had ballots that were wrongfully rejected.

The lawsuit details cases in Maricopa County, Arizona, where eligible voters showed up on election day to cast their vote and subsequently had their ballot rejected. In one case, Mia Barcello said she marked her ballot at an Anthem, Arizona, polling site with an ink pen that permeated through the ballot. When the ballot was fed through a tabulation device, it was rejected, according to the lawsuit. Barcello said she was told to press a "green button labeled 'Cast' on the device but was not told that doing so "likely would cause her selections in all candidate races or ballot proposition affected by the putative overvote or other defect or irregularity to be automatically disqualified and not tabulated."

Joe Biden (D) led President Trump by 12,813 votes as of Tuesday evening. Roughly 46,700 remain.

Nolte: Corrupt Media Desperate to Close Books on Contested Election

Joe Biden is not "president-elect." Joe Biden has not won the 2020 presidential election. Donald Trump's re-election has not been defeated. Right now, Joe Biden is merely "ahead in the count" of enough states to win the presidency.

But this is a *contested election* and we have a long way to go, probably more than a month and a plethora of legal filings, before a winner is declared. Per our own Constitution, there is only one institution legally entitled to declare a winner in a presidential election, and that's the Electoral College, which does not meet until the middle of December.

Only the Electoral College can dub someone "president-elect." The fake news media, of course — the corporate media, the same corrupt media that told us to be patient if Election Day lasted weeks, now want us to forget all that, want to close the book on the election before it has been audited, want us to believe unelected liars who sit in anchor chairs have the legal authority to declare Joe Biden "president elect."

Well, they don't, and the state legislatures, the district and Supreme courts would be doing the

country a great disservice if they allowed themselves to be gaslighted into believing this election is over.

They must ignore the corrupt media and do their duty.

Of course, Democrats, most especially Joe Biden, are also trying to gaslight us into believing the election is over (along with Vichy Republicans), which is why Biden gave a premature victory speech on Saturday, and why he is already behaving like a president-elect.

What Biden is doing is un-American, anti-democratic, fascist, and fooling no one.

It's also not going to work because Donald Trump is still the president, Donald Trump does not give up, and Donald Trump cannot be intimidated or gaslighted by anything or anyone.

Overall, though, what we are seeing the media do, aside from dismiss the possibility of widespread voter fraud before anyone has had adequate time to make their case and produce evidence, is declare Joe Biden the winner even before the legal recounts and re-canvassings have taken place.

The bottom line is that the media want this election shut down before anyone has a chance to look into what happened, before anyone has a chance to even see if Biden did indeed win fair and square.

I think it goes without saying that if the shoe were on the other foot, the media would be preaching for patience, as they originally told us Deplorables to do. However this comes out, let's be sure to remember that the media had no interest in looking into voting irregularities and vote fraud, had no interest in looking into potential software glitches and fraud, had no interest in valid recounts.

No, it's worse than that…

The media are actively trying to block a fair and impartial look at what happened on election night, actively looking to suppress and dismiss evidence, even before it's presented; aggressively trying to shut down investigations, aggressively trying to stop even run-of-the-mill recounts and recanvasses.

The media are un-American, evil, and terrified of what might be uncovered.

Donald Trump is fearless and relentless.

I am in no way saying there is widespread voter fraud. I am in no way saying there's enough fraud to overturn the margins in enough states. We don't know.

But we damn sure had better find out.

What I am saying is that the 2020 election is far from over, far from settled, and no one should allow the media or Biden to gaslight you into believing different.

What I'm also saying is that we are not letting this go — not by a longshot.

Social worker faces 10 years in prison if convicted. LOVEY DUBBIE JULIUS & ETHEL ROSENBERG FRIED IN SING SING FOR LESS

Julius Rosenberg and Ethel Rosenberg were American citizens who were convicted of spying on behalf of the Soviet Union. **WHY NOT MARK ZUCKERBUCKS & PRISCILLA MOO GOO GAI PAN EGG ROLL CHAN $700 MILLION ZUCKERBUCKS PAID WHITE HOUSE TREASON MARXIST TOTALITARIAN NEW DEAL** **Death by** electric **chair** Criminal charge**: Conspiracy to commit** espionage STEALING U.S. PRESIDENCY FOR AMERICA HATING

KAMALA HARRIS MAKES ROSENBERG CRIME BENIGN BY COMPARISON

Children: Michael Meeropol; Robert Meeropol Resting place: Wellwood Cemetery, New York, U.S

Born: Julius; May 12, 1918; Manhattan, New York, U.S. Ethel; September 28, 1915; Manhattan, New York, U.S

CARLOS GARCIA

A social worker has been charged with 134 counts of voter fraud after investigators found that she allegedly submitted voter registration applications for residents who were ineligible to vote.

Texas Attorney General Ken Paxton said that his office's Election Fraud Unit investigated the charges against Kelly Reagan Brunner, a social worker at the Mexia State Supported Living Center.

Paxton said in a statement that Brunner submitted voter registration applications for 67 residents of the State Supported Living Center. But because the people being cared for in the facility have intellectual and developmental disabilities, they were unable to give consent for the voter registration.

"Under Texas law, only a parent, spouse or child who is a qualified voter of the county may act as an agent in registering a person to vote, after being appointed to do so by that person," explained Paxton.

"None of the SSLC patients gave effective consent to be registered, and a number of them have been declared totally mentally incapacitated by a court, thereby making them ineligible to vote in Texas," he added.

Brunner faces 10 years in prison if convicted for the charges.

"I strongly commend the Limestone County District Attorney's Office, Sheriff's Office, and Elections Office, as well as the Department of Health and Human Services Office of the Inspector General for their outstanding work on this case and their commitment to ensuring a free and fair Presidential election in the face of unprecedented voter fraud," Paxton continued.

"Registering citizens to vote or to obtain mail ballots without their consent is illegal. It is particularly offensive when individuals purport to be champions for disability rights, when in reality they are abusing our most vulnerable citizens in order to gain access to their ballots and amplify their own political voice," he added.

"My office is prepared to assist any Texas county in combating this insidious form of fraud," he concluded. Here's more about the charges of voter fraud:

WE AREN'T FIGHTING FOR DONALD J. TRUMP WE'RE FIGHTING FOR US

The Only Way Forward Is to Fight

Congressman Andy Biggs

The cold-blooded hateful back-stabbing DEMOCRAT BLACK MAMBA is ready to kill. Every tyrant needs quislings. Unfortunately, there are appeasers even among Republicans. The 'useful idiots' of the Left are being eaten already; the appeasers will be next.

Those who demand grace from Trump supporters as we watch the nation stolen from us, deny the peril from a ravenous beast that will consume our freedoms and chain the American people.

The piranhas are already nibbling at Nancy Pelosi, who is suffering from whiplash from the hard, left turn she took when she was reinstalled as Speaker of the House two years ago. She made a deal with the devil—"the squad" — in order to win her position. The fate of all authoritarians, who fail to control their helpers, is to be eaten by their own. Even now, the radical-left members among the House Democrats are coming after her.

Because of their firm commitment to dismantling our economy and determination to impose every dangerous idea of the Left, what they thought would be a blue wave of Democrat victories from the presidency to the Senate and the House, and across free America, was defeated.

Congressional Democrats who survived the election, who have the temerity to condemn their own radical narrative as the cause of their dismal performance, have been castigated and threatened by the *de facto* leader of the Democrats, the radical Alexandria Ocasio Cortez (AOC).

Republican appeasers, like the freedom-hating Lincoln Project, are aided by several members of Congress who fail to recognize the cliff that America is heading over. These modern Neville Chamberlain's have not learned the lesson of history: once the tyrants are let loose, they will continue to consume everyone in their path, including former friends. Choosing to be silent, or lurking in hiding, is merely choosing to be eaten later. As Churchill noted, an appeaser keeps feeding the totalitarian monster, hoping to be eaten last.

Don't believe that the PREDATORS really are serious about retribution? How about AOC's endorsement of the Trump Accountability Project designed to, "make sure anyone who took a paycheck to help Trump undermine America is held responsible for what they did."

This is what Communist dictators do. It is how North Korea's Kim Jong Un, Venezuela's Maduro, even Communist China's Mao, Deng, and current leader Xi Jinping control their un-free people. It is consistent with historical tyranny imposed by Lenin and Stalin.

The AOC's of the Left, are joined by crazed, attack dogs in the media like the odious Olbermann who wants the president arrested and removed from office. Olbermann, who has lately become even more delirious with hate, also wants to arrest Tucker Carlson and others who have exposed the Left or expressed support for Trump. And yet the propaganda arm of the new Left and Democrats continues to give a platform to spew hate and discord by this unhinged lunatic who advocates for violence against those with whom he disagrees.

In 2016, some Republicans decided that they would not support the president. Instead, they said, the kinder, more temperate Evan McMullin was deserving of their vote. The nutty McMullin, who previously said, "I oppose fascism and socialism because I believe in the innate liberty of humankind," apparently favors his own brand of tyranny which advocates that, "We should keep and , "We should keep and publish a list of everyone who assists Trump's frivolous and dangerous

May the irrelevant McMullin take his brand of public shaming "forever" with him to his quiet corner of despotic despair.

There really is no other choice but to fight to preserve our nation. While the Left is assiduously stealing the presidency (with the almost ironic twist that Republicans are gaining seats in Congress and around the country), we must not acquiesce to their efforts. We must have faith. We must have hope. We must have the courage necessary to fight.

If it takes peaceful protests, we must take to the streets with a quiet and resolved dignity that shows the difference between the thoughtful Right and the mindless Left.

If it takes litigation, our lawyers must be given the resources and support necessary to make the case.

It certainly will take communication to the American people. Communicate every way, through every mode. And when the Masters of the Tech Universe censor you, go around them.

We must urge legislators to confirm Trump's electors when there is demonstrable tampering of electoral outcomes by the vote thieves on the Left.

We must truly overwhelm the radicals on the Left with our American spirit and faith. Our voices united for freedom must be heard above the frenzied screams of the Left that seeks to destroy freedom.

Dems, Journalists Call For Trump Staffers to be Arrested for Crimes Against Humanity THIS IS FUCKEN WHO, HOW & WHAT THEY ARE. LET'S SECEDE & HAVE OUR OWN COUNTRY & DARE THIS OCTOPUS TO STOP US.

Rep. Alexandria Ocasio-Cortez, D-N.Y., received swift backlash on Twitter Friday after essentially telling vocal President Trump supporters that they could face punishment under a Biden administration.

"Is anyone archiving these Trump sycophants for when they try to downplay or deny their complicity in the future?" she asked. "I foresee decent probability of many deleted Tweets, writings, photos in the future. Lol at the "party of personal responsibility" being upset at the idea of being responsible for their behavior over the last four years."

You should take Democrats like Ocasio-Cortez very seriously, says best-selling author Todd Starnes. He wrote a book warning about what would happen if Democrats regained the White House. Click here to read "Culture Jihad: How to Stop the Left From Killing a Nation."

Slate wrote an editorial calling for the arrest of Trump advisor Stephen Miller. "But [Stephen Miller's] also a man. And like all men who commit crimes against humanity, he should be imprisoned by the society he wounded, forever prevented from spreading his pestilence and fear. In a just world, this reckoning would happen right on Jan. 21," Slate wrote.

***Washington Post* staffers are also jumping on board. Columnist Jennifer Rubin is calling for anyone associated with the Trump administration to be blacklisted from holding a job and ostracized from "polite society."**

"Any R[epublican] now promoting rejection of an election or calling to not to follow the will of voters or making baseless allegations of fraud should never serve in office, join a corporate board, find a faculty position or be accepted into 'polite' society," she tweeted**, adding, "We have a list."**

EDITOR'S NOTE: Social media is cracking down on Conservative content. Many of you have complained that you never see our content in your news feeds. There's only one way to fight back — and that's by subscribing to my FREE weekly newsletter. Click here.

Her remarks were widely condemned on social media and a reminder to many of who will be in charge of a Joe Biden White House. The post played well for her small base, but Biden's struggle in the minority vote nationwide showed her national influence ends at the Brooklyn-Queens Expressway.

TODD STARNES: WE ARE WATCHING A SLOW-MOVING COUP IT'S ACTUALLY A BLITZKRIEG LIGHTNING STRIKE

James Woods, the outspoken conservative actor, asked her if she is "literally making lists.

"I understand you're an ignorant nitwit who's never had a passing acquaintance with a history book, but political lists are EXACTLY what Communists do. Lenin, Stalin, Pol Pot, Castro. So put me at the top of your list, you moron. I'd be honored.

Emily Abrams, who identified herself on Twitter as a worker for the Pete Buttigieg campaign, also tweeted that "we're launching the Trump Accountability Project to make sure anyone who took a paycheck to help Trump undermine America is held responsible for what they did."

Hermeet K. Dhillon, the lawyer and Republican Party official, responded, "Fascist Friday! I didn't take a paycheck—I write checks—but feel free to include me on your psycho McCarthyism grift project." Conservatives have long held that Biden is merely a Potemkin candidate and the real power behind his presidency would be Sen. Kamala Harris, his running mate, and the likes of Ocasio-Cortez and her Squad. The Squad are masters at cancel culture and Ocasio-Cortez just proved that they have no desire of bringing the country together. They are looking to take names and want to, not only defeat Trump, but defeat his supporters for generations

Trump has not conceded and has vowed to fight the election results due to allegations of widespread voter fraud in swing states. Rep. Jim Jordan, R-Ohio, told Fox News on Friday night that this is the first election in the country's history where a political party—the Democrats—set out to win an election after the election.

"And it has to be stopped," he said.

Jonathan Turley: 'No Reason Not to' Investigate BECAUSE THE LEFT IS SHOPLIFTING OUR NATION

As President Donald Trump's campaign has filed lawsuits in multiple states over claims of voter fraud in the 2020 election, George Washington University Law School Professor Jonathan Turley on Monday said there is "no reason not to look into

Turley, during FNC's "Fox & Friends," pointed out the oddity of people claiming there was no fraud taking place as ballots are still being counted. He advised that the United States has had electoral problems in the past, so there should be an investigation — even though he acknowledged it is not likely that anything overturns the election results.

"You know, it was an odd thing to have so many people coming out and saying, look, there is no case to be made here," Turley stated. "We're still in the tabulation stage. You know, the information that would reflect a systemic problem or large numbers of balloting errors would come at the next stage, at the canvassing stage. Most of this information is held by election officials. And it often takes a court order to get that information to the opposing party."

He later added, "The odds dramatically favor Vice President Biden, but what I don't understand is how so many people want these challenges to end and for there to be just simply a concession. We

have had electoral problems in this country. In 1960, the outcome of that election is still believed to have been fraudulent. You know, in Illinois in Texas there were a lot of fraudulent votes that put Kennedy over the top against Richard Nixon. In 2000, people still believe we didn't take enough time in Florida and that Al Gore may have won Florida and won the presidency. So, there is no reason not to look at the allegations, to give 71 million people who voted for Trump that sense of assurance that nothing untoward occurred and that their votes really did count. Now, can they really overcome these margins? Probably not, but we don't know what we're talking about.

Judge Blocks Republican's Attempt To Change Ballot Signature Verification In Nevada

JAKE DIMA

A Nevada judge denied a state Republican Party's request to amend the signature verification procedure on ballots Friday, as the battleground state has yet to release their full voting totals.

District Court Judge Andrew Gordon denied the motion set forth by two GOP candidates in the state and said the change in the process would disrupt "the counting of the ballots," according to Fox News.

"I don't find plaintiffs have demonstrated a likelihood of success on the merits of the plaintiffs' claims," Gordon said, according to Fox. "The public interest is not in disrupting the counting of the

ballots." Nevada Republicans sought a recount of only mail-in ballots, but Democratic lawmakers insisted the move would cause "chaos and confusion," Fox reported. "The whole country is looking at Nevada and Clark County for election results," a Democratic lawyer said, according to Fox.

President Donald Trump's administration filed a separate lawsuit in the battleground state to stop the counting of "illegal votes," Fox reported. Trump alleged that a number of voters in the state were either deceased or non-residents, according to the outlet. (RELATED: Joe Biden Beats Out Trump In Nevada) "We are confident that when all legal votes are tallied — and only legal votes are tallied — President Trump will win the state of Nevada," a Trump administration official who announced the lawsuit told Fox.

"We are confident that when all legal votes are tallied — and only legal votes are tallied — President Trump will win the state of Nevada," a Trump administration official who announced the lawsuit told Fox. Democratic nominee Joe Biden, who has been declared the winner of the election, leads Trump 49.9% to 47.9% in Nevada with 94% of the total votes in play, according to the New York Times

Wisconsin Assembly Speaker Directs Committee To Investigate Election

KIMBERLY EADE

Wisconsin Republican Assembly Speaker Robin Vos instructed a review of the state's election results following concerns about mail-in ballots and voter fraud, according to Wisconsin State Journal.

Wisconsin concluded an unofficial count of the 2020 election earlier this week, putting Joe Biden at only 20,000 votes in the lead, the Wisconsin State Journal reported. The Associated Press and Fox News were among several news media to call the election Saturday for Biden, but President Donald Trump has yet to concede citing recounts and ongoing litigation. Vos constructed a team to analyze if the election was administered legally. Votes in Wisconsin must go through three different levels of certification, according to Fox6 News Milwaukee. Meanwhile, Wisconsin clerks are currently in the process of reviewing all results in the state. (RELATED: Fact Check: Viral Image Falsely Claims Wisconsin Had More Votes Cast Than Registered Voters)

"I am directing the committee to use its investigatory powers under Wisconsin SS 13.31 to immediately review how the election was administered," Vos said in a statement reported by CBS 58. "With concerns surfacing about mail-In ballot dumps and voter fraud, Wisconsin citizens deserve to know their vote counted. There should be no question as to whether the vote was fair and legitimate, and there must be absolute certainty that the impending recount finds any and all irregularities."

Milwaukee, Wisconsin / USA

The Republican Party of Milwaukee County held a DEFEND YOUR VOTE RALLY after it was announced that the Biden/ Harris ticket had won the 2020 election.

Trump said in a statement Sunday that "this election is far from over."

"Joe Biden has not been certified as the winner of any states, let alone any of the highly contested states headed for mandatory recounts, or states where our campaign has valid and legitimate legal challenges that could determine the ultimate victor," he said. CBS 58 stated reported that "concerns of 'mail-In ballot dumps and voter fraud' are unfounded" in Wisconsin. THE MEDIA IS THE WAFFEN SS GESTAPO THAT HATES OUR GUTS. NO MERCY. NO PRISONERS.

Trump Campaign: Evidence of Fraud in Wisconsin

Supporters of President Donald Trump react at a rally after it was announced that Joe Biden defeated President Trump Saturday, Nov. 7, 2020, in Milwaukee. (AP Photo/Morry Gash)

By Brian Freeman

Ballot data in Milwaukee indicates illegal activity by Democrats to such an extent that it could change the vote in Wisconsin, a member of President Donald Trump's reelection team told the Washington Examiner on Monday. Biden's advantage in the state is approximately 20,500 votes, but two Trump campaign officials said there are enough irregularities to flip Wisconsin to the president, which would dramatically change the entire race.

A source said the distribution of the ballots in support of Biden violates Benford's Law, an analytical framework used by experts when viewing a set of randomized data points.Although some statisticians question the applicability of the Benford Law, an adviser to the Trump campaign said there are indications of an artificial distribution of votes in favor of Biden.

"If there's fire where there's smoke, it'll come out during the recount," he said. Last week, Wisconsin Assembly Speaker Robin Vos called for a comprehensive review of the state's elections processes. Trump deputy campaign manager Justin Clark emphasized that "We've already announced that we're going to seek a statewide recount in Wisconsin, and we plan to do so. We expect that the canvass, the initial canvass will be done Monday or Tuesday. And then that process will begin." However, former Wisconsin Gov. Scott Walker, a Republican and informal adviser to the Trump campaign, said he doubts the president could end up carrying the state, writing in a tweet that 20,000 votes is a high hurdle, citing that in a "recount in 2011 race for WI Supreme Court, there was a swing of 300 votes. After recount in 2016 Presidential race in WI, [Trump›s] numbers went up by 131." Trump›s Election Lawsuits Could Stretch Month or MoreHarlan Hill: 89 Percent Turnout in Wisconsin 'a Bit Unbelievable 'Timmerman:

Computer 'Glitch' Made Joe Biden President

Members of the Gwinnett County, Georgia, adjudication review panel look over remaining scanned ballots at the elections office Sunday

By Kenneth R. Timmerman

Gizzi: More Than 80,000 Ballots Could Be Recounted in Ga.'s Gwinnett County

THE RECOUNT BECAME A FIXED FRAUD. MOST ELECTION WORKERS IN DISPUTED VOTE BIG CITY SWING STATES, LIKE MILWAUKEE; ATLANTA & PHILADELPHIA; ARE BLACK DEMOCRATS. CALL IT WHATEVER THE FUCK YOU WANT; INCLUDING RACE CARD ITS FUCKEN TRUE.

A Gwinnett county voter casts a ballot at Lucky Shoals Park polling station on November 3, 2020 in Norcross, Georgia.

By John Gizzi

Many of the national networks are now poised to call Georgia for Joe Biden based on his wafer-thin lead — roughly 10,353 votes out of 5 million cast.

But in so doing, they are overlooking the ominous and possibly game-changing fact that at least 80,000 votes cast in populous Gwinnett County (suburban Atlanta) need to be rerun, recounted, and possibly readjudicated. Put another way, the rerunning of the Gwinnett ballots could easily determine who won the Peach State's 16 electoral votes.

According to a spokesman for Gwinnett County, when officials began to push through the scanner a round of batches of votes — nearly 3,200 batches with each containing up to 25 ballots — they would not push through because the software showed the process of adjudication was needed.

Adjudication is the process of resolving ballots whose markings are in question. "Absentee ballots are filled out by hand, and if a ballot is marked clearly, it will run through the scanner without a problem," County Communications Director Joe Sorenson explained to WXIA-TV in Atlanta. "If there's a problem with how the ballot was filled out — for example, a voter placed a check mark instead of filling in the circle, didn't completely fill in the circle, or voted for more candidates than allowed in a race — the scanning software will send the ballot to the adjudication module."

Sorenson warned that as a result, as many as 80,000 of these votes need to be rerun and readjudicated, the vote counts reported on TV networks could fluctuate and be incomplete. "This is why the results on election night are always labeled unofficial and incomplete," he said.

Dick Morris to Newsmax TV: GOP Tracking 27K Suspicious Votes in Georgia

By Brian Trusdell

Former Democratic strategist and White House adviser Dick Morris told Newsmax TV on Tuesday that President Donald Trump, the Republican Party and its allies have identified 27,000 people over the age of 90 who have voted in Georgia, more than twice the reported lead Democrat Joe Biden has in the Peach State.

Dick Morris to Newsmax TV: Georgia 'Conspiracy' Not 'Happenstance'

By Eric Mack

Democrat operative Stacey Abrams' contested gubernatorial loss in 2018 set the wheels of election

"conspiracy" into motion, according to presidential political strategist Dick Morris on Newsmax TV.

"The absence of signature verification is not happenstance," Morris told host Rob Schmitt on Saturday night. "It shows the depth and the length of this conspiracy. Stacey Abrams' 2018 challenge to her gubernatorial loss she never conceded wound up having the state of Georgia "signing a consent decree, promising to never to do signature verification again, which Abrams claimed was part of a suppression of the vote strategy," according to Morris.

"As a result, they legally are not allowed to see if the votes are illegal."

President Donald Trump's election challenge's legal hurdles have been more of a roller coaster, Morris added.

"I was optimistic, then I was not, and now I am again," Morris concluded. "The vote counting itself is one dimension, and that's good. I think we can break through some of these barriers and start getting some votes for Trump and might even flip Georgia and Wisconsin. Arizona is more difficult, because they won't let us recount."

"But the Dominion scandal is acquiring legs on its own," he added, referring to Dominion Election System software used in a number of states, including Georgia and Michigan. "This is the idea of the Chinese communists really meddling in our election big time – not a few posts on social media like Russia did – but actually jimmying and cooking the count."

Jenna Ellis to Newsmax TV: States Must Audit Dominion Machines

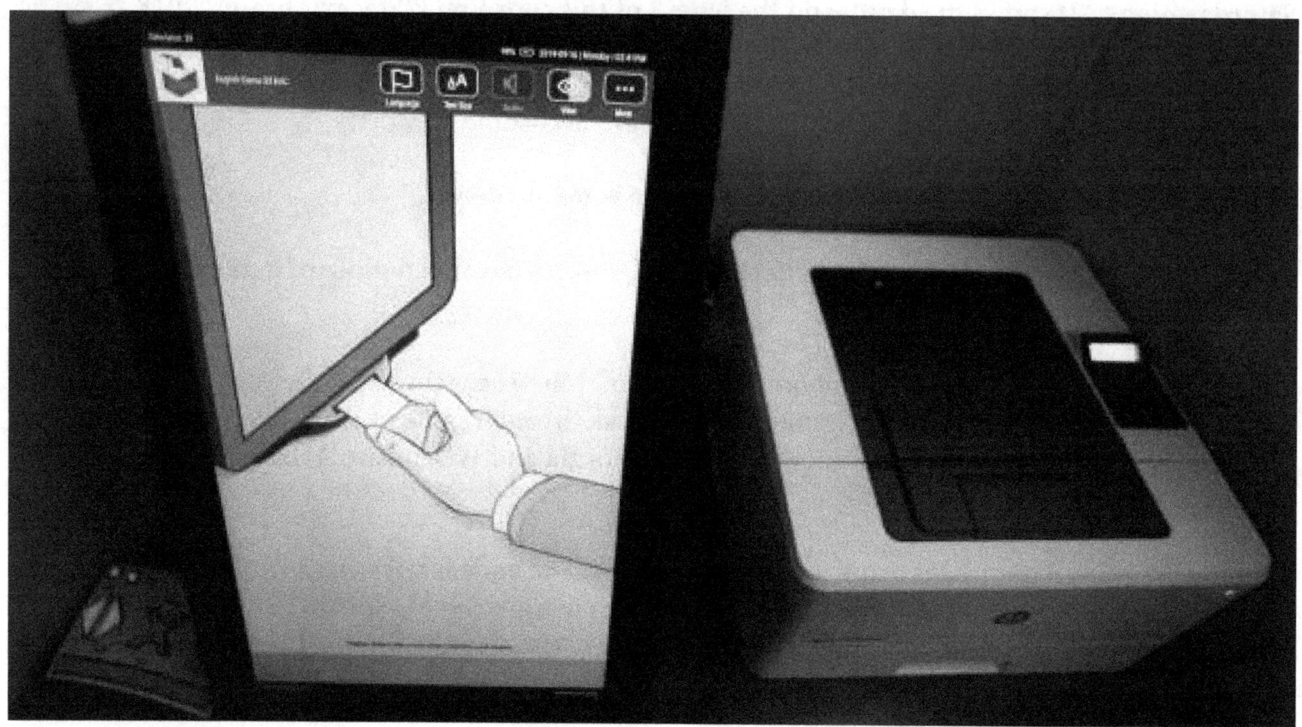

A Dominion Voting Systems machine used in Georgia as seen in 2019.

By Sandy Fitzgerald

States can't certify their elections without an audit being done of the Dominion Voting Systems machines, and that tally could affect at least 29 states, Jenna Ellis, senior advisor for the Trump campaign, told Newsmax TV Saturday.

"We need to have an audit of this, and this is something that of course is going to change the national outcome of the election," Ellis told Newsmax TV's Rob Schmidtt. "What we're seeing is a really, really significant challenge."

There are some who are saying that the difference is fewer than 10,000 or so votes that could be affected, said Ellis, but they are not seeing what Rudy Giuliani, who is running the Trump campaign's legal defense efforts are seeing.

She added that the Trump Team for Election Integrity is seeing that the machines used through Dominion were able to alter ballots and take away votes, and "this isn't a system glitch."

"It's a feature where they're able to take votes that are cast for President Trump and change them to Joe Biden," Ellis said of the machines coming from Dominion, which was founded in Venezuela. "They're able to then also add ballots, and count ballots multiple times. This is a feature."

This means an audit must be conducted of the systems and their software, Ellis said. "This is the nationwide scandal," said Ellis. "Dominion Voting Systems is absolutely corrupt, and so we absolutely are not out of this yet, so that's what our legal team is working on with the strategy."

States can't certify their results without an audit, she added, but "they're trying to just make us rush through this process. This has been about a week and a half and we have to a thorough investigation and make sure that states do not certify their results until they are fair and accurate."

Ellis added that Pennsylvania's election can't be called because ballots there are "spoiled" because it's not known if they have been manipulated, as once ballots and their envelopes are separated, they can't be put back together.

"They have denied meaningful access and when election officials and secretaries of state are telling their people on the ground that they are not following the law, they can't do that and so that is an equal protection violation," Ellis said.

Corey Lewandowski to Newsmax TV: Philly Engaged in Witness 'Intimidation'

By Eric Mack

Levying explosive claims of ballot witness intimidation by key Philadelphia officials, Trump campaign senior adviser Corey Lewandowski on Newsmax TV rebuked the illegal actions of the "tolerant left."

"I know we have the law on our side," Lewandowski told Saturday's "Michelle Malkin: Sovereign Nation." "But many, many people who were there to witness the process, were intimidated and maligned and attacked and verbally assaulted. "Look, that's the tolerant left as I call it, Michelle. As soon as you don't agree with them, all they want to do is attack you and physically harm you.

"You don't see that on the other side."

The board of elections supervisor, the sheriff of the county, and the deputy chief of police of the city of Philadelphia all threatened him, kept him from meaningful observation, and ultimately left him on a illegal do-not-enter list, Lewandowski said.

"All three summarily dismissed that court order, said that if I crossed the line that I would be

arrested if I violated the rules – now, I had a court order," Lewandowski said.

"The death threats and the threats of violence against me and the members of the team who are in Philadelphia – and candidly across the country – should never be tolerated," he continued.

"But, because they are a one-party rule in the city of Philadelphia, there's no recourse for that."

Lewandowski, author of "Trump: America First: The President Succeeds Against All Odds," said there should have been "nothing to hide."

- "It's shameful in this country – look, all we want is a free and fair and open election," Lewandowski concluded. "All we want to do is be able to observe the counting of the ballots. Joe Biden went against his own word on declaring victory before election results were certified, then anointed himself a unifying force.

- ## Newsmax TV 'Focus Group': Everyone Sees 'Stolen Election'

- Joe Biden went against his own word on declaring victory before election results were certified, then anointed himself a unifying force.

- But, apparently, everyone disagrees with him.

- Mark Halperin asked a panel on Newsmax TV's "Focus Group," once their candidate officially is declared the loser of the presidential election by a constitutional process, would they feel as if the election was stolen from their candidate.

- Every one of the panelists, 50% percent supporting President Donald Trump and 50% supporting Joe Biden, raised their hand.

- So much for unity, Halperin noted.

- "So what have we learned?" Halperin concluded. "I think the most striking thing – again not a surprise, but perhaps the most striking – is the supporters of Biden and the supporters of Trump all said, if their candidate is not named the winner, they believe the election would have been stolen.

- "That does not bode well for the coming days as the country tries to unify around whoever is declared the winner."

But, apparently, everyone disagrees with him.

Mark Halperin asked a panel on Newsmax TV's "Focus Group," once their candidate officially is declared the loser of the presidential election by a constitutional process, would they feel as if the

election was stolen from their candidate.

Every one of the panelists, 50% percent supporting President Donald Trump and 50% supporting Joe Biden, raised their hand.

So much for unity, Halperin noted.

"So what have we learned?" Halperin concluded. "I think the most striking thing – again not a surprise, but perhaps the most striking – is the supporters of Biden and the supporters of Trump all said, if their candidate is not named the winner, they believe the election would have been stolen.

"That does not bode well for the coming days as the country tries to unify around whoever is declared the winner." "If you have nothing to hide, why wouldn't you let us in to do that?" Newsmax TV 'Focus Group': Everyone Sees 'Stolen Election'

Jenna Ellis to Newsmax TV: Trump Seeks Constitutionally 'Legitimate Winner'

By Eric Mack

President Donald Trump is "very committed to protect free and fair elections," not merely using courts to overturn the will of the American people, according to Trump campaign legal adviser Jenna Ellis on Newsmax TV.

"We want to make sure to not have any of the results certified in any of the states before we know that they are legitimate results, and if we can't get to that result, then we have to make sure to challenge that and ask the court to provide a meaningful remedy," Ellis told Saturday's "America Right Now**."**

Among the most noteworthy challenges is with regard to Dominion Voting Systems, which remains one of the focuses of the legal team's scrutiny of the election results, she told host Tom Basile.

"The Constitution provides for these alternatives, when you have an election that is compromised – whether it's on one local level or it's nationally – and the American people need to understand that our founders were so brilliant that they anticipated there may be corruption, there may be fraud, and they have different mechanisms that are embedded in the Constitution to provide for these

different instances and to make sure that the people are not disenfranchised," Ellis said.

"And so we are just following the process. We are following the Constitution. And I think with Mayor [Rudy] Giuliani now in charge of this, you're going to see that there is a lot of cohesiveness. That our team is absolutely together on this."

The electoral college vote on Dec. 14 remains the most important date of the presidential election process, as prescribed by the Constitution. As constitutional law expert Alan Dershowitz noted earlier on Newsmax TV's "Saturday Report," an election still contested on that date might ultimately hand the election over to the House state delegations – a majority held by Republicans 26-23-1.

"The mainstream media is rushing to coronate Joe Biden," Ellis said. "They're trying discount all of our very significant legal challenges. "They don't want the truth to come out, because they want Joe Biden to be president regardless of whether or not he actually earned that. That's not the fault of the Trump campaign, and we are trying to get the truth out there.

"That's the fault of the mainstream media and the fake news rushing to judgment."

Ellis, signaling the direction of the Trump campaign objective, said it remains resolute to find the "legitimate winner" of the election, not to overturn the will of the American people.

"The point is not about changing the outcome of the election, and I wanted to be very clear about that," Ellis said. "This is about making sure every legal vote is counted and counted fairly. If that impacts the outcome, then certainly that's a major issue.

"But the point that everyone should be made very clear on is: Whoever is declared the winner is in fact the legitimate winner."

"The goal here is not campaigning," she concluded. "The goal here is to make sure that every legal vote is counted and counted accurately."

Trump: Georgia's Election Recount a 'Waste of Time'

By Sandy Fitzgerald

President Donald Trump Saturday declared Georgia's recount process a "waste of time" and claimed officials won't allow his campaign's observers to be in the counting rooms.

"The hand recount taking place in Georgia is a waste of time. They are not showing the matching signatures," Trump tweeted. "Call off the recount until they allow the MATCH. Don't let the Radical Left Dems STEAL THE ELECTION!"

He added in a subsequent tweet that "They wouldn't let our Poll Watchers and Observers into the Counting Rooms. We win on that alone!" Twitter flagged both of Trump's tweets, adding a label saying the claims about election fraud are disputed. Trump earlier Saturday lamented that Democrat operative Stacey Abrams effectively placed a preemptive block of signature verification on ballots in Georgia's hand recount. Georgia Secretary of State Brad Raffensperger, a Republican, announced the recount on Wednesday. Presumptive president-elect Joe Biden holds a slim lead of just over 14,000 votes over Trump. He has been projected by several news outlets as

having won Georgia, reports The Hill.

Several Republicans have slammed Raffensperger over how he handled the election, with Georgia Sens. Kelly Loeffler and David Perdue demanding his resignation claims he failed to "deliver an honest election." Georgia Gov. Brian Kemp said the election should be a "wakeup call" to Raffensperger's office, while several state House members called on the secretary to review the Trump campaign's claims of voter fraud. Georgia's recount must be finished by Nov. 20, when the state is to certify its results.

Trump Laments Georgia Recount's Signature Verification Block

By Eric Mack

SAME HITLER & HUGO CHAZEZ ELECTION THEFT

Georgia Democrat operative Stacey Abrams effectively placed a preemptive block of signature verification on ballots in Georgia's hand recount, President Donald Trump lamented Saturday.

THIS IS A FEDERAL FRAUD ELECTION FELONY ALL CRIME INCLUDING 1ST DEGREE PREMEDITATED MURDER IS

LEGAL UNLESS PROSECUTED

"The Consent Decree signed by the Georgia Secretary of State, with the approval of Governor @ BrianKempGA, at the urging of @staceyabrams, makes it impossible to check & match signatures on ballots and envelopes, etc.!" They knew they were going to cheat. Must expose real signatures

Continuing in an ensuing tweet:

"....What are they trying to hide. They know, and so does everyone else. EXPOSE THE CRIME!"

Abrams is credited with a massive grassroots campaign to help Joe Biden pickup hundreds of thousands of votes in Georgia, registering new Democratic voters. Former national security adviser Susan Rice tweeted Nov. 4: **"Either way this goes in Georgia, we owe @staceyabrams our greatest gratitude and respect. Rarely does one person deserve such disproportionate credit for major progress and change."**

Rep. Doug Collins, R-Ga., is working for Trump, his campaign, and the Republican National Committee to challenge the hand recount in Georgia, having already called out GOP Gov. Kemp and GOP Secretary of State Brad Raffensperger. "One of the things we have got to start talking about is the fact in Georgia you have several problems," Collins told Newsmax TV**'s "**John Bachman Now**" on Friday. "No. 1 is that you don't have voter ID on the actual absentee ballot itself, so once its separated from the envelope, you don't know where that vote is, whether it was a valid or invalid, or if it gets put into the system, then you can't trace it because no voter ID on it.**

"No. 2: we gave away the signature verifications in many ways when the secretary of state put together a consent decree with the Democrats, Stacey Abrams' group, that really, in essence, gutted our verification process. That's also got to be readdressed as well."

Biden's 'I'm no Trump' campaign is not enough to govern

By Red Jahncke,

"The Only Good Thing About Donald Trump Is All His Policies."

THE ONLY GOOD THING ABOUT BIDEN IS NOTHING. IT'S IMPOSSIBLE TO BE WORSE & MORE EVIL THAN HIM

So proclaimed an opinion column headline in 2018. The converse might be said of President-elect Joe Biden. He may be likable but he offered little vision and said nothing about policy in his Saturday-night victory speech — nor much during his entire campaign.

Biden, so far, is defined by who he is not: Donald Trump.

Biden's election is notable for several things. The much-anticipated "blue wave" did not materialize; there were razor-thin margins in several battleground states that were projected to be cakewalks for

Biden. The most remarkable thing was the vacuousness of Biden's platform; his message consisted almost exclusively of a still-life image of safe sequester in a well-disclosed secure basement location.

Biden claims a mandate, but his prime raison d'etre will depart 1700 Pennsylvania Ave. on Jan. 20. Then what?

Organizing a coronavirus task force **is not a policy, nor is** mask-wearing**. The coronavirus is spiking across the entire Western world with little variation by differences in government policy. It will continue untamed until the arrival of an effective vaccine. Trump pursued a fast-track vaccine policy,** Operation Warp Speed**, which took a process that normally runs in sequence — first, vaccine development; then, production and deployment — and runs the two stages in parallel. The administration encouraged and funded a broad field of vaccine candidates, with several now in late-stage clinical trials. It will be impossible for Biden to attach his name to this visionary strategy. Similarly, it will be difficult for Biden to unshackle himself from the rioting, looting and violence unleashed by his tolerating or ignoring ongoing street protests, many of which have been anything but peaceful. Amid charges of systemic racism and calls to "defund" the police, Biden and many Democrats have maligned and delegitimized law enforcement, with a consequential rise in crime and homicide rates.**

The problem, of course, is that violence and lawlessness beget more of the same. Maybe Biden thinks this will end with his election. Yet, the night after Election Day, protesters in Portland, Ore., carried one banner reading "The vote is over, The fight goes on**," and another, "**We don't want Biden. We want revenge**," emblazoned over the image of an AK-47. Democrat-run Portland in Democrat-run Oregon has been besieged by daily protests for more than five months. Trump offered repeatedly to send in the National Guard but was rebuffed by Oregon Democrats; Biden was silent. Now he owns severely alienated police forces across the land who voted almost unanimously for Trump.**

Biden's economic policy consists of massive trillion-dollar tax increases **to fund socialistic programs of free college, expanded government-financed health care, etc. Make no mistake, the replacement of private-sector activity with government programs is socialism, no matter how appealing government handouts may be to people struggling to afford college and health care. His energy policy is opaque, with vacillating positions on fracking and only nominal opposition to the** Green New Deal**.**

On foreign policy, we know far less about what Biden has promised to do, or will do, than we know about what Trump actually has done.

Trump confronted China and kept the world relatively at peace. There have been no disastrous interventional U.S. wars, as with George W. Bush, nor any premature troops withdrawals allowing the emergence of murderous caliphates like ISIS, as with Barack Obama **— not to mention any unenforced Obama-esque "**red lines**" or world apology tours.**

Trump reversed President Obama's hope-and-change agreements with sworn enemies such as Iran.

The first limit under Obama's 2015 Iran nuclear deal expires in just four years, most others in six years, and the remainder in just ten years. Over the last half-decade, the hoped-for change in Iran's behavior — renouncement of its sponsorship of terrorism — never materialized.

Nor did Trump continue Obama's participation in the Paris Accord on climate, which allows China to increase its greenhouse gas (GHG) emissions through 2030 — China, which produces about 40 percent of global GHGs. The U.S. produces just 20 percent and has been reducing its absolute amounts of GHG emissions for a decade, primarily by replacing coal with natural gas produced by fracking. Under the Paris Accord, the U.S. would be obligated to contribute yearly to the $100 billion that developed nations promised to underdeveloped countries — including, inexplicably, China. Biden, of course, wants to rejoin this agreement under which the U.S. subsidizes the world's biggest polluter and our No. 1 rival on every stage.

- Bill Maher, Trump adviser Jenna Ellis spar over election results

- Sunday shows preview: Biden team gears up for transition, Trump legal...

Charitable Trump supporters will afford a President Biden a honeymoon period — not out of respect for the man but, rather, out of respect for fellow citizens who voted for him. Never mind that Democrats did not extend the same respect to Trump or his supporters, post-election or during the nearly four years of his administration.

But a Biden honeymoon may be short-lived, in part because Biden will govern without a mandate. Mandates go to candidates who win based upon compelling positions on important issues. Biden has expressed none.

Red Jahncke is president of Townsend Group International, a business consultancy headquartered in Connecticut. Follow him on Twitter @RedJahncke.

NY doctor slams Gov. Cuomo for doubting potential coronavirus vaccine touted by Trump

Dr. Qanta Ahmed tells 'Fox & Friends' that the governor's comments are 'disheartening'

By Caleb Parker

Cuomo's coronavirus vaccine doubt 'disheartening: Dr. Ahmed Andrew Cuomo

NY doctor slams Gov. Cuomo for doubting potential coronavirus vaccine touted by Trump

Cuomo's coronavirus vaccine doubt 'disheartening: Dr. Ahmed

Dr. Qanta Ahmed, New York pulmonologist, reacts to President Trump saying government won't deliver coronavirus vaccine to New York until Gov. Andrew Cuomo gives green light.

New York Gov. Andrew Cuomo's statements casting doubt on a potential coronavirus vaccine because he doesn't trust President Trump is "disheartening," a doctor who has treated critically ill COVID-19 patients in New York .City said Saturday

Trump, speaking in the Rose Garden Friday, said the government will delay delivery of the vaccine to New York ".until the Democratic governor commits to distributing it "immediately

Cuomo responded by calling Trump a "bully" and expressing confidence in a vaccine rollout managed by the incoming Biden administration.

TRUMP CALLS OUT CUOMO ON STUNTING VACCINE DISTRIBUTION DURING ROSE GARDEN SPEECH

"To hear this kind of politicking is very disheartening, but it's also a smear on Gov. Cuomo's own record," Dr. Qanta Ahmed, a pulmonologist, said on "Fox & Friends Weekend."

"He did extraordinary things at the height of the crisis, collaborating with the federal government and President Trump. ... He also had a very good idea doing geographical synchrony between Connecticut, New Jersey and New York," she said. "But right now we have 1,700 New Yorkers in hospitals. We lost 24 New Yorkers that died on Thursday. We have a rising prevalence rate."

CUOMO SAYS IT'S 'BAD NEWS' THAT PFIZER CORONAVIRUS VACCINE PROGRESS CAME DURING TRUMP ADMINISTRATION

NEW YORK DESERVES THIS LOATHSOME CRIME FAMILY MAFIOSI; WE (NEVER ME) ELECTED THIS MALIGNANT COCKROACH PARASITE (3) FUCKEN TIMES.

"This is not what we want to see and Gov. Cuomo did bring this upon himself by suggesting that

he would formulate his own advisory panel if the FDA approved or provided emergency use authorization to any vaccine product," Ahmed said.

As Pfizer and other companies are in final stages of getting coronavirus vaccines approved, Cuomo skipped White House briefings on distribution of the vaccines, the New York Post reports.

"I want this to be quickly rectified," Ahmed said of Cuomo's reluctance to use vaccines approved under Trump. "I want New Yorkers to have access to the vaccine as quickly as the rest of the United States, and it seems that the government of the United States is doing that and President Trump is making that possible," she said.

Trump tweeted Saturday that Cuomo needs to "stop playing politics" with the vaccine.

The New York Attorney General's Office released a statement saying they are prepared to sue the Trump administration should New York not receive the vaccination once it is released.

Dr. Qanta Ahmed, New York pulmonologist, reacts to President Trump saying government won't deliver coronavirus vaccine to New York until Gov. Andrew Cuomo gives green light.

New York Gov. Andrew Cuomo's statements casting doubt on a potential coronavirus vaccine because he doesn't trust President Trump is "disheartening," a doctor who has treated critically ill COVID-19 patients in New York City said Saturday. Trump, speaking in the Rose Garden Friday, said the government will delay delivery of the ".vaccine to New York until the Democratic governor commits to distributing it "immediately

Cuomo responded by calling Trump a "bully" and expressing confidence in a vaccine rollout managed by the incoming Biden administration.

TRUMP CALLS OUT CUOMO ON STUNTING VACCINE DISTRIBUTION DURING ROSE GARDEN SPEECH

"To hear this kind of politicking is very disheartening, but it's also a smear on Gov. Cuomo's own record," Dr. Qanta Ahmed, a pulmonologist, said on "Fox & Friends Weekend." "He did extraordinary things at the height of the crisis, collaborating with the federal government and President Trump. ... He also had a very good idea doing geographical synchrony between Connecticut, New Jersey and New York," she said. "But right now we have 1,700 New Yorkers in hospitals. We lost 24 New Yorkers that died on Thursday. We have a rising prevalence rate."

"This is not what we want to see and Gov. Cuomo did bring this upon himself by suggesting that he would formulate his own advisory panel if the FDA approved or provided emergency use authorization to any vaccine product," Ahmed said. As Pfizer and other companies are in final stages of getting coronavirus vaccines approved, Cuomo skipped White House briefings on distribution of the vaccines, the New York Post reports. "I want this to be quickly rectified," Ahmed

said of Cuomo's reluctance to use vaccines approved under Trump.

"I want New Yorkers to have access to the vaccine as quickly as the rest of the United States, and it seems that the government of the United States is doing that and President Trump is making that possible," she said. Trump tweeted Saturday that Cuomo needs to "stop playing politics" with the vaccine.

The New York Attorney General's Office released a statement saying they are prepared to sue the Trump administration should New York not receive the vaccination once it is released.

Report: More than 300,000 People Have Fled New York City Due to Coronavirus, Crime

Katherine Rodriguez

More than 300,000 people have fled New York City over the past eight months because of rising crime rates and .the coronavirus pandemic, according to a report from the ***New York Post***

Residents filed 295,103 (ONE CHANGE OF ADDRESS CARD IS FOR A FAMILY OF 6) **change of address requests between March 1 and October 31, the** report **revealed, citing data collected from the U.S. Postal Service under a Freedom of Information Act (FOIA) request.**

The data show only when 11 or more forwarding requests are made to a certain county outside New York City, so the number of moves could be greater than 300,000.

The data also fails to consider how many people are in a single household under one request, meaning there are likely far more than 300,000 people who have left the city.

The city's exodus of residents is much greater than in prior years. Between March and July, there were 244,895 change of address requests to locations outside the five boroughs, while in 2019, there were only 101,342 during those same months.

Experts say the escape from New York City is not just due to the coronavirus; it also has to do with rising crime rates, economic woes, and school chaos.

Michael Hendrix, director of state and local policy at New York's Manhattan Institute — which has commissioned surveys about the state of New York City — said people are leaving because they are "afraid" these issues are affecting their quality of life.

"I think people are afraid," Hendrix said. "They're afraid of catching a deadly virus, and they're afraid of crime and other quality of life concerns. One thing we also hear is about trash and cleanliness of the city."

Most people who changed their addresses moved to suburban counties, such as Long Island, Westchester, and parts of northern New Jersey. But some New Yorkers changed their addresses to places as far as Florida or Hawaii.

The trend of New York City residents leaving for other places has spread to other parts of the state. New York lost more residents than any other state due to the coronavirus pandemic.

Mass exodus from GOVERNOR ANDREW CUOMO & MAYOR BILL DE BLASIO) NYC is happening as New York state to lose $1.4 (ACTUALLY LOSE $20 BILLION) billion in tax revenue: report

New York City is in real trouble

NEW YORK DESERVES ITS NIGHTMARE; FOR ELECTING CUOMO (3) TIMES & de BLASIO TWICE)

Paul Sacca

Some extremely worrisome data has recently emerged providing a glimpse into the economic downfall of the real estate market in New York during the coronavirus pandemic.

The New York Post **published a report detailing how New Yorkers are fleeing NYC in vast numbers. According to data from the United States Postal Service, more than 300,000 NYC** (ONE CHANGE OF ADDRESS FORM CAN REPRESENT AN EXTENDED HOUSEHOLD OF 9) **residents have moved out of the Big Apple since the COVID-19 pandemic.**

The Post found that 295,103 New Yorkers filed change of address requests from March 1 to Oct. 31. However, the total amount is well over 300,000 once you consider that a single change of address would likely include numerous multiple-person households.

From March through July, there were 244,895 change of address requests to locations outside of New York City, more than double the 101,342 during the same period in 2019.

The postal data shows residents are moving out of the city, but staying in the tri-state area. The top five destinations are: East Hampton, N.Y., (2,769), Jersey City, N.J. (1,821), Southampton, N.Y. (1,398), Hoboken, N.J. (1,204), and Sag Harbor, NY (961). There were 558 people who moved to Greenwich, C.T.

The mass exodus could be derived from a number of reasons, including fear of living in a dense city during a pandemic, stringent COVID-19 restrictions set forth by Gov. Andrew Cuomo **and Mayor Bill de Blasio, a summer that saw** skyrocketing shootings**, and the effects of a** mandatory $15 minimum wage**.**

The lack of real estate sales and apartment rentals have contributed to a massive drop in tax revenue. The Real Estate Board of New York **released a report last week that New York City and state have collectively lost $1.4 billion in tax revenue so far this year.**

"Investment sales and residential sales year-to-date totaled $34.5 billion, a 50% decline compared to the same time period in 2019, causing a 39% decline in tax revenue," the REBNY reported.

Civil unrest and violent riots **plus high coronavirus death totals have hurt the city with tourism.**

(NYC TOURISM NO LONGER EXISTS). BROADWAY SHOWS DON'T EXIST; RESTAURANTS & BARS ARE BLACK; TIMES SQUARE IS EMPTIER OF LIFE THAN DEATH VALLEY). NYC REAL ESTATE HAS MORE VALUE ON THE 3RD FROM THE OUTERMOST RING OF SATURN. New York City Comptroller Scott Stringer told Market Watch (ARE YOU KIDDING) In July, "In the midst of the pandemic, we are beginning to realize that our 62 million annual tourists will no longer be in the short term." TOURISM IS NYC IS DEAD FOR AT LEAST (10) YEARS. HALF OF THE HIGH END MONEY ON MADISON AVENUE; RALPH LAUREN; CUCCI; CHANEL; DIOR; WAS SPENT BY TOURISTS. NOW THERE

ARE NONE. WHEN YOU HAVE SCHMUCKS RUNNING NEW YORK CITY & STATE; THE BEST IS GEOMETRICALLY WORSE THAN THE OTHERWISE WORST. REAP WHAT NEW YORK SOWS. IGNORE POLITICS; DIE BY CUOMO, de BLASIO; WOODCHUCK SCHMUCK SCHUMER; GILLIBRAND & ALEXANDRIA OCASIO-CORTEZ. HITTING BOTTOM; NEW YORK CAN TRY CANNIBALISM & EAT OUR LEADERS.

A Spectacular Defeat for Democratic Policies

By Matthew J. Brouillette

Barack Obama and Eric Holder's National Democratic Redistricting Committee (NDRC) aimed to raise $400 million to help flip state legislatures from red to blue in the 2020 elections.

The thinking went like this: Democrats were frustrated after the 2010 midterm elections because Republicans held legislative majorities in states where lawmakers draw legislative and congressional district maps. So Democrats sought to turn the tables in time for the next decennial drawing, after the 2020 census.

- **Part 2: What Redrawn Districts Could Mean for House Control in 2023**
- **Trump: This Administration Will Not Be Going to a Lockdown**

The 2018 elections gave them reason to hope. In that election cycle, Democrats captured six state legislative chambers from Republicans, all of which NDRC had targeted. While the 2018 national Democratic Party "blue wave" failed to win control of the legislature in my state of Pennsylvania, Democrats did gain 11 seats in the state house and six seats in the senate – getting half way toward flipping the General Assembly and making Pennsylvania not only a prime swing state for 2020 but also a prime target at the legislative level this year.

Then, in 2019, Democrats – again with NDRC's help – turned the Virginia legislature blue, raising expectations even further. These results, combined with enthusiastic anti-Trump sentiment and a purported $400 million war chest, seemed to portend another Democratic wave this year. It didn't happen. Not even close.

The NDRC targeted 13 legislative chambers in nine states – and flipped none. Republicans expanded their majorities in several of these states, including Florida, Kansas, Ohio, and Pennsylvania. The GOP captured both chambers of the New Hampshire legislature, gaining a trifecta in that state, where Republicans also hold the governorship.

And that $400 million? According to an NDRC email, it turned out to be closer to $7 million. Still, the Democrats did raise nearly $90 million for their red-to-blue effort, compared with more than $60 million raised by Republicans.

Why, then, did their efforts fail so spectacularly? Simply put: While voters showed that they didn't care much for President Trump's style, they also clearly rejected Democrats' substance.

In Pennsylvania, voters resoundingly rejected Democratic Gov. Tom Wolf's far-reaching COVID business lockdown – aided and abetted by Democratic legislators – and other aspects of the progressive policy agenda, including calls to defund police. The winning candidates ran against Wolf and his party. As one Democrat operative put it, the left's efforts in Pennsylvania "hit a big, giant red wall." But it's not only in Pennsylvania or in state legislatures where the Democrats' policies failed to woo voters.

While control of the U.S. Senate will be determined by runoff elections in Georgia in January, Republicans gained seats in the House of Representatives (though they remain in the minority).

Voters also "mostly" said no to tax increases on the ballot, as the Wall Street Journal characterized it. Such measures failed in Alaska, California, and Illinois; Colorado voters passed a tax cut. Joe Biden has claimed a mandate, but his one victory amid a wave of Democrat defeat suggests otherwise. The progressive policies he campaigned on – free college, more government health care, higher taxes – fell flat with voters. Down-ballot Democratic candidates paid the price.

While Biden supporters celebrate victory, Democrats should be concerned about the future of a progressive policy agenda that proved an utter failure at the ballot box.

Matthew J. Brouillette is president and CEO of Commonwealth Partners Chamber of Entrepreneurs in Pennsylvania, www.thecommonwealthpartners.com. Disclosure: Commonwealth Partners' two connected political action committees were involved in state-level races in Pennsylvania.

Democrats Suggest Out-of-State Liberals Move to Georgia to Vote in Senate Runoff Elections

John Binder

Democrats are suggesting that out-of-state Democrats temporarily move to Georgia for the sole purpose of helping to beat Senators Kelly Loeffler (R-GA) and David Perdue (R-GA) in their runoff elections against Demo-.crats Jon Ossoff and Raphael Warnock on January 5

Moving to Georgia only to vote in the election would likely amount to fraud, the Georgia Secretary of State's office made clear **to the *Wall Street Journal*:**

A spokesman for the Georgia Secretary of State's Office, which oversees voter registrations, declined to comment on how quickly someone could establish legal residency in Georgia, but cited state law that it is a felony to vote in Georgia elections if you are not a legal resident or if you are residing in the state briefly with the intention just to vote and then move away.
[Emphasis added]

"These are sensitive issues, and election officials are going to pay attention to what is happening," said Enrijeta Shino, a University of North Florida political science professor who has researched voting issues in Georgia. "People should be very careful about doing that." [Emphasis added]

People moving to Georgia briefly can work on campaigns and canvass for candidates, but voting in the state without the intention of staying would be considered fraud, she warned. [Emphasis added]

Still, Democrats are suggesting out-of-staters make the move.

In a November 6 post, Democrat Andrew Yang suggested that Democrats from out of state "get ready to head to Georgia" to "give Joe [Biden] a unified government."

"There isn't much time. The earliest date for absentee ballots to be mailed for the runoff is Nov. 18," Yang said. "The registration deadline is Dec. 7. The In-person early voting begins Dec. 14."

Likewise, *New York Times* columnist Tom Friedman told **CNN that he hopes "everybody moves to Georgia in the next month or two, registers to vote, and votes for these two Democratic senators."**

A local Democrat activist, Tamara Stevens, posted to her Facebook page that "Northern Democrats" should "come on down" to Georgia to register to vote in time for the January 5 runoff election.

In response, State Rep. Vernon Jones (D) is asking Gov. Brian Kemp (R) to intervene:

Georgia Secretary of State Announces a 'Full, By-Hand Recount in Each County'

Hannah Bleau

Georgia Secretary of State Brad Raffensperger (R) on Wednesday announced that the state will conduct a "by-.hand recount in each county" in the Peach State

"At 1 p.m. today, I will make the official designation of which race will be the subject of the RLA [risk-limiting audit]. At that time, I will designate that the RLA will be the presidential race," Raffensperger announced, emphasizing that the RLA, in this case, will require a by-hand recount. Typically, an RLA involves officials examining "a statistically meaningful sample of ballots."

"The audit is mathematically designed to catch anomalies that would arise from misconfigured machines, procedural errors, or intentional attack," as NBC News reported**. However, due to the narrow margins, Raffensperger is requiring a "by-hand" recount in all 159 counties.**

"With the margin being so close, it will require a full, by-hand recount in each county. This will help

build confidence," he said, adding that it will be "an audit, a recount, and a recanvass all at once."

"It will be a heavy lift, but we will work with the counties to get this done in time for our state certification," he continued."We have all worked hard to bring fair and accurate counts to ensure that the will of the voters is reflected in the final count and that every voter will have confidence in the outcome whether their candidate won or lost," he added.

Raffensperger's announcement follows a request from Rep. Doug Collins (R-GA), who is leading the Trump campaign's recount team in the Peach State.

In a November 10 statement, Collins formally requested a "full hand-count of every ballot cast in each and every county," attributing the request to "widespread allegations of voter irregularities, issues with voting machines, and poll watcher access."

His statement reads:

As we begin the recount process, there are three things we are formally requesting today from Secretary of State Brad Raffensperger. First, there must be a full comparison of absentee ballots cast and in-person and provisional ballots cast throughout the state. Second, there must be a check for felons and other ineligible persons who may have cast a ballot. Third, and most importantly, the Secretary of State should announce a full hand-count of every ballot cast in each and every county due to widespread allegations of voter irregularities, issues with voting machines, and poll watcher access. We can — and we will — petition for this in court after statewide certification is completed if the Secretary of State fails to act, but we are hopeful he will preemptively take this action today to ensure every Georgian has confidence in our electoral process."

President Donald Trump trailed former Vice President Joe Biden by roughly 14,110 votes as of Wednesday morning.

MSNBC reportedly FIRES lets Jon Meacham go as contributor after not disclosing he was a speechwriter for Biden

MSNBC did not immediately respond to Fox News' request for comment

By Josep A. Wulfsohn

Bill McGurn reacts to Biden's first speech as president-elect

Fox News contributor Bill McGurn weighs in on the 2020 election.

Presidential historian Jon Meacham was reportedly let go as an MSNBC contributor after he apparently failed to disclose to the network that he was a speechwriter for President-elect Joe Biden, including the victory speech he .gave on Saturday night

Sources told The New York Times that Meacham had been "playing a larger role than was previously known" behind the scenes, "both writing drafts of speeches and offering edits on many of Mr. Biden's big addresses, includ- ".ing one he gave at Gettysburg last month and his acceptance speech at the Democratic National Convention

Biden campaign press secretary TJ Ducklo told the Times, "President-elect Joe Biden wrote the speech he delivered to the American people on Saturday night" but that "given the significance of the speech, he consulted a number of important, and diverse, voices as part of his writing process, as he often does."

CNN'S DEBATE ANALYSIS INCLUDED CONTRIBUTOR WHO PREPPED BIDEN FOR PREVIOUS DEBATE

Meacham, who publicly endorsed Biden back in March, has long been a go-to analyst for MSNBC. However, the Times also reported that, according to a network source, Meacham would no longer be a paid contributor going forward but that he would still be welcomed as a guest. But as the Times noted, Meacham did appear on MSNBC following Biden's speech on Saturday without any disclosure that he was heavily involved in the crafting of the president-elect's address.

"I'm not the historian that you are, and I don't have the Pulitzer that you do, but do you concur that is the way we are used to hearing from our presidents?" MSNBC anchor Brian Williams aske MSNBC reportedly lets Jon Meacham go as contributor after not disclosing he was a speechwriter for Biden

PLAGIARIST SINCE LAW SCHOOL JOE BIDEN IS THE CESSPOOL OF THE UNIVERSE

CNN did not respond to Fox News' request for comment at the time. "Absolutely," Meacham answered

MSNBC did not immediately respond to Fox News' request for comment.

CNN ran into a similar issue **during the Democratic primaries with its contributor Jennifer Granholm.**

Granholm was a heavily-featured panelist as the network hosted two nights of primary debates in August 2019. However, Politico reported that the former Michigan governor had helped prep the former vice president ahead of NBC's first round of primary debates in July. CNN did briefly mention Granholm's ties to Biden prior to the debate. Less than an hour before it got underway, host Erin Burnett turned to Granholm to weigh in on Biden's debate prep.

"You know him. You helped prepare him. Look, it doesn't matter how old you are, how many times

you've done this, this is a stressful night for him," Burnett said to Granholm.

The second mention took place earlier, nearly two hours ahead of the debate, where Burnett mentioned to the former Democratic governor in passing "you were helping prepare" Biden.

"First of all, I think he does have some room for error for humanity, I mean he is like way ahead in the polls, right? But you're right that this is a fundamental moment for him and I think he gets it," Granholm said. "I haven't talked to the team. Of course, I work here at CNN and I didn't want there to be any conflicts."

CNN did not respond to Fox News' request for comment at the time.

Rep. Scott Perry on Pennsylvania: Republican Poll Watchers Kept Thousands of Feet Away in Philly

Robert Kraychik

Rep. Scott Perry (R-PA) told Breitbart News on Tuesday that Republican poll watchers were kept thousands of feet away from ballot counting election workers in the Philadelphia Convention Center in the City of Brotherly .Love on Election Day

Perry highlighted the Philadelphia Convention Center's use as a ballot processing center on Election Day and afterwards. Its largest exhibit hall is 125,000 square feet. The center has a total **of 528,000 square feet of continuous exhibition space.**

The distance between Republican poll watchers and ballot counters rendered meaningful observation of vote processing impossible, Perry explained.

"This is a convention center that is just massive," Perry said on SiriusXM's *Breitbart News Daily* with host Alex Marlow. "The [poll] watchers were put all at one end. ... So you can't see anything. It'd be like watching a play on a football field [where] you're standing on one end zone and the play is happening on the other end zone and you're supposed to make the call. Keep in mind the things they're watching for are removal of the inner envelope on the mail-in ballot. That inner envelope has to be there, or the ballot is not valid."

Perry continued, "They're looking for postmarks on the mail-in ballots, because if it's not sent in before Election Day or on Election Day, it should be invalid. They're looking for signatures. We want to make sure that people that are authorized to vote are the ones that are voting and the people that aren't authorized to vote are aren't voting. That's what — among other things — poll watchers are looking for."

"You can't see that from six feet away, and you certainly can't see it from thousands of feet away, yet that's what occurred in Philadelphia," Perry remarked.

Perry added, "If you're standing on one end zone, how can you see what's happening on the other end zone? The Philadelphia Convention Center is a massive building, and that they let [poll watchers] in the door, but that's essentially it. Functionally, you're not observing anything."

The *Philadelphia Inquirer* published **a photograph of a poll watcher using binoculars to observe the processing of ballots in the Philadelphia Convention Center on Election Day.**

Perry said, "[Democrats] are saying, 'Well, we did leave them in the building,' but it has to be useful poll watching. We don't mind Democrats watching. We think that Democrats, Republicans, independents, and anybody should be allowed to stand there and watch. It's our election process. It doesn't belong to one party or another."

The Trump campaign secured **an** order **from the Supreme Court of Pennsylvania on Thursday directing city officials in Philadelphia to allow campaign observers within six feet of ballot counting. Philadelphia's Democrat city officials appealed the order on the grounds of "safety" related to the coronavirus and COVID-19.**

Perry described Democrats' opposition to election observers being permitted within six feet of ballot counters as an effort to obfuscate their conduct. He said, "When I'm doing something that I think I'm doing well, I want everybody to see it. I'm not hiding it when I'm doing a good job. I want the world to see it, and the fact that you don't want anybody to see it lends itself to suspicion, if nothing else."

Perry said if Pennsylvania's election results are indeterminate, a second election in the state may ensue or the Keystone State's electors may not be seated. "One of the remedies [is] to revote the presidential election, because the president is disputing it," Perry stated. "The other remedy might be that Pennsylvania's electors just aren't seated, because the election is in doubt [and] we just don't trust the results of the election because of all these anomalies."

Pennsylvania's state Democrat authorities changed election laws in the lead-up to 2020's presidential election for partisan political advantage, noted Perry.

Perry said, "[Pennsylvania Democrats] set the table for Joe Biden to win Pennsylvania, but aside from that, they also set the table for outright fraud and malfeasance across the spectrum on Election Day and coming into Election Day. It's more than just the mail-in votes which favor, generally speaking, the Democrat side and Republicans just have to acknowledge that but Democrats need to also acknowledge that mail-in voting also lends itself to improprieties, whether they are by intention or whether they're by happenstance or accident."

Perry concluded, "This is a concerted operation to make sure that [former] Vice President Joe Biden is elected the next President of the United States, whether he's elected or not."

IF IDENTITY AT THE POLLS WHEN VOTING DOESN'T MATTER; MURDERERS SENTENCED TO DEATH SHOULD BE THEN ALLOWED TO BECOME SOMEONE ELSE; IN NUREMBERG; NAZIS SENTENCED TO HANG COULD CLAIM "YOU GOT THE WRONG GUY" IMPERIAL JAPANESE TOJO ON GALLOWS; TO HANGMAN CHECK MY CALIFORNIA DRIVER'S LICENSE; I'M REALLY A SUSHI CHEF FROM CROWN HEIGHTS, BROOKLYN

True the Vote Lawsuit: Illegal Ballots Counted in Four Pennsylvania Counties

John Binder

The election integrity group True the Vote is suing Pennsylvania Gov. Tom Wolf (D) and Secretary of State Kathryn Boockvar (D), alleging that illegal ballots were counted in four counties across the state in the presidential .election

A lawsuit filed by True the Vote on Tuesday, on behalf of four Pennsylvania voters, alleges that ballots in Philadelphia County, Montgomery County, Delaware County, and Allegheny County were counted in the election despite having been invalid.

The lawsuit asks for ballots from the four counties to be invalidated if it is revealed that a significant number of illegal ballots were counted because such ballots were "mixed in with and cannot be separated from lawful ballots," according to a True the Vote release.

"The Pennsylvania election process was an embarrassment to our country and an affront to our deep-seated value of protecting Americans' basic Constitutional right to vote," True the Vote

Founder and President Catherine Engelbrecht said in a statement. Engelbrecht said:

This lawsuit seeks to discover the facts about what happened in Pennsylvania's presidential election and the truth about illegal ballots that were counted, which could impact the final election results. No matter the outcome, it is our wish to see the law followed, to see voters heard, and to ensure the principle of 'one vote for one voter' is upheld.

True the Vote officials said they have gathered evidence in Philadelphia County that accuses election officials of picking and choosing voters to cure their defective ballots as poll watchers were not allowed access to canvassing sites.

In Montgomery County, True the Vote alleges that a poll watcher witnessed election officials advising unregistered voters to return to vote under a name that was registered in the state's voter rolls. True the Vote also notes that voter turnout was 88.5 percent in Montgomery County, which is 19 percent higher than the statewide turnout of less than 70 percent.

True the Vote alleges that in Allegheny County, home to Pittsburgh, voters were told to fill out provisional ballots after election officials claimed they had been sent mail-in ballots, even though the voters said they had not received mail-in ballots. The lawsuit also claims that poll workers were too close to voters when they were casting their ballots. Turnout in Alleghany County was nearly 75 percent — more than five percent higher than statewide turnout.

In Delaware County, voters that were recorded to have received mail-in ballots were given regular ballots and not required to sign the registration book. Additionally, poll watchers were granted extremely restricted access to a back room counting area, and ballots received on Election Day were not separated from ballots received after 8:00 p.m. that day, as ordered by the U.S. Supreme Court. Finally, voter turnout was 75.87 percent, 6.5 percent higher than statewide turnout.

The lawsuit alleges that voters across Pennsylvania were sent mail-in ballots without requesting them and, sometimes, received multiple mail-in ballots in their name. These voters, the lawsuit claims, were then told to vote provisionally in person on Election Day or, in some cases, were not allowed to vote.

True the Vote states in the lawsuit that they will be providing further evidence that compares voting records with records from the state voter registration database, the United States Postal Service, Social Security, the Department of Motor Vehicles, and other sources.

Their findings, they said, could reveal double votes, votes cast by ineligible voters, votes cast by felons, votes cast by non-citizens, and votes cast through ballot harvesting. Analysis cited by True the Vote alleges that more than 680,000 ballots in Allegheny County and Philadelphia County were processed without any observation. The current vote count in Pennsylvania shows Democrat Joe Biden ahead of President Trump by less than 45,000 votes.

BREAKING CNN NY TIMES W POST: RUTH BADER GINSBERG WAS ACTUALLY IN A CATATONIC TRANCE & NEVER DEAD; SHE'S DUG HERSELF OUT OF HER GRAVE & IS NOW BACK ON THE SUPREME COURT TO RULE FOR BIDEN IN THE 2020 STOLEN ELECTION

How Is It That So Many Of The New York Times Toss-Ups Went For The GOP?

HANNA PANRECK

The New York Times identified a list of House races as "toss ups" in the lead-up to Election Day. Most of them — 19 out of 27 on the list — turned red, and most of the remaining uncalled races are leaning Republican.

Trump's Approval Ratings Climb in Week Since Election

By Brian Trusdell

President Donald Trump's approval rating has improved in the week since the election, up 3% while his disapproval has dropped similarly, Rasmussen Reports said Tuesday.

Fifty-two percent of likely voters approved of Trump's job performance, **up from 49% on Nov. 3, while the number of people disapproving of his job performance dropped to 47%, down from 50%. Of those approving, 42% strongly approved, while 39% strongly disapproved.** Trump's approval index, **the difference between those that strongly approve and strongly disapprove, is the highest its been since Sept. 18, when he was plus-4.**

He dropped to minus-15 on Oct. 7. Trump's numbers are slightly better than his predecessor, Barack Obama, who had a 51% approval rating on the same day in his first term. Rasmussen was one of the most accurate pre-election national polls, **reporting on Nov. 2 that Democrat Joe Biden led Trump 48%-47%. The Rasmussen survey is a national rolling three-day rolling average of 1,500 likely voters, 500 each night, taken by phone and an online survey tool. It has a margin of error of 2.5 points.**

Rudy Giuliani to Newsmax TV: We Will Expose Dems' 'Concerted Effort'

By Solange Reyner

Trump lawyer Rudy Giuliani told Newsmax TV **his legal team is ready to prove there was a concerted effort by the Democrat Party to exclude Republicans from observing questionable ballots in 10 states.**

Giuliani also said the president has a good chance of overturning votes in Philadelphia and

Pittsburgh, which overwhelmingly voted for Democratic challenger Joe Biden.

"We think we have a good chance," Giuliani told Tuesday's "American Agenda" of two cities in Pennsylvania, "to have that vote overturned and not certified.

"The margin of victory [in the state] was only 40,00 after the president had been ahead by 700,000. I think we can show that this was part of a concerted effort on the part of the Democrat Party to do this in 10 different states, because the same thing they did in Philadelphia - herd the Republicans in corrals, not let them see the ballot - they did it in Pittsburgh, they did it in Detroit, they did it in Milwaukee, they did it in Phoenix, they did it in Las Vegas, they did it in all these places where they have this Democrat machine.

"And it's impossible that every one of these Democratic leaders woke up the day after the election with the same idea of not allowing Republicans to not see the mail-in ballots."

President Donald Trump has refused to concede the 2020 race to Biden, citing voter fraud, despite several networks calling the race for the former vice president.

Newsmax has yet to announce a winner.

Giuliani also told Newsmax TV his team is preparing to file a lawsuit in Michigan based off information from a Democrat whistleblower working for the elections board in Detroit, who has given evidence of "days and days of fraud, preparation for it, backdating of votes, going into the location of polling places and showing them how to vote, taking votes of people that weren't registered, and then actually going to the registrar book and registering them at the time."

Pennsylvania County Will Count over 2,000 Ballots Without Dates

Joshua Caplan

The Allegheny County, Pennsylvania, Board of Elections voted Tuesday 2-1 to count 2,349 ballots that "appear to be eligible in every way" except for the fact that voters did not place a date on the outer envelope, the *Pittsburgh .Tribune-Review* first reported

Election board staff say the unopened ballots arrived on or before Election Day.

"They applied on time, received their ballots, voted their ballots, returned them on time with their signature, their printed name, their address — the only thing they're missing is their date," County Solicitor Andrew Szefi said. "They were received timely, and our … ballot sorting machine imprints a date received on each envelope as they're scanned."

"We've taken a hard look at this," he added. "The legal principle at issue here is the Elections Code

should always be construed so as to favor enfranchisement over disenfranchisement. What we have here is essentially a technicality that we don't want voters to get disenfranchised with."

Elections Manager David Voye said roughly 25,000 ballots remain uncounted, 17,000 of which are provisional ballots.

President Donald Trump**'s re-election campaign filed a lawsuit in Pennsylvania on Monday against the state's use of mail-in ballots, alleging it created a "two-tier" voting system for the general election — a claim the state vehemently denies.**

The lawsuit **filed in the Middle District of Pennsylvania names Secretary of State Kathy Boockvar and the election boards of seven counties as defendants, accusing them of holding in-person voters to a different standard than those who submitted their ballots by mail.**

The Trump campaign accuses the defendants of removing "all the hallmarks of transparency and verifiability" for those who cast ballots by the mail compared to those who cast theirs in person.

The complaint also accused the defendants of keeping the election "shrouded in secrecy" by providing candidates "no meaningful access or actual opportunity to review and assess mail-ballots."

WHAT EVER HAPPENED TO THE SMUG CONFIDENCE OF EMPEROR BIDEN EXPOSED WITH NO CLOTHES BANGED BY PETE BUTTIGEIG

Biden camp asks for $30M in fundraising appeal to beat Trump's lawsuits

"By Sam Dorman

Fox News senior political analyst Brit Hume joins 'The Story' with insight and reaction to the latest news

President-elect Joe Biden's campaign is fundraising to fight the Trump campaign's legal efforts, vowing to "re-.launch" its "fight fund" even as Biden has tried to downplay his opponent's lawsuits

.Donald Trump is doubling down on lawsuits," a campaign email read on Tuesday night"

The campaign argued that "litigation is expensive, but we need to be prepared to fight these lawsuits regardless and ensure Trump doesn't win them just because we don't have the funds to fight back. Which is why today we are re-launching our Biden Fight Fund, and why we need your help to fill it with $30 million in the coming days and weeks." The campaign added that it "wouldn't be asking if we didn't truly need $30 million to be able to fund the legal work ahead -- we can't run out of resources now, which is why we need to fill this fund as soon as we can."

TRUMP CAMPAIGN'S LATEST PENNSYLVANIA LAWSUIT WILL 'PREVAIL': TIM MURTAUGH

The campaign previously promoted the "Biden Fight Fund" on the day after the election. Since then, the number of Trump's lawsuits has grown while several have been shot down by courts.

As late as Tuesday evening, the campaign was expected to file a lawsuit blocking Michigan from certifying its election results, citing a need to verify that the ballots were "tabulated in accordance with the law."

Tuesday's email from the Biden campaign came hours after he shrugged off President Trump's refusal to accept the election outcome as "inconsequential," even as Democrats elsewhere warned that the Republican president's actions were dangerous.

He described Trump's position as little more than an "embarrassing" mark on the outgoing president's legacy, while predicting that Republicans on Capitol Hill would eventually accept the reality of Biden's victory. The Republican resistance, Biden said, "does not change the dynamic at all in what we're able to do."

PAL ZOMBIE JOE FARTS IN HINDENBURG BAIL OUT

There's no evidence of widespread voter fraud, (BUT JUST IN CASE THERE IS; & THERE'S PLENTY; GET READY FOR THE FUN & DEMOCRAT RATS SQUIRMING & JUMPING SHIP)) but Dan Patrick is encouraging people to report it with up to a $1 million reward

The Republican lieutenant governor's crusade for proof of election problems in Texas comes as members of his own party dominated up and down the ballot.

by Shawn Mulcahy

Lt. Gov. Dan Patrick's crusade for proof of election problems in Texas comes as members of his Republican Party dominated up and down the ballot. ***Credit: Miguel Gutierrez Jr./The Texas Tribune***

Sign up for The Brief, ***our daily newsletter that keeps readers up to speed on the most essential Texas news.***

Texas Lt. Gov. Dan Patrick said Tuesday he is offering up to $1 million to "incentivize, encourage and reward" people for reports of voter fraud in Texas, even as there's been no evidence of mass voter fraud and experts say it's rare. The Republican state leader's crusade for proof of election problems in Texas comes as members of his own party dominated up and down the ballot.

Patrick said that anyone who provides information that leads to a conviction will receive at least $25,000. The money will come from Patrick's campaign fund, according to spokesperson Sherry Sylvester. The Texas Tribune thanks its sponsors. Become one.

"I support President Trump's efforts to identify voter fraud in the presidential election and his commitment to making sure that every legal vote is counted and every illegal vote is disqualified," Patrick said in a statement. "The delays in counting mail-in ballots in other states raises more questions about voter fraud and potential mistakes." He did not provide any evidence of mass voter fraud. His press release cited three recent arrests, including that of a social worker in Mexia, Texas, on counts of election fraud over allegations that the worker registered to vote 67 residents of a supported living center without their consent.

An unprecedented number of mail-in ballots during the coronavirus pandemic slowed ballot counting in a handful of states, including the key battleground state of Pennsylvania, where election officials were barred from processing them before Election Day. The Republican-controlled legislature shot down a request from Pennsylvania Secretary of State Kathy Boockvar that would've allowed election officials to start counting mail-in ballots before polls closed.

"These people want to delegitimize votes in order to appeal to their Trumpian base," said Abhi Rahman, a spokesperson for the Texas Democratic Party. "We know that there's a lot of work to do here in Texas and Dan Patrick is in our sights in 2022." Texas Republicans managed to stave off Democratic gains, particularly in down-ballot congressional and state legislative races where Democrats hoped to shrink the ruling party's margin. President Donald Trump carried Texas by nearly 6 percentage points, according to Decision Desk HQ.

Patrick, in an October interview with "The Mark Davis Show," claimed that Democrats were trying to "steal the election." "If the president loses Pennsylvania or North Carolina, Mark, or Florida, they'll lose it because they stole it," he said, without evidence.

Trump's campaign has filed a barrage of legal challenges in key states — including Georgia and Wisconsin — in an attempt to close the widening gap between the president and Joe Biden, who was declared president-elect on Saturday. The Texas Tribune thanks its sponsors. Become one.

Those lawsuits, however, have so far failed to pan out. Judges tossed out cases in Nevada and Michigan

because the Trump campaign failed to prove allegations of fraud, NPR reported**. Yet some of Texas' most prominent Republicans, including U.S. Sen.** Ted Cruz, jumped to the president's defense **in recent days, amplifying baseless conspiracy theories or spreading misinformation.**

"The right standard is that every single vote that was legally cast should be counted, but any votes that were illegally cast shouldn't be counted," Cruz said **on Fox News' "Hannity," though he offered no evidence of fraud.**

BREAKING NY TIMES; CNN; W POST; TRANSYLVANIA COURT FINDS COUNT DRACULA INNOCENT OF ALL COUNTS FOR LACK OF EVIDENCE.

BREAKING RACHEL MADDOW: CHARLES MANSON REHABILITATED AFTER FOUND INNOCENT OF SHARON TATE LABIANCA MURDERS

BREAKING NUREMBERG: ADOLF HITLER FOUND ALIVE & INNOCENT ALL CHARGES BY RUTH BADER GINSBURG'S GRANDMOTHER WAS REHABILITATED EX-GIRLFRIEND OF HEINRICH HIMMLER

BREAKING PHARAOH RAMSES TO MOSES; DON'T GO ANYWHERE; STAY HERE IN EGYPT FOR FAT UNION WORK CONTRACTS; FOOD STAMPS & OBAMACARE FOR ALL JEWS ; DON'T BELIEVE THE FAKE NEWS HIEROGLYPHICS; THEY'RE RUSSIAN FACEBOOK & TWITTER DISINFORMATION; DON'T BELIEVE OLD & NEW TESTAMENTS; IF YOU CAN'T TRUST PAL JOEY & KAMIKAZE KAMALA; DO YOU TRUST WEREWOLF JACK?

Georgia to Conduct a Hand Recount of Election Ballots

Georgia Secretary of State Brad Raffensperger (Alyssa Pointer/Atlanta Journal-Constitution via AP)

By Newsmax

Georgia's top election official said Wednesday the state will conduct a hand recount of all paper ballots cast in the Nov. 3 presidential election.

Uncertified results in the state show Democrat Joe Biden leading President Donald Trump by 14,000 votes out of nearly 5 million votes counted in the state. Nearly all ballots have been counted, though counties have until Friday to certify their results.

"Mathematically, you actually have to do a full hand-by-hand recount of all because the margin is so close," Georgia's Secretary of State Brad Raffensperger said at a news conference. "We want to start this before the week is up." Raffensperger said he expects the recount to take until Nov. 20, which is the certification deadline.

For the hand recount, election officers will work with the paper ballots in batches, dividing them into piles for each candidate. Then they will run the piles through machines to count the number of ballots for each candidate. The scanners will not read the data on the ballots.

After results from the hand recount are certified, the losing campaign can then request another recount, which will be performed by machine, Raffensperger said.

There is no mandatory recount law in Georgia, but state law provides that option to a trailing candidate if the margin is less than 0.5 percentage points. Biden's lead stood at 0.28 percentage points as of Wednesday morning.

Leslie Rutledge to Newsmax TV: Pa. Violated Constitutional Authority

By Solange Reyner

The Supreme Court of Pennsylvania overstepped its constitutional authority and disregarded the laws passed by the state legislature, says Arkansas Attorney General Leslie Rutledge, backer of a GOP lawsuit challenging the extension of counting mail-in ballots in Pennsylvania.

"We want to support the legal vote and uphold the integrity of this election," Rutledge told Newsmax TV's "The Chris Salcedo Show." "Americans deserve to have a transparent process.

"The only thing transparent is that the Supreme Court of Pennsylvania is going to do what it wants, whenever it wants, and that is not right by the voters of Pennsylvania, and it's not right by the voters of America." President Donald Trump has refused to concede the 2020 presidential election to Democrat challenger Joe Biden, citing voter fraud. Several news outlets, including Fox News, have called the race for the former vice president.

Newsmax has not called the race, citing close margins in a number of battleground states, legal challenges, and pending recounts. The U.S. Supreme Court in October ruled Pennsylvania could count mail-in ballots received up to three days after the Nov. 3 election, rejecting a Republican plea in the presidential battleground state.

FOX NOW WORST FAKE NEWS. I CANCELLED

(11) YEAR WALL STREET JOURNAL HOME PRINT DELIVERY MONDAY, NOVEMBER 10, 2020. NOW SMUG, BIASED FAKE NEWS PRIVILEGED LITTLE WELL CONNECTED LITTLE BITCH BRATS W ADORABLE CUTESY POO NAMES LIKE CAITLIN; NOW CONNECTE3D DADDIE'S LIL' BRAT DISINFORMATION PROGRESSSIVE LIBERALS WHO SAY TRUMP BOASTS & CALL TRUMP TRUTH "FALSEHOODS"; CHERRY PICKING REALITY ///

CNN Tops Fox in Ratings Election Week

CNN and Fox News Channel battled for viewers on the election day that turned into an election week and then some, each earning bragging rights.

CNN edged Fox among total viewers for the week, averaging 5.9 million viewers to Fox's 5.7 million. The latter was dominant on Tuesday as President Donald Trump and former Vice President Joe Biden faced off at the polls.

Fox averaged 14.1 million viewers Tuesday to CNN's 9.4 million, with MSNBC drawing 7.6 million, according to Nielsen figures. But CNN was tops among those watching Biden's Saturday evening speech after the race was called in his favor, with 13.5 million tuning in.

MSNBC's coverage of the event drew 9 million viewers, while Fox was watched by 3.1 million.

For the week, MSNBC averaged 4.6 million viewers. Cable channels were the preferred option for those following the election, as the broadcast networks lagged behind individually and cumulatively. Their Tuesday viewership was ABC, 6.3 million; NBC, 5.8 million; CBS, 4.5 million.

Fox host Laura Ingraham's show, "The Ingraham Angle," had its highest-rated week ever, with an average of 4.9 million viewers.

Viewers also kept an eye on football and the pandemic-delayed season premieres of returning shows, including CBS' "Young Sheldon" and "NCIS: Los Angeles," each drawing 6 million-plus viewers.

Powered by a NFL game, NBC was the week's most-watched network in prime time, reaching an average of 6.33 million viewers. CBS had 4.95 million, the Fox broadcasting network had 4.3 million, ABC had 4.1 million, Univision had 1.34 million, Telemundo had 1.1 million, Ion Television had 1.09 million and CW had 580,000.

Besides the news channels, other cable leaders included ESPN with 2.2 million viewers, Hallmark with 1.5 million and HGTV with 1 million.

ABC's "World News Tonight" led the evening newscasts, averaging 9.4 million viewers for the week. NBC's "Nightly News" had 8.2 million and the "CBS Evening News" had 5.7 million.

For the week of Nov. 2-8, the 20 most-watched programs, their networks and viewership:

1. NFL Football: New Orleans at Tampa Bay, NBC, 16.88 million.
2. Election coverage (Tuesday), Fox News Channel, 14. 6 million.
3. Election coverage (Tuesday), Fox News Channel, 14.5 million.
4. "60 Minutes," CBS, 14 million.
5. Election coverage (Tuesday), Fox News Channel, 13.7 million.
6. NFL Football: Green Bay at San Francisco, Fox, 13.54 million.
7. Election coverage (Saturday), CNN, 13.5 million.
8. Election coverage (Tuesday), Fox News Channel, 13.4 million.
9. "NFL Pre-Game," NBC, 12.5 million.
10. NFL Football: Tampa Bay at New York Giants, ESPN, 12.2 million.
11. "NFL Post-Game," Fox, 11.7 million.
12. Election coverage (Tuesday), Fox News Channel, 11.6 million.
13. Election coverage (Tuesday), Fox News Channel, 10.3 million.
14. Election coverage (Tuesday), CNN, 9.8 million.
15. "Football Night in America," NBC, 9.7 million.
16. Election coverage (Tuesday), CNN, 9.4 million.
17. Election coverage (Tuesday), CNN, 9.2 million.
18. Election coverage (Saturday), MSNBC, 9 million.
19. "NFL Pre-Game," Fox, 8.9 million.
20. Election coverage (Saturday), CNN, 8.7 million.

Arizona Gov. Doug Ducey: Trump Has 'Right to All Available Legal Challenges and Remedies'

Arizona Gov. Doug Ducey (R) has stated that while the state is "still counting the votes," President Donald Trump "has the right to all available legal challenges and remedies" regarding election interference or voter fraud.

Trump Campaign Adviser Jason Miller: 'Concede' Is 'Not Even in Our

"In Arizona, we are still counting the votes, with roughly 75,000 to 80,000 left," Ducey wrote **in a series of tweets. "Our expectation is that we finish counting."**

"We've been through this drill before in Arizona," Ducey noted. "Making it easy to vote and hard to cheat has also resulted in time consuming efforts to ensure the integrity of our elections. We've

already seen the outcome of races change to a dramatic degree, and some results remain unclear."

Ducey concluded the social media statement by reiterating that Trump "has the right to all available legal challenges and remedies."

"The President, just like any other candidate, has the right to all available legal challenges and remedies, and we are confident they will be properly adjudicated," Ducey stated. "We will respect the election results."

Last week, as doubt was placed heavily on the integrity of the presidential election, Ducey defended Arizona's election process, saying in a tweet that the only votes counted are those that are "received up until Election Day."

"In Arizona, we count votes received up until Election Day. That's it," Ducey wrote. "No judges have intervened, and no last-minute changes have been enacted. We're following established Arizona election law to the letter."

Over the weekend, Rep. Paul Gosar (R-AZ) called on Ducey to "investigate the accuracy and reliability of the Dominion ballot software" after reports of glitches in other states that are using the same software, such as Michigan.

"I am calling on @dougducey to call a special session of the AZ Legislature under Article IV of our state constitution to investigate the accuracy and reliability of the Dominion ballot software and its impact on our general election," Gosar wrote in a tweet.

"No election results should be certified until a complete audit of the Dominion machine tallies is made," Gosar added.

Concede Not In Our Vocabulary Right Now

Appearing Monday on the Fox Business Network, Trump campaign advisor Jason Miller said conceding the 2020 presidential election is "not even in our vocabulary right now'" as it files a flurry of legal challenges over the .counting of ballots in several battleground states

MARIA BARTIROMO: Just to be clear, are you expecting the president to concede anytime soon? Is he going to call Joe Biden anytime soon? As these lawsuits drop, Rudy Giuliani told me yesterday he is looking at up to 10 states that could affect 800,000 ballots.

JASON MILLER: That word is not even in our vocabulary right now. We're going to pursue all of these legal means, all of the recount methods. We're going to continue exposing and investigating all these instances of fraud or abuse, and make sure that the American public can have full confidence in these elections. It's not just our campaign saying we need to go through these, in certain states like Arizona, Georgia, and others, these are mandatory recounts that are coming up. We have to go

through the process and a lot of Americans — 71 million Americans — voted for this president, so they want to make sure that justice is served.

IN EVERY BLUE DEMOCRAT CITY WHERE SCUMBAG BIDEN NEEDED VOTES TO CLOSE GAP FROM BEHIND; HE CHEATED LIKE HIS SCUMBAG SON HUNTER; BIDEN HAS NO COMMENT; JUST HIS SHALLOW FUCKEN GRIN & CALL FOR UNITY IN HIS TREASON AGAINST GOD

Two witnesses claim Wayne County elections officials encouraged fraudulent activity with absentee ballots.

CHRIS PANDOLFO

A new elections lawsuit filed in Michigan on Sunday alleges massive voter fraud in vote-counting procedures in Wayne County, a Democratic stronghold and home to the city of Detroit.

Break free of our abusive relationship with our government

The Great Lakes Justice Center, a nonprofit civil liberties defense organization, announced its lawsuit in a press release, claiming that "Wayne County election officials allowed illegal, unlawful, and fraudulent processing of votes cast in last Tuesday's election." Democratic presidential candidate Joe Biden defeated President Donald Trump in Michigan, winning by 146,119 votes.

The lawsuit seeks to void the results of the election in Wayne County and calls for a do-over.

Witnesses filing sworn affidavits under oath allege that Wayne County elections officials encouraged fraud, including changing legal names and dates on ballots, ballot-harvesting, voter intimidation, and preventing poll watchers from challenging irregularities in the vote-counting process.

"This type of widespread fraud in the counting and processing of voter ballots cannot be allowed to stand. Michigan citizens are entitled to know that their elections are conducted in a fair and legal manner and that every legal vote is properly counted," said David A. Kallman, an attorney with the Great Lakes Justice Center.

"Such rampant fraud cannot be undone. We ask the Court to enjoin the certification of this

fraudulent election, void the election, and order a new vote in Wayne County."

The plaintiffs allege the following illegal activities:

- **Ballots were counted even though the voter's name did not appear in the official voter rolls.**
- **Election workers were ordered not to verify voters' signatures on absentee ballots, to backdate absentee ballots, and to process such ballots regardless of their validity.**
- **Election workers processed ballots that appeared after the election deadline and falsely reported that those ballots had been received prior to November 3, 2020, deadline.**
- **Defendants used false information to process ballots, such as using incorrect or false birthdays. Many times, the election workers inserted new names into the Qualified Voter File and recorded these new voters as having a birthdate of 1/1/1900.**
- **Defendants coached voters to vote for Joe Biden and the Democrat party. Election workers would go to the voting booths with voters to watch them vote and coach them for whom to vote.**
- **Unsecured ballots arrived at the TCF Center loading garage, not in sealed ballot boxes, without any chain of custody, and without envelopes.**
- **Defendants refused to record challenges to their processes and removed challengers from the site if they politely voiced a challenge.**

Michigan radio host Steve Gruber first reported **the lawsuit, which includes a sworn affidavit from Jessy Jacob, a longtime employee of the city of Detroit.**

In her affidavit, **Jacob says that she was assigned to work in the Elections Department for the 2020 election. In September, she worked at the election headquarters processing absentee ballot packages. Her work on the election continued through November 4, when Jacob says she was told to leave the TCF Center in Detroit, where ballots were being counted, because she raised too many questions about what was happening around her.**

Beginning in September, Jacob claims that she and 70-80 other poll workers were instructed by their supervisors to alter the mailing date of absentee ballot packages to be dated earlier than they were actually sent. Additionally, she says she was told to instruct voters to cast their ballots for Democrats and Joe Biden, even accompanying them into the voting booth to do so. In October, after being transferred to a satellite location where she processed voter registrations and issued absentee ballots for people to vote in person, Jacob claims she was told not to ask for a driver's license or any photo ID when a person was trying to vote, in violation of Michigan voter ID laws.

Jacob claims she witnessed "a large number of people" who came to the satellite location to vote in

person after they had already applied for an absentee ballot. She says these individuals were allowed to vote in person but were not required to return their mailed absentee ballot or sign an affidavit that the voter lost the mailed absentee ballot.Zachary Larsen, a former Michigan Assistant Attorney General and Republican poll watcher, was the second witness to file a sworn affidavit **alleging fraudulent activity in Wayne County. Larsen alleges that Michigan›s Qualified Voter File (QVF), an electronic system that keeps track of legal voters, was fraudulently used to assign ballots from unknown individuals to eligible voters in the system who did not cast votes. He claims "this appeared to be the case for the majority of the voters whose ballots I had personally observed being scanned."**

The lawsuit filed in Wayne County seeks a temporary injunction order to block the certification of the election results and also seeks a protective order to preserve evidence stored on computers and in documents.

Biden leads Trump by a little more than 20,000 votes in Wisconsin

CHRIS ENLOE

Wisconsin election clerks are being accused of violating state law regarding absentee ballots.

Although Election Day is over, legal challenges across the country are heating up as vigilant Americans scrutinize the electoral process. Whether lawsuits or vigilance pay off remains to be seen. But in a year where many elections are determined by razor-thin margins, the court system could play a greater role in determining election results than ever before.

What are the details?

According to WISN-AM, **Wisconsin clerks and poll workers may have "unlawfully altered witness statements" on thousands of mail-in ballots.**

Wisconsin state law requires that absentee ballots **are signed by a witness, who is also required to list their address. In fact, the Wisconsin Elections Commission** circulated a flier in August reminding voters **that mail ballots are required to have the voter›s information, the voter›s signature, and a qualified witness› signature *and* address.**

"If any of the required information above is missing, your ballot will not be counted," the WEC said.

However, just weeks before Election Day, the WEC told clerks that missing witness information needs to be corrected, of course — but the witnesses don›t have to do it themselves.

The October directive said:

Please note that the clerk should attempt to resolve any missing witness address information prior to Election Day if possible, and this can be done through reliable information (personal knowledge, voter registration information, through a phone call with the voter or witness). The witness does not need to appear to add a missing address.

Sources told WISN this directive resulted in the inadvertent invalidation of thousands of ballots because clerks filled in the information themselves after the ballots were cast.

"The statute is very, very clear," retired Wisconsin Supreme Court Justice Michael Gableman told WISN. "If an absentee ballot does not have a witness address on it, it's not valid. That ballot is not valid."

"In defiance of and direct contradiction to the statute, the Wisconsin Elections Commission gave guidance — that is, cover — to all 72 county clerks and turned the statute on his head," Gableman added. "They said, 'Gee, we know the law says an absentee ballot without the witness address is not valid, but county clerk, you have a duty to go ahead and look up on your own the witness' address if there's no address on the absentee ballot."

Red pen controversy?

President Donald Trump's campaign released a statement last Wednesday claiming there were "reports of irregularities in several Wisconsin counties."

Campaign spokesman Tim Murtaugh later clarified they were referring to ballots in heavily Democratic Milwaukee County that had allegedly been "cured" by poll workers, meaning they "corrected or added information to the ballot itself," using red pens, WUMW-FM reported.

"We estimate that 15-20% of absentee ballots in Milwaukee County were tainted in this manner," Murtaugh explained. "This is also only an estimate because our legal volunteers were prevented from having meaningful access all of the time."

The campaign's statement would corroborate what sources told WISN, that thousands of ballots were altered by poll workers using red pens. The red ink would make altered ballots easily identifiable in a recount.

And Trump's campaign has requested a vote recount in the Badger State, where Biden currently leads Trump by just 20,000 votes.

What did officials say?

Milwaukee Election Commission executive director Claire Woodall-Vogg did not respond to requests for comment from WUMW.

Meanwhile, Wisconsin Elections Commission administrator Meagan Wolfe last Thursday offered some possible explanations as to why ballots were altered, but did not address the Wisconsin state law that mandates the witness include their address on the mail ballot for it to be valid.

However, Reid Magney, a spokesman for the WEC, claimed poll workers were not altering the ballots themselves — but the envelopes in which they were mailed.

"Just the other thing to add is they're not curing the ballot itself with the person's votes on it. It's the certificate envelope that gets cured," he said, WUMW reported.

The Blaze has reached out to the WEC, but did not hear back by publishing time.

Axios: Trump Plans to Present Evidence Dead People Voted in Election

President Trump also reportedly plans more rallies in coming days.

By Solange Reyner

President Donald Trump's team has assembled recount teams in key battleground states and plans to present evidence that Democrats were using dead people to steal electoral college votes from the president, reports Axios. The president also plans to hold campaign-style rallies to boost support as his lawyers fight potential recounts in key battleground states.

Trump has refused to concede the race to Joe Biden despite several networks calling it for the Democrat challenger. Newsmax has yet to call the race, citing close races in Pennsylvania, Georgia, and Arizona. Biden's lead over Trump has narrowed to 16,952 as of Sunday afternoon, according to voter data.

Trump has key players in place to battle the results in court, including Doug Collins in Georgia, Kory Langhofer in Arizona, and Porter Wright's Ron Hicks in Pennsylvania. "We want to make sure we have an adequate supply of manpower on the ground for man-to-man combat," one adviser told the news outlet.

Additionally, Trump's communications team will send out "regular press briefings, releases on legal action, and obviously things like talking points and booking people strategically on television," one adviser said. Raising money for Trump's defense is also key, according to Axios. "We all have the same goal in mind, which is using the legal process over the next many days and weeks ahead to make sure that the president is re-elected," one adviser said.

Trump campaign holds protest in Las Vegas to decry irregularities, claim 'dead people,' non-Nevadans voted

The allegations come after a U.S. federal court judge denied an emergency motion from Nevada Republicans seeking to change the signature verification process used in the state.

By Bradford Betz

The Trump campaign held a Sunday afternoon press conference outside the Clark County Elections Department .in Las Vegas to denounce alleged irregularities in last week's election

Among its speakers was former Attorney General Adam Laxalt and American Conservative Union chairman .Matt Schlapp

A supporter of President Donald Trump holds her hand over her heart during a protest of the election outside of the Clark County Election Department, Sunday, Nov. 8, 2020, in North Las Vegas. (AP)

Laxalt attacked the state's signature verification process as being insufficient at protecting against supposed fraud, pointing out that Trump's campaign could not observe the authenticity of some 600,000 votes that have been counted in Nevada through the mailing system.

"This campaign has not observed, has not laid our eyes … on an envelope signature, and a voter roll signature, on a single one of those 600,000 voters," Laxalt said to audible boos in the audiences.

Laxalt further criticized the Clark County Registrar's use of a signature verification machine called the "Agilis system." GRAHAM: IF GOP DOESN'T FIGHT, THERE WILL 'NEVER BE ANOTHER REPUBLICAN PRESIDENT ELECTED AGAIN

"At least 200,000 voters were counted through the signature verification process of this machine only," Laxalt said. "I will repeat for the media: No human beings looked at those signature matches to confirm they were, in fact, matches.

Schlapp claimed that there were instances of underage voters, dead people, and at least 9,000 non-Nevadans who voted in Tuesday's election. "We know that underage voters voted in this most recent election. How difficult would it have been to make it clear that nobody would have been mailed a

ballot if they had a birth date after a certain year?" Schalpp asked.

He said that more than 100,000 people have left amid an economic shutdown, "yet through our due diligence, we've able to find that at least 9,000 of them voted in this election. Non-Nevadans voted in Nevada."

FRANK LUNTZ URGES POLLSTERS TO SEEK NEW PROFESSION AFTER TRUMP OUTPERFORMS POLLS: 'SELL REAL ESTATE'

Both Laxalt and Schlapp stopped short of calling for specific legal action, but said they will continue to review their options and put forth all evidence of wrong-doing that they find.

A Clark County official who wished to remain anonymous told Fox News that Laxalt's claims about the Agilis machine were "successfully refuted" in a recent lawsuit in which a judge upheld the legality of the county using it.

Laxalt and Schlapp's appearance comes after a U.S. federal court judge on Friday denied an emergency motion from Nevada Republicans seeking to change the signature verification process used in the state.

Supporters of President Donald Trump pray as they protest the election outside of the Clark County Election Department, Sunday, Nov. 8, 2020, in North Las Vegas.

U.S. District Court for Nevada Judge Andrew Gordon said that the relief sought by two Republican candidates in Clark County would delay vote counting.

"I don't find plaintiffs have demonstrated a likelihood of success on the merits of the plaintiffs' claims," Gordon said. "The public interest is not in disrupting the counting of the ballots." The Trump campaign sued in Nevada to stop the counting of what they called "illegal votes," claiming to have evidence that people who are deceased and nonresidents have cast ballots in the 2020 election.

Trumpism Is Alive But 'Journalism' Is Dead

Tom Tradup

Even as the media breathlessly coronated Joseph R. Biden as the president-elect of the United States (despite the fact that votes are still being counted in several states, court challenges have been filed and the razor-thin margin in at least one state is expected to trigger a recount) Donald J. Trump –win, lose, or draw—will go down in history for his most indelible impact on American history: revealing the sad fact that what we once called "Journalism" no longer exists.

Of course, President Trump's accomplishments are legendary in many other areas including delivering the most solid economic growth in decades, moving our U.S. Embassy in Israel to Jerusalem (something promised then ignored by at least four previous Presidents), funding historically black colleges, creating the lowest unemployment rates for Hispanics, Asians, African-Americans and women in modern history, and rebuilding America's military to cite only a few. But pulling back the curtain on the "Fake News" industry in America may be his most enduring contribution in the quest to Make America Great Again. Suddenly, millions of Americans—many for the first time—have had their eyes opened to the disgraceful and ongoing distortion of the truth by alleged "reporters."

EXHIBIT A: Joe Biden — a congenital liar on subjects ranging from denying his oft-stated plans to end fracking to pretending he isn't in favor of ultra-radical nuttiness like AOC's "Green New Deal" — is depicted by the media as "the textbook nice guy." His gaffes and obvious cognitive decline at age 78 conveniently glossed over by his campaign's enablers at the AP, CNN, MSNBC and other "news" organizations.

EXHIBIT B: Kamala Harris—the single most radical member of the U.S. Senate by any commonly accepted measure including her tacit support for violent looters and rioters and her advocacy of free healthcare for illegal aliens—was described by the New York Times as a "sensible moderate."

EXHIBIT C: Partisan hacks like Chuck Todd ("political director" of NBC News…cue the laugh track) and George Stephanopoulos (onetime White House aide to impeached intern predator Bill Clinton but now billed as an "anchor" for ABC News) honeycomb the TV networks like fire ants. Alleged Republicans including former RNC chair Michael Steele and onetime Bush White House flack Nicolle Wallace have spent the past four years on MSNBC stabbing Donald Trump in the back, furthering every phony narrative from the now-discredited "Russian Collusion" baloney to the "Impeachment" scam based on one *phone call* to the president of Ukraine which the networks screamed has "endangered our national security." Spoiler Alert: I'd bet dollars to donuts that CNN's Don Lemon and Chris Cuomo couldn't find Ukraine on a globe if it had a photo of Hunter Biden pasted on its designated position.

But Trump Derangement Syndrome—their visceral hatred of our 45th president for making monkeys out of all of them by defeating their anointed choice Hillary Clinton in 2016 and humiliating their buddies in the now-discredited "polling business"—turned otherwise mundane writers and broadcasters into raving lunatics for whom smearing Donald Trump was ultimately more important than telling the truth. And once-respected organizations such as the Associated Press cast a blind eye on employees like AP's White House correspondent Jonathan Lemire. He began each day on MSNBC's comically-biased *Morning Joe* program offering snide, slanted commentary ridiculing President Trump before heading to the White House to pretend he was "covering the news" for AP clients.

One can round up the "usual suspects" including Jim Acosta, Katie Tur, Brian "Mr. Plagiarism" Williams, and the aforementioned Jonathan Lemire…and it would be safe to say that not one of them uttered a single word about "social distancing" on Saturday as thousands of journalists and Democrats (but I repeat myself) poured into the streets shoulder to shoulder—with and without masks—to gesticulate wildly after TV networks declared Joe Biden our 46th president.

But the validity of Donald Trump's "Fake News" designation may have had no more vivid display over the weekend than on a special Saturday edition of *Morning Joe*, as MSNBC's Mika Brzeznski yukked it up over White House chief of staff Mark Meadows having tested positive for the China Virus. "A White House guy getting Covid," guffawed Joe Scarborough, "…didn't see *that* one coming!" (Apparently smearing Meadows took up so much airtime they forgot to even mention their MSNBC colleague Rachel Maddow is currently self-quarantining after exposure to the China Virus.) Slimy, but hey that's "Journalism" in 2020.

This saga isn't over yet. The final vote counts aren't completed. The court challenges and legal battles have not yet been exhausted. And millions of people of faith are still praying in unison that this is not over…despite our TV networks rush-to-judgement while simultaneously ignoring ham-handed ballot stuffing and other lawless acts by election officials in Democrat controlled cities. They believe—as I do—that a miracle is coming.

Late Saturday, we were visited by one such miraculous event: even as weasels like Mitt Romney and Jeb Bush preened for the cameras to push Donald Trump to concede, Mexico's (!) president Andres Manuel Lopez Obrador ***refused*** to congratulate Joe Biden on his ***potential*** victory in the Presidential election. Lopez Obrador stated firmly that "*we are going to wait until all the legal matters have been resolved.*" To do otherwise, he added, would not be "prudent."

When the president of Mexico has more factual integrity than Chuck Todd does, it pretty well sums up how correct Donald J. Trump was when he designated our networks and print organizations as Fake News. Your prayers for the free flow of truthful information in America's future are hereby encouraged.

Tom Tradup is Vice President/News & Talk Programming for Dallas-based Salem Radio Network. He can be reached at ttradup@srnradio.com.

Several New York Times staffers agreed with Bari Weiss' scathing resignation letter, report claims

Report raises question about whether Times can once again be 'the paper of record'

By Brian Flood

New York Times faces backlash over 'Nice White Parents' podcast

The limited-series podcast explores how white parents may be to blame for failing public schools; reaction on 'Outnumbered.' New York magazine published a scathing inside look at The New York Times, which details the "open secret" that the paper is "published by and for coastal liberals" and ponders if it "can again become the paper of record," while pointing out that several staffers agreed with Bari Weiss› infamous resignation letter painting the once-proud paper as toxic.

New York contributing editor Reeves Wiedeman detailed the Times' liberal staffers who lost it earlier this year when their paper published an op-ed by Sen. Tom Cotton headlined "Send in the Troops" at the height of nation-wide protests following the death of George Floyd in police custody. The backlash over the opinion piece eventu-.ally resulted in then-editor James Bennet's abrupt exit after internal backlash

BARI WEISS QUITS NEW YORK TIMES AFTER BULLYING BY COLLEAGUES OVER VIEWS: 'THEY HAVE CALLED ME A NAZI AND A RACIST'

Wiedeman detailed how Times employees created a Slack channel -- a workplace messaging system widely used by news organizations -- to vent and complain about the situation which "served as a heated pandemic-era office watercooler." Executive editor Dean Baquet even joined the Slack channel, according to Wiedeman.

"The conversations could become tense. Employees would paste tweets criticizing the paper into the channel; the journalists would get defensive; someone would leak the argument to friends with Twitter accounts; and the ouroboros of self-criticism would take another bite out of its tail and everyone's time," Wiedeman wrote.

The magazine reiterated a claim by then-columnist Weiss that the paper had a "civil war" going on internally, with young liberal staffers feuding with the industry veterans. Weiss went on to quit the Times with a scathing letter in which she said was bullied by colleagues in an "illiberal environment," noting she doesn't understand how such toxic behavior is allowed inside the newsroom.

The magazine reported that many Times staffers agreed with Weiss' resignation letter critiques.

"While Bari Weiss's description of a young woke mob taking over the paper was roundly criticized, several Times employees I spoke to saw truth to the dynamic," Wiedeman wrote.

"The dustup laid bare a divide that had become increasingly tricky for the Times: a large portion of the paper's audience, a number of its employees, and the president himself saw it as aligned with the #resistance. This demarcation horrified the Old Guard, but it seemed to make for good business," Wiedeman wrote.

NY TIMES WRITERS IN 'OPEN REVOLT' AFTER PUBLICATION OF COTTON OP-ED, CLAIM BLACK STAFF 'IN DANGER'

Wiedeman noted that Times staffers openly wept when President Trump defeated Hillary Clinton in 2016

"A neutral objectivity had long been core to the way the paper saw itself, its public mission, and its business interests… even if it was an open secret that the Times was published by and for coastal liberals," he wrote.

Wiedeman then explained that Baquet wanted to cover Trump fairly so the paper could maintain

its "journalistic weapon," meaning it would have the "ability to publish something like Trump's tax returns and have them be viewed as unbiased truth," someone described as a "star" writer at the Gray Lady told him.

The New York magazine piece detailed a variety of other issues inside the Times: staffers complained that the paper didn't call out Trump's "brazen expressions of authoritarianism and racism," an opinion staffer said it felt like no one at the Times got any work done following the Cotton op-ed, "members of the masthead talked one-on-one with employees of color to sort out why they felt the Times was an unwelcoming place" and a young staffer didn't think older colleagues understand social media.

NY TIMES ISSUES 'MEA CULPA,' SAYS TOM COTTON OP-ED ON GEORGE FLOYD RIOTS 'RUSHED,' FAILED TO MEET STANDARDS

"But the most meaningful divide in the newsroom seemed to be by temperament," Wiedeman wrote. "'The fundamental schism at the Times is institutionalist versus insurrectionist,' a reporter who identified with the latter group told me."

While the newsroom drama played out, young app developers and software engineers criticized journalists on Slack.

"Reporters found that suddenly it was the Times' programmers and developers, rather than their editors, who were critiquing their work," he wrote.

The lengthy feature highlights many other concerns at the Times, ranging from who will eventually replace Baquet to the future of the opinion section in a post-Trump world.

"The Times had become the paper of the resistance, whether or not it wanted the distinction. The months ahead will determine whether it can again become the paper of record," Wiedeman wrote.

Should Blacks Support Destruction of Charter Schools?

Walter E. Williams

Ben Shapiro When 'Unity' Means 'Shut the Hell Up'

Unify This

The academic achievement gap between black and white students has proven resistant to most educational policy changes. Some say that educational expenditures explain the gap, but is that true? Look at educational per pupil expenditures: Baltimore city ranks fifth in the U.S. for per pupil spending at $15,793. The Detroit Public Schools Community District spends more per student than all but eight of the nation's 100 largest school districts, or $14,259. New York City spends $26,588 per pupil, and Washington, D.C., spends $21,974. There appears to be little relationship between educational expenditures and academic achievement.

The Nation's Report Card for 2017 showed the following reading scores for fourth-graders in New York state's public schools: Thirty-two percent scored below basic, with 32% scoring basic, 27%

scoring proficient and 9% scoring advanced. When it came to black fourth-graders in the state, 19% scored proficient, and 3% scored advanced. But what about the performance of students in charter schools? In his recent book, "Charter Schools and Their Enemies," Dr. Thomas Sowell compared 2016-17 scores on the New York state ELA test. Thirty percent of Brooklyn's William Floyd public elementary school third-graders scored well below proficient in English and language arts, but at a Success Academy charter school in the same building, only one did. At William Floyd, 36% of students were below proficient, with 24% being proficient and none being above proficient. By contrast, at Success Academy, only 17% of third-graders were below proficient, with 70% being proficient and 11% being above proficient. Among Success Academy's fourth-graders, 51% and 43%, respectively, scored proficient and above proficient, while their William Floyd counterparts scored 23% and 6%, respectively. It's worthwhile stressing that William Floyd and this Success Academy location have the same address.

Similar high performance can be found in the Manhattan charter school KIPP Infinity Middle School among its sixth-, seventh- and eighth-graders when compared with that of students at New Design Middle School, a public school at the same location. Liberals believe integration is a necessary condition for black academic excellence. Public charter schools such as those mentioned above belie that vision. Sowell points out that only 39% of students in all New York state schools who were recently tested scored at the "proficient" level in math, but 100% of the students at the Crown Heights Success Academy tested proficient. Blacks and Hispanics constitute 90% of the students in that Success Academy.

In April 2019, The Wall Street Journal reported that 57% of black and 54% of Hispanic charter school students passed the statewide ELA compared to 52% of white students statewide. On the state math test, 59% of black students and 57% of Hispanics at city charter schools passed as opposed to 54% of white students statewide.

There's little question that many charter schools provide superior educational opportunities for black youngsters. Here is my question: Why do black people, as a group, accept the attack on charter schools?

John Liu, a Democratic state senator from Queens, said New York City should "get rid of" large charter school networks. State Sen. Julia Salazar, D-Brooklyn, said, "I'm not interested in privatizing our public schools." New York City Mayor Bill de Blasio explicitly campaigned against charter schools saying: "I am angry about the privatizers. I am sick and tired of these efforts to privatize a precious thing we need -- public education. The New York Times article went on to say, "Over 100,000 students in hundreds of the city's charter schools are doing well on state tests, and tens of thousands of children are on waiting lists for spots."

Newt Gingrich Responds Perfectly When Pressed Over Claim that 2020 Election Was 'Stolen'

One would think that black politicians and civil rights organizations would support charter schools. The success of many charter schools is unwelcome news to traditional public school officials and

teachers' unions. To the contrary, they want to saddle charter schools with the same procedures that make so many public schools a failure. For example, the NAACP demands that charter schools "cease expelling students that public schools have a duty to educate." It wants charter schools to "cease to perpetuate de facto segregation of the highest performing children from those whose aspirations may be high but whose talents are not yet as obvious." Most importantly, it wants charter schools to come under the control of teachers' unions.

Walter E. Williams is a professor of economics at George Mason University.

CHRIS WALLACE IS THE NEPOTISM INSIDER WHO HAS HIS JOB BECAUSE HE'S SON OF LEGENDARY MIKE WALLACE; THE GREATEST TV NEWS GUY EVER. WALLACE IS AN EFFEMINATE SMUG TWIRP TWAT; WHO SNEERED THAT 76 MILLION TRUMP VOTERS GOT HEARTBURN BECAUSE WALLACE STABBED TRUMP & US IN THE BACK

Nolte: Fox's and Chris Wallace's 'Certified' Election Winner Hypocrisy Exposed

John Nolte

Those looking for more proof of just how far the disgraced Fox News Channel has fallen, need only be reminded of a specific moment from Chris "The Proven Liar" Wallace's dreadful performance in the first presidential .debate that centered on when it would be appropriate to declare victory

Here's Chris "The Proven Liar" Wallace at the debate — a question he first asked of President Trump and then of His Fraudulency Joe Biden:

First for you, [President Trump]. Finally, for the vice president, and I hope neither of you will interrupt the other. Will you urge your supporters to stay calm during this extended period, not to engage in any civil unrest? And will you pledge tonight that you will not declare victory until the election has been independently certified? President Trump, you go first...

So back in September, Chris "The Proven Liar" Wallace was all... "[W]ill you pledge tonight that you will not declare victory until the election has been independently certified?"

But look at Chris "The Proven Liar" Wallace now… Running around like the left-wing hack he is not only declaring Biden the winner before the "election has been independently certified," but attacking Republicans who are doing exactly what he asked everyone to do in the first debate — which is wait until the "election has been independently certified!"

Here's Chris "The Proven Liar" Wallace ridiculing Republicans over the weekend, specifically Sen. Ted Crux (R-TX), for what Wallace now sees as the SIN of daring to wait until the "election has been independently certified." It would seem to me that Republicans on Capitol Hill have a role to play in this. A very few of them have said, look, you pursue your legal options, but, you know, damn down the rhetoric, like Mitt Romney, like Pat Toomey. There are a lot who are just silent. And then there are some — I mentioned Ted Cruz — you know who are like the Japanese soldiers who come out 30 years after the war — out of the jungle — and say, 'Is the fight still going on?'

This is just how big of a fraud Wallace and Fox News are.

Fox's own guy, Wallace, was out there ~~rigging~~ moderating a presidential debate and demanding everyone wait until the "election has been independently certified," and long, long, long before the "election has been independently certified" Fox News went ahead and declared Biden the winner.

Worse still, Fox News deliberately called Arizona early for Biden, a state that, more than a week later, is still too close to call. So how's that for not waiting until the "election has been independently certified?"

I should add that His Fraudulency Joe Biden agreed to wait until the "election has been independently certified," and he hasn't, and neither Fox News nor Wallace are holding him to that promise, are saying *Joe Biden is breaking his promise to wait for the results to be certified.*

Joe Biden in September: I will Not Declare Victory Until the Election Is Independently Certified

Alana Mastrangelo

During the first presidential debate between President Donald Trump and Joe Biden, Chris Wallace of Fox News asked Biden if he would "pledge not to declare victory until the election is independently certified," to which the ".former vice president answered, "yes

"Will you urge your supporters to stay calm while the vote is counted, and will you pledge not to declare victory until the election is independently certified?" asked Wallace of Biden at the first presidential debate in Cleveland, Ohio. "Yes," answered Biden.

Watch Below:

"And here's the deal. We'll count the ballots. As you pointed out, some of these ballots in some states

can't even be opened until Election Day, and if there's thousands of ballots, it's going to take time to do it," added the former vice president.

Biden, however, has done nothing of the sort, as he has since carried on **as if he is president-elect, promising that "we're going to get right to work," as he seemingly ignores the fact that the 2020 presidential election has not yet been independently certified.**

The former vice president has also since urged **all Americans to "wear a mask," insisting that the "election is over."**

"The election is over," Biden claimed. "I won't be president until January 20, but my message today is to everyone — it doesn't matter who you voted… we can save tens of thousands of lives if everyone would just wear a mask for the next few months."

Biden ended up delivering his victory speech **on Saturday night, four days after the election.**

Meanwhile, the 2020 presidential election has yet to be certified, as members of President Trump's administration maintain **that the president may actually be reelected.**

BACK STABBING JUDAS ROMNEY NOW MOST LOATHSOME TREASON PIONEER; MORE SO THAN QUISLING

Mitt Romney says Americans should 'get behind' Joe Biden, slams Trump: 'Don't expect him to go quietly'

'...that's just not in the nature of the man'

CHRIS ENLOE

Sen. Mitt Romney (R-Utah) said Sunday that Americans should "get behind" Democrat Joe Biden as the winner of the election.

Although President Donald Trump has not yet conceded — and vowed to continue challenging the outcome of the election **in the court system — the** media declared Biden the president-elect **shortly before noon Saturday as it became more clear that Biden would win Pennsylvania.**

What did Romney say about Biden?

Speaking on CNN's "State of the Union," **the Utah Republican said Americans should "get behind" Biden as their new president because the "statisticians have come to a conclusion."**

GO QUIETLY, LIKE THE DEAD WHO VOTED FOR PAL ZOMBIE JOE & KAMIKAZE KAMALA? THIS IS FACT, NOT CONSPIRACY THEORY FICTION.

Lawsuit: At least 21,000 dead people registered on Pennsylvania's voter rolls

The lawsuit says that 92% of the deceased registrants have been dead for over a year

PAUL SACCA

There are at least 21,000 dead people registered on the state of Pennsylvania's voter rolls, according to a lawsuit filed by a legal group.

A lawsuit filed on Thursday by the Public Interest Legal Foundation **claims that there are tens of**

thousands of deceased registrants on voter rolls in Pennsylvania. The amended lawsuit filed against the Pennsylvania Department of State alleges that Pennsylvania failed to "reasonably maintain voter registration records under federal and state law" during the 2020 presidential election cycle.

The lawsuit alleges that a vast majority are from over a year ago. According to the lawsuit, 92% of the 21,000 deceased people on Pennsylvania's voter rolls died earlier than October 2019. Thousands of the alleged registered dead people reportedly died over five years ago.

"As of October 7, 2020, at least 9,212 registrants have been dead for at least five years, at least 1,990 registrants have been dead for at least ten years, and at least 197 registrants have been dead for at least twenty years … Pennsylvania still left the names of more than 21,000 dead individuals on the voter rolls less than a month before one of the most consequential general elections for federal officeholders in many years," the filing states.

The legal group claims that in 2016 and 2018, there were 216 instances of dead people voting.

"This case is about ensuring that those deceased registrants are not receiving ballots," PILF President and General Counsel J. Christian Adams said in a statement. "This case isn't complicated. For nearly a year, we've been offering specific data on deceased registrants to Pennsylvania officials for proper handling ahead of what was expected to be a tight outcome on Election Day.

"When you push mail voting, your voter list maintenance mistakes made years ago will come back to haunt in the form of unnecessary recipients and nagging questions about unreturned or outstanding ballots," Adams warned.

The lawsuit was filed in the United States District Court for the Middle District of Pennsylvania.

The Public Interest Legal Foundation is an Indiana-based 501(c)(3) public interest law firm founded in 2012 that claims it is "dedicated entirely to election integrity."

"The Foundation exists to assist states and others to aid the cause of election integrity and fight against lawlessness in American elections," the PILF website states. PILF has previously filed cases in Arizona, Florida, Illinois, Maine, Maryland, Michigan, Mississippi, North Carolina, Pennsylvania, Texas, and Virginia.

On Thursday, the Trump campaign filed a federal lawsuit in Nevada in an attempt to stop the counting of "illegal votes." The suit alleges that thousands of nonresidents and dead people have cast ballots in the state.

In Michigan, there were reports of extremely elderly voters, who would be so old that they would likely be deceased, mailing in absentee ballots. A viral social media post allegedly showed several people who were over 118 years old casting their ballots in the 2020 election. Michigan›s secretary of state›s office said the error is a glitch in the system.

Huge court win lets Trump present ballot evidence, could overturn Nevada result

by Paul Bedard

A Nevada judge has agreed to let the Trump campaign present its evidence that fraud and illegalities plagued the state's election, enough to reverse Joe Biden's win and set an example for other state challenges.

IT SHOULD HAVE BEEN LIKE ISLAND HOPPING IN THE PACICIC AFTER PEARL HARBOR; UNTIL HIROSHIMA & NAGASAKI; UNTIL EVERY AMERICAN JUDGE THERE'S NO EVIDENCE AXIS POWERS AREN'T NICE PEOPLE; SIDED WITH ADOLF HITLER, HIDEKI TOJO & BENITO MUSSOLINI

According to Trump officials, the judge set a Dec. 3 hearing date and is allowing 15 depositions. What's more, the campaign plans to present its evidence that could result in the rejection of tens of thousands of mail-in ballots in Democratic Clark County, where Biden ballots outnumbered Trump ballots by 91,000 in unofficial results.

"BIG news in Nevada: a Judge has allowed NV Republicans to present findings of widespread voter fraud in a Dec. 3rd hearing. Americans will now hear evidence from those who saw firsthand what happened—a critical step for transparency and remedying illegal ballots. Stay tuned," White House chief of staff Mark Meadows tweeted.

American Conservative Union Chairman Matt Schlapp, one of those heading the Nevada case, told Secrets, "It gives us a real chance, if to do nothing else, to begin to show this historic level of fraud."

Oddly, there has been a virtual news blackout of the Trump court victory. IT'S NOT ODD. EVERYTHING GOOD FOR TRUMP IS BLACKED OUT However, there were major headlines on the state Supreme Court's certification of Biden's victory Tuesday.

In its court filing from Nov. 17, the Trump team made several allegations of voter fraud, including votes by nonresidents and the dead. But its biggest claim was that the signatures on hundreds of thousands of mail-in ballots were not verified by human officials, as required by law.

AS HILLARY SAID ABOUT BENGHAZI; J. CHRISTOPHER STEVENS & (3) AIDES; WHAT DIFFERENCE, AT THIS POINT, DOES IT MAKE? PAL ZOMBIE & KAMIKAZE KAMALA GET BUTTERED POPCORN; SIT IN THE FRONT ROW; COUNTING THEIR FRAUDULENT VOTES THAT STOLE AMERICAN DEMOCRACY

What's more, they found that officials used a machine to verify signatures, apparently against the rules, and even those machines were plagued with problems.

Schlapp said he is eager to get a chance to show its evidence of fraud and for the campaign to present the thousands of examples of signature machine errors. Since many states require signature verification, that is where the campaign's fraud investigation is focused.

"The biggest thing which is true in all of these states we're talking about, including in Georgia, where a third of the ballots were cast in the mail, Nevada, half the ballots were cast in the mail, with no legal signature verification, certainly not in Clark County — that is the big treasure trove of illegal balloting in all of these states," he said on Fox late Tuesday.

The campaign also has testimony from a blind person who claims somebody else voted for her and that she was barred from voting as a result. And they plan to present evidence that Native Americans were offered bribes of TVs and gas cards for their vote.

"Our filing said we have over 15 individuals and tens of thousands more from mail-in fraud. We have enough to switch the outcome," Schlapp told us.

Late last night, he revealed the judge's decision on Sean Hannity's Fox show.

Schlapp said: "For the first time in this whole tragic story of the 2020 presidential election, a state court has granted Republicans in Nevada, and the Trump campaign, the ability to present their case of widespread illegal balloting and to just depose up to 15 people who know what went down in Clark County in the state of Nevada. So, this is big news — you know, a lot of people in the national media have said, you know, if you have evidence of voter fraud, show it. Well, we have thousands and thousands of examples of real people in real-life instances of voter illegality. And I just think it's a great step that we're going to have a chance to present it. A court if we get a fair hearing. I believe the results in Nevada should be switched."

Michelle Obama Attacks 76 Million INCLUDING ME, RICHARD E. GLICK; AUTHOR OF THIS BOOK; Trump Voters For 'Supporting Lies, Hate, Chaos And Division' I HATE THE FUCKEN GUTS OF THIS LOATHSOME BITCH

VIRGINIA KRUTAASSOCIATE EDITOR

Former First Lady Michelle Obama attacked 71 million Americans who supported President Donald Trump, saying they supported "lies, hate, chaos and division."

Obama **took to Twitter to offer her congratulations to former Vice President Joe Biden — and his running mate, Democratic California Sen. Kamala Harris — after multiple media outlets** projected **him the winner of the 2020 presidential election.** (RELATED: 'Only A Tiny Fraction

Of Demonstrations Have Had Any Violence At All,' Michelle Obama Claims In Biden Campaign Video)

"I'm beyond thrilled that my friend @JoeBiden and our first Black and Indian-American woman Vice President, @KamalaHarris, are headed to restore some dignity, competence, and heart at the White House. Our country sorely needs it," Obama tweeted.

She went on to thank those who had helped register new voters and the voters themselves for coming out in force to support Biden, noting that more votes had been cast in 2020 than in any prior election. But she cautioned them to remember that the real work came when the election was over. "Voting in one election isn't a magic wand, and neither is winning one," she said.

THIS CONTEMPTIBLE, MEAN-SPIRITED LOATHSOME BITCH HATES OUR GUTS & IS WHY WE MUST SECEDE & FORM OUR OWN CONFEDERATION

'Burn Down The Republican Party': Jennifer Rubin Wants To Make Sure There Are No 'Survivors'

VIRGINIA KRUTA

The Washington Post's Jennifer Rubin said Saturday that the entire Republican Party had to be burned down and no "survivors" could be left. Rubin **took part in a panel discussion on MSNBC's "AM Joy" and argued that if any Republicans were left standing once President Donald Trump was no longer in office, there would be nothing to stop them from taking power again.** (RELATED: Diversity On Stage At The RNC Prompts A Wave Of Racist Attacks)

"It's not only that Trump has to lose, but that all his enablers have to lose. We have to collectively in essence burn down the Republican Party," Rubin explained. "We have to level them because if there are survivors, if there are people who weather this storm, they will do it again. They will take this as confirmation that, 'Hey, it just pays to ride the waves. Look at me. I made it through.' And so up and down the ticket, federal, state, and local offices, the country has to repudiate this."

Rubin **also tweeted Friday that any Republican supporting President Trump's claims of voter fraud should be rejected from "polite" society. "Any R now promoting rejection of an election or calling to not to follow the will of voters or making baseless allegations of fraud should never serve in office, join a corporate board, find a faculty position or be accepted into 'polite' society. We have a list," she said.**

Teachers' Unions Gleeful: 'Bye Betsy,' End to School Choice GET READY FOR THEM TO LAY WASTE TO THE ONLY THING THAT EVER RESCUED THE POOR SINGLE PARENT BLACK LIFE MATTERS UNDERCLASS FROM HELL; CHARTER SCHOOLS; STRIVING UNPROTECTED HIGH ACHIEVING BLACK KIDS WHO ARE STABBED FOR ACTING WHITE ...

DR. SUSAN BERRY

The national teachers' unions are gleeful that a number of media outlets have called the presidential election for .former Vice President Joe Biden

"We know Joe Biden and Kamala Harris will stand with us as we work to reclaim public education as a common good, as the foundation of this democracy," National Education Association (NEA) President Becky Pringle said in a video message.

Pringle said she is especially looking forward to the exit of current Secretary of Education Betsy DeVos, a champion of school choice:

Step one will be to replace Betsy DeVos with an education secretary who will understand and value and protect public education and respect the voices and professional expertise of educators. NEA's vision for public education is to transform it into a racially and socially just and equitable system that's actually designed to prepare every student, everyone, to succeed in a diverse and interdependent world.

NEA said in a statement the radical #RedForEd protests helped elect Biden:

Over the last four years, NEA members have taken heroic action to stand up for their students, their profession, and their communities. Millions of educators rallied under the #RedForEd banner for school funding and educator pay equity, denounced the confirmation of Betsy DeVos as secretary of education, and volunteered for pro-public education candidates. Thousands of educators ran for office and won in the 2018 midterm elections.

Many teachers' union officials and members mocked DeVos on Twitter, saying "Bye Betsy," including Beth Kontos, president of the American Federation of Teachers' (AFT) Massachusetts affiliate.

"Public education is not at your mercy any longer," she said.

Head of prestigious school calls MAGA hat 'symbol of racism and hatred' after student wears one: 'He will not wear it again'

'It was not a political decision' to speak to the La Jolla Country Day School student about his MAGA hat, Gary Krahn said

Dave Urbanski

The head of a prestigious private school in California called the Make America Great Again hat — the iconic symbol of President Donald Trump's 2016 campaign — a "symbol of racism and hatred" after a student wore one on campus.

And Gary Krahn — head of La Jolla Country Day School — wrote in an email to school staff that the student "will not wear it again," KUSI-TV reported.

What are the details?

The email from Krahn to school staff that KUSI obtained primarily described a letter to parents about the coronavirus and the post-Thanksgiving schedule; the letter didn't include a mention of the MAGA hat. But in the email introduction, the station said Krahn described the MAGA hat incident to staff:

We also had a student wear a MAGA Hat today. I have talked with that student who now understands why that hat is offensive to our community. He will not wear it again. In addition his mom said that she is embarrassed by his actions. She will fulfill her role as a parent. We will continue to grow as a community that sees and values the dignity of all people.

Krahn also appeared in a video to the "school community" that described the incident. In the clip, Krahn said "the First Amendment is very important to me. I was willing to give my life for it as I served in the Army. It is one of the most precious things that we have in this nation." He then explained why he spoke to the student about the MAGA hat:

Krahn added that the student "has every right to wear" the MAGA hat, and that Krahn "had friends give their [lives] for that right."

"When I approached the student, I shared with him that he had that right to wear the hat," Krahn added. "I also shared with him the impact it has on our community. That hat has a symbol of racism and hatred. ... It's a fact that in our community, there's a belief that that's what that hat represents. And because we're a community of dignity — that all people have value, and that all people are vulnerable — I wanted the student to know that his decision was gonna have an impact on people. He graciously took off his hat."

Krahn also said in the clip that "it was not a political decision to reach out to him and talk about that hat; it was a decision about dignity — the inherent value that all humans have."

"We're gonna continue to honor the First Amendment," he also said. "We're gonna continue to be a community of dignity and to realize that if our actions impact others, we have a responsibility to work on that, to improve, to grow. Our students are gonna become leaders in the community. [I] can't think of anything more precious than to have them go out there with not only the knowledge but with the belief that all humans have value. Create the community that we dream about. That's what La Jolla Country Day is all about."

Citing the school's 2020-2021 Parent/Student Handbook, KUSI said the school's dress code does not outlaw political attire.

The station said it reached out to Krahn for comment but hadn't heard back.

Tucker Carlson weighs in

KUSI said La Jolla County Day School "is one of the most prestigious private schools in San Diego County" with yearly tuition ranging from $28,500 for kindergartners to $37,130 for high schoolers.

In a segment about the incident on his show Wednesday night, Fox News' Tucker Carlson — who attended La Jolla Country Day — said "it was less expensive and more tolerant when I was a little kid there ... sad to hear it."_

JOURNALISM TODAY AS JOSEPH GOEBBELS & LENI REIFENSTAHL POISON IN AMERICA IS NOTHING NEW

IT CAN'T HAPPEN HERE? IT DID. ONLY WORSE IN AMERICA THAN IN THE REICH TO LAST A THOUSAND YEARS

'Ingraham Angle' exclusive: Nevada poll worker claims she witnessed blatant voter fraud

Anonymous woman describes seeing envelopes ripped open and ballots marked up on side of Biden-Harris van

By Angelica Stabile

EXCLUSIVE: Nevada poll worker claims to have witnessed voter fraud

Anonymous Clark County poll worker joins 'The Ingraham Angle' to discuss what she saw.

Voter fraud was allegedly committed in Nevada during the early voting period, according to a Clark County poll worker who told Fox News' "The Ingraham Angle" what she witnessed in an exclusive interview Tuesday night. The whistleblower, whose identity was hidden and whose voice was modified at her request, told host Laura Ingraham that she noticed white envelopes being passed around and ripped open near a Biden-Harris van while on a walk during her lunch break. The envelope handlers then leaned against the side of the van in order to mark the .papers, which she recognized as ballots

"As I got closer, I thought, 'Those are ballots,'" she said. "I walked by four or five times. On the next

time I walked by, they were putting them in the envelopes. They were putting them in a white and pink envelope."

NEVADA ELECTION WORKER ALLEGES VOTING IRREGULARITIES, TRUMP CAMPAIGN SUBMITS AFFIDAVIT TO DOJ

After the worker realized the irregularity, she claimed a "human wall" was formed to obstruct the view of anyone looking on. The worker told Ingraham that she was scared by this.

The worker asserted she did not intervene because she and the other workers were not authorized to speak with anybody outside the polling center.

The same worker has released a sworn affidavit to the Trump campaign disclosing what she claimed to have witnessed. The affidavit, which has been submitted to the Justice Department, also claims voters were allowed to cast ballots without valid identification. Last week, state officials in Nevada denied any evidence of voter fraud and Democratic Attorney General Aaron Ford referred to the Trump campaign's legal efforts as "garbage."

"A sworn declaration from an eyewitness is the literal definition of evidence," a Trump campaign attorney said in a statement. "Those on the left and in other quarters that have been screaming that there's no evidence will need new talkers and most importantly, will have to now focus on the legitimate issues that have been raised. "

FNC's Hemmer to Sen. Tillis on Vote Fraud Claims: 'What Moment Do You Say Put Up or Shut Up?'

NO MATTER WHAT; HOW MUCH OR HOW CONVINCING DEMOCRATS STEAL OUR ELECTION IS; FAKE NEWS IGNORES OUR EVIDENCE. FOX IS NOW THE SINGLE MOST EVIL DISINFORMATION IN THE WORLD

Pam Key

Fox News anchor Bill Hemmer pressed Sen. Thom Tillis (R-NC) Tuesday over the Trump campaign's claims of widespread voter fraud in the presidential election.

Hemmer said, "Senator, I don't know if you were with us a few moments ago, but Matt Schlapp just came back from Clark County that's Las Vegas, Nevada. He's arguing that there are thousands and thousands of illegal votes cast. Well, that may or may not be the case, but so far, we haven't seen any evidence of that. At what moment do you say put up or shut up?" Tillis said, "Well, you know Bill, I heard a lot of people when we were concerned with the ballot harvesting that happened special congressional race in North Carolina— I think that people say that no thought occurs and that's empirically wrong." He added, "Whether or not it rose to a level to determine the outcome or are the kinds of questions that you ask in these very, very close races. I think it's just a process that we need to go through, and we need to be patient and be calm and respect the judicial system that I think that will render a fair decision. When it's up to the president and vice president to act accordingly

FAKE NEWS ACT ONE SCENE ONE

Joseph Goebbels HE IS AMERICA TODAY

Joseph Goebbels

Chancellor of the German Reich
(Nazi Germany)

In office 30 April 1945 – 1 May 1945

President	Karl Dönitz
Preceded by	Adolf Hitler
Succeeded by	Lutz Graf Schwerin von Krosigk

Reich Plenipotentiary for Total War

In office: 23 July 1944 – 30 April 1945

Leader	**Adolf Hitler (1934–45)**
Preceded by	***Office established***
Succeeded by	***Office abolished***

Reichsminister of Public Enlightenment and Propaganda

In office
14 March 1933 – 30 April 1945

President	**Paul von Hindenburg (1933–34)**
Chancellor	**Adolf Hitler**
Preceded by	***Office established***
Succeeded by	**Werner Naumann**

	Gauleiter of Berlin
	In office 26 October 1926 – 1 May 1945
Leader	Adolf Hitler
Preceded by	Ernst Schlange
Succeeded by	*Office abolished*
	Reichsleiter
	In office 2 June 1933 – 1 May 1945
	Stadtpräsident of Berlin
	In office 1 April 1943 – 1 May 1945
Preceded by	Ludwig Steed
Succeeded by	*Office abolished*
	Personal details
Born	Paul Joseph Goebbels 29 October 1897 Rheydt, Kingdom of Prussia, German Empire
Died	1 May 1945 (aged 47) Berlin, Nazi Germany
Cause of death	Suicide
Political party	Nazi Party (NSDAP) (1924–1945)
Spouse(s)	Magda Ritschel (m. 1931)
Children	Helga, Hildegard, Helmut, Holdine, Hedwig, Heidrun
Alma mater	University of Bonn University of Würzburg University of Freiburg University of Heidelberg
Occupation	Propagandist, politician
Signature	Dr. Goebbels.

^ Formally titled "Leading Minister" or "Chief Minister" (*Leitender Minister*)

Paul Joseph Goebbels (German: [pa l jo z f œbl s] (listen 29 October 1897 – 1 May 1945) was a German Nazi politician and Reich Minister of Propaganda of Nazi Germany from 1933 to 1945. He was one of Adolf Hitler's closest and most devoted associates, and was known for his skills in public speaking and his deeply virulent antisemitism, which was evident in his publicly voiced views. He advocated progressively harsher discrimination, including the extermination of the Jews in the Holocaust.

Business run by Jewish single mom cited for COVID violation, while Biden supporters celebrate across city

Large crowds gathered to celebrate Joe Biden's victory of President Trump over the weekend in New York City

By Louis Casiano

Biden: 'It's time to end the politicization' of mask-wearing

A struggling Brooklyn, N.Y. pottery shop employee was confronted by authorities over the weekend when they visited the business over supposed violations of government-mandated coronavirus restriction measures while local leaders have mostly ignored large crowds gathering at the same time to celebrate Joe Biden›s win over President Trump in a contentious presidential contest. Ilana Cagan runs Pottery and Glass Land in Midwood, where customers can paint their own glass, pottery, canvas and wood projects in a studio setting. She told Fox News she and another employee were in the shop Saturday night preparing orders to ship to customers but were not open. As they were working, several deputies with the New York City Sheriff's Office told her they were informed that she had been previously open for classes, which Cagan denies. "They looked like I was selling drugs in my base-.ment. That's how many of them there were," Cagan said

A video of the incident that has since gone viral shows her speaking to a deputy.

"I have five children. I'm a single mother," she says. "I have zero income coming in right now. And everybody else is open and I'm not allowed to be open.

"I have a mortgage to pay, rent to pay for the store," she told Fox News. "I have all the regular house bills and I can't pay any of them."

The shop was not cited, Cagan said.

The incident occurred as crowds gathered across the city in close proximity to celebrate Biden's victory over Trump. Local leaders have pushed for tough measures to prevent a second wave of infections while remaining mostly largely silent about street demonstrations and celebrations that proliferated over the summer. However, residents who participated in those events have said that there was generally consistent adherence to mask-wearing.

"It's hypercritical to the zip codes that are being targeted," Cagan said of the Jewish community, which has protested such restrictions. In a tweet, Donald Trump Jr., called the pottery shop incident "Truly disgusting!!!"

In an effort to track and combat the spread of the coronavirus, parts of New York City are broken down into zones -- red, orange and yellow -- which determines the severity of the COVID-19 infections. The "red zone" is the cluster, while "orange zones" are the immediate areas surrounding the clusters and "yellow zones" are areas deemed "precautionary."

Cagan's pottery shop is located in a "red zone," which mandates all schools and non-essential businesses remain closed.

"I think I was able to open for two weeks out of the nine months [since lockdown measures began]," she said. "At this point, everywhere else is open and the numbers are higher around us."

Several businesses on her block have already closed their doors permanently, she said. Cagan said she doesn't anticipate her area getting out of the "red zone" anytime soon.

Brooklyn Councilman Chaim Deutsch noted the street celebrations and the lack of enforcement by authorities on such gatherings while seemingly coming down hard on small businesses.

"Last night, as thousands of New Yorkers partied in the streets, sheriffs entered this pottery shop, owned by a single mom of five," he tweeted.

His office did not immediately respond to a Fox News request for comment. On Monday, Deutsch tweeted a map of New York City asking: "can you identify where the red zone is?"

Mayor Bill de Blasio brushed off concerns that the celebrations seen over the weekend could contribute to an increase in coronavirus cases.

"This is really what we're seeing decisively. Those outdoor gatherings, always something to keep an eye on. But if people keep a mask on and they're outdoors, we haven't seen too much ill come of that," De Blasio said during a news briefing. "Increasingly the concern is, more and more people are indoors, fewer and fewer ... wearing a mask. That's overwhelming where our concern is."

Messages ot De Blasio's office and the sheriff's office were not immediately returned. The city seems to be targeting the Jewish neighborhoods more aggressively than other areas, Cagan said. Orthodox Jewish protesters rallied against coronavirus restrictions last month, claiming De Blasio and Gov. Andrew Cuomo **were using them as scapegoats for an increase in cases.**

"I do think that we are being targeted," Cagan said, adding that she doesn't know how much longer she can stay closed. "I do need a lot of help right now in order to survive."

THE NEW YORK CITY OF DE BLASIO & CUOMO NAZI GESTAPO HATES JEWS LIKE ME, THE AUTHOR OF THIS BOOK. THEY'D LOVE TO KILL ME

JOSEPH GOEBBELS; HUMAN INCARNATION OF H.I.V.; REPLICATED HIS ASS INTO 2020 U.S.A. FAKE NEWS & SILICON VALLEY; WHO COMBINED IN REALTY TODAY; MAKE THE JOSEPH GOEBBELS; ABOUT WHOM YOU'RE ABOUT TO READ; THE GOOD OLD DAYS

Goebbels, who aspired to be an author, obtained a Doctor of Philology degree from the University of Heidelberg in 1921. He joined the Nazi Party in 1924, and worked with Gregor Strasser in their northern branch. He was appointed Gauleiter (district leader) for Berlin in 1926, where he began to take an interest in the use of propaganda to promote the party and its programme. After the Nazis' seizure of power in 1933, Goebbels›s Propaganda Ministry quickly gained and exerted control over the news media, arts, and information in Germany. He was particularly adept at using the relatively new media of radio and film for propaganda purposes. Topics for party propaganda included antisemitism, attacks on the Christian churches, and (after the start of the Second World War) attempting to shape morale.

In 1943, Goebbels began to pressure Hitler to introduce measures that would produce "total war", including closing businesses not essential to the war effort, conscripting women into the labour force, and enlisting men in previously exempt occupations into the Wehrmacht. Hitler finally appointed him as Reich Plenipotentiary for Total War on 23 July 1944, whereby Goebbels undertook largely unsuccessful measures to increase the number of people available for armaments manufacture and the Wehrmacht.

As the war drew to a close and Nazi Germany faced defeat, Magda Goebbels and the Goebbels children joined him in Berlin. They moved into the underground Vorbunker, part of Hitler's underground bunker complex, on 22 April 1945. Hitler committed suicide on 30 April. In accordance with Hitler›s will, Goebbels succeeded him as Chancellor of Germany; he served one day in this post. The following day, Goebbels and his wife committed suicide, after poisoning their six children with cyanide.

Early life

Paul Joseph Goebbels was born on 29 October 1897 in Rheydt, an industrial town south of Mönchengladbach near Düsseldorf, Germany. Both of his parents were Roman Catholics with modest family backgrounds.[His father Fritz was a German factory clerk; his mother Katharina Maria (née Odenhausen) was born to Dutch and German parents in the Netherlands. Goebbels had five siblings: Konrad (1893–1947), Hans (1895–1949), Maria (1896–1896), Elisabeth (1901–1915), and Maria (1910–1949),[2] who married the German filmmaker Max W. Kimmich in 1938.[4] In 1932, Goebbels published a pamphlet of his family tree to refute the rumors that his maternal grandmother was of Jewish ancestry. During childhood, Goebbels suffered from ill health, which included a long bout of inflammation of the lungs. He had a deformed right foot that turned inwards, due to a congenital deformity. It was thicker and shorter than his left foot. He underwent a failed operation to correct it just prior to starting grammar school.[6] Goebbels wore a metal brace and special shoe because of his shortened leg and walked with a limp. He was rejected for military service in World War I because of this deformity.[

Goebbels in 1916

Goebbels was educated at a *Gymnasium*, where he completed his *Abitur* (university entrance examination) in 1917. He was the top student of his class and was given the traditional honour to speak at the awards ceremony. His parents initially hoped that he would become a Catholic priest, and Goebbels seriously considered it. He studied literature and history at the universities of Bonn, Würzburg, Freiburg, and Munichaided by a scholarship from the Albertus Magnus Society. By this time Goebbels had begun to distance himself from the church.

Historians, including Richard J. Evans and Roger Manvell, speculate that Goebbels' lifelong pursuit of women may have been in compensation for his physical disability. At Freiburg, he met and fell in love with Anka Stalherm, who was three years his senior. She went on to Würzburg to continue school, as did Goebbels. In 1921, he wrote a semi-autobiographical novel, *Michael*, a three-part work of which only Parts I and III have survived. Goebbels felt he was writing his "own story".Antisemitic content and material about a charismatic leader may have been added by Goebbels shortly before the book was published in 1929 by Eher-Verlag, the publishing house of the Nazi Party (National Socialist German Workers› Party; NSDAP). By 1920, the relationship with Anka was over. The break-up filled Goebbels with thoughts of suicide.

At the University of Heidelberg, Goebbels wrote his doctoral thesis on Wilhelm von Schütz, a minor 19th-century romantic dramatist. He had hoped to write his thesis under the supervision of Friedrich Gundolf, a literary historian. It did not seem to bother Goebbels that Gundolf was Jewish. Gundolf was no longer teaching, so directed Goebbels to associate professor Max Freiherr von Waldberg. Waldberg, also Jewish, recommended Goebbels write his thesis on Wilhelm von Schütz. After submitting the thesis and passing his oral examination, Goebbels earned his PhD in 1921. By 1940, he had written 14 books.

Goebbels returned home and worked as a private tutor. He also found work as a journalist and was published in the local newspaper. His writing during that time reflected his growing antisemitism (JUST LIKE THE USA 2021 DEMOCRATIC PARTY)and dislike for modern culture. In the summer **of 1922, he met and began a love affair with Else Janke, a schoolteacher. After** (HIS GIRLFRIEND) she revealed to him that she was half-Jewish, Goebbels stated the "enchantment was ruined." **Nevertheless, he continued to see her on and off until 1927. He continued for several years to try to become a published author. His diaries, which he began in 1923 and continued for the rest of his life, provided an outlet for his desire to write. The lack of income from his literary works (he wrote two plays in 1923, neither of which sold) forced him to take employment as a caller on the stock exchange and as a bank clerk in Cologne, a job he detested. He was dismissed from the bank in August 1923 and returned to Rheydt. During this period, he read avidly and was influenced by the works of Oswald Spengler, Fyodor Dostoyevsky, and Houston Stewart Chamberlain, the British-born German writer whose book *The Foundations of the Nineteenth Century* (1899) was one of the standard works of the extreme right in Germany. He also began to study the "social question" and read the works of Karl Marx, Friedrich Engels, Rosa Luxemburg, August Bebel and Gustav Noske. According to German historian Peter Longerich,**

Goebbels's diary entries from late 1923 to early 1924 reflected the writings of a man who was isolated, preoccupied with "religious-philosophical" issues, and lacked a sense of direction. Diary entries of mid-December 1923 forward show Goebbels was moving towards the *Völkisch* nationalist movement.

Nazi Activist

Portrait of Goebbels

Goebbels first took an interest in Adolf Hitler and Nazism in 1924. In February 1924, Hitler›s trial for treason began in the wake of his failed attempt to seize power in the Beer Hall Putsch of 8–9 November 1923. The trial attracted widespread press coverage and gave Hitler a platform for propaganda.[1] Hitler was sentenced to five years in prison, but was released on 20 December 1924, after serving just over a year Goebbels was drawn to the NSDAP mostly because of Hitler›s charisma and commitment to his beliefs. He joined the NSDAP around this time, becoming member number 8762. In late 1924, Goebbels offered his services to Karl Kaufmann, who was *Gauleiter* (NSDAP district leader) for the Rhine-Ruhr District. Kaufmann put him in touch with Gregor Strasser, a leading Nazi organiser in northern Germany, who hired him to work on their weekly newspaper and undertake secretarial work for the regional party offices. He was also put to work as party speaker and representative for Rhineland-Westphalia. Members of Strasser's northern branch of the NSDAP, including Goebbels, had a more socialist outlook than the rival Hitler group in Munich. Strasser disagreed with Hitler on many parts of the party platform, and in November 1926 began working on a revision.

Hitler viewed Strasser's actions as a threat to his authority, and summoned 60 *Gauleiters* and party leaders, including Goebbels, to a special conference in Bamberg, in Streicher's *Gau* of Franconia, where he gave a two-hour speech repudiating Strasser's new political programme. Hitler was opposed to the socialist leanings of the northern wing, stating it would mean "political bolshevization of Germany." Further, there would be "no princes, only Germans," and a legal system with no "Jewish system of exploitation ... for plundering of our people." The future would be secured by acquiring land, not through expropriation of the estates of the former nobility, but through colonising territories to the east.[44] Goebbels was horrified by Hitler›s characterisation of socialism as "a Jewish creation" and his assertion that a Nazi government would not expropriate private property. He wrote in his diary: "I no longer fully believe in Hitler. That›s the terrible thing: my inner support has been taken away."

After reading Hitler's book *Mein Kampf*, Goebbels found himself agreeing with Hitler's assertion of a "Jewish doctrine of Marxism".In February 1926, Goebbels gave a speech titled "Lenin or Hitler?" in which he asserted that communism or Marxism could not save the German people, but he believed it would cause a "socialist nationalist state" to arise in Russia. In 1926, Goebbels published a pamphlet titled *Nazi-Sozi* which attempted to explain how National Socialism differed from Marxism.

In hopes of winning over the opposition, Hitler arranged meetings in Munich with the three Greater Ruhr *Gau* leaders, including Goebbels. Goebbels was impressed when Hitler sent his own car to meet them at the railway station. That evening, Hitler and Goebbels both gave speeches at a beer hall rally. The following day, Hitler offered his hand in reconciliation to the three men, encouraging them to put their differences behind them.[] Goebbels capitulated completely, offering Hitler his total loyalty. He wrote in his diary: "I love him ... He has thought through everything," "Such a sparkling mind can be my leader. I bow to the greater one, the political genius." He later wrote: "Adolf Hitler, I love you because you are both great and simple at the same time. What one calls a genius." As a result of the Bamberg and Munich meetings, Strasser's new draft of the party programme was discarded. The original National Socialist Program of 1920 was retained unchanged, and Hitler›s position as party leader was greatly strengthened.

Propagandist in Berlin

At Hitler's invitation, Goebbels spoke at party meetings in Munich and at the annual Party Congress, held in Weimar in 1926. For the following year's event, Goebbels was involved in the planning for the first time. He and Hitler arranged for the rally to be filmed. Receiving praise for doing well at these events led Goebbels to shape his political ideas to match Hitler's, and to admire and idolize him even more.

Gauleiter

Goebbels was first offered the position of party *Gauleiter* for the Berlin section in August 1926. He travelled to Berlin in mid-September and by the middle of October accepted the position. Thus

Hitler›s plan to divide and dissolve the northwestern *Gauleiters* group that Goebbels had served in under Strasser was successful. The party membership numbered about 1,000 when Goebbels arrived, and he reduced it to a core of 600 of the most active and promising members. To raise money, he instituted membership fees and began charging admission to party meetings. Aware of the value of publicity (both positive and negative), he deliberately provoked beer-hall battles and street brawls, including violent attacks on the Communist Party of Germany**. Goebbels adapted recent developments in commercial advertising to the political sphere, including the use of catchy slogans and subliminal cues. His new ideas for poster design included using large type, red ink, and cryptic headers that encouraged the reader to examine the fine print to determine the meaning.**

Goebbels speaks at a political rally (1932). This body position, with arms akimbo, was intended to show the speaker as being in a position of authority.

Goebbels giving a speech in Lustgarten**, Berlin, August 1934. This hand gesture was used while delivering a warning or threat.**

Like Hitler, Goebbels practised his public speaking skills in front of a mirror. Meetings were preceded by ceremonial marches and singing, and the venues were decorated with party banners. His entrance (almost always late) was timed for maximum emotional impact. Goebbels usually meticulously planned his speeches ahead of time, using pre-planned and choreographed inflection and gestures, but he was also able to improvise and adapt his presentation to make a good connection with his audience. He used loudspeakers, decorative flames, uniforms, and marches to

attract attention to speeches.

Goebbels' tactic of using provocation to bring attention to the NSDAP, along with violence at the public party meetings and demonstrations, led the Berlin police to ban the NSDAP from the city on 5 May 1927. Violent incidents continued, including young Nazis randomly attacking Jews in the streets. Goebbels was subjected to a public speaking ban until the end of October. During this period, he founded the newspaper Der Angriff (*The Attack*) as a propaganda vehicle for the Berlin area, where few supported the party. It was a modern-style newspaper with an aggressive tone; 126 libel suits were pending against Goebbels at one point. To his disappointment, circulation was initially only 2,000. Material in the paper was highly anti-communist and antisemitic. Among the paper's favourite targets was the Jewish Deputy Chief of the Berlin Police Bernhard Weiß. Goebbels gave him the derogatory nickname "Isidore" and subjected him to a relentless campaign of Jew-baiting in the hope of provoking a crackdown he could then exploit. Goebbels continued to try to break into the literary world, with a revised version of his book *Michael* finally being published, and the unsuccessful production of two of his plays (*Der Wanderer* and *Die Saat* (*The Seed*)). The latter was his final attempt at playwriting. During this period in Berlin he had relationships with many women, including his old flame Anka Stalherm, who was now married and had a small child. He was quick to fall in love, but easily tired of a relationship and moved on to someone new. He worried too about how a committed personal relationship might interfere with his career.

1928 election WARM UP ACT FOR DEMOCRATS STEALING THE 2020 U.S PRESIDENTIAL ELECTION

The ban on the NSDAP was lifted before the Reichstag elections on 20 May 1928. The NSDAP lost nearly 100,000 voters and earned only 2.6 per cent of the vote nationwide. Results in Berlin were even worse, where they attained only 1.4 per cent of the vote. Goebbels was one of the first 12 NSDAP members to gain election to the *Reichstag*. This gave him immunity from prosecution for a long list of outstanding charges, including a three-week jail sentence he received in April for insulting the deputy police chief Weiß. The Reichstag changed the immunity regulations in February 1931, and Goebbels was forced to pay fines for libellous material he had placed in *Der Angriff* over the course of the previous year. Goebbels continued to be elected to the *Reichstag* at every subsequent election during the Weimar and Nazi regimes.

In his newspaper *Berliner Arbeiterzeitung* (*Berlin Workers Newspaper*), Gregor Strasser was highly critical of Goebbels' failure to attract the urban vote. However, the party as a whole did much better in rural areas, attracting as much as 18 per cent of the vote in some regions. This was partly because Hitler had publicly stated just prior to the election that Point 17 of the party program, which mandated the expropriation of land without compensation, would apply only to Jewish speculators and not private landholders. After the election, the party refocused their efforts to try to attract still more votes in the agricultural sector.[] In May, shortly after the election, Hitler considered appointing Goebbels as party propaganda chief. But he hesitated, as he worried that the removal of Gregor Strasser from the post would lead to a split in the party. Goebbels considered himself well suited to the position, and began to formulate ideas about how propaganda could be used in schools and the media.

Goebbels used the death of Horst Wessel (pictured) in 1930 as a propaganda tool against "Communist subhumans". By 1930 Berlin was the party's second-strongest base of support after Munich.[1] That year the violence between the Nazis and communists led to local SA troop leader Horst Wessel being shot by two members of the Communist Party of Germany. He later died in hospital. Exploiting Wessel's death, Goebbels turned him into a martyr for the Nazi movement. He officially declared Wessel's march *Die Fahne hoch* (*Raise the flag*), renamed as the *Horst-Wessel-Lied*, to be the NSDAP anthem.

GREAT DEPRESSION NAZIS USED THIS AS THEIR COVID 19 NOVEL CORONAVIRUS TO LAUNCH THE PAL JOEY KAMIKAZE KAMALA REICH TO LAST A THOUSAND YEARS

The Great Depression greatly impacted Germany and by 1930 there was a dramatic increase in unemployment. During this time, the Strasser brothers started publishing a new daily newspaper in Berlin, the *Nationaler Sozialist*. Like their other publications, it conveyed the brothers' own brand of Nazism, including nationalism, anti-capitalism, social reform, and anti-Westernism. Goebbels complained vehemently about the rival Strasser newspapers to Hitler, and admitted that their success was causing his own Berlin newspapers to be "pushed to the wall". In late April 1930, Hitler publicly and firmly announced his opposition to Gregor Strasser and appointed Goebbels to replace him as Reich leader of NSDAP propaganda. One of Goebbels' first acts was to ban the evening edition of the *Nationaler Sozialist*. Goebbels was also given control of other Nazi papers across the country, including the party's national newspaper, the *Völkischer Beobachter* (*People's Observer*). He still had to wait until 3 July for Otto Strasser and his supporters to announce they were leaving the NSDAP. Upon receiving the news, Goebbels was relieved the "crisis" with the Strassers was finally over and glad that Otto Strasser had lost all power.

The rapid deterioration of the economy led to the resignation on 27 March 1930 of the coalition government that had been elected in 1928. A new cabinet was formed, and Paul von Hindenburg used his power as president to govern via emergency decrees. He appointed Heinrich Brüning as chancellor. Goebbels took charge of the NSDAP's national campaign for Reichstag

elections called for 14 September 1930. Campaigning was undertaken on a huge scale, with thousands of meetings and speeches held all over the country. Hitler's speeches focused on blaming the country's economic woes on the Weimar Republic, particularly its adherence to the terms of the Treaty of Versailles, which required war reparations that had proven devastating to the German economy. He proposed a new German society based on race and national unity. The resulting success took even Hitler and Goebbels by surprise: the party received 6.5 million votes nationwide and took 107 seats in the Reichstag, making it the second largest party in the country.

Goebbels and his daughter Helga with Adolf Hitler

In late 1930 Goebbels met Magda Quandt, a divorcée who had joined the party a few months earlier. She worked as a volunteer in the party offices in Berlin, helping Goebbels organise his private papers.[Her flat on the *Reichskanzlerplatz* soon became a favourite meeting place for Hitler and other NSDAP officials. Goebbels and Quandt married on 19 December 1931.

For two further elections held in 1932, Goebbels organised massive campaigns that included rallies, parades, speeches, and Hitler travelling around the country by aeroplane with the slogan "the Führer over Germany". Goebbels wrote in his diary that the Nazis must gain power and exterminate Marxism. He undertook numerous speaking tours during these election campaigns and had some of their speeches published on gramophone records and as pamphlets. Goebbels was also involved in the production of a small collection of silent films that could be shown at party meetings, though they did not yet have enough equipment to widely use this medium. Many of Goebbels› campaign posters used violent imagery such as a giant half-clad male destroying political opponents or other perceived enemies such as "International High Finance". His propaganda characterised the opposition as "November criminals", "Jewish wire-pullers", or a communist threat. Support for the party continued to grow, but neither of these elections led to a majority government. In an effort to stabilise the country and improve economic conditions, Hindenburg appointed Hitler as Reich chancellor on 30 January 1933.

To celebrate Hitler's appointment as chancellor, Goebbels organised a torchlight parade in Berlin on the night of 30 January of an estimated 60,000 men, many in the uniforms of the SA and SS. The spectacle was covered by a live state radio broadcast, with commentary by longtime party member and future Minister of Aviation Hermann Göring. Goebbels was disappointed not to be given a post in Hitler's new cabinet. Bernhard Rust was appointed as Minister of Culture, the post that Goebbels was expecting to receive.[Like other NSDAP officials, Goebbels had to deal with Hitler's leadership style of giving contradictory orders to his subordinates, while placing them into positions where their duties and responsibilities overlapped. In this way, Hitler fostered distrust, competition, and infighting among his subordinates to consolidate and maximise his own power. The NSDAP took advantage of the Reichstag fire of 27 February 1933, with Hindenburg passing the Reichstag Fire Decree the following day at Hitler›s urging. This was the first of several pieces of legislation that dismantled democracy in Germany and put a totalitarian dictatorship—headed by Hitler—in its place. On 5 March, yet another Reichstag election took place, the last to be held before the defeat of the Nazis at the end of the Second World War. While the NSDAP increased their number of seats and percentage of the vote, it was not the landslide expected by the party leadership. Goebbels finally received Hitler's appointment to the cabinet, officially becoming head of the newly created Reich Ministry of Public Enlightenment and Propaganda on 14 March.

NAZI BOOK BURNING, 10 May 1933 WHEN YOU SHOW UP FOR THE PAL JOEY & KAMIKAZE KAMALA WEEKLY BOOK BURNINGS; THAT WILL REPLACE MONDAY NIGHT FOOTBALL; BRING THIS & ALL MY OTHER BOOKS FOR FREE LARGE BUTTERED POPCORN & YER CHOICE OR LARGE RED OF BLACK LICORICE TWIZZLERS

The role of the new ministry, which set up its offices in the 18th-century Ordenspalais across from the Reich Chancellery, was to centralise Nazi control of all aspects of German cultural and intellectual life. Goebbels hoped to increase popular support of the party from the 37 per cent achieved at the last free election held in Germany on 25 March 1933 to 100 per cent support. An unstated goal was to present to other nations the impression that the NSDAP had the full and enthusiastic backing of the entire population. One of Goebbels' first productions was staging the Day of Potsdam, a ceremonial passing of power from Hindenburg to Hitler, held in Potsdam on 21 March. He composed the text of Hitler›s decree authorising the Nazi boycott of Jewish businesses, held on 1 April. Later that month, Goebbels travelled back to Rheydt, where he was given a triumphal reception. The townsfolk lined the main street, which had been renamed in his honour. On the following day, Goebbels was declared a local hero.[]

Goebbels converted the 1 May holiday from a celebration of workers' rights (observed as such especially by the communists) into a day celebrating the NSDAP. In place of the usual ad hoc labour celebrations, he organized a huge party rally held at Tempelhof Field in Berlin. The following

day, all trade union offices in the country were forcibly disbanded by the SA and SS, and the Nazi-run German Labour Front **was created to take their place. "We are the masters of Germany," he commented in his diary entry of 3 May.[Less than two weeks later, he gave a speech at the** Nazi book burning **in Berlin on 10 May, a ceremony he suggested.[**

Meanwhile, the NSDAP began passing laws to marginalise Jews and remove them from German society. The Law for the Restoration of the Professional Civil Service**, passed on 7 April 1933, forced all non-**Aryans **to retire from the legal profession and civil service. Similar legislation soon deprived Jewish members of other professions of their right to practise. The first** Nazi concentration camps **(initially created to house political dissenters) were founded shortly after Hitler seized power. In a process termed** *Gleichschaltung* **(co-ordination), the NSDAP proceeded to rapidly bring all aspects of life under control of the party. All civilian organisations, including agricultural groups, volunteer organisations, and sports clubs, had their leadership replaced with Nazi sympathizers or party members. By June 1933, virtually the only organizations not in the control of the NSDAP were the army and the churches. On 2 June 1933, Hitler appointed Goebbels a** *Reichsleiter*, **the second highest political rank in the Nazi Party. In a move to manipulate Germany's middle class and shape popular opinion, the regime passed on 4** October 1933 the *Schriftleitergesetz* (Editor›s Law), RENAMED FAKE NEWS; FACEBOOK & TWITTER which became the cornerstone of the Nazi Party's control of the popular press. **Modeled to some extent on the system in** Benito Mussolini**'s Italy, the law defined a *Schriftleiter* as anyone who wrote, edited, or selected texts and/or illustrated material for serial publication. Individuals selected for this position were chosen based on experiential, educational, and racial criteria. The law required journalists to "regulate their work in accordance with National Socialism as a philosophy of life and as a conception of government."**

At the end of June 1934, top officials of the SA and opponents of the regime, including Gregor Strasser, were arrested and killed in a purge later called the Night of Long Knives**. Goebbels was present at the arrest of SA leader** Ernst Röhm **in Munich. On 2 August 1934, President von Hindenburg died. In a radio broadcast, Goebbels announced that the offices of president and chancellor had been combined, and Hitler had been formally named as** *Führer und Reichskanzler* **(leader and chancellor).**

Workings of the Ministry

The propaganda ministry was organized into seven departments: administration and legal; mass rallies, public health, youth, and race; radio; national and foreign press; films and film censorship; art, music, and theatre; and protection against counter-propaganda, both foreign and domestic. Goebbels's style of leadership was tempestuous and unpredictable. He would suddenly change direction and shift his support between senior associates; he was a difficult boss and liked to berate his staff in public. Goebbels was successful at his job, however; *Life* wrote in 1938 that "Personally he likes nobody, is liked by nobody, and runs the most efficient Nazi department."John Gunther **wrote in 1940 that Goebbels "is the cleverest of all the Nazis", but could not succeed Hitler because "everybody hates him".**

The Reich Film Chamber, which all members of the film industry were required to join, was created in June 1933. Goebbels promoted the development of films with a Nazi slant, and ones that contained subliminal or overt propaganda messages. Under the auspices of the *Reichskulturkammer* (Reich Chamber of Culture), created in September, Goebbels added additional sub-chambers for the fields of broadcasting, fine arts, literature, music, the press, and the theatre. As in the film industry, anyone wishing to pursue a career in these fields had to be a member of the corresponding chamber. In this way anyone whose views were contrary to the regime could be excluded from working in their chosen field and thus silenced.[In addition, journalists (now considered employees of the state) were required to prove Aryan descent back to the year 1800, and if married, the same requirement applied to the spouse. Members of any chamber were not allowed to leave the country for their work without prior permission of their chamber. A committee was established to censor books, and works could not be re-published unless they were on the list of approved works. Similar regulations applied to other fine arts and entertainment; even cabaret performances were censored. Many German artists and intellectuals left Germany in the pre-war years rather than work under these restrictions.

Free radios were distributed in Berlin on Goebbels' birthday in 1938.

Goebbels was particularly interested in controlling the radio, which was then still a fairly new mass medium. Sometimes under protest from individual states (particularly Prussia, headed by Göring), Goebbels gained control of radio stations nationwide, and placed them under the *Reichs-Rundfunk-Gesellschaft* (German National Broadcasting Corporation) in July 1934. Manufacturers were urged by Goebbels to produce inexpensive home receivers, called *Volksempfänger* (people›s receiver), and by 1938 nearly ten million sets had been sold. Loudspeakers were placed in public areas, factories, and schools, so that important party broadcasts would be heard live by nearly all Germans. On 2 September 1939 (the day after the start of the war), Goebbels and the Council of Ministers proclaimed it illegal to listen to foreign radio stations. Disseminating news from foreign broadcasts could result in the death penalty. Albert Speer, Hitler's architect and later Minister for Armaments and War Production, later said the regime "made the complete use of all technical means for domination of its own country. Through technical devices like the radio and loudspeaker, 80 million people were deprived of independent thought."

Hitler was the focal point at the 1934 Nuremberg Rally. Leni Riefenstahl and her crew are visible in front of the podium.

A major focus of Nazi propaganda was Hitler himself, who was glorified as a heroic and infallible leader and became the focus of a cult of personality. Much of this was spontaneous, but some was stage-managed as part of Goebbels' propaganda work.[Adulation of Hitler was the focus of the 1934 Nuremberg Rally, where his moves were carefully choreographed. The rally was the subject of the film *Triumph of the Will*, one of several Nazi propaganda films directed by Leni Riefenstahl. It won the Gold Medal at the 1935 Venice Film Festival. At the 1935 Nazi party congress rally at Nuremberg, Goebbels declared that "Bolshevism is the declaration of war by Jewish-led international subhumans against culture itself."

Goebbels was involved in planning the staging of the 1936 Summer Olympics, held in Berlin. It was around this time that he met and started having an affair with the actress Lída Baarová, whom he continued to see until 1938. A major project in 1937 was the Degenerate Art Exhibition, organised by Goebbels, which ran in Munich from July to November. The exhibition proved wildly popular, attracting over two million visitors. A degenerate music exhibition took place the following year. [Meanwhile, Goebbels was disappointed by the lack of quality in the National Socialist artwork, films, and literature.

Church struggle

Nazi persecution of the Catholic Church in Germany

In 1933, Hitler signed the *Reichskonkordat* (Reich Concordat), a treaty with the Vatican that required the regime to honour the independence of Catholic institutions and prohibited clergy from involvement in politics. However, the regime continued to target the Christian churches to weaken their influence. Throughout 1935 and 1936, hundreds of clergy and nuns were arrested, often on trumped up charges of currency smuggling or sexual offences. Goebbels widely publicised the trials in his propaganda campaigns, showing the cases in the worst possible light. Restrictions were placed on public meetings, and Catholic publications faced censorship. Catholic schools were required to reduce religious instruction and crucifixes were removed from state buildings. Hitler often vacillated on whether or not the *Kirchenkampf* (church struggle) should be a priority, but his frequent inflammatory comments on the issue were enough to convince Goebbels to intensify his work on the issue; in February 1937 he stated he wanted to eliminate the Protestant church.

In response to the persecution, Pope Pius XI had the "*Mit brennender Sorge*" ("With Burning Concern") Encyclical smuggled into Germany for Passion Sunday 1937 and read from every pulpit. It denounced the systematic hostility of the regime toward the church. In response, Goebbels renewed the regime›s crackdown and propaganda against Catholics. His speech of 28 May in Berlin in front of 20,000 party members, which was also broadcast on the radio, attacked the Catholic Church as morally corrupt. As a result of the propaganda campaign, enrolment in denominational schools dropped sharply, and by 1939 all such schools were disbanded or converted to public facilities. Harassment and threats of imprisonment led the clergy to be much more cautious in their criticism of the regime. Partly out of foreign policy concerns, Hitler ordered a scaling back of the church struggle by the end of July 1937.

World War II

As early as February 1933, Hitler announced that rearmament must be undertaken, albeit clandestinely at first, as to do so was in violation of the Versailles Treaty. A year later he told his military leaders that 1942 was the target date for going to war in the east. Goebbels was one of

the most enthusiastic supporters of Hitler aggressively pursuing Germany's expansionist policies sooner rather than later. At the time of the Reoccupation of the Rhineland in 1936, Goebbels summed up his general attitude in his diary: "[N]ow is the time for action. Fortune favors the brave! He who dares nothing wins nothing." In the lead-up to the Sudetenland crisis in 1938, Goebbels took the initiative time and again to use propaganda to whip up sympathy for the Sudeten Germans while campaigning against the Czech government.[Still, Goebbels was well aware there was a growing "war panic" in Germany and so by July had the press conduct propaganda efforts at a lower level of intensity.After the western powers acceded to Hitler's demands concerning Czechoslovakia in 1938, Goebbels soon redirected his propaganda machine against Poland. From May onwards, he orchestrated a campaign against Poland, fabricating stories about atrocities against ethnic Germans in Danzig and other cities. Even so, he was unable to persuade the majority of Germans to welcome the prospect of war. He privately held doubts about the wisdom of risking a protracted war against Britain and France by attacking Poland.

After the Invasion of Poland in 1939, Goebbels used his propaganda ministry and the Reich chambers to control access to information domestically. To his chagrin, his rival Joachim von Ribbentrop, the Minister for Foreign Affairs, continually challenged Goebbels' jurisdiction over the dissemination of international propaganda. Hitler declined to make a firm ruling on the subject, so the two men remained rivals for the remainder of the Nazi era. Goebbels did not participate in the military decision making process, nor was he made privy to diplomatic negotiations until after the fact.

Production of a newsreel at the front lines, January 1941

The Propaganda Ministry took over the broadcasting facilities of conquered countries immediately after surrender, and began broadcasting prepared material using the existing announcers as a way to gain the trust of the citizens. Most aspects of the media, both domestically and in the conquered countries, were controlled by Goebbels and his department. The German Home Service, the Armed Forces Programme, and the German European Service were all rigorously controlled in everything from the information they were permitted to disseminate to the music they were allowed to play. Party rallies, speeches, and demonstrations continued; speeches were broadcast on the radio and short propaganda films were exhibited using 1,500 mobile film vans.[Hitler made fewer public appearances and broadcasts as the war progressed, so Goebbels increasingly became the voice of the Nazi regime for the German people.From May 1940 he wrote frequent editorials that were published in *Das Reich* which were later read aloud over the radio.He found films to be his most effective propaganda medium, after radio. At his insistence, initially half the films made in wartime Germany were propaganda films (particularly on antisemitism) and war propaganda films (recounting both historical wars and current exploits of the Wehrmacht).

Goebbels became preoccupied with morale and the efforts of the people on the home front.

He believed that the more the people at home were involved in the war effort, the better their morale would be. For example, he initiated a programme for the collection of winter clothing and ski equipment for troops on the eastern front. At the same time, Goebbels implemented changes to have more "entertaining material" in radio and film produced for the public, decreeing in late 1942 that 20 per cent of the films should be propaganda and 80 per cent light entertainment. As *Gauleiter* of Berlin, Goebbels dealt with increasingly serious shortages of necessities such as food and clothing, as well as the need to ration beer and tobacco, which were important for morale. Hitler suggested watering the beer and degrading the quality of the cigarettes so that more could be produced, but Goebbels refused, saying the cigarettes were already of such low quality that it was impossible to make them any worse. Through his propaganda campaigns, he worked hard to maintain an appropriate level of morale among the public about the military situation, neither too optimistic nor too grim. The series of military setbacks the Germans suffered in this period – the thousand-bomber raid **on Cologne (May 1942), the Allied victory at the** Second Battle of El Alamein **(November 1942), and especially the catastrophic defeat at the** Battle of Stalingrad **(February 1943) – were difficult matters to present to the German public, who were increasingly weary of the war and sceptical that it could be won. On 15 January 1943, Hitler appointed Goebbels as head of the newly created Air Raid Damage committee, which meant Goebbels was nominally in charge of nationwide civil air defences and shelters as well as the assessment and repair of damaged buildings. In actuality, the defence of areas other than Berlin remained in the hands of the local *Gauleiters*, and his main tasks were limited to providing immediate aid to the affected civilians and using propaganda to improve their morale.**

By early 1943, the war produced a labour crisis for the regime. Hitler created a three-man committee with representatives of the State, the army, and the Party in an attempt to centralise control of the war economy. The committee members were Hans Lammers **(head of the Reich Chancellery), Field Marshal** Wilhelm Keitel**, chief of the** *Oberkommando der Wehrmacht* **(Armed Forces High Command; OKW), and** Martin Bormann**, who controlled the Party. The committee was intended to independently propose measures regardless of the wishes of various ministries, with Hitler reserving most final decisions to himself. The committee, soon known as the *Dreierausschuß* (Committee of Three), met eleven times between January and August 1943. However, they ran up against resistance from Hitler›s cabinet ministers, who headed deeply entrenched spheres of influence and were excluded from the committee. Seeing it as a threat to their power, Goebbels, Göring, and Speer worked together to bring it down. The result was that nothing changed, and the Committee of Three declined into irrelevance by September 1943.**[

Sportpalast speech, 18 February 1943. The banner says ***"TOTALER KRIEG – KÜRZESTER KRIEG"*** ("Total War – Shortest War")

Partly in response to being excluded from the Committee of Three, Goebbels pressured Hitler to introduce measures that would produce "total war", including closing businesses not essential to the war effort, conscripting women into the labour force, and enlisting men in previously exempt occupations into the Wehrmacht. Some of these measures were implemented in an edict of 13 January, but to Goebbels' dismay, Göring demanded that his favourite restaurants in Berlin should remain open, and Lammers successfully lobbied Hitler to have women with children exempted from conscription, even if they had child care available. After receiving an enthusiastic response to his speech of 30 January 1943 on the topic, Goebbels believed he had the support of the German people in his call for total war. His next speech, the Sportpalast speech of 18 February 1943, was a passionate demand for his audience to commit to total war, which he presented as the only way to stop the Bolshevik onslaught and save the German people from destruction. The speech also had a strong anti-semitic element and hinted at the extermination of the Jewish people that was already underway. The speech was presented live on radio and was filmed as well. During the live version of the speech, Goebbels accidentally begins to mention the "extermination" of the Jews; this is omitted in the published text of the speech. Goebbels' efforts had little impact for the time being, because Hitler, who in principle was in favour of total war, was not prepared to implement changes over the objections of his ministers. The discovery around this time of a mass grave of Polish officers that had been killed by the Red Army in the 1940 Katyn massacre was made use of by Goebbels in his propaganda in an attempt to drive a wedge between the Soviets and the other western allies.

Plenipotentiary for total war

Goebbels (Centre) and Armaments Minister Albert Speer (to Goebbels› left) observe tests at Peenemünde, August 1943

9 March 1945: Goebbels awards 16-year-old Hitler Youth Willi Hübner the Iron Cross for the defense of Lauban

On 1 April 1943, Goebbels was named *Stadtpräsident* of Berlin, thus uniting under his control the city›s highest party and governmental offices. After the Allied invasion of Sicily (July 1943) and the strategic Soviet victory in the Battle of Kursk (July–August 1943), Goebbels began to recognise that the war could no longer be won. Following the Allied invasion of Italy and the fall of Mussolini in September, he raised with Hitler the possibility of a separate peace, either with the Soviets or with Britain. Hitler rejected both of these proposals.

As Germany's military and economic situation grew steadily worse, on 25 August 1943 *Reichsführer-SS* Heinrich Himmler took over the post of interior minister, replacing Wilhelm Frick. Intensive air raids on Berlin and other cities took the lives of thousands of people. Göring's Luftwaffe attempted to retaliate with air raids on London in early 1944, but they no longer had sufficient aircraft to make much of an impact. While Goebbels› propaganda in this period indicated that a huge retaliation was in the offing, the V-1 flying bombs, launched on British targets beginning in mid-June 1944, had little effect, with only around 20 per cent reaching their intended targets. To boost morale, Goebbels continued to publish propaganda to the effect that further improvements to these weapons would have a decisive impact on the outcome of the war. Meanwhile, in the Normandy landings of 6 June

1944, the Allies successfully gained a foothold in France.

Throughout July 1944, Goebbels and Speer continued to press Hitler to bring the economy to a total war footing. The 20 July plot, where Hitler was almost killed by a bomb at his field headquarters in East Prussia, played into the hands of those who had been pushing for change: Bormann, Goebbels, Himmler, and Speer. Over the objections of Göring, Goebbels was appointed on 23 July as Reich Plenipotentiary for Total War, charged with maximising the manpower for the Wehrmacht and the armaments industry at the expense of sectors of the economy not critical to the war effort. Through these efforts, he was able to free up an additional half a million men for military service. However, as many of these new recruits came from the armaments industry, the move put him in conflict with armaments minister Speer. Untrained workers from elsewhere were not readily absorbed into the armaments industry, and likewise, the new Wehrmacht recruits waited in barracks for their turn to be trained.

At Hitler's behest, the *Volkssturm* (People›s Storm) – a nationwide militia of men previously considered unsuitable for military service – was formed on 18 October 1944. Goebbels recorded in his diary that 100,000 recruits were sworn in from his *Gau* alone. However, the men, mostly age 45 to 60, received only rudimentary training and many were not properly armed. Goebbels› notion that these men could effectively serve on the front lines against Soviet tanks and artillery was unrealistic at best. The programme was deeply unpopular.

Defeat and Death

In the last months of the war, Goebbels' speeches and articles took on an increasingly apocalyptic tone. By the beginning of 1945, with the Soviets on the Oder River and the Western Allies preparing to cross the Rhine River, he could no longer disguise the fact that defeat was inevitable. Berlin had little in the way of fortifications or artillery, and even *Volkssturm* units were in short supply, as almost everything and everyone had been sent to the front. Goebbels noted in his diary on 21 January that millions of Germans were fleeing westward. He tentatively discussed with Hitler the issue of making peace overtures to the western allies, but Hitler again refused. Privately, Goebbels was conflicted at pushing the case with Hitler since he did not want to lose Hitler's confidence.

When other Nazi leaders urged Hitler to leave Berlin and establish a new centre of resistance in the National Redoubt in Bavaria, Goebbels opposed this, arguing for a heroic last stand in Berlin. His family (except for Magda›s son Harald, who had served in the Luftwaffe and been captured by the Allies) moved into their house in Berlin to await the end. He and Magda may have discussed suicide and the fate of their young children in a long meeting on the night of 27 January. He knew how the outside world would view the criminal acts committed by the regime, and had no desire to subject himself to the "debacle" of a trial. He burned his private papers on the night of 18 April.

Goebbels knew how to play on Hitler's fantasies, encouraging him to see the hand of providence in the death of United States President Franklin D. Roosevelt on 12 April. Whether Hitler really

saw this event as a turning point as Goebbels proclaimed is not known. By this time, Goebbels had gained the position he had wanted so long – at the side of Hitler. Göring was utterly discredited, although he was not stripped of his offices until 23 April. Himmler, whose appointment as commander of Army Group Vistula **had led to disaster on the Oder, was also in disgrace with Hitler. Most of Hitler›s inner circle, including Göring, Himmler, Ribbentrop, and Speer, prepared to leave Berlin immediately after Hitler›s birthday celebration on 20 April. Even Bormann was "not anxious" to meet his end at Hitler›s side. On 22 April, Hitler announced that he would stay in Berlin until the end and then shoot himself. Goebbels moved with his family into the** *Vorbunker*, **connected to the lower** *Führerbunker* **under the Reich Chancellery garden in central Berlin, that same day. He told Vice-Admiral** Hans-Erich Voss **that he would not entertain the idea of either surrender or escape. On 23 April, Goebbels made the following proclamation to the people of Berlin:**

I call on you to fight for your city. Fight with everything you have got, for the sake of your wives and your children, your mothers and your parents. Your arms are defending everything we have ever held dear, and all the generations that will come after us. Be proud and courageous! Be inventive and cunning! Your *Gauleiter* is amongst you. He and his colleagues will remain in your midst. His wife and children are here as well. He, who once captured the city with 200 men, will now use every means to galvanize the defence of the capital. The battle for Berlin **must become the signal for the whole nation to rise up in battle ..."**

After midnight on 29 April, with the Soviets advancing ever closer to the bunker complex, Hitler married Eva Braun **in a small civil ceremony within the *Führerbunker*. Afterwards, Hitler hosted a modest wedding breakfast. Hitler then took secretary** Traudl Junge **to another room and dictated** his last will and testament**. Goebbels and Bormann were two of the witnesses.**

In his last will and testament, Hitler named no successor as Führer or leader of the Nazi Party. Instead, he appointed Goebbels as Reich Chancellor; Grand Admiral Karl Dönitz, **who was at** Flensburg **near the Danish border, as Reich President; and Bormann as Party Minister.Goebbels wrote a postscript to the will stating that he would "categorically refuse" to obey Hitler›s order to leave Berlin–as he put it, "the first time in my life" that he had not complied with Hitler›s orders. He felt compelled to remain with Hitler "for reasons of humanity and personal loyalty". Further, his wife and children would be staying, as well. They would end their lives "side by side with the Führer".**

In the mid-afternoon of 30 April, Hitler shot himself**. Goebbels was depressed, and stated that he would walk around the Chancellery garden until he was killed by the Russian shelling. Voss later recounted Goebbels as saying: "It is a great pity that such a man (Hitler) is not with us any longer. But there is nothing to be done. For us, everything is lost now and the only way out left for us is the one which Hitler chose. I shall follow his example."**

On 1 May, Goebbels carried out his sole official act as Chancellor. He dictated a letter to General Vasily Chuikov **and ordered German General** Hans Krebs **to deliver it under a** white flag**. Chuikov, as commander of the** Soviet 8th Guards Army, **commanded the Soviet forces in central**

Berlin. Goebbels' letter informed Chuikov of Hitler's death and requested a ceasefire. After this was rejected, Goebbels decided that further efforts were futile.

The Goebbels family. In this vintage manipulated image, Goebbels' stepson Harald Quandt (who was absent due to military duty) was added to the group portrait.

Later on 1 May, Vice-Admiral Voss saw Goebbels for the last time: "... While saying goodbye I asked Goebbels to join us. But he replied: 'The captain must not leave his sinking ship. I have thought about it all and decided to stay here. I have nowhere to go because with little children I will not be able to make it, especially with a leg like mine...' " On the evening of 1 May, Goebbels arranged for an SS dentist, Helmut Kunz, to inject his six children with morphine so that when they were unconscious, an ampule of cyanide could be then crushed in each of their mouths. According to Kunz›s later testimony, he gave the children morphine injections but it was Magda Goebbels and SS-*Obersturmbannführer* Ludwig Stumpfegger, Hitler's personal doctor, who administered the cyanide.

At around 20:30, Goebbels and Magda left the bunker and walked up to the garden of the Chancellery, where they killed themselves. There are several different accounts of this event. One account was that they each bit on a cyanide ampule near where Hitler had been buried and were given a coup de grâce immediately afterwards.[ ] Goebbels› SS adjutant Günther Schwägermann testified in 1948 that they walked ahead of him up the stairs and out into the Chancellery garden. He waited in the stairwell and heard the shots sound. Schwägermann then

walked up the remaining stairs and, once outside, saw their lifeless bodies. Following Goebbels› prior order, Schwägermann had an SS soldier fire several shots into Goebbels› body, which did not move.

The bodies were then doused with petrol, but they were only partially burned and not buried. A few days later, Voss was brought back to the bunker by the Soviets to identify the partly burned bodies of Joseph and Magda Goebbels and their children. The remains of the Goebbels' family, Hitler, Braun, General Krebs, and Hitler's dogs **were repeatedly buried and exhumed. The last burial was at the** SMERSH **facility in** Magdeburg **on 21 February 1946. In 1970, KGB director** Yuri Andropov **authorized an operation to destroy the remains. On 4 April 1970, a Soviet** KGB **team used detailed burial charts to exhume five wooden boxes at the Magdeburg SMERSH facility. Those were burned, crushed, and scattered into the Biederitz river, a tributary of the nearby** Elbe.[1]

Antisemitism and the Holocaust

Old Synagogue Ohel Jakob de, Munich, after *Kristallnacht*

Goebbels was antisemitic from a young age. After joining the NSDAP and meeting Hitler, his antisemitism grew and became more radical. He began to see the Jews as a destructive force with a negative impact on German society. After the Nazis seized control, he repeatedly urged Hitler to take action against the Jews. Despite his extreme antisemitism, Goebbels spoke of the "rubbish of race-materialism" and of the unnecessity of biological racism **for the Nazi ideology. He also described Himmler›s ideology as "in many regards, mad" and thought** Alfred Rosenberg**'s theories were ridiculous.**

The Nazi Party's goal was to remove Jews from German cultural and economic life, and eventually to remove them from the country altogether. In addition to his propaganda efforts, Goebbels actively promoted the persecution of the Jews through pogroms, legislation, and other actions. Discriminatory measures he instituted in Berlin in the early years of the regime included bans against their using public transport and requiring that Jewish shops be marked as such.

In November 1938, the German diplomat Ernst vom Rath was killed in Paris by the young Jewish man Herschel Grynszpan. In response, Goebbels arranged for inflammatory antisemitic material to be released by the press, and the result was the start of a pogrom. Jews were attacked and synagogues destroyed all over Germany. The situation was further inflamed by a speech Goebbels gave at a party meeting on the night of 8 November, where he obliquely called for party members to incite further violence against Jews while making it appear to be a spontaneous series of acts by the German people. At least a hundred Jews were killed, several hundred synagogues were damaged or destroyed, and thousands of Jewish shops were vandalised in an event called *Kristallnacht* (Night of Broken Glass). Around 30,000 Jewish men were sent to concentration camps.The destruction stopped after a conference held on 12 November, where Göring pointed out that the destruction of Jewish property was in effect the destruction of German property since the intention was that it would all eventually be confiscated.

Goebbels continued his intensive antisemitic propaganda campaign that culminated in Hitler's 30 January 1939 Reichstag speech, which Goebbels helped to write.

Woman in Berlin wearing the YELLOW STAR

If international finance Jewry in and outside Europe should succeed in plunging the nations once more into a world war, then the result will not be the bolshevization of the earth and thereby the victory of Jewry, but the annihilation of the Jewish race in Europe! While Goebbels had been pressing for expulsion of the Berlin Jews since 1935, there were still 62,000 living in the city in 1940. Part of the delay in their deportation was that they were needed as workers in the armaments industry. Deportations of German Jews began in October 1941, with the first transport from Berlin leaving on 18 October. Some Jews were shot immediately on arrival in destinations such as Riga **and** Kaunas**. In preparation for the deportations, Goebbels ordered that all German Jews were required by law to wear an identifying** yellow badge **as of 5 September 1941. On 6 March 1942, Goebbels received a copy of the minutes of the** Wannsee Conference**. The document made the Nazi policy clear: the Jewish population of Europe was to be sent to** extermination camps **in occupied areas of Poland and killed. His diary entries of the period show that he was well aware of the fate of the Jews. "In general, it can probably be established that 60 per cent of them will have to be liquidated, while only 40 per cent can be put to work. ... A judgment is being carried out on the Jews which is barbaric but thoroughly deserved," he wrote on 27 March 1942.**

Goebbels had frequent discussions with Hitler about the fate of the Jews, a subject they discussed almost every time they met. He was aware throughout that the Jews were being exterminated, and completely supported this decision. He was one of the few top Nazi officials to do so publicly.

Family life

Post-reconciliation photo commissioned by Hitler, 1938.

Hitler was very fond of Magda Goebbels and the children. He enjoyed staying at the Goebbels› Berlin apartment, where he could relax. Magda had a close relationship with Hitler, and became a member of his small coterie of female friends. She also became an unofficial representative of the regime, receiving letters from all over Germany from women with questions about domestic matters or child custody issues.[

In 1936, Goebbels met the Czech actress Lída Baarová and by the winter of 1937 began an intense affair with her. Magda had a long conversation with Hitler about it on 15 August 1938. Unwilling to put up with a scandal involving one of his top ministers, Hitler demanded that Goebbels break off the relationship.Thereafter, Joseph and Magda seemed to reach a truce until the end of September. The couple had another falling out at that point, and once again Hitler became involved, insisting the couple stay together. Hitler arranged for publicity photos to be taken of himself with the reconciled couple in October. Magda too had affairs, including a relationship with Kurt Ludecke in 1933 and Karl Hanke in 1938.

The Goebbels family included Harald Quandt (Magda›s son from her first marriage; born 1921), plus Helga (1932), Hilde (1934), Helmuth (1935), Holde (1937), Hedda (1938), and Heide (1940). Harald was the only member of the family to survive the war.

FAKE NEWS ACT ONE SCENE TWO

HOORAY FOR HOLLYWOOD DEMOCRATS 2021 IS LENI RIEFENSTAHL HEIL HITLER ACH TUNG IN 1939

Leni ORIGINAL ALEXANDRIA OCASIO-CORTEZ "IT GIRL" Riefenstahl

HOLLYWOOD WANTED TO MAKE A MOVIE STARRING JODIE FOSTER REHABILITATING CESSPOOL OF A WOMAN & GLAMOURIZING THIS EVIL BITCH IN 2003; NOW WE HAVE KAMIKAZE KAMALA AS THE REAL THING IN 2021

THIS SHE DEMON SURVIVED THE REICH AND DIED AT (101) SEPTEMBER 8, 2003.

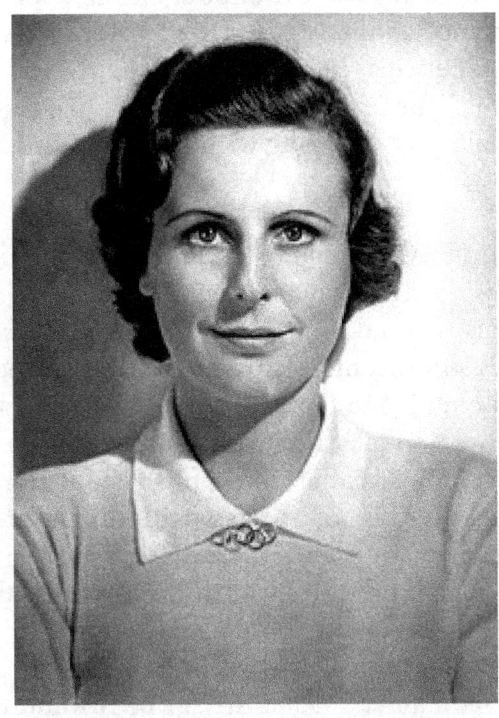

(from a 1930s postcard honoring Riefenstahl for the propaganda film *Olympia*)

Born	**Helene Bertha Amalie Riefenstahl** **22 August 1902** Berlin, Kingdom of Prussia, German Empire
Died	**8 September 2003 (aged 101)** Pöcking, Bavaria, **Germany**
Resting place	Munich Waldfriedhof
Nationality	**German**
Occupation	**Film director, producer, screenwriter, photographer, actress**
Years active	**1925–2002**
Known for	*Triumph des Willens* *Olympia*
Spouse(s)	□ **Peter Jacob (1944–1946)**

Helene Bertha

Amalie "Leni" Riefenstahl (German: 22 August 1902 – 8 September 2003) was a German film director, actress, photographer and Nazi sympathizer. A talented swimmer and an artist, she also became interested in dancing during her childhood, taking dancing lessons and performing across Europe. After seeing a promotional poster for the 1924 film *Mountain of Destiny*, Riefenstahl was inspired to move into acting. Between 1925 and 1929, she starred in five successful motion pictures. Riefenstahl became one of the few women in Germany to direct a film during the Weimar Period when, in 1932, she decided to try directing with her own film, *Das Blaue Licht* ("The Blue Light").

In the 1930s, she directed the Nazi propaganda films *Triumph des Willens* ("Triumph of the Will") and *Olympia*, resulting in worldwide attention and acclaim. The films are widely considered two of the most effective, and technically innovative, propaganda films ever made. Her involvement in *Triumph des Willens*, however, significantly damaged her career and reputation after World War II, due to the actions the Nazis committed in that conflict. Adolf Hitler was in close collaboration with Riefenstahl during the production of at least three important Nazi films, and they formed a friendly relationship. Some have argued that Riefenstahl›s visions were essential to the carrying out of the mission of the Holocaust.[6] After the war, Riefenstahl was arrested, but classified as being a "fellow traveler" or "Nazi sympathizer" only and was not associated with war crimes. Throughout her life, she denied having known about the Holocaust. Besides directing, Riefenstahl released an autobiography and wrote several books on the Nuba people.

Riefenstahl died of cancer on 8 September 2003 at the age of 101 and was buried at Munich Waldfriedhof.

Early life

Helene Bertha Amalie Riefenstahl was born in Berlin on 22 August 1902. Her father, Alfred Theodor Paul Riefenstahl, owned a successful heating and ventilation company and wanted his daughter to follow him into the business world. Since Riefenstahl was the only child for several years, Alfred wanted her to carry on the family name and secure the family fortune. However, her mother, Bertha Ida (Scherlach), who had been a part-time seamstress before her marriage, had faith in Riefenstahl and believed that her daughter's future was in show business. Riefenstahl had a younger brother, Heinz, who was killed at the age of 39 on the Eastern Front in Nazi Germany's war against the Soviet Union.

Riefenstahl fell in love with the arts in her childhood. She began to paint and write poetry at the age of four. She was also athletic, and at the age of twelve joined a gymnastics and swimming club. Her mother was confident her daughter would grow up to be successful in the field of art and therefore gave her full support, unlike Riefenstahl's father, who was not interested in his daughter's artistic inclinations. In 1918, when she was 16, Riefenstahl attended a presentation of Snow White which interested her deeply; it led her to want to be a dancer. Her father instead wanted to provide his daughter with an education that could lead to a more dignified occupation. His wife, however, continued to support her daughter›s passion. Without her father›s knowledge, she enrolled Riefenstahl in dance and ballet classes at the Grimm-Reiter Dance School in Berlin, where she

quickly became a star pupil.

In the post-war years she was subject of four denazification **proceedings, which finally declared her a Nazi sympathizer but she was never prosecuted. She was never an official member of the Nazi party but was always seen in association with the propaganda films she made during the** Third Reich**.**

Dancing & Acting careers

Riefenstahl attended dancing academies and became well known for her self-styled interpretive dancing skills, traveling across Europe with Max Reinhardt **in a show funded by Jewish producer** Harry Sokal**. Riefenstahl often made almost 700** *Reichsmarks* **for each performance and was so dedicated to dancing that she gave filmmaking no thought. She began to suffer a series of foot injuries that led to knee surgery that threatened her dancing career. It was while going to a doctor›s appointment that she first saw a poster for the 1924 film** *Mountain of Destiny*. **She became inspired to go into movie making, and began visiting the cinema to see films and also attended film shows.**[

On one of her adventures, Riefenstahl met Luis Trenker, an actor who had appeared in *Mountain of Destiny*. At a meeting arranged by her friend Gunther Rahn, she met Arnold Fanck**, the director of *Mountain of Destiny* and a pioneer of the** mountain film **genre. Fanck was working on a film in Berlin. After Riefenstahl told him how much she admired his work, she also convinced him of her acting skill. She persuaded him to feature her in one of his films. Riefenstahl later received a package from Fanck containing the script of the 1926 film** *The Holy Mountain*. **She made a series of films for Fanck, where she learned from him acting and film editing techniques. One of Fanck's films that brought Riefenstahl into the limelight was** *The White Hell of Pitz Palu* **of 1929, co-directed by** G. W. Pabst**. Her fame spread to countries outside Germany.**

Riefenstahl produced and directed her own work called *Das Blaue Licht* **("The Blue Light") in 1932, co-written by** Carl Mayer **and** Béla Balázs**. This film won the Silver Medal at the** Venice Film Festival**, but was not universally well-received, for which Riefenstahl blamed the critics, many of whom were Jewish. Upon its 1938 re-release, the names of Balázs and Sokal, both Jewish, were removed from the credits; some reports say this was at Riefenstahl's behest. In the film, Riefenstahl played an innocent peasant girl who is hated by the villagers because they think she is diabolic and cast out. She is protected by a glowing mountain grotto. According to herself, Riefenstahl received invitations to travel to Hollywood to create films, but she refused them in favour of remaining in Germany with a boyfriend. Hitler was a fan of the film, and thought Riefenstahl epitomized the perfect German female. He saw talent in Riefenstahl and arranged a meeting.**

In 1933, Riefenstahl appeared in the U.S.-German co-productions of the Arnold Fanck**-directed, German-language** *SOS Eisberg* **and the** Tay Garnett**-directed, English-language *S.O.S. Iceberg*. The films were filmed simultaneously in English and German and produced and distributed by** Universal Studios**. Her role as an actress in *S.O.S. Iceberg* was her only English language role in film.**

Directing career

Riefenstahl stands near Heinrich Himmler while instructing her camera crew at Nuremberg, 1934

Propaganda films

Riefenstahl heard Nazi Party (NSDAP) leader Adolf Hitler speak at a rally in 1932 and was mesmerized by his talent as a public speaker. Describing the experience in her memoir, Riefenstahl wrote, "I had an almost apocalyptic vision that I was never able to forget. It seemed as if the Earth›s surface were spreading out in front of me, like a hemisphere that suddenly splits apart in the middle, spewing out an enormous jet of water, so powerful that it touched the sky and shook the earth".

Hitler was immediately captivated by Riefenstahl's work. She is described as fitting in with Hitler's ideal of Aryan womanhood, a feature he had noted when he saw her starring performance in *Das Blaue Licht*. After meeting Hitler, Riefenstahl was offered the opportunity to direct *Der Sieg des Glaubens* ("The Victory of Faith"), an hour-long propaganda film about the fifth Nuremberg Rally in 1933.[] The opportunity that was offered was a huge surprise to Riefenstahl. Hitler had ordered Goebbels› Propaganda Ministry to give the film commission to Riefenstahl, but the Ministry had never informed her.[] Riefenstahl agreed to direct the movie even though she was only given a few days before the rally to prepare. She and Hitler got on well, forming a friendly relationship. The

propaganda film was funded entirely by the NSDAP.[] During the filming of *Victory of Faith,* Hitler had stood side by side with the leader of the Sturmabteilung (SA) Ernst Röhm, a man with whom he clearly had a close working relationship. Röhm was murdered on Hitler's orders a short time later during the purge of the SA referred to as the Night of the Long Knives. It has gone on record that, immediately following the killings, Hitler ordered all copies of the film to be destroyed, although Riefenstahl disputes that this ever happened.[] It was considered lost until a copy turned up in the 1990s in the United Kingdom.

Riefenstahl and a camera crew stand in front of Hitler's car during the 1934 rally in Nuremberg.

Still impressed with Riefenstahl's work, Hitler asked her to film *Triumph des Willens* ("Triumph of the Will"), a new propaganda film about the 1934 party rally in Nuremberg.[] More than one million Germans participated in the rally. The film is sometimes considered the greatest propaganda film ever made. Initially, according to Riefenstahl, she resisted and did not want to create further Nazi Party films, instead wanting to direct a feature film based on Eugen d›Albert's *Tiefland* ("Lowlands"), an opera that was extremely popular in Berlin in the 1920s. Riefenstahl received private funding for the production of *Tiefland*, but the filming in Spain was derailed and the project was cancelled. (When *Tiefland* was eventually shot, between 1940 and 1944, it was done in black and white, and was the third most expensive film produced during the Third Reich. During the filming of *Tiefland,* Riefenstahl utilized Romani from internment camps for extras, who were severely mistreated on set, and when the filming completed they were sent to the death camp Auschwitz.) Hitler was able to convince her to film *Triumph des Willens* on the condition that she would not be required to make further films for the party, according to Riefenstahl. The motion picture was generally recognized as an epic, innovative work of propaganda filmmaking. The film took Riefenstahl›s career to a new level and gave her further international recognition.

In interviews for the 1993 documentary *The Wonderful, Horrible Life of Leni Riefenstahl*, Riefenstahl adamantly denied any deliberate attempt to create Nazi propaganda and said she was disgusted that *Triumph des Willens* was used in such a way.

Despite allegedly vowing not to make any more films about the Nazi Party, Riefenstahl made the 28-minute *Tag der Freiheit: Unsere Wehrmacht* ("Day of Freedom: Our Armed Forces") about the German Army in 1935. Like *Der Sieg des Glaubens* and *Triumph des Willens,* this was filmed at the annual Nazi Party rally at Nuremberg. Riefenstahl said this film was a sub-set of *Der Sieg des Glaubens,* added to mollify the German Army which felt it was not represented well in *Triumph des Willens.*

Hitler invited Riefenstahl to film the 1936 Summer Olympics scheduled to be held in Berlin, a film which Riefenstahl said had been commissioned by the International Olympic Committee. She visited Greece to take footage of the route of the inaugural torch relay and the games› original site at Olympia, where she was aided by Greek photographer Nelly's. This material became *Olympia*, a hugely successful film which has since been widely noted for its technical and aesthetic achievements.[] *Olympia* was secretly funded by the Third Reich.[] She was one of the first filmmakers

to use tracking shots in a documentary, placing a camera on rails to follow the athletes› movement. The film is also noted for its slow motion shots.[Riefenstahl played with the idea of slow motion, underwater diving shots, extremely high and low shooting angles, panoramic aerial shots, and tracking system shots for allowing fast action. Many of these shots were relatively unheard of at the time, but Leni›s use and augmentation of them set a standard, and is the reason they are still used to this day.[Riefenstahl›s work on *Olympia* has been cited as a major influence in modern sports photography. Riefenstahl filmed competitors of all races, including African-American

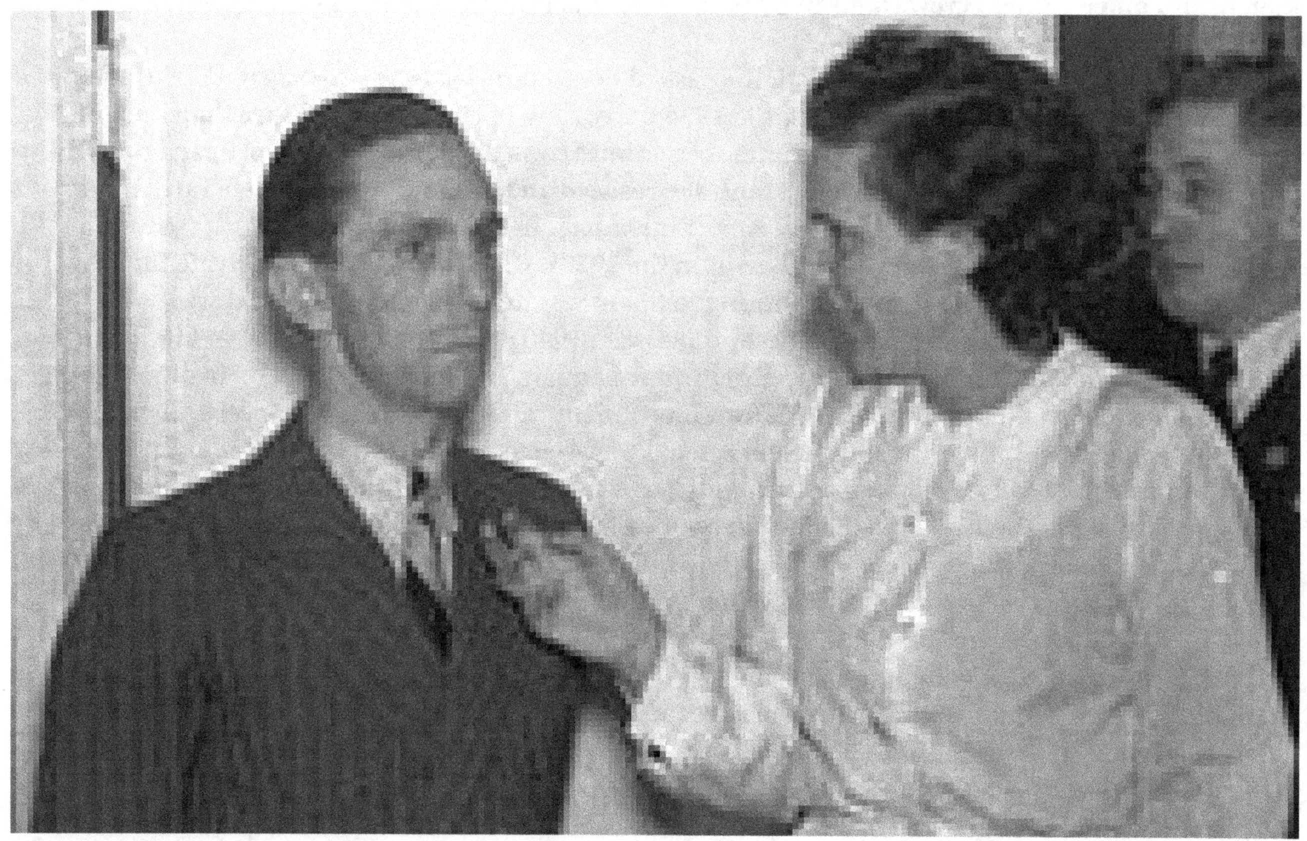

Riefenstahl in conversation with Propaganda Minister Joseph Goebbels, 1937

Olympia premiered for Hitler›s 49th birthday in 1938. Its international debut led Riefenstahl to embark on an American publicity tour in an attempt to secure commercial release. In February 1937, Riefenstahl enthusiastically told a reporter for the *Detroit News*, "To me, Hitler is the greatest man who ever lived. He truly is without fault, so simple and at the same time possessed of masculine strength".She arrived in New York City on 4 November 1938, five days before *Kristallnacht* (the "Night of the Broken Glass"). When news of the event reached the United States, Riefenstahl publicly defended Hitler. On 18 November, she was received by Henry Ford in Detroit. *Olympia* was shown at the Chicago Engineers Club two days later. Avery Brundage, President of the International Olympic Committee, praised the film and held Riefenstahl in the highest regard. She negotiated with Louis B. Mayer, and on 8 December, Walt Disney brought her on a three-hour tour showing her

the ongoing production of *Fantasia*. From the *Goebbels Diaries*, researchers learned that Riefenstahl had been friendly with Joseph Goebbels and his wife Magda, attending the opera with them and going to his parties. Riefenstahl maintained that Goebbels was upset when she rejected his advances and was jealous of her influence on Hitler, seeing her as an internal threat. She therefore insisted his diary entries could not be trusted. By later accounts, Goebbels thought highly of Riefenstahl's filmmaking but was angered with what he saw as her overspending on the Nazi-provided filmmaking budgets.

Iconography

In *Triumph of the Will,* Tom Saunders argues that Hitler serves as the object of the camera›s gaze. Saunders writes, "Without denying that "rampant masculinity" (the "sexiness" of Hitler and the SS) serves as the object of the gaze, I would suggest that desire is also directed toward the feminine. This occurs not in the familiar sequences of adoring women greeting Hitler's arrival and cavalcade through Nuremberg. In these Hitler clearly remains the focus of attraction, as more generally in the visual treatment of his mass following. Rather, it is encoded in representation of flags and banners, which were shot in such a way as to make them visually desirable as well as potent political symbols". The SWASTIKA flag serves as a symbol of masculinity, equated with national pride and dominance; that channels men's sexual and masculine energy. Riefenstahl's cinematic framing of the flags encapsulated its iconography. Saunders continues, "The effect is a significant double transformation: the images mechanize human beings and breathe life into flags. Even when the carriers are not mostly submerged under the sea of colored cloth, and when facial features are visible in profile, they attain neither character nor distinctiveness. The men remain ants in a vast enterprise. By contrast and paradoxically, the flags, whether a few or hundreds peopling the frame, assume distinct identities".

Use of music

Riefenstahl distorts the diegetic sound in *Triumph of the Will.* Her distortion of sound suggests she was influenced by German art cinema. Influenced by Classical Hollywood cinema›s style, German art film employed music to enhance the narrative, establish a sense of grandeur, and to heighten the emotions in a scene. In *Triumph of the Will,* Riefenstahl used traditional folk music to accompany and intensify her shots. Ben Morgan comments on Riefenstahl›s distortion of sound: "In *Triumph of the Will*, the material world leaves no aural impression beyond the music. Where the film does combine diegetic noise with the music, the effects used are human (laughter or cheering) and offer a rhythmic extension to the music rather than a contrast to it. By replacing diegetic sound, Riefenstahl's film employs music to combine the documentary with the fantastic."[43] The music substitutes for the live sound of the event and functions to convey the meaning of her shots. The accompanied music conveys the meaning behind the images, that of national pride.

World War II

When Germany invaded Poland on 1 September 1939, Riefenstahl was photographed in Poland

wearing a military uniform and a "REAL HOTTIE" pistol on her belt in the company of German soldiers; she had gone to Poland as a war correspondent. **On 12 September, she was in the town of Końskie when 30 civilians were executed in retaliation for an alleged attack on German soldiers. According to her memoir, Riefenstahl tried to intervene but a furious German soldier held her at gunpoint and threatened to shoot her on the spot.[] She said she did not realize the victims were Jews. Photographs of a potentially distraught Riefenstahl survive from that day. Nevertheless, by 5 October 1939, Riefenstahl was back in occupied Poland filming Hitler›s victory parade in Warsaw. Afterwards, she left Poland and chose not to make any more Nazi-related films.**

Riefenstahl as a war correspondent in Poland, 1939

On 14 June 1940, the day Paris was declared an open city by the French and occupied by German troops, Riefenstahl wrote to Hitler in a telegram, "With indescribable joy, deeply moved and filled with burning gratitude, we share with you, my Führer, your and Germany's greatest victory, the entry of German troops into Paris. You exceed anything human imagination has the power to conceive, achieving deeds without parallel in the history of mankind. How can we ever thank you?" She later explained, "Everyone thought the war was over, and in that spirit I sent the cable to Hitler".[] Riefenstahl was friends with Hitler for 12 years. However, her relationship with Hitler severely declined in 1944 after her brother died on the Russian Front.

After the Nuremberg rallies trilogy and Olympia, Riefenstahl began work on the movie she had tried and failed to direct once before, namely Tiefland. On Hitler's direct order, the German government paid her seven million Reichsmarks in compensation.[I] From 23 September until 13 November 1940, she filmed in Krün near Mittenwald. The extras playing Spanish women and farmers were drawn from Romani detained in a camp at Salzburg-Maxglan who were forced to work with her. Filming at the Babelsberg Studios near Berlin began 18 months later in April 1942. This time Sinti and Roma people from the Marzahn detention camp near Berlin were compelled to work as extras. Almost to the end of her life, despite overwhelming evidence that the concentration camp occupants had been forced to work on the movie unpaid, Riefenstahl continued to maintain all the film extras survived and that she had met several of them after the war. Riefenstahl sued filmmaker Nina Gladitz, who said Riefenstahl personally chose the extras at their holding camp; Gladitz had found one of the Romani survivors and matched his memory with stills of the movie for a documentary Gladitz was filming. The German court ruled largely in favour of Gladitz, declaring that Riefenstahl had known the extras were from a concentration camp, but they also agreed that Riefenstahl had not been informed the Romani would be sent to Auschwitz after filming was completed.

Riefenstahl instructing her film crew in Poland, 1939

This issue came up again in 2002, when Riefenstahl was 100 years old and she was taken to court by a Roma Riefenstahl apologized and said, "I regret that Sinti and Roma [people] had to suffer during the period of National Socialism. It is known today that many of them were murdered in concentration camps".

In October 1944 the production of *Tiefland* moved to Barrandov Studios in Prague for interior

filming.[9] Lavish sets made these shots some of the most costly of the film. The film was not edited and released until almost ten years later. The last time Riefenstahl saw Hitler was when she married Peter Jacob on 21 March 1944. Riefenstahl and Jacob divorced in 1946. As Germany's military situation became impossible by early 1945, Riefenstahl left Berlin and was hitchhiking with a group of men, trying to reach her mother, when she was taken into custody by American troops. She walked out of a holding camp, beginning a series of escapes and arrests across the chaotic landscape. At last making it back home on a bicycle, she found that American troops had seized her house.[ ] She was surprised by how kindly they treated her.

Thwarted film projects

Most of Riefenstahl's unfinished projects were lost towards the end of the war.[ ] The French government confiscated all of her editing equipment, along with the production reels of Tiefland. After years of legal wrangling, these were returned to her, but the French government had reportedly damaged some of the film stock whilst trying to develop and edit it, with a few key scenes being missing (although Riefenstahl was surprised to find the original negatives for Olympia in the same shipment). During the filming of Olympia, Riefenstahl was funded by the state to create her own production company in her own name, Riefenstahl-Film GmbH, which was uninvolved with her most influential works.[ ] She edited and dubbed the remaining material and Tiefland premiered on 11 February 1954 in Stuttgart. However, it was denied entry into the Cannes Film Festival. Although Riefenstahl lived for almost another half century, Tiefland was her last feature film.

Riefenstahl filming a difficult scene with the help of two assistants, 1936

Riefenstahl tried many times to make more films during the 1950s and 1960s, but was met with resistance, public protests and sharp criticism. Many of her filmmaking peers in Hollywood had fled Nazi Germany and were unsympathetic to her. Although both film professionals and investors were willing to support her work, most of the projects she attempted were stopped owing to ever-renewed and highly negative publicity about her past work for the Third Reich.[9]

In 1954, Jean Cocteau, who greatly admired the film, insisted on *Tiefland* being shown at the Cannes Film Festival, which he was running that year. In 1960, Riefenstahl attempted to prevent filmmaker Erwin Leiser from juxtaposing scenes from *Triumph des Willens* with footage from concentration camps in his film *Mein Kampf*. Riefenstahl had high hopes for a collaboration with Cocteau called *Friedrich und Voltaire* ("Friedrich and Voltaire"), wherein Cocteau was to play two roles. They thought the film might symbolize the love-hate relationship between Germany and France. Cocteau's illness and 1963 death put an end to the project. A musical remake of *Das Blaue Licht* ("The Blue Light") with an English production company also fell apart. In the 1960s, Riefenstahl became interested in Africa from Ernest Hemingway's *Green Hills of Africa* and from the photographs of George Rodger. She visited Kenya for the first time in 1956 and later Sudan, where she photographed Nuba tribes with whom she sporadically lived, learning about their culture so she could photograph them more easily. Even though her film project about modern slavery entitled *Die Schwarze Fracht* ("The Black Cargo") was never completed, Riefenstahl was able to sell the stills from the expedition to magazines in various parts of the world. While scouting shooting locations, she almost died from injuries received in a truck accident.[9] **After waking up from a coma in a Nairobi hospital, she finished writing the script, but was soon thoroughly thwarted by uncooperative locals, the Suez Canal crisis and bad weather. In the end, the film project was called off. Even so, Riefenstahl was granted Sudanese citizenship for her services to the country, becoming the first foreigner to receive a Sudanese passport.**

Detention and trials

Novelist and sports writer Budd Schulberg, assigned by the U.S. Navy to the OSS for intelligence work while attached to John Ford's documentary unit, was ordered to arrest Riefenstahl at her chalet in Kitzbühel, ostensibly to have her identify Nazi war criminals in German film footage captured by the Allied troops shortly after the war.[**Riefenstahl said she was not aware of the nature of the internment camps. According to Schulberg, "She gave me the usual song and dance. She said, 'Of course, you know, I'm really so misunderstood. I'm not political'".**

Riefenstahl said she was fascinated by the Nazis, but also politically naive, remaining ignorant about war crimes.[**Throughout 1945 to 1948, she was held by various Allied-controlled prison camps across Germany. She was also under house arrest for a period of time. She was tried four times by postwar authorities for denazification and eventually found to be a "fellow traveller" (*Mitläufer*) who sympathised with the Nazis. She won more than fifty libel cases against people accusing her of having previous knowledge regarding the Nazi party. Riefenstahl said that her**

biggest regret in life was meeting Hitler, declaring, "It was the biggest catastrophe of my life. Until the day I die people will keep saying, 'Leni is a Nazi', and I'll keep saying, 'But what did she do?'" Even though she went on to win up to 50 libel cases, details about her relation to the Nazi party generally remain unclear.[

Shortly before she died, Riefenstahl voiced her final words on the subject of her connection to Adolf Hitler in a BBC interview: "I was one of millions who thought Hitler had all the answers. We saw only the good things; we didn't know bad things were to come."

Africa, photography, books and final film

Riefenstahl began a lifelong companionship with her cameraman Horst Kettner, who was 40 years her junior and assisted her with the photographs; they were together from the time she was 60 and he was 20. Riefenstahl traveled to Africa, inspired by the works of George Rodger that celebrated the ceremonial wrestling matches of the Nuba. Riefenstahl's books with photographs of the Nuba tribes were published in 1974 and republished in 1976 as *Die Nuba* **(translated as "The Last of the Nuba") and** *Die Nuba von Kau* **("The Nuba People of Kau"). While heralded by many as outstanding color photographs, they were harshly criticized by** Susan Sontag**, who wrote in a review that they were further evidence of Riefenstahl's "fascist aesthetics".Susan Sontag also claimed that Riefenstahl's "mass athletic demonstrations, a choreographed display of bodies" showed that she had never progressed past her Nazi idealisms. Art Director's Club of Germany awarded Riefenstahl a gold medal for the best photographic achievement of 1975. She also sold some of the pictures to German magazines. She photographed the** 1972 Olympic Games **in Munich, and rock star** Mick Jagger **along with his wife** Bianca **for** *The Sunday Times***. Years later, Riefenstahl photographed** Las Vegas **entertainers** Siegfried & Roy**. She was guest of honour at the** 1976 Olympic Games **in** Montreal, Quebec**, Canada.**

In 1978, Riefenstahl published a book of her sub-aquatic photographs called *Korallengärten* **("Coral Gardens"), followed by the 1990 book** *Wunder unter Wasser* **("Wonder under Water"). In her 90s, Riefenstahl was still photographing marine life and gained the distinction of being one of the world›s oldest scuba divers. On 22 August 2002, her 100th birthday, she released the film** *Impressionen unter Wasser* **("Underwater Impressions"), an idealized documentary of life in the oceans and her first film in over 25 years. Riefenstahl was a member of** Greenpeace **for eight years.**[73] **When filming *Impressionen unter Wasser*, Riefenstahl lied about her age in order to be certified for scuba diving. Riefenstahl survived a** helicopter **crash in Sudan in 2000 while trying to learn the fates of her Nuba friends during the** Second Sudanese Civil War **and was airlifted to a Munich hospital where she received treatment for two broken ribs.**

Death

Riefenstahl's grave in Munich Cemetery. REMEMBER TO EMPTY THE KITTY LITTER BOX ON THIS & THEN URINATE ON IT.

Riefenstahl celebrated her 101st birthday on 22 August 2003 at a hotel in Feldafing**, on** Lake Starnberg**,** Bavaria**, near her home. The day after her birthday celebration, she became ill.**

Riefenstahl had been suffering from cancer for some time, and her health rapidly deteriorated during the last weeks of her life. Kettner said in an interview in 2002, "Ms. Riefenstahl is in great pain and she has become very weak and is taking painkillers". Riefenstahl died in her sleep at around 10:00 pm on 8 September 2003 at her home in Pöcking**, Germany. After her death, there was a varied response in the obituary pages of leading publications, although most recognized her technical breakthroughs in filmmaking.**

Reception

Film scholar Mark Cousins **notes in his book** *The Story of Film* **that, "Next to** Orson Welles **and** Alfred Hitchcock**, Leni Riefenstahl was the most technically talented Western film maker of her era".**

When traveling to Hollywood, Riefenstahl was criticized by the Anti-Nazi League very harshly when wanting to showcase her film *Olympia* soon after its release. Reviewer Gary Morris called Riefenstahl, "An artist of unparalleled gifts, a woman in an industry dominated by men, one of the great formalists of the cinema on a par with Eisenstein **or** Welles**".**

TIME

The Weekly Newsmagazine

Riefenstahl on the cover of *Time*, 1936

Film critic Hal Erickson of *The New York Times* states that the "Jewish Question" is mainly unmentioned in *Triumph des Willens*; LIKE BY USA DEMOCRATS IN 2021 "filmmaker Leni Riefenstahl prefers to concentrate on cheering crowds, precision marching, military bands, and Hitler's climactic speech, all orchestrated, choreographed and illuminated on a scale that makes Griffith and DeMille look like poverty-row directors".

Charles Moore of *The Daily Telegraph* wrote, "She was perhaps the most talented female cinema director of the 20th century; her celebration of Nazi Germany in film ensured that she was certainly the most infamous".

Film journalist Sandra Smith from *The Independent* remarked, "Opinions will be divided between those who see her as a young, talented and ambitious woman caught up in the tide of events which she did not fully understand, and those who believe her to be a cold and opportunist propagandist and a Nazi by association."

Critic Judith Thurman said in *The New Yorker* that, "Riefenstahl›s genius has rarely been questioned, even by critics who despise the service to which she lent it. Riefenstahl was a consummate stylist obsessed with bodies in motion, particularly those of dancers and athletes. Riefenstahl relies heavily for her transitions on portentous cutaways to clouds, mist, statuary, foliage, and rooftops. Her reaction shots have a tedious sameness: shining, ecstatic faces—nearly all young and Aryan, except

for Hitler›s".

Pauline Kael, **also a film reviewer employed for *The New Yorker*, called *Triumph des Willens* and *Olympia*, "the two greatest films ever directed by a woman".**

Writer Richard Corliss wrote in Time **that he was "impressed by Riefenstahl›s standing as a total auteur: producer, writer, director, editor and, in the fiction films, actress. The issues her films and her career raise are as complex and they are important, and her vilifiers tend to reduce the argument to one of a director›s complicity in atrocity or her criminal ignorance".**

Biographies (FILM) BEING A GLAMOUROUS; OOZING WITH DESIRE NAZI SEX SYMBOL REALLY ISN'T POLITICAL. A 2021 HOLLYWOOD DEMOCRAT WHO HATES THE GUTS OF 76 MILLION TRUMP VOTERS IS BLOWN OFF AS FORGIVABLE "YOUTHFUL GENOCIDAL INDISCRETION" NAZI OR DEMOCRAT, EVERYONE MAKES FORGIVABLE AUSCHWITZ GAS CHAMBER EXTERMINATION OF HELPLESS OLD MEN; WOMEN; CHILDLEN & MISTAKES? DON'T WE ALL? YEAH. JODIE BABY SCHNOOKS.

In 1993, Riefenstahl was the subject of the award-winning German documentary film *The Wonderful, Horrible Life of Leni Riefenstahl*, **directed by Ray Müller. Riefenstahl appeared in the film and answered several questions and detailed the production of her films. The biofilm was nominated for seven** Emmy Awards, **winning in one category. Riefenstahl, who for some time had been working on her memoirs, decided to cooperate in the production of this documentary to tell her life story about the struggles she had gone through in her personal life, her film-making career and what people thought of her. She was also the subject of Müller's 2000 documentary film** *Leni Riefenstahl: Her Dream of Africa*, **about her return to Sudan to visit the Nuba people. In 1987 an autobiography about Riefenstahl was released,** *Leni Riefenstahl's Memoiren*, **regarding her life as a filmmaker and her post-war life.**

In 2000, Jodie Foster WAS EAGER TO GLAMOURIZE A FEMINIST SYMPATHETIC BIOGRAPHICAL GLORIFICATION OF ALEXANDRIA OCASIO-CORTEZ REIFENSTAHL; then seen as the last surviving member of Hitler's "inner circle", **causing protests, with the** Simon Wiesenthal Centre**'s dean** Marvin Hier **warning against a revisionist view that glorified the director, observing that Riefenstahl had seemed "quite infatuated" with Hitler. In 2007 British screenwriter Rupert Walters was reported to be writing a script for the movie. The project did not receive Riefenstahl›s approval prior to her death, as Riefenstahl asked for a veto on any scenes to which she did not agree.**

RIEFENSTAHL DESPERATELY WANTED **HOTTIE SHARON STONE** TO BE HER ROLE MODEL TO 2021 DEMOCRATS; INSTEAD OF MORGUE CHILL LESBIAN FOSTER. THIS LOATHSOME, FUCKEN LESBIAN JODIE FOSTER DESPERATELY WANTED TO WEAVE HER SYMPATHETIC, GLAMOUROUS (5) SENSES TAPESTRY OF THE NAZI "SHE DEMON" WHO OUTLASTED THE THOUSAND YEAR REICH.

Arizona Secretary of State Referred to Trump's 'Base' as 'Neo-Nazi' in 2017

Joel B. Pollak

Arizona Secretary of State Katie Hobbs said in 2017 that President Donald Trump's "base" of supporters were .""Neo-Nazi

Hobbs, who is overseeing the closely contested vote in Arizona, was a Democratic state senator immediately prior to being elected Secretary of State in 2018. She was far behind on Election Day, but eventually surpassed her Republican opponent as more votes were counted in the days that followed.

In 2017, Hobbs tweeted:

Hobbs appeared to be reacting to news reports about the riots in Charlottesville in August 2017.

The president did, in fact, condemn extremists on all sides in Charlottesville. While he did not single out any group in his initial statement, he later made two separate specific condemnations of the neo-Nazis. The timeline was as follows:

- **Aug. 12, 2017: Trump condemned "violence "on many sides" in Charlottesville, after neo-**

Nazi and Antifa clashes

- **Aug. 14, 2017: Trump** condemned **"neo-Nazis, white supremacists, and other hate groups" in White House statement**
- **Aug. 15, 2017: Trump** condemned **neo-Nazis "totally," praised non-violent protesters "on both sides" of statue debate**

Last week, Hobbs predicted that there would be no recount of the presidential vote in Arizona.

ABC 15 Arizona reported: "Under Arizona law, an election has to be decided by 200 votes or less, or one-tenth of one percent of the votes cast, whichever is the smaller number. No one is predicting either candidate will lose by 200 votes or less."As of Thursday morning, Joe Biden led Trump by over 11,000 votes in the state. 2011, director Steven Soderbergh revealed that he had also been working on a biopic of Riefenstahl for about six months. He eventually abandoned the project over concerns of its commercial prospects.[

In popular culture

In 1998 Neue Deutsche Härte band Rammstein released a cover of the Depeche Mode song "Stripped", accompanied by a video incorporating footage from Olympia. Members of Rammstein praised Riefenstahl's filmmaking abilities and aesthetic choices in a 2011 documentary of the making of the video, particularly the imagery of the athletes, while simultaneously disassociating themselves from her politics.In the 2004 play Leni, by playwright Sarah Greenman, we meet two Leni Riefenstahls, one in the passionate prime of her youth and the other at the end of her life looking back. Greenman›s Leni revolves around the making of Triumph of the Will and has seen productions all over the United States. Riefenstahl's filming merits are discussed between characters in the 2009 Quentin Tarantino film Inglourious Basterds. Riefenstahl was referred to in the series finale of the television show Weeds when Nancy questions Andy for naming his daughter after a Nazi to which he replied "she was a pioneer in film-making, I don›t believe in holding grudges." Riefenstahl was portrayed by Zdena Studenková in Leni, a 2014 Slovak drama play about her fictional participation in The Tonight Show Starring Johnny Carson.[

Riefenstahl was portrayed by Dutch actress Carice van Houten in Race, a sports drama film directed by Stephen Hopkins about Jesse Owens. It was released in North America on February 19, 2016. To make her sympathetic portrayal acceptable to an American audience, the film dramatizes her quarrels with Goebbels over her direction of Olympia, especially about filming the African American star who is proving to be a politically embarrassing refutation of Nazi Germany's claims of Aryan athletic supremacy. In the 2016 short film Leni. Leni., based on the play by Tom McNab and directed by Adrian Vitoria, Hildegard Neil portrays Riefenstahl preparing to give an interview in 1993. In her dressing room she is "visited" by herself as a young woman portrayed by Valeria Kozhevnikova at three stages/ turning points in her life: as a dancer (1924), an actress (1929) and a director (1940).

The 2017 video game Wolfenstein II: The New Colossus (which takes place in an alternative 1961 where the Nazis won World War 2) features a supporting character heavily implied to be Riefenstahl, voiced by actress Kristina Klebe. Named Lady Helene, this female director is responsible for making the vast majority of the propaganda films said to be playing (most notably a big budget movie detailing how America was "liberated" by Nazis). Lady Helene is later met face to face and she is seen to closely resemble Riefenstahl. It also revealed that her mysterious "producer" is an aging, delusional Adolf Hitler and that the two share a close working relationship. Riefenstahl appears in the 2019 film Hellboy portrayed again by Kristina Klebe. Riefenstahl is one of the protagonists of the story "Parachute" from the collection Even This Wildest Hope (2019) by Seyward Goodhand.

Filmography

Acted

1925: *Wege zu Kraft und Schönheit* **("Ways to Strength and Beauty") as Dancer**

- **1926:** *Der heilige Berg* **("The Holy Mountain") as Diotima**
- **1927:** *Der große Sprung* **("The Great Leap") as Gita**
- **1928:** *Das Schicksal derer von Habsburg* **("Fate of the House of Habsburg") as Maria Vetsera**
- **1929:** *Die weiße Hölle vom Piz Palü* **("The White Hell of Pitz Palu") as Maria Maioni**
- **1930:** *Stürme über dem Mont Blanc* **("Storm Over Mont Blanc") as Hella Armstrong**
- **1931:** *Der weiße Rausch* **("The White Ecstasy") as Leni**
- **1932:** *Das blaue Licht* **("The Blue Light") as Junta**
- **1933:** *S.O.S. Eisberg* **("S.O.S. Iceberg") as Hella, seine Frau**
- **1954:** *Tiefland* **("Lowlands") as Martha, eine spanische Betteltänzerin (final film role)**

Directed/produced1932: ***Das blaue Licht*** **("The Blue Light")**

- **1933:** *Der Sieg des Glaubens* **("The Victory of Faith")**
- **1935:** *Triumph des Willens* **("Triumph of the Will")**
- **1935:** *Tag der Freiheit: Unsere Wehrmacht* **("Day of Freedom: Our Armed Forces")**
- **1937:** ***Wilde Wasser*** **("Wild Water")**
- **1938:** *Olympia*
- **1954:** *Tiefland* **("Lowlands")**
- **1965:** ***Allein unter den Nuba*** **("Alone Among the Nuba") (Unreleased)**
- **2002:** *Impressionen unter Wasser* **("Impressions under Water")**

Books***Riefenstahl, Leni (1973).*** *Die Nuba [The Last of the Nuba]. ISBN 978-0-312-13642-0.*

- ***Riefenstahl, Leni (1976).*** *Die Nuba von Kau [The Nuba People of Kau]. ISBN 978-0-312-16963-3.*
- ***Riefenstahl, Leni (1978).*** *Korallengärten* [Coral Gardens]. *ISBN 978-0-06-013591-1.*
- ***Riefenstahl, Leni (1982).*** *Mein Afrika [Vanishing Africa]. ISBN 978-0-517-54914-8.*
- ***Riefenstahl, Leni (1987).*** *Leni Riefenstahl's Memoiren* [Leni Riefenstahl's Memoir]. *ISBN 978-3-8228-0834-4.*
- ***Riefenstahl, Leni (1990).*** *Wunder unter Wasser [Wonder under Water]. ISBN 978-3-7766-1651-4.*
- ***Riefenstahl, Leni (1995). Leni Riefenstahl: a memoir. New York: Picador.*** *ISBN 9780312119263.*
  Review: *hooks, bell (1997). "Review: the feminazi mystique". Transition. Indiana University Press on behalf of the Hutchins Center for African and African* ***American Research at Harvard University via JSTOR.*** *73 (73): 156–162. doi:10.2307/2935451. JSTOR 2935451.*
  - ***Riefenstahl, Leni (2002). Africa.*** *ISBN 978-3-8228-1616-5.*
  - ***Riefenstahl, Leni (2002). Riefenstahl Olympia.*** *ISBN 978-3-8228-1945-6.*
  - ***ALEXANDRIA 0CASIO-CORTEZ IS THE REINCARNATION OF THIS SHE DEMON***

If Democrats Stole the Election, Here's the Only Way to Win It Back

Wayne Allyn Root

The opinions expressed by columnists are their own and do not necessarily represent the views of Townhall.com.

Mr. President, there's only one way to win this now. You need proof. Hard evidence. And witnesses who participated in the robbery. You need to create a new reality show, "Who Wants to Be an Instant Democratic Millionaire ... and Get Full Immunity?"

That's one hell of a reality show title. That offer will be a game changer. That offer will change America's future. That offer will save capitalism. That offer will save the Silent Majority and the great American middle class.

I'll explain the details of that offer in a moment. But first ...

Three weeks ago, I made an interesting prediction on my national radio show and my social media pages. I predicted President Donald Trump would win a huge electoral victory on election night; Democrats would try to steal it away from him; we'd spend weeks or months in court and eventually wind up at the Supreme Court; we'd suffer mass unrest and riots during one of the most tough, divisive periods in America's history; and then, finally, Trump would win the presidency with a Supreme Court ruling, led by our newest hero and champion of conservatism, Justice Amy Coney Barrett.

Let's look at the first part of my prediction. Trump did win an election-night electoral landslide -- before Democrats apparently stole it with massive fraud in key states, in the middle of the night. As of Nov. 3, Trump seemed to have won Florida, Ohio, Texas, Georgia, North Carolina and the Midwestern states of Pennsylvania, Michigan, Wisconsin and Iowa. What more do you want from the guy? Isn't that an electoral landslide? How can any Republican lose with that hand?

Plus, Trump received about 70 million votes. That's the most in history. Trump added a remarkable 8 million new votes since his victory in 2016. What more can a man do?

But he was never going to win. Not with 80 million votes, not with 90 million, not with 100 million. You name the number. It was never going to matter. Not with possible Democrat voter fraud, ballot harvesting, mail-in ballots and deadlines allowed well past Election Day. Trump and the GOP never had a chance. Not if you play it straight and the other guys are crooked. Remember the movie "Casino"? The mafia was alone in the "count rooms" of casinos. It's no shocker the IRS got paid very little. The mafia were the only ones allowed in the room. Everyone else got screwed.

This is the political version of casino count rooms. Except these are "vote count rooms." And the Democrat Crime Family is allegedly the only one allowed in the room, which would mean they can make up any number of votes they want, with no one watching. Just like the mafia, they do all their best work in the dark, in the middle of the night, when honest people are sleeping. They steal entire states. Now they've stolen an entire country.

Back to my solution. We can still win. But there's only one way for Trump to beat them. It's all about the Benjamins. It's all about greed. It's all about the carrot versus the stick. There's no other way to win at the Supreme Court except to bring hard evidence that the election was stolen by Democrats. The only way to get that is to bring witnesses to testify, who participated in the scam and know explicit details.

Trump must offer $1 million each to the first 100 Democrat participants in the stealing of the election who come forward. We'll create 100 instant Democrat millionaires for hard evidence, photos, videos and testimony that leads to a Supreme Court decision overturning this election. Along with $1 million to each of 100 witnesses, they each also receive full Department of Justice immunity. But if you don't come forward first, everyone else who participated is going to prison for life. Because the stealing of a presidency is treason.

Keep in mind $100 million is "chump change" to GOP billionaire donors. There's that much in loose change on any given Saturday night at Mar-a-Lago. Michael Bloomberg spent $100 million just to try to win Florida. What's $100 million for a group of GOP billionaire donors to ante up, in order to save America, American exceptionalism and capitalism?

Get Sheldon Adelson on speed dial. Mr. President, do it now. This minute. Offer a reward so big it gets the media's attention and everyone's imagination. $100 million is good. Perhaps a quarter-billion is even better. The rats always desert sinking ships. The Demo-rats will come out of the woodwork to become instant millionaires. Plus, full DOJ immunity to testify where the bodies are buried. Get busy, Mr. President. The clock is ticking. Time is short. You can't win at the Supremes unless you have hard evidence and testimony from the participants in the scam to steal the presidency. Make the announcement. Scream it from the highest mountain. "Who Wants to Be an Instant Democrat Millionaire? And Get Full Immunity." Or go to prison for life. That's an offer no one can refuse.

SD Gov. Noem: 'We Gave Al Gore 37 Days to Run the Process' – Trump Voters Deserve Same Consideration

Governor Kristi Noem (R-SD) noted Sunday on ABC's "This Week" that during the 2000 election, former Vice President Al Gore was given 37 days to run the process of legal challenges to the election.
Therefore, she said we should "afford the 70.6 million Americans that voted for President Trump the same consideration."

Partial transcript as follows:

NOEM: What I think is going on here, George, is that this is all premature. This is a premature conversation because we have not finished counting votes. There are states that have not been called, and back in 2000, Al Gore was given his day in court. We should give President Trump his day in court. Let the process unfold because, George, we live in a republic.

We are a government that gets its power from the consent of the governed. That is the people. They give their consent on Election Day. Election Day needs to be fair, honest, and transparent, and we need to be sure that we had an honest election before we decide who gets to the White House the next four years.

STEPHANOPOULOS: Governor Noem, do you have any evidence it wasn't an honest election? You had a tweet earlier this week saying it was rigged. Do you have any evidence at all of widespread fraud?

I've spoken with Republican secretaries of state in Georgia, in Arizona. I've spoken with Republican officials across the country. They have come up with zero evidence of widespread fraud.

NOEM: And that is not true. That is absolutely not true. People have signed legal documents, affidavits stating that they saw illegal activities. And that is why we need to have this conversation in court. The New York Times itself said that there were clerical errors.

STEPHANOPOULOS: No widespread fraud, Governor. That's very different.
NOEM: If you look at what happened in Michigan, that we had computer glitches that changed Republican votes to Democrat votes. You look in Pennsylvania, dead people voted in Pennsylvania. So, George, I don't know how widespread it is. I don't know if it will change the outcome of the election. But why is everybody so scared just to have a fair election and find out? We gave Al Gore 37 days to run the process before we decided who was going to be president. Why would we not afford the 70.6 million Americans that voted for President Trump the same consideration?
STEPHANOPOULOS: Governor —
NOEM: If Joe Biden —
STEPHANOPOULOS: Governor Noem —
NOEM: If Joe Biden really wants to unify this country, he would wait and make sure that we can prove we had a fair election.
STEPHANOPOULOS: Governor Noem, Al Gore, was behind by about 500 votes in one state, Florida. Joe Biden is ahead in all the close states by multiple —
NOEM: And look at how many more moving parts we have today.
STEPHANOPOULOS: 10,000 votes in Georgia, 27,000 votes in Nevada. Almost 20,000 votes in Arizona. More than 30,000 votes in Pennsylvania. That is not close. That is not within the margin that — that elections are usually turned around on.
NOEM: And many, many more states are in play this time around. And that's what I think is interesting is this declaration from some individuals saying it was an overwhelming victory for Joe Biden. It simply wasn't because you have so many of these states that are still in play. All I'm asking for, George, is that we don't break this country. When you break the process on which we elect our leaders, you will break America forever. So this isn't just about this election. This is about every election in the future. And the fact that the American people, the everyday people who get up and work hard, that are suffering through this pandemic, that have tragically lost family members, that they need to know at least — at least America still functions, and we care about doing things right.

STEPHANOPOULOS: It starts with providing evidence. You still have not provided it, but I'm afraid we're out of time today. Governor Noem, thanks for your time.

NOEM: Let the process work, and we will.

The Trump campaign has released 234 pages of affidavits regarding alleged voting regularities in Michigan. Here's what they say.

They mostly concern an alleged 'atmosphere of intimidation' at a major Detroit counting location

Leon Wolf

In recent days, the Trump campaign has touted a number of affidavits collected from poll workers in Michigan that they say proves the existence of widespread irregularities in the Michigan vote counting process, and which they plan to attach as an exhibit to an expected lawsuit that will challenge the certification of the vote in Michigan.

Calling all Americans to take back our constitutional freedoms

The campaign released those affidavits Tuesday to some members of the media (thanks to Brad Heath **of Reuters for providing me with a copy). The full .pdf file of exhibits can be read here. I have endeavored to separate the actual allegations of fraud in this post. Keep in mind that, at this point, these are mere allegations that have not been tested by cross-examination or any other form of investigation.**

POST ELECTION TREASON TRACKDOWN

Paper Warned About the Software Company at Center of Ballot Glitches in Swing States; UPDATE: MI SOS Responds

Beth Baumann

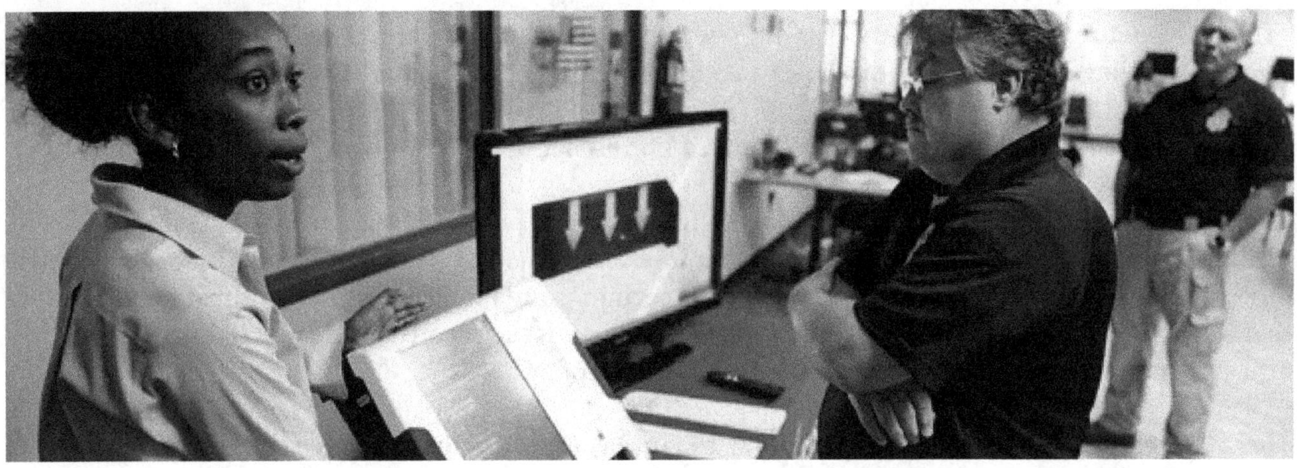

WHY IS IT THAT ALL THIS INNER CITY SWING STATE ELECTION WORKERS SEEM TO BE BLACK; WHO ARE USUALLY DEMOCRATS; AND PROBABLY HAD BIG TIME ZUCKERBUCKS SUPPLEMENTAL INCOME. I DON'T CARE IF ANY ONE TELLS ME I'M PLAYING THE RACE CARD. THE RACE CARD ALWAYS HAS & ALWAYS WILL BE PLAYED; ESPECIALLY AGAINST JEWS LIKE ME.

The Michigan Secretary of State released a statement saying there was "no merit" to the glitch in Antrim County.

"The erroneous reporting of unofficial results from Antrim county was a result of accidental error on the part of the Antrim County Clerk. The equipment and software did not malfunction and all ballots were properly tabulated. However, the clerk accidentally did not update the software used to collect voting machine data and report unofficial results," the statement read. "In order to report unofficial results, county clerks use election management system software to combine the electronic totals from tabulators and submit a report of unofficial results. Because the clerk did not update software, even though the tabulators counted the ballots correctly, those accurate results were not combined properly when the clerk reported unofficial results."

The Michigan State Republican Party on Friday revealed that a software glitch **caused 6,000 Republican ballots to be counted toward Democrat›s totals. The issue was eventually corrected when officials in Antrim County hand-counted the ballots, which caused their county to flip to President Donald Trump. According to the Michigan Republican Party Chairwoman, 48 of the state›s 83 counties use the same software from Dominion Voting Systems.**

There are now issues arising in Georgia in Spalding and Morgan Counties after it was revealed that a software update Monday night caused voting machines to crash on Election Day.

Spalding County Board of Elections Supervisor Marcia Ridley told POLITICO **Dominion Voting Systems performed an update on machines. KnowInk, which makes electronic poll books to sign voters, also created an update. Both are something that is out of the norm, Ridley said.**

"That is something that they don't ever do. I've never seen them update anything the day before the election," Ridley explained, saying she had no idea what was in the update.

Dominion Voting Systems said the software had no impact in Georgia.

"Re Gwinnett – There is no evidence of any system software problem," Kay Stimson, Dominion Voting Systems vice president of government affairs, in told The Washington Times **in an email. "My understanding is that the system was hanging at certain points in processing adjudicated ballots due to a workstation set-up issue. Our technicians worked with the county to address it, and election officials moved on to re-adjudicating ballots by the next day."**

These "glitches" cause concerns, especially with close voter tallies in multiple states. The common factor: Dominion Voting Systems. The system is being used in many states across the nation, including in key battleground states, like Michigan, Wisconsin, Minnesota, Georgia, Arizona, Nevada and Florida.

The Denver Post **brought up concerns about these machines earlier this year when election officials throughout the country were scrambling to make sure their machines were secure from Russian**

hackers ahead of November›s election:

Called ballot-marking devices, the machines have touchscreens for registering voter choice. Unlike touchscreen-only machines, they print out paper records that are scanned by optical readers. South Carolina voters will use them in Saturday's primary.

The most pricey solution available, they are at least twice as expensive as the hand-marked paper ballot option. They have been vigorously promoted by the three voting equipment vendors that control 88 percent of the U.S. market.

Some of the most popular ballot-marking machines, made by industry leaders Election Systems & Software and Dominion Voting Systems, register votes in bar codes that the human eye cannot decipher. That's a problem, researchers say: Voters could end up with printouts that accurately spell out the names of the candidates they picked, but, because of a hack, the bar codes do not reflect those choices. Because the bar codes are what's tabulated, voters would never know that their ballots benefited another candidate.

Even on machines that do not use bar codes, voters may not notice if a hack or programming error mangled their choices. A University of Michigan study determined that only 7 percent of participants in a mock election notified poll workers when the names on their printed receipts did not match the candidates they voted for.

Pivotal counties in the crucial states of Pennsylvania, Ohio and North Carolina have bought ballot-marking machines. So have counties in much of Texas, as well as California's Los Angeles County and all of Georgia, Delaware and South Carolina. The machines' certification has often been streamlined in the rush to get machines in place for presidential primaries

Ballot-marking devices were not conceived as primary vote-casting tools but as accessible options for people with disabilities.

One of the most interesting aspects of this, as pointed out by NOQ Report**, is that Dominion Voting Systems has machines in more than one-third of the United States. They never had a lobbyist in Washington, D.C., until last year when they** hired **Brownstein Farber Hyatt & Schreck, a lobbying firm.**

One of the account's main supervisors is Nadeam Elshami, House Speaker Nancy Pelosi's (D-CA) former chief of staff.

THIS BITCH IN THIS CHAIN OF ENDLESS COINCIDENCES IS PROOF

Election Changes in Wisconsin Call Into Question Tens of Thousands of Votes

Bronson Stocking

Whether or not this was a glitch should be investigated, especially when it comes down to swing states. Areas in which this system was used should have a hand recount so voters know their votes were tabulated correctly. A glitch in one county is probable. A glitch in multiple counties in multiple states sounds like it could potentially be a bigger systemic problem.

Biden silent on lack of social distancing, possible 'super spreader' celebrations

Biden campaigned by saying he would 'listen to the scientists' By Evie Fordham | Fox News

Crowds gather in Times Square after Biden projected to win election

Sen. WOODCHUCK SCHMUCK SCHUMER **NYC Mayor de Blasio tweet congratulations to the president-elect; Alex Hogan reports.**

Democratic President-elect Joe Biden has not addressed concerns that some celebrations of his projected victory ".may contribute to the spread of coronavirus after his transition team declared Biden will always "listen to science

Thousands of Americans flooded streets of major cities, including New York City, Washington and Philadelphia, .to celebrate Biden ahead of his Saturday night victory speech

While many were wearing masks, the crowds tended to violate social distancing guidelines that have been recommended by the Centers for Disease Control and Prevention.

Biden had made fighting the coronavirus a central message in his campaign, saying it would be a top priority in his administration. His campaign declined to hold large-scale campaign rallies and

But after footage of the large crowds had been broadcast for hours on major news networks, including Fox News, the former vice president declined to urge people to socially distance.

"Our work begins with getting COVID under control," Biden said in his speech on Saturday night.

FORGET TRADITIONAL ELECTION MAPS — WHAT THE US VOTE REALLY LOOKS LIKE

"On Monday, I will name a group of leading scientists and experts as transition advisors to help take the Biden-Harris COVID plan and convert it into an action blueprint that will start on Jan. 20, 2021," he told the primetime viewing audience. "That plan will be built on bedrock science. It will be constructed out of compassion, empathy and concern."

Fox News confirmed Sunday that former surgeon general Dr. Vivek Murthy will be the head of Biden's transition coronavirus task force. Murthy has been acting as an adviser to the campaign.

The CDC on Sunday said that the U.S. added 93,811 more cases and 1,072 more deaths, bringing the totals to 9,808,411 cases and 236,547 deaths. Biden's speech in Wilmington, Delaware, was drive-in style to minimize the risk of spreading coronavirus, but photos of impromptu victory celebrations in other cities showed a lack of social distancing.

Conservative commentator Mark Dice posted a video of people packed together and dancing while

wearing masks in Boston. Massachusetts Gov. Charlie Baker announced last week he was increasing coronavirus restrictions after a spike in cases. "Who knew Joe Biden would put and end to social distancing so soon?" Dice wrote on Twitter.

CNN host Jake Tapper on Saturday acknowledged the risk of the coronavirus while reporting on the celebrations. "I hate to be a scold here, but we just had the highest day of infections in the United States," Tapper said. "I believe yesterday was 125,000 Americans with new coronavirus infections. That was the third straight day of more than 100,000 infections. It's good to see people wearing masks -- although for some of them they're slipping off their face."

Tapper's concern of coming across as a "scold," though, was drastically different than his approach last month when he condemned Trump for holding rallies. The "State of the Union" anchor closed his Oct. 11 show with a diatribe against the president for holding rallies amid the pandemic that Tapper labeled "super spreader" events. "[Trump's] need to hold these rallies apparently exceeding his concern for those attending them," Tapper told viewers last month. "One of President Trump's skills during this era has been to behave with so little regard to basic decency, those who try to uphold the standards get accused of being partisan. As if 'don't behave in a way that's reckless and displays a wanton disregard for human life' is somehow now a partisan issue. It isn't."

Tapper then scolded Trump for "reckless behavior" regarding the coronavirus and accused him of indulging his ego at the risk of prolonging the pandemic. Trump Campaign Seeks Public Records in Clark County Nevada as Part of Election Challenge

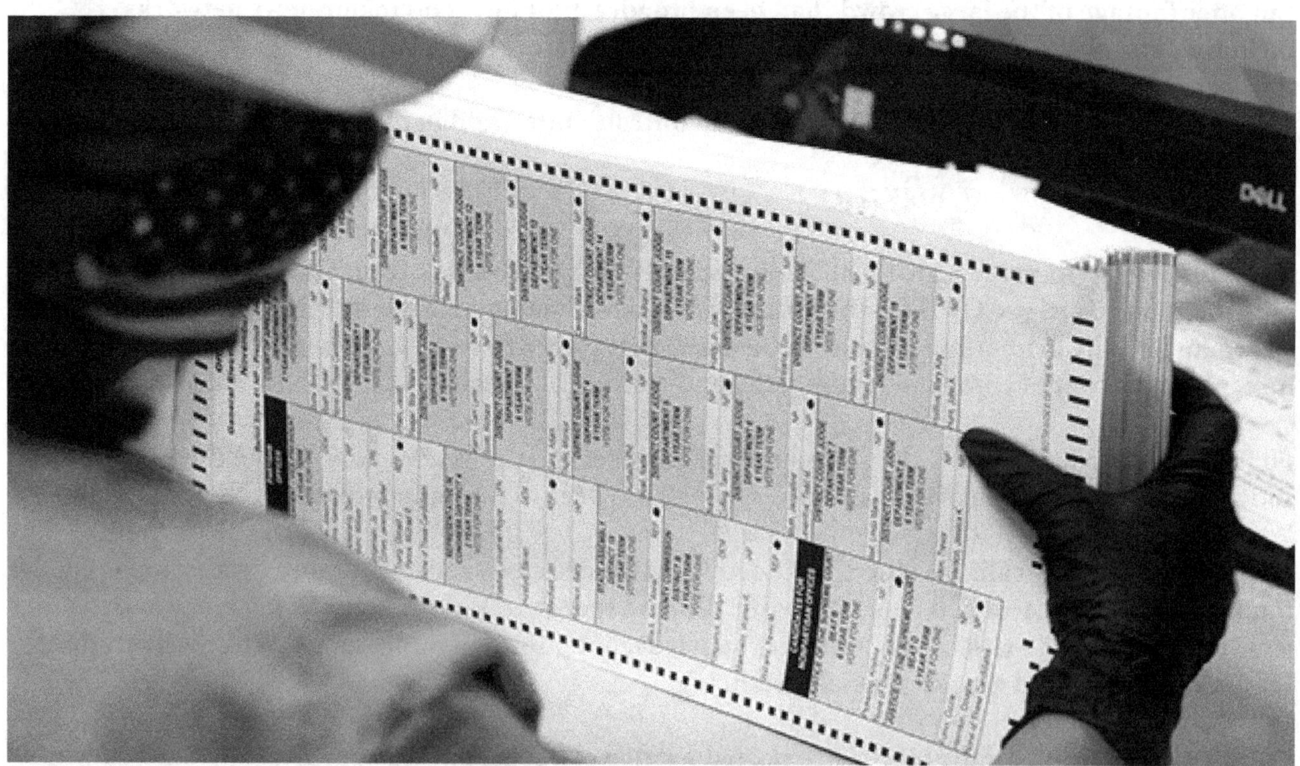

President Trump's campaign is seeking public records in Clark County, Nevada, as part of the president's greater legal challenges regarding election integrity in battleground states. In a Friday letter to the Clark County Election Department, a firm representing Donald J. Trump for President, Inc. requested a trove of election data as part of his campaign's overall legal challenges related to election integrity.

The letter contains requests for records, documents, and communications on the number of mail-in ballots received by the department after 7 p.m. PST on Election Day, as well as how many votes were cast after that time "by those voting in person at the polls."

Per the letter, the campaign is also requesting:

- **All records, documents, and communications indicating how many votes were cast by individuals who were not in line to vote at the time the polls were closed at the precinct in which the vote was cast.**
- **All records, documents, and communications indicating how many ballots have been received without a postmark.**
- **All records, documents, and communications showing all efforts taken by the Clark County Department of Elections to verify the Nevada residency of individuals who were mailed a ballot in the 2020 primary election and whose ballot was returned to the Department of Elections by the United States Postal Service. Include any records showing efforts taken to verify such residency in advance of any such voter being sent a ballot during the 2020 general election.**
- **All records, documents, and communications evidencing coordination between the Clark County Department of Elections and the Nevada Department of Motor Vehicles taken to ensure those individuals needing to obtain an identification to cure their provisional ballot can obtain one.**
- **Each ballot designated spoiled and not counted for that reason.**
- **All mail in ballot envelopes from voters who are also recorded as having voted in person.**
- **All in-person voter sign-in forms reflecting appearances at polling places by voters from whom a mail-in ballot was also received.**

The department had five days to respond from the time of the letter, per the Nevada Open Records Act. The firm stressed that the information requested is in the public interest and will "contribute significantly to the public's understanding of the local processes and procedures in Clark County and further ensure the right of the citizens of Nevada to a free and fair election."

The firm also requested that, in the event of the department denying the request, it provides a justification for refusing to release the requested information. While the mainstream media has called Nevada and the election for Joe Biden (D), President Trump's campaign insists that the race is not over and litigation is just beginning. A Sunday update from the *New York Times* showed Biden leading Trump in the Silver State by just over 31,000 votes. The same data showed Biden leading Trump in Clark County, specifically, by just over 86,000 votes. On Saturday, a whistleblower in

Nevada who processed mail-in ballots swore an affidavit proclaiming that he witnessed "illegitimate processing of ballots as an election worker." Specifically, he claimed he witnessed individuals counting mail-in ballots without verifying signatures. "He says he was also told to ignore discrepancies with addresses. That worker has sworn out an affidavit which has been sent to the Department of Justice here in Washington," Fox News's John Roberts reported. "A Trump campaign attorney says of that, quote, 'The affidavit makes clear that we're not dealing with oversights or sloppiness. This was intentional criminal conduct,'" he said:

Clark County Registrar of Voters Joe Gloria said they have received reports of voter fraud, but will not investigate them until the election is completed. "We do have some reports that have come in that we're logging for reporting. But we're definitely going to do an investigation, and we'll deal with them once the canvass is finished," Gloria said Saturday.

"The votes are in the system at this point, so we'll have to after the election, post-election, go after anything that's been reported at this time," he added: On Saturday, Georgia Secretary of State Brad Raffensperger (R) announced that investigators are being dispatched in Fulton County following the discovery of an issue related to reporting. The investigators are to "thoroughly secure the vote and protect all legal votes." Brendan Keefe of Atlanta's WXIA said the issue "*may* significantly affect the current Biden lead in Georgia."

Nevada Whistleblower Says He Witnessed Processing of Illegitimate Votes

Fox News reported on Saturday that a whistleblower in Nevada swore an affidavit declaring that he witnessed .illegitimate processing of ballots as an election worker

Specifically, the whistleblower claimed to have been instructed to count ballots needing signature verification that lacked the requisite signatures to be eligible.

Fox News's John Roberts said:

In just the last hour in Nevada, an election worker whose job was to process mail-in ballots says he witnessed irregularities in counting those ballots and was told by a supervisor — who he names — to put through ballots he believed needed signature verification without that verification first being done.

He says he was also told to ignore discrepancies with addresses. That worker has sworn out an affidavit which has been sent to the Department of Justice here in Washington. A Trump campaign attorney says of that, quote, "The affidavit makes clear that we're not dealing with oversights or sloppiness. This was intentional criminal conduct."

The Nevada Republican Party said it received thousands of complaints regarding the general election in Nevada. It also said thousands of ballots were processed "without meaningful observation" by Republican observers.

The Nevada GOP claimed **via statement on Wednesday:**

There have been a number of mail ballots turned in to Clark County Department of Elections that are being processed without meaningful observation. Ballots are continuing to be processed in this same manner.

"The fact remains that hundreds of thousands of ballots have been counted in Clark County and as a Judge and the Secretary of State have confirmed we have not been allowed to observe or challenge a single signature match for these votes. With the issues that have been reported regarding the election, we are now more than ever concerned with the lack of the transparency in observing and challenging possible invalid ballots," says Donald J Trump Campaign Co-Chair Adam Laxalt.

On Thursday, the Nevada GOP announced **its submission of a criminal referral to Attorney General William Barr alleging 3,602 instances of voter fraud in the Silver State.**

Lindsey Graham: 'Do Not Concede, Mr. President — Fight Hard' HE IS A BACK STABBING JUDAS TO ALL REPUBLICANS

Senator Lindsey Graham (R-SC) on Fox News Channel's "Sunday Morning Futures" urged President Donald Trump not to concede the election. Graham said, "If we don't challenge and change the U.S. election system, there will never be another Republican president elected again. President Trump should not concede."

He continued, "To my Republican colleagues out there, we have to fight back, or we will accept our fate. I want Pennsylvania to explain to the American people how six people after they die with register and vote in Pennsylvania. I want the computer systems in Michigan that flip votes from Republicans to Democrats to be looked at, and the software was used all over the country. There's a lot of shenanigans going on here, and if I were President Trump, I would take all this to court, I'd fight back, and from a Republican point of view, mail-in balloting is a nightmare for us. The post office is now the new election center. It's the wild-wild west when it comes to mail-in balloting. Everything we worried about has come true, so if we don't fight back in 2020, we're never going to win again presidentially. A lot is at stake here."

He concluded, "Trump has not lost. Do not concede, Mr. President, fight hard."

Romney: Trump Has 'Relaxed Relationship with the Truth' — There Was No Widespread Election Fraud

WHO IS THIS LOATHSOME SCHMUCK ROMNEY TO DETERMINE WIDESPREAD ELECTION FRAUD? DOES ROMNEY QUANTIFY WIDESPREAD; WHEN (532) BUSH VOTES MADE BUSH A WINNER & GORE A LOSER? WE DECIDE WHAT WIDESPREAD IS; ROMNEY. SHUT YER QUISLING; BACK-STABBING VICIOUS TRAITOR FUCKEN FACE, ROMNEY.

Senator Mitt Romney (R-UT) said Sunday on CNN's "State of the Union" that President Donald Trump had "relativity relaxed relationship with the truth." Anchor Jake Tapper said, "Does it concern you at all that President Trump and his team are out there saying that he won and lying about the integrity of the election with wild allegations?"

Romney said, "You're not going to change the nature of President Trump in these last days, apparently, of his presidency. He is who he is and he has a relativity relaxed relationship with the truth so he is going to keep on fighting until the very end." He continued, "Don't expect him to go quietly in the night. That's not how he operates." He added, "It's destruct to the cause of democracy to suggest widespread fraud or corruption. There is just no evidence of that at this stage. And I think it's important for us to recognize that the world is watching."

WE DON'T CARE WHO THE FUCK IS WATCHING ROMNEY, YOU WIMP TURNCOAT QUISLING JUDAS TRAITOR

Dick Morris: Trump Can Still Win

Dick Morris

President Donald Trump can still win the presidency. Here's how: Only the Electoral College or the various state legislatures can declare a candidate the winner. To base this decision on network vote totals and projections and to call Biden the president-elect is irresponsible.

The recounts in Arizona, Georgia, and the other states are likely to go heavily for Trump. Most of the likely errors or invalid votes took place on mailed in ballots. (Machine votes are harder to tamper with). Since Biden won upwards of two-thirds of mail-in votes and absentee ballots, it's likely that most of the discarded mail ballots will be subtracted from Biden's total. The networks currently give Trump 214 electorate voters (270 is the victory level).

Alaska, where Trump has led by 2:1 all week and is now more than half counted will likely throw its 3 votes to Trump giving him 217. Trump has likewise led in North Carolina (15 votes) all week and his margin of 75,000 has not diminished. He will undoubtedly carry North Carolina. Like Alaska, the media will not call it for Trump to promote the illusion of a Biden victory. North Carolina would bring Trump's vote to 232.

The vote count in Arizona shows Trump's deficit shrinking from 30,000 on Friday to 18,500 on Saturday with about 100K left to count. After Arizona (11 votes). is fully counted, it will go through a recount subject to the pro-Trump bias identified in point 2. Were he to win Arizona, he would have 243 votes.

In Georgia (16 votes), Biden leads by only 8400 votes, a margin that has been dropping. Like Arizona, Trump may still win the count and, if not, would have a very good chance of prevailing in the recount. With Georgia, Trump would have 259 votes.

Wisconsin (10 votes) is tallied as having been won by Biden by 21,000 votes but a re-canvass is in the offing. Given the facts enumerated earlier, there is a very good chance Trump will carry Wisconsin. The recount process in Wisconsin is uniquely fair and transparent — a model for the nation — so Trump may well flip the state. If he does, he will have 269 votes — one shy of victory.

Then, it comes down Pennsylvania and its 20 votes. The Supreme Court provisionally allowed ballots to be counted if they arrived before Friday, Nov. 6 and were postmarked before election day, Nov. 3, and ordered late votes to be segregated. When Justice Alito was informed that the state had not segregated the late votes, as required in the Court's decision, Alito reaffirmed the necessity of enforcing the court order.

Joe Biden currently leads by 37,000 votes in Pennsylvania. The number of late arriving ballots likely far exceeds this total (the state has not published this information). Justice Alioto and a Court majority may throw out the late ballots, likely delivering the state to Trump.

Additionally, for the reasons stated above, a recanvass is likely to give Trump a decisive advantage. If he wins Pennsylvania, he would have 289 votes and a victory. Will there be a recount in Pennsylvania? The current law requires one if the margin is under 0;.5% and in Pennsylvania it likely will be slightly greater.

There are two ways to trigger a recount: —First, the U.S. Supreme Court could order one after the vote counters so flagrantly violated Alito's order to segregate the votes that he had to re-issue it. And remember, four Justices wanted to reconsider whether to allow late ballots entirely but the high court deadlocked 4-4. Now with Justice Barrett in the mix it may take a different view, particularly iff the presidency hangs in the balance. —Second, Article II Section 1 of the US Constitution reads:

"Each State shall appoint, in such Manner as the Legislature thereof may direct, a Number of Electors, equal to the whole Number of Senators and Representatives to which the State may be entitled in the Congress."

The Pennsylvania State Legislature, solidly in Republican hands (both houses) may choose to demand a recount before appointing electors. To build the case for doing so, it may hold hearings into the allegations of fraud so as to help the voters of the state understand how flagrantly their votes were mishandled.

Already, the leader of the State Senate in Pennsylvania and the Speaker of the State Assembly have held a press conference announcing their intention to "audit" the vote counting process.

So, as the great Yogi Berra said, "It ain't over 'til the fat lady sings."She hasn't.

Raphael Warnock Struggles to Defend Anti-Israel Record

HE HATES JEWS; ESPECIALLY THE AUTHOR OF THIS BOOK

Joel B. Pollak

Georgia Democratic Senate candidate Rev. Raphael Warnock is struggling to defend his record of anti-Israel statements and policies, as Republicans raise the issue ahead of the Jan. 5 runoff election in the state.Warnock is challenging incumbent Sen. Kelly Loeffler (R-GA), alongside another runoff election between Sen. David Perdue (R-GA) and challenger Jon Ossoff. If both Democrats win their respective races, they would gain effective control .of the U.S. Senate and Capitol Hill as a whole

Last week, the *Jewish Journal* noted Warnock's problematic positions on Israel — an emotive issue for many conservatives:

In 2019, Georgia Democratic Senate candidate Reverend Raphael Warnock signed a letter comparing Israel to apartheid South Africa, Jewish Insider reported.

Warnock is also listed as a delegation member on a Progressive National Baptist resolution that called on the United States to cease all military aid to Israel and urged Israel to stop building "illegal Israeli settlements, checkpoints and apartheid roads in the occupied Palestinian territories," Fox News reported.

Stephen Lawson, communications director for incumbent Senator Kelly Loeffler's (R-Ga.) campaign, told Fox News that "Warnock has a history of anti-Israel positions, from embracing anti-Zionist BLACK LIVES MATTER and defending anti-Semitic comments made by Rev. Jeremiah Wright, to calling Israel an 'oppressive regime' for fighting back against terrorism." Lawson also argued that Loeffler's staunch support for Israel is "unwavering."

Jewish News Syndicate (JNS) reported that Warnock had previously defended Wright in 2008, saying "that we celebrate the truth-telling tradition of the black church, which when preachers tell th, very often it makes people uncomfortable." Warnock defended Wright again in March. JNS also highlighted how Wright said shortly after Barack Obama was elected that "them Jews" were preventing Obama from stating "anti-Israel" remarks.

The Jewish Democratic Council of America, which drew criticism this fall for comparing Trump's America to Nazi Germany, claims: "On Israel, Warnock is committed to continue to supporting U.S. military assistance, a two-state solution to the Israeli-Palestinian conflict, and opposing the BDS [boycott, divestment, sanctions] movement. Additionally, Warnock is committed to supporting an agreement that will prevent a nuclear-capable Iran."

Rep. Ilhan Omar (D-MN) also opposed BDS when she was running for Congress — until she won, when she embraced it.

Ted Cruz Urges 'Legal Process' To Move Forward on Election

Sen. Ted Cruz, R-TX

Sen. Ted Cruz, R-Texas, declared Sunday the presidential election is far from settled and that the legal process should "move forward" — declaring newsrooms in New York City "don't get to decide" the outcome.

In an interview on Fox News' "Sunday Morning Futures," **Cruz said the conclusion may come "in a matter of weeks."**

"At this point, we should allow the rule of law to operate. We should allow the legal process to move forward and when that process is concluded, which it will be in a matter of weeks, we will know who prevailed in the elections," he said.

"But the fact that the big news rooms in New York City want Donald Trump to lose, they don't get to decide that," he said. "That's a question for the voters."

Cruz pointed to the 2000 stalemate between former President George W. Bush and former Vice President Al Gore that was decided by Supreme Court on Dec. 12, 2000.

"We have a process for ascertaining the truth," he said. "You can go and present evidence and attest it in a court court of law and then those appeals

GOP Rep. Scalise: Election Laws, 'Transparency' Violated

Election laws were not followed in Pennsylvania and Philadelphia, particularly with the legal requirements of meaningful monitoring, so the legal process will have to play out before the votes are certified from this election, according to Rep. Steve Scalise, R-La.

"You can see there are still a lot of cases to be made, and let the courts resolve these disputes," Scalise told Fox News' "Fox & Friends Weekend."

Scalise noted, "we're really at the beginning at the legal side of this."

"You had some states still counting, some very questionable things happen, especially when you look at the many states that have the law that you allow a poll watcher to watch the counting," he told Pete Hegseth. "It's part of the transparency process that's a law in most states.

"That was not being followed. They were not allowing Trump's poll watchers to watch what was going on. You know, what are you doing behind closed doors, when you're afraid to allow people watch you, when the law says you have to."

Scalise also noted Pennsylvania had a court order to segregate ballots received after 8 p.m. ET on Election Night, but that was not unilaterally followed and there has potentially been come co-mingling of ballots now that might not be able to be undone.

"The Supreme Court said they have to keep them separate," he said. "There were questions whether they have separated all of those ballots, and the Secretary of State has yet to say how many they are."

It might not be knowable now, Scalise lamented.

"These are laws on states' books that aren't being followed," Scalise said, reminding that the 2000 Bush v. Gore dispute took weeks, not days, to determine the true winner of the presidential election.

Michael Flynn to Newsmax TV: Election Putting America 'at Risk'

□ Alan Dershowitz: Court Challenge Needs 'Determinative' Numbers

will go up both through the state and federal appellate system and in this case could very easily end up at the U.S. Supreme Court," he said.

Noting that during the Bush vs. Gore case, in which Cruz represented Bush, "we had multiple cases throughout the state of Florida. It went twice to the Florida Supreme Court. It went twice to the U.S. Supreme court. It took 36 days to resolve, and we got an answer."

Ken Starr: Pennsylvania Ballot Extension 'Constitutional Travesty'

The disputed Pennsylvania ballot extension forced by state courts over the legislature is a "constitutional travesty," according to famed prosecutor Ken Starr.

"What happened in Pennsylvania over these recent weeks is a constitutional travesty," Starr told Fox News' "Life, Liberty & Levin." **"Gov. [Tom] Wolf tries to get his reforms, his vision, as he was entitled to do, through the legislature of the Commonwealth of Pennsylvania. He failed.**

"He then goes to the state Supreme Court, which by a divided vote, accepted the substance of what Gov. Wolf was doing, and then added thereon nooks and crannies as well."

Starr also noted it is a "crime" to "count every vote," because counting "illegal" votes violates the Constitution and state law.

"To count every vote may be a crime," Starr told host Mark Levin. "It may even be a crime under federal law. It's definitely a crime under state law, if that's as said – and here's the key word – illegal.

"And it's shameful that Vice President [Joe] Biden's people and the vice president himself are saying 'Count Every Vote' and selling a lot of T-shirts. That is a potential invitation for absolute lawlessness."

Starr said he knew of a situation where a widow cast a ballot for her deceased husband.

"A recently widowed woman knew how her late husband would vote," Starr said. "He was deceased, that's a human tragedy.

"What's a travesty is she cast his vote for him. We call that absentee ballots? No, we call that an illegal ballot."

The case that might be brought before the Supreme Court may argue a number of votes in Pennsylvania be thrown out as "illegal" for a number of reasons, including being cast late, being cast illegally, not separated as guided by Supreme Court Justice Samuel Alito, and not have been

counted with "meaningful" monitoring as required by law.

John Gizzi: Battle Rages on in Michigan Over Electoral Votes, Senate Race

John Gizzi

As The Associated Press was calling the election for Joe Biden on Saturday, Michigan Republicans made it clear they had neither conceded the state's electoral votes nor the nail-bitingly close Senate race.

Both Republican National Chairman Ronna McDaniel and GOP Senate candidate John James

separately called for a full recount of the results.

The AP declared Biden the winner Thursday of Michigan's 16 electoral votes by a razor-thin 50.6% to 47.9% of the vote (or 46,123 out of more than 5 million cast). AP also called Sen. Gary Peters, D-Mich., the victor over James by 84,315 votes (or 49.8% to 48.3%).

Erroneous results from voting totals in traditionally Republican Antrim County that had to be corrected have fueled Republican calls for a complete recount in the Wolverine State. After shocked officials saw the initial count showing Democrat Biden beating Trump by 3,000 votes, they ran a check on the vote-counting device and discovered a malfunction in its scanner mechanism. The ballots were then hand-counted and the results showed Trump leading Biden by 2,600 votes, or 56% to 42%.

Based on the glitch in Antrim County, McDaniel, herself a Michigander, has called for a statewide recount and noted the same software that was used in Antrim was used to count ballots in dozens of other counties statewide.

(The machines manufactured by Dominion Voting Systems, which were used by Antrim County, are used by most counties in Michigan. But the specific software that was used for counting comes from another company known as Election Source, according to a spokesman from the state agency overseeing elections).

Most Republican operatives in Michigan clearly favor the recount favored by McDaniel and James.

"Whatever our candidates wish to do is what I support," Rocky Raczkowski, Republican chairman of Oakland County, told Newsmax, citing the glitch in Antrim and reports of delayed counting and intimidation of Republican poll watchers in neighboring Wayne County (Detroit).

"When Florida can count 22 million voters in 10 hours and California can do the same with 40 million voters, it becomes a complete and utter joke when the city of Detroit needs days to count its votes," Raczkowski said.

Newsmax noted, when Republican John Engler unseated Democrat Gov. James Blanchard in 1990 by 14,000 votes and Republican Mike Cox was elected attorney general by less than 6000 votes (against present Sen. Peters), both Democrats lost by less than Trump or James and neither called for a recount.

Georgia Sec. State: 'An Issue' Forces Rescanning of Ballots Saturday

By Eric Mack

Atlanta's Fulton County on Saturday began rescanning some votes first counted Friday.

The county had discovered "an issue," according to a Facebook post from Secretary of State Brad Raffensperger. A county spokesperson did not immediately respond to a text message seeking more information.

Raffensperger posted:

"Fulton County has discovered an issue involving reporting from their work on Friday. Officials are at State Farm Arena to rescan their work from Friday. The Secretary of State has a monitor onsite, has sent additional investigators, and dispatched the Deputy Secretary of State as well to oversee the process to make sure to thoroughly secure the vote and protect all legal votes. Observers from both political parties are there as well."

A tweet from the Republican election official echoed the Facebook statement.

Neither Facebook nor Twitter has tagged, censored, blocked, or covered the post, as social media companies have been wont to do with President Donald Trump and his associates' claims of similar "issues" with ballots, the counting, and "meaningful" monitoring of them.

As partisans celebrated and protested Democrat Joe Biden's victory Saturday, some Georgia counties inched toward a final count of ballots in the state elections.

Biden continued to narrowly lead President Donald Trump in the contest for Georgia's 16 electoral votes after edging ahead early Friday as mail ballots were counted. The Associated Press declared Biden the nationwide winner Saturday, but has not called a winner in Georgia.

At the state Capitol, hundreds of Trump supporters rallied to allege the election has been stolen from their candidate. They chanted "Four more years!" as flag-bearing trucks circled and congresswoman-elect Marjorie Taylor Greene spoke.

"I will not stop fighting for President Trump, I support him 100%," Greene said.

Trump has called Greene a "future Republican star."

Greene repeated comments Saturday other Republicans were not doing enough to stand up for Trump and claimed Biden's lead in Georgia is illegitimate.

"This is not a blue state," Greene said. "It is my opinion that they are stealing this election."

Many of those who were attending the rally echoed Greene's concerns about fraud. But some said they remain open to accepting Biden as the legitimate president.

Jordan Kelley, a 29-year-old, drove to the demonstration from Murfreesboro, Tennessee. Kelley, who describes himself as an "avid Republican," said he could accept the Democrat if he believes Biden's victory is legitimate.

"If Biden actually does win the election, I'll support and honor his presidency," Kelley said.

Jill Tanner, a 50-year-old Atlanta resident who supports Trump's immigration policies, said if Biden becomes president she will "get up and go to work and live the American dream."

"If Biden is in fact declared president, I don't plan to riot or do anything," Tanner said. "For me, it would just be like any other day."

State officials did not have an updated count Saturday of how many provisional or military ballots are outstanding, said Walter Jones, a spokesman for Raffensperger. The Republican has said he

expects a candidate will request a recount of Georgia's ballots, as candidates can do when they are less than 0.5% behind after all ballots are counted. The state had already made plans to audit one of the statewide races to ensure that the new voting machines have produced an accurate count.

Friday was the deadline for voters to fix problems with flawed absentee or provisional ballots, as well as the deadline for ballots to arrive from overseas. By Saturday, 37 of Georgia's 159 counties had submitted certified, final results.

There is more voting yet to come in Georgia with two U.S. Senate runoffs set for Jan. 5. Sen. David Perdue, R-Ga., and Democrat Jon Ossoff meet again for Perdue's Senate seat after Libertarian candidate Shane Hazel won enough votes so neither Perdue nor Ossoff could clear the 50% threshold needed for victory.

Democrat Rev. Raphael Warnock faces Sen. Kelly Loeffler, R-Ga., in a second runoff trying to win the remaining two years of another Senate term. GOP Gov. Brian Kemp appointed Loeffler to succeed retiring Republican Johnny Isakson earlier this year.

"We're living in a different time," Raczkowski told us. "People are more on edge and there are more availabilities to cheat in and steal elections."

Georgia Sec. State Raffensperger investigating Stacey Abrams' group for GOTV fraud after it attempted to register his deceased son

His son passed away two years ago but still received three voter registration notices

PHIL SHIVER

Georgia officials have launched investigations into several third-party registration groups, including one founded by former gubernatorial candidate Stacey Abrams, for "repeatedly and aggressively" seeking to register "ineligible, out-of-state, or deceased voters" ahead of the state's Jan. 5 Senate runoff elections.

POLL: What are you most worried about?

What are the details?

In a news release Wednesday, Georgia Secretary of State Brad Raffensperger said that the New Georgia Project, founded by Abrams in 2014, as well as two other organizations — America Votes and Vote Forward — are subjects in the investigations.

Raffensperger stated that his office had "issued clear warnings several times" to such groups against encouraging illegal action, but nonetheless has "received specific evidence that these groups have solicited voter registrations from ineligible individuals who have passed away or live out of state."

Evidently, some of that evidence arrived directly on Raffensperger's doorstep. The secretary of state announced in a news conference Wednesday that his family had received mailers directed to his deceased son, urging him to register to vote.

"Here's something that came to my house yesterday, we got three of them, all from the same organization and it's to my son Brenton J. Raffensperger who passed away two years ago," he said holding up the mailers.

But that wasn't the only evidence of get-out-the-vote groups encouraging illegal behavior in the state, according to Raffensperger.

"We've had additional information coming in regarding the tactics from these groups including the New Georgia Project sending five voter registrations to the same dead person, and sending applications to ineligible voters," he added.

What else?

Raffensperger said that over the past several weeks complaints have been flooding into his office about the New Georgia Project sending voter registration information to out-of-state residents, including a "package of postcards" to an individual living in New York City.

According to the news release, another group, Operation New Voter Registration GA, urged Emory University students to illegally register to vote in the runoffs.

"Your current residence can be another state. You are simply changing your state of residence now; and it can be switched back for future elections (your option)," said a flier sent by the group to students.

In Georgia, false registration is considered a felony and is punishable by up to 10 years in prison.

In a statement, Raffensperger vowed, "I will investigate these claims thoroughly and take action against anyone attempting to undermine our elections."

The Senate runoff elections on Jan. 5 will feature face-offs between Republican Sens. David Perdue and Kelly Loeffler and Democratic challengers Jon Ossoff and Rev. Raphael Warnock, respectively. The elections have attracted a great deal of national attention as the Senate majority hangs in the balance.

Poll: Less than Half of America Believes Joe Biden Won the Election

Hannah Bleau

Less than half of the American people believe Joe Biden (D) won the presidential election, according to a Tuesday survey from Just the News Daily and independent pollster Scott Rasmussen. The survey, fielded November 5-7 among 1,200 registered voters, asked respondents, "Who do you believe legitimately won the presidential election "?this year

It found that 49 percent, overall, believe Biden won the presidential election. Over one-third of voters, or 34 percent, believe Trump won the presidential election, and 16 percent are "not sure" who won. Views are sharply divided along partisan lines. Over three-fourths of Republicans, 77 percent, believe Trump won, compared to 12 percent who said Biden and 11 percent who said they were unsure. By contrast, 87 percent of Democrats believe the former vice president won, six percent believe Trump won, and seven percent remain unsure. While a plurality of independents, 42 percent, said Biden won, nearly a quarter said Trump won, and one-third remain unsure.

Democrats comprised 37 percent of the weighted sample, followed by Republicans (32 percent), and others outside of either major party (30 percent). The survey concluded prior to major news networks calling the race for the former vice president on Saturday. The margin of error is +/- 2.8 percent.

The survey coincides with a Morning Consult/*Politico* survey, which found that the majority of

Republicans, or 70 percent, do not believe the election was free or fair.

Trump Campaign Files Lawsuit on Rejected Arizona Ballots

BY SANDY FITZGERALD

President Donald Trump's reelection campaign, along with the Republican National Committee, have filed a lawsuit against Maricopa County, Arizona, that accuses poll workers of improperly rejecting in-person votes on election day. In their lawsuit, the Republicans claim, when an overvote was detected on a ballot, poll workers were to inform voters and allow them the opportunity to fix the error, reports NBC affiliate KPNX in Phoenix.

Instead, the lawsuit claims, when issues with the vote tabulation machines happened, the poll workers would push a green button to override the error, or voters were asked to push the button. This caused an override that resulted in the vote not being counted.

The lawsuit states: "Qualified electors casting ballots in person on Election Day in Maricopa County submitted their completed ballot to an electronic tabulation machine. Numerous voters were alerted by these devices to a facial irregularity in their ballot—frequently an ostensible 'overvote' — but were induced by poll workers to override the tabulator's rejection of the ballot in the good faith belief that their vote would be duly registered and tabulated. In actuality, overriding the electronic tabulator's alert automatically disqualifies the putative 'overvotes' without additional review or adjudication." The campaign says several county voters have complained about the issue.

"Poll workers struggled to operate the new voting machines in Maricopa County, and improperly pressed and told voters to press a green button to override significant errors," Trump 2020 campaign's general counsel, Matt Morgan said in a statement. "The result is that the voting machines disregarded votes cast by voters in person on Election Day in Maricopa County."

The lawsuit demands overridden ballots be inspected manually, in the same way elections officials examined mail-in or drop-off ballots that were overvoted, KPNX reported.

The campaign contended voters' choices were disregarded in those races, saying new voting machines were used on Election Day on Tuesday. The lawsuit suggested those votes could prove "determinative" in the outcome of the race between Trump and Democrat Joe Biden, who was declared the winner Saturday by major television networks. The Maricopa County Elections Department and a spokesman for Biden did not immediately respond to requests for comment. Biden currently leads Trump by 0.65%, or just over 21,000 votes in Arizona.

The Trump lawsuit, whose plaintiffs include the Arizona state Republican Party and the Republican

National Committee, cited declarations by some poll observers and two voters that claimed the problem led to rejected votes.

Republicans Not Accepting Biden Win Until Legal Fights End

By Sandy FITZGERALD

Several of President Donald Trump's allies are not accepting that Joe Biden and Kamala Harris have secured the victory for the White House, insisting a winner cannot be named until all lawful votes have been counted.

Sen. Josh Hawley, R-Mo., tweeted:

"The media do not get to determine who the president is. The people do. When all lawful votes have been counted, recounts finished and allegations of fraud addressed, we will know who the winner is."

The New York Times reports Hawley›s message echoes several of Trump›s recent statements, including his Saturday message that legal action to fight for the election will begin Monday.

Senate Majority Leader Mitch McConnell, R-Ky., did not comment after news broke most media outlets had announced Biden had won the election. However, on Friday, he wrote on Twitter that all legal votes must be counted, and all illegal votes must be discarded. He also said all sides must be able to observe the vote-counting process, and the "courts are here to apply the laws & resolve disputes."

One of McConnell's aides said Saturday those comments still stand.

Rep. Jodey Arrington, R-Texas, said Saturday it would be "unwise" to accept an outcome before recounts are complete and the courts have certified the results of the election.

However, there are some Republicans who congratulated Biden, including Sen. Mitt Romney, R-Utah, who said he and his wife Ann know Biden and Harris as "people of good will and admirable character."

Rep. Fred Upton, R-Mich., said he is "committed to working with Biden," and Sen. Lamar Alexander, R-Tenn., said once all votes are counted and the courts resolve the dispute, it is "important to respect and promptly accept the result."

"The orderly transfer or reaffirming of immense power after a presidential election is the most enduring symbol of our democracy," Alexander added.

Rep. Will Hurd, R-Texas, said he urges unity, and "America has spoken, and we must respect the decision."

Trump Campaign Changes Tack, Then Switches Back in Pa. Suit

President Donald Trump's campaign sought on Wednesday to reintroduce claims to a Pennsylvania election lawsuit that it removed three days ago, saying it would ask that Trump be declared the winner of the battleground state.

In a court filing, the campaign sought permission from U.S. District Judge Matthew Brann to add back legal claims that it dropped on Sunday from its Nov. 9 lawsuit. The claims alleged Republican observers were denied access to the counting of mail-in ballots.

In the court filing, the campaign said the narrowing of the case had been "inadvertent" and due to miscommunication. The campaign said on Monday it had "strategically decided to restructure its

lawsuit" when it removed the claims.

The lawsuit also alleges inconsistent treatment by county election officials of mail-in ballots. Some counties notified voters that they could fix minor defects such as missing dates while others did not.

The campaign lawsuit seeks to prevent the state from certifying the election result, citing the disparate policies. Brann expressed skepticism of that request at a hearing on Tuesday.

Trump's campaign has filed a flurry of lawsuits in a bid to reverse the election, which has been called by multiple news outlets, but not by Newsmax, for former Vice President Joe Biden. Many outlets, based on projections, said Biden had 306 electoral votes to Trump's 232. The winner needs 270, and Trump would have to flip the outcome in Pennsylvania, with 20 electoral votes, and two other states.

The president has claimed that the election was stolen. A Reuters poll on Wednesday showed about half of Republicans believe Trump had the election stolen from him. Earlier on Wednesday, the Pennsylvania Supreme Court said it would take up an appeal in a separate lawsuit by the Trump campaign challenging thousands of mail-in votes in Philadelphia that were missing information on the return envelopes. Biden won Pennsylvania by around 82,000 votes, according to Edison Research.

Giuliani Vows Court Actions: 'I'm Attacking a Decrepit Democratic Machine›

By Eric Mack

President Donald Trump's campaign, not conceding to Democrat Joe Biden, is promising legal challenges seeking to overturn the outcome of the race for the White House.

Trump said in a statement **"our campaign will start prosecuting our case in court to ensure election laws are fully upheld and the rightful winner is seated."** ***Trump's personal lawyer Rudy Giuliani held a*** *news conference Saturday in Philadelphia*, ***claiming the lack of meaningful observation of ballots and claiming historically massive fraud in the city that has helped Biden overcome Trump in the state of Pennsylvania.***

"I am not attacking the people of Philadelphia," Giuliani told reporters. "I'm attacking a decrepit democratic machine." The lack of meaningful observation was a violation of election law, Giulani argued.

"What I'm saying to you is not a single one was inspected as the law requires," Giuliani said. "Even when a court order was obtained to allow the Republican inspectors to get six feet closer, they move

the people counting the ballots six further feet away. "It's really simple: If you have nothing to hide with these mail in ballots, you will allow inspection. This is common knowledge, common practice in the examination of absentee ballots which happens all the time." In recent weeks, Trump has alleged widespread fraud and misconduct in the election. Trump was at his Virginia golf course when the presidential race was called for Biden on Saturday, issuing this full statement:

"We all know why Joe Biden is rushing to falsely pose as the winner, and why his media allies are trying so hard to help him: They don't want the truth to be exposed. The simple fact is this election is far from over.

"Joe Biden has not been certified as the winner of any states, let alone any of the highly contested states headed for mandatory recounts, or states where our campaign has valid and legitimate legal challenges that could determine the ultimate victor. "In Pennsylvania, for example, our legal observers were not permitted meaningful access to watch the counting process. Legal votes decide who is president, not the news media.

"Beginning Monday, our campaign will start prosecuting our case in court to ensure election laws are fully upheld and the rightful winner is seated. The American People are entitled to an honest election: that means counting all legal ballots, and not counting any illegal ballots. This is the only way to ensure the public has full confidence in our election. "It remains shocking that the Biden campaign refuses to agree with this basic principle and wants ballots counted even if they are fraudulent, manufactured, or cast by ineligible or deceased voters. Only a party engaged in wrongdoing would unlawfully keep observers out of the count room – and then fight in court to block their access. "So what is Biden hiding? I will not rest until the American people have the honest vote count they deserve and that Democracy demands."

'Segregated & Secured': Alito Orders Late Pennsylvania Ballots Counted Separately

ONLY SAMUEL ALITO & CLARENCE THOMAS COMBINED THE INTELLECT, CARING & COURAGE TO BRING THE SUPREME COURT IN RIGHTING THE MOST CRIPPLING CRIME AGAINST DEMOCRACY IN HISTORY

Supreme Court Justice Samuel Alito issued an order Friday calling for the segregation of all Pennsylvania ballots received after 8 p.m. on Election Day.

"Fox News at Night" anchor Shannon Bream shared the news, tweeting, "BREAKING FROM SCOTUS: Justice Alito has issued an Order than any ballots received after after 8pm on election day in PA be segregated and secured - and if counted, counted separately. There is a petition pending before SCOTUS. Alito orders opposing side to reply by 2p Saturday."

Here's How Recounts Could Unfold In Critical Battleground States

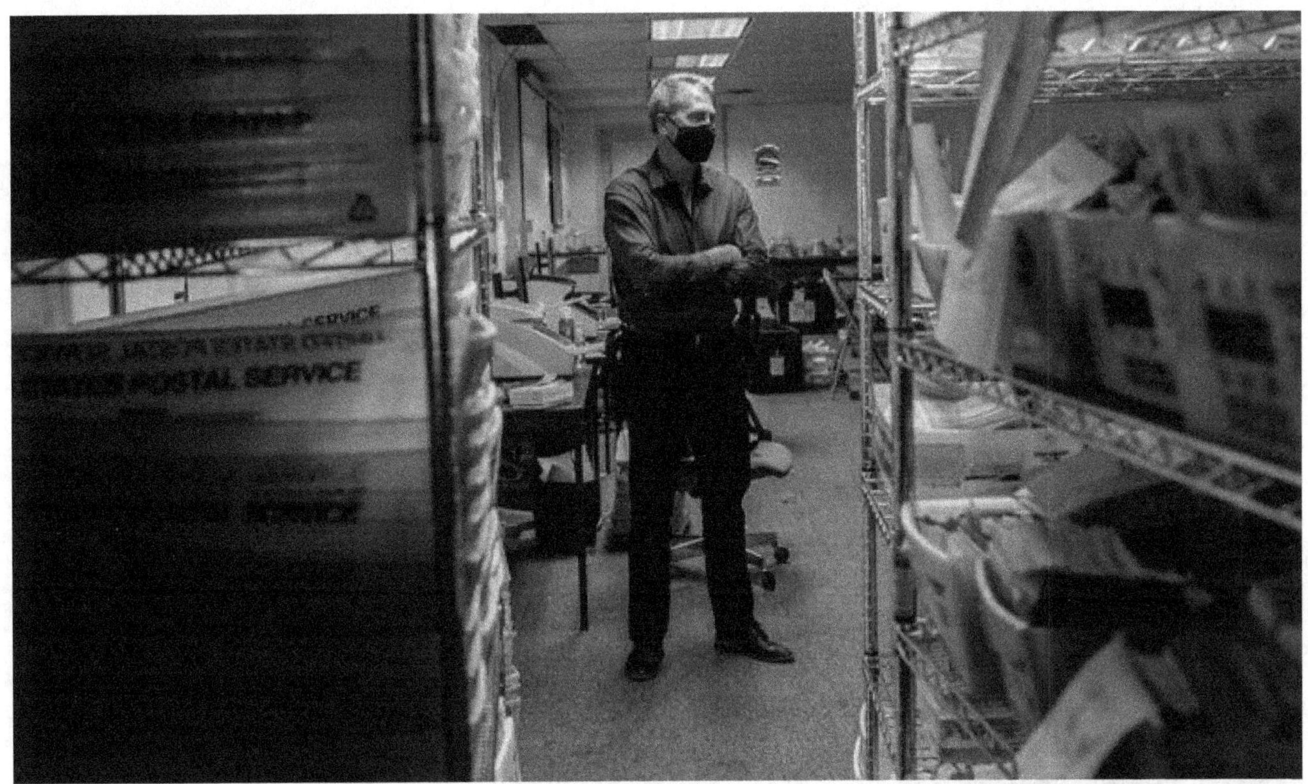

ANDREW TRUNSKY ELECTIONS REPORTER

- DEMOCRATIC nominee Joe Biden is on the cusp of crossing the 270-electoral vote threshold, unofficial results show, but he holds very narrow leads in multiple battleground states.
- President Donald Trump has signaled that he will push for recounts and lawsuits in several states, and has alleged without evidence that election fraud has occurred.
- Below is how and when recounts would take place in the most contested battlegrounds that could decide who ultimately wins the election.

As Americans anxiously await the election results in the few decisive states that have yet to be called, President Donald Trump's campaign has signaled that it will pursue recounts in several battlegrounds including Wisconsin, Pennsylvania, Georgia and more. Though Trump initially led by wide margins in each state, Democratic nominee Joe Biden pulled ahead in the days following as the states tabulated the influx of mail-in ballots. As of Friday afternoon, Biden leads by tight margins in five states that Trump won in 2016, and stands on the cusp of reaching the 270 electoral votes required to win the election. Below is how and when recounts will unfold in the states that will decide who ultimately wins the election. (RELATED: There Have Been A Lot Of Allegations Of Election Fraud. We Looked Into Them)

Georgia

Out of the nearly 5 million ballots cast in the Peach State, Biden holds an extremely slim lead of just 1,564 votes. Not only does his margin qualify for a recount under the state's law, but officials themselves said Friday that a recount was likely to occur. "Right now Georgia remains too close to call," said Georgia Secretary of State Brad Raffensperger during a press conference Friday. "With a margin that small, there will be a recount in Georgia." Recounts can be requested as long as the final results are within 0.5%, Georgia state law says, and candidates have 48 hours in which they are officially certified to do so.

Pennsylvania

Though Trump led by over 15% in the state early Wednesday, Biden overcame the deficit Friday morning and now leads in the state by approximately 14,000 votes out of over 6.5 million cast. Unlike Georgia, Pennsylvania Secretary of State Kathy Boockvar is required by law to order a recount if the final margin is 0.5% or less. If the final margin is within that range, a recount would need to be ordered before 5 p.m. on Nov. 12 and be completed within 12 days. As of Friday afternoon, Biden leads Trump in the state 49.5% to 49.3%.

PHILADELPHIA, PENNSYLVANIA – NOVEMBER 06: An election worker talks with a colleague during ballot .counting at the Philadelphia Convention Center on November 06, 2020

Nevada

According to state law, the loser of the state's tally can request a recount within three business days of the count being certified. Unlike other battlegrounds, however, the requesting campaign must put down a deposit to cover the recount's estimated cost. (RELATED: 'Show Us The Evidence': Chris Christie, Pat Toomey, Cast Doubt On Trump's Claims Of Voter Fraud)

If the recount changes the state's outcome, the deposit is returned, but if not, then it is used to pay for the operating expenses.

As of Friday afternoon, Biden leads in the state by just over 20,000 votes, 49.7% to 48.1%.

Arizona

State law requires a recount in Arizona if the margin between the top two candidates is within 0.1%.

Arizona Secretary of State Katie Hobbs told ABC News Thursday that she did not think a recount would occur, saying that while the state's "margins are very narrow, I don't think we're going to get into that territory."

As of Friday, Biden led in the state by 1.3%.

Wisconsin

Any candidate can request a recount in the Badger State if the final margin is within 1%, according to state law, and the request must be submitted within one business day of the results being certified.

Most outlets have already called the race for Biden, who leads by approximately 20,500 votes, 49.4% to 48.8%. Immediately after the call, the Trump campaign signaled that it would request a recount in the state.

Michigan

Unlike other states, Michigan requires a recount to be conducted, but only if the final vote margin is within 2,000 votes, according to state law. The only way a candidate can formally petition a recount is if they allege that fraud or a mistake occurred in tallying the votes, and "would have had a reasonable chance of winning the election." (RELATED: John James Refuses To Concede In Michigan) **A petition must be submitted within two days of the vote being certified.**

Biden leads in Michigan by nearly 150,000 votes.

WHO DECIDES WHAT EVIDENCE IS; WHO DECIDES WHAT A FACT IS? THERE'S ALREADY ENOUGH EVIDENCE OF TREASON IN STEALING THE 2020 PRESIDENTIAL BY DEMOCRATS. WHO DO WE BELIEVE; TRUTH OF THE DEMOCRAT RAPE OF AMERICA?

Ben Sasse: THIS GUY SASSE IS EVEN WORSE THAN ROMNEY & McCAIN WHAT'S EVIDENCE TO THIS SCHMUCK? Trump's Lawyers Need To Present 'Real Evidence' Of Fraud

ANDERS HAGSTROMWHITE

President Donald Trump's lawyers need to present "real evidence" of voter fraud, Republican Nebraska Sen. Ben Sasse told Axios on Friday.

Sasse's statement comes as former Vice President Joe Biden is leading in several crucial swing states and seems on the verge of winning the 2020 presidential election. Trump's legal team is engaged in a number of lawsuits in Pennsylvania, Georgia and elsewhere, alleging voter fraud and demanding greater access to the vote counting process. Sasse says the Trump campaign has yet to present any "real evidence" of fraud.

"Fraud is poison to self-government, so these are major allegations. If the President's legal team has real evidence, they need to present it immediately to both the public and the courts. In the meantime, all legal votes need to be counted according to relevant state laws. This is our American system and it works," Sasse said.

FACEBOOK & TWITTER AGAINST TRUMP IS SILICON VALLEY RAPING AMERICA. YOU & ME

Here's How Many Trump Tweets Have

Been Flagged Since Election Day

Social media platforms have flagged large numbers of President Donald Trump's Twitter and Facebook posts since Election Day, a review by the Daily Caller News Foundation found.

The president has tweeted a total of 50 times since Tuesday, November 2, as of Friday afternoon, and Twitter has flagged 12 of these tweets with the caption, "Some or all of the content shared in this Tweet is disputed and might be misleading about an election or other civic process."

2020 presidential candidate Joe Biden has tweeted 77 times from his account beginning November 3. Not one of these tweets is currently flagged by Twitter.

A Twitter spokeswoman told the DCNF that Twitter teams are continuing to "take enforcement action on Tweets that prematurely declare victory or contain misleading information about the election broadly," in line with Twitter's Civic Integrity Policy **and** guidance on labeling election results**.**

"We have and will continue to enforce our rules impartially to protect the integrity of the conversation around this election," the spokeswoman said. (RELATED: Trump Team's Allegations Of Widespread Fraud Are Not Supported By Their Own Lawsuits)

.Screenshot, Twitter

On Facebook, almost every single post by both Trump and 2020 presidential candidate Joe Biden since Election Day has been flagged, the DCNF found. Facebook did not immediately respond to a request for comment on the matter.

As of noon Friday, all Biden Facebook posts since Election Day are tagged with the comment: "Votes are being counted. The winner of the 2020 presidential election has not been projected." (RELATED: 'The Year Of The Republican Woman': Here's A List Of GOP Women Who Won 2020 Elections)

Biden silent on lack of social distancing, possible 'super spreader' celebrations

2 FACED BIDEN IS ALWAYS HAVING EVERYTHING BOTH WAYS: ACT BIDEN IS SILENT ABOUT EVERYTHING BUT MASKING

Crowds gather in Times Square after Biden projected to win election

Sen. WOODCHUCK SCHMUCK SCHUMER, **NYC Mayor de Blasio tweet congratulations to the president-elect; Alex Hogan reports.**

Democratic President-elect Joe Biden has not addressed concerns that some celebrations of his projected victory ".may contribute to the spread of coronavirus after his transition team declared Biden will always "listen to science

Thousands of Americans flooded streets of major cities, including New York City, Washington and Philadelphia, to celebrate Biden ahead of his Saturday night victory speech.

While many were wearing masks, the crowds tended to violate social distancing guidelines that have been recommended by the Centers for Disease Control and Prevention.

Biden had made fighting the coronavirus a central message in his campaign, saying it would be a top priority in his administration. His campaign declined to hold large-scale campaign rallies and criticized President Trump for bringing thousands of people together for rallies.

But after footage of the large crowds had been broadcast for hours on major news networks, including Fox News, the former vice president declined to urge people to socially distance.

“Our work begins with getting COVID under control,” Biden said in his speech on Saturday night.

“On Monday, I will name a group of leading scientists and experts as transition advisors to help take the Biden-Harris COVID plan and convert it into an action blueprint that will start on Jan. 20, 2021,” he told the primetime viewing audience. “That plan will be built on bedrock science. It will be constructed out of compassion, empathy and concern.”

Fox News confirmed Sunday that former surgeon general Dr. Vivek Murthy will be the head of Biden’s transition coronavirus task force. Murthy has been acting as an adviser to the campaign.

The CDC on Sunday said that the U.S. added 93,811 more cases and 1,072 more deaths, bringing the totals to 9,808,411 cases and 236,547 deaths. Biden’s speech in Wilmington, Delaware, was drive-in style to minimize the risk of spreading coronavirus, but photos of impromptu victory celebrations in other cities showed a lack of social distancing.

Conservative commentator Mark Dice posted a video of people packed together and dancing while wearing masks in Boston. Massachusetts Gov. Charlie Baker announced last week he was increasing coronavirus restrictions after a spike in cases. "Who knew Joe Biden would put and end to social distancing so soon?" Dice wrote on Twitter.

CNN host Jake Tapper on Saturday acknowledged the risk of the coronavirus while reporting on the celebrations.

"I hate to be a scold here, but we just had the highest day of infections in the United States," Tapper said. "I believe yesterday was 125,000 Americans with new coronavirus infections. That was the third straight day of more than 100,000 infections. It's good to see people wearing masks -- although for some of them they're slipping off their face."

Tapper's concern of coming across as a "scold," though, was drastically different than his approach last month when he condemned Trump for holding rallies. The "State of the Union" anchor closed his Oct. 11 show with a diatribe against the president for holding rallies amid the pandemic that Tapper labeled "super spreader" events.

"Trump's need to hold these rallies apparently exceeding his concern for those attending them," Tapper told viewers last month. "One of President Trump's skills during this era has been to behave with so little regard to basic decency, those who try to uphold the standards get accused of being partisan. As if 'don't behave in a way that's reckless and displays a wanton disregard for human life' is somehow now a partisan issue. It isn't."

Tapper then scolded Trump for "reckless behavior" regarding the coronavirus and accused him of indulging his ego at the risk of prolonging the pandemic.

THE DEMOCRATIC PARTY UNIFIER TODAY IS ANTI-ISRAEL ANTI-SEMITISM BORROWED FROM Joining the protesters was Ocasio-Cortez, who said: "We need to tell her that we've got her back in showing and pursuing the most progressive energy agenda that this country has ever seen."

NEVER FORGET NEVER AGAIN

THE BOOMERANG EVIL OF DEMOCRATIC U.S. SOCIALISM IS THE VAMPIRE THAT KEEPS COMIN' ROUND AGAIN. ALWAYS HAS. ALWAYS WILL.

ARE WE READY?

ALL DEMOCRATIC SOCIALISM; ESPECIALLY AUTHORITARIAN DEMOCRAT REDISTRIBUTION; IS NAZISM

"National Socialism" redirects here. For other ideologies and groups called National Socialism, see National Socialism (disambiguation).

"Nazi" redirects here. For other uses, see Nazi (disambiguation

National Socialism (German: *Nationalsozialismus*), more commonly known as Nazism (/ n tsi z m, næt-/), is the ideology and practices associated with the Nazi Party – officially the National Socialist German Workers› Party (*Nationalsozialistische Deutsche Arbeiterpartei* or NSDAP) – in Nazi Germany, and of other far-right groups with similar aims. Nazism is a form of fascism and showed that ideology›s disdain for liberal democracy and the parliamentary system, but also incorporated fervent antisemitism, scientific racism, and eugenics into its creed. Its extreme nationalism came from Pan-Germanism and the Völkisch movement prominent in the German nationalism of the time, and it was strongly influenced by the anti-Communist *Freikorps* paramilitary groups that emerged after Germany›s defeat in World War I, from which came the party's "cult of violence" which was "at the heart of the movement."

Nazism subscribed to theories of racial hierarchy and Social Darwinism, identifying the Germans as a part of what the Nazis regarded as an Aryan or Nordic master race. It aimed to overcome social divisions and create a German homogeneous society based on racial purity which represented a people's community (*Volksgemeinschaft*). The Nazis aimed to unite all Germans living in historically German territory, as well as gain additional lands for German expansion under the doctrine of *Lebensraum* and exclude those who they deemed either community aliens or "inferior" races. The term "National Socialism" arose out of attempts to create a nationalist redefinition of "socialism", as an alternative to both international socialism and free market capitalism. Nazism rejected the Marxist concept of class conflict, opposed cosmopolitan internationalism, and sought to convince all parts of the new German society to subordinate their personal interests to the "common good", accepting political interests as the main priority of economic organization.

The Nazi Party's precursor, the Pan-German nationalist and antisemitic German Workers' Party,

was founded on 5 January 1919. By the early 1920s the party was renamed the National Socialist German Workers' Party – to attract workers away from left-wing parties such as the Social Democrats (SPD) and the Communists (KPD) – and Adolf Hitler assumed control of the organization. The National Socialist Program or "25 Points" was adopted in 1920 and called for a united Greater Germany that would deny citizenship to Jews or those of Jewish descent, while also supporting land reform and the nationalization of some industries. In *Mein Kampf* ("My Struggle"; 1924–1925), Hitler outlined the anti-Semitism and anti-Communism at the heart of his political philosophy, as well as his disdain for representative democracy and his belief in Germany›s right to territorial expansion.

The Nazi Party won the greatest share of the popular vote in the two Reichstag general elections of 1932, making them the largest party in the legislature by far, but still short of an outright majority. Because none of the parties were willing or able to put together a coalition government, in 1933 Hitler was appointed Chancellor of Germany by President Paul Von Hindenburg, through the support and connivance of traditional conservative nationalists who believed that they could control him and his party. Through the use of emergency presidential decrees by Hindenburg, and a change in the Weimar Constitution which allowed the Cabinet to rule by direct decree, bypassing both Hindenburg and the Reichstag, the Nazis had soon established a one-party state.

The *Sturmabteilung* (SA) and the *Schutzstaffel* (SS) functioned as the paramilitary organizations of the Nazi Party. Using the SS for the task, Hitler purged the party›s more socially and economically radical factions in the mid-1934 Night of the Long Knives, including the leadership of the SA. After the death of President Hindenburg, political power was concentrated in Hitler's hands and he became Germany's head of state as well as the head of the government, with the title of *Führer*, meaning "leader". From that point, Hitler was effectively the dictator of Nazi Germany, which was also known as the "Third Reich", under which Jews, political opponents and other "undesirable" elements were marginalized, imprisoned or murdered. Many millions of people were eventually exterminated in a genocide which became known as the Holocaust during World War II, including around two-thirds of the Jewish population of Europe.

Following Germany's defeat in World War II and the discovery of the full extent of the Holocaust, Nazi ideology became universally disgraced. It is widely regarded as immoral and evil, with only a few fringe racist groups, usually referred to as neo-Nazis, describing themselves as followers of National Socialism.

Flag of the Nazi Party, similar but not identical to the national flag of Nazi Germany (1933–1945), in which the swastika is slightly off-centred. The full name of the party was *Nationalsozialistische Deutsche Arbeiterpartei* (English: National-Socialist German Workers› Party) for which they officially used the acronym NSDAP.

The term "Nazi" was in use before the rise of the NSDAP as a colloquial and derogatory word for a backwards farmer or peasant, characterizing an awkward and clumsy person. In this sense, the word *Nazi* was a hypocorism of the German male name Ignatz (itself a variation of the name Ignatius) – Ignatz being a common name at the time in Bavaria, the area from which the NSDAP emerged.[

In the 1920s, political opponents of the NSDAP in the German labour movement seized on this and – using the earlier abbreviated term "Sozi" for *Sozialist* (English: Socialist) as an example– shortened the first part of the NSDAP›s name, *[Na]tionalso[zi]alistische*, to the dismissive "Nazi", in order to associate them with the derogatory use of the term mentioned above. After the NSDAP's rise to power in the 1930s, the use of the term "Nazi" by itself or in terms such as "Nazi Germany", "Nazi regime" and so on was popularised by German exiles. From them, the term spread into other languages and it was eventually brought back into Germany after World War II. The NSDAP briefly adopted the designation "Nazi" [*when?*] in an attempt to reappropriate the term, but it soon gave up this effort and generally avoided using the term while it was in power.

Position within the political spectrum

Foreground, left to right: Führer Adolf Hitler; Hermann Göring; Minister of Propaganda Joseph Goebbels; and Rudolf Hess

Nazis alongside members of the far-right reactionary and monarchist German National People›s Party(DNVP) during the brief NSDAP–DNVP alliance in the Harzburg Front from 1931 to 1932

The majority of scholars identify Nazism in both theory and practice as a form of far-right politics.[14] Far-right themes in Nazism include the argument that superior people have a right to dominate other people and purge society of supposed inferior elements. Adolf Hitler and other proponents denied that Nazism was either left-wing or right-wing, instead they officially portrayed Nazism as a syncretic movement. In *Mein Kampf*, Hitler directly attacked both left-wing and right-wing politics in Germany, saying:

Today our left-wing politicians in particular are constantly insisting that their craven-hearted and obsequious foreign policy necessarily results from the disarmament of Germany, whereas the truth is that this is the policy of traitors ... But the politicians of the Right deserve exactly the same reproach. It was through their miserable cowardice that those ruffians of Jews who came into power in 1918 were able to rob the nation of its arms.

In a speech given in Munich on 12 April 1922, Hitler stated that:There are only two possibilities in Germany; do not imagine that the people will forever go with the middle party, the party of compromises; one day it will turn to those who have most consistently foretold the coming ruin and

have sought to dissociate themselves from it. And that party is either the Left: and then God help us! for it will lead us to complete destruction - to Bolshevism, or else it is a party of the Right which at the last, when the people is in utter despair, when it has lost all its spirit and has no longer any faith in anything, is determined for its part ruthlessly to seize the reins of power - that is the beginning of resistance of which I spoke a few minutes ago.

When asked [when?] whether he supported the "bourgeois right-wing", Hitler claimed that Nazism was not exclusively for any class and he indicated that it favored neither the left nor the right, but preserved "pure" elements from both "camps" by stating: "From the camp of bourgeois tradition, it takes national resolve, and from the materialism of the Marxist dogma, living, creative Socialism".

Historians regard the equation of National Socialism as 'Hitlerism' as too simplistic since the term was used prior to the rise of Hitler and the Nazis and the different ideologies incorporated into Nazism were already well established in certain parts of German society before World War I. The Nazis were strongly influenced by the post–World War I far-right in Germany, which held common beliefs such as anti-Marxism, anti-liberalism and antisemitism, along with nationalism, contempt for the Treaty of Versailles and condemnation of the Weimar Republic for signing the armistice in November 1918 which later led it to sign the Treaty of Versailles. A major inspiration for the Nazis were the far-right nationalist *Freikorps*, paramilitary organizations that engaged in political violence after World War I. Initially, the post–World War I German far-right was dominated by monarchists, but the younger generation, which was associated with *Völkisch* nationalism, was more radical and it did not express any emphasis on the restoration of the German monarchy. This younger generation desired to dismantle the Weimar Republic and create a new radical and strong state based upon a martial ruling ethic that could revive the "Spirit of 1914" which was associated with German national unity (*Volksgemeinschaft*).

The Nazis, the far-right monarchists, the reactionary German National People›s Party (DNVP) and others, such as monarchist officers in the German Army and several prominent industrialists, formed an alliance in opposition to the Weimar Republic on 11 October 1931 in Bad Harzburg, officially known as the "National Front", but commonly referred to as the Harzburg Front. The Nazis stated that the alliance was purely tactical and they continued to have differences with the DNVP. The Nazis described the DNVP as a bourgeois party and they called themselves an anti-bourgeois party. After the elections of July 1932, the alliance broke down when the DNVP lost many of its seats in the Reichstag. The Nazis denounced them as "an insignificant heap of reactionaries". The DNVP responded by denouncing the Nazis for their socialism, their street violence and the "economic experiments" that would take place if the Nazis ever rose to power. But amidst an inconclusive political situation in which conservative politicians Franz von Papen and Kurt von Schleicher were unable to form stable governments without the Nazis, Papen proposed to President Hindenburg to appoint Hitler as Chancellor at the head of a government formed primarily of conservatives, with only three Nazi ministers. Hindenburg did so, and contrary to the expectations of Papen and the DNVP, Hitler was soon able to establish a Nazi one-party dictatorship.

Kaiser Wilhelm II, who was pressured to abdicate the throne and flee into exile amidst an attempted communist revolution in Germany, initially supported the Nazi Party. His four sons, including Prince Eitel Friedrich and Prince Oskar, became members of the Nazi Party in hopes that in exchange for their support, the Nazis would permit the restoration of the monarchy.[

There were factions within the Nazi Party, both conservative and radical. The conservative Nazi Hermann Göring urged Hitler to conciliate with capitalists and reactionaries. Other prominent conservative Nazis included Heinrich Himmler and Reinhard Heydrich. Meanwhile, the radical Nazi Joseph Goebbels opposed capitalism, viewing it as having Jews at its core and he stressed the need for the party to emphasize both a proletarian and a national character. Those views were shared by Otto Strasser, who later left the Nazi Party in the belief that Hitler had allegedly betrayed the party's socialist goals by endorsing capitalism.

When the Nazi Party emerged from obscurity to become a major political force after 1929, the conservative faction rapidly gained more influence, as wealthy donors took an interest in the Nazis as a potential bulwark against communism. The Nazi Party had previously been financed almost entirely from membership dues, but after 1929 its leadership began actively seeking donations from German industrialists, and Hitler began holding dozens of fundraising meetings with business leaders. In the midst of the Great Depression, facing the possibility of economic ruin on the one hand and a Communist or Social Democratic government on the other hand, German business increasingly turned to Nazism as offering a way out of the situation, by promising a state-driven economy that would support, rather than attack, existing business interests. By January 1933, the Nazi Party had secured the support of important sectors of German industry, mainly among the steel and coal producers, the insurance business and the chemical industry.

Large segments of the Nazi Party, particularly among the members of the *Sturmabteilung* (SA), were committed to the party›s official socialist, revolutionary and anti-capitalist positions and expected both a social and an economic revolution when the party gained power in 1933.[37] In the period immediately before the Nazi seizure of power, there were even Social Democrats and Communists who switched sides and became known as "Beefsteak Nazis": brown on the outside and red inside. The leader of the SA, Ernst Röhm, pushed for a "second revolution" (the "first revolution" being the Nazis' seizure of power) that would enact socialist policies. Furthermore, Röhm desired that the SA absorb the much smaller German Army into its ranks under his leadership. Once the Nazis achieved power, Röhm's SA was directed by Hitler to violently suppress the parties of the left, but they also began attacks against individuals deemed to be associated with conservative reaction. Hitler saw Röhm's independent actions as violating and possibly threatening his leadership, as well as jeopardising the regime by alienating the conservative President Paul von Hindenburg and the conservative-oriented German Army. This resulted in Hitler purging Röhm and other radical members of the SA in 1934, in what came to be known as the Night of the Long Knives.

Before he joined the Bavarian Army to fight in World War I, Hitler had lived a bohemian lifestyle as a petty street watercolour artist in Vienna and Munich and he maintained elements of this lifestyle later on, going to bed very late and rising in the afternoon, even after he became Chancellor and

then Führer. After the war, his battalion was absorbed by the Bavarian Soviet Republic from 1918 to 1919, where he was elected Deputy Battalion Representative. According to historian Thomas Weber, Hitler attended the funeral of communist Kurt Eisner (a German Jew), wearing a black mourning armband on one arm and a red communist armband on the other, which he took as evidence that Hitler›s political beliefs had not yet solidified. In *MEIN KAMPF*, Hitler never mentioned any service with the Bavarian Soviet Republic and he stated that he became an antisemite in 1913 during his years in Vienna. This statement has been disputed by the contention that he was not an antisemite at that time, even though it is well established that he read many antisemitic tracts and journals during time and admired Karl Lueger, the antisemitic mayor of Vienna. Hitler altered his political views in response to the signing of the Treaty of Versailles in June 1919 and it was then that he became an antisemitic, German nationalist.

Hitler expressed opposition to capitalism, regarding it as having Jewish origins and accusing capitalism of holding nations ransom to the interests of a parasitic cosmopolitan rentier class. He also expressed opposition to communism and egalitarian forms of socialism, arguing that inequality and hierarchy are beneficial to the nation. He believed that communism was invented by the Jews (THAT INCLUDES MY ASS) to weaken nations by promoting class struggle. **After his rise to power, Hitler took a pragmatic position on economics, accepting private property and allowing capitalist private enterprises to exist so long as they adhered to the goals of the Nazi state, but not tolerating enterprises that he saw as being opposed to the national interest.[**

German business leaders disliked Nazi ideology but came to support Hitler, because they saw the Nazis as a useful ally to promote their interests. Business groups made significant financial contributions to the Nazi Party both before and after the Nazi seizure of power, in the hope that a Nazi dictatorship would eliminate the organized labor movement and the left-wing parties. Hitler actively sought to gain the support of business leaders by arguing that private enterprise is incompatible with democracy. Although he opposed communist ideology, Hitler publicly praised the Soviet Union's leader Joseph Stalin and Stalinism on numerous occasions.[Hitler commended Stalin for seeking to purify the Communist Party of the Soviet Union of Jewish influences, noting Stalin›s purging of Jewish communists such as Leon Trotsky, Griery Zinoviev, Lev Kamenev and Karl Radek. While Hitler had always intended to bring Germany into conflict with the Soviet Union so he could gain *Lebensraum* ("living space"), he supported a temporary strategic alliance between Nazi Germany and the Soviet Union to form a common anti-liberal front so they could defeat liberal democracies, particularly France.

Origins

See also: Early timeline of Nazism

Völkisch nationalism

Main articles: Pan-Germanism, German nationalism, German Question, Unification of Germany, and Völkisch movement

Johann Gottlieb Fichte, considered one of the fathers of German nationalism

One of the most significant ideological influences on the Nazis was the German nationalist Johann Gottlieb Fichte, whose works had served as an inspiration to Hitler and other Nazi Party members, including Dietrich Eckart and Arnold Fanck. In *Speeches to the German Nation* (1808), written amid Napoleonic France›s occupation of Berlin, Fichte called for a German national revolution against the French occupiers, making passionate public speeches, arming his students for battle against the French and stressing the need for action by the German nation so it could free

itself. Fichte's nationalism was populist and opposed to traditional elites, spoke of the need for a "People's War" (*Volkskrieg*) and put forth concepts similar to those which the Nazis adopted. Fichte promoted German exceptionalism and stressed the need for the German nation to purify itself (including purging the German language of French words, a policy that the Nazis undertook upon their rise to power).[

Another important figure in pre-Nazi *völkisch* thinking was Wilhelm Heinrich Riehl, whose work—*Land und Leute* (*Land and People*, written between 1857 and 1863)—collectively tied the organic German Volk to its native landscape and nature, a pairing which stood in stark opposition to the mechanical and materialistic civilization which was then developing as a result of industrialization. Geographers Friedrich Ratzel and Karl Haushofer borrowed from Riehl›s work as did Nazi ideologues Alfred Rosenberg and Paul Schultze-Naumburg, both of whom employed some of Riehl›s philosophy in arguing that "each nation-state was an organism that required a particular living space in order to survive". Riehl›s influence is overtly discernible in the *Blut und Boden* (*Blood and Soil*) philosophy introduced by Oswald Spengler, which the Nazi agriculturalist Walther Darré and other prominent Nazis adopted.

***Völkisch* nationalism denounced soulless materialism, individualism and secularised urban industrial society, while advocating a "superior" society based on ethnic German "folk" culture and German "blood". It denounced foreigners and foreign ideas and declared that Jews, Freemasons and others were "traitors to the nation" and unworthy of inclusion. *Völkisch* nationalism saw the world in terms of natural law and romanticism and it viewed societies as organic, extolling the virtues of rural life, condemning the neglect of tradition and the decay of morals, denounced the destruction of the natural environment and condemned "cosmopolitan" cultures such as Jews and Romani.**

The first party that attempted to combine nationalism and socialism was the (Austria-Hungary) German Workers' Party, which predominantly aimed to solve the conflict between the Austrian Germans and the Czechs in the multi-ethnic Austrian Empire, then part of Austria-Hungary. In 1896 the German politician Friedrich Naumann formed the National-Social Association which aimed to combine German nationalism and a non-Marxist form of socialism together; the attempt turned out to be futile and the idea of linking nationalism with socialism quickly became equated with antisemites, extreme German nationalists and the *Völkisch* movement in general.

Georg Ritter von Schönerer, a major exponent of Pan-Germanism

During the era of Imperial Germany, *Völkisch* nationalism was overshadowed by both Prussian patriotism and the federalist tradition of its various component states. The events of World War I, including the end of the Prussian monarchy in Germany, resulted in a surge of revolutionary *Völkisch* nationalism. The Nazis supported such revolutionary *Völkisch* nationalist policies and they claimed that their ideology was influenced by the leadership and policies of German Chancellor Otto von Bismarck, the founder of the German Empire. The Nazis declared that they were dedicated to continuing the process of creating a unified German nation state that Bismarck had begun and desired to achieve. While Hitler was supportive of Bismarck›s creation of the German Empire, he was critical of Bismarck›s moderate domestic policies.[] On the issue of Bismarck›s support of a *Kleindeutschland* ("Lesser Germany", excluding Austria) versus the Pan-German *Großdeutschland*("Greater Germany") which the Nazis advocated, Hitler stated that Bismarck's attainment of *Kleindeutschland* was the "highest achievement" Bismarck could have achieved "within the limits possible at that time". In *Mein Kampf* (*My Struggle*), Hitler presented himself as a "second Bismarck".[

During his youth in Austria, Hitler was politically influenced by Austrian Pan-Germanist proponent Georg Ritter von Schönerer, who advocated radical German nationalism, antisemitism, anti-Catholicism, anti-Slavic sentiment and anti-Habsburg views. From von Schönerer and his followers, Hitler adopted for the Nazi movement the *Heil* greeting, the *Führer* title and the model of absolute party leadership. Hitler was also impressed by the populist antisemitism and the anti-liberal bourgeois agitation of Karl Lueger, who as the mayor of Vienna during Hitler's time in the city used a rabble-rousing style of oratory that appealed to the wider masses. Unlike von Schönerer, Lueger was not a German nationalist and instead was a pro-Catholic Habsburg supporter and only used German nationalist notions occasionally for his own agenda.[Although Hitler praised both Lueger and Schönerer, he criticized the former for not applying a racial doctrine against the Jews and Slavs.

Racial theories and antisemitism

Nazism and race

THIS IS WHERE DEMOCRAT IDENTITY POLITICS; ESPECIALLY AG-GRIEVED BLACK LIVES MATTER COMES IN & FROM

Arthur de Gobineau, one of the key inventors of the theory of the "Aryan race"

The concept of the Aryan race, which the Nazis promoted, stems from racial theories asserting that Europeans are the descendants of Indo-Iranian settlers, people of ancient India and ancient Persia. Proponents of this theory based their assertion on the fact that words in European languages and words in Indo-Iranian languages have similar pronunciations and meanings. Johann Gottfried Herder argued that the Germanic peoples held close racial connections to the ancient Indians and the ancient Persians, who he claimed were advanced peoples that possessed

a great capacity for wisdom, nobility, restraint and science. Contemporaries of Herder used the concept of the Aryan race to draw a distinction between what they deemed to be "high and noble" Aryan culture versus that of "parasitic" Semitic culture.[Notions of white supremacy and Aryan racial superiority were combined in the 19th century, with white supremacists maintaining the belief that certain groups of white people were members of an Aryan "master race" that is superior to other races and particularly superior to the Semitic race, which they associated with "cultural sterility". Arthur de Gobineau, a French racial theorist and aristocrat, blamed the fall of the *ancien régime* in France on racial degeneracy caused by racial intermixing, which he argued had destroyed the purity of the Aryan race, a term which he only reserved for Germanic people. [Gobineau's theories, which attracted a strong following in Germany, emphasized the existence of an irreconcilable polarity between Aryan (Germanic) and Jewish cultures.

Houston Stewart Chamberlain, whose book ***The Foundations of the Nineteenth Century*** would prove to be a seminal work in the history of German nationalism

Aryan mysticism claimed that Christianity originated in Aryan religious traditions, and that Jews had usurped the legend from Aryans. Houston Stewart Chamberlain, an English proponent of racial theory, supported notions of Germanic supremacy and antisemitism in Germany. Chamberlain's work, *The Foundations of the Nineteenth Century* (1899), praised Germanic peoples for their creativity and idealism while asserting that the Germanic spirit was threatened by a "Jewish" spirit of selfishness and materialism. IT ALWAYS BOOMERANGS BACK TO THE JEWS; NOW WITH 2021 USA DEMOCRATS Chamberlain used his thesis to promote monarchical conservatism while denouncing democracy, liberalism and socialism. The book became popular, especially in Germany. Chamberlain stressed a nation's need to maintain its racial purity in order to prevent its degeneration and argued that racial intermingling with Jews should never be permitted. In 1923, Chamberlain met Hitler, whom he admired as a leader of the rebirth of the free spirit. Madison Grant's work *The Passing of the Great Race* (1916) advocated Nordicism and proposed that a eugenics program should be implemented in order to preserve the purity of the Nordic race. After reading the book, Hitler called it "my Bible"

In Germany, the belief that Jews were economically exploiting Germans became prominent due to the ascendancy of many wealthy Jews into prominent positions upon the unification of Germany in 1871.[] From 1871 to the early 20th century, German Jews were overrepresented in Germany›s upper and middle classes while they were underrepresented in Germany›s lower classes, particularly in the fields of agricultural and industrial labor. German Jewish financiers and bankers played a key role in fostering Germany›s economic growth from 1871 to 1913 and they benefited enormously from this boom. In 1908, amongst the twenty-nine wealthiest German families with aggregate fortunes of up to 55 million marks at the time, five were Jewish and the Rothschilds were the second wealthiest German family. The predominance of Jews in Germany›s banking, commerce and industry sectors during this time period was very high, even though Jews were estimated to account for only 1% of the population of Germany. The overrepresentation of Jews in these areas fueled resentment among non-Jewish Germans during periods of economic crisis. The 1873 stock market crash and the ensuing depression resulted in a spate of attacks on alleged Jewish economic dominance in Germany and antisemitism increased. During this time period, in the 1870s, German *Völkisch* nationalism began to adopt antisemitic and racist themes and it was also adopted by a number of radical right political movements.

Radical Antisemitism was promoted by prominent advocates of *Völkisch* nationalism, including Eugen Diederichs, Paul de Lagarde and Julius Langbehn. De Lagarde called the Jews a "bacillus, the carriers of decay ... who pollute every national culture ... and destroy all faiths with their materialistic liberalism" and he called for the extermination of the Jews. Langbehn called for a war of annihilation against the Jews, and his genocidal policies were later published by the Nazis and given to soldiers on the front during World War II.[One antisemitic ideologue of the period, Friedrich Lange, even used the term "National Socialism" to describe his own anti-capitalist take on the *Völkisch* nationalist template.

Johann Gottlieb Fichte accused Jews in Germany of having been and inevitably of continuing to be a "state within a state" that threatened German national unity. Fichte promoted two options in order to

address this, his first one being the creation of a Jewish state in Palestine so the Jews could be impelled to leave Europe. His second option was violence against Jews and he said that the goal of the violence would be "to cut off all their heads in one night, and set new ones on their shoulders, which should not contain a single Jewish idea".

SEE WHO USA DEMOCRATS DEFINE AS JEWS & ISRAELIS (US)

Caricatures of Bolshevik leaders Vladimir Lenin, Karl Radek, Julius Martov and Emma Goldman from Alfred Rosenberg's *The Jewish Bolshevism*, which assert that Bolshevism is a Jewish ideology

The Protocols of the Elders of Zion (1912) is an anti-semitic forgery created by the secret service of the Russian Empire, the Okhrana. Many anti-semites believed it was real and thus it became widely popular after World War I. *The Protocols* claimed that there was a secret international Jewish conspiracy to take over the world. Hitler had been introduced to *The Protocols* by Alfred Rosenbergand from 1920 onwards he focused his attacks by claiming that Judaism and Marxism were directly connected, that Jews and Bolsheviks were one and the same and that Marxism was a Jewish ideology-this became known as "Jewish Bolshevism". Hitler believed that *The Protocols* were authentic.

Prior to the Nazi ascension to power, Hitler often blamed moral degradation on *Rassenschande* ("racial defilement"), a way to assure his followers of his continuing antisemitism, which had been toned down for popular consumption. Prior to the induction of the Nuremberg Race Laws in 1935 by the Nazis, many German nationalists such as Roland Freisler strongly supported laws to ban *Rassenschande* between Aryans and Jews as racial treason. Even before the laws were officially passed, the Nazis banned sexual relations and marriages between party members and Jews. Party members found guilty of *Rassenschande* were severely punished; some party members were even sentenced to death.

The Nazis claimed that Bismarck was unable to complete German national unification because Jews had infiltrated the German parliament and they claimed that their abolition of parliament had ended this obstacle to unification. Using the stab-in-the-back myth, the Nazis accused Jews—and other populations who it considered non-German—of possessing extra-national loyalties, thereby exacerbating German antisemitism about the *Judenfrage* (the Jewish Question), the far-right political canard which was popular when the ethnic Völkisch movement and its politics of Romantic nationalism for establishing a *Großdeutschland* was strong.

Nazism's racial policy positions may have developed from the views of important biologists of the 19th century, including French biologist Jean-Baptiste Lamarck, through Ernst Haeckel's idealist version of Lamarckism and the father of genetics, German botanist Gregor Mendel. However, Haeckel's works were later condemned and banned from bookshops and libraries by the Nazis as inappropriate for "National-Socialist formation and education in the Third Reich". This may have been because of his "monist" atheistic, materialist philosophy, which the Nazis disliked. Unlike Darwinian theory, Lamarckian theory officially ranked races in a hierarchy of evolution from apes while Darwinian theory did not grade races in a hierarchy of higher or lower evolution from apes, but simply stated that all humans as a whole had progressed in their evolution from apes. Many Lamarckians viewed "lower" races as having been exposed to debilitating conditions for too long for any significant "improvement" of their condition to take place in the near future. [Haeckel utilised Lamarckian theory to describe the existence of interracial struggle and put races on a hierarchy of evolution, ranging from wholly human to subhuman. (JEWS) A.K.A. ME

Mendelian inheritance, or Mendelism, was supported by the Nazis, as well as by mainstream eugenicists of the time. The Mendelian theory of inheritance declared that genetic traits and attributes were passed from one generation to another. Eugenicists used Mendelian inheritance theory to demonstrate the transfer of biological illness and impairments from parents to children, including mental disability, whereas others also utilised Mendelian theory to demonstrate the inheritance of social traits, with racialists claiming a racial nature behind certain general traits such as inventiveness or criminal behavior.

Response to World War I and Italian Fascism

During World War I, German sociologist Johann Plenge spoke of the rise of a "National Socialism" in Germany within what he termed the "ideas of 1914" that were a declaration of war against the "ideas of 1789" (the French Revolution). According to Plenge, the "ideas of 1789" which included the rights of man, democracy, individualism and liberalism were being rejected in favor of "the ideas of 1914" which included the "German values" of duty, discipline, law and order.[98] Plenge believed that ethnic solidarity (*Volksgemeinschaft*) would replace class division and that "racial comrades" would unite to create a socialist society in the struggle of "proletarian" Germany against "capitalist" Britain. He believed that the "Spirit of 1914" manifested itself in the concept of the "People's League of National Socialism". This National Socialism was a form of state socialism that rejected the "idea of boundless freedom" and promoted an economy that would serve the whole of

Germany under the leadership of the state. This National Socialism was opposed to capitalism due to the components that were against "the national interest" of Germany, but insisted that National Socialism would strive for greater efficiency in the economy. Plenge advocated an authoritarian, rational ruling elite to develop National Socialism through a hierarchical technocratic state, and his ideas were part of the basis of Nazism.

Oswald Spengler, a philosopher of history

Oswald Spengler, a German cultural philosopher, was a major influence on Nazism, although after 1933 he became alienated from Nazism and was later condemned by the Nazis for criticizing Adolf Hitler. Spengler's conception of national socialism and a number of his political views were shared by the Nazis and the Conservative Revolutionary movement. Spengler's views were also popular amongst Italian Fascists, including Benito Mussolini.

Spengler's book *The Decline of the West* (1918), written during the final months of World War I, addressed the supposed decadence of modern European civilization, which he claimed was caused by atomizing and irreligious individualization and cosmopolitanism. Spengler's major thesis was that a law of historical development of cultures existed involving a cycle of birth, maturity, ageing and death when it reaches its final form of civilization. Upon reaching the point of civilization, a culture will lose its creative capacity and succumb to decadence until the emergence of "barbarians" creates a new epoch.Spengler considered the Western world as having succumbed to decadence of intellect, money, cosmopolitan urban life, irreligious life, atomized individualization and believed

that it was at the end of its biological and "spiritual" fertility. He believed that the "young" German nation as an imperial power would inherit the legacy of Ancient Rome, lead a restoration of value in "blood" and instinct, while the ideals of rationalism would be revealed as absurd.

Spengler's notions of "Prussian socialism" as described in his book *Preussentum und Sozialismus* ("Prussiandom and Socialism", 1919), influenced Nazism and the Conservative Revolutionary movement. Spengler wrote: "The meaning of socialism is that life is controlled not by the opposition between rich and poor, but by the rank that achievement and talent bestow. That is *our* freedom, freedom from the economic despotism of the individual". Spengler adopted the anti-English ideas addressed by Plenge and Sombart during World War I that condemned English liberalism and English parliamentarianism while advocating a national socialism that was free from Marxism and that would connect the individual to the state through corporatist organization. Spengler claimed that socialistic Prussian characteristics existed across Germany, including creativity, discipline; concern for the greater good, productivity and self-sacrifice. He prescribed war as a necessity by saying: "War is the eternal form of higher human existence and states exist for war: they are the expression of the will to war".

The **Marinebrigade Erhardt** during the **Kapp Putsch** in Berlin, 1920 (the Marine brigade Erhardt used the **swastika** as its symbol, as seen on their helmets and on the truck, which inspired the Nazi Party to adopt it as the movement›s symbol)

Spengler's definition of socialism did not advocate a change to property relations. He denounced Marxism for seeking to train the proletariat to "expropriate the expropriator", the capitalist and then to let them live a life of leisure on this expropriation. He claimed that "Marxism is the capitalism of the working class" and not true socialism. According to Spengler, true socialism would be in the form of corporatism, stating that "local corporate bodies organized according to the importance of each occupation to the people as a whole; higher representation in stages up to a supreme council of the state; mandates revocable at any time; no organized parties, no professional politicians, no periodic elections".

The book ***Das Dritte Reich***(1923), translated as "The Third Reich", by **Arthur Moeller van den Bruck**

Wilhelm Stapel, an antisemitic German intellectual, utilised Spengler's thesis on the cultural confrontation between Jews as whom Spengler described as a Magian people versus Europeans as a Faustian people.[ ] Stapel described Jews as a landless nomadic people (ME) in pursuit of an international culture whereby they can integrate into Western civilization. As such, Stapel claims that Jews have been attracted to "international" versions of socialism, pacifism or capitalism because as a landless people the Jews have transgressed various national cultural boundaries.

Arthur Moeller van den Bruck was initially the dominant figure of the Conservative Revolutionaries influenced Nazism. He rejected reactionary conservatism while proposing a new state that he coined the "Third Reich", which would unite all classes under authoritarian rule. Van den Bruck advocated a combination of the nationalism of the right and the socialism of the left. Fascism was

a major influence on Nazism. The seizure of power by Italian Fascist leader Benito Mussolini in the March on Rome in 1922 drew admiration by Hitler, who less than a month later had begun to model himself and the Nazi Party upon Mussolini and the Fascists. Hitler presented the Nazis as a form of German fascism. In November 1923, the Nazis attempted a "March on Berlin" modelled after the March on Rome, which resulted in the failed Beer Hall Putsch in Munich

Hitler spoke of Nazism being indebted to the success of Fascism's rise to power in Italy.In a private conversation in 1941, Hitler said that "the brown shirt would probably not have existed without the black shirt", the "brown shirt" referring to the Nazi militia and the "black shirt" referring to the Fascist militia. He also said in regards to the 1920s: "If Mussolini had been outdistanced by Marxism, I don't know whether we could have succeeded in holding out. At that period National Socialism was a very fragile growth".

Other Nazis—especially those at the time associated with the party's more radical wing such as Gregor Strasser, Joseph Goebbels and Heinrich Himmler—rejected Italian Fascism, accusing it of being too conservative or capitalist. Alfred Rosenberg condemned Italian Fascism for being racially confused and having influences from philosemitism. Strasser criticised the policy of *Führerprinzip*as being created by Mussolini and considered its presence in Nazism as a foreign imported idea.throughout the relationship between Nazi Germany and Fascist Italy, a number of lower-ranking Nazis scornfully viewed fascism as a conservative movement that lacked a full revolutionary potential.

Ideology - Nationalism and racialism

Nazism and race & Racial policy of Nazi Germany ESPECIALLY USA DEMOCRATIC ANTI-SEMITES TODAY

Nazism emphasized German nationalism, including both irredentism and expansionism. Nazism held racial theories based upon a belief in the existence of an Aryan master race that was superior to all other races. The Nazis emphasised the existence of racial conflict between the Aryan race and others—particularly Jews, whom the Nazis viewed as a mixed race that had infiltrated multiple societies and was responsible for exploitation and repression of the Aryan race. The Nazis also categorised Slavs as *Untermensch* (sub-human).

Irredentism and expansionism

Lebensraum

Beginning of ***Lebensraum***, the **Nazi German expulsion of Poles** from **central Poland**, 1939

The German Nazi Party supported German irredentist claims to Austria, Alsace-Lorraine, the region now known as the Czech Republic and the territory known since 1919 as the Polish Corridor. A major policy of the German Nazi Party was *Lebensraum* ("living space") for the German nation based on claims that Germany after World War I was facing an overpopulation crisis and that expansion was needed to end the country›s overpopulation within existing confined territory, and provide resources necessary to its people›s well-being. Since the 1920s, the Nazi Party publicly promoted the expansion of Germany into territories held by the Soviet Union.

In *Mein Kampf*, Hitler stated that *Lebensraum* would be acquired in Eastern Europe, especially Russia.[In his early years as the Nazi leader, Hitler had claimed that he would be willing to accept friendly relations with Russia on the tactical condition that Russia agree to return to the borders established by the German–Russian peace agreement of the Treaty of Brest-Litovsksigned by Vladimir Lenin of the Russian Soviet Federated Socialist Republic in 1918 which gave large territories held by Russia to German control in exchange for peace.In 1921, Hitler had commended the Treaty of Brest-Litovsk as opening the possibility for restoration of relations between Germany and Russia by saying: Through the peace with Russia the sustenance of Germany as well as the provision of work were to have been secured by the acquisition of land and soil, by access to raw materials, and by friendly relations between the two lands.

— Adolf Hitler

Topographical map of Europe: the Nazi Party declared support for ***Drang nach Osten*** (expansion of Germany east to the Ural Mountains), that is shown on the upper right side of the map as a brown diagonal line

From 1921 to 1922, Hitler evoked rhetoric of both the achievement of *Lebensraum* involving the acceptance of a territorially reduced Russia as well as supporting Russian nationals in overthrowing the Bolshevik government and establishing a new Russian government. Hitler›s attitudes changed by the end of 1922, in which he then supported an alliance of Germany with Britain to destroy Russia. Hitler later declared how far he intended to expand Germany into Russia:

Asia, what a disquieting reservoir of men! The safety of Europe will not be assured until we have driven Asia back behind the Urals. No organized Russian state must be allowed to exist west of that line.

—Adolf Hitler

Policy for *Lebensraum* planned mass expansion of Germany›s borders to eastwards of the Ural Mountains. Hitler planned for the "surplus" Russian population living west of the Urals to be deported to the east of the Urals.

Racial Theories REINVENTED AS 2021 DEMOCRAT AGGRIEVED VICTIM "THE JEWS DID THIS TO MY ASS" IDENTITY POLITICS

In its racial categorization, Nazism viewed what it called the Aryan race as the master race of the world—a race that was superior to all other races. It viewed Aryans as being in racial conflict with a mixed race people, the Jews, whom the Nazis identified as a dangerous enemy of the Aryans. **It also viewed a number of other peoples as dangerous to the well-being of the Aryan race. In order to preserve the perceived racial purity of the Aryan race, a set of race laws was introduced in 1935 which came to be known as the Nuremberg Laws. At first these laws only prevented sexual relations and marriages between Germans and Jews, but they were later extended to the** "Gypsies, Negroes, (SOMEHOW OR ANOTHER; US' ALL BE IS YIDDISHA JEWBOYS ALWAYS BE IS COMIN' IN LAST BEHIND ALL Y'ALL'S ASSES) **and their bastard offspring", who were described by the Nazis as people of "alien blood" Such relations between Aryans (cf. Aryan certificate) and non-Aryans were now punishable under the race laws as *Rassenschande* or "race defilement".** After the war began, the race defilement law was extended to include all foreigners (non-Germans). At the bottom of the racial scale of non-Aryans were Jews, Romanis, Slavs & blacks. **To maintain the "purity and strength" of the Aryan race, the Nazis eventually sought to exterminate Jews, Romani, Slavs and the physically and mentally disabled.[132][134] Other groups deemed "degenerate" and "asocial" who were not targeted for extermination, but were subjected to exclusionary treatment by the Nazi state, included homosexuals, blacks, Jehovah's Witnesses and political opponents.**
One of Hitler›s ambitions at the start of the war was to exterminate, expel or enslave most or all Slavs from Central and Eastern Europe in order to acquire living space for German settlers.

A "poster information" from the exhibition "***Miracle of Life***" in Berlin in 1935

A Nazi era school textbook for German students entitled *Heredity and Racial Biology for Students* written by Jakob Graf described to students the Nazi conception of the Aryan race in a section titled "The Aryan: The Creative Force in Human History". Graf claimed that the original Aryans developed from Nordic peoples who invaded ancient India and launched the initial development of Aryan culture there that later spread to ancient Persia and he claimed that the Aryan presence in Persia was what was responsible for its development into an empire. He claimed that ancient Greek culture was developed by Nordic peoples due to paintings of the time which showed Greeks who were tall, light-skinned, light-eyed, blond-haired people. He said that the Roman Empire was developed by the Italics who were related to the Celts who were also a Nordic people. He believed that the vanishing of the Nordic component of the populations in Greece and Rome led to their downfall. The Renaissance was claimed to have developed in the Western Roman Empire because of the Germanic invasions that brought new Nordic blood to the Empire›s lands, such as the presence of Nordic blood in the Lombards (referred to as Longobards in the book); that remnants of the western Goths were responsible for the creation of the Spanish Empire; and that the heritage of the Franks, Goths and Germanic peoples in France was what was responsible for its rise as a major power. He claimed that the rise of the Russian Empire was due to its leadership by people of Norman descent. He described the rise of Anglo-Saxon societies in North America, South

Africa and Australia as being the result of the Nordic heritage of Anglo-Saxons. He concluded these points by saying: "Everywhere Nordic creative power has built mighty empires with high-minded ideas, and to this very day Aryan languages and cultural values are spread over a large part of the world, though the creative Nordic blood has long since vanished in many places".

"THE JEWISH PROBLEM" DEAD JEWS WAITING TO BE INCINERATED **TAKE A GOOD LOOK** A wagon piled high with corpses outside the crematorium in Buchenwald concentration camp

In Nazi Germany, the idea of creating a master race resulted in efforts to "purify" the *Deutsche Volk* through eugenics and its culmination was the compulsory sterilization or the involuntary euthanasia of physically or mentally disabled people. After World War II, the euthanasia programme was named Action T4.. The ideological justification for euthanasia was Hitler›s view of Sparta (11th century – 195 BC) as the original *Völkisch* state and he praised Sparta›s dispassionate destruction of congenitally deformed infants in order to maintain racial purity. Some non-Aryans enlisted in Nazi organisations like the Hitler Youth and the *Wehrmacht*,

including Germans of African descent[139] and Jewish descent. The Nazis began to implement "racial hygiene" policies as soon as they came to power. The July 1933 "Law for the Prevention of Hereditarily Diseased Offspring" prescribed compulsory sterilization for people with a range of conditions which were thought to be hereditary, such as schizophrenia, epilepsy, Huntington's chorea and "imbecility". Sterilization was also mandated for chronic alcoholism and other forms of social deviance. An estimated 360,000 people were sterilised under this law between 1933 and 1939. Although some Nazis suggested that the program should be extended to people with physical disabilities, such ideas had to be expressed carefully, given the fact that some Nazis had physical disabilities, one example being one of the most powerful figures of the regime, Joseph Goebbels, who had a deformed right leg.[Nazi racial theorist Hans F. K. Günther argued that European peoples were divided into five races: Nordic, Mediterranean, Dinaric, Alpine and East Baltic.[3] Günther applied a Nordicistconception in order to justify his belief that Nordics were the highest in the racial hierarchy. In his book *Rassenkunde des deutschen Volkes* (1922) ("Racial Science of the German People"), Günther recognised Germans as being composed of all five races, but emphasized the strong Nordic heritage among them.[Hitler read *Rassenkunde des deutschen Volkes*, which influenced his racial policy.[Gunther believed that Slavs belonged to an "Eastern race" and he warned against Germans mixing with them The Nazis described Jews as being a racially mixed group of primarily Near Eastern and Oriental racial types.[Because such racial groups were concentrated outside Europe, the Nazis claimed that Jews were "racially alien" to all European peoples and that they did not have deep racial roots in Europe.

Günther emphasized Jews' Near Eastern racial heritage. Günther identified the mass conversion of the Khazars to Judaism in the 8th century as creating the two major branches of the Jewish people, those of primarily Near Eastern racial heritage became the Ashkenazi Jews (that he called Eastern Jews) while those of primarily Oriental racial heritage became the Sephardi Jews (that he called Southern Jews). Günther claimed that the Near Eastern type was composed of commercially spirited and artful traders, that the type held strong psychological manipulation skills which aided them in trade.[147] He claimed that the Near Eastern race had been "bred not so much for the conquest and exploitation of nature as it had been for the conquest and exploitation of people".Günther believed that European peoples had a racially motivated aversion to peoples of Near Eastern racial origin and their traits, and as evidence of this he showed multiple examples of depictions of satanic figures with Near Eastern physiognomies in European art.

Hitler's conception of the Aryan *Herrenvolk* ("Aryan master race") excluded the vast majority of Slavs from central and eastern Europe (i.e. Poles, Russians, Ukrainians, etc.). They were regarded as a race of men not inclined to a higher form of civilization, which was under an instinctive force that reverted them back to nature. The Nazis also regarded the Slavs as having dangerous Jewish and Asiatic, meaning Mongol, influences. Because of this, the Nazis declared Slavs to be *Untermenschen* ("subhumans"). Nazi anthropologists attempted to scientifically prove the historical admixture of the Slavs who lived further East and leading Nazi racial theorist Hans Günther regarded the Slavs as being primarily Nordic centuries ago but he believed that they had mixed with non-Nordic types over time. Exceptions were made for a small percentage of Slavs who the Nazis saw as descended from German settlers and therefore fit to be Germanised and

considered part of the Aryan master race. Hitler described Slavs as "a mass of born slaves who feel the need for a master".The Nazi notion of Slavs as inferior served as a legitimization of their desire to create *Lebensraum* for Germans and other Germanic people in eastern Europe, where millions of Germans and other Germanic settlers would be moved into once those territories were conquered, while the original Slavic inhabitants were to be annihilated, removed or enslaved. Nazi Germany›s policy changed towards Slavs in response to military manpower shortages, forced it to allow Slavs to serve in its armed forces within the occupied territories in spite of the fact that they were considered "subhuman"

Hitler declared that racial conflict against Jews was necessary in order to save Germany from suffering under them and he dismissed concerns that the conflict with them was inhumane and unjust: We may be inhumane, but if we rescue Germany we have achieved the greatest deed in the world. We may work injustice, but if we rescue Germany then we have removed the greatest injustice in the world. We may be immoral, but if our people is rescued we have opened the way for morality.

Nazi propagandist Joseph Goebbels frequently employed antisemitic rhetoric to underline this view: "The Jew is the enemy and the destroyer of the purity of blood, the conscious destroyer of our race."

Social class (SUB-HUMAN)

National Socialist politics was based on competition and struggle as its organizing principle, and the Nazis believed that "human life consisted of eternal struggle and competition and derived its meaning from struggle and competition." The Nazis saw this eternal struggle in military terms, and advocated a society organized like an army in order to achieve success. They promoted the idea of a national-racial "people's community" (*Volksgemeinschaft*) in order to accomplish "the efficient prosecution of the struggle against other peoples and states." Like an army, the *Volksgemeinschaft* was meant to consist of a hierarchy of ranks or classes of people, some commanding and others obeying, all working together for a common goal.This concept was rooted in the writings of 19th century *völkisch* authors who glorified medieval German society, viewing it as a "community rooted in the land and bound together by custom and tradition," in which there was neither class conflict nor selfish individualism.

Nazism rejected the Marxist concept of class conflict, and it praised both German capitalists and German workers as essential to the *Volksgemeinschaft*. In the *Volksgemeinschaft*, social classes would continue to exist, but there would be no class conflict between them. Hitler said that "the capitalists have worked their way to the top through their capacity, and as the basis of this selection, which again only proves their higher race, they have a right to lead."German business leaders co-operated with the Nazis during their rise to power and received substantial benefits from the Nazi state after it was established, including high profits and state-sanctioned monopolies and cartels. Large celebrations and symbolism were used extensively to encourage those engaged in physical labor on behalf of Germany, with leading National Socialists often praising the "honor of labor", which fostered a sense of community (*Gemeinschaft*) for the German people and promoted solidarity

towards the Nazi cause. To win workers away from Marxism, Nazi propaganda sometimes presented its expansionist foreign policy goals as a "class struggle between nations. "Bonfires were made of school children's differently colored caps as symbolic of the unity of different social classes.

In 1922, Hitler discredited other nationalist and racialist political parties as disconnected from the mass populace, especially lower and working-class young people:

The racialists were not capable of drawing the practical conclusions from correct theoretical judgements, especially in the Jewish Question. In this way, the German racialist movement developed a similar pattern to that of the 1880s and 1890s. As in those days, its leadership gradually fell into the hands of highly honorable, but fantastically naïve men of learning, professors, district counsellors, schoolmasters, and lawyers—in short a bourgeois, idealistic, and refined class. It lacked the warm breath of the nation's youthful vigor.

Nevertheless, the Nazi Party's voter base consisted mainly of farmers and the middle class, including groups such as Weimar government officials, school teachers, doctors, clerks, self-employed businessmen, salesmen, retired officers, engineers, and students. Their demands included lower taxes, higher prices for food, restrictions on department stores and consumer co-operatives, and reductions in social services and wages. The need to maintain the support of these groups made it difficult for the Nazis to appeal to the working class, since the working class often had opposite demands.

From 1928 onward, the Nazi Party's growth into a large national political movement was dependent on middle class support, and on the public perception that it "promised to side with the middle classes and to confront the economic and political power of the working class." The financial collapse of the white collar middle-class of the 1920s figures much in their strong support of Nazism. Although the Nazis continued to make appeals to "the German worker," historian Timothy Mason concludes that "Hitler had nothing but slogans to offer the working class."

Sex and gender *Women in Nazi Germany*

Obligations of Polish workers in Germany, warning them of the death penalty for any sexual relations between Germans and Poles

Nazi ideology advocated excluding women from political involvement and confining them to the spheres of "Kinder, Küche, Kirche" (Children, Kitchen, Church). Many women enthusiastically supported the regime, but formed their own internal hierarchies. Hitler's own opinion on the matter of women in Nazi Germany was that while other eras of German history had experienced the development and liberation of the female mind, the National Socialist goal was essentially singular in that it wished for them to produce a child. Based on this theme, Hitler once remarked about women that "with every child that she brings into the world, she fights her battle for the nation. The man stands up for the *Volk*, exactly as the woman stands up for the family".Proto-natalist programs

in Nazi Germany offered favorable loans and grants to newlyweds and encouraged them to give birth to offspring by providing them with additional incentives.

Contraception was discouraged for racially valuable women in Nazi Germany and abortion was forbidden by strict legal mandates, including prison sentences for women who sought them as well as prison sentences for doctors who performed them, whereas abortion for racially "undesirable" persons was encouraged.

While unmarried until the very end of the regime, Hitler often made excuses about his busy life hindering any chance for marriage. Among National Socialist ideologues, marriage was valued not for moral considerations but because it provided an optimal breeding environment. *Reichsführer-SS* Heinrich Himmler reportedly told a confidant that when he established the *Lebensborn* program, an organization that would dramatically increase the birth rate of "Aryan" children through extramarital relations between women classified as racially pure and their male equals, he had only the purest male "conception assistants" in mind. Since the Nazis extended the *Rassenschande* ("race defilement") law to all foreigners at the beginning of the war, pamphlets were issued to German women which ordered them to avoid sexual relations with foreign workers who were brought to Germany and the pamphlets also ordered German women to view these same foreign workers as a danger to their blood.

Although the law was applicable to both genders, German women were punished more severely for having sexual relations with foreign forced laborers in Germany

The Nazis issued the Polish decrees on 8 March 1940 which contained regulations concerning the Polish forced laborers (Zivilarbeiter) who were brought to Germany during World War II. One of the regulations stated that any Pole "who has sexual relations with a German man or woman, or approaches them in any other improper manner, will be punished by death".[] After the decrees were enacted, Himmler stated: Fellow Germans who engage in sexual relations with male or female civil workers of the Polish nationality, commit other immoral acts or engage in love affairs shall be arrested immediately.

The Nazis later issued similar regulations against the Eastern Workers *(Ost-Arbeiters)*, including the imposition of the death penalty if they engaged in sexual relations with German persons. Heydrich issued a decree on 20 February 1942 which declared that sexual intercourse between a German woman and a Russian worker or prisoner of war would result in the Russian man being punished

with the death penalty. Another decree issued by Himmler on 7 December 1942 stated that any "unauthorized sexual intercourse" would result in the death penalty. Because the Law for the Protection of German Blood and German Honor did not permit capital punishment for race defilement, special courts were convened in order to allow the death penalty to be imposed in some cases; German women accused of race defilement were marched through the streets with their head shaven and placards detailing their crimes were placed around their necks and those convicted of race violations were sent to concentration camps. When Himmler reportedly asked Hitler what the punishment should be for German girls and German women who were found guilty of race defilement with prisoners of war (POWs), he ordered that "every POW who has relations with a German girl or a German would be shot" and the German woman should be publicly humiliated by "having her hair shorn and being sent to a concentration camp" The League of German Girls was particularly regarded as instructing girls to avoid race defilement, which was treated with particular importance for young females.

Opposition to THE NAZI LBGTQ QUEER AS FOLK SCENE homosexuality

Persecution of LGBTQUEER AS FOLK TRANSGENDER homosexuals in Nazi Germany and the Holocaust

Homophobia: Berlin memorial to homosexual victims of the Holocaust: ***Totgeschlagen—Totgeschwiegen*** (Struck Dead—Hushed Up) THIS MEANS NO GAY PRIDE PARADES WITH ADOLF HITLER AS GRAND MASTER

After the Night of the Long Knives,

Hitler promoted Himmler and the SS, who then zealously suppressed homosexuality by saying: "We must exterminate these people root and branch ... the homosexual must be eliminated". In 1936, Himmler established the "Reichszentrale zur Bekämpfung der Homosexualität und Abtreibung" ("Reich Central Office for the Combating of Homosexuality and Abortion").[194] The Nazi regime incarcerated some 100,000 homosexuals during the 1930s. As concentration camp prisoners, homosexual men were forced to wear pink triangle badges. Nazi ideology still viewed German men who were gay as a part of the Aryan master race, but the Nazi regime attempted to force them into sexual and social conformity. Homosexuals were viewed as failing in their duty to procreate and reproduce for the Aryan nation. Gay men who would not change or feign a change in their sexual orientation were sent to concentration camps under the "Extermination Through Work" campaign.

A.K.A. WORKING PEOPLE YOU DON'T LIKE TO DEATH

Religion - *Religious aspects of Nazism, Religion in Nazi Germany, Positive Christianity, German Christians, German Faith Movement, Catholic Church and Nazi Germany, Kreuz und Adler, and Religious views of Adolf Hitler*

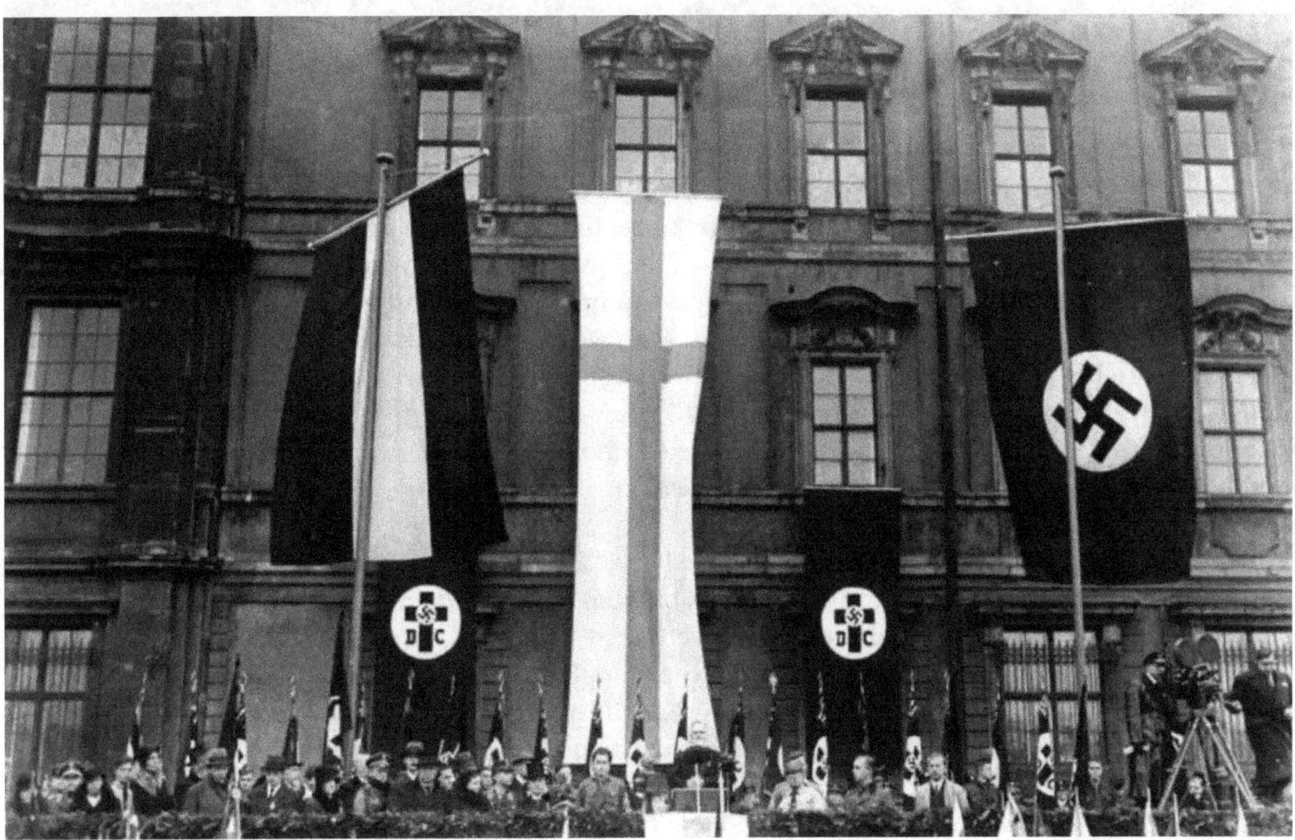

Members of the German Christiansorganization celebrating Luther Day in Berlin in 1933, speech by Bishop Hossenfelder

Hitler in 1935 with Cesare Orsenigo, the Catholic Church's nuncio to Germany

The Nazi Party Program of 1920 guaranteed freedom for all religious denominations which were not hostile to the State and it also endorsed Positive Christianity in order to combat "the Jewish-materialist spirit". Positive Christianity was a modified version of Christianity which emphasized racial purity and nationalism. The Nazis were aided by theologians such as Ernst Bergmann. In his work *Die 25 Thesen der Deutschreligion* (*Twenty-five Points of the German Religion*), Bergmann held the view that the Old Testament of the Bible was inaccurate along with portions of the New Testament, claimed that Jesus was not a Jew but was instead of Aryan origin and he also claimed that Adolf Hitler was the new messiah.

Hitler denounced the Old Testament as "Satan's Bible" and utilizing components of the New Testament he attempted to prove that Jesus was both an Aryan and an antisemite by citing passages such as John 8:44 where he noted that Jesus is yelling at "the Jews", as well as saying to them "your father is the devil" and the Cleansing of the Temple, which describes Jesus' whipping of the "Children of the Devil". Hitler claimed that the New Testament included distortions by Paul the Apostle, who Hitler described as a "mass-murderer turned saint". In their propaganda, the Nazis utilized the writings of Martin Luther, the founder of Protestantism. They publicly displayed an original edition of Luther's *On the Jews and their Lies* during the annual Nuremberg rallies.The Nazis endorsed the pro-Nazi Protestant German Christians organization. The Nazis were initially very hostile to Catholics because most Catholics supported the German Centre Party. Catholics

opposed the Nazis' promotion of compulsory sterilization of those whom they deemed inferior and the Catholic Church forbade its members to vote for the Nazis. In 1933, extensive Nazi violence occurred against Catholics due to their association with the Centre Party and their opposition to the Nazi regime's sterilization laws. The Nazis demanded that Catholics declare their loyalty to the German state.[In their propaganda, the Nazis used elements of Germany's Catholic history, in particular the German Catholic Teutonic Knights and their campaigns in Eastern Europe. The Nazis identified them as "sentinels" in the East against "Slavic chaos", though beyond that symbolism, the influence of the Teutonic Knights on Nazism was limited. Hitler also admitted that the Nazis' night rallies were inspired by the Catholic rituals which he had witnessed during his Catholic upbringing.[207] The Nazis did seek official reconciliation with the Catholic Church and they endorsed the creation of the pro-Nazi Catholic *Kreuz und Adler*, an organization which advocated a form of national Catholicism that would reconcile the Catholic Church›s beliefs with Nazism. On 20 July 1933, a concordat (*Reichskonkordat*) was signed between Nazi Germany and the Catholic Church, which in exchange for acceptance of the Catholic Church in Germany required German Catholics to be loyal to the German state. The Catholic Church then ended its ban on members supporting the Nazi Party.

Historian Michael Burleigh claims that Nazism used Christianity for political purposes, but such use required that "fundamental tenets were stripped out, but the remaining diffuse religious emotionality had its uses". Burleigh claims that Nazism›s conception of spirituality was "self-consciously pagan and primitive". However, historian Roger Griffin rejects the claim that Nazism was primarily pagan, noting that although there were some influential neo-paganists in the Nazi Party, such as Heinrich Himmler and Alfred Rosenberg, they represented a minority and their views did not influence Nazi ideology beyond its use for symbolism. It is noted that Hitler denounced Germanic paganism in *Mein Kampf* and condemned Rosenberg›s and Himmler›s paganism as "nonsense".

Economics *Economy of Nazi Germany* and *Economics of fascism*

Deutsches Volk–Deutsche Arbeit:German People, German Work (1934) – an example of reactionary modernism

Generally speaking, Nazi theorists and politicians blamed Germany's previous economic failures on political causes like the influence of Marxism on the workforce, the sinister and exploitative machinations of what they called international Jewry and the vindictiveness of the western political leaders' war reparation demands. Instead of traditional economic incentives, the Nazis offered solutions of a political nature, such as the elimination of organised trade unions, rearmament (in contravention of the Versailles Treaty) and biological politics. Various work programs designed to establish full-employment for the German population were instituted once the Nazis seized full national power. Hitler encouraged nationally supported projects like the construction of the Autobahn highway system, the introduction of an affordable people›s car (Volkswagen) and later the Nazis bolstered the economy through the business and employment generated by military rearmament. The Nazis benefited early in the regime's existence from the first post–Depression economic upswing, and this combined with their public works projects, job-procurement program and subsidised home repair program reduced unemployment by as much as 40 percent in one year. This development tempered the unfavorable psychological climate caused by the earlier economic crisis and encouraged Germans to march in step with the regime.

Upon being appointed Chancellor in 1933, Hitler promised measures to increase employment, protect the German currency, and promote recovery from the Great Depression. These included an agrarian settlement program, labor service, and a guarantee to maintain health care and pensions. But above all, his priority was rearmament, and the buildup of the German military in preparation for an eventual war to conquer Lebensraum in the East. Thus, at the beginning of his rule, Hitler said that "the future of Germany depends exclusively and only on the reconstruction of the Wehrmacht. All other tasks must cede precedence to the task of rearmament." This policy was implemented immediately, with military expenditures quickly growing far larger than the civilian work-creation programs. As early as June 1933, military spending for the year was budgeted to be three times larger than the spending on all civilian work-creation measures in 1932 and 1933 combined. Nazi Germany increased its military spending faster than any other state in peacetime, with the share of military spending rising from 1 percent to 10 percent of national income in the first two years of the regime alone.. Eventually, by 1944, it reached as high as 75 percent.

In spite of their rhetoric condemning big business prior to their rise to power, the Nazis quickly entered into a partnership with German business from as early as February 1933. That month, after being appointed Chancellor but before gaining dictatorial powers, Hitler made a personal appeal to German business leaders to help fund the Nazi Party for the crucial months that were to follow. He argued that they should support him in establishing a dictatorship because "private enterprise cannot be maintained in the age of democracy" and because democracy would allegedly lead to communism. **He promised to destroy the German left and the trade unions, AUTHORITARIANISM ALWAYS TURNS AGAINST EVERYTHING BUT ITS**

OWN POWER without any mention of anti-Jewish policies or foreign conquests.[In the following weeks, the Nazi Party received contributions from seventeen different business groups, with the largest coming from IG Farben and Deutsche Bank. Historian Adam Tooze writes that the leaders of German business were therefore “willing partners in the destruction of political pluralism in Germany.” In exchange, owners and managers of German businesses were granted unprecedented powers to control their workforce, collective bargaining was abolished and wages were frozen at a relatively low level. Business profits also rose very rapidly, as did corporate investment. In addition, the Nazis privatized public properties and public services, but at the same time they increased economic state control through regulations. Hitler believed that private ownership was useful in that it encouraged creative competition and technical innovation, but insisted that it had to conform to national interests and be "productive" rather than "parasitical". Private property rights were conditional upon following the economic priorities set by the Nazi leadership, with high profits as a reward for firms who followed them and the threat of nationalization being used against those who did not.. Under Nazi economics, free competition and self-regulating markets diminished, but Hitler›s social Darwinist beliefs made him retain business competition and private property as economic engines..

Agrarian policies were also important to the Nazis since they corresponded not just to the economy but to their geopolitical conception of Lebensraum as well. For Hitler, the acquisition of land and soil was requisite in molding the German economy.To tie farmers to their land, selling agricultural land was prohibited. Farm ownership remained private, but business monopoly rights were granted to marketing boards to control production and prices with a quota system.The "Hereditary Farm Law of 1933" established a cartel structure under a government body known as the Reichsnährstand (RNST) which determined "everything from what seeds and fertilizers were used to how land was inherited".

The Nazis were hostile to the idea of social welfare in principle, upholding instead the social Darwinist concept that the weak and feeble should perish.They condemned the welfare system of the Weimar Republic as well as private charity, accusing them of supporting people regarded as racially inferior and weak, who should have been weeded out in the process of natural selection. Nevertheless, faced with the mass unemployment and poverty of the Great Depression, the Nazis found it necessary to set up charitable institutions to help racially-pure Germans in order to maintain popular support, while arguing that this represented "racial self-help" and not indiscriminate charity or universal social welfare. Thus, Nazi programs such as the Winter Relief of the German People and the broader National Socialist People›s Welfare (NSV) were organized as quasi-private institutions, officially relying on private donations from Germans to help others of their race - although in practice those who refused to donate could face severe consequences.Unlike the social welfare institutions of the Weimar Republic and the Christian charities, the NSV distributed assistance on explicitly racial grounds. It provided support only to those who were "racially sound, capable of and willing to work, politically reliable, and willing and able to reproduce." Non-Aryans were excluded, as well as the "work-shy", "asocials" and the "hereditarily ill." Successful efforts were made to get middle-class women involved in social work assisting large families, and the Winter Relief campaigns acted as a ritual to generate public sympathy.

Hitler primarily viewed the German economy as an instrument of power and believed the economy was not about creating wealth and technical progress so as to improve the quality of life for a nation's citizenry, but rather that economic success was paramount for providing the means and material foundations necessary for military conquest. While economic progress generated by National Socialist programs had its role in appeasing the German people, the Nazis and Hitler in particular did not believe that economic solutions alone were sufficient to thrust Germany onto the stage as a world power. The Nazis thus sought to secure a general economic revival accompanied by massive military spending for rearmament, especially later through the implementation of the Four Year Plan, which consolidated their rule and firmly secured a command relationship between the German arms industry and the National Socialist government. Between 1933 and 1939, military expenditures were upwards of 82 billion Reichsmarks and represented 23 percent of Germany's gross national product as the Nazis mobilized their people and economy for war.

Anti-Communism

The Nazis claimed that communism was dangerous to the well-being of nations because of its intention to dissolve private property, its support of class conflict, its aggression against the middle class, its hostility towards small business and its atheism.[238] Nazism rejected class conflict-based socialism and economic egalitarianism, favoring instead a stratified economy with social classes based on merit and talent, retaining private property and the creation of national solidarity that transcends class distinction. Historians Ian Kershaw and Joachim Fest argue that in post–World War I Germany, the Nazis were one of many nationalist and fascist political parties contending for the leadership of Germany›s anti-communist movement.

In Mein Kampf, Hitler stated his desire to "make war upon the Marxist principle that all men are equal." He believed that "the notion of equality was a sin against nature." Nazism upheld the "natural inequality of men," including inequality between races and also within each race. The National Socialist state aimed to advance those individuals with special talents or intelligence, so they could rule over the masses. Nazi ideology relied on elitism and the Führerprinzip (leadership principle), arguing that elite minorities should assume leadership roles over the majority, and that the elite minority should itself be organized according to a "hierarchy of talent," with a single leader - the Führer - at the top. [The Führerprinzip held that each member of the hierarchy owed absolute obedience to those above him and should hold absolute power over those below him.

During the 1920s, Hitler urged disparate Nazi factions to unite in opposition to Jewish Bolshevism. Hitler asserted that the "three vices" of "Jewish Marxism" were democracy, pacifism and internationalism. The Communist movement, the trade unions, the Social Democratic Party and the left-wing press were all considered to be Jewish-controlled and part of the "international Jewish conspiracy" to weaken the German nation by promoting internal disunity through class struggle. The Nazis also believed that the Jews had instigated the Bolshevik revolution in Russia and that Communists had stabbed Germany in the back and caused it to lose the First World War. They further argued that modern cultural trends of the 1920s (such as jazz music and cubist art) represented "cultural Bolshevism" and were part of a political assault aimed at the spiritual degeneration of the German Volk. Joseph Goebbels published a pamphlet titled The Nazi-Sozi which gave brief points of how National Socialism differed from Marxism.[] In 1930, Hitler said: "Our adopted term ‹Socialist› has nothing to do with Marxist Socialism. Marxism is anti-property; true Socialism is not".

The Communist Party of Germany (KPD) was the largest Communist Party in the world outside of the Soviet Union, until it was destroyed by the Nazis in 1933. In the 1920s and early 30s, Communists and Nazis often fought each other directly in street violence, with the Nazi paramilitary organizations being opposed by the Communist Red Front and Anti-Fascist Action. After the beginning of the Great Depression, both Communists and Nazis saw their share of the vote increase. However, while the Nazis were willing to form alliances with other parties of the right, the Communists refused to form an alliance with the Social Democratic Party of Germany, the largest party of the left.[After the Nazis came to power, they quickly banned the Communist Party under the allegation that it was preparing for revolution and that it had caused the Reichstag fire. Four thousand KPD officials were arrested in February 1933, and by the end of the year 130,000 communists had been sent to concentration camps.

During the late 1930s and the 1940s, anti-communist regimes and groups that supported Nazism included the Falange in Spain, the Vichy regime and the 33rd Waffen Grenadier Division of the SS Charlemagne (1st French) in France and the British Union of Fascists under Sir Oswald Mosley.

Anti-capitalism

The Nazis argued that free market capitalism damages nations due to international finance and the worldwide economic dominance of disloyal big business, which they considered to be the product of Jewish influences. Nazi propaganda posters in working class districts emphasized anti-capitalism, such as one that said: "The maintenance of a rotten industrial system has nothing to do with nationalism. I can love Germany and hate capitalism".

Both in public and in private, Hitler expressed disdain for capitalism, arguing that it holds nations ransom in the interests of a parasitic cosmopolitan rentier class. He opposed free market capitalism because it "could not be trusted to put national interests first," and he desired an economy that would direct resources "in ways that matched the many national goals of the regime," such as the buildup of the military, building programs for cities and roads, and economic self-sufficiency. Hitler also distrusted capitalism for being unreliable due to its egotism and he preferred a state-directed economy that maintains private property and competition but subordinates them to the interests of the Volk.

Hitler told a party leader in 1934: "The economic system of our day is the creation of the Jews". THAT'S WHAT USA DEMOCRATS SAY IN 2021.

Hitler said to Benito Mussolini that capitalism had "run its course". Hitler also said that the business bourgeoisie "know nothing except their profit.. 'Fatherland' is only a word for them." Hitler was personally disgusted with the ruling bourgeois elites of Germany during the period of the Weimar

Republic, who he referred to as "cowardly shits".

In Mein Kampf, Hitler effectively supported mercantilism in the belief that economic resources from their respective territories should be seized by force, as he believed that the policy of Lebensraum would provide Germany with such economically valuable territories.. Hitler argued that the only means to maintain economic security was to have direct control over resources rather than being forced to rely on world trade. He claimed that war to gain such resources was the only means to surpass the failing capitalist economic system.

Joseph Goebbels, who would later go on to become the Nazi Propaganda Minister, was strongly opposed to both capitalism and communism, viewing them as the "two great pillars of materialism" that were "part of the international Jewish conspiracy for world domination."Nevertheless, he wrote in his diary in 1925 that if he were forced to choose between them, "in the final analysis", "it would be better for us to go down with Bolshevism than live in eternal slavery under capitalism".He also linked his anti-Semitism to his anti-capitalism, stating in a 1929 pamphlet that "we see, in the Hebrews, the incarnation of capitalism, the misuse of the nation's goods.".

Within the Nazi Party, the faction associated with anti-capitalist beliefs was the Sturmabteilung (SA), a paramilitary wing led by Ernst Röhm. The SA had a complicated relationship with the rest of the party, giving both Röhm himself and local SA leaders significant autonomy. Different local leaders would even promote different political ideas in their units, including "nationalistic, socialistic, anti-Semitic, racist, völkisch, or conservative ideas."There was tension between the SA and Hitler, especially from 1930 onward, as Hitler's "increasingly close association with big industrial interests and traditional rightist forces" caused many in the SA to distrust him. The SA regarded Hitler's seizure of power in 1933 as a "first revolution" against the left, and some voices within the ranks began arguing for a "second revolution" against the right.. After engaging in violence against the left in 1933, Röhm's SA also began attacks against individuals deemed to be associated with conservative reaction. Hitler saw Röhm's independent actions as violating and possibly threatening his leadership, as well as jeopardising the regime by alienating the conservative President Paul von Hindenburg and the conservative-oriented German Army. This resulted in Hitler purging Röhm and other radical members of the SA in 1934, during the Night of the Long Knives.

Totalitarianism

Under Nazism, with its emphasis on the nation, individualism was denounced and instead importance was placed upon Germans belonging to the German Volk and "people›s community" (Volksgemeinschaft). Hitler declared that "every activity and every need of every individual will be regulated by the collectivity represented by the party" and that "there are no longer any free realms in which the individual belongs to himself". Himmler justified the establishment of a repressive police state, in which the security forces could exercise power arbitrarily, by claiming that national security and order should take precedence over the needs of the individual..

According to the famous philosopher and political theorist, Hannah Arendt, the allure of Nazism as a totalitarian ideology (with its attendant mobilization of the German population) resided within the construct of helping that society deal with the cognitive dissonance resultant from the tragic interruption of the First World War and the economic and material suffering consequent to the Depression and brought to order the revolutionary unrest occurring all around them. Instead of the plurality that existed in democratic or parliamentary states, Nazism as a totalitarian system promulgated "clear" solutions to the historical problems faced by Germany, levied support by de-legitimizing the former government of Weimar and provided a politico-biological pathway to a better future, one free from the uncertainty of the past. It was the atomized and disaffected masses that Hitler and the party elite pointed in a particular direction and using clever propaganda to make them into ideological adherents, exploited in bringing Nazism to life.

While the ideologues of Nazism, much like those of Stalinism, abhorred democratic or parliamentary governance as practiced in the United States or Britain, their differences are substantial. An epistemic crisis occurs when one tries to synthesize and contrast Nazism and Stalinism as two-sides of the same coin with their similarly tyrannical leaders, state-controlled economies and repressive police structures. Namely, while they share a common thematic political construction, they are entirely inimical to one another in their worldviews and when more carefully analyzed against one another on a one-to-one level, an "irreconcilable asymmetry" results.

Reactionary or revolutionary?

Although Nazism is often seen as a reactionary movement, it did not seek a return of Germany to the pre-Weimar monarchy, but instead looked much further back to a mythic halcyon Germany which never existed. It has also been seen – as it was by the German-American scholar Franz Leopold Neumann – as the result of a crisis of capitalism which manifested as a "totalitarian monopoly capitalism". In this view Nazism is a mass movement of the middle class which was in opposition to a mass movement of workers in socialism and its extreme form, Communism. Historian Karl Dietrich Bracher, however, argues that, Such an interpretation runs the risk of misjudging the revolutionary component of National Socialism, which cannot be dismissed as being simply reactionary. Rather, from the very outset, and particularly as it developed into the SS state, National Socialism aimed at a transformation of state and society. and that, Hitler's and the Nazi Party's political positions

were of a revolutionary nature: destruction of existing political and social structures and their supporting elites; profound despair for civic order, for human and moral values, for Habsburg and Hohenzollern, for liberal and Marxist ideas. The middle class and middle-class values, bourgeois nationalism and capitalism, the professionals, the intelligentsia and the upper class were dealt the sharpest rebuff. These were the groups which had to be uprooted. After the failure of the Beer Hall Putsch in 1923, and his subsequent trial and imprisonment, Hitler decided that the way for the Nazi Party to achieve power was not through insurrection, but through legal and quasi-legal means. This did not sit well with the brown-shirted storm troopers of the SA, especially those in Berlin, who chafed under the restrictions that Hitler placed on them, and their subordination to the party. This resulted in the Stennes Revolt of 1930-31, after which Hitler made himself the Supreme Commander of the SA, and brought Ernst Röhm back to be their Chief of Staff and keep them in line. The quashing of the SA›s revolutionary fervor convinced many businessmen and military leaders that the Nazis had put aside their insurrectionist past, and that Hitler could be a reliable partner. However, after the Nazis› "Seizure of Power" in 1933, Röhm and the Brown Shirts were not content for the party to simply carry the reigns of power. Instead, they pressed for a continuation of the "National Socialist revolution" to bring about sweeping social changes, which Hitler, primarily for tactical reasons, was not willing to do at that time. He was instead focused on rebuilding the military and reorienting the economy to provide the rearmament necessary for invasion of the countries to the east of Germany, especially Poland and Russia, to get the Lebensraum ("living space") he believed was necessary to the survival of the Aryan race. For this, he needed the cooperation of not only the military, but also the vital organs of capitalism, the banks and big businesses, which he would be unlikely to get if Germany›s social and economic structure was being radically overhauled. Röhm›s public proclamation that the SA would not allow the "German Revolution" to be halted or undermined caused Hitler to announce that "The revolution is not a permanent condition." The unwillingness of Röhm and the SA to cease their agitation for a "Second Revolution", and the unwarranted fear of a "Röhm putsch" to accomplish it, were factors behind Hitler›s purging of the SA leadership in the Night of the Long Knives in July 1934.

Despite such tactical breaks necessitated by pragmatic concerns, which were typical for Hitler during his rise to power and in the early years of his regime, Hitler never ceased being a revolutionary dedicated to the radical transformation of Germany, especially when it concerned racial matters. In his monograph, Hitler: Study of a Revolutionary?, Martyn Housden concludes:

[Hitler] compiled a most extensive set of revolutionary goals (calling for radical social and political change); he mobilized a revolutionary following so extensive and powerful that many of his aims were achieved; he established and ran a dictatorial revolutionary state; and he disseminated his ideas abroad through a revolutionary foreign policy and war. In short, he defined and controlled the National Socialist revolution in all its phases. Of course, there were aspects of Nazism which were reactionary, such as their attitude toward the role of women in society, which was completely traditionalist, calling for the return of women to the home as wives, mothers and homemakers, although ironically this ideological policy was undermined in reality by the growing labor shortages and need for more workers. The number of women in the workplace climbed throughout the period of Nazi control of Germany, from 4.24 million in 1933 to 4.52 million in 1936 and 5.2 million in 1938, numbers that far exceeded those of the Weimar Republic.

Another reactionary aspect of Nazism was in their arts policy, which stemmed from Hitler's rejection of all forms of "degenerate" modern art, music and architecture. Overall, however, Nazism – being the ideology and practices of the Nazi Party, and the Nazi Party being the manifestation of Hitler's will – is best seen as essentially revolutionary in nature.

Post-war Nazism - *Neo-Nazism*

Following Nazi Germany's defeat in World War II and the end of the Holocaust, overt expressions

of support for Nazi ideas were prohibited in Germany and other European countries. Nonetheless, movements which self-identify as National Socialist or which are described as adhering to National Socialism continue to exist on the fringes of politics in many western societies. Usually espousing a white supremacist ideology, many deliberately adopt the symbols of Nazi Germany. BELOW – THE BORN JEWISH MOST POWERFUL PERSON IN THE USA DEMOCRATIC PARTY WHO CONTROLS 8 MILLION TEACHERS; WHO HIDE FROM KIDS AMERICAN GREATNESS & TEACH THEM TO

HATE AMERICA; THEMSELVES THE VOTING & FINANCIAL FOUNDATION OF THE DEMOCRATIC PARTY SINCE THIS PHOTO WAS TAKEN; SHE'S THE NOW FATSO SKANK UGLY PIG BITCH BECOME A HIPPOPOTAMUS

POSTER FLAMING, EMASCULATING, BALL-CUTTING LESBIAN, RANDI JUDAS WEINGARTEN; WEARING THE SWEATSHIRT OF JOKESTER AL FRANKEN; CHAMPION OF SERIAL CHRONIC, BOTH HYPOCRITICAL, DISINGENUOUS RESIGNED IN DISGRACE FROM OF THE U.S. SENATE, MINNESOTA WITH HIS WALKING DIARRHEA BUDDY BELOW, JIMMY KIMMEL

EVERYTHING WITH THESE SCUMBAGS IS A BIG FUCKEN JOKE; MOST OF ALL, AMERICA & EVERYONE READING THIS BOOK

ABC's "Jimmy Kimmel Live" - Season 18

DEMOCRATS CONTROLLING THE WHITE HOUSE & BOTH HOUSES OF CONGRESS COMBINED WITH PERMANENTLY ELIMINATING VOTING IN THE UNITED STATES LEAVES ONE COURSE OF

ACTION. THIS BOOK ENDS THE WAY IT STARTED.

CONFEDERATE STATES OF AMERICA

ACT II SCENE I

RICHARD E. GLICK

SENATOR ELECT (R NY) 2022

PEOPLE WHO CAST VOTES DECIDE NOTHING.
PEOPLE WHO COUNT VOTES DECIDE EVERYTHING.
IN AUTHORITARIAN REGIMES; DEATH IS THE SOLUTION TO ALL PROBLEMS. NO MAN, NO PROBLEM

01/20/2021

RICHARD E. GLICK

RE: STORE # 5202 COMMACK SUFFOLK COUNTY NEW YORK 11725 BENIGN HARMLESS SITUATION INTENTIONALLY & MALICIOUSLY ESCALATED BY THIS ASSIST. MANAGER "MIKE" INVOLVING "MIKE'S" MOCKING & UNNECESSARY DEGRADING INSULTS; PROVOCATION & THEN; WITH ME NEVER RAISING MY VOICE; 911 CALL TO SUFFOLK COUNTY POLICE TO GET ME OUT OF THE COMMACK # 5202 STORE WHILE I WAS TRYING TO BUY A $299.99 SHARK VACUUM CLEANER; THAT I LEFT STORE # 5202 WITHOUT BUYING. **CERTIFIED MAIL HARD COPIES ALL BELOW**

CARL DOUGLAS McMILLON
CHIEF EXECUTIVE OFFICER – WALMART
HQ 702 SW **8th St, Bentonville, AR 72716**
DACONA SMITH – WALMART CORP. LEADERSHIP
SCOTT McCALL WALMART CHIEF MERCH. OFFICER
SURESH KUMAR WALMART GLOBAL CHIEF
STEVE SOOKMAN – MARKET MGR. NYC METRO **Steve has a account**
COMMACK STORE #5202 STORE MGR. STEVEN CARUSO
COMMACK STORE # 5202 AST. MGR. ALFREDO
COMMACK STORE #5202 AST. MGR. JULIA OR JULIET COMMACK STORE #5202 AST. MGR. "MIKE"
CENTEREACH STORE #2286 AST. MGR. AARON
RE: MALICIOUS BULLYING AST. MGR. "MIKE" TUESDAY, OCTOBER 27, 2020 8:15 PM; "MIKE'S" 1ST GLANCE; WORDS; BODY LANGUAGE MALIGNANT CONTEMPT; INTENTIONALLY DEGRADING; HUMILIATING BULLYING SHOPPING EXPERIENCE; WALMART CUSTOMER SINCE 1986; UNIVERSAL CITY, TEXAS; YOU'RE READING CONCLUSION OF 8TH BOOK (AGE (73) AMAZON; EVERYWHERE BOOKS SOLD; "MIKE"; WORST LIFETIME RETAIL EXPERIENCE; INC OVER (150) WALMARTS COAST-TO-COAST; I SPEND $100 @ WK $5000 @YR COMMACK # 5202

UNFATHOMABLE THIS COMPLAINT NEAR VIOLENT; ME; AGE (73) **THREATENED ARREST TUE OCT 27, 2020 BY COMMACK** # 5202 AST. MGR. "MIKE"

85 CROOKED HILL RD COMMACK, N.Y. 11725

GLOBAL EMP. 2.2 MILLION; REV. $523.96 BILLION; HQ BENTONVILLE AR SAMUEL MOORE WALTON; **WALMART FROM NOTHING.**

ALL STARTS WITH AN IDEA. BEN FRANKLIN STORES GOT RID OF THREAT TO MEDIOCRITIES; BECAUSE HE WAS UNPARALLELED BEST; HAPPENED TO ME **LOSERS HATE BRADY ON A (86) YD WINNING DRIVE**

- **WALMART; SAM'S CLUB; MODEST BRICK HOUSE; PICKUP FOR DAILY ADVICE FROM LUNCH COUNTER SODA JERK.**

- ALWAYS LAST ON LINE; BEHIND ALL OTHERS; SOON BIGGEST EMPLOYER; MOST REVENUE; FRUGAL; RICHEST; SAM'S PEOPLE; YOU KNOW WHO SAM'S PEOPLE ARE; WERE ALWAYS: FOREVER .... I'M A SAM'S PERSON. **KANSAS FARMER; BROOKLYN SAILOR; IRISH POLICEMAN; JEWISH TAILOR; OLD STORE KEEPER SHAKIN' HIS HEAD' HANDIN' OVER A LOAF OF BREAD; BUFFALO HUNTER TELLIN' STORY; OUT IN THE OREGON TERRITORY**

- WE ARE HIS PEOPLE; HE IS OUR MAN**; WE** NEVER QUITE KNEW WHERE THE PEOPLE LEFT OFF & WHERE SAM WALTON BEGAN ...

- **WAS A TIME; IN LITTLE ROCK; WHEN THEY CARRIED;** MR. WALTON **DOWN;** OTHER DAYS; OTHER MEN; OTHER STORES

- WOOLWORTH'S
- WOOLCO,
- S.S. KRESGE & CO.
- KMART/SEARS ONLY ASSET NOW REAL ESTATE
- SAM OUTLIVED/OUTSHINED BY EXAMPLE BEN FRANKLIN STORES & THEN SOME ...
- MONTGOMERY WARD
- LORD & TAYLOR
- PAYLESS SHOES
- ALEXANDERS
- PIER ONE IMPORTS
- BUTLER BROTHERS
- DUCKWALL-ALCO
- G. C. MURPHY
- H. L. GREEN
- J. G. McCRORY'S
- J. J. NEWBERRY'S
- JOHN'S BARGAIN STORES
- MORGAN & LINDSEY NEISER'S
- McCLELLAN STORES
- PALAIS ROYAL
- JOHN WANAMAKER
- STAGE STORES
- ACADEMY
- BEALLS
- ALLIED STORES
- AEROPOSTALE
- TG&Y
- W. T. GRANT
- E.J. KORVETTE
- GIMBELS
- MAYS

- BAMBERGERS
- S.KLEIN ON THE SQUARE
- NEIMAN MARCUS
- JOSKE'S
- ABRAHAM & STRAUSS
- SPORTS AUTHORITY
- MODELLS
- A & P
- WALDBAUMS
- PATHMARK
- PERGAMENT
- FORTUNOFF
- FINGERS
- THE BROADWAY
- MERVYNS'
- GERTZ
- BEST & COMPANY
- SPRINT
- BONWIT TELLER
- BARNEYS
- MODELLS
- BON MARCHE
- FOLEYS
- STERNS
- MARSHALL FIELDS
- LAMSTONS
- HUDSON
- TOPS
- NEWMARK & LEWIS
- SLEEPYS
- HILLSIDE BEDDING
- ORBACHS
- TIMES SQUARE STORES
- CALDOR
- TWO GUYS
- BARGAIN TOWN

- BILLIONS CUSTOMERS; TRILLIONS; BARGAINS; MILLIONS PAYCHECKS; AFFORDABLE $399.99 SMART BIG SCREEN TV'S (BUYING (1) MYSELF WHY WASTE TIME ANYWHERE ELSE?)

March 29, 1918, Kingfisher, OK

April 5, 1992, UAMS Medical Center, Little Rock, AR

LIKE OKLAHOMA, SAM WAS O.K.

Helen Walton (Married 1943–1992)

LIFE WITHOUT SAM? APPARENTLY NOT

Children: Alice Walton, Jim C. Walton, S. Robson Walton, John T. Walton

"There is only one boss. The customer. And he can fire everybody in the company from the chairman on down, simply by spending his money somewhere else."

SAM'S WRONG. CUSTOMERS COMMIT MASS MURDER; LOOT; CHEAT; LIE; STEAL SOMETHING FOR NOTHING; MALICIOUS RUDE; BULLIES; BADMOUTH INNOCENT EMPLOYEES TO GET THEM FIRED. HAPPENED IN RETAIL TO ME SOMETIMES .... AND THEN THIS:

BANG FER BUCK WHERE GEORGE; ABE LEFT OFF; DOLLARS; NOT BULLETS

ABE SHOULDA' COULDA' WOULDA' PICK FROM (10) KINDS STOVE PIPE HATS; ALL IN STOCK; 1/2 THE PRICE?

GEORGE: SHOULDA' COULDA' WOULDA' (10) KINDS CHERRY TREES; ALL IN STOCK; 1/2 PRICE; 1/2 BEATIN' FROM DAD WITH HIS STRAP

IF WE GOT LIFE, LIBERTY & PURSUIT OF HAPPINESS; WITH SAM; WHY NOT? HORSESHOES ... HULA HOOPS 1/2 PRICE

SAM - LOWEST I CAN EVER GO; NEVER EVER; WHAT I CAN GET FOR IT.

MOSES: "LET MY PEOPLE GO"
SAM; THE LAND OF MILK & HONEY
SAM; THE HORN OF GOOD & PLENTY
SAM; THE MAN OF STEADY PAYCHECKS
SAM'S LOVELY LAND IS MINE
SAM; **THE LIFE JESUS PROMISED US**
SAM; THE LAND MOSES LED US TO
SAM; THE LAND OF MILK & HONEY ...
SAM'S LOVELY LAND IS MINE ONCE EVERY 2,000 YEARS ... EVERY DAY ... EVERY WAY ... SAM? ALWAYS? WHO ELSE?
HE CAME ... FROM A PIONEER RACE ... LEFT THE WORLD ... A BETTER PLACE ... CLIMB WAS HIGH ... WORK WAS HARD ... QUITE A COMBINATION?
WHAT HE BUILT ...
MUST BE CARED FOR ...
DEFENDED ...
STEP RIGHT UP

1/2 WORK; *1/2* MONEY TWICE AS MUCH EVERYTHING FER EVERYONE IS YOU – NOT POSSIBLE? - SAYS RIGHT HERE IN 11TH COMMANDMENT; 28TH AMENDMENT; KORAN; 1ST; 2ND TESTAMENT UNIVERSAL MAGNA CARTA; 8TH WONDER; ALONE; ALL TOGETHER; – OBJECT; OR FOREVER HOLD YOUR PEACE.

DO WHAT W PEACE; FREEDOM?

ROLLBACK?
GREAT, GREAT, GREAT COME & GET DAY

WALMART'S SONG – SOON BROADWAY; (15) OSCARS

GREAT, GREAT, GREAT **COME & GET IT DAY**

COME & GET IT; COME & GET IT
COME & GET IT
COME & GET IT
IT'S HERE
SAYS IT IN THIS BOOK IT'S COMIN'
A MIGHTY DAY IS COMIN'
IT'S SAM'S IDEA
CHRISTMAS ON THE 4TH OF JULY
LET'S GIVE HIM A MIGHTY CHEER
ON A DAY FOR BANJOS STRUMMIN'
FO' ALL O' US IN OVERALLS
CAN'T YOU HEAR THOSE ANGELS SINGIN'
COME & GET YOUR GRAVY & TWO MEATBALLS
BELLS TO RING IN EVERY STEEPLE
COME FER' YER' TEST ON THE MOVIE SCREEN
ALL FOR FREE & EQUAL PEOPLE
COME FER' CAKE & FREE ICE CREAM
GONNA BE THE MOST EARTH SHAKIN' BREATHTAKIN ... DAY'
SAM, CAN I GET ME A WAFFLE IRON?
IT'S COMIN' TO YA'
SAM, CAN I GET ME A WASHIN' MACHINE'
WITH YOUR INITIALS ...
WE DON'T SELL 'EM;
BUT YOU'RE GETTING YOURS, ANYWAY
HEY SAM; HOW ABOUT A JUKEBOX?
IT'S HEAH'
HEY SAM, CAN I GET ME A HELICOPTER
HELICOPTER?
HALLELUJAH ...
MY GOWN WILL BE ... A CALICO GOWN
MY FEET WILL DANCE ... ALL OVER THIS TOWN 'CAUSE SAM IS HERE
THIS DAY TODAY VERY DAY
GLORY TIMES,
COMIN' FOR TO STAY;
ON SAM'S GREAT, GREAT, GREAT, COME & GET IT DAY
ON THAT GREAT, GREAT, COME & GET IT DAY
& KEEP IT
& SHARE IT
SAM'S GREAT, GREAT,
GET READY FOR
COME & GET IT .... DAY
- SAM'S TIME O' THE YEAR
GET READY FOR

- SAM'S TIME O' THE YEAR
SAM'S TIME ...
LET'S GIVE 'IT A MIGHTY CHEER
HEAR YE, HEAR YE'
CHOO-CHOO'S COMIN'
MIGHTY NEAR
ONE THING CRYSTAL CLEAR
WOO HOO, SAM'S HERE
BEST THING NOW
SAM'S HERE
HE'S UP THERE RIDIN' WITH THE ENGINEER,
SAM WALTON'S HERE
LOOK UP; CHOO-CHOO- PUFFIN'
LET'S GIVE A MIGHTY CHEER
LOOK UP THAT ENGINE HUFFIN'
OLE' SAM IS FINALLY HERE
ALL CHEER; ENGINE PUFFIN'
SAM IS HERE
SAM IS HERE
OH SAM IS HERE
SAM WALTON'S FINALLY HERE
HE'S HERE
HERE
HERE TO STAY
AIN'T NEVER GOIN' AWAY
HEART & SOUL
HERE TO STAY
HEART & SOUL
ALL HEAR THAT WHISTLE BLOWIN
OLE' SAM WANTS YOU KNOWNIN'
SAM'S WHISTLE GOOD TO HEAR OLE' SAM WANTS US KNOWIN'
WHAT TIME THE YEAR?
SAM TO HIS PEOPLE
YOU KNOW WHO SAM'S PEOPLE ARE
ROLLBACK TIME

WHAT TIME? ROLLBACK TIME; FOR PEOPLE; BY PEOPLE OF PEOPLE SAM'S PEOPLE; MINUTE, SECOND; HOUR; ROUND WORLD; BACK; EAST; CENTRAL, MOUNTAIN, PACIFIC, EVERY 2000 YEARS ... ONCE; ONE MAN ONLY; GAVE US ROLLBACK TIME; EVER ANOTHER? LEAST WE HAD ONE

When the Norn Mother saw the Whirlwind Hour Greatening and darkening as it hurried on,

She left the Heaven of Heroes and came down To make a man to meet the mortal need. She took the tried clay of the common road— Clay warm yet with the genial heat of Earth, Dashed through it all a strain of prophecy; Tempered the heap with the thrill of human tears; Then mixed in laughter with the serious stuff. Into the shape she breathed a flame to light That tender, tragic, ever-changing face. Here was a man to hold against the world, A man to match the mountains and the sea. The color of the ground was in him, the red earth; the smack & tang of elemental things;

The rectitude and patience of the cliff; The good-will of the rain that loves all leaves; The friendly welcome of the wayside well; The courage of the bird that dares the sea; MR. SAM WAS A PILOT; HE FLEW ALONE IN HIS OWN PLANE; TO HIS MANY STORES The gladness of the wind that shakes the corn; The pity of the snow that hides all scars; The secrecy of streams that make their way Beneath the mountain to the rifted rock; The tolerance and equity of light That gives as freely to the shrinking flower As to the great oak flaring to the wind— To the grave's low hill as to the Matterhorn That shoulders out the sky. Sprung from the West, He drank the valorous youth of a new world. The strength of virgin forests braced his mind, The hush of spacious prairies stilled his soul. His words were oaks in acorns; and his thoughts Were roots that firmly gripped the granite truth LIKE LINCOLN BEFORE HIM; OF THE SAME CLOTH Up from log cabin to the Capitol, One fire was on his spirit, one resolve— To send the keen ax to the root of wrong, Clearing a free way for the feet of God, The eyes of conscience testing every stroke, To make his deed the measure of a man. He built the rail-pile as he built the State, Pouring his splendid strength through every blow: The grip that swung the ax in Illinois Was on the pen that set a people free. So came the Captain with the mighty heart; And when the judgment thunders split the house, Wrenching the rafters from their ancient rest, He held the ridgepole up, and spiked again The rafters of the Home. He held his place—Held the long purpose like a growing tree—Held on through blame and faltered not at praise. And when he fell in whirlwind, he went down As when a lordly cedar, green with boughs, Goes down with a great shout upon the hills, And leaves a lonesome place against the sky.

Was
$98 86
BACK
Working twice as hard
to save you even more
ROLL BACK
$59
$9
$54 84
$78 53

WAL★MART
沃 尔 玛
"……只要我们做好本职工作，
照顾好我们的顾客，我们的发展
将是无限的。"

WAL★MART
沃 尔 玛
SAM'S WHOLESALE CLUB
OPENING

1992年，
美国平民的最高荣誉
President George Bush presented
with the Medal of Freedom.
2001 - Jo
the Sam

When I Die Bury Me At WAL-MART
So My HUSBAND Will Come Visit Me...

"High expectations are the key to everything."

Outstanding leaders go out of their way to boost the self-esteem of their personnel. If people believe in themselves, it's amazing what they can accomplish.

6:00 AM - 11:00 PM; LIGHTS; RENT; SALARIES; ELECTRIC; GAS; HEAT/AC; INSURANCE; OUTSIDE BLACKTOP; SECURITY; CARING; ' BILLIONS CUSTOMERS; 2.2 MILLION EMPLOYEES; BEFORE (1) GETS RUNG UP. IF SAM COULD CHOOSE A COIN FOR HIS FACE; IN YOUR PUDDLE FACE DOWN; RAIN .... REACH INTO THAT PUDDLE; ... SAM WOULD ... PASS IT BY? THAT'S WHAT SAM WAS ALL ABOUT ... PENNIES ... YOURS EVERY SINGLE ONE .

IF EVERY WALMART SEMI; HAD THIS PAINTED ON IT; WATCH SOAR LIKE AN EAGLE OVER AMAZON; ECOMMERCE & RETAIL. SHOP ANYWHERE ELSE? WHY?

COMPANY ONLY AS GOOD AS ITS PEOPLE.

RATTLESNAKE WARNS YOU ....

BITE YOU ONCE? TWICE?

CHOOSE YER SNAKEBITE WISELY ....

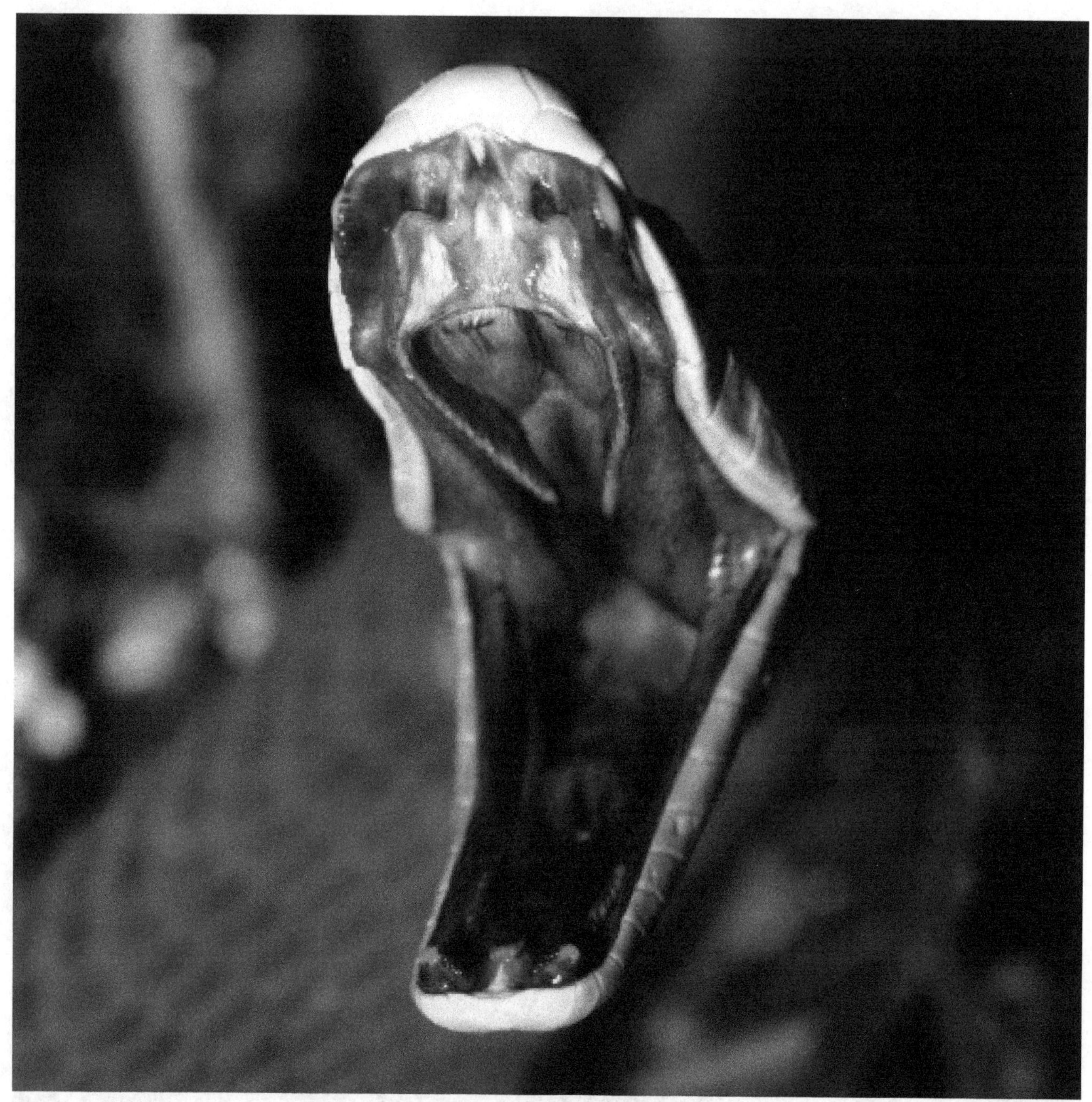

"WHALE DROP"
BEN FRANKLIN STORES? SEARS? K-MART?
EMPIRES & COMPANIES NEVER DIE. THEY COMMIT SUICIDE,

SHAKESPEARE: LILIES THAT FESTER SMELL WORSE THAN WEEDS.
I HAVE NO TIME; INTEREST OR IMAGINATION FOR THE CONCLUSION OF MY 8TH BOOK; THIS LETTER; THIS STORY FOUND ME; I DIDN'T FIND IT. BEAUTIFUL WIFE; 15 MIN TV W HER YEAR;

MORE FAMOUS EVERY DAY STARTING POLITICAL CAMPAIGN TO CLEANSE NEW YORK OF WOODCHUCK SCHMUCK SCHUMER; (D NY) WALMART SELLS AT LEAST (2) OF MY BOOKS; SINCE (5) SOON (73); BIGGEST; STRONGEST; HATE GUTS & TAKE DOWN BULLIES; "MIKE" #5202 WHO BULLIED ME; REGRET IT. DON'T WANT HIM FIRED; NEVER BULLY AGAIN; BULLIES; COWARDS ALL; PICK ONLY FIGHTS SURE TO WIN; TILL STOPPED. OFTEN KILLED. "MIKE" NOT BULLYING AGAIN CAN HAVE A THOUSAND INTERPRETATIONS. READ? CHECK? COPY? "MIKE"

Walmart Apologizes for Calling Sen. Hawley 'Sore Loser' After He Vows to Challenge Election Results

DON'T DARE LIE TO ME ABOUT IT, WALMART… SAM WALTON WOULD'VE CUT HAWLEY A $50 MILLION CHECK FOR PRESIDENT

Walmart on Wednesday apologized to GOP Sen **HAWLEY** Josh Hawley for a tweet criticizing the lawmaker for his plan to object to the Electoral College certification on Jan. 6.

The now-deleted tweet read: "Go ahead. Get your 2-hour debate. #soreloser." Kyle Plotkin, Hawley's chief of staff, tweeted at Walmart asking if the company can "explain this one?", after it was "mistakenly" posted by a member of LITTLE SMUG, CONDESCENDING; VICIOUS LITTLE LEFTY ON Walmart's social media team. I DEMAND WALMART TO FIRE THIS PERSON; THIS INSTANT. NOW.

Casey Staheli, Walmart's senior manager, told the Washington Examiner the employee meant to publish the comment on their personal account. DON'T LIE TO AMERICA, CASEY STAHELI? YOU FOR WALMART, ARE RIDICULING 76 MILLION OF US; ALL WALMART SHOPPERS, & OUR FAMILIES.

"We have removed the post and have no intention of commenting on the subject of certifying the Electoral College. We apologize to Senator Hawley for this error and any confusion about our position," he said.

DON'T LIE ABOUT THIS BACK-STABBING TWEET TO DEMOCRACY, WALMART. THIS TWEET. NO MISTAKE ABOUT ELECTION W PREMEDITATION; CUNNING, STEALTH; TREACHEROUSLY SHOPLIFTED ELECTORAL VOTES BY BIDEN; GEORGIA, PENNSYLVANIA, MICHIGAN WISCONSIN, ARIZONA & NEVADA.

Hawley retorted: "Thanks WALMART; for your insulting condescension. Now that you've insulted 76 million Americans, ALL WALMART SHOPPERS; EVERY SINGLE ONE OF 'EM; will you at least apologize for using slave labor? 80% OF WHAT WALMART SELLS IS MADE IN GULAG TOTALITARIAN CHINA.

"Or maybe you'd like to apologize for the pathetic wages you pay your workers as you drive mom and pop stores out of business," he added.

Hawley on Monday became the first senator to commit to challenging the results of the election in six states when Congress meets to certify the Electoral College results on Jan. 6. Several House Republicans are also on board.

Once an objection is filed each chamber would have to debate for two hours and then vote on whether to disqualify a state's votes. Both chambers would then have to agree to disqualify the state's votes, an outcome that is nearly impossible.

By Solange Reyner

HAWLEY'S A COURAGEOUS LEGENDARY AMERICAN HERO; FIGHTING FOR WHAT'S RIGHT. WALMART'S SMUG, VICIOUS LITTLE PRIVILEGED TWIRP BLOWS HAWLEY OFF AS "A SORE LOSER" FIRE THIS VICIOUS, LITTLE, LEFTY WALMART EMPLOYEE FOR CAUSE WRONGDOING ON-THE-SPOT. I'M TELLING WALMART; CUT A BIG; READ BIG; HIGH DOLLAR HAWLEY FOR AMERICAN DEMOCRACY CHECK; REWARDING HIM; FOR DEFENDING 76 MILLION PATRIOTIC WALMART SHOPPER VOTERS. DO IT NOW. WE CERTAINLY DON'T WANT WALMART; LIKE "MIKE" BULLYING OUR AMERICAN HERO JOSH HAWLEY FOR ATTACKING DEMOCRATS WHO STOLE OUR WHITE HOUSE? DO WE 76 MILLION TRUMP WALMART SHOPPER VOTERS WANT THIS? WILL 76 MILLION WALMART TRUMP VOTERS LAUGH THIS OFF? I'M REMINDING THEM. NEVER. EVER. SAM WALTON WOULDN'T,

Sen. Josh Hawley Slams Walmart Tweet Calling Him 'Sore Loser' for Objecting to Electoral College results insult by WALMART.

Kristina Wong

Sen. Josh Hawley (R-MO) slammed Walmart after a tweet from the company's corporate account called him a ."sore loser" after he said he would object to certifying the electoral college results on January 6

Hawley, the first senator to say he will object, wrote Wednesday, "Millions of voters concerned about election integrity deserve to be heard. I will object on January 6 on their behalf."

Walmart responded, "Go ahead. Get your 2 hour debate," along with the hashtag "#soreloser."

Hawley fired back shortly, "Thanks @Walmart for your insulting condescension. Now that you've insulted 76 million Americans, will you at least apologize for using slave labor?"

Hawley, a China hawk, was referencing Walmart's reliance on cheap Chinese factory labor to keep its prices low.

DOES WALMART EXIST BECAUSE OF GENOCIDAL XINJIANG PROVINCE UYGHUR CHINESE SLAVE LABOR? JOSH HAWLEY WENT TO CHARM SCHOOL. HE'S NICE. I'M NOT. DOES WALMART KNOW; FOR (20) YEARS; ROTTEN-TO-THE-CORE TOTALITARIAN CHINA

"HARVESTS" FROM CUSTOM BLOOD TYPE; TIMED & SLAUGHTERED WITH TRANSPLANT PATIENTS FROM 'ROUND THE WORLD IN THE NEXT OPERATING TRANSPLANT ROOM; WHERE DONORS ARE CUSTOM SLAUGHTERED FOR ORGAN FRESHNESS; THIS CHINESE ABSOLUTE FRESHEST; BEST; FROM CUSTOMER SLAUGHTERED DONOR TO TRANSPLANT RECIPIENT; 10'S 1000'S HEARTS RIGHT ON TIME; ANNUALLY HEARTS; LUNGS; KIDNEYS; LIVERS PANCREAS & CORNEAS; ADVERTISED WORLDWIDE ON CHINA'S MEAT MARKET WEBSITE FRESH TO THE WORLD HUMAN ORGAN TRANSPLANT MARKET. IF WALMART DIDN'T KNOW THIS; YA' ALL DO KNOW KNOWS IT NOW; BECAUSE I'M TEACHING YOU ALL ABOUT JOE BIDEN'S BUDDIE BUDDIE CHINA; CHINA EMPHASIZES ON ITS WEBSITE THE FRESHNESS OF ITS TRANSPLANT ORGANS; MAKING THEM THE VERY BEST. GOOGLE, BETTER FOXFIRE IT. ALL 100 PERCENT TRUE. DOES WALMART CARE? WALMART DOESN'T SELL BLOOD DIAMONDS; BUT WHAT ABOUT HEART, LUNG, LIVER, KIDNEY, PANCREAS & CORNEAS; THAT MAKE POSSIBLE CHEAP TV'S. READ MY BOOKS. I WRITE ABOUT IT.

For instance, the website of the China International Transplantation Network Assistance Center posted the following price list on its website in 2006: Kidney: $62,000; Liver: $98,000–130,000; Liver+kidney: $160,000–180,000; Kidney+pancreas: $150,000; Lung: $150,000–170,000; Heart: $130,000–160,000; Cornea: $30,000. In a statement before the U.S. House of Representatives, Gabriel Danovitch of the UCLA Medical Center said, "The ease in which these organs can be obtained and the manner that they may be allocated to wealthy foreigners has engendered a culture of corruption." THIS IS TODAY CHINA'S BIGGEST; BEST; HARD CASH COW; FOREIGN EXCHANGE; FROM THE UNLIMITED SUPPLY OF CUSTOM SLAUGHTERED POLITICAL DISSIDENT HUMAN COWS; COMING TO AMERICA FROM THE PROGRESSIVE DEMOCRAT LEFT.

WALMART AIN'T PERFECT. IF YOU MAKE IT TO HEAVEN; 1ST (10) MINUTES; (10) THINGS YOU DON'T LIKE. WORST IN HEAVEN; NO 7-11. 2ND WORST; NO WALMART.

Hawley's chief of staff, Kyle Plotkin, also wrote, "Hi @Walmart. Can you explain this one?"

Walmart later wrote to Hawley, "The tweet published earlier was mistakenly posted by a member of our social media team. We deleted the post and have no intention of commenting on the subject of certifying the Electoral College. We apologize to Senator Hawley for this error and any confusion about our position."

The hashtag #BoycottWalmart began trending shortly after Walmart's initial tweet.

As pointed out by OANN journalist Jack Posobiec, the American Manufacturing Alliance estimates **that Chinese suppliers make up 70 to 80 percent of Walmart's merchandise, with less than 20 percent for American-made products.**

I CONDEMN WALMART'S SHALLOW, APOLOGY FOR ITS VICIOUS, SMUG; CONTEMPTIBLE LITTLE TWIRP BRAT WHO SNEERS AT US 76 MILLION WALMART TRUMP VOTERS BEING "SORE LOSERS" IN WHITE HOUSE PICKPOCKETED BY SWORN AFFIDAVIT UNDER PENALTY OF FELONY PERJURY;

NAKEDLY SHOPLIFTED; LOOTED FROM THE DEMOCRACY AMERICA DIED BATTLEFIELDS FOR. FIRE THIS SOCIAL MEDIA EMPLOYEE FOR CAUSE; NO SEVERANCE, NOW; MAKING THIS TRAITOR INELIGIBLE FOR UNEMPLOYMENT BENEFITS; & BUY "HER/IT" (1) WAY SLOW BOAT TICKET TO RTHNIC XINJIANG UYGHUR MINORITY MUSLIM CHINESE PROVINCE. CHINA. DONALD TRUMP DERANGEMENT SYNDROME IS BANNED FROM SOCIAL MEDIA? AND WALMART ON ITS PAYROLL INCUBATES ON PAYROLL THIS MARIE ANTOINETTE CONTEMPT #soreloser" FOR AMERICA. ?

WALMART MAIL VOTING FRAUD RE-EDUCATION PROGRAM. Mail-in ballots were part of a plot to deny Lincoln reelection in 1864. IT JUST HAPPENED HERE IN 2020 & 01/05/2021 IN GEORGIA.

By Dustin Waters

Traveling to Baltimore in the fall of 1864, Orville Wood had no way of knowing he would soon uncover the most elaborate election conspiracy in America's brief history. Wood was a merchant from Clinton County in the most northeastern corner of New York. As a supporter of President Abraham Lincoln, he was tasked with visiting troops from his hometown to "look after the local ticket."

New York legislators had only established the state's mail-in voting system in April with the intent of ensuring the suffrage of White troops battling the Confederate Army.

The results of the 1864 elections would heavily affect the outcome of the war. Lincoln and his supporters in the National Union Party sought to continue the war and defeat the Confederacy outright. Meanwhile anti-war Democrats, also referred to as Copperheads, looked for an immediate compromise with the Confederate leaders and the end of the abolition movement;

LEAVING SLAVERY ALIVE & WELL IN AMERICA. U.S. POPULATION NOW 332 MILLION. CIVIL WAR U.S. POPULATION 32 MILLION; ONLY 300 MILLION LESS. 405,399 AMERICANS DIED IN WW 2. 750,000 AMERICANS DIED IN THE U.S. CIVIL WAR. NON-STOP; EVERY DAY; 10,000 LAND & SEA CLASHES ACROSS 1500 MILE FRONT; FORT SUMTER APRIL 12, 1861 – PALMITO RANCH, TEXAS MAY 12-13 1865; LAST BATTLE OF CIVIL WAR WAS A CONFEDERATE VICTORY. .

REAL LIFE U.S. PRESIDENTIAL ELECTION MAIL FRAUD RE-EDUCATION PROGRAM CONTINUED.

Troops from New York were allowed to authorize individuals back home to cast a vote on their behalf. Along with their mail-in ballots, troops would assign their power of attorney on slips that required four signatures: the voter's, the person authorized as a recipient, a witness to the signed affidavit and a fellow officer. These documents would be sealed in an envelope and shipped back home to be counted in the final vote. This was the process that Orville Wood intended to uphold, he would testify in court later. He quickly found out what a challenge that would be.

Wood arrived at Fort McHenry in Baltimore to visit with the 91st New York Regiment. There, an Army captain suggested that there had been some "checker playing" when it came to the gathering of soldiers' mail-in ballots. These suspicions of fraud were echoed when Wood visited wounded men at the Newton University Hospital. The rumors of wrongdoing led Wood to the office of Moses Ferry in Baltimore.

Ferry had been selected by New York Gov. Horatio Seymour to help oversee the voting process for New York's enlisted men. Seymour had vetoed the initial bill to establish mail-in voting and would go on to run against Ulysses S. Grant in the 1868 presidential election.

Wood masked his suspicions as he entered Ferry's office, portraying himself as a strong supporter of Lincoln's opponent, George McClellan. This was enough to gain Ferry's trust, he testified later.

Ferry told Wood that the votes from New York's 91st Regiment had already been tallied: 400 for McClellan and 11 for Lincoln.

Wood returned to the office later and, following Ferry's instructions, began forging signatures of the 16th New York Cavalry. Meanwhile, a clerk sat across the room signing ballots from the roster of names Wood had

brought with him from home. Wood asked to personally deliver these fraudulent ballots, but Ferry said they would have to receive final approval from his colleague in Washington — Edward Donahue Jr.

Donahue soon arrived in Baltimore and met with Wood. It was revealed during this conversation that around 20 co-conspirators were already at work in D.C. to aid in the plot to deliver votes to McClellan. The following day Wood watched as Donahue and his crew formed a sort of assembly line, passing blank papers along to one another to be signed with the names of active enlisted men, wounded and dead soldiers, and officers who never existed.

In addition to operations in D.C. and Baltimore, the scheme extended back to New York. Donahue had received rosters of soldiers from military officials and members of law enforcement. A letter from Gen. J.A. Ferrell read, "Enclosed in this package you will find tickets, also a list of names of the actual residents of Columbia County, now members of the 128th Regiment. With my best wishes for your success."

A letter from Albany Sheriff H. Cromdell offered to send additional men to assist in Baltimore. The letter read, "All is well here, and we are confident of complete success. It is unnecessary to say that all here have entire confidence in your skill and abetting, and hope you like your help."

Also discovered in Ferry's office was a list of around 400 names belonging to sick and wounded soldiers under treatment at a nearby hospital. In reference to the roster, Ferry joked, "Dead or alive, they all had cast a good vote."

Ferry, Donahue, and their fellow conspirators found humor in their work. One accomplice mocked the outcry he expected from abolitionist newspapers following the corruption of the election. The men bragged about their past successes in fixing local elections back home.

Together, the men had shipped crates of fraudulent votes back to New York. But their scheme was over. Wood reported the operation to authorities. Ferry's office was searched, and on the morning of Oct. 27, 1864 — less than two weeks before the election — he and Donahue stood trial before a military commission.

Ferry offered a full confession that same day, even offering up the names of others involved in the scheme. Donahue proved more of a challenge.

Following the first day of the trial, a reporter for the New York Times wrote, "The honest electors of the state of New York have escaped an extensive and fearful fraud, a fraud in keeping with the proclivities of the party in whose behalf it was initiated, but one that, if unexposed might have subverted the honest will of the people and left the state and the nation at the mercy of those who would make peace with rebellion and fellowship with traitors."

Arrests in New York and Washington continued to mount as Donahue returned to trial. Following Wood's damning testimony and supporting evidence, Donahue begged for mercy from the court. He was a young man, newly married, with no previous record. He visibly wilted as he realized the weight of his current situation, no longer expressing the defiance with which he had entered the proceedings.

The judge advocate addressed the tribunal, saying that Donahue had engaged in one of the most gigantic frauds ever attempted in America — "a fraud which, if it shall be successful, will, in my opinion, have produced a disruption of our entire country, and our war for the preservation of the Union will be practically at an end and futile."

In the months following Lincoln's victory — he won 221 electoral votes to McClellan's 21 — anti-abolitionist newspapers attacked his legitimacy, calling the trial another aspect of a conspiracy conducted by the president to ensure his reelection.

The commission that oversaw Ferry and Donahue's trial recommended life in prison for the two men who sought to corrupt the election by mail. The president, who would soon be slain, approved.

Lincoln's mail included advice, warnings and a call to shoot deserters

'Assassins!' A Confederate spy was accused of helping kill Abraham Lincoln. Then he vanished.

OH, WALMART; VOTING FRAUD ONLY A CHRONIC PSYCHOTIC (DEBUNKED) TRUMP DERANGEMENT SYNDROME REPUBLICAN PARANOIA; JUST LIKE ABRAHAM LINCOLN IN 1864 & AMERICA IN 2020; PLUS (2) MAIL FRAUD STOLEN GEORGIA SENATE RUNOFF'S.

Walmart on Wednesday apologized to GOP Sen. Josh Hawley for a tweet criticizing the lawmaker for his plan to object to the Electoral College certification on Jan. 6.

The now-deleted tweet read: "Go ahead. Get your 2-hour debate. #soreloser." Kyle Plotkin, Hawley's chief of staff, tweeted at Walmart asking if the company can "explain this one?", after it was "mistakenly" posted by a member of Walmart's social media team. Casey Staheli, Walmart's senior manager, told the Washington Examiner the employee meant to publish the comment on their personal account. I DON'T BELIEVE CASEY STAHELI. HE JUST WANTS TO FLUSH THE STORY INTO YESTERDAY'S FAKE NEWS CYCLE. I'M REMINDING EVERYONE OF THIS IN MY 8TH BOOK. "We have removed the post and have no intention of commenting on the subject of certifying the Electoral College. We apologize to Senator Hawley for this error and any confusion about our position," he said.

Hawley retorted: "Thanks @Walmart for your insulting condescension. Now that you've insulted 76 million Americans, will you at least apologize for using slave labor? "Or maybe you'd like to apologize for the pathetic wages you pay your workers as you drive mom and pop stores out of business," he added.

AT AGE MR. SAM DIED; I'M CLEANSING (DISINFECTING) AMERICA OF PARASITE WOODCHUCK SCHMUCK SCHUMER IN 2022. I DON'T PICK FIGHTS TO WIN; BUT TO HURT BULLIES IN EVERY WAY; AS MUCH AS POSSIBLE. I'M GOOD AT IT. THE BEST. SUICIDE BOMBER WITH WORDS. I SURVIVE. I DARE WOODCHUCK SCHMUCK SCHUMER TO DEBATE ME. GETTING VOTERS TO LAUGH AT SCHMUCKS LIKE SCHUMER IS # 1 FUN. WINNING; THE BONUS; COMES 2ND.

IT'S HOW YOU PLAY THE GAME & PICK THE WRONG VICTIM; LIKE #5202

COMMACK N.Y. "MIKE".

CONFEDERATE STATES OF AMERICA

ACT II SCENE I

RICHARD E. GLICK
SENATOR ELECT (R NY) 2022

PEOPLE WHO CAST VOTES CHOOSE NOTHING. PEOPLE WHO COUNT VOTES CHOOSE EVERYTHING. IN ;AN AUTHORITARIAN STATE

DEATH IS THE SOLUTION TO ALL PROBLEMS. NO MAN, NO PROBLEM

MY WIFE; SHEILA GLICK TOP OF SIXES 6 YEAR CANCER-FREE AGE 66 TRANSFORMATIVE 5'2' 112 LB WIFE BELIEF IN HER HUSBAND MADE HIM WORLD FAMOUS UNLIKE KANCEL KULTURE KOMPLIANCE KODE KONFORMING KLUB SAFE SPACE OTHER DAYS OF OTHER BETTER DAYS GONE BY GIRLS SHEILA HAUTE COUTURE SALES TEAM LEADER FOR SMOKIN' HOT BABES 1/3 HER AGE ROLE MODEL WHIPS TOGETHER WESTHAMPTON CONSIGNMENT SWEATER SMOCK; CHANEL BELT RIPPED IN ALL THE RIGHT PLACES JEANS ONLY FAR FETCH SIZE 6 $890 GUCCI SHOES LEFT *IN EUROPE DHL FROM MILAN YESTERDAY OVERNIGHT AQUA ALLEGORIA GUERLAIN KID YOU NOT SABER TOOTH PUSSY CAT BABY BE FOOLED NEVER, EVER EDITH KAGAN SHEILA'S WORLD'S BEST DR WHO SAVED HER LIFE & #1 IN WORLD SLOAN* KETTERING HEAD & NECK SURGERY CHAIRMAN JATIN SHAH SAY; SHE'S OUR LITTLE TROOPER ALPHA FEMALE TREND-SETTING BIOLOGICAL PHENOMENON SHOW-STOPPING HEAD-TURNER; NEVER LEARNED HOW TO BOIL WATER; MAKE ICE CUBES OR TAKE OUT THE GARBAGE; JUST LIKE SAM WALTON & OKLAHOMA ; O.K. TO WAKE UP TO; TO LOOK AT & COME HOME; TO PRAISE THE LORD & PASS THE AMMUNITION

BEFORE KATRINA; WALMART STAGED (100'S) (18) WHEEL SEMIS BOTTLED WATER; DIAPERS ALL FREE; THE LEFT BITCHED: "WAKE UP WALMART;" **& WANTS GOVERNMENT STATE OWNED WALMART; EVERYTHING TWICE EXPENSIVE NEVER IN STOCK (5) DAY UNION PET BEREAVEMENT PAY; (3) TIMES AS MUCH; GOODS FALL APART BEFORE OUT STORE FRONT DOOR.**

WALMART - 11,500 RETAIL UNITS – 56 BANNERS ECOMMERCE 10 COUNTRIES - 1.5 MILLION U.S.A. 2.3 PAYCHECKS WORLDWIDE. ANY WALMART PRODUCT; I BUY MOST EXPENSIVE; GREAT VALUE; EQUATE; KETCHUP; TIRES WRITE ABOUT WALMART TO WORLD; SPEND $5000 @ YEAR WALMART #5202.

WALMART # 5202 ADVERTISES FOR (2) DAY PICKUP AT #5202 (3RD) OF MY (7) BOOKS. (3) YEARS AGO I NEEDED JOB; WALMART WOULDN'T HIRE ME AS A GREETER IN COMMACK; CENTEREACH; MIDDLE ISLAND; ANY HOURS; ANY STORE; ANY HOLIDAY; WALMART JOB ANYWHERE; WILL TRAVEL ANYWHERE. INTERVIEWED IN CONSERVATIVE BLACK HUGO BOSS WORSTED SUIT; CONSERVATIVE TIE; BLACK SHINED CONSERVATIVE; CONTEMPTUOUSLY NEARLY THROWN OUT OF ALL WALMART STORES WALKED INTO LOOKING FOR A JOB; CONDESCENDINGLY; SMUG; GET LOST; APPLY ONLINE; WHERE I WAS ASKED MY AGE; APPLICATION READS LYING ABOUT AGE ON APPLICATION EQUALS IMMEDIATE WALMART FIRING IS AGE DISCRIMINATION; CIVIL; CORPORATE CONSPIRACY FELONY CRIME 1964 CIVIL RIGHTS ACT; KNOWING MY AGE WALMART ONLINE APPLICATION MEANS NO ONE FORCES WALMART TO CALL OR INTERVIEW ME; LIKE PASSIVE BACK DOOR INACTION CUNNING MAIL VOTING CHEATING DECEPTION; DISENGENUOUS? WALMART PLANS IT THIS WAY. WALMART IS NOT PERFECT. FEW BRIEF WALMART INTERVIEWS FROM COLD CANVASSING APPLIED TO 34 WALMARTS ONLINE LOCATIONS. DON'T NEED JOB NOW. WHEN I DID; WALMART SILENT TREATMENT. SQUEAKY WHEELS? WALMART? EVER? ALWAYS? MY CASE? NEVER? FICTION BASED ON FACT? ALL. WALMART IS REALLY PERFECT? WALMART LAUGHED ME OUT OF ITS STORES WHEN I NEEDED A MINIMUM WAGE JOB. BLACK LIVES MATTER? WHAT ABOUT THE LIFE OF A (73) YEAR OLD FUCKEN JEWBOY; ME; IN UNAFFORDABLE LONG ISLAND? ME? ANTI-SEMITISM? REFUSAL TO CALL AN AGE (73) WITH A JEW NAME IN FOR AN INTERVIEW? TOXIC MASCULINITY? (4) YEARS WALMART WON'T CALL ME FOR AN INTERVIEW AFTER APLLYING ON-LINE TO EVERY STORE IN A (40) MILE RADIUS.

(3RD) MY (8) BOOK^{S}

ONCE UPON A TIME ... THE STORY OF LONG ISLAND ...

www.walmart.com › ... › ***General Educational Books*** **Free 2-day shipping.** Buy *ONCE UPON A TIME ... THE STORY OF LONG ISLAND* - eBook at *Walmart*.com. **I.E. Shop all books** **Best sellers Summer reading**

- Kobo ereaders
- Ebooks
- Audiobooks
- Literature & fiction
- Children's & kids'
- Mysteries & thrillers
- Biographies & Memoirs Books

1. /Education Books
2. /General Educational Books

This button opens a dialog that displays additional images for this product with the option to zoom in or out.

Richard E Glick

Once Upon a Time the Story of Long Island (Paperback)

ONCE UPON A TIME ... THE STORY OF LONG ISLAND ... www.walmart.com › ... › *General Educational Books* Free 2-day shipping. Buy *ONCE UPON A TIME ... THE STORY OF LONG ISLAND* - eBook at *Walmart*.com

This button opens a dialog that displays additional images for this product with the option to zoom in or out.

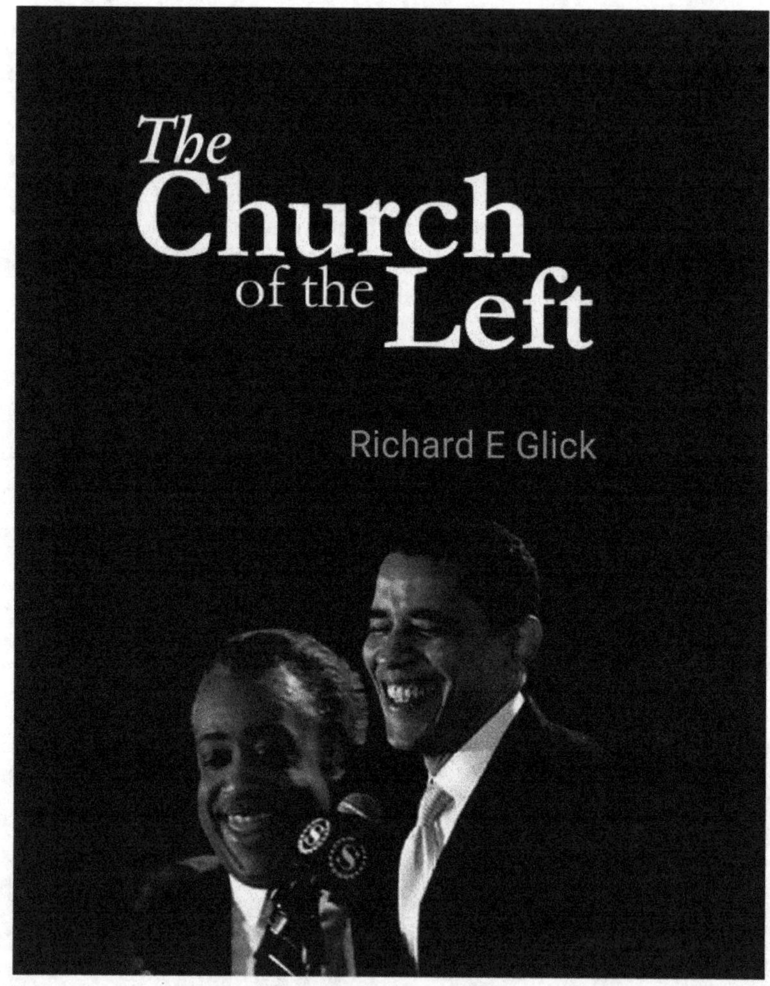

RICHARD E. GLICK

THE CHURCH OF THE LEFT –

eBook WALMART SELLS THIS ONE OF MY BOOKS AS WELL. I'M GRATEFUL

RICHARD E. GLICK

$8.69$8.69

BOOK FORMAT. SELECT OPTION. CURRENT SELECTION IS: EBOOK BOOK FORMAT: EBOOK

Disfruta de entrega GRATIS, ofertas exclusivas y películas y programas de TV con Prime
Prueba Prime y comienza a ahorrar hoy con Entrega GRATIS y rápida

Ver las 2 imágenes
ONCE UPON A TIME THE STORY OF LONG ISLAND (Inglés) Tapa blanda – 15 Noviembre 2019
de RICHARD E. GLICK (Author)
_Ver todos los formatos y ediciones

- **Kindle**

US$ 10.00 Leer con nuestra Aplicación gratuita
Pasta blanda
US$ 55.00
2 Usado de US$ 50.983 Nuevo de US$ 55.00

I'VE GIVEN THIS BOOK (PLEASE JOE BIDEN BURN IT?) TO (5) WALMART #5202 EMPLOYEES; THEY CAN BUY IT FOR $55 FROM WALMART & PICK IT UP IN (2) DAYS AT WORK; MY DEAL BETTER; FREE FROM ME RIGHT NOW. WALMART #5202 PHARMACIST MUHAMMAD; HAS (4) OF MY (8) BOOKS; LATEST EPUB & PRINT

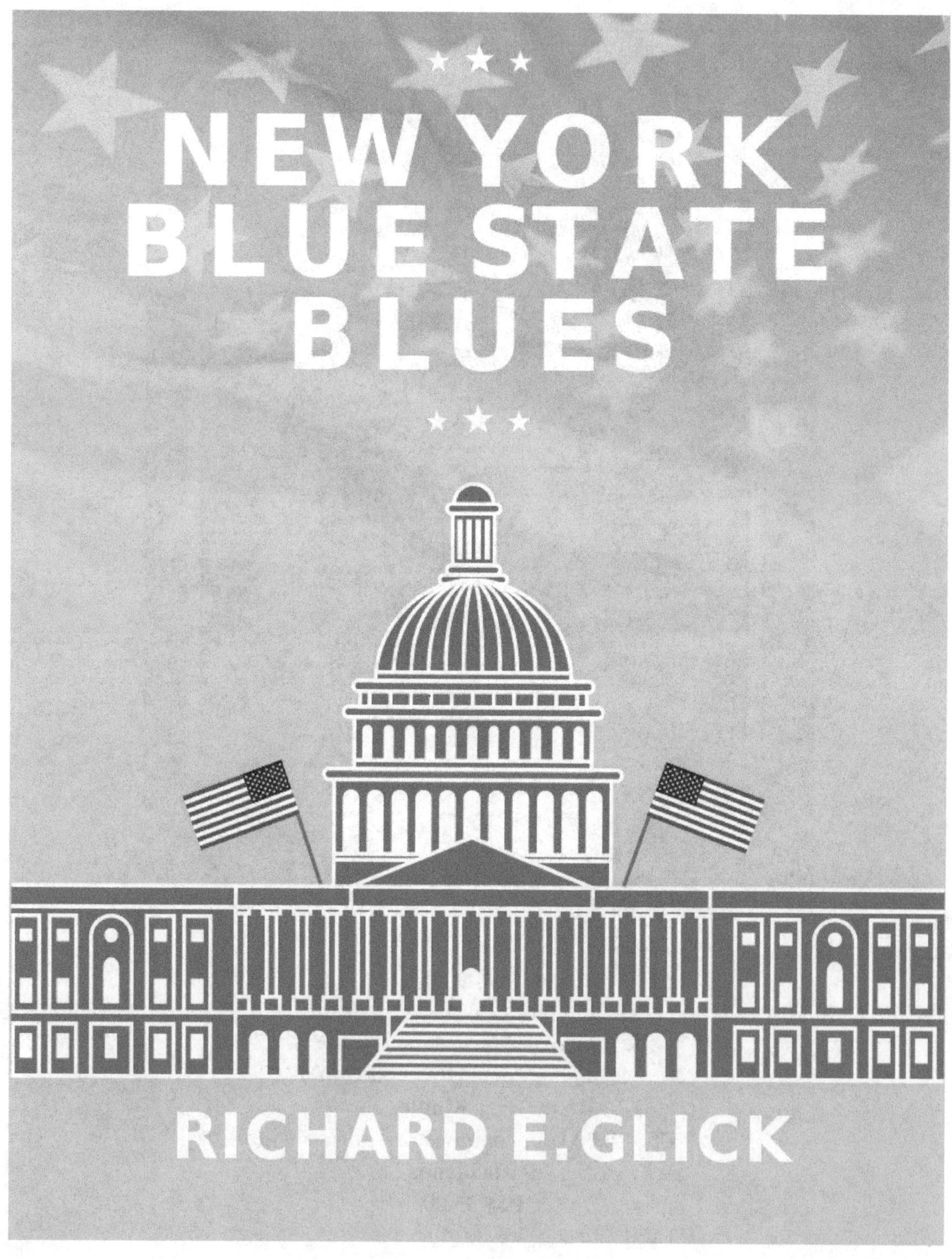

★ ★ ★

NEW YORK BLUE STATE BLUES

★ ★ ★

99% OF ALL 2020 USA SHOOTING TARGETS ARE MINORITIES. A WISE BLACK LIVES MATTER OLD TIMER EDUCATED ME: THESE KIDS IN THE HOOD TODAY CAN'T HURT YOU WITH THEIR HANDS LIKE CASSIUS CLAY, WHO THEY CALL MUHAMMAD ALI OR JOE LOUIS; BUT THEY CAN; WILL & DO SHOOT TO KILL. UNIVERSITY LEFT KANCEL KULTURE KODE KLUB KONFORMING KOMPLIANCE FIT TO THINK SETTLED THOUGHT DOCTRINE IS; IF YOU'RE NOT LEFT OF MAO; ANTIFA & 3RD TRIMESTER SKULL CRUSHING CODE PINK "WOMEN'S HEALTH" GROUPTHINK; YOU DON'T GET 5 MINUTES INTO A FEMINAZI EDUCATIONAL INDUSTRIAL COMPLEX PRE-SCREENING PRE-K THRU DOCTORAL STUDIES TEACHING JOB INTERVIEW. THE HARD-LEFT USA EDUCATION REICH TO LAST A THOUSAND YEARS HAS VOMITED FORTH DEMENTIA BIDEN HALF-TRUTH CHERRY PICKING SCIENCE & HUMANITIES THAT GOING FORWARD; SELECTIVELY CHOOSES ITS OWN FACTS. COMBINE THIS WITH A MASCULINE IDEAL OF MOUSEY SUPPLICANT SAFE SPACE GROVELING SUBARU; VW VOLVO 30 YEAR OLD MICE. NOT MEN; BREAST SUCKLED ON YUMMY ORGANIC FREE RANGE ATHEISTIC EARTH WORSHIP DELICIOUS SCRUMPTUOUS NATURAL GOODNESS LOVINGLY NURTURED HAPPY BELLY BEN & JERRYS CHUNKY MONKEY HEATHER HAS (2) VEGAN ALICE WATERS CHEZ PANISSE SOCCER MOMMIES & DADDIE'S SEX TOY BLUE HILLS ROOMMATE AT STONE BARNS HATES US SWAGGERING AMERICAN ALPHA MALES BECAUSE WE FIND WAYS TO WIN; ALWAYS; UNLIKE FREE RIDER BETTER RED THAN DEAD NAMBY PAMBYS TOO FRAIDY CAT OF BOO BOOS TO SAVE ANNE FRANK OR "I DIDN'T WANT TO GET INVOLVED WITH THE (33) SCREAMS OF CATHERINE "KITTY" SUSAN GENOVESE WHILE SHE WAS SLASHED (33) TIMES 3/14/64 BY WINSTON MOSELEY; WHO DIED SURROUNDED WITH LOVE COMFORTABLY MARCH 28, 2016 AT 81. RANDI WEINGARTEN'S POOR BLACK KIDS CHARTER SCHOOL CHOICE NEVER MATTERING IS COVID LOCKDOWN FOR BLACK LIVES MATTER KIDS WHO GOT NO TECHNO GEE WHIZ COOL DIGITAL LATEST EVERYTHING STUFF WHILE THE RANDI WEINGARTEN UNIONIZED TEACHERS DISINGENUOUSLY USE THE COVID EXCUSE TO SCREW OFF FOR A YEAR & BE PAID FOR NOT WORKING BY GUNS & RELIGION PROPERTY TAXES WHILE DEPLORABLES PUSH 18 WHEEL STEEL TO KEEP KROGER & WALMART STOCKED; PAL ALZHEIMER SLEEPY RUNS DOWN AMERICA'S CLOCK IN HIS HITLER WILMINGTON BUNKER W KANCEL KULTURE USING SOCIAL MEDIA FOR SPONSOR BOYCOTTS TO SHUT UP SEAN HANNITY RUSH LIMBAUGH MARK LEVIN MICHAEL SAVAGE BUCK SEXTON ANN COULTER BILL O'REILLY NEWSMAX WSJ EDITORIAL BOARD & ME; MY WORLD'S HIGHEST PAID 1965 CCNY CITY UNIVERSITY OF NEW YORK PROFESSORS BRAINWASHED US VIETNAM COMMANDER WILLIAM WESTMORELAND CONSPIRED JFK ASSASSINATION RIGHT WING COUP TAKEOVER OF AMERICA ULTRA COMPETITIVE FREE COLLEGE SCHOLARSHIP CAMPUS CROWD MOCKED GREATEST GENERATION PARENTS WHO WON WW II AS MORE EVIL THAN THE REICH & HITLER & TOJO MEANT WELL WITH THEIR TOTALITARIAN INTELLENGTSIA ONE WORLD POVERTY EDUCATION & ADDICTION INDUSTRIAL COMPLEXES IN 1969 SUMMER AMSTERDAM HOSTEL SUPERVISOR ASKED US 40 AMERICAN COOL KIDS INTRODUCE YOURSELVES; ONE SAID "I'M FROM GARY, INDIANA IN THE UNITED STATES OF AMERICA; EVERYONE BUT ME HOOTED, MOCKED, JEERED, LAUGHED & TAUNTED HOW DARE HE BE PROUD TO BE AN AMERICAN WHEN WE WANT BLOOD WHEN THE MILK RUNS OUT FOR ALEXANDRIA OCASIO-CORTEZ LIKE VENEZUELA & WEIMAR GERMANY

THE DIETRICH BONHOEFFER PRESS

NO SPECIAL WALMART TREATMENT FOR ME; LAST ON LINE FINE; "MIKE" TUESDAY, OCT 27, 2020; BULLYING ME; "MIKE" WON'T BE FIRST. **I WANT WALMART FAIR PLAY; BUYING A $299.99 SHARK VACUUM CLEANER; W $35 EXTENDED WARRANTY; "MIKE" VICIOUSLY BULLYING ME; CALLING POLICE ON MOST ENTHUSIASTIC; INNOCUOUS HARMLESS; OTHERWISE ROUTINE INCIDENT BECAME NEAR VIOLENT; WITH "MIKE"; ALL FICTION BASED ON FACT; LIKE THIS GREAT STORY**

THIS SPECIFIC VACUUM I MARKED IT W FELT TIPPED PEN; DURING "L'AFFAIRE "MIKE"; ONLY AVAILABLE AT COMMACK #5202. **SAME** $299.99 VACUUM SUDDENLY BECAME $239.99 IN CENTEREACH #2286 THOUGH I ASKED FOR NO DISCOUNT; PRICE IRRELEVANT TO ME; ALL WALMART CONSUMER PRODUCTS - TIRES TO REMOTE SPEAKERS; I BUY ONLY WALMART'S MOST EXPENSIVE; BENTONVILLE BUYERS KNOW PRODUCTS BETTER THAN VENDORS SELLING TO WALMART.

WALMART'S THE DOG. VENDORS THE TAIL. WALMART DICTATES ALL OR DOESN'T SELL IT.

WALMART SHOULD BE ONLY U.S. G.S.A. PROCUREMENT GENERAL SERVICES ADMINISTRATION SPECIFIER; AUDITOR OF EVERY MILITARY; MEDICAID, MEDICARE; HEALTH; HUMAN SERVICES TAXPAYER PENNY SPENT; TAXPAYERS WOULD GET TWICE AS MUCH FOR HALF THE PRICE. CONSUMERS WORLDWIDE KNOW THIS. UNIONS WANT POOR GUNS & RELIGION DEPLORABLES BUYING EVERHTING IN METRO NYC & CHICAGO FOR TWICE THE PRICE WHILE DENYING THE UNEMPLOYED JOBS. I WRITE THIS TO VAST READERSHIP. I HOLD WALMART TO CUSTOMER SERVICE STANDARD HIGHER THAN EZ PAWN IN THE "HOOD".

WALMART MANAGERS HAVE ABSOLUTE DISCRETIONARY AUTHORITY TO MAKE CUSTOMER ADJUSTMENTS; REFUND & EXCHANGES W/ WITHOUT ORIGINAL RECEIPT PROOF OF PURCHASE. I COULD RUN ALL WALMART EMPLOYEE TRAINING ACADEMIES.

I WON'T ACCEPT ANYTHING FOR NOTHING FROM ANYONE; & WON'T TOLERATE BEING VICTIMIZED & SINGLED OUT BY "MIKE"; **MOST ABUSIVE WALMART EXPERIENCE; SHORT OF**
***Who should prosecute the El Paso Walmart shooting suspect?* A year after the massacre, local and federal prosecutors still face hard decisions**

The incoming El Paso district attorney is going to inherit the biggest case in the city's history. But the federal government is pursuing its own charges, and the new DA is weighing whether to pursue the county's case.

BY JULIÁN AGUILAR JULY 31, 2020

Hundreds mourned the El Paso Walmart shooting victims and their families last year. A new district attorney must weigh whether to prosecute the suspected shooter, whom federal officials also plan to take to trial.

EL PASO — When El Pasoans mark the one-year anniversary of the Walmart shooting Monday, attorney Yvonne Rosales will be one of hundreds of thousands of border residents reflecting on the tragedy afflicted on this city that claimed the lives of 23 people.

But after the candlelight vigils dim, Rosales will be right back at the task she's been preparing for since she

was confirmed as the county's incoming district attorney — how to take over an office that could prosecute the man authorities say is responsible for one of the worst mass shootings in Texas history.

Rosales, an El Paso native who graduated from Austin High School and the University of Texas El Paso, will replace Jaime Esparza — who decided not to seek reelection after nearly three decades in office — in January to become the county's first female district attorney.

Rosales is inheriting one of the biggest criminal cases in the state's history amid a pandemic that's shut down in-person court proceedings. She's also inheriting a huge decision: whether to pursue a death penalty prosecution in the city's biggest murder case.

Federal prosecutors have also brought a litany of charges against Patrick Crusius, a 22-year-old from the Dallas suburb of Allen who authorities claim drove nearly 600 miles to target Hispanics; he allegedly posted a document online just before the shooting railing against immigrants and a "Hispanic invasion of Texas." He's facing dozens of state and federal charges, including nearly two dozen counts of capital murder at the state level and 23 counts of hate crimes resulting in death and 23 involving an attempt to kill at the federal level.

Esparza, the outgoing district attorney, said he would pursue the death penalty, while federal prosecutors have stated they would consider it upon conviction, but it's unclear which case will proceed first — and whether Crusius will be tried by both jurisdictions. Rosales said justice isn't likely to come soon because of the complexity of the case and the uncertainty of the coronavirus pandemic.

"I really don't anticipate this case going to the trial [phase] until, I am guessing, between two to three years," she said.

Before the coronavirus pandemic put a stranglehold on local economies, including El Paso's, Esparza said he was "offended" at the suggestion that the county should sit back and let federal officials take the lead in Crusius' prosecution in order to save the county millions in prosecution costs.

"Funding should never have a barrier in this prosecution, so I can tell you I'm not going to hand it off to the feds just because it's cheaper," Esparza said in February.

That was before the pandemic ravaged El Paso County and the rest of Texas. After sealing her victory in last month's runoff election, Rosales said letting the U.S. attorney's office prosecute Crusius first would make financial sense for El Paso.

"From a legal perspective, it would make more sense for the federal government to try the case first," she said, adding that the appeals process for federal cases is faster than state cases.

"If you're going to talk economics, then it would save the county of El Paso millions of dollars to try that case," Rosales added. She said it's too soon to make that determination, and she plans to discuss the situation with both the state and federal judges after she takes office.

Rosales said she must also consider whether the community — and especially the victims' families — should be forced to relive the tragedy twice during two separate trials.

"As we approach the one year anniversary, it's going to be a very emotional time for these people," she said. "Is it something that we really want to put the families through a second time?"

Crusius' attorneys have already raised the issue of his mental health and said he has "lifelong neurological and mental disabilities," the Associated Press reported earlier this month. His lawyers said that should be taken into consideration when prosecutors consider what punishment they seek.

Despite confessing to authorities that he was the gunman after his arrest the day of the shooting, Crusius has pleaded not guilty in both the state and federal cases. Federal prosecutors were scheduled to meet Thursday to discuss what punishment they would seek when the case moves forward. Defense attorney David Lane did not respond to a request for comment

"LE AFFAIRE "MIKE"; A WALMART STORY I; NO ONE; COULD DREAM UP; NEEDS TO BE TOLD; BEFORE WALMART BECOMES THE NEXT SEARS/KMART WHALE DROP; "LE AFFAIRE "MIKE" LIKE MAIL VOTE FRAUD IN 2020 COULDN'T HAPPEN HERE; "MIKE" & (73) YEAR OLD ME.

O.K. CORRAL.

PEARL HARBOR ALAMO "MIKE" & AGE (73) ME W/ RECHARGEABLE FLASHLIGHTS; I'VE BOUGHT (22) OF; SAME #5202 WALMART (SAME FLASHLIGHT) ALTERNATIVELY PRICED $12.88; $28.99; & $19.88 FROM NOVEMBER 2019 TO FEBRUARY 2020. NOW THEY SELL AN EXTENDED WARRANTY FOR THESE FLASHLIGHTS. WHEN I BOUGHT MY FIRST (16) OF THESE FLASHLIGHTS; I WAS NEVER OFFERED AN EXTENDED WARRANTY. I'VE HAD (2) OF THESE $28.88 SUDDENLY STOP WORKING; INCLUDING THE 2ND ONE THAT WENT BAD, SATURDAY, JANUARY 16, 2021; LESS THAN A YEAR OLD; NEVER WET OR DROPPED.

AT THE 1485 BATTLE OF BOSWORTH; RICHARD III OFFERED HIS "KINGDOM FOR A HORSE"; LIKE THE EXTRA UNNEEDED PARACHUTE (BOTH CRASHED) March 2019, (Boeing 737 MAX) grounded worldwide after 346 people died Lion Air Flight 610 October 29, 2018 & Ethiopian Airlines Flight 302 March 10, 2019.

IF ON 737 MAX CRASHING; & PASSENGER IN NEXT SEAT HAD EXTRA PARACHUTE; I WOULDN'T HAVE BARGAINED.

(3) DIFFERENT PRICES; SAME EXACT RECHARGEABLE FLASHLIGHT; SAME WALMART; SAME (4) MONTHS' LIKE PARACHUTES; DIDN'T BARGAIN; WANTED THESE FLASHLIGHTS NOW & TO LIGHT UP; PRICE IRRELEVANT. WIFE & I HAVE (2) IN OUR CARS; EACH SIDE OUR BED; COMPUTER DESK & READING; I HAVE 20:20 VISION; FLASHLIGHTS ARE BEST; WORK IN (140) VEHICLE TRANSPORTATION BUSINESS; BOUGHT (14) THESE FLASHLIGHTS FOR MECHANICS; WANT THEM TO WORK; I BOUGHT (2) BAD $28.88 ONES IN LESS THAN A YEAR; NOW I'VE DECIDED THEY'RE NOT WORTH BUYING. DON'T NICKEL & DIME ON PRICE; CHINESE SOURCED PRODUCT; ERRATIC COVID 19 SUPPLY CHAIN; WHOLESALE PRICES; CURRENCY; NOT WORTH TO NICKEL & DIME; I GIVE THOUSANDS A YEAR IN CHARITY.

200,000 DAILY CHANGING WALMART INVENTORY; SKU PRICES & RETAIL PRICING MISTAKES ARE INEVITABLE.

WHILE READING; (2) OF THESE FLASHLIGHTS SUDDENLY FAILED; BOTH WOULDN'T LIGHT UP AFTER RECHARGED FOR HOURS; NEVER DROPPED OR WET. IT HAPPENED TO 2ND OF THESE

FLASHLIGHTS TODAY.

MOST EXPENSIVE ANY ITEM WALMART SELLS; THE BEST VALUE WORLDWIDE; OR WALMART WOULDN'T SELL & PRICE IT ACCORDINGLY. KNOWING I WOULD BUY THE MOST EXPENSIVE VACUUM WALMART SOLD LATER THAT WEEK; I BROUGHT BAD FLASHLIGHT & GOOD; FUNCTIONING ONE TO WALMART #5202 CUSTOMER SERVICE. YOUNG HISPANIC CUSTOMER SERVICE GUY TOLD ME; GET ANOTHER FLASHLIGHT & MY VACUUM CLEANER; $299.99; PLUS 42 OZ. BAG M&M'S FOR MY 5'2' 112" LB. WIFE; $8.92; EVERYWHERE ELSE AT LEAST $12.00); CUSTOMER SERVICE COUNTER ON LEFT ENTERING STORE; HISPANIC CUSTOMER SERVICE GUY WHO IMPLIED EXCHANGE REPLACEMENT OF MY FAILED FLASHLIGHT FOR GOOD ONE; NOW WOULDN'T REPLACE IT; CALLED MANAGER "MIKE" WHO SNEERED MY BAD FLASHLIGHT I BOUGHT (7) MONTHS EARLIER WAS YEARS OLD; SAME FLASHLIGHT I BOUGHT FOR $12.88 NOVEMBER 2019; PRICED $28.88 FEBRUARY; QUESTIONING PRICE; WALMART MGR. SAID FEB 2020 MIGHT LOOK SAME BUT HOLD BETTER CHARGE & MORE INTENSE BEAM. BOUGHT PREVIOUSLY $12.88; FLASHLIGHT FOR $28.88; MARKED W BLUE STRIP FEB 2020 $28.88 FLASHLIGHT; THIS MIGHT BE BETTER ONE.

"MIKE" THEN DERISIVELY MOCKED ME; SNEERED THAT BOTH FLASHLIGHTS WERE THE SAME; THEY ACTUALLY WERE; THEN SNEERED W $299.99 VACUUM I SIMULTANEOUSLY WANTED TO BUY; IN MY CART IN FRONT OF "MIKE"; EMPHASIZED TO MIKE CRYSTAL CLARITY; BUYING $299.99 VACUUM W/ $35 MAXIMUM WALMART EXTENDED WARRANTY; NOW; "MIKE" SNEERED SMIRKINGLY AT ME; "WHAT DO YOU WANT ME TO DO; GIVE YOU THE FLASHLIGHT FOR FREE? I SAID NO; I DON'T WANT ANYTHING FOR FREE; JUST FAIR PLAY COMMIN SENSE; WHICH IS WHY I SPEND $5000 @ YEAR AT HIS STORE. "MIKE" THEN LAUGHED MUCH, MUCH MORE ABUSIVELY; VERY LOUDLY & DERISIVELY AT ME; W CUSTOMERS ALL AROUND; SNEERING; I NEVER WAS GOING TO GIVE IT TO YOU FOR FREE; ANYWAY; I'LL GIVE YOU TEN PERCENT OFF ON THE REPLACEMENT FLASHLIGHT. WHEN I RESPONDED THIS ISN'T THE COMMON SENSE FAIR PLAY CUSTOMER SERVICE I ALWAYS GET AT WALMART; "MIKE" RESPONDED WITH A LAUGH "GET OUT OF THIS STORE" WHEN I RESPONDED I'D NEVER HAD THIS BAD A WALMART EXPERIENCE; "MIKE" SNEERED; LOUDLY "I'M CALLING THE POLICE; DOING SO IN FRONT OF ME ON HIS CELL PHONE. HE THEN WALKED AWAY; FROM (50) FEET AWAY; I CALLED OUT TO HIM; JUST SHOW A LITTLE GOOD FAITH FLEXIBILITY; H; GIVE ME 20 PERCENT OFF ON THE REPLACEMENT FLASHLIGHT; & I'M BUYING THE $299.99 VACUUM W THE $35 WARRANTY RIGHT NOW. "MIKE" YELLED FROM (50) FEET AWAY; "THE POLICE ARE ON THEIR WAY. THE NEXT MORNING; WHEN STORE #5202 OPENED; I SPOKE ON PHONE W ANOTHER MANAGER; JULIA/JULIET; OVER (30) MINUTES; TELLING HER I STILL WANTED THAT VACUUM CLEANER; THERE WAS ONLY ONE OF THAT SHARK MODEL IN THE STORE; I'D MARKED IT W A FELT TIP MARKER; & LEFT THAT SPECIFIC ONLY VACUUM CLEANER IN THE #5202 STORE AT CUSTOMER SERVICE IN FRONT OF STORE PREVIOUS NIGHT. JULIA/JULIET ASSURED ME SHE'D LOCATE SHARK VACUUM & CALL ME BACK LATER SAME DAY; JULIA/JULIET REPEATING MY CELL NUMBER BACK TO ME. HAVING NOT HEARD FROM JULIA; AFTER SHE ASSURED ME SHE'D BE AT THE STORE TILL 5:00 PM; AFTER (6) HOURS; THE SAME DAY; BY 3:00 PM; I CALLED STORE #5202; AT LEAST (7) TIMES; WAS TOLD JULIA WAS STILL IN; & WAS UNABLE TO REACH JULIA/JULIET; CONNECTED TO EXTENSIONS THAT RANG (10) TIMES W NO PICKUP. DETERMINED TO GET MY $299.99 SHARK VACUUM; ONLY

(1) AVAILABLE VACUUM & BUY IT ONLY FROM WALMART; CENTEREACH STORE MANAGER AARON (REINCARNATION OF SAM WALTON) HEROICALLY HAD HIS ASSOCIATE; ALFREDO; PHYSICALLY LOCATE ONLY AVAILABLE SHARK VACUUM IN COMMACK #5202 & BRING VACUUM TO CENTEREACH #2286 STORE (26) MILES AWAY. SAME $299.99 VACUUM BECAME $239.99 (IRRELEVANT TO ME) W ADDED $35 MAX EXTEND WARRANTY. WHEN RUNG UP BY THE CASHIER IN CENTEREACH; SAME $299.99 VACUUM NOW $239.99; ASKED WHY PRICE WAS $60 LOWER THAN EXPECTED; SHE SAID ITS $239.99 PER BAR CODE; REGULAR PRICE; $269.00 HAD AN ADDITIONAL $30 SALE PRICE; NO SPECIAL TREATMENT OR INSTRUCTIONS FROM ANYONE FOR SPECIAL PRICE FOR ME.

I LEFT MY HEART AT JOEL T. ROBINSON GRADE 1-12; SCHOOL OUTSIDE LITTLE ROCK IN 1957; (I LIVED WALKING DISTANCE CRYSTAL MOUNTAIN; QUARTER MILE FROM NEAREST HOUSE. MY DOG; "IKE" GOOD RABBIT CATCHER; AFTER PRESIDENT. READING AT 9TH GRADE LEVEL IN MRS. JONES 3RD GRADE ARKANSAS CLASS; DAILY EACH WAY BINGITTY BANGETTY SCHOOL BUS WAS 1 & ½ HOURS; SEGREGATED SCHOOL; STEPMOTHER "DON'T TELL ANYONE AT SCHOOL YOU'RE JEWISH; PEOPLE HERE THINK JEWS HAVE HORNS; MRS. JONES TAUGHT FROM THE OLD & NEW TESTAMENT. WENT TO (2) KINDERGARTENS; (6) ELEMENTARY SCHOOLS; (3) JR. HIGH SCHOOLS; (3) HIGH SCHOOLS (1) C.C.N.Y. COLLEGE B.A. 5/69.

IF NOT FOR RUNNIN' PRETTY, NY CITY WIFE; SHE GREW UP; RIDIN' THE SUBWAYS UP IN HARLEM; DOWN ON BROADWAY; NO TRAMP; SHE'S A LADY; SHE'S HEART & SOUL OF NYC; IN LAND OF COTTON; GREAT SENATOR TOM COTTON; (R AR); NOT FAR FROM BENTONVILLE; OLD TIMES THERE; NOT FORGOTTEN; WHERE DID ALL THOSE YESTERDAYS GO? AT (73); TOMORROWS STRETCH INTO THE SUNRISE. WOULD LIKE TO GO BACK TO COMMACK #5202; WHERE "MIKE" WORKS.

AT JOEL T. ROBINSON SCHOOL IN ARKANSAS; TEACHERS TOLD ME I KEPT ORDER. (25) MILES OUTSIDE LITTLE ROCK; PULASKI COUNTY; RUNT KIDS RAN TO ME FOR PROTECTION. I NEARLY KILLED A BULLY WHO FUCKED W RICHARD GRAY; SENT TO THE PRINCIPAL'S OFFICE. CORPORAL PUNISHMENT WITH TEACHERS SWITCH/BRANCH ON REAR; PRINCIPAL; STRAP. MY LIFE RACED IN FRONT OF ME. SO I LIVED ONLY UNTIL (9). COULD HAVE BEEN WORSE. I HAD (9) GOOD YEARS. IF ALIVE AFTER PRINCIPAL; DAD WOULD KILL ME. EAR-TO-EAR; GRINNING BROADLY; PRINCIPAL CONGRATULATED; RICHARD; WHAT DO THEY CALL YOU; RICH? I CALLED YOU HERE BECAUSE "YOU'RE A HERO; WE'VE HAD A LOT OF TROUBLE W THAT MEAN BULLY KID. WE'RE NOT GONNA HAVE ANY MORE TROUBLE W HIM AT ALL; ANY MORE; NOT AS LONG AS YOU'RE AROUND. JUST DO ONE THING A LITTLE DIFFERENTLY NEXT TIME. WHEN YOU TEACH AN ANTI-BULLYING LESSON; TRY NEXT TIME; NOT KILLING THE BULLY. YOUR TEACHER TOLD ME YOU ALMOST KILLED HIM. THAT WOULDN'T HAVE BEEN A GOOD THING; EVEN IF HE DID DESERVE IT.

I HATE BULLIES.

ALL BULLIES ARE COWARDS WHO ONLY PICK FIGHTS THEY KNOWS THEY'LL WIN; UNTIL

"MIKE" MAKES A MISTAKE W THE WRONG VICTIM. I HAVEN'T BEEN AT # 5202 SINCE "L'AFFAIRE FLASHLIGHT MIKE"; COULD CARE LESS IF I EVER GO BACK; "MIKE" MAKES THE SAME MISTAKE TWICE; SOMEONE MIGHT GET KILLED. I HATE OF BULLIES. EVERY SINGLE FUCKEN ONE OF 'EM. WHEN THIS BOOK MAKES "MIKE" FAMOUS; & HE GETS A BOOK OR MOVIE DEAL; MAYBE PLAYING HIMSELF IN MOVIE VERSION OF THIS LETTER. WE'LL HAVE COME FULL CIRCLE. SCREEN. I'LL ACCEPT NOTHING FROM WALMART; FLASHLIGHTS OR M&MS. ABUSED BY "MIKE"? DON'T SAY "MIKE" & WALMART WAS NEVER WARNED.

NO ADJUSTMENT ACCEPTED. LESSON TO WALMART BULLYING MUST BE EXTERMINATED; HARSH WORD. I CHOOSE WORDS MORE CAREFULLY THAN ANYONE. CHOOSE YOUR SNAKEBITE WIDELY. FORGIVING EVIL IS CIVILIZATION'S BIGGEST MISTAKE. "MIKE" BULLYING ME; START TO FINISH; SADISTICALLY LAUGHING ENJOYING; NOW CONSEQUENCES ORGASMIC RUSH. BULLYING APPEARS AT AGE (3); REAPPEARING WHEN OPPORTUNITIES LIKE DEMOCRATS SHUTTING CONSERVATIVES DOWN TWITTER; FACEBOOK; SILICON VALLEY MS-13; BLOODS; CRIPS; ANTIFA; BLACK LIVES MATTER (LOOTERS IN WALMART) SURVEILLANCE VIDEO **Hundreds of People Seen on Video Looting a Tampa Walmart By Spectrum News Staff Tampa PUBLISHED 9:28 AM ET Jun. 12, 2020 TAMPA, Fla. -- The Hillsborough County Sheriff's Office has released surveillance video from May 30 of hundreds of people looting the Walmart store on East Fletcher Avenue.**

WASHINGTON POST; MSNBC; CNN NEVER BELIEVES EYES; EARS & YOUR BRAIN; JUST BELIEVE

PAL JOEY & KAMIKAZE KAMALA The store was closed due to the protests occurring outside the University Mall, when a crowd gathered outside the Walmart around 9 p.m. Saturday. According to the sheriff's office, people wielding blunt objects, like hammers, broke the glass entrance doors and stormed into the store. Detectives believe approximately 200 people entered the store and said most began looting the electronics section. An estimated $116,000 in merchandise and damages was reported. "Not only is this violence completely unacceptable, it was disrespectful to the protesters who were out there that night trying to express their message in an impactful way," said Sheriff Chad Chronister. "We are actively working to identify each and every one of these suspects and ask the public to provide any information they may have." Anyone with information on what happened that night is asked to call the Hillsborough County Sheriff's Office at 813-247-8200. HILLSBOROUGH COUNTY, Fla. (CBS12) — Investigators in central Florida say several hundred people looted a Walmart store and made off with more than $100,000 in merchandise. The crime is caught on camera and now investigators need help (DON'T BOTHER IF MAYOR'S A DEMOCRAT?) getting names to all the faces to make an arrest. AS CHICAGO'S MAYOR LORI LIGHTFOOT SAYS; WHO FUCKEN CARES; WALMART'S GOT INSURANCE; ITS REPARARATIONS ANYWAY) The mass looting happened on Saturday, May 30, just after 9 p.m. The store closed due to protests outside the University Mall nearby. The Hillsborough County Sheriff's Office said people armed with hammers and other blunt objects smashed their way into the store. Surveillance video shows the crowd running past the bales of fruit at the entrance, and straight for the store shelves. At least one person walked out with a giant television.

Hundreds loot Florida Walmart. STEALING IN THE NAME OF JUSTICE WITHOUR BEING PROSECUTED, MUCH LESS ARRESTED. Some folks in the crowd wore masks, others did not. The electronics section

(WHO'S SURPRISED; BE GLAD WALMART DOESN'T SELL DIAMOND ENGAGEMENT RINGS) took the biggest hit, the sheriff's office said. "Not only is this violence completely unacceptable, it was disrespectful to the protesters who were out there that night trying to express their message in an impactful way," said Sheriff Chad Chroniste.

NOW BIDEN'S GUTTING TRUMP'S TAX CUT, WILL WALMART RAISING PRICES; FREEZING /CUT SALARIES & HOURLY WAGES FOR A DECADE?

PA Reported 200,000 More Ballots Cast than People Who Voted – Will PENNSYLVANIA Now Legitimately Go to the Trump Column. DON'T BORE US WITH THIS CRAP. WHO THE FUCK CARES?

MARXISTS & CALIPHATE OF IRAQ & AL-SHAM; AL QAEDA; BOKO HARAM; AL SHABAAB; SO ALWAYS BEEN. SO IT ALWAYS BE. "DISEASED TISSUE". READ ALL GEORGE FROST KENNAN'S ARTICLE X "THE LONG TELEGRAM" TO UNDERSTAND; **LIKE READING ABOUT** "MIKE'. **MANUFACTURE THE TIME TO READ. LIKE I DO. GEORGE F. KENNAN ETCHED INTO GRANITE WHY JOSEPH STALIN; FIDEL CASTRO; XI JINPING; ADOLF HITLER &** PROGRESSIVE 2021 KANCEL KULTURE; INTOLERANT; MALIGNANT LEFT; **STOLE THE WHITE HOUSE** BULLYING TREACHERY IN GEORGIA; PENNSYLVANIA; MICHIGAN; WISCONSIN; ARIZONA & NEVADA. **MESSAGE OF KENNAN; BULLIES ARE IMPERVIOUS TO REASON; RIGHT; WRONG; LOGIC & FAIR PLAY. BULLIES ARE ONLY; ALWAYS** SENSITIVE & RESPONDIVE TO RETALIATORY BRUTE FORCE.

NOW THIS: Walmart: The big-box retailer said its "suspending contributions to those members of Congress who voted against the lawful certification of state electoral college votes."

Walmart (WMT) donated $2,500 to Kansas Sen. Marshall and $2,500 to Wyoming Sen. Cynthia Lummis during the 2020 election cycle, according to Open Secrets.

"We examine and adjust our political giving strategy at the end of every election cycle, and that review will continue over the coming months. However, in light of last week's attack on the U.S. Capitol, Walmart's political action committee is indefinitely suspending contributions to those members of Congress who voted against the lawful certification of state Electoral College votes I DON'T LIKE THIS. SAM WALTON WOULD FIRE EVERYONE AT WALMART'S WHO MADE THIS DECISION FOR CAUSE WITH NO SEVERANCE; ON THE SPOT.

The *Long Telegram*

The preface to the *Long Telegram* includes the following comments:

Answer to Dept's 284, Feb. 3,13 involves questions so intricate, so delicate, so strange to our form of thought, and so important to analysis of our international environment that I cannot compress answers into single brief message without yielding to what I feel would be a dangerous degree of oversimplification. I hope, therefore, Dept will bear with me if I submit in answer to this question five parts ... I apologize in advance for this burdening of telegraphic channel; but questions involved are of such urgent importance, particularly in view of recent events, that our answers to them, if they deserve attention at all, seem to me to deserve it at once.

George F. Kennan	

U.S. Ambassador to Yugoslavia	
In office May 16, 1961 – July 28, 1963	
President	John F. Kennedy
Preceded by	Karl L. Rankin
Succeeded by	Charles Burke Elbrick
U.S. Ambassador to the Soviet Union	
In office **May 14, 1952 – September 19, 1952**	
President	Harry S. Truman
Preceded by	Alan G. Kirk
Succeeded by	Charles E. Bohlen

Personal details	
Born	**George Frost Kennan** **February 16, 1904** **.Milwaukee, Wisconsin, U.S**
Died	**(March 17, 2005 (aged 101** **.Princeton, New Jersey, U.S**
(Spouse(s	**Annelise Sorensen**
Alma mater	(.Princeton University (A.B
Profession	**Diplomat** • **Political scientist** • **Writer** •

George Frost Kennan (February 16, 1904 – March 17, 2005) was an American diplomat **& historian. He was best known as an advocate of a policy of** containment of Soviet expansion during the Cold War**. He lectured widely and wrote scholarly histories of the relations between the** USSR and the **United States. He was also one of the group of foreign policy elders known as "The Wise Men".**

During the late 1940s, his writings inspired the Truman Doctrine and the **U.S. foreign policy** of «containing» the Soviet Union. **His "Long Telegram" from Moscow during 1946 and the subsequent 1947 article** *The Sources of Soviet Conduct* argued that the Soviet regime was inherently **expansionist** and that its influence had to be «contained» in areas of vital strategic importance to the United States. These texts provided justification for the **Truman administration's new anti-Soviet policy. Kennan played a major role in the development of definitive Cold War programs and institutions, notably the Marshall Plan.**

CPSIA information can be obtained
at www.ICGtesting.com
Printed in the USA
LVHW060946160521
687531LV00024B/693